DIVINE INTIMACY

MEDITATIONS ON THE INTERIOR LIFE FOR EVERY DAY OF THE LITURGICAL YEAR

By

Father Gabriel of St. Mary Magdalen, O.C.D.

Translated from the seventh Italian edition by the
Discalced Carmelite Nuns of Boston

TAN BOOKS AND PUBLISHERS, INC.
Rockford, Illinois 61105

IMPRIMI POTEST:
Fr. Christophorus a SS. Sacramento, O.C.D.
Provincialis
                                        July 19, 1963

NIHIL OBSTAT:
Fr. Christophorus a SS. Sacramento, O.C.D.
Fr. Joannes a Jesu Maria, O.C.D.
Censores Ordinis
                                        July 19, 1963

IMPRIMATUR:
✢ Richard Cardinal Cushing
  Archbishop of Boston
                                        July 16, 1964

The original edition of *Divine Intimacy* was published in Italian by the Carmel of St. Joseph in Rome under the title: *Intimitá Divina*, del P. Gabriele di S. M. Maddalena, O.C.D. Originally published in English circa 1964 by Desclée Company, New York, Paris, Tournai, Rome and printed in Belgium by Desclée & Co., Éditeurs, S.A., Tournai.

Acknowledgements. Courtesy of: Sheed and Ward Inc., New York, N.Y.—most quotations from St. Teresa, taken from *The Complete Works of St. Teresa*, translated and edited by E. Allison Peers from the critical edition of P. Silverio de Santa Teresa, O.C.D., published in three volumes; The Newman Press, Westminster, Md. and Burns and Oates Ltd., London—most quotations from St. John of the Cross, taken from *The Complete Works of St. John of the Cross*, edited and translated by E. Allison Peers.

Library of Congress Control Number: 93-61593

ISBN 0-89555-676-6

Printed and bound in the United States of America.

TAN BOOKS AND PUBLISHERS, INC.
P. O. Box 424
Rockford, Illinois 61105

1996

Reverend Mother,

The Reigning Pontiff accepts with pleasure the copy of the fifth edition of *Intimità Divina*, a book of meditations following the course of the liturgical year, inspired by the late Fr. Gabriel of St. Mary Magdalen, which you humbly offer Him. It should be added that several Religious of the Monastery of St. Joseph, Rome, collected and diligently arranged the material furnished by the Author, who had not the consolation of seeing his work, an effective compendium of Carmelite spirituality, published.

The meditations are substantial and solid, adapted to the various degrees of spirituality, and within reach of every person of good will. Priests, seminarians, contemplative souls, those dedicated to the apostolate, and finally the laity of every social class have meditated these pages and found encouragement and spiritual profit. This has been so, not only in Italy, but, it may be said, throughout the world, thanks to the translations into all the principal languages.

The Holy Father is glad to know that a new edition in Italian is being prepared. He is pleased that the book has been so successful; He hopes that it will have an ever wider diffusion, so that the innumerable souls in every state of life who long above all things for God, and aspire to an intimate life with Him, may draw light and strength from it to persevere with increased fervor in the work of their salvation.

Finally, His Holiness is happy to impart to you, and to all the Religious of your Monastery, in token of Divine Grace, the Apostolic Benediction.

Yours devotedly in Our Lord,

✠ ANGELLO DELL'ACQUA
Substitute

Reverend Mother
Prioress of the Discalced Carmelites
Monastery of St. Joseph
Rome

N. 63314

Reverenda Madre,

Ella ha umiliato al Regnante Pontefice copia della quinta edizione del volume "Intimità Divina", meditazioni per l'anno liturgico, dovute al cuore e alla penna del compianto P. Gabriele di S.Maria Maddalena. Bisogna aggiungere che è merito di alcune Religiose di codesto Monastero aver diligentemente raccolto ed ordinato il materiale fornito dall'Autore stesso, il quale non ebbe la consolazione di vedere pubblicata l'opera, efficace compendio della spiritualità carmelitana.

Di fatto, il libro è sostanzioso, adatto a tutti i gradi della vita spirituale e alla portata di ogni anima volonterosa. Sacerdoti, seminaristi, anime di contemplativi o di persone dedite all'apostolato, laici infine di ogni categoria sociale hanno meditato su queste pagine e si sono sentiti incoraggiati a migliorarsi. Ciò non solo in Italia ma, si può dire, in tutto il mondo, per le traduzioni che di esso sono state fatte nelle principali lingue.

Il Santo Padre, Che ha gradito l'omaggio, ha appreso con soddisfazione che si prepara una nuova edizione italiana; e mentre Si compiace per il successo dell'opera, fa voti per una sua larga diffusione, affinchè quelle innumerevoli anime, che, in tutti gli stati di vita, desiderano soprattutto Dio ed aspirano alla vita intima con Lui, possano attingervi luce e forza per meglio attendere alla propria santificazione.

Sua Santità è lieta, infine, d'impartire a Loi e alle Religiose tutte di codesto Monastero, l'Apostolica Benedizione, auspicio della divina grazia.

Con sensi di religiosa stima mi confermo

di Lei
dev.mo nel Signore

Rev.da Madre Priora
del Monastero di S.Giuseppe
delle Carmelitane Scalze
Roma

INTRODUCTION

In these times when the lines of battle are being drawn more and more clearly between the forces of religion and those of atheism, we see the devotees of each of these systems calling upon every resource at their disposal. Before one can really fight for a cause, he must be fully convinced of the truth of it. He must ponder its ideals and adapt his thoughts and actions to it.

We can be sure that the fervent Communist gives serious thought and frequent consideration to the ideals for which he is sacrificing himself. Only in this way can he fire his zeal to continue the struggle. But we, as Christians, have a much greater cause to fight for. It is greater precisely because it is true and divine. How mistaken we are if we neglect to increase our knowledge of and zeal for our Faith. We can hardly expect to remain fervent and apostolic Christians unless we make it a practice to ponder the truths of our holy religion, to strive to identify our thoughts with those of Christ, our Leader, and to transform those thoughts into effective action in His service.

This book is a mine of inspirational thoughts, an excellent book of meditations which aims at helping us to review and concentrate on the treasures of our Faith, so that an intelligent appreciation thereof will become a significant factor in our thinking and acting. It should also prompt us to be one with Christ and to bring about the most intimate union that is possible in this life between souls and God. The author of *DIVINE INTIMACY*, Father Gabriel of St. Mary

Magdalen, O.C.D., was one of the outstanding Discalced Carmelite authors and lecturers of modern times.   A devout son of St. John of the Cross, he devoted himself generously and tirelessly to the task of promoting that desired union, both in himself and in others.   His book of meditations for each day of the year is an outstanding part of his effort.   Faithful to these meditations from day to day, we shall know Christ and live Christ, absorb His teachings more fully and become more dedicated to His service.   Our zeal for the cause of Christ will then equal — nay, far outstrip — that of the atheistic Communist.   He meditates on false doctrines, the work of Godless men, which lead him to become less than a man. The Christian meditates on the Gospel of Christ, which leads him to become something more than a man—to share in an intimate manner in the life of God Himself—to become Godlike, or in the words of St. John of the Cross, " God by participation. "

✠ Richard Cardinal Cushing
Archbishop of Boston

FOREWORD

The extraordinary success with which the volume, DIVINE INTIMACY, has been received among clergy and religious, as well as among those in the world who are consecrated to God, those engaged in Catholic Action, and the faithful in general, is a fitting crown to the author's life, one which was permeated with the desire for intimate union with God and the apostolate of fostering the interior life.

The late Father Gabriel of St. Mary Magdalen entered the Order of Discalced Carmelites in Bruges, Belgium, in 1910, at the age of seventeen.

The First World War (1914-18) forced him to continue his study of philosophy and theology in Ireland. He was ordained priest in 1919. From 1919 to 1926, while teaching philosophy in the Seminary of the Order at Courtrai in Belgium, he had the opportunity of completing his own studies at the nearby University of Louvain, and finally in Rome, where he attended the Pontifical Institute, the "Angelicum."

From 1926 to 1936 Father Gabriel was spiritual director of the young theologians at the International College of St. Teresa in the city where, at the same time, he was teaching theology. From 1931 until his death (March 15, 1953), he dedicated himself especially to the study of spiritual theology. During this last period of his life, his remarkable talents as a teacher and spiritual director were clearly evidenced, both in the conferences on Carmelite spirituality, which he gave in Rome and in the larger cities of Italy, as well as in his numerous publications on St. Teresa of Avila, St. John of the Cross, St. Thérèse of the Child Jesus, and St. Teresa Margaret of the Heart of Jesus.

He was also a member of the Roman Academy of St. Thomas Aquinas and a Consultor of the Sacred Congregation of Rites.

By his lectures and writings, this great religious and eminent spiritual director became an ardent leader in the spiritual movement in Italy.

In 1941 he founded the review Vita Carmelitana, *the title of which was changed in 1947 to* Revista di Vita Spirituale. *This review continues to propagate the sound doctrine of the spiritual life that is needed more than ever today.*

Father Gabriel was profoundly aware of the spiritual needs of our times, and he also understood the special mission of Carmel in the Church, that of leading souls to a life of intimate union with God by means of the practice of mental prayer. Thus he conceived the idea of a book which, taking its inspiration from the great teachers of Carmel, would set forth the whole doctrine of the spiritual life in the form of simple, but solid, meditations—a book which would introduce souls to intimate prayer.

Divine Intimacy, *therefore, seeks to arrange daily meditations " in such a way that in the course of one year the most important problems of the spiritual life and all the supernatural realities met with in the interior life will have been reviewed " (Preface).*

To promote his work, Father Gabriel asked the assistance of the Discalced Carmelite Nuns of the Monastery of St. Joseph in Rome. To this end, he furnished them with the vast amount of material at his disposal (his publications, the texts of his conferences, instructions, sermons, and so forth). He then outlined the plan for the whole book and directed the work on it. This collaboration with his spiritual daughters in Carmel proved truly providential. After the untimely death of the renowned master, the Nuns, who were in possession of all his manuscripts, were able to bring to a happy conclusion the publication of their venerated Father's work.

The first edition of Divine Intimacy, *received with great enthusiasm by Christians everywhere, was quickly exhausted. Translations into several languages were requested. Numerous letters from prelates, directors of seminaries, superiors of religious houses, priests, and the laity have testified to the benefit received from this work.*

May this English edition of Divine Intimacy *awaken many souls to the need of a solid interior life and lead them to close union with God, the source of a really fruitful apostolate in the Church.*

Fr. Benjamin of the Holy Trinity, O.C.D.
First Definitor General of the Discalced Carmelites

PREFACE

Mental prayer is indispensable to the spiritual life; normally it is, so to speak, its very breath. However, this spontaneity in prayer is usually realized only if the soul applies itself to meditation for some time by its own personal effort. In other words, one must learn how to pray. It is to teach souls this devout practice that various meditation books have been published. There are many methods, each with its own merit; among them is the Teresian method, so called because it is based on the teachings of St. Teresa of Jesus, the Foundress of the Discalced Carmelites and the great mistress of the spiritual life.

Some years ago, we outlined this method in a pamphlet called the *Little Catechism of Prayer*, [1] which has since been translated into many European languages and into some of the Asiatic tongues. It is a simple exposition of the Teresian method according to the writings of many Carmelite authors; its widespread circulation shows very clearly that this method answers the needs and the desires of many prayerful souls. Hence we judged it timely to offer souls aspiring to advance in the interior life, a collection of subjects for meditation for each day of the year, according to the Teresian idea and method of mental prayer.

* * *

[1] FATHER GABRIEL OF ST. MARY MAGDALEN, O.C.D., *Little Catechism of Prayer*, translated by the Discalced Carmelite Nuns of Concord, New Hampshire, 1949.

The idea of mental prayer which St. Teresa has left us is well known in our day. In her *Autobiography* she defines it as " friendly intercourse and frequent solitary converse with Him who we know loves us " (*Life*, 8).

In these words St. Teresa reveals the affective spirit of mental prayer which is its special characteristic. It is " friendly intercourse, " and exchange of " mutual benevolence " between the soul and God, during which the soul " converses intimately " with God—intimacy, as we know, is the fruit of love—and the soul speaks with Him whose love she knows. Each element of the definition contains the idea of love, but at the end the Saint mentions that the soul ought also to " know " and be conscious of God's love for her : this is the part which the intellect plays in prayer. Therefore, according to St. Teresa, there is an exercise of both the intellect and the will in mental prayer : the intellect seeks to convince the soul that God loves her and wishes to be loved by her; the will, responding to the divine invitation, loves. That is all. There could be no clearer concept of prayer. But how translate it into practice? This is the task of the *method*.

* * *

In order to understand the structure of the Teresian method clearly, we must keep in mind the definition of prayer given above; then we shall easily see that it is fully realized by such a method, that it truly means conversing lovingly with Our Lord, once we understand that He loves us.

We cannot speak to God intimately unless we are in contact with Him. For this reason, we make use of the " preparation, " which consists in placing ourselves more directly in the *presence of God*, turning to Him by means of a good thought.

In order to convince ourselves that God loves us, we choose for the subject of meditation one of the truths of faith which can make His love evident : this is the purpose of the *reading* of an appropriate passage.

However, it does not suffice merely to read the matter; we must examine it thoroughly, and there is no better way of doing this than by reflecting upon it—by *meditating*.

All revealed truth can manifest God's love for me, but today I try to understand it by reflecting on the theme I have chosen in my *reading*. I make use of the good thoughts contained in the subject of the meditation to actually convince myself of His love, so that love for Him will come spontaneously into my heart, and words perhaps, to my lips.

Thus my *colloquy* with God begins; I tell Him in every way possible (using the words which come to me most spontaneously) that I love Him, that I want to love Him, that I want to advance in His holy love, and that I wish to prove my love for Him by my actions, by doing His holy will.

And now we are at the center, *the heart of prayer*. For many souls, nothing more is needed. Some, however, prefer greater variety; therefore, to facilitate the prolonging of our loving conversation with God, the three final steps of the method are offered. These, however, are *optional*.

Thanksgiving : After having told Our Lord again that we love Him, we thank Him for all the benefits we have received from Him and show Him that we are grateful.

Offering : Aware of having received so many favors, we try to repay our debt as far as we can by making some good resolution. It is always useful to end our prayer in this way.

Petition : The consciousness of our weakness and frailty urges us to implore the help of God.

This is the whole Teresian method, divided into seven steps :

Two *introductory* : the preparation (presence of God) and reading.

Two *essential* : the meditation and the colloquy.

Three *optional*, to help in prolonging the colloquy : the thanksgiving, the offering, and the petition.

* * *

The meditations in this book are based on this method.

We begin with the *presence of God*, an appropriate thought which brings us into contact with our Creator and orientates us toward Him.

The *reading* provides the subject for the meditation. And as many spiritual persons apply themselves to meditation twice a day, each meditation offers two points.

The soul then begins to *reflect*, using freely the text already read. In this way it will pass spontaneously to the *colloquy* which, according to the Teresian concept, is the " heart, " the center of mental prayer.

That is why our meditations are directed toward helping souls especially on this point. To this end we have tried to give the colloquies a form that is sufficiently ample; nevertheless, they may be used freely as desired, each soul choosing whatever corresponds to the need of the moment. To make the colloquies more efficacious, we have selected suitable ardent expressions and thoughts taken by preference from the writings of the saints and other loving souls. Very often we have been obliged to make slight modifications in these texts, in order to adapt them to the intimate form of a colloquy. However, we always indicate their source in parentheses. [1]

The colloquies consist of expressions of love, alternating with petitions, acts of thanksgiving, and transports of the soul toward God; these are made concrete in the resolutions.

We hope that these meditations, written in this way, will help souls to apply themselves to mental prayer according to the Teresian idea and method.

* * *

Teresian spirituality is the spirituality of divine intimacy, [2] that is, it tries to nourish in souls the ideal of intimacy with God and it directs them toward this ideal, principally by means of mental prayer. Mental prayer should be attuned, therefore, to this great and lofty aspiration.

This is the " tone " we have tried to give our meditations, and the title, DIVINE INTIMACY, indicates our intention to help souls as far as possible to attain this great end.

In addition, Teresian spirituality is also doctrinal. St. Teresa of Jesus, the great " mistress of the spiritual life, " always desired—and endeavored to put her desire into practice — that the ascetical and mystical life of those who were dear to her be based on solid doctrine, for the Saint greatly loved theology. That is why we have desired to build these meditations upon a sound theological basis.

---

[1] In spite of the modifications we have made, we have not used the customary " cf., " so as to avoid constant repetition. We have used this sign only when the colloquies were merely inspired by the writings of the saints and not quoted from them.

[2] See our work, *Carmelite Spirituality*, Rome, College of St. Teresa 1943.

We have attempted to arrange them in such a way that, in the course of one year, the most important problems of the spiritual life and all the supernatural realities met with in the interior life will have been reviewed.

The meditations begin with the opening of the liturgical year, and are arranged in the following order :

December – The Ideal : Holiness, Intimacy with God, The Apostolate - The Mystery of the Incarnation.

January – Jesus : His Person, His Works, Our Relations with Him - The Church - The Sacraments.

February and *March* – Interior Purification and the Exercice of Abnegation - The Passion of Jesus.

April – The Life of Prayer.

May – Our Blessed Lady - The Holy Spirit.

June – Jesus in the Holy Eucharist - The Sacred Heart of Jesus - The Most Holy Trinity.

July – The Divine Perfections - The Theological Virtues.

August and *September* – The Moral Virtues - The Gifts of the Holy Spirit - The Beatitudes.

October and *November* – The Apostolate - Union with God. [1]

* * *

We should like to call attention to one last point.

Precisely because Teresian spirituality is the spirituality of divine intimacy, the spirit impregnating the exercises by which we hope to attain this lofty ideal must be the *spirit of love*. We have tried to keep in mind this special mark of the spirit of Carmel. Not all meditation books are adapted to souls thirsting for divine intimacy, simply because they are too much imbued with a spirit of fear. Not, indeed, that fear is not profitable for certain souls, but since there are so many books of this type, we judged it timely to publish a collection of meditations in which love would be united to filial, reverential fear, instead of servile fear, while not denying that this latter can be very salutary. This is also the reason we have

---

[1] Because of the desire of many to facilitate the use of the work, it was decided to abolish the division into months, leaving only the order of the liturgical weeks.

by preference emphasized the positive topics of virtue and spiritual progress rather than the negative ones of vice and sin.

May the Holy Spirit, the Spirit of love, who deigns to dwell in our souls in order to bring them gradually under His complete influence and direction, kindle in us, " with abundant effusion, " that love of charity which will lead us to intimacy with God! May the Blessed Virgin Mary, Mother of fair love, whose soul, filled with grace, was ever moved by the Holy Spirit, obtain for us from this divine Spirit the favor of remaining docile to His invitations, so that we may realize, with the help of an assiduous, effective practice of mental prayer, the beautiful ideal of intimate union with God.

Fr. Gabriel of St. Mary Magdalen, O.C.D.
Rome, Feast of the Sacred Heart, 1952.

CONTENTS

THE FIRST SUNDAY OF ADVENT TO THE FIFTH SUNDAY AFTER THE EPIPHANY

THE IDEAL : SANCTITY, INTIMACY WITH GOD, THE APOSTOLATE -- THE MYSTERY OF THE INCARNATION — JESUS : HIS PERSON, HIS WORK, OUR RELATIONS WITH HIM — THE CHURCH — THE SACRAMENTS.

Meditation   *Page*

SEPTUAGESIMA SUNDAY TO HOLY SATURDAY

THE PURIFICATION OF THE SENSES AND THE PRACTICE OF
ABNEGATION — THE STRUGGLE AGAINST SIN —
HUMILITY, OBEDIENCE, AND ACCEPTANCE OF
THE CROSS — THE PASSION OF JESUS.

Meditation   *Page*

Meditation   *Page*

EASTER SUNDAY TO THE FEAST OF THE MOST HOLY TRINITY

THE LIFE OF PRAYER : VOCAL AND MENTAL PRAYER,
DEVELOPMENT OF CONTEMPLATIVE PRAYER, LITURGICAL
PRAYER — OUR BLESSED LADY : HER PRIVILEGES AND
VIRTUES — THE HOLY SPIRIT AND HIS ACTION
IN US.

Meditation   *Page*

THE FEAST OF CORPUS CHRISTI TO THE NINTH SUNDAY AFTER PENTECOST

THE HOLY EUCHARIST — THE SACRED HEART OF JESUS — THE MOST HOLY TRINITY — THE DIVINE PERFECTIONS — THE THEOLOGICAL VIRTUES.

THE TENTH TO THE EIGHTEENTH SUNDAY
AFTER PENTECOST

FRATERNAL CHARITY — THE MORAL VIRTUES — THE GIFTS
OF THE HOLY SPIRIT — THE BEATITUDES.

Meditation   *Page*

THE NINETEENTH TO THE LAST SUNDAY AFTER PENTECOST

THE APOSTOLATE : DUTY, FORMATION, PREPARATION,
PRACTICE — UNION WITH GOD : PURIFICATION OF THE
SPIRIT, DEVELOPMENT OF LOVE, UNION OF WILL,
COMPLETE UNION.

IMMOVABLE FEASTS

ABBREVIATIONS

Ep	=	Epistle
Gosp	=	Gospel
RB	=	Roman Breviary
RM	=	Roman Missal
J.C.	=	ST. JOHN OF THE CROSS
AS	=	Ascent of Mt. Carmel
CR	=	Counsels to a Religious
DN	=	Dark Night of the Soul
LF	=	Living Flame of Love
P	=	Precautions (Cautions)
SC	=	Spiritual Canticle
SM	=	Spiritual Maxims :
l	=	Words of Light
ll	=	Points of Love
lll	=	Other Counsels
T.J.	=	ST. TERESA OF JESUS
Con	=	Conceptions of the Love of God
Exc	=	Exclamations of the Soul to God
F	=	Foundations
Int C	=	Interior Castle (Mansions)
Life	=	Life
M	=	Maxims for her Nuns
SR	=	Spiritual Relations
Way	=	Way of Perfection
T.M.	=	ST. TERESA MARGARET OF THE HEART OF JESUS
Sp	=	Spirituality of St. Teresa Margaret of the Heart of Jesus (Not yet translated)
T.C.J.	=	ST. THERESE OF THE CHILD JESUS
C	=	Counsels and Souvenirs
NV	=	Novissima Verba
St	=	Story of a Soul
E.T.	=	SR. ELIZABETH OF THE TRINITY
I	=	First Retreat (Heaven on Earth)
II	=	Last Retreat
III	=	Elevation to the Most Holy Trinity
ALL AUTHORS		
L	=	Letters

THE FIRST SUNDAY OF ADVENT

TO

THE FIFTH SUNDAY

AFTER THE EPIPHANY

THE IDEAL: SANCTITY, INTIMACY WITH GOD, THE APOSTOLATE —
THE MYSTERY OF THE INCARNATION — JESUS: HIS PERSON,
HIS WORK, OUR RELATIONS WITH HIM — THE CHURCH —
THE SACRAMENTS.

I

THE LORD COMETH FROM AFAR

PRESENCE OF GOD - The Lord is coming; I place myself in His presence and go to meet Him with all the energy of my will.

MEDITATION

1. " The Name of the Lord cometh from afar.... I look from afar, and behold I see the power of God coming.... Go out to meet Him, and say, ' Tell us if You are He who shall rule.... ' " These words are taken from today's liturgy, and in reply, it invites us, " Come, let us adore the King, the Lord who is coming!.. " *(RB)*.

This coming was expected for long ages; it was foretold by the prophets, and desired by all the just who were not granted to see its dawn. The Church commemorates and renews this expectation with each recurring Advent, expressing this longing to the Savior who is to come. The desire of old was sustained solely by hope, but it is now a confident desire, founded on the consoling reality of the Redemption already accomplished. Although historically completed nineteen centuries ago, this longing should be actualized daily, renewed in ever deeper and fuller reality in every Christian soul. The spirit of the Advent liturgy, commemorating the age-long expectation of the Redeemer, will prepare us to celebrate the mystery of the Word made Flesh by arousing in each one of us an intimate, personal expectation of the renewed coming of Christ to our soul. This coming is accomplished by grace; to the degree in which grace develops and matures in us, it becomes more copious, more penetrating, until it transforms the soul into an *alter Christus*. Advent is a season of waiting and of fervent longing for the Redeemer : " Drop down dew, ye heavens, and let the clouds rain the Just One! " *(ibid.)*.

2. In today's Epistle *(Rom* 13,11-14), St. Paul exhorts us, " Brethren, it is now the hour...to rise from sleep. " During Advent, the " springtime " of the Church, we must

3

arouse ourselves and bring forth new fruits of sanctity.
Even now, the Apostle shows us the great fruits of Advent :
" Let us therefore cast off the works of darkness and put
on the armor of light...put ye on the Lord Jesus Christ. "
If we have been somewhat drowsy and languid in Our
Lord's service, now is the time to arouse ourselves to a new
life, to strip ourselves generously of our meanness and
weakness, and to " put on Jesus Christ, " that is, His holiness.
In order to help us attain this end, Jesus encourages us by
reminding us of His love in coming as our Redeemer : He
comes to meet us with His grace; it is infinite mercy that
inclines to us.

On the other hand, the Church, in today's Gospel
(*Lk* 21,25-33), puts before us the last coming of Jesus as
supreme Judge, " and then they shall see the Son of Man
coming in a cloud, with great power and majesty. " He came
with love to Bethlehem; He comes with grace into our souls;
He will come with justice at the end of the world : Christ's
triple coming, the synthesis of Christianity, an invitation
to a vigilant, trusting expectation, " Lift up your heads, for
your redemption is at hand! "

COLLOQUY

O my God, Word of the Father, Word made flesh for
love of us, You assumed a mortal body in order to suffer
and be immolated for us. I wish to prepare for Your coming
with the burning desires of the prophets and the just who in
the Old Testament sighed after You, the one Savior and
Redeemer. " O Lord, send Him whom You are going
to send.... As You have promised, come and deliver us! "
I want to keep Advent in my soul, that is, a continual longing
and waiting for this great Mystery wherein You, O Word,
became flesh to show me the abyss of Your redeeming,
sanctifying mercy.

O sweetest Jesus, You come to me with Your infinite
love and the abundance of Your grace; You desire to engulf
my soul in torrents of mercy and charity in order to draw
it to You. Come, O Lord, come! I, too, wish to run to
You with love, but alas! my love is so limited, weak, and
imperfect! Make it strong and generous; enable me to
overcome myself, so that I can give myself entirely to You.

Yes, my love can become strong because " its foundation is the intimate certainty that it will be repaid by the love of God. O Lord, I cannot doubt Your tenderness, because You have given me proofs of it in so many ways, with the sole purpose of convincing me of it. Therefore, trusting in Your love, my weak love will become strong with Your strength. What a consolation it will be, O Lord, at the moment of death to think that we shall be judged by Him whom we have loved above all things! Then we can enter Your presence with confidence, despite the weight of our offenses! " (T.J. *Way*, 40).

O Lord, give me love like this! I desire it ardently, not only to escape Your stern eye at Judgment, but especially in order to repay You in some degree for Your infinite charity.

O Lord, do not, I beseech You, permit that this exceeding great love which led You to become incarnate for my salvation, be given in vain! My poor soul needs You so much! It sighs for You as for a compassionate physician, who alone can heal its wounds, draw it out of its languor and tepidity, and infuse into it new vigor, new enthusiasm, new life. Come, Lord, come! I am ready to welcome Your work with a docile, humble heart, ready to let myself be healed, purified, and strengthened by You. Yes, with Your help, I will make any sacrifice, renounce everything that might hinder Your redeeming work in me. Show Your power, O Lord, and come! Come, delay no longer!

2

INVITATION TO SANCTITY

PRESENCE OF GOD - I place myself in the presence of Jesus in the Most Blessed Sacrament, contemplating Him as the Redeemer and Sanctifier of my soul.

MEDITATION

1. " Where sin abounded, grace did more abound " (*Rom* 5,20). Adam's fall brought about the destruction of God's plan for man's sanctification. Our first parents,

created to the image and likeness of God, in a state of grace
and justice, and raised to the dignity of children of God,
were hurled into an abyss of misery, drawing with them the
whole human race. For centuries man groaned in his sin,
he could no longer call God by the sweet name of Father,
he did not even dare to pronounce His name, regarding the
Most High with a sense of terror : " He is a powerful and
terrible God, the God of justice and vengeance. " Sin made
an insurmountable abyss between man and God, and man
groaned in the depths of the abyss, utterly incapable of
rising from it.

To do what man could not do, to destroy sin and
restore divine sonship to the human race, a Savior was
promised. The most merciful God, " so loved the world,
as to give His only-begotten Son " (*Jn* 3,16) for its salvation.
The Word, the splendor of the Father, and the figure of His
substance became flesh in order to destroy sin and restore
grace to us, that " we might once again be called, and really
be the children of God " (cf. 1 *Jn* 3,1).

God wants us " all to be saved "; for this reason He gave
us His Son, and with Him and through Him, all the means
necessary for our salvation. Therefore, if a soul is not
saved, it alone will be responsible.

2. Jesus was not satisfied with destroying sin and meriting
only a sufficient amount of grace for our salvation. He did
much more and He Himself declared it, " I am come that
they may have life, and may have it more abundantly "
(*Jn* 10,10). This plenitude of life is the plenitude of grace,
the supernatural life which causes sanctity to blossom.

Sanctity is not reserved for a few; Jesus, by His Incarnation and by His death on the Cross, merited the means of
salvation and sanctification for all who believe in Him.
He, the All-holy, came to sanctify us, and has taught us,
" Be you therefore perfect, as also Your heavenly Father
is perfect " (*Mt* 5,48).

Jesus did not give this precept to a chosen group of
persons, nor did He reserve it for His Apostles and close
friends; He proclaimed it to the multitude who were following
Him. St. Paul received His message and announced it to
the Gentiles, " This is the will of God, your sanctification "
(1 *Thes* 4,3). And in our times the Church, speaking through
the great Pope Pius XI, has repeated it strongly and on many

occasions to the modern world : " Christ has called the whole human race to the lofty heights of sanctity.... There are some who say that sanctity is not everyone's vocation; on the contrary, it is everyone's vocation, and all are called to it.... Jesus Christ has given Himself as an example for all to imitate. " And elsewhere : " Let no one believe that sanctity belongs to a few chosen people, while the rest of humanity can limit itself to a lesser degree of virtue. Everyone is included in this law; no one is exempt from it. "

Jesus comes not only to save me, but to sanctify me. He is calling me to sanctity and has merited for me all the graces I need to attain it.

COLLOQUY

" It grieves me, my God, that I should be so wicked and that I am able to do so little in Your service. I well know that it is my own fault that You have not granted me the favors which You gave to those who went before me.... I grieve over my life, Lord, when I compare it with theirs; and I cannot say this without weeping. When I meditate, my God, upon the glory which You have prepared for those who persevere in doing Your will, and when I think how many trials and pains it cost Your Son to gain it for us, and how little we have deserved it, and how bound we are not to be ungrateful for this wondrous love which has taught us love at such a cost to itself, my soul becomes greatly afflicted. How is it possible, Lord, that all this should be forgotten, and that, when they offend You, mortal men should be so forgetful of You? O my Redeemer, how forgetful are men! They are forgetful even of themselves. And how great is Your goodness that You should remember us when we have fallen and have tried to strike You a mortal blow, and that You forget what we have done and give us Your hand again and awaken us from our incurable madness so that we seek and beg You for salvation. Blessed be such a Lord, blessed be such great mercy and praised be He forever for His merciful pity! O my soul, bless forever so great a God! How can a soul turn against Him? " (T.J. *F*, 4 – *Exc*, 3).

O Lord, although I know how much this poor soul of mine has cost You, yet how often have I offended You,

resisted Your grace, been unfaithful to Your love, and deaf
to Your invitation to a more perfect life, to sanctity.

You, my God, have given everything, You have given
Yourself entirely for me; therefore, it is not seeking too much
in return to ask me to give myself entirely to You, to give
You everything in order to match Your love for me. Yes,
I know that You are not satisfied with my thinking only of
saving my soul, just as You were not satisfied to acquire for
me only the means necessary for my salvation, but willed
also to acquire the means necessary for my sanctification.
You have already purchased and paid for all of them;
therefore, if I do not become a saint, it is entirely my own fault.

But, O Lord, how can a soul as weak and miserable
as mine, one so full of faults, selfishness and meanness aspire
to an ideal as high as that of sanctity? Oh yes, my pretensions
would certainly be the greatest temerity if You Yourself
had not shown me that this is exactly what You will. You
have even given me a precious commandment concerning
it, " Be you therefore perfect as also Your heavenly Father
is perfect " (*Mt* 5,48).

I beseech You, O Lord, repeat this sublime invitation
to my poor soul, pressingly, compellingly, so that held by
this ideal, it may be urged to greater generosity, stronger
resolutions, and more complete confidence in Your merciful
work of redemption and sanctification.

3

SANCTITY AND THE PLENITUDE OF GRACE

PRESENCE OF GOD - I draw near to Jesus, the " fountain of life and
holiness, " with an ardent desire to drink from this inexhaustible
fount.

MEDITATION

I. If Jesus came to sanctify all, if it is God's will
that " all should be saints, " then sanctity cannot consist in
extraordinary gifts of nature and grace, which depend solely
upon God's liberality.

Sanctity, therefore, must consist in something that all souls of good will, even the simplest and most humble, can attain, sustained by the divine assistance. Sanctity is the perfection of the Christian life. It is the full development in us of the supernatural life, whose beginnings are sanctifying grace, the infused virtues, and the gifts of the Holy Spirit.

Baptism has deposited within us this seed of sanctity, which is grace, a seed capable of blossoming into precious fruits of supernatural and eternal life for the soul which zealously cultivates it.

By elevating us to the supernatural state, grace makes us capable of entering into relations with the Blessed Trinity, that is, capable of knowing and loving God as He is in Himself, as He knows and loves Himself. Grace, therefore, engenders and nourishes a new life of knowledge and love in us, a life which is a participation in the divine life. What could be holier or more sanctifying than these intimate relations with the Blessed Trinity? Such are the lofty heights to which grace raises us, and this gift is bestowed on all who have been baptized.

2. This supernatural life, proceeding from grace, must permeate our entire human life in such a way that the latter will be supernaturalized in all its activities, in every detail, as well as in its totality. As grace grows and flourishes in our soul, its influence becomes deeper and wider; and when this influence extends effectively to all our actions, directing them solely to God's glory and uniting us wholly to Him by means of charity, then we have reached the fullness of Christian life, sanctity.

Grace is a wholly gratuitous gift bestowed on us by God through the infinite merits of Jesus. He merited it for us by His death on the Cross, and not in a limited measure, but superabundantly. St. John says that He is " full of grace... and of His fullness we all have received, and grace for grace " (*Jn* 1,14.16). Hence, we can all become saints.

This does not mean, however, that we are all called to the same degree and kind of sanctity. Besides those we call the " great " saints, those who had a special mission to accomplish and therefore received singular gifts of nature and grace, there have always been the humble, hidden saints, who were sanctified in obscurity and silence.

Sanctity does not consist in the greatness of the works accomplished or of the gifts received, but in the degree of sanctifying grace and charity to which the soul has attained by faithful correspondence with God's invitations. I, too, can aspire to this kind of sanctity with no fear of rashness or self-deception.

COLLOQUY

O my sweet Savior, it was not only for certain privileged souls, but also for me, that You willed to merit the fullness of the life of grace which is sanctity. I understand that the infinite love which made You become incarnate for us and become one of us, which made You who are God, suffer death on the Cross and shed Your precious Blood for us, is more than sufficient to merit not only the salvation, but even the sanctification of the whole human race.

Why then are there so few who really become saints? Why am I so backward on the way of sanctity, I who, because I have received from You not only the gift of holy Baptism, but also that of so many confessions and Holy Communions, should already have greatly increased my treasure of grace; I who have received so many actual graces, inspirations, and invitations, and have been called by Your infinite love to a state of consecrated life?

O my Lord, make me understand it well : You created me without any help from me, but You will not save me, You will not sanctify me, without my help. You have already merited all that serves for my sanctification; Your gifts are unnumbered, but I shall not become a saint unless I cooperate with You.

You alone are holy and You alone can make me holy, and yet You demand my full cooperation to such a degree that, if I refuse it, You will not make me a saint, despite Your omnipotence and infinite love.

O Jesus, by my sloth, my scanty love, my coldness, I can nullify all Your merits, all the Blood which You shed on the Cross. How could a miserable creature who owes everything to his God, be so bold as to oppose and hinder His action in his soul? Shall I, a little worm, have the audacity to do this? O Lord, never allow me to act thus; pursue me with Your grace until I give myself entirely to You.

To prove to You that I am sincere, I intend, with Your help, to be generous, to overcome myself in the things which cost me most, and to say " yes " to You, even when it is most repugnant to my evil nature. Help me with Your all-powerful aid, assist and sustain my poor efforts, for You know that I am weakness itself. Grant, O Lord, that I may drink from the fountain of living water which has its source in You, the fountain of life and grace, of strength and holiness, so that when my thirst is quenched, I can once again continue with fresh ardor along the way You point out to me.

4

CHARITY THE ESSENCE OF SANCTITY

PRESENCE OF GOD - I place myself in the presence of God, considering that He is infinite charity : " Deus caritas est, " God is charity.

MEDITATION

1. " Be you therefore perfect, as also Your heavenly Father is perfect " (*Mt* 5,48). Before we can begin to imitate God, we must know who He is, and in what His perfection consists. Holy Scripture tells us, *God is charity* (1 *Jn* 4,16). It does not say, " in God there is charity, " but " God *is* charity, " that is, everything in God is love, God is essentially love. Now love, even human love, is a desire for what is good; to love is to desire the good of another; it is the act by which the will is drawn toward the good. In God, the infinite Being, love is an infinite will for good, and is directed toward infinite good, the divine essence which God possesses and in which He delights. This love, which is God, is therefore an infinite, complacent love of His own infinite goodness. Yet His embrace extends even to the creatures whom He creates, to communicate to them His own goodness and happiness. Infinite charity, which is God, turns therefore to creatures, bringing them into existence by an act of love which does not stop at the limited good they possess, but brings them back to the infinite good,

the Trinity. In other words, God creates and loves them for His own glory.

We, poor creatures, are called to share in this sublime life of love which is God, and grace has been given us for this express purpose. St. Paul exhorts us, " Be ye, therefore, followers of God, as most dear children, and walk in love " (*Eph* 5,1.2).

If we are to imitate God, our supernatural life must be essentially love, that is, a love of benevolence for God and a will directed toward good, loving that infinite good which He is, and loving all creatures for Him and in Him.

2. Charity is so essential in the supernatural life that on its presence or absence depends the Christian's state of life or death. He who does not possess charity, does not possess sanctifying grace either, because they are absolutely inseparable, " He that loveth not, abideth in death " (1 *Jn* 3,14). On the other hand, he who possesses charity, also possesses grace and shares in the life of God. " He that abideth in charity, abideth in God, and God in him " (*ibid.* 4,16), and according to St. Thomas, " Charity... unites man with God so that he no longer lives for himself but for God " (IIª IIªe, q.17, a.6, ad 3).

The three theological virtues, faith, hope, and charity, are infused into the soul together with sanctifying grace. God is the object of all three, but " the greatest of these is charity " (1 *Cor* 13,13). It is the greatest, because without charity there can be no Christian life; the greatest, because it will never end. Further, it is the unitive force which binds us to God and is a participation in that infinite charity which is God Himself. In fact, to the Pharisee who asked which was the greatest commandment of the law, Jesus answered, " Thou shalt love the Lord thy God with thy whole heart, and with thy whole soul, and with thy whole mind. This is the greatest and the first commandment " (*Mt* 22,37.38).

When our charity is perfect, it will keep us completely united to God and will direct all our activity to Him. Hence, in the measure that a soul is dominated by charity, it is mature in the supernatural life, and is holy, to a greater or lesser degree.

COLLOQUY

O my God, make me understand, even in a small degree, Your infinite charity. You are all charity and everything in you is charity. Charity is Your Being, Your Essence, Your Life. You are that sovereign charity by which You love Yourself *ab aeterno*, from all eternity, and take pleasure in Yourself. O Father, You love the Word, the figure of Your substance. O Word, You love the Father from whom you proceed. This reciprocal charity by which You, O God, love Yourself is so perfect that it constitutes a Person, the third Person of the Most Holy Trinity, the Holy Spirit.

" O my soul, reflect on the great delight and the great love which the Father has in knowing His Son and the Son in knowing His Father and the ardor with which the Holy Spirit unites with Them, and how none of These can cease from this love and knowledge since They are One and the same. These sovereign Persons know each other, love each other and delight in each other. What need, then, have They of my love? Why do You seek it, my God, or what do You gain by it? " (T. J. *Exc*, 7)

Yet, O Most Holy Trinity, You who are all—because You are infinite charity and enjoy from all eternity the reciprocal love of Your divine Persons—have willed, in time, to diffuse Your love, and to communicate Your infinite good to us Your creatures. By an act of Your love You brought us out of nothing; Your love is our first principle, the first principle of all things. Everything receives life from it; it is the cause of our existence and we, like little fishes, swim and live in the ocean of Your infinite love.

But, Lord, of what use can we, poor creatures, be to You, who possess within Yourself all love, all felicity, all glory? I understand : You have created us to share with us Your infinite goodness, to bring us back to the bosom of the infinite charity which is You Yourself, from whom we have received life. You have created us for the glory of the Most Holy Trinity, to communicate to us Your life of infinite love and to give us a part in it.

" O my God and my mercy! What shall I do, so as not to destroy the effect of the wonders which You deign to work in me? O Lord, how smooth are Your paths! Yet who will walk them without fear? I fear to live without serving You, yet when I set out to serve You I find no way of doing so that satisfies me or can pay any part of what I owe. I feel that I would gladly spend myself wholly in Your service, and yet when I consider my wretchedness, I realize that I can do nothing good unless You help me " (T.J. *Exc*, 1).

Without Your help, indeed, how can I obtain a treasure as precious as charity? O my God, if You want my whole life to be one of charity, it is absolutely necessary that You, charity itself, come to transform my poor soul. My faults —selfishness, pride, sensuality, coldness, avarice, sloth—all are obstacles to Your charity which should triumph in me. Give me grace to remove these obstacles with generosity, so that Your infinite charity may take entire possession of my nothingness.

5

SANCTITY AND GOD'S WILL

PRESENCE OF GOD - I place myself in the presence of Jesus in the Eucharist, asking Him to penetrate my soul with His words, " He that doth the will of My Father who is in heaven, he shall enter into the kingdom of heaven " (*Mt* 7,21).

MEDITATION

1. The path which leads to sanctity, that is, to God, can be marked out only by God Himself, by *His will*. Jesus expressed this very strongly when He said, " Not everyone that saith to Me, Lord, Lord, shall enter into the kingdom of heaven, but he that doth the will of My Father who is in heaven, he shall enter into the kingdom of heaven " (*Mt* 7,21). And to show that the souls who are most closely united to Him, the ones He loves most, are precisely those who do the will of God, He does not hesitate to say : " Whosoever shall do the will of My Father, that is in heaven, he is my brother, and sister, and mother " (*ibid.* 12,50).

The saints learned in the school of Jesus. St. Teresa of Avila, after having received the most sublime mystical communications, did not hesitate to declare, " The highest perfection consists not in interior favors, or in great raptures, or in visions, or in the spirit of prophesy, but in the bringing of our wills so closely into conformity with the will of God that, as soon as we realize He wills anything, we desire it ourselves with all our might, and take the bitter with the sweet " (*F*, 5). St. Thérèse of the Child Jesus echoes this statement, " The more joyfully [souls] do His will, the greater is their perfection " (*St*, 1).

True love of God consists in adhering perfectly to His holy will, not desiring to do or be other than what God indicates for each of us, to the point of becoming, as it were, " a living will of God. " Seen in this light, sanctity is possible for every soul of good will; it is not impossible that a soul which leads a humble, hidden life, may adhere to the divine will as well and perhaps even better than a " great " saint who has received from God an exterior mission and has been enriched with mystical graces. The perfection of a soul may be measured by the degree to which it does the will of God, and finds its happiness in doing it.

2. To become saints we must have total conformity of our will with God's. It is necessary, then, that there should be nothing in our soul which is not in harmony with the divine will, and that our actions be motivated by His will alone. " Divine union consists in the soul's total transformation, according to the *will*, in the will of God, so that there may be naught in the soul that is contrary to the will of God, but that, in all and through all, its movement may be that of the will of God alone " (J.C. *AS I*, 11,2).

In all our actions we are always impelled by love, love of ourselves, love of creatures, or love of God. As long as the soul clings to the least thing contrary to God's will, that is, to some irregular attachment to self or creatures, it will often act, not under the impulse of God's love, but through a desire for personal satisfaction, or because of a disordered love of creatures, and therefore, will walk apart from God's will. Sin is not the only thing which is opposed to God's will; even the slightest imperfection or deliberate attachment prevents the soul from acting under the motion of God's will alone.

But when the soul no longer has any attachments, and is entirely free from love of self and of creatures, it can adhere to God alone, acting only according to His will,

and living moment by moment according to His good
pleasure. The soul thus transformed has lost its will in the
will of God and therefore is perfectly united to God Himself.
This is the essence and the apex of sanctity.

COLLOQUY

O my God, You make me understand that the only
thing necessary is Your holy will, that it is my one and only
treasure. In this life, what can be more beautiful, more safe,
more perfect and more holy than to do Your will? You have
given me free will; to what better use can I put it than to
make it adhere to Your divine will? If I should perform
great works and carry out marvelous undertakings which
are not fully in accordance with Your will, they would have
no value for eternity and would therefore be destined to
perish; whereas the slightest works done according to Your
will have an eternal value.

O Lord, I know that I am nothing, I acknowledge the
weakness of my poor will which now turns to one good,
now to another, and considers as good what is really imperfection, fault, sin. But Your will is indefectible; You can
desire nothing but the true, sovereign good; hence, You
desire only my good, my salvation, my sanctification.
Nothing, then, can be more advantageous to me than to
consecrate my will to Yours, O my God.

" At this moment, O Lord, I freely consecrate my will
to You without reserve.... Grant that Your will may
always be fulfilled in me, in the way which is most pleasing
to You. If You wish me to do this by means of trials, give
me strength and let them come. If by means of persecutions
and sickness and dishonor and need, here I am, my Father,
I shall not turn my face away " (T.J. *Way*, 32).

So many times I have made You the offering of my will,
consecrating it to You and declaring that I wanted nothing
but Your divine will. But an equal number of times, alas,
I have taken back my offering, and in my actions, labors,
and apostolic works; instead of allowing myself to be guided
by You, I have been led more or less by pride and personal
satisfaction. How far I am, O Lord, from losing my will
in Yours! How attached I still am to my own ideas and
tastes! How many things still remain in me which are

contrary to Your will! Give me light to recognize them, and strength to free myself from them! I confess that every time I draw away from Your will, even if only in little things, to act according to my own will, I feel remorse, and a lessening of peace in my soul. Only in Your will is my good, my peace, my salvation, my sanctification.

O Lord, hear my poor prayer : once more I offer You my will; take it, keep it a prisoner, so that I shall never be able to withdraw my offering.

With St. Thérèse of the Child Jesus, I repeat, " My God...I will not be a saint by halves, I am not afraid of suffering for You. One thing only do I fear, and that is to follow my own will. Accept, then, the offering I make of it, for I choose *all* that You will " (T.C.J. *St*, 1).

6

SANCTITY AND MY DUTIES

PRESENCE OF GOD - I place myself in the presence of God, ardently beseeching Him to help me know and fulfill His holy will.

MEDITATION

1. Jesus has said, " If you love Me, keep My commandments.... If you keep My commandments, you shall abide in My love; as I also have kept My Father's commandments, and do abide in His love " (*Jn* 14,15 – 15,10).

The perfection of charity consists in the perfect conformity of our wills with the divine will; this divine will is expressed, first of all, in the commandments of God and the precepts of the Church. Moreover, it is expressed in a more concrete and detailed way in the duties of my state and the various circumstances of life. The *duties of my state* determine particularly how I must act in daily life, so as to be always in conformity with the divine will : if I am a religious, these duties are set forth in my Rule, the customs of my Institute, the commands of my superiors, and the tasks imposed by obedience. If I am a priest, my duty is the care of souls; if I am a lay person, my duties are those required by my family life, my profession or occupation, my social activities and by good citizenship.

God's will is also marked out for me by the *circumstances of my life*, whether important or not, down to the smallest detail, health or sickness, poverty or wealth, aridity or interior consolation, success or failure, misfortunes, losses, and struggles. From time to time, God asks me to fulfill special tasks of charity, patience, activity, or renouncement, detachment, submission, generosity, sacrifice. But everything is permitted by God, all is ordered by Him for my sanctification, " To them that love God, all things work together unto good " (*Rom* 8,28); " everything is a grace! " (T.C.J. *NV*).

2. " Sanctity properly consists only in conformity to God's will, expressed in a constant and exact fulfillment of the duties of our state in life " (Benedict XV). This statement confirms my knowledge that sanctity does not consist in doing extraordinary things, but is *essentially* reduced to the *fulfillment of duty;* therefore, it is possible for me.

For this reason I must be punctual and persevering in the fulfillment of my duties : *punctual*, that is, diligent, being careful to please God in all my actions, in order to do His holy, sanctifying will. Hence, I must accustom myself to see the expression of God's will in every one of my duties, for then everything I do will be an opportunity to submerge myself in God's love and to unite myself to Him; *persevering*, that is, fulfilling my duties faithfully, not only when I feel great fervor, but also when I am sad, tired, or in aridity; constancy calls for generosity. " It takes uncommon virtue to fulfill with exactitude, that is, without carelessness, negligence, or indolence... but with attention, piety, and spiritual fervor, the whole combination of ordinary duties which make up our daily life! " (Pius XI).

This untiring, generous fidelity will not always be easy; however, I must not become discouraged by my failures, but begin again every day, fully confident that some day, God will make my poor efforts fruitful.

COLLOQUY

O my God, in spite of my unworthiness, I have a fervent longing to become a saint. I desire this not for my own satisfaction, nor to obtain the esteem and praise of others, but solely because You desire it; for You have said : " Be ye holy, because I am holy " (*Lev* 19,2). My one aim is to conform entirely to Your will and Your desire, to please You, to give You glory, to correspond to Your infinite love, to give You all the love You expect of me and of which I am capable. You teach me more and more clearly that sanctity does not demand of me great exterior works, but only a strong, generous love which will lead me to fulfill Your holy will perfectly.

O my God, when I consider that You, the Creator and Lord of the universe, have deigned to make known Your will to me, who in comparison with You, am less than a little worm, I am filled with confusion. A King so great and so powerful speaks to the least of His servants with the goodness with which He would speak to a beloved son! Yes, O my God, You speak to me thus, and manifest Your will by Your commandments, the duties of my state, and all the circumstances of my life. Everything that surrounds me—every incident, event, sorrow and joy—all express Your will and tell me at every moment what You desire of me.

O my God, how I wish I had that profound spirit of faith to help me recognize each circumstance of my life as a messenger of Your divine will!

Yes, even at difficult moments and in painful experiences, it is You who come to me and ask a special act of charity, patience, sweetness, humility, or self-sacrifice. O my God, how this changes my point of view! Creatures, circumstances, causes, and human motives, all disappear, and I see only You and Your holy will, which always envelops me and urges me to greater generosity. Seen in this light, even the duties that are hardest and most repugnant to human nature, the " terrible daily duties, " become sweet and lovable, everything seems easy and agreeable. All I have to do at every moment and under all circumstances is to say a generous " Yes " to Your sweet, lovable will.

I beseech You, O Lord, give me the fidelity I need to persevere with humility and constancy in this path of continual adherence to Your will. With Your help, I will make this practice the center of my interior life.

O my God, shall I ever fall again? Yes, for I am frailty itself; but I know that You will be even more eager to help me rise again than I shall be prone to fall. My firm resolution and my perseverance will be to " begin again " every day, every instant, humbling myself profoundly for my weakness, but having utter confidence in Your will to sanctify my soul.

7

THE MOUNT OF PERFECTION

PRESENCE OF GOD - " Who shall ascend into the mountain of the Lord? " (Ps 23,3). I beg my God to permit me to approach the holy mountain on which He dwells, where His honor and glory alone reign.

MEDITATION

1. St. John of the Cross has left us a drawing which sums up, expresses in synthesis the whole spiritual life. It is the outline of a mountain whose summit, symbolized by a circle, represents the state of perfection. The ascent is symbolized by three paths, all leading toward the summit, but only one of them, the narrowest, reaches it. This is the way of the " nothing " (nada), the way of total abnegation. It leads directly to the summit of the mount, where there is an inscription : " Only the honor and glory of God remain. "

The soul arrives at this supreme height, when dominated by perfect charity, it adheres totally to the divine will, and moved by that divine will alone, tends solely to the glory of the Most Holy Trinity. On the periphery of the circle are the words : " And here there is no way, as for the just man there is no law... " In fact, the soul which is completely dominated by the love of God no longer needs the stimulus of an external law obliging it to keep on the right road; God's

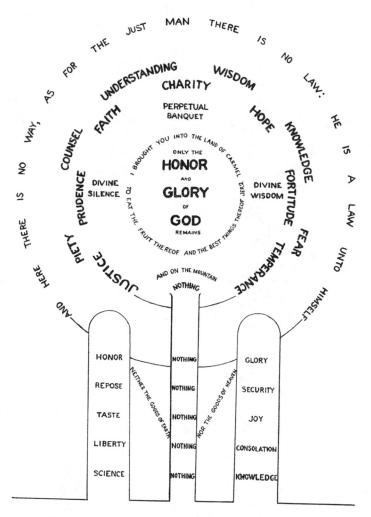

GRAPH OF THE MOUNT OF PERFECTION
OF ST. JOHN OF THE CROSS

will has become the one " principle of activity " which moves and directs it in all its actions. This is why the Saint says that, in this state, the two wills—the will of God and the will of the soul—have become one, and this one will is the divine will which has now become the will of the soul, which, losing itself in this divine will, has abandoned all other choice.

All the infused virtues, together with the gifts and fruits of the Holy Spirit, flourish abundantly in this soul, making it enjoy intimacy with God in a " perpetual banquet, divine silence, and divine wisdom. "

Thus, by following the rugged path of the " nada " (nothing) the soul reaches the immense " All " of God, its only treasure, in which it loses itself.

2. The only road that can bring us to the summit of perfection is the rugged path of " nothing " which leaves aside the two easy roads of the " imperfect spirit "; these end half-way up the mountain and go no farther. The imperfect spirit is one that is " attached " to the things of earth, or even to spiritual goods, using these goods in a disordered way and with a view to personal satisfation.

In order to leave the " road of the imperfect spirit, " we must no longer love anything, unless it be in perfect conformity with God's will. In fact, every object which we love for itself and not according to God's will, becomes for us a source of preoccupation, desires, distress, and anxiety; it moves our hearts and makes us act only for our own satisfaction. In a soul attached to created things, how many principles of action there are which are not conformable to God's will! Such a soul finds itself on these " paths of the imperfect, " which will never take it to the goal. This is why next to them is written : " Neither the goods of earth, nor the goods of heaven "; therefore *nothing*. A few lines inscribed at the foot of the mountain stress this fundamental idea : " In order to enjoy, know, possess, and be *everything*, desire to enjoy, know, possess, and be *nothing*. You must continue on the way without *enjoying*, without *knowing*, without *possessing*, you must follow the path on which you are nothing. " It is the arid, desolate path of the purification of the senses and of the spirit, the path which reduces the soul to nothing in order to prepare it for meeting God, for the " all " of perfect conformity of its will to His.

COLLOQUY

O my God, behold me at the foot of the sublime mountain of perfection! How shall I be able to follow such a long, rugged road?

To encourage my faintheartedness, I must consider that Your beloved Son came down to earth expressly to show us the one way that leads to You, and to walk before us on that way. He said, " If any man will come after Me, let him deny himself, and take up his cross, and follow Me " (*Mt* 16,24). Does this not mean the path of the *nothing?* When He said, " Be you therefore perfect, as also your heavenly Father is perfect " (*ibid.* 5,48), was He not inviting me too, to attain that high perfection in which only God's honor and glory are sought?

If You, O Lord, call me to sanctity, You are ready to provide me with the graces necessary to reach it. Your divine assistance always goes before me and gently urges me on. With You, even the most difficult things become easy and pleasant.

" O my God, how abundantly do You manifest Your power! There is no need to seek reasons for what You will, for You transcend all natural reason and make all things possible, thus showing clearly that we have only to love You truly, and truly to forsake everything for You, and You, my Lord, will make everything easy.

" It is well said with regard to this, that ' You feign labor in Your law '; for I do not see, Lord, and I do not know how the road that leads to You can be narrow. To me it seems a royal road, not a pathway; a road upon which anyone who sets out in earnest will travel securely. Mountain passes and rocks that might fall upon him—I mean occasions of sin—are far distant.... He who truly loves You, my God, travels by a broad and royal road and travels securely. It is far away from any precipice, and hardly has such a man stumbled in the slightest degree when You, Lord, give him Your hand. One fall—and even many falls, if he loves You and not the things of the world—will not be enough to lead him to perdition : he will be traveling along the valley of humility. I cannot understand why it is that people are afraid to set out upon the way of perfection.... Our eyes must be fixed upon You, and we must not be afraid that You, the Sun of Justice, will set, or that You will allow us to travel by night, and so be lost, unless we first forsake You.

" People are not afraid to walk among lions, each of which seems to be trying to tear them to pieces – I mean among honors, delights, and pleasures of that kind...but when it is a question of virtue, the devil frightens us with scarecrows!... How sad this makes me! Fain would I weep ten thousand times!... You, whose goodness is all powerful, open my eyes and never let them become blind again. Amen " (T.J. *Life*, 35).

8

THE LORD WILL NOT DELAY

SECOND SUNDAY OF ADVENT

PRESENCE OF GOD - I place myself in the presence of Jesus in the Blessed Sacrament, to receive His two-fold invitation to confidence and repentance, contained in today's liturgy.

MEDITATION

1. After we have considered the sublime program of sanctification which we should follow, it is very consoling to consider the magnificent texts of today's liturgy. They invite us to have complete trust in God's help. " Thy salvation cometh quickly : why art thou wasted with sorrow?... I will save thee and deliver thee, fear not.... As a mother comforteth her sons, so will I comfort thee, saith the Lord " *(RB)*. God does not want anxiety or discouragement. If He proposes to us an exalted way of sanctity, He does not leave us alone, but comes to help and sustain us.

Today's Mass shows clearly how Jesus comes not only for the people of Israel, for a small number of the elect, but also for the Gentiles, for all men. " Behold the Lord shall come to save the nations " *(Introit)*, Therefore, let us have confidence and rejoice, as St. Paul exhorts us : " Now

may the God of hope fill you with all joy and peace in
believing that you may abound in hope " (*Ep : Rom* 15,4-13).
And in order to stimulate our hope in Christ, the Gospel
(*Mt* 11,2-10) presents His wonderful works : " The blind see,
the lame walk, lepers are cured, the deaf hear, the dead rise
again, the poor have the gospel preached to them. "

There is no physical or moral misery which Jesus cannot
cure. He asks only that we go to Him with a heart dilated
by faith, and with complete trust in His all-powerful, merciful
love.

2. In today's Gospel Jesus directs our attention to the
strong, austere figure of John the Baptist. " What went you
out to see? A reed shaken by the wind?... A man clothed
in soft garments? "

If we want to prepare our hearts for Jesus' coming,
we, like St. John the Baptist, must detach ourselves from all
the goods of earth. John had left everything and gone into
the desert to lead a life of penance. His example invites us
to retire into the interior desert of our heart, far from creatures,
to await the coming of Jesus in deep recollection, silence, and
solitude, insofar as the duties of our state in life permit.
We must persevere in this waiting, in spite of aridity and
discouragement. " The Lord shall appear and shall not
deceive us : *if He make any delay, wait for Him*, for He will
come and will not tarry " *(RB)*.

To our interior recollection, let us add a greater spirit
of penance and mortification. Let us examine our generosity
in practicing the penances and mortifications prescribed by
our Rule, and those which we have imposed upon ourselves
with the approval of our confessor or superior. If we discover
that we are lax in this regard, it would be well to resolve to
do something more : some mortification at meals, in our
rest, or in our clothing, some work that is hard or painful
to nature.

If we wish to taste the sweet joys of Christmas, we
should know how to prepare ourselves with these dispositions
which the Church invites us to pray for today : " We beseech
You, O Lord, to teach us...to despise the things of earth
and to love those of heaven " *(RM)*.

COLLOQUY

O my Savior, Word of God, how can I doubt that You are coming upon earth to save and sanctify me? Why do I not go to You with complete, loving confidence, when You have spared nothing to show me Your infinitely merciful love? Your Incarnation, Your infant tears, Your humble, hidden life, Your apostolate, Your miracles, Your sorrowful Passion and death, all Your precious Blood poured out, shall they not be enough to make me believe in Your love, to open my heart in the most complete confidence?

" I repeat with all confidence the humble prayer of the publican. Most of all do I imitate the behavior of Magdalen, for her amazing—rather I should say her loving—audacity, which delighted Your heart. . . . I am certain that even if I had on my conscience every imaginable crime, I should lose nothing of my confidence, but would throw myself, my heart broken with sorrow, into Your arms, for I remember Your love for the prodigal son who returns to You " (T.C.J. *St*, 12).

With this confidence, O my Jesus, I will resume my way and begin again my poor efforts.

During this Advent You invite me to greater recollection, to greater interior and exterior silence, so that I may be able to hear Your voice and prepare for Your coming. Help me, then, to quiet my continual chatter about useless things, the discordant voices of nature, self-love, sensitiveness, the distracting prattle of my fantasies, imaginations, thoughts and useless preoccupations.

I acknowledge that often my mind and heart are like a raging sea in which the waves thunder continually; and yet, if You wish, a sign from You will be enough to make calm return and all be silent.

Yes, You teach me that interior silence exacts detachment from self and from creatures, exacts interior and exterior mortification. For love of You I will mortify my curiosity, curiosity of my eyes, ears, thoughts, and imagination. I also want to silence my passions and, therefore, I resolve to be more generous in the practice of corporal mortification.

O eternal Word, my Savior, draw all my powers to Yourself; fasten my interior gaze upon Yourself, so that I shall no longer seek or hear anything or anyone but You alone, eternal Word of my eternal God!

9

THE IMMACULATE CONCEPTION
OF THE BLESSED VIRGIN MARY

DECEMBER EIGHTH

PRESENCE OF GOD - I place myself in the presence of Mary Immaculate, my loving Mother, and listen to her invitation : " Come over to me all you who desire me, and I will declare to you what great things God has done for my soul " (*RB*).

MEDITATION

1. The Feast of the Immaculate Conception is in perfect harmony with the spirit of Advent; while the soul is preparing for the coming of the Redeemer, it is fitting to think of her, the all-pure one, who was His Mother.

The very promise of a Savior was joined to, or rather, was included in the promise of this peerless Virgin. After having cursed the insidious serpent, God proclaimed : " I will put enmities between thee and the woman, and thy seed and her seed : she shall crush thy head " (*Gen* 3,15). And behold, the Virgin whose coming was foretold, approaches, " white as snow, more beautiful than the sun, full of grace, and blessed above all women " *(RB)*.

Precisely in view of the sublime privilege which would make her the Mother of the Incarnate Word, Mary alone, among all creatures, was preserved from original sin. Yet in Mary Immaculate we see not only her preservation from original sin, and the complete absence of the slightest shadow of an imperfection, but we also see the positive side of this mystery which made her, from the very first moment of her existence, " full of grace. "

Theologians teach that the Most Blessed Virgin Mary began her spiritual life with grace much more abundant and perfect than that which the greatest saints have acquired at the end of their lives. When we consider also that during her whole life, the Blessed Virgin corresponded fully and most perfectly to every movement of grace, to every invitation from God, we can understand how charity and grace increased in her with incessant and most rapid progress, making her the holiest of creatures, the one most completely united to God and transformed in Him.

2. St. John of the Cross, in describing the marvels of the state of perfect union with God, presents Mary Immaculate to us as the prototype and model. " Such were those [works and prayers] of the most glorious Virgin our Lady, who, being raised to this high estate of union from the beginning, never had the form of any creature imprinted in her soul, neither was she moved by such, but was invariably guided by the Holy Spirit " (AS III, 2,10).

The two essential conditions for achieving divine union are found in their fullness in Mary. The first condition, which is a negative one, is that there be nothing in the soul's will which is contrary to the divine will; that is, no attachment which would cause it to be subject to a creature, so that this creature would rule in its heart in any way, or impel it to act for love of this same creature; all such attachments must be eliminated. The second condition, which is positive and constructive, and is the consequence of the first, is that the human will be moved in all and through all, only by the will of God. This was realized so perfectly in the most pure soul of Mary Immaculate that she never had even the faintest shadow of an attachment to a creature; in her soul there was never any impression of a creature which could move her to act; she was so completely seized by divine love that she could act only under the inspiration and " motion of the Holy Spirit. "

Thus we see Mary as the most pure spouse of the Holy Spirit, not only in relation to her divine maternity, but also in relation to her whole life in which she was moved only by His impulse.

COLLOQUY

O Mary, Mother of God and my Mother, what light and strength your sweet image brings me! The most beautiful, the holiest, the purest of all creatures, so " full of grace " that you were worthy to bear within you the Author and Source of all grace, you do not disdain to give yourself to me—a poor creature, conscious of my sin and misery—as a model of purity, love, and holiness.

The privileges of your Immaculate Conception and divine maternity are inimitable, but you have hidden them within such a simple, humble life that I am not afraid to approach you, and ask you to take me by the hand and help me to ascend the mountain of perfection with you. Yes, you are Queen of heaven and earth; but because you are more Mother than Queen, you encourage me to have recourse to you, saying, " O my child, hear me; blessed are they who keep my ways.... He who finds me, finds life, and will obtain salvation from the Lord " *(RB)*. And I answer you in the words of the Church, " Draw me, O Immaculate Virgin, I will run after you in the odor of your ointments" *(ibid.)*.

Yes, draw me, Immaculate Mother, draw me above all by the luminous charm of your spotless purity! I feel so impure and stained by the things of earth compared with you, the all-pure, so detached from everything, so forgetful of yourself that nothing moves you to act apart from the divine will, apart from the inspiration of the Holy Spirit.

If I see you always docile and ready to respond to every least divine invitation, even though it be hidden under the most human, ordinary circumstances; if I hear you gently repeating your " yes, " *Ecce ancilla Domini...fiat*, in all the happenings of your life, big and little, agreeable and disagreeable, it is because you are the Immaculate. No shadow of creatures or purely human interests or affections touches your heart; and therefore, nothing can delay your most rapid course toward God.

O Immaculate Virgin, I am so reluctant, indolent, and miserly in giving myself to God, so immersed in the things of earth! Teach me how pure my heart ought to be, so that I will never refuse anything to the Lord, and will always be able to repeat with you my sweet, prompt *fiat*.

Illumine my mind, then, with the light which emanates from your resplendent purity, so that no attachment, no earthly affection may remain hidden in me to prevent my leading a life truly and fully consecrated to my God.

To you I entrust, in a very special way, my vow of chastity; guard it and make me pure, not only in body, but also in mind and heart. With your help, O Mother, I am ready to renounce any affection, even if slight, which could still bind me to creatures. I want my heart to belong wholly to God, for whom I would keep its every throb in a spirit of perfect chastity.

10

INVITATION TO DIVINE INTIMACY

PRESENCE OF GOD - I recollect myself in the presence of my God living in me by grace, and I ardently desire to come close to Him.

MEDITATION

1. " If any one love Me, he will keep My word, and My Father will love him, and We will come to him, and make Our abode with him " (*Jn* 14,23). This is the great mystery of the divine indwelling, which assures us, in Jesus' own words, that the one, triune God is not far away from a soul who loves Him, but rather lives in it and makes His abode in it.

Catholic doctrine teaches that God is necessarily present in all His creatures. In fact, in order to exist, they need not only to be created by Him, but also to be kept in existence by Him. God conserves them by operating in them, that is, by continually communicating existence to them. Since He operates by His substance, He is present wherever He operates, and therefore, in all His creatures. Thus God is everywhere, even in the souls of unbelievers and sinners.

However, in the case of a soul filled with sanctifying grace and charity, there is a special presence of God, which was promised by Jesus, and which is called *indwelling*. " The divine Persons are said to be indwelling in as much as They are present to intellectual creatures in a way that lies beyond human comprehension, and are known and loved by them in a purely supernatural manner alone, within the deepest sanctuary of the soul " *(Enc. Mystici Corporis)*. In other words, the three divine Persons are present in the soul that is in the state of grace, so that it may know Them by faith, and love Them by charity, and that They may even make Themselves known to the soul by the intimate illumination of the gifts of the Holy Spirit.

2. The three Persons of the Blessed Trinity are present in a soul in the state of grace to invite it to live in Their society, in intimate friendship with Them. Jesus

states this clearly and authoritatively : " Abide in Me and
I in you " (*Jn* 15,4); " I in you and the Father in Me, that
you may be perfect in one " (cf. *ibid.* 17,23); " as Thou, Father,
in Me, and I in Thee; that they also may be one in Us "
(*ibid.*, 21).   But wherever the Father and the Son are, the
Holy Spirit is there also, and Jesus has expressly said :
" The Spirit of Truth...shall abide with you, and shall
be in you " (*ibid.* 14,17).

To every soul in the state of grace may be repeated
in all truth the words which made such an impression
on Sr. Elizabeth of the Trinity, " The Father is in you; the
Son is in you; the Holy Spirit is in you. "

God is within you as your Father and as the sweet Guest
of your soul, to invite you to live, not only *by* Him, but *with*
Him and *in* Him.   He is within you to manifest Himself to
your soul, just as a friend manifests himself to his friend,
according to the word of Jesus, " He that loveth Me...I will
love him and will manifest Myself to him.   I will not now
call you servants...but I have called you friends " (*Jn* 14,21—
15,15).   God Himself—God the Father, God the Son,
God the Holy Spirit—offers you the invitation to live with
Him; He offers you His friendship.

What a tremendous gift!   " If thou didst know the gift
of God! " (*ibid.* 4,10).

COLLOQUY

O my God, adorable Trinity, make me know Your
gift, the immense gift by which You dwell in my poor soul,
You, One and Three, You, the Immense, the Omnipotent!

" O Deity eternal, O high, eternal Deity, O sovereign,
eternal Father, O ever-burning fire!...   What do Your
bounty and Your grandeur show?   The gift You have given
to man.   And what gift have You given?   Your whole self,
O eternal Trinity.   And where did You give Yourself?   In the
stable of our humanity which had become a shelter
for animals, that is, mortal sins " (St. Catherine of Siena).

" O my Lord and my good!   I cannot say this without
tears and great delight of soul!   Is it possible, O Lord, that
You love us so much that You wish to be with us?   If our
faults do not impede us, we may rejoice in You and You will
take Your delight in us, since You say that Your delight is

to be with the children of men. O my Lord! What is this? Whenever I hear these words they are a great comfort to me. But is it possible, Lord, that after realizing You take delight in it, the soul would turn again to offend You, and to forget so many favors and such signal marks of love that it cannot doubt them, since it sees Your work so clearly? Alas, yes, O Lord, I am this soul. And I have done this, not once, but many times.

" I knew perfectly well that I had a soul, but I did not understand what that soul merited or who dwelt within it. If I had understood then as I do now that You dwell in this little palace of my soul, You who are so great a King, it seems to me I would not have left You alone so often, but would have kept You company from time to time and would have been more diligent to keep it spotless. There is nothing more wonderful than to see You, my God, whose greatness could fill a thousand worlds and still more worlds, confine Yourself within so small a thing! You are the Lord of the world, free to do what You will, and yet, because You love us, You fashion Yourself to our measure " (T.J. *Life*, 14 – *Way*, 28).

O Blessed Trinity, my God, I shall no longer close my ears to Your loving invitation. I do not wish You to be any longer the " great abandoned One " in my soul. Help me to establish all my faculties in You, especially my intellect and my will, so that I shall live in intimate, perpetual union with You. Grant that I may seek You and You alone, that my gaze may always be turned toward You, and that I may suffer, pray, and work with You and in You.

O eternal Trinity, my sweet love! O Father, draw me by the power of Your omnipotence! O Son, enlighten me by the brilliance of Your wisdom! O Holy Spirit, inflame me with the burning fire of Your charity!

11

IN SEARCH OF GOD

PRESENCE OF GOD - I recollect myself in the interior sanctuary of my soul to seek God there, living in me by grace.

MEDITATION

1. " The kingdom of God is within you" (*Lk* 17,21), Jesus taught us, and St. Teresa of Avila comments, " If a soul wishes to speak with its Father and enjoy His company, it does not have to go to heaven.... It needs no wings to go in search of Him but only to find a place where it can be alone and look upon Him present within itself" (T.J. *Way*, 28).

But if God is within us, why do we have so much difficulty in finding Him and recognizing His presence? St. John of the Cross answers, " It is to be observed that the Word, the Son of God, together with the Father and the Holy Spirit, is hidden, in essence and in presence, in the inmost being of the soul. Wherefore, the soul that would find Him must go forth from all things according to the affection and will, and enter within itself in deepest recollection, so that all things are to it as though they were not.... God, then, is hidden within the soul and there the good contemplative must seek Him with love " (J.C. *SC*, 1,6).

The answer is clear : God is within us but He is *hidden. If we wish to find Him, we must go forth from all things, according to the affection and will.* To " go forth, " according to the terminology of the Saint, signifies to *detach oneself, deprive oneself, renounce oneself, annihilate oneself, to die* spiritually to oneself and to all things. This is the path of the " nothing, " of complete detachment : it is the death of the old man, the indispensable condition for life in God. St. Paul too has said, " You are dead; and your life is hid with Christ in God " (*Col* 3,3).

The loving search for God hidden within us goes hand in hand with this dying to the world and to ourselves. The more we die to ourselves, the more we find God.

2. St. John of the Cross continues, " He that has to find some hidden thing must enter very secretly even into that same hidden place where it is, and when he finds it, he too is hidden like that which he has found. And since thy beloved Spouse is the treasure hidden in the field of thy soul, for which treasure the wise merchant gave all that he had, it will be fitting that, in order to find it, thou *forget all that is thine, withdraw thyself from all creatures,* and hide in the interior closet of thy spirit " (J.C. *SC,* 1,9). This is a new invitation to detachment—to *forget* everything, to *withdraw* from everything—in order *to enter into* the depths of your soul, the place where God hides Himself.

We live too much in the exterior. Too often there is in us a host of inclinations, ideas, and strong passions which make us turn to creatures and induce us to give them our hearts, build our hopes on them, and find consolation in thinking about them. We live in this superficial world which absorbs us so completely that it makes us forget the more profound life, the really interior life where a soul may live in intimate union with its God. The Lord waits for us, so to speak, in the depths of our soul, but we do not go into these depths, taken up as we are with our affairs, to which we give all our interest.

We must then *go forth* from ourself and from all things, *forget* ourself and everything else; we must escape from the exterior world, from the superficial life, in order to hide ourself with the hidden God.

COLLOQUY

" O my God, make me understand that I am Your dwelling-place, the hiding place where You conceal Yourself. Have courage and rejoice, my soul, knowing that the object of your hope is so near to you that He dwells in you and you cannot exist without Him. What more could I desire, and what do I seek outside of myself, O my Lord and my God, when You have deigned to put Your kingdom, Your dwelling-place, in my very soul? Here, then, in the innermost sanctuary of my heart, I wish to love, desire, and adore You; no, I shall no longer go to seek You outside myself " (cf. J.C. *SC,* 1,7.8).

Exterior things, creatures and their discourse, may perhaps speak to me of You, but they are not You Yourself; therefore, they weary and distract me, whereas here, in the little heaven of my soul, I can find You as You really are, in Your whole essence, Your substance, Your charity.

But I understand, O my God, that in order to find You, I must *go forth* from all things : *go forth* from the confusion and turbulence of the exterior life, from the noise of earthly things, from the curiosity which draws me outside to see, to hear, to know. I must *go forth* by my will, from all this exterior world which ever tries to attract my attention, thoughts, and affections. Help me to subdue my vain curiosity, my excessive loquacity; help me to pass through the vicissitudes of earthly life, its ostentatious attractions, its affairs, its whirling activity, without letting my eyes or my heart rest on these things, seeking for satisfaction, comfort and personal interest in them.

To *go forth* from all things means to die—to die to the superficial life, to the purely human life, to the old man with all his passions. To *go forth* is to free oneself, to detach oneself from everything, to seek You alone. Does not this " going forth " call to mind that steep ascent of the mountain of perfection, that narrow path of the " nothing " which leads to the " all " of the life of perfect union with You?

What a new light, O my God! How well I see that this ascent, this mountain of perfection, is the same magnificent summit on which the soul is perfectly united to You, and is found, not outside, but wholly within myself. The summit is Your secret hiding-place, and if I would find You, I must also hide myself with You, always walking in the way of the " nothing " of total detachment from all things.

Will it be too much for me to detach myself from everything, to leave all things in order to find You, O my God? It is a comfort to my weakness to know that I am not alone on this rough road of complete renouncement—You are always with me. O Father, be my strength; O Word, be my light; O Holy Spirit, be my love!

O Most Holy Trinity, be my great treasure, for to find You, it is very little to sell all the things of this earth!

SEEKING GOD IN PRAYER

PRESENCE OF GOD - I leave all my duties and all earthly cares, to recollect myself in the little heaven of my soul, to place myself in intimate contact with God.

MEDITATION

1. " When thou shalt pray, enter into thy chamber, and having shut the door, pray to thy Father in secret " (*Mt* 6,6). Exterior solitude, withdrawing physically from the noise, from the occupations and preoccupations of this world is a great means, and even, at least to a certain point, an indispensable means for leading a serious interior life.

Every Rule of religious life, even of a simple secular institute, prescribes certain hours for prayer, during which every occupation must be firmly laid aside, and one must retire into solitude in order to renew one's spirit by means of a more direct and more intense contact with God.

Without these prayerful intervals, it is a real illusion to pretend to live a spiritual life—not only a serious one, but even the most elementary one.

Every activity, no matter how important or urgent it is, must therefore be suspended at the prescribed time, so that all the strength of the soul may be concentrated in the supreme activity of prayer. These hours are sacred. A soul consecrated to God cannot, of its own initiative, subtract even a small part of this time under pain of seeing its spiritual life weaken. The time of prayer is the time to apply Jesus' great commandment : " Seek ye therefore first the kingdom of God " (*ibid*. 6,33), this kingdom that we now know is within us. In order to find it, we must have these moments of retirement, solitude, total avoidance of creatures, of business and occupations. During these blessed minutes we can and should effectively " go forth " from all things and " withdraw ourselves " from all creatures to seek God hidden within us.

2. When the Samaritan woman asked Jesus where the Lord should be adored, He answered, " God is a spirit,

and they that adore Him, must adore Him in spirit and in truth " (*Jn* 4,24). The Divine Master tells us that more important than the *place* in which we pray, is the interior spirit with which we pray, for from it alone can flow the " true adoration " of God, who is " spirit " and truth. Although retirement and material solitude are of great importance in prayer, they will not suffice if they are not accompanied by interior recollection.

St. John of the Cross says, " . . . shutting the door upon thee (that is to say, *shutting thy will upon all things*), pray to thy Father in secret " (*SC*, 1,9). This does not mean to shut only the material door of our room, but that it is necessary to close our will to everything, that is, as the Saint again says, to " shut all thy faculties upon all creatures. "

If we wish to find God in prayer, we must begin by making this very firm decision of our will : to put aside everything—all care, all preoccupation with human things— and concentrate all the powers of our souls on God alone.

St. Teresa of Jesus offers the following advice, " Since we have resolved to devote to Him this very brief period of time. . . let us give it to Him freely with our minds unoccupied by other things and with a firm resolve never to take it back again, whatever we may suffer through trials, annoyances, or aridities " (*Way*, 23).

We often give the prescribed time to prayer, but we do not give our hearts to it; they are still preoccupied with earthly cares. We go to the chapel or our room, but do not know how to withdraw ourselves from the thoughts and cares of life; therefore, we cannot reach that intimate interior hiding-place where God conceals Himself.

COLLOQUY

O my God, teach me how to seek You in prayer, to put my heart in contact with Yours, to learn how to withdraw, not only materially, but also spiritually, from all the attractions which this world offers. How many times I am kneeling, but my mind is wandering all over the world!

And You, O Blessed Trinity, are here in the depths of my soul, waiting to manifest Yourself to me in the intimacy of prayer; You are here to draw me to Your secret hiding-place, but Your efforts are of no avail because my mind remains without, still immersed in human things and preoccupations.

If, because of my natural weakness and the deficiencies of my poor human nature, I am not always able to silence my memory and imagination, it is, however, always possible for me to seek You with my heart and will, and this is exactly what You ask of me.

Make me understand that the essence of prayer does not consist in " thinking much, but in loving much " (T.J. *Int C IV*, 1). Help me to set my heart free from creatures, so that in prayer I may devote it wholly to seeking and loving You alone. O Lord, strengthen my will so that it can leave all things and apply itself only to You; give me the strength to resist temptations and to continue to seek You in spite of the distressing wanderings of my thoughts, aridity, and powerlessness. " The kingdom of heaven suffereth violence " (*Mt* 11,12); by these words You emphasize the fact, O my God, that even to attain the kingdom of heaven which is within me, in other words, to find You within me, I must do violence to myself.

When You Yourself attract me, O Lord, all difficulties disappear; but when You hide Yourself, my poor soul wanders about restlessly, not knowing where to stay, and the slightest remembrance of creatures is sufficient to distract it. O my God, deign to fix my mind and my heart on You!

" O my God, Trinity whom I adore, help me to become entirely forgetful of self, that I may establish myself in You, as changeless and as calm as though my soul were already in eternity! May nothing disturb my peace nor draw me forth from You, O my immutable Lord! but may I penetrate more deeply every moment into the depths of Your mystery. Give peace to my soul, make it Your heaven, Your cherished dwelling place, Your home of rest. Let me never leave You alone, but keep me ever there, all absorbed in You, in living faith, adoring You and wholly yielded up to Your creative action! " (E.T. *III*).

13

SEEKING GOD IN OUR DAILY DUTIES

PRESENCE OF GOD - O my soul, withdraw into yourself and, forgetting all things, persevere in seeking God with all the affection of your heart.

MEDITATION

1. " Whatsoever you do in word or in work, do all in the name of the Lord Jesus Christ, giving thanks to God and the Father by Him " (*Col* 3,17). We must seek God, not only during the hours prescribed for prayer, but in all the acts and occupations of life. Jesus said in this regard, " We ought always to pray " (*Lk* 18,1). There are employments and contacts with creatures required by the duties of our state in life; these are expressions of God's will, and we should not think that we must avoid them in order to seek Him. If they are regulated exactly according to God's will, these contacts with others can never, of themselves, be obstacles to the union of our soul with God. However, we must always keep ourselves within the limits of God's will. In other words, in our contacts with creatures and in our various activities, we must have but one end in view, the fulfillment of our duties. When, on the contrary, the " affection " of our will fixes itself upon such things, seeking in them a little personal satisfaction, gratifying our curiosity or our natural desire for affection, trying to gain recognition for ourself or looking for esteem from others, then our will strays away from the path of God's will; our heart becomes attached to creatures, and thus meets a real obstacle—the greatest—to its continual seeking for God. St. John of the Cross expressly requires that we " go forth from all things *according to the affection and will* " (*SC*, 1,6). He demands not only the detachment that is material withdrawal from the world, but much more, the detachment of the heart.

2. " Whether you eat or drink or speak or converse with persons in the world, or whatever else you do, be ever

desiring God and having your heart affectioned to Him, for this is a thing most necessary for *interior solitude*, which demands that the soul have no thought that is not directed toward God " (J.C. *CR*, 9). In order to be able to seek God and live in close union with Him, even in the midst of our occupations and contacts with the world, we must have *interior solitude*; that is " the inner cell " of which St. Catherine of Siena speaks. If this foundation is lacking, solitude itself, just like the material cell, would be useless. This " inner solitude " is detachment. A heart which is not completely detached will always and everywhere find something to distract it from seeking God, to enslave it and make it more or less a prisoner of creatures, and to fill it with worldly affections and desires. But once the soul becomes detached, it acquires the great, supreme liberty of being able to seek God and to tend only toward Him through all things, having become capable of *desiring God and having its heart affectioned to Him* in all its occupations and activities.

Here on earth our search for God and our union with Him are accomplished by means of the will, rather than by the intellect. Even when duty—study, work, teaching, the apostolate—requires intense application of the mind and dedication to the work, the soul can still remain oriented to God by the affection of the heart, that is, with the " desire of charity, " which unceasingly urges it to seek God, His will and His glory. If the charity of Christ urges us, nothing will be able to separate us from Him.

COLLOQUY

As the thirsty stag pants for the spring of living water, so does my heart long for You, O God. My soul thirsts for You; it desires, seeks and wants nothing but You alone.

" O compassionate and loving Lord of my soul! You also say : ' Come unto Me, all ye that thirst and I will give you to drink. ' O Life, who giveth life to all, deny me not this precious water which You have promised to those who desire it. I desire it, Lord, and I ask for it and I come to You : hide not Yourself from me, Lord, for You know my need and how this water is true medicine for the soul You have wounded.... O living streams, issuing from the wounds of my God! How abundantly do you ever flow for our succor and how safely will one pass through the perils of this miserable life who can draw sustenance from this divine water!" (T.J. *Exc*, 9).

Only You, O Lord, can satisfy my soul's thirst for supreme truth, infinite charity, and eternal beauty. When my heart becomes fixed upon any created thing, seeking a little satisfaction in it; when it lets itself be taken up, even to a slight degree, by some earthly affection, and without discretion becomes immersed in the business and cares of life, very soon it has to withdraw from them, weary and exhausted, empty and oppressed. O Lord, create in me a pure, upright heart which seeks You always and in all things; set in order charity within me, so that my affections and desires may remain constantly directed toward You.

"Who can free himself from base and mean ways, if Thou, O my God, wilt not lift him up to Thee in pure love? How shall a m. raise himself up to Thee, for he is born and bred in misery, if Thou wilt not lift him up with the hand that made him?... Thou wilt not take away from me, O my God, what Thou hast once given to me in Thy only-begotten Son, Jesus Christ, in whom Thou dost give me all I desire. I will therefore rejoice, Thou wilt not tarry if I wait for Thee. Wait in hope, then, O my soul, for from henceforth thou mayst love God in thy heart.

"The heavens are mine, the earth is mine, and the nations are mine; mine are the just, and the sinners are mine; mine are the angels, the Mother of God, and all things are mine : God Himself is mine and for me, because Christ is mine, and all for me. What dost thou, then, ask for, what dost thou seek for, O my soul? All is thine, all is for thee, do not take less, nor rest with the crumbs which fall from the table of thy Father. Go forth and exult in thy glory, hide thyself in it, and rejoice, and thou shalt obtain all the desires of thy heart " (J.C. *SM I*, Prayer of the Enamoured Soul).

14

THE VIRGIN OF THE INCARNATION

PRESENCE OF GOD - I draw near you, O Virgin Mary, with a lively desire to enter into the secret depths of your interior life, so that you may be my light and my model.

MEDITATION

1. " It seems to me that Our Lady's attitude during the months that intervened between the Annunciation and the Nativity is the model for interior souls, for those whom God has chosen to live *within,* in the depths of the unfathomable abyss " (E.T. *I*, 10).

If Mary's whole life was one of recollection and concentration on God, it must have been especially such at the time when, overshadowed by the power of the Most High, the Word became incarnate within her.

The Angel Gabriel found Mary in solitude and recollection. *The Angel being come in,* says the Gospel; the expression " come in, " leads us to believe that Mary was " within " her house. The Angel reveals to her in God's name what will take place in her. " The Holy Ghost shall come upon thee, and the power of the Most High shall overshadow thee. And therefore also the Holy which shall be born of thee shall be called the Son of God " (*Lk* 1,35). From that moment God made Himself present in Mary in a very special way, present not only by essence, knowledge, and power, as He is in all creatures; present not only by grace as He is in the souls of the just; but, far more, the Word of God was in Mary by " corporal presence, " as St. Albert the Great says.

Although retaining her humility, Mary was perfectly conscious of the " great things " that were taking place within her; her sublime canticle, the *Magnificat,* is proof of this. Nevertheless, she kept the great mystery hidden in her soul, hidden even from Joseph, and lived recollected in the intimacy of her spirit, adoring and meditating : she " kept all these words, pondering them in her heart " (*ibid.* 2,19).

2. God never " gave " Himself to any creature more fully than He did to Mary, but no one ever understood better than Mary the grandeur of the divine " Gift "; nor has there ever been a more loving, more faithful guardian and adorer of it. Sister Elizabeth of the Trinity says, " If you but knew the gift of God!... There is one created being who knew this gift of God, one who never lost a particle of it... the faithful Virgin, who kept all things in her heart.... The Father, inclining toward this creature so beauteous, so unaware of her beauty, decreed that she should be the Mother in time of Him who is His Son in eternity. Then the Spirit of Love, who presides at all the workings of God, came upon this Virgin and she uttered her *Fiat!* ' Behold the handmaid of the Lord : be it done unto me according to Thy word. ' The greatest of mysteries was accomplished, and through the descent of the Word into her, Mary was forever seized upon and held by God.

" In what peace, what recollection, Mary went to and lent herself to everything! How the most commonplace things were divinized by her—for she remained ever in adoration of the Gift of God!—yet that did not hinder her from spending herself externally when there was question of practicing charity. The Gospel tells us that ' Mary... went into the hill country with haste into a city of Juda...and saluted Elizabeth. ' Never did the unspeakable vision which she contemplated within herself diminish her exterior charity for, says a spiritual writer, ' If contemplation is directed to the eternal praise of God, it possesses unity and will not lose it ' " (E.T. *I*,10).

COLLOQUY

O Mary, I love to contemplate you as you adore in profound recollection the great mystery which is taking place within you. You are the first temple of the Blessed Trinity, the first adorer of the Incarnate Word, the first tabernacle of His sacred humanity.

" O Mary, temple of the Trinity! Mary, you bore the divine fire; Mother of Mercy, from you has blossomed forth the fruit of life, Jesus! O Mother, you are that new plant from which we have the fragrant flower, the Word, the only-begotten Son of God, because in you, fertile land, was sown this Word. O Mary, fiery chariot, you bore a hidden fire which was concealed beneath the ashes of your humanity. If I look at you, O Mary, I see that the hand of the Holy Spirit has inscribed the Trinity in you, by forming within you the Incarnate Word, the only Son of God. O Mary, I see this Word given to you, within you " (St. Catherine of Siena).

" O Mary, nearer than all to Jesus Christ, although at a distance that is infinite, you are the great ' praise of glory ' of the Blessed Trinity. You were always holy, unspotted, blameless in the sight of the thrice-holy God. Your soul is so simple, its movements are so deeply hidden, that we cannot detect them. Your whole life may be summed up in these words from the Gospel, ' His Mother kept all these words in her heart. ' You lived within your heart : so deeply did you enter therein that human eyes cannot follow you. When I read in the Gospel that you ' went into the hill country with haste into a city of Juda, ' to perform an act of charity for your cousin Elizabeth, I picture you to myself as you pass by—beautiful, serene, majestic, absorbed in communion with the Word of God within you. Like Him, your prayer was always, ' Behold, here I am. ' Who? The handmaid of the Lord; the last of His creatures, you, His Mother! Your humility was so genuine because you were always forgetful and disregarding of self, free from self. Therefore, you could sing, ' Behold from henceforth all generations shall call me blessed. Because He that is mighty hath done great things to me ' " (E.T. *II*, 15).

O my Mother, teach me the secret of your interior life; teach me to live recollected with God present in my soul. Teach me your silence, communicate to me your spirit of adoration; close to you, in your school, I too wish to be the little temple of the Trinity. Help me to detach myself from creatures and to live in silent, loving adoration of the Trinity in the innermost depths of my soul.

15

THE LORD IS NIGH

THIRD SUNDAY OF ADVENT

PRESENCE OF GOD - The Lord is always drawing nearer to my soul by the solicitations of His grace; I too wish to draw near to Him by a renewal of my faith and my desires.

MEDITATION

1. " O Lord, we have patiently waited for Thee : Thy name and Thy remembrance are the desire of the soul. My soul hath desired Thee in the night; yea, and with my spirit within me in the morning early I will watch for Thee " *(RB)*.

If you also, O consecrated soul, are preparing to commemorate the Incarnation of the Word in loving, watchful expectation, today's happy announcement will resound in your ears more joyfully than ever : " Rejoice in the Lord always; again I say, rejoice. . . the Lord is nigh. "   Thus today's Mass begins and the Epistle *(Phil* 4,4-7) repeats the theme. It is one of exultant joy : " The Lord is nigh! "   For the soul who waits for Jesus and seeks Him alone, sincerely and ardently, with lively desire and love, there can be only one motive for its joy, to know that Jesus is near, nearer with each day.   Even St. Paul admonishes us to have no other desire, " The Lord is nigh.   Be nothing solicitous. . . .   And may the peace of God, which surpasseth all understanding, keep your hearts and minds. . . " *(Ep)*.

The more a soul concentrates its desires and affections on God, the more it will be freed from earthly cares.   It will no longer be troubled about anything, knowing that only one thing is necessary, " to seek God, " and that in God it will find everything it needs.   Hence to draw near to God, is to find not only true joy, but also peace.   In Him it has everything, and God alone suffices.

2. " The Lord is in the midst of you. "   This is the second joyful message in today's liturgy.   It is St. John the Baptist

who speaks to us in the Gospel (*Jn* 1,19-28), " There is one in the midst of you whom you know not. "   John, a man of faith, was telling the Jews with full conviction that Jesus had been living among them for thirty years and that they did not know Him because He had not yet manifested Himself by miracles.

His words have value for us, too; Jesus is really present in our midst : present in our tabernacles by the Eucharist, present in our souls by grace.   But who recognizes Him? Only those who believe.   Revive, then, your faith; you will find Jesus, and will know Jesus according to the measure of your faith in Him.   Sometimes He conceals Himself from you, and you think that you will never find Him, never feel Him again.   This is the time to redouble your faith, to walk " in pure faith. "   " Blessed are they that have not seen, and have believed " (*Jn* 20,29).   Such was the faith of St. John the Baptist, who had not seen Jesus' miracles, and nevertheless believed.   Such was Mary's faith, to which the Vesper antiphon refers, " Blessed art thou, O Mary, that hast believed the Lord; those things will be fulfilled in thee, which were spoken to thee. "   Even Mary lived by faith; she had to *believe* in the words of the Angel, and when she agreed to become the Mother of God, she had to accept a mystery which she did not understand.   But Mary did believe, and by her faith, God's words were accomplished in her.   And so shall they be in you; you will see all your hopes fulfilled, you will be able to realize your ideal of intimate union with God—if you have faith in Him and in His promises.

COLLOQUY

" O God, my God, to Thee do I watch at break of day. In a desert land, and where there is no water, my soul thirsts for Thee; my flesh hath thirsted for Thee.   It is Thou I seek, O Lord; without Thee the world is a desert burned by the sun where nothing can quench my thirst.   Thou alone art my salvation, my refuge, my Savior, and my Redeemer. Day and night I sigh for Thee; to Thee I direct all my desires and affections.   As the eyes of the handmaid are on the hands of her mistress, so are my eyes always on Thy face.   Show me Thy face, O Lord, and illumine my path; be Thou my light and my strength.

" Come, Lord, and tarry not; reveal Thy power and come to save us. Come and be our salvation, according to Thy promise! Thou art our Savior; Thou wilt free us from all our iniquities and cast our sins into the depths of the sea. Thou wilt descend like rain upon the fleece and wilt bring us justice and peace.... Thou wilt be my guide and my shepherd; Thou wilt teach me Thy ways and I shall walk in Thy paths. Thy coming fills me with joy and my soul rejoices in Thee, my God and my Savior. O Lord, I rejoice in all Thy deeds and I exult in Thy works. How admirable are Thy works and how great is Thy mercy " *(RB)*!

My God and my Savior, I believe in You, I trust in You. I seek for You, yet I know that You are near me, and in me : near me, hidden under the Eucharistic veil; in me, by grace. O Lord, make me know You! Do not permit it to happen to me as to the Jews : You were living in the midst of them and they knew You not. Grant that my soul may always have a lively faith; increase my faith, for faith is the light by which I can know You on earth. You are within me, Lord, I know it, I believe it, even if I cannot feel You. But if You wish, You can illumine my soul with Your light and make me know Your divine, mysterious presence.

" You are the light surpassing all other light; You give supernatural light to the eye of the intellect with such abundance and perfection that You clarify the light of faith. My soul has life in faith, and in faith it receives You and knows You. In the light of faith, I acquire wisdom in the wisdom of the Word. In the light of faith, I am strong, constant and persevering. This light will never fail me in my way; it teaches me the path, and without it, I would walk in darkness. Therefore I beg You, O Lord, to illumine me with the light of holy faith " (St. Catherine of Siena).

16

GUARD OF THE SENSES

PRESENCE OF GOD - O my God, I recollect my senses and faculties in Your presence, withdrawing them from all exterior occupations, in order to fix my attention wholly on You.

MEDITATION

1. To live a serious interior life, one that is wholly concentrated on seeking God, it is necessary to prevent the outside world from entering the soul and filling it with distractions and noise; it is necessary, therefore, to guard its doors assiduously. The senses are precisely the doors which open to earthly things : sight permits its images to enter; hearing, its sounds, and so forth, so that, without a discreet mortification of the senses, the soul, the living temple of the Blessed Trinity, becomes like a market-place, open to all kinds of traffic, open to every wind of rumor. Then Jesus might well say to us what He once said to the profaners of the temple, " Make not the house of My Father a house of traffic " *(Jn* 2,16). A temple of the Blessed Trinity by Baptism, the consecrated soul is doubly so by reason of its vows and promises, and is, therefore, doubly obliged to guard the recollection of its spirit, in order to make it really a " house of prayer. " According to St. Teresa Margaret of the Heart of Jesus, " It suffices to keep well closed the outside doors, that is, the senses, so that the soul and the heart cannot go elsewhere than to their center, which is God. " This was her method : " I shall fix my gaze on my heart and I shall raise my heart to God " *(Sp)*.[1] Mortification of the senses should not be limited to Carthusians and to those

---

[1] St. Teresa Margaret of the Heart of Jesus, a young Carmelite nun who died in the Carmel of Florence, March 7, 1770, had an extraordinary interior life which might be epitomized in her motto : " hidden with Christ in God. " A true contemplative, she knew how to unite the office of Mary to that of Martha, displaying surprising activity in caring for the sick sisters. For further details about her, consult our work, *La Spiritualità di S. Teresa Margherita Redi del Cuore di Gesù*, Libreria Fiorentina, 1950.

in cloisters, as it is an indispensable exercise for all souls, that they may become recollected and wholly concentrated upon God.

2. St. John of the Cross says that we should use our exterior senses in such a way as not to disturb our recollection. " The faculties and senses must not be employed wholly upon things, but only insofar as in unavoidable. With this exception all must be left free for God " (J.C. *SM II*, 38). The " unavoidable " is indicated by what duty requires, and when we use the powers of our soul only to this degree, which is that determined by God's will, the soul cannot be harmed in any way. But the Saint continues : " If there present itself to a man the pleasure of listening to things that tend not to the service and honor of God, let him not desire that pleasure, nor desire to listen to them; and if there present itself the pleasure of looking at things that help him not Godward, let him not desire the pleasure or look at these things; and if in conversation or in aught else, such pleasure present itself, let him act likewise " (J.C. *AS I*, 13,4). This means that we should not use our senses for anything that is not required by duty or which cannot serve to raise our mind to God. However, those who are obliged to have almost continual contact with the world will not always be able to keep strictly to this rule, because by doing so they might become disagreeable to others, or appear eccentric. Therefore, St. John adds that " if by reason of necessity or expedience he cannot avoid seeing or hearing such things, it suffices that he desire not to have this pleasure " *(ibid.)*. In other words, it is necessary to learn how to pass over such sense satisfactions, without stopping at the pleasure we find in them, nor allowing them to take full possession of our senses, thus always maintaining that interior liberty which permits the soul to elevate itself to God in all things. Make use of the senses only insofar as is necessary; the rest must be " left free for God. "

COLLOQUY

O Lord, guard my senses, so that I may never be separated from You. With Your help, I will keep a vigilant watch over the doors of my soul, and apply myself more fervently to a perfect observance of the rules of modesty which apply to my state in life. I will make the spirit of mortification the guardian of my senses, exercising myself in not wishing to see, hear, or discuss anything but what is required for the fulfillment of my duties. "But if You, O Lord, do not keep my house, I shall watch it in vain" (cf. *Ps* 126); therefore, with my whole heart I beg You to restrain and moderate my tongue, guard my eyes so that they will not be fed by vanity. "Lord God, King of heaven and earth, deign to direct and sanctify, rule and govern my heart, my body, my thoughts, words, and deeds in Your law and in the works of Your commandments, so that now and forever, by Your help, I may attain salvation and freedom from all evil" *(RB)*.

O my God, place a guard on my eyes, my ears, my lips—on all my senses—and may this guard be Your love. Your love does not permit me to occupy my senses voluntarily with useless, unnecessary, or frivolous things; Your love does not permit the rumors, images, or the vain curiosity of earthly things to enter the sanctuary of my soul.

May Your love be the weight which draws me continually toward you. Thus my eyes will always seek Your face; my ears, Your word; all my senses will ever tend toward You, to seek, enjoy, and possess You alone. Grant that this love may always attract my senses and faculties; Lord, fill them completely with Your beauty, Your words, the knowledge of Your mysteries, so that when they are obliged by necessity to turn to creatures, they will feel uneasy and be anxious to return in haste to recollect and fix themselves in You.

But if, through frailty and misfortune, I relax the watch over my senses and allow them to stray far away from You amongst the things of the world, I beg You, Lord, come to my aid at once! "Do not permit my senses to go astray, but do You Yourself deign to call them back to You, like the good shepherd who, with his flute, calls his sheep dispersed in the valley. You, more than any other shepherd, have a call so sweet and so powerful that the senses, as soon as they hear it, cannot resist, and quickly come back into the sanctuary of the soul where You await them and to which You call them. O loving Shepherd of my soul, do not refuse to show me this mercy, so necessary for my weakness" (cf. T.J. *Int C IV*, 3).

17

INTERIOR SILENCE

PRESENCE OF GOD - O Lord, hush all the voices of the world, of creatures, and of self, so that I may listen to no voice but Yours.

MEDITATION

1. Holy Scripture says, " In the multitude of words there shall not want sin. He that hath no guard on his speech shall meet with evils " (*Prv* 10,19 – 13,3). The rule of life of a consecrated soul, even if she lives in the world, should always provide for the practice of silence; and if, because of the demands of her duties, it is absolutely impossible for her to observe fixed times of silence, it is indispensable that she hold fast to this principle : to speak as little as possible with creatures in order to be able to speak as much as possible with God. She must, therefore, accustom herself to keeping control over her words, thus avoiding loquaciousness, idle chatter, prolonged conversations, and excessive exchange of confidences. The same norm which governs the use of the senses governs also the use of speech—it is to be used only in the measure required by duty or charity. Of course, it is certainly licit to talk for the purpose of taking some just alleviation or recreation, but always with moderation and within reasonable limits.

However, it is not enough to observe exterior silence; we must also strive for interior silence, that is, silence of the interior senses—the memory, imagination, sensitive feelings, thoughts, recollections of the past and useless conjectures about the future.

" If any man think himself to be religious, not bridling his tongue...this man's religion is vain " (*Jas* 1,26), which is to be understood, says St. John of the Cross, " no less of inward speech than of outward " (*P*, 9).

2. God Himself says to the soul desirous of divine intimacy, " Hearken, O daughter, and see, and incline thy

ear, and forget thy people and thy father's house " (*Ps* 44,11).
Sister Elizabeth of the Trinity makes the following comment
on this verse, " In order to listen we must forget our ' father's
house '; that means, whatever pertains to the natural life....
To forget our ' people ' seems to me more difficult; for by
' people ' is meant that world which forms, as it were, part
of ourselves. It includes our feelings, memories, impressions,
and so forth. In a word, it is *self*. We must forget it, give
it up, and when the soul has broken with it, and is wholly
delivered from all it means, ' the King greatly desires its
beauty ' " (E.T. *II*, 10).

The beauty of a recollected soul is the unity of her spirit,
which is not divided and dissipated among creatures but is
entirely concentrated on God. Then God takes pleasure
in her and often manifests Himself to her, transforming her
recollection, that is, her " silence " and making it divine, for
" the knowledge of Him is in divine silence " (J.C. *SM I*, 26).

This total silence, both exterior and interior, disposes
the soul to know and listen to God who dwells within her :
" One word spoke the Father, which Word was His Son, and
this Word He speaks ever in eternal silence, and in silence
must it be heard by the soul " (J.C. *SM II*, 21); and Sister
Elizabeth of the Trinity exclaims : " O eternal Word,
utterance of my God, I desire to spend my life in listening
to You! " This is the fundamental occupation of a soul
who wishes to be a " perfect praise of glory " of the Blessed
Trinity : to live interiorly in continual silence, listening to
and adoring God present within her, and exteriorly, being
and doing only what the divine Word indicates from moment
to moment.

COLLOQUY

O my God, teach me the secret of the silence which
reaches unto interior silence.

I have often had this experience : when I pour myself
out on creatures and waste my time in long, useless
conversations, my spirit becomes dry, dissipated and empty;
and then, if I want to be recollected in prayer, I am unable
to silence that little world of impressions, talk, imaginings,
and idle thoughts which continually brings me back to
creatures.

O Lord, I know that You want greater fidelity to silence
and more care to avoid spending myself on creatures. Yes,
O God, I will be silent with creatures so that I can hear
Your voice which speaks in silence.

"But whenever I dally with my 'self,' preoccupied
with my sensitiveness; when I pursue useless trains of thought
or any sort of useless desire, I am wasting my strength, and
my soul is not perfectly ordered toward You, O Lord. My
lyre is not in tune, and when You, my divine Master, strike it,
You cannot bring forth the divine harmonies. It is still too
human and there is discord. If I am keeping anything for
myself in my interior kingdom, my powers are not all
'enclosed' in You, my God, and I cannot be a perfect
praise of glory...because unity does not reign in me, and
instead of persevering in praise, in simplicity, no matter
what happens, I am continually obliged to tune the strings of
my instrument (the powers of my soul), because they are all
a little discordant" (E.T. *II*, 2).

Help me, O Lord, to attain this beautiful interior unity
which unites all my faculties in silence in order to concentrate
them on You, which makes my soul attentive to every one
of Your words, capable of perceiving the slightest inspiration
and motion of the Holy Spirit.

"You, O Lord, wakeneth in the morning, in the morning
You wakeneth my ear, that I may hear You as a master"
(cf. *Is* 50,4), but Your word is light as a whisper and sounds
without noise; a profound silence is necessary, therefore,
in order to hear it. O loving Incarnate Word who once,
with one movement of Your hand, silenced the winds and
calmed the waves on Genesareth, deign to repeat this action
in my soul, so that a great calm, a great silence will reign
in it.

"O eternal Word, utterance of my God! I long to
spend my life in listening to You; to become wholly
'teachable,' that I may learn all from You" (E.T. *III*).

18

SEEKING GOD IN FAITH

PRESENCE OF GOD - I recollect myself in the presence of God living in my soul, to learn how to seek Him by the light of faith.

MEDITATION

1. " He that cometh to God, must believe " (*Heb* 11,6), says St. Paul, and he gives us this definition of faith : " Faith is the substance of things to be hoped for, the evidence of things that appear not " (*ibid.* 11,1). In heaven we shall see God by the light of glory, but on earth we know Him by the light of faith.

We must not base our interior life, our search for God, on sentiment or spiritual consolations, but on an intensive practice of the theological virtues. St. John of the Cross gives this advice to a soul seeking God, " Hear a word full of substance and unapproachable truth : it is that thou seek Him in faith and in love, without desiring to find satisfaction in aught " (*SC*, 1,11). Therefore, we must learn to seek God without any desire for pleasure, consolation, satisfaction, even though it be purely spiritual; we must learn to walk in the path of " naked faith. " Faith, more than any kind of knowledge or of reasoning, puts the soul into direct contact with God. Faith is " the proximate and proportionate means whereby the soul is united with God; for such is the likeness between itself and God, that there is no other difference save that which exists between seeing God and believing in Him " (J.C. *AS II*, 9,1). Faith places us before God as He is; it does not make us see Him, but it makes us believe in Him, and thus puts our intellect in contact with Him. By means of faith, " God manifests Himself to the soul in divine light which passes all understanding. And therefore, the greater the faith of the soul, the more closely is it united with God " (*ibid.*). Faith unites the soul with God, even though it experiences no spiritual consolation; on the contrary, God often deprives the soul of all spiritual consolation that it may exercise itself more in faith and grow in it.

2. " Faith and love are like the guides of the blind
which will lead thee by a way which thou knowest not to
the hidden place of God " (J.C. *SC*, 1,11).   Faith is an
obscure but firm adherence to the divine Word which reveals
the supreme greatness of our God, who is so sublime, so
omnipotent, but also so good and merciful.   Faith says
to the Christian soul, " You are the temple of the living
God "; and the more lively the soul's faith, the more it
believes Jesus' words, " If any one love Me...My Father
will love him and We will come to him, and will make Our
abode with him " (*Jn* 14,23).   By faith the soul believes
in the infinite love of God, who deigns to lower Himself
to His creature even to making His dwelling within it,
inviting it to live in intimate union with Him.   " And we
have known and have believed the charity which God
hath to us " (1 *Jn* 4,16).   This is our great act of faith,
by which, although we do not see or experience by our
senses, we proceed with the confidence of one who does see.
" When the soul finally comes to believe in this ' excessive
love ' of God, we may say of it what was said of Moses,
' For he endured as seeing Him that is invisible ' (*Heb* 11,27).
" What does it matter to the soul that is recollected in itself...
whether it feel or does not feel, whether it be in light or
in darkness, in sensible joy or not? " (E.T. *II*, 4).   It believes
in His love.   " For I know whom I have believed, and I am
certain that He is able to keep that which I have committed
unto Him " (2 *Tm* 1,12).   This is the cry of a soul of faith
who perseveres in its search for God in spite of darkness
and aridity.   But to attain such unshakeable faith, we
must practice it and pray : " I do believe, Lord : help my
unbelief " (*Mk* 9,23).   " Increase my faith " (*Lk* 17,5)!

COLLOQUY

O Lord, give me a pure, ardent, strong faith to sustain
and guide me in my continual search for You, and to make
me adhere to You with perfect confidence although You
remain hidden from my sight.

Only by faith can my soul adhere to You, as You
really are—infinite, omnipotent, and merciful, unity in
Trinity : thus faith presents You to my soul.   Faith
comprehends You as You are, in Your divinity, Your

mysteries, and Your works—all of which it proposes to my belief, so that in faith I find You completely, and in the act of faith, even though I do not see You, I possess You truly. If faith holds You hidden and veiled, if it permits me to see You only " through a glass in a dark manner " (1 *Cor* 13,12), I am certain, however, that it does not deceive me; it proposes You to me as You have revealed Yourself. How shall I not believe, Lord, in Your word, since You have spoken to us not only by the mouths of the prophets, but by the mouth of Jesus, Your Incarnate Word? Even if faith presents mysteries and wonders to believe which my poor mind cannot understand, I shall not be bewildered. What mystery is greater than that of Your infinite charity which has loved me from all eternity, created me by an act of love, redeemed me by the Blood of Your Son, and made my poor soul the temple of the Most Holy Trinity? " On Your word alone, I believe with full certitude. I believe everything the Son of God has said; there is nothing more true than the Word of Truth " (St. Thomas).

" O God, far from being astonished by Your works, they are for me but one more reason for praising You. The more difficult they are to understand, the more they arouse devotion in me; and the greater they are, the greater is the devotion. . . . So the less of a natural foundation these truths of the faith have, the more firmly I hold them and the greater is the devotion they inspire in me. Since You are almighty, I accept all the wondrous works which You have done as most certain, and in this respect I have never harbored a doubt" (T.J. *Life*, 28 – 19).

I want to seek You, O God, in this ardent faith, and cling to You always, even if such faith is " naked " and stripped of every consolation. " Nothing shall affright me, neither wind nor rain; and should impenetrable clouds come, O Jesus, to conceal You from my eyes, I shall not change my place, knowing that beyond the dark clouds the sun of Your love is still shining and that its splendor cannot be eclipsed for a single instant " (T.C.J. *St*, 13).

19

SEEKING GOD IN LOVE

PRESENCE OF GOD - Help me, O God, to concentrate all my affections on You, so that my heart will be satisfied with You alone.

MEDITATION

1. Faith " is like the feet wherewith the soul journeys to God, and love is the guide that directs it " (J.C. *SC*, 1,11). Charity follows faith; in this life, faith and charity, as it were, go at an equal pace : the one depends on the other, one progresses with the progress of the other, and both of them immerse the soul deeper and deeper into God. A soul who believes with its whole strength that God is truly God, that He is the supreme Being to whom we all belong and that He is worthy of all our love, will have an ardent desire for Him, and in it will be fulfilled the words of St. John of the Cross : " The soul will merit the revelation by love of that which faith holds within itself " *(ibid.)*. That is, faith will make us believe in the greatness, mercy and infinite charity of God, but love will make us taste and experience them : this happens especially during contemplative prayer in which God draws the soul to Himself. However, even prescinding from this experience, we ought to exercise ourselves in love in order to go to God " by steps of love. "

Jesus Himself commanded us to practice this virtue in the highest degree : " Thou shalt love the Lord thy God with thy whole heart, and with thy whole soul, and with thy whole mind, and with thy whole strength " (*Mk* 12,30). St. Paul exhorts us to " walk in love " (*Eph* 5,2), and St. Thomas teaches that " love is the life of the soul. " However, the love that is charity is pure benevolence toward God; its intensity depends upon its purity, that is, this love must consist in the one desire of pleasing God and doing His will, without seeking personal satisfaction.

2. The love which will lead us to God does not consist in sentiment; it is an act of the will. To love is to " will

good "; to love God, is to " will good to God. "   The good
which we can desire for God is that which Jesus Himself
taught us to ask of our heavenly Father : " Hallowed be
Thy name; Thy will be done. "   Since God is the infinite
good upon which everything depends, the good that He
desires and that by which He is pleased is none other than
His own glory and the accomplishment of His holy will.

    We love God, then, to the degree in which we apply
ourselves to do His will, without any personal preoccupations
or self-seeking.   St. John of the Cross says that if a soul
looks for sweetness and delight in God, " it would not then
love God purely, above all things " (*L*, 11).   In fact, together
with Him the soul would also be seeking some personal
satisfaction, because its heart would be divided between
love of God and love of itself; and therefore, it would be
unable to " set the strength of the will upon Him. "   Hence,
the Saint concludes, it should " have that hunger and thirst
for God alone, and desire not to be satisfied with aught
else " *(ibid.)*.   A soul which, moment by moment and
in all its actions, seeks nothing but the will of God, is really
seeking God in love and is uniting itself effectively to Him,
even though it feels no consolation.   But because it is
always true that " if a soul is seeking God, its Beloved is
seeking it much more " (J.C. *LF*, 3,28), He may sometimes
draw it to Himself, making it taste the sweetness of His
love and the joy of belonging entirely to Him.   However,
not even then may the soul stop to relish these consolations,
but humbly accepting them, it should use them to give
itself to God with greater resolution and generosity.

COLLOQUY

    O Lord, grant me this pure, strong love which seeks
You alone, by a continuous and generous adherence to
Your holy will!   Grant that Your divine will may be my
food and drink, as it was for Jesus; grant that like Jesus
I may hunger and thirst for nothing but the fulfillment
of Your will, and apply all my faith to recognize it and all
my love to fulfill it in every circumstance of my life.

    When I have learned how to see my duties in the light
of faith, I shall realize that my daily duties, as they present
themselves to me moment by moment, and under various

aspects, are the expression of Your will, which asks of me at this moment that certain task, that duty, that pious practice, that act of charity. If I know how to do this with fidelity and constancy, I shall really know how to " seek You in love, " and You will not delay in letting Yourself be found by my soul.

But how weak, O Lord, is my love, how feeble it is, and how easily it comes to a standstill in the face of difficulties, vanishes in time of trial, and is dismayed in aridity!

" O my God, how can I have a love worthy of You, if the love You have for me is not united with it?... Love alone gives value to all things and the most needful thing is that it should be so great that nothing can hinder its operation. But alas! I have only words and am unable to give You more. May my desires, my God, be availing in the sight of Your divine presence : consider not my slight deserving.... Lord, since we have to live, let us live for You and let our own desires and interests disappear. What greater good can we gain than to please You? Lord I desire to please You. Well do I know that my pleasure can be found in no mortal being; since this is so, You will not blame my desire. Behold me here, Lord; if it is needful for me to suffer in order to do You some service, I refuse none of the trials that may come to me on earth.... Oh, my pleasure and my God! What shall I do to please You? Since I can serve You in nothing, I must needs console myself with any little service. Blessed are they who serve You by doing great deeds! If I could accomplish anything by merely envying them and desiring to imitate them I should not be backward in pleasing You. But I am of no worth, my Lord. Do You put worth in what I do, since You have such love for me " (T.J. *Exc*, 5 - 15 – *Life*, 39).

O Lord, in my weakness I cannot ask to do great things for You, nor do I wish to ask You for consolations and sweetness. I only desire that I may prove my love for You and know how to " seek You in love, " doing Your will from moment to moment.

20

SEEKING GOD IN CREATURES

PRESENCE OF GOD - I place myself in the presence of Jesus in the tabernacle, asking Him to teach me how to seek Him and to find Him in others.

MEDITATION

1. The relations with our neighbor which duty imposes cannot distract the soul in its search for God if it has learned to consider creatures with a wholly supernatural view, that is, with a deep spirit of faith. When the eye is illumined by the light of faith, the soul seeks and finds God, not only present in itself, but also in all creatures and especially in its neighbor.

" Creatures are, as it were, traces of the passing of God, whereby are revealed His greatness, power, wisdom, and divine virtues "; in fact, every one of them has been created by God " through His wisdom, which is the Word, His only-begotten Son " (J.C. *SC*, 5,3.1). If this is true of all creatures, even of those that are inanimate, it is especially so of man, whom God expressly created " to His image and likeness " (*Gen* 1,26). The soul living by faith always relates its acts to God when dealing with its neighbor; and rather than detain itself on outward appearances, sees, serves, and loves God alone in all creatures indiscriminately. For the soul of faith, men, of whatever race, nationality, position or social standing, have only one aspect : the image of God; only one name : child of God.

Unfortunately, vice, sin, and faults can more or less disfigure the divine image in man, but the image remains and the spirit of faith knows how to find it. Furthermore, even those who live far from God are still His children, if not effectively by grace, at least by their vocation to grace. In other words, they too are always capable of being elevated to a supernatural state. When the soul sees God in all creatures, nothing can distract it from its spirit of recollection and its search for God.

2. Only when our relations with our neighbor remain on a purely human level can they disturb our interior recollection in various ways. This happens, first of all, because the soul easily becomes attached to creatures : not knowing how to see God in them, it stops at their human qualities, at the feelings of congeniality and affection which they arouse in it, and looks to these for consolation and the satisfaction of its natural need to love and be loved. In this way, creatures more or less invade it, preoccupying its mind and heart, and robbing its spirit of the precious liberty of remaining oriented toward God and recollected in Him. And even when its relations with the neighbor cease, the soul will remain occupied with him, and will therefore be unable, even in the very hours of prayer, to recollect itself in God.

Furthermore, if we see in creatures only human persons who disturb us with their requests and needs, who often besiege us from morning till night, not giving us a moment's rest or peace, who irritate us by their faults—when we see creatures in this manner, our relations with them, although required by our duties, will weary and bore us; and we shall often be tempted to evade them, even under the pretext of defending our interior recollection. When, on the other hand, the soul is fixed in the simple glance of faith, every creature is for it a messenger from God; it brings God to the soul and takes the soul to Him. Thus, through visible creatures, the soul goes to the invisible God and speaks familiarly with Him.

COLLOQUY

O Lord, how I want to learn to see You and recognize You in every creature! You have created all men to Your image and likeness; all therefore bear Your impression, Your mark. Teach me not to stop at human appearances, which might allure my heart, making it give to a simple creature that affection which, in virtue of my consecration, should be reserved for You alone, O my God! Whenever my glance and my heart stop at creatures and look for satisfaction, contentment, and understanding in them, I get lost, distracted, and tormented; I always come away from them more tired and weary, because, after much seeking and loving, I find nothing to satisfy my infinite need for love.

Yes, I know that as long as I do not look upon creatures with that simple, profound glance of faith which enables me to find You in all of them, O my God, to deal with them—even when duty requires it—will always be an obstacle and an impediment to my interior recollection.

O my God, grant me the single eye mentioned in the Gospel, that eye which can pierce through exterior appearances and fix its gaze on that divine mark which You Yourself have imprinted on every man. Then I shall make no distinction between those who are congenial and attractive and those who are mean, disagreeable, or repulsive; all these " externals " will disappear and I shall recognize Your face in everyone, and shall serve and love You, my God. Shall I then be able to complain that the relations with my neighbor which duty imposes or the things I have to do for him distract me from You? Does not faith tell me that in treating with my brethren I am treating with You, and that when I serve them I am serving You? Did not Jesus say, " As long as you did it to one of these My least brethren, you did it to Me" (*Mt* 25,40)? You dwell in the soul of everyone who is in the state of grace, just as You dwell in mine and if, unfortunately, all men are not in the state of grace, all are capable of receiving grace; all are the objects of Your merciful love; all are called, by vocation, to be temples of the Blessed Trinity. Then, O Lord, if I wish to seek You within myself, why do I not seek You also in my brethren?

O my God, purify my sight which is so easily deceived by human appearances, and make it capable of discovering You and finding You in every creature.

21

SEEKING GOD IN ACTIVITY

PRESENCE OF GOD - I leave all exterior activity to become recollected before Jesus, and I beg Him to teach me how to preserve this interior spirit, even in the midst of my occupations.

MEDITATION

1. St. John of the Cross teaches the soul that would attain quickly to holy recollection: "Never undertake anything, however good and full of charity it may seem... without being ordered by obedience" (*P*, 11).   In this way one is certain of acting solely according to the will of God; and God's will cannot permit the duties which it requires of us—even though they are absorbing and disturbing—to become a hindrance to the recollection of the soul in Him. "If one acts only by obedience and under obedience, it is God who commands, and it does not seem to me that He can destroy His own work," that is, His intimate union with the soul, affirms St. Teresa Margaret. When exterior activity is wholly regulated by obedience, not only is the risk of acting through self-love lessened, but also that of exposing oneself temporarily to distractions, for in every occupation one has the certainty of embracing the holy will of God. And if one embraces the holy will of God, there can be no danger of separation from Him, no danger of distracting the mind from its continual orientation toward Him.

Union of the soul with God is not accomplished so much in the sweetness of prayer, as in embracing perfectly the holy will of God.

2. "We must needs be careful, in doing good works, even those of obedience and charity, not to fail to have frequent inward recourse to our God" (T.J. *F*, 5).   This is a further condition to be observed in order to prevent external activity from disturbing interior recollection.   "I will never do anything with haste or agitation."   This was the constant resolution of St. Teresa Margaret who, in the midst of

a surprising amount of activity, always maintained " a peaceful, calm attitude, which showed her perfect self-control in each one of her actions " *(Sp)*. Such an attitude implies keeping complete control of oneself and of one's activity so as to avoid the danger of being dominated and carried away by this activity. Those who rush headlong into action, without taking precautions, will soon lose their calm, become agitated, unable to recollect themselves, and their activity will become ever more and more absorbing and demanding.

Jesus chided Martha, not because she gave herself to activity, but because she was too anxious about it : " Martha, Martha, thou art careful, and art troubled about many things " *(Lk* 10,41). God wants activity, but not anxiety, for even in activity, the soul should attend to " the one thing necessary, " that is, union with Him. Therefore, as soon as a soul perceives that it is beginning to lose its interior calm, it should interrupt its work, if possible, at least for an instant, and retire into its interior with God. These brief moments of pause, frequently repeated, will accustom it, little by little, to keep calm and recollected in God, even in the most absorbing activity.

COLLOQUY

O Lord, here at Your feet, in the light of Your divine presence, I wish to examine my occupations sincerely, to find out if they are really all regulated by holy obedience. You have made me understand that when I act solely on my own initiative, with no real motive of obedience or charity, my actions can very easily draw me away from You; I am drawn away either because I occupy in activity that time which I ought to dedicate to prayer, or because in doing what pleases me, I often do nothing but follow my self-love, my natural tendency toward activity, my own ideas, my own will. In these cases, I am united not to Your will but to mine; not to You, but to my self-love. O my God, I beseech You, free me from such great danger! To weary myself, to suffer in order to do Your will, to unite myself to You—yes, with Your help I wish to do this always, O Lord. But to weary myself and to suffer in order to do my own will, would be truly foolish, and all the more so because my soul would pay dearly for it.

Guard me, O Lord, from such foolishness, and do not permit me to be so blind as to squander my strength uselessly, to the detriment of my interior life.

O Lord, give me a " passion " for Your will, so that I may never will or do anything except what You will, what You ask of me in the commands and wishes of my superiors or in the advice of my spiritual director.   Nothing else should exist for me, for I want You and Your will alone.

O my God, help me also not to let myself be dominated and carried away by activity.   Help me, O peaceful One, to keep myself always calm and recollected, always at peace in Your presence, even in the midst of the most intense activity.   This continual calm and interior peace alone will permit me to gather all the powers of my soul and to keep them fixed on You, despite the many demands of exterior activity.   O my Jesus, is not this what You meant to say when You spoke to Magdalen about the *one thing necessary?*   " How well this great Saint understood!   Illumined by the light of faith, she recognized her God beneath the veil of His humanity, and in silence and in the union of her powers, she listened to His word; she could chant, ' My soul is always in my hands ' and also that little word *Nescivi!* I knew not.   Yes, she knew nothing but You, my God! No matter what noise or disturbance went on around her, *Nescivi!*   She could have accusations made against her, *Nescivi!* "   (E.T. *II*, 2).   Even when she was obliged to leave Your adorable feet to perform some task, her heart remained fixed on You.   And after she had finally found You risen again, she had to leave You, at Your command, to run to announce Your resurrection to the Apostles, but her soul remained established in an attitude of profound calm, recollected and concentrated upon You.

With Your help, may I too so live!

22

BEHOLD THE SAVIOR COMES

FOURTH SUNDAY OF ADVENT

PRESENCE OF GOD - I place myself at the feet of Jesus and ask Him to prepare my heart for His imminent coming.

MEDITATION

1. " Call together the nations, tell it among the people and say : Behold our Savior cometh! " *(RB)*. The message becomes more and more urgent : in a few days, the Word of God made flesh will show Himself to the world. We must hasten our preparations and make our hearts worthy of Him.

The incarnation of the Word is the greatest proof of God's infinite love for men; today's liturgy very appropriately recalls to our mind the wonderful words : " I have loved thee with an everlasting love, therefore have I drawn thee, taking pity on thee " *(Jer* 31,3). Yes, God has loved man from all eternity, and in order to draw him to Himself, He did not hesitate to send " His own Son in the likeness of sinful flesh " *(Rom* 8,3). With hearts full of love, we must run to meet Love who is about to appear " incarnate " in the Infant Jesus. May it be a love that is faithful in great things as well as in small, an ingenious love that is always seeking opportunities to repay God's infinite love. " Love is repaid by love! " This is the motto which has made saints, and spurred a multitude of souls to greater generosity.

With this love prepare for Christmas, be in this love faithful, for as St. Paul says in the Epistle (1 *Cor* 4,1-5), " What we desire is that everyone may be found faithful. "

2. " Prepare the way of the Lord, make straight His paths. Every valley shall be filled; and every mountain and hill shall be brought low. " The voice of John the Baptist, the great Advent preacher, is heard again in today's Gospel *(Lk* 3,1-16), inviting us to prepare " the way of the Lord. "

This invitation is especially a call to humility; John was not only the herald of this virtue, but its model too. We know, by the testimony of Jesus Himself, that he was " more than a prophet " and that " there hath not risen among them, that are born of women, a greater than John the Baptist " (*Mt* 11,9.11).   John claimed to be nothing more than a mere voice, " the voice of one crying in the wilderness : Make straight the way of the Lord, " and declared that he baptized only with water, while another would come who would baptize in the Holy Spirit, another of whom John protested himself unworthy to loose " the latchet of His shoe " (*Jn* 1,23.27).   And further, speaking of the Savior's coming, John adds, " He must increase, but I must decrease " (*ibid.* 3,30).   Today's Office gathers up all this magnificent testimony of St. John the Baptist, as if to give us a concrete idea of the profound sentiments of humility with which, in our heart, we ought to make smooth " the way of the Lord. "   If the valleys, that is, our deficiencies, are to be filled up by love, then the mountains and hills, that is, the vain pretenses of pride, must be made low by humility.

A heart filled with self-love and pride cannot be filled with God, and too small will be the place reserved in it for the sweet Babe of Bethlehem.

COLLOQUY

O almighty, omnipotent, eternal God, what greater proof of love could You give Your poor creatures than the gift of Your Word, Your only-begotten Son?   For our sake, You clothed with human flesh, like the flesh of sin, Him who is eternal splendor, the perfect image of Your substance!

" God of goodness, who art above all goodness, You alone art sovereign good!   You gave us the Word, Your only Son, to live with us, to assume our evil, corrupt nature. Why did You make us such a gift?   Out of love, because You loved us even before we existed.

" O eternal Greatness, O fathomless Bounty, You lowered Yourself to ennoble mankind!   Wherever I turn, I can see nothing but the abyss and fire of Your charity " (St. Catherine of Siena).

"Whenever I think of Christ, I should remember...
how great is Your love, O Father, which in Jesus has given
us a pledge of such great tenderness; for love begets
love and although I am only a beginner and very wicked,
I shall strive ever to bear this in mind and awaken my own
love. Once You, O Father, do me the favor of implanting
this love in my heart, everything will become easy for me
and I shall get things done in a very short time and with
very little labor. O my God, give me this love, since You
know how much I need it, for the sake of the love You
bore us and through Your glorious Son who revealed it to us,
at such great cost to Himself" (T.J. *Life*, 22).

Love will fill the valleys in my heart, and humility
will level its mountains and hills. Destroy my pride, arrogance, and vanity, O Lord, by the powerful fire of Your
love. By the might of Your all-powerful arm, tear out
of my heart every fiber which is infected with the poison
of self-love, and which, therefore, does not belong to You.
O Lord, I, too, wish to decrease, decrease that You may
increase in me, so that on Christmas day You may find my
heart entirely empty and free and therefore ready for the
total invasion of Your love.

23

THE CALL TO THE APOSTOLATE

PRESENCE OF GOD - I place myself in the presence of Jesus, the
Head of the Mystical Body, the Church, begging Him to show me
how to collaborate with Him in the work of saving souls.

MEDITATION

1. "Prepare ye the way of the Lord" (*Lk* 3,4). This
cry of St. John the Baptist is implicitly a call to
the apostolate, to that apostolate practiced by St. John
himself, when he tried to prepare the hearts of his brethren
for the coming and for the work of the Messiah. This
invitation is addressed to us, too, not only by St. John,

but also by Jesus, who wants to make of every Christian
a collaborator in His work of Redemption.

We know that Jesus alone has merited the vast, precious
treasury of grace necessary to redeem and sanctify the whole
human race. Yet He has not disdained our humble
cooperation; rather, He has positively willed " to have
need of us. " Pope Pius XII says in his Encyclical, *Mystici
Corporis* : " It is manifestly clear that the faithful need the
help of the divine Redeemer.... Yet this, too, must be
held...Christ requires the help of His members.... This
is not because He is indigent and weak, but rather because
He has so willed it for the greater honor of His spotless
Spouse. "

The Spouse of Christ is the Church; the Church is
the " company " of His faithful, that is, we ourselves.
Certainly, Jesus had absolutely no need of us. As He alone
merited grace for us, so He alone can apply it directly to
each soul. " It was quite possible for Him personally to
impart these graces immediately to men; but He wished
to do so through a visible Church that would be formed
by the union of men, and thus through that Church every
man would perform a work of collaboration with Him in
dispensing the graces of Redemption " *(ibid.)*. Jesus then,
in His infinite goodness, has willed to associate us with Him,
to give us the honor and joy of being His collaborators
in the greatest work to be is accomplished in the world :
the salvation of souls.

2. Since Jesus, in His infinite love for us, has willed
to associate us with Him in His redemptive work, reserving
in it a place for our activity, we must say that now, in the
actual economy of the Redemption, our collaboration is
necessary. Henceforth, to bring His work to a successful
end, *Jesus has need of us*. We should have a holy pride
in this, but we must not forget that it entails a tremendous
responsibility : the salvation of our brethren depends also
on the generosity with which we collaborate in Christ's
work. " A tremendous mystery certainly, and one never
sufficiently meditated, that the salvation of many souls
depends on the prayers and voluntary mortifications offered
for this end, by the members of the Mystical Body of Christ,
and on the collaboration of both pastors and the faithful "
(Mystici Corporis). A " tremendous " mystery, because of the

responsibility which it puts on us, and one " never sufficiently meditated. " Hence, it is necessary to be profoundly convinced that " the salvation of many *depends* " also on us, upon our collaboration. If this fact ought to incite the faithful to a generous apostolate, how much more should it spur on a soul consecrated to God! She has left all to give herself to Him; therefore her interests should, in a very special way, be the interests of God. She is a spouse of Christ, and, as such, is bound to collaborate in the work of her divine Spouse : the salvation of souls and the glory of the heavenly Father.

Souls are the " patrimony " of a spouse of Christ; their salvation is her " passion "; the welfare and growth of the Church are her " interests "; she lives only for Jesus and for His work.

COLLOQUY

" O my God, You give me the keenest desire not to displease You in any respect whatsoever, however trivial, or to commit so much as an imperfection if I could avoid doing so. For this reason alone, if for no other, I would like to flee from other people, and I envy those who live, or have lived, in deserts. On the other hand, I would like to plunge right into the heart of the world, to see if by doing this I could help even one soul to praise God more. I am distressed at being prevented from doing this by my natural weakness and am very envious of those who are free to cry aloud and proclaim abroad this great God of Hosts.

" Have pity on me, O my God, and dispose things so that I may be able to do something toward fulfilling my desires for Your honor and glory. Remember not my want of merit or the baseness of my nature. Did not You, O Lord, order the sea to be divided, and the great Jordan to recede, and allow the children of Israel to pass over them?

" Stretch out Your mighty arm, O Lord; let Your greatness appear in this unworthy creature, so that men may realize that I can do nothing and may give You praise. Cost what it may, this is what I desire, and I would give a thousand lives if I had them, so that one soul might praise You more. I would consider them all well spent, because I know that in actual fact I do not deserve to suffer the very smallest trial for You, still less to die for You.

" Lord, do not forget that You are a God of mercy; have mercy on this poor sinner, this miserable worm who is so bold with You. Behold my desires, my God, and the tears with which I beg this of You; forget my deeds, for Your Name's sake and have pity upon all these souls that are being lost, and help Your Church. Do not permit more harm to be done to Christendom, Lord; give light to this darkness " (T.J. *Int C VI*, 6 – *Way*, 3).

O Lord, grant me, too, a great love for souls; kindle in me an ardent thirst for their salvation, and grant that I may use my feeble powers to collaborate in Your great redemptive work.

24

THE INTERIOR APOSTOLATE

PRESENCE OF GOD - I place myself before Jesus, my sweet Savior and Redeemer, asking Him to teach me how to collaborate with Him in the salvation of souls.

MEDITATION

1. The apostolate, considered in its totality, consists in everything we can do in collaboration with Christ to diffuse the supernatural life in souls. The apostolate is always a collaboration with Jesus, and attains its end only when it helps to bring God's grace to souls and to develop it in them. Catholic doctrine gives us two fundamental means for our collaboration with Christ : prayer and sacrifice. Even the Encyclical *Mystici Corporis* speaks first of " prayer and voluntary mortification " and only then speaks of the exterior activity of the clergy and the faithful. Our cooperation with Jesus for the salvation of souls must be deeply rooted in prayer and sacrifice, for it was mainly by prayer and sacrifice that Jesus Himself redeemed the world.

Jesus saved us not only by His exterior activity of preaching, teaching, instituting and administering the Sacraments, but also by the obedience and silence of His hidden life, by His prayer which is expressly mentioned so often in the Gospel, and above all by the Sacrifice of the Cross, in which all His work of redemption reached its culmination.   St. John of the Cross says, " Just then He wrought the greatest work that He had ever wrought. . .which was the reconciliation and union of mankind with God through grace " (*AS II*, 7,11). The " interior apostolate " of prayer and immolation, then, holds the first place. Upon it is founded the exterior apostolate of action which draws its strength and efficacy from the interior one.

2. The apostolate does not consist in doing " in a little way " all that Christ did " in a big way " for the salvation of the world, but in " taking part in His work. " The more our action participates in what is deepest and most fruitful in Christ's work, the more efficacious it will be; this is accomplished precisely by means of prayer and sacrifice, embraced with generosity and constancy, and united to that of Christ's, offered for the salvation of souls. This is why the Church—although recognizing the urgent need of the exterior apostolate—continues to desire and support that form of contemplative life which is consecrated to the interior apostolate : " The Religious Orders which are vowed to contemplation are, in a certain way, *necessary* to the Church. " [1]

But if the interior apostolate is to be truly the most fruitful, the soul dedicated to it must nourish within itself a burning apostolic fire, as did St. Teresa of Avila, who used to say to her daughters, " If your prayers and desires, disciplines and fasts are not performed for the intentions of which I have spoken (the salvation of souls), you are not fulfilling the object for which the Lord has brought you here " (T.J. *Way*, 3). The apostolic ideal should urge the soul to embrace, with complete generosity, a life of continual, hidden immolation in order that it may be a powerful means of salvation for its brethren; and this same ideal should, on the other hand, urge the soul to make rapid

---

[1] Address of Pius XII to the International Congress for the modernization of the States of Perfection, December 8, 1950.

progress in the way of sanctity, so as to very soon become worthy to obtain from God all the graces that it desires for the Church. "And for them do I sanctify Myself, that they also may be sanctified" (*Jn* 17,19). The holier a soul is, the greater is the influence that it exercises in the Church.

COLLOQUY

"To be Your spouse, O my Jesus...and by my union with You to be the mother of souls, should not all this content me? Yet other vocations make themselves felt, and I would wield the sword, I would be a priest, an apostle, a martyr, a Doctor of the Church, I would fain accomplish the most heroic deeds — the spirit of the crusader burns within me, and I wou.' gladly die on the battlefield in defense of the Church.... Like the prophets and doctors, I would be a light to souls. I would travel the world over to preach Your name, O my Beloved, and raise on heathen soil the glorious standard of the Cross.... But the greatest of all my desires is to win the martyr's palm. Martyrdom was the dream of my youth! Yet this too is folly, since to slake my thirst for suffering, not one, but every kind of torture would be needful. O Jesus, to folly such as this, what answer will You make?... Is there on earth a soul more feeble than mine? Yet precisely because of my feebleness You have been pleased to grant my least, my most childish desires, and now You will to realize those others, more vast than the universe.

"I understand that love alone imparts life to all the members of the Church, so that should love ever fail, apostles would no longer preach the Gospel and martyrs would refuse to shed their blood. I realize that love includes every vocation, that love is all things, that love is eternal, reaching down through the ages and stretching to the uttermost limits of earth!

"O Jesus, my Love, my vocation is found at last — my vocation is love! Yes, I have found my place in the bosom of the Church, and this place, O my God, You Yourself have given to me : in the heart of the Church, my Mother, I will be Love!... Thus I shall be all things and my dream will be fulfilled" (T.C.J. *St*, 13).

O Lord, love alone will give value to my prayers, efficacy to my works. Love will make me eager to embrace all the mortifications and penances which the faithful observance of my rule continually offers and demands of me, as well as every opportunity for sacrifice which the actual circumstances of my life present. Give me this love, I beseech You, O Lord, so that in the bosom of the Church and in union with You I may exercise a fruitful, efficacious apostolate. " A very little of this pure love is more precious in the sight of God and of the soul, and of greater profit to the Church than are all other works together " (J.C. *SC*, 29,2). O my God, how I want to have this " pure love! " How I desire to strip myself generously of all selfishness and self-love; how I would like to forget myself entirely, so that I may attain to possessing a love which is so efficacious for the Church and souls!

25

APOSTOLIC ACTION

PRESENCE OF GOD - I place myself in the presence of Jesus, in order to learn from Him, the first Apostle, the Apostle par excellence, the qualities I need to make my activity of real value to souls.

MEDITATION

1. During the three years of His public life, Jesus carried out an exterior apostolate on a large scale, but His activity was never separated from His intimate union with the Father; rather, it blossomed from it : a union not limited to His hours of prayer, but a permanent, indissoluble union embracing every moment of His life. Such a union, a substantial union with God, could exist only in Christ because of the hypostatic union and the Beatific Vision which He enjoyed. Nevertheless, as far as is possible for mere creatures, we should strive to imitate this conduct of Jesus and to live in constant union with God, even while working for our brethren. In this sense the interior life is the soul of the

apostolate; a really efficacious activity, the bearer of grace
to souls, can proceed only from one who lives intimately
united to God. Jesus Himself has proclaimed it, " As the
branch cannot bear fruit of itself, unless it abide in the vine,
so neither can you, unless you abide in Me " (*Jn* 15,4).

Union with God, union with Jesus, is the preliminary
and indispensable requisite for the efficacy of any apostolic
life. This union is accomplished by means of sanctifying
grace, it grows with the fervent reception of the sacraments
and with the generous practice of the virtues; it is established
more firmly and strengthened by prayer, and is consolidated
and preserved by recollection and detachment. The more
one's union with God increases, the more the action which
flows from it will bear fruit for souls. An apostolic activity
which is purely external, one which under the pretext of
having important duties, neglects the exercises of the interior
life—prayer and the quest for union with God—condemns
itself to sterility.

2. Jesus' apostolic work, which was thoroughly
impregnated with sacrifice, culminated in the supreme
sacrifice of the Cross. So, too, our apostolic works, if they
are to bear fruit, must sink their roots into the fertile soil
of self-immolation. Apostolic action in itself demands
sacrifice, either because of the fatiguing life it imposes, or
because of the continual contacts with people of different
mentalities, tastes, and habits, or because it can expose
one to the possibility of failure and of becoming an object
of derision. The apostle must accept all these difficulties
with a generous heart, convinced that from them, if they
are endured in union with Jesus Crucified, will come the
fruit of his works. Furthermore, to be really supernatural,
the exterior apostolate requires *rectitude of intention :* that is,
the works must be undertaken *solely* for God's glory, and
in a manner that is conformable to His will, as expressed
by the superiors of one's Institute and the ecclesiastical
hierarchy. To attain to this purity of intention, the apostle
must die, day by day, to self-love and vainglory, to the
tendency to draw upon himself the praises of others or to
take complacency in his successes; he must die to his personal
views and initiatives, to his own interests. This means
a real immolation of the *ego* and will bear fruit in the
apostolate in proportion to its depth. " Unless the grain

of wheat falling into the ground die, itself remaineth alone; but if it die, it bringeth forth much fruit " (*Jn* 12,24.25).

COLLOQUY

O Jesus make me understand that the greatest works of the apostolate are only useless agitation, if they do not proceed from a profound interior life. You are the true vine through which the sap of divine grace flows, and only the branch which is grafted onto You can distribute it to souls by bringing forth for them fruits of grace. What illusion is mine if, allowing myself to be carried away by the urgency of my works, I squander myself on them, neglecting to nourish and strengthen my union with You! Yet your warnings are ever before me : " Without Me, you can do nothing. "   Only " he who abides in Me bears much fruit. "   O vain agitation!   O the uselessness of so many of my works, undertaken only by human activity, as if their fruit depended on my industry and ability!   O my God, preserve me from such stupidity.   No, I do not wish to waste my energy and lose my time in this way. What would be the value of being consecrated to You and dedicated to the apostolic life if afterwards I confined myself to a purely human activity which could be done by any professional or workman?   Even those who do not believe in You devote themselves to social work : they open schools and hospitals, they print books and newspapers, and spread propaganda....   My activity must be distinguished from theirs by the interior spirit which animates it : the spirit of union with You, the spirit of prayer, of sacrifice.   Only this spirit has the great power to transform poor human activity into supernatural action, into apostolate.   Grant, O Lord, that my activity may be that of a vigorous branch which is firmly grafted onto You; grant that it may be impregnated with prayer, permeated with sacrifice.

Make me understand, O my Jesus, how necessary it is for me to die to myself in order to attain that complete purity of intention which should animate every true apostolate!   How often I think I am moved by zeal for Your glory and the welfare of souls, when perhaps, on the contrary, I am moved, at least in great part, by my pride. I want that initiative, that work, because I find in it an outlet for my natural tendency toward activity, for my secret hankering to put myself forward, to make myself important, to obtain praise and success. And is it not for just such motives that I so often resist obedience, the wishes, and even the expressed will of my superiors, thinking that they do not understand me, and that therefore, I can follow my own opinion in preference to theirs?

O my God, when I consider all these possible errors of my ego seen thus in Your light, how ugly, mean, hateful, and profoundly unworthy of a consecrated soul they seem! Yet if they arouse in me a feeling of horror, I do not ask You, O my God, to diminish Your light; on the contrary, I beg You to make it always more penetrating, so that I may be able to see clearly into my soul and, with the help of Your all-powerful grace, to fight energetically against these base inclinations of my ego which, like gnawing worms, threaten to ruin and destroy my apostolate. Grant me purity of intention, humility of heart, and the truth of love. Draw me to You, my God, and I shall seek none but You!

26

THE MYSTERY OF THE INCARNATION

DECEMBER TWENTY-SECOND

PRESENCE OF GOD - I place myself in the presence of Jesus in the Blessed Sacrament, with an ardent desire to penetrate the infinite mystery of divine love which impelled God Himself to become " one of us. "

MEDITATION

1. God is Love; everything He does, both in Himself and outside of Himself, is a work of love. Being the infinite good, He cannot love anything outside of Himself from the desire of increasing His happiness, as is the case with us; in Himself He possesses *all*. Therefore, in God, to love, and

hence to will creatures, is simply to extend, outside of Himself, His infinite good, His perfections, and to communicate to others His own Being and felicity. *Bonum diffusivum sui*, St. Thomas says. Thus God loved man with an eternal love and, loving him, called him into existence, giving him both natural and supernatural life. Through love, God not only brought man out of nothing, but chose him and elevated him to the state of divine sonship, destining him to participate in His own intimate life, in His eternal beatitude. This was the first plan of the immense charity of God with regard to man. But when man fell into sin, God, who had created him by an act of love, willed to redeem him by an even greater act of love. See then, how the mystery of the Incarnation presents itself to us as the supreme manifestation of God's *exceeding* charity toward man. " By this hath the charity of God appeared toward us, because God hath sent His only-begotten Son into the world, that we may live by Him. In this is charity...He hath first loved us, and sent His Son to be a propitiation for our sins " (1 *Jn* 4,9.10). After having given man natural life, after having destined him for the supernatural life, what more could He give him than to give Himself, His Word made flesh, for his salvation?

2. God is Love. It is not surprising, therefore, that the story of His benevolent action on behalf of man is all a poem of love, and of merciful love. The first stanza of this poem was our eternal predestination to the vision and to the fruition of the intimate life of God. The second stanza relates, in an even more touching way, the sublimity of His mercy : the mystery of the Incarnation.

The sin of our first parents had destroyed God's original plan for our elevation to a supernatural state; we had forfeited our claim, and we could never atone for the sin. God could have pardoned all, but it was becoming to His holiness and infinite justice to exact an adequate satisfaction; man was absolutely incapable of providing this. Then the most sublime work of God's mercy was accomplished : one Person of the Blessed Trinity, the second, came to do for us what we could not do for ourselves. Behold the Word, God's only-begotten Son, " who for us men and for our salvation, descended from heaven and became incarnate " *(Credo)*. The merciful love of God thus attains its highest manifestation : if there is no ingratitude and misery greater than sin, there can be no love greater than that of Him who inclines over so much ingratitude and abjection to restore it to its primal splendor.   God did this, not by the intervention of a prophet or the most sublime of the angels; but He did it personally : all three Persons of the Blessed Trinity acted in the Incarnation, the end of which was to unite a human nature with the Person of the Word.   In this mystery, the immensity of the love and mercy of God for man appears and shines forth.

COLLOQUY

" O my God! make me worthy to understand something of the mystery of the burning charity which is in You, which impelled You to effect the sublime act of the Incarnation, the root and source of our salvation.   O ineffable Incarnation! which brings to man, with the outpouring of love, the assurance of salvation.   How ineffable is this charity!   Truly, there is no greater than this, that the Word was made flesh in order to make me like unto God!   You became nothing in order to make me something; You clothed Yourself like the lowliest slave to give me the garments of a King and a God!   Although You took the form of a slave, You did not lessen Your substance, nor injure Your divinity, but the depths of Your humility pierce my heart and make me cry out : ' O incomprehensible One, made comprehensible because of me!   O uncreated One, now created!   O Thou who art inaccessible to mind and body, become palpable to thought and touch, by a prodigy of Thy power!... '

" O happy fault! not in itself, but by the power of divine mercy.   O happy fault, which has disclosed the sacred, hidden depths of the abyss of love!   Truly, a higher form of charity cannot be imagined....   O ineffable love! Sublime, transforming love!   Blessed art Thou, O Lord, because Thou teachest me that Thou wert born for me! Oh! how glorious it is to see and feel, as I believe and feel, that Thou wert born for me!   To feel this, is indeed, a delight, and the joy of joys!...   O admirable God, how marvelous are Thy mercies!   O uncreated God, make me worthy to know the depths of Thy love and the abyss of Thy mercy!   Make me worthy to understand Thy ineffable charity, which was transmitted to us when the Father gave Jesus Christ to us in the Incarnation " (St. Angela of Foligno).

Permit me to say, O Lord, that my mind and heart are bewildered before the abyss of Your charity! It is a mystery in which I lose myself without being able to see it to its depths. Give me, O Lord, the grace to believe firmly, unshakably in Your exceeding charity; grant that I, too, may say with complete conviction : " I have known and I have believed in the charity of God for me! " The stronger my conviction, the more shall I trust wholly in Your charity, in Your infinite merciful love.

This immense charity, this ineffable mercy, by means of Your Incarnate Word, inclines over all men without distinction. You incline over me too; Your love surrounds me, nourishes me, gives me life, and brings me to You, O my God! O Lord, may Your love invade my soul; or rather, give me the grace to know and believe in that love, which from the first moment of my existence has surrounded and possessed me.

27

THE WORD WAS MADE FLESH

DECEMBER TWENTY-THIRD

PRESENCE OF GOD - O Jesus, eternal Word, permit me to penetrate more deeply into the sublime mystery of Your Incarnation, so that my heart may always be held captive by Your infinite love.

MEDITATION

1. The Word is the second Person of the Blessed Trinity. In the bosom of the one divine nature, there are three Persons, three subsistent relations. We too, are " subsistent " : " subsistence " is that which permits me to say " I, " and to attribute to this " I " the various acts that I perform as a person. In God, in the divine nature, there are three relations who can say " I " in regard to the divine operations, operations which are common to all

three, because they proceed from the one single nature, possessed by all and each one of the three divine Persons. The Word possesses the same divine nature as the Father and the Holy Spirit; He possesses the same divine attributes, such as infinity, eternity, omnipotence, omniscience—all the divine grandeur and perfections belong to the Word as well as to the other two Persons. The Word performs the same divine actions as the Father and the Holy Spirit : the intimate actions of knowledge and love which constitute the very life of the Blessed Trinity, and the external acts such as creation and preservation of creatures. The Word is God! St. John the Evangelist, in the beginning of his Gospel, before speaking of the temporal birth of Jesus, presents to us the eternal generation of the Word, existing *ab aeterno* (from all eternity), in the bosom of the Father, equal to the Father in all things, but distinct from Him. " In the beginning was the Word, and the Word was with God, and the Word was God " (*Jn* 1,1). The Word is the one utterance of the Father—He expresses the Father *completely*. The Father, in giving the Word His whole essence and divine nature, also communicates to Him all the divine activity. Thus the Word is the efficient *cause*, the first principle of all natural and supernatural life : " All things were made by Him, and without Him was made nothing that was made " (*ibid*. 1,3). But the Word, the splendor of the Father, is not only life; He is also light, the *light* which reveals the greatness and mystery of God to men : " In Him was life, and the life was the light of men " (*ibid*. 1,4). Natural life and the life of grace, light and knowledge of God—all come from the Word, who is God, together with the Father and the Holy Spirit.

2. " The Word was made flesh. " As God, the Word is eternal and immutable; therefore, of necessity, He always remains what He was : *manet quod erat!* But nothing prevented Him, together with the Father and the Holy Spirit, from creating in time a *human nature*, which instead of having a limited, weak *ego* like ours, was completely governed by its divine *Person*. And so it was done : the human nature assumed by Him is the same as ours, but instead of belonging to a *human person*, it belongs to a *divine Person*, to the subsistent Person of the Word; therefore, even the operations and passions of this human nature belong to the Word. Since

the Incarnation, the Word has a *two-fold nature :* the unique divine nature, which He possesses in common with the Father and the Holy Spirit, and the human nature, which is of the same quality and has the same properties as ours.

The Word remains what He was—perfect God. Nevertheless, He does not disdain to assume our poor human nature, fallen through sin, " but emptied Himself, taking the form of a servant, being made in the likeness of men and in habit found as a man " (*Phil* 2,7). This is the work of the immense charity of God, who being full of mercy for His poor creatures who had fallen into the abyss of sin, did not hesitate to decree the redemptive Incarnation of His only-begotten Son. Thus the eternal Word comes to us like the good shepherd who leaves everything and goes down into the valley to look for the lost sheep. This is the fruit of the exceeding charity with which God has loved us!

COLLOQUY

" O eternal Word! O my Savior! Thou art the divine eagle whom I love and who allurest me. Thou who, descending to this land of exile, didst will to suffer and to die, in order to bear away each single soul and plunge it into the very heart of the Blessed Trinity — Love's eternal Home! Thou who, returning to Thy realm of light, dost still remain hidden here in our vale of tears under the appearance of the white Host, to nourish me with Thy own substance. Forgive me, O Jesus, if I tell Thee that Thy love reacheth even unto folly, and at the sight of such folly what wilt Thou but that my own heart should leap up to Thee? How could there be any limit to my trust?

" I know well that for Thy sake the saints have made themselves foolish—being ' eagles ' they have done great things. Too little for such mighty deeds, my folly lies in the hope that Thy love accepts me as a victim, and in my confidence that the angels and saints will help me to fly unto Thee with Thy own wings, O my divine Eagle! As long as Thou willest I shall remain with my gaze fixed upon Thee, for I long to be *fascinated* by Thy divine eyes, I long to become Love's prey " (T.C.J. *St*, 13).

Yes, my Jesus, I have a burning desire to become the prey of Your love; I desire it to take entire possession of me, to purify and transform me, so that You will have the joy of fully accomplishing Your sanctifying, merciful work of redemption in me.

You come to us to cure all our ills, to transform us from children of sin into children of God. But alas! how often Your infinite charity is obliged to stop before our ungrateful hearts, which close the door to You! " You came unto Your own, and Your own received You not " (cf. *Jn* 1,11). Those do not receive You who do not believe in Your love, who doubt Your infinite mercy, and do not trust in You. Your exceeding charity brought You down from heaven to us; You did not find it unbecoming, O eternal Word, to take on our poor human nature; yet, You continue to find an obstacle to Your course in that same creature, Your creature, upon whom You have showered Your favors!

O eternal Word, my Savior, grant that I may never place any obstacle to Your work. Grant that my soul may always be ready to receive Your infinitely merciful love, so that You may be able to wholly accomplish in me Your work as Savior and Sanctifier.

28

THE GREAT MYSTERY IS ACCOMPLISHED

DECEMBER TWENTY-FOURTH

PRESENCE OF GOD - O Incarnate Word, my Savior, teach me the lessons of wisdom contained in the mystery of Your Incarnation.

MEDITATION

1. Of all the works done by God in time and outside of Himself, the redemptive Incarnation of the Word is the greatest. It is the greatest because it has for end not a mere creature, however sublime, but God Himself, the eternal Word who, in time, assumed a human nature. It is the greatest because it is the supreme manifestation of the

merciful love of God, and the work which above all others
glorifies Him; and it glorifies Him precisely in reference
to charity which is His very essence.   It is also the
greatest of His works because of the immense good it brings
to mankind.   The salvation, sanctification, and eternal
happiness of the whole human race depend wholly upon
the Incarnation of the Word, upon Jesus, the Incarnate
Word.   God the Father " chose us in Him before the
foundation of the world, that we should be holy and
unspotted. . . .   Who hath predestined us unto the adoption
of children through Jesus Christ unto Himself. . . .   In whom
we have redemption. . .the remission of sins according
to the riches of His grace. . . .   God hath quickened us together
in Christ. . .and hath raised us up together, and hath made
us sit together in the heavenly places, through Christ Jesus "
(*Eph* 1,4.5.7 – 2,5.6).   Jesus, the Incarnate Word, is the
one source of our salvation and our sanctification.   Without
Him, man would not be able to call God by the sweet name
of Father; he could not love Him as a son loves his father,
nor could he hope to be admitted to His intimacy : there
would be no grace, no Beatific Vision.   Without Jesus,
man would be imprisoned within the limits of a purely
human life, deprived of every supernatural horizon, in time
and in eternity.

  2. God's greatest work, the Incarnation of the Word,
destined to enlighten and save the whole world, takes place
in obscurity and silence, and under the most humble and
most human conditions.   Caesar's edict obliges Mary and
Joseph to leave their little home in Nazareth and undertake
a journey.   They travel on foot like the poor, in spite of the
discomfort of Mary's condition.   They do not think of
objecting to the trip; they make no complaint, but obey
with promptness and simplicity.   He who commands is
a man, but their profound spirit of faith discovers God's
will in the command of the pagan emperor.   And they
go, trusting in God's Providence; God knows, God will
provide : " To them that love God, all things work together
unto good " (*Rom* 8,28).   In Bethlehem there is no room
for them; they are obliged to take shelter in a hillside
cave.   The poverty of this refuge for animals does not
dismay or scandalize them.   They know that the Child
who is about to be born is the Son of God; but they

also know that God's works are entirely different from man's! And if God wishes His greatest work to be accomplished here, in this wretched stable, in utter poverty, Mary and Joseph embrace His will! The least bit of human reasoning would be enough to confuse and disturb them, and arouse doubts. Mary and Joseph are extremely humble; hence, they are docile and filled with faith in God. And God, as is His custom, made use of what is humble and despicable in the eyes of the world to accomplish the greatest of His works : the Incarnation of the Word.

COLLOQUY

O my God, what a luminous, sublime contrast! O eternal Word, Incarnate Word, source of life, salvation, grace, and sanctity! O Redemption and Light of all mankind! You are about to show Yourself to the world! All creation should exult, all nature should tremble with joy, all men should run to You, their God, their King and Savior! Instead, You choose to be born in secret, solitude, and silence, and all is pre-arranged to this end. " While all things were in quiet silence, and the night was in the midst of her course, Thy almighty Word leapt down from heaven, from Thy royal throne...into the midst of the land " (*Wis* 18,14.15). O my God, You came down from heaven to save the world, and the world which is Yours, the work of Your hands, has not even a lodging to offer You! Who is this Child who has no house, however poor and wretched, to be born in? There was the humble little house at Nazareth ready to welcome You; Mary had prepared it with much love, but You did not want even that, and You dispose everything in such a way that You have not even a place to lay Your Head. Bethlehem is crowded with visitors; there is a little corner for everyone except You, the royal Guest, the Creator, the King of the universe. For You, there is no place. You come to us like a poor pilgrim, walking the streets, not knowing where to spend the night. No one notices You, no one is aware of Your imminent appearance, no one could suppose that this humble woman from Nazareth is about to give the world its Savior, its King and its God. Only Mary and Joseph know and adore in silence. Nothing disturbs them; their hearts are firm in faith, anchored in perfect confidence; they are sure of You and of Your promises.

O Incarnate Word, impress this lesson deeply in my heart and help me to understand the mysterious ways of Your love. You are coming to save and sanctify me, but You want to accomplish Your work in me by means of the most humble, ordinary, and insignificant circumstances. Give me the humility, faith, and blind trust of Mary and Joseph, that I may know how to recognize and adore Your work, adhere to it with docility and love, and know that You love to surround Your works with humility, silence and secrecy.

29

THE NATIVITY OF OUR LORD

CHRISTMAS DAY — THE SAVIOR HAS APPEARED

PRESENCE OF GOD - Behold, I am at the feet of my Incarnate God, who has become a Child for love of me! I adore, I thank, I love!

MEDITATION

1. God is charity : He has loved us with an everlasting love! "I think God must have said to Himself : Man does not love Me because he does not see Me; I will show Myself to him and thus make him love Me. God's love for man was very great, and had been great *from all eternity*, but this love had not yet become visible.... Then, it really appeared; the Son of God let Himself be seen as a tiny Babe in a stable, lying on a little straw" (St. Alphonsus). This is the mystery of the Nativity; this is St. Paul's exultant cry : "The grace of God our Savior hath appeared to all men.... The goodness and kindness of God our Savior appeared" (*Ep* 1st and 2nd Masses : *Ti* 2,11-15 – 3,4-7). These are the blessed tidings " of great joy " brought by the Angel to the shepherds; " This day is born to you a Savior, who is Christ the Lord! "

(*Gosp* 1st Mass : *Lk* 2,1-14). The texts in today's liturgy, following each other in tones of increasing exultation, sing the praises of the sweet Child Jesus, the Word made Man, living and breathing among us : " Whom have you seen, O shepherds? Speak and tell us who has appeared on earth? We saw the new-born Child and choirs of angels loudly praising the Lord " *(RB)*. " Let the heavens rejoice, let the earth exult in the presence of the Lord! *(RM)*. Our God is here in the midst of us, He has become one of us. " A Child is born to us, a Son is given to us.... His name is Admirable, God, Prince of peace, Father of the world to come!... Rejoice, O daughter of Sion, sing, O daughter of Jerusalem.... Rejoice, ye inhabitants of the earth! Come, ye nations, adore the Lord! *(RB)*. Come! Come, adore, listen, and rejoice! Jesus, the Word of the Father, speaks to us a wonderful word : God loves you!

2. The three Christmas Masses place before us a majestic picture : the touching description of the birth of Jesus as man alternates with the sublime one of the eternal birth of the Word in the bosom of the Father; and there are also allusions to Christ's birth in our souls by grace. However, this three-fold birth is but one single manifestation of God who is Charity. No one on earth could know God's love; but the Word, who is in the bosom of the Father, knows it and can reveal it to us. The Word was made flesh and has shown to us the love of God. Through the Word, God's incomprehensible, invisible charity is made manifest and tangible in the sweet little Babe, who from the manger holds out His arms to us. Today's Preface solemnly declares it : " O eternal God, because of the mystery of the Word made flesh, the light of Thy glory hath shone anew upon the eyes of our mind : that while we acknowledge Him to be God visible, He may draw us to the love of things invisible. " Yes, this " Child, wrapped in swaddling clothes and laid in a manger " is our God, who, for us, has made Himself visible : our God, who shows us in the most concrete way His infinite charity. One cannot contemplate little Jesus without being captivated and enraptured by the infinite love which has given Him to us. The Infant Jesus reveals to us God's love, He manifests it in the clearest, most touching way. St. Paul says in the Epistle of the Third Mass (*Heb* 1,1-12) : " God, in these days hath spoken

to us by His Son...the brightness of His glory, and the figure of His substance. " Jesus, the Incarnate Word, in His silence as a helpless Child, speaks to us and reveals to us the substance of God : His charity.

COLLOQUY

" O all-powerful and eternal Trinity! O sweet, ineffable charity! Who would not be inflamed by such love? What heart could keep itself from being consumed by You?

" O abyss of charity! You have so closely bound Yourself to Your creatures that it seems that You cannot live without them! Nevertheless You are our God! You have no need of us. Our good adds nothing to Your greatness, for You are immutable. Our misfortune cannot harm You, O God, sovereign, eternal Goodness! Then what urges You to such mercy? Love—for You have no obligation toward us and no need of us. Then, O infinite God, who brings You to me, a little creature? No one but Yourself, O Fire of Love! Love alone has always urged You, and love still urges You!

" O sovereign sweetness, You have deigned to unite Yourself to our bitterness; You, brilliance, with our darkness; You, wisdom, with our stupidity; You, life, with death; You, who are infinite, with us who are finite! " (St. Catherine of Siena).

O sweet Incarnate Word, O most amiable Infant Jesus, behold me at last at Your feet; let me contemplate You; permit me to delight in Your beauty, Your goodness, Your immense charity! In this little Child who smiles, and holds out His baby arms to me, I find Your infinite love, living, breathing—for this Babe is You, O my God! How can I ever thank You for Your exceeding love? How can I ever make You a return of love?

" You, who are so great and rich, have made Yourself little and poor for us! You chose to be born far from home, in a stable, to be wrapped in swaddling clothes, to be nourished at Your Virgin Mother's breast, to be laid in a manger between an ox and an ass. Today is the dawn of the new redemption, of the old restoration, of eternal happiness; today, the heavens have distilled honey throughout the whole world! Then, O my soul, kiss this divine manger,

press your lips to the Infant's feet and embrace them.
Meditate on the shepherds watching their flocks, contemplate
the angelic hosts, prepare to join in the heavenly melody,
singing with your lips and with your heart : ' Glory to God
in the highest, and peace on earth to men of good will ' "
(St. Bonaventure) !

30

BELIEVING IN LOVE

DECEMBER TWENTY-SIXTH

PRESENCE OF GOD - O most sweet Infant Jesus, permit me to enter
into the abyss of Your infinite love, so that I may believe in it with
all my strength.

MEDITATION

1. When creating us, God loved us so much that He
made us to His own image and likeness; when redeeming
us, He loved us so much that He made Himself to our image!
Christmas is pre-eminently the feast of love—the love
which was revealed, not in the sufferings of the Cross, but
in the lovableness of a little Child, our God, stretching
out His arms to make us understand that He loves us.

If the consideration of God's infinite justice can rouse
us to greater fidelity in His service, how much more does
the consideration of His infinite love incite us! St. Thérèse
of the Child Jesus used to say, " Fear makes me shrink,
while under love's sweet rule I not only advance, I fly "
(T.C.J. *St*, 8). Jesus, the divine Infant, is here in the midst
of us, to replace the old law of fear with the new law of love.

To run in the path of God's commandments, we must
be thoroughly convinced of God's infinite love for us, and
precisely in order to reach this conviction, we immerse
ourselves in contemplation of the mystery of the Nativity.
In fact, when we see Jesus, the eternal Word, become
a child for us, and from the very first moment of His earthly
life, gladly taking on all our miseries, even to the point

of having nothing but a manger for a cradle, with a little
hay for bedding, and poor swaddling clothes for covering...
Oh, we can no longer doubt His love. God loves us! Jesus
loves us! Yes, let us repeat it again and again, " We
have known and have believed the charity which God
hath to us " (1 *Jn* 4,16). Lord, I believe in Your love for
me! Lord, increase my faith!

2. God is Love! An immense treasure is contained in
these words, and it is the treasure which God discloses to
souls who devoutly contemplate the Incarnate Word. Until
we comprehend that God is infinite love and infinite benevolence, who gives Himself and extends Himself to all
men in order to communicate to them His goodness and His
happiness, our spiritual life has still just begun; it has not
yet developed or deepened. Only when the soul, enlightened
by the Holy Spirit, has penetrated the mystery of divine
charity, only then does its spiritual life attain to full maturity.
We cannot better understand the infinite love of our
God, than by drawing near to the humble manger where
He lies, made flesh for us. " The virtues and attributes
of God are known in God, through the mysteries of God
made man, " says St. John of the Cross (cf. *SC*, 37,2); and
among these attributes the first is charity, which constitutes
the very essence of God. From the silent, loving contemplation of the Infant Jesus, there is easily aroused in us a more
profound and penetrating *sense* of His infinite love : we no
longer merely believe, but in a certain way, we know by
experience God's love for us. Then our will fully accepts
what faith teaches; it accepts it with love, with all its strength,
and our soul believes unreservedly in God's infinite love.
God is Love; this truth, fundamental for all Christian life, has
penetrated to the depths of the soul; it feels it, it lives
it, because it has, so to say, almost touched it in its Incarnate
God. One who so believes in infinite love will know how to
give itself to Him without measure : to give itself totally.

COLLOQUY

Lord, I believe in Your love for me! How could I still
doubt it?

"You have come down from the great height of Your divinity to the mire of our humanity, because the lowness of my intellect could neither understand nor behold such height. In order that my littleness might see Your greatness, You became a little child, concealing the greatness of Your Deity in the littleness of our humanity. And so You manifest Yourself to us in the Word, Your only-begotten Son; thus have I known You, O abyss of charity! O blush with shame, blind creature, so exalted and honored by your God, not to know that God, in His inestimable charity, came down from the height of His infinite Deity to the lowliness of your humanity! O inestimable love! What do you say, O my soul? I say to You, eternal Father, I beseech You, most benign God, that You give us and all Your servants a share in the fire of Your charity" (St. Catherine of Siena).

O God, how great is my need to know Your infinite love! To know in order to believe, to believe in order to love, to love in order to give myself entirely to You, with no reservation, just as You have given Yourself entirely to me.

O my God, how much I want to repay You for this inestimable gift! Alas! You who are all, have given me all, whereas I, who am nothing, can give You only this nothing! Yet how slow, indolent, and miserly I am in giving You this nothing, how much I try to spare myself, to give myself with measure, with prudence.... Oh, Your love knew no measure; it did not calculate the infinite distance between the Creator and the creature, but surpassed, exceeded, and engulfed this distance by uniting indissolubly human nature with the divine Person of the Word. How true it is that love knows no obstacles, overcomes everything, and adapts itself to everything in order to attain its end! O loving Infant Jesus, my God, my Savior, give me the grace of an ever-increasing understanding of the greatness and depth of Your love; make me penetrate this boundless abyss, whose bottom no creature can ever touch! The more I enter into it, the more I feel new strength born in me, a new impulse which urges me irresistibly to give myself wholly to you. You know how necessary it is for this strength to grow and become established in me, so as to make me truly generous, ready for every sacrifice, every gift of myself. O Lord, grant that I may understand Your infinite charity! Give me a firm faith in it, and never let me refuse anything to Your love : this is the gift I beg of You on the day of Your Nativity!

31

RETURNING LOVE FOR LOVE

DECEMBER TWENTY-SEVENTH

PRESENCE OF GOD - I recollect myself before the humble manger : I contemplate the divine Infant, begging Him to teach me how to give Him love for love.

MEDITATION

1. To assume human nature and hence unite Himself to it, the eternal Word concealed His divinity, majesty, power, and infinite wisdom : behold the divine Infant who can neither speak nor move by Himself, who in all things depends entirely upon His Mother, His creature, to whom He looks for everything.

Let us try to understand this mystery in order to apply it to our poor lives. True love overcomes every obstacle, accepts every situation, and makes any sacrifice in order to unite itself with Him whom it loves. If we wish to be united to God, we must do exactly what the Word did to become united to human nature; He followed a path of prodigious self-abasement, of infinite humility! Here there opens before us the path of the " nothing, " of total abnegation. " All, nothing; all, nothing! " This was the lullaby sung by St. John of the Cross to his God made man. " In order to possess everything, desire to possess nothing " (*AS I*, 13,11). Compared to the infinite humiliations of the eternal Word made flesh, this path should not seem to us too austere and exacting. To repay His infinite love, to prove our love for Him, let us resolve to strip ourselves generously of everything that could hinder our union with Him; above all, let us divest ourselves of self-love, pride, vanity, all our righteous pretensions. What a striking contrast between these vain pretenses of our " ego " and the touching humility of the Incarnate Word! *Sic nos amantem, quis non redamaret?* Who would not love Him who loves us so much? *(Adeste Fidelis).*

2. Out of love for us, Jesus not only stripped Himself of all His greatness and majesty, but from the very first moment of His earthly life, He embraced every possible privation. Let us also strip ourselves voluntarily for love of Him. Let us strip ourselves of our love of riches, of our attachment to our material well-being, our comforts, and everything that is superfluous. We are already under obligation to do this by our vow or promise of poverty, but even without this obligation, how can we calmly lead a life of ease when our God has voluntarily embraced so much poverty and hardship? Let us consider how the Holy Child Jesus lived : rough straw, insufficient coverings, a stable for His house, a manger for His cradle.... Looking at the manger, one feels that the way of " nothing " does not ask too much : " Strive to seek not the best of temporal things, but the worst. Strive thus to desire to enter into complete detachment and emptiness and poverty, with respect to everything that is in this world, for Christ's sake " (J.C. *AS I,* 13,6).

If we want to repay Jesus' infinite love, let us strip ourselves generously of everything for Him, not only material goods, but also every attachment to creatures, for, as St. John of the Cross teaches, " To love is to labor, to detach and strip oneself for God's sake, of all that is not God " (J.C. *AS II,* 5,7). The way of " nothing " takes us quickly to Bethlehem, where God has united Himself to our human nature in the most intimate, personal way, there where He awaits us to unite our souls to Himself.

COLLOQUY

O my sweet Jesus, grant that I, even in a small way, may be able to repay You for Your infinite love. Out of love for me, my God, You became man; from Lord, a slave; from rich, poor; from omnipotent, a little helpless Babe....

Oh! grant that for love of You, I may courageously and generously follow the path of the " nothing, " of total despoliation.

For love of me You are stripped of Your majesty and grandeur. You conceal every sign of Your divinity, You make Yourself little and humble, in order to become " mine, " so that I may not only know You, but that I may possess You *entirely*, since You give me—not only in Bethlehem, but every day in the Holy Eucharist—all Your divinity, all Your humanity! I, Your miserable creature, who am so loved and favored by You, shall I not know how, for love of You, to become wholly Yours and strip myself of my self-love?

" O divine Word, become a Child for love of me, teach me to become a child for love of You. Oh! what great love and power You show me by becoming a little Babe, willing to keep silence, and to have need of everything, like other children! You were like unto us in all things—sin excepted. To show me my misery, the first sound You uttered was a cry, fulfilling the words of Wisdom : *Primam vocem simile omnibus emisi plorans*, like all others I came into the world crying. And what an example You give me! When You place Your tiny limbs on the manger straw and rest Your head on a stone, You teach me the lesson of Your humility and poverty. O most sweet Infant Jesus, grant that I may be like unto You in all things " (cf. St. Mary Magdalen dei Pazzi).

O God, infinite, eternal wealth, how You have abased Yourself for love of me! And I, who have promised You poverty, how far I still am from being really poor, from fervently practicing this poverty which You love so much!

O Lord, sweet Incarnate Word, I wish to return by my love Your infinite love. I wish to prove by my actions that I really love You. What shall I do for You, O sweet Jesus? Out of love for You, I will strip myself of everything that is not You, for I desire nothing but You, and I want to become like You, who being God, became man. Make me, who am proud, become humble. You, who are the Ruler and Lord of the whole universe, became poor and needy; make me, who love my comfort, become a sincere lover of true poverty. Humility and poverty will start me on the road of the " nothing, " and then, emptied of myself and all things, I shall at last be able to love You with all my strength, and to say with perfect sincerity :

" Lord, I love You more than myself and above all things. "

32

GLORY TO GOD

DECEMBER TWENTY-EIGHTH

PRESENCE OF GOD - I unite myself in spirit to the angelic choir singing the glory of the Lord over the fields of Bethlehem.

MEDITATION

1. The Word was made flesh for our salvation and happiness. However, the primary end of the Incarnation is God's glory, which is the end of all His works. He, the one absolute good, cannot will anything apart from His glory. By sending His only Son to save men, He wished to glorify His infinite goodness, to glorify Himself in our salvation, accomplished by means of this supreme act of His infinitely merciful love. The work of creation glorifies God in His wisdom and omnipotence; the work of the Incarnation glorifies Him in His charity. And as God could not manifest greater mercy and charity than by giving His Son for our salvation, so none of His works can give Him greater glory than the Incarnation of the Word. Hence, the angels sang at the birth of the Redeemer, " Glory to God in the highest! " The Church takes up this hymn and amplifies it in the Gloria which is sung in every feast-day Mass; " We praise You, we bless You, we glorify You, we give You thanks for Your great glory. " At no time more than at Christmas do we feel the need of repeating this song, more with our heart than with our lips. The soul feels more than ever incited to praise its God, so immense, so great, so beautiful, but also so good, so merciful, so full of charity. Song does not suffice : the soul would wish to be transformed into an incessant " praise of His glory. "

2. We have been predestinated in Christ " that we may be unto the praise of His glory " (*Eph* 1,11.12). As Christians, we are, of ourselves, proofs of Christ's glory; our elevation to a supernatural state, our sanctification, and eternal happiness have for their supreme end the glory of Him who has redeemed us.   Christians, and with greater reason, consecrated souls, must act in such a way that all their works and their whole lives may be a praise of glory to the Trinity and to Christ Our Lord.   Today the Church presents to us the " first fruits " of these " true Christians, " those who by their works, and even by their death, have sung the glory of the Redeemer.   We see them in the retinue of the divine Child, like angels on earth, who unite their hymn to that of the angels in heaven.   St. Stephen, the protomartyr, teaches us that a faithful, loving soul must be ready to give up everything, itself and even its life, for the glory of its God.   St. John the Evangelist, " the blessed Apostle to whom heavenly secrets were revealed " and who penetrated so deeply into the mystery of God as infinite charity, shows us that love for our neighbor " is the precept of the Lord; if this only be done, it is enough " *(RB)* to give glory to Him who is infinite Love.

The Holy Innocents, " the first tender buds of the Church, " demonstrate that the voice of innocence is a hymn of glory to God, resembling that of the angels : " From the mouths of babes and sucklings you have perfected praise, O God! "   But this hymn becomes much more powerful and eloquent when it is united to the sacrifice of their blood : " The martyred Innocents confessed God's glory, not in word but by their death " *(RB)*.   May our life also be a hymn of praise to God, " not by words, but by works. "

COLLOQUY

" May my voice loudly resound : with attentive mind may I contemplate You, my God, and with my words sing Your praises; it is right that a creature praise its Creator, for You created and redeemed us that we might praise You, although You do not need our praise.   You are incomprehensible Power and have no need of anyone, but are sufficient in Yourself.   You are great, O Lord, my God, Your power is great and the works of Your wisdom are

without number. You are great, O Lord, my God, and
worthy of all praise. May my soul love You, my tongue
praise You, my hand write of You, and may my whole
soul be occupied in these holy exercises. Satisfy me ever
with this sweet food, so that I may praise You with a mighty
voice, with all my heart and all my powers, singing Your
praise sweetly, joyfully, and fervently, O God!

" ' O my soul, bless the Lord, and let all that is within
me bless His holy Name. Bless the Lord, O my soul, and
never forget His innumerable favors!' Let us praise this
God whom the angels praise, before whom the Dominations
prostrate to adore, who is feared by the Powers and in whose
honor the Cherubim and Seraphim continually sing : Holy!
Holy! Holy! Let us join our voices to those of the angels
and saints, and let us praise the Lord with the fullness of
our powers " (St. Augustine).

Yes, my God, my Redeemer, and my Savior, I desire
to praise You eternally, and until I go to praise Your glory
with the angels and saints in heaven, I want to begin to
praise You here below, not only with my tongue, but with
my deeds, with my whole life. " In order to be a praise
of glory, I must love You with a pure, disinterested love,
without seeking myself in the sweetness of Your love; I must
love You above all Your gifts. Now, how shall I desire
and effectively will good to You, except by fulfilling Your
will, since this will orders all things for Your greater glory?
I ought, therefore, to surrender myself completely, blindly,
to that will, so that I cannot possibly will anything but
what You will " (E.T. *I*, 10). When Your will or Your
laws ask me to sacrifice myself for love of You and for Your
glory, grant that I may never shrink from it, but be ever
ready to give myself wholly, even to the supreme sacrifice of
my life.

33

PEACE TO MEN

DECEMBER TWENTY-NINTH

PRESENCE OF GOD - I place myself at the feet of the Infant Jesus to meditate on the angels' hymn : " Peace on earth to men of good will " (*Lk* 2,14).

MEDITATION

1. At Bethlehem the angels announced two things : glory to God and peace to men; the one corresponds to the other. No one glorifies God as much as that little Babe lying on the straw. He alone, being the eternal Word, can give God the perfect, infinite praise that is worthy of Him. And no one more than Jesus, our Savior, brings peace to men; making reparation for sin, He reconciles man with His Creator and establishes a new covenant between them : the Creator will become Father, and man, His son.

Something similar is verified in our daily life. Those who obey God's law enjoy peace; observing the divine law they also glorify God. The glory of God corresponds perfectly to the peace of men. But we are treating of that peace which comes only from Jesus, from His grace, peace which we will seek in vain elsewhere.

" Peace is the tranquillity of order. " Order is established by the law and will of God. Those who respect this order fully, possess the plenitude of interior peace; those who depart from it, even in a slight degree, lose their peace in proportion to their deviation from it. Peace is the refreshment and repose of the soul in the midst of the struggles and sorrows of life, but this is not the only reason for which we should try to obtain and possess it. We should desire it above all because it gives glory to God.

2. The angels promised peace " to men of good will. " Our will is " good " when it is upright, docile, and resolute. It is *upright* when it is sincerely and entirely oriented toward

good; *docile*, when it is always ready to follow every indication of God's will; *resolute*, when it is prompt to adhere to the will of God, even though difficulties and obstacles arise, and sacrifices are required. The Lord is continually urging us to generosity and abnegation in all the circumstances of life, even the smallest ones. We must give ourselves to God without hesitation, certain that if God asks anything of us He will also give us the strength to carry out His wishes. Such was the conduct of the shepherds; as soon as they heard the message of the angel, they left all, their flocks and their rest, and " came with haste [to Bethlehem] where they found... the Infant lying in the manger" (*Lk* 2,16). They were the first to find Jesus and to taste His peace.

St. Teresa of Jesus says, " Holy peace consists in a union with God's will, of such a kind that no dissension arises between the will of God and the soul, but they are both one — not in words or in desires alone but in works. When a soul finds that by doing something it can serve its Spouse better, it listens to no objections raised by its mind, nor to any fears... but allows faith to act, and considers not its own profit nor its own tranquillity " (T.J. *Con*, 3). This is perfect " good will. " Mary and Joseph are unsurpassable models of it. Despite the obscurity of the mystery and the great sacrifices entailed, they clung to the divine plan in total abandonment, and had the supreme joy of receiving the King of Heaven in their arms. To the greatest good will corresponds the greatest union with God, and the deepest peace and joy.

COLLOQUY

I give You thanks, O Jesus, for the infinite glory which You give to Your divine Father, making up for all the inability and insufficiency of Your poor creatures! You are the perfect praise of glory of the Blessed Trinity, the splendor of Their glory : praise and thanksgiving I render to You, O Lord! You could have glorified Your Father without caring for us who had offended Him. What need did God have of our happiness and welfare? But You, the most merciful, wanted to glorify Your Father precisely by obtaining salvation for us and giving us peace. Oh! how much I long for that peace which You came to bring into the world!

You alone can give it to me, You alone can wholly pacify my poor heart, which is too often torn between the demands of Your divine love and the violence of my passions or the attractions of the world.

O Lord, give me Your peace; let it establish Your kingdom in me and make me a praise of glory of Your Holy Name. But it is Your will that, while I hope for everything from Your grace and mercy, I should not fail to labor assiduously to obtain this Your great gift.

You will give me peace if I have " good will " : a sincere will, which clings strictly to the good, without duplicity or artifice, without secondary ends or compromises. O Lord, give me this upright will which never wanders from the good and true; even when the truth stings, and discloses all my weaknesses, give me courage to love it, to accept it wholly, just as it is, and to act accordingly. O Lord, I also want my will to be submissive to the smallest sign from You, like a light sailboat which follows every breath of wind with docility. Alas, my will is still so tenacious, so obstinate and hard to bend, so firm in its stand! Make it supple, O sweetest Jesus, who came down from heaven to earth to carry out Your Father's will.

Strengthen my will also, so that I may be enabled to conquer every repugnance, every vacillation and hesitation, especially when I have to overcome difficulties and face sacrifice. O Lord, I desire to have an upright, resolute will, that I may go straight to You, with the swiftness of an arrow; a will as supple as a wave which obeys the wind, that I may follow every indication of Your will. Then there will be no division between my will and Yours; there will be perfect union, perfect peace. O Jesus, what a high ideal You have given man, whom You have redeemed! Man was living in sin, and was therefore as far away from God as sin is from infinite perfection. By your precious merits You not only raised him from the abyss in which he lay, but called him to union with God. By Your mediation, the Master and Judge becomes the Father, Friend, and Spouse of the soul of good will!

O Jesus, how much You have given us, how much You have given me! Eternal praise be to You!

34

A SIGN OF CONTRADICTION

PRESENCE OF GOD - The world is made up of friends and enemies of Jesus. O Lord, grant that I may be one of the former, and one of the most loving of them.

MEDITATION

1. Today's Mass is an echo of Christmas, but while it speaks of peace and joy, it also has a note of deep sadness. The Gospel (*Lk* 2,33-40) suddenly transports us to the presentation of Jesus in the Temple, forty days after His birth, and repeats Simeon's prophecy, " Behold this Child is set for the fall and for the resurrection of many in Israel, and for a sign which shall be contradicted. "

The Son of God became man for all men; He brings and offers salvation to all, but many will not receive it. This is the great mystery of human freedom. God has made man intelligent and free; He offers him all the treasures of salvation and sanctity contained in the infinite merits of Jesus Christ; man is free to accept or refuse. This is our tremendous responsibility. Jesus came to save us, to sanctify us, to give Himself entirely to our souls. He is ready to do it, He wants to do it, and yet He will not do it until we *freely* accept His infinite gift, until we correspond to His loving solicitation with the *free* gift of our will. " God never forces anyone; He takes what we give Him, but does not give Himself wholly until He sees that we are giving ourselves wholly to Him " (T.J. *Way*, 28).

The prophecy of Simeon was addressed directly to the Virgin Mother. " And thy own soul a sword shall pierce. " The bloody vision of the Cross is thus mingled unexpectedly with the charming scene of the Nativity, reminding us that the tender Babe of Bethlehem is the divine Lamb who will one day be immolated for the salvation of the world.

2. Among all those present when the Child Jesus was presented in the Temple, there were only two who recognized

the Savior, the aged Simeon and the prophetess Anna. Of Simeon it is said : " He was just and devout, waiting for the consolation of Israel; and the Holy Ghost was in him " (*Lk* 2,25); and of Anna : " She departed not from the Temple, by fastings and prayers serving night and day. " Behold the characteristics of souls well disposed to accept the redemptive work of Jesus : rectitude of mind and will, sincere longing for God, recollection, prayer, mortification. The more profound these dispositions become, the more the soul opens itself to the divine action. The light of the Holy Spirit enables it to recognize in Jesus its Redeemer and its Sanctifier, and Jesus can wholly accomplish His work in it. St. Paul's magnificent words in today's Epistle (*Gal* 4,1-7) apply to such souls in a special way : " And because you are sons, God hath sent the Spirit of His Son into your hearts, crying : Abba, Father! " And the Apostle says to every Christian, to every soul redeemed by Jesus' Blood, " Now you are not a servant, but a son. And if a son, an heir also through God. " Unfortunately, not all Christians live as true sons of God; in Baptism they have received the " adoption of sons, " but they do not make their deeds correspond to this immense, gratuitous gift, the fruit of the merits of Jesus.

When, on the other hand, a soul generously corresponds with God's action, He takes total possession of it, and the Holy Spirit, the Spirit of Jesus, cries out from the depths of its heart, " Abba, Father. "

COLLOQUY

O my God, what responsibility men have when they consider Your great gifts, and especially the Incarnation of Your only-begotten Son, who became man for our salvation!

" Oh, how the very greatness of His favor will condemn those who are ungrateful! Do come to the help of such, my God! O children of men, how long will you be hard of heart and fight against this most gentle Jesus? What is this? Is it possible that our wickedness will prevail against Him? No, for human life is cut short like the flower of the grass, and the Son of the Virgin will come and pass that terrible sentence.... Blessed are they who at that dread moment shall rejoice with You, O my Lord and my God.

"O my Lord, how shall I ask You for favors, I who have served You so ill and have hardly been able to keep what You have already given? How can You have any confidence in one who has so often betrayed You? What, then, shall I do, Comfort of the comfortless, and Help of all who seek help from You? Can it be better to keep silence about my necessities, hoping that You will relieve them? No, indeed, for You, my Lord and my Joy, knowing how many they are, and how it will alleviate them to speak to You about them, bid us to pray to You and promise that You will not fail to give.

"What, then, can one who is as wretched as I, ask of You? 'That Thou wilt give to me, my God,' as St. Augustine said, 'so that I may give to Thee, to repay Thee some part of all that I owe Thee; that Thou wilt remember that I am Thy handiwork; and that I may know who my Creator is, and so may love Him'" (T.J. *Exc*, 3-5).

But it is I, O Lord, above all, who am forgetful and do not correspond as I should to Your infinite gifts!

O gentle pilgrim of love, You stand at the door and wait! How many doors in Bethlehem were closed to You : there was no room for You except in a wretched stable. And is not my heart still more wretched, more squalid, more unworthy of You than that poor stable? And yet, if I open it to You, You will not disdain to make it Your dwelling and the place of Your repose, as You did the stable where You were born. O my Jesus, give me the grace to open my heart wide to You, to adhere with all the strength of my will to Your grace, to give You all my liberty, because henceforth I desire but one liberty : the liberty to love You with all my strength, to give myself wholly to You. O Lord, how much You have loved us, and how few are those that love You! Grant that at least these few may be truly faithful to You, and that I also may be of their number.

35

LET US MAKE GOOD USE OF TIME

DECEMBER THIRTY-FIRST

PRESENCE OF GOD - On the last day of the year, I recollect myself in the presence of the Child Jesus, to examine in the light of eternity the value of time.

MEDITATION

1. Time passes and does not return. God has assigned to each of us a definite time in which to fulfill His divine plan for our soul; we have only this time and shall have no more. Time ill spent is lost forever. Our life is made up of this uninterrupted, continual flow of time, which never returns. In eternity, on the contrary, time will be no more; we shall be established forever in the degree of love which we have reached now, in time. If we have attained a high degree of love, we shall be fixed forever in that degree of love and glory; if we possess only a slight degree, that is all we shall have throughout eternity. No further progress will be possible when time has ended. " Therefore, whilst we have time, let us work good to all men " (Gal 6,10). " We must give every moment its full amount of love, and make each passing moment eternal, by giving it value for eternity " (Sr. Carmela of the Holy Spirit, O.C.D.). ¹ This is the best way to use the time given us by God. Charity allows us to adhere to God's will with submission and love and thus at the close of life we shall

¹ Sr. Carmela of the Holy Spirit, a Discalced Carmelite Nun who died July 23, 1949, was a soul of an exceptional interior life, some of whose writings were published by FATHER GABRIEL OF ST. MARY MAGDALEN, O.C.D. toward the end of 1950 in his *Revista di vita spirituale* (See Nos. 1 and 2). In 1954 her life was published together with more of her writings and some notes of direction from Father Gabriel, who had been her spiritual director in Carmel. Cf. *Sr. Carmela of the Holy Spirit*, Carmel of St. Joseph, Rome.

have realized God's plan for our soul; we shall have reached
the degree of love which God expects from each one of us and
with which we shall love and glorify Him for all eternity.

2. The growth of charity depends upon meritorious
acts, that is, good works done under the influence of charity.
Every good act merits an increase of charity, which may
be given to the soul at once or withheld until the end of life,
according to whether the act had been performed with
all the love of which the soul was capable, or whether,
on the contrary, it was performed with less vigor, generosity,
and carefulness than was possible at that moment. In the
first case, the increase of charity comes like interest which
is immediately accrued to the capital, and which then
bears interest together with it. In the second case, it is
like interest which is kept separate from the capital and
hence does not increase with it, even though it remains the
property of the one who has acquired it.

In order that the merit of our good works, that is,
the increase of charity which we have merited by them,
be granted immediately, it is necessary that these works
be done with all the love possible, that is, with all the good
will and generosity of which the soul is capable. Then it is as
if the soul opens to receive the increase of love it has merited;
and this is added at once to the capital of charity already
possessed, immediately increasing its degree and intensity.

We have only the short day of this earthly life in which
to grow in love, and if we wish to derive from it the greatest
possible profit, we must overcome our natural inertia and
carry out our good works " with our whole heart. " Then
love will increase immeasurably and we shall be able to say
to Our Lord like St. Thérèse of the Child Jesus : " Your
love has grown with me and now it is an abyss, the depth
of which I am unable to sound " (*St,* 12). We must, then,
make haste while we still have time, for " the night cometh
when no man can work " (*Jn* 9,4).

COLLOQUY

O Lord, as I look back on the year just passed, a year
given me by Your divine Providence in which to increase
my love of You, I can only grieve over myself and say to

You : " How little I have loved You, my God! How badly I have spent my time! "

"How late have my desires become enkindled, and how early, Lord, did You go in search of me, calling me to spend myself wholly in Your service! Did You perchance, Lord, forsake the wretched or turn from the poor beggar who sought to approach You? Can it be, Lord, that there is any limit to Your wonders or to Your mighty works? O my God and my Mercy! Now will You be able to show Your mercies in Your handmaiden. How powerful You are, great God! Now it will become clear, Lord, if my soul, looking upon the time it has lost, is right in its belief that You, in a moment, can turn its loss to gain. I seem to be talking foolishly, for it is usual to say that time lost can never be recovered.

" Blessed be my God! O Lord, I recognize Your great power. If You are mighty, as indeed You are, what is impossible for You who can do all things?

" Well do You know, my God, that in the midst of all my miseries I have never ceased to recognize Your great power and mercy. May it prove of avail to me that I have not offended You in this. Restore the time I have lost, my God, by granting me Your grace both in the present and in the future, that I may appear before You wearing the wedding garment, for You can do this if You so will " (T.J. *Exc*, 4).

On my part, O Lord, I can think of no better way to make up for the time I have lost than to try with all my might to increase my love. Yes, my love will grow if, for Your sake, I fulfill all my duties and perform all my good works " with all my heart " and " with all my good will. " Alas! I am so weak, so careless, so indolent! I am inclined to flee from exerting myself; I try to avoid making sacrifices. My nature always seeks what is easiest, what is least tiring, and soon falls into negligence and laziness. Help me, O Lord, and strengthen my love by Your almighty power. What I do for You is so little; grant, O my God, that I may at least do it with all the love possible.

36

THE OCTAVE OF THE NATIVITY OF OUR LORD

JANUARY FIRST

PRESENCE OF GOD - I draw near You, Divine Babe, in order to receive the first drops of Your most Precious Blood in my soul.

MEDITATION

1. The *Magnificat antiphon* of First Vespers of the Feast sums up perfectly the spirit of this day : " For His great love, wherewith God loved us, He sent His own Son in the likeness of sinful flesh. "   This liturgical solemnity unites to the consideration of God's immense charity, which illumines and dominates all the feasts of the Christmas cycle, this vision of the Incarnate Son of God in the likeness of sinful man.   In order to transform us from sinners into children of God, the only Son of the Father willed to be clothed in human nature, thereby putting on our sinful flesh and submitting to all its most humiliating consequences.   The law of circumcision could in no way affect Jesus, the Son of God, the Most Holy One; but Jesus willed to submit to it as the least of the sons of Abraham, for as St. Paul says, " It behooved Him in all things to be made like unto His brethren... that He might be a propitiation for the sins of the people " (*Heb* 2,17).   The rite, which Joseph may have performed in the intimacy of the family, caused the first drops of the Precious Blood to be shed from the immaculate flesh of Jesus.   Thus eight days after His birth, He is beginning His redemptive mission.   He has not yet spoken; the world does not know Him; but He is already shedding His Blood for the salvation of mankind.

Contemplating Him, we shall learn that deeds are better than words, that the greater the sacrifices they require, the greater the proof they give of real love.   Furthermore, every undertaking must receive its baptism of blood in order to be fruitful.

2. This Feast coincides with the beginning of the civil year; the first drops of Jesus' Blood seal and consecrate

each new year, making it really the "annus Domini," the year of Our Lord, which it actually is, since time belongs to God.   Our life too is God's; it has been redeemed and sanctified by the Blood of Christ.

Let us, then, begin the year by circumcising our hearts, for as St. Ambrose says, "He who has been circumcised of every vice will be judged worthy of the Lord's attention.... See how all the events which followed one another in the Old Testament prefigured what was to happen later, for the circumcision also represents purification from sins" *(RB)*.

A new year, a new life!   A new life indeed!—for if we circumcise in ourselves the "old man" with his vices and passions, the "Christian" can grow in us : we can become new creatures, purified by the Blood of Christ, vivified and nourished by His grace, so that it may no longer be we who live, but Christ who lives in us.   The new year which begins today will acquire value only if lived in this light.   Only by this daily circumcision of the heart will grace triumph in us, thus making the Christ-life an ever-increasing reality in our souls.

Jesus' humble submission to His Father's will, manifested by His obedience to the law, is another lesson to be learned from today's Feast.   It is an invitation to us to be docile to God's will, whatever it may be.   None of us knows what awaits us in this new year, but God knows.   His will has already prepared our path; every detail of our life is already determined in His mind.   Let us be ready to accept, or rather to embrace with courage and readiness, everything that God wishes or permits, certain that in His holy will we shall find our peace and our sanctification.

COLLOQUY

"O Word Incarnate, You are but eight days old and already You are giving Your Blood for me.   What lesson do I draw from this?... Obedience.   By Your circumcision You reveal to me Your obedience to God, Your meekness, and Your humility" (St. Mary Magdalen de Pazzi).

O Jesus, permit the first drops of Your most pure Blood to purify and inebriate my poor soul!   I understand that from the very first days of Your life You hastened to shed

Your Blood because You wanted to show us at once that You are our Savior and Redeemer. This shedding of Blood was not necessary for You, O Son of God, who art holy with the holiness of Your Father; but it was necessary for me, a poor creature born in sin. You wished to humble Yourself, even to submitting Yourself to a law which was made for sinners. O my Lord, teach me to be humble and obedient. You did not refuse circumcision, You the innocent Lamb, who taketh away the sins of the world... and I, a sinner, want to be considered just? I resent it when I am considered imperfect; I try to conceal my faults under a cloak of false excuses. Oh! teach me that I can neither follow You, nor become like You, if I do not welcome opportunities of humbling myself with You!

You also teach me to obey and to submit to my heavenly Father's will, no matter what it demands or what sacrifice it requires. " I think of this new year as a white page given to me by Your Father, on which He will write, day by day, whatever His divine good pleasure has planned. I shall now write at the top of the page, with complete confidence : *Domine, fac de me sicut vis*, Lord, do with me what You will, and at the bottom I already write my *Amen* to all the proposals of Your divine will. *Yes* Lord, *yes* to all the joys, the sorrows, the graces, the hardships prepared for me, which You will reveal to me day by day. Grant that my *Amen* may be the Paschal *Amen*, always followed by the *Alleluia*, uttered wholeheartedly, in the joy of a complete gift. Give me Your love and Your grace, and I shall be rich enough " (Sr. Carmela of the Holy Spirit, O.C.D.).

37

FEAST OF THE MOST HOLY NAME OF JESUS

SUNDAY FROM JANUARY SECOND TO FIFTH
OTHERWISE, JANUARY SECOND

PRESENCE OF GOD - O Jesus, make me understand the mysteries and the treasures contained in Your most sweet Name.

MEDITATION

1. This Feast complements the circumcision mystery, since it was during the rite of circumcision that the name Jesus was given to the Child. On the first day, the Church directed our attention to the humility of the Son of God; today she invites us to meditate upon and celebrate the glories of His Name.

That these glories flow especially from His prodigious humiliations is clearly affirmed by St. Paul : " Brethren, Christ humbled Himself, becoming obedient unto death, even to the death of the Cross. For which cause God also hath exalted Him and hath given Him a Name which is above all names : that at the Name of Jesus every knee should bow " *(Phil* 2, 8-10). The Church, by placing on our lips this theme from today's Office, invites us, her children, to render grateful, pious homage to Him who humbled Himself so profoundly for us.

The heart of every Christian should respond to this invitation and exalt the most Holy Name of Our Savior, that is, His very Person, for the Name of Jesus expresses what He is : Savior, Redeemer. This sacred Name, announced by the Angel to both Mary and Joseph, was given to Our Lord by God Himself. " Thou shalt call His Name Jesus, for He shall save His people from their sins " *(Mt* 1,21). This Name expresses and synthesizes the great mysteries of the Incarnation and the Redemption; it is at the center of the universe like a point of contact, like a bridge between God and all mankind. Man can reach God only by means of Jesus and in the Name of Jesus : " for there is no other name under heaven whereby we must be saved " *(Ep : Acts* 4,8-12).

2. Today's Mass, continuing St. Paul's thought, offers us a majestic picture of the glory which is due the holy Name of Jesus : " That at the Name of Jesus, every knee should bow, of those that are in heaven, on earth, and under the earth; and that every tongue should confess that the Lord Jesus Christ is in the glory of God the Father " (Introit). The entire Church—triumphant, militant, and suffering—is prostrate in adoration; the whole of creation seems to be silent, having stopped in its course for a moment to hear this most holy Name which gives glory to God and salvation to mankind. Truly, " neither tongue can tell, nor pen express " the inestimable treasures contained in the Name of Jesus. " Nothing sweeter can be sung, nothing more agreeable can be heard, nothing more delightful can be imagined than Jesus, the Son of God " *(RB)*. " Thy name is as oil poured out " *(Ct* 1,2), says Holy Scripture, and St. Bernard comments, " Oil gives light, it nourishes, it anoints. . . . See how well this applies to the Name of the true Bridegroom. It is light when it is preached; it is food in meditation; it is balm and healing when it is invoked for aid. . . . All food is as dry husks to the soul unless it is steeped in this oil; insipid unless seasoned with this salt. If you write, it has no savor for me, unless I read there the Name of Jesus. If you discourse or converse, it has no taste unless the Name of Jesus shall sound. The Name of Jesus is honey to the mouth, music to the ear, gladness to the heart. It is healing " *(RB)*. Let us lovingly bless and invoke this most sweet Name which contains all our hope and our salvation, all our life and our glory. Only he who loves can penetrate the mysterious sweetness contained in it; only he who loves can praise it suitably, not by words alone but by deeds; only he who loves can bear witness to it by his entire life. " May Thy Name, O Jesus, resound in our voices! May our actions express Thy life and our hearts love Thee now and forever! " *(ibid.)*.

COLLOQUY

" O glorious Name! Gracious Name! Name full of love and virtue! Through You, sins are forgiven, enemies overcome, the sick healed, and sufferers strengthened in adversity! You are the honor of believers, the master of preachers, the comfort of those who toil, the support of the weak. Holy desires are nourished by the ardor of Your fire; and by it, necessary suffrages are obtained, contemplative souls are inebriated, and the triumphant are glorified in heavenly glory! By Your most Holy Name, O sweet Jesus, You make us reign with the Blessed, You, their glory, You who triumph gloriously with the Father and the Holy Spirit, in perfect Unity and Trinity, forever and ever.

" O Name of Jesus, exalted above every other Name! O triumphant Name! O joy of Angels! O terror of hell! All hope of pardon, of grace and of glory is found in You! O sweetest Name, You pardon the guilty, You reform evil habits, You fill the timid with divine sweetness and drive away terrifying visions! O glorious Name! By You, the mysteries of eternal life are revealed, souls are inflamed with divine love, strengthened in time of struggle, and freed from all dangers. O desirable Name! Delightful Name! Admirable Name! Venerable Name! Little by little You raise the souls of the faithful by Your gifts and graces to the heights of heaven. All to whom You communicate Your ineffable grandeur, by Your power attain to salvation and glory! " (St. Bernardine of Siena).

How good is Your Name, O Lord! Grant that its goodness may make me, unworthy creature that I am, capable of loving and praising You with all my heart.

I want to begin and end all my works by invoking Your Name, and to mark all my affections, desires, undertakings, joys, and sorrows with this sacred seal. But O Lord, I beg You, above all, imprint Your Name on my heart and mind, so that I may always love You and think of You.

38

JESUS OUR MEDIATOR

PRESENCE OF GOD - Grant, O Jesus, that I may enter still further into the great mystery of Your Incarnation.

MEDITATION

1. During the Christmas days our thoughts, centered on Jesus, have revealed to us a little of the great " mystery which hath been hidden from eternity in God " (*Eph* 3,9), the mystery we now wish to consider in synthesis, in order to arouse in ourselves greater admiration for its " unfathomable riches. "

The infinite distance between God and man, the impassable abyss, the breaking of every bond of friendship—all this was the tremendous consequence of sin. Then between God and man appeared the sweet Babe of Bethlehem; suddenly and completely the whole situation changes : distance is overcome, and across the abyss a wonderful bridge is erected which unites earth with heaven and re-establishes relations of intimacy between God and men. This bridge is Jesus, the " only Mediator between God and man, " who " joins earth to heaven in a truly remarkable manner " (*Mystici Corporis*). In His office as Mediator, Jesus is really " at the center " : He is the point of union between divinity and humanity. His mediation has all the qualifications necessary for perfectly pleasing God, since He Himself is true God; at the same time, because He is true man and, as such, represents the whole human race, Jesus can make worthy satisfaction to God for the entire debt of sinful mankind.

The divinity possessed by Jesus as the Word is united in His Person with the humanity He possesses as man. These two natures are not merely in juxtaposition, but they embrace each other; even more, they are united in one Person, the Person of the Incarnate Word, Jesus Christ, Our Lord. In Him and through Him, all mankind is readmitted to friendship with the heavenly Father. In

Him all can find again the way to reach union with the Trinity.

The eternal Father deigned to reveal this wonderful mystery to St. Catherine of Siena : " It is My wish that you consider the bridge I have built in the Person of my only-begotten Son, and that you notice that it reaches from earth to heaven, because in Him the majesty of the divinity is united with the lowliness of your human nature. It was necessary to construct this bridge in order to repair the road which had become impassable and to open a passage across the trials of this world to eternal life " (Dialogue).

2. " For it hath well pleased *the Father* that in [Jesus] all fullness should dwell, and that through Him He should reconcile all things unto Himself, making peace through the blood of His Cross, both as to the things that are on earth, and the things that are in heaven " (*Col* 1,19.20). Jesus accomplished His work as Mediator on Calvary, where He shed all His Blood as the price of our redemption. But His work began at Bethlehem, where the Word took, so to speak, that ineffable " giant's step " which brought Him from heaven to earth, which made Him true Man as well as true God.

The terrible abyss which sin had produced between God and man has been filled up by the Child who opens His arms to us from the manger. All that sin had spoiled and destroyed is now, by the will of God, saved, " re-established in Christ " (cf. *Eph* 1,10). Oh! how spontaneous is the need to praise and adore when the Child Jesus is contemplated in this light! Here, tenderness and admiration are one!

The grace which Adam had received directly from God, we now receive only through Jesus, our Mediator; our whole supernatural life always comes through Him. If we wish to be united to God, we have no other means than to attach ourselves to Jesus, to pass through Him, our Mediator, our Bridge, our Way. Jesus has said, " I am the way " (*Jn* 14,6); " I am the door. By Me, if any man enter in, he shall be saved " (*ibid.* 10,9). Behold the only condition, the only way of salvation, of sanctity.

COLLOQUY

"O eternal God, O high eternal Father, in You I find inestimable love, the love which made You cast a glance of pity on Your poor creatures. It made You send us the Word, Your only Son, the Incarnate Word, veiled in flesh and clothed in our mortality. And You, O Jesus Christ, our Peacemaker, Reformer, and Redeemer, You, the Word, Love, became our Mediator, and signed the peace treaty of the great battle which man had been waging against God. He punished our iniquity and Adam's disobedience in Your Body, when You were obedient even unto Your ignominious death on the Cross.

"Whatever way I turn, I meet nothing but ineffable love. I cannot excuse myself for not loving You, because it is You alone, God and man, who loved me without any return of love on my part, because when I did not exist, You created me. In You I find all that I want to love.... If I want to love God, I have Your ineffable Deity; if I want to love man, You are man.... If I want to love the Lord, You paid my ransom with Your Blood, and lifted me up from the slavery of sin. You are our Lord, Father, and Brother by Your benignity and Your incommensurable charity.... You are God, supreme wisdom, I am only a poor ignorant creature. You are sovereign, eternal goodness. I am death, You are life; I am darkness, You are light; I am stupidity, You are wisdom; You are infinite, I am finite. I am sick, You are the physician; I am a weak sinner that has never loved You; You are purest beauty, and I a most vile creature. In Your ineffable love, You have drawn me to You; You draw us all to You by grace, not by force, and this, only if we are willing to be drawn to You, that is, if our will does not rebel against Yours" (St. Catherine of Siena).

"O Christ, O God, sweet Lover of mankind, I implore You; I beg and beseech You to be my Way, to let me reach You, and rest in You, the Way, the Truth, and the Life; without whom no one reaches the Father" (St. Augustine).

39

JESUS THE FIRST-BORN OF ALL CREATURES

PRESENCE OF GOD - Give me light, O Lord Jesus, to see in the lowliness of the Child, the indescribable Majesty of the Son of God.

MEDITATION

1. Jesus " is the image of the invisible God, the first-born of every creature; for in Him were all things created in heaven and on earth, visible and invisible...all things were created by Him and in Him. And He is before all, and by Him all things consist " (*Col* 1,15-17). This text from St. Paul summarizes the infinite greatness of Jesus. As the Word, He is the perfect, substantial image of the Father, having the same divine nature as the Father and proceeding from Him by eternal generation. As the Word He is the first-born of all creatures, begotten of the Father before all creation; furthermore, the Father created everything through Him, His Word, His eternal Wisdom. St. John of the Cross teaches, " God looked at all things in this image of His Son alone, which was to give them their natural being and to communicate to them many natural gifts and graces.... To behold them...was to make them very good in the Word, His Son " (J.C. *SC*, 5,4). But the Word is not only the first-born of all creatures. Possessing the same divine nature as the Father, He is also their Creator, for " without Him was made nothing that was made " (*Jn* 1,3).

All these splendors, which belong by nature to the Word, became the splendors of Jesus, the Man-God, by reason of His Incarnation and His hypostatic union. In fact, St. Paul declares that " in Him dwelleth all the fullness of the Godhead corporeally " (*Col* 2,9).

Jesus was pleased to conceal all the infinite riches of His divinity in the obscurity of the manger; yet, guided by faith and love, we shall not be slow to recognize and praise Him in this lowly guise.

2. Jesus, the first-born, is the source of our being, not only in the natural order, the order of creation, but also

and especially in the supernatural order, the order of grace. In fact, " ...in this image of His Son alone He left them clothed with beauty, communicating to them supernatural being. This was when He became man, and thus exalted man in the beauty of God " (J.C. *SC*, 5,4).

The Word became incarnate in order to give us super-natural being; Jesus came precisely to make us children of God. He, God's only Son by nature, became thus the first-born of many brethren who, in Him and through Him, become children of God by grace. This is the wonderful, mysterious plan of our elevation to the supernatural state : " Blessed be the God and Father...who hath blessed us with spiritual blessings in heavenly places, in Christ...who hath predestinated us unto the adoption of children through Jesus Christ " (*Eph* 1,3.5).

From all eternity, God the Father willed to raise men to the dignity of sons; therefore, He gave our first parents, not merely natural life, but also supernatural life, which they lost by sin. God, however, had foreknown their fall, had even permitted it in view of a still more wonderful plan than the first, a plan which would manifest in an incomparable manner His infinite charity and mercy toward man : the Incarnation of His Son, that through Him " we might receive the adoption of sons " (*Gal* 4,5).

In this marvelous plan we contemplate two sublime mysteries : Jesus, the first-born of every creature in the order of nature as well as in the order of grace; we, the children of sin, becoming in Him and through Him the adopted sons of God.

COLLOQUY

" Thou hast multiplied Thy wonderful works, O Lord, my God; and in Thy thoughts there is no one like to Thee " (*Ps* 39,6). " It is good to give praise to the Lord : and to sing to Thy Name, O Most High, to show forth Thy mercy in the morning, and Thy truth in the night. For Thou hast given me, O Lord, a delight in Thy doings; and in the works of Thy hands I shall rejoice. O Lord, how great are Thy works! Thy thoughts are exceeding deep " (*ibid.* 91, 2.3.5.6).

What work could be more wonderful than the Incarnation of Your only-begotten Son? Is there any masterpiece more sublime than Jesus Christ, true God and true man, " in whom are hid all the treasures of wisdom and knowledge " (*Col* 2,3)?

O Jesus, You make me understand that You are really God made man and You manifest Yourself to my soul with such majesty that I can no longer doubt Your infinite greatness. O Lord, who can comprehend the depths of Your great Majesty, You who are the absolute Ruler of heaven and earth?

" O Christ, my God, my hope, lover of mankind, the light, the way, the life; the salvation, honor, and glory of all Your servants, You live eternally, reigning now and for all eternity.... You are my living and true God, my holy Father, my loving Lord, the great King, the good Shepherd, my only Teacher, my incomparable helper, my guide to heaven, my straight path...my immaculate Victim, my holy Redeemer, my firm hope, my perfect charity, my true resurrection, my eternal life. I long for You, my sweetest, most beautiful Lord!...

" O splendor of the Father's glory, who sit above the Cherubim and scrutinize the abyss, true light, shining light, unfailing light, on whom the angels desire to gaze, behold my heart before You; drive away the darkness from it that it may be more abundantly inundated with the splendors of Your holy love.

" Give me Yourself, O my God, give me Yourself, that I may love You; and if my love is not very fervent, make me love You more ardently.

" I cannot measure what is wanting in my love to make it what it ought to be, to make it run to meet Your embrace, and not to leave it until my life is hidden in the light of Your face; this I know, that all is a source of evil for me except You, O Lord, and not only what is outside of me, but also what is within me. All wealth which is not my God is poverty and misery for me " (St. Augustine).

40

JESUS THE UNIVERSAL KING

PRESENCE OF GOD - O Lord, Your greatness is unfathomable; enable me to adore and love You in a manner worthy of Your infinite Majesty.

MEDITATION

1. Since Jesus is all things to us, it is fitting that we honor Him as our King. He Himself proclaimed, " I am a king " (*Jn* 18,37). " All power is given to Me in heaven and in earth " (*Mt* 28,18).

In the Encyclical *Quas Primas*, Pius XI teaches that " Jesus is King by right of nature and by conquest. " By right of nature, " He possesses...power over all creatures, not that He seized it by violence, nor received it from another, but He possesses it by His own nature and essence; His power comes from that wonderful union which is called by theologians *hypostatic*. For this reason Christ is to be adored not only as God by angels and men, but these angels and men owe submission and obedience to Him also as man. " In fact, Christ as man participates fully in the royalty and sovereign majesty of Christ as God; since, as man and as God, Christ is one Person, the second Person of the Blessed Trinity. He is at the summit of all creation : the beginning and the end, the King of all things; He holds " the primacy in all things " (cf. *Col* 1,18).

" What could be more pleasing and agreeable than the thought that Christ is our Ruler, not only by right of nature, but by a right of conquest, which He acquired when He became our Redeemer! O that ungrateful men would remember how much we have cost our Savior! We were not redeemed at the price of gold or silver...but by Christ's precious Blood. We no longer belong to ourselves, because Christ has paid a precious ransom for us" *(Quas Primas)*. Jesus has every right to rule over us; He *must* reign; *oportet Illum regnare!* (1 *Cor* 15,25).

2. From all eternity, God the Father beheld in Christ —His only-begotten Son, made man for the redemption

of sinful humanity—the masterpiece of His hands, and therefore He decreed that *all* should be created by Him, given to Him as His royal allotment. St. Paul states that God the Father has set Christ " on His right hand in the heavenly places, above all principality and power, and virtue and dominion, and every name that is named, not only in this world, but also in that which is to come " (*Eph* 1,20.21). Behold Christ the King set above the angels, above those pure spirits who also were created for His glory.

As for mankind, we must repeat with the Apostle that we have been chosen and predestined in Christ, " that we may be unto the praise of His glory " (*ibid.* 1,12). Like the angels, we have been created for the glory of Christ, the universal King. By glorifying Him on earth, we unite our praise with that of the angels in heaven.

To glorify Jesus as our King is to acknowledge His sovereign rights over us, that is to say, to live in docile submission to His gentle rule.

His reign is one of love : out of love for us and to save us, He came down from heaven and became one of us. He died on the Cross for the same reason, shedding all His sacred Blood for us. Jesus reigns in the crib; He reigns from the height of the Cross. Behold the price He paid to win our poor hearts, He who by His very nature was already our absolute ruler. Let us not resist the gentle violence of His infinite love; let us give ourselves entirely to Him, allowing Him to reign in our minds, in our wills, and in our hearts.

COLLOQUY

" O my Lord and my King! If one could but picture Your Majesty! It is impossible not to see that in Yourself, You are a great Emperor, for to behold Your Majesty strikes terror. But my terror is greater, my Lord, when together with Your Majesty I behold Your humility and the love that You bestow on such a creature as I.

" When I have overcome the first feeling of terror which is aroused at the sight of Your great Majesty, I can converse with You, and speak freely about my interests.... Although You are God, I can talk with You as with a friend, for You are not like those whom we call lords on earth, all of whose power rests upon an authority conferred on them by others. Your Kingdom, O Lord of glory and King of kings, is without end. How little we need any intermediaries to reach You. I have only to see You to realize that You alone deserve the name of Lord; Your Majesty is so great that You need neither guard nor escort to convince us that You are King " (T.J. *Life*, 37).

O Lord, grant that I may always acknowledge You as the King and sovereign Ruler of my soul. Everything I have I have received from You; how, then, could I fail to understand that You hold all rights over me? Yet You are a King who seems to take no account of His sovereign rights. Why did You have to abase Yourself to the obscurity of Bethlehem, to humiliate Yourself even to dying on the Cross, even to shedding all Your Blood in order to win my heart? My heart, my whole life, and all my being already belonged to You, because You are my Creator and because I was created for Your glory. But You willed to forget all Your rights and You came to me like a beggar, seeking my poor heart.

O Jesus, how can I still resist Your infinite love? Take my heart; take my whole being; and make me a living praise of Your glory.

41

THE EPIPHANY OF OUR LORD

JANUARY SIXTH

PRESENCE OF GOD - I recognize in You, O little Jesus, the King of heaven and earth; grant that I may adore You with the faith and love of the Magi.

MEDITATION

1. " He whom the Virgin bore is acknowledged today by the whole world.... Today is the glorious Feast of His *Manifestation* " *(RB)*. Today Jesus shows Himself to the world as God.

The Introit of the Mass brings us at once into this spirit, presenting Jesus to us in the full majesty of His divinity. " Behold the sovereign Lord is come; in His hands He holds the kingdom, the power, and the empire. " The Epistle (*Is* 60,1-6) breaks forth in a hymn of joy, announcing the vocation of the Gentiles to the faith; they too will acknowledge and adore Jesus as their God : " Arise, be enlightened, O Jerusalem : for thy light is come.... And the Gentiles shall walk in thy light, and kings in the brightness of thy rising.... All they from Saba shall come, bringing gold and frankincense, and showing forth praise to the Lord. " We no longer gaze upon the lowly picture of the shepherds at the manger; passing before us now is the resplendent procession of the Wise Men from the East, representing the pagan nations and all the kings of the earth, who come to pay homage to the Child-God.

Epiphany, or *Theophany*, means the *Manifestation of God;* today it is realized in Jesus who manifests Himself as God and Lord of the world. Already a prodigy has revealed His divinity—the extraordinary star which appeared in the East. To the commemoration of this miracle, which holds the primary place in the day's liturgy, the Church adds two others : the changing of water into wine at the wedding feast of Cana, and the Baptism of Jesus in the Jordan, when a voice from heaven announced, " This is My beloved Son. " The Magnificat Antiphon says, " Three miracles adorn this holy day "—three miracles which should lead us to recognize the Child Jesus as our God and King, and to adore Him with lively faith.

2. The verse at the Gradual of the Mass continues the story of the Magi : " We have seen His star in the East and are come with gifts to adore Him. " They saw the star and immediately set out. They had no doubts : their unbounded faith was strong and sure. They did not hesitate at the prospect of the trials of a long journey : they had generous hearts. They did not postpone the journey : their souls were ready.

A star often appears in the heaven of our souls; it is an inspiration from God, clear and intimate, urging us to greater generosity and calling us to a life of closer union with Him. Like the Magi, we too must always follow our star with faith, promptness, and selfless generosity. If we allow it to guide us, it will certainly lead us to God; it will bring us to the One whom we are seeking.

The Magi did not give up their quest, although the star—at one point—disappeared from their sight. We should follow their example and their perseverance, even when we are in interior darkness. This is a trial of faith which is overcome only by the exercise of pure, naked faith. I know that He wills it, I know that God is calling, and this suffices for me : *Scio cui credidi et certus sum* (2 *Tm* 1,12); I know whom I have believed. No matter what happens, I shall trust Him.

In this spirit let us accompany the Magi to adore the new-born King. " And as they brought forth from among their treasures mystical gifts, let us *from our hearts* bring forth something fit to offer Him " *(RB)*.

COLLOQUY

O Jesus, I adore You, for You are the Lord my God. " For You, my Lord, are a great God, and a great King above all kings. For in Your hand are all the ends of the earth, and the heights of the mountains are Yours. For the sea is Yours, and You made it; and Your hands formed the dry land.... We are the people of Your pasture and the sheep of Your hand " (cf. *Ps* 94). Yes, O Jesus, I am one of Your lambs, one of Your creatures; and I am happy to acknowledge my nothingness in Your presence, and still happier to adore You, O lovely Infant, as my God and my Redeemer. O that all nations would acknowledge You for what You are, that all might prostrate before You, adoring You as their Lord and God!

O Lord, You can do this. Reveal Your divinity to all mankind, and just as once You drew the Magi from the East to You, now in like manner unite all peoples and all nations around Your manger.

You have shown me that You want my poor cooperation in order to bring about the coming of Your Kingdom. You wish me to pray, suffer, and work for the conversion of those who are near and of those who are far away. You wish that I, too, place before the manger the gifts of the Wise Men : the incense of prayer, the myrrh of mortification and of suffering borne with generosity out of love for You, and finally, the gold of charity, charity which will make my heart wholly and exclusively Yours, charity which will spur me on to work, to spend myself for the conversion of sinners and infidels, and for the greater sanctification of Your elect.

O my loving King, create in me the heart of an apostle. If only I could lay at Your feet today the praise and adoration of everyone on earth!

O my Jesus, while I beg You to reveal Yourself to the world, I also beseech You to reveal Yourself more and more to my poor soul. Let Your star shine for me today, and point out to me the road which leads directly to You! May this day be a real Epiphany for me, a new manifestation to my mind and heart of Your great Majesty. He who knows You more, loves You more, O Lord; and I want to know You solely in order to love You, to give myself to You with ever greater generosity.

42

FEAST OF THE HOLY FAMILY, JESUS, MARY, AND JOSEPH

FIRST SUNDAY AFTER THE EPIPHANY

PRESENCE OF GOD - I beg the Blessed Virgin Mary to allow me to enter in spirit the humble home at Nazareth, to contemplate Jesus' most admirable life there.

MEDITATION

1. On this day for the last time in the cycle of the liturgical year, the Church invites us to contemplate the mystery of Jesus' humble, hidden life. A feeling of close intimacy and tenderness characterizes this Feast and is expressed in the liturgy of the day : " ...it is good for us to recall the little home at Nazareth and the humble life of those who lived there.... In it, Jesus learned Joseph's humble trade, and grew in age, and was happy sharing the work of a

carpenter : ' Let the sweat, ' He seemed to say, ' trickle over My limbs before they are drenched with the torrent of My Blood, and the pain of this labor shall go to atone for the sins of men! ' " *(RB)*. Let us enter the little house; in the presence of such humility, which conceals Jesus' infinite Majesty, let us repeat the words of the sacred text : " Thou art indeed a hidden King, O God the Savior, King of Israel " *(ibid.)*.

Today's liturgy particularly emphasizes one typical aspect of the humble life of this hidden God : obedience. " Although He was the Son of God...He learned to obey; He humbled Himself, becoming obedient even unto death " *(ibid.)*. From Bethlehem to Calvary obedience was His companion. The Gospel *(Lk* 2, 42-52) stresses this obedience of Jesus at Nazareth in words which carry for all time the strength of their first utterance, " He was subject to them. " Let us ask ourselves with St. Bernard, " Who obeyed? Whom did He obey? " The Saint replies, " God obeyed man! Yes, the God to whom the angels are subject...was subject to Mary, and not only to Mary, but also to Joseph. For God to obey a woman is humility without parallel.... Learn then, man, to obey; learn, O earth, to be submissive. God subjected Himself to men; and do you, desiring to rule others, place yourself above your Creator? "

2. " Did you not know that I must be about My Father's business? " Jesus, who was so humble and submissive, did not hesitate to make this reply to Mary when she gently questioned Him about having remained behind in the Temple without her or Joseph's knowledge, while they in anguish had been seeking Him for three days.

These are the first words of Jesus which we find recorded in the Gospel. He spoke them in order to declare His mission and to affirm the primacy of the rights of God. When hardly an adolescent, Jesus taught us that God and the things of God must always come first. He must hold the first place in our lives, and we must obey Him regardless of all other considerations, even if it means sacrificing the rights of nature and of blood. Yielding to relatives and friends is no longer a virtue—and may even be sinful—if it leads us away from the will of God or hinders its fulfillment.

Giving precedence to the rights of God does not imply that we neglect our duties toward our neighbor. Today's

Feast calls our attention to these obligations, and especially to those concerning our family, natural or religious, inviting us to follow the example of the Holy Family of Nazareth. To this end, the Epistle (*Col* 3,12-17) shows us the virtues we should practice : " Clothe yourself... with mercy, benignity, humility, modesty, and patience, bearing with one another, and forgiving one another. "

COLLOQUY

O Jesus, how I love to contemplate You as a Child, in the poor house at Nazareth, with Mary and Joseph! Your simple, humble life was just like that of any other child of Your age. You, the splendor of the Father, did not wish anything to distinguish You from the children of men; You, uncreated wisdom, wished to learn from Mary and Joseph, Your creatures, the ordinary little details of life. Joseph showed You how to handle his tools and You watched Him attentively, You learned, You obeyed. Mary taught You holy hymns and recounted tales from the Sacred Scriptures; You listened to her like a humble disciple, You who are the one true Teacher, You who are Truth itself. No one, neither Your relatives nor Your fellow townspeople, knew who You really were. Everyone believed You to be the carpenter's son and paid no more attention to You than they would have paid to an ordinary apprentice.

Only Mary and Joseph knew; they knew by divine revelation that You were the Son of the Most High, the Savior of the world, and yet they knew it more by faith than by experience. Your ordinary way of life concealed Your majesty and divinity from them so completely that when, without their knowledge, You remained among the doctors in the Temple, they could not understand the reason for Your unusual behavior.

That incident, however, was an isolated one; immediately afterward, You wished to return to the hiddenness of Your most humble life. You went back with them, and were subject to them. And this, day by day, until You were thirty years old.

O most sweet Jesus, grant that I may imitate, at least to some degree, Your infinite humility! You, the Creator, were obedient to Your creatures. Teach me to bow my proud head and willingly obey my superiors. You came down from heaven to earth. Give me the grace to humble myself, to come down, once and for all, from the pedestal of my pride! How can I bear the sight of Your humility and self-effacement, O my God and my Creator, when I, who am nothingness and sin, use the gifts I have received to set myself above others, to prefer myself even to my superiors?

43

JESUS THE TRUE VINE

PRESENCE OF GOD - O my Lord and Redeemer, grant that I may understand the deep intimate ties that bind You to us, whom You have redeemed.

MEDITATION

1. Jesus is the " one Mediator between God and men " (1 *Tm* 2,5); however, He did not will to effect the work of our redemption independently of us, but used it as a means of strengthening the bond between Himself and us. This is the wonderful mystery of our incorporation in Christ, the mystery which Our Lord Himself revealed to His apostles the night before His Passion. " I am the true vine; and My Father is the husbandman.... Abide in Me, and I in you. As the branch cannot bear fruit of itself, unless it abide in the vine, so neither can you, unless you abide in Me " (*Jn* 15,1.4).

Jesus strongly affirms that there is no redemption, no supernatural life, no grace-life for one who does not live in Him, who is not grafted onto Him. He points to the vine : the shoots will not live and bear fruit unless they remain attached to the trunk. Jesus wishes to actualize this close connection between Himself and us, a connection which is necessary for our salvation and sanctification. We cannot receive the least degree of grace except through

Christ's mediation, even as the smallest drop of sap cannot reach a branch which is detached from the tree.

Moreover, Jesus declares that, if we abide in Him, we shall not only have supernatural life, but we shall become the recipients of special attention from our heavenly Father, the " Husbandman " of the mystical vine.   In fact, our heavenly Father acknowledges us as His adopted children, loves us as such, and takes care of us, precisely to the degree in which He sees in us Christ, His only-begotten, His well-beloved Son. The grace of adoption, then, is wholly dependent upon our union with Christ, a union so close that we form, as it were, a " living part " of Him, as the branch forms a living part of the vine.

2. " Abide in Me. " We can only abide in a place where we are already. Jesus tells us to " abide " in Him because we have been grafted onto Him.   This spiritual engrafting, an accomplished fact, was made possible for all men by Christ's death on the Cross, and it became effective for each one of us at the time of our Baptism.   Christ grafted us into Himself at the cost of His precious Blood.   Therefore, we " are " in Him, but He insists further that we " abide " in Him and bring forth fruit.

Baptism is sufficient to graft us into Christ, and one degree of grace will permit us to abide in Him like living branches, but we should not be content with this union only.   We must show our gratitude for the immense gift we have received by endeavoring to become more and more firmly grafted into Christ.   We must " live " this union with Christ, making Him the center, the sun of our interior life.   " Abide in Me " is not a chance expression.   Christ wished to show us that our life in Him requires our personal collaboration with Him, that we are to employ all our strength, our mind, our will, and our heart that we may live in Him and by Him.   The more we try to abide in Christ, the deeper our little branch will grow into Him, because it will be nourished more abundantly by the sap of grace.

" Abide in Me and I in you. "   The more closely we are united to Christ by faith, charity, and good works done with the intention of pleasing God, the more intensely will He live in us and bestow on us continually a new life of grace.   Thus we shall become, not merely living branches,

but branches laden with fruit, the fruit of sanctity destined
to bring joy to the Heart of God, for Jesus has said : " In this
is My Father glorified, that you bring forth very much
fruit " (*Jn* 15,8).

COLLOQUY

"O most high and eternal Trinity, Deity, Love, we are
trees of death, and You are the tree of Life.   O infinite God!
How beautiful was Your creature when a pure tree in Your
light!   O supreme purity, You endowed it with branches,
that is, with the faculties of the soul, memory, intellect,
and will. . . .   The memory, to recall You; the intellect,
to know You; the will, to love You. . . .   But this tree fell,
because by disobeying it lost its innocence.   Instead of
a tree of life, it became a tree of death and brought forth
only fruits of death.

"This is why, O eternal, most high Trinity, in a sublime
transport of love for Your creature, seeing that this tree
could produce only fruits of death because it was separated
from You, who are Life, You gave it a remedy with that
very same love by which You had created it, grafting Your
Deity into the dead tree of our humanity.   O sweet, gentle
grafting!. . .   Who constrained You to do this, to give
back life to it, You who have been offended so many times
by Your creature?   Love alone, whence by this grafting
death is dissolved.

"Was Your charity content, having made this union?
No, eternal Word, You watered this tree with Your Blood.
This Blood by its warmth makes it grow, if man with his
free will grafts himself onto You, and unites and binds his
heart and affections to You, tying and binding this graft
with the bond of charity and following Your doctrine.
Since it is through You, O Life, that we bring forth fruits
of life, we wish to be grafted onto You.   When we are
grafted onto You, then the branches which You have given
to our tree bear fruit " (St. Catherine of Siena).

How encouraging it is to think, O Jesus, that my longing
to be united to You is not a vain fantasy, but is already
a reality!   It is a reality because You have willed to graft
me onto You as a shoot is grafted onto the vine, so that
I live wholly by this union with You.   Oh! grant that my

soul may become always more closely united to You, and may always be ready to receive the vital sap of grace which You produce in me, Your branch!

44

THE MYSTICAL BODY OF CHRIST

PRESENCE OF GOD - O Holy Spirit, grant that I may be rich with the " fullness of understanding, unto the knowledge of the mystery... of Christ Jesus " (*Col* 2,2).

MEDITATION

1. " I am the vine; you, the branches. " On these words of Jesus, which describe our union with Him, the whole doctrine of the Mystical Body of Christ is founded. Only the figure is changed : instead of the vine, we speak of the Body of which Christ is the Head and we are the members. In explaining this doctrine, St. Paul aptly paraphrases what Jesus had previously said. " As the body is one, and hath many members; and all the members of the body, whereas they are many, yet are one body, so also is Christ.... Now you are the Body of Christ, and members of member " (1 *Cor* 12,12.27).

The thought in both descriptions is evidently identical : as the branches are part of the vine on which they grow and from which they are nourished with one sap; as the parts of the human body form one body and have a single life; so we, being incorporated in Christ, make but one body with Him and live of His Life. This is the Mystical Body of Christ " which, " St. Paul teaches, " is the Church " (*Col* 1,24).

Christ is the Head of this Body. " Christ is the Head of the Church.... He is the Savior of the Body " (*Eph* 5,23). The Father " hath made Him Head over all the Church, which is His Body...and His fullness " (cf. *ibid.* 1,22.23). One Body, one life which comes to each of its members from the Head. " Christ Our Lord vivifies the Church with His own supernatural life; by His divine power He permeates the whole Body and nourishes and sustains each of the members...very much as the vine nourishes and makes fruitful the branches which are joined to it " *(Mystici Corporis)*. The fact that every Christian has life in Christ and lives of the very life of Christ is reaffirmed in these words.

2. Our union with Christ, the Head of the Mystical Body, is certainly not to be understood as being identical with the union that exists among the various members of a physical body. In fact, although we are incorporated in Him, each one of us preserves " intact his own personality " *(ibid.)*. But neither should we understand this union to be a mere moral union, such as exists, for example, among members of the same organization. No, it is something much more profound, it is a mysterious union, and in this sense is called *mystical*, but it is no less *real* and *vital*. It is a union which comes from there being present in all the parts of the Body of the Church " a distinct internal principle, which exists effectively in the whole and in each of its parts, and whose excellence is such, that of itself it is vastly superior to whatever bonds of union may be found in a physical or moral body. This principle is...not of the natural but of the supernatural order. Essentially it is something infinite, uncreated : it is the Spirit of God, who, as the Angelic Doctor says, ' one and the same for all, fills and unifies the whole Church ' " *(ibid.)*.

The Holy Spirit, " the soul of the Church " *(ibid.)*, is the bond which intimately and really unites and vivifies all the members of Christ, diffusing grace and charity in them. He has been " given to the Church with most copious effusion, so that its members from day to day might become always more like the Redeemer " *(ibid.)* Therefore, it is not a question of a symbolical, metaphorical union, but of a real union, so real that it surpasses all the others " as grace surpasses nature, and immortal realities surpass perishable realities " *(ibid.)*. It is a reality so great that it embraces not only our earthly life but, provided we preserve it, it continues to be the source of our happiness for all eternity. Indeed, " grace is the seed of glory. "

We are members of Christ. This is our greatness and our glory, infinitely surpassing all earthly dignity and glory.

COLLOQUY

" O my beloved Spouse and loving Word, You engender the Body of the Holy Church in a way which You alone know and understand.... By means of Your Blood, You make a well-organized, well-formed Body of which You are the Head. The angels delight in its beauty, the archangels admire it, the seraphim are enraptured by it, all the angelic spirits marvel at it, and all the souls of the blessed in heaven rejoice in it. The Blessed Trinity takes delight in it in a manner beyond our comprehension " (St. Mary Magdalen dei Pazzi).

Behold at Your feet, O Lord, a very poor creature : weak, feeble, inclined to evil, and capable of every sin, a worthless creature, like the grass of the field, which is today and tomorrow is not, a wretched creature, who has nothing good in itself and is unable to do anything that is good. Yet, O Jesus, true Son of God, image of the Father, the beginning and the end of all things, Ruler of the universe, Savior of the world, You bend down to me, miserable as I am. You take me, and unite me to Yourself, so closely that I become one of Your members. Then you give me Your life, You make me live Your very life. O Lord, O infinite beauty and holiness, how can You bear to have as one of Your members such a wretched, unworthy creature? You not only do this, but You want to do so, for You have said, " Abide in Me. "

Can I refuse to accept Your invitation and Your command, O Lord, when I know that You Yourself wish to make me an integral part of Your Mystical Body? O Lord, if I could only realize the greatness, the value of this infinite gift which You offer me, and understand the meaning of this sublime reality—to live in You and by You, as the branch lives in the vine, as the member in the body! What do I lack, O Lord, for my sanctification, for my life of union with You? You have already given me much more than I ever could have desired.

O Lord, make me sense the profound reality of this great mystery which brings me into such close union with You. Let it dominate, illumine, and direct my whole life; let everything else fade before it. Grant that I may never seek or desire anything except this reality, and let the deceptive vanities of the world have no attraction for me. Make me have a deep, lively sense of the duty and sweet necessity of being a member worthy of You, and grant that my actions and my life may be such as to do honor to You.

45

" I AM THE LIFE "

PRESENCE OF GOD - O Jesus, Fount of life, may Your life ever increase in my soul.

MEDITATION

1. Jesus explained His mission in these words : " I am come that they may have life, and may have it more abundantly " (*Jn* 10,10). What is this life which He gives us? It is the life of grace, which is a participation in His divine life.

Jesus is the Incarnate Word; in His divine nature as the Word, He possesses divine life in the same way and to the same degree that His Father possesses it. " As the Father hath life in Himself, so He hath given to the Son also to have life in Himself " (*ibid.* 5,26).

This plenitude of divine life reverberates in Christ's humanity by reason of the hypostatic union. His sacred humanity, placed in direct contact with His divinity, to which it is united in one Person, is inundated with divine life; that is, it receives the greatest possible participation in it through " such plenitude of grace that no greater amount can be imagined " (*Mystici Corporis*). The sanctifying grace which fills the soul of Jesus is so plentiful, perfect, intense, and superabundant that theologians do not hesitate to call it " infinite grace. " " Because in Him [Christ], it hath well pleased the Father that all fullness should dwell " (*Col* 1,19), affirms St. Paul; and St. John describes Him as being " full of grace and truth " (*Jn* 1,14). But Jesus does not wish to keep all this immense wealth for Himself alone; He wishes to have brethren with whom He can share it. For this reason He embraced His sorrowful Passion;

by dying on the Cross, He merited for us His members that grace which He possesses in such great plenitude. Thus Christ becomes the one and only source of grace and supernatural life for us. He is so " full of grace and truth " that " of His fullness we have all received " (*ibid.* 1,14.16). Here, then, is how divine life comes to us : from the Father to the Word; from the Word to the humanity which He assumed in His Incarnation, and from this humanity, which is the sacred humanity of Christ, to our souls.

2. Grace, like everything that exists, apart from God, is also created by God. Jesus as God, that is, as the Word, is, together with the Father and the Holy Spirit, the Creator of grace. Let us now contemplate Jesus as our Redeemer, therefore, as Man, and as such, the Mediator of grace, the One who merited grace for us, in virtue of His own infinite treasure of grace, and who also bestows it upon us. He not only merited it for us once for always by His death on the Cross, but He is continually applying it to our souls and producing it in us. Thus grace is infused and made to grow in us by means of His living and ever-present action. In this way, Jesus gives us life; He *is* Life for us, the one source of our supernatural life. For this reason the grace of Jesus is called " capital grace, " that is, grace belonging to the Head, who both merited it and dispenses it to His members.

Two precious, practical consequences follow from this. One who desires to possess grace and supernatural life must go to Christ. He must become incorporated in Him and live in Him. " He that hath the Son hath life. He that hath not the Son, hath not life " (1 *Jn* 5,12).

The grace which sanctifies our souls is, in its essence, identically the same as that which adorns the sacred soul of Jesus (St. Thomas, III[a], q.8, a.5). Of course, they differ immensely in measure and perfection, but the nature of the grace is the very same. Hence grace in us has the same sanctifying power, the same tendencies as it has in the soul of Jesus. Thus it can sanctify us, making us live in union with God and for His glory. By giving us grace, Jesus has truly communicated His life to us; He has planted in us the seed of His sanctity, so that we can live a life similar to His own.

COLLOQUY

O Jesus, how delightful it is to contemplate Your sacred humanity which contains all the treasures of the divine life! I cannot gaze directly at Your divinity, O eternal Word, but it is easy for me to contemplate it in Your humanity; there my thoughts rest, and never cease admiring Your immensity. O Jesus, Your soul is so rich in grace, so luminous, so filled with divine life that Your glory as the only-begotten Son of the Father is fully reflected in it. Your humanity seems to me to be the one mediator and the source of all grace and of all divine life which can be given to mankind. But then I contemplate this sacred humanity as it was lacerated in the bitter torment of the Cross, this humanity which is so glorious and so closely united to God. All its glory is hidden; I see nothing but sorrow, death, and total annihilation. Yet, from those bleeding wounds there gushed forth a marvelous fountain of life : by Your death, O Jesus, You merited grace for us and have become Yourself its one and only source.

I run to You, O Jesus; as one who is thirsty runs toward a spring, I draw near You. Give me, O Lord, of Your water, and I shall thirst no more because " the water You give me will become in me a fountain which will spring up into life everlasting " (cf. *Jn* 4,14). The Apostle, who did not wish to go away from You, once said, " Thou hast the words of eternal life " (*ibid*. 6,69). Oh! You have much more than words of life. You are Life itself, and You give life to us!

But Jesus, let me ask one question. If that sanctifying grace which comes from You and gives life to my soul is, by its very nature, the same kind of grace that fills Your sacred soul, why am I so unlike You, so far from sanctity?

I know the answer. You give me Your grace gratuitously, but You do not make it increase in me without the cooperation of my free will. There is very often a bitter struggle in me between the demands of grace and the claims of my evil nature. Alas! How often nature conquers! O Lord, I beg You, give me the grace to overcome and sacrifice myself, no matter what the cost. Let Your grace and Your life triumph in me for Your glory, and for the glory of Your work of redemption.

" May my mind, my heart, my body, my life, be wholly

animated by You, my sweet Life! I will love You Lord, my strength; I will love You, and will live, no longer through my own efforts, but through You " (St. Augustine).

46

THE INFLUENCE OF JESUS

PRESENCE OF GOD - O Jesus, give me the grace to understand that my soul is always under the powerful, sanctifying influence of Your sacred humanity.

MEDITATION

1. " Virtue went out from Him, and healed all " (*Lk* 6,19), the Gospel says in speaking of Jesus and the astonishing miracles which He worked. At the touch of His hand, the blind saw, the deaf heard, the dumb spoke. The power which went forth from Him was so great that the poor woman suffering from the issue of blood had only to touch the hem of His garment to feel herself instantly cured. It was just as easy for Him to purify and sanctify souls and to forgive sins, as it was to heal bodies. " Which is easier to say : Thy sins are forgiven thee, or to say : Arise and walk? But that you may know that the Son of Man hath power on earth to forgive sins (He saith to the paralytic), I say to thee : Arise, take up thy bed, and go into thy house " (*ibid.* 5,23.24). To remit sins is the prerogative of God alone. If, then, Jesus, says of Himself, who is visibly a man, that He has the power to forgive sins, He affirms that He is God and that the divinity works in His humanity. Indeed, His sacred humanity, full of grace and power, is precisely the instrument which His divinity uses to bestow all grace and life.

The sacred humanity of Jesus, now glorified in heaven, continues to impart the same power and virtue it once did in the districts of Palestine, and this power, being imparted to our souls, influences them from within, purifies, transforms, and sanctifies them. " The interior influence from which grace comes to our souls belongs...to Christ, whose humanity, because it is united to His divinity, has the power to justify " (St. Thomas, III^a, q.8, a.6, co.).

2. We distinguish two phases in Jesus' work of redemption and sanctification. The first phase is His sorrowful life on earth, which ended with His death on the Cross; by it He merited grace for us. The second is His glorious life, which began at His resurrection and still continues, since Jesus Himself is always bestowing upon our souls the grace He merited for us on Calvary. " But to every one of us is given grace, according to the measure of the giving of Christ " (*Eph* 4,7). Day after day, Jesus applies grace to each of us and He causes it to increase and develop in us, so that we live continually under His influence. " As the head rules the members, " says the Council of Trent, " as the vine sends its s. through all its branches, so does Jesus Christ exert His influence at every moment over all the just. This influence precedes, accompanies, and crowns their good works and makes them pleasing to God and meritorious in His sight " (Sess. VI, Can. 16).

Jesus is " always living to make intercession for us, " says St. Paul (*Heb* 7,25). He is living in the most holy Sacrament of the Altar and He is living in heaven, where, seated in glory at the right hand of His Father, He shows Him the reddened wounds of His passion, thereby making continual intercession for us. In addition, " He is Himself choosing, determining, and distributing graces to each one according to the measure of His gift " (*Mystici Corporis*). Christ is then—in the fullest sense, in the most actual sense—the source of all our life. " Christ is our life " (cf. *Col* 3,4), St. Paul exclaims, because, as St. Thomas says : " He is the source of our life. "

COLLOQUY

O Lord, how much I love Your most sacred humanity! O eternal Word, did You not become man in order to be closer to us, to encourage us to come to You fearlessly, in order to lead us to Your Father? Then, how could I, O Jesus, be willing to depart from You or forget You, even for a short time?

" O Lord of my soul, my only Good, my Crucified Jesus, whence have all good things come to me save from You? With so good a Friend, so good a Captain at my side, who came forward first of all to suffer, I can bear everything. You help and give strength; You never fail; You are a faithful Friend. I see clearly that if we are to please God and He is to grant us great favors, He wills that this should be done through Your most sacred humanity, O Christ, for in You, as the Father has said, He is well pleased. Blessed the soul who loves You in truth and has You always at its side. When I see You near me, I have seen all blessings " (T.J. *Life*, 22).

O Jesus, my dearest Redeemer, if I could not follow You along the roads of Palestine, if I cannot behold You in heaven where You are seated in glory at the right hand of Your Father, always interceding for me, I can, nevertheless, every time I so desire, find You living in the most holy Sacrament of the Altar. What an immense gift You have bestowed on me by leaving Your sacred humanity in the Holy Eucharist! As God, You are everywhere, it is true, but as man and my Redeemer I find You in the Sacred Host. My poor human nature needs to find You in the integrity of Your Person as God made man; it needs to be able to approach You and possess You, not only spiritually, but even in a physical reality. I am thinking especially of those precious moments after Holy Communion, when Your sacred humanity is in direct physical contact with my soul. At that time I am not merely touching the hem of Your garment, like the poor woman in the Gospel, but my human nature is touching Yours, and not only touching it, but is being nourished by it, for You come to me as Food. O Jesus! if the influence of Your humanity was so powerful that it could heal and justify all who drew near to You, what can it not effect in my soul during those moments of close, profound contact? O Jesus, forgive me my sins; heal, purify, and sanctify my soul; give me those dispositions of profound humility, lively faith, and ardent love which will enable me to receive the fullness of Your divine influence.

47

THE SOUL OF JESUS

PRESENCE OF GOD - O Jesus, permit me to contemplate Your soul, the chosen temple of the Holy Spirit, and grant that, following Your example, I, too, may become a temple worthy of Him.

MEDITATION

1. Although grace was created equally by the three Persons of the Blessed Trinity, without any difference or distinction, its diffusion in souls is usually attributed especially to the Third Person, the Holy Spirit, to whom everything that concerns the work of sanctification is referred by appropriation. In this sense the tremendous gift of grace which filled the soul of Jesus must be attributed to the work of the Holy Spirit. The soul of Jesus possesses every supernatural gift because " the Holy Spirit dwells in Christ with such plenitude of grace that no greater plenitude can be imagined " *(Mystici Corporis)*. This plenitude of grace, which is a created gift, corresponds to the plenitude of the Holy Spirit, who is the uncreated Gift. Jesus, the only One who " received this Spirit in an unlimited degree " *(ibid.)*, has received from Him the immense capital of grace which permits Him to merit it for all of us.

The soul of Jesus is uniquely beautiful, holy, intimately united to the divinity, and all this to such a degree that the Holy Spirit " takes delight in abiding in it as His chosen temple " *(ibid.)*. He dwells in it with such plenitude and sovereignty that He inspires, directs, and guides all the actions of Jesus, and that is why the Holy Spirit " is correctly called the Spirit of Christ or the Spirit of the Son " *(ibid.)*.

The Gospel tells us several times that Jesus " acted under the influence of the Holy Spirit " (cf. *Lk* 4,1). This happened, not under certain special conditions, but always; the sacred soul of Jesus was not moved by any other impulse, by any spirit other than the Holy Spirit.

2. Jesus, by His Passion and death, merited for us, not only grace, but even the very Author of grace, the Holy Spirit, whom He had promised to the Apostles and whom He

had sent to them at Pentecost. We too receive the Holy Spirit through Jesus; it is always He who, together with the Father, sends us the Holy Spirit. This divine Spirit " is bestowed from the fullness of Christ Himself according to the measure of the giving of Christ " *(Mystici Corporis)*. We receive the Holy Spirit according to the measure of our union with Christ; the Holy Spirit, in turn, unites us to Christ. In fact, as St. Paul says, " Now if any man does not have the Spirit of Christ, he is none of His. And if Christ be in you...the Spirit liveth, because of justification " *(Rom* 8,9.10).

To live in Christ is to live in the Holy Spirit, it is to be a member of His Mystical Body, to be a temple of His Spirit. The grace merited for us by Christ and dispensed to us by Him is diffused in us at the same time by the Holy Spirit. Each increase of grace is caused simultaneously by the creative action of the Holy Spirit and the mediation o Christ. " Christ is in us by His Spirit whom He communicates to us and by means of whom He acts in us in such a way that it may be said that everything that is divine is accomplished in us by the Holy Spirit and also by Christ " *(Mystici Corporis)*.

COLLOQUY

O Jesus, You are so rich, so divine, and so all-powerful that Your gifts are not limited to created things, however sublime they may be, but reach their culmination in the uncreated Gift, in the gift of the Holy Spirit.

It is conformable with Your dignity as God-Man, O Lord Jesus, that the Spirit of Love, the substantial Love which proceeds from the Father and the Son, should be Your Spirit. But that You have wished to give me, a poor creature, this divine Spirit, is a mystery so sublime that I am lost in it. I can only understand, O my dear Redeemer, that I owe this Gift to You!

What return shall I make You, O Jesus, for Your infinite Gift? Oh! if I could at least live and act in such a way that Your Spirit, the Holy Spirit, would find in my soul a temple not too unworthy of Him!

I know that Your Spirit dwells within me, because You have given Him to me. Yet, He cannot fully possess

me, nor lead me swiftly to sanctity, nor hasten my journey
to God, because He often finds resistance in me instead
of docility. O my Jesus, do not permit me to resist Your
Spirit; do not let me grieve Him by my blindness and
obduracy!

"O power of the eternal Father, come to my aid!
Wisdom of the Son, illumine the eye of my intellect! Sweet
clemency of the Holy Spirit, inflame my heart and unite
it to Yourself. I confess, O sweet, eternal Goodness of
God, that the mercy of the Holy Spirit and Your burning
charity are trying to inflame my heart and unite it to You,
together with the hearts of all rational creatures. . . . Burn
with the fire of Your Spirit, consume and destroy, down
to the very roots, all love and affection of the flesh, in the
hearts of the new plants which You have deigned to graft
onto the Mystical Body of Holy Church. Deign, O God,
to carry us away from worldly affection into the garden
of Your love, and create in us a new heart and a clear understanding of Your will, so that, despising the world, ourselves,
and our pride, and filled with the true fervor of Your love
. . . we may follow You for Yourself alone, in chaste purity
and fervent charity! . . .

"O Holy Spirit, come into my heart; by Your power
draw it to You, O God of truth; grant me charity with
fear . . . warm me and inflame me with Your most sweet
love" (St. Catherine of Siena).

48

LIVING IN CHRIST

PRESENCE OF GOD - Grant me, O Lord, to understand the joy and
the responsibility You have given me, in communicating Your
life to me : that I may die to self and live solely for Thee.

MEDITATION

1. "Unless a man be born again of water and the Holy
Ghost, he cannot enter into the kingdom of God" (*Jn* 3,5).
We can attain to God and His kingdom only through Christ,

through our incorporation in Him. This was effected in us by " water and the Holy Spirit, " on the day of our holy Baptism. Jesus said to Nicodemus, " You must be born again "; and this means truly a new birth, because in Baptism we receive the seed of a new life. Before we receive this Sacrament, we have only a human life; afterwards, we participate in divine life. Because we have become incorporated in Christ as His members, we receive the Holy Spirit, who diffuses Christ's grace in us. St. Paul wrote to the Galatians, " For as many of you as have been baptized in Christ, have put on Christ " (*Gal* 3,27). On the day of our Baptism, we are born in Christ and in Him we have become that " new creature " born not of the flesh, but of the Spirit, " born not of blood...nor of the will of man, " but solely " of God " (*Jn* 1,13).

Being born in Christ, we are to live in Christ and walk in Christ, following the exhortation of the Apostle, " Walk ye in Him, rooted and built up in Him, and confirmed in the faith " (*Col* 2,6.7). Baptism gives us our birth in Christ; the other sacraments are not only to restore, but also to root, invigorate, and build up our life in Christ.

2. " O God...grant that we may be made *partakers of His divinity*, who has condescended to become partaker of our humanity. " We may say that this prayer, which the Church repeats at the Offertory of every Mass, has been answered beforehand, because, from the day of our Baptism, we have been made partakers in Christ's divinity. However, this gift, bestowed on us without any merit on our part, requires our cooperation. " Recognize your dignity, O Christian, " St. Leo exclaims, " and having become a sharer in the divine nature, beware lest you return to your former baseness by unworthy conduct. Remember the Head and Body to which you belong. "

Every sin, fault, or voluntary negligence dishonors Christ, our Head, and grieves the Holy Spirit who dwells in us. A consecrated soul, however, cannot remain content with merely avoiding sin; we must also strive to make Christ's life increase in us. In the life of nature, we grow without the help of our own wills; but this is not true of the life of grace. Without our cooperation, it is possible for this life to remain stationary in us for twenty, thirty, fifty years after our baptism, after hundreds of confessions and Holy Communions. What a tremendous disproportion! We may be adults, or even aged in years, but children according to grace!

We must grow in Christ; and He must increase in us. The words of St. John the Baptist form our program, " He must increase, but I must decrease " (*Jn* 3,30). See what the development of grace in us exacts—the death of the " old man " with his bad habits, faults, and imperfections, so that the " new man, " the Christ-life in us, may grow to perfection.

COLLOQUY

" O Lord, how little we profit from all the blessings Thou hast granted us! Thy Majesty seeks methods and ways and inventions by which to show us Thy love; yet we, inexperienced in loving Thee, set so little store by them that, unpracticed as we are, our thoughts pursue their habitual path and cease pondering on the great mysteries of Thy infinite love.

" How miserable is the wisdom of mortal man! How uncertain is His foresight! Do Thou, who foreseest all, provide the necessary means whereby my soul may serve Thee according to Thy will, and not its own.... May this self of mine die, and may Another, greater than myself and better for me than myself, live in me, so that I may serve Him. May He live and give me life; may He reign and may I be His captive, for my soul desires no other freedom.

" How can one be free who is separated from the Most High? What harder or more miserable captivity is there than for the soul to have escaped from the hand of its Creator? Happy are they who find themselves laden with the strong fetters and chains of the gifts of God's mercy, so that they are unable to gain the power to set themselves free.... O free will, thou art the slave of thine own freedom, unless thou be pierced through with fear and love for Him who created thee! " (T.J. *Con*, 1 – *Exc*, 17).

O Lord, when I think that I have the terrible power to paralyze the action of grace, the action of the Holy Spirit within me, I realize that the greatest mercy You can show me is to captivate my freedom by Your love, so that it may be Your willing prisoner forever.   O my Jesus, I beseech You to take away from me the freedom to frustrate Your graces, to live a purely human life, as though no seed of divine life were implanted in me.   Oh! I know that I am very distracted, very forgetful; I am superficial, I allow myself to be ensnared by all kinds of attractions and preoccupations with exterior material things, and I forget the supernatural realities which my senses do not perceive, although they are the beautiful realities.

Your love alone, O Lord, can conquer the great inconstancy of my mind and heart, and establish them in You, so that my life may become interior, rather than exterior, centered on You and Your grace instead of on myself and the things of earth.

49

THE FIRST MIRACLE OF JESUS

SECOND SUNDAY AFTER THE EPIPHANY

PRESENCE OF GOD - O Jesus, I beg You to transform my soul as You once transformed the water for the bride and bridegroom at Cana.

MEDITATION

1. Now that the cycle of Jesus' childhood has ended, the liturgy begins to speak of His public life.   During the days following the Epiphany, it recalled Our Lord's baptism in the Jordan, the event which marked the beginning of His apostolate.   Today it tells us about His first miracle, destined, like the Epiphany and His baptism, to manifest to the world His glory as the Son of God.

" And the third day, there was a marriage in Cana of Galilee; and the Mother of Jesus was there.   And Jesus also was invited...to the marriage " (*Gosp: Jn* 2,1-11). For the first time, we see the Blessed Virgin in her maternal function as mediatrix of all graces.   The Cana miracle,

Jesus' first, was worked precisely because of her inter-cession which was so powerful that it made Jesus anticipate His hour. "My hour is not yet come," the Savior had answered His Mother, and Mary was neither dismayed by this apparent refusal nor did she insist on her request. Secure in the knowledge of her Son and full of loving confidence in Him, she says to the servants, "Whatsoever He shall say to you, do ye." Her humility, consideration for others, faith, and trustful abandonment win Jesus, and to show us the greatness of her power over His divine heart, He grants her wish; the miracle takes place.

Mary's faith is admirable; and also worthy of admiration is the faith and prompt obedience of the servants who, following Mary's advice, immediately carry out the orders of Jesus; they fill the waterpots with water and then pour from them. Not a moment of doubt, not a protest—they simply obey. May we not learn from them how to believe, how to obey? Shall we not have recourse to Mary's powerful intercession?

2. "The water was made wine." A miracle much more wonderful than the one which Jesus performed at Cana is repeated daily on our altars; a little bread and wine are changed into the Body and Blood of Christ, and given to us as the Food of our souls. The Communion antiphon of today's Mass repeats the passage in the Gospel which speaks of the water made wine. Yes, for us pre-eminently, Jesus has "kept the good wine until now." It is the precious wine of the Holy Eucharist, inebriating our souls with His Body and Blood.

There is another wonderful transformation which Jesus accomplishes in our souls by means of grace; the water of our poor human nature becomes a sharer in God's divine nature; it is transformed into the sacred wine of the life of Christ Himself. Man becomes a member of Christ, the adopted child of God, the temple of the Holy Spirit. Today our Lady tells us how we can and should foster this precious transformation; she says to us as she once did to the servants at the Cana feast, "Whatsoever He shall say to you, do ye." In these words, Mary invites us to that complete transformation in Christ which is effected by the generous practice of all that He teaches and commands. Let us, then, with humble, docile hearts, with lively faith and perfect abandonment, entrust ourselves to Jesus through Mary's hands.

COLLOQUY

How encouraging it is, O Lord, for me to find Your sweet Mother beside You today! Everything becomes simple and easy near Mary, beneath her maternal eye, under the protection of her powerful intercession. How good You were, O Jesus, to give us Your dear Mother to be the Mother of our spiritual life! I will follow Mary's precious advice and do everything You tell me, everything You wish me to do.

I want to imitate the blind, prompt obedience of the servants at the wedding feast : to obey You as they did, always and in everything, Your instructions, counsels, and precepts—to obey You likewise in the person of my superiors, even when I do not see the reason for their orders and arrangements, even when they expect difficult things of me or something which seems to me absurd. Furthermore, I want to imitate Your Mother's complete abandonment when, in her great thoughtfulness, she confided to You her wish to help the bride and bridegroom in their difficulty. Your apparent refusal did not trouble her; she did not persist in her request, but she was sure, absolutely sure, that Your infinitely good and tender heart would provide, and provide abundantly.

O Lord, with a like confidence and trust, I lay my needs before You today. Do You see them? My soul is like the waterpots at the feast : full of water, the cold, insipid water of my frailty and weakness, which I never seem to overcome completely. I can say with the Psalmist : " The waters have come even unto my soul " (*Ps* 60,1), and they submerge me and I am as one drowned in incompetence and weakness. O Lord, I believe that, if You will, You can change all this water into the precious wine of Your love, Your grace, and Your life. You are so powerful, so merciful, that my wretchedness, great as it is, does not astonish You, because in comparison with You, who are infinite, it is always very small. Just as in the Mass the few drops of water which are poured into the chalice are changed with the wine into Your Blood, O Lord, take my wretchedness, plunge it into Your heart, make it disappear in You.

50

" I AM THE TRUTH "

PRESENCE OF GOD - O Jesus, Incarnate Word, splendor and brightness of the Father, instruct and illumine my soul.

MEDITATION

    1. Jesus came to give us life and to show us the way which leads to it. He, the Teacher of life, is also its source.

    At the beginning of Jesus' apostolate, the heavenly Father presented Him to the world as its divine Teacher. The Holy Spirit, descending upon Jesus in the form of a dove immediately after His baptism, and the voice from heaven saying, " This is My beloved Son in whom I am well pleased " (*Mt* 3,17) are, as it were, the divine credentials guaranteeing His teaching and giving the basic reasons for it. Who could refuse to believe His doctrine if He is the Son of God and the Holy Spirit is with Him? Two years later on Mt. Thabor, the same presentation is renewed : the same voice, the same words, " This is My beloved Son in whom I am well pleased, " but this time an explicit mandate is given us : " Hear ye Him! " (*ibid.* 17,5). By these words an even greater light is cast upon the teaching mission of Christ.

    Jesus revealed Himself as Teacher, as the one and only Teacher : " You call Me Master...and you say well, for so I am " (*Jn* 13,13). " Neither be ye called masters; for one is your Master, Christ " (*Mt* 23,10). Strengthening the validity of this claim, Jesus declared that He was the Life and the Truth. He even equates the latter with His origin and mission, as when He declared to Pilate : " For this was I born, and for this I came into the world, that I should give testimony to the truth " (*Jn* 18,37). Those who listen to His word, hear the truth : " If you continue

in my word...you shall know the truth, and the truth shall
make you free " (*ibid*. 8,31.32).

2. A man may or may not be a teacher; in either case,
he remains a man. Jesus, on the other hand, is Teacher
by nature, because He is the Incarnate Word. God is
Truth; all the truth which is in the Father is communicated
to the Word, and comes to us through Christ. Jesus is
Teacher because He is the Word, the substantial Word
of the Father, and as such, He possesses and manifests all
truth, all wisdom, all knowledge; indeed, He Himself is the
Truth, the Wisdom, the Splendor, the Light of the Father.
It is because of this that Jesus could say that He was the one
and only Master. Other teachers know only a part of the
truth; Jesus not only knows all truth, but because He is
the Word, He *is* the Truth. Other teachers set forth truths
which are superior to them, truths which exist outside themselves, and of which they can have but an imperfect
knowledge. Jesus, on the contrary, teaches the truth
which He Himself *is* by nature. His teaching, therefore,
is supreme, unique, and infallible. This is why He said,
" I am come a light into the world, that whosoever believeth
in Me may not remain in darkness " (*ibid*. 12,46), and even
more explicitly, " I am the light of the world " (*ibid*. 8,12).
Jesus alone could call Himself the light of the world, because
the Word alone is the light.

The teaching of Jesus does not consist then in mere
human words, however sublime and elevated they might
be, but it is the revelation of God Himself. This is the
Word to which He invites us to open our minds and hearts.

COLLOQUY

" O divine Father, You have opened the Book of Life,
Jesus Christ, before us, Your children. In Him, the God-
Man, we find all that we could wish to know. Reading
in Him, we shall be filled with holy knowledge; we shall
find all the doctrine we need for ourselves and for others.
But, O my soul, if you want to be enlightened and instructed,
you must not read this Book of Life hastily or superficially,
but slowly and attentively; then you will be inflamed with
divine love and you will know the truth.

" Above all, O my soul, try to have a true knowledge of God and yourself; you can obtain this only by reading, meditating, and studying the Book of Life, Christ, Our Lord " (St. Angela of Foligno).

O my Jesus, true light, drive away the clouds of ignorance which come from my evil nature, and give me the grace to seek the truth with a sincere heart and to love it; for You, the Incarnate Word, are the Truth.

Be the only light on my path, the only Master to guide my steps. I need You, eternal Truth, to liberate me from the slavery of my frailty and wretchedness, and from the passions which often blind my conscience and hinder me from complete adherence to the good and the true which You teach me.

Your truth teaches me that You are He who is, and that I am one who is not; that You alone have worth, and that I have no value; that You are All, and I am nothing, and if there is any good in me, it is a wholly gratuitous gift from You.

O Jesus, grant that I may seek Your truth and love it, even when it is painful, or when, like a two-edged sword, it lays bare my miseries, my faults, my sins. Let Your truth penetrate my whole being and all my acts; make me courageously reject every light which does not emanate from You!

O my only Master, make me comprehend the vanity of all knowledge and thought which does not reflect Your truth. O Lord, submerge my soul in Your light, penetrate my mind and heart with Your truth. Unite me to You, O eternal Truth! O Jesus, Incarnate Word, Incarnate utterance of my God, instruct my soul. I wish to learn everything from You, to " spend my life in listening to You " (E.T. *III*).

51

THE DOCTRINE OF JESUS

PRESENCE OF GOD - Behold me at Your feet, O Lord, that I may hear Your doctrine, the doctrine of eternal life.

MEDITATION

1. The truths Jesus taught are so important and essential that, to know them or not, to believe them or not, is a matter of life or of death. His doctrine is not optional; rather, it is so essential that we cannot attain eternal life without it. " Whosoever believeth in Him...may have life ever-lasting....but he that doth not believe is already judged : because he believeth not in the Name of the only-begotten Son of God " (*Jn* 3,16.18). Compared to the truths taught by Jesus, all others are insufficient.

Because the doctrine of Jesus is absolutely indispensable, He proved its truth by miracles in order to help our weak faith to adhere to it. To the blindly obstinate Jews who refused to believe in Him, He said, " The works which the Father hath given Me to perfect; the works themselves which I do, give testimony of Me " (*ibid.* 5,36). When the disciples of John the Baptist asked Him if He were the Messiah in whom they were to believe, He answered simply, " Go and relate to John what you have heard and seen : the blind see, the lame walk, the lepers are cleansed, the deaf hear, the dead rise again " (*Mt* 11,4.5). The Gospel almost always concludes a recital of the wonders performed by Jesus with such words as : " and His disciples believed in Him " (*Jn* 2,11); " All wondered and glorified God " (*Mk* 2,12). Jesus is the only Teacher who can guarantee with miracles the truth of His doctrine.

2. Jesus wants everyone, even the simple and the ignorant, to understand His doctrine; He often said that He came especially to evangelize the poor. Jesus is not a teacher seeking glory and praise; He seeks only the good of His disciples. He uses simple language which can be understood

by all, and He illustrates the most sublime truths by very
ordinary things.   Thus, for example, He uses the water
in the well to represent the living water of grace, and the
vine to explain the mystery of our union with Him, the true
Vine.   Further, Jesus does not wait for us to seek Him;
He is the Master who goes Himself in search of His disciples,
and He seeks them everywhere—in the tax-collectors' office,
in the homes and haunts of the publicans, in the streets
and squares, in the country.   He teaches in the synagogues
and from the porch of the Temple as well as in Peter's boat
or on the grassy slopes of the hillsides.   He welcomes
Nicodemus at night and stops at the well of Sichem to
wait for the Samaritan woman.

Jesus explains His doctrine in a manner which is adapted,
not only to the mentality and needs of the people of Palestine,
but also to that of all future generations.   His words are
always living and timely, suited to the needs of every age
and every people.

His hearers were divided into two groups : the proud,
obstinate hearts who refused to believe, even when they
saw the most astounding miracles, and of whom Jesus said,
" If I had not come, and spoken to them, they would not
have sin; but now they have no excuse for their sin "
(*Jn* 15,22); and the upright hearts, sincerely eager for the
truth, who accepted His words with faith and love.   Jesus
rejoiced because of them, saying, " I confess to Thee, O
Father, Lord of heaven and earth, because Thou hast hid
these things from the wise and prudent, and hast revealed
them to little ones " (*Mt* 11,25).

COLLOQUY

" O Lord, my God, Thou hast indeed the words of life,
wherein, if we will seek it, we mortals shall all find what we
desire.   But what wonder is it, my God, that we should
forget Thy words, when our evil deeds have made us so
infirm and foolish?...   What is this, Lord?...   How
blind of us to seek repose where it cannot possibly be
found!...   Reflect that we do not understand ourselves,
or know what we desire, nor are we able to ask as we should.
Give us light, Lord.   Behold, we need it more than the man
who was blind from his birth, for he wished to see the light

and could not, whereas nowadays, Lord, no one wishes to see it. "

" You alone, O Lord, teach us truth and show us the way of salvation. O unhappy are we, for well do we know and believe these truths, yet our inveterate habit of not reflecting upon them makes them so strange to our souls that we neither know them nor seek to know them.

" Grant, then, Lord, that Your words may never be absent from my thoughts " (T.J. *Exc,* 8-13).

O Jesus, do not permit me to allow myself to be attracted by maxims and doctrines which do not come from You.

What will it profit me to possess every kind of knowledge, if I do not know You, O Lord, and the truths which You came to teach us? Do not permit me, O Jesus, to be content with superficial knowledge, but give me the light and the intelligence I need to penetrate the profound meaning of Your teachings. Your words will not be made clear by reasoning and eager studying, but by humility, love, and an ardent desire to possess You. Create in me, O Lord, a heart that is upright, humble, sincere, and able to love and understand the meaning of Your divine words.

O my dear Master, I lay open my soul before You, as I would expose a piece of linen to the rays of the sun. I kneel before the tabernacle, knowing that I shall learn much more from You in prayer and recollection than in perusing learned books. But, O Lord, I shall never leave Your book, the Gospel : " I find in it all that my poor soul needs, and I am always discovering there new lights and hidden, mysterious meanings " (T.C.J. *St,* 8).

O Lord, grant that I may understand the words of Your Gospel, and I shall be sufficiently wise.

52

JESUS SHOWS US THE FATHER

PRESENCE OF GOD - O Jesus, You are the Word who reveals the Father. You alone can teach me who God is. Speak, Lord, for Your servant heareth!

MEDITATION

1. " Now this is eternal life : that they may know Thee, the only true God " (*Jn* 17,3), Jesus tells us; and St. John the Evangelist says, " No man hath seen God at any time; the only-begotten Son who is in the bosom of the Father, He hath declared Him " (*ibid.* 1,18). Only Jesus, the Son of God, can give us knowledge of the Father : He alone, as God's Word, is by nature the Revealer of God.

Our words express our thoughts; likewise, the Word, the substantial utterance of the Father, expresses the Father and reveals the nature of God. When the Word was made flesh, He continued to be what He was, the Word, the Splendor of God, the Revealer of God. Becoming incarnate, He made Himself known to men, and accessible to our human capacity, but that implied no lessening of His divine nature.

Even when Jesus does not speak, His very Person and actions reveal God to us. He often remarked sadly, in the face of misunderstanding, " If you knew Me, you would know My Father also " (cf. *ibid.* 8,19; 14,7). To Philip who, at the Last Supper, asked Him to show them the Father, He replied in a tone of gentle reproach, " Have I been so long a time with you, and have you not known Me? Philip, he that seeth Me seeth the Father also.... Do you not believe that I am in the Father, and the Father in Me? " (*ibid.* 14,9.10).

Jesus is " the image of the invisible God " (*Col* 1,15) : it is sufficient to look upon Him with faith and love in order to know God. From no other master, through no other way can we acquire such knowledge, indispensable for eternal life. " Neither doth anyone know the Father, but the Son, and he to whom it shall please the Son to reveal Him " (*Mt* 11,27).

2. When by reason we trace creatures back to their first cause, we are able to know that God exists, that He is the Creator and Ruler of the universe. The knowledge obtained thus, however, is always mediate, indirect, and far from perfect. It is arrived at only with great difficulty and often after many errors.

There are other divine truths which cannot be reached by the human intellect alone, for example, the Trinity, the Incarnation, the universal Fatherhood of God, our incorporation in Christ and our elevation to the supernatural state. We would never be able to arrive at these profound truths, which disclose so many things about God and His intimate life, and which at the same time are concerned with our supreme destiny, if Jesus had not come to reveal them to us. He does this with the highest possible authority : " We speak what We know, and We testify what We have seen... " (*Jn* 3,11); " I speak that which I have seen with My Father " (*ibid.* 8,38). " You do not know Him; but I know Him, because I am from Him " (*ibid.* 7,28.29). Jesus made use of the parables of the prodigal son and the lost sheep to describe in touching words the goodness of His heavenly Father, who " maketh His sun to rise upon the good and bad " (*Mt* 5,45), and who " feedeth the birds of the air and giveth raiment to the lilies of the field " (cf. *ibid.* 6,26.28), thus revealing God's infinite mercy toward us, and His fatherly Providence, which receives us and provides for us as His children. The revelation of these great truths is further clarified by the works of Jesus : His concern for material and spiritual misery, His love which keeps Him continually seeking souls to be saved, even to giving His life for them. The good tidings that Jesus brought to the world consist above all in this revelation of God as infinite charity, of God as our loving Father; the New Testament and the whole Christian life are based entirely on this revelation.

COLLOQUY

" O Jesus Christ, Son of God, Word and Wisdom of the Father, You are the Book of Life; You came into the world to teach us, by Your life, Your death, and Your doctrine.... O uncreated God, make me worthy to understand You, as Your Son revealed You, His Father, to us" (St. Angela of Foligno).

O Jesus, I, too, ask with Philip : " Show me the Father, " but I quickly add : Show Him to me in You, for the Father is in You, and You in Him, so that looking at You, I see and find Your Father. Your humanity is a veil which hides and conceals the divinity of the Father, divinity which is also Yours because You are God, like the Father and the Holy Spirit. You are the Word, O Jesus, but the Incarnate Word; and the utterance of the Father is, so to speak, written in Your flesh, so that I can read it in You, the one, true Book of Life. You reveal God to me by Your whole Being, Your Person, Your actions, and Your words. Always and in every way You repeat one great truth to me : God is Love. Eternal life consists in knowing You, O Jesus, and through You knowing God. No one but You can give me this knowledge; I can learn it only from You. How necessary it is, then, and how much I want You to teach me! " O my Lord and true God! He who knows You not, loves You not. Oh, what a great truth is this! But alas, alas, Lord, for those who seek not to know You!" (T.J. *Exc*, 14). O Jesus, it is surely deplorable that the world is not interested in knowing You and Your Father; but the offense would be beyond imagination if a soul who is consecrated to You should act in this way, or should be satisfied to know You only superficially!

O Lord, reveal Yourself to my soul, because I want to know You, to know You in order to love You, to serve You and to regulate my life according to Your wishes. " O God, when a woman in the world is about to marry, she knows beforehand whom she is to marry, what sort of a person he is and what property he possesses. Shall not we, then, who are already betrothed, think about our Spouse...who is His Father, what is the country to which He will take us, what are the riches with which He promises to endow us, what is His character, how we can best make Him happy, what we can do to give Him pleasure, and how we can conform our character to His? O my Spouse, must we, then, make less account of You than is made of men?" (T.J. *Way*, 22).

53

JESUS THE TEACHER OF SANCTITY

PRESENCE OF GOD - I need You always, my divine Master, because You alone are holy and can show me the true way of holiness.

MEDITATION

1. The knowledge of God in which eternal life consists, as Jesus has said, is not the kind of knowledge which stops at the enlightenment of our intellects, but knowledge which stirs up our wills to love the God whom we know, and which regulates our whole life so that it will be pleasing to Him. Consequently, when Jesus has brought us to the knowledge of the Father, He then teaches us what we must do to please Him : " Be you therefore perfect as also your heavenly Father is perfect " (*Mt* 5,48). In this brief formula, the divine Teacher reveals two great truths : God is the model of sanctity, because He alone is the fullness of perfection, free from every shadow of fault or failing; secondly, God's will in our regard is that we also be perfect, which we shall be according to the degree in which we try to imitate God's perfection.

Yet how can a mere creature imitate divine perfection? Jesus, our Life and our Teacher, makes it possible for us. The grace which Jesus merited for us and which He is continually giving us, together with the infused virtues and the gifts of the Holy Spirit, raises us from the human level to the supernatural, divine level; we are made sharers in the divine nature, the divine life. Faith also makes us sharers in God's truth and in the knowledge which He has of Himself and of all things. Charity gives us a participation in the infinite love with which God loves Himself and His creatures.

However, we cannot see God's perfection and holiness, because He " inhabiteth light inaccessible, whom no man hath seen, nor can see " (1 *Tm* 6,16). But Jesus reveals God to us : He manifests Him to us in Himself, His works, and His words.

Hence, Jesus is the perfect Teacher of holiness. He teaches us that God wants us to be holy, shows us God as the supreme, infinite ideal of holiness, and enables us to start out toward this sublime ideal.

2. When Jesus says to us : " Be you perfect, as also your heavenly Father is perfect, " He gives us a model of perfection that we can never exhaust. The perfection of the very greatest saints when compared with God's perfection is nothing. Jesus teaches us, then, not to rest complacent in the degree of perfection we have attained, nor to be satisfied with our progress or even our efforts. Compared with the lofty ideal He sets before us, we are nothing. This is why He tells us never to stop, never to say, " This is enough. " No matter how much progress we make, we never advance far enough. Who, indeed, can become as just, as merciful as God? As long as we are on earth, our holiness will always consist in a continual tending toward divine perfection. " Strive for it untiringly and uninterruptedly, " says St. Augustine.

Among the perfections of God which Jesus has revealed, charity has first place. It is so important that, when He asks us to imitate God, His first requirement is an intense practice of charity toward God and our neighbor. The precept of charity, like that of striving for perfection, has no limits : however much we love God we shall never succeed in loving Him as much as He is capable of being loved, that is, as much as He deserves; and however much we love our neighbor we shall never love him as God loves him.

Jesus thus invites us to rise to perfection, to a holiness which has no limits and which requires of us a continual advancement, progress and ascension. Although we always do little, a mere nothing compared with so lofty an ideal, Our Lord is satisfied with this little, provided we put all our good will into it.

COLLOQUY

O my divine Master, what a sublime ideal of perfection You set before my soul! With Your help, I shall go on in this way with the one desire of following Your teaching, of doing the will of God, and of pleasing our heavenly Father. If in comparing myself to the saints, I see so many defects, how shall I ever put my misery before the infinite perfection of God? But, O Jesus, there is no question about it, for Your words resound clearly in my mind : " Be you perfect, as Your heavenly Father is perfect. "

I can do nothing better, then, than to imitate St. Thérèse's charming, audacious method. Instead of becoming discouraged, I shall say to You as she did, " O Lord, You would not inspire me with a desire which could not be realized; therefore, in spite of my littleness, I can aim at being a saint. It is impossible for me to become great, so I must bear with myself and my many imperfections; but I will seek out a means of reaching heaven by a little way—very short, very straight, and entirely new. We live in an age of inventions : there are now lifts which save us the trouble of climbing stairs. I will try to find a lift by which I may be raised unto God, for I am too small to climb the steep stairway of perfection.... O Jesus, Your arms, then, are the lift which must raise me even to heaven. To reach heaven I need not become great; on the contrary, I must remain little, I must become even smaller than I am " (T.C.J. *St*, 9).

These are Your two arms, O Jesus : the Holy Spirit whom You have sent to me, and the grace which You have given me : sanctifying grace and actual grace, by which You continually sustain the steps of those who trust in You. I must admit that if I am often discouraged, finding the path of perfection too difficult and wearisome; if I give up at last, because I think that a certain effort or act of generosity is too much for me, it is simply because I forget to have recourse to You, to cast myself into Your arms and implore You to help me. O my loving Master, You who never abandon us, but are always ready to help us if we have recourse to You, teach me to fly to You for refuge continually, with full confidence, asking Your help in every difficulty.

54

WHAT JESUS' TEACHING EXACTS

PRESENCE OF GOD - O Jesus, I beg You to make me understand all Your instructions and then give me strength to put them into practice.

MEDITATION

In calling us to imitate the holiness of His heavenly Father, Jesus summons us to an unrelenting war against sin, which is in direct opposition to God's infinite perfection and is the greatest offense against Him. In all His teachings He tries to inculcate in us a deep hatred of sin, especially of pride, hypocrisy, and obstinate willful malice, all of which constitutes a state of complete opposition to God. Jesus, who shows such great mercy toward sinners, has scathing words for the Pharisees : " Woe to you scribes and Pharisees, hypocrites : because you are like to whited sepulchres.... You serpents, generation of vipers, how will you flee from the judgment of hell? " (*Mt* 23,27.33). Again, He describes the ugliness of sin and its disastrous effect on man, lowering him to a state of complete moral degradation, such as that of the prodigal son who, because he had left his father's house, was reduced to " feeding swine " (*Lk* 15,15).

" Whosoever committeth sin, is the servant of sin " (*Jn* 8,34); a slave of sin cannot be a servant of God; hence, the words of the Master : " No man can serve two masters. For either he will hate the one, and love the other : or he will sustain the one, and despise the other " (*Mt* 6,24).

Jesus, our Savior, came to destroy sin by His death; it is precisely by His death that He shows us most clearly the terrible malice of sin. Sin is such a great enemy of God and has such a destructive power that it brought about the death of the divine Master.

2. Only mortal sin is completely opposed to God; this opposition is so great that it separates the soul from God. However, every sin, even venial sin, and every fault and imperfection, is in opposition to God's infinite holiness.

Our nature, wounded as a consequence of original sin, bears within itself the seed of sin, in the form of evil tendencies or habits. If we desire to follow Jesus, who offers us the perfection of His heavenly Father as a norm for our life, we must engage in an intense struggle against sin in order to destroy its deepest roots and even its slightest traces in us. This is just what Jesus teaches us with the brief words : " Deny thyself. " We must deny " self" with all its imperfect habits and inclinations; and we must do so continually. Such a task is fatiguing and painful, but it is indispensable if we wish to attain sanctity. Jesus says : " How narrow is the gate, and strait is the way that leadeth to life, and few there are that find it ! " (*Mt* 7,14). We approach the infinite perfection of God only in the measure in which we take upon ourselves the work of complete self-denial. Hence, all the masters of the spiritual life insist so strongly on detachment and self-renunciation as the indispensable foundation of the spiritual life. St. John of the Cross offers a soul who is desirous of attaining union with God the harsh way of the " nothing. "

But, first and foremost, Jesus, the divine Teacher, has pointed out to us the absolute necessity of passing through this way : " If any man will come after Me, let him deny himself " (*ibid.* 16,24).

COLLOQUY

O Jesus, I beseech You to fill my soul with a sincere and profound hatred of sin, of every kind of sin, so that I shall always be ready to prefer any suffering, even death, to offending God. Make me see, O divine Master, that the only real evil which can befall me and from which I must always pray to be delivered, is sin; for sin is such an enemy of Yours that it caused You to be scourged, crowned with thorns, and nailed to the Cross. Sin made You shed all Your Blood and die in terrible torment. O Jesus, You taught us to ask our heavenly Father to " deliver us from evil "; make use of Your power of intercession; show Your Father, who is ours, too, the still-bleeding wounds of Your Passion, and obtain for me and for all faithful souls, the grace to be freed from the terrible evil of sin. O Jesus, must one make a distinction between serious sin and venial sin, between sin and imperfection?

"From any sin, however slight, committed with full knowledge, may God deliver us, especially since we are sinning against so great a Sovereign and realizing that He is watching us! That seems to me a sin committed of malice aforethought : it is as though one were to say : ' Lord, although this displeases You, I shall do it. I know that You see it and I know that You would not have me do it; but, though I understand this, I would rather follow my own whim and desire than Your will ' " (T.J. *Way*, 41).

With Your help, O Jesus, I want to fight more strongly against sin and try to overcome all my evil tendencies, inclinations, and habits. This exacts constant self-denial, but with Your help, I am ready to begin. Of course, I shall have to give up my own desires, but I shall do so in order to please God; I shall have to say " No " to my evil nature, and prefer our heavenly Father's will, His inspirations and wishes. It will mean dying to myself in order to live by You, O Jesus! If I really love You, shall I find this total self-denial hard? Oh! grant that I too may say with St. Paul, " I count all things to be but loss...and count them but as dung, that I may gain Christ and may live in Him " (cf. *Phil* 3,7.9).

55

THE POWER OF THE DIVINE TEACHER

PRESENCE OF GOD - O Jesus, I beg You, not only to instruct me, but to move my soul to accept Your teaching and to put it into practice.

MEDITATION

1. Jesus not only imparts truth to us, He also helps us to accept it. This is the task of any teacher, but he can work only from the exterior, trying to clear his pupil's mind of the errors which obscure it and to present the truth in

a clear and convincing manner. Jesus, however, does much more than this; His activity is far more intimate and profound. He is the only Teacher capable of acting directly on the souls, the minds and the wills of His pupils. Jesus moves our souls *interiorly* to accept His teachings and to put them into practice.

The truths Jesus teaches are divine mysteries; therefore, we cannot master them by the art of human reasoning. To accept them, our minds must be equipped with a new supernatural light and power, the light and power of faith. Faith comes to us through Jesus; not only did He merit it for us, together with grace, the other infused virtues, and the gifts, but He is continually obtaining it for us and producing it in us. " He is always the author of faith... He infuses the light of faith into the faithful " *(Mystici Corporis)*. Therefore, while Jesus is revealing eternal truths to us, He is also filling our souls with the light of faith, until He produces in us, by means of the gifts of the Holy Spirit, a profound, mysterious knowledge giving us an intuition, a *sense* of divine things. He acts on our wills in the same way by the virtue of charity, drawing us to love Him and our heavenly Father, impelling us to put His teachings into practice. While Jesus is teaching us, He is kindling in us the fire of divine love just as He did in the two disciples from Emmaus. After they had heard His explanation of the events that had taken place in Jerusalem, they said to each other : " Was not our heart burning within us, whilst He spoke in the way? " *(Lk* 24,32).

2. " Our Master, " writes St. Thérèse of the Child Jesus, " has no need of book or teacher to instruct a soul. The Teacher of teachers instructs without sound of words, and though I have never heard Him speak, yet I know He is within me, always guiding and inspiring me; and just when I need them, lights, hitherto unseen, break in upon me " *(St,* 8). Jesus interiorly teaches souls who are willing to listen to Him, and He teaches them above all by His Spirit, the Holy Spirit, thus carrying out His promise to the Apostles : " The Holy Ghost, whom the Father will send in My Name, He will teach you all things, and bring all things to your mind, whatsoever I shall have said to you " *(Jn* 14,26). Jesus and the Father are always sending the Holy Spirit from heaven into our souls; this Divine Spirit makes us

understand the profound meaning of Our Lord's teaching and suggests practical applications for our daily life. Jesus teaches us through the authority of the Church, to which He has entrusted the task of preserving His doctrine and transmitting it unchanged to all the faithful.

When we accept Jesus as our Teacher, we must also accept all His teachings : the written words of the Gospel, the living word of the Church, and the mysterious, secret word by which He teaches our souls individually, making us perceive intuitively the way He wishes us to live. If His word is to be truly a treasure, it is not enough for us merely to hear it; we must sound its depths. This demands silence and interior recollection. We must imitate Mary, who "kept all these words, pondering them in her heart" (*Lk* 2,19), meditating on everything her divine Son said and did.

COLLOQUY

O Lord Jesus, I need You to exercise all Your power as divine Master over me! I dearly love Your words of instruction, but only too often these divine words fail to bring forth in me the fruit I desire. Why is this, O Lord? Could it be because, after I have listened to You in prayer and made a resolution to put into practice what You have deigned to make me understand, I forget it all at the opportune moment and allow myself to be overcome by my habitual frailty? Perhaps, O Lord, it is because I do not know how to retain and deeply penetrate Your words in interior recollection, but allow them to be stifled by distractions and useless preoccupations, just as the careless farmer allows the good grain to be choked by weeds. Oh! in times of difficulty, when I should be carrying out Your instructions, if I only knew enough to turn to You, my divine Teacher, always present and operating in me by Your grace! Oh! if I would place myself, were it only for an instant, at Your feet and implore Your help, how I should profit! I know You are always ready to receive me and to increase my spirit of faith, so that I may see everything in Your light and regard all circumstances and things according to their value for eternity. You are always eager to kindle in my heart a more ardent flame of charity and to draw me gently to the practice of what You have taught me.

People weary themselves seeking learned teachers; they spend a great deal of money; they take long journeys and make many sacrifices to consult them even for a few brief moments. And I, who have always at hand the divine Master, do I not know enough to take advantage of His teaching? O Jesus, infinite wisdom and knowledge, You do not hesitate to come down to me to be my Guide and Master; do not permit me to be so foolish as to forget You! May I always listen to Your word and continually seek Your light and strength!

56

JESUS WELCOMES EVERYONE

THIRD SUNDAY AFTER THE EPIPHANY

PRESENCE OF GOD - O divine Savior, I, too, am a poor leper; receive me : " If Thou wilt, Thou canst make me clean! "

MEDITATION

1. Today's Gospel (*Mt* 8,1-13) places before us two miracles of Jesus, two profound lessons in humility, faith, and charity.

Observe the humble faith of the leper : " Lord, if Thou wilt, Thou canst make me clean. " He is so certain that Jesus can heal him that he feels nothing else is necessary for his cure other than the Lord's will. Christian faith does not wander about in subtle reasonings; its logic is simple : God can do all that He wills; therefore, His will alone is necessary. Yet the leper does not insist; one who lives by faith knows that God always wills whatever is best for him, even if it brings him suffering. Therefore, instead of insisting, he prefers to abandon himself to God's good pleasure.

Next comes the centurion. The strong, proud Roman soldier is not ashamed to personally beg Jesus, a Galilean, to help his paralyzed servant. Our Lord is touched by this humble, charitable act, and says at once, " I shall go and heal him! " But the centurion continues, " I am not worthy that Thou shouldst enter under my roof, but only say the word, and my servant shall be healed. " At this point humility becomes still more profound, and faith reaches its maximum : it is not necessary for the Lord to go; His power is so great that a word spoken from afar suffices to perform any miracle. Jesus Himself " marveled and said : ' Amen I say to you, I have not found so great faith in Israel! ' " Is this not a complaint against those who live so close to Him, who perhaps live in His own house, receiving constant favors from Him, while their faith remains very weak and therefore inefficacious?

2. According to Jewish law, lepers were kept apart from society and no one was allowed to go near them; likewise, the pagans were to be shunned because they did not belong to the chosen people. Jesus goes beyond the old law and in the name of universal charity He welcomes and heals the leper, listens to the foreign centurion and cures his pagan servant. Thus Christ teaches us to make no distinction of persons, not to despise sinners and infidels, but to welcome all with loving kindness. He does not wish the good to enclose themselves in a little circle, but to open the doors to everyone, doing good to all without concerning themselves about the traits and opinions of others. All men are children of God; and our charity, like the mercy of our heavenly Father, should extend to all. This is the dominant thought of today's Epistle (*Rom* 12, 16-21), where St. Paul exhorts us to practice charity, especially toward our enemies. " To no man rendering evil for evil.... If it be possible, as much as in you, have peace with all men. Revenge not yourselves ...but if thy enemy be hungry, give him to eat.... Be not overcome by evil, but overcome evil by good. "

Jesus conquered evil, both physical and moral evil, by His mercy and love. This must be our strategy too. Whatever the evil around us, whatever the suffering it may cause us, we shall never overcome it by arguments and discussions or by taking a stand and adhering rigidly to it. This can only be accomplished by a delicate charity which understands intuitively the mentality, the tastes, and the needs of others, and which knows precisely when to intervene, to condescend and to sacrifice itself for the good of another, even if that other is unfriendly toward us—only such charity can triumph over evil.

COLLOQUY

" Being what we are and having our free will, when we do not receive what pleases us, we sometimes refuse what the Lord gives us, even though the gift might be the best one possible.... But no, my God, no, no more trust in anything which I can desire for myself: do You desire for me that which You are pleased to desire; for that is my desire, since all my good consists in pleasing You. And, if You, my God, should be pleased to please me, by fulfilling all that my desire asks of You, I know that I should not be lost " (T.J. *Way*, 30 – *Exc*, 17).

O my Jesus, I trust You, I abandon myself to You, dispose of me, of my health and of all that concerns me, according to what You know is best for my spiritual advancement. I beg but one thing : heal my poor soul. I too, spiritually, am a poor leper, a poor paralytic. My pride and vanity are always ready to impair and vitiate the little good I accomplish. Sloth and inertia seek to paralyze my efforts toward perfection. Behold me at Your feet, O Lord; I need Your help like the leper and the paralytic servant. I too, O Lord, believe that, if You will, You can heal me.

" Miserable though I am, I firmly believe that You can do what You will; and the greater are Your marvels that I hear spoken of, and the more I reflect that You can work others still greater, the stronger grows my faith and the greater is the resolution with which I believe that You will hear my requests " (T.J. *Exc*, 4).

O sweet Jesus, I beg for a little of Your overflowing charity, which is so universal, so kind. You well know the difficulties I sometimes encounter when practicing this virtue, especially toward those whose ways of acting and thinking are so different from mine. O Lord, fill my heart with warm, sincere kindness toward them. Only the charity which comes from You will give me strength to overcome all the conflicts which arise from differences in temperament, education and ideas. Only this charity can enable me to sacrifice myself generously for those who hurt me and to continue to act kindly toward those whom I naturally dislike.

O Jesus, You came on earth to enkindle the fire of charity : enkindle in me an ardent love for my neighbor.

57

" I AM THE WAY "

PRESENCE OF GOD - O Jesus, my beloved Master, take my hand and lead me to the Father : You alone are the way of salvation and sanctity.

MEDITATION

1. Jesus is not only the Master who teaches us how to attain to the perfection of His heavenly Father, but He is also the living model of that perfection. Men, on the other hand, are by their very nature so limited and imperfect that they can never serve as perfect models for us. At the same time, we cannot see God, who is holiness itself. But the Son of God, His living image, by becoming man, has made infinite perfection incarnate in Himself. In Jesus, we see, we know, we touch, so to say, the sanctity of God. The divine perfections, which were beyond our grasp and inaccessible to our senses, we find as a living, concrete, tangible reality in Christ Our Lord. The Father has presented Him to the world as His beloved Son in whom He is well pleased, because He sees in Him His own perfect image and all His own infinite perfections. The Father gives Christ to us, not only as our Master, but as our Model, since from all eternity He predestinated us " to be made conformable to the image of His Son " (*Rom* 8,29).

Jesus Himself has told us that He is our only model : " I am the way.... No man cometh to the Father but by Me " (*Jn* 14,6). By His example, He shows us how we can approach God's perfection, and He says very definitely that we must imitate Him : " I have given you an example, that as I have done to you, so you do also " (*ibid.* 13,15). " Learn of Me because I am meek and humble of heart " (*Mt* 11,29).

When we imitate Jesus, we are imitating our heavenly Father; when we endeavor to practice the virtues as He did, we are drawing nearer to God's infinite perfection. When we become conformable to the image of Christ, we become conformable to the image of God.

2. In the Acts of the Apostles we are told that " Jesus began to do and to teach " (1,1). All His acts are the model for ours. All the virtues which Jesus recommended to us, He Himself practiced first, perfectly and in the highest degree. He then told us to do as He had done. His doctrine shows us exactly what our conduct should be in order to resemble His. Therefore, all Christian tradition declares that the way to attain sanctity is to imitate Christ. St. John of the Cross gives the following advice : " First, let us have a habitual desire to imitate Christ in everything that we do, conforming ourselves to His life; upon which life we must meditate, so that we may know how to imitate it and to behave in all things as Christ would behave " (*AS I,* 13,3).

This must not be a merely exterior and material imitation of Jesus' acts; we must endeavor to enter into the interior dispositions of His soul, so as to make these dispositions our own, according to the counsel of St. Paul : " Let this mind be in you, which was also in Christ Jesus " (*Phil* 2,5). In this way, the imitation of Jesus is based on what is most profound and vital, that is, His intimate dispositions, which constitute the interior principle of all His actions. This putting on the " mind " of Christ is within the reach of all, whatever our state or condition of life, whereas the exterior imitation of the life of Jesus can never be complete, since it always varies according to the circumstances in which each one finds himself.

COLLOQUY

" O Christ, eternal Truth, what is Your doctrine? And by what path do You direct us to the Father? I can find no other way but the one which You have marked out in virtue of the fire of Your charity. The path, O eternal Word, which You have marked with Your Blood is the way.

" O loving, tender Word of God, You tell me : ' I have marked the path and opened the gate with My Blood; do not be negligent in following it, but take the same road which I, eternal Truth, have traced out with My Blood. ' Arise, my soul, and follow your Redeemer, for no one can go to the Father but by Him. O sweet Christ, Christ-Love, You are the way, and the door through which we must enter in order to reach the Father " (St. Catherine of Siena).

O Jesus, be truly my model, my way! All that You have revealed to us of the Father's infinite holiness, all that You have taught us I see incarnate in Your life, in Your acts. What an excellent Master You are, and how well You adapt Yourself to my weakness, which needs not only to understand, but also to see concretely what it should do! If I find it painful to humble myself, You show Yourself to me as a poor, helpless Babe, lying in a manger, in a poor stable; You also show me the long years You spent in the carpenter's shop at Nazareth, and Your humiliations before the tribunals and on the Cross. Is obedience repugnant to me? I behold You, my God, obeying Mary and Joseph, Your creatures, and submitting, with the meekness of a lamb, to Your judges and executioners. When I find it hard to practice charity toward my neighbor, I have but to contemplate You, showing the most loving solicitude to hardened sinners and to Your bitterest enemies. I can find everything in You, O Jesus : life, teaching, and example. In You, I see and possess my God; You are the Mediator who brings me to the Father, my Master and my model of holiness.

O Jesus, in You alone I find my pleasure. You are all I desire; You alone can captivate me.

Grant, O Lord, that Your image may always be imprinted on my mind and in my heart, that my interior glance may always be directed toward You, so that I may be conformed in everything to You, my Master, my Model, my Way!

58

"*I AM IN THE FATHER*"

PRESENCE OF GOD - O Jesus, grant that I may enter into the interior dispositions of Your soul, into its continual personal union with the Father.

MEDITATION

1. The intimate dispositions of Jesus toward God and His relations with Him are of the utmost importance to us. Jesus is the Son of God; herein lies all His greatness and holiness. By His very nature, He is the only Son of God; we, who are made to His image, have become children of God by His mediation. This divine sonship, which belongs to Him by nature, is communicated to us by grace; hence, like Him, all our greatness and holiness consist in our living as true children of God. Therefore, as far as is consistent with our human nature, we should try to reproduce in ourselves the interior attitude of Jesus toward His heavenly Father.

First of all, we note an attitude, or rather a state, o, intimate union. It is as the Word that Jesus declares. "The Father is in Me, and I in the Father" (*Jn* 10,38)f He is referring, of course, to the substantial, incommunicable union of the Word with the Father, which no one can ever imitate; this union is the prerogative of the Son of God alone. But He also made the statement as Man, because, as Man, all His love is concentrated on the Father and dominated by the Father. His whole mind is directed toward Him in an effort to please Him. This union of Jesus with His divine Father is the model for our union, precisely because it is a union of grace. Grace in Jesus is "infinite," in the language of the theologians, and in this respect it differs from ours; yet even the grace we possess enables us to keep our souls directed toward the Father and our affections centered in Him. Jesus gives us the example Himself, and asks of the Father this close union for us : "As Thou, Father, in Me, and I in Thee; that they also may be one in Us " (*ibid.* 17,21).

2. The soul of Jesus is completely immersed in the Blessed Trinity. His human intellect enjoys the Beatific Vision, in which He sees God, whose nature He possesses; He knows the Person of the Word as the subject of all His human activity. He sees the Father and knows that He is His Son; He sees the Holy Spirit who dwells within Him. His heart is filled with created charity, as infinite as the grace which adorns His soul. This charity continually ascends toward His heavenly Father with a very rapid movement, thence to pour itself out upon our souls. Whether Jesus is busy in the workshop at Nazareth, walking the roads of Palestine, preaching, teaching, debating with the Pharisees, healing the sick, or talking with the multitudes—while giving Himself to all, He never interrupts that life of wonderful union with the three divine Persons which goes on in the depths of His soul.

By means of grace, our souls have become the temples of the Blessed Trinity. The three divine Persons are really present within us, continually offering and giving Themselves to us, so that we, even here on earth, may begin to know, love, and possess Them. It is by faith that we can know Them, by charity that we can love and live in union with Them. It was to enable us to possess this life of close union with God that Jesus merited for us the grace and charity which He is continually bestowing upon us. This grace and charity are identically the same as that which fills the soul of Jesus, although given to us in a lesser degree and with far less perfection. Jesus sees God face to face, in the Beatific Vision; we " see " Him through the obscure, yet certain, knowledge of faith.

In this way we, too, can have a share in Christ's interior life which is completely immersed in the Blessed Trinity. Did not St. Paul say, " Your life is hid with Christ in God " (*Col* 3,3)? With St. Teresa Margaret, we can aspire to " emulate, by faith, insofar as it is possible for a creature, the hidden, *interior* life and activity of the intellect and will of the sacred humanity of Jesus Christ, hypostatically united to the Word " (*Sp*).

COLLOQUY

O Jesus, what great treasures are hidden in Your words : " As Thou, Father, in Me, and I in Thee; that they also may be one in Us! " It is not enough for us to imitate Your exterior life; You want more than that. You want us to imitate, as far as mere creatures can, Your interior life, Your intimacy and Your unceasing union with the Father! It would be folly and arrogant temerity even to think of doing this, had You not commanded us to do so. But You have commanded it, and these words of Yours are particularly sacred because they form part of Your last prayer to Your Father, a prayer which contains Your spiritual testament.

You, O Jesus, are indissolubly united to the Father by nature, and I may always be united to God by grace. Your most holy soul is always immersed in the Beatific Vision of the Most Blessed Trinity; and I by faith know that the Trinity lives within me. Under the motion of the Holy Spirit, an infinite love of charity is continually rising up from Your heart toward the Father; and in me the fire of charity, kindled and diffused by the divine Paraclete, desires only to grow, to expand, and to be seized by the Holy Spirit and drawn into His flame of love, so as to mount again toward the Father, toward the Blessed Trinity.

Aided by Your grace, O Jesus, I live in You and You live in me. But I do not live in You alone, for wherever You are, O Word, there are the Father and the Holy Spirit also. Thus You, O Christ, draw me to live in the Trinity and my poor human life remains hidden with You in God. O Lord, do not permit me to become so absorbed by exterior activities, even good ones, that I forget or neglect the wonderful life of union with God to which You are calling and inviting me. In the innermost depths of my heart, hidden from all human gaze, dwells the Trinity; help me to dwell with Them! Help me to be silent and recollected, to hide myself with God who is hidden within me! Grant that, like a true child of God, I may always live in union with my Father, always remain at His feet to love and adore Him, and to listen to His divine words.

59

THE PRAYER OF JESUS

PRESENCE OF GOD - O Jesus, grant that I may enter the sanctuary of Your most holy soul where You reveal to me the secrets of Your prayer.

MEDITATION

1. Although Jesus was always indissolubly united to His Father by the Beatific Vision and the plenitude of charity, He willed to consecrate to Him exclusively a part of His human activity : the time of prayer. The long years spent at Nazareth and the forty days in the desert were especially consecrated to prayer, and during His apostolic life Jesus usually prayed during the whole or part of the night. The Gospel clearly notes this prayer of Christ at the more solemn moments of His life : before He chose the twelve Apostles, Jesus "went out into a mountain to pray, and He passed the whole night in the prayer of God" (*Lk* 6,12). He prayed before Peter's confession, before the Transfiguration, at the Last Supper, in Gethsemane, on Calvary. Moreover, He frequently interrupted His apostolic activity to retire into the desert to pray, and St. Matthew tells us that, often, before performing a miracle, He would raise His eyes to heaven and call upon His Father; he also tells us that "having dismissed the multitude, He went into a mountain alone to pray" (*Mt* 14,23).

We cannot imagine a more intimate and profound prayer than the prayer of Jesus. Only in heaven, where it will be given us also to see God face to face, shall we be able to understand it and really participate in it. But even here on earth we can imitate the conduct of Jesus by readily interrupting any activity, even apostolic work, in order to devote to prayer the time assigned to it, leaving everything else to focus our attention on God alone.

2. Only the prayer of Jesus is perfect praise and adoration of the Trinity, perfect thanksgiving and always efficacious supplication; He alone can offer infinite homage to the

Trinity. Our prayer has value only insofar as we unite it to that of Jesus and try to make it an echo and extension of His.

The prayer of Jesus was completed in sacrifice; sacrifice was its logical accompaniment as well as its culmination : the sacrifice of nights spent in vigil; the sacrifice of penance, which for forty days accompanied His prayer in the desert; the sacrifice of a laborious life, without having even a place to lay His head. This rhythm of sacrifice progressively increased, until it reached its maximum in His agony in the Garden and on the Cross. At this point, the prayer of Jesus became the total sacrifice of His life for the glory of the Father and the salvation of souls.

Our prayer must also be impregnated, substantiated with sacrifice; it must be based on a true generous offering of our whole being with Christ, until we become, with Him and in Him, a sacrifice of praise and of propitiation. While we are on earth, prayer, even contemplation itself, cannot consist solely in the enjoyment of God; it must always be united with sacrifice—only thus is it true. Authentic prayer and contemplation incite the soul to generosity, disposing it to accept for God any labor or toil, and to give itself entirely to Him. On this earth, the gift of self is always realized in sacrifice.

St. Teresa of Jesus says that the purpose of the graces of contemplation is " to strengthen our weakness, so that we may be able to imitate our Lord in His great sufferings " (*Int C VII*, 4).

COLLOQUY

O Jesus, how different Your prayer is from mine! Yours is so profound and intense; mine is so superficial, distracted, and hurried. How often, alas, I allow myself to be hurried on account of my work and to become so absorbed in my activity that I cannot put it aside!

But You make me understand that my activity is fruitless and my works sterile unless they are impregnated and imbued with prayer and union with God.

You also teach me by Your example that, if I really wish to live in union with God and to nourish that union, I must frequently pause in my occupations in order to

concentrate all my powers on Him alone.   O Lord, I want to
follow Your example and to leave everything at the prescribed
time to become recollected in prayer.   You chose to go up
on a mountain to pray, thus teaching me that in order
to pray well, I must detach myself from the things of earth
and rise above human thoughts and anxieties.   When
a soul is thus recollected in solitude far from creatures and
from self, and desires nothing but to converse with You,
O Lord, You do not delay in letting Yourself be found.

O my God, Most Holy Trinity, grant that, at least
in time of prayer, I may be aware of Your presence in my
soul and may make my union with You real.   Grant that,
at least in this hour, I may not leave You alone in the depths
of my heart, but entering within, " returning home, " let me
enclose myself in the temple of my soul where You are
waiting for me!

O Jesus, teach me and grant me that intense prayer
which immerses the soul in God and which, by living
contact with Him, inflames and strengthens it.   I desire
to share in Your prayer, which is the only adoration
worthy of God.   Therefore, dear Lord, take my poor
prayer; unite it to Yours and offer it to the Blessed Trinity.
Only in this way can I too become one of those " true adorers
...in spirit and in truth " (*Jn* 4,23) whom the Father
seeks and desires.

That my prayer may be really like Yours, teach me how
to nourish it by true, generous sacrifice—renouncing some
well-earned repose, detaching myself from creatures, being
silent and interiorly recollected.   Grant that I may be faithful
in performing my duties, that I may prove my love by little
voluntary mortifications, and may joyfully accept Your
will in all the circumstances of my life.

O Lord, grant that each day I may finish my prayer
with dispositions of greater generosity and that I may be
ready to accept, for love of You, every sacrifice that I find
on my way.

60

JESUS AND HIS FATHER'S WILL

PRESENCE OF GOD - O Jesus, teach me to follow You in Your
life of total, perfect adherence to the Father's will.

MEDITATION

1. " Wherefore when He cometh into the world, He
saith [to the Father] : ' Sacrifice and oblation Thou wouldst
not; but a body Thou hast fitted to me.... Behold,
I come... that I should do Thy will, O God '" (*Heb* 10,5-7).
These words reveal the constant interior disposition of Jesus
with regard to His Father's will. When the Apostles begged
Him to take a little food, the divine Master replied, " I have
meat to eat, which you know not.... My meat is to do the
will of Him that sent Me " (*Jn* 4,32.34). The only desire of
Jesus and the source of His strength is the fulfillment of His
Father's will. The human will of Jesus is so perfectly
transformed and so completely lost in the will of God, that
He acts only under the influence of this will. " I came down
from heaven, not to do my own will, but the will of Him that
sent me " (*ibid.* 6,38). " I seek not My own will, but the
will of Him that sent Me " (*ibid.* 5,30). In these words
Jesus reveals the dispositions of His soul, the profound
reason for all His acts and the rule which guided His whole
life on earth, even to His sorrowful Passion, when He repeated,
in spite of all the repugnance of His human nature,
" Father...not My will, but Thine be done " (*Lk* 22,42).

2. For us also, the adopted children of God, the way to
sanctity, the rule of our actions must be our heavenly Father's
will. Like Jesus we must be nourished by this holy,
sanctifying will; we must feed on it at every moment, we
must seek it and desire to live by it alone, making it the
one great motive for all our actions. " We must fully
conform our will to God's, " so that, as St. John of the
Cross says, " there will be nothing in our thoughts or actions
which is contrary to the divine will " (cf. *AS I*, 11,2).
Conformity to God's will and the growth of grace in

us are the two constituent elements of sanctity and of a life of union with God. These two elements are inseparable, for one depends upon the other. Our increase in grace corresponds to our degree of conformity to God's will. Jesus said, " If anyone love Me, he will keep My word...and We will come to him, and will make Our abode with him " (*Jn* 14,23). " Keeping His word, " that is, obeying God's will as manifested in the commandments, is the condition necessary for living in the state of grace and, hence, for enjoying the presence of the Blessed Trinity in our soul. The more complete our conformity to God's will becomes, embracing not only the grave precepts, but also the smallest details of the divine law, so as to exclude not only mortal sins, but even venial sins and the slightest voluntary imperfection, and the more we try to seek God's good pleasure in everything and accept all the circumstances of our lives as His will, the more the life of grace grows and develops within us. The three divine Persons, on Their part, give Themselves more and more to our souls, establishing their in-dwelling ever more fully and profoundly, thus drawing us to greater union with Themselves.

Then is fulfilled in us the word of Jesus : " He that sent Me is with Me, and He hath not left Me alone, for I do always the things that please Him " (*ibid.* 8,29).

COLLOQUY

O Jesus, would that I could understand, however slightly, Your perfect union with Your Father's will! It is a union, not only profound, but unchangeable, for I know that You, as God, can have no will but Your Father's, and as Man, Your will does not depend on a human ego, but belongs directly to Your divine Person. Such union can exist only in You, the Incarnate Word; yet the more I contemplate it, the more I desire to reproduce in myself at least a few of its characteristics. O Jesus, it is You who fill me with this desire, for You became our Brother and Model, that we might become like You. Did You not teach us to say to the Father : " Thy will be done on earth as it is in heaven ?" Just as the divine will is realized perfectly in the heaven of Your holy soul, so may it also be accomplished in the little heaven of mine!

" O good Master, You know that nothing is of more profit to me than to consecrate my will to the Father's. You teach me to do this, knowing that it will win Your Father's heart, and You also teach me how to serve Him. You have made Yourself my intermediary and have even said in my name : ' Thy will be done. '

" O Divine Father, after Your Son has consecrated to You my will, together with the wills of all, it would be unreasonable for me to refuse to give what He has offered.

" O Lord, what power there is in this gift of my will! If made with due determination, it cannot fail to draw You, Almighty God, to become one with our lowliness, to transform us into Yourself, and to unite the creature with the Creator.... O my God, the more You see by our actions that the words we use when speaking to You are not words of mere politeness, the more You draw us to Yourself and raise us above all petty earthly things. Not content with having made our soul one with Yourself, You begin to cherish it and to reveal Your secrets to it....

" At this very moment, O Lord, I consecrate my will to You, freely and unreservedly! " (cf. T.J. *Way*, 32).

61

THE WORKS OF JESUS

PRESENCE OF GOD - Grant, O good Jesus, that I may learn how to act as You did, with the one purpose of accomplishing the work entrusted to me by the Father, allowing Him to direct me in everything.

MEDITATION

1. " The works which the Father hath given Me to perfect, the works themselves...I do " (*Jn* 5,36). " I must do the works of Him that sent Me " (*ibid.* 9,4). Jesus has no other aim than to accomplish the mission entrusted to Him by the Father, and to accomplish this mission for the glory of the Father Himself and for the redemption of mankind. Burning with desire, " *desiderio desideravi* "

(*Lk* 22,15), to perform this work perfectly, He goes to face His Passion and to embrace the Cross.

God has entrusted to each one of us a share in the great redemptive work of Jesus. As consecrated souls, we are especially called to cooperate in Christ's work. First of all, we must cooperate with grace, so that the fruits of the redemption can be fully applied to our souls. This is the work of our own personal sanctification. It is not limited to this one aspect, however. We are called to sanctify ourselves in order to be able to bring others to sanctity. Each one of us has a mission to fulfill for the good of others and for their sanctification. We must collaborate with Christ in extending the fruits of the Redemption to as many souls as possible. This work is entrusted to us by the heavenly Father, and we must apply ourselves to it with the interior disposition of Christ : a total, generous, exclusive dedication, a dedication capable of making even the greatest sacrifices. All actions are of value only insofar as they help toward the accomplishment of this work. Anything that does not contribute to our own sanctification or to the sanctification of others is useless, a waste of time, and should be courageously eliminated.

Let us repeat with Jesus : " I must do the works which the Father has entrusted to Me. "

2. " I am not alone, because the Father is with Me. " " My Father worketh...and I work.... I cannot of Myself do anything. " " I do nothing of Myself, but as the Father hath taught Me, these things I speak " (*Jn* 16,32 – 5,17.30 – 8,28).

Jesus not only devoted Himself completely to the mission entrusted to Him by the Father, but in accomplishing this mission, and in every detail of it, He always acted in union with the Father and in perfect harmony with Him, always depending upon Him and regulating His whole life according to what He heard and saw in Him. His acts were but the human, tangible expression of the unceasing, invisible work of the Father : " What He seeth the Father doing...these the Son also doth in like manner " (*ibid.* 5,19). " The things...that I speak, " affirms Jesus, " even as the Father said unto Me, so do I speak " (*ibid.* 12,50).

Every soul which is in the state of grace can say, " I am not alone, for the Trinity is in me : the Father, Son, and

Holy Spirit. " Our attitude should mirror the attitude of Jesus : we must work in continual dependence upon God present within us, listening to His voice, to the interior motion of grace, and acting in accordance with it. We must conform our judgment to God's will, trying to see everything in His light, and working in such a way that our actions will always be in harmony with His views, designs, and good pleasure. In all our actions we, too, should be able to say, " I do nothing by myself, I act according to God's inspiration, in order to do what is most pleasing to Him. " Any work, no matter how exalted, which deviates from this line of conduct is, from a supernatural point of view, vain and sterile.

COLLOQUY

O Jesus, I place my poor soul before You. Fill me with the zeal which You had for the Father's works, with Your wholehearted, unconditional dedication to the mission He gave You. Oh, that I could perform with Your zeal and love the small part assigned to me in Your great redemptive work! But I need You to teach me how to make this zeal genuine and fruitful!

You make me understand that I should strive for perfection, correcting my faults, and overcoming my evil tendencies; this is the first field for my zeal. Then You teach me to give myself generously for the good of souls. You offer me the same arms that You Yourself used : prayer and sacrifice. You will not be satisfied with vague dreams of helping souls who are far away; You wish me first of all to do good in a concrete way to those who are near me. O Jesus, give me the zeal and courage to sacrifice myself for my neighbor; give me the strength to renounce my own tastes in order to adapt myself to the tastes of others and place myself at their disposal and service. O Jesus, meek and humble of heart, make my heart like Yours, for I can do no true apostolic work unless I am meek, humble, and patient.

You also tell me that You do not wish merely human works, undertaken more by natural activity than by the influence of grace. O Jesus, even as You, in all Your works, depended on the Father and acted according to what You heard and saw in Him, so make me depend on divine light and inspiration in all my works. I receive this light and inspiration from You, who, as the Word, are within me together with the Father and the Holy Spirit. Being the Word, the utterance of the Father, You cannot remain silent but You are in me that I may listen to You. " O eternal Word, utterance of my God, I wish to spend my life in listening to You! " (E.T. *III*), listening to You in order to act according to Your instructions. O Word of God, You are the light in which I should judge all things, consider all things; You are the Word which should direct all my actions. You are the interior Master always ready to instruct me if I but listen to You! Oh! grant that even in the midst of my occupations I may listen to Your voice within me. I am not alone, for You are always with me and in me; do not permit me to act as if I were alone, but help me always to act with You, always depending on Your light and word.

O Jesus, I want to look at You always, to listen to You, and to act according to what I see in You and hear from You, even as You always listened to Your Father and kept Your eyes upon Him.

62

JESUS AND THE GLORY OF THE FATHER

PRESENCE OF GOD - O Jesus, increase within me Your love and Your zeal for the glory of the Father; teach me to despise all personal glory and to flee from it.

MEDITATION

1. " I honor My Father.... I seek not My own glory. " " I receive not glory from men " (*Jn* 8,49.50 – 5,41).

Jesus ever sought His Father's glory, and to this end He chose for Himself utter humiliation, even to becoming " the reproach of men and the outcast of the people " (*Ps* 21,7). Bethlehem, Nazareth, Calvary—the three great stages of the humble, hidden life of Jesus, in which He veiled His glory as the Son of God. Even during His public life, when His divinity was more openly manifested, Jesus tried to flee as much as possible from human glory. Many times after performing a miracle, He imposed silence on those who had witnessed it. He forbade the three Apostles who had been present at the Transfiguration " to tell any man what things they had seen, till the Son of Man shall be risen again from the dead " (Mk 9,8). After the first multiplication of the loaves, " when He knew that they would come to take Him by force and make Him king [He] fled again into the mountain Himself alone " (Jn 6,15).

The glory of Jesus lies in the fact that He is the Son of God; He desires no other glory. It is as though He would relinquish this essential glory by accepting any other. Therefore He said : " If I glorify Myself, My glory is nothing; it is My Father that glorifieth Me " (ibid. 8,54). Jesus knows that after His death He will be glorified and acknowledged as the Son of God and the Savior of the world, but He desires that even this glory may be for the glorification of His Father : " Father, the hour is come, glorify Thy Son, that Thy Son may glorify Thee " (ibid. 17,1).

2. Following Christ's example, a Christian must seek only the glory of God. He must desire no other glory save that of being a child of God, a brother of Jesus Christ, and a member of His Mystical Body—a singular glory, indeed!

We must be on our guard against that tendency of pride which inclines us to seek a little satisfaction, praise, and personal glory even in our most spiritual actions. If we seek glory for ourselves, though it be only in insignificant matters, this glory is of no value; it elevates us in the eyes of men, but lowers us in God's eyes; it lessens and may even endanger our glory as children of God.

Seeking human glory and taking pleasure in it hinder and blind us on our way to perfection. Jesus said to the proud, haughty Pharisees, " How can you believe, who receive glory one from another, and the glory which is from God alone, you do not seek? " (ibid. 5,44). Only profound humility will enable us to overcome the allurements of pride, to silence the interior voices of self-esteem and vain complacency in order to seek always and in everything

the glory of God. St. John of the Cross urges us to fix our
eyes on the interior dispositions of Jesus and to renounce
everything " which does not lead to the honor and glory
of God, and this for the love of Jesus Christ, who sought
no satisfaction in this life but the accomplishment of His
Father's will " (J.C. *AS I*, 13,4).

COLLOQUY

O Lord, give me Your love for Your Father's glory,
so that I too, wretched and poor though I am, may serve
my God in some small way and give Him glory.

" May it be Your pleasure, my God, that the time may
come when I shall be able to pay at least a small part of
the immense debt I owe You; do You ordain it, Lord,
according to Your pleasure, that I may in some way serve
You. There have been others who have done heroic
deeds for love of You; I myself am capable of words only;
and therefore, my God, it is not Your good pleasure to
test me by actions. All my will to serve You amounts to
nothing but words and desires, and even here I have
no freedom, for it is always possible that I may fail
altogether. Strengthen and prepare my soul, Good of all
good, my Jesus, and then ordain means whereby I may
do something for You, for no one could bear to receive
as much as I have and pay nothing in return. Cost what
it may, Lord, permit me not to come into Your presence
with such empty hands, since a man's reward must be
according to his works! O Lord, here is my life, my
honor, and my will! I have given it all to You; I am
Yours; dispose of me according to Your desire. Well do
I know, Lord, how little I am capable of, but keep me
near You. I shall be able to do all things, provided You
do not withdraw from me. If You should withdraw, for
however short a time, I should go where I have already
been—namely, to hell " (T.J. *Life*, 21).

Make me understand, O Lord, that if I wish to work
for Your glory and the glory of Your Father, I must be
entirely detached from every desire for personal glory;
otherwise I shall deceive myself, thinking that I am working
for You, whereas in reality I am but serving my own
ego.

You know, O Jesus, that herein lies the greatest danger for me, that which I fear most in my good works, especially in the works of my apostolate. Therefore, I beg You, Lord, to use every means to save me from it. And if this requires humiliations, failure, criticism, use them, and use them abundantly. Do not consider my repugnance, pay no attention to my tears, for I do not want to lessen Your glory or ruin Your works by my pride.

63

JESUS CALMS THE TEMPEST

FOURTH SUNDAY AFTER THE EPIPHANY

PRESENCE OF GOD - O Lord, I adore You in the little boat of my soul. Since You are with me, I shall not fear.

MEDITATION

1. In today's liturgy, especially the Gospel (*Mt* 8,23-27), Jesus appears in our midst as the ruler of the elements, the conqueror of all tempests. " And behold a great tempest arose in the sea, so that the boat was covered with waves. " Let us think of all the persecutions which have beaten against Peter's barque, the Church, down through the ages; or we can think of the trials which God still permits individual souls to undergo. Whatever happens, the spirit of faith tells us that every struggle and tempest is willed, or at least permitted by God : " Everything is grace " (T.C.J. *NV*); everything is the result of His infinite love. God is not a tyrant who crushes us, but a Father, who tests us because He loves us. If He permits sorrow, interior or exterior trials, personal or public vicissitudes, it is only to draw out of them some greater good. Virtue and goodness are strengthened in time of difficulty; the efforts made in bearing trials tend to make us surpass what we would have done had we enjoyed perfect calm.

Jesus was sleeping peacefully in the stern of the boat when the terrified Apostles awakened Him : " Lord, save us, we perish! " He answered them reproachfully, " Why are you fearful, O ye of little faith? "

If we are disturbed and upset by trials, it means that we lack faith. Even when God conceals Himself, when everything seems to fail us and we feel terribly alone, we can be absolutely certain that God will never abandon us if we do not first abandon Him. Instead of becoming bitter or falling into despair, it is the moment to intensify our faith, to make strong acts of faith. St. Thérèse of the Child Jesus used to say, " I count on Him. Suffering may go to its limit, but I am sure He will never abandon me " (*St*).

2. The Apostles were saved only when they called upon Jesus. As long as they labored and struggled alone, they had no success. Many times we fail to surmount interior difficulties because we work alone. God wants us to experience our own insufficiency; therefore, He lets us struggle until we have recourse to Him with full confidence. Certainly God wants our efforts, but He does not want us to place all our hope in them. This accounts for the small progress so many make on the road to sanctity— too much reliance on their own resources, too little on God's help. We must be firmly convinced that " our sufficiency is from God " (2 *Cor* 3,5). We must have less confidence in ourselves and more in God. Jesus can do all things, and confidence works miracles. " We receive from God as much as we hope for " (J.C. *DN II*, 21,8).

There are other kinds of tempests, too, such as those provoked by the difficulties we sometimes experience in our relations with our neighbor. St. Paul in the Epistle (*Rom* 13,8-10) gives us the remedy : " Owe no man anything, but to love one another. " Love conquers all. Our love for God overcomes our interior storms; our love for our neighbor, in whom we love Christ, overcomes the tempests which arise from dissensions, misunderstandings, and clashes of temperaments. If from certain people we receive only pain and trouble, let us follow the precious advice of St. John of the Cross : " Where there is no love, put love, and you will find love " (*L*, 22).

COLLOQUY

" O my Lord, how true a friend You are, and how powerful! For You can do all You will and never do You cease to love! Let all things praise You, Lord of the world! Oh, if someone would but proclaim throughout the world how faithful You are to Your friends! All things fail, but You, Lord of them all, never fail. How little is the suffering that You allow to those who love You! O my Lord, how delicately and skillfully and tenderly do You deal with them! Oh, happy are they who have never loved anyone save You! You seem, Lord, to give severe trials to those who love You, but only that in the excess of their trials they may learn the greater excess of Your love. O my God, had I but understanding and learning to find new words with which to exalt Your works as my soul knows them! These, my Lord, I lack, but if You forsake me not, I shall never fail You. Let all learned men rise up against me, let all created things persecute me, let the devils torment me; but You, Lord, do not fail me; for I have already experienced the benefits which come to him who trusts only in You! " (T.J. *Life*, 25).

Take away from me, O Lord, all trust in my own strength. Make me see that I can do nothing without You. Show it to me in a practical way, even if it causes me sorrow and humiliation. O Lord, I no longer desire to rely on my own strength; in You alone do I place all my trust. With Your help I shall continue to strive to practice virtue and to advance in Your ways, but with my eyes always fixed on You, O divine Sun, who alone can make my feeble efforts bring forth fruits of virtue! When storms arise, I will take refuge in You; I will call upon You with all the strength of my heart and with all my faith, certain that You will give me that peace and that victory which I would seek in vain apart from You.

64

JESUS AND MANKIND

PRESENCE OF GOD - O Jesus, teach me to love others as You love them.

MEDITATION

1. The sacred soul of Jesus always remains in closest union with the Blessed Trinity and therefore in the most profound contemplation, yet He is ever mindful of the needs of mankind. It was for men that Jesus came—to save them and bring them to the Father; and He gives Himself to them with the utmost solicitude and abandon. The same charity which unites Jesus to His Father descends through the Father upon the men whom Jesus loves so tenderly. He wills to redeem them all because they belong to the Father, to whose image and likeness they were created. In a most touching manner Jesus expressed His tender love for men comparing Himself to the Good Shepherd : " I am the Good Shepherd; and I know Mine, and Mine know Me. As the Father knoweth Me and I know the Father : and I lay down My life for My sheep " (*Jn* 10,14.15). Jesus likens His union with us to the union He enjoys with His Father, the terms of comparison being knowledge and love. Certainly it is only a simple similitude and yet Jesus delights to speak of it. He sees and knows the Father in the splendor of His glory, but He also sees and knows each one of us in the reality of our poverty, sorrows, and longings. He loves the Father, and gives Himself totally for His glory, and at the same time He loves each one of us and gives Himself wholly for our salvation; or rather Jesus sees and knows us only in the Father and in relation to Him. This is the very reason for His love and for everything He has done for us; His infinite love for the Father has made Him the Good Shepherd who gives His life for His sheep.

2. Our love and contemplation of God, our desire for intimate union with Him, should not make us strangers to our brethren, should not lessen our sensitivity to their

needs and sufferings; it should not prevent us from giving ourselves to them with true supernatural charity, as far as our state in life permits. No state of life, even the most contemplative, can excuse us from the duty and necessity of caring for our neighbor : if external works are reduced to a minimum, we must devote ourselves to our neighbor by prayer and apostolic immolation.

When love for God is genuine and intense, it does not confine the soul within itself, but in one way or another it always leads it to embrace all those who belong to God because they are His creatures, His children, and the object of His love.

Although Jesus was God, He did not hold Himself aloof from men. He willed to feel and experience all their needs, even their temptations, " without sin " (*Heb* 4,15). He shared with them a life of privation, fatigue, painful poverty, and suffering. Therefore, if we wish to attain to an effective fraternal charity, we must feel the sorrows, the poverty, and the material and spiritual needs of our neighbor; we must feel these in order to sympathize with him, help him, and even share in his trials. We must sacrifice ourselves, our ease and comfort, in order to give ourselves to others. We shall be able to do this only if our love for our neighbor resembles the love of Jesus, that is, if it springs from our love of God. Only one who loves others for the love of God will have that strong, persevering, fraternal charity which never fails.

COLLOQUY

O Jesus, why am I not moved by Your solicitude and tender love for us, Your poor creatures? You enjoy the uninterrupted vision of the Most Holy Trinity, finding in it all Your beatitude and glory, but you do not will that this glory and beatitude should be exclusively Yours; You want to give us a share in it. O Jesus, I see You sharing our poor human life of misery and suffering, so that, making Yourself like to us in sorrow, we might be made like to You in glory.

Men have not understood You; they have not returned Your love...they have crucified You. Yet You still love them because Your love is not for Your own personal satisfaction, but only for the glory of the Blessed Trinity. O Jesus, out of love for Your Father You have loved us to the point of sacrificing Yourself entirely for us; grant that, out of love for You and for Your glory, I may know how to love my brethren and to give myself to them most generously.

" O my Jesus, how great is the love that Thou hast for the children of men! The greatest service that we can render Thee is to leave Thee for love of them and for their advantage. By doing this, we possess Thee the more completely; for, although the will has less satisfaction in the enjoyment of Thee, the soul is glad that Thou art pleased, and sees that, while we live in this mortal life, earthly joys are unsure, even though they seem to be bestowed by Thee, unless they are accompanied by the love of our neighbor. He who loves not his neighbor, loves not Thee, my Lord; for in all the Blood Thou didst shed, we see the exceeding great love which Thou bearest for the children of Adam " (T.J. *Exc*, 2).

O Jesus, grant that like You I may live in continual union with God and at the same time give myself to my neighbor. May I lead a life of continual recollection, prayer, and contemplation, yet a life wholly devoted to the service of others.

65

LIVING CHRIST

PRESENCE OF GOD - O Jesus, deign to imprint Your likeness on my poor soul, so that my life may be a reflection of Yours.

MEDITATION

1. The imitation of Christ should not be limited to some particular aspect of His life; it means living Christ and becoming completely assimilated to Him. The life-giving principle of our resemblance to Christ is grace : the more grace we possess, the greater our resemblance to Him. The principal characteristic of Christ's soul is the unlimited charity which urges Him to give Himself entirely for the glory

of His Father and the salvation of souls. This same charity increases in our souls in the measure in which we grow in grace and live under the influence of Jesus, who is the source of grace, and to the degree in which our souls are directed by the same divine Spirit that directed the soul of Jesus. Each one of us will be an *alter Christus* (another Christ) in the measure in which he receives Christ's influence, His grace, His virtues, the gifts of the Holy Spirit and, above all, the motion of the Holy Spirit, which urges us to make a complete gift of self for the glory of God and the good of our neighbor. However, in order to accomplish this fully, we must continually die to ourselves, " always bearing about in our body the mortification of Jesus, that the life also of Jesus may be made manifest...in our mortal flesh " (2 *Cor* 4,10.11). Jesus lived a life of total abnegation in order to save us; we too must follow in His footsteps that He may live in us and we in Him. " For to me, to live is Christ" (*Phil* 1,21) is the cry of the Apostle who had so lived Christ that He was able to say, " I live, now not I but Christ liveth in me " (*Gal* 2,20).

2. " My God, I desire to seek but one thing, and that is to become a perfect copy of Yourself. Since Your life was a hidden life of humiliation, love, and sacrifice, such shall henceforth be mine " (T.M. *Sp*). If we truly desire to " live Christ, " we must make St. Teresa Margaret's resolution our own. However, the Saint did not intend to be merely a detached copy of Christ, the divine model; rather, she wanted to live His very life : with Him, by Him, and in Him. We are to imitate Jesus by conforming and identifying ourselves with Him by grace and love, until each one of us becomes, as Sr. Elizabeth of the Trinity expresses it, " another humanity, wherein He may renew all His mystery " (E.T. *III*).

As the word *Christian* is an extension of the word *Christ*, so the life of a Christian should be an extension of Christ's life. St. Paul said, " I fill up those things that are wanting of the sufferings of Christ, in my flesh " (*Col* 1,24). The life and Passion of Jesus are perfect in themselves; nothing can be added to His infinite merits. However, it is His will to continue to live and suffer in us, the members of His Mystical Body, so that through us He may continue His redemptive work until the end of time—that work of applying the fruits of the redemption to every new soul that comes into the world. Yet there are very few souls whom Jesus can freely use to carry out His lofty plans. Therefore, let us give ourselves wholly to Him, that in our humanity He may continue to immolate Himself for the glory of the Father and the salvation of souls, continue to adore His Father, love mankind, and make all souls share in the solicitude of His most merciful heart. Let us give ourselves to Him, " so that the life of Jesus may be made manifest in our mortal flesh. "

COLLOQUY

" O my Christ, whom I love! Crucified for love! I long to be the bride of Your heart! I long to cover You with glory and love You...even until I die of love! Yet I realize my weakness and beg You to clothe me with Yourself, to identify my soul with all the movements of Your own. Immerse me in Yourself; possess me wholly; substitute Yourself for me, that my life may be but a radiance of Your life. Enter my soul as Adorer, as Restorer, as Savior!

" O consuming Fire, Spirit of Love, descend upon me and reproduce in me, as it were, an incarnation of the Word; that I may be to Him a super-added humanity wherein He may renew all His mystery! " (E.T. *III*).

O my Jesus, this is my great desire : to be an extension of Your humanity, so that You can use me with the same freedom with which You used the humanity that You assumed on earth. Now in Your glory in heaven, You continue to adore the Father, implore Him on our behalf, give grace to our souls; You continue to love us and offer the merits of Your passion for us; but You can no longer suffer. Suffering is the only thing that is impossible for You, who are glorious and omnipotent, the only thing which You do not have and which I can give You. O Jesus, I offer You my poor humanity, that You may continue Your passion in me for the glory of the Father and the salvation of mankind. Yes, Jesus, renew in me the mystery of Your love and suffering; continue to live in me by Your grace, by Your charity, by Your Spirit. I want my humble life to be a reflection of Yours, to send forth the perfume of Your virtues, and above all the sweetness of Your charity.

You know O Jesus, that the world needs saints to convert it—saints in whom it will be able to recognize and experience Your love and infinite goodness, saints in whom it will find You again. O Lord, although I am so miserable, I also want to be of the number of these Your faithful followers in order that through me You may continue to win souls for the glory of the Blessed Trinity. O Jesus, give us many saints and grant that many priests may be counted among them.

66

JESUS OUR ALL

PRESENCE OF GOD - O Jesus, my God and my Redeemer, make me understand that You are my All and that in You I may find all that my soul needs.

MEDITATION

1. Jesus is both true God and true Man. As Man, He is our *Way* : He came to take us by the hand and lead us back to our Father's house. He is the source of our life because He merited grace for us and still continues to dispense it to us; He is the Master who shows us the way to go to God, the Model who, by His example, teaches us how we should live as children of God. Having merited our participation in the divine life, which He as the Word possesses in its full plenitude, Jesus has made us worthy to be readmitted to the intimacy of the family of God. In His last prayer, as if summing up His work as Redeemer, Jesus said to the Father, " And the glory which Thou hast given Me, I have given to them, that they may be one, as We also are one " (*Jn* 17, 22). Yes, He has given us His grace, His Spirit, and has thus made us sharers in the glory of His divine Sonship, true children of God and temples of the Holy Spirit. In Jesus, the one perfect Mediator between God and man, we find everything we need for our sanctification and our life of union with the Triune God.

We belong to Christ, we live in Him, " who, of God is made unto us wisdom and justice, and sanctification, and redemption " (1 *Cor* 1,30).

2. As God, Jesus is our *End* : He is the Incarnate Word and, as the Word, He is in all things equal to the Father and the Holy Spirit. Equally with the Father and the Holy Spirit He is our Beginning, the Creator of everything in the natural and supernatural order. He is also our last end, the End toward which we must move in this life with faith, love, generosity, and perseverance, in expectation of the joy of eternal union with Him and the Father and the Holy Spirit in heaven. Jesus, as Man, merited grace for us; as the Word He bestows it upon us. He creates it in union with the other two Persons of the Blessed Trinity. If, as Man, Jesus merited the coming of the Holy Spirit, as the Word, He, together with the Father, is continually sending the Spirit into our souls, because the Holy Spirit proceeds from Him as well as from the Father.

In Jesus, therefore, we find our Mediator and our God. When as Mediator He guides us, He is also drawing us to Himself as God; and when we are united to Him as Man we are also united to Him as the Word of God. Whether we fix our gaze on the humanity of Jesus or on His divinity, we shall always behold Him in the Word. To go to Jesus is to go to the Word; and to go to the Word, to the Son, is to go also to the Father, to the Trinity. That is why St. Teresa of Jesus insists so strongly that we must never separate ourselves from Christ : " It is by this door [Jesus] that we must enter.... Let us seek no other way : that way alone is safe. It is through this Lord of ours that all blessings come " (*Life*, 22). St. Paul says the same : " And you are filled in Him " with all good things; " Christ is all, and in all " (*Col* 2,10 – 3,11).

COLLOQUY

O Jesus, my God and my All! You are everything to me, and I want to belong entirely to You, consecrating my whole self to Your love and service.

" Now do I see, my Spouse, that You are mine; I cannot deny it. For my sake You came into the world; for my sake You suffered such great trials; for my sake You endured to be scourged; for my sake You have remained with us in the Most Holy Sacrament.... I have seen clearly that it is by this door that we must enter if we wish Your sovereign Majesty to show us great secrets. He who loses You will be unable to find his way.

"What am I, Lord, without You? And what am I worth if I am not near You? If once I stray from Your Majesty, where shall I find myself?

"Blessed is he who loves You in truth and has You always at his side. What more do we need than to have at our side so good a Friend who will never leave us? O my Lord, my mercy and my good, what more do I want in this life than to be so near You that there is no division between You and me? In such company what can become difficult? What can one not undertake for You, with You so near? Never, with Your help and favor, will I turn my back on You.

"What can I do for my Spouse? How can I be Yours, my God? What can a person do for You who has contrived such evil things as I? I can only lose the favors You have granted me. From such a one what services could be hoped for? And even if, by Your favor, I should accomplish something, consider how little a miserable worm can do. How can a powerful God have need of it? Only love allows us to think that this true Lover needs us.

"But if You come to me, Lord, can I doubt that I can render You great services? From this moment, Lord, I will forget myself and look solely at the ways in which I can serve You; I will have no will but Yours. But my will is powerless, my God; it is You that are powerful. All I can do is to resolve to serve You, and this resolve I make and will henceforth carry into action " (cf. T.J. *Con*, 4 – *Life*, 22 – *Int C VI*, 7).

67

THE CHURCH

PRESENCE OF GOD - O Jesus, You have given me the Church as my Mother; grant that I may love her with true filial love.

MEDITATION

1. Jesus loves us so much that He wills to remain with us until the end of time. Therefore, He abides with us in the Blessed Sacrament as the Companion of our earthly pilgrimage, as the Food of our souls, but He also remains with us in the Church as our Guide, our Shepherd, and our Teacher. Jesus formed the first nucleus of the Church by His preaching, by choosing and instructing the Apostles; He gave life to her by dying on the Cross. " The Church, " as the Holy Father notes, " came forth from the side of our Savior on the Cross like a new Eve, Mother of all the living " *(Mystici Corporis)*. Jesus sanctified her by shedding His Blood for her. He gave her His power; He made her His spouse and collaborator, continuing through her His work of sanctifying and directing souls. Today Jesus no longer dwells among us as He did nineteen hundred years ago; His *Physical Body* is gloriously enthroned in Heaven at the right hand of the Father. But He does abide with us in His *Mystical Body*, the Church, His Spouse and our Mother. Jesus is the living Head of the Church; it is always He who rules her invisibly by His Spirit, the Holy Spirit. He sustains and vivifies her unceasingly, gives her life, and distributes graces to each of her members " according to the measure of His giving " (cf. *Eph* 4,7). The Church lives by Christ alone; she is holy with His holiness; she is the Mother of souls through her union with Him. This union of Christ with the Church is so intimate and vital that the Church can be regarded as a prolongation of Christ. Indeed, Pope Pius XII teaches that " Christ sustains the Church in a divine manner; He lives in her to such a degree that she is, as it were, another Christ " *(Mystici Corporis)*. Even as it is through the Eucharist that we unite ourselves to Jesus and are nourished with His immaculate Flesh, so it is through His Church that guided and ruled by Him, we are vivified by His grace and

nourished by His doctrine. And as we cannot become more one with Christ in this life than by uniting ourselves to Him in the Eucharist, so we can have no greater assurance of living according to His Spirit, of being directed and taught by Him, than by uniting ourselves to the Church and following her directives.

2. To be a " Child of the Church " is the most glorious title for a Christian and second only to that of " Child of God. " These two titles can never be separated — one depends upon the other; for, as St. Cyprian has said, " He who does not have the Church for a Mother, cannot have God for a Father. " Jesus wishes to save and sanctify us, but He wishes to do it by means of the Church. He gave His life and shed His Blood for us; He put His most precious merits at our disposal; He gave us the Holy Eucharist and left us the heritage of His doctrine, but He wished the Church to be the sole depository and dispenser of these inestimable benefits, so that all who wish to enjoy them must have recourse to her. Let us go, then, to the Church with the complete confidence of children, certain to find Jesus in her, Jesus who sanctifies, nourishes, teaches, rules, and directs us by means of His representatives. If the thought of being a Child of the Church does not make our hearts vibrate, if our love for the Church is weak, if our recourse to her is not confident, this indicates a lack of the spirit of faith : we have not sufficiently understood that the Church is Christ, continuing to live in our midst to sanctify and sustain us and to lead us to eternal beatitude. " We can think of nothing more glorious, more noble, and more honorable than membership in the Holy Roman Catholic Church, by which we become members of such a holy Body [the Mystical Body of Christ], are guided by one and so sublime a Head [Jesus Christ], are filled with one divine Spirit [the Holy Spirit], and finally, are nourished in this earthly exile with one doctrine and one same heavenly Bread until we are permitted to share the one eternal beatitude in heaven " *(Mystici Corporis)*. Let us love the Church, " the most perfect Image of Christ " *(ibid.)*; let us love the Church, the most pure Spouse of Christ and our Mother; and as He loved her whom " He hath purchased with His own Blood " *(Acts* 20,28), so let us love her with a true spirit of obedience and filial devotion, offering ourselves completely to serve, glorify and defend her.

COLLOQUY

" O Christ, our Lord, You have transmitted to Your Church the sovereign power which You have received. By virtue of Your dignity, You have made her Queen and Spouse. You have given her supreme power over the entire universe. You have commanded all men to submit to her judgment. She is the Mother of all the living, and her dignity increases with the number of her children.

" Every day she gives birth to new children by the operation of the Holy Spirit. As a vine, her branches cover the whole world. Her boughs are upheld by the wood of the Cross and they reach up to the Kingdom of heaven.

" Your Church, O Christ, is a strong city built on a mountain, visible to all and enlightening all. You are her Founder and fore most Citizen, O Jesus Christ, Son of God and our Lord.

" We beseech You, eternal King of souls, Christ our Lord, stretch Your omnipotent Hands over Your holy Church and the holy people who belong to You; defend them, guard them, preserve them; combat, challenge, subdue all their enemies.

" May Your Church always remain pure and living! May she chant Your praises under the guidance of the holy angels! We pray to You for all her members; grant them pardon and remission of all their sins; grant that they may sin no more. Be their defense; take away from them all temptation. Have pity on men, women, and children; reveal Yourself to all, and let the knowledge of Your Holy Name be written in their hearts " (from an ancient Liturgy).

68

THE PRIESTHOOD

PRESENCE OF GOD - O Lord, give to Your Church many holy priests.

MEDITATION

1. The Church, the Mystical Body of Christ, is not to be regarded merely as a spiritual institution which can be neither touched nor seen; it is a concrete organism which is visible in its members, the faithful, who are joined together under the leadership of their pastors. " For as in one body we have many members, but all the members have not the same office " (*Rom* 12,4), so in the Church there are members of diverse importance, having various functions : there are the faithful and there are the shepherds, the priests appointed by Christ to guide souls. To state that Jesus sanctifies and governs us by means of the Church, is to say that He sanctifies and governs us by means of the Bishops and the Pope. Jesus has placed all the powers given to His Church in the hands of the priests, who have been chosen by Him from among the people to become His ministers. " As the Father hath sent Me, I also send you " (*Jn* 20,21); " He that heareth you, heareth Me, and he that despiseth you, despiseth Me " (*Lk* 10,16). The priestly dignity depends upon this investiture by Christ, this appointment as His representative and minister. Priests must be thoroughly aware of the great dignity of their call if they wish to live at the height of their vocation. " They must be holy, says St. Pius X, because they are the friends and representatives of a holy God. "

The faithful on their part should see and venerate Christ Himself in their priests. St. Paul, writing to the Christians of Corinth, gave them the exact meaning of his priestly authority : " For Christ, therefore, we are ambassadors, God, as it were, exhorting by us " (2 *Cor* 5,20). And St. Catherine of Siena cautioned her disciples to see priests only as " the dispensers of the Blood of the humble, Immaculate Lamb " and to overlook the faults which they might notice in them. A priest is a man, and therefore always remains fallible and capable of making mistakes, but

this does not prevent him from being the Anointed of the
Lord, marked forever with an indelible sign and having the
power to consecrate the Body of Christ, to administer the
sacraments, and to preach to the people in the name of God.

2. Without the priesthood we would be deprived of the
Holy Eucharist; we would never have the consolation of
hearing, in the name of God, " Thy sins are forgiven thee "
(*Mt* 9,2). If there were no priests, the churches would be
deserted, schools would become secularized, there would
be no nuptial blessings, the dying would be deprived of final
consolation, children would be abandoned to evil; all men
would become totally immersed in misery, with no one to
raise them up and lead them to God, with no one to pray to
Him in their name and for their welfare. But Jesus, the
sole Mediator between God and man, willed to institute
the priesthood to perpetuate among us, in a visible manner,
His work of mediation, salvation, and sanctification. The
priest accompanies us at every step of our life. Soon after
our birth, he welcomes us at the baptismal font; he administers the Sacraments to us, He helps us to understand divine
truths, he shows us how to lead a good life, blesses our efforts,
sustains our footsteps, and strengthens us in our last agony.
He often works unseen and unknown, misunderstood, never
sufficiently appreciated; yet his apostolic work is priceless,
indispensable. Every Christian ought to be grateful for
the gift of the priesthood : in the first place, we should
be grateful to Jesus who instituted it, and then to those
who perform its sublime duties. We must express this
gratitude, not only by showing reverent respect and filial
docility to God's ministers, but also by assiduously offering
our prayers and good works for priestly vocations. " Pray
ye therefore the Lord of the harvest, that He send forth
laborers into His harvest " (*ibid.* 9,38). " What prayer, "
comments Pius XI, " can be more pleasing to the Sacred Heart
of the Redeemer?... Ask, and it shall be given to you :
ask for good, holy priests, and the Lord will not refuse to
send them to His Church " *(Ad Catholici Sacerdotii)*. To our
prayers we must add good works " to awaken, foster and
help vocations to the priesthood " *(ibid.)*. Blessed are the
families that have had the honor of giving a priest to God;
blessed are all those who by their prayers, sacrifices, and
good works help in the formation of holy priests!

COLLOQUY

" Lord, do not look upon my sins, but hear Your servant through the mercy of Your inestimable charity. You did not leave us orphans when You departed from us, but You left us Your Vicar and Your ministers to baptize us in the Holy Spirit. By Your sacred power, they cleanse our souls from sin, not once, but again and again.

" O eternal Mercy, grant that Your Vicar and Your ministers may hunger for souls, may burn with an ardent desire for glory, and in all things seek You alone, O supreme, eternal Goodness.

" Sanctify these Your servants, O eternal God, that they may follow You alone, in simplicity of heart and with a perfect will; look not upon my wretchedness, but receive my prayer and establish them in Your will.

" O eternal God, I know that Your arm is powerful and strong, that it will deliver the Church and Your people, rescue them from the hands of the demon, and put an end to persecution. I know that the Wisdom of Your Son, who is one with You, can illumine our intellects and scatter the clouds which hover around Your dear Spouse, the Church.

" Then, eternal Father, I beg and implore Your power, the Wisdom of Your only-begotten Son and the clemency of the Holy Spirit, abyss and fire of charity, to show mercy to the world and restore the warmth of charity so that peace and union may reign in the holy Church. Alas, I do not want to wait any longer : I pray that Your infinite goodness may constrain You not to close the eye of Your mercy on Your holy Spouse, O sweet Jesus, Jesus-love " (St. Catherine of Siena).

69

THE SACRAMENTS

PRESENCE OF GOD - Grant, O Lord, that the grace You give me so generously may not be given in vain.

MEDITATION

1. Just as the human body is endowed with organs capable of " providing for the life, health, and development of each of its members, so the Savior of the human race... has provided in a marvelous way for His Mystical Body, endowing it with the Sacraments, so that by so many consecutive, graduated graces, as it were, its members should be supported from the cradle to life's last breath " *(Mystici Corporis)*. The Church, the Mystical Body of Christ, is a living organism possessing elements which are capable of propagating, conserving, and nourishing life in all her members. This vital force emanates from her divine Head and is the fruit of the grace merited for Her by this most loving Redeemer when He died on the Cross, that grace which He still diffuses in all His members by means of the Sacraments. In fact, " when the Church administers the Sacraments by means of exterior rites, it is He who produces their interior effect " *(ibid.)*. Jesus is the author of grace and has complete dominion over it; He created it as God, merited it as Man, and can dispense it as He wills and to whom He wills, even without the medium of the Sacraments. However, He ordinarily communicates grace to us through these sensible signs which He Himself has instituted, thus giving us greater assurance of having received it.

But we must not forget that, if the exterior rite is indispensable for the reception of the corresponding grace, this grace is always produced by Jesus, who, in cooperation with His ministers, intervenes with His sanctifying power each time a Sacrament is administered. This shows the deep, inseparable union between Jesus and His Church. He wills to make use of her exterior acts in sanctifying souls, but He reserves for Himself the power to vivify these acts and make them effective. When we receive a Sacrament, it is not the priest alone who is attending to the good of our soul, but with him is Jesus, whose all-powerful action penetrates and vivifies the inmost fibers of our spirit. This is why the Sacraments, when administered to those who are capable of receiving them, have of themselves an infallible efficacy : in them is the action of God Himself.

2. The Sacraments act *ex opere operato*, that is, they always give the grace that corresponds to the outward sign, for it is Christ by His all-powerful action who is producing it in them. This is the profound motive for the great esteem and respect which we should have for the Sacraments.

The frequency and ease with which we can receive certain Sacraments often make us approach them with negligence, inattentiveness, or even with that superficiality with which we treat things of little value. This attitude is the result of a lack of right knowledge and appreciation, and a weak spirit of faith. How necessary it is to awaken and revive our faith, to place ourselves actually and sincerely in the presence of God in order to open our souls to His action! When we approach a Sacrament, we are approaching Christ; we are putting ourselves in contact with Him to receive the effusion of His grace, to welcome a renewed communication of His divine life. " It is true," Pius XII teaches, " that the Sacraments have an intrinsic power, inasmuch as they are the acts of Christ Himself who communicates and diffuses grace from the divine Head to the members of the Mystical Body; but to have their due efficacy, they require good dispositions in our souls " *(Mediator Dei)*. In other words, every time we approach a Sacrament, Jesus infallibly offers us the gift of His grace, but the Sacrament will produce its sanctifying effect only in proportion to the intensity of our good dispositions. Just as the very best seed, sown in uncultivated ground, brings forth little or no fruit, so divine grace, although in itself sanctifying, fructifies in us only in the measure of our good will. Oh! how Jesus desires that His grace, so generously given by means of the Sacraments, should find our hearts well disposed, open to His coming, docile to His action!

Each Sacrament brings us a gift of sanctifying grace, either an initial grace or an increase of grace; in addition it offers us the sacramental grace which is proper to it alone. Thus God puts at our disposal His immense riches — immea-

surable possibilities of sanctity. Let us endeavor with
all our strength that such great gifts may not be given in vain.

COLLOQUY

" O eternal Word made flesh, You have given us the
Sacraments endowed with the virtue of Your Blood and
Your Passion. Through them our souls are bathed in
Your Blood, nourished by Your Blood.

" Your Sacred Side is the fount of water and of Blood,
from which flow the waters of Baptism and the Blood of the
Sacraments. We are bathed in the waters of this fountain
when we receive holy Baptism, which enables us to glorify God
and receive His gifts. We drink the Blood from this fountain
when we receive the sacraments, especially Penance and the
Sacrament of the Altar, by which the soul is fed and nourished,
taking refuge, O Christ, in the fount of Your Sacred Side.

" Oh! how great is the dignity of priests! They are the
ministers of this fount, they bathe us in the water of Baptism
and then nourish us with Your Blood! Oh! how great is
their dignity! They are, O Lord, Your secretaries and
treasurers, for in transmitting Your word to us, they reveal
Your secrets and, in administering the Sacraments, they
give us Your treasures " (St. Mary Magdalen dei Pazzi).

" O good, sweet Jesus! Father of lights, from whom every
perfect gift proceeds, look upon us with mercy, upon us who
know You, who truly understand that we can do nothing
without You. You gave Yourself as the price of our redemption. Although we are unworthy of such a precious gift,
grant that we may correspond with Your grace entirely,
perfectly, and in all things, so that, being conformed to the
likeness of Your Passion, we may recover what we have lost
by sin, the likeness of Your divinity " (St. Bonaventure).

70

THE BOND OF PERFECTION

FIFTH SUNDAY AFTER THE EPIPHANY

PRESENCE OF GOD - O my God, grant that I may desire and seek above all else the perfection of love.

MEDITATION

1. The Epistle for this Sunday (*Col* 3,12-17) recalls to our mind the fundamental duty of a Christian : charity. All programs and resolutions of the spiritual life are of little value if they are not animated by love and directed to the perfection of love.   Detachment, mortification, humility, and all the other virtues are of little worth if they do not incline the heart to a wider, more complete and more expansive charity.   " But above all these things, " St. Paul recommends, " have charity, which is the bond of perfection "; not only love for God, but also for our neighbor.   It is under this aspect that the Apostle speaks of charity in today's Epistle, carefully pointing out that all our relations with our neighbor should be inspired by love.   " Put ye on therefore, as the elect of God, holy and beloved, the bowels of mercy, benignity, humility, modesty, patience : bearing with one another and forgiving one another, if any have a complaint against another. "   Fraternal charity is the mark of God's elect. If we do not have this distinctive mark, Jesus does not reconize us as His disciples; our heavenly Father does not love us as His children, nor will He take us into His Kingdom. The spiritual life requires the use of so many means, calls for the exercise of so many virtues that care must be taken lest we become lost in details, forgetting the love which should be the foundation and end of all.   Of what value is the spiritual life, consecration to God, or even the vows of religion, if they do not help the soul to tend to the perfection of love?

Consider the perfect love which the Apostle asks us to have for our neighbor : mercy, compassion, mutual forgiveness, and that love which leaves no room for divisions or dissensions, which overcomes strife and forgets offenses.   This is long-suffering charity which makes every sacrifice and overcomes all difficulties in order to be in harmony with all, because we all form " one body " in Christ, because we are all children of the same heavenly Father.

Fraternal charity of this kind is the surest guarantee of a spiritual life that is advancing toward sanctity.

2. The Epistle has presented us with the ideal of the Christian life, an ideal of love which should unite all the faithful in singleness of heart; the Gospel (*Mt* 13,24-30) shows us the practical way to live this ideal.

" The kingdom of heaven is likened to a man that sowed good seed in his field. But...his enemy came and oversowed cockle among the wheat. " God has sown the good seed generously in His field, the world; He has sown grace and love, and the desire for total oblation, the ideals of an apostolic, religious, saintly life. But, in the midst of all this good, the enemy comes to sow evil. Why does God permit this? To sift His servants as we sift grain, to test them.

Sometimes we are scandalized, seeing evil working its way even into the best places, seeing that even among God's friends, among those who should be a source of edification to others, there are some who behave unworthily. Then we are filled with zeal, like the servants in the parable. We want to remedy this evil and root up the cockle. " Wilt Thou that we go and gather it up? " But God answers, " No, lest perhaps gathering up the cockle, you root up the wheat also together with it. " The cockle is spared, not because it is good, but in order to save the wheat. In the same way God spares the wicked and does not destroy them, for the sake of the elect. When God asks us to endure with patience certain situations, as inevitable as they are deplorable, He asks for one of the greatest exercises of charity, compassion, and mercy. He does not tell us to fraternize with evil, to make a league with the cockle, but He tells us to endure it with the longanimity with which He Himself endured it. Was there not a traitor among the Apostles? Yet Jesus wanted him among His intimates — and with how much love He treated him! Indeed one of the greatest opportunities for the practice of charity is offered us by those who by their evil conduct give us so many occasions for forgiving them, for returning good for evil, and for suffering injustice for the love of God. Moreover, we should consider that, whereas cockle cannot be changed into wheat, it is always possible for the wicked to be converted and become good. Were not Magdalen, the good thief, and Peter, who had denied Jesus, converted? This is one of the strongest motives to incite us to do good to all. When our love is perfect, we are able to live among the wicked without being harsh or contentious, without being influenced by them, but rather doing them good.

COLLOQUY

" O most noble, most beautiful, most innocent Lord Jesus, You have loved me, a vile, ugly creature, deformed by sin; teach me to imitate Your great charity, so that I will love my neighbor with sincere, brotherly love, however imperfect and sinful he may be.

" Teach me to love all men for love of You, and then I shall never lack motives for benevolence, even if I have to deal with those who are coarse, ill-mannered, and full of imperfections. Only by keeping my eyes fixed on You, my God, who are infinite love, shall I be able to surmount all the annoyances and difficulties I meet in my contacts with my neighbor.

" O Jesus, who took on my wretchedness in becoming man and in clothing Yourself with my weak nature, teach me how to accommodate myself to my neighbor and to bear with his faults patiently; help me to do my best to correct my own faults and to eliminate from my conduct everything that might be displeasing to others " (Ven. John of Jesus Mary).

" See, Lord, how far I still am from true charity and humility! You show me that there is nothing wonderful about living in peace with kind, good people; nothing is more natural. We all love peace and prefer those who love peace also. But it takes great virtue to live in peace with obstinate, perverse, intractable people whose ideas are not like our own.

" I beseech You, Lord, grant me that grace without which I shall never be at peace with my neighbor, but will ever be prompt to take offense. It would be far better for me to correct my own faults than to criticize the actions of others! If I expect others to bear with my defects, I must likewise bear with theirs " (cf. *Imit. II*, 3,2).

71

BAPTISM

PRESENCE OF GOD - O God, who without any merit on my part, have made me Your child, grant that my life may be worthy of this divine Sonship.

MEDITATION

1. The Church, like a mother anxious for the salvation of her children, and eager to rescue them from the slavery of Satan, to make them living temples of God, does not wait until a child is able to appreciate the value of Baptism, but hastens to confer it upon him in the first days of his life. Thus Baptism is the only Sacrament which is given without the consent of the recipient. However, the Church requires that competent sponsors represent the newborn child in order that God's gift may not be lost through the child's unawareness in receiving it. As soon as the child has attained the age of reason, it is the sacred duty of these sponsors to see that it understands and appreciates this great Sacrament and lives accordingly. Indeed, we are all bound to cultivate during the entire course of our life that knowledge and appreciation which we could not take personally to the baptismal font; we are bound to live in such a way as to place no obstacle to the development of baptismal grace, thus making ourselves more worthy of the sacramental character we have received. We must live up to the pledges of our Baptism, that is, we must conform our lives to the petitions, renouncements, and promises which our godparents made in our name. Through our godparents we asked for faith; we renounced Satan and all his works and pomps; we requested to be baptized, so that we might be received into God's great and holy family.

God, by means of the Church, has delivered us from the bonds of sin; He has taken us into His arms and marked us with an indelible sign as His children. The passing years, the vicissitudes of life, our failures to cooperate with grace, even the most serious sins, if we have been so unfortunate as to commit any, can never destroy that indelible mark of a child of God. Think what an honor it is, how glorious and blessed, to be for all eternity the child of God! " Behold what manner of charity the Father hath bestowed on us, that we should be called and should be the sons of God " (1 *Jn* 3,1). We are children of God, not through any merit on our part, but only through His infinite goodness anticipating, as it were, our request and desire.

2. Baptism is the seed, the cause of our whole Christian life and of all the graces which we have received and will receive until we die. Furthermore, beyond the limits of this earthly life, Baptism is the cause and beginning of our eternal glory. This was prefigured by the white robe and the lighted candle which the Church presented to us at the sacred fount : " Receive this white garment and wear it without spot until you come to the judgment seat of our Lord Jesus Christ, in order to have eternal life. Receive this burning candle and preserve untarnished the grace of your Baptism...so that, when the Lord comes to conduct you to the eternal nuptials, you may go to meet Him with all the saints of heaven and may have eternal life " *(Roman Ritual)*. These profoundly significant words should be engraved upon our hearts, reminding us continually of our duty to preserve our baptismal grace. As the years go by, many obligations and duties will claim our time and attention. These duties are sacred, because they are closely connected with our state in life and are therefore willed by God. Nevertheless, we must never forget that our first duty is always the one imposed by holy Baptism : to preserve intact the garment of grace. Before everything else, we have the great obligation of living our Baptism.

If we had not been baptized, we would be unable to nourish our soul with the Body of the Lord; we would not be an apostle; we would not be consecrated to God as a priest or as a religious. Everything is attached to that first link in the chain of sanctifying grace. If we do not strive to live our Baptism according to the perfection demanded by our state in life, our piety will be vain, our Communions without fruit; our apostolic works and even our consecration to God or our priestly ministry will be futile.

We should often reflect on the words which the Church pronounced over us on that day : " Depart from him, unclean spirit, and give place to the Holy Spirit, the consoler.... So live that you will indeed be a temple of God " *(Roman Ritual)*.

COLLOQUY

" O Lord, I beseech You, keep my faith pure and grant that, until my last sigh, I may feel the testimony of a good conscience. Grant that I, who have been baptized in the name of the Father, the Son, and the Holy Spirit, may always believe what I professed in the Sacrament of my regeneration. Let me adore You, my Father, and Your Son with You; let me be worthy of the Holy Spirit who proceeds from You and Your only-begotten Son. Truly I have a worthy pledge of faith to guarantee what I believe, and it is He who said, ' Father, all that is Mine is Yours, and all that is Yours is Mine, ' Jesus Christ, my Lord, who lives in You and who, remaining God, proceeds from You, is always near You, and is blessed forever and ever " (St. Hilary).

" I renounce satan! O my God, this was my baptismal promise, a solemn promise made in the presence of the Church, a promise so explicit that no one can dispense me from it, a promise recorded by angelic hands, a promise on which I shall be judged at the hour of my death.

" O my God, I desire to renew very fervently that promise today. Therefore, with all my heart and all my strength, I renounce you, O Satan; I renounce you, abominable sin; I renounce you, detestable world!

" O Lord Jesus Christ, I give myself entirely to You forever. I desire to adhere to Your holy doctrine by faith, to Your sacred promises by hope, to Your divine commandments and counsels by love and charity. I desire to follow You by the practice of all the virtues. I desire to follow You as my Head, as a living member of Your Body " (St. John Eudes).

72

CONFIRMATION

PRESENCE OF GOD - O Holy Spirit, come, work in me again and enable me to live like a true soldier of Christ.

MEDITATION

1. Baptism is the *Sacrament of Christian initiation.* It introduces us into the Church, God's great family, and infuses into our souls the new life of sanctifying grace by which we become children of the Most High and brothers of Jesus Christ. Confirmation *confirms* and strengthens this supernatural life which Baptism has engendered in us. Baptism is our Christian birth; *Confirmation* brings us to Christian maturity. " Confirmation, " according to the catechism, " is the Sacrament through which the Holy Spirit comes to us in a special way to enable us to profess our faith as strong and perfect Christians and soldiers of Jesus Christ. "

At Baptism we become temples of the Holy Spirit; in Confirmation, this divine Spirit comes to us in greater plenitude and sets us apart as knights of Christ, capable of fighting to defend our faith and the Church. We have very great need of this Sacrament, especially today when God's enemies and the snares and enticements of evil are increasing to such an extent that it often requires great courage, and sometimes even heroism, to stand firm in our Catholic faith and morality. Confirmation imprints an indelible mark on our soul, the glorious character of a " soldier " of Jesus Christ. It endows us with the corresponding strength and confers on us the right to receive, at the opportune moment, the actual graces necessary to remain faithful to God, in spite of the difficulties and obstacles we may encounter. This is the " sacramental grace " of Confirmation.

Therefore we may say that, at least virtually, Confirmation is the Sacrament that consecrates the heroes and the martyrs of duty, for it gives man the strength to live in open profession of his faith, even at the cost of great sacrifices, not excluding the sacrifice of his life, if this were necessary.

When cowardice or human respect tempts us to waver, we should repeat St. Francis of Assisi's daring words : " Knight of Christ, are you afraid? "   And recalling the happy day of our Confirmation when we were solemnly consecrated a soldier of Christ, we shall find the strength to continue the battle and to win.

2. Writing about her confirmation, St. Thérèse of the Child Jesus said, " It was with the greatest care that I made ready for the coming of the Holy Ghost, and I could not understand how anyone could do otherwise before receiving this Sacrament of Love.... Like the Apostles, I looked with joy for the promised Comforter, gladdened by the thought that I should soon be a perfect Christian " (T.C.J. *St*, 4). Unfortunately, there are very few who, like this young saint, can say that they prepared themselves for the reception of Confirmation with a true comprehension of it. Very few give any thought to the Holy Spirit, the great uncreated Gift, who gives Himself to the soul as its Paraclete, that is, as its strength, support, and guide; very few think of Him or if they do, it is in passing, and superficially, so that there is little possibility of their coming to a deep understanding of this ineffable mystery. Let us try to make up now for our own lack of preparation for the reception of this Sacrament. Let us meditate on the beautiful prayer recited by the Bishop during the imposition of hands : " Almighty, everlasting God... send forth upon them the Author of Thy sevenfold Gifts, the Paraclete, Thy Holy Spirit, the Spirit of wisdom and understanding, the Spirit of counsel and fortitude, the Spirit of knowledge and piety; fill them with the Spirit of Thy holy fear, and sign them with the sign of the Cross of Christ unto eternal life " *(Roman Ritual)*.   The Holy Spirit came down upon us with the abundance of His Gifts.   He confirmed us in the faith; He gave us the strength we need to live as perfect Christians, in complete accord with the holy requirements of God's law.   Jesus said to the Apostles, " You shall receive the power of the Holy Ghost coming upon you, and you shall be witnesses unto Me in Jerusalem... and even to the uttermost part of the earth " *(Acts* 1, 8).   In these words He predicted the coming of the divine Paraclete.   We too received this power when we were confirmed, and if our

conduct has not always borne witness to Christ, this is not due to a defect in the Sacrament, but to our lack of correspondence with the grace it conferred. If we are weak in the struggle against our passions, the world, and the devil, it is precisely because we have not made profitable use of the grace of fortitude which the Holy Spirit lavished upon us when we were confirmed.

Let us implore this divine Spirit to pardon our negligence and to help us henceforth to make up for our past deficiencies.

COLLOQUY

" I recognize You as the one true God, O Holy Spirit, proceeding from the Father and the Son, consubstantial and coeternal with them, the Paraclete and our Advocate, who came down in the form of a dove upon our Lord Jesus Christ and appeared in the form of tongues of fire over the Apostles. From the beginning You have taught all the saints and the elect of God by the gift of Your grace; You opened the mouths of the prophets so that they could speak of the wonders of God's kingdom. You, together with the Father and the Son, are adored and glorified by all the saints of God. And I too, the child of your handmaid, glorify Your Name with my whole heart because You have enlightened me, You who are the true light, the Fire of God, and the director of souls, teaching us all truth by Your unction. Without Your help, we cannot be pleasing to God, because You are God of God, Light proceeding from Light, that is, proceeding ineffably from the Father of lights and from His Son, our Lord Jesus Christ, with whom You are glorified and reign, consubstantial, equal and coeternal with Them, existing in the essence of one indivisible Trinity!

" O Holy Spirit, quench my thirst at the torrent of Your delights, so that I will no longer wish to taste the poisonous delights of the world " (St. Augustine).

" O Holy Spirit, infinite Love, proceeding from the Father and the Son, give me the spirit of adoption; teach me to act always like a true child of God. Abide in me and grant that I may abide in You, that I may love as You love. Without You, I am nothing : *Sine tuo numine nihil est in homine...* I am worth nothing, but keep me united to You;

fill me with Your love, so that, with Your help, I may remain
united to the Father and the Son " (Dom Marmion).

73

PENANCE (1)

PRESENCE OF GOD - O Jesus, You who are ever seeking the prodigal
son, despise not my contrite and humble heart, but purify it in
Your precious Blood.

MEDITATION

1. Grace, which has been given to us so abundantly
in Baptism and Confirmation, has of itself the infallible
power to sanctify. It does not force us, however, to do good
nor does it sanctify us without our voluntary cooperation.
Man always remains free to cooperate or not with this
divine gift; unfortunately, it is always possible for him to
resist grace and condescend to evil, thus failing in his duty
as a child of God and a soldier of Christ. Jesus, foreseeing
these possible defections and falls, has instituted a special
Sacrament for the sole purpose of healing the wounds of
sin, of restoring sinners to grace and of providing strength
for their weakness. Our Lord said to the Apostles, " Whose
sins you shall forgive, they are forgiven them; and whose
sins you shall retain, they are retained " (*Jn* 20,23). By
these words Christ conferred on them and on their successors
the formidable power of forgiving sins in His Name. This
power was not given to the angels nor even to the most
Blessed Virgin Mary, but was reserved for His ministers.
Scandalized at seeing Jesus absolve sinners, the scribes
asked one another, " Who can forgive sins, but God only? "
(*Mk* 2,7). Wavering between unbelief and derision, the
world still considers the Sacrament of Penance with a like
attitude; it cannot and will not recognize in the priest a
minister commissioned by God to remit sin. But for those
who believe, there is perhaps no other Sacrament which

----

(1)   Also see Meditation 104.

so rouses our piety, devotion and gratitude. How powerful are the Sacraments by which we are raised to the dignity of children of God and soldiers of Jesus-Christ; how ineffable is the Sacrament by which we are nourished with the immaculate Flesh; yet is it not more touching still that in the Sacrament of Penance Jesus goes in search of the Christian who has betrayed Him, of the soldier who has deserted the camp, of the son who, after having been nourished at His table, has gone far away to eat even the husks of swine? Instead of being indignant or repelling one who has made such poor use of His boundless gifts, Jesus through the Sacrament of Penance offers him pardon and mercy; He heals this soul which, though formerly clothed in the wedding garment of grace and regenerated in His precious Blood, has fallen into sin, making itself His enemy.

2. Although the Sacrament of Penance is necessary only to remit mortal sins, the Church has always recommended and praised the frequent use of it even for those who have only venial sins to confess. " We heartily recommend, " says Pius XII, " the pious custom introduced by the Church, through the inspiration of the Holy Spirit, of frequent confession. It gives us a more thorough knowledge of ourselves, stimulates Christian humility, helps us to uproot our evil habits, wages war on spiritual negligence and tepidity, purifies our consciences, strengthens our wills, encourages spiritual direction and, by virtue of the Sacrament itself, increases grace " (Mystici Corporis). Frequent confession has always been considered, in authentic Catholic tradition, as a school of perfection, an effective way to correct faults and evil tendencies and to advance in virtue. When a penitent sees Our Lord Jesus Christ in the person of the confessor, and discloses with humble sincerity his sins and weaknesses, accompanying his accusation with true repentance and a firm purpose of amendment, the Sacrament will have most efficacious results. Not only will he be absolved from his infidelities and receive an increase of sanctifying grace, but he will also receive the " sacramental grace, " which assures him of divine assistance in correcting his weak points, overcoming the temptations to which he is most often exposed, and surmounting the particular difficulties he encounters in the practice of virtue. There is no better medicine for the ills and wounds of the soul than frequent confession when it is made with a humble, sincere,

and contrite heart. Jesus awaits us in this Sacrament of His merciful love, not only to cleanse our soul in His precious Blood, but also to strengthen it in this salutary bath, fortify it, and guard it against future attacks of temptation and evil. Confession applies to our soul all the merits of the Passion of Jesus, all the infinite value of His Blood; we shall always return from this Sacrament renewed, sanctified, and strengthened in good in the measure in which we have approached it with a contrite and humble heart.

COLLOQUY

" If you have sinned, my soul, and are wounded, behold your God, your physician, waiting to heal you. His omnipotence permits Him to remit all your sins in one moment; His goodness and mercy urge Him to forgive you.

" Are you terrified, perhaps, because He is your judge? Have confidence, my soul, because if He is your judge, He is also your defender. He is your defender to excuse you and justify you if you repent; and He is your judge, not to condemn you, but to save you, if you are humble. His mercy is infinitely greater than all your iniquities. And I tell you this, not that you will remain in sin and make yourself unworthy of His pity, but that you will drive away evil, and not despair of His clemency and pardon " (Bl. Louis de Blois).

" O fountain of love, most loving Lord Jesus Christ, filled with so much and such ineffable goodness, You always forestall us with Your love; if we seek You, You present Yourself to us and come to meet us. Your love, Your immense charity extends even to Your enemies. You do not refuse to give Yourself to anyone; You despise no one, but You call and welcome all as Your friends. Your superabundant charity is so limitless that You call to repentance those who miserably lie in sin; and often, even though they rebel, You constrain them to return to You.

" Deign then, to help me, O most merciful Lord Jesus Christ, fire and light of love; enkindle and illumine my cold, rebellious heart by Your charity, so that, for love of You, I may grieve for my sins, do penance, and with a pure, loving, and humble heart give myself to the practice of the works which are pleasing to You. Thus, prevented, aided, and followed by Your grace, I may live the present life in Your love, and at its close may obtain by your mercy life eternal where I shall love You forever in glory " (Ven. Raymond Jourdain). [1]

74

EXTREME UNCTION
(Anointing of the Sick)

PRESENCE OF GOD - May Your grace, O Lord, cleanse me from all my faults, so that I may be without spot when admitted to Your presence.

MEDITATION

1. Extreme Unction (or the anointing of the sick) has been significantly defined by the Council of Trent as the " *sacramentum exeuntium* " that is, the Sacrament of those about to leave this world to enter eternity. The life of a Christian, begun at Baptism, perfected by Confirmation, nourished by the Holy Eucharist, restored by Penance, is, at its close, crowned, as it were, by Extreme Unction. This Sacrament completes the work of purifying the soul, giving it strength to face the difficulties of the last hour. It prepares the soul to appear in the sight of God. The special effect of this Sacrament, according to the Council of Trent, is the infusion into the soul of " the grace of the Holy Spirit, whose unction takes away the residue of sin, and animates and revives courage in the sick, arousing great trust in God's mercy, so that the soul bears more calmly the sufferings of illness and resists more easily the temptations of the devil. " Undoubtedly, Extreme Unction has also the power to " cancel the venial and mortal sins which the dying person, although he has attrition, may not be able to confess " *(Catechism of Pius X)*. However, this is not the special grace of this Sacrament, but is the effect proper to the Sacrament of Penance. Extreme Unction destroys the last

---

An ancient author, known in ascetical literature under the pseudonym " Idiota. "

consequences of sin, curing the soul of the lassitude and weakness which are the natural effects of all the sins committed during life, sins which have already been forgiven in confession. Just as Confirmation strengthens and perfects the grace received in Baptism, so Extreme Unction perfects the purification of the soul already accomplished by the sacrament of Penance. " O our Redeemer, " says the Church, in administering Extreme Unction, " by the grace of the Holy Spirit, cure all the ills of this sick person, heal his wounds, pardon his sins, and drive away all his pains of soul and body. In Your mercy restore him to perfect spiritual and bodily health. " Perfect spiritual health, that is, the total remission, not only of sin, but also of all its consequences, is the effect of this Sacrament, by which the dying person, relieved of all the weight of his sins, can go serenely to God in peace.

2. St. Thomas teaches that Extreme Unction is the last Sacrament and, in a certain way, the " consummation " of all the work of purifying the soul; it prepares man for participation in glory.

A dying person who receives this Sacrament with the proper dispositions obtains the full remission of all his sins and of the penalty due to them, so that he can go directly from this earthly exile to eternal glory without passing through purgatory. But although this is the normal effect of Extreme Unction, very few actually receive all its fruit because very few have the proper dispositions. There is perhaps no Sacrament which is so little understood, it is often received in haste, without preparation, and in a state of complete or partial unconsciousness. The result is that its precious fruits are lost in great part. How necessary it is, therefore, to do all that is possible to see that the sick receive Extreme Unction in time, with full consciousness and with deep piety, so that they may derive all possible profit from the grace being offered to them. The fear of distressing the sick person or his family should not deter us from fulfilling this pious duty with charity and tact. Some day we ourselves shall have the same need, and how fortunate we shall then be if there is someone who will render us this assistance at the proper moment. Moreover, in order to remove the prejudice which people often have against this Sacrament, it is useful to mention that it is ordered not only to the health of the soul, but even to that of the body, when this enters into God's designs and would be beneficial to the soul. What is of most importance, however, is to try to procure for the dying person perfect tranquillity of conscience and divine assistance and support in the painful sufferings and bitter struggle of the agony of death, so that he may courageously face the final attacks of the enemy, accept death with resignation, abandon himself with confidence to God's mercy, and at last reach the heavenly country. Then the touching prayer of the Church will become a living reality for him : " Go forth from this world, O Christian soul, in the name of God the Father who created you, in the name of Jesus Christ who died for you, in the name of the Holy Spirit who has been poured forth upon you " *(Roman Ritual)*.

COLLOQUY

" You have softened the terrors of death for us, Lord; You have made the end of our life the beginning of true life. You make our body rest for a short time, but only for a short time. Then You will awaken us with the sound of the last trumpet. You commit us to the earth which You have made, that it may preserve us; some day You will restore our mortal remains and make them beautiful forever.

" For us You became malediction and sin to save us from the curse of sin. You prepared our resurrection when you burst the gates of hell and destroyed by Your death the one who had empire over death.

" You have given to the fearful the Sign of the Cross to destroy their enemies; and you have assured us that we will have life, O eternal God, to whom I was offered as a babe and whom I have loved with all my strength.

" O Master, send me an angel of light to conduct me to that place of refreshment, whence flows the spring which quenches our thirst.

" You gave paradise to the man who was crucified with You and who implored pardon. Be mindful also of me in Your kingdom, for I am crucified with You, and the fear of Your judgment has pierced my flesh. Grant that the abyss may not separate me from Your elect! Remember not my sins. If, because of the weakness of my nature, I have failed in thought, word, or deed, pardon me, for You have the power to forgive sins. May my soul be found without guilt when I lay aside the garment of my body. At that moment, deign to receive it without spot or blemish into Your hands as an offering pleasing to You " (St. Macrina).

75

VOCATION

PRESENCE OF GOD - Grant, O Lord, that I may accept with a humble and generous heart the honor of Your call.

MEDITATION

1. In a general sense, any invitation of God to the soul may be called a " vocation "; thus we speak of a " vocation to the Christian life. " " Blessed be the God and Father of our Lord Jesus Christ, " exclaims St. Paul, " who chose us in Him before the foundation of the world, that we should be holy and unspotted in His sight, in charity; who hath predestined us unto the adoption of children through Jesus Christ unto Himself... " (*Eph* 1,3-5). How exalted is the Christian vocation, a vocation for which we can never adequately thank God, and to which we can never fully correspond. Within this universal vocation which is proper to all Christians, there are more specific calls to the various states in life—to matrimony, and to the single and religious states; thus the term " vocation " is often used restrictively. A person is said to *have a vocation* when he is called by God to that higher state of life indicated by the counsels and implying a special relationship with God which sets him apart as one " consecrated, " that is, reserved for God alone. This is precisely why God asks these souls to renounce that life in which individuals contract bonds which establish a close union between them, and a mutual belonging to one another. Instead of binding itself to another creature, a consecrated soul binds itself to God by the pure bond of perfect chastity. It therefore belongs neither to itself nor to creatures, but only to God. This total *belonging* to God is the characteristic

mark of a consecrated soul, whether it is sealed by sacramental charismatic consecration to the priesthood, by religious profession, or by a private vow of perfect chastity. It is not only its characteristic mark, but also its glory and the profound reason for its dignity, for just as God is superior to His creatures, so the honor of belonging to Him alone far surpasses that of belonging to a creature.

2. Vocation, or the call to consecrate oneself to God, is a *privilege* : a privilege which does not depend on personal merit, but on God's good pleasure alone. God chooses whom He wills, when He wills, and as He wills. " All men take not this word, " said Jesus, speaking of perfect chastity, " but only they to whom it is given " (*Mt* 19,11). This prerogative has been given only because it pleased God and He so willed. " You have not chosen Me, but I have chosen you " (*Jn* 15,16). God's choice is the basis of every vocation; it is wholly gratuitous, inspired solely by His love. Each one so chosen should justly consider himself as a privileged one of God, privileged without any merit on his own part, privileged only because the Most High has so decreed in the unfathomable designs of His will. Each one so chosen can and should feel that God might have selected others far more deserving, more virtuous, more gifted; and confronted with the mystery of God's choice and his own insufficiency, he should be unable to do otherwise than prostrate himself in gratitude and humility. Together with Mary, the most privileged of all creatures, every consecrated soul can sing its *Magnificat* : " My soul doth magnify the Lord, and my spirit hath rejoiced in God my Savior, because He hath regarded the humility of His handmaid " (*Lk* 1,46-48). The story of every vocation can be summarized by saying that God's glance has rested with special love on one of His creatures. That this creature is poor, weak, and wretched does not matter. God knows what it is made of. He sees its poverty and draws it to Himself : " I have loved thee with an everlasting love; therefore, have I drawn thee, taking pity on thee " (*Jer* 31,3). God's choice is absolutely free and cannot be determined either by the merits or by the characteristics of His creatures. On the other hand, because He is infinite Wisdom and Omnipotence, He has no need of the gifts of His creatures, nor does He seek them; rather, His choice often falls on the weakest, on those whom the word

despises. God only seeks hearts capable of corresponding to His love of predilection, hearts capable of giving themselves to Him without reserve and with complete generosity.

COLLOQUY

" O infinite Goodness, You chose us to be Your creatures even before You gave us being; therefore, You could well say, ' You have not chosen Me, for since you are nothing, you had no power to choose, but I have chosen you. '

" You chose to make us Your creatures and to create us to Your own image and likeness, moved by Your goodness alone. You chose us again at our Baptism, and made us Your children, while we, born in sin, could never have hoped to be Your children if You had not chosen us.

" Still moved by Your infinite bounty alone, O my God, You chose me and so many others to be consecrated wholly to You, choosing us in so many, many ways, by Your interior inspirations and by other means. You chose us especially to enable us to raise ourselves up to You, so that You could make us know Your Being and permit us to share Your Life.

" Oh, the grandeur of a creature who has been chosen by You! To what a sublime state it has been raised, and how abject it becomes when it falls into sin, instead of corresponding with Your choice!

" O my dear Spouse, I ask this grace of You always : grant that all chosen souls may receive perfect light and knowledge of their state, so that they may gladly renounce themselves and devote themselves to Your service.

" O Lord, how necessary this prayer is! How necessary it is for You to grant us this grace, that Your chosen ones may serve You perfectly! " (St. Mary Magdalen dei Pazzi).

" I come to You, O most loving Jesus, whom I have loved, sought, and always desired. I come because of Your sweetness, Your pity, Your charity. I come with all my heart, all my soul, all my strength. I follow You because You have called me. Do not reject me, but treat me with forbearance, in accordance with Your great mercy " (St. Gertrude).

76

CORRESPONDENCE TO VOCATION

PRESENCE OF GOD - O Lord, You call me unceasingly, drawing me to Yourself; grant that I may respond to Your call with ever-increasing generosity.

MEDITATION

1. God calls us but He does not constrain us. He grants man full liberty to accept or to refuse His divine invitation. " If thou wilt be perfect...come, follow Me " (*Mt* 19,21), says the Lord to every soul that He chooses, but as with the young man in the Gospel, He leaves to each soul the responsibility of answering or rejecting His call. However, when God calls us, it would be rash to close our heart to His voice and spurn His invitation. Who would dare turn away from the glance of predilection which the Most High casts on one whom He calls to follow Him?

We ought to answer God's call with great humility and joy, with gratitude and readiness, saying with all our heart, *Ecce venio,* " Behold, I come...that I should do Thy will, O God " (*Heb* 10,7). The creature should respond to God's eternal choice of its soul, by choosing God to be its only good, its only love, by rising above all creatures and earthly affections. " He that loveth father or mother more than Me, is not worthy of Me " (*Mt* 10,37). God, our Creator and absolute Ruler, has the full right to ask of us the renunciation of even the holiest affections and to exact that, for love of Him, we abandon father and mother, brothers and sisters, home, and all our possessions. Furthermore, if God has decreed that " a man shall leave father and mother and shall cleave to his wife " (*Gn* 2,24), would it be extravagant to do the same thing when we give ourselves, not to another creature, but to the Creator Himself?

The first duty one who has received the divine call, is therefore to renounce all earthly affections, possessions, and joys, so that freed from all ties, he may follow the Lord. Actually, what is to be given up will not be the same for all; more is required of the religious than of the secular priest, of the nun than of a person consecrated to God in the world.

But from the point of view of affection, the renunciation, or rather the detachment of the heart, must be the same for all; it attains its full measure when it is complete, with no reservation.

2. In order to correspond to one's vocation, it is not enough to leave the world, nor to enter the seminary or the convent, nor even to be ordained a priest or make the vows of religion; we must strive, day by day, to live up to our vocation and to adapt our lives more and more to the exigencies of the divine call. Everything in us, as long as we live, is capable of becoming more perfect. Thus we can say that although our consecration to God becomes stabilized by receiving Holy Orders or by pronouncing vows, it is, nevertheless, subject to the law of growth and should become ever deeper and more perfect. Ordinarily, when we first bind ourselves to God—although we have a sincere intention of giving ourselves definitively to Him—we have not yet realized a full and total consecration. In reality, we are not yet entirely " consecrated "; we still have inclinations, tendencies, and affections not wholly under God's sway. There is still much of " self, " much of the purely natural which is not perfectly submissive to God, not entirely sacrificed to Love. Each day should mean progress in the realization of one's vocation, until not a single fiber of the soul remains which does not belong entirely to God.

There is nothing static about vocation, not even on God's part, because, adapting Himself to our nature, He calls us in a progressive way. If we are faithful to His first invitation, others, increasingly pressing and definite, will follow, which will bind us more and more to our divine Master. Basically, there is but one call to the priesthood, the religious life, or consecration to God in the world; but God, through the various circumstances of life, and especially, through new occasions for sacrifice, repeats this invitation more precisely, more definitely, each time letting the soul see how far the gift of self must be extended in order to reach the plenitude of its consecration. If the soul is faithful, and answers these progressive calls generously, God will continue to send new invitations, which will open up wider and more luminous horizons, until the soul lives its consecration in a perpetual renewal of fervor and love.

COLLOQUY

" My love holdeth Thee, O loving Jesus, nor will I let Thee go. O Love, who art Life, Thou art also the living Word of God; kindle anew Thy life within me; make amends for all the losses my love has suffered. O God who art love, who hast created me, create me anew in love. O Love who hast redeemed me, redeem and give back to me all that I have lost of Thy love through my negligence. O Love who hast purchased me for Thyself with Thy precious Blood, sanctify me in charity. O God who art Love, who hast adopted me as Thy child, train and fashion me according to Thine own heart. O Love, who hast chosen me for Thyself, and not for another, grant that I may be wholly Thine, Thine alone. O God who art Love, Thou hast loved me freely, gratuitously; grant that I may love Thee with all my heart, with all my soul, with all my strength.

" O Jesus, my Brother and my Spouse, supreme King, set Thy mark on the face of my soul, and engrave it so deeply, that no creature may attract my choice, nor excite my desire, nor possess my love. Thou art dearer to me than all that is dearest; deign that I may ever be Thy true and faithful spouse in that love which is stronger than death.

" O Love, Thou art dear to me above all things; oh, let Thy love teach me always to be faithful to my promises.

" Grant that I may have a place among the wise virgins. There will I await the heavenly Bridegroom, having my lamp lighted and filled with oil. So I shall not be confounded at the sudden coming of my King; but all peaceful and clothed with light, I shall join with songs of gladness the choirs of virgins who have gone before me. O Lamb without spot, grant that I may not be excluded with the foolish virgins, but in humble confidence, may enter the banquet hall of the great King, where in virtue of my patient and persevering fidelity, I shall dwell forever with the heavenly Lamb " (St. Gertrude).

NOTICE - *When there are six Sundays after Pentecost, it is suggested to use Meditation N°. 357* : The Grain of Mustard Seed.

SEPTUAGESIMA SUNDAY

TO

HOLY SATURDAY

THE PURIFICATION OF THE SENSES AND THE PRACTICE OF
ABNEGATION — THE STRUGGLE AGAINST SIN —
HUMILITY, OBEDIENCE, AND ACCEPTANCE OF
THE CROSS — THE PASSION OF JESUS

77

A NEW PROGRAM

SEPTUAGESIMA SUNDAY

PRESENCE OF GOD - O Lord, I come to You with a keen desire to learn how to respond to Your invitations.

MEDITATION

1. The time of Septuagesima is somewhat like a prelude to Lent, the traditional time for spiritual reform. That is why the liturgy presents us today with a program which we must put into effect in order to bring about within ourselves a new, serious conversion, so that we may rise again with Christ at Easter. The Collect of today's Mass, while reminding us that we are sinners, invites us to sentiments of profound humility, " to the end that we, who are justly afflicted because of our sins, may through Thy mercy, be freed from them. " The first step toward conversion always consists in humbly recognizing that we need to be converted. The lukewarm must become fervent, the fervent must reach perfection, the perfect must attain heroic virtue. Who can say that he does not need to advance in virtue and in sanctity? Each new step effects a new conversion to God, *conversio ad Deum.* In the Epistle (1 *Cor* 9,24-27—10,1-5) St. Paul urges us to undertake this ceaseless spiritual labor. To reach sanctity and heavenly glory we must never tire of running and striving, as those who run in the stadium struggle and exert themselves " to receive a corruptible crown, but we an incorruptible one. I, therefore, so run... not as one beating the air, " says the Apostle, " but I chastise my body and bring it into subjection! " This is the first point in the program : a generous struggle to overcome ourselves, to conquer evil and achieve goodness; denial of self by humility; denial of the body by physical mortification. Only those who struggle and exert themselves will win the prize. Therefore let us also run in such a way as to obtain the reward.

2. The Gospel (*Mt* 20, 1-16) gives us the second part of the program for this liturgical season : not to remain idle, but to labor assiduously in the Lord's vineyard. The first vine to be cultivated is our own soul. God comes to meet us with His grace, but He does not will to sanctify us without our cooperation. On this Sunday the great invitation to sanctity is repeated to every soul. God in His love seeks out His scattered, idle children and gently reprimands them : " Why stand you here idle? " St. Mary Magdalen dei Pazzi says that " God calls us at various times, because creatures differ in state. In this variety we see God's greatness and benignity, which never fail to call us by means of His divine inspirations, in no matter what stage or situation we may be. " Blessed are those who, ever since their youth, have always heard and followed the divine invitation! But each hour is God's hour; and He passes by and calls us, even to the very last hour. What a consolation, and at the same time what an incentive to respond at last to the Lord's appeal : " Today if you shall hear His voice, harden not your hearts! " (*Ps* 94,8).

In addition to the vineyard of our soul, we must also consider the vineyard of the Church, where so many souls are waiting to be won to Christ. No one can consider himself dispensed from thinking of the welfare of others. However lowly our place in the Mystical Body of Christ, we are all members of it; consequently, each one of us must work for the welfare of the others. It is possible for everyone to carry on an efficacious apostolate by example, prayer, and sacrifice. If, up to now, we have done but little, let us listen today to the words of Jesus : " Go you also into My vineyard. " Let us go and embrace generously the work which the Lord offers us; let us consider nothing too difficult when there is question of winning souls.

COLLOQUY

Bless, O Lord, this new liturgical season which opens today. By penetrating its spirit may I be disposed, with Your aid, for a serious reform of my spiritual life. Grant me sincere humility, that I may know my misery and see myself as I am in Your eyes, free from those false lights which arise from self-love, deceiving me and leading me to think I am better than I am. If I wish to consider my wretchedness

at Your feet, it is by no means in order to become discouraged :
" In my trouble I call upon You, my God, and from Your
holy temple, You hear my prayer.... You are my strength,
O Lord, my support, my refuge, my Redeemer. You are my
help in time of trouble. He who knows You, hopes in You,
for You do not abandon the one who seeks You. From the
depths of the abyss, I cry to You, O Lord; Lord, hear my
voice. If You will mark our iniquities, O Lord, who can
stand it? But with You there is mercy, and by reason of
Your law, I trust in You, O Lord!" (Mass of the day).

Infuse into me, O Jesus, new strength to take up more
eagerly the course which will lead me to win the incorruptible
crown of sanctity. " And since nature opposes what is good,
I promise to declare a merciless war against myself. My
weapons for the battle will be prayer, the practice of the
presence of God, and silence. But, O my Love, You know
that I am not skilled in handling these arms. Nevertheless,
I will arm myself with sovereign confidence in You, with
patience, humility, conformity to Your divine will, and
supreme diligence. But where shall I find the aid I need to
fight against so many enemies in such a continual battle?
Ah! I know! You, my God, proclaim Yourself my Captain,
and raising the standard of Your Cross, You lovingly say,
'Come, follow Me; do not fear' " (T.M. *Sp*).

O my Lord, I will no longer resist Your invitation. May
today sound for me the decisive hour of a response filled with
generosity and perseverance. You call me. Here I am.
I come to Your vineyard, O Lord, but if You are not with me
to sustain me in my work, I shall accomplish nothing. O You
who invite me, help me to do what You ask of me.

78

THE NECESSITY FOR INTERIOR PURIFICATION

PRESENCE OF GOD - Purify my soul, O Lord, so that it may be filled completely with Your light and Your love.

MEDITATION

1. St. John of the Cross compares the soul to a glass window with a ray of sunlight shining on it. If the glass is dirty, " the ray cannot illuminate it, nor transform it completely into its light; its illumination will be in proportion to its clearness. If, on the other hand, it is absolutely clean and spotless, it will be illuminated and transformed in such a way as to appear to be the luminous ray itself, and to give the same light " (AS II, 5,6). God is the divine Sun shining upon our souls, desiring to invade them and penetrate them, completely transforming them into His light and love. Before He does this, however, He waits until the soul resolves to free itself from every " creature stain, " that is, the stains of sin and inordinate attachments. As soon as God finds that a soul is free from mortal sin, He immediately fills it with His grace. This precious gift is the first step in the great transformation which the Lord desires to bring about in us. The more we become purified of all sin and imperfection, and of even the slightest attachment; that is, in proportion as we conform our will to the will of God, not only in serious matters of obligation but even in the least details of perfection, the more capable we become of being entirely penetrated and transformed by divine Grace.

Grace, the gift of God which makes the soul a participant in the divine nature, is poured forth into the soul in proportion to its degree of interior purity, which always corresponds to its degree of conformity with God's will. Therefore, the soul that wishes to be totally possessed and transformed by divine Grace, must in practice strive to conform fully to the will of God, according to the teaching of St. John of the Cross, " so that there may be nothing in the soul that is contrary to the will of God, but that in all and through all its movement may be that of the will of God alone " (AS I, 11,2).

2. God not only illumines our soul with the rays of His divine Grace, but He Himself, Unity and Trinity, takes up His abode within us, according to the promise of Jesus : " If anyone love Me...We will come to him, and will make our abode with him " (*Jn* 14, 23).

Even if we possess but one single degree of grace, God dwells in us and invites us to live in real union with Him; nevertheless, He does not give Himself completely to us; He does not consummate us in His unity nor transform us completely into Himself as long as He finds in us the slightest thing contrary to His will.   The smallest imperfection is opposed to the will of God because God cannot desire the slightest imperfection and, *a fortiori*, He cannot admit to perfect union with Himself a soul who keeps any trace—no matter how insignificant—of opposition to His infinite perfection.   The basis of all perfect union is total conformity of will and affection.   As long as we love and desire, even in small details, anything that God cannot love or desire, our will is not fully conformed to the divine will, and these two wills, God's will and our own will, cannot become one, " that is, the will of God become also the will of the soul " (J.C. *AS I*, 11,3).

As long as we do not attain this perfect union of wills, God, although He dwells in us, will not communicate Himself fully to our soul.   Hence St. John of the Cross teaches that " the soul disposes itself for union...by purity and love, that is, by renouncement and perfect detachment from all things for God's sake alone. "   When the soul is thus disposed, God bestows on it " that supernatural favor by which all the things of God and the soul are one in participant transformation, and the soul seems to be God rather than soul, and is indeed God by participation, although its natural being is as distinct from the Being of God as it was before...even as the window has a nature distinct from that of the ray by which it is illumined " (*AS II*, 5, 8-7).

COLLOQUY

O my God, for what great things have You created me! You have created me to know You, to love You, to serve You — and not as a slave, but as Your child, Your friend, living in intimacy with You, sitting at Your table, enjoying Your presence.   O Jesus, You have said, " I will not now call you servants, for the servant knoweth not what his lord doth. But I have called you friends, because all things whatsoever I have heard of My Father, I have made known to you" (*Jn* 15,15).

You have revealed to me the great mystery of a God who deigns to love me as His child, to establish His dwelling in my soul, to invite me to a more intimate friendship and union with Him. You Yourself asked for this union for me at the Last Supper : " As Thou, Father, in Me and I in Thee, that they also may be one in Us " (*ibid.* 17,21). To be one with God, to be consumed in the Unity of the Most Holy Trinity! O Jesus, how sublime is the ideal You propose to me, how wonderful the invitation you offer me! Yes, Your words apply also to me, a creature of sin and misery. Why should I delay, remaining among the base things and vanities of this earthly life? Why should I, like a reptile, be content to crawl on the ground, when You invite me to soar like an eagle and give me wings with which to do so? Alone I can do nothing and would struggle in vain to free myself from the bonds of sin, to detach myself from creatures and from myself; all my efforts would be useless because my natural weakness constantly tends to drag me down. But Your grace and love are the wings on which I can fly to perfect union with You. With such an ideal, how could I think it hard to undertake and carry out a work of profound purification and total detachment?

O God, make me understand clearly that " real love consists in detaching oneself from everything that is not You " (J.C. *AS II*, 5,7). From everything, not only from this thing or that, but from everything, for love is by nature totalitarian, and perfect union demands perfect harmony of wills, desires, and affections.

My God, what profound purification I must undergo in order that You may be able to unite me to Yourself, who art infinite perfection!

79

VOLUNTARY ATTACHMENTS

PRESENCE OF GOD - O Lord, I place myself in Your presence, begging You to enlighten my soul so that I may see what are the obstacles to my union with You.

MEDITATION

1. " To be perfectly united to God by love and will, the soul must first be cleansed of all appetites of the will, even the smallest " (J.C. *AS I*, 11,3). In the language of St. John of the Cross, *appetites* are disordered inclinations or affections for oneself or creatures, tendencies which are, according to their seriousness, more or less contrary to the divine will. God wishes us to love ourselves, as well as all created things, in the measure assigned by Him, with a view to His pleasure and not to our own selfish satisfaction. These inclinations or appetites always give rise to venial sins, or at least to deliberate imperfections, when one willingly yields to them, even though it be only in matters of slight importance. The will of the soul which freely assents to these failings, slight though they be, is stained by this opposition to the will of God; for this reason a perfect union cannot exist between its will and God's. Moreover, if these imperfections become habitual and the soul does not try to correct them, they form a great obstacle to divine union; and according to St. John of the Cross, " they prevent not only divine union but also advancement in perfection " *(ibid.)*. He gives a few examples of these unmortified " habitual imperfections " : the habit of talking too much, unrestrained curiosity, attachment to little things—whether persons or objects—such as food and so forth, which the soul refuses to give up. There is also the attachment to one's comfort, to certain sensible satisfactions, little vanities, foolish self-complacency, attachment to one's own opinion or reputation. There is a real mushroom-bed of " appetites " and disordered inclinations from which the soul will not free itself, precisely because it is attached to the meager selfish satisfaction which it finds in these wretched things. It is " attached " to them; that is why it cannot make

the decision to give them up completely.   These are precisely
the " habitual voluntary appetites " of which St. John of the
Cross says, " One single unmortified appetite is sufficient to
fetter the soul " *(ibid.)*.

On the other hand, when it is a question of imperfect
inclinations arising solely from human weakness, of those
which do not get beyond the stage of " first movements " in
which the will has no part, " either before or after, " but
rather tries to repress as soon as it notices them, " these do
not prevent one from attaining divine union " *(ibid.*, 11,2).   It
is the will that counts and it must be completely free from the
slightest attachment.

2. " The least of these imperfections to which the soul is
attached or accustomed is more of a barrier to increasing and
advancing in virtue than if one fell every day into several
imperfections and isolated venial sins not the result of bad
habits " *(ibid.*, 11,4).   It is not so much these " isolated
falls, " due to inadvertence or weakness, which hinder the
soul's advancement, as it is the little venial faults and even
simple imperfections caused by habitual voluntary attachments which the soul does not take the trouble to uproot.
Even though they are slight, they nevertheless constitute
bonds which attach it to earth.   " For it comes to the same
thing whether a bird be held by a slender cord or by a stout
one, since, even if it be slender, the bird will be as well held as
though it were stout for so long as it breaks it not and flies
not away.   It is true that the slender one is the easier to
break; still, easy though it be, the bird will not fly away if it
be not broken.   And thus the soul that has attachment to
anything, however great its virtue, will not attain to the
liberty of divine union " *(ibid.)*.

St. John of the Cross has only one thing to say about
renouncement and detachment : renounce everything, be
detached from everything.   If this demand seems unreasonable, let us remember that it is pure evangelical
doctrine, that it asks nothing more than what Jesus proposes
to us when He says, " Renounce thyself. "   He asks us to
renounce ourselves not only in this or that matter, but in
everything that might prevent us from following Him :
" For he that will save his life shall lose it, and he that shall
lose his life for My sake, shall find it.   If thy hand or thy
foot scandalize thee, cut it off, and cast it from thee " *(Mt* 16,

25 - 18,8). Jesus teaches us in these words that, for the salvation and sanctification of our soul, we must give up everything that might become a stumbling block to us. It is precisely in this thorough renunciation, in this " losing " of self in everything—even in what is dearest to us and if it were necessary, even to the extent of sacrificing our life—that we find the road to salvation and sanctity.

COLLOQUY

" Late have I loved Thee, O Beauty ever ancient, ever new, late have I loved Thee. Thou wert within me, and I looked outside; I sought Thee, and miserable as I was I longed for creatures, I was detained by the wonderful works of Thy hands. Thou wert with me, but I was not with Thee, though that which kept me far from Thee could exist only in Thee. Thou hast called and cried to me in my deafness. Thou hast shone as lightning, brilliant enough to drive away my blindness. Thou hast scattered Thy perfume; I breathed it, and now I sigh for Thee. I have tasted Thee, and now I hunger and thirst for Thee. Thou hast touched me, and I burn with desire for Thy peace " (St. Augustine).

My God, give me the light necessary to recognize in myself all that keeps me from union with You. Grant me the light to recognize all the attachments which still bind me to creatures, and especially those which are most displeasing to You because they proceed directly from pride and self-love. In the secrecy of my heart You teach me sweetly and gently, You show me clearly that I am still far from conforming my will to Yours, in all things and for all things. I love and desire so many trifles, so many imperfections which You neither love nor desire because they are contrary to Your infinite perfection. Give me strength to wage a constant and courageous battle against them. You know, O Lord, that I have great need of Your help, for I am too attached to myself to be capable of struggling against my disordered affections, of giving up so many little pleasures which feed my egotism. I love myself too much to sacrifice what separates me from You. Then, let me present myself to You, O Lord, as a sick person to a surgeon; plunge the knife into my soul, cut away and destroy all that displeases You and that is not in accord with Your will.

80

THE ESSENCE OF DETACHMENT

PRESENCE OF GOD - Help me, O Lord, to understand the meaning of that total detachment which is the indispensable condition for perfect union with You.

MEDITATION

1. " The soul has only one will, and if it occupies itself or encumbers itself with anything, it will not remain free, solitary, and pure, as is required for divine transformation " (AS I, 11,6). This teaching of St. John of the Cross is in perfect harmony with the fundamental precept of Jesus : " Thou shalt love the Lord thy God with thy whole heart, and with thy whole soul, and with all thy strength and with all thy mind " (Lk 10,27). If the heart is occupied with inordinate attachments to self or creatures, it is clear that it cannot love God with all its strength, which is divided between God and self, between God and creatures. The precept of charity proposed to all Christians requires the radical renunciation of every attachment which is not conformable to the will of God, or which is not consistent with the love of God. Total detachment is the logical result of Jesus' commandment and the indispensable means of perfectly fulfilling it.

This is why St. John of the Cross insists that if the soul wishes to possess God, it must strip itself of all that is not God.. This is why it must give up every satisfaction or attachment which does not lead to God. This is the meaning of his statements : " In order to enjoy everything [that is, to enjoy God, who is everything], do not seek to enjoy anything [do not seek any inordinate pleasure]. In order to possess everything, do not desire to possess anything. When you stop at anything, you do not reach the *all* " (AS I, 13,11.12). When the soul, through some disordered attachment, stops at any creature, it interrupts its progress toward God : the nothingness of the creature prevents it from reaching the *all* of God.

2. The essence of total detachment does not consist in effective material separation from creatures, a thing which,

in its absolute form, would be impossible on this earth. Those who are cloistered, and even hermits, cannot escape certain dealings with their neighbors, nor get along without the necessities of life. Besides, wherever one is he carries with him his own person, his " self "; nevertheless, detachment from self is always the point of departure. It is clear, however, that it can never be a question of complete material detachment, but only of affective, spiritual detachment.

The doctrine of total detachment does not require that everyone abandon all things materially, but that each one, in whatever surroundings he finds himself, know how to keep his heart free from all attachment. " In order to enter into this divine union, all the affections living in the soul must die, whether they are many or few, large or small; and the soul must remain free from them, and as detached as if it were not made for them, nor they for it " (J.C. *AS I*, 11,8).

However, it will be impossible to attain this affective detachment, that is, the death of all inordinate affection for self and creatures if, at least to a certain degree, we do not practice effective or material detachment. If we cannot give up all useless preoccupation with creatures, we shall never reach interior detachment. Likewise, the soul who, by consecrating itself to God, has separated itself materially from people dear to it or has already given up so many things, must not think that all is accomplished. It will always have to be vigilant in order to keep itself free from all attachments. Whether we live in the world or in solitude, whether we possess much or little, we must always strive for the essence of detachment, which is detachment of heart and mind.

This is the teaching of St. Paul : " Let those who have wives be as if they had none...those who buy, as though they possessed not, and those who use this world, as if they used it not " (1 *Cor* 7,29-31).

COLLOQUY

O Lord, why should the idea of total detachment frighten me since it is the means of finally arriving at loving You with all my heart, with all my soul, and with all my strength, since it is the path which leads me to union with You, infinite beauty and charity, Triune God, the beginning and end of all things?

"O blessed detachment from all that is mean and perishable, to what a sublime state will you not raise me? You love me, my God, and for those who love You, Your love is no insignificant thing! Why, then, should I not return Your love with all my strength? It would really be a happy exchange, O my God, giving You my love and receiving Yours. I know indeed that You can do everything, and that I can do only what You enable me to do. But what do I do for You, my Lord and Creator? I make some feeble resolutions which really amount to nothing. But if You wish me to gain everything by this nothing, I shall not be so foolish as not to listen to You!" (T.J. *Way*, 16).

O Lord, with Your help I wish to set to work immediately to refuse no sacrifice, to spare no fiber of my heart in order to detach myself completely from everything that might tie me to earth. These sacrifices and detachments will pain my weak human nature, but You will enable me to see that, even though they make my heart bleed, it is nothing in comparison with the immense treasure which they purchase for me, which is the attainment of You, my God, You who are *All*.

O Lord, do not permit my cowardly heart to tarry amid earthly things; do not permit me to divide my affection, little as it is, between You who are All and creatures who are nothing, between You, my God, and my egoism, which is nothing but sin and misery. Perhaps I think "it is a small favor to have the grace to consecrate myself wholly, without reservation, to You who are the All" (*ibid.*, 8)? Oh! how I long, O Lord, for this supreme favor of total detachment which will give me the liberty of loving You with all my strength!

If You, O Lord, have already granted me the grace to renounce earthly things, to abandon life in the world and to consecrate myself to Your service, what gratitude I owe You! Do not permit me, I beg of You, to be so blind as to believe that because I have left the world, I have nothing else to do. What a mistake it would be, after making such big sacrifices, to attach myself to miserable trifles, which are not worthy of a soul consecrated to You!

81

THE WAY OF THE " NOTHING "

PRESENCE OF GOD - Show me, O Lord, the narrow path that leads to true life, to union with You.

MEDITATION

1. If you wish to start resolutely on the road of total detachment—the only sure road to divine union—you must " put the axe to the root of the tree "; that is, you must break off and pull up the root of your attachments—that inordinate tendency to enjoy, or to seek satisfaction in yourself, in your pride, or in other creatures. It is true that you were created to enjoy, but *to enjoy God*. However, God is not present to your senses, while your " self " and the things of earth are so close to you. Hence instead of looking beyond yourself and all creation in order to reach God, instead of making use of creatures to help you rise toward the Creator, you pause and seek your happiness in them. You pause with an inordinate affection, and for this grain of satisfaction, you bind your heart to earth and become incapable of union with God, the only source of real happiness. This inordinate desire for pleasure is the thing which turns your desires and affections toward creatures, instead of fixing them on God. This is the root of every attachment, no matter how slight.

In order to mortify completely this inordinate tendency, St. John of the Cross says, " If something is presented to the senses, which is not solely for the honor and glory of God, give it up, and deprive yourself of it for the love of Jesus Christ, who, while on earth, had and desired nothing but to do the will of His Father " (*AS I*, 13,4). The Saint does not mean that you must live without any pleasure or satisfaction; this would be impossible, as man is created for happiness. However, he does tell you to renounce all the pleasures which are displeasing to God and to put all your pleasure and satisfaction solely into accomplishing the will of God, giving Him pleasure and procuring His glory. This was Jesus' life; He could say, "I do always the things that please Him " (*Jn* 8,29).

2. If your way of acting or speaking satisfies your self-love, but you know that it does not please God, then you must give it up. If a conversation, a friendship, or a comfort pleases you, but you doubt whether it is pleasing to God, you must give it up. If your will urges you to do anything which may be even slightly contrary to the will of God, you must refrain from doing it. In all these cases St. John of the Cross continually says : " nothing, nothing, nothing. " Nothing for the satisfaction of pride or selfishness, nothing for the pleasure of the senses, or even of the mind or will—if it is not in perfect agreement with the will of God. There is only one choice : to live for self or to live for God.

If you act for your own selfish satisfaction, even in small matters, you will never be able to live totally for God. If, for example, you are unwilling to combat and overcome your pride which has been offended, and you are impatient or cross with someone, it is evident that you prefer to act for the satisfaction of self rather than to please God, for God loves virtue and not defects. You must always substitute for the tendency to seek your own satisfaction the desire to seek God's satisfaction and pleasure. This is what St. John of the Cross means when he suggests detachment, not as an end in itself, but as a means of becoming more closely united with God, not to leave you in a vacuum, but to direct you quickly to God. The same line of conduct was proposed by Jesus : " Renounce thyself, " He says to you. And to what purpose? To walk in His path, to follow Him until you have attained perfect union with Him. The end is union, the road is abnegation or total detachment; we must not forget that it was of this road that Jesus said, " How narrow is the gate and strait is the way that leadeth to life " (*Mt* 7,14).

COLLOQUY

" O Lord, You have created me for Yourself, to love You and to enjoy You, infinite Good, ineffable Beauty; do not permit me to lose sight of this sublime end toward which I must tend; do not permit me to wander among the wretched satisfactions that vain, feeble creatures can offer me.

" O my Lord, what poor use I have made of creatures! Pardon me, O Lord! Henceforth I do not want to use anything unless it is for Your glory and according to Your holy will, as Your Son Jesus did. O my God, if in the past I have turned aside from You, who are my Beginning, my End, and my supreme Good; if I have turned toward myself and creatures, preferring their will and mine to Yours, I here and now promise to renounce, entirely and forever, the world and myself, and to give myself wholly and forever to You. O my God, I give myself to You as my Beginning; take complete possession of me. May I always abide in You! Be the beginning and end of all my actions. O my God, I give myself to You as my End, my Center, my supreme Good. Draw me to You! Make me tend continually toward You. Be my delight, my glory, my treasure, my all! "   (St. John Eudes).

O Lord, teach me to make use of all things with perfect purity of intention, without desiring to draw any selfish satisfaction from them.

" But how harsh it sounds to say that we must take pleasure in nothing, unless we also speak of the consolations and delights that this renunciation brings in its train. Oh, what a great gain it is, even in this life " (T.J. *Way*, 12). Yes, Lord, I understand Your words; I must surrender my own will and many little personal satisfactions; but in exchange I shall know the joy of doing Your will, of giving You pleasure and satisfaction, You who are my God and my All.

82

RULES FOR DETACHMENT

PRESENCE OF GOD - O Lord, my blindness and weakness have further need of Your light and strength, in order that I may follow generously the way of " nothing. "

MEDITATION

1. Jesus said, " The kingdom of heaven is like to a merchant seeking good pearls, who when he had found one pearl of great price, went his way and sold all that he had, and bought it " (*Mt* 13,45.46). The pearl of great price is

union with God; if we wish to acquire it, we must sell *all* that we possess; that is, we must detach ourselves from every inordinate appetite. Hence St. Teresa of Avila, in speaking of detachment, says that " when it is practiced perfectly, it is *everything* " (*Way*, 8). Of course, the spiritual life is not simply detachment, nor does it end there; but detachment practiced with perfection leads effectively to its goal : union with God. God alone can bring us to this union, but He will not do so unless, like the merchant in the Gospel, we *sell* everything, that is, unless we renounce even the smallest attachment to self or to creatures.

These are the golden rules proposed by St. John of the Cross for total detachment : The soul must always be inclined " not to the easiest thing, but to the hardest; not to the tastiest, but to the most insipid; not to things that give the greatest pleasure, but to those that give the least; not to restful things, but to painful ones; not to consolation, but to desolation; not to more, but to less; not to the highest and dearest, but to the lowest and most despised; not to the desire for something, but to having no desires " (*AS I*, 13,6). In this way we shall gradually become accustomed to subduing this inordinate desire for pleasure, which is at the base of all attachments. It is like going against a current; hence it is a hard, tiring task which can be accomplished only by strength of will. We must oppose the inclinations of nature and make ourselves do what is repugnant to nature. This is, however, a sweet task for a soul in love with God; it knows that everything it refuses to self is given to God and that, when it has reached the point of renouncing self in everything—of *selling* everything—God Himself will give it the precious pearl of divine union.

2. " The soul must *embrace* these acts wholeheartedly and strive to subject its will thereto. For if it undertakes them wholeheartedly, in a short time it will find great delight and consolation in them, working with *order* and *discretion* (*ibid.*, 13,7). St. John of the Cross asks two things of the soul that desires to enter upon the way of the " nothing. " First of all, he demands decision and generosity; for anyone who has not the courage to renounce himself in everything will never reach total detachment and union with God. At the same time, he also demands " order and discretion. " The Saint does not expect us always and in everything to choose what

is most difficult, painful, or tiring—which would be impossible, both because of the circumstances in which we live and because of our physical constitution, which always needs a certain amount of relaxation—but he does ask that we be disposed to this choice, that is, we must cultivate a desire for it. He wants us to develop within ourselves the inclination and habit of doing what is opposed to our own tendencies, so that when the opportunity occurs, we can do so without being hindered by our natural repugnance. At the beginning of the spiritual life it is especially necessary to proceed with discretion and to act according to the advice of the confessor and superior, particularly with regard to corporal mortification. It is most important that we make a firm decision to bend our will by this practice of renunciation, that we never give up on account of cowardice, and that, when we have to allow ourselves a little relaxation, because of expediency or duty, we do so with detachment, that is, with a will detached from the pleasure we may find in it.

It is clear that we shall never attain the goal if we do not gain mastery over our attachments and resolve, once and for all, to put them all to death. It means real death to selfish and worldly satisfactions, but this death will give birth to life. Jesus said, " unless the grain of wheat falling into the ground die, itself remaineth alone. But if it die, it bringeth forth much fruit. . . . He that hateth his life in this world, keepeth it unto life eternal " (*Jn* 12,24.25).

COLLOQUY

O Lord, in the light of Your teachings even the hard and bitter way of total detachment becomes desirable, and everything invites me to undertake it courageously. You know, however, that I am weak and that my nature rebels at everything that is difficult, wearisome, or disagreeable; You know that it is always inclined to the things that require the least effort, to all that is easy, agreeable, and consoling. But Your love is all powerful, O Lord, and You, who through love made me out of nothing, can once again by the same love change my tastes, my inclinations. I well know that nothing but Your love can inspire me to enter upon this road and give me the courage to undertake this fundamental reform of myself. Your love alone, O Lord, is the magnet

which draws me toward total renunciation. Your love alone
will attract me and will be my reward. O God, deign to
draw me ever more powerfully, because my weakness tends
to stop me, to hold me back; this is exactly what I fear.

" Why, O Lord, should I be preoccupied with my fears
and lose courage in the face of my weakness? You give me to
understand that I must fortify myself in humility, and
convince myself that I can do very little alone, and that
without your help I am nothing. I shall put all my confidence
in your mercy, and shall distrust my own strength, convinced
that my weakness is caused by my self-reliance. You teach
me not to be astonished at my struggle, for when a soul
wishes to give itself over to mortification, it encounters
difficulties on all sides. Does it wish to give up its ease?
What a hardship! To scorn a point of honor? What a
torture! To endure harsh words? Intolerable suffering!
In short, it becomes filled with extreme sadness, but as soon
as it is resolved to die to the world, every anguish is at an
end " (T.J. *Con*, 3).

You died for me, O Lord. For love of You make me die
to myself, to my desires, to my satisfactions. I shall die to
myself in order to live for You, to attain to union with You.

83

THE NIGHT OF THE SENSES

PRESENCE OF GOD - O Lord, strengthen my desire for union with You,
so that I may have the courage to face, for love of You, the total
purification of my senses.

MEDITATION

1. " In order to attain to divine union with God, the soul
must pass through the dark night of mortification of the
appetites and the denial of pleasure in all things "
(J.C. *AS I*, 4,1). St. John of the Cross calls the total
mortification of the senses the " dark night, " because the soul
that renounces every irregular attachment to creatures and

to the pleasure it might find in them, remains " unoccupied and in darkness " (*ibid.*, 3,1) as far as the senses are concerned.

It is to help us enter this night, through which we must pass in order to attain to union with God, that the Saint tells us to mortify our inordinate tendencies toward sensible satisfactions.

However, it is evident that even if we sincerely wish to mortify our senses, we cannot always avoid seeing agreeable things, listening to interesting news, eating appetizing food, and so forth. Sometimes sensible satisfactions will be imposed on us by the necessities of life, by the duties of our state, or even by our superiors. It is absolutely necessary, even in these cases, that our soul remain wholly free from all attachment to creatures and to sensible satisfactions. It will suffice to desire not to have this pleasure, and promptly to " mortify our senses, voiding them of such pleasure, " depriving them of everything, " as though they were in darkness " (cf. *ibid.*, 13,4).

In other words, we should not stop at the selfish enjoyment of what pleases our senses, but try to raise our heart at once to God by offering Him the enjoyment we feel and which He permits for the renewal of our strength, so that we may be able to take up again with greater generosity the practice of mortification. In this way even natural joys will help to bring us to God and to increase our love. This is what St. Thérèse of the Child Jesus called " to rejoice for Love. "

This is the pure doctrine of St. Paul, who said, " Rejoice in the Lord always "; and again, " Whether you eat or drink, or whatsoever else you do, do all to the glory of God " (*Phil* 4,4 — 1 *Cor* 10,31). If, on the contrary, we stop at the enjoyment of sensible things, we shall never be able to enter the night of the senses.

2. " The soul ordinarily enters this night of the senses in two ways : the one is active, the other passive. The active way consists in that which the soul can do, and does of itself, in order to enter therein. The passive way is that wherein the soul does nothing, and God works in it, and it remains, as it were, patient " (J.C. *AS I*, 13,1). The active way inludes everything that we can do on our own initiative to rid ourselves of every affection for and attachment to creatures. For example, it is in our power to apply

ourselves to the practice of poverty, corporal mortification, penance, and chastity—all of which are virtues that detach the soul from the goods of earth and the satisfaction of the senses. If we want to do all that we can to enter the night, we must practice these virtues generously, keeping our eyes fixed on Jesus, our divine model, who wished to give us an example in everything.

But no matter how much we do, our own practices will never be sufficient to destroy completely all the roots of attachments. If we examine ourselves carefully, we shall see that, even in the practice of voluntary mortification, a little complacency may enter in because of what we have chosen, which is to our liking and according to our wishes. In order that our purification be complete, the work of God must intervene, that work which will bring us passively into the night of the senses. He does this by means of trials and contradictions both exterior and interior. It is a time of submission rather than of action; we must be as a patient in the hands of the surgeon; we must accept with humility and docility all that God permits, without trying either to escape the trial or to lessen or change it.

In the *Ascent of Mt. Carmel* St. John of the Cross gives the picture of a soul which, " kindled in love with yearnings, sings of the happy fortune which befell it to pass through the dark night. " In fact, to be brought into the passive night is one of the greatest graces the soul can receive, because then God himself is preparing and disposing it for divine union. If we wish to obtain this grace, we must do everything we can to enter the active night, that is, we must practice renunciation and total detachment.

COLLOQUY

O Lord, deign to come to me with Your grace and inflame me with Your love, that I may be able to plunge enthusiastically into the dark night which is to prepare me for union with You. Night does not please my nature which loves the light, the sun, the full radiant daylight. But with Your help, and for love of You, why should I not be willing to deprive my senses of all satisfactions and to annihilate them in the night, when all it amounts to is the giving up of a few worthless trifles in order to have the enjoyment of You, in whom are all light, all joy, all happiness? Can I not then, O Lord, for love of You, bear a little darkness, cold, want, or poverty? Alas! How often have I been so blind as to prefer the wisp of immediate pleasure which creatures give me and which vanishes as quikly as darkness before the sun, to the less obvious but much more profound, true, and lasting satisfaction which is found in You by one who is firmly determined to put all his pleasure in You alone!

" O Lord, Father most merciful, receive, I beg You, Your prodigal child! I have suffered enough; I have long enough been the slave of Your enemies, which You put beneath Your feet; I have been long enough the plaything of false flatterers. I know that I must turn to You. When I knock at Your door, let me find it open; show me the way to come to You. All I know is that I must despise unstable and temporary goods to seek those that are stable and eternal.

" O Lord, keep far from the heart of Your servant the thought that any kind of joy will bring happiness! On the contrary, there is a joy which is not granted to the wicked, but to those who honor You unselfishly. You are their joy. All happiness consists in this : to rejoice in You, because of You and through You; there is no other. He who believes that any other happiness exists is pursuing a strange and false joy " (St. Augustine).

84

THE DIVINE SEED

SEXAGESIMA SUNDAY

PRESENCE OF GOD - O Lord, I am here before You. Grant that my heart may be the good ground, ready to receive Your divine word.

MEDITATION

1. Today Jesus, the divine Sower, comes to scatter the good seed in His vineyard the Church. He wishes to prepare our souls for a new blossoming of grace and virtue.

"The seed is the word of God." Jesus Christ, the Word
Incarnate, eternal Utterance of the Father, came to sow
this word in the hearts of men; it is, as it were, a reflection of
Himself. The divine word is not a sound which strikes
the air and disappears rapidly like the word of men; it
is a supernatural light which reveals the true value of things;
it is grace, the source of power and strength to help us live
according to the light of God. Thus it is a seed of
supernatural life, of sanctity, of eternal life. This seed is
never sterile in itself; it always has a vital, powerful strength,
capable of producing not only some fruits of Christian life,
but abundant fruits of sanctity. This seed is not entrusted to
an inexperienced husbandman who, because of his ignorance,
might ruin the finest sowing. It is Jesus Himself, the Son of
God, who is the Sower.

Then why does the seed not always bring forth the
desired fruit? Because very often the ground which receives
it does not have the requisite qualities. God never stops
sowing the seed in the hearts of men; He invites them, He
calls them continually by His light and His appeals; He
never ceases giving His grace by means of the Sacraments;
but all this is vain and fruitless unless man offers God a good
ground, that is, a heart, well prepared and disposed. God
wills our salvation and sanctification, but He never forces
us; He respects our liberty.

2. Today's Gospel (*Lk* 8,4-15) mentions four categories
of people who receive the seed of the divine word in different
ways. It compares them to the hard ground, to the stony soil,
to the earth choked with thorns, and lastly, to the good
fertile field.

The hard ground : souls that are frivolous, dissipated, open
to all distractions, rumors, and curiosity; admitting all kinds
of creatures and earthly affections. The word of God hardly
reaches their heart when the enemy, having free access,
carries it off, thus preventing it from taking root.

The stony ground : superficial souls with only a shallow
layer of good earth, which will be rapidly blown away, along
with the good seed, by the winds of passion. These souls
easily grow enthusiastic, but do not persevere and "in time of
temptation fall away." They are unstable, because they
have not the courage to embrace renunciation and to make
the sacrifices which are necessary if one wishes to remain

faithful to the word of God and to put it into practice in all circumstances. Their fervor is a straw fire which dies down and goes out in the face of the slightest difficulty.

The ground covered with thorns : souls that are preoccupied with worldly things, pleasures, material interests and affairs. The seed takes root, but the thorns soon choke it by depriving it of air and light. Excessive solicitude for temporal things eventually stifles the rights of the spirit.

Lastly, *the good ground* is compared by Jesus to those " who, with a good and upright heart, hearing the word, keep it, and bring forth fruit in patience. " The good and upright heart is the one which always gives first place to God, which seeks before everything else the kingdom of God and His justice. The seed of the divine word will bear abundant fruit in proportion to the good dispositions it finds in us : recollection, a serious and profound interior life, detachment, sincere seeking for the things of God above and beyond all earthly things, and finally, perseverance, without which the word of God cannot bear its fruit in us.

COLLOQUY

O Jesus, divine Sower, rightly do You complain of the arid, sterile ground of my poor heart! What an abundant sowing of holy inspirations, interior lights, and grace You have cast into my heart! How many times You have invited me to come to You by special appeals, and how many times have I stopped, after following You for a short time! O Lord, if only I could understand the fundamental reason for my spiritual sterility, my instability and inconstancy in good! Will Your light fail me? No, for You are continually instructing and admonishing my soul in a thousand ways. Oh! if so many souls living in error and not knowing You had received but a hundredth part of the light which You have given me so profusely, how much fruit would they not have drawn from it!

Will Your grace fail me? Is not Your grace my strength? O Lord, I see that neither Your light nor Your strength will fail me; what I lack is the perseverance which can faithfully withstand temptations, difficulties, and darkness; which can face courageously the sacrifices and austerity of the Christian life. It is easy to make sacrifices and to renounce oneself for a day, but it is hard to keep on doing it always, every day of our life. Is this not the reason that You said, O Lord, that the good heart brings forth fruit " in patience "?

O Jesus, who endured with invincible patience Your most sorrowful Passion and death, give me the patience I need to keep up the struggle against my passions and my self-love, patience to embrace with perseverance all the sacrifices required by total detachment, to be able to live without personal satisfactions and pleasures, to do everything that is repugnant to me, that hurts me, that crosses me and is displeasing to my self-love.

O Lord, You know that I desire total purification because I long for union with You; but You cannot purify me entirely if I cannot accept patiently Your work : the trials, humiliations and detachments that You prepare for me. O Jesus, divine Sufferer, give me Your patience; make me, like Yourself, humble and patient.

85

EVANGELICAL POVERTY

PRESENCE OF GOD - O Jesus, for my sake You embraced a life of extreme poverty; make me realize the great value of this virtue.

MEDITATION

1. One day a scribe approached Jesus and said to Him, " Master, I will follow Thee whithersoever Thou shalt go. " Jesus answered him, " The foxes have their holes, and the birds of the air have their nests; but the Son of Man has nowhere to lay His head " (Mt 8,19.20).

To one who is willing to follow Him, Jesus immediately presents a picture of His life, a life that is extremely poor and without the smallest comfort. Anyone who has not the courage to share, at least to a certain degree, His earthly poverty will have no part in His eternal wealth. No one can serve two masters at the same time : God and riches. " You cannot serve God and mammon " (*Mt* 6,24). If you are attached to wealth, ease and material comfort, in vain will you try to give your whole heart to God; it will always be the slave of worldly goods. That is why the rich young man, after asking what he should do to obtain eternal life, went away sadly when Jesus answered, " Go, sell whatsoever thou hast, and give to the poor, " for " he had great possessions. " He was a good young man; from his youth he had kept the commandments and he sincerely longed for eternal life, so much so that, " Jesus looking on him, loved him " (*Mk* 10,21.22). And yet, attachment to his possessions kept him from following Jesus. This is the story of many souls who, after having accomplished much in the service of God, stop and turn back because they lack the courage to detach themselves from the goods of earth. In commenting on this fact and speaking to His disciples, Jesus said, " How hard it is for them that trust in riches to enter into the kingdom of God! It is easier for a camel to pass through the eye of a needle, than for a rich man to enter into the kingdom of God " (*ibid.* 10,24.25). Reflect that in these words Jesus was speaking not only of the man who is " rich " because he has great possessions, but more especially of the one who is " rich " because he is attached to what he possesses.

2. Riches do not in themselves constitute an obstacle to eternal salvation and sanctity, but they become an obstacle when a person makes himself their slave. We do not have to own very much in order to be the slave of worldly goods; it is necessary only to possess something with " attachment, " even if the object in question is of little or no value. The Apostles were poor and possessed very little; yet when Jesus invited them to follow Him, He required them to give up even that little. The soul is freed from slavery to earthly goods not so much by material poverty as by " poverty of spirit, " that is, poverty of affections, of attachments, however slight.

St. John of the Cross tells us that this poverty alone constitutes the " night of the soul, " that is, permits the soul to enter the night of the senses : " for we are not treating here of the lack of things, since this implies no detachment on the part of the soul if it has a desire for them; but we are treating of detachment from them with respect to taste and desire, for it is this that leaves the soul free and void of them, although it

may have them " (*AS I*, 3,4). For this reason the Saint teaches
that we should " not seek the best of temporal things, but the
worst "; yet this material poverty which is good, and even
necessary to a certain degree, is not sufficient.   He at once
adds that we must " desire to enter into complete detachment
and emptiness and poverty, with respect to everything
that is in the world, for Christ's sake " (*ibid.*, 13,6). This
is the spiritual poverty which, by freeing the soul from
all desire and affection for worldly goods, completes and gives
value to material poverty.   In fact, if after renouncing the
superfluous, the comforts and the conveniences of life, we
still remain attached to them by affection, our material
renunciation will amount to very little.   " For it is not the
things of this world that either occupy the soul or cause it
harm, since they enter it not, but rather the will and desire
for them, for it is these that dwell within it " (*ibid.*, 3,4).

COLLOQUY

" O gentle Lord Jesus Christ, most rich in love, experience
has taught me that there is nothing in life more wearisome
than to burn with earthly desires, for the love of riches is an
insatiable hunger which so tortures the soul by the ardor
of desire that it does not find solace even when it obtains what
it covets.   The acquisition of wealth causes great fatigue; the
possession of it brings great fear; its loss occasions great sorrow.

" One who loves riches cannot love You, O Lord, but
perishes with the things that are perishable, and he who relies
on them with affection, vanishes with them in sadness.   He
who finds them, loses his peace; when he lies awake at night,
he tries to think of ways to add to them; if he sleeps, he
dreams of thieves; during the day he is anxious and troubled;
at night his fears increase, and thus he is always miserable "
(Ven. Raymond Jourdain).

How unfortunate I should be, O Lord, if the love of
worldly things prevented me from following you closely!   Oh!
how little does my life resemble Yours!   What a difference in
our tastes and desires!   You, the King of heaven and earth,
could have surrounded Yourself with grandeur, since all
riches were created by You.   You could have had many
servants to carry out Your orders, yet You wanted none of
these; instead You chose, for the first place of Your stay on

earth, a stable, and for the last, a hard cross. And I, who am but dust and ashes, with no right to possess anything, because I have nothing of myself and receive everything from Your generosity, would I claim a life of comfort, filled with so many desires for material well-being?

O Lord, do not permit the love of temporal goods to be an obstacle, to become a wall between You and me. Union of love demands resemblance; love either finds two beings similar or makes them so. I love You, O Lord, but my love is still weak; strengthen it, so that it may be able to destroy every attachment which hinders me from following You closely and becoming like You.

86

VOLUNTARY POVERTY

PRESENCE OF GOD - O Lord, deign to show me the treasures concealed in voluntary poverty and the duties which proceed from it.

MEDITATION

1. St. Thomas teaches that in order to arrive at the perfection of charity it is necessary for the heart to be completely detached from the things of the world, that it may concentrate all its affections on God. " He who possesses temporal goods, by the very fact that he possesses them, is inclined to love them. Consequently, the fundamental basis for the acquisition of perfect charity is voluntary poverty, that is, the free renunciation of all one's possessions, as the Master said in St. Matthew : ' If thou wilt be perfect, go sell what thou hast, and give it to the poor, and come, follow Me! ' " (IIª IIae, q.186, a.3).

This is particularly realized in the religious life by the vow of poverty. However, even those who are living a life of consecration to God in the world may embrace voluntary poverty as a means of tending to perfection. The Church makes it a matter of obligation for all who belong to Secular Institutes precisely because the state of perfection requires a

serious obligation of poverty. The members of these Institutes
" must make a vow or a promise of poverty, by which they
relinquish the free use of their material goods " (Apostolic
Constitution, *Provida Mater Ecclesia*). The essence of voluntary poverty consists in this renunciation of the *free and
independent use* of temporal goods. In fact, only one who
renounces the free use of temporal goods can, according to
St. Thomas, " live without possessing anything of his own. "
By making the vow of poverty, man attains the freedom
necessary to follow Jesus in the way of perfection.

2. If you have made a vow of voluntary poverty, you
know that you have given up the freedom to use temporal
goods as you wish. Even if the Rule of your Institute permits
you to have certain things, you cannot use them as an owner;
the vow of poverty has taken this power away from you.
You cannot dispose of anything on your own authority, not
even what is necessary for life, but you must govern yourself
in all things according to the norms of your Constitutions and
must depend on your superiors.

The Rules of the various Orders and Religious or Secular
Institutes are not equally strict concerning the use of
temporal goods. Some more austere Rules forbid the free
use of objects, even if they are of very little value; others, less
rigorous, allow a greater liberty. But if you wish to practice
your vow to perfection, adopt the rule of *never using or disposing
of anything with a spirit of ownership*. The more you live as if
you really owned nothing—even a book, or a piece of clothing,
or a bit of bread—the more you will become like Jesus and
be free to follow Him as one of His intimate friends.

Another consequence of the vow or promise of voluntary
poverty is the spontaneous acceptance for the love of God of
living conditions like those of the really poor. The poor
person is obliged to do without comforts, to economize, to
work for his living. You, therefore, should readily and
willingly renounce what is superfluous or merely convenient;
you should not allow anything to be wasted; and, above all,
you should subject yourself to a life of hard work. This is
to be done, not in a spirit of avarice, nor in view of gain,
but purely as an exercise of virtue.

If some day it happens that you lack something necessary, thank Our Lord, who thus offers you a choice occasion
for practicing real poverty.

COLLOQUY

O Lord, what great treasures are contained in holy poverty. " Poverty is a good which contains within itself all the good things in the world. It is a great domain—I mean that he who cares nothing for the good things of the world has dominion over them all. What do kings and lords matter to me if I have no desire to possess their money or to please them, especially if by so doing, I should cause the least displeasure to You, my God? And what do their honors mean to me if I have realized that the chief honor of a poor man consists in his being truly poor? True poverty, which is embraced for love of You, O Lord, brings with it a great dignity; it impresses everyone because its only care is to be pleasing to You " (T.J. *Way*, 2).

I praise You, O Lord, because You have given me the grace to embrace holy poverty, which frees me from all preoccupation with material things and delivers me from earthly slavery! Thus I, miserable creature that I am, have the great honor of serving You alone, the King of heaven and earth.

O Lord, grant me the favor of preserving the sweet bonds of holy poverty which draw me away from the world to bind me to You. Grant that, in conformity with the obligations undertaken by my profession, poverty may really be " the arms inscribed on my banner; grant that I may observe it in all things and everywhere : in my dwelling, my dress, my words, and much more in my thoughts " *(ibid.)*. Yes, even in my thoughts, so that my desires will not, if only for a single moment, bring me back to the things I have given up for love of You.

I understand and confess, O my God, that every time I have complained about some privation or hardship, every time that I have been demanding or have desired a life of greater ease, I have withdrawn from the ideal and the effective practice of voluntary poverty. In the same way, I have also withdrawn from You and have returned to the slavery of material things. How foolish, O Lord, to divide my heart between You, who are All, and the nothingness of earthly creatures!

87

THE SPIRIT OF POVERTY

PRESENCE OF GOD - O Jesus, I contemplate You on the mountain, instructing the crowds on the spirit of poverty. I, too, approach You, eager to hear Your words.

MEDITATION

1. " Opening His mouth, He taught them, saying : Blessed are the poor in spirit, for theirs is the kingdom of heaven " (*Mt* 5,2.3).

Thus begins the Sermon on the Mount; then Jesus explained several times how this poverty of spirit is to be understood. " Lay not up to yourselves treasures on earth : where the rust and moth consume, and where thieves break through and steal. But lay up to yourselves treasures in heaven : where neither the rust nor moth doth consume, and where thieves do not break through nor steal. For where thy treasure is, there is thy heart also " (*ibid.*, 6,19-21).

Consider that Jesus addressed these words not only to the Apostles, but also to His disciples and the crowds that followed Him, proving that although everyone is not called to make the vow of poverty—family life does not permit this— the practice of the " spirit of poverty " is incumbent upon all, namely, that affective detachment from the goods of earth which enables one to use these goods with moderation and detachment. Those who, like fathers and mothers of families, have the obligation to administer goods and to increase them by honest work, must do so rightly, taking care that these material affairs do not make them neglect their own spiritual good and their duties to God. " What doth it profit a man if he gain the whole world, and suffer the loss of his own soul " (*ibid.*, 16,26)? The spirit of poverty also demands that they who have few possessions and live in material want accept their condition serenely and patiently, seeing in it an invitation to imitate Jesus' life of poverty more closely.

Consider furthermore that when the divine Master said, " Sell what thou hast and give it to the poor, " He joined the exercice of charity to that of poverty. If we detach our hearts from earthly goods, the spirit of poverty will make us generous toward the needy.

2. " Be not solicitous for your life, what you shall eat, nor...what you shall put on. Is not the life more than the meat : and the body more than the raiment? Behold the birds of the air, for they neither sow, nor do they reap, nor gather into barns; and your heavenly Father feedeth them.... And for raiment, why are you solicitous? Consider the lilies of the field, how they grow.... And if the grass of the field, which is today, and tomorrow is cast into the oven, God doth so clothe : how much more you, O ye of little faith? " (*Mt* 6,25-30). Jesus does not forbid our providing for the morrow; on the contrary, He says through His Apostle, " If any man will not work, neither let him eat " (2 *Thes* 3,10). But Jesus does not wish the solicitude which would engulf us entirely in temporal affairs; this would indicate not only an excessive attachment to earthly things, but also a lack of confidence in divine Providence. The divine Master tells us that, if God has given us the more essential things — our life and our body — He will also give us the less essential things, that is, food and clothing, which are the means of preserving our life and our body.

The spirit of poverty will not be lasting and profound unless it is based on confidence in divine Providence. It is only when we trust in God and in His word, which will never fail, that we shall have the courage to put aside all excessive preoccupation with temporal affairs. Then the words of Jesus will be accomplished in us : " Seek ye therefore first the kingdom of God and His justice, and all these things shall be added unto you " (*Mt* 6,33).

In every state of life and in the practice of every profession, the principal care of the Christian must be to serve God and to tend toward Him; everything else is secondary. St. Teresa of Jesus said to her daughters, " You have given up a regular income; give up worry about food as well, or you will lose everything.... Let us not fail God, and let us have no fear that He will fail us " (*Way*, 2).

COLLOQUY

"O Lord, the spirit of poverty is such a great treasure! When we possess it, we rely not on human means, but we place all our trust in Your divine Providence. I beg You to give me a great love for this precious treasure. It is so noble that it has You, O sovereign God," for its servant (cf. St. Francis).

O Lord, cure me of my excessive solicitude for the necessities of life. In the silence of my heart I seem to hear Your gentle reproach : "For after all these things do the heathens seek. For your Father knoweth that you have need of all these things . " (*Mt* 6,32).

Yes, Lord, You know my needs, and since You are no stranger to me, but a Father, You are bound to provide for all my wants. O Lord, strengthen my faith in Your word. May my confidence equal that of St. Francis of Assisi, who was so certain of You that he did not hesitate to give his father not only his money, but even his clothes and to go about the world deprived of everything, happier and more secure in his poverty than the rich in their wealth. O blessed poverty! You do not abandon, O Lord, him who trusts in You; You are kind and generous to him who has given up everything for love of You, and who trusts completely in your heavenly Providence.

O Jesus, if I cannot actually leave all material goods and concerns, grant that I may at least renounce all exaggerated solicitude for them and preoccupation with them. May my only concern be to love and serve You with all my strength, to seek friendship, intimacy, and union with You.

One day You said to St. Catherine of Siena, "Think of Me and I will think of you. " Deign to repeat these words to me and fix them in my mind and heart, so that no care for material things will be able to distract me from You.

88

CHASTITY

PRESENCE OF GOD - O Jesus, lover of virgins, make me understand the beauty of perfect chastity.

MEDITATION

1. " Know you not that you are the temple of God, and that the Spirit of God dwelleth in you? But if any man violate the temple of God, him shall God destroy. For the temple of God is holy, which you are " (1 *Cor* 3,16.17).

The grace of Baptism consecrates the body of a Christian, makes it the temple of the living God and a member of Christ. Hence every Christian has the duty of respecting his body, a duty which demands the virtue of chastity according to his state in life. Sins of impurity profane the body, the temple of God, and make the members of Christ " the members of a harlot " (*ibid.* 6,15).

Outside of marriage, absolute continence is demanded of everyone without distinction. Conjugal chastity limits marital pleasure to the ends of marriage itself. Even as poverty frees us from slavery to earthly goods and regulates their use, so chastity frees us from the slavery of our senses and moderates their use. Hence the virtue of chastity is not restricted to those who are consecrated to God, but is a serious obligation for every Christian. Chastity of the body is not enough; we must also practice chastity of thought, desire, and heart, for Jesus has said, " The things that come forth from the heart...defile a man. From the heart come forth evil thoughts, murders, adulteries " (*Mt* 15,18.19). Chastity of body, therefore, calls for chastity of heart. Jesus strongly insists on this interior purity. " The light of thy body is thy eye. If thy eye be single, thy whole body shall be lightsome. But if thy eye be evil, thy whole body shall be darksome " (*ibid.* 6,22.23).

2. " He that is without a wife, is solicitous for the things that belong to the Lord, how he may please God.... The virgin thinketh of the things of the Lord, that she may be

holy both in body and in spirit" (1 *Cor* 7,32.34). Perfect chastity, chosen as a state of life and embraced by a vow, frees one from the cares and solicitude which are inevitable in married life and which divide the heart between God and human affections.

Jesus said that there are some who have renounced having a family " for the sake of the kingdom of heaven " (*Mt* 19,12). The essential value of the vow of chastity consists precisely in this renunciation which a person voluntarily imposes on himself in order to give himself wholly to God—body and soul, heart and mind—all must be consecrated to Him and reserved for Him alone.

One who embraces the married state becomes a collaborator with God in the transmission of life to others; one who consecrates himself to God by a vow of chastity becomes His collaborator in the transmission of the life of grace to others. The person who is consecrated to God sacrifices material fecundity for a far superior, spiritual fecundity, natural paternity or maternity for supernatural paternity or maternity. St. Thérèse of the Child Jesus described her vocation to Carmel thus : " To be Thy spouse, O my Jesus...and by my union with Thee to be the mother of souls " (*St*, 13).

Such is the fruitfulness of virgins, the " chaste generation " whom Jesus calls to the total renunciation of the licit joys of marriage in order to make them intimate collaborators in His work of redeeming and sanctifying the world. The vow of chastity does not shut souls up in a sterile life, but by binding them wholly to God, it opens up to them the sublime fertility of the apostolate. " Perpetual virginity is a pure host offered to God, a holy victim; it is a flower which gives honor and joy to the Church, and it is a great source of power " (Pope Pius XII, *Allocution*, September 1951).

COLLOQUY

" O Lord, all my hope is based on Your great mercy. Give me what You command, and command what You will. You command that we be continent. Someone has said that no one can be continent unless God grants it, but it is true wisdom to know from whom this gift comes. Continence brings us recollection and the restoration of that unity which we have lost in giving ourselves to too many things. He loves You less who loves, together with You, anything which he does not love for You. O love, ever burning and never extinguished, O charity, O my God, inflame me! You command me to be continent; give me what You command and command what You will " (St. Augustine).

O Jesus, make me understand that there is no greater honor for man than the one You do him when You deliver him from the " tribulation of the flesh " (1 *Cor* 7,28) and invite him to give himself entirely to You in the bond of perfect chastity. O holy bond which unites to God, who is infinite purity, a base creature, and raises him to the level of sharing in the immaculate splendor of divine virginity! O holy bond, which establishes an indissoluble union between God and man, which presents souls " as pure virgins to the one Man, Christ " (cf. 2 *Cor* 11,2), to be espoused to Him in faith and love!

O Jesus, Spouse of virgin souls, You who have said, " All men take not this word, but they to whom it is given " (*Mt* 19,11), give me a better understanding of the great value of perfect chastity. What more sublime gift could I ask for and receive from You?

O Jesus, You who by calling me to perfect chastity have freed me from the cares of a family and from earthly affections, grant that I may not become egotistical, but may share in the most direct and intense way Your solicitude and Your life of immolation and sacrifice for the salvation of men and the glory of the Father. You want me to be a virgin that I may collaborate more intimately with You in the sublime work of redemption; and in the measure in which I give myself fully and generously to You, You will give me the gift of spiritual fecundity. O Jesus, tighten the bonds of my union with You, for this union will enable me to bring forth many souls to Your love and grace!

89

MODESTY

PRESENCE OF GOD - O Jesus, Spouse of Virgins, teach me how a soul consecrated to You should live.

MEDITATION

1. Perfect chastity presupposes an absolute dominion of spirit over matter. However, there is in us a disordered tendency toward sensible pleasure which is opposed to this dominion; even souls consecrated to God bear the treasure of chastity *in earthen vessels* (2 *Cor* 4,1), in the fragile vessel of flesh, which is attracted by satisfactions of the senses. The vow of chastity does not remove these tendencies; consequently, it does not dispense us from continual vigilance. "One who makes a vow to God of perfect chastity must struggle by prayer and penance, in order to preserve its integrity" (Pope Pius XII)—by prayer because no one can be chaste unless God grants it to him, by penance and mortification because the body must be subject to the spirit.

It is modesty which *moderates* and regulates all our actions, both interior and exterior, according to our vocation. St. Paul recommends this virtue to all Christians : " Let your modesty be known to all men " (*Phil* 4,5). Souls consecrated to God are obliged to observe modesty more strictly, because they are called by their state in life to preserve the treasure of absolute chastity intact; therefore, they need to practice *mortification* of the senses more assiduously and delicately. They must be like men who, possessing material treasures of great value, take all necessary measures and precautions to protect them from thieves. " Brethren, be sober and watch, " says St. Peter (1 *Pt* 5,8), for the enemy is always lying in wait.

The vow of chastity, by consecrating the body to God, also consecrates the senses. For this reason they must be freed from the base things of earth in order to be wholly employed in the service of God.

2. The more a soul aspires to the total gift of self and intimate union with God, the more its conduct must be

imbued with perfect modesty—modesty of countenance, gait, gesture, and manner. " Be modest in every action or conversation " (*M*, 4), St. Teresa of Avila instructs her daughters. St. Teresa Margaret of the Heart of Jesus " kept such a perfect restraint and guard over her faculties and senses that she refused herself every glance and every word which did not in some way have reference to God " (T.M. *Sp*). The golden rule of St. John of the Cross was *to use the senses solely for the service and glory of God and to raise the heart to Him* (cf. *AS I*, 13,4), which, in practice, means using them only as they are required for the accomplishment of one's duties or for an honorable and just purpose; " with this exception all must be left free for God " (*SM II*, 38). Therefore the soul must carefully guard its sight and hearing from vain curiosity, images, and news; for these encumber it uselessly and give entrance toimpressions which are not entirely pure and holy.

One who without necessity desires to see, hear, and taste everything is like a man who leaves the door of his house open to any intruder. The senses are the doors of the soul; we must guard them and not endanger the treasure of chastity.

Modesty, however, is not only a weapon of defense for chastity; it is the bulwark of the interior life. Only a soul who knows how to guard the senses is capable of recollecting itself interiorly in order to live in intimacy with God. By detaching the senses from earthly things, modesty concentrates and fixes them on God. " We put to death the curiosity of our eyes when, turning them away from all useless things, we fix them on ourselves, on the movements of our heart, and on the heart of Jesus " (T.M. *Sp*). This is the positive value of modesty. Only one who loves God very much can impose such a discipline on himself.

COLLOQUY

" If I could only love You more ardently, O my God, my Help, my Defense, my sweet Hope! Let me embrace You, O Sovereign Good, without whom nothing good exists for me; let me find all my delight in You, the source of perfection, without whom nothing is perfect!

" Open my ears to Your words, more penetrating than a two-edged sword, that I may hear Your voice. So illumine my eyes, O incomparable light, that they will never again turn toward earthly vanities, but may seek You alone, O invisible Good! Draw me, O sweetest perfume of my life, so that I may run in the fragrance of Your ointments! Purify my sense of taste, that I may know and savor Your great sweetness, O Lord, that sweetness which You have reserved for those who are filled with Your holy love. By Your sweetness, dissipate and destroy my concupiscence, so that I may desire nothing but You, and not be seduced and deceived by worldly vanities, so as to regard what is bitter as sweet and what is sweet as bitter, darkness as light and light as darkness. Let me escape the snares set by the enemy of our souls, who fills the world with his deceits.

" O my sweet Lord, the world is filled with the snares of concupiscence. Who can avoid them all? Only he from whom You remove the pride of life, the concupiscence of the flesh, irreverence, and obstinacy of soul. Oh! how happy is the soul to whom You give this grace, for he will pass unharmed through the midst of so many enemies! " (St. Augustine).

O my sweet Lord, I renew with all my heart the consecration of my senses to You. I consecrate to You my eyes, that they may seek only Your Face and the things that lead to You; I consecrate to You my tongue, that it may be worthy to sing Your praises and may never utter a word displeasing to You; I consecrate to You my ears, that they may listen to Your voice alone and hear only what is necessary for Your service; I consecrate to You my sense of smell, of taste, of touch, that they may take delight in You alone, O Spouse of virgins! I repeat with St. Agnes, " In loving You, O Christ, I am chaste; in touching You, I am pure; in possessing You, I am a virgin! " (RB).

90

CHASTITY OF HEART

PRESENCE OF GOD - O Lord, show me how pure my heart must be if I am to be admitted to intimacy with You.

MEDITATION

1. The heart of a person consecrated to God should be " a garden enclosed, a fountain sealed up " (*Ct* 4,12), because it cannot admit any other affection than one which has God for its object or one which refers to Him. Of course this does not exclude the love of neighbor in general, nor that which one owes to one's own family, but it does exclude all purely natural love. In other words, the affections of a soul consecrated to God must be wholly supernaturalized; that is, it must love creatures in reference to God, because they are His and belong to Him. When instead, it allows itself to be guided in its affections by human motives, such as congeniality, sympathy, or self-interest, it is not for God that it loves these creatures, but for itself, for the satisfaction it finds in them; its love is not supernatural, but human. These human affections ravage a heart that has been consecrated to God, just as the little foxes, spoken of in the Canticle, ravage the vines.

After having broken, for the love of God, our sacred family ties, after having renounced the right to have families of our own, is it not the height of folly to let our heart be chained by creatures who have no claim to it, or by affections which are not holy? We must reply to their invitations with the fortitude of St. Agnes : " God has put a sign on my face, that I may admit no other lover. It is to Him alone that I plight my troth " (*RB*).

" It is sad, " says St. John of the Cross, " to see certain souls...that are laden with wealth...and spiritual exercises...and yet, because they have not the resolution to break with some whim or attachment or affection... they never make progress or reach the port of perfection.... God has granted them to break other and stouter cords of affection, but they have not shaken off some childish thing, and fail to attain to so great a blessing " (*AS I*, 11,4.5).

2. God is jealous of a heart which has been consecrated to
Him and He will not admit it to intimacy with Himself as
long as He finds it occupied with some affection which prevents
it from concentrating on Him all the love of which He has
rendered it capable. St. Teresa of Jesus says, " As He refuses
to force our will, He takes what we give Him but does not
give Himself wholly to us until He sees that we are giving
ourselves wholly to Him " (*Way*, 28). " God will not have a
divided heart; He wants all or nothing " (T.M. *Sp*).

If we do not give our hearts entirely to God, we cannot
enjoy divine intimacy. Jesus said, " Blessed are the clean of
heart : for they shall see God " (*Mt* 5,8). This vision, this
enjoyment of God, is in a certain way anticipated even in
this life for those who keep the integrity and purity of their
heart for Him. St. Thomas says, " A heart which is free from
thoughts and affections alien to God is like a temple
consecrated to the Lord, in which we can contemplate Him
even in this world " *(Commentary on St. Matthew)*. A pure
heart, like a limpid eye, can comprehend God and to a certain
degree penetrate the depths of His infinite mystery. For
this reason theologians teach that the gift of understanding
corresponds to the beatitude " blessed are the clean of heart. "
By this gift the Holy Spirit enables the soul to read within,
" *intus legere*, " that is, to penetrate divine truths. One who
loves ardently, desires to know the loved one more and more,
not only exteriorly, but also intimately, sharing his thoughts
and secrets; he is willing to sacrifice every other satisfaction
in order to attain his end.

If you wish to know your God, if you wish to enter into
an intimate and deep friendship with Him, you must offer
Him a pure heart, free from all human affection. " Take
no heed of creatures if thou wilt keep the image of God
clearly and simply in thy soul, but empty thy spirit of them
and withdraw far from them, and thou shalt walk in the
divine light " (J.C. *SM I*, 25).

COLLOQUY

O Jesus, divine sweetness, change all the consolation of
earth into bitterness for me, for I do not wish creatures to
possess even a single atom of my heart. If I knew that a single
fiber of my heart vibrated for human affection, I would

hasten to tear it out and throw it away, no matter how much suffering it might cost.

But You know my weakness and how tempted I feel in moments of discouragement, of loneliness, of abandonment to seek a little understanding and affection from creatures. " Oh! then, I beg You, grant that I may find nothing but bitterness in earthly friendships; otherwise, with a heart like mine, I could easily be caught and my wings clipped (T.J.C. *St*, 4).

O Lord, illumine the hidden and innermost recesses of my heart; if You find there the least affection which is not for You, reveal it to me and give me the grace to renounce it forever.

You want all, and I want to give You all. In giving all to You, my heart is only returning what is already Yours, for You have given it to me, and I should be incapable of loving if You had not put a spark of Your infinite charity in me. O Lord, it is only just that this spark should return to You, and that it should requite Your love, O infinite Love, who have created me out of nothing and enabled me to return love for love. By reaching up to You and coming in contact with You, O immense furnace of Charity, my love insignificant as it is, will increase immeasurably and pour itself out over all the earth, embracing all creatures in the munificence of a pure, supernatural love, so that it may bring them to You, their beginning and their end.

O Jesus, guardian of virgins, guard my heart, make it so pure and transparent that it will become worthy to gaze upon the splendor of Your Face.

I do not know You yet, my Lord, for, since I still love and enjoy creatures, my interior eye has not the clearness necessary for contemplating You. And because I do not know You, I do not love You as much as I should, and I have very little enjoyment of You. Behold how great is my misery! Come Yourself and purify my heart, so that I may know You fully, and knowing You fully, really love You with all my strength.

91

PREDICTION OF THE PASSION

QUINQUAGESIMA SUNDAY

PRESENCE OF GOD - O Jesus, give me light to understand the mystery and the value of Christian suffering.

MEDITATION

1. Lent is approaching and our thoughts turn spontaneously to the sorrows of Jesus. Today's Gospel (*Lk* 18,31-43) brings us an announcement of the Passion.

The prediction is clear : " The Son of Man...shall be delivered to the Gentiles, and shall be mocked and scourged and spit upon, and after they have scourged Him, they will put Him to death; and the third day He shall rise again. " However, as on other occasions, the Apostles " understood none of these things, and this word was hid from them. " They did not understand because they imagined that Jesus' mission was like an earthly conqueror's and that He would re-establish the kingdom of Israel. Since they dreamed only of triumphs and of occupying the first places in the kingdom, any allusion to the Passion upset and scandalized them.

To those who dream only of prosperity and earthly glory, the language of the Cross is incomprehensible. Those who have a purely material ideal of life find it very difficult to understand any spiritual significance, and especially that of suffering. St. Paul said that Christ Crucified was " unto the Jews indeed a stumbling block, and unto the Gentiles foolishness " (1 *Cor* 1,23). Rebuking St. Peter, who at the first mention of the Passion had exclaimed, " Lord, be it far from Thee, this shall not be unto Thee, " Jesus had said, " Go behind Me, Satan...because thou savorest not the things that are of God, but the things that are of men " (*Mt* 16,22.23). To human wisdom, suffering is incomprehensible; it is disconcerting; it can lead one to murmur against divine Providence and even to lose all trust in God. However, according to the wisdom of God, suffering is a means of salvation and redemption. And as it was necessary " for Christ to have suffered these things, and so to enter into His glory " (cf. *Lk* 24,26), it is also necessary for the Christian to be refined in the crucible of sorrow in order to attain to sanctity, to eternal life.

2. It was not until after the descent of the Holy Spirit that the Apostles fully understood the meaning of the Passion; then, instead of being scandalized, they considered it the greatest honor to follow and to preach Christ Crucified.

The human eye has not sufficient light to comprehend the value of the Cross; it needs a new light, the light of the Holy Spirit. It is not by chance that in today's Gospel, immediately after the prediction of the Passion, we find the healing of the blind man of Jericho. We are always somewhat blind when faced with the mystery of suffering; when it strikes us in what we hold most near and dear, it is easy to get lost and to grope our way like blind men through uncertainty and darkness. The Church invites us to repeat today the blind man's prayer of faith : " Jesus, Son of David, have mercy on me! "

The world is often astonished at the sufferings of the good, and instead of encouraging them in their reliance on God, seeks to turn them from Him by urging them to defiance and false fear. Our passions themselves, our innate tendencies toward pleasure, often cry out to us and try, by a thousand pretexts, to prevent us from following Jesus Crucified. Let us remain steadfast in our faith, like the poor blind man. He was not disturbed by the crowd that tried to keep him from approaching Jesus, and he did not give up when the disciples remonstrated with him and wanted him to be quiet; he only shouted his prayer " even more loudly. "

Let us cry to the Lord from the bottom of our hearts : " *De profundis clamo ad te, Domine; Domine audi vocem meam!* " (*Ps* 129). Let us ask, not to be exempt from suffering, but to be enlightened as to its value. " Lord, that I may see! " As soon as the blind man recovered his sight, he immediately followed Jesus, " glorifying God! " The supernatural light which we seek from the Lord will give us the strength to follow Him and to carry our cross as He did.

COLLOQUY

"O Jesus Christ, Son of the eternal Father, our Lord, true King of all things! What didst Thou leave in the world for Thy descendants to inherit from Thee? What didst Thou ever have, my Lord, save trials, pains, and insults? Indeed Thou hadst only a beam of wood to rest upon while drinking the bitter draught of death. Those of us, then, my God, who desire to be Thy true children and not to renounce their inheritance, must never flee from suffering. Thy crest is five wounds!... So that too must be our device if we would inherit His kingdom! Not by ease, nor by comfort, nor by honor, nor by wealth can we gain that which He purchased for us by so much Blood. O you who come of illustrious lineage, for the love of God open your eyes. Behold those true knights of Jesus Christ, the princes of His Church, St. Peter and St. Paul : never did they travel by the road you are taking. Can you be imagining that a new road is to be built for you? Do not think that for a moment" (T.J. *F*, 10).

O my Jesus, the Cross is Your standard; I should be ashamed to ask to be delivered from it. From one evil only I ardently beg You to preserve me : from any deliberate sin, however slight. O Lord, I beg You by the merits of Your sacred Passion to keep all sin far from me. But as for other evils— bodily or spiritual sufferings, physical pain or mental anguish—I beg Your light and strength : light to understand the hidden meaning which they have in the plans of Your divine Providence, light to believe firmly that every sorrow or trial, every pain or disappointment, is planned by You for my greater good; strength not to let myself be influenced by the false maxims of the world or led astray by the vain mirage of earthly happiness, strength to accept suffering of any kind with courage and love.

92

CORPORAL MORTIFICATION

PRESENCE OF GOD - O Jesus Crucified, grant that my love for You may make me willing to crucify my flesh with You and for You.

MEDITATION

1. As a result of original sin, man no longer has complete dominion over his senses and his flesh; therefore he is filled with evil tendencies which try to push him toward what is base. St. Paul humbly admits : " I know that there dwelleth not in me, that is to say, in my flesh, that which is good.... For the good which I will, I do not; but the evil which I will not, that I do " (Rom 7,18.19).

God certainly gives us the grace to overcome our evil tendencies; but we must also use our own efforts, which consist in voluntary mortification : " They that are Christ's have crucified their flesh, with the vices and concupiscences " (Gal 5,24). The purpose of corporal mortification is not to inflict pain and privation on the body for the pleasure of making it suffer, but to discipline and control all its tendencies which are contrary to the life of grace. The Apostle warns us : " If you live according to the flesh, you shall die : but if by the Spirit you mortify the deeds of the flesh, you shall live " (Rom 8,13). We must curb ourselves in order to avoid falls; we must prune the useless or harmful branches in order to avoid deviation; we must direct toward good the forces which, left to themselves, might lead us into sin. For these reasons mortification, although it is not an end in itself nor the principal element in the Christian life, occupies a fundamental place in it and is an absolutely indispensable means toward attaining a spiritual life. No one can escape this law without closing off all access to eternal salvation, to sanctity. St. Paul, who had done and suffered much for Christ, did not consider himself dispensed from it, and said, " I chastise my body and bring it into subjection : lest perhaps, when I have preached to others, I myself should become a castaway " (1 Cor 9,27).

2. St. Teresa warns us that " if prayer is to be genuine it must be reinforced with this practice [of mortification] : for prayer and self-indulgence do not go together " (*Way*, 4). It would be an illusion to think that we can reach intimacy with God without the serious exercise of physical mortification. In this regard, we must take care that love of our own body and of our physical welfare does not cause us to reject all penitential practices under the pretext that they will ruin our health. In reality, there are many corporal mortifications which, without the slightest danger to our health, have the great advantage of keeping our spirit of generosity on the alert by the voluntary acceptance of a little physical suffering. If we are to be generous in this respect, we must " rid ourselves of all inordinate love for our body " (*ibid.*, 10), that is, of all excessive preoccupation about our health; and we must put aside all anxiety about food, clothing, rest and comfort. " This body of ours, " says St. Teresa, " has one fault : the more you indulge it, the more things it discovers to be essential to it... and if there is any reasonable pretext for indulgence, however little necessity for it there may be, the poor soul is deceived and prevented from making progress " (*ibid.*, 11).

Anyone who wants to advance on the road to sanctity and union with God must be ready to sacrifice everything, even in the physical order, to the point of " giving up his skin and everything else for Christ, " as St. John of the Cross says. He teaches, however, that in these matters we must always depend on our superiors or confessors; " corporal penance without obedience is no more than the penance of beasts " (*DN I*, 6,2), because it prefers a material practice to obedience " which is penance of the reason and discretion, " and is, therefore, the sacrifice most pleasing to God.

COLLOQUY

" This servant of Thine, my God, can no longer endure such trials as come when she finds herself without Thee; for if she is to live, she desires no repose in this life, nor would she have Thee give her any. This soul would fain see itself free : to eat is a torment; to sleep brings only anguish. It finds itself in this life spending its time upon comforts, yet nothing can comfort it but Thee; it seems to be living against nature,

for it no longer desires to live to itself, but only to Thee "
(T.J. *Life*, 16).

O Lord, help me, I beg You, to free myself from the
slavery of the body! Teach me to conquer its extravagant
demands and to mortify its pretensions. You have given me
this body of flesh, in order that I may serve You on earth.
Grant that it may not become an obstacle to me and hinder
the generous, total gift of my whole self to You.

How far I am, O God, from the austerities and mortifications of the saints! " Do I, perhaps, think they were
made of iron? No : they were as frail as I. O Lord, help
me to understand that once I begin to subdue my miserable
body, it will give me much less trouble " (*Way*, 11). Why
should I be terrified by the fear of losing my health?

Sickness and health, life and death, all are in Your
hands, my God; everything depends on You. I now make
a firm resolution to entrust all solicitude to You, and to keep
but one occupation : to love You and serve You with all
my strength. Help me, O Lord, to gain the mastery over
my body and to conquer it completely, so that I may attain
that magnificent liberty of spirit which allows the soul
to devote itself undisturbed to the exercise of a deep interior
life.

93

WITH JESUS CRUCIFIED

PRESENCE OF GOD - O Jesus, I place myself at the foot of the Cross,
help me to understand how necessary it is to suffer in order to
resemble You.

MEDITATION

1. For the soul who aspires to union with God, penance
is not only a means of subjecting the flesh to the spirit, but
also a means of being assimilated to Christ Crucified, in order
to reproduce and prolong His Passion in its own body.

" Love makes equality and similitude " (J.C. *AS I*, 4,4) :
he who truly loves has a spontaneous desire to share in the
sufferings of the loved one; it is the same with real lovers
of the Crucified. St. Mary Magdalen dei Pazzi exclaims,
" It is not fitting to be a delicate member of a Head crowned
with thorns and crucified, nor the unmortified bride of
a suffering Spouse. " It is an honor for a wife to be able
to share in the entire life of her spouse. For a soul consecrated to God, it is an honor to be able to share, even in
a small way, in the Passion of Christ; such a soul glories
in it. " But God forbid that I should glory, save in the Cross
of our Lord Jesus Christ, by whom the world is crucified
to me, and I to the world " (*Gal* 6,14).

Although mortification of the spirit is certainly more
important than that of the body, we must not forget that, in
order to save the world, Jesus was willing to embrace both in
the most complete manner. His whole life was a cross and a
martyrdom; it ended with the sacrifice of Calvary, where His
spiritual and physical immolation reached its height. As for
the mortification of the senses, " It is certain, " says St. John
of the Cross, " that He died as to sense, spiritually, during His
life, besides dying naturally, at His death. For...in life He
had not where to lay His head, and at His death, this was
even truer.... Wherefore, as it seems to me, any spirituality
that would fain walk in sweetness and with ease, and flees
from the imitation of Christ, is worthless " (*AS II*, 7,10.8).

2. St. Teresa Margaret of the Heart of Jesus wrote :
" Remember that when you entered religion, you proposed
to express in yourself the life of the Crucified " *(Sp)*. To
express the life of the Crucified means to live His Passion,
to associate ourselves with His sufferings, to unite ourselves to
His intentions—the glory of the Father and the salvation
of souls. " I...fill up those things that are wanting of the
sufferings of Christ in my flesh, for His Body, which is the
Church " (*Col* 1,24). This is another motive which has
urged the saints to generous corporal mortification. Nothing is
lacking in the Passion of Christ; He Himself said on the Cross,
" all is consummated " (*Jn* 19,30). All was accomplished
in Him, our Head, but it must now be accomplished in us,
His members. Jesus wills to continue His Passion in us so
that we may be associated with Him in the work of redemption; He wills to make us His collaborators in the most

sublime of His works, the salvation of souls. Jesus, who could have accomplished His work alone, willed to need us in order to apply the infinite merits of His Passion to many souls.

Mortification, and even physical suffering, is therefore a requirement of a life of union with Christ; the more generous the soul is, the more it will participate intimately in the interior life and apostolic work of Jesus. We cannot be intimate with Christ if we do not suffer with Him, if we do not ascend the Cross with Him. " Let Christ Crucified be sufficient for thee, and with Him suffer and rest " (J.C. *SM II*, 13).

Suffering has a supernatural value only when it is borne with Christ and for Christ. It is Jesus who sanctifies suffering; apart from Him it is worth nothing and is of no use. But if it is embraced for love of Him, it becomes precious coin, capable of redeeming and sanctifying souls; it becomes a continuation of the Passion.

COLLOQUY

" O much desired Passion! Who desires you, loves you and is glorified in you? O eternal Truth, You tell me that Your Passion is neither desired nor loved by anyone who loves himself, but only by one who has stripped himself of self and clothed himself with You, O Crucified Christ; by means of Your light he sees in the Cross the greatness of Your charity. O gentle, quiet Passion, which in the calmness of peace allows the soul to traverse the waves of the angry sea! O delectable, sweet Passion! O wealth of the soul, true joy, our glory and our beatitude; the soul which is glorified in you acquires your fruit. O Word, the soul which takes shelter in Your Passion is dead to sensuality and tastes the sweetness of Your charity.

" O my God, my Love, permit me one question : When the world was languishing in sickness, You sent Your only Son to be its physician...and now what means will You use to revive again this world which lies once more in death? I see that You give the name of Christ to Your servants and that by means of them You want to take away death and give back life to the world. And in what way? They must walk bravely in the footprints of the Word and work for

Your honor and the salvation of souls with love and burning
desire; to this end they should bear patiently all pains,
anxieties, reproaches, and disgrace. O wonderful Restorer,
give us many ' Christs ' who will spend their lives in vigils,
tears, and prayers for the salvation of the world " (St. Catherine of Siena).

O Lord, You know the profound desire of my heart :
to assimilate and unite myself to You in order to live Your
life alone. If sublime states of prayer and flights of the
spirit are not for me, the Cross is my share. You offer
it to me, and I embrace it with all my heart. I know that
what is easily within my reach, what I encounter every day,
what is most suitable and proportioned to my misery, is
suffering, for no human life is without sorrow. Lord, grant
that in every suffering, physical as well as moral, I may
recognize and embrace Your Cross, so that I may be
intimately associated with Your Passion, for the salvation
of souls. Now that You are glorified at the right hand of
the Father, You can no longer suffer. Deign, then, to suffer
in me and to use my poor humanity to continue Your work
of redemption.

94

ASH WEDNESDAY

PRESENCE OF GOD - I place myself in Your presence, O Lord; illumine
with Your light the eternal truths, and awaken in my soul a sincere
desire for conversion.

MEDITATION

1. " Dust thou art, and into dust thou shalt return "
(*Gn* 3,19). These words, spoken for the first time by God
to Adam after he had committed sin, are repeated today by
the Church to every Christian, in order to remind him of
two fundamental truths—his nothingness and the reality of
death.

Dust, the ashes which the priest puts on our foreheads
today, has no substance; the lightest breath will disperse it.
It is a good representation of man's nothingness : " O Lord,

my substance is as nothing before Thee " (*Ps* 38,6), exclaims the Psalmist.   Our pride, our arrogance, needs to grasp this truth, to realize that everything in us is nothing.   Drawn from nothing by the creative power of God, by His infinite love which willed to communicate His being and His life to us, we cannot—because of sin—be reunited with Him for eternity without passing through the dark reality of death.   The consequence and punishement of sin, death is, in itself, bitter and painful; but Jesus, who wanted to be like to us in all things, in submitting to death has given all Christians the strength to accept it out of love.   Nevertheless, death exists, and we should reflect on it, not in order to distress ourselves, but to arouse ourselves to do good.   " In all thy works, remember thy last end, and thou shalt never sin (*Sir* 7,40).   The thought of death places before our eyes the vanity of earthly things, the brevity of life— " All things are passing; God alone remains "—and therefore it urges us to detach ourselves from everything, to scorn every earthly satisfaction, and to seek God alone.   The thought of death makes us understand that " all is vanity, except to love God and serve Him alone " (*Imit. I*, 1,4).

" Remember that you have only one soul; that you have only one death to die...then there will be many things about which you care nothing " (T.J. *M*, 68), that is, you will give up everything that has no eternal value.   Only love and fidelity to God are of value for eternity.   " In the evening of life, you will be judged on love " (J.C. *SM I*, 57).

2. Today's liturgy is an invitation to penance.   During the imposition of the ashes we chant : " Let us change our garments, and cover ourselves with sackcloth and ashes; let us fast and weep before the Lord. "   It is an invitation to the corporal penance which is especially prescribed for this season; but it is immediately followed by the invitation to be converted : " Let us atone for the sins we have committed. "   The end of physical mortification is spiritual penance— humility, recognition of our faults, compunction of heart, and the reform of our lives.

This is the predominant thought of the day.   We read in the Epistle (*Jl* 2,12-19), " Thus saith the Lord : be converted to Me with all your heart, in fasting and in weeping and in mourning.   And rend your hearts, and not your garments. " Compunction and conversion of heart hold the first place, because the corporal penance that does not proceed from a contrite heart has no value. On the other hand, corporal penance prepares the soul for conversion, insofar as it is the means of reaching it. We read in the Preface, " O God, by fasting You repress sin, elevate the soul, and give it strength and recompense. " One who wishes to reach the goal, which is the renewing of the spirit, must embrace willingly the means which leads to it, namely, corporal penance. At the same time, he must remember that compunction of heart gives value to corporal penance, which in its turn engenders and gives expression to compunction of heart. These two elements are never separated.

The Gospel (*Mt* 6,16-21) says further that all penance must be accomplished sincerely and joyfully, without vain ostentation, " When you fast, be not as the hypocrites, sad. For they disfigure their faces, that they may appear unto men to fast. " Vanity and pride make even the most austere penitential practices useless and sometimes even sinful; they destroy their substance and value, and reduce them to mere externals, empty of all content. Hence when you mortify your body, take care to mortify your self-love still more.

COLLOQUY

" O Jesus, how long is man's life, although we say that it is short! It is short, O my God, since by it we are to gain a life without end; but it seems very long to the soul who aspires to be with You quickly.... O my soul, you will enter into rest when you are absorbed into the sovereign Good, when you know what He knows, love what He loves, and enjoy what He enjoys. Then your will will no longer be inconstant nor subject to change...and you will forever enjoy Him and His love. Blessed are they whose names are written in the Book of Life! If yours is there, why are you sad, O my soul, and why are you troubled? Trust in God, to whom I shall still confess my sins and whose mercies I shall proclaim. I shall compose a canticle of praise for Him and shall not cease to send up my sighs toward my Savior and my God. A day will come, perhaps, when my glory will praise Him, and my conscience will not feel.the bitterness of compunction, in the place where tears and fears have ceased forever.... O Lord, I would rather live and die in hope, and in the effort to gain eternal life, than to possess all creatures and their perishable goods. Do not abandon me, O Lord! I hope in You, and my hope will not be confounded. Give me the grace to serve You always and dispose of me as You wish " (T.J. *Exc*, 15 – 17).

If the remembrance of my infidelities torments me, I shall remember, O Lord, that " as soon as we are sorry for having offended You, You forget all our sins and malice. O truly infinite goodness! What more could one desire? Who would not blush with shame to ask so much of You? But now is the favorable time to profit from it, my merciful Savior, by accepting what You offer. You desire our friendship. Who can refuse to give it to You, who did not refuse to shed all Your Blood for us by sacrificing Your life? What You ask is nothing! It will be to our supreme advantage to grant it to You " (*ibid.*, 14).

95

DEATH

PRESENCE OF GOD - O Lord, You have created me for Yourself; grant that I may live and die for love of You.

MEDITATION

1. Today, the Thursday following Ash Wednesday, we find in the liturgy another reference to death. " Take order with thy house, for thou shalt die " (*Is* 38,1-6). The Church wishes us to become familiar with this thought, " less being suddenly surprised by the day of death, we should seek time for penance and not find it " *(RM)*. In the Gospel Jesus spoke of death as coming like a thief in the night, when we least expect it; but for the watchful Christian who lives according to the words, " Be you then also ready " (*Lk* 12,40), death will not be a surprise, because it will always find him " with his loins girt and lamp burning, " like those faithful servants who were waiting for their master,

" that when he cometh and knocketh, they may open to him
immediately " (*ibid.* 12,35.36). At that moment there
will be no complaint, no fear or anxiety, because one who
has always lived in expectation of the coming of the Lord
will not be afraid to open the door to Him at His arrival.
He will go to meet Him with great joy, give Him a loving
welcome, and with all the ardor of his soul pronounce his
last " Ecce venio, " behold, I come (*Ps* 39,8).

Although death is the last, it is not the only coming
of the Lord in the life of a Christian; it is preceded by many
other comings whose special purpose is to prepare us for this
last. Death will then be for us in the fullest sense a coming
of grace. From the moment of our Baptism until the end of
our life, we experience a continual succession of comings or
visits from our Lord; each Sacrament we receive, each
inspiration, each increase of grace is a divine visit to the
soul, by means of which God always possesses it more and
more, dwelling in it more fully and intimately. One who
has never hesitated to open his heart to all these visits from
our Lord, who has always welcomed them faithfully and
lovingly, who has followed all the impulses of grace with
docility, has nothing to fear from this last coming. Then
the words of Jesus will sound sweetly in his ears : " Well
done, good and faithful servant... enter thou into the joy of
thy Lord " (*Mt* 25,21).

2. St. John of the Cross, in speaking of those who have
reached the state of transforming union by love, declares
that their death is caused more by the impetus of divine love
than by natural causes. " Although they seem to die from
an illness or because of old age, their spirits are wrested away
by nothing less than some loving impulse and encounter,
far loftier and of greater power and strength than any in
the past, for it has succeeded in breaking the web and
bearing away the precious jewel of the soul " (*LF* 1,30).
This is indeed " dying of love, " a precious, blessed death,
the true nuptial meeting of the soul with God which brings
it immediately into the Beatific Vision. It is the way holy
souls die, those souls who are prevented from seeing God
face to face only because they are still imprisoned in their body.

Closely related to this death of love which is so glorious
and blessed, there is another, accessible to all who sincerely
love God and His holy will. As the essence of sanctity consists

in always doing the will of God lovingly, even when it imposes great sacrifices and painful renouncements, so too, the essence of a holy death consists in submitting oneself lovingly to this supreme sacrifice, accepting it willingly as the last expression of God's will. The deeper and more wholehearted the loving resignation with which we accept death, the more truly can it be called a death of love, precisely because it is embraced out of love for God.

God is the absolute master of our life; as we should live for love of Him, striving to conform in everything to His holy will, so that it becomes in everything and for everything the supreme norm of all our actions, so should we know how to die for love of Him, and accept death from His hand at the hour and under the circumstances ordained by Him. " For whether we live, we live unto the Lord, " said St. Paul; " or whether we die, we die unto the Lord. Therefore, whether we live, or whether we die, we are the Lord's " (*Rom* 14,8). Whether we are in life or in death, we are the Lord's, and because we are His, we should have no desire but to live and die according to His holy will. If during our life we try to carry out God's will with the greatest love, we can surely hope that God will give us the final grace to accept death with great love also.

COLLOQUY

" O Jesus, agonizing on the Cross, be my model at the hour of death. Although You are the Creator and Restorer of life, You willed to undergo death and accepted it willingly in order to expiate my sins. Death had no claim on You; You are the fountain of life and immortality, in whom and by whom all creatures have life; yet You willed to subject Yourself to death in order to resemble me and to sanctify my death.

" O death, who will henceforth fear you, since the Author of life bears you in His bosom, and without doubt, everything in Him is life-giving. I embrace you, I clasp you in my divine Savior's heart; there, like a chick under the wing of the mother hen, I shall peacefully await your coming, secure in the knowledge that my most merciful Jesus will sweeten your bitterness and defend me against your rigors.

" O Jesus, from this moment I wish to employ all my powers in accepting all the circumstances and pains of my death; from this moment I desire to accept death in the place, hour, and manner in which it may please You to send it. I know very well that I must suffer and be ground by the teeth of tribulations, sorrows, privations, desolations, and sufferings in order to become bread worthy to serve at Your celestial banquet, O Christ, on the day of the general resurrection. I well know that if the grain of wheat does not fall into the ground and die, it brings forth no fruit; therefore, with all my heart, I accept the annihilation of death in order to become a new man, no longer mortal and corruptible, but immortal and glorious " (St. Francis de Sales).

96

THE PROOF OF LOVE

PRESENCE OF GOD - O Jesus Crucified, make me understand that the Cross is the greatest proof of love.

MEDITATION

1. After the Incarnation, the Cross of Jesus is the greatest proof of His love for man.   Similarly, mortification, which is suffering eagerly accepted for the love of God, is one of the greatest proofs of love that we can give Him.   It means freely giving up a satisfaction or a pleasure in order to impose on ourselves, for love of God, something which is contrary to our own natural inclinations; we thus prove that we prefer to satisfy God rather than ourselves.   Every act of voluntary mortification, whether physical or moral, says to God, " Lord, I love You more than myself! "   And since a soul in love has an ardent desire to give proof of its love, it is very vigilant not to miss a single opportunity for renunciation.

It was in this sense that St. Teresa Margaret of the Heart of Jesus resolved " not to let a single occasion for suffering escape, as far as she was able—and always in silence between God and herself. "   In fact, she made every effort " to find at each moment some occasion for suffering or bodily pain, so as never to satisfy the slightest appetite or desire, and she sought ways to make even what was necessary, painful and wearying to her body" *(Sp)*. Her ardent love for God found an outlet in this generous, untiring exercise of mortification.

Using a different expression, St. Thérèse of the Child Jesus called this practice "scattering flowers," that is, profiting by every least opportunity to suffer in order to give God a proof of her love. Knowing that the value of mortification depends upon the generosity of the dispositions with which it is done, the Saint said, "I shall always sing, even should my flowers be gathered from the midst of thorns" (*St*, 13).

2. The value of voluntary mortification consists much more in the good will with which it is practiced than in the intensity of the suffering which is imposed, although the latter may contribute to it in the sense that a more painful mortification requires more good will.

The amount of suffering must be wisely proportioned, and limited to the physical strength of each one; but what must never be limited is the love, the spirit of generosity with which we perform each act of sacrifice. From this point of view, a slight mortification done with all the love of which a soul is capable has greater value than a painful penance performed in a material way, with no interior spirit. Hence before performing an act of mortification, especially when it concerns certain customary practices such as those which are used in Religious Institutes, it is necessary to arouse our good will and our sincere desire to suffer willingly for the love of God. This will prevent a mere mechanical performance of the act that has little or no value.

Loving contemplation of the Crucified was the soul of all the austerities of St. Teresa Margaret. "This humiliated, suffering God, of whom she was constantly thinking, was the One who gave her the interior strength to overcome every difficulty, however arduous, and to take on spontaneously so many labors and works of charity and mortification; it was He who gave her an insatiable desire for suffering" (T.M. *Sp*).

Contemplating Jesus Crucified, the soul feels that, even if it is mortifying itself much for love of Him, its sacrifices and renunciations amount to very little, and instead of

conceiving sentiments of vain complacency for the mortifications already practiced, it feels the need of humbling itself
and of always doing more. " Have great love for suffering, "
says St. John of the Cross, " and consider it very little to
attain the favor of the Spouse, who hesitated not to die for
thee " (*SM II*, 15).

COLLOQUY

" O my Beloved, how shall I show my love, since love
proves itself by deeds? I have no other means of proving
my love than to strew flowers, and these flowers will be each
word and look, each little daily sacrifice. I wish to make
profit out of the smallest actions and to do them all for Love.
For Love's sake I wish to suffer and to rejoice : so shall I strew
my flowers. Not one that I see but, singing all the while,
I will scatter its petals before You. Should my roses be
gathered from amid thorns, I will sing notwithstanding; and
the longer and sharper the thorns, the sweeter will grow my
song " (T.C.J. *St*, 13).

" O Lord, dispose of me according to Your will, for
I am content with everything if only I am following You
on the road to Calvary. The more thorns there are on this
road and the heavier the Cross is, the more consoled shall
I be, for I desire to love You with an effective love, with a
patient love, with a love which is dead to self and entirely
surrendered to You. O Lord, You on the Cross for me and
I on the Cross for You! Oh! if I could but once understand
how sweet and precious it is to suffer : to suffer in silence for
You, O Jesus! O dear suffering! O good Jesus! " (T.M. *Sp*).
Yes, suffering is dear to me because it permits me to give
God proofs of my love; because in the darkness of faith, in
which I must live here below, it gives me the assurance of
loving not only in words, but with a strong, effective love.
O Jesus, now I understand why St. Teresa of Avila asked for
only one thing : " to die or to suffer, " professing to have no
other reason for living except to suffer for love of You
(*Life*, 40).

O Lord, may I too have such strong, true, and ardent
love! Grant it to me, You who can give me all things, and
who can, in one instant, transform this dry, cold heart into
a furnace of charity.

97

THE SPIRIT OF MORTIFICATION

PRESENCE OF GOD - I come back to Your feet, O Crucified Jesus, desirous of understanding more thoroughly the spirit of mortification.

MEDITATION

1. The spirit of mortification has more than a purely physical aspect of mortification; it also includes renunciation of the ego, the will, and the understanding. Just as in our body and in our senses we have unruly tendencies toward the enjoyment of material things, so also in our ego there are inordinate tendencies toward self-assertion. Love of self and complacency in our own excellence are often so great that, even unconsciously, we tend to make " self " the center of the universe.

The spirit of mortification is really complete when, above all, we seek to mortify self-love in all its many manifestations. The Pharisee who fasted on the appointed days, but whose heart was so puffed up with pride that his payer amounted to nothing more than praise of himself and scorn of his neighbor, did not have the spirit of mortification and hence was not justified before God. There is little value in imposing corporal mortifications on ourselves if we then refuse to yield our opinion in order to accommodate ourselves to others, if we cannot be reconcilied with our enemies, or bear an injury and a cutting word with calmness, or hold back a sharp answer.

" Why, " asks St. Teresa of Jesus, " do we shrink from interior mortification [of our ego, our will, and judgment] since this is the means by which every other kind of mortification may become much more meritorious and perfect, and may be practiced with greater tranquillity and ease? " (*Way*, 12). As long as mortification does not strike at our pride, it remains at the halfway mark and never reaches its goal.

2. The true spirit of mortification embraces, in the first place, all the occasions for physical or moral suffering

permitted by divine Providence. The sufferings attendant
on illness or fatigue; the efforts required by the performance
of our duties or by a life of intense labor; the privations
imposed by the state of poverty—all are excellent physical
penances. If we sincerely desire to be guided by divine
Providence in everything, we will not try to avoid them, or
even to lighten them, but will accept wholeheartedly whatever
God offers us. It would be absurd to refuse a single one of
those providential opportunities for suffering and to look
for voluntary mortifications of our own choice. Likewise,
it would be foolish for those in religious life to omit the
least exercise imposed by the Rule in order to do a penance
of their own choosing.

It is exactly the same in the moral order. Do we not
sometimes try to avoid a person whom we do not like, but
with whom the Lord has brought us into contact? Do we
look for every means of avoiding a humiliation or an act of
obedience which is painful to nature? If we do, we are
running away from the best opportunities for sacrificing
ourselves and for mortifying our self-love; even if we substitute
other mortifications, they will not be as effective as those
which God Himself has prepared for us. In the mortifications
offered to us by divine Providence, there is nothing of our
own will or liking; they strike us just where we need it
most, and where, by voluntary mortification, we could
never reach.

In order to arrive at sanctity, a certain specified amount
of voluntary penance is not required of all; this varies
according to the inspiration of the Holy Spirit, the advice
of superiors, and each one's physical strength. All, however,
must have that truly deep spirit of mortification which can
embrace with generosity every opportunity for renunciation
prepared or permitted by God.

COLLOQUY

O Lord, You who have sought for adorers in spirit and in
truth, preserve me, I beg You, from the pharisaic spirit
against which You fought while on earth, and which is so
opposed to You, who are infinite Truth and Simplicity.
Grant that while mortifying my body, I may mortify my pride
even more, or better, mortify it Yourself.

You who know the secret places in my heart, the most deeply hidden instincts of my self-love, prepare for me the most effective medicine for purifying, healing, and transforming me. You alone know where this most harmful microbe nests; You alone can destroy it. But how often, alas, in the varying circumstances of my life, I have not recognized Your hand, Your work; and I have tried in so many ways to escape the physical and moral sufferings, the mortifications, humiliations, and difficulties which You Yourself had prepared for me.

How blind I am, O Lord, and how poorly do I recognize Your ways, which are so different and remote from my limited human views. Give me, O God, that supernatural sight which can judge events in Your light, and which can penetrate the true meaning of the sufferings which You place in my path. Intensify this light in proportion to the obstacles You prepare for me to strike my " ego , " my pride, my opinions, my rights, because it is then above all that I am terribly blind, and groping in the dark, I reject the medicine You offer. I may lack, O Lord, the means of carrying out the purification of my ego, so foolish and so proud. But nothing is lacking to You, You who are the All, and whose infinite mercy utterly surpasses my misery. I confess, O Lord, that I have often strayed like a lamb which, leaving its shepherd, has taken a wrong path. But I desire to return once more, and I come back with complete confidence because I know that You never tire of waiting and of pardoning. Here I am, Lord; I place myself in Your hands. Mortify me, purify me as You wish, for whenever You afflict, it is to heal, and wherever You mortify, life increases.

98

THE GREAT COMBAT

FIRST SUNDAY OF LENT

PRESENCE OF GOD - O Jesus, I withdraw in spirit with You into the desert; teach me how to fight the triple concupiscence of the flesh, pride, and avarice.

MEDITATION

1. On this day, which is the real beginning of Lent, the Church invites us to the great combat, the struggle against sin which will bring us to the Easter resurrection. Our model is Jesus, who although exempt from the incitements of concupiscence, willed to be tempted by the devil *for us*, in order to have " compassion on our infirmities " (*Heb* 4,15).

After forty days of rigorous fast, while He is feeling the pangs of hunger, Jesus is tempted by Satan to change stones into bread. No one can undertake a serious program of penance or mortification without feeling its discomforts; but that is the time to resist the insinuating voices which invite us to condescend to the demands of nature; that is the time to reply with Jesus, " not in bread alone doth man live, but in every word that proceedeth from the mouth of God " (Gosp. : *Mt* 4,1-11). Man's life is far more dependent on the will of God than on material food. If we are convinced of this truth, we shall have the courage to submit to privations, trusting in divine Providence for our sustenance.

Jesus was next tempted to pride. " If thou be the Son of God, cast thyself down...and in their hands the angels shall bear thee up. " Such a miracle would have aroused the admiration and enthusiasm of the people, but Jesus knew that His Father had chosen an entirely different way for Him—the way of humiliations rather than of triumphs, the way of the Cross and of death. Because He had no desire to escape from this way, He resolutely rejected the suggestion to pride. The best means of conquering temptations to pride and vanity is to choose exactly what humiliates us and makes us appear little in the eyes of others.

The devil returns to the attack and tempts Jesus to

avarice : " All these will I give thee, if falling down thou wilt adore me. " But Jesus replies, " The Lord thy God shalt thou adore and Him only shalt thou serve! " He whose heart is firmly anchored in God will never let it be drawn away from His service by an attraction for, or envy of, earthly things. But if this strong adherence to God is weakened or lost, the temptations to avarice will often succeed in making even those stray who have a special vocation to be " serving God alone. "

2. Jesus was tempted because He willed it. We, however, are tempted without willing it, and often against our will. The temptation of Jesus was wholly exterior, for it found no echo within Him; on the contrary, our nature, wounded by the triple concupiscence of the flesh, of pride, and of avarice, is not only an easy prey for the assaults of the devil, but is itself the source of many temptations. It is impossible for us to live without temptations; our virtue does not consist in being exempt from them but in being able to overcome them. It is a struggle which none can escape; God even wishes this struggle to be the price of eternal life. " Blessed is the man that endureth temptation; for when he hath been proved, he shall receive the crown of life " (*Jas* 1,12).

Let us learn from Jesus how to conduct ourselves in temptations. Primarily, He teaches us to have a great confidence in God. Jesus would not satisfy His hunger, nor impress men by means of a brilliant miracle, nor accept kingdoms and wealth because, in a spirit of perfect filial confidence, He had entrusted everything to the Father's care—His life, His mission, and His glory. Those who will fully trust in God and who rely on His divine Providence, will not be easily enticed by the vain flattery of the devil, the world, or the flesh, because they know that only God can give true blessings and real happiness.

We should extend the practice of this confidence to the moment of temptation. If God permits us to be tempted, He does not permit us to be tempted beyond our strength, and, accompanying every temptation, there is always a special actual grace sufficient to overcome it. Therefore, instead of being disturbed by the violence of the struggle, let us use faithfully the grace God always gives and turn to Him in humble, confident prayer.

COLLOQUY

" Lord God, our Father, Life by which all live, without which everything would be as dead, do not abandon me to evil thoughts and to pride; take away from me all concupiscence and do not give me as prey to an irreverent and foolish spirit; but take possession of my heart, that I may always think of You.... Help me now, my Redeemer, I beseech You, so that I will not fall before my enemies, caught in the snares which they set for my feet to abase my soul; but save me, strength of my salvation, that I may not become a laughing-stock to Your enemies who hate You. Rise, O Lord, my God, my strength, and Your enemies will be dispersed; those who hate You will flee before Your face.

" As wax melts in the fire, so do sinners vanish before Your face. I shall hide myself in You, and rejoice with Your children, satiated with all Your good things. And You, O Lord God, Father of orphans, protecting Mother, spread your wings, that under them we may take refuge from our enemies " (St. Augustine).

I entrust myself to You, my God and Savior! I wish, particularly in times of struggle, to take refuge in You with redoubled confidence, for " You are my defense and will deliver me from the nets of the fowler and from all misfortune. You will cover me with Your wings and I shall be safe. Your fidelity will surround me like a shield, and I shall fear neither the terrors of the night nor the arrow that flies by day, nor the plague that roams in darkness, nor the attacks of the noonday devil. You are my hope, Lord; You are my refuge, O Most High! You have commanded Your angels to watch over all my paths, and they will bear me in their hands lest my feet strike againt a stone " (cf. *Ps* 90,3-12).

99

CONVERSION

PRESENCE OF GOD - O Lord, You have created me for Yourself; grant that, with all my strength, I may tend toward You, my last end.

MEDITATION

1. In the Epistle of today's Mass (*Ez* 34,11-16), we read : " For thus saith the Lord God : Behold I Myself will seek My sheep, and will visit them...and will deliver them out of all the places where they have been scattered in the cloudy and dark day.... I will bring them to their own land, and I will feed them in the mountains of Israel.... There shall they rest on the green grass. " This is the program which the Lord wishes to accomplish in our souls during the holy season of Lent, in order to lead us by means of it to a life of higher perfection and closer intimacy with Him. He stretches out His hand to us, not only to save us from dangers, but also to help us climb to those higher places where He Himself will nourish us.

The point of departure which will make the realization of this divine plan possible is a new conversion on our part : we must collect our powers, desires, and affections, which have been scattered and are lingering in the valley of the purely human; putting them all together, we must make them *converge* on God, our one last end. In this sense, our Lenten *conversion* should consist in a generous determination to put ourselves more resolutely in the way of perfection. It means a new *determination to become a saint.* The desire for sanctity is the mainspring of the spiritual life; the more intense and real this desire is in us, the more it will urge us to pledge ourselves totally. In this first week of Lent, we must try to arouse and strengthen our resolution to become a saint. If other efforts in the past have been unsuccessful or have not entirely reached the goal, this is no reason for discouragement. *Nunc coepi*—" now have I begun, " or rather : " now I begin "; let us repeat it humbly, and may the experience of our past failures make us place our trust in God alone.

2. St. Thomas teaches that " in the pursuit of the end,
no limits should be set " (II^a II^{ae}, q.184, a.3). Sanctity
is the end of the spiritual life; that is why we must propose
it to ourselves, not in a reduced, restricted manner, but
in all its fullness—fullness which speaks to us of intimate
union with God, of the complete invasion of grace, and of
entire conformity to the divine will, to the extent that it
becomes the only motive of all our actions; for when the
soul becomes totally purified of everything contrary to
God's will, " then the Lord will communicate His supernatural
Being to it, in such a way that it will seem to be God Himself
and to have what God possesses " (*AS II*, 5,7). Sanctity is
the plenitude of love and grace; it is transformation in God
by love, it is deification by grace.

What measure of love and grace must we attain?
That depends primarily upon God's designs on our soul
and then on our cooperation. Now on our part, the secret
of reaching the goal is never to stop : first, because even
if we were to grow in love indefinitely, we would never
be able to love God as musch as He is to be loved; secondly
because we do not know to what degree of sanctity God
is calling us. Furthermore, God does not let Himself be
outdone in generosity, and the more we give ourselves
to Him in the exercise of intense love, the more He will
give Himself to us by grace.

The measure of loving God is to love Him " without
measure "; if we should not set a limit to love, neither
should we set one to our *conversion*. The Lord said, " Be
converted to Me with all your heart " (*Jl* 2,12). This
is the indispensable condition for loving God with our
whole heart. The cases where total conversion is reached
in an instant by a very special grace are rare; ordinarily,
we do not arrive at it except by a daily progressive conversion.
And if, in this conversion—as in the whole work of sanctification—the initiative is always from God, who prevents us
with His grace, our cooperation is nevertheless required;
hence we must strive every day with renewed diligence to
" be converted to God with all our heart. " Let this be
our program for Lent.

COLLOQUY

"O Lord of my soul and my only good! Why do You not wish that the soul should enjoy at once the consolation of arriving at this perfect love as soon as it has decided to love You and is doing all it can to give up everything in order to serve You better? But I am wrong : I should have made my complaint by asking why we ourselves have no desire to arrive at it, for it is we alone who are at fault in not at once enjoying so great a dignity. If we attain to the perfect possession of this true love of God, it brings all blessings with it. But so niggardly and so slow are we in giving ourselves wholly to God that we do not prepare ourselves to receive this benefit.... So it is that this treasure is not given to us in a short time because we do not give ourselves to God entirely and forever.... O my God, grant me the grace and the courage to determine to strive after this good with all my strength. If I persevere, You, who never refuse Your help to anyone, will strengthen my courage until I come off with victory. I say courage, because the devil, with so many obstacles, tries to make us deviate from this path" (cf. T.J. *Life*, 11).

Grant, O Lord Jesus, by the infinite merits of Your passion, that I may be converted to You with all my heart. Do not permit me to be discouraged by the continual return of my egotistical tendencies, or by the incessant struggle which I must maintain against them. Make me clearly understand that, if I wish to be completely converted to You, I can never make peace with my weaknesses, my faults, my self-love, my pride. Make me understand that I must sacrifice everything to Your love, and even when I have sacrificed everything I must still say : " I am an unprofitable servant, " O Lord, because everything is as nothing, compared with the love which You deserve, O infinitely lovable One!

100

SIN

PRESENCE OF GOD - O Jesus Crucified, give me the grace to understand the great malice of sin.

MEDITATION

1. The essence of Christian perfection consists in union with God by charity. While charity, by conforming our wills to God's, unites us to Him, grave sin, which directly opposes His will, produces the opposite effect. In other words, charity is the force uniting man to God, and sin the force drawing him away. Serious sin is therefore the greatest enemy of the spiritual life, since it not only injures it, but destroys it in its constituent elements : charity and grace. This destruction, this spiritual death, is the inevitable result of sin, the act by which man voluntarily detaches himself from God, the one source of life, charity, and grace. As the branch cannot live if it is separated from the trunk, neither can the soul live if separated from God.

God, the cause of every being, is always present in the soul of the sinner in the same way in which He is present in all creatures; yet He is not there as a Father, as a Guest, as the Trinity which offers Itself to the soul to be known and loved. Hence, the sinner, though created to be the temple of the Blessed Trinity, has voluntarily made himself incapable of dwelling with the three divine Persons and has barred his own road to union with God. He has, so to speak, obliged God to break all ties of friendship with him because he has preferred the temporal, fleeting good of a miserable creature—a selfish satisfaction, an earthly pleasure—instead of the sovereign good. This is the malice of sin which rejects the divine gift and betrays its Creator, Father, and Friend. " Oh! why can we not realize that sin is a pitched battle fought against God with all our senses and the faculties of the soul; the stronger the soul is, the more ways it invents to betray its King " (T.J. *Exc*, 14).

2. If we wish to have a better understanding of the evil of mortal sin, we must consider its disastrous effects. One

single sin instantly changed Lucifer, the angel of light, into an angel of darkness, into the eternal enemy of God. A single sin deprived Adam and Eve of the state of grace and friendship with God, taking away all their supernatural gifts and condemning them to death together with the rest of mankind. One single sin was enough to make an abyss between God and man, to deprive the whole human race of any possibility of union with God.

The Passion of Jesus is a further proof of the great malice and the destructive power of sin. The lacerated members of Christ, His sorrowful death on the Cross, proclaim that sin is a form of deicide. Jesus, the most beautiful of the sons of men, through sin, became the " despised and the most abject of men, a man of sorrows. . . . He was bruised for our sins, " so that " from the sole of His foot unto the top of His head, there is no soundness therein " (*Is* 53,3-5 – 1,6). Sin made Christ a martyr and brought Him to His death; still we must understand that Christ went to His Passion and death " because it was His own will " (*ibid.* 53,7), for by means of it, He wished to vanquish death and restore divine friendship to man.

Jesus, our Head, invites us, His members, to unite with Him in His work of destroying sin : to destroy it in ourselves down to the very roots, that is, in our evil inclinations, and to destroy it likewise in His other members by allowing Him to work in us. This is the law of solidarity, for the misfortune of one is the misfortune of the others; each sin is a burden on the whole world and disturbs the equilibrium of God's plan. Therefore, every Christian, and more especially, every soul consecrated to God, must throw himself ardently into the battle against sin and fight it with the proper weapons : penance, expiatory prayer, and most of all, love. When the love of charity is perfect, it destroys sin more efficaciously than the fire of purgatory. In this we see why the saints were able to convert so many souls. God used the fire of their charity to do away with sin in sinners.

COLLOQUY

" O my God and my true Strength! How is it, Lord, that we are cowards in everything save in opposing Thee?

To this the children of Adam devote all their energies. Were not reason so blind, the combined energies of all men put together would not suffice to make them bold enough to take up arms against their Creator and maintain a continual warfare against One who in a moment could plunge them into the depths. But because reason is blind, they act like madmen courting death, for they imagine that this death will bring them new life : they act, in short, like people bereft of reason. O incomprehensible Wisdom! In truth Thou needest all the love which Thou hast for Thy creature to enable Thee to endure such folly, and to await our recovery, and to seek to bring it about by a thousand kinds of means and remedies.

" It amazes me when I consider how we lack the effort to take in hand a very small thing, and how we really persuade ourselves that, even if we so desire, we cannot flee from some occasion of sin and avoid something which imperils our soul, and yet that we have effort and courage enough to attack so great a Sovereign as art Thou. How is it, my Good? How is this? Who gives us this strength?

" O Lord, what hardness of heart! Oh, what folly and blindness! We are distressed if we lose anything, the merest trifle. Then why are we not distressed at losing that great Treasure which is the Majesty of God, and a kingdom in which our fruition of Him will be endless. Why is this? Why is this? I cannot understand it. Do Thou, my God, cure such great folly and blindness.... The loss of so many souls hurts me so much that I am beside myself. I cry to Thee, Lord, and beseech Thee to give me the means of contributing to the winning of souls by my prayers, since I am not good for anything else.... It seems to me that I would willingly sacrifice a thousand lives to save even one of the many souls which are being lost! I believe, Lord, that You treasure one soul that we gain for You by our prayers and works, thanks to Your mercy, more than all other services that we can render You " (T.J. *Exc*, 12 – 14 – *F*, 1 – *Way*, 1).

IOI

VENIAL SIN

PRESENCE OF GOD - O Lord, inflame me with Your holy zeal, so that I will no longer be able to tolerate in myself the slightest thing which is displeasing to You.

MEDITATION

1. Venial sin, like mortal sin, goes counter to God's will, although with less serious deviation. While it does not destroy charity, it is opposed to it and therefore diminishes its fervor and vigor, hindering its development. This is the disastrous effect of deliberate venial sin committed with the realization that it is displeasing to God.

Once venial sins of this kind become habitual, they decrease the soul's tendency toward God, and increase, on the other hand, its leaning toward self-satisfaction and creatures. Thus, little by little the soul loses its fervor, its sense of sin, and falls into tepidity, which is characterized by a certain indifference to venial sin. This puts it in danger of offending God in serious matters also. In this sense, venial sin may be compared to a disease of insidious languor, a kind of spiritual tuberculosis, which undermines the organism slowly but fatally. It is not unusual to meet souls who having at first surrendered themselves to God with sincere fervor, afterwards let themselves fall into continual carelessness, indifference, voluntary omissions, and laziness, because they have given in to selfishness and sought their own comfort. They become incapable of making the generous efforts required to advance on the way they have started. Their spiritual life is reduced to a king of lethargy which is not yet death, but which has none of the freshness and vigor of a strong, healthy life. It lacks the fervor of charity, for this is continually being lessened by deliberate concessions to venial sin.

To put us on our guard against such a state, St. Teresa of Jesus declares, " Always be fearful if you do not feel sorry for the faults you commit, for even venial sin ought to fill you with sorrow to the very depths of your soul.... For the

love of God, take care not to commit any deliberate venial
sin, even the smallest.... And can anything be small if it
offends God? " (*Con* 2 – *Way* 41).

2. Quite different are the venial sins which we commit
through frailty or inadvertence. Very often the soul is
determined not to give in at any price; due to its weakness,
however, it falls when temptation comes, especially if the
attack is unexpected. Nevertheless, once aware of it, the
soul feels sincere sorrow, repents at once, asks God's pardon,
rises, and sets out again. Such sins cause no great harm
to the soul; they are signs of its frailty and show that it has
not yet reached spiritual maturity. Moreover, if the soul
sincerely humbles itself after these falls, it will draw profit
from them and a more profound knowledge of its own
misery, which will make it mistrust its own strength entirely
and place all its confidence in God alone. It will experience
in a practical way the profound truth of the words of Jesus,
" Without Me you can do nothing " (*Jn* 15,5). It is not
unusual for God to permit these falls, and He does so precisely
to give the soul this practical knowledge of its nothingness,
and to anchor it firmly in humility, the foundation of all
our spiritual life.

In regard to faults of this kind, St. Thérèse of the Child
Jesus felt that we can be sure " they do not grieve the good
God, " because they are not caused by a will intent on sin,
by indifference or by coldness; they spring from the weakness
of human nature.

If because of our weakness it is impossible for us to
avoid these little daily venial faults of inadvertence or frailty,
it is important to know how to detest them and to make
generous reparation. As to deliberate venial sins, we should
be firmly resolved not to commit them for anything in
the world.

COLLOQUY

" *Peccavi, Domine, miserere mei!* Pardon, Father, pardon
me, a miserable ingrate. I owe it to Your goodness that
I am still Your spouse, even though I am unfaithful to You
by my faults. *Peccavi, Domine, miserere mei.* O my soul,
what are you doing? Are you not aware that God sees

you always? You can never hide yourself from His sight,
for nothing is hidden from Him. . . .   O eternal God, Father
of all goodness and mercy, have pity on us because we are
blind and in darkness, and I, more than anyone else, am
miserable and to be pitied. . . .   O true Sun, enter my soul
and illumine it with Your brightness.   Drive out the darkness
and give me light; melt the ice of my self-love and kindle
in me the fire of Your charity.   *Peccavi, Domine, miserere mei*"
(St. Catherine of Siena).

"May His Majesty be pleased to make us fear Him
whom we ought to fear and understand that one venial
sin can do us greater harm than all the forces of hell
combined" (T.J. *Life*, 25).   Indeed the real evil, the only
one I have to fear, is neither temptation, nor trial, nor
interior or exterior contradictions, nor the loss of material
things or of health, but only what is contrary in any way
at all to my union with You, my sovereign Good!   This
evil, I see, can be caused by one single venial sin, committed
deliberately.   O Jesus, I beseech You, through the merits
of Your Passion, deliver me from this great evil, take away
from me the wretched power to offend You, and if, because
of my innate weakness, it is impossible for me to avoid
these faults, grant that they may never be the consequence
of my bad will.   May my faults serve only to humiliate me,
not to offend You.

Because of my weakness, I often fall.   "Often I lose
sight of what is my only care, and straying from Your side,
allow my wings to be draggled in the muddy pools of this
world.   Then 'I cry like a young swallow,' and my cry
tells You all, and You remember, O infinite Mercy, that
You 'did not come to call the just, but sinners'" (T.C.J.
St, 13).

102

IMPERFECTIONS

PRESENCE OF GOD - O my God, make me understand how necessary it is for the soul to be pure in order to be united to You who are infinite Perfection!

MEDITATION

1. While venial sin always consists in a more or less slight transgression of one of God's laws, imperfection is the omission of some good act to which we are not obliged by any law, but one which charity invites us to do. To illustrate : when I am aware of the possibility of performing a better act suited to my state, in accord with my actual capabilities, in harmony with my duties, and for the accomplishment of which I may reasonably believe that I am inspired by the Holy Spirit, I cannot deliberately refuse to do it without real actual imperfection. In this case, my *refusal* to perform a better act cannot be judged to be good, nor can it be justified by the thought that I am free to omit this better action since no law or commandment obliges me. This would be an *abuse* of that liberty which was given me by God for the sole purpose of making me capable of adhering to the good, uninfluenced by my passions. In fact, in the last analysis, my *refusal* to perform the better act always implies a lack of generosity, motivated by a little selfishness, laziness, meanness, or fondness for my own comfort, all of which are evidently contrary to perfection.

Viewed from this angle, it is clear that voluntary imperfection can never be conformable to the will of God, and that consequently, like sin, it is contrary to charity which tends to full conformity with the divine will. Hence, it is important for a soul striving for union with God to eliminate from its conduct every voluntary imperfection. In this sense, St. John of the Cross admonishes us : " For the soul to come to unite itself perfectly with God through love and will...it must not intentionally and knowingly consent with the will to imperfections. " Furthermore, he teaches that attachment to even one habitual voluntary imperfection suffices to impede the soul " not only from divine union, but also from progress in perfection " (*AS I*, 11,3).

2. If we wish to go into further detail, we can think of other types of imperfection. Let us consider, first of all, the breaking of a law which of itself does not bind us under pain of sin, as is generally the case with the Constitutions or Statutes of the various Religious Orders and Institutes. In this respect we must note that if there is no reasonable motive—proportionate and sufficient—to exempt us from one of these laws, these transgressions may very easily become venial sins through the absence of a morally good end. Indeed, St. Thomas teaches that man is always bound to act through a reasonable motive and for a good end. If the end is vitiated—as would be the case, for example, in breaking the rule of silence, of solitude, or of religious modesty, through curiosity, through regarding one's own convenience, or similar motives—the act becomes sinful; and in general there will be a question of " sins, at least slight ones, such as spiritual sloth, inconstancy, ingratitude and a certain hardness of heart which does not sufficiently esteem the help God gives us to do better " (Salamanticenses). Another form of imperfection is found in a certain lack of completeness in an act which is substantially good, but which is done, for example, with some reluctance, or without putting into it all the good will and fervor of spirit of which we are capable.

Every kind of imperfection in fact always comes from a want of effort, energy, and fervor in the spiritual life. It is always selfishness which, in one way or another, takes something away from God to satisfy the ego. We are too calculating, afraid of giving too much, and so selfishness clips our wings and keeps us from reaching full union with God.

COLLOQUY

Grant me, I beg You, O my God, a strong, generous charity, capable of destroying my selfishness down to its very roots. Oh! how well I understand that this self-love is the cause of so many of my little infidelities, of so many imperfections into which I habitually fall and which I do

not take care to correct, under the pretext that they are
not sins!

These faults, however, are not without importance
to a soul consecrated to You and bound to strive for perfection,
to a soul called by You to sanctity and one whom You
invite to complete union with Yourself. How can I pretend
to be united to You, infinite Perfection, if I voluntarily
commit so many and such great imperfections in my life?
How can my will be entirely conformed to Yours, when
I desire and love things that You do not desire and absolutely
cannot love?

O Lord, I feel the weight of my egoism which drags
me down. This self-love would like to possess everything
without effort and flees with all its might from fatigue,
sacrifice, and complete generous giving! I feel the weight
of the flesh which is ever trying to lessen the measure of my
giving, which postpones until tomorrow anything that is
painful or distasteful, which makes a thousand excuses
for avoiding an act of generosity!

I know all that, O Lord, and You know better than
I these secret compromises of my self-love. But You also
know that I want to love You with my whole heart and to
give myself entirely to You. You know that my poor desires
are sincere, even if they are not efficacious. Give me a real,
effectual love, capable of overcoming all the opposition
of self-love, and of demolishing all its plans. You who are
infinite charity, consuming fire, kindle in my soul a spark
of Your love that will destroy and consume my selfishness.
If self-love is the weight which slows my progress toward
You, grant that Your love will be a weight still heavier
to draw me incessantly to You through a total gift of self,
without reserve or limit.

103

EXAMINATION OF CONSCIENCE

PRESENCE OF GOD - O Lord, cast a ray of light on my soul, so that I may be able to see myself as You see me and as You judge me.

MEDITATION

1. To insure an orderly and progressive growth in the spiritual life, *we must know ourselves.* We have to consider our sins, our weak points, our evil tendencies, as well as the progress we have already made, the favorable results we have attained, and our inclinations to good. This knowledge of our interior state is obtained through the *examination of conscience.* The examen considered in this way becomes one of the most important exercises of the spiritual life, since its object is to help the soul to rid itself of everything that might obstruct or delay its journey to God, and to stimulate it to quicken its pace toward Him. Just as we cannot wage war with an unknown enemy, or make conquest of an unknown region, in the same way it is impossible to fight the evil in ourselves if we have not previously identified it. We can never attain sanctity if we have not looked for an efficacious means of acquiring it. In other words, the examination of conscience attains its end when the soul who has faithfully practiced this exercise can say to itself : these are the inclinations which I must watch more carefully to avoid falling into sin; these, the weak points which I must strengthen; these are the virtues that I must practice most of all. In this way the soul will be able to formulate practical, firm resolutions which will then become the special subject of its subsequent examinations.

It is clear that we must first recognize and combat any tendencies which could lead us to mortal sin, but then, those that could bring us to venial sin or to simple voluntary imperfections must be similarly treated. Everything that constitutes a deliberate fault must be progressively and energetically rooted out of the soul which aspires to divine union.

2. Instead of trying to seek out all the faults it has committed, the soul living an interior life—one we assume to be free by now from mortal sin—should fix its attention on the degree to which its faults have been voluntary, even in the case of slight imperfections, because it is these deliberate faults that present the greatest obstacle to spiritual progress and to union with God. The soul must carefully investigate the cause of and the motive for these failures. It must realize that while its exterior faults are of various kinds—faults against charity, for example, or patience, or obedience, or sincerity—all of them, nevertheless, have one and the same cause, one common root which may be, for example, pride or sloth. It is precisely against this root of our sins and imperfections that we must direct our efforts, not simply to lessen it by mortification, but rather to fight it directly by the increase of the opposite virtues in ourselves. In other words, we must struggle against our dominant passion or fault; this is very important, for by aiming to destroy the evil at its root, we eliminate at the same time many actual faults.

When the soul has reached the point where it no longer has to reproach itself for deliberate faults and imperfections, it should turn its attention to those failures of surprise or inadvertence from which it has not yet succeeded in freeing itself, in spite of its sincere and often renewed resolutions. In these cases the soul, besides continuing the struggle against the root of its faults, will find it very useful to continually reinforce its firm purpose to overcome self. The more determined the soul is to correct its faults, the less voluntary will those be which escape it. They grow slighter and slighter and are often only the residue or the purely natural movement of habits once contracted but now detested.

Another important point that must not be overlooked in the examination of conscience is the remembrance of our duty to sustain and guard the desire for sanctity and to enliven our determination to do always what is most pleasing to God; here is the heart of the spiritual life, of generosity. It is also an excellent method to examine ourselves from God's point of view instead of our own, to ask ourselves if God is pleased with us and how He will judge our conduct.

COLLOQUY

" O God of my soul, what am I in Your presence! Have my acts ever been free from faults—my words, my will? But You, O Lord, are good and Your right hand is merciful.

" O Physician of my soul, show me the fruits of my avowal. I confess because the admission of my miseries awakens my heart and keeps it from slumber; but even while saying I am incapable of doing good, my soul awakes again in the love of Your mercy and the sweetness of Your grace, by which every sick soul feels strong and becomes aware of its weakness.

" I shall love You, O Lord, and return thanks to You and exalt Your Name because You have pardoned so many of my guilty acts. If my sins have melted away like ice, it is the work of Your grace and mercy. All the evil that I have not committed was likewise the work of Your grace. Was there any sin that I could not have committed, I who have loved evil with so light a heart? I confess that all my sins have been forgiven, both those that I committed as well as those that, with Your help, I did not commit " (St. Augustine).

O my God, You who by one single act of Your will created light—and light was made—speak again Your all-powerful creative word : *fiat lux*, and light will be created in my soul; and in Your light I shall be able to see myself as I really am in Your sight.

But light is not enough for me who am so weak and cowardly; I need strength, O Lord; I need a strong, resolute will to hate evil in all its forms, to have a horror of my self-love, my pride, my sloth, to renew and strengthen my resolution to overcome myself for love of You.

Yes, Lord, with Your help I wish to conquer myself, not for the vain satisfaction of thinking that I am doing better, but solely to give You pleasure, to avoid even the smallest thing that displeases You, to grow in Your love, to enter into closer union with You. O my God, infinite Perfection, envelop and penetrate my soul with the reflection of Your holiness, and just as the sun illumines, purifies and makes the earth fruitful with its rays, illumine, purify, and sanctify my whole being. Teach me to look at myself with Your eyes, to know myself as You know me, to consider my miseries in the light of Your infinite perfections, to open my soul to Your purifying, sanctifying light.

104

CONFESSION [1]

PRESENCE OF GOD - At the foot of Your Cross, O Jesus, I confess my sins. Pour over me Your Precious Blood that it may purify my soul.

MEDITATION

1. Penance is the sacrament of Christ's Precious Blood in which God—according to the eloquent words of St. Catherine of Siena—" has bathed us in order to cleanse the face of our souls from the leprosy of sin. " If mortal sin only is the *necessary* matter of this sacrament, venial sin is sufficient matter, since all Catholic tradition insists on frequent confession, even when one has only venial sins to confess. However, those who confess weekly must take great care lest their confessions become a mere routine, instead of the really *vital acts* which would enable these souls to profit fully from all the graces offered by the sacrament.

" Do not despise the Blood of Christ! " exclaims St. Catherine of Siena. Certainly anyone who appreciates it will not approach the sacrament of penance lightly. To this end it is useful to recall that absolution is truly the pouring forth of the Precious Blood which, inundating and penetrating the soul, purifies it from sin, and restores sanctifying grace if it has been lost, or increases this gift if it is already present in the soul. The remission of sin and the imparting of grace are the fruits of the action of Jesus, expressed by the formula the priest pronounces in His Name : " I absolve thee. " At that moment it is Jesus who is acting in the soul, either by remitting sin or by producing or increasing grace. It is well to remember that the efficacy of the absolution is not limited merely to sins that have already been committed, but that it even extends into the future. By means of the particular sacramental grace, the soul is strengthened beforehand against relapses and it is offered the fortitude to resist temptations and to carry out its good resolutions. The Blood of Christ is, in this sense, not only a remedy for the past, but also a

-----
[1] See also Meditation **73.**

preservative and a strengthening help for the future. The soul which plunges into it, as into a healthful bath, draws from it new vigor and sees the strength of its passions extinguished little by little. We see then the importance of frequent confession for a soul desirous of union with God, a soul which must necessarily aspire to total purification.

2. When the soul in the tribunal of penance has only venial sins to confess, it is not necessary that it preoccupy itself with confessing all of them, either as to their number or their kind. This completeness is necessary only when there is question of mortal sin. In other cases, however, it is much more profitable to fix the attention on deliberate faults first, then on those which are semi-deliberate—even if they are only simple imperfections—telling not only the faults themselves but also the motives behind them. Although this method is not required for the validity of the confession, it is certain that the soul will draw much profit from it since the accusation will have exposed the root of the evil. The soul will benefit too by its act of humility, which will be a stimulus to deeper repentance and will arouse in it a more ardent desire to amend its life, for this is the logical result of considering the motives—usually not noble ones!—from which our faults arise. Furthermore, an accusation of this kind helps the confessor to have a better knowledge of the penitent's weak points, and to suggest the most suitable remedies, a matter of special importance when direction is given with confession.

In addition to its accusation, the soul must also occupy itself with sorrow for its sins because they offend God, who is infinite Goodness. This should be a sorrow *ex amore*, springing from love, the repentance of the child who is more disconsolate over the displeasure given to a father who loves it so much and to whom it should return love for love, than over the thought of its guilt and the punishment it deserves. For the validity of the sacrament, sorrow is necessary; if it is lacking, the absolution will be null. However, the more perfect the contrition, the more effectively will the absolution erase not only the sin but also the temporal punishment which it has incurred. The Blood of Jesus will purify, renew, and enrich the heart of the penitent with fortitude, charity, and grace, in the measure of his contrition.

COLLOQUY

" Sweet Jesus, in order to clothe us again with the life of grace, You stripped Yourself of the life of Your body. The body which You stretched on the wood of the holy Cross is like a lamb which has been sacrificed and which is shedding its blood from every part of its body. In Your Blood, You have created us anew to the life of grace.

" Sweet Jesus, my soul ardently desires to be bathed and entirely submerged in Your Blood ... since in Your Blood I find the source of all mercy; in Your Blood are clemency, fire, piety. In Your Blood, mercy abounds for our faults. In Your Blood, justice is satisfied and our hardness is melted; what is bitter becomes sweet and what is heavy becomes light. And since all virtues reach maturity in Your Blood, O Christ, inebriate my soul, engulf it in Your Blood, so that it will be adorned with real and solid virtues " (St. Catherine of Siena).

O Jesus, if just one drop of Your Precious Blood has the power to wipe out all the crimes of the world, what will it not do in me when You pour it so abundantly over my poor soul at the moment of absolution! O Jesus, revive my faith and give me a complete understanding of the immense value of the sacrament of Your Blood. Only Your Blood can wash away my sins, purify the stains on my soul, and heal and vivify it. Oh! grant that this salutary bath may cleanse my whole being and restore it entirely to Your grace and love!

Through the merits of Your passion, grant, O Lord, that I may always bring to the tribunal of penance a truly humble and contrite heart, an increasingly perfect sorrow for my faults, and a deeper and more sincere horror of anything that offends You, my God. Only if it finds no attachment to sin in me, will Your Precious Blood be able to penetrate the depths of my soul, renew it and vivify it wholly. O Jesus, grant that Your Precious Blood may bear its full fruit in me.

105

THE TRANSFIGURATION

SECOND SUNDAY OF LENT

PRESENCE OF GOD - O Jesus, grant that Your grace may triumph in me and make me worthy to participate in Your glorious Transfiguration!

MEDITATION

1. The soul of Jesus, personally united to the Word, enjoyed the Beatific Vision, which has as its connatural effect the glorification of the body. But this effect was impeded by Jesus, who, during the years of His life on earth, wanted to resemble us as much as possible by appearing " in the likeness of sinful flesh " (*Rom* 8,3). However, in order to confirm the faith of the Apostles who were shaken by the announcement of His Passion, Jesus permitted some rays from His blessed soul to shine forth for a few brief instants on Thabor, when Peter, James, and John saw Him transfigured : " His face did shine as the sun and His garments became white as snow. " The three were enraptured by it, and yet Jesus had revealed to them only one ray of His glory, for no human creature could have borne the complete vision.

Glory is the fruit of grace : the grace possessed by Jesus in an infinite degree is reflected in an infinite glory transfiguring Him entirely. Something similar happens to us : grace will transform us " from glory to glory " (2 *Cor* 3, 18), until one day it will bring us to the Beatific Vision of God in heaven. But while grace transfigures, sin, on the other hand, darkens and disfigures whoever becomes its victim.

Today's Gospel (*Mt* 17,1-9) brings out the close connection between the Transfiguration and the Passion of Jesus. Moses and Elias appeared on Thabor on either side of the Savior. They conversed with Him, and as St. Luke explains, talked specifically about His coming Passion : " They spoke of His decease, that He should accomplish in Jerusalem " (*Lk* 9,31).

The divine Master wished to teach His disciples in this
way that it was impossible—for Him as well as for them—to
reach the glory of the Transfiguration without passing
through suffering.   It was the same lesson that He would
give later to the two disciples at Emmaus : " Ought not
Christ to have suffered these things and so to enter into
His glory? " (*Lk* 24,26).   What has been disfigured by sin
cannot regain its original supernatural beauty except by
way of purifying suffering.

2. In ecstasy before the vision on Thabor, Peter cried
out with his usual eagerness, " It is good for us to be here, "
and offered to make three tabernacles : one for Jesus, one
for Moses, and one for Elias.   But his proposal was interrupted
by a voice from heaven : " This is My beloved Son, in
whom I am well pleased; hear ye Him! " and the vision
disappeared.
    Spiritual consolations are never an end in themselves,
and we should neither desire them nor try to retain them
for our own satisfaction.   Joy, even that which is spiritual,
should never be sought for itself.   Just as in heaven, joy
will be the necessary concomitant of possessing God, so
too on earth, it should be nothing but a means, enabling
us to give ourselves with greater generosity to the service
of God.   To Peter, who wanted to stay on Thabor in the
sweet vision of the transfigured Jesus, God Himself replied
by inviting him to listen to and follow the teachings of His
beloved Son.   The ardent Apostle would soon learn that
following Jesus meant carrying the Cross and ascending
Calvary with Him.
    God does not console us for our entertainment but
rather for our encouragement, for our strengthening, for
the increase of our generosity in suffering for love of Him.
    The vision disappeared; the Apostles raised their eyes
and saw nothing " *nisi solum Jesum*, " save Jesus alone, and with
" Jesus alone, " they came down from the mountain.   This
is what we must always seek and it must be sufficient for
us : Jesus alone, God alone.   Everything else—consolations,
helps, friendships (even spiritual ones), understanding
esteem, encouragement (even from Superiors)—may be good
to the extent that God permits us to enjoy them.   He very
often makes use of them to encourage us in our weakness;
but if, through certain circumstances, His divine hand

takes all these things away, we should not be upset or disturbed. It is precisely at such times that we can prove to God more than ever—by deeds and not by words only—that He is our *All* and that *He alone suffices*. On these occasions the loving soul finds itself in a position to give God one of the finest proofs of its love : to be faithful to Him, to trust in Him, and to persevere in its resolution to give all, even if, by removing His gifts, He has left it alone. The soul may be in darkness, that is, subject to misunderstanding, bitterness, material and spiritual solitude combined with interior desolation. The time has come to repeat, " Jesus alone, " to come down from Thabor with Him, and to follow Him with the Apostles even to Calvary, where He will suffer, abandoned not only by men, but even by His Father.

COLLOQUY

" You only do I love, my God. You only do I wish to seek and to follow; I am ready to follow You alone. I wish to be entirely at Your disposal. I beg You to order and command whatever You will, but cure me, open my eyes, that I may see Your slightest gesture. Cure me completely, that I may recognize You. Tell me which way to turn my attention in order to see You; and I hope that I shall be able to do all that You command me " (St. Augustine).

Permit me to follow you, O Jesus, not only to Thabor, but especially to Calvary. I am attracted by the light and splendor of Thabor; I want to see Your face, O my God, if only for an instant! Calvary is night, solitude, mournful sorrow which terrifies me, but in the darkness there stands a Cross on which I contemplate You, crucified for love. I glimpse Your face, not transfigured by glory, but disfigured by sorrow, the result of our sins!

O Jesus, destroy sin in me, the sin which has disfigured Your face and disfigured my soul created to Your image and likeness. But to bring about this destruction, I must share Your Calvary, Your Cross. Deign then, O Lord, to unite to Your Passion all the sufferings, little or great, of my life, that they may purify me and prepare me to rise from light to light, until I am completely transformed in You.

The light and glory of Thabor encourage me. Thank You, O Lord, for having allowed me, if only for a few moments, to contemplate Your splendor and to enjoy Your divine consolations. Fortified and encouraged by this, I come down from the mountain to follow You, *You alone*, to Calvary.

106

HUMILITY

PRESENCE OF GOD - O Jesus, You who were so humiliated for us, teach me how to practice true humility.

MEDITATION

1. Charity is the essence of Christian perfection, for charity alone has the power to unite man to God, his last end. But for us poor, miserable creatures, whom God wishes to raise to union with Himself, is charity the ultimate basis of the spiritual life? No. There is something deeper still which is, so to speak, the *basis* of charity, and that is humility. Humility is to charity what the foundation is to a building. Digging the foundation is not building the house, yet it is the preliminary, indispensable work, the condition *sine qua non*. The deeper and firmer it is, the better the house will be and the greater assurance of stability it will have. Only the fool " built his house upon the sand, " with the inevitable consequence of seeing it crumble away very soon. The wise man, on the contrary, " built...upon a rock " (*Mt* 7,24-26); storms and winds might threaten, but his house was unshakable because its foundation was solid.

Humility is the firm bedrock upon which every Christian should build the edifice of his spiritual life. " If you wish to lay good foundations, " says St. Teresa of Jesus to her daughters, " each of you must try to be the least of all " that is, you must practice humility. " If you do that...your foundation will be so firmly laid that your Castle will not fall " (cf. *Int C VII*, 4)

Humility forms the foundation of charity by emptying the soul of pride, arrogance, disordered love of self and of one's own excellence, and by replacing them with the love of God and our neighbor.

The more humility empties the soul of the vain, proud pretenses of self, the more room there will be for God. " When at last [the spiritual man] comes to be reduced to nothing, which will be the greatest extreme of humility, spiritual union will be wrought between the soul and God " (J.C. *AS II*, 7,11).

2. The soul who desires to reach the sublime heights of union with God must walk in the path of profound humility, for as the divine Master taught, only " he that humbleth himself shall be exalted " (*Lk* 18,14).

The higher the ideal of sanctity to which we aspire, the more sublime the end toward which we tend, the more we will have to descend and excavate in ourselves the fertile abyss of humility. " *Abyssus abyssum invocat* " (*Ps* 41,8); the abyss of humility calls to the abyss of infinite mercy, of grace and of the divine gifts, for " God resisteth the proud, but to the humble He giveth grace " (1 *Pt* 5,5). We must humble ourselves therefore under the mighty hand of God, sincerely recognize our nothingness, take account of our poverty; and if we wish to glorify ourselves, we must glory, like St. Paul, solely in our infirmities. It is only in our weakness, humbly acknowledged, that grace and divine virtue work and triumph (cf. 2 *Cor* 12,9). Even if we are of the number of those good souls who sincerely desire to advance on the road to perfection, but who are relying too much on their own powers and personal initiative, we can apply to ourselves to great advantage the valuable warning that St. Thérèse of the Child Jesus gave a novice : " I see clearly that you are taking the wrong road; you will never reach the end of your journey. You want to scale a mountain, and the good God wills to make you descend.... It is Jesus who takes upon Himself to fill your soul according as you rid it of imperfections " *(C)*.

The sublime ideal of union with God totally exceeds our capacities, which are those of weak creatures. If we aspire to it, it is not because we expect to reach it by our own efforts and initiative, but because we trust that God Himself, according to His promise, will come and lead us by the hand. But God will not act thus with a proud

soul. He stoops only to the humble; the more lowly He
finds a soul, the closer He draws it to Himself. Humility
deepens the soul's capacity to receive the fullness of divine gifts.

COLLOQUY

"O my God, You make me realize how far I must
descend in order that my heart may serve as a dwelling-place
for You : I must become so poor that I have no place whereon
to lay my head. My heart is not wholly emptied of self,
and that is why You order me to descend. Oh! I want to
descend much lower, so that You will be able to rest Your
divine head in my heart and know that there You are
loved and understood. O sweet, divine Guest, You know
my misery; that is why You come to me in the hope of
finding an *empty tabernacle*, a heart wholly emptied of self.
This is all You ask " (cf. T.C.J. *L*).

O Lord, help me to excavate in my poor soul that abyss
of humility which will attract the abyss of Your infinite
mercies. Help me to descend, although my pride seeks
to rise. Help me to recognize and humbly confess my
nothingness and my weakness, although my pride desires
so much to have me esteemed as something great. Help
me to glory in my infirmities, although my pride always
tends to glory in what is not mine, but Your free gift. How
true it is, O God, that grace follows an entirely different
road from that of nature! Give me the strength to travel
on this way with courage, to swim against the current,
the muddy, treacherous current of my pride. How can
I succeed if You do not come to help me? But I trust in You,
Lord, because I know that You are always ready to uphold
the weak who have recourse to You with trust; because
I know that, if my pride is great, Your mercy is infinite and
Your omnipotence is invincible; because I know that if
" anyone is an inactive man that wants help, is very weak in
ability and full of poverty, Your eye looks upon him for
good, and lifts him up from his low estate and exalts his
head " (cf. *Sir* 11,12.13).

O Lord, who is more " full of poverty " than I, who
have not yet conquered my pride? Who then is in greater
need of Your help?

107

OUR PLACE

PRESENCE OF GOD - O my God, help me to know You and to know myself! I know that You are He who is, and I am he who is not!

MEDITATION

1. Among all the creatures in which we take pleasure and toward which our nature seems to be attracted the most, *self* undoubtedly holds the first place. There is no one, no matter how limited in talents and good qualities, who does not love his own excellence, and who does not try, in one way or another, to make it shine forth to himself and to others. It is for this reason that we often spontaneously exaggerate our own worth, and as a result are demanding and pretentious. This makes us haughty and arrogant, as well as difficult in our relations with others. Humility is the virtue which keeps within just limits the love of one's own excellence. Whereas self-esteem often induces us to make ourselves too evident, or to occupy a place which is higher than our due, humility keeps us *in our own place*. Humility is truth : it tends to establish in truth both our intellect—by making us know ourselves as we really are—and our life, by inclining us to take, in relation to God and to men, our proper place and no other.

Humility makes us realize that, in the sight of God, we are only His little creature, entirely dependent upon Him for our existence and for all our works. Having received life from God, we cannot subsist even one moment independently of Him. He who gave us existence by His creative action, maintains life in us by His conserving action. In addition we cannot perform the slightest act without God's cooperation, in the same way that a machine—even a perfect one—cannot make any motion until it is started by the one who made it. It is very true that, unlike the machine, our acts are neither mechanical nor compulsory, but are conscious and free; yet, we cannot move even a finger without the concurrence of the divine Artist.

It follows then that everything we possess in the order of being—qualities, gifts, capacities—and everything we have accomplished in the order of action, is not ours, but all, in one way or another, are gifts of God, all are acts performed with God's help. " What hast thou that thou hast not received? And if thou hast received it, why dost thou glory, as if thou hadst not received it? " (1 Cor 4,7).

2. In the supernatural order, where everything depends on grace, the words of Jesus, " Without Me you can do nothing " (Jn 15,5), are more strictly verified. Although in Baptism, sanctifying grace raised us to the supernatural order, and the infused virtues made us capable of producing supernatural acts, still St. Paul says : " No man can say the Lord Jesus, but by the Holy Ghost " (1 Cor 12,3). In order to perform even the tiniest supernatural act we need God's help; we need actual grace which prevents us by its inspirations and accompanies us in the act until it is accomplished.

The great theologian, who has profoundly studied Catholic doctrine, has as absolute a need of actual grace in order to put into practice the most insignificant point of Catholic doctrine or to produce a single act of the love of God as does the peasant who knows nothing beyond his catechism. Even a saint, one who has received so many favors and divine lights and has attained to heroic virtue, cannot perform the smallest virtuous act without the help of actual grace. How total then must be our dependence upon God! We are very far from the truth if, trusting in our own knowledge or long practice in the spiritual life, we believe that our lights or our virtues are sufficient to make us act like good Christians. No, St. Paul warns us : " sufficientia nostra ex Deo est, " our sufficiency is from God (2 Cor 3,5). Without God we cannot think, or speak, or desire any good, " for it is God who worketh in you both to will and to accomplish, according to His good will " (Phil 2,13).

Of ourselves, then, we have only the one capacity which belongs to our limited nature, injured by original sin : the capacity to fail in our duties and to sin. If we take away from ourselves what is of God, we will find that of ourselves we are nothing, or rather less than nothing, for nothingness is incapable of offending God, while we have this sad capability.

COLLOQUY

"O omnipotent Father, God of truth, God of love, permit me to enter into the cell of self-knowledge. I admit that of myself I am nothing, but that all the being and goodness in me comes solely from You. Show me my faults, that I may detest my malice, and thus I shall flee from self-love and find myself clothed again in the nuptial robe of divine charity, which I must have in order to be admitted to the nuptials of life eternal" (St. Catherine of Siena).

"Give me, O my God, a thorough knowledge of myself! Let me be really convinced that I am nothing and that You are everything! Do not let me think that I am anything more than the nothing I am. Let me do nothing more for myself, but all for You! Grant that no creature may think any more about me, do anything more for me, give me anything more, but let all be done for You and given to You. And may my nothingness be reduced to nothing in the eyes of all creatures and in Yours, my God, that You, the All, may be all, in all and through all" (St. John Eudes).

Reveal my nothingness to me, O Lord, reveal it so well that, not only shall I understand it, but I shall also have a practical, profound conviction of it. You know how painful that is to my proud nature! My intellect cannot resist the evidence of truth and is obliged to admit that I am nothing, have nothing, and can do nothing without You, yet my ego is always trying to attribute something to itself, to take the credit for this or that and to take as much pleasure in it as if it were its own. Help me, O Lord, to triumph over this pride which, as You see, steals Your gifts and makes my life sterile by preventing me from receiving the abundance of Your graces.

Grant that I may know my nothingness, O Lord, for the more I recognize it with simplicity and humility of heart, the more You will take pleasure in being my All—You are All, I am nothing; You, He who is and I, he who is not! Glorify Yourself then in my nothingness! May Your love and grace triumph in this nothing, but may Your mercy also triumph, for I am a nothing which has sinned. *Peccavi, Domine, miserere mei!*

108

HUMILITY AND CONFIDENCE

PRESENCE OF GOD - Out of the depths of my misery I have cried to Thee, O Lord; Lord, hear my voice.... I trust in Thee.

MEDITATION

1. Christian humility does not lower, it elevates; it does not cast down, but gives courage, for the more it reveals to the soul its nothingness and abjection, the more it moves it toward God with confidence and abandonment. The very fact that in everything—in essence as in act, in the natural as in the supernatural order—we depend on Him, and that we can do nothing without Him, shows us that God wants to sustain us continually by His help and His grace. Consequently, the relations of a humble soul with God will be those of a child who confidently expects everything from its father. This is the lesson that Jesus wished to give His Apostles when they asked Him who would be the greatest in the kingdom of heaven : " Amen, I say to you, unless you be converted and become as little children, you shall not enter into the kingdom of heaven. Whosoever therefore shall humble himself as this little child, he is the greater in the kingdom of heaven " (*Mt* 18,3.4). " To remain little, " explains St. Thérèse of the Child Jesus, " is to acknowledge one's nothingness and to expect everything from the good God, as the child expects everything from its father.... Even among the poor, a child, while he is very little, is given everything that is necessary, but when he has grown, his father no longer wants to support him, and says ' Go to work now! You can rely on yourself. ' It is that I might never hear those words that I never wanted to grow up, because I felt incapable of earning my own living : *eternal life* " (*NV*).

To the soul who humbly acknowledges its poverty and turns toward God with complete confidence, He is a very tender Father who delights in showering His gifts upon it and in doing for it what it cannot accomplish by itself. Then the smallest soul—that is, the one most thoroughly convinced of its own nothingness—becomes the greatest, since it has the greatness of God Himself at its command.

2. God does not introduce a soul to a higher spiritual life, nor admit it to deeper intimacy with Himself, as long as it is not completely despoiled of all confidence in itself. When a soul practically forgets its nothingness, and still relies on its own strength, knowledge, initiative, or virtues—be it ever so little—God leaves it to itself. The failures which follow, the falls, the fruitlessness of its works—all reveal its insufficiency; and the more a soul insists upon trusting in itself, so much the more will the Lord prolong this experience of its nothingness.

In speaking of her definite, total conversion, St. Teresa of Jesus confesses that what prevented her from overcoming the last obstacles was really a remnant of confidence which she still had in herself. " I must have failed to put my whole confidence in His Majesty and to have a complete distrust of myself" (*Life*, 8). Confidence in God increases in proportion to our mistrust of ourselves; it becomes total when the soul, having acquired a thorough comprehension of its nothingness, has lost all faith in its own resources. The soul then realizes the truth of Jesus' words : " When you shall have done all these things that are commanded you, say : We are unprofitable servants " (*Lk* 17,10). Even if the soul has had much experience in the interior life, in prayer and in virtue, it knows that it cannot rely on its own strength at all. It realizes that even if it has worked for the glory of God, it cannot depend on its own works; hence it will rely wholly and solely on God's mercy and grace : *Non habeo fiduciam nisi in tua misericordia*. All its confidence rests on the infinite merits of Jesus, on the merciful love of the heavenly Father and on the workings of grace; and this confidence makes it more courageous, more daring than ever, because it knows that with God it can do everything.

" What pleases Jesus, " says the Saint of Lisieux, " is to see me love my littleness and poverty, the blind hope that I have in His mercy. This is my only treasure " *(L)*.

COLLOQUY

"I admit, O Lord, that I am very weak; I have salutary proof of it every day. But You deign to teach me the knowledge which makes me glory in my infirmities. This is a very great grace, and only in it do I find peace and contentment of heart, for now I understand Your ways : You give as God, but You want humility of heart " (T.C.J. L).

O Lord, Your light penetrates my soul and makes me understand how far from Your ways are mine! Instead of being disturbed on account of my miseries and discouraged by my falls and failures, instead of pretending to succeed in everything and to accomplish great things, I must humbly accept the fact that I am weak, needy, and absolutely unable to get along without Your help.

How sweet it is, O my God, for a soul who loves You, to need You so much that it can do nothing without You! It is sweet for me, for in this way I learn that You wish constantly to take part in my poor life, that You want to sustain me always by Your grace, and that You will never of Yourself abandon me. To give me the fullness of Your divine help, You are only waiting for me to come before You with the humble, trusting attitude of a child who, not being able to rely on his own strength and resources, expects everything from his father. You wish me to be thoroughly convinced of my nothingness and to accept with love the fact that I am nothing so that You may be my All.

Deprive me, O Lord, of every remnant of confidence in myself. Every man is like the grass of the field which springs up today and tomorrow is not, and what greater foolishness is there than to rely on the strength of a blade of grass! Free me, O Lord, from such stupidity and place me, I beg of You, in the way of truth. O You who are Truth, sanctify me in the Truth, in the truth of my nothingness.

You alone are good, my God, and You alone can make me good. You alone are just and You alone can justify me. You alone are holy and You alone can make me holy. The less I expect from myself, the more I can and will expect from You : good-will and constancy, strength and patience, purity and goodness, virtue and sanctity. Hasten, O Lord, to come to my aid! My nothingness implores You, my misery sighs for You!

109

HUMILITY IN OUR FALLS

PRESENCE OF GOD - " I am a beggar and poor, but the Lord is careful for me. In the shadow of Thy wings will I hope " (*Ps* 39,18 – 56,2).

MEDITATION

1. If we contemplate our misery without raising our eyes to God, the Father of mercies, we will easily become discouraged. By examining ourselves thoroughly, we will see that discouragement always comes from two closely related causes. The first is that we depend upon our own strength; through it our pride is wounded and deceived when we fall. The second is that we lack reliance on God; we do not think of referring to Him in times of prosperity, nor do we have recourse to Him when we fail Him. In short, we act by ourselves : we try to succeed alone, we fall alone, and alone we contemplate our fall. The result of such conduct can only be discouragement. Indeed, how could we expect to find in ourselves the strength to rise again, when it was our very want of strength that made us fall? God does not want us to act by ourselves. " Woe to him that is alone, " says Sacred Scripture, " for when he falleth, he hath none to lift him up " (*Eccl* 4,10). Woe to him who relies only on his own strength to put his good resolutions into execution. When he falls, he will not have the aid of God's might to lift him up; thus he will remain in his misery, confused and discouraged.

Just as we should not make good resolutions without counting on God's help to keep them, by the same token we should not view our failures without considering God's mercy at the same time, for as God is the only One who can help us persevere in good, so He alone can raise us up from evil.

That is why all the saints have taught that the knowledge of oneself must never be separated from the knowledge of God and vice versa. St. Teresa of Jesus says, " The soul must sometimes emerge from self-knowledge and soar aloft in meditation upon the greatness and the majesty of its God. Doing this will help it to realize its own baseness better than thinking of its own nature, and it will be freer from the reptiles which enter the first rooms, that is, the rooms of self-knowledge " (*Int C I*, 2).

2. " True humility, however deep it may be, neither disquiets, nor troubles, nor disturbs the soul; it is accompanied by peace, joy, and tranquility.... It enlarges it, and makes it fit to serve God better. " On the other hand, " false humility only disturbs and upsets the mind and troubles the soul, so grievous is it. I think the devil is anxious for us to believe that we are humble and, if he can, he will lead us to distrust God " (T.J. *Way*, 39).

Distress and lack of confidence lessen our capacity for loving and the devil's aim is to hold back souls on the road to love. He tries in this way to overcome those especially who would never give in to open temptations to sin. In this case we must react in a positive way and recall, as St. Thérèse of the Child Jesus teaches, that " what offends God and wounds His heart most is want of confidence " *(L)*.

To be wanting in confidence in God's mercy, even after a grave fall, is never a sign of true humility but of insidious pride and diabolical temptation. If Judas had been humble he would have asked pardon and wept for his sins like Peter, instead of despairing. Humility is the virtue which keeps us in our place; and our place in God's sight is that of children who are weak and miserable, yes, but confident children.

When we fall into the same imperfections after so many good resolutions; when after many efforts we still do not succeed in correcting certain faults or in overcoming certain difficulties, and we find ourselves in one way or another far beneath what we ought or would like to be, let us have recourse to the infallible remedy of humility. " Humility, " says St. Teresa of Jesus is " the ointment for our wounds " (*Int C III*, 2). Even if we seem to have used up all our strength, if we feel unable to do anything and see ourselves always prostrate, powerless to rise, there is still one possibility for us : to humble ourselves. Let us humble ourselves sincerely and with confidence; and humility will supply for all our miseries; it will heal all our wounds because it will attract divine mercy to them.

COLLOQUY

O Lord, my misery " does not surprise me. Nor does my utter helplessness distress me. I even glory in it, and expect every day to reveal some fresh imperfection. Indeed these lights on my nothingness do me more good than lights on matters of faith.

" What an illusion!.... We wish never to fall? What difference does it make, O Lord, if I fall at every instant? It will make me realize my weakness and I shall derive great profit from it. You see what I am capable of, O my God, and so You will be obliged to carry me in Your arms. If You do not do so, it will mean that You are pleased to see me on the ground...but I shall not be disturbed. Full of love, I shall always lift up my suppliant arms to You. I cannot believe that You will abandon me.

" O Jesus, it is true that I am not always faithful, but I never become discouraged, I cast myself into Your arms, and like a little dewdrop, I sink deeper and deeper into Your chalice, O divine Flower of the field, and there I find all I have lost and much more besides.

" Yes, O my God, I am happy to feel little and weak in Your presence, and my heart remains in peace.... I am glad to feel so imperfect and to need Your mercy so much! When we calmly accept the humiliation of being imperfect, Your grace, O Lord, returns at once " (T.C.J. *St – L – NV*).

110

HUMILIATIONS

PRESENCE OF GOD - O Jesus, humbled to abjection for me, teach me to humble myself for love of You.

MEDITATION

1. Many souls would like to be humble, but few desire humiliation; many ask God to make them humble and fervently pray for this, but very few want to be humiliated.

Yet is is impossible to gain humility without humiliations;
for just as studying is the way to acquire knowledge, so it
is by the way of humiliation that we attain to humility.

As long as we only desire this virtue of humility, but
are not willing to accept the means thereto, are we not
even on the true road to acquiring it. Even if in certain
situations we succeed in acting humbly, this may well be
the result of a superficial and apparent humility rather
than of a humility that is real and profound. Humility
is truth; therefore, let us tell ourselves that since we possess
nothing of ourselves but sin, it is but just that we receive only
humiliation and scorn. If we were really convinced of
this truth, we would find it very just that all should humiliate
us, treat us without consideration, and despise us. In
fact, what honor and consideration does one deserve who
has offended his Creator, when a single sin—even a venial
one—is more deplorable and worthy of more contempt
than the most miserable earthly condition, the poorest
and lowest estate? The saints were so firmly convinced
of this truth that they never found the humiliations which
came to them too painful; they considered them, on the
contrary, always less than they deserved. " I never heard
anything bad said of me, " said St. Teresa of Jesus, " which
I did not clearly realize fell short of the truth. If I had
not sometimes—often, indeed—offended God in the ways
they referred to, I had done so in many others, and I felt
they had treated me far too indulgently in saying nothing
about these " (*Way*, 15).

Bear your humiliations patiently, for man is tried
in this crucible as gold in the fire (cf. *Sir* 2,4.5). If we
feel the weight of our pride and wish to be rid of it, we must
accept humiliations calmly—through them the Lord will
crush our pride.

2. Before seeking humiliations on our own initiative,
we should prepare to accept those which will come to us
against our will. Whereas subtle pride might work its
way into the lowly acts we impose upon ourselves—for
example, the desire to appear humble—this danger is absolutely excluded from those which come from others in
spite of ourselves. However, even in this case they must
be willingly accepted in order to bear fruit. It is not the
humiliation itself which makes us humble, but the act

of the will by which we accept it. St. Bernard teaches that being humble and being humbled are two different things. We can say that everyone, in one way or another, receives humiliations in this life. Not many, however, become humble because very few accept humiliation and submit to it patiently.

What profit do we draw from humiliations, if instead of accepting them, we oppose and resist them with resentment and vexation and become angry with the person who gives them to us?

It is true that these occasions are not agreeable to proud, sensitive nature; nevertheless, although we feel their bitterness, we must force ourselves to accept them graciously, making the words of the Psalmist our own : " It is good for me that Thou hast humbled me. " If, in spite of all the repugnance and resistance of nature, we accept a humiliation by an act of the will, and assure God that we want to be content with it and to savor it thoroughly, we will gradually become humble. The hard, bitter bread of abasement will become, little by little, sweet and pleasant, but we will not find it agreeable until we have been nourished by it for a long time. Moreover, the most important thing is not the sweetness, but the willingness to accept everything that is humiliating. " Allow thyself to be taught, allow thyself to be commanded, allow thyself to be enslaved and brought into submission and despised, and thou shalt be perfect! " (J.C. *SM II*, 33).

COLLOQUY

" O Lord, how can a person like me, who deserves to be tortured by demons for eternity, be insulted? If I am badly treated in this world, is it not just? Really, Lord, I have nothing to offer You in this regard.... I know that I am so guilty in Your eyes that I feel that those who insult me are treating me too well, although they think they are offending me, not knowing me as well as You do " (T.J. *Way*, 36).

How true it is, O God, that the only thing that I, a sinner, receive by right is humiliation, insults, scorn. And yet, how troubled and excessively sensitive I am when anything hurts my pride; You know, O my God, how much I wish to get rid of this propensity. I can truthfully say that with the help of Your grace I detest it, and that nothing is more hateful to me. Nevertheless, I have not the strength to accept the remedy You offer me. How shall I have the courage, Lord, to ask You for humiliations, when I have rejected them so often, changing them from medicine into occasions for new acts of pride?

Instead of seeing in humiliations the remedy You provide to cure my pride, how many times have I looked only at the creatures You used to humble me, and irritated by them, I have been indignant and rebellious, as if treated unjustly. How blind I am, O Lord, how far have I wandered from Your ways! Come to bring the light again into my soul, come to place me in the truth, come to set my feet anew on the good, safe way of humiliation.

I do not ask You for particular humiliations, but I do ask You to dispose my heart to accept those which, in Your infinite love and mercy, You have prepared for me from all eternity. In them, I see Your remedy, adapted to my pride; if up to the present I have often refused to taste it, help me now not to lose the smallest drop of it. I am ill, O Lord, and like the patient who wants the medicine which will cure him and who swallows it, bitter though it be, I too, with the help of Your grace, wish to accept and to drink to the very dregs every humiliation. But help me, O sweet Jesus, You who willed to know every form of abasement, for without You I shall only fail in my good resolutions.

III

HUMILITY OF HEART

PRESENCE OF GOD - O Jesus, meek and humble of heart, make my heart like unto Thine.

MEDITATION

1. Jesus expressed Himself only once in these words : " Learn of Me," and this was when He was speaking of humility. " Learn of Me, for I am meek and humble

of heart " (*Mt* 11,29). Knowing how much the practice of real humility would cost our proud nature, He seemed to want to give us special encouragement. The example He gave in the extraordinary humiliations which made Him " the reproach of men, and the outcast of the people " (*Ps* 21,7), those humiliations by which, out of love for men, He was " made sin " (2 *Cor* 5,21) and the bearer of all our iniquities, even to being " reputed with the wicked " (*Mk* 15,28), is certainly the strongest stimulus and the most urgent invitation to the practice of humility.

Jesus speaks directly to us about humility of heart, because every virtue, every reform of life, if it is to be sincere, must come from the heart, whence come our thoughts and our actions. The exterior attitude and the humility of our words are useless unless accompanied by lowliness of heart; many times they are but the mask of a refined—and therefore all the more dangerous—pride. " First make clean the inside, " said Jesus when He was branding the Pharisees' hypocrisy, " that the outside may become clean " (*Mt* 23,26). St. Thomas teaches that " an interior disposition to humility puts its seal upon the words, gestures, and acts, by means of which that which is hidden within is manifested on the outside " (II^a II^ae, q.161, a.6).

Therefore, to be truly humble, we must apply ourselves first of all to humility of heart and continue to deepen the sincere recognition of our nothingness, of our weakness. Let us acknowledge our faults and failings without trying to assign any other case for them than our misery; let us recognize the good that is in us as a pure gift of God and never claim it for our own.

2. Humility of heart is a virtue which is at the same time both difficult and easy. It involves hardship because it is totally opposed to pride, which is always urging us to exalt ourselves; it is easy because we do not have to look very far to find grounds for it; we find them—and how abundantly—in ourselves, in our own misery. However, it does not suffice to be wretched in order to be humble—only he is humble who sincerely acknowledges his own unworthiness and acts accordingly.

Man, proud by nature, cannot reach this acknowledgment without God's grace, but since God never refuses necessary grace to anyone, we have only to turn to Him

and ask Him with confidence and perseverance for humility
of heart.   Let us ask for it in the Name of Jesus who humbled
Himself so much for the glory of His Father and for our
salvation; " ask for it in His Name, and you will receive it "
(cf. *Jn* 16,24).   If in spite of our sincere desire to become
humble, movements of pride, vain glory, or idle complacency
arise in us, we must not become discouraged, but know and
admit that they are the fruit of our fallen nature and use
them as a new motive for abasing ourselves.

We should remember that we can practice humility of
heart, even when we are not able to perform special exterior
acts of humility, even when no one humiliates us and we
are, on the contrary, the object of confidence, esteem, and
praise.   St. Thérèse of the Child Jesus said in like circumstances : " The remembrance of my weakness is so constantly
present to me that there is no room for vanity " (*St*, 11).
Let us remember, then, that " reproaches do not make
us more guilty, and neither does praise add anything to
our holiness " (*Imit. II*, 6,3).   We must humble ourselves
within, the more we are praised by others.   If humility
of heart is practiced in this way, it will give us such a low
opinion of ourselves that we will not be able to prefer ourselves
to anyone; we will consider others better and more worthy
of esteem, respect, and consideration than we are.   Thus
we will be in peace, undisturbed by the desire to be better
than others, undisturbed by the humiliations which may
come to us.   The fruit of humility is interior peace, for
Jesus has said : " Learn of Me, for I am meek and
humble of heart, and you shall find rest to your souls "
(*Mt* 11,29).

COLLOQUY

O Jesus, meek and humble of heart, cure me of my
pride, make my heart humble, infuse a little of Your profound
humility into my soul.   Since You know me better than I
know myself, how could I, with my proud will, make my
heart humble?   A poor man cannot give wealth to himself,
nor can a proud man give humility to his heart.   Only
Your infinite goodness can heal pride.

" This is the remedy to fix my gaze on You, Incarnate
Word, hanging on the Cross.   As soon as You see a humble

soul looking at You in this way, You are quickly moved to look at it, and the effect of Your divine glance is like that of a ray of sunshine on the earth : it warms it and prepares it to bring forth fruit.   This is the way You act, O divine Word, who by the light of Your glance, drain my soul of all its pride, and consume it in Your fire.   No one can acquire humility if he does not fix his gaze on You, O Word, on the Cross " (St. Mary Magdalen dei Pazzi).

   " O divine Word, You humbled Yourself even unto death and willed to be treated as the least of men by sinners, by demons, and even by the Holy Spirit and by Your eternal Father.   You did all this to glorify Your Father, to make reparation for the offenses committed against Him by our pride, to confound and destroy our arrogance and to teach us to detest vanity and to love humility.   Oh! how truly can we see that pride dishonors God and is very displeasing to Him, since it was necessary for You, the Son of God, to be so humiliated in order to atone for such dishonor! We can truly say also that vanity is a monstrous thing, since in order to destroy it, You were willing to be reduced to such humiliation!   Oh! how firmly must we believe that in the eyes of God humility is an infinitely precious treasure and a jewel most pleasing to Him, since You, His divine Son, willed to be so humiliated to make us love this virtue, and to urge us to imitate You in the practice of it, and thus merit the grace to perform its works! " (St. John Eudes).

112

THE POWER OF JESUS

THIRD SUNDAY OF LENT

PRESENCE OF GOD - O Jesus, divine Strength, I come to You to seek support for my weakness, and infirmity.

MEDITATION

   1. On the first Sunday in Lent, the Church showed us Jesus in His struggle with the devil, but while she presented

Him to us then in an attitude of humble defense before the devil's temptations, today we see Him in an attitude of attack which culminates in a glorious victory.

The Gospel (*Lk* 11,14-28) tells us that there was a poor man possessed by the devil and he " was dumb. " By a single act of His divine power Jesus " cast out the devil, " and when he went out, " the dumb spoke, and the multitudes were in admiration at it. " But the enemy, as if to avenge his defeat, insinuates into the minds of the Pharisees the shameful calumny : " He casteth out devils by Beelzebub, the prince of devils. " Jesus is accused of being possessed by the devil and of having received from the devil power to free the possessed man. Our Lord, however, wills to completely unmask the enemy and with clear logic replies that Satan cannot give Him such power, because thereby Satan himself would be helping to destroy his own kingdom. No, it cannot be so : Jesus drives out devils by " the finger of God, " by divine virtue. If Satan is powerful and his satellites join with him in the struggle to rule over man, Jesus is still more powerful and will overcome him and snatch away his prey. He has come to destroy the kingdom of Satan and to establish the kingdom of God.

If in these days God still permits the devil to carry on his evil work against individuals and society, Jesus by His death on the Cross has already paid the price of our victory. This treasure is at our disposal. Through the virtue and grace of Christ, every Christian has the power to overcome the enemy's attacks. The triumph of evil should not disturb us, for it is only an apparent victory. The might of Jesus is stronger and He is the one and only victor.

2. We must work in union with Jesus that His victory over evil may be our own. In today's Gospel the Master Himself shows us several aspects of this collaboration.

" Every kingdom divided against itself shall be brought to desolation "; in these words Our Lord tells us that union is the secret of victory—union with Him above all, for without Him we can do nothing, but also union with our neighbor. If we would work for the triumph of good, let us collaborate — one heart and one soul — with our superiors and our fellow religious. We can often labor with much more efficacy in achieving good if we give up our own personal ideas and act in perfect harmony with others. It may even be necessary sometimes to renounce opinions, plans, and ways which are better in themselves. Let us not be deceived; unity is always to be preferred. Division never leads to victory.

" He that is not with Me is against Me, " Jesus adds. Christianity does not tolerate indifference. He who is not firmly on Christ's side, working with Him for the extension of His kingdom, by this very fact is opposed to Him and to what is good. He is an enemy of Christ and a partisan of evil. To omit the good one could do and ought to do is evil, and is consenting to the extension of evil.

The first condition necessary for victory over evil is active cooperation in the work of Christ in union with our brethren. The second condition is vigilance. Jesus warns us that the enemy of good is lying in wait. Even after he leaves a soul, he is ready to return, more powerful than before, " with seven other spirits more wicked than himself " if he finds the soul empty and open to his snares. To halt the approach of evil we must watch in prayer, filling our heart with God so that there will be no place in it for the enemy. And there is no place when the soul is wholly united to God through the acceptance and observance of His word, of His will. In fact, Jesus answered to the woman who praised His Mother : " Yea rather, blessed are they who hear the word of God and keep it. " Of course, the Virgin Mary is blessed because she gave birth to the Redeemer, but she is still more blessed through her perfect union with Him in the observance of His word. This blessedness is not reserved for Mary alone; it is offered to every soul of good will and constitutes the greatest guarantee of victory over evil, for one united to God becomes strong with His strength.

COLLOQUY

" My eyes are ever toward the Lord, for He shall pluck my feet out of the snare. Look Thou upon me, and have mercy on me; for I am alone and poor. Keep Thou my soul and deliver me : I shall not be ashamed, for I have hoped in Thee " (Ps 24,15-20).

" O eternal Trinity, O most high and eternal Trinity, You give us the Word, full of sweetness and love. O sweet and loving Word, Son of God, if our nature is weak and capable of every evil, Yours is strong and disposed to good, because You have received it from Your eternal, all-powerful Father. O sweet Word, You have strengthened our weak nature by uniting it to Yourself. Our nature is fortified by this union, for the power of Your Blood takes away our weakness. We are also strengthened by Your doctrine, for he who follows it in truth, perfectly clothing himself with it, becomes so strong and capable of good, that he loses, as it were, the rebellion of the flesh against the spirit and can overcome every evil. So You, O eternal Word, substituted for our human weakness the strength of Your divine nature which You received from the Father; and this strength You have given to us by Your Blood and Your doctrine.

"O sweet Blood, You fortify and illumine the soul; in You it becomes angelic, because You cover it with the fire of Your charity so that it forgets itself entirely and can no longer see anything except You.

"O divine Truth, You give so much strength to the soul which clothes itself with You, that it never falters under the weight of adversity or beneath the burden of troubles and temptations, but in every struggle it gains a great victory. I am wretched because I have not followed You, O eternal Truth; hence I am so weak that in every least tribulation I fall" (St. Catherine of Siena).

113

THE LOWEST PLACE

PRESENCE OF GOD - O Jesus, You who said, " The Son of man is not come to be ministered unto, but to minister " (*Mt* 20,28), teach me to love the lowest place.

MEDITATION

1. Jesus has proved to us not only in words, but also by example, that He came not to be ministered unto but to minister. This example He gave on the eve of His Passion,

as if to leave it to us as a testament, together with His last and most precious instructions. Before instituting the Holy Eucharist, Jesus like a common slave, " began to wash the feet of the disciples, " and when He had finished, said : " I have given you an example, that as I have done to you, so you do also, " for " the servant is not greater than his lord; neither is the apostle greater than He that sent him " (*Jn* 13,15.16). The instruction is clear : to be true disciples of Jesus, we must humble ourselves as He did. Note that here it is not only a question of humbling ourselves before God, but also before our neighbor. To consider ourselves servants in our relations with God is not difficult, but to do so in dealing with others will call for real effort. It is harder still to let ourselves be treated like servants without any attention or consideration, and even by those who are our inferiors. Yet Jesus, infinitely superior to all, willed to be treated not only as a servant, but as a slave and even as a malefactor.

Just as humility makes us recognize our place of inferiority and absolute dependence before God, so too does it assign us to the " lowest place " in relation to our neighbor. " Woe to you, because you love the uppermost seats in the synagogues " (*Lk* 11,43), said Jesus to the Pharisees, condemning their desire for the first places, for honorable duties and positions, and He added, " When thou art invited, go, sit down in the lowest place " (*Lk* 14,10). As far as we are able, wherever we are, we must seek the last place doing so with such simplicity and naturalness that no one who notices us will come and invite us to go up to the first place. We must expect that invitation only from God, and not in this life but in the next.

2. At the Last Supper, Jesus wanted to give the Apostles a further lesson in humility. While they were arguing about which of them should be considered the greater, He warned them : " He that is the greater among you, let him become as the younger; and he that is the leader, as he that serveth, " since I also " am in the midst of you as he that serveth " (*Lk* 22,26.27). Whenever Jesus speaks of our relations with our neighbor, He always insists that each of us should take the place of him who ministers, considering himself the servant of the others. When He showed them a little child as a model of perfection He said, " If any man

desire to be first, he shall be the last of all, and the minister of all " (*Mk* 9,34). This teaching He repeated when He put His disciples on guard, lest they imitate the proud attitude of the Pharisees : " He that is the greatest among you shall be your servant " (*Mt* 23,11). The idea is clear : for those who follow Christ the privileged place of honor is that of servant, and the divine Master insists that those who occupy important positions must be the most zealous to become the servants of all.

If we hold some authority, we must remember that it has been given not to honor us, but for the service of others. If we are not elevated above the common level, we should do nothing to exalt ourselves to a prominent position. Finally, if our status is an inferior one, we should occupy it gladly, never attempting to leave it. By assigning us to a lowly position, God Himself has taken care to make us practice humility, and this is one of the greatest graces He has given us. Let us try to correspond to it by exercising this virtue faithfully.

" The only thing for which you will not be envied, " said St. Thérèse of the Child Jesus, " is the lowest place; therefore, the lowest place is the only one where there is no vanity and affliction of spirit " *(C)*.

COLLOQUY

" O Lord, when You were a pilgrim here below, You said, ' Learn of Me, for I am meek and humble of heart, and you will find rest for your souls. ' My soul finds its rest in seeing You, the powerful Monarch of the Heavens, clothed in the form and nature of a slave, humbling Yourself to wash the feet of Your Apostles. Then I recall the words You spoke to teach me how to practice humility : ' I have given you an example, that as I have done to you, so you do also.... The servant is not greater than his lord.... If you know these things, you shall be blessed if you do them ' (*Jn* 13,15-17). With the help of Your grace, O Lord, I understand these words which came from Your gentle, humble heart; and with the help of Your grace I wish to put them into practice. " I want to abase myself humbly and submit my will to others, not contradicting them nor asking if they have the right to give me orders. No one had this right over You and yet You were obedient, not only to the Blessed Virgin and St. Joseph but even to Your executioners.

"O Lord, You could not humble Yourself any more in order to teach me humility. That is why I want to respond to Your love by putting myself in the lowest place and by sharing Your humiliations, so as to be able to share the kingdom of heaven with You hereafter. I beg You, divine Jesus, send me a humiliation every time I try to put myself above others. But Lord, You know my weakness; every morning I make a resolution to practice humility, and every evening I acknowledge that I still have many failures. I am tempted to be discouraged by this, but I know that discouragement also has its source in pride. That is why I prefer to put my trust in You alone, O my God. Since You are all-powerful, deign to create in my soul the virtue for which I long " (T.C.J.).

114

THE HIDDEN LIFE

PRESENCE OF GOD - O Jesus, hidden God, teach me the secret of the hidden life.

MEDITATION

1. During His life on earth, Jesus chose to conceal His divinity under the veil of His humanity. Except on very rare occasions—and this is especially true during the thirty years preceding His apostolate—He never allowed His greatness, His wisdom, or His omnipotence to be manifest. Later, during the years of His public life, He willed to adapt Himself to the Apostles' imperfect way of living and acting, He who was infinitely superior to them. Jesus is truly the hidden God and teaches us by His example the value of the hidden life.

To imitate Jesus' humility perfectly, we must share in His hidden life, veiling, as He did, everything, in us that might attract attention or praise from others, whatever might single us out or make us noticed, fleeing as far as we are able from every mark of distinction. " *Ama nesciri et pro nihilo reputare,* " love to live unknown and reputed as nothing (*Imit.* I, 2,3); by doing this we will become more like Jesus who, being God, willed to take " the form of a servant, being made in the likeness of men, and in habit found as a man " (*Phil* 2,6.7). Jesus Himself has taught us how to practice the hidden life, insisting that we do our good works in secret, only to please God, and without ostentation. He tells us also to guard the secret of our interior life and our relations with Him : " When thou shalt pray, enter into thy chamber and shut the door "; to conceal our mortifications and penances : " When thou fastest, anoint thy head and wash thy face "; not to display our good works : " When thou dost give alms, let not thy left hand know what thy right hand doth, " for those who do their good works before men, to be seen by them, " have received their reward " and will receive no further one from their heavenly Father (cf. *Mt* 6,1-18).

2. " Work for the sole end of pleasing God, never looking for any human praise " (*Sp*). This was the program of St. Teresa Margaret of the Heart of Jesus, the saint of the hidden life. Because she wanted to reserve for God alone the gift of her whole being, she tried to hide from the eyes of others the riches of her interior, her heroic virtues; and she succeeded in this to such an extent that her life was the perfect realization of the maxim : " To live alone with God alone. " The soul who is ever looking for approbation, praise, and the esteem of creatures does not live alone with God. Its interior life cannot be very profound, nor its relations with God very intimate. Such a soul is still living on the surface. Thus, preoccupied as it is with the effect it is producing and with what others may be thinking or saying about it, it easily lets itself be influenced in its actions by human respect and the desire to attract the good will and the esteem of others. As a result, simplicity will often be lacking in its conduct as well as a pure intention and perhaps even sincerity. The supernatural is still too bound up with the natural to be able to dominate its life, and indeed it very often acts not to please God and to give Him glory, but to please others, to win their affection, to gain a more or less honorable position.

When " we observe in ourselves a desire for something brilliant, " said St. Thérèse of the Child Jesus, " let us humbly take our place with the imperfect and know that we are weak souls who must be sustained every instant by God " (cf. *C*). The Saint also asked : " O Jesus, grant that no one may think about me, that I be forgotten and trodden underfoot like a little grain of sand " (*St*, 8). The interior soul wishes to be known and loved by God alone; therefore, it hides itself from creatures.

COLLOQUY

" O Jesus who has said, ' My kingdom is not of this world, ' You teach me that the only kingdom worth coveting is the grace of being ' unknown and esteemed as naught ' and the joy that comes from self-contempt.... Ah! like You, I want my face to be hidden from all eyes; I want no one here below to esteem me! You wanted ' neither beauty nor comeliness.... Your look was as it were hidden and despised, whereupon we esteemed You not. ' I too, wish to be like You, without comeliness and beauty, unknown to every creature.

" Yes, all must be kept for You with jealous care, because it is so sweet to work for You alone! Then the heart is filled with joy and the soul with gladness! Grant that no one may think of me, that my very existence may be, as it were, unknown to all; only one thing do I desire : to be forgotten and counted for nothing. Yes, I want to be forgotten, not only by creatures, but even by myself, so as to be totally reduced to nothingness and to have no other desire than Your glory, my Jesus—that is all! My own, I abandon to You " (T.C.J. *St*, 7 – *NV* – *L*).

O Lord, to be forgotten by people, to work without having my labor known, to spend in silence and self-effacement a humble life in which nothing appears great, nothing is worthy of attention—all this will thoroughly mortify my pride. This will be a powerful remedy for my innate desire to make myself important.

I confess, O Lord, and You already know, that unlike the saints, I am far from desiring to be forgotten and ignored. I often use little ways of drawing attention to myself and of putting myself forward. But You know, Jesus, that I am ill, and You also know that I wish to be cured by modeling my life on Yours. It is only in order to be like You that I can accept and love effacement; it is only to merit Your love, Your glance, Your intimacy, that I can renounce the good will and esteem of creatures. O Jesus, increase my desire to live for You alone, and I will find it sweet to live unknown to men.

115

TO BE HIDDEN FROM MYSELF

PRESENCE OF GOD - O Jesus, totally consecrated to the glory of the Father through complete forgetfulness of Yourself, teach me how to forget myself.

MEDITATION

1. In order to enter the fullness of the hidden life, it is not enough to hide oneself from the attention of others; we must also hide from ourselves, that is, forget ourselves, avoiding all excessive concern about ourselves. We can be preoccupied with self not only from a material point of view, but also from a spiritual point of view. To be overly concerned about one's spiritual progress, about the consolations which God gives or does not give, about the state of aridity in which one may be—all this is often the sign of a subtle spiritual egoism, a sign that the soul is more occupied with itself than with God. We must learn to forget ourselves, to hide from ourselves, by refusing to examine too minutely what is happening within our soul, and by not attaching too much importance to it, renouncing even the satisfaction of wanting to know the exact condition of our own spiritual life. It is well to understand that God often permits painful, obscure states just because He wants the soul to live hidden from itself. This was the aim of St. Teresa Margaret's program of self-effacement; she intended not only " to live, as it were, hidden and unnoticed " among her sisters, but " to be, in a certain manner, hidden and

unknown to herself, to die to herself without knowing it and without feeling any pleasure in this mystical spiritual death, burying in Christ, in a very subtle way, every thought and personal reflection, even in the spiritual and eternal order. " This is what complete forgetfulness of self explicitly proposes to one who renounces even the spiritual satisfaction of recognizing his own immolation. But in order to avoid turning one's thoughts inward, the soul must focus its aspirations elsewhere; hence the *negative* exercise of not thinking of itself must accompany the *positive* exercise of fixing its *center* in Christ, of " burying in Christ " every thought, every preoccupation with self, even in the spiritual order. No one can succeed in turning away from himself unless he concentrates all his attention on the object of his love. St. Teresa Margaret completely forgot herself; her thoughts were absorbed " in Christ, " her one Well-Beloved.

2. A soul entirely oblivious of self is also completely disinterested. It no longer serves God in a mercenary spirit, with more regard for the reward which it may receive than for His glory, but it is " at His service, " according to St. Teresa's beautiful expression, " *gratuitously*, as great lords serve their king " *(L)*. This should be the attitude of an interior soul called by God to a life of intimacy with Him. Such a one should act not as a hireling, but as a daughter or a spouse. Here we have one of the most beautiful fruits of the hidden life. St. John of the Cross teaches that " more pleasing to God is one good work, however small it be, that is done in secret with no desire that it be known, than a thousand that are done with the desire that they be known to men. For he that with purest love does such works for God's sake, not only cares nothing to have men see him, but does them not even that God Himself may see him. Such a man, even though God were never to know it, would not cease to render Him the same services, with the same joy and purity of love " *(SMI,* 20). We find this same delicate thought in St. Thérèse of the Child Jesus : " If the good God Himself were not to see my good deeds (which is impossible), I would not be disturbed. I love Him so much that I would want to please Him, without His knowing that it is I who am doing it " *(C)*.

This total purity of intention makes the soul act for God alone and never for personal interest, even of a spiritual

nature.   God will certainly reward our good works, but
concern about this is wholly abandoned to Him as long
as the soul is intent only on giving Him pleasure.   The
hidden life thus finds its culminating point in a complete
disinterestedness, not only concerning human rewards and
praises, but also in regard to spiritual consolations; our
soul seeks God alone and God alone is sufficient for us.
Even if, apparently unaware of our love and our services,
He leaves us in aridity and abandonment, we do not
worry nor stop on this account, since the one motive which
actuates us is to please God alone.

COLLOQUY

O my God, teach me how to forget myself, to bury
every preoccupation, all excessive care of myself in You.
Why do I wish to serve You, O Lord?   Why do I desire
to love You and to advance in the paths of sanctity?   Would
it be for my own interest or foolish self-complacency?   Oh!
how mean the spiritual life which would have such vain and
low aims!   No, my God, You have created me for Your
glory, and I humbly ask to be able to live for it alone, without
personal interest or satisfaction!

Is not the honor You do me sufficiently great when
You allow such a miserable, wretched creature to consecrate
its life to glorifying You—when a poor worm like me can
procure glory for You, O God most high, O infinite
Perfection?   What more could I wish, O Lord?   Would
it be better to please creatures than the Creator, to satisfy
myself rather than God?   O Lord, I wish to serve and please
You alone, to give pleasure to You alone; this will be my
only satisfaction, the only reason for my joy.   I understand
that if You lead me by an obscure and arid road, if You
often permit the darkness to deepen around me, it is only
because You want to teach me to serve You with a pure
intention, seeking nothing but Your satisfaction, not my
own.   If You allow me to continue to practice the interior
life and virtue without seeing any results, if You veil my
eyes to my slight progress, it is to establish my soul in humility.
If I had more light, or if the workings of Your grace were
more evident in me, perhaps I would glorify myself and
halt my progress toward You, the one object of my affection.

O Lord, how admirable are Your ways! Blessed be this interior obscurity which protects me from the dangers of spiritual pride! No, my God, I do not ask You to change my path; on the contrary, I beg You to continue to lead me in the same way, the road of complete self-effacement, veiled not only from the eyes of others, but even from my own. And if, by Your grace, there is anything good in me, it will be for Your pleasure and not mine; if I were to take satisfaction in it, everything could be ruined in a moment. Keep me, then, in the shadow of Your wings, teach me how to serve You out of pure love; show me how to forget myself entirely, to hide all concern for myself in You, to put my soul into Your hands with complete abandon. In order to gain it for You, I give it up to You, I want to lose it in You; in You I shall find it again clothed in Your beauty.

116

TO BE HIDDEN WITH CHRIST IN GOD

PRESENCE OF GOD - O Jesus, help me to hide from creatures in order to enter into intimacy with You.

MEDITATION

1. When we speak of the hidden life of Jesus, we do not mean only His self-effacement in the eyes of men, from whom He concealed His divinity, thus avoiding their praise. Besides these exterior relations with creatures, we must penetrate into the secret places of His heart where, hidden from human eyes, another life goes on, a secret one of much greater sublimity. It is His interior life, a life of intimacy with the Trinity. Jesus' sacred soul, personally united to the Word, unceasingly enjoys the Beatific Vision. It sees the Word, the subject of all its activity. It sees the Father, the cause of its Being. It sees the Holy Spirit, who dwells in it as " His chosen temple, " and who, by covering it with the flame of His love, draws it toward God in the perfect accomplishment of His will. Exteriorly Jesus lives with

men, deals with them as if He were one of them, but His real life, His existence as the Son of God, is lived hidden from all human sight, with the Trinity and in the Trinity. The imitation of Jesus' hidden life has for its ultimate end the participation in His interior life; that is, to be hidden " with Christ in God, " in order to enter with Him the sanctuary of the Most Holy Trinity.   St. Teresa Margaret expressed this in her ardent desire to " emulate by faith, insofar as it is possible for a creature, the hidden, *interior* life and activity of the intellect and will of the sacred humanity of Jesus Christ, hypostatically united to the Word " *(Sp)*.

The practice of the hidden life has, therefore, two aspects : the first, negative and mostly exterior, consists in hiding ourselves from the eyes of others and even from our own and in dying to glory and worldly honors.   The second, which is positive and entirely interior, consists in concentrating on God in a life of intimate relations with Him. The first aspect is the condition and measure of the second : the more a soul is able to hide from creatures, and even from itself, the more capable it will be of living " with Christ in God, " according to the beautiful expression of St. Paul : " You are dead : and your life is hidden with Christ in God " *(Col* 3,3).

2. " My God, I desire to enclose myself forever within Your most loving Heart, as in a desert, so that in You, with You, and for You I may live a hidden life of love and sacrifice. "   In these words St. Teresa Margaret expressed her ideal of a life hidden with Christ.   After long practicing the exterior, negative aspect of effacement, concealing itself from the eyes of creatures with constant fidelity, the soul is free and ready to hide itself with Christ in God. It no longer wastes its energy looking for esteem or human satisfactions; from this point of view creatures have become as nothing to it.   It can say that " created things, its own as well as others', no longer give it the least worry or trouble; it is just as if they did not exist " (T.M. *Sp*).   Thus the soul arrives at that sovereign liberty of spirit which permits it to concentrate itself wholly upon God.   Exteriorly its conduct shows nothing extraordinary, or rather, the very care it takes to hide from the eyes of others makes it very often go unnoticed, and most people consider it a soul of little worth.   But in its secret heart a very rich interior

life, known only to God, is developing. United to Jesus—in Him, with Him, by Him—it participates in His Trinitarian life. This means that it attains the plenitude, the end of the Christian life—for grace has been given to us in order to make us sharers in the divine nature, in the life of the Triune God. To this end the Word became Incarnate. By dying on the Cross, Jesus merited grace for us. He grafted us into Himself so that He could take us with Him into the bosom of the Trinity, from which sin had barred us. Not through our own merit or ability, but only through our union with Christ—our Mediator, our Bridge, our Way—can we penetrate with Him and by Him into the intimate life of God, into the life of the Trinity. Faith and charity which Jesus merited for us together with grace, enable us to enter into relations with the three divine Persons, to the extent that we can really live " hidden with Christ in God. "

A life hidden in God is the great attraction of interior souls, and to attain it, they are very happy to hide from their own eyes and the eyes of others, fleeing every shadow of earthly glory. O blessed self-effacement which introduces the soul to the " *vita abscondita cum Christo in Deo!* "

COLLOQUY

" O Jesus, I wish to strive solely to become a perfect copy of You, and since You lived a hidden life of humiliations, love, and sacrifice, henceforth mine must be the same; therefore I now wish to enclose myself forever in Your most lovable Heart, as in a desert, so as to live there in You, with You, and by You, that hidden life of love and sacrifice.... Since You inspire me to become as much as possible like You, all my efforts will tend toward that end. I shall imitate You especially in those virtues which are most pleasing to Your most lovable Heart—humility and purity of intention, interior as well as exterior—always working with a spirit of simplicity " (T.M. *Sp*).

O Jesus, deign to open Your loving Heart to me too, and permit me to take refuge in it, so that I may live hidden in God with You. Exterior things, fame, earthly glory, have no longer any attraction for me; is it not all vanity, a simple succession of circumstances which will soon cease to be? The only life which attracts me and which will last forever, beyond all earthly contingencies, is that of intimate union with You. And this is the great treasure which You offer me by the merits of Your Passion. I contemplate You on the Cross, O Jesus, Your side rent by the lance, as if to tell me that Your death has opened the door of Your Heart to admit me into the sanctuary of Your interior life. Your death has, in fact, grafted my poor human life onto Yours and made it share in Your divine life, a life of intimate relations with the Trinity. This is true living and life eternal! I aspire to it, not by my merits, but by those of Your Passion. O Jesus, grant that I may seek my joy, my good, only in this participation in Your interior life, and put all my glory in it. Yes, let all my glory be within, in the secrecy of my life hidden with You in God.

117

TRUE GLORY

PRESENCE OF GOD - O Jesus, who, for love of me, accepted the disgrace of death on the Cross, teach me what true glory is, and grant that for love of You I may learn how to overcome my desire for honor.

MEDITATION

1. St. Teresa of Jesus declares, " However slight may be our concern for our reputation, " if we " wish to make progress in spiritual matters, " we must " put this attachment right behind us, " for " if questions of honor " prevail, we " will never make great progress or come to enjoy the real fruit of prayer, " which is intimacy with God. The Saint also says that the reason why many people who have devoted themselves to the spiritual life, and are deserving on account of so many good works, " are still down on earth " and never succeed in reaching " the summit of perfection, " is " punctiliousness about their reputation. And the worst

of it is that this sort of person will not realize that he is guilty of such a thing, the reason being that the devil tells him that punctiliousness is incumbent upon him " (*Life*, 31 – *Way*, 12).

Attachment to our honor is expressed in all those susceptibilities, large or small, arising from our attitude of soul that wishes to affirm our personality, hold on to the esteem we receive from others and make our own point of view prevail. This shows up concretely in various schemes—more or less conscious and petty—to obtain or to keep certain privileged and honorable positions where our own views, which we always think are good, will prevail. By this means, we hope to make manifest our capabilities, our works, and our personal merits—so great and worthy of consideration in our own eyes. All this remains more or less disguised by the fact that we have—or think we have—the intention of acting with an eye to good. We decide, therefore, that what we do is legitimate. Yet we are not aware that this way of acting, though apparently done to defend the good, prevent scandals, and further good works, is only a defense of our own pride. This truth is made evident, for on similar occasions, when like circumstances have been resolved, we do not take as much trouble to defend the honor and the works of others as we would have done if these had been our own. A soul that allows itself to be preoccupied with such things is, as St. Teresa of Jesus says, bound to earth by " a chain which no file can sever. Only God can break it, with the aid of prayer and great effort on our part " (*Life*, 31).

2. To find out if we are really detached from sensitiveness about honor, we should not rely on the desires which sometimes come to us during prayer and make us think that we are ready to bear any kind of humiliation or scorn. Instead we must find out what our attitude is at the critical moment when something wounds our pride. Then it will be easy to see that " we refuse to be thwarted over the very smallest matter of precedence : apparently such a thing is quite intolerable " (T.J. *Way*, 16). These more or less sharp reactions of our sensitiveness show us clearly that we are very far from crushing underfoot our concern about honor. Our awareness of these failings will be the starting point for correcting them, for the greatest obstacle to acquiring

the virtues is the belief that we have already gained them and that it is no longer necessary, therefore, to practice them.

" God, deliver us, " exclaims St. Teresa, " from people who wish to serve You yet who are mindful of their own honor " (*ibid.*, 12). We are trying to serve two incompatible masters at the same time—God and our own pride. Everything that a soul does to serve its ego and to defend its honor is taken away from the service of God, from the pure, sincere seeking of His honor and glory. Even if we sometimes seem to have real rights, it is only by sacrificing them, at least as far as our own person is concerned, that we shall attain to the liberty of spirit necessary for a deep interior life. Preoccupation with the defense of our rights continually distracts us from our ideal of union with God, deprives us of interior peace, and finally, involves us in so many worldly cares that it will often be an occassion of failing in charity and even in justice toward our neighbor. For it is very difficult, if not impossible, to keep up the defense of our own rights without more or less injuring the rights of others.

COLLOQUY

" O Lord, art Thou our example and our Master? Thou art, indeed. And wherein did Thy honor consist, O Lord, who hast honored us? Didst Thou perchance lose it when Thou wert humbled even to death? No, Lord, rather didst Thou gain it for all.... God grant that no soul be lost through its attention to these wretched niceties about honor, when it has no idea wherein honor consists.... O Lord, all our trouble comes from not having our eyes fixed upon Thee, we stumble and fall a thousand times and stray from the way " (*ibid.*, 36 – 16).

" We are trying to attain to union with God. We want to follow the counsels of Christ on whom were showered insults and false witness. Are we, then, really so anxious to keep intact our own reputation and credit? We cannot do so and yet attain to union, for the two ways diverge. When we exert our utmost efforts and try in various ways to forego our rights, the Lord comes to the soul " (T.J. *Life*, 31).

O Jesus, grant that my honor may consist solely in intimate union with You, in the effort to become more and more like You. Although You were God and had the right to be treated and honored as God, You willed to be treated like the lowest of men! You wished no other right than to fulfill the will of the Father, to die on the Cross for His glory and our salvation. In the light of Your example, I have a better understanding of the meanness of my pride which, in order to defend foolish rights, loses itself in so much confusion and so many fruitless discussions. O Lord, why should I confine myself to crawling on the ground among the thorny roots of my passions, when You have created me to soar in the heavens? Oh! help me to free myself from the vain pretenses of my ego which, like a heavy weight, continually try to drag me down; help me to get rid of this great load, and to rise toward You, my God, in a sure flight!

118

NOT EXCUSING ONESELF

PRESENCE OF GOD - O Jesus, who willed to be silent before him who condemned You to death, teach me the art of not excusing myself.

MEDITATION

1. In any failure, fault, or personal error, our ego instinctively tries to excuse itself. It is the tactic of pride—which is not willing to admit its mistakes and schemes—to hide them under more or less false pretexts, always finding some way to blame them on other people or on circumstances. Adam and Eve acted in this way after their sin; it is also the instinct of anyone who commits a fault. Herein lies great danger for the soul, because it is impossible for us to correct our faults if we are not willing to acknowledge them. It requires great courage to tear down these ingenious but inconsistent constructions of self-love, to expose our failings and look them squarely in the face, just as they are, without blaming them on anyone but ourselves. " When we commit a fault, " said St. Thérèse

of the Child Jesus, " we must not attribute it to a physical
cause, such as illness or the weather, but we must attribute
it to our own lack of perfection. . . .   Occasions do not make
man weak, but they do show what he is " *(C)*.

Excusing our faults may satisfy our pride; but in reality,
it is voluntarily blinding oneself and making oneself incapable
of seeing the true situation.   Thus our poor soul is not
only unable to advance, but is condemned to grope in the
dark with no possibility of escape.   On the other hand,
if we sincerely recognize our faults, we have already taken
the first step toward correcting them.   Yet it is not enough
to avoid excusing ourselves interiorly; we must also guard
against exonerating ourselves before others.   In other words,
after acknowledging our failings before God, we must also
confess them before men, accept a correction humbly,
and repair the bad example we may have given.   At the
same time, it would be of little value to receive an accusation
or a reproach silently, if the soul—even at the cost of great
struggle and effort—did not also avoid excusing itself
interiorly.

2. Rebukes very often annoy us because we think
they are not entirely in proportion to our faults and failings.
We do not realize that this is one of the inevitable
consequences of human limitations; only God who reads
our hearts can judge our acts with perfect justice.   Men
see but the exterior, and therefore, even when it is their
duty to correct us, they do not always evaluate correctly,
but may often make mistakes either by excess or by deficiency.
If we are willing to accept only the observations which
perfectly correspond to our faults, we will very often be
in danger of making excuses, protesting, giving explanations,
and if we cannot do this outwardly, we shall do it at least
interiorly.   Thus we will lose the benefit we could have
derived from the corrections, had we received them with
humility of heart.

St. Teresa of Jesus urges souls eager to arrive at union
with God to great generosity on this point, telling them to
accept, without excusing themselves, every correction or
rebuke, even if not wholly deserved, and even if wholly
unjust.   " It takes great humility, " said the Saint, " to find
oneself unjustly condemned and be silent, and to do this
is to imitate the Lord, who set us free from all our sins. . . .

The truly humble person will have a genuine desire to be thought little of, and persecuted, and condemned unjustly, even in serious matters. For if we desire to imitate the Lord, how can we do so better than in this? And no bodily strength is necessary here, nor the aid of anyone save God. " And then she adds very shrewdly : " Properly speaking, we can never be blamed unjustly, since we are always full of faults.... If we are not to blame for the thing that we are accused of, we are never wholly without blame in the way that our good Jesus was " (*Way*, 15).

"But Jesus held His peace" (*Mt* 26,63), says the Evangelist, in showing us Our Lord before the Tribunal. A soul who aspires to intimate union with Jesus must know how to unite itself to His silence even when accused most unjustly. When special reasons — such as avoiding scandal or causing displeasure to someone — require that excuses be made, they will be limited to what is strictly necessary, with careful weighing and pondering so that the grace of the humiliation may not be lost.

COLLOQUY

O Lord, I pray that Your light will be so abundant in me that it will disperse, like fog before the sun, all those excuses by means of which my self-love tries to cover my failings and faults. Enable me to recognize all my defects and to judge them as You do. Rule over my heart so that it will not try to find subtle reasons for manufacturing excuses for my faults. And if, because of my weakness, I fall easily, grant that I may at least confess it humbly to You and to others. Take away from my conscience the mask of vain, pitiful excuses which prevents me from seeing myself as You see me and know me, as I really am in Your eyes. Then, O Lord, give me the humility necessary to accept with good will the corrections of others. With Your gentleness extinguish my sensitiveness which is ever ready to burst into flame and to be resentful, and grant me the grace to imitate Your meekness and humility in the presence of Your judges.

"O Lord, when I think in how many ways Thou didst suffer, and in all of them undeservedly, I know not what to say for myself or what I am doing when I make

excuses for myself. Thou knowest, my God, that if there
is anything good in me it comes from no other hands than
Thine own. Should I desire that no evil be spoken of a thing
so evil as myself, when they have said such wicked things
of Thee, who art good above all other good? It is intolerable,
my God; nor would I that Thou shouldst have to tolerate
anything displeasing to Thine eyes being found in Thy
handmaiden. For see, Lord, I am blind, and I content
myself with very little. Do Thou give me light and make
me truly desire that all should hate me, since I have so
often left Thee, who hast loved me with such faithfulness.

" What is this, my God? What does it matter to us
if we are blamed by all, provided we are without blame
in the sight of the Lord? " (T.J. *Way*, 15).

119

THE MULTIPLICATION OF THE LOAVES

FOURTH SUNDAY OF LENT

PRESENCE OF GOD - O Jesus, true Bread of eternal life, appease
my hunger.

MEDITATION

1. Today there is a pause of holy joy and spiritual
comfort which the Church, like a good mother, gives us
in the middle of the Lenten austerity so that we may renew
our strength. " Rejoice, O Jerusalem, " the Introit of
today's Mass sings, " and all you who love her, leap with
joy and be filled with the abundance of her delights. "
What are these delights? The Gospel (*Jn* 6,1-15) answers
the question by the narrative of the multiplication of the
loaves, the great miracle by which Jesus meant to prepare
the people for the announcement of a much more startling
miracle, the institution of the Holy Eucharist, in which
He, the Master, would become our Bread, the " living
Bread which came down from Heaven " (*ibid.* 6,41) to nourish
our souls. This is the cause of our joy, the source of our

delight. Jesus is the Bread of life, always at our disposal to appease our hunger.

Although Jesus appreciates spiritual values much better than we, He does not forget or despise the material necessities of life. Today's Gospel shows Him surrounded by the crowd which had followed Him to hear His teachings. Jesus thinks of their hunger, and to provide for it, performs one of His most outstanding miracles. With His blessing, five loaves of bread and two fishes suffice to feed five thousand people, with twelve basketfuls left over.

Jesus knows that when a person is tormented by hunger or material needs, he is unable to apply himself to the things of the spirit. Charity likewise requires of us this understanding of the bodily necessities of others, a practical understanding which translates itself into efficacious action. " If a brother or sister be naked and want daily food, and one of you say to them, ' Go in peace ' ...yet give them not those things that are necessary for the body, what shall it profit? " (*Jas* 2,15.16).

The Apostles had suggested to the Master that He dismiss the crowd " that they may buy themselves victuals " (*Mt* 14,15). Jesus did not agree but provided for them Himself. We, too, must strive, as far as we are able, to show ourselves solicitous for the needs of others.

2. Before performing this miracle, Jesus asked Philip, " Whence shall we buy bread wherewith to feed these people? " And the Evangelist observes, " He said that to try him, for He knew what He was about to do. " There is no difficulty in our lives for which God does not know the solution. From all eternity He has foreseen it and has the remedy for each case, no matter how complicated the situation may be. However, sometimes in difficult circumstances He seems to leave us alone as if the outcome were to depend on us, but He does this only to test us. He wants us to measure our strength against the difficulty—which makes us more aware of our weakness and insufficiency—and He wants us also to exercise our faith and our confidence in Him. The Lord never really abandons us unless we forsake Him first. He only hides Himself and covers His actions with a dark veil. This is the time to believe, to believe firmly, and to wait with humble patience and complete confidence.

The Apostles tell Jesus that a young boy has five loaves and two fishes, that this is very little, in fact, nothing at all for feeding five thousand men. But the Lord asks for this nothing and uses it to accomplish a great miracle. It is always thus : the all-powerful God, who can do everything and create from nothing, when dealing with His free creatures, will not act without their help. Man can do but very little; yet God wants, asks for, and requires this little as a condition of His intervention. Only the Lord can make us saints, as only He could multiply the small supplies of the young boy; still He asks for our help. Like the boy in the Gospel, we too must give Him everything in our power; we must offer Him each day our good resolutions, renewed faithfully and lovingly, and He will bring about a great miracle for us also, the miracle of our sanctification.

COLLOQUY

"Lord Jesus Christ, Son of the living God, who, on the Cross, with Your arms extended for the redemption of all men, drank the chalice of unspeakable sorrows, deign to help me today. Poor am I, but I come to You who are rich; in my wretchedness I present myself to You, the All-merciful. Ah! grant that I may not leave You, empty and deceived. I come to You hungry; do not let me go away fasting. Weak, I approach You; do not turn me away unstrengthened! And, if I sigh with hunger, grant me the grace to be nourished " (St. Augustine).

Yes, I hunger for You, true Bread, living Bread, Bread of life. You know what my hunger is—hunger of the soul, hunger of the body—and You will to provide for the one as well as for the other. By Your teaching, by Your Body and Blood, You strengthen my spirit; You strengthen it abundantly, withholding nothing, except what I myself keep by the coldness of my love, the smallness of my heart. You have set a rich and abundant table for me, beyond anything imaginable, which I have only to approach in order to be fed. You not only welcome me, but You Yourself become my food and drink when You give Yourself wholly to me, wholly in Your divinity, wholly in Your humanity.

In Your infinite goodness, You have even set a table for my body, and Your Providence feeds it, clothes it, and maintains it in life like the lilies of the field and the birds of the air. You know my needs, my pains, my preoccupation with the past, the present, and the future; and You provide for everything with a paternal love. O Lord, why do I not confide in You, why do I not cast all my cares on You, certain that You will find a remedy for all of them? I entrust my life to You, the life of my body, my earthly life with all its needs and its labors, as well as the life of my soul with all its necessities, its pains, its hunger for the infinite. Only You can fill up the emptiness in my heart, only You can make me happy. You alone can bring about my ideal of sanctity— union with You.

120

THE VALUE OF OBEDIENCE

PRESENCE OF GOD - O Jesus most obedient, make me understand the value of obedience.

MEDITATION

1. St. John of the Cross has said, " God wants from us the least degree of obedience and submission, rather than all the works we desire to offer Him " (*SM I*, 13). Why? Because obedience makes us surrender our own will to adhere to God's will as expressed in the orders of our superiors; and the perfection of charity, as well as the essence of union with God, consists precisely in the complete conformity of our will with the divine will. Charity will be perfect in us when we govern ourselves in each action— not according to our personal desires and inclinations—but according to God's will, conforming our own to His. This is the state of union with God, for " the soul that has attained complete conformity and likeness of will (to the divine will), is totally united to and transformed in God supernaturally " (*AS II*, 5,4).

The will of God is expressed in His commandments, in the precepts of the Church, in the duties of our state in life; beyond all that, there is still a vast area for our free choice, where it is not always easy to know with certitude exactly what God wants of us. In the voice of obedience, however, the divine will takes on a clear, precise form; it comes to us openly manifest and we no longer need to fear making a mistake. Indeed, as St. Paul says, " There is no power but from God " (*Rom* 13,1), so that by obeying our lawful superiors, we can be certain that we are obeying God. Jesus Himself, when entrusting to His disciples the mission of converting the world, said, " He that heareth you, heareth Me; and he that despiseth you, despiseth Me " (*Lk* 10,16).

He teaches us here that ecclesiastical superiors represent Him and speak to us in His Name. Furthermore, St. Thomas points out that every lawful authority—even in the natural order, such as the civil and social spheres—when commanding within the just limits of its powers manifests the divine will. In this very sense, the Apostle does not hesitate to say, " Servants, be obedient to them that are your lords...as to Christ...doing the will of God from the heart " (*Eph* 6,5.6).

2. One of the greatest obstacles to full conformity of our will to God's is our attachment to our own desires and inclinations. Obedience, because it asks us to be governed by the will of another, is the best way of accustoming ourselves to renounce our own will, of detaching us from it, and of making us cling to the divine will as revealed in the orders of our superiors. The stricter the form of obedience to which we submit—that is, the more it tends to govern not only some particular detail but our whole life—the more intense will its practice be, and the more surely will it make us conform to the will of God. This is the great value of obedience : to unite man's life with the will of God : to give man in every circumstance, the opportunity to govern himself, not according to his weak, fragile will, which is so subject to error, blindness, and human limitations, but according to the will of God. This divine will has such goodness, perfection, and holiness that it can never be mistaken nor will what is evil; it aims only at the good—not the transitory good, which today is and tomorrow is not—but the eternal, imperishable good.

Obedience makes us this happy exchange : renunciation of our own will for God's will. For this reason the saints loved obedience. It is said of St. Teresa Margaret of the Heart of Jesus that, not only did she obey orders promptly, but she experienced intense pleasure in doing so—her whole aspect expressing the joy she found in obeying. If it is costly to nature to give up one's own will, to renounce a plan, a project, or a much cherished work, the interior soul will not stop at this act of renunciation, but will realize that by suffering and struggling to overcome itself, it will be carried much further. The soul is fixed in the will of God which comes hidden in the voice of obedience and it tends toward this will with all its strength, for to embrace the will of God is to embrace God Himself.

COLLOQUY

" Oh! how sweet and glorious is this virtue of obedience, which contains all the other virtues! Because it is born of charity, and on it the rock of holy faith is founded, it is a queen, and he who espouses it knows no evil, but only peace and rest. The tempestuous waves of evil cannot hurt him because he sails in Your holy will, O my God.... He has no wish which cannot be satisfied because obedience makes him desire You alone, O Lord, who know his desires and can and will fulfill them. Obedience navigates without fatigue, and without danger comes into the port of salvation. O Jesus, I see that obedience conforms itself to You; I see it going with You into the little boat of the holy Cross. Grant me, then, O Lord, this holy obedience anointed with true humility. It is straightforward and without deceit; it brings with it the light of divine grace. Give me this hidden pearl trampled underfoot by the world, which humbles itself to submit to creatures for love of You " (St. Catherine of Siena).

O Lord, I have only one life; what better way could I use it for Your glory and my sanctification, than to submit it directly to obedience? Only by doing this shall I be certain that I am not wasting my time or deceiving myself, for to obey is to do Your will. If my will is very imperfect, Yours is holy and sanctifying; if mine has only the sad power to lead me astray, Yours can make holy my life and all my acts—even the simplest and most indifferent—if they are accomplished at its suggestion. O Lord, the desire to live totally in Your will urges me to obedience and compels me to love and embrace this virtue, in spite of my great attachment to my liberty and independence.

O holy, sanctifying will of my God, I want to love You above everything else; I want to embrace You at every moment of my life; I do not want to do anything without You or outside of You.

121

COME, FOLLOW ME

PRESENCE OF GOD - O Jesus, obedient even unto the death of the Cross, teach us to follow Your example.

MEDITATION

1. Jesus said to the young man who was aspiring to perfection, " If thou wilt be perfect, go sell what thou hast, and give to the poor, "—the evangelical counsel of poverty— " and come follow Me " (*Mt* 19,21),—the counsel of voluntary obedience, according to St. Thomas. To follow Jesus means to imitate His virtues, among which obedience certainly ranks first. Jesus came into the world to accomplish the will of His Father : " It is written of Me that I should do Thy will, O God " (*Heb* 10,7). Several times during His life He said it expressly : " I came down from heaven, not to do My own will, but the will of Him that sent Me " (*Jn* 6,38); and He declared that His food, His sustenance, the support of His life, was the fulfilling of His Father's will (cf. *ibid.* 4,34). But Jesus also wanted to express concretely His dependence on His heavenly Father, by submitting Himself to those creatures who in the natural order had authority over Him as man. Thus he lived for thirty years subject in all things to Mary and Joseph, recognizing His Father's authority in theirs. " He was subject to them, " the Gospel says (*Lk* 2,51), as it summarizes in these few

words the long years of the private life of the Savior.   Later, during His public life, and especially during His Passion, Jesus always gave an example of obedience to constituted authority, civil as well as religious, even subjecting Himself to His judges and executioners and making Himself, according to the words of St. Paul, " obedient unto death, even to the death of the Cross " (*Phil* 2,8).   Having come into the world through obedience, Jesus wanted to live in obedience and through obedience.   He embraced death, repeating in the Garden of Olives : " Father...not My will but Thine be done " (*Lk* 22,42).   To follow Jesus in the life of perfection means that we must voluntarily embrace a life of total dependence.   St. Thomas concludes from this that obedience belongs to the essence of the state of perfection.

2. To follow Jesus means to carry out fully His invitation : " If any man will come after Me, let him deny himself " (*Mt* 16,24).   Now the greatest act of renunciation that man can make is just this sacrifice of his liberty by submission to obedience in all things.   In fact, " nothing is dearer to man than the freedom of his own will, for this is what makes him master over others; because of this freedom, he can use and enjoy other goods and is master of his acts.   Even as a man by abandoning his wealth or his kinsfolk renounces them, so by surrendering the freedom of his own will, by which he is master of himself, he renounces himself " (St. Thomas, *The Perfection of the Spiritual Life*). For this reason the vow of obedience is the greatest and most meritorious sacrifice man can offer to God.

To permit our life to be ruled by another—in this the sacrifice of obedience consists.   Every man is free, having received his liberty from God; therefore, he has the right to govern himself according to his own judgment and personal views. [1]   Hence anyone who promises obedience uses his freedom to renounce this right, *voluntarily* offering it as a free holocaust for the service, worship, and glory of God. As the holocaust of the chosen people was a victim entirely consumed in honor of God, no part of it being spared, similarly the vow of obedience immolates the *whole* man to the honor of God.   Obedience then makes a sacrifice

---

[1] This does not dispense him from conforming his personal views and his own judgment to God's.

of our being to its depths, or to be more exact, it sacrifices everything selfish in it—our attachments to our opinions, inclinations, and our personal demands. In this sense, nothing helps to free us from love of self, to strip us of ourselves as much as obedience. At the same time, far from destroying our personality, obedience makes use of it in a most glorious and sublime way, by enabling it to surrender itself in order to adhere entirely to God, to His holy, sanctifying will.

COLLOQUY

"O Jesus, You would not have one that loves You well take any other road than that which You Yourself took" (cf. T.J. *F*, 5). And now I have decided to follow You, to walk in Your footsteps on the path of holy obedience, a way hollowed out in the solid rock of Your example, of Your most humble submission, of Your ineffable subjection. "O God, You who reign over the angels, You whom the principalities and powers obey, were subject to Mary, and not only to Mary, but also to Joseph because of Mary. For God to obey a creature is humility without a parallel. O Lord, You abase Yourself, and I, shall I exalt myself? O my soul, if you disdain to imitate the example of a man, it will certainly not be unworthy of you to imitate your Creator. If perhaps you cannot follow Him wherever He goes, at least follow Him to the point to which He willed to descend for you" (cf. St. Bernard).

O Jesus, grant that I may follow You in the way of obedience; give me a profound spirit of faith so that I shall always be able to recognize Your voice and will in the command of obedience. "Teach me, O Lord, to abandon myself with confidence to Your words : ' He who hears you, hears Me. ' Teach me to forget my own will; You appreciate this sacrifice very greatly because it makes You Master of the free will which You Yourself have given me. I wish to offer You this gift in its plenitude, with no reservation whatever. Grant that I may be faithful to this resolution and then, in spite of the repugnances and opposition of nature, I shall succeed in conforming myself to what You command; in short, whether it costs me pain or not, I shall succeed in submitting myself. I know indeed, O Lord, that You will not fail to help me, and in subjecting my reason and will for love of You, You will teach me how to become master of them. Once I am master of myself, I shall be able to consecrate myself perfectly to You by offering You a pure will, for You to unite to Your own" (cf. T.J. *F*, 5).

122

FREE SACRIFICE OF LIBERTY

PRESENCE OF GOD - O Jesus, divine Lamb, immolated voluntarily for the glory of the Father, make me understand the great value of voluntary immolation.

MEDITATION

1. The vow of obedience has been excellently defined as the "free immolation of liberty" (Pius XII, *Alloc. Congr. Relig.*, Dec., 1950). This definition stresses the idea of the *freedom* of our immolation. It involves no nonchalant passivity, but an intense, noble activity, consisting in the *voluntary* renunciation of one's own will by *voluntarily* submitting oneself to the will of God as expressed in the commands of our superiors. This is very far from the idea of a mechanical, material, or forced obedience, submitted to from necessity—an obedience by which man acts like a machine, or like a servant who submits himself to his master only because he cannot do otherwise. Under these circumstances, there is only the name and the outward appearance of obedience. What is wholly lacking is the inner content : the formal act which consists precisely in the free, and therefore conscious, renunciation of our own wills, in order to adhere to God's will manifested in the orders of our superiors. Obedience will not be a perfect holocaust unless it contains this double element : *free renunciation of self and free adherence to the divine will*. This offering will be pleasing and precious in the eyes of God far more than the "oblation of victims" (1 *Sm* 15,22). If this twofold interior element is lacking, the exterior act of obedience can suffice to keep us

from breaking the vow or the promise made, but it loses its
profound value and will never succeed in detaching a man
from his own will and casting him into God's will.

When we are satisfied with material, forced obedience,
we do not complete the interior act of self-renunciation;
though there is the external fulfillment of an order, we are
keeping our own will interiorly.   Therefore, we cannot say
that we have realized the immolation of our liberty, and not
even that we have freely embraced the divine will.   Such
obedience is senseless for a soul that aspires to union with
God; it is an attempt to attain the end without making use of
the means, to exchange the precious metal of true obedience
for a cheap pewter coin.   St. Teresa of Jesus tells us that
there is " no path which leads more quickly to the highest
perfection than that of obedience....   Obedience brings us
the sooner to that happy state of union with God " (*F*, 5).
She is evidently speaking only of that obedience which is
" the free immolation of liberty, " which has no desire
for any other liberty than to do God's will.

2. A " free immolation " always implies full knowledge
and awareness on the part of the one who makes it; it is the
same with the act of obedience.   If we make a vow or
promise of obedience, we must try always to keep alive the
sense of responsibility for this contract we have made.

When we pronounced the formula of our profession,
we intended to offer our will as a holocaust to God, and
to be guided by His representative.   Therefore, when given
commands—and especially those most unlike our own
personal ideas or orders which for one reason or another are
more painful to us—we should be vigilant lest it happen that
we take back in practice what we have offered by our
vow, which would be to commit robbery in our holocaust.
Our will has been consecrated, sacrificed on the altar of the
Lord, it is no longer ours, hence we have no freedom to
take it back.   We should, instead, use our liberty to live
our offering in its totality day by day, that is, to constantly
renew the immolation of our freedom before every disposition
of obedience.   Blessed obedience, which permits us to
actualize our holocaust!   " If you give Him your will
in any other way, " wrote St. Teresa of Jesus to her daughters,
" you are just showing Him a jewel, pretending to give it to
Him and begging Him to take it; and then, when He puts

out His hand to do so, taking it back and holding on to it tightly " (*Way*, 32). Unfortunately, this inconsistency is always possible. Although we have sacrificed our will by our vow, it still remains in our hands, and our fidelity to our vow depends on our own will. It is necessary then to have great determination to overcome our repugnance to embrace the will of God as expressed in the commands of our superiors.

" Obedience is the burden of the strong " (Pius XII, *Allocution to the Discalced Carmelites*, September, 1952), and rightly so, because it requires strength to renounce oneself; but this burden of sacrifice is sweet to the soul enamored of God's will, for in His love it will always find the strength to renounce itself.

COLLOQUY

O Lord, is there any finer or greater ideal than that of attaining total conformity of my will with Yours, so that it is no longer my own will but Yours that directs, guides, and governs me in all my movements and actions?

Oh! how sublime is this state of perfect conformity to Your divine will! You tell me through St. Teresa : " There is no better way of acquiring this treasure than to dig and toil in order to get it from this mine of obedience. The more we dig, the more we shall find; and the more we submit to men for love of You, and have no other will than that of our superiors, the more completely we shall become masters of our wills and bring them into conformity with Yours. This is true union with You, my God, the union which I desire; I do not covet those delectable kinds of absorption which it is possible to experience and which are given the name of union. They may be union if the result of them is what I have described; but if such suspension leaves behind it little obedience and much self-will, it seems to me that it will be a union with love of self, not with the will of God. May His Majesty grant that I myself may act according to my belief " (T. J. *F*, 5).

O Lord, You know my will's dislike of submission, of renouncing itself in subjection to the will of another. There is in me a very strong love of liberty and independence, which inclines me to seek a thousand pretexts and means for avoiding the necessity of submitting. But You also know that there is nothing in the world that I love, seek for and desire as much as Your will. In order to live in Your will, to have the certitude and joy of acting in all things according to Your divine will, I am ready with Your help to make every sacrifice to immolate my liberty fully. O Lord, increase my love for Your holy will, enkindle in me a passion for Your will, and then increase in my soul a love for obedience, that golden channel through which the precious treasure of Your will comes to me.

123

SUPERNATURAL OBEDIENCE

PRESENCE OF GOD - O Jesus, teach me to see only You in my superiors.

MEDITATION

1. An excellent instruction from St. John of the Cross says : " Never look upon your superior, whoever he may be, with less regard than upon God Himself" *(P)*. If we do not have this supernatural spirit which makes us see God in the person of our superior, our obedience cannot be supernatural. It is necessary to be animated by this motive alone : I obey because my superior represents God for me and speaks to me in His Name; my superior is another *Christ* to me : *Hic est Christus meus*. This is my Christ.

We should not obey through the motive of human confidence in the person of our superior : because he is intelligent, prudent, capable, because he understands or likes us, and so forth. That is human obedience, the fruit of human prudence—an act good in itself but not supernatural. Neither should we obey because what we are told to do is the most perfect; again this is not the real reason for obedience. We must obey only because God wills whatever our superior commands. The one exception is an order involving sin, which of course God cannot want, or a command not conformable to the Rule or Constitutions which we have embraced. In either case, obedience would be unlawful. Apart from these exceptions no limit should be put to our obedience. We need not hesitate through fear that the superior is asking something less perfect. Even if he commands what is objectively less perfect than its alternative (for instance, to take some rest instead of working), it would nevertheless be the more perfect thing for us. By the simple fact that the superior has expressed an order, it is clearly the fulfillment of that, and not something else, that God wants from us at the moment. It could very well be that in the abstract we see the possibility of performing an action more perfect than what we have been told to do, and that our idea is better than our superior's. But in reality there is no doubt about it : nothing can be more perfect for us than what God commands by means of our superior.

2. Since the motive of human confidence in our superior is a defective basis for our obedience, we must found it on supernatural confidence, on trust that springs from the recognition of the divine government working through the superiors God has given us. Even if our superiors were less upright or less virtuous, we would have no reason to fear. Faith teaches us that God controls and rules everything and that no human will can escape His divine dominion. Let us suppose that our superior is wrong and orders us to do something—either good in itself or indifferent—from a less upright motive. God always knows how to make use of him for the benefit of our soul; even his imperfect intentions are utilized by God to make us do what He wants of us. This is certain : God directs us by means of our superiors and they are not independent of Him. He uses them as instruments which He employs at His pleasure. Hence we must have recourse to our superior with confidence, since through him we contact God, and we are obeying God when we obey him. Such obedience is entirely supernatural and places us in direct contact with the divine will.

By acting otherwise, St. John of the Cross warns us, " you would do yourself the immense harm of lowering your obedience from the divine plane to the human.... And your obedience will be all the more vain and sterile, the more you feel irritated at the hostile attitude of your superior

or more pleased with his easy or pleasant disposition. For
I tell you that the devil has ruined the perfection of a great
multitude of religious by causing them to consider these
characteristics, and their obedience is of very little worth in
the eyes of God, because they have considered these things
and not paid sole respect to obedience.

" If you want your obedience to have full value, fasten
your glance only on God, whom you are serving in your
superior " *(P, 12)*.

COLLOQUY

O Lord, increase my spirit of faith, so that I will see
You in the soul of my superior. May I repeat, spontaneously
and sincerely, in his presence, *Hic est Christus meus!* Only by
this way of obedience will a life of continual contact and
uninterrupted intimacy with You be possible. If I find You
present and living in the Sacrament of the Altar under the
veil of the Eucharistic species, always ready to welcome and
nourish my soul, I can also, but in a different way, find You
hidden in the person of my superior, through whom You
speak to me, always ready to disperse my doubts, to manifest
Your holy will, and to direct and guide me along the road
You have chosen from all eternity for my sanctification.

O Lord, why should I stop at the human appearances of
my superiors? Such an attitude will only serve to keep me
from finding You in them and recognizing Your will in
theirs. Help me, O God, to pass over all the human aspects
of obedience and to put myself in contact with You and Your
divine will. Just as in the Eucharist I do not halt at the
created species of bread and wine, so I ought not in obeying
to consider the person of my superior, but only Your will,
which reaches me under the appearance of a human order
or command. O Jesus, what a great mystery! The Eucharist
gives me Your Body, Your Blood, Your divinity—such is
the power of the Sacrament which You have instituted.
Obedience gives me Your will and makes me communicate
with it—such is the power of the authority which You have
established.

Once I have understood this profound truth, how can
I still dare to argue or hesitate at the commands of my
superiors? " It would be a terrible thing if God were to be

telling us plainly to go about His business in some way, and we would not do it but stood looking at Him because that gave us greater pleasure. A fine way it is of advancing in the love of God to tie His hands by thinking that there is only one way in which He can benefit us " (T.J. *F*, 5). No, Lord, grant that I may never act thus. I shall follow You wherever You lead me by means of holy obedience.

124

BLIND OBEDIENCE

PRESENCE OF GOD - O Jesus, who out of love for me were willing to submit to Your own creatures, teach me to obey blindly.

MEDITATION

1. When we see God in our superior we obey without argument or futile reasoning and with no delay : *Christus jubet, sufficit*, Christ commands, that is enough. What more do I want, when I know that the orders of my superior are those of God Himself? Even if the thing commanded is hard or painful, my certitude that Our Lord expects it of me will give me the strength to undertake it promptly, without offering the least resistance.

Of course there may be cases where there is good reason to think an order has been imposed without taking into consideration facts which, if overlooked, might be prejudicial to the superior himself; then it is well and sometimes even necessary to bring it to his attention. Neither is there any imperfection in asking for explanations when the order does not seem clear or when it places us in a very embarrassing position; however, this must be done with humility, without insistence and with readiness to submit oneself to the decision of the superior. We must have the firm determination not to reason or debate about an order, not to inquire into the motives which might have made the superior give a certain command. If we begin to argue about obedience, we put difficulties in the way of obeying; therefore, we must stop all rationalizing, even interiorly, if we wish our obedience to be a pleasing sacrifice to God. It would be worse still to discuss our feelings with others or to criticize the superior's decisions; acting in such a way, we should create difficulties in obedience for others as well as for ourselves.

If we want to offer our entire being to Our Lord, we must completely renounce our own way of thinking, for however good it may be, it will always be infinitely inferior to God's, and God will accomplish His will in us only when we carry out the orders of our superior.

2. In declaring that our superior manifests the will of God for us, we certainly do not mean that everything he thinks, says, or wishes is thought, said, or wished by God. Certainly not. But we must understand that when the superior—in virtue of his office—gives a legitimate order, the command is a sure manifestation of God's will. Blind obedience is obedience which goes beyond all personal judgment or opinion and adheres to the superior's orders, solely because in them is recognized the divine will. This obedience is *blind* because the intellect is deprived of its own light when it is not permitted to consider its personal judgment, to inquire into the superior's reasons, or to discuss his orders; it is *blind* because it is based only on a motive of faith, for by faith we know God's will is manifested through our superior. Even as faith is an " obscure " knowledge, we can say that the obedience it inspires is " deprived of natural light " and is therefore blind. In other words, blind obedience is not based on reasoning that involves human motives, but it is based on the unique motive of faith which knows that one who hears the superior hears God. " He who hears you, hears Me. "

In a case where the opinion of the subject might be better than the superior's, blind obedience does not require the denial of one's own judgment to the point of affirming the contrary—an affirmation which would not be conformable to truth. It simply demands that we give up the right to direct our actions according to our own opinion; we decide that we must obey *just the same*, because it is certain that God wants what the superior has ordered and not what seems better to us, and perhaps is so objectively.

One who, under the pretext of doing the more perfect thing, departs from the way of obedience, leaves at the same

time the sure path of God's will to enter upon the perilous
and treacherous road of his own will. It is certain that a soul
consecrated to God can do nothing agreeable to Him outside
of holy obedience. " The actions of a religious, " says
St. John of the Cross, " are not his own but belong to
obedience, and if he withdraw them from obedience,
he wilt have to account them as lost " (*P*, 11).

COLLOQUY

" O Lord, how different are Thy ways from our clumsy
imaginings! When once a soul has resolved to love Thee
and has resigned itself into Thy hands, Thou wilt have
nothing of it save that it shall obey Thee and find out for
itself how it may best serve Thee and desire to do so. It has
no need to look for paths or to choose them, for its will is
Thine. Thou, my Lord, takest upon Thyself the task of
guiding it in the way which is the greatest benefit to it.
And even though our superior has no mind to our soul's
profit...Thou, my God, hast a mind to our profit, and
dost dispose the soul and prepare things for it to do in such
a way that, without knowing how, we find ourselves so
much more spiritual and so greatly benefited that we are
astonished " (T.J. *F*, 5).

" O my God, from how much disquiet do we free
ourselves when we make the vow of obedience! Having
nothing for a compass but the will of our superior, we are
always sure of following the right path, and need not fear
that we will be misled, even when it may appear that our
superiors are mistaken. But when we cease to consult the
unerring compass, immediately our soul goes astray in barren
wastes, where the waters of grace quickly fail. O Jesus,
obedience is the compass You have given me to direct me
safely to the eternal shore. What a joy it is for me to fix my
glance upon You and then to accomplish Your will "
(cf. T.C.J. *St*, 9).

O Lord, I want to apply myself to obedience with
unshakable confidence in Your divine Providence which
rules, guides and directs everything, making all things work
together in an ineffable manner for the good of my soul.
I wish to apply myself to obedience without the slightest
hesitation, binding myself to You and to Your divine will.

125

DIFFICULTIES IN OBEDIENCE

PRESENCE OF GOD - O Jesus, teach me the secret of humble obedience which submits to every superior and every command.

MEDITATION

1. Although obedience is precious because it places our whole life in God's will, nevertheless, in practice it has its difficulties and these arise chiefly because the command itself does not come directly from God but through His representatives. Thus it often happens that we fail to see God in our superiors and to recognize His authority in them. For example, when, as often happens in religious life, we have as our superior a former colleague or perhaps even a former pupil, younger and less experienced than we, one whose weaknesses and defects we know only too well, we could easily be tempted to have insufficient respect for his authority and his commands. Then a life of obedience becomes especially difficult : it is hard for us to obey, we do not have recourse to the superior with childlike trust, and what is worse, we justify this attitude to ourselves. Here we are making a great mistake in perspective; we forget that, no matter who the superior is, he is invested with authority which comes from God, authority placed on him solely because he has been called to this office. This authority is unchangeable and has the same force whether the superior is old or young, experienced and virtuous or inexperienced and less virtuous. Basically, if we find ourselves in these difficulties, we must lay the blame on our lack of a supernatural spirit, a spirit of faith. We are judging spiritual matters according to natural standards and from the point of view of human values, which makes it impossible for us to live a life of real obedience, a life entirely based on supernatural values and motives. We must learn how to rise above human views concerning the person of our superior—his good qualities or his faults, his actions in the past, and so forth—to look upon him only as the representative of God and of His divine authority. It is true, we often

find it absolutely necessary to use all our strength and efforts to do this if we do not wish to lose the fruit of a life of obedience. It is certain that the more we force ourselves to see in our superiors the authority which comes from God, so much the more perfect and meritorious our obedience will be, and God Himself will guide us by through them.

2. Very often, if not always, a want of supernatural spirit is accompanied by a want of humility. It is painful to self-love to depend upon and submit to others; it is hard to subject our own affairs to the judgment and rule of someone else and to acquiesce to his decisions. It is particularly difficult if the superior seems to be, at least in some respects, our inferior in age, culture, experience, or ability; then the " ego, " its pride hurt, rebels vigorously, hiding its resistance under a thousand excuses. This, too, is a grave error because, although it is true that the superior may be our inferior in some ways, we must not consider this, but only the fact that he is always superior in relation to us—because God has made him so. He is superior because God has placed him over us; he is superior because God has given him the mission to direct us in His place; his personal qualities or defects do not affect the office of superior which God has conferred upon him. Certainly a superior, on his part, should endeavor to acquire, if he does not already possess them, the virtue and capability required by his office. But this is his affair; our duty, as subjects, is to do but one thing : to submit with filial humility, to allow ourselves to be guided and governed. It is strictly a question of humility, because after all, humility means humbling ourselves, putting ourselves in the right place, the place of a subject in relation to a superior, which is always that of humble dependence. Let us reflect on the obedience of Jesus, and in it we shall see the attitude of humility carried to its utmost : although He was God, " He emptied Himself, taking the form of a servant, being made in the likeness of men.... He humbled Himself, becoming obedient unto death, even to the death of the Cross " (*Phil* 2,7.8). What is our self-abasement, our submission to our superiors and our dependence on them compared to this profound humiliation of Jesus, who although He was God willed to become man, to live as man, subjecting Himself to His own creatures?

Let us be convinced that if our obedience is faulty, it is almost always because we are wanting in humility.

COLLOQUY

" My sweet Savior, can I see You obedient to Your
creatures for love of me, and refuse to be obedient out of love
for You to those who represent You? Can I see You obedient
unto death, the death of the Cross, out of love for me, without
lovingly embracing this virtue and the Cross on which You
consummated it?

" I will force myself to the utmost of my power to
imitate Your example, and for love of You, obey all
creatures—my superiors, equals, or inferiors—in all things,
without argument, murmuring, or delay, but joyfully and
lovingly. Therefore, I will not question the reasons why I am
told to do this or that; I will not think about the way in
which the order is given to me, or the person who gives it.
I will consider Your will alone, letting myself be moved like
You in any direction, by anyone, in agreeable or disagreeable,
suitable or unseemly circumstances. It matters not! Grant
me the obedience You desire.

" O Jesus, who willed to make reparation for Adam's
disobedience and mine at the cost of Your life; O Jesus who
by Your death acquired for me the grace of knowing how to
obey, I wish to live longer only to sacrifice my life by perfect,
continual obedience " (St. Francis de Sales).

" O Lord, You desire to infuse obedience into our hearts,
but You cannot because we will not recognize that You
speak and work through our superiors, and also because we are
attached to our own will " (St. Mary Magdalen dei Pazzi).

126

JESUS PERSECUTED

PRESENCE OF GOD - O Jesus, help me to enter into the mystery of Your Passion; deign to associate me with it, so that I may participate in Your Resurrection.

MEDITATION

1. Today Passiontide begins, a time especially consecrated to the remembrance and loving contemplation of the sorrows of Jesus. The veiled crucifix and statues, the absence of the *Gloria* in the Mass and the *Gloria Patri* in the responsories of the Divine Office,—are all signs of mourning by which the Church commemorates Our Lord's Passion. Pope St. Leo exhorts us to participate " in the Cross of Christ, in order that we also may do something which will unite us to what He has done for us, for as the Apostle says, ' if we suffer with Him, we shall be glorified with Him.' " Therefore, we must not only meditate on Jesus' sufferings, but also take part in them; only by bearing His Passion in our heart and in our body (cf. 2 *Cor* 4,10) shall we be able to share in its fruits. So it is that in the liturgy of this season the Church repeats more insistently than ever : " If you hear the voice of the Lord, harden not your hearts. " The voice of the Lord makes itself heard these days, not by words, but by the eloquent testimony of deeds, by the great events of the Passion—a mystery which gives us the most convincing proof of His infinite love for us. Let us, therefore, open our heart to the sublime lessons of the Passion : let us see how much Jesus has loved us and how much we ought to love Him in return; let us learn that, if we wish to follow Him, we, too, must suffer and bear the Cross with Him and after Him. At the same time, let us open our heart to a lively hope; for our salvation is in the Passion of Jesus. In today's Epistle (*Heb* 9,11-15) St. Paul presents to us the majestic figure of Christ, the Eternal High Priest, who " by His Blood, entered once into the holies,

[that is, heaven] having obtained eternal redemption. "
The Passion of Jesus has redeemed us; it has opened once
again our Father's house to us; it is then the motive for our
hope.

2. The Gospel (*Jn* 8,46-59) narrates an instance of the
pressing hostility of the Jews, an evident prelude to the Passion
of Jesus.   In their hardened hearts they had absolutely
refused to acknowledge the mission of the Savior; as a result,
they schemed in a thousand ways to oppose His teachings
and to belittle Him before the people by declaring Him a liar
and one possessed by the devil.   Their animosity had increased
to the point where they decided to stone Him : " They took
up stones therefore to cast at Him. "   Jesus' death was
already decreed by the Jews, but the hour fixed by His
Father had not yet come, so " Jesus hid Himself, and went out
of the Temple. "

This passage in the Gospel allows us to consider the
conduct of Jesus in the presence of His persecutors : we see
zeal for their souls, meekness, personal disinterestedness,
and total abandonment to God.   St. Gregory the Great
wrote : " Consider, beloved brethren, the meekness of the
Lord.   He, who had come to remit sins, said, ' Which of you
will convince Me of sin? '   He, who by virtue of His divinity,
could justify sinners, does not disdain to prove by reasoning
that He is not a sinner. "

The calumnies continued : " Thou art a Samaritan and
hast a devil. "   The divine Master answered, always with
meekness, only what was necessary to testify to the truth :
" I have not a devil, but I honor My Father, and you have
dishonored Me. "   Then He placed His reputation and His
cause in the hands of God.   " I seek not My own glory;
there is One that seeketh and judgeth. "   In the meantime,
throughout all the discussions, He did not cease to instruct
and to enlighten minds, attempting to draw them away from
error.   Always forgetful of Himself, He thought only of the
good of souls.   It was precisely in these painful circumstances
that Jesus gave us precious instruction : " He that is of God,
heareth the words of God. . . .   If any man keep My word,
he shall not see death forever. "   Let us gather these lessons
from the lips of our persecuted Master, and keep them in our
heart with a jealous care.   In our day, too, the world is
filled with His enemies, those who oppose His doctrine and

despise His Passion.   Let us, at least, believe in Him and be His faithful friends.

COLLOQUY

"Praise be to You, O most merciful God, who willed to redeem us and restore us by the Passion, the sufferings, the scorn, and the poverty of Your Son, when we were wretched outcasts and condemned prisoners.   I run to Your Cross, O Christ—to suffering, scorn, and poverty; with all my strength I desire to be transformed in You, O suffering God-Man, who loved me so much that You endured a horrible, shameful death for the sole purpose of saving me, and to give me an example, so that I would be able to endure adversity for love of You.   It is the perfection and true proof of love to conform myself to You, O Crucified One, who for my sins willed to undergo a cruel death, delivering Yourself entirely to tortures, as a victim.   O my suffering God, only by reading the book of Your life and death shall I be able to know You and to penetrate Your mystery.   Grant me, then, a profound spirit of prayer, a pious, humble, attentive prayer, springing not only from my lips, but also from my heart and soul, so that I shall be able to understand the lessons of Your Passion!

"In this book, I see Your infinite goodness and mercy, which made You take upon Yourself our condemnation, our scorn, our sufferings, rather than leave us in such a wretched state.   I see the unlimited bounty, the care, the diligence You showed to save us and lead us back to the heavenly kingdom.   I see the infinite wisdom by which You redeemed us, saved us, and glorified us in an ineffable manner, through Your mercy, without harming Your justice.   While You died a painful death, You vivified everything and destroyed that death common to us all.

"Yet more, in the book of Your Cross I see Your infinite meekness, by which, although being cursed, You did not curse nor avenge Yourself, but on the contrary, You pardoned and won heaven for the very ones who were crucifying You" (St. Angela of Foligno).

127

THE VALUE OF SUFFERING

PRESENCE OF GOD - O Jesus Crucified, teach me the science of the Cross; make me understand the value of suffering.

MEDITATION

1. The Passion of Jesus teaches us in a concrete way that in the Christian life we must be able to accept suffering for the love of God.   This is a hard, repugnant lesson for our nature, which prefers pleasure and happiness; however, it comes from Jesus, the Teacher of truth and of life, the loving Teacher of our souls, who desires only our real good.   If He commends suffering to us, it is because suffering contains a great treasure.

Suffering in itself is an evil and cannot be agreeable; if Jesus willed to embrace it in all its plenitude and if He offers it to us, inviting us to esteem and love it, it is only in view of a superior good which cannot be attained by any other means—the sublime good of the redemption and the sanctification of our souls.

Although man, by his twofold nature, is subject to suffering, God willed to exempt our first parents from it by their preternatural gifts; but through sin, these gifts were lost forever, and suffering inevitably entered our life.   The gamut of sufferings which has harassed humanity is the direct outcome of the disorder caused by sin, not only by original sin, but also by actual sins.   Yet the Church chants : *O happy fault!*   Why?   The answer lies in the infinite love of God which transforms everything and draws from the double evil of sin and suffering the great good of the redemption of the human race.   When Jesus took upon Himself the sins of mankind, He also assumed their consequences, that is, suffering and death; and this suffering, embraced by Him during His whole life, and especially in His Passion, became the instrument of our redemption. Pain, the result of sin, becomes in Jesus and with Jesus, the means of destroying sin itself.   Thus a Christian may not consider pain only as an undesirable burden from which he must necessarily recoil, but he must see in it much more—a means of redemption and sanctification.

2. Suffering is the disagreeable feeling which we experience when something—a situation, a circumstance, —does not correspond to our inclinations, our needs, or our hopes, which does not harmonize with them or gratify them, but on the contrary, contradicts and opposes them. Whereas all men are subject to this misery, the Christian alone possesses the secret of accepting it into his life without destroying the harmony or the happiness which he can enjoy on earth. This secret consists precisely, for a Christian, in attuning all kinds of suffering to his personal aspirations, which, for him, can never be limited to an ideal of earthly happiness. This harmony is possible, for that which appears to be opposition and disagreement from one point of view, often turns into profit when seen in a different light. Thus, for example, physical suffering, cold, hunger, illness, while unpleasant to the body, can be very useful for the attainment of a moral or supernatural good, such as the acquisition of virtue, or progress in holiness. If, from a purely human viewpoint, some sufferings seem inopportune and useless, they are never so when regarded supernaturally. " To them that love God, all things work together unto good " (*Rom* 8,28). Even the greatest calamity, private or public, can become a precious and most effective means of elevating the soul. Every kind of suffering can then be made conformable to the highest ideals of the Christian : eternal salvation, sanctity, the glory of God, the good of souls. But this congruity is impossible without love; or rather, it will be possible only in proportion to our love, for it was by love alone that Jesus transformed the Cross, a terrible instrument of torture, into a most efficacious instrument for the glory of God and the salvation of mankind. It is the same for us : charity, the love of God and of souls, will enable us to accept any kind of suffering, harmonizing it with our loftiest aspirations. In this way, suffering finds a place, a very important place, in our life, without destroying our peace and serenity. On the contrary, our spirit is dilated under an increasingly generous inspiration, unto an ever greater love. As a result, we shall be happy, even while we are experiencing pain. Behold how Jesus has transformed suffering; behold the value conferred on it by His Passion.

COLLOQUY

" O Lord, You do not like to make us suffer, but You
know it is the only way to prepare us to know You as You
know Yourself, to prepare us to become like You.   You know
well that if You sent me but a shadow of earthly happiness,
I should cling to it with all the intense ardor of my heart,
and so You refuse me even this shadow...because You wish
that my heart be wholly Yours.

" Life passes so quickly that it is obviously better to have
a most splendid crown and a little suffering, than an ordinary
crown and no suffering.   When I think that, for a sorrow
borne with joy, I shall be able to love You more for all
eternity, I understand clearly that if You gave me the entire
universe, with all its treasures, it would be nothing in
comparison to the slightest suffering.   Each new suffering,
each pang of the heart, is a gentle wind to bear to You, O
Jesus, the perfume of the soul that loves You; then You smile
lovingly, and immediately make ready a new grief, and fill
the cup to the brim, thinking the more the soul grows in
love, the more it must grow in suffering too.

" What a favor, my Jesus, and how You must love me to
send me suffering!   Eternity itself will not be long enough to
bless You for it.   Why this predilection?   It is a secret which
You will reveal to me in our heavenly home on the day when
You will wipe away all our tears.

" Lord, You ask me for this suffering, this sorrow....
You need it for souls, for my soul.   O Jesus, since You have
made me understand that You would give me souls through
the Cross, the more crosses I meet, the more ardent my thirst
for suffering becomes.

" I am happy not to be free from suffering here; suffering
united with love is the only thing that seems desirable to me
in this vale of tears " (T.C.J. *L*, 32,50,23,40,58,224 - *St*).

128

PATIENCE

PRESENCE OF GOD - O Jesus, meek and divinely patient, teach me the secret of true patience.

MEDITATION

1. Patience is the virtue which makes us accept for love of God, generously and peacefully, everything that is displeasing to our nature, without allowing ourselves to be depressed by the sadness which easily comes over us when we meet with disagreeable things.

Patience is a special aspect of the virtue of fortitude which prevents our deviating from the right road when we encounter obstacles. It is an illusion to believe in a life without difficulties. These are usually all the greater and the more frequent as our undertakings are more generous. Great works, magnanimous and heroic virtues, always grow in the midst of difficulties. In the presence of these, fortitude has a double function : to *face* them and to *bear* them. Many difficulties are surmounted and overcome by an act of courage; others, on the contrary, cannot be mastered. We must learn to *bear* with them, and this is the role of patience—an arduous task, because it is easier to face obstacles directly, than to support the inevitable oppositions and sufferings of life, which, in time, tend to discourage and sadden us.

Only by fixing our glance on Jesus, the divinely patient One, can we learn to practise patience. When we see Him who came into the world to save us, living from the first moment of His earthly existence in want, privation, and poverty, and later in the midst of misunderstanding and persecution; when we see Him become the object of the hatred of His own fellow citizens, calumniated, doomed to death, betrayed by a friend, and tried and condemned as a malefactor, our souls are stirred : we realize that we cannot be His disciples unless we follow the same road. If Jesus, the Innocent One *par excellence*, bore so much for love of us, can we, sinners who are deserving to suffer, not endure

something for love of Him? Whatever the total of suffering
in our lives, it will always be very small, and even
nothing, compared with the infinite sufferings of Jesus; for in
His Passion Christ not only endured the suffering of one
life or of several human lives, but that of *all* mankind.

2. Whoever wishes to become patient, must, first of all,
look at the motives for suffering in the profound light of faith.
This superior illumination will make the soul understand that
everything that happens in life is always permitted by God,
and is solely for its good. It is true that very often suffering
and hardships come to us through secondary causes; but that
makes little difference when we realize that everything comes
from our loving Father in Heaven, who uses these painful
circumstances to help us to become more virtuous. If we
wish to live only for God, we must never stop to consider the
human causes of our sufferings, we must accept all from
His hands, simply repeating : " *Dominus est!* " It is the Lord!

This acceptance does not prevent us from feeling, even
deeply feeling, the weight of suffering—Jesus, also, felt
it in His agony in the Garden of Olives—but it does help us
to be undisturbed, to preserve peace and serenity, to maintain
self-control and, consequently, to be patient.

In order to begin to practice patience, we must try to bear
daily annoyances and sufferings resignedly, without complaint,
knowing that divine Providence does not permit any trial
that will not be a source of good for us. In the beginning,
and even for a long time, we may experience a great
repugnance for suffering. Nevertheless, if we try to accept
it as we should, with constancy, peace, and submission to the
divine will, we shall gradually be cognizant of the great
spiritual profit that flows from it; we shall feel more detached
from creatures and from ourselves, and closer to God. Then
shall we come to value suffering spontaneously; and later,
having experienced its spiritual fruitfulness more completely,
we shall finally come to love it.

But let us have no illusions : the love of suffering is the
summit of patience; it is the fruit of patience brought to
perfection. To reach this height, we must begin with a much
humbler practice; that is, the peaceful and uncomplaining
acceptance of everything that makes us suffer.

COLLOQUY

O Jesus, for love of You and with Your help, I wish to
suffer in peace all the contradictions of my life. " Your
thoughts are not our thoughts, Your ways are not our ways.
You offer us a cup so bitter that our feeble nature cannot
bear it. But I do not want to draw back my lips from the cup
prepared by Your hand. You have taught me the secret
of suffering in peace. *Peace* does not mean *joy*, at least not
sensible joy; to suffer in peace, all I have to do is to will all
that You will.

" To be Your spouse, I must be like You; and You are all
covered with blood and crowned with thorns. You wish
to make me like You; then, should I fear that I cannot carry
the Cross without weakening? On the way to Calvary,
You fell three times; and I, a poor little child, do I not wish
to be like You? Should I not wish to fall a hundred times
to prove to You my love, rising up again with more strength
than before my fall?

" It is very consoling for me to remember that You,
the God of might, knew our weaknesses, that You shuddered
at the sight of the bitter cup which earlier You had so ardently
desired to drink.

" O Jesus, what it costs to give You what You ask!
But what happiness that it does cost! Far from complaining
to You of the crosses You send me, I cannot fathom the
infinite love which has moved You to treat me so. O Lord,
do not let me waste the trial You send me, it is a gold mine
I must exploit. I, a little grain of sand, want to set myself
to the task, without joy, without courage, without strength,
and all these conditions will make the enterprise easier;
I want to work for love.

" In spite of this trial which robs me of all sense of
enjoyment, I can still say : ' You have given me, O Lord,
a delight in Your doings. ' For is there any greater joy than
to suffer for Your love, O my God? The more intense and the
more hidden the suffering, the more do You value it. And
even if, by an impossibility, You should not be aware of my
affliction, I should still be happy to bear it, in the hope that
by my tears I might prevent or atone for one sin against
faith " (T.C.J. *L*, 63,51,184,59 - *St*, 9).

129

THE DAILY CROSS

PRESENCE OF GOD - O Jesus Crucified, help me, by the merits of Your Cross, to carry my cross daily.

MEDITATION

1. " He that taketh not up his cross, and followeth Me, is not worthy of Me " (*Mt* 10,38). By these words, the divine Master expressly declares that one of the indispensable conditions for being His disciple is to carry the cross. The word *cross*, however, should not make us think only of special sufferings, which, while not excluded, are not generally our portion. First of all, we must think of those common daily disagreeable things which are part of everyone's life and which we must try to accept as so many means to progress and spiritual fruitfulness.

It is often easier to accept, in a burst of generosity, the great sacrifices and sufferings of singular occurence, than the little, insignificant sufferings, closely connected with our state of life and the fulfillment of our duty : sufferings which occur daily under the same form, with the same intensity and insistence, among endless and unchanging circumstances. These may include physical ailments caused by poor health, economic restrictions, the fatigue attendant upon overwork or anxiety; they may be moral sufferings resulting from differences of opinion, clash of temperaments, or misunderstandings. Herein lies the genuine cross that Jesus offers us daily, inviting us to carry it after Him—an unpretentious cross, which does not require great heroism, but which does demand that we repeat our *Fiat* every day, meekly bowing our shoulders to carry its weight with generosity and love. The value, the fruitfulness of our daily sacrifices comes from this unreserved acceptance, which makes us receive them just as God offers them to us, without trying to avoid them or to lessen their weight. " Yea, Father, for so hath it seemed good in Thy sight " (*Mt* 11,26).

2. Jesus calls our sufferings a *cross* because the word cross signifies instrument of salvation; and He does not want

our sorrows to be sterile, but to become a cross, that is, a means of elevating and sanctifying our souls. In fact, all suffering is transformed, changed into a cross as soon as we accept it from the hands of the Savior, and cling to His will which transforms it for our spiritual advantage. If this is true for great sufferings, it is equally true for the small ones; all are part of the divine plan, all, even the tiniest, have been predisposed by God from all eternity for our sanctification. Therefore, let us accept them with calmness, and not allow ourselves to be submerged by things which are unpleasant; let us leave them where they belong, in the place they really occupy in the divine plan, that is, among the instruments by means of which we can attain our ideal of sanctity and union with God. If these annoyances are an evil because they make us suffer, they are also a good, because they give us an opportunity of practicing virtue; they purify us and bring us near to the Lord. However, to understand the value of the cross is not equivalent to bearing it; we need fortitude as well. If we let ourselves be guided by Jesus, He will certainly give it to us and will support us in our daily struggles and sufferings, leading us by the path He Himself has chosen, and to the degree of sanctity He has determined for each one of us. We must have an immense confidence, advance with our eyes closed, and forget ourselves completely. We must accept the cross which Our Lord offers us and carry it with love. If, with the help of grace, we succeed in sanctifying all our daily sufferings, great and small, without losing our serenity and confidence, we shall become saints. Many souls are discouraged at the thought of suffering, and try in every way to avoid it because they do not have enough confidence in the Lord, and are not fully convinced that *all* is planned by Him, down to the last detail, for their real good. Every suffering, whatever its dimensions, always conceals a redemptive, a sanctifying grace; and this grace becomes ours from the moment we accept the suffering in a spirit of faith, for love of God.

COLLOQUY

" I see You, O Jesus, my Guide, raising the standard of the Cross and saying lovingly to me : ' Take the cross I hold out to you, and no matter how heavy it seems to you, follow

Me and do not doubt. ' In response to Your invitation,
I promise You, O my heavenly Spouse, to resist Your love
no longer. I see You as You once made Your way to Calvary,
and I long to follow You promptly.

" As a spouse will not be pleasing to her bridegroom if
she does not apply herself very diligently to the work of
becoming like him, so, O Jesus, my Bridegroom, I resolve,
now and forever, to take every care to imitate You and to crucify myself wholly with You.... I shall consider the cloister,
my Calvary; the regular observance, my cross; and the three
vows, my nails. I do not wish for any consolation except
what comes from You, not now, but in heaven; what does
it matter whether I live a happy life, so long as I live a
religious life. I willingly surrender my heart to affliction,
sadness, and labor. I am happy in not being happy, because
fasting in this life precedes the eternal banquet which awaits
me.

" All this is very little, O my God, to gain You, who
contain every good. No trial should seem hard nor should
I turn back because of the difficulties I might find; I wish to
accept bitterness and all kinds of crosses with readiness "
(cf. T.M. *Sp*).

" O Lord, is there, among all Your works, one which
would not be directed toward the greatest good of the soul
whom You consider as Yours, since she put herself at Your
service, to follow You everywhere, even to the death of the
Cross, resolved to help You bear Your burden and never
to leave You alone?.... I shall trust in Your goodness....
Lead me wherever You wish; I no longer belong to myself,
but to You. Do with me, O Lord, what You wish; I ask
only the grace never to offend You. I want to suffer, O Lord,
because You, too, have suffered " (cf. T.J. *Life*, 11).

130

SUFFERING AND ABANDONMENT

PRESENCE OF GOD - O Lord, teach me to suffer with simplicity, without useless concentration on self, but in total abandonment to Your divine will.

MEDITATION

1. The secret of learning to suffer in a virtuous way consists chiefly in forgetting oneself and one's sorrows and in abandoning oneself to God.

The soul that is absorbed in its own sufferings and concentrates its whole attention on them, becomes unable to bear them serenely and courageously. " Sufficient for the day is the evil thereof" (*Mt* 6,34), said Jesus, thus teaching us to bear calmly, day by day, moment by moment, whatever sorrows and crosses God places in our path, with no thought of what we suffered yesterday, no worry about what we shall have to endure tomorrow. Even when our suffering is intense, let us not exaggerate it, nor attach too much importance to it; let us not foster a morbid tendency to nurture our sorrow, to ponder over it, weighing and analyzing it under every aspect. To act in this way would result in the paralysis of our spirit of sacrifice, of our ability to accept and to act, and would make us useless to ourselves and to others. One who is oversensitive and preoccupied with his own suffering, often becomes insensible and indifferent to the suffering of others.

In order to resist these selfish tendencies which have been rightly defined by Father Faber as " the worm of Christian sorrow, " we must forget ourselves, go out of ourselves and our own sufferings, become interested in the sufferings of others and endeavor to alleviate them. This is a very effective way to regain in times of discouragement the strength to bear our own crosses. We should be mindful of the truth that we are never alone in suffering; that if our sufferings are great, there are always those who suffer incomparably more than we. Our troubles, often enough, are but a drop compared to the sea of sorrows in which mankind is engulfed, and are practically nonentities in comparison with the Passion of Jesus.

Those who are overly concerned with their own troubles eventually become exasperated by them. Drowned in their sorrows, they stifle every impulse to generosity. By contrast, those who know how to forget themselves, maintain their equilibrium, and take greater thought for others than for themselves. They are always open to charity and generosity toward God and their neighbor. These are simple souls who, because they are unmindful of themselves, can bear suffering magnanimously and derive much profit for their own sanctification.

2. Despite all our efforts to escape our own misery and to forget our troubles, we may go through moments of such profound anguish, such impenetrable darkness, that our poor soul does not know how to emerge from it—especially when the horizon, instead of becoming brighter, grows darker and more threatening. At such times there is only one thing to do : to make a leap in the dark, abandoning ourselves entirely into God's hands. We are so helpless and weak that we always need some place of refuge; if we are to forget ourselves and stop thinking about our own concerns, we shall need someone who will sustain and think of us. This Someone is God, who never forgets us, who knows all about our sufferings and our needs, who sees how weak we are, and who is always ready to come to the aid of those who take refuge in Him. Of course, we can look for a certain amount of consolation and help from creatures, but let us not deceive ourselves; people will not always understand us, nor will they always be at our disposal. But if we turn to God, we shall never be disappointed; even if He does not alter our situation or take away our troubles, He will console our hearts interiorly, in secret and in silence, and will give us the strength to persevere.

" Cast thy care upon the Lord, and He shall sustain thee " (Ps 54,23). This is the attitude of abandonment which we should have in times of suffering, and which we should intensify as our sorrows increase. If our spirit of abandonment is proportionate to the depth of our sufferings, then we shall not lose their merit.

Many souls exaggerate their sufferings, dramatizing them because they cannot see God's paternal hand in them, because their faith in His divine Providence is not sufficiently strong; and therefore, they are unable to abandon themselves to Him with complete trust. If our life and all its events, even the most painful ones, did not rest in God's hands, we should have reason to fear; but since everything is *always in His hands,* our fears are groundless and we should not be dismayed. A soul who is confident in God and abandons itself to Him can remain calm in the midst of great trials, can accept even tragic occurrences with simplicity, and suffer serenely and courageously, because it is always supported by God.

COLLOQUY

" O Lord, grant that I may never cease to turn to You, and to look only at You. In consolation or desolation I shall run to You, stopping at nothing else; I shall run so quickly that I shall have no time to look at anything, nor to see the things of earth, because my pace will be so rapid. Therefore, out of love for You, I shall spurn pleasure, repose, dependence upon the judgment of men, satisfaction in their approval, dread of physical discomfort, sadness of spirit, and success or failure. In a word, I shall spurn everything that is not God.

" I realize that my crosses have been permitted and willed by You, my God, to teach me to trust in You in spite of everything.

" O God, be my sole strength in fear, weakness, and distress; be my confidant, or rather my confidence. Divine Guest, dwelling within me, on the throne of my heart, abide with me as my protector; You alone have dominion and power over my whole being; You alone are its love!

" Why should I worry or fear? All is Yours, O God, and You will take care of my wants and provide for them. You are infinite Love, and You love the works of Your hands more than they can know and love themselves. Who would dare question Your power, or the loving, providential care You bestow on Your creatures from all eternity, and with the efficacy of Your love?

" I believe that all You do and permit is for my good and my salvation, and I abandon myself to Your guidance with love and trust, and without anxiety, fear, or calculation " (Bl. M. Thérèse Soubiran).

131

THE SEVEN SORROWS OF MARY

PRESENCE OF GOD - Permit me, O Mary, to remain near the Cross, that I may share with you in the Passion of Jesus.

MEDITATION

1. We find in Simeon's prophecy the first explicit announcement of the part the Blessed Virgin was to have in the Passion of Jesus : " Thy own soul a sword shall pierce " (*Lk* 2,35). This prophecy was fulfilled on Calvary. " Yes, O Blessed Mother, " says St. Bernard, " a sword has truly pierced your soul. It could penetrate Your Son's flesh only by passing through your soul. And after Jesus had died, the cruel lance which opened His side did not reach His soul, but it did pierce yours. His soul was no longer in His body, but yours could not be detached from it. " This beautiful interpretation shows us how Mary, as a Mother, was intimately associated with her Son's Passion.

The Gospel does not tell us that Mary was present during the glorious moments of the life of Jesus, but it does say that she was present on Calvary. " Now there stood by the Cross of Jesus, His Mother, and His Mother's sister, Mary of Cleophas, and Mary Magdalen " (*Jn* 19,25). No one had been able to keep her from hastening to the place where her Son was to be crucified, and her love gave her courage to *stand* there, erect, near the Cross, to be present at the sorrowful agony and death of the One whom she loved above all, because He was both her Son and her God. Just as she had once consented to become His Mother, so she would now agree to see Him tortured from head to foot, and to be torn away from her by a cruel death.

She not only accepted, she offered. Jesus had willingly gone to His Passion, and Mary would willingly offer Her well-beloved Son for the glory of the Most Holy Trinity and the salvation of men. That is why the sacrifice of Jesus became Mary's sacrifice, not only because Mary offered it together with Jesus, and in Him, offered her own Son; but also because, by this offering, she completed the most profound holocaust of herself, since Jesus was the center of her affections and of her whole life. God, who had given her this divine Son, asked, on Calvary, for a return of His gift, and Mary offered Jesus to the Father with all the love of her heart, in complete adherence to the divine will.

2. The liturgy puts on the lips of Our Lady of Sorrows these touching words : " O you who pass by the way, attend and see if there be any sorrow like to my sorrow " *(RM)*. Yes, her grief was immeasurable, and was surpassed only by her love, a love so great that it could encompass that vast sea of sorrow. It can be said of Mary, as of no any other creature, that her love was stronger than death; in fact, it made her able to support the cruel death of Jesus.

" Who could be unfeeling in contemplating the Mother of Christ suffering with her Son? " chants the *Stabat Mater*; and immediately it adds, " O Mother... make me feel the depth of your sorrow, so that I may weep with you. May I bear in my heart the wounds of Christ; make me share in His Passion and become inebriated by the Cross and Blood of your Son. " In response to the Church's invitation, let us contemplate Mary's sorrows, sympathize with her, and ask her for the invaluable grace of sharing with her in the Passion of Jesus. Let us remember that this participation is not to be merely sentimental—even though this sentiment is good and holy—but it must lead us to real *compassion*, that is, to *suffering with* Jesus and Mary. The sufferings God sends us have no other purpose.

The sight of Mary at the foot of the Cross makes the lesson of the Cross less hard and less bitter; her maternal example encourages us to suffer and makes the road to Calvary easier. Let us go, then, with Mary, to join Jesus on Golgotha; let us go with her to meet our cross; and sustained by her, let us embrace it willingly, uniting it with her Son's.

COLLOQUY

" O Mary, Mother of Jesus Crucified, tell me something about His Passion, for you felt and saw it more than all the others who were present, having contemplated it with the eyes of your body and soul, and given it all the attention

possible, O you who love Him with such great love "
(St. Angela of Foligno).

" O Mary, grant that I may stand with you near the
Cross; permit me to contemplate with you the Passion of
your Jesus, and to have a share in your sorrow and tears.
O holy Mother, impress deeply in my heart the wounds of
the Crucified; permit me to suffer with Him, and to unite
myself to your sorrows and His " (cf. *Stabat Mater*).

" O Queen of Virgins, you are also the Queen of
Martyrs; but it was within your heart that the sword
transpierced you, for with you everything took place within
your soul.

" Oh, how fair you are to behold during your long
martyrdom, enveloped in a majesty both strong and gentle;
for you have learned from the Word how those should suffer
who are chosen as victims by the Father, those whom He
has elected as associates in the great work of the redemption,
whom He has known and predestinated to be conformed
to His Christ, crucified for love.

" You are there, O Mary, at the foot of the Cross,
standing, in strength and courage; and my Master says to me,
" *Ecce Mater Tua.* " Behold your Mother. He gives you to
me for my Mother! And now that He has returned to
His Father, and has put me in His place on the Cross so that
I may fill up those things which are wanting of the sufferings
of Christ in my flesh for His Body, which is the Church, you
are still there, O Mary, to teach me to suffer as He did,
to let me hear the last song of His soul which no one but
you, O Mother, could overhear " (E.T. *II*, 15).

That my desire for suffering will not be sterile, help
me, O sweet Mother, to recognize in each daily suffering
the Cross of your Jesus and to embrace it with love.

132

LOVE OF THE CROSS

PRESENCE OF GOD - Again I come to You, O my Crucified God, with the desire to penetrate more deeply into the mystery of the Cross.

MEDITATION

1. The Cross is suffering viewed in the supernatural light of faith as an instrument of salvation and sanctification, and therefore, as an instrument of love. Seen in this light, the Cross is certainly worthy of love; it is the outstanding means of our sanctification. Our union with God cannot be accomplished except through suffering. St. John of the Cross has explained the means by which the soul is to be purified, *scraped* to the bottom in order to reach this life of divine union. A program of total mortification is required to break all our bonds, for we have within us many obstacles which keep us from being entirely moved by God; and the accomplishment of this work is impossible without suffering. But *active suffering*, that is, the mortifications and penances inspired by our personal initiative, is not sufficient. We especially need *passive suffering*. In other words, the Lord Himself must make us suffer, not only in our body, but also in our soul, because we are so *covered with rust*, so full of miseries that our total purification is not possible unless God Himself intervenes directly. To plunge us into passive suffering is, therefore, one of His greatest works of mercy, a proof of His exceeding love.

When God acts in a soul in this way, it is a sign that He wants to bring it to very high perfection. It is precisely in these passive purifying sufferings that the concept of the cross is realized preeminently. In *The Living Flame of Love* (2,27), St. John of the Cross asks why there are so few souls who reach the plenitude of the spiritual life; and he answers : " It is not because God wants to reserve this state for a few privileged souls, but because He finds so few souls disposed to accept the hard task of purification. Therefore, He stops purifying them, and they condemn themselves to mediocrity and advance no farther. " It is impossible to become united to God without these spiritual sufferings, without bearing this " burden " of God.   Suffering and interior desolation alone enlarge the powers of the soul and make it capable of embracing God Himself.

2. " O souls that seek to walk in security and comfort in spiritual things!   If you did but know how necessary it is to suffer and endure in order to reach this security! " (J.C. *LF*, 2,28).   Suffering is requisite not only for the good of the soul, but also that the soul may be able to glorify God and prove its love for Him.   It is not a question of attaining perfection in order to enjoy it—for the perfect soul never thinks of self—but that the soul may be wholly dedicated to the glory of God.   It is in this sense that we read on the summit of the *Mount of Perfection* : Only the honor and glory of God dwell on this mountain. "   Even as the Cross of Jesus was for Him the great means of rendering to the Father the glory that sinful man had refused Him, so should it be in regard to our cross : by means of suffering, we should expiate and repair our faults and the faults of others, in order to give God all the glory due Him.

In addition, as the Cross of Jesus was the supreme proof of His love for us, our cross too, should be the finest proof of our love for Him.   The Son of God has revealed His infinite love for us by His death on the Cross; in like manner, the reality of our love is made apparent by the acceptance of sufferings out of love for Him.   The Cross is, therefore, both the instrument and the work of love, as much that of God's love for us as that of our love for Him.

The more God sanctifies us, the more He proves His love for us and gives us the opportunity of glorifying Him; but He sanctifies us only by means of the Cross—the great Cross of Jesus to which we must unite our little cross.

Our sanctification, then, is proportionate to our experience of the Passion of Christ.   Sufferings are, even in this sense, a proof of God's love for us.   If we understood all this, how we should love the Cross!

COLLOQUY

" O Lord, the road of trials is the way by which You lead those You love, and the more You love them, the more trials You send them, since You admit to Your friendship only souls that love the Cross.... If You asked me whether I should prefer to endure all the trials in the world up to the end of time, and afterwards to gain a little more glory, or to have no trials and to attain one degree less of glory, I should answer that I would most gladly accept all the trials in exchange for a little more fruition in the understanding of Your wonders, for I see that the more we know You, the more we love and glorify You.

" No, I do not wish to make anything of passing troubles, when it is a question of procuring some glory for You who suffered so much for us.

" If I want to know, O my God, how You act toward those who beg You from the bottom of their heart to accomplish Your will in them, I have only to ask Your glorious Son, who addressed the same prayer to You in the Garden of Olives.... You fulfilled this wish in Him by giving Him up to all kinds of sorrows, insults, and persecutions, leaving Him finally to die on the Cross. This is what You gave the One whom You loved above all others. As long as we are in this world, these are Your gifts. You proportion them according to Your love for us; You give more to those You love more, and less to those You love less. You also give according to the courage You find in each of us, and according to our love for You, for if we love You much, we shall be able to suffer much for You; whereas if we love You only a little, we will suffer little " (T.J. *Way*, 18 – *Life*, 37 – *Way*, 3;32).

O my God, increase my love, dilate my poor heart and make it able to endure much for love of You. I shall willingly accept suffering, in order to prove to You the reality of my love.

¹33

THE TRIUMPH OF JESUS

THE SECOND SUNDAY OF THE PASSION OR PALM SUNDAY

PRESENCE OF GOD - O Jesus, I want to follow You in Your triumph, so that I may follow You later to Calvary.

MEDITATION

1. Holy Week begins with the description of the triumphal entrance of Jesus into Jerusalem on the Sunday before His Passion. Jesus, who had always been opposed to any public manifestation and who had fled when the people wanted to make Him their king (cf. *Jn* 6,15), allows Himself to be borne in triumph today. Not until now, when He is about to die, does He submit to being publicly acclaimed as the Messiah, because by dying on the Cross, He will be in the most complete manner Messiah, Redeemer, King, and Victor. He allows Himself to be recognized as King, but a King who will reign from the Cross, who will triumph and conquer by dying on the Cross. The same exultant crowd that acclaims Him today will curse Him in a few days and lead Him to Calvary; today's triumph will be the vivid prelude to tomorrow's Passion.

Jesus enters the holy city in triumph, but only in order to suffer and die there. Hence, the twofold meaning of the Procession of the Palms : it is not enough to accompany Jesus in His triumph; we must follow Him in His Passion, prepared to share in it by stirring up in ourselves, according to St. Paul's exhortation (*Ep : Phil* 2,5-11), His sentiments of humility and total immolation, which will bring us, like Him and with Him, " unto death, even to the death of the Cross. " The palms which the priest blesses today have not only a festive significance; they also " represent the victory which Jesus is about to win over the prince of death " *(RM)*. For us too, they must be symbols of triumph, indicative of the victory to be won in our battle against the evil in ourselves and against the evil which roams about us. As we receive the blessed palm, let us renew our pledge to conquer with

Jesus, but let us not forget that it was on the Cross that He conquered.

2. Jesus submits to being borne in triumph, but with what meekness and humility! He knows that His enemies are hiding among the people who are singing the hosanna, and that they will succeed in changing that hosanna into *crucify Him!* He knows it, and He could impose Himself upon them in all the power of His divinity; He could unmask them publicly and disclose their plans. However, Jesus does not wish to conquer or to rule by force; His kingdom is founded on love and meekness. The Evangelist says this very aptly : " Tell ye the daughter of Sion : Behold, thy King cometh to thee, meek, and sitting upon an ass " (*Mt* 21,5). With the same meekness, He, the Innocent One, the only true King and Conqueror, will consent to appear as a criminal, a condemned and conquered man, a mock king. In this way, however, from the throne of the Cross He will draw all things to Himself.

As the joyful procession advances, Jesus sees the panorama of Jerusalem spread out at His feet. St. Luke says (19,41-44) : " When He drew near, seeing the city, He wept over it, saying, ' If thou also hadst known, and that in this thy day, the things that are to thy peace!... Thy enemies...shall not leave in thee a stone upon a stone because thou hast not known the time of thy visitation. ' " Jesus weeps at the obstinacy of the holy city which, because it has not recognized Him as the Messiah and has not accepted His Gospel, will be destroyed to its foundations. Jesus, true God, is also true man, and as man He is moved with compassion because of the sad fate which Jerusalem has prepared for itself by its obstinate resistance to grace. He goes to His Passion and will even die for the salvation of Jerusalem, but the holy city will not be saved because it has not wished to be, " because it did not know the time of its visitation. " This is the story of so many souls who resist grace; it is the cause of the most profound and intimate suffering of the benevolent heart of Jesus. Let us give Our Lord the joy of seeing us profit to the full by the merits of His sorrowful Passion, by all the Blood which He has shed. When we resist the invitations of grace, we are resisting the Passion of Jesus and preventing it from being applied to us in its plenitude.

COLLOQUY

" O Jesus, I contemplate You in Your triumphant
entrance into Jerusalem. Anticipating the crowd which
would come to meet You, You mounted an ass and gave
an admirable example of humility in the midst of the
acclamations of the crowd who cut branches of trees and
spread their garments along the way. While the people
were singing hymns of praise, You were filled with pity
and wept over Jerusalem. Rise now, my soul, handmaid
of the Savior, join the procession of the daughters of Sion
and go out to meet your King. Accompany the Lord of
heaven and earth, seated on an ass; follow Him with olive
and palm branches, with works of piety and with victorious
virtues " (cf. St. Bonaventure).

O Jesus, what bitter tears You shed over the city which
refused to recognize You! And how many souls, like
Jerusalem, go to perdition on account of their obstinate
resistance to grace! For them I pray with all my strength.
" My God, this is where Your power and mercy should
be shown. Oh! what a lofty grace I ask for, O true God,
when I conjure You to love those who do not love You, to
answer those who do not call to You, to give health to those
who take pleasure in remaining sick!... You say, O my
Lord, that You have come to seek sinners. Here, Lord, are the
real sinners. But, instead of seeing our blindness, O God,
consider the precious Blood which Your Son shed for us.
Let Your mercy shine out in the midst of such great malice.
Do not forget, Lord, that we are Your creatures, and pour
out on us Your goodness and mercy " (T.J. *Exc*, 8).

Even if we resist grace, O Jesus, You are still the Victor;
Your triumph over the prince of darkness is accomplished,
and humanity has been saved and redeemed by You. You
are the Good Shepherd who knows and loves each one
of His sheep and would lead them all to safety. Your loving
heart is not satisfied with having merited salvation for the
whole flock; it ardently desires each sheep to profit by this
salvation.... O Lord, give us then, this good will; enable
us to accept Your gift, Your grace, and grant that Your
Passion may not have been in vain.

134

THE SUPPER AT BETHANY

MONDAY OF HOLY WEEK

PRESENCE OF GOD - O Lord, with Mary of Bethany I wish to pay my humble, devout homage to Your sacred Body before it is disfigured by the Passion.

MEDITATION

1. The Gospel for today (*Jn* 12,1-9) tells us of this impressive scene : " Jesus therefore, six days before the Pasch, came to Bethany . . . and they made Him a supper there; and Martha served. . . . Mary, therefore, took a pound of ointment of right spikenard, of great price, and anointed the feet of Jesus, and wiped His feet with her hair. " Martha, as usual, was busy about many things. Mary, however, paid attention only to Jesus; to show respect to Him, it did not seem extravagant to her to pour over Him a whole vase of precious perfume. Some of those present murmured, " Why this waste? Could not the ointment have been sold. . . and the price given to the poor? " And they murmured against her (cf. *Mk* 14,4.5). Mary said nothing and made no excuses; completely absorbed in her adored Master, she continued her work of devotion and love.

Mary is the symbol of the soul in love with God, the soul who gives herself exclusively to Him, consuming for Him all that she is and all that she has. She is the symbol of those souls who give up, in whole or in part, exterior activity, in order to consecrate themselves more fully to the immediate service of God and to devote themselves to a life of more intimate union with Him. This total consecration to the Lord is deemed wasteful by those who fail to understand it—although the same offering, if otherwise employed, would cause no complaint. If everything we are and have is His gift, can it be a waste to sacrifice it in His honor and, by so acting, to repair for the indifference of countless souls who seldom, if ever, think of Him?

Money, time, strength, and even human lives spent in the immediate service of the Lord, far from being wasted, reach therein the perfection of their being. Moreover, by this consecration, they conform to the proper scale of values. Giving alms to the poor is a duty, but the worship and love of God is a higher obligation. If urgent works of charity sometimes require us to leave His service for that of our neighbor, no change in the hierarchy of importance is thereby implied. God must always have the first place.

Jesus Himself then comes to Mary's defense : " Let her be, that she may keep this perfume against the day of My burial. " In the name of all those who love, Mary gave the sacred Body of Jesus, before it was disfigured by the Passion, the ultimate homage of an ardent love and devotion.

2. In St. John's Gospel it is clearly stated that the murmurings about Mary's act were uttered by Judas Iscariot. The sinister face of the traitor appears darker still beside that of the loyal Mary : physically, he is still numbered among the Twelve, but spiritually, he has been cut off from them for a long time. Ever since the previous year, when the Master had told them about the Eucharist, Judas was lost. Referring to him on one occasion, Jesus had said, " Have not I chosen you twelve; and one of you is a devil" (*Jn* 6,71). Judas had been chosen by Jesus with a love of predilection; he had been admitted to the group of His closest friends and, like the eleven others, had received the great grace of the apostolate. In the beginning, he must have been faithful; but later, attachment to worldly things and avarice began to take possession of him, so as to completely chill his love for the Master and transform the Apostle into a traitor. Because of His divine foreknowledge, Jesus had expected the treachery; and yet, since Judas had been originally worthy of His trust, He had placed him on an equal footing with the other members of the apostolic college. Subsequently, although he had already become a liar, Jesus continued to treat him like the others, showing him the same love and esteem. This was very painful to the sensitive heart of Jesus, but He would not act otherwise, He wished that we might see with what love, patience, and delicacy He treats even His most stubborn enemies. How many times must the Master have tried to enlighten that darkened mind! Certainly, He was thinking of Judas when He

mind! Certainly, He was thinking of Judas' worldly goods : " You cannot serve God and mammon.... What doth it profit a man if he gain the whole world, and suffer the loss of His own soul? " (*Mt* 6,24—16,26). However, these words, which should have been an affectionate reprove to the traitor, did not touch him. Judas represents those souls who have received from God graces of predilection, but who prove to be unworthy of them, because of their infidelities. Consecrated souls must, therefore, be very faithful to the grace of their vocation and must not permit the slightest attachment to take root in their hearts.

COLLOQUY

Here are two paths, Lord, as diametrically opposed as possible : one of fidelity and one of betrayal, the loving fidelity of Mary of Bethany, the horrible treachery of Judas. O Lord, how I should like to offer You a heart like Mary's! How I should like to see the traitor in me entirely dead and destroyed!

But You tell me : " Watch ye, and pray that you enter not into temptation! " (*Mk* 14,38). Oh! how necessary it is for me to watch and pray, so that the enemy will not come to sow the poisonous germs of treason in my heart! May I be faithful to You, Lord, faithful at any cost, in big things as well as in small, so that the foxes of little attachments will never succeed in invading and destroying the vineyard of my heart!

" Lord Jesus, when I meditate on Your Passion, the first thing that strikes me is the perfidy of the traitor. He was so full of the venom of bad faith that he actually betrayed You—You, his Master and Lord. He was inflamed with such cupidity that he sold his God for money, and in exchange for a few vile coins delivered up Your precious Blood. His ingratitude went so far that he persecuted even to death Him who had raised him to the height of the apostolate.... O Jesus, how great was Your goodness toward this hard-hearted disciple! Although his wickedness was so great, I am much more impressed by Your gentleness and meekness, O Lamb of God! You have given me this meekness as a model. Behold, O Lord, the man whom

You allowed to share Your most special confidences, the
man who seemed to be so united to You, Your Apostle, Your
friend, the man who ate Your bread, and who, at the Last
Supper, tasted with You the sweet cup, and this man committed this monstrous crime against You, his Master! But, in
spite of all this at the time of betrayal, You, O meek Lamb,
did not refuse the kiss of that mouth so full of malice. You
gave him everything, even as You gave to the other Apostles,
in order not to deprive him of anything that might melt the
hardness of his evil heart " (cf. St. Bonaventure).

O Jesus, by the atrocious suffering inflicted on Your
heart by that infamous treachery, grant me, I beg of You,
the grace of a fidelity that is total, loving, and devoted.

135

THE MEEK LAMB

TUESDAY OF HOLY WEEK

PRESENCE OF GOD - O Jesus, give me the grace to penetrate the
abyss of sorrow made by sin in Your heart, so full of meekness.

MEDITATION

1. In the Epistle of today's Mass, Jeremias (11,18-20)
speaks to us as the suffering Savior : " I was as a meek lamb
that is carried to be a victim. " This sentence expresses the
attitude of Jesus toward the bitterness of His Passion. He
knew every one of these sufferings in all their most concrete
particulars; His heart had undergone them by anticipation,
and the thought of them never left Him for an instant during
the course of His life on earth. If the Passion, in its historical
reality, took place in less than twenty-four hours, in its
spiritual reality it spanned His entire life.

Jesus knew what was awaiting Him, His heart was
tortured by it; and yet He not only accepted but ardently
desired that hour, " His hour "; and He gave Himself into

the hands of His enemies with the meekness of a lamb being led to the slaughter. " I have left My house, " He says again through the mouth of Jeremias. "...I have delivered My beloved soul into the hands of My enemies " *(RB)*. Judas betrayed Him, His enemies dragged Him before the tribunal, they condemned Him to death, they tortured His body horribly; but Jesus, even in His Passion, remained always God, remained always the Master, the Lord. " I have power to lay down My life and to take it up again, " says the liturgy in today's Vespers *(RB)*. Jesus went to His Passion " because it was His own *will* " *(Is* 53,7). He willed it because, as He Himself said, " This is the command which I have received from My Father " *(Jn* 10,18).

However, His ardent desire for the Passion did not prevent Him from tasting all its bitterness. " The sorrows of death have encompassed me.... Insults and terrors I have suffered from those who called themselves my friends.... God of Israel, because of You, I have suffered opprobrium, and shame has covered my face " *(RB)*. Let us try to sound the depths of these sacred texts which we read in today's liturgy, in order that we may have a better understanding of the most bitter Passion of Christ.

2. Today at Mass we read the Passion as recounted by Mark, Peter's disciple (14,32-72—15,1-46). No other Evangelist has described so minutely the denial of Peter; it is the humble confession which the chief of the Apostles makes of himself through the mouth of his disciple. During the Last Supper, when Jesus predicted that the Apostles would desert Him that very night, Peter had protested with all the vigor of his ardent temperament : " Although all shall be scandalized in Thee, yet not I! " In vain did the Master foretell his desertion, outlining it in detail : " Even in this night, before the cock crows twice, thou shalt deny Me thrice. " An overweening confidence in himself had blinded Peter to the truth of Jesus' words, to the possibility of his own weakness. " Although I should die together with Thee, I will not deny Thee. " Peter was sincere in his protestation, but he sinned through presumption; the practical experience of human misery and frailty, by which no one, even the most courageous, can remain faithful to duty without divine aid, was lacking to him. His initial steps along this road would be taken in Gethsemane,

when he, like the others, would be unable to watch " one
hour " with the Master. Further, at the time of Jesus'
arrest, he would flee away trembling with fear. But these
two episodes would not be enough to cure him of his
presumption; he would need a third, the saddest of all.

In the courtyard of Caiphas' palace, where, having
recovered from his first fright, Peter had gone to watch
the turn of events, he was recognized by a maid as a disciple
of Jesus. Seized by the fear of being involved in the Master's
trial, he denied the accusation immediately, saying, " I know
Him not. " Having fallen once, he had difficulty in
recovering himself, and when questioned again, he made
a second, even a third denial. " As he was yet speaking,
the cock crew, and the Lord turning, looked on Peter. "
That crowing of the cock, and much more, that look full
of love and sorrow, made him enter into himself, " and
going out, he wept bitterly " (Lk 22,62). The blindfold
of presumption fell from his eyes; and Peter, who sincerely
loved Jesus, acknowledged his weakness, his fault. The
loving glance of the Master had saved him. Because Peter
no longer relied on himself, Jesus could rely upon him and
would entrust His flock to him. The lesson is clear. As long
as a soul depends solely upon itself, it is not ready to be
sanctified, nor to cooperate efficaciously in the sanctification
of others.

COLLOQUY

" O Lord of my soul, how quick we are to offend You!
But how much quicker are You to forgive us! What am
I saying, Lord! ' The sorrows of death have encompassed
me. ' Alas! What a great evil is sin, since it could put
God Himself to death with such terrible sufferings! And
these same sufferings surround You today, O my Lord!
Where can You go that You are not tortured? Men cover
You with wounds in all Your members.

" Christians, this is the hour to defend your King and
to keep Him company in the profound isolation in which
He finds Himself. How few, O Lord, are the servants who
remain faithful to You!... The worst of it is that there
are some who profess to be Your friends in public, but who
sell You in secret. You can scarcely find one in whom You

can trust. O my God, true Friend, how badly does he repay You who betrays You!

"O true Christians, come to weep with your God! It was not only over Lazarus that He shed tears of compassion, but over all those who, in spite of His call, would never rise from the dead. At that time, my Love, You saw even the sins that I would commit against You. May they be at an end, and with them, those of all sinners. Grant that these dead may come to life. May Your voice, Lord, be strong enough to give them life, even if they do not ask it of You. Lazarus did not ask You to bring him back to life, and yet You restored life to him at the prayer of a sinner. Here is another sinner, my God, and much more culpable than she was. Let, then, Your mercy shine forth! I ask it of You in spite of my wretchedness, for those who will not ask " (T.J. *Exc*, 10).

136

THE MAN OF SORROWS

WEDNESDAY OF HOLY WEEK

PRESENCE OF GOD - O suffering Jesus, grant that I may read in Your Passion Your love for me.

MEDITATION

1. Today's Mass contains two lessons from Isaias (62,11 – 63,1-7 – 53,1-12) which describe in a very impressive way the figure of Jesus, the Man of Sorrows. It is the suffering Christ who presents Himself to us, covered with the shining purple of His Blood, wounded from head to foot. "Why then is Thy apparel red, and Thy garments like theirs that tread in the winepress? I have trodden the winepress alone, and of the Gentiles there is not a man with Me." All alone Jesus trod the winepress of His Passion. Let us think of His agony in the Garden of Olives, where the vehemence of His grief covered all His members with a bloody sweat. Let us think of the moment when Pilate,

after having Him scourged, brought Him before the mob, saying : " Behold the Man! " Jesus stood there, His head crowned with thorns, His flesh lacerated by the whips; the brilliant red of His Blood mingled with the purple of His cloak, that cloak of derision with which the soldiers had clothed their mock king. Christ was offering Himself as a sacrifice for men, shedding His Blood for their salvation, and men were abandoning Him. " I looked about and there was none to help; I sought, and there was none to give aid " *(RM)*. Where were the sick whom He had cured, the blind, who at the touch of His Hand had recovered their sight, the dead who were raised to life, the thousands whom He had miraculously fed with bread in the wilderness, the wretched without number who in countless ways had experienced His goodness? Before Jesus there was only an infuriated mob clamoring : *Crucify Him! Crucify Him!* Even the Apostles, His most intimate friends, had fled; indeed one of them had betrayed Him : " If he that hated Me had spoken great things against Me, I would perhaps have hidden Myself from him! But thou, a man of one mind, My guide, and My familiar, who didst take sweetmeats together with Me " (*Ps* 54,13.14). We read these words today, as on all the Wednesdays of the year, in the psalms of Terce. To this text which is so deeply expressive of the bitterness Jesus felt when betrayed and abandoned by His own, there is a corresponding response at Matins : " Instead of loving Me, they decried Me, and returned evil for good, and hate in exchange for My love " *(RB)*.

As we contemplate Jesus in His Passion, each one of us can say to himself, *dilexit me, et tradidit semetipsum pro me*, He loved me, and delivered Himself for me (*Gal* 2,20); and it would be well to add, " How have I repaid His love? "

2. Jesus is singularly worthy of the gratitude and fidelity of men. No one has ever done more for them than He; yet no one has suffered more than He the bitterness of ingratitude and treachery.

Let us review for a moment the prologue of St. John's Gospel, which presents Jesus to us in all His divine Majesty, in the eternal splendor of the Word, the " true light which enlighteneth every man that cometh into this world. " Compare it then with the lesson from Isaias (2nd lesson of the Mass), which describes the opprobrium and ignominy to which His Passion has reduced Him. The result should be a deeper understanding of the two great truths that emerge : the exceeding charity with which Jesus has loved us, and the enormous gravity of sin.

Of Him, the Son of God, it was written : " There is no beauty in Him, nor comeliness : and we have seen Him, and there was no sightliness that we should be desirous of Him : despised and the most abject of men, a man of sorrows.... His look was, as it were, hidden. " He has no beauty, He who is the splendor of the Father. He seeks to hide His face, He, the sight of whose face is the beatitude of the angels and saints. He is so disfigured that He seems like a leper, so abject that no account is made of Him. To this pitiable condition our sins have reduced Him. " Surely He hath borne our infirmities and carried our sorrows "—infirmities and sorrows are the consequences of sin— " He was wounded for our iniquities and bruised for our sins.... The Lord took all our iniquity upon Himself. "

The consideration of the horror of sin should throw into relief the other great truth of the Passion; namely, the inexpressible love of Christ. This love made Him willingly accept His Passion; and having accepted it because " He willed it, " He did not evade His enemies, but freely gave Himself into their hands. Let us recall the moment when Jesus, by His divine power, cast to the ground the soldiers who had come to arrest Him, and having said that, if He wished, He could have legions of angels to defend Him, allowed them to take and bind Him without any resistance. Let us remember that, when He was taken prisoner and condemned, He did not hesitate to say to the Roman governor, " Thou shouldst not have any power against Me, unless it were given thee from above " (*Jn* 19,11). Jesus is the victim. He goes willingly to be sacrificed; He immolates Himself lovingly, with sovereign liberty. We touch here the summit of love, the summit of liberty, for we speak of the love and the liberty of God.

COLLOQUY

" O sweet Jesus, I understand what You must be feeling! O good Jesus, meek and loving! You suffered martyrdom by the many wounds caused by the scourging and the nails.

You were crowned with thorns. How many, O good Jesus, were they who struck You! Your Father struck You, since He did not spare You, but made You a victim for all of us. You struck Yourself when You offered Your soul to death, that soul which cannot be taken from You against Your will. The disciple who betrayed You with a kiss struck You too. The Jews struck You with their hands and feet, and the Gentiles struck You with whips and pierced You with nails. Oh! how many people, how many humiliations, how many executioners!

"And how many gave You over! The heavenly Father gave You for us, and You gave Yourself, as St. Paul joyfully says : ' He loved me and delivered Himself up for me. '

"What a marvelous exchange! The Master delivers Himself for a slave, God for man, the Creator for the creature, the innocent One for the sinner. You put Yourself into the hands of the traitor, the faithless disciple. The traitor handed You over to the Jews. The wicked Jews delivered You to the Gentiles to be mocked, scourged, spit upon, and crucified. You had said these things; You had foretold them, and they came to pass. Then, when all was accomplished, You were crucified and numbered among the wicked. But it was not enough that You were wounded. To the pain of Your wounds, they added other ignominies and, to slake Your burning thirst, they gave You wine mixed with myrrh and gall.

"I weep for You, my King, my Lord, and Master, my Father and Brother, my beloved Jesus " (St. Bonaventure).

137

THE GIFT OF LOVE

HOLY THURSDAY

PRESENCE OF GOD - O Jesus, grant that I may fathom the immensity of that love which led You to give us the Eucharist.

MEDITATION

1. " Having loved His own...He loved them unto the end " (*Jn* 13,1-15), and in those last intimate hours spent in their midst, He wished to give them the greatest proof of His love. Those were hours of sweet intimacy, but also of most painful anguish. Judas had already set the price of the infamous sale; Peter was about to deny his Master; all of them within a short time would abandon Him. The institution of the Eucharist appeared then as the answer of Jesus to the treachery of men, as the greatest gift of His infinite love in return for the blackest ingratitude. The merciful God would pursue His rebellious creatures, not with threats, but with the most delicate devices of His immense charity. Jesus had already done and suffered so much for sinful man, but now, at the moment when human malice is about to sound the lowest depths of the abyss, He exhausts the resources of His love, and offers Himself to man, not only as the Redeemer, who will die for him on the Cross, but also as the food which will nourish him. He will feed man with His own Flesh and Blood; moreover, death might claim Him in a few hours, but the Eucharist will perpetuate His real, living presence until the end of time. " O You who are mad about Your creature! " exclaimed St. Catherine of Siena, " true God and true Man, You have left Yourself wholly to us, as food, so that we will not fall through weariness during our pilgrimage in this life, but will be fortified by You, celestial Nourishment! "

Today's Mass is, in a very special way, the commemoration and the renewal of the Last Supper, in which we are all invited to participate. Let us enter the Church and gather close around the altar as if going into the Cenacle to gather around Jesus. Here we find, as did the Apostles at Jerusalem, the Master living in our midst, and He Himself, through the person of His minister, will renew once again the great miracle which changes bread and wine into His Body and Blood; He will say to us, " Take and eat...take and drink. "

It was Jesus Himself who made the arrangements for the Last Supper, choosing " a large room " (*Lk* 22,12), and bidding the Apostles to prepare it suitably. Our hearts, dilated and made spacious by love, must also be a " large " cenacle, where Jesus may come and worthily celebrate His Pasch.

2. During the Last Supper and coincident with His gift of the Sacrament of love, Jesus also left us His testament of love—the living, concrete testament of His admirable example of humility and charity in the washing of the Apostles' feet, and His oral testament in the proclamation of His " new commandment. " The Gospel of today's Mass (Jn 13,1-15) shows us Jesus, as the Master, washing the Apostles' feet; it ends with His words : " I have given you an example, that as I have done, you also may do. " It is an urgent invitation to that fraternal charity which should be the fruit of union with Jesus, the fruit of our Eucharistic Communion. He mentioned it in precise words at the Last Supper : " A new commandment I give unto you : ' that you love one another ' as I have loved you, that you also love one another " (*ibid.* 13,34).

If we cannot imitate the love of Jesus by giving our body as food to our brethren, we can imitate Him at least by giving them loving assistance, not only in agreeable circumstances, but also in difficult and disagreeable ones. By washing His disciples' feet, the Master shows us how far we should humble ourselves to render a service to our neighbor, even were he most lowly and abject. The Master, who, by unceasing proofs of His love, advances to meet ungrateful men and even those who have betrayed Him, teaches us that our charity is far from His unless we repay evil with good, forgive everything, and are even willing to repay with kindness those who have done us harm. The Master, who gave His life for the salvation of His own, tells us that our love is incomplete if we cannot sacrifice ourselves generously for others. His " new commandment, " which makes the love of Jesus Himself the measure of our fraternal love, opens up unlimited horizons for the exercise of charity, for it means charity without limits. If there is a limit, it is that of giving, like the Master, one's life for others, for " greater love than this no man hath, that a man lay down his life for his friends " (*ibid.* 15,13).

Jesus revealed to us the perfection of fraternal charity on the same evening that He instituted the Eucharist, as if to indicate that such perfection should be both the fruit of the Sacrament of the Eucharist and our response to this great gift.

COLLOQUY

" O Lord, Lord, how small and narrow is the house of my soul for You to enter! Enlarge it Yourself. It is in ruins; repair it. I know and admit that there are things in it that are offensive in Your sight. But who will cleanse it? Or to whom but You shall I cry, purify me, Lord, from my hidden sins? " (St. Augustine).

" O good Jesus, to sustain our weakness and to stir up our love, You have chosen to remain always in our midst, although You well foresaw the way that men would treat You and the shame and outrages from which You would have to suffer. O eternal Father, how could You permit Your Son to live with us, to endure fresh insults every day? O my God! What great love in that Son! and also, what great love in that Father!

" But how, eternal Father, couldst Thou consent to this? How canst Thou see Thy Son every day in such wicked hands?... How canst Thy mercy, day by day, and every day, see Him affronted? And how many affronts are being offered today to this most Holy Sacrament! How often must Thou see Him in the hands of His enemies!

" O eternal Father! Surely all these scourgings and insults and grievous tortures will not be forgotten.... Could it be that He failed to do something to please Thee? No, He fulfilled everything.... Has He not already more than sufficiently paid for the sin of Adam?

" O Holy Father who art in Heaven, if Thy divine Son has left nothing undone that He could do for us in granting sinners so great a favor as that of the Blessed

Sacrament, do not permit Him to be so ill-treated. Since
Thy holy Son has given us this excellent way in which we
can offer Him up frequently as a sacrifice, let us make use
of this precious gift so that it may stay the advance of such
terrible evil and irreverence as in many places is paid to this
most holy Sacrament " (cf. T.J. *Way*, 33-3-35).

138

THE MYSTERY OF THE CROSS

GOOD FRIDAY

PRESENCE OF GOD - O Jesus, permit me to penetrate with You into
the depths of the mystery of the Cross.

MEDITATION

1. Good Friday is the day which invites us more than
any other to " enter into the thicket of the trials and
pains...of the Son of God " (J.C. *SC**, 35,9), and not only
with the abstract consideration of the mind, but also with
the practical disposition of the will to accept suffering
voluntarily, in order to unite and assimilate ourselves to the
Crucified. By suffering with Him, we shall understand His
sufferings better and have a better comprehension of His
love for us, for " the purest suffering brings with it the most
intimate and the purest understanding " (*ibid.*, 36,12);
and " no one feels more deeply in his heart the Passion of
Christ than one who has suffered something similar " (*Imit.
II*, 12,4). With these dispositions let us accompany our
Lord during His last day on earth.

The atrocious martyrdom, which within a few hours
will torture His body, has not yet begun, and yet the agony
of Jesus in the Garden of Olives marks one of the most
sorrowful moments of His Passion, one which best reveals the
bitter sufferings of His soul. His most sacred soul finds
itself immersed in inexpressible anguish; it is extreme
abandonment and desolation, without the slightest consola-

---

* Asterisk indicates first redaction of the *Spiritual Canticle*.

tion, either from God or from man. The Savior feels the weight of the enormous burden of all the sins of mankind; He, the Innocent One, sees Himself covered with the most execrable crimes, and made, as it were, the enemy of God and the target of the infinite justice which will punish all our wickedness in Him. Of course, as God, Jesus never ceased, even in the most painful moments of His Passion, to be united to His Father; but as man, He felt Himself rejected by Him, " struck by God and afflicted " (*Is* 53,4). This explains the utter anguish of His spirit, much more sorrowful than the dreadful physical sufferings which await Him; explains the cruel agony which made Him sweat blood; explains His complaint, " My soul is sorrowful even unto death " (*Mt* 26,38). Whereas before He had so ardently desired His Passion, now that His humanity finds itself facing the hard reality of the fact, deprived of the sensible help of the divinity, which seems not only to withdraw, but even more, to be angry with Him, Jesus groans : " My Father, if it be possible, let this chalice pass from Me! " But this anguished cry of human nature is immediately lost in that of the perfect conformity of Christ's will to the Father's : " Nevertheless not as I will, but as thou wilt " (*ibid.* 26,39).

2. The Agony in the Garden is followed by the treacherous kiss of Judas, the arrest, the night passed in the interrogations by the high priests and insults from the soldiers who strike Jesus, spit in His face and blindfold Him, while in the outer court, Peter is denying Him. At dawn they commence anew the questionings and accusations; the going back and forth from one tribunal to another begins—from Caiphas to Pilate, from Pilate to Herod, and back again to Pilate—followed by the horrible scourging and the crowning with thorns. Finally, clothed as a mock king, the Son of God is presented to the mob which cries out : " Away with this man, and release unto us Barabbas "; for Jesus, the Savior, the crowd can only shout : " Crucify Him, crucify Him! " (*Lk* 23,18-21). Loaded down with the wood for His torture, Jesus is led away to Calvary where He is crucified between two thieves. These terrible physical and mental sufferings reach their climax when the Savior, in agony on the Cross, utters the cry : " My God, My God, why hast Thou forsaken Me? " (*Mt* 27,46).

Here again we are in the presence of the inner struggle which tortures the soul of Christ, and now accompanies, with rapid crescendo, the intense increase of His physical sufferings. Jesus had said to His Apostles at the Last Supper, in speaking of His approaching Passion : " Behold, the hour cometh... [when] you shall be scattered... and shall leave Me alone; yet I am not alone, because the Father is with Me " (*Jn* 16,32). Union with the Father is everything to Jesus; it is His life and His strength, His comfort and His joy. If men desert Him, the Father is always with Him, and that is sufficient for Him. This fact gives us a better understanding of the intensity of His sufferings when, in the course of His Passion, the Father withdraws from Him. Yet, even in His agony and death on the Cross, Jesus is always God, and therefore always indissolubly united to the Father. However, He has taken upon Himself the heavy burden of our sins, which stand like a moral barrier between Him and the Father. Although personally united to the Word, His humanity is, by a miracle, deprived of all divine comfort and support, and feels instead the weight of all the malediction due to sin : " Christ, " says St. Paul, " has redeemed us from the curse ... being made a curse for us " (*Gal* 3,13). Here we touch the most profound depths of the Passion of Jesus, the most atrocious bitterness which He embraced for our salvation. Yet, even in the midst of such cruel torments, the last words of Jesus are an expression of total abandonment : " Father, into Thy Hands I commend My spirit " (*Lk* 23,46). Thus Jesus, who willed to taste to the dregs all that is bitter for man in suffering and dying, teaches us to overcome the anxieties and anguish caused in us by sorrow and death, by acts of complete submission to the will of God and trustful abandonment into His hands.

COLLOQUY

" O Christ, Son of God, as I contemplate the great sufferings You endured for us on the Cross, I hear You saying to my soul : ' It is not in jest that I have loved you! ' These words open my eyes, and I see clearly all that Your love has made You do for me. I see that You suffered during Your life and death, O Man-God, suffered because of that profound, ineffable love.   No, O Lord, it was not in jest that You loved me, but Your love is perfect and real. In myself, I see the opposite, for my love is lukewarm and untrue, and this grieves me very much.

" O Master, You did not love me in jest; I, a sinner, on the contrary, have never loved You except imperfectly. I have never wanted to hear about the sufferings You endured on the Cross, and thus I have served You carelessly and unfaithfully.

" Your love, O my God, arouses in me an ardent desire to avoid anything that might offend You, to embrace the grief and contempt that You bore, to keep continually in mind Your Passion and death, in which our true salvation and our life are found.

" O Lord, Master, and eternal Physician, You freely offer us Your Blood as the cure for our souls, and although You paid for it with Your Passion and death on the Cross, it costs me nothing, save only the willingness to receive it. When I ask for it, You give it to me immediately and heal all my infirmities.   My God, since You agreed to free me and to heal me on the one condition that I show You, with tears of sorrow, my faults and weaknesses; since, O Lord, my soul is sick, I bring to You all my sins and misfortunes. There is no sin, no weakness of soul or mind for which You do not have an adequate remedy, purchased by Your death.

" All my salvation and joy are in You, O Crucified Christ, and in whatever state I happen to be, I shall never take my eyes away from Your Cross " (St. Angela of Foligno).

139

THE VICTORY OF THE CROSS

HOLY SATURDAY

PRESENCE OF GOD - O Jesus, crucified for love of me, show me the victory won by Your death.

MEDITATION

1. As soon as Jesus expired, " the veil of the Temple was torn in two...the earth quaked, the rocks were rent. And the graves were opened; and many bodies ... arose, " so that those who were present were seized with a great fear and said : " Indeed this was the Son of God " (*Mt* 27,51-54). Jesus willed to die in complete ignominy, accepting to the very end the mocking and ironic challenges of the soldiers, " If Thou be Christ, save Thyself " (*Lk* 23,39); but scarcely had He drawn His last breath, when His divinity revealed itself in such a powerful manner that it impressed even those who, up to that moment, had been jeering at Him.   Christ's death began to show itself for what it really was, that is, not a defeat but a victory : the greatest victory that the world would ever witness, the victory over sin, the victory over death, which was the consequence of sin, the victory, which restored to man the life of grace.

In offering us the Cross for adoration yesterday, the Church sang : " Behold the wood of the Cross, on which hung the salvation of the world, " and after the mournful alternations of the *Improperia,* or tender reproaches, she intones a hymn of praise in honor of the Cross : " Sing, my tongue, the noble triumph whose trophy is the Cross, and the victory won by the immolation of the Redeemer of the world! " Thus consideration of the Lord's sufferings and compassion for them alternate with the hymn of victory.   The supreme paradox of death and life, of death and victory reach a unity in Jesus, in such a way that the first is the cause of the second.   St. John of the Cross, describing the agony of Jesus on the Cross, affirms : " He wrought herein the greatest work that He had ever wrought, whether in miracles or in mighty works, during the whole of His life, either upon earth or in Heaven, which was the reconciliation and union of mankind, through grace, with God. And this, as I say, was at the moment and the time when this Lord was most completely annihilated in everything. Annihilated, that is to say, with respect to human reputation; since, when men saw Him die, they mocked Him rather than esteemed Him; and also with respect to nature, since His nature was annihilated when He died; and further with respect to the spiritual consolation and protection of the Father, since at that time He forsook Him.... " And he concludes : " Let the truly spiritual man understand the mystery of the gate and of the way of Christ, and so become united with God, and let him know that, the more completely he is annihilated for God's sake, according to these two parts, the sensual and the spiritual, the more completely he is united to God and the greater is the work which he accomplishes " (*AS II*, 7,11).

2. " In peace in the selfsame I will sleep, and I will rest. " These opening words of Matins of Holy Saturday refer to the peace of the tomb, where, after so many torments, the sacred Body of Jesus rests. Indeed, this day is meant to be one of recollection in silence and prayer beside the sepulcher of the Lord.

After the death of Jesus, frightened by the earthquake and the darkness, all had left Calvary except the little group of faithful ones : Our Lady and St. John, who were never away from the Cross, and Mary Magdalen and the other pious women who " had followed Jesus from Galilee ministering unto Him " (*Mt* 27,55). Although Our Lord had died, they could not tear themselves away from Him, their adored Master, the object of all their love and hope. It was their love that kept them near the lifeless Body. This is a sign of real fidelity, to persevere even in the darkest and most painful moments, when all seems lost, and when a friend, instead of triumphing, is reduced to defeat and profound humiliation. It is easy to be faithful to God when everything goes smoothly, when His cause triumphs; but to be equally faithful in the hour of darkness, when, for a time, He permits evil to get the upper hand, when everything that is good and holy seems to be swept away and irrevocably lost—this is hard, but it is the most authentic proof of real love.

Two disciples, Joseph of Arimathea and Nicodemus, took charge of the burial. The sacred Body was taken down from the Cross, wrapped in a sheet with spices, and laid " in a new tomb " which Joseph " had hewed out in a rock [for himself] " (*Mt* 27,60). Together with Mary, who must certainly have been present at the scene and received the lacerated Body of her divine Son into her arms, let us also draw near to the sacred remains; let us gaze on these wounds, on these bruises, on this Blood, all of which speak so eloquently of Jesus' love for us. It is true that these wounds are no longer painful, but glorious; and tomorrow, at the Easter dawn, we shall celebrate the great victory which they have won. However, though glorified, they remain and will remain forever the indelible marks of the exceedingly great charity with which Christ loves us.

May this Saturday, a day of transition between the agony of Friday and the glory of the Resurrection, be a day of prayer and recollection near the lifeless body of Jesus; let us open wide our heart and purify it in His Blood, so that renewed in love and purity, it can vie with the " new sepulcher " in offering the beloved Master a place of peace and rest.

COLLOQUY

" Hail, O Cross, our only hope! You increase grace in the souls of the just and remit the faults of sinners. O glorious resplendent tree, decked in royal purple, on your arms hangs the price of our Redemption, in you is our victory, our ransom! " (cf. *RB*).

" O Christ, I glance again at Your bloodstained face, and I raise my tear-filled eyes to see Your wounds and bruises. I lift my contrite, afflicted heart, to consider all the tribulations You have endured in order to seek me and to save me.

" O good Jesus, how generously have You given us, on the Cross, all You had! To Your executioners, Your loving prayer; to the thief, Paradise; to Your Mother, a son, and to the son, a Mother; to the dead, You gave back life, and You placed Your soul in Your Father's hands; You showed Your power to the entire world, and shed, through Your wide and numerous wounds, not a few drops, but all

Your Blood, to redeem a slave!... O meek Lord and Savior of the world, how can we thank You worthily?

"O good Jesus, You bow Your crowned Head, pierced by many thorns, inviting me to the kiss of peace. 'See,' You say to me, 'how disfigured, torn, and annihilated I am! Do you know why? To lift you up, O wandering sheep, to put you on My shoulder, and bring you to the heavenly pasture in Paradise. Now return My Love. Behold Me in My Passion. Love Me. I gave Myself to you; give yourself to Me.' O Lord, I am grief-stricken at the sight of Your wounds; I want You to rule over me, just as You are, in Your Passion. I want to set You as a seal upon my heart, as a seal on my arm, to make me conformable to You and Your martyrdom in all I think and do.

"O good and gentle Jesus! You who gave Yourself to us as a ransom for our redemption, grant that we, unworthy though we be, may correspond with Your grace, entirely, perfectly, and in all things" (St. Bonaventure).

EASTER SUNDAY TO THE FEAST
OF THE MOST HOLY TRINITY

THE LIFE OF PRAYER : VOCAL AND MENTAL PRAYER,

DEVELOPMENT OF CONTEMPLATIVE PRAYER,

LITURGICAL PRAYER – OUR BLESSED

LADY : HER PRIVILEGES AND

VIRTUES – THE HOLY

SPIRIT AND HIS

ACTION IN

US.

THE RESURRECTION OF THE LORD

EASTER SUNDAY

PRESENCE OF GOD - O risen Jesus, make me worthy to share in the joy of Your Resurrection.

MEDITATION

1. "This is the day which the Lord hath made; let us be glad and rejoice therein" *(RB)*. This is the most excellent day, the happiest day in the whole year, because it is the day when "Christ, our Pasch, has been sacrificed." Christmas, too, is a joyous feast, but whereas Christmas vibrates with a characteristic note of sweetness, the Paschal solemnity resounds with an unmistakable note of triumph; it is joy for the triumph of Christ, for His victory. The liturgy of the Mass shows us this Paschal joy under two aspects : joy in truth *(Ep : 1 Cor 5,7.8)* and joy in charity *(Postcommunion)*.

Joy in truth : According to the vibrant admonition of St. Paul, "Let us celebrate the feast, not with old leaven... but with the unleavened bread of sincerity and truth." In this world there are many ephemeral joys, based on fragile, insecure foundations; but the Paschal joy is solidly grounded on the knowledge that we are in the truth, the truth which Christ brought to the world and which He confirmed by His Resurrection. The Resurrection tells us that our faith is not in vain, that our hope is not founded on a dead man, but on a living one, the *Living One* par excellence, whose life is so strong that it vivifies, in time as in eternity, all those who believe in Him. "I am the Resurrection and the Life; he that believeth in Me, although he be dead, shall live" *(Jn 11,25)*. Joy in truth : for only sincere and upright souls who seek the truth lovingly and, still more, "do the truth" can fully rejoice in the Resurrection. We are sincere when we recognize ourselves for what we are, with all our faults, deficiencies, and need for conversion. From this knowledge of our miseries springs the sincere resolve to purify ourselves of the old leaven of the passions in order to be renewed completely in the risen Christ.

Truth, however, must be accomplished in charity—*veritatem facientes in caritatem*, doing the truth in charity (*Eph* 4,15); therefore the Postcommunion prayer that is placed on our lips is more timely than ever : " Pour forth upon us, O Lord, the spirit of Thy love, to make us of one heart. " Without unity and mutual charity there can be no real Paschal joy.

2. The Gospel (*Mk* 16,1-7) places before our eyes the faithful holy women who, at the first rays of the Sunday dawn, run to the sepulcher, and on the way, wonder : " Who will roll back the stone from the door of the sepulcher for us? " This preoccupation, although it is well justified on account of the size and weight of the stone, does not deter them from proceeding with their plans; they are too much taken up with the desire of finding Jesus! And behold! hardly have they arrived when they see " the stone rolled back. " They enter the tomb and find an Angel who greets them with the glad announcement : " He is risen; He is not here. " At this time, Jesus does not let Himself be found or seen; but a little later when, in obedience to the command of the Angel, the women leave the tomb to bring the news to the disciples, He will appear before them saying, " All hail! " (*Mt* 28,9), and their joy will be overwhelming.

We, too, have a keen desire to find the Lord; perhaps we have been seeking Him for many long years. Further, this desire may have been accompanied by serious preoccupation with the question of how we might rid ourselves of the obstacles and roll away from our souls the stone which has prevented us thus far from finding the Lord, from giving ourselves entirely to Him, and from letting Him triumph in us. Precisely because we want to find the Lord, we have already overcome many obstacles, sustained by His grace; divine Providence has helped us roll away many stones, overcome many difficulties. Nevertheless, the search for God is progressive, and must be maintained during our whole life. For this reason, following the example of the holy women, we must always have a holy preoccupation about finding the Lord, a preoccupation which will make us industrious and diligent in seeking Him, and at the same time confident of the divine aid, since the Lord will certainly take care that we arrive where our own strength could never bring us, because He will do for us what we cannot do for ourselves.

Every year Easter marks a time of renewal in our spiritual life, in our search for God; every year we reascend the path toward Him *in novitate vitae*, in newness of life (*Rom* 6,4).

COLLOQUY

"Lord Jesus, good and gentle Jesus, who deigned to die for our sins and to rise for our justification, I beg You, by Your glorious Resurrection, to bring me out of the sepulcher of my vices and sins, so that I may merit to have a real share in Your Resurrection. O most kind Lord, who ascended to Heaven in the triumph of Your glory and are seated at the right hand of the Father, You who are all-powerful, raise me up to You, so that I may run in the odor of Your ointments, run without slackening, while You call and guide me. My soul thirsts; draw me to the divine spring of eternal satiety; lift me out of the abyss toward this living spring, so that I may drink as much as I can of it, and live on it forever, O my God, my Life.

"I pray You, Lord, give my soul the wings of an eagle, that I may fly without weakening, fly, until I reach the splendor of Your glory. There, You will feed me on Your secrets at the table of the heavenly citizens, in the place of Your Pasch, near the celestial fount of eternal satiety. Let my heart rest in You, my heart which resembles a great ocean, agitated by tumultuous waves.

"When shall I see You, O precious, long-desired, amiable Lord? When shall I appear before Your face? When shall I be satiated with Your beauty? When will You take me out of this dark prison, that I may confess Your Name, without being confused any longer? What shall I do, a wretch loaded down with the chains of my human condition? What shall I do? As long as we are in the body, we are journeying toward the Lord. We have not here a lasting dwelling, but we seek a future city, for our homeland is in heaven.

"As long as I carry about with me these fragile members, give me the grace, O Lord, to cling to You, for he who adheres to the Lord is one spirit with Him" (St. Augustine).

141

STAY WITH US

EASTER MONDAY

PRESENCE OF GOD - Do not leave me, O Jesus, gentle Pilgrim; I have need of You.

MEDITATION

1. God has made us for Himself, and we cannot live without Him; we need Him, we hunger and thirst for Him; He is the only One who can satisfy our hearts. The Easter liturgy is impregnated with this longing for God, for Him who is from on high; it even makes it the distinctive sign of our participation in the Paschal mystery. " If you be risen with Christ, seek the things that are above, where Christ is sitting at the right hand of God; mind the things that are above, not the things that are upon the earth" (*Col* 3,1.2). The more the soul revives itself in the Resurrection of Christ, the more it feels the need of God and of heavenly truths; it detaches itself more and more from earthly things to turn toward those of heaven.

Just as physical hunger is an indication of a living, healthy organism, so spiritual hunger is a sign of a robust spirit, one that is active and continually developing. The soul which feels no hunger for God, no need to seek Him and to find Him, and which does not vibrate or suffer with anxiety in its search, does not bear within itself the signs of the Resurrection. It is a dead soul, or at least one which has been weakened and rendered insensible by lukewarmness. The Paschal *alleluia* is a cry of triumph at Christ's Resurrection, but at the same time it is an urgent invitation for us to rise also. Like the sound of reveille, it calls us to the battles of the spirit, and invites us to rouse and renew ourselves, to participate ever more profoundly in Christ's Resurrection. Who can say, however advanced he may be in the ways of the spirit, that he has wholly attained to his resurrection?

2. We read in today's Gospel the very beautiful story of the disciples at Emmaus (*Lk* 24,13-35). Here we find the earnest supplication : " Stay with us, because it is towards evening, and the day is now far spent. "

Stay with us, Lord! It is the cry of the soul who has found its God and never again wishes to be separated from Him. Let us too, as the disciples at Emmaus, go in search of the Lord. Our whole life is a continuous journey toward Him, and we are often sad, even as they were, because we do not succeed in finding Him, because, not understanding His mysterious ways, it seems that He has abandoned us. " We hoped that it was He that should have redeemed Israel...but..., " said the two disciples, frustrated by the death of Jesus, and not perceiving that Jesus, at the very moment when they were about to relinquish all hope, was there close to them, disguised as their fellow traveler. We have often shared this experience of Him. Hidden in the obscurity of faith, God draws near our soul, makes Himself our traveling companion, and still more, lives in us by grace. It is true that here below He does not reveal Himself in the clarity of the " face to face " vision which is reserved for eternity; we see Him only as " through a glass in a dark manner " (1 *Cor* 13,12); nevertheless, God knows how to make Himself known. To us as to the disciples at Emmaus, His presence is revealed in an obscure manner; yes, but unmistakably, because of the unique ardor which He alone can kindle in our hearts. " Was not our heart burning within us whilst He spoke in the way? " The soul who has found the Lord, even but once in this manner, not outside itself, but within itself, living and acting in its heart, cannot fail to direct to Him the cry : " Stay with me! "

Yet this cry is already heard, it is already a permanent reality, because God always dwells with a soul in the state of grace. God is always with us, even when we do not feel Him, even when we do not notice His presence. God is there, God remains with us; it is for us to remain with Him. If at certain moments He permits Himself to be recognized by our soul, He does so just to invite us to dwell with Him in His intimacy. Let us, therefore, beg Him ardently : teach us, O Lord, to stay with You, to live with You.

COLLOQUY

" O my hope, my Father, my Creator, true God and Brother, when I think of what You said—that Your delights are to be with the children of men—my soul rejoices greatly. O Lord of heaven and earth, how can any sinner, after hearing such words, still despair? Do You lack souls in whom to delight, Lord, that You seek so unsavory a worm as I?.... O what exceeding mercy! What favor far beyond our deserving!

" Rejoice, O my soul . . . and since the Lord finds His delights in you, may all things on earth not suffice to make you cease to delight in Him and rejoice in the greatness of your God.

" I desire neither the world, nor anything that is worldly; and nothing seems to give me pleasure but You; everything else seems to me a heavy cross.

" O my God, I am afraid, and with good reason, that You may forsake me; for I know well how little my strength and insufficiency of virtue can achieve, if You are not always granting me Your grace and helping me not to forsake You. It seems to me, my Lord, that it would be impossible for me to leave You . . . . But as I have done it so many times I cannot but fear, for when You withdraw but a little from me I fall utterly to the ground. But blessed may You be forever, O Lord! For though I have forsaken You, You have not so completely forsaken me as not to raise me up again by continually giving me Your hand . . . . Remember my great misery, O Lord, and look upon my weakness, since You know all things " (T.J. *Exc,* 7 – *Life,* 6).

142

WHOM SEEK YOU?

PRESENCE OF GOD - O Lord, may I always seek You alone, and seeking You, may I have the grace to find You.

MEDITATION

1. In the Masses of Easter week the Gospels recount the various apparitions of the risen Jesus; the first, and one of the most moving, is that to Mary Magdalen (*Jn* 20,11-18). In this episode Mary appears with her characteristic trait, that of a soul completely possessed by the love of God. When she reaches the sepulcher, she has scarcely seen " the stone rolled away, " before she is seized with one only anxiety : " They have taken away my Lord. " Who could have taken Him? Where could they have put Him? She repeats these questions to everyone she meets, supposing that they are filled with a like apprehension. She tells it to Peter and John who come running to see for themselves; she tells it to the Angels, and she tells it even to Jesus. The other women, finding the sepulcher open, go in to find out what has happened, but Magdalen runs off quickly to bring the news to the Apostles. Then she returns. What will she do near that empty tomb? She does not know, but love has impelled her to return, and it keeps her at the place where the body of the Master had been, the body that she wants to find at any cost.

She sees the Angels, but she does not marvel or become frightened like the other women; she is so possessed by her grief that there is no room in her soul for other emotions. When the Angels ask her : " Woman, why weepest thou? " she has only one answer : " Because they have taken away my Lord, and I know not where they have laid Him. " Later, Jesus asks her the same question and Mary, absorbed in her same thoughts, does not even recognize Him, but " thinking that it was the gardener, " she says to Him : " Sir, if thou hast taken Him hence, tell me where thou hast laid Him, and I will take Him away. " The thought of finding Jesus so occupies her mind that she does not even feel the need of giving His name; it seems to her that everyone must be thinking of Him, that everyone would understand immediately—as though everyone were in the same state of mind as she.

When love of God and desire for Him have taken full possession of a soul, there is no longer room in it for other loves, other desires, other preoccupations. All its movements are directed to God, and through all things the soul does nothing but seek God alone.

2. " If a soul seeks for God, her Beloved seeks for her even more " (J.C. *LF*, 3,28). Mary sought with much love, and lo! the Lord Himself seeks her, and seeks her calling, " Mary! " Although He has risen gloriously, Jesus is always the Good Shepherd who knows His sheep individually; and He " calleth His own sheep by name... and the sheep follow Him because they know His voice " (*Jn* 10,3.4). When Mary hears her name, she recognizes the Lord and cries : " Rabboni! Master! "

Once again Mary is at the feet of Jesus, her favorite place. We saw her in the same attitude at Bethany, while Martha was busy preparing the meal. We remember her in the house of Simon the leper, the Saturday before the Passion, when she broke the vase of precious ointment, pouring it over the feet of Jesus, bathing those feet with her tears and wiping them with her hair. We met her again at the foot of the Cross, unwilling to tear herself away from the Crucified. Always it is the same ardent love which makes her forgetful, makes her indifferent to everything else. Mary seeks only the Lord, she wants Him and Him alone; the rest does not interest her, does not concern her.

She wanted to clasp those sacred feet again and remain there in loving contemplation, but Jesus said to her gently : " Do not touch Me! " Without doubt the Lord reveals Himself and gives Himself to the soul that seeks Him, but at the same time He always remains God, the Most High, the Inaccessible : " Do not touch Me! " Although admitted to divine intimacy, the soul should not lose the sense of the transcendence of God, and of the infinite distance that lies between the creature and the Creator, between the one who is not and the One who is. Thus, the nearer the soul comes to God, the more it realizes this infinite distance, and together with confidence and love, there is born in it a profound sentiment of reverence for the supreme majesty of God.

" Whom seekest thou? " It is to each one of us, as to Mary Magdalen, that Jesus addresses this question today. Can we reply that we are seeking Him alone? Jesus appeared to Mary who " loved Him much " before appearing to the other holy women. If we wish to find the Lord quickly, we must love Him much and seek Him with great love.

COLLOQUY

" O Lord Jesus Christ, how good, blissful and desirable it is to feel the violence of Your love! Ah! enlighten my heart every day with the rays of this love, dissipate the darkness of my mind, illuminate the secret places in my heart, strengthen and inflame my intellect, and rejoice and fortify my soul! Oh! how tender is Your mercy, how great and sweet Your love, O Lord Jesus Christ. You lavish Your love to be enjoyed by those who love none but You, and who think of nothing but You! Loving us first, You invite us to love You; You delight us and draw us, so great is the power of Your love. Nothing invites us, nothing delights and attracts us more than this kind attention of love; the heart, which at first was torpid, feels itself inflamed; and the heart that is fervent, when it knows it is loved and has been loved by You, it becomes still more ardent.

" O most loving Lord Jesus Christ, although You have loved me inexpressibly, I, a wicked sinner, enclosing in my bosom a heart of stone and iron, have not recognized Your burning love; and even though I desired Your affection, I did not want to love You. Deign, then, to come to my aid, O most merciful Lord Jesus Christ, and by the violence of Your most sweet love, force my rebellious soul to love You, so that I may serve You in peace and attain the unending life of love " (Ven. R. Giordano).

143

THE LIVING WATER

PRESENCE OF GOD - O Jesus, my soul thirsts for You, the source of living water; grant that I may draw near You and drink!

MEDITATION

1. Jesus stated on several occasions that He was the fountain of living water for all who believed in Him, and He invited souls to draw near this spring because, as He said to the Samaritan woman, " He that shall drink of the water that I will give him, shall not thirst forever " (*Jn* 4,13). The most solemn invitation to drink from this fountain, however, was given by Jesus, during the last year of His ministry, to the crowd which thronged the Temple on the Feast of Tabernacles. Standing erect in the midst of the crowd, He said in a loud voice : " If any man thirst, let him come to Me and drink. He that believeth in Me ... within him shall flow rivers of living water " (*ibid.* 7,37-38). The thirst of which Jesus was speaking is the thirst for truth, for justice, the thirst for peace and true happiness, and above all the thirst for God, the keen, ardent desire for Him. The soul who has tried to drink at the spring of earthly delights has found that they do not serve to quench its thirst; instead, if they have given the soul a tiny drop of truth, justice, peace, and joy, they have left it more thirsty than before. Only then does the soul understand that God alone is the fountain which can quench its thirst. But what is this water of which Jesus declares that He is the source and which He promises to all? It is the life-giving water of grace, the only water capable of quenching our thirst for the infinite, because, by making us sharers in the divine nature, it permits us to enter into intimate relations with God; it permits us to live with the Trinity dwelling in our soul; in a word, it opens the door to divine intimacy.

St. John Chrysostom teaches : " When the grace of the Holy Spirit enters a soul and is established there, it gushes forth more powerfully than any other spring; it neither ceases, dries up, nor is exhausted. And the Savior, to

signify this inexhaustible gift of grace, calls it a spring and
a torrent; He also calls it gushing water, to indicate its force
and impetus. " The power of grace is so great that it can
cast the soul into God and bring it to divine intimacy and
union, first in this life, by faith and love, and then in heaven,
by the Beatific Vision.

2. Mortification frees the soul from every obstacle which
might retard the growth of grace, which might hinder the
soul's love for God and its flight toward Him; whereas
prayer which consists essentially in intimate conversation
with God feeds this love and quickens this flight. Mortification prepares a suitable place for a loving meeting with
God; prayer effects this meeting, and by placing the soul
in real contact with God, the source of living water, it
quenches its thirst and reanimates it. It is in this sense
that the saints, and particularly the contemplative saints,
have always seen in the living water promised by Jesus,
not only sanctifying grace, but also those special graces of
light and love which are its consequences and which the
soul attains to in prayer, in the moments of intimate contact
with God. This light and love are not the fruit of the
activity of the soul alone; but rather, God Himself, by means
of the actuation of the gifts of the Holy Spirit, infuses them
into the soul, causing it to acquire a completely new " sense "
of God. This does not mean new ideas and concepts, but
rather an experimental knowledge derived from love—
especially from the love which God Himself awakens in the
soul. It means a profound " sense " of the divinity, by
means of which the soul becomes aware—not by reasoning
or demonstration, but more by way of experience—that God
is so different from creatures, so unique, so great, that He
truly deserves all the love of the heart. This new way of
loving God, this new experience of God and divine things
is really living water which quenches the soul's thirst. It is
the living water of prayer, which, as a result of divine action,
has now become deeper, more intimate, more contemplative;
it is the living water of contemplation. This contemplation
is a gift of God. " He gives it, " says St. Teresa of Jesus,
" when and as He wishes " (*Life*, 34). Although He offers
it to all, in one form or another, He will grant it only to
those souls who apply themselves generously to mortification
and prayer.

COLLOQUY

" O Truth, light of my soul, do not permit the darkness
to frighten me. You have allowed me to walk in it, and
now I am in obscurity. But even from the darkness, yes,
even from there, I have loved You. I have sinned, and
I have remembered You. I have heard Your voice behind
me, inviting me to come back; I heard it with difficulty
because of the noise of my rebellious passions. Here I am
again at Your spring, burning with thirst. Let nothing
hold me back henceforth! Let me drink at Your spring,
and live....

" ' As the heart pants after the fountain, so does my soul
sigh for You, Lord! My soul thirsts for You, O God, the
living source; when shall I go to appear in Your presence? '
O fount of life, vein of living water, when shall I reach the
waters of Your sweetness in this desert land, dry and full
of rocks, and see Your power and glory, and quench my
thirst with the waters of Your mercy? I thirst, O Lord,
I thirst for You, living fountain....

" O fire that ever burns and is never consumed, enkindle
me! O Light that shineth ever and is never veiled, illumine
me! Oh! if I could only burn with Your flame, O sacred
fire! How gently You burn; how secretly You shine; how
wonderful it is to be enkindled by You! Woe to those who
do not burn with Your love! Woe to those who are not
illumined by You, O true Light that enlighteneth every
man, O Light that filleth the world with Your brightness!

" I give You thanks, who illumine me and deliver me,
for You have enlightened me and I have known You. Late
have I known You, O ancient Truth; late have I known
You, O eternal Truth! You were in the light and I was
in darkness, and I did not know You, for I had no light
without You, and without You, there is no light! "
(St. Augustine).

144

GOD INVITES ALL SOULS

PRESENCE OF GOD - O Lord, I answer Your invitation, I run to Your fountain : quench my thirst!

MEDITATION

1. Commenting on the invitation of Jesus : " If any man thirst, let him come to Me, and drink " (*Jn* 7,37), St. Teresa of Avila says, " Consider that the Lord calls everyone. Now, He is Truth itself, we cannot doubt His word. If His invitation were not addressed to all, He would not call all of us.... But, as He puts no restriction on it... I am certain that all who do not stop on the way will drink this living water " (*Way*, 19). Therefore, it is not amiss for an interior soul to aspire to contemplation; in fact, it would be logical, since the Lord offers it to everyone, and since contemplation is a great means of introducing us into divine intimacy, of making us understand and enjoy the infinite greatness of God, of filling us with love for Him, and of quenching all thirst for earthly things. If Jesus has offered this living water to all souls, and if it is so precious, why should we not desire it?

However, the Saint instructs us to desire it without pretension, in humility and full abandonment to the divine will. God alone is Master of His gifts, and it is His privilege to distribute them to souls in the form and amount, and at the time He wishes. " God gives them as He wishes, when He wishes, and to whom He wishes, without prejudice to anyone " (*Int C IV*, 1). St. Teresa clarifies any mistaken ideas we may have in this regard. To demand the favor of contemplation from God, would be exposing ourselves to illusions and deceptions. Besides, it would be a true sin of pride to interfere with the divine plans. Nevertheless, when a soul gives itself generously to God, He, who never lets Himself be outdone in generosity, will not refuse it at least a few sips of the living water which He offers to everyone.

2. " God does not force anyone, " says St. Teresa of Jesus, " but to those who follow Him, He gives them to drink in

many ways, so that none may lack comfort or die of thirst"
(*Way*, 20). This tells us that there are many forms and
degrees of contemplation. In order to give us a better
understanding of this, the Saint compares contemplation to
" an abundant fountain from which spring many streams,
some small, others large, and there are also little pools "
(*ibid.*). The Lord invites everyone and gives water to all,
but He does not reveal to us from what kind of stream
we are called to drink. He does not tell us at what moment
of our life we shall drink, and much less is He obliged to
make us drink from a big stream rather than from a little
one. There have been saints, like Teresa of Jesus, who
drank abundantly; there have been others, like Thérèse of
Lisieux, who have partaken only of a tiny rivulet, and yet
both types have attained sanctity. Just as several streams
may rise from the same source and all contain the same
water, although they are not all of the same size, so there
are many varied forms of contemplation : some are sweet,
others arid; some give great clarity and ineffable sweetness,
while others are obscure, even painful, although no less
useful to the soul. Despite the varying degrees, it is
essentially the same life-giving water which plunges the soul
into God, makes it penetrate the divine mystery, and makes
it understand the All of God and the nothingness of the
creature; it is the same life-giving water which opens the way
to divine intimacy and conducts the soul to sanctity.

Yes, God gives " to whom He wishes, as He wishes,
when He wishes. " This statement concerns the form and
the degree of contemplation, as well as the time when it
will be granted, all of which depends solely on God. However,
St. Teresa assures us that God never refuses this life-giving
water to anyone who " seeks it in the right way. " Therefore,
it depends on us, too, and our part consists in disposing
ourselves in such a way that God will not find us unworthy
of His gifts. [1]

---

[1] For a complete treatise on this subject, see the posthumous work
of FR. GABRIEL OF ST. MARY MAGDALEN. *La via dell'orazione*, Carmelo
S. Giuseppe, Rome, 1955.

COLLOQUY

"O compassionate and tender Sovereign of my soul! You also say : ' If anyone thirst, let him come to Me, and I will give him to drink.'

"Oh! how our souls need this water! I know, O my God, that out of Your bounty You will give it to us. You Yourself have promised it, and Your words cannot fail. Knowing our weakness, You, in Your mercy, have increased Your help. But You have not said, ' Let some come this way and others that way.' On the contrary, Your bounty is so great that You have not forbidden anyone to drink from this fountain of life. Be forever blessed for this! How justly could You have forbidden me! But since you dit not bid me go away from this fountain when I had begun to slake my thirst there, nor cast me into the abyss, You certainly will not drive anyone away from it. You call all souls with a loud voice.

"O Lord, You told the Samaritan woman that he who drinks of this water will not thirst forever. Oh! How true are these words spoken by You, Truth itself! The soul who drinks this water never thirsts for the things of this life, but it does thirst more and more with the desire to possess You and a desire for eternal things. How it thirsts to have this thirst which brings with it a sweetness which softens its difficulties, for as it quenches the desire for the things of earth, it fills the soul with celestial goods. When, O God, You condescend to quench our thirst with this water, one of the greatest graces You can give the soul is to still leave it thirsting. Every time it drinks this water, it always ardently desires to drink still more of it.

"This water is so potent that it always increases the fire of Your love. O great God! how marvelous is the fire which is enkindled more and more by water, a water which activates the fire of love in souls!

"O Lord, give me to drink of this water, and I shall never thirst again! O my Lord! How good it is for me to be engulfed in this living water, and to lose my life in it! O You who have promised it to us, give us the grace to seek it as we should " (T.J. *Exc,* 9 – *Way,* 20 – 19).

145

OUR PREPARATION

PRESENCE OF GOD - O Lord, make me generous and faithful in Your service; grant that I may never put an obstacle to Your action in me.

MEDITATION

1. The fount of living water, from which springs the loving experience of God and contemplative light, is really the operation of the Holy Spirit acting in the soul by the actuation of His gifts. Since at Baptism we have all received the gifts of the Holy Spirit—those supernatural dispositions that make us capable of receiving the divine activity—it is clear that God has given them to us, not that they may remain inoperative, but that they may be put into action. Hence their actuation cannot be considered extraordinary, but connatural; and this to such a point that the loving experience of God and the contemplative light which comes from it cannot be considered extraneous to the full development of grace. In other words, if a soul opens itself generously to the action of grace, if it seconds this action with all good will, it can well think that the Lord will not refuse to give it at least a few drops of living water, that is, some form of contemplative knowledge. St. Teresa strongly affirms this and says, " We must not be afraid that we shall die of thirst. On this road, the water of consolation never fails " (*Way*, 20); but we must understand that the " road " of which the Saint speaks is the road of total giving, of unlimited generosity which never says, " This is too much, " of generosity which gives itself without counting the cost, and perseveres in spite of the hardships on the road, the interior aridity, and the exterior difficulties.

If it be right that a soul who feels itself called to divine intimacy appreciate and long for contemplation, it cannot be wrong for it to try to prepare itself for it. Many souls are refused this grace by God simply because He does not find them suitably disposed. It is, therefore, necessary for us to work, so that we shall not be deprived of contemplation through our own fault. On the other hand, if we have done all that depends on us as best we can, we should not fear that our work will be wasted; sooner or later, in one way or another, the Lord will always give us to drink.

2. In speaking of the spiritual atmosphere in which contemplation usually flourishes, Teresa of Jesus suggests, first of all, an intense practice of virtue, especially total detachment and profound humility. We must note that she does not mean any kind of practice, but exacts that it be a very generous practice, and even requires that it be really heroic. The reason is this : as contemplation is a free gift of God, it requires generosity on our part. Souls who are not generous are precisely the ones who will never experience it. This is always the great principle which the Saint inculcates : " God refuses to force our will; He takes what we give Him. But He will not give Himself wholly until we have given ourselves wholly to Him " (*Way*, 28).

In addition to this atmosphere of generosity, there is also required a gentle and constant application to recollection and prayer. The more a soul knows how to be recollected in God, making its prayer and its vital contact with Him always more intimate and profound, the more apt it will be to receive the divine motions. Here then, in synthesis, is what our preparation ought to be : on the one hand, an intense exercise of mortification, abnegation, and detachment —and this is the practice of the virtues[1]—and on the other hand, an intense application to the life of prayer.

Of course, in preparing for contemplation, we do not intend to make it the end of our spiritual life. The goal is always love, for sanctity consists essentially in the perfection of charity. Nevertheless, contemplation is a very potent means of bringing us quickly to the plenitude of love, and it is for this reason that we desire it. Our life is a journey toward God, a continual tending, a continual directing of all our energies toward Him. Happy the soul who is strongly attracted to God! Her way is much quicker and easier. This is the great help which contemplation, properly speaking,

---

[1] This subject was fully treated in the first part of this work; here we shall take up the subject of prayer.

gives us. Summarily then, we understand that we must prepare ourselves for it, not to enjoy its sweetness, but to enter fully into the way of divine intimacy, into the way of perfect love, since nothing can direct us toward God and His glory as much as this loving experience and contemplative light which are the essence of contemplation.

COLLOQUY

"My God, if You desire to enter my soul to find Your delight in it and to shower it with blessings, there is only one thing necessary : the soul must be simple, pure, and desirous of receiving You. But if, instead of clearing the way, we place many obstacles in it, how can You enter? How do we expect You to give us Your graces?

"It is really astonishing! We are still full of faults and imperfections, virtue has scarcely taken root in us—and please God that it has begun!—we are barely able to walk; yet we are not ashamed to complain about aridity and to look for consolation in prayer!

"But Lord, You know better than I what is good for me; I do not have to advise You what to give me, because You could justly tell me that I do not know what I am asking. I want to give myself to prayer and to prepare myself to receive Your gifts; my one ambition must be to work, with all the diligence possible, to strengthen this resolution and to be ready to conform my will to Yours. O my God, You have taught me that the highest perfection to be attained in the spiritual way consists in this. The more perfect this conformity is, the more You will overwhelm me with favors and the more progress I shall make" (T.J. *Life*, 8 – *Int C II*, 1). Grant, then, O Lord, that I may make generous resolutions, and give myself unreservedly to You, without any division. You are waiting for this, so that You may come and finish Your work.

"I am Yours, O my God! Do what You wish with me and lead me by whatever path suits You. If, with Your help, I am really humble and detached from everything, You will not fail to grant me the gift of prayer, and many others in addition, which will far exceed my desires " (cf. T.J. *Int C IV*, 2).

146

PRAYER

PRESENCE OF GOD - O Lord, I come to ask of You the true spirit of prayer.

MEDITATION

1. Prayer is essentially an intimate conversation with God in which the soul seeks His presence, so that it may speak with Him in a friendly and affectionate way. It is a child talking with its Father, a friend conversing with his Friend. From its very nature, then, prayer is something intimate and interior. " For me, " said St. Thérèse of the Child Jesus, " prayer is an uplifting of the heart, a glance toward heaven, a cry of gratitude and of love in times of sorrow as well as of joy " (*St*, 11). In this perspective we must understand the traditional definition of prayer : *elevatio mentis ad Deum*, the raising of the mind to God, and not only the mind, but also, and especially, the heart. Prayer may be a silent movement of the mind, or simply a cry, a request, a colloquy; in these latter motions are verified the other aspects of prayer : *pia locutio ad Deum*, a pious conversation with God, and *petitio decentium a Deo*, a confident request for His graces.

Whatever form it takes, true prayer is not complicated or constrained; it is the breath of the soul that loves its God, the habitual attitude of the heart which tends toward God. The soul seeks Him, wants to live with Him, knows that every benefit, every help, comes from Him. Thus, spontaneously, without even thinking about it, the soul passes from the simple elevation toward God to the prayer of petition or to intimate colloquy, to arrive finally at the transport of the heart, the glance toward heaven. Prayer understood in this way is always possible, in all kinds of circumstances and in the midst of varying occupations; furthermore, for a soul who really loves God, it would be as impossible for it to interrupt prayer as it would be for it to stop breathing. We can thus understand how everyone, even those living in the world, can fulfill the words of the Gospel : " Pray always " (*Lk* 18,1). The one condition necessary is to have a heart capable of loving; the stronger and more vigorous this love is, the deeper and more continuous will the prayer be.

2. Although it may be a simple matter, it is not always easy to pray and to pray well. It is an art to be learned by studying the various forms and methods of prayer, or better still, by diligently applying ourselves to prayer itself. While the essence of prayer is always the interior movement, the elevation of mind and heart to God, the forms of it differ : there is vocal prayer and mental prayer, discursive prayer and affective prayer, private prayer and liturgical prayer. We employ one or another of these, in conformity with what is required by our duties. Thus, for example, all Christians are bound to certain vocal and liturgical prayers, such as morning and evening prayers, attendance at Mass on Sundays and holy days of obligation; but after that, we are free to choose, according to the particular attraction of the moment, special circumstances, or individual needs. All these forms are good and serve to nourish our love for God, provided that we really put ourselves in touch with Him. We should always be careful about this point, because it is the substance of prayer; and if this were lacking, the form would be useless, and God could say of us : " This people honor Me with their lips, but their heart is far from Me " (*Mt* 15,8).

However, a soul aspiring to divine intimacy will turn spontaneously toward a wholly interior form of prayer, a form which will facilitate an intimate contact with God, a silent, profound union. All forms of prayer will assume this special characteristic of interiority. Therefore, through vocal and liturgical prayer, as well as through mental prayer, the soul will make its way toward God and dispose itself for an ever-increasing intimacy with Him, until God Himself, by means of the loving experience and the contemplative light, will introduce it into a prayer which is more profound and capable of immersing it in Him.

COLLOQUY

"Grant, O good Jesus, that my soul may always fly toward You, that my entire life may be one continual act of love. Make me understand that any work which is not done in Your honor is a dead work. Grant that my piety may not become just a habit, but a continual elevation of my heart!

"O my Jesus, supreme Goodness, I ask of you a heart so enraptured with You that nothing can distract it. I wish to become indifferent to everything that goes on in the world, and to want You alone, to love everything that refers to You, but You above everything else, O my God! And my spirit, O Lord, my spirit—grant that it may be zealous in seeking You and may succeed in finding You, O sovereign Wisdom!" (St. Thomas).

O Lord, give me a heart which will love You, seek You uncompromisingly, always long for You, and have no other desire than to be closely united to You.

"May my soul languish and sigh for You; my heart and my senses cry eagerly for You, O living God. As the sparrow has found herself a house, and the turtledove a nest, so do I long to dwell near Your altars, O Lord of hosts, my King and my God! Blessed are they that dwell in Your house, O Lord, and who pray to You always!" (cf. *Ps* 83,1-5). I also, from morning until night, wish to chant in the temple of my heart hymns of praise and love in Your honor, O Most High God, who condescend to dwell in me. If my tongue is silent or occupied with other discourses, if my mind and body are busy working, my heart is always free to love You and to turn toward You at every instant, in every action. O Lord, I beg this great grace of You : may I always seek You in the depths of my soul and unite myself to You in the affection of my heart.

147

THE PASCHAL HARVEST

LOW SUNDAY

PRESENCE OF GOD - O Jesus, I come to You like Thomas; grant that I may not be unbelieving, but faithful.

MEDITATION

1. Today's liturgy is concerned in a very special way with the newly baptized, who, at the close of Easter week, laid aside the white garments which they had received at the baptismal font. It is actually to them that St. Peter addressed his affectionate recommendation which we read in the Introit of the Mass : " As newborn babes, desire the pure spiritual milk. " These words continue to express the maternal solicitude of the Church for the children whom she has regenerated in Christ, and especially for the newly born. We, too, are the object of this solicitude. Although we were baptized as infants, we can say that every Easter regenerates us in Christ by means of our spiritual resurrection in Him. Therefore, we also must be like " newborn babes, " in whom there is no malice, deceit, pride, or presumption, but only candor and simplicity, confidence and love. This is a wonderful invitation to the spiritual childhood which Jesus told us is an indispensable condition for attaining salvation : " Unless you be converted and become as little children, you shall not enter into the kingdom of heaven " (*Mt* 18,3). Each wave of grace purifies and cleanses our soul from sin and its roots, giving us rebirth to a new life in Christ, a pure, innocent life, which craves only " the pure spiritual milk " of the doctrine of Christ, His love and His grace. Today, however, the Church wishes to turn our desires in a very special way toward faith : that faith which makes us cling to Jesus so as to be taught by Him, and nourished and guided toward eternal life. The Master's words upon which we meditated last week are equally appropriate here : " He that believeth in Me... from within him shall flow rivers of living water...

springing up into life everlasting" (*Jn* 7,38-4,14). Let us draw near to Jesus with the simple, sincere faith of a little child, and He will give us the abundance of His grace as a pledge of eternal life.

2. Today's Gospel (*Jn* 20,19-31) has the particular value of strengthening us in our faith.

Thomas' doubt confirms us in the faith, for as St. Gregory says, " His disbelief was more useful to us than the faith of the other Apostles. " If he had not doubted, no man would have " put his finger in the wounds of the nails, nor his hand into the side " of Our Lord. Jesus had pity on the tottering faith of the Apostle, and on ours, too; and He allowed him not only to see Him, as He had allowed the others, but also to touch Him, thereby permitting Thomas, the incredulous, to do what He had not permitted Mary Magdalen, the most faithful one. From this incident we derive a better understanding of God's ways. Whereas He gives sensible consolations and more or less palpable signs of His presence to souls who are still wavering in the faith, He often leads by very obscure paths those who have irrevocably given themselves to Him and on whose faith He can count. God is a Father. He never denies to any soul who seeks Him with sincerity the necessary props to support its faith, but He often refuses to the strong what He grants to the weak. Is this not Jesus' own teaching : " Blessed are they that have not seen, and have believed "? Blessed are they who, in order to believe in God, do not need to see Him or to touch Him and do not require sensible signs, but who can unreservedly affirm : *Scio cui credidi*, " I know whom I have believed " (2 *Tm* 1,12), and I am sure of Him. Faith such as this is more meritorious for us, because, being founded solely on the word of God, it is entirely supernatural. It shows greater honor to God, because it gives Him full credence, without demanding any proof, and because it perseveres even in obscurity and in the midst of the most disconcerting events—even when it seems that heaven is closed and the Lord is deaf to our groanings.

Such a strong faith as this is certainly the fruit of divine grace, but we must prepare ourselves to receive it, both by asking for it in prayer, and by exercising ourselves in this same faith.

COLLOQUY

My God, give me a simple, pure heart, free of malice and hypocrisy. " O Lord, grant me true purity and simplicity : in my looks, words, heart, intentions, works, and in all my interior and exterior acts. I should like to know, O Lord, what there is in me that impedes these virtues. I shall tell you, O my soul, since I cannot make anyone else understand. Do you know that the obstacle is the smallest glance that is not directed to God, and all the words that are not spoken in praise of Him or for the benefit of your neighbor. Do you know how you drive these virtues out of your heart? You banish them every time you fail to have the pure intention of honoring God or helping your neighbor; you also expel them when you try to cover up and excuse your faults, forgetting that God sees everything, including your heart. O Lord, give me real purity and true simplicity, for You cannot find Your rest in a soul which is without them " (cf. St. Mary Magdalen dei Pazzi).

O Lord, cleanse my heart and lips in the fire of Your charity, so that I may love You and seek You with the purity and simplicity of a child. Give me also the simple faith of a child, faith without a shadow, without uncertainty or useless reasoning; an upright, pure faith which finds its satisfaction in Your word, in your testimony, for in this it is at peace and desires nothing else.

" O Lord, what is it to me whether I feel or do not feel, whether I am in darkness or in light, whether I have joy or suffering, when I can be recollected in the light created in me by Your words? I feel a kind of shame in differentiating between such matters, and while I feel that I am still affected by them, I heartily despise myself for my want of love, but I quickly turn my gaze upon you, my divine Master, to be delivered by You.... I will exalt You above Your sweetness and sensible consolations, for I am resolved to pass by all else in order to be united with You " (cf. E.T. *II*, 4).

148

VOCAL PRAYER

PRESENCE OF GOD - Lord, teach me to pray!

MEDITATION

1. When one of His disciples said to Jesus, " Lord, teach us to pray " (*Lk* 11,1), He taught them a very simple vocal prayer : the *Our Father*. It is certainly the most sublime formula possible and contains the whole essence of the most elevated mental prayer. However, Jesus gave it as a formula for vocal prayer : " When you pray, say... " (*ibid.* 11,2). This is enough to make us understand the value and importance of vocal prayer, which is within the reach of everyone— even children, the uneducated, the sick, the weary.... But we must realize that vocal prayer does not consist only in the repetition of a certain formula. If this were true, we should have a recitation but not a prayer, for prayer always requires a movement, an elevation of the soul toward God. In this sense, Jesus instructed His disciples : " When thou shalt pray, enter into thy chamber, and having shut the door, pray to thy Father in secret.... And when you are praying, speak not much as the heathens " (*Mt* 6,6.7). It is interesting to note that in St. Matthew these prescriptions concerning the exterior and interior dispositions necessary for well-made prayer immediately precede the teaching of the *Pater Noster*.

Therefore, in order that our vocal prayer be real prayer, we must first recollect ourselves in the presence of God, approach Him, and make contact with Him. Only when we have such dispositions will the words we pronounce with our lips express our interior devotion and be able to sustain and nourish it. Unfortunately, inclined as we are to grasp the material part of things instead of the spiritual, it is only too easy in our vocal prayer to content ourselves with a mechanical recitation, without taking care to direct our heart to God; hence we should always be vigilant and alert. Vocal prayer made only by the lips dissipates and wearies the soul instead of recollecting it in God; it cannot be said that this is a means of uniting us more closely to Him.

2. St. Teresa wanted to educate souls and to dispose them for intimate converse with God. Thus, she orientates vocal prayer to this end by saying: " I shall always recommend you to join vocal prayer with mental prayer " (*Way*, 22). She explains her idea in this way : " If while I am speaking with God, I have a clear realization that I am doing so, and if this is more real to me than the words I am uttering, then I am uniting mental prayer to vocal prayer " *(ibid.)*. The Saint does not mean that we should disregard the care which is demanded by the recitation, and which is of great importance—especially in liturgical prayer like the Divine Office—but she does mean that the most important thing is to be always attentive to God. Especially when we are saying prayers of some length, it is almost impossible to give our attention to the meaning of all the words, but it is always possible to keep ourselves in the presence of God while reciting them. We can nourish the desire to praise God, or to unite ourselves to Him, to implore His help in general, or to ask for a particular grace, each according to his own actual dispositions. A general thought about the meaning of the words might be sufficient, or a simple glance at God to whom we are addressing our prayer. In short, it is not only a question of reciting words, but also of being with God. This is why the Saint insists : " You should consider [before praying] who it is that you are addressing, and who you are, if only that you may speak to Him with respect... " *(ibid.)*; and this, she concludes, is already to make mental prayer. This does not mean, of course, intense mental prayer, such as we make at the time devoted exclusively to this prayer, without any attempt to recite vocally. Still it is mental prayer in the sense that the mind and heart are orientated to God and that we are trying to get into close contact with Him by means of it.

Vocal prayer practiced in this way has great value : first, because it is made in a manner very becoming and respectful toward the majesty of God, and secondly, because it gradually accustoms the soul to mental prayer, to intimate converse with Him.

COLLOQUY

"Never permit it to be thought right, my God, that those who come to speak with You do it with their lips alone.

"I must not be unmannerly because You are good, addressing You in the same careless way I might adopt in speaking to a peasant. If only to show You my gratitude for enduring my foul odor and allowing one like myself to come near You, it is well that I should try to realize who You are....

"O my Emperor, Supreme Power, Supreme Goodness, Wisdom itself, without beginning, without end, and without measure in Your works; infinite are these and incomprehensible, a fathomless ocean of wonders, O Beauty, containing within Yourself all beauties. O very Strength. God help me. Would that I could command all the eloquence of mortals and all wisdom, so as to understand, as far as is possible here below, that to know nothing is everything, and thus to describe some of the many things on which we may meditate in order to learn something of Your nature, my Lord and my God.

"When we approach You, then, let us try to realize who You are with whom we are about to speak. If we had a thousand lives we should never fully understand what are Your merits, Lord, and how we should behave before You, before whom the angels tremble.... We cannot approach a prince and address him in a careless way. Shall less respect be paid then to You, my Spouse, than to men?... I cannot distinguish mental prayer from vocal prayer when faithfully recited with a realization that it is You, O Lord, that we are addressing. Further, are we not under the obligation of trying to pray attentively?" (T.J. *Way*, 22-24).

149

MEDITATIVE READING

PRESENCE OF GOD - O Lord, teach me to seek You, even when my heart is dry and my mind distracted.

MEDITATION

1. The simplest way of conversing with God is certainly vocal prayer, properly made; but as the soul progresses in the spiritual life, it is natural for it to feel the need of a more interior prayer, of one that is more intimate; and so it spontaneously turns toward mental prayer. If the divine attraction takes hold of the soul by giving it some sensible devotion, no difficulty is experienced in becoming recollected in God; on the contrary, this exercise becomes extremely easy and pleasant. But it is quite different when the soul is left to itself, especially if an excessive activity of the imagination makes thoughts on a definite subject almost impossible. St. Teresa remarks that there are many who suffer from these continual wanderings of the mind, in which " they go here and there, and are always upset, whether the fault is in their own nature, or whether God permits it " (*Way*, 19).

Those who are in this condition are easily tempted to give up mental prayer, which has become so painful that they find it almost impossible. The Saint has an entirely different opinion, and insists that even these can apply themselves to mental prayer with profit, although they ought to do it in a somewhat special way. This way consists in helping themselves by reading a book, which, she says, " will be a great help to recollection, and is practically indispensable; let them read, therefore, even if only a little, but let them read " (*Life*, 4).

This does not mean that we are to spend the time allotted to mental prayer in continual reading. Rather, we should use some devout book in which we can find, from time to time, a good thought which serves to recollect us in God, to put us in contact with Him. St. Thérèse of the Child Jesus, who suffered habitually from aridity, often used this method. " In my helplessness, " she said, " the Holy Scriptures and the *Imitation* are of the greatest assistance. . . . It is from the Gospels, however, that I derive most help in the time of prayer; I find in their pages all that my poor soul needs, and I am always discovering there new lights and hidden, mysterious meanings " (*St*, 8).

2. St. Teresa of Jesus, who before she was raised to the highest states of contemplation had long known aridity and the torment of importunate thoughts during prayer, confesses : " I passed more than fourteen years unable to meditate, except with the help of a book. . . . With this help, I was able to collect my wandering thoughts, and the book acted like a bait to my soul. Often, I only needed to open the book; sometimes I read a little, at other times much, according to the favor which the Lord showed me " (*Way*, 17 – *Life*, 4).

It is important to choose a book which will arouse devotion, such as, in general, the writings of the saints. It will usually be preferable to take a book we have already read and one which we know will be helpful. We may even have marked some passages in it which have made an impression on us, whereas with a new book we would be somewhat lost, and perhaps exposed to the temptation of reading out of curiosity. We must avoid selecting authors who are too speculative, and choose instead those who are more practical and affective, since we are not interested in studying or learning but in *praying*, which consists much more in the exercise of love than in the work of the mind. Hence we should read, from time to time, only what is necessary to put the soul in a proper mood for conversing with God. As soon as we have read enough—and it may be only a sentence—to arouse in us good thoughts and holy affections which will occupy our mind devoutly, we must stop reading and turn our attention directly to God : meditating in His presence on the thoughts we have read, or savoring in silence the devotion they have awakened in our heart, or even speaking to Him the loving words inspired by the reading. Like birds, who, when they drink, bend their heads toward the water, take a few drops, and raising their beaks toward the sky, swallow gradually, and then begin again, let us also bend our heads toward the devout book to gather a few drops of devotion, and then let us raise them to God, so that our minds may be fully impregnated with these thoughts. In this way, it will not be difficult to finish the prayer which we have begun by reading in an intimate colloquy with God.

COLLOQUY

O Lord, teach me how to seek You! Do not hide from my eyes, for I need to find You, to converse with You, to approach You, O infinite Love, to be inflamed and attracted by You.

"Although I am but dust and ashes, shall I speak to You, O Lord? Yes, from this vale of tears, from this place of exile, I dare to raise my eyes and fix them on You, supreme Goodness! Just as faithful servants and handmaids watch attentively for the slightest sign from their masters, so my eyes are on Your hands, O Lord. I beg You, have mercy on me.

"O good God, have pity on the work of Your hands. I am incapable, Lord, of formulating by myself any good thought, since all my sufficiency comes from You; nor can I worthily invoke Your Name without the help of the Holy Spirit. May it please You, then, to send me Your Spirit, in order that the rays of Your light may shine down upon me from the height of heaven. Come, O sweet Holy Spirit; come, Father of the poor; come, dispenser of graces; come, light of hearts; come, wonderful comforter; come, sweet guest and refreshment of our souls. You are rest in toil, dew on a summer morning, consolation in sorrow. O blessed Light! fill the inmost places of my heart" (cf. St. Peter of Alcantara).

O Lord, enlighten my heart, for without Your light, without Your Spirit, even the holiest books leave me cold and dry and do not speak to me of You. When, on the contrary, You come to my aid and give me Your interior grace, then everything is illumined with a new light, and even the simplest words are food for my soul. Grant me then, O Lord, this grace, without which no reading, however sublime, can inspire me with devotion; no reasoning, however lofty, can move my heart to love You and my will to accomplish good.

150

MEDITATION

PRESENCE OF GOD - Inspire me, O Lord, with piety, so that I may learn how to converse with You in a spirit of real filial love.

MEDITATION

1. The teachings of St. John of the Cross and St. Teresa of Jesus suggest a method of meditation which is especially well adapted for bringing souls to divine intimacy and preparing them for contemplation.

St. John of the Cross gives us the distinctive note of this method : " The end of meditation and mental consideration of divine things is ," he says, " to obtain some knowledge and love of God " (*AS II*, 14,2). We see at once that the emphasis is not placed on the work of the intellect, nor on the " speculative knowledge " of God and of the truths of faith. Rather, it rests on " loving knowledge, " which, of course, has its support in thought, but thought that is affectionate, permeated with love, and that surges from a loving heart. When we love a person, we come to know him intuitively, and thus, better and more easily than those who might study him more minutely, but without love.

St. Teresa of Jesus speaks in the same sense and says that prayer consists " not in thinking much, but in loving much " (*Int C IV*, 1). Thought is always subordinated to love. While we do think during the meditation, our purpose is not to become more learned, but to increase our ability to love God more. Consequently, the work of the mind will be orientated especially to the realization of God's love for us; and this, by reflection on the various manifestations of infinite love. It can well be said that there is no divine mystery or truth of faith which does not, in some way, speak of the excessive love of the Lord. The more we are convinced of this love, the more profound will be our " loving knowledge " of God; and at the same time, we shall feel an ever increasing impulse to return love to Him who has first loved us so greatly. Thus, meditation, the discourse of the intellect, will bring us spontaneously to the exercise of love. For this

reason we do not give the principal place in our prayer to
reflection and reasoning, however lofty and sublime they
may be; but we make use of them only insofar as is necessary
to awaken love within us, to place us and maintain us in the
actual exercise of love.

2. If in meditation we should not give first place to
thought, neither should we go to the opposite extreme and
neglect the necessary effort and application. We should
apply the following method :

Even before reading the point of the meditation, we
should take great care to put ourselves in the presence of
God, seeking by means of an energetic act of the will to put
aside all alien thoughts, all preoccupation and haste.

Mental prayer is an intimate conversation with God;
but it is clear that we cannot treat intimately with Him if
He is far from our minds and hearts. It is true that God is
always present to us, but it is we who are not always present
to Him. Therefore, we must establish contact with Our Lord,
and place ourselves near Him, by a conscious realization of
His presence. Each one of us can do this in the way which
seems most suitable—either by considering the Most Holy
Trinity dwelling in our heart, or by drawing near to Jesus
present in the tabernacle, or perhaps by picturing to ourselves
interiorly some episode in the life or the Passion of our
Savior. Thus, in the presence of God and beneath His
gaze, we read the point of the meditation tranquilly, and
reflects upon it calmly and gently, not as if reasoning with
ourselves, but rather as if speaking to God in whose presence
we are. The more the soul becomes accustomed to this
way of reflecting, that is, treating and developing the
subject of our meditation with God, the more quickly will this
method attain its end, which is to enable the soul to converse
with the Lord, to speak affectionately with Him as a son
speaks with its father, as a friend with a friend. Throughout
the time of prayer application and effort are certainly needed;
but these must be directed more to the sustaining of the soul
in loving contact with God than to its preoccupation with
abstract, narrow reasoning. The thoughts drawn from the
meditation—and we may refer to the text whenever we feel
the need of doing so—will serve to nourish this contact and
to give the soul a subject for conversation with God. The
work of the intellect must not make us forget that the essence

of prayer consists in an intimate communing with God in which an interchange of love, not reasoning, predominates.

COLLOQUY

" Teach me, O Lord, how to meditate; teach me to pray, for I can do neither the one nor the other as I should, and You alone can teach me.   Give me ears to hear You in the reading and in the meditation; give me a tongue to speak with You in prayer.   Inspire me with Your divine Spirit, so that He may enable me to know the subject on which I should reflect, what I should say and ask, and how I should ask in order to obtain it.   Let the Holy Spirit teach me to groan in Your presence; or rather, may He Himself form in me those holy groanings which You always hear and never reject.   Inspire me, O Lord, with a great love for Your divine truths and doctrines, so that when I read of them, I shall understand and relish them.   Open my mind and my heart; make me faithfully believe what You teach and practice what You command " (an ancient author).

Above all, O Lord, grant that meditation on Your mysteries may serve to inflame me with Your holy love, so that I shall become more capable of loving You and more disposed to give myself generously to Your service.   Teach me to meditate, not only with my mind, but especially with my heart; teach me to reflect devoutly and lovingly.   Then, indeed, meditation will strike new sparks of love in my heart, and, as I hope, with Your grace, a flame will rise from it, ever stronger and more ardent, more and more able to purify my soul and to urge me ardently to accomplish Your will. How happy shall I be, O Lord, if at the powerful breath of the Holy Spirit, this flame should burst forth into a conflagration of divine love!   My coldness, my meanness, my selfishness make me unworthy and incapable of this, but You who can raise up sons of Abraham even from stones, break my heart, so hard and cold, and light in it the living flame of Your love.

" O eternal God, You are eternal and infinite Goodness, no one can understand You or know You wholly, except insofar as You give him the grace to do so.   And You give as much of this knowledge as we prepare our souls to receive.   O sweet Love, all my life I have never loved You.

But my soul always longs for You; and the more it possesses
You, so much the more it seeks You; the more it desires You,
so much the more it finds You and relishes You, O sovereign,
eternal fire, abyss of charity " (St. Catherine of Siena).

151

INTIMATE CONVERSE WITH GOD

PRESENCE OF GOD - O Lord, although I am so unworthy, deign to
admit me to intimacy with You.

MEDITATION

1. Meditation, like meditative reading, is a means to
attain to the heart of prayer which, according to St. Teresa
of Jesus, is " nothing but friendly intercourse, and frequent
solitary converse with Him who we know loves us " (*Life*, 8).
It makes no difference whether we attain this end by means
of meditation, or reading, or even by the slow, pious recitation
of a vocal prayer.   All these ways are good; the best for each
one, however, will be that which will lead him more quickly
to the end, that is, to intimate converse with God.   Once we
reach the heart of prayer, we must learn how to persevere
in it, in other words, to converse " in friendly intercourse
with the Lord. "   Here, likewise, the manner will differ
according to one's attraction and personal dispositions, which
will often vary with the days and with circumstances.   Sometimes, as soon as we are sufficiently convinced of God's love
for us, we feel incited to express our gratitude to Him,
desiring to return love for love, and we spontaneously begin
an intimate conversation with the Lord.   We express our
gratitude, protesting that we want to be more generous in
giving ourselves to Him; we beg His pardon for not having
done so in the past; finally, we go on to make practical
resolutions and to ask His help to keep them faithfully.
Of course, this means an intimate colloquy, wholly personal
and spontaneous, without preoccupation about form or order,
and proceeding only from the superabundance of the heart.
In this way, having interrupted the reading or the meditation

which has aroused in us so many good thoughts, we " stop to have solitary converse with God, " returning to the book or the reflection when we feel the need of seeking new reasons or of arousing new affections to maintain our colloquy with God. Here is a genuine colloquy, because not only does the soul speak, but God often answers—not audibly, of course, but by sending it graces of light and love through which the soul will have a better understanding of the divine ways, and will feel more eager to advance in them with generosity. It is well, therefore, not to make use of many words in the colloquy, but to stop often and listen interiorly in order to perceive the movements of grace, which are really God's answer.

2. We must not believe that in order to treat intimately with God and to show Him our love, it is always necessary to do so by means of words. On the contrary—and this happens spontaneously with progress in the spiritual life—we will often prefer to be silent in order to fix our gaze calmly on the Lord, to listen to Him, the interior Master, and to return Him love in silence. The manifestation of our love thus becomes less lively and impetuous, but it gains in depth what it loses in emotion and outward appearance. We express our love more tranquilly, but the movement of our will toward God is much firmer and more serious. Leaving aside reasonings and words, we concentrates all in a loving, intuitive look on God, and this gaze, far more than reasonings and colloquies, allows us to penetrate the depths of the divine mysteries. Before reaching this point, we have read, meditated, analyzed; now, enjoying as it were the fruit of our investigation, we stop to contemplate God in silence and love. Our colloquy now becomes silent, contemplative, according to the traditional idea of " contemplation, " *simplex intuitus veritatis*, that is, a simple look which penetrates truth. But let us repeat, this is not a speculative look, but a look of love which keeps the soul in intimate contact with God, in a real exchange of friendship with Him. The more the soul contemplates God, and the more it falls in love with Him, the greater need it feels to concentrate its love in total generosity. The Lord in turn answers this seeking love of the soul. He lets Himself be found and felt by illuminating the soul with His light and drawing it more intensely to Himself by His grace.

The soul will not always be able to continue long in this contemplative look, this silent colloquy; now and again it will need to come back to reflection, to the verbal expression of its thoughts, and—especially when it is not yet accustomed to this manner of prayer—it will be well for it to do so rather often, in order to avoid vagueness and distractions. Nevertheless, it must be remembered that more is gained in these silent pauses at the feet of Our Lord than in a thousand reasonings and discourses.

COLLOQUY

" Grant, O Lord, that the purpose of my prayer may be to occupy my heart with loving You; and since I can find no better way to practice love than by this intimate recollection in silence and detachment from all creatures, I beg You, my God, to take away my life rather than deprive me of this interior exchange with You, my paradise on earth " (cf. St. Leonard of Port Maurice).

" O Lord, there is no profit for You in staying with us; and yet You love us enough to say that Your delight is to dwell in our company. Why do You love us so much as to give Yourself to us more freely than the things we ask of You? It is certain that I no longer desire to possess anything else; since, if I ask You properly, I can receive You, my God, and converse intimately with You. I shall adorn myself with the jewels of the virtues, and invite You to the nuptial couch of my heart where I shall rest with You. I know that You neither ask nor wish for anything else than to visit my soul, that You want to enter, and have been knocking at its door for a long time, and I regret that I have so long deprived myself of this great gift. So I shall come near You in the secret place of my heart and say to You : I know that You love me more than I love myself, I shall no longer be concerned for myself, but shall have no thought save for You alone, and You will take care of me. I cannot pay attention to You and to myself at the same time; therefore, in a loving mutual exchange, You will think of me, comforting my infirmity, and I shall think of You, finding my joy in Your goodness. Whereas I have much to gain from You, You have nothing to gain from me; yet I know that You are with me very willingly, and more desirous of helping me than

I am of remaining with You and enjoying Your goodness. Whence does this come? Certainly it arises from this : that I love myself poorly, and You love me well.... But if You wished, O Lord, to set before my eyes all the marks of Your love, I would faint away, for even if I had all the tongues of men and of angels, I could never express all the gifts of nature, grace, and glory which You have given me.... How then, O Lord, can I think or meditate on anything except Your love? What is sweeter than that? Why should I desire anything else? And how does it happen that I am not seized and bound by Your love? It surrounds me on all sides, and yet I do not comprehend it " (cf. St. Bonaventure).

152

PRAYER OF RECOLLECTION

PRESENCE OF GOD - May I find You within me, O my God, in the little heaven of my soul!

MEDITATION

1. St. Teresa of Jesus warmly recommends to interior souls another kind of prayer, much simpler and more profitable—the prayer of recollection. The foundation of this prayer is the divine presence in our souls : the *presence of immensity*, by which God is in us as Creator and Preserver in so real and essential a manner that " in Him we live, and move, and are " (*Acts* 17,28), so that if He ceased to be present in us, we should cease to exist; the *presence of friendship*, by which in a soul in the state of grace, God is present as a Father, as a Friend and as a sweet Guest, who invites that soul to dwell with the three divine Persons : with the Father, the Son and the Holy Spirit. This is the consoling promise of Jesus to the soul who loves Him : " If anyone love Me... My Father will love him, and We will come to him, and will make our abode with him " (*Jn* 14,23).

The prayer of recollection consists in the realization of this great truth : God is in me, my soul is His temple; I recollect myself in the intimacy of this temple to adore Him,

love Him, and unite myself to Him. " O soul, most beautiful
of all creatures, " exclaims St. John of the Cross, " that so
greatly desireth to know the place where your Beloved is,
in order to seek Him and be united with Him. . . . It is
a matter of great contentment and joy for you to see that
He is so near you as to be within you. Rejoice and be glad
in your inward recollection with Him, since you have Him
so near. There desire Him, there adore Him, and do not
go to seek Him outside yourself " (*SC*, 1,7.8). The soul who
has the sense of the presence of God within it, possesses one
of the most efficacious means of making prayer. " Do you
believe, " says St. Teresa of Jesus, " that it is of little
importance for a soul who is easily distracted, to understand
this truth [that God is in it] and to know that, in order to
speak with its heavenly Father and to enjoy His company,
it does not have to go up to heaven or even to raise its
voice? No matter how softly it speaks, He always hears
it, because He is so near. It does not need wings to go
to contemplate Him in itself " (*Way*, 28).

2. Although the prayer of recollection is the highest of
the active forms of prayer, St. Teresa notes that we can
obtain it for ourselves, " for this is not a supernatural state
[a passive recollection which can only be produced by divine
motion], but depends upon our volition; and by God's favor,
we can enter it of our own accord " (*ibid.*, 29).

Therefore, it is important to know what the soul should
do in order to practice this prayer, and this can be reduced
to two things : " The soul collects together all its faculties and
enters within itself to be with its God " (*ibid.*, 28). Our
senses, imagination, and intellect tend spontaneously toward
exterior things, on which they are dispersed; therefore, the
soul, by a prolonged, resolute act of the will, ought to withdraw
them from these exterior things in order to concentrate them
on interior things—in this little heaven of the soul where the
Blessed Trinity dwells. This exercise, especially in the
beginning, requires effort and energy and it will not be easy
at first. However, the Saint teaches, " let the soul try to
cultivate the habit, despite the fatigue entailed in recollecting
itself and overcoming the body which is trying to reclaim
its rights. " Little by little, " as a reward for the violence
which it has previously done to itself " (*ibid.*), recollection

will become easy and delightful; the senses will obey promptly; and even if the soul is not entirely free from distractions, it will not be so hard to overcome them.

In this way, we shall be able to concentrate entirely on God present within us, and there at His feet will be able to converse with Him to our heart's delight. It will not be difficult to spend even the whole time of prayer in acts of faith, love, and adoration, admiring and contemplating the great mystery of the indwelling of the Trinity in our poor heart, and offering our humble homage to the three divine Persons. But if this is not enough, we can also use other practices : " Hidden there within our soul, we can think about the Passion, and picture the Son, and offer Him to the Father, without tiring the mind by going to seek Him on Mount Calvary, or in the Garden, or at the Column "; or else, more simply, we can " speak with Him as with a Father, a Brother, a Lord, and a Spouse—sometimes in one way, sometimes in another...we can tell Him our troubles, beg Him to put them right, and yet realize that we are not worthy to be called His child " *(ibid.)*. And the Saint concludes with these words : " Those who are able to shut themselves up in this way within this little heaven of the soul, where dwells the Maker of heaven and earth...may be sure that they are walking on an excellent road and will come without fail to drink of the water of the fountain " *(ibid.)*.

COLLOQUY

" Give me the grace to recollect myself in the little heaven of my soul where You have established Your dwelling. There You let me find You, there I feel that You are closer to me than anywhere else, and there You prepare my soul quickly to enter into intimacy with You. Then, the soul, understanding that all the things of the world are but toys, seems all of a sudden to rise above everything created and escape it.... My God, if I could only recall often that You are dwelling within my soul, I think that it would be impossible for me to give myself up to the things of the world, for compared with what I have within me, they seem to me to have no value at all.

" Help me, O Lord, to withdraw my senses from exterior things, make them docile to the commands of my will, so that when I want to converse with You, they will retire at once, like bees shutting themselves up in the hive in order to make honey " (cf. T.J. *Way*, 28).

" O Lord, You say to my soul, ' My kingdom is within you. ' It is very comforting to know that You never leave me, and that I cannot exist without You. What more do you want, O my soul, and what do you seek elsewhere, since you possess within yourself your wealth, your love, your peace, your plenitude, and your kingdom, that is, the Beloved whom you desire and for whom you sigh? " (cf. J.C. *SC*, 1,7.8).

" O my God, You are in me and I am in You. I have found my heaven on earth, since heaven is You, O Lord, and You are in my soul. I can find You there always; even when I do not feel Your presence, You are there nevertheless, and I like to seek You there. Oh! if only I could never leave You alone! " (cf. E.T. *L*).

153

ARIDITY

PRESENCE OF GOD - O Lord, help me to be faithful to You, so that the spirit of prayer will not be extinguished in me through my own fault.

MEDITATION

1. At the beginning of a more intense spiritual life the soul usually enjoys a sensible fervor which makes spiritual exercises easy and agreeable. Good thoughts, sentiments of love, and outpourings from the heart arise spontaneously. To be recollected and alone with God in prayer is a joy; time passes quickly, and frequently the presence of God becomes almost perceptible; there is a like facility in the practice of mortification and the other virtues. However, this state does not ordinarily last long, and there comes a time when the soul is deprived of all sensible consolation. This suppression of sensible devotion is the state of aridity, which may have various causes.

Sometimes it is the result of infidelity on the part of those who little by little have become lax, allowing themselves many slight satisfactions and pleasures and giving in to their curiosity, selfishness, or pride—which they had previously renounced. If they only realized what benefits they were losing by such conduct, they would be ready for any kind of sacrifice rather than yield to these weaknesses. The habit of mortification, which was acquired at great cost, is quickly lost, and they again become the slaves of their own passions. Self-love, which was not dead, but only sleeping, becomes active again and may become not only the cause of many voluntary imperfections which had previously been overcome, but even of deliberate venial sins. It may ultimately reduce to lukewarmness a once fervent soul. The unfaithful one who has fallen back into mediocrity cannot protest to the Lord in prayer that it loves Him and desires to advance in His love; still less can it taste the joy of knowing that it truly loves God. Hence such a soul inevitably falls into aridity. In this condition the only remedy is to return to its first fervor. This will cost it dearly, but far from becoming discouraged, the soul should begin anew as soon as possible. Besides, Our Lord loves so much to forgive!

2. On the other hand, aridity sometimes arises from physical or moral causes which are entirely independent of ourselves : indisposition, illness, fatigue, or depression caused by troublesome preoccupations or excessive work. These are things which can make all feeling of spiritual consolation disappear, and this often occurs with no way of remedying it. It is a trial which may last a long time, but one in which we must, with good reason, see the hand of God which disposes everything for our good, and realize that He cannot fail to give us the grace necessary to profit by our suffering. Although not feeling any consolation nor experiencing any attraction for prayer, the soul should apply itself to it *through duty*, while trying by some ingenuity to remedy its own powerlessness. St. Teresa of Jesus says that " anyone who cannot make mental prayer should turn to vocal prayer, or reading, or colloquies with God, but should never fail to consecrate to prayer the time set apart for it " (*Way*, 18).

If, in spite of everything, the soul does not succeed in moving its heart, let it love God by the will alone. This requires a great effort, but by it this faculty is strengthened.

Almost without realizing it, the soul is made capable of a more active, generous love. This love will be deprived of feeling, it is true, but we must remember that the substance of love does not consist in *feeling*, but in *willing* to give pleasure, at any cost, to the person loved. One who, in order to please God, perseveres in prayer although he finds no consolation in it, but rather repugnance, gives Him a beautiful proof of true love. Progress in the spiritual life is not measured by the consolation the soul feels; for this is unnecessary, since true devotion consists solely in the promptness of the will in God's service. The will can be very prompt and firmly resolved to serve God, although at the same time it is arid and even forced to struggle against its natural repugnance.

COLLOQUY

" Lord, my God, You who are holy, look and see my affliction! Have pity on the child whom You have engendered in sorrow and do not consider my sins, lest You forget Your power over them. What father will not liberate his son? And what son has not been chastised by his father's compassionate rod? O Father and Lord, although I am a sinner, I am nonetheless Your child, because You have created and recreated me. Can a mother forget the fruit of her womb? If she should forget—You, Father, have promised to remember. Behold! I cry, and You do not hearken to me, I am torn with grief, and You do not console me. What shall I say, what shall I do, miserable creature that I am? Deprived of Your consolation, I am far away from Your sight.

" O Lord Jesus, where are Your ancient mercies? Shall You be angry with me forever? Be appeased, I beg You, and do not turn Your face away from me.... I confess that I have sinned, but I am certain that Your mercy surpasses all my offenses!

" Weep, my soul, and complain, miserable one; groan because You have sent away Your Spouse, Jesus Christ, the All-powerful God; do not be angry with me, O Lord, for I could never withstand Your anger. Have pity on me, so that I may not fall into despair. Although I am worthy of condemnation, do not withhold that which can save sinners.

" I hope for much from Your bounty, O Lord, because You Yourself teach us to ask, to seek, and to knock; at Your word, I ask, I seek, I knock.   O Lord, You who tell us to ask, grant that I may receive; You who tell us to seek, grant that I may find; You who teach us to knock at the door, open to the one who is knocking!   I am weak; strengthen me.   Bring me back, because I have wandered away, and revive me, because I am dead.   According to Your good pleasure, direct and govern my senses, my thoughts, and my actions, that I may live by You and give myself entirely to You "   (St. Augustine).

154

THE GOOD SHEPHERD

SECOND SUNDAY AFTER EASTER

PRESENCE OF GOD - I come to You, O Jesus, my Good Shepherd; lead me to the pastures of eternal life.

MEDITATION

1. The liturgy today sums up in the gentle figure of the Good Shepherd all that Jesus has done for our souls.

The shepherd is everything to his flock; their life, their sustenance, and their care is entirely in his hands, and if the shepherd is good, they will have nothing to fear under his protection, and they will want for nothing.

Jesus is preeminently the Good Shepherd : He not only loves, feeds, and guards His sheep, but He also gives them life at the cost of His own.   In the mystery of the Incarnation, the Son of God comes to earth in search of men who, like stray sheep, have wandered away from the sheepfold and have become lost in the dark valley of sin.   He comes as a most loving Shepherd who, in order to take better care of His flock, is not afraid to share their lot.   Today's Epistle (1 Pt 2,21-25) shows Him to us as He takes our sins upon Himself that He may heal us by His Passion : " Who His own self bore our sins in His Body upon the tree that we, being dead to sin,

should live to justice; by whose stripes you were healed.
For you were as sheep going astray; but you are now
converted to the Shepherd and Bishop of your souls "
(1 *Pt* 2,24-25). Jesus said, " I am the Good Shepherd, and
I give my life for my sheep " and in the Office for Paschal time,
the Church chants many times : " The Good Shepherd is
risen, He who gave His life for His sheep and who died for
His flock. " What could be a better synthesis of the whole
work of the Redemption? It seems still more wonderful
when we hear Jesus declare : " I am come that they may
have life and may have it more abundantly " (*Jn* 10,10).
In truth, He could well repeat to each one of us : " What
more could I have done for you that I have not done? "
(cf. *Is* 5,4). Oh, would that our generosity in giving ourselves
to Him had no limits, after the pattern of His own liberality
in giving Himself to us!

2. Again Jesus said : " I know Mine, and Mine know Me,
even as the Father knows Me and I know the Father "
(*Gosp : Jn* 10,11.16). Although there is no question here of
equality, but merely that of a simple comparison, it is
nevertheless very consoling and glorious for us to see how
Jesus likes to compare His relations with us to those He has
with His Father. At the Last Supper also, He said : " As the
Father hath loved Me, I also have loved you, " and again :
" as Thou, Father, in Me, and I in Thee; that they also may
be one in Us " (*Jn* 15,9 – 17,21). This shows that between
us, the sheep, and Jesus, our Shepherd, there is not only
a relation of acquaintance, but also one of love, and better
still, of a communion of life, similar to that which exists
between the Son and the Father. It is by means of the
grace, faith and charity, which the Good Shepherd acquired
for us by His death, that we arrive at such intimacy with our
God—so deep that it makes us share in His own divine life.
A close relationship of loving knowledge is here
established between the Good Shepherd and His sheep—one
so intimate that the Shepherd knows His sheep one by one
and can call them by name; and they recognize His voice
and follow Him with docility. Each soul can say : " Jesus
knows me and loves me, not in a general abstract way, but
in the concrete aspect of my needs, of my desires, and of my
life; for Him to know me and to love me is to do me good,
to encompass me more and more with His grace, and to

sanctify me.   Precisely because He loves me, Jesus calls me by name : He calls me when in prayer He opens to me new horizons of the spiritual life, or when He enables me to know my faults and weaknesses better; He calls me when He reprimands me or purifies me by aridity, as well as when He consoles and encourages me by filling me with new fervor; He calls me when He makes me feel the need of greater generosity, and when He asks me for sacrifices or gives me joys, and still more, when He awakens in me a deeper love for Him.   Hearing His call, my attitude should be that of a loving little sheep who recognizes the voice of its Shepherd and follows Him always.

COLLOQUY

" O Lord, You are my Shepherd, I shall not want; You make me lie down in green pastures, You lead me to the water of refreshment, You convert my soul and lead me on the paths of justice.   Even though I walk in the ravines, in the dark valleys, I shall fear no evil, for You are with me. Your rod and Your staff are my comfort.   You prepare a table before me in the presence of my enemies.   You anoint my head with oil, my cup runs over " (cf. *Ps* 22). O Lord, my Good Shepherd, what more could You have done for me that You have not done?   What could You have given to me that You have not given?   You willed to be my food and drink.   What more delightful and salutary, nourishing and strengthening pasture could You have found than Your own Body and Blood?

" O good Lord Jesus Christ, my sweet Shepherd, what return shall I make to You for all that You have given me? What shall I give You in exchange for Your gift of Yourself to me?   Even if I could give myself to You a thousand times, it would still be nothing, since I am nothing in comparison with You.   You, so great, have loved me so much and so gratuitously, I who am so small, so wicked and un-grateful!   I know, O Lord, that Your love tends toward the immense, the infinite, because You are immense and infinite.   Please tell me, O Lord, how I ought to love You.

" My love, O Lord, is not gratuitous, it is owed to You. . . .   Although I cannot love You as much as I should,

You accept my weak love. I can love You more when You condescend to increase my virtue, but I can never give You what You deserve. Give me then, Your most ardent love by which, with Your grace, I shall love You, please You, serve You, and fulfill Your commands. May I never be separated from You, either in time or in eternity, but abide, united to You in love, forever and ever " (Ven. R. Jourdain).

155

ARIDITY AND PROGRESS

PRESENCE OF GOD - O Lord, help me to seek for You and to unite myself to You, even through the aridity and powerlessness of my spirit.

MEDITATION

1. Even without the presence of the physical or moral causes which we have mentioned before, it is possible to pass from a state of sensible fervor to one of absolute aridity. This happens by the direct work of God which makes it impossible for the soul to pray with the help of the imagination, or to practice acts of sensible love as before. The fact is that, whereas meditation or affectionate converse with God was formerly made with ease and comfort, the soul now finds it impossible to connect two ideas. Thoughts or reading which once moved the soul now leave it in-different—the heart remains cold and hard as a stone. Even though watching over itself carefully in order to be faithful in mortification and generosity; even though intens-ifying its preparation for prayer and fervently beseeching the Lord for help, it no longer succeeds in wringing one drop of devotion from its heart. Then the poor soul worries and is afraid, thinking that the Lord has abandoned it because of some fault or other. What she does not realize is that this kind of aridity conceals a great grace—the grace of purification and of progress in the ways of prayer. In fact, by means of aridity, the Lord intends to free it from childish

feelings and to raise it to the purer, firmer level of the will. When it was experiencing so much comfort in prayer, the soul, unknown to itself, was becoming somewhat attached to these sensible consolations. Hence it loved and sought prayer not purely for God, but also a little for itself. Now, deprived of all attraction for prayer, the soul will henceforth learn to apply itself to it solely to give pleasure to the Lord. Furthermore, finding no help in beautiful thoughts and sweet emotions, it will learn to walk by strength of will alone, exercising itself in acts of faith and love which, it is true, are wholly arid, but are all the more meritorious because they are more voluntary. In this way, its love for God will become purer, because it is more disinterested; and stronger, because it is more voluntary.

2. Through aridity, the soul also makes progress in humility. The inability to meditate, to fix its attention, to awaken good sentiments in its heart—all these convince the soul more and more of its nothingness. This state makes it realize, without effort or reasoning, that, apart from God's help, it can really do nothing. Thus, little by little, that high opinion of self, that feeling of confidence in its own strength, which had more or less secretly insinuated itself into the soul when all was easy and pleasant in prayer, now vanishes.

At the same time, seeing how poor and wretched it is in the presence of God, there is born in the soul a feeling of more profound respect and greater reverence before the infinite majesty of God. When it could speak heart to heart with Him in prayer, the soul may have forgotten somewhat the infinite distance which always separates God from His creature. It is true that God wants us to act toward Him with great confidence and He invites us in thousands of ways to His intimacy; however, He always remains the inaccessible one, and we, nothingness and misery. It is very precious, this feeling of greater reverence which ripens in the soul through the experience of its own nothingness, and which always, even in moments of the greatest loving intimacy, will permit it to approach God with true humility of heart.

If, therefore, during the time of prayer we can do nothing but humble ourselves before God, by recognizing our own nothingness and showing Him our impotence, our incapacity, yes, even offering God this very nothingness in adoration

of His infinite majesty, we will have made very good use of
our time. Certainly, in this state of aridity, especially when
suffering greatly from distractions, we will often feel that we
have done nothing during prayer. Let us not be disturbed,
however, because as St. Peter of Alcantara says : " He who
does the little he can, does much before God. It is not difficult
to persevere in prayer when we find consolation in it, but
there is great merit in doing so when sensible devotion is
reduced to a minimum. Yet it is precisely then that prayer
becomes more meritorious and humility is increased, as well
as patience and perseverance. "

COLLOQUY

" O Lord, blessed be Your Name forever, because You
willed me to suffer this tribulation. I cannot escape it, so
I have recourse to You, that You may help me to profit
by it. O Lord, I am deeply afflicted, my heart can find no
rest, and it suffers much on account of this hard trial. What
can I say to You, O beloved Father? I am in anguish;
Lord, save me! This happens to me in order to glorify You
by my very humiliation, but later, You will deliver me.
May it please You to deliver me, O Lord, for alone and
wretched, what can I do or where can I go without You?
    " Give me once more the grace of patience! Help me,
O God, and I shall fear nothing, even if the burden is heavy.
And now, what shall I say in all these misfortunes? Lord,
Your will be done. I well deserve the tribulation which is
crushing me. I must bear it. May I do so patiently, until
the storm is past and calm re-established " (*Imit. III*,
29,1.2).
    " O my Jesus, nothing from You but dryness. But
I am very happy to suffer that which You want me to suffer.
I am happy to see that You show me that I am not a
stranger by treating me like this.
    " O Lord, make my darkness serve to enlighten souls.
I consent, if such is Your will, to continue walking all my
life in the darkness of faith, provided that one day I arrive
at the goal of the mountain of love.
    " I am very happy to have no consolation, for thus my
love is not like that of the world's brides who are always
looking at their bridegroom's hands to see if they bear a gift,

or at his face in the hope of glimpsing a smile of love to enchant them. . . . O Jesus, I want to love You for Yourself alone. . . . I do not desire love that I feel, but only love that You feel " (T.C.J. *L*, 51,90,93,89).

156

ENERGETIC RESOLVE

PRESENCE OF GOD - O Lord, make me persevere in seeking You and in serving You, in spite of all the difficulties which I may encounter.

MEDITATION

1. St. Teresa says that anyone who wishes to give himself to prayer with profit must make " an earnest and most determined resolve not to halt " on the way he has chosen. This means that we must give ourselves to prayer, not for a stated time only, but at all times, every day, all our life; let us not be dissuaded from prayer for any reason whatsoever. " Come what may, happen what will, let those complain who will, tire yourself as you must, but even if you die half-way along the road. . . tend always toward the goal " (*Way*, 21). Let us ever remember that this goal is the living water promised by Jesus to those who sincerely thirst for Him and His love.

Without a strong, determined resolve, the soul will too often find more or less plausible reasons for neglecting prayer. Sometimes aridity will make the soul think that it is a waste of time to devote itself to an exercise from which it seems to draw no fruit, and that it would be better to use this time in good works. Sometimes, too, our numerous employments will seem to justify this idea. At other times, the feeling of our wretchedness—especially when we consider our want of fidelity to grace—will make us think ourselves unworthy of divine intimacy and that, therefore, it is useless to persevere in prayer. It should be evident that all these pretexts are suggestions of the enemy who, sometimes under the pretext of zeal for exterior works, sometimes under that of false humility or of waste of time, does all he can to draw souls away from prayer. " No temptation, " declares St. Teresa, " is more serious " than this one, " and the devil does us the very greatest harm by it " (cf. *Life*, 7 – 8). Therefore, she insists : " One who has begun to make mental prayer must never give it up, in spite of the sins into which he may fall. Prayer is the means which will help him to rise. Without prayer, this would be more difficult. He should not allow himself to be deceived by the devil to abandon prayer under the pretext of humility " (*ibid.*, 8).

2. Even if the soul has fallen into aridity through its own fault, it should not neglect prayer, but should persevere in it in spite of the violence it will have to do to itself and the strong repugnances which must be overcome. " If that soul perseveres, notwithstanding the sins, temptations, and falls of a thousand kinds into which the devil leads it, the Lord, I am certain, will bring it to the harbor of salvation " *(ibid.)*. Accept the torture of having to spend the time of prayer in complete aridity, and moreover, with the pain of feeling yourself so unlike to God and so unworthy of Him in whose presence you are; accept the reproaches of your conscience for your infidelities, and offer them all to the Lord in expiation for your faults and omissions, and to obtain the grace to amend your life. Never weary of repeating with a sincere heart the prayer of the publican : " Lord, be merciful to me, a sinner " (*Lk* 18,13); and God, who loves those who humbly recognize their own wretchedness, will not fail to come to your aid. However, you must learn to wait patiently for the time fixed by Him. St. Teresa of Jesus spent nearly eighteen years in such aridity. " Many times " says the Saint, " I would have gladly endured the most severe penances rather than try to recollect myself to make prayer. I needed to summon all my courage to force myself, so unbearable was the temptation of the devil to leave off prayer. " But, she concludes, " the Lord Himself helped me " (*Life*, 8). This was the reward of her fidelity.

The Saint has, therefore, all the authority which comes from experience, to insist that never, for any motive, should we give up prayer. And she strongly recommends it, saying : " Do not tarry on the way, but strive like strong men until you die in the attempt, for you are here for nothing else than to strive " (*Way*, 20).

We can likewise apply the words of Jesus to prayer : " The kingdom of heaven suffereth violence, and the violent bear it away " (*Mt* 11,12).

COLLOQUY

" O Lord, I know that in order that love be true and friendship lasting, equal conditions must exist between the two friends.   I also know that there can be nothing wrong in You; while my nature, on the contrary, is vicious, sensual, and ungrateful...Hence I cannot love You as You deserve.

" O infinite goodness of my God!   I see who You are and who I am, and seeing how different You are from me, O joy of the angels, I long to be wholly consumed in love for You!   How true it is that You bear with those who permit You to be with them!   How good a friend You are to them! How You lavish Your favors upon them and bear with them, and wait until their ways become more like Yours.   You remember the time spent in loving You, and at the first sign of repentance, You forget all their offenses.   This I know from experience, and I do not understand, O my Creator, why the whole world does not strive to draw near You in this intimate friendship.   The wicked, who are not like You, ought to come so that You may make them good, allowing You to be with them, at least two hours each day, even though they are not with You but with a thousand cares and thoughts of the world, as I used to be.   In exchange for the effort which it costs them to want to be in such good company (for You know that in the beginning they cannot do more, nor afterwards sometimes) You force the devils not to attack them, and make the devils every day less strong against them, and give these souls strength to conquer them.   Yea, Life of all lives, You slay none of those who put their trust in You and desire You for their Friend " (T.J. *Life*, 8).

O Lord, give me also that holy audacity which will make me always persevere in prayer, in spite of exterior and interior difficulties, aridities, weakness, and lack of correspondence with Your grace....   You will remedy all my ills.

157

ARIDITY AND CONTEMPLATION

PRESENCE OF GOD - Draw me to You, O Lord, by the road You choose and in any way You will; I ask only for grace to know how to follow You always.

MEDITATION

1. The aridity which comes from God not only has the advantage of making us go forward in virtue, but it also brings us to a higher form of prayer. St. John of the Cross teaches that it is by means of this kind of aridity that God calls souls to a simpler and more profound form of prayer which he terms " initial contemplation. " To distinguish this aridity from that which is caused by other things, he gives three signs. The first sign is : " the soul finds no pleasure or consolation in the things of God, it also fails to find pleasure in anything created " (*DN I*, 9,2). This loss of delight in the things of God may occur, too, when aridity is caused by the soul's own faults; but then it looks for human satisfactions, whereas in the former case, although it no longer experiences the joy of being with God, it does not return to creatures, but rather, remains firm in its decision to keep its heart detached from them. The second sign is that, in spite of aridity, " the memory is ordinarily centered upon God with painful care and solicitude, fearing that it is not serving God " (*ibid.*, 3). In other words, the soul suffers from its spiritual insensibility, fearing that it does not love God and is not serving Him; and at the same time, it continues to seek Him with the anxiety of one who does not succeed in finding its treasure. The soul remains then always occupied with God, although in a negative, painful way, as if suffering because of the absence of a loved one. On the contrary, when the aridity is culpable, especially if it is caused by a state of habitual lukewarmness, the soul is not at all grieved about not loving God; it has become indifferent. The last sign consists in the fact that " the soul can no longer meditate or reflect in the imaginative sphere of sense as it was wont, however much it may of itself endeavor to do so "

(*ibid.*, 8). The soul would like to meditate; it applies itself, tries as hard as possible, and still does not succeed. When this state continues—for if it lasted only a short time it might have arisen from special conditions, either physical or moral—although it may have days of greater or less intensity, it tends to invade the whole soul in such a way as to make meditation habitually impossible. This aridity then means a call from God to more profound prayer.

2. By plunging the soul into aridity, God wishes to elevate it, to make it pass from a too human and low way of treating with Him, to a higher and more supernatural way. In meditation the soul went to God through intellectual effort—an excellent method, but one that is necessarily limited and inadequate in bringing us to know God who, being infinite, immensely exceeds the capacity of our mind. Now when God puts aridity into the soul, He makes meditation impossible for her, and forces her, so to speak, to go to Him by another way.

According to St. John of the Cross, this road is the way of initial contemplation, which consists in the soul's beginning to know God, no longer through the intellect alone, but by means of the experience of love. This experience will not give the soul any new ideas about God, but it will give the " sense " of His greatness. In fact, we have already seen that it is precisely in the midst of aridity that the torturing pain of no longer loving Our Lord, of not feeling this love any longer, is born in the soul. This feeling would not exist if the soul had not acquired a profound sense of the greatness of God and of His worthiness to be loved. This realization is not the result of any reasoning on the part of the soul, but of its experience of love. In fact, although unaware of it, the soul now loves God much more than previously; the best proof of this is that great anxiety which torments it with the fear of not loving Him. See, then, that it is precisely through this painful experience of love, which consists in the preoccupation about not loving and serving its God, that there is born in the soul contemplative knowledge, that is, the " sense " of God. We speak here of a knowledge which for the moment brings no comfort to the soul, but which nevertheless is most precious because, far better than any meditation, it infuses into the soul the " sense " of the divinity and fills it more and more with love for this God, whose infinite lovableness it now perceives by intuition. These advantages are so precious that, in order to obtain them, the soul not only ought to accept courageously the aridity which God sends, but also should recognize in it one of the greatest benefits He can bestow.

COLLOQUY

"O Jesus, how burdensome and bitter is life when You hide Yourself from our love! What are You doing, my Friend? Do You not see my anguish and the weight which is crushing me? Where are You? Why do You not come to console me, since I have no friend but You?

"But if it pleases You to leave me in this state, help me to accept it for love of You. Make me love You enough to suffer for You whatever You choose—sorrow, aridity, anguish, or even, seeming coldness of heart. Ah! that is indeed a great love, to love You without feeling the sweetness of Your love.

"Many serve You, O Jesus, when You console them; but few are willing to keep You company when You sleep on the raging waters or suffer in the garden of agony. Who, then, will serve You for Yourself? Oh! grant that it may be I!

"The Gospel tells me, O divine Shepherd, that You leave the *faithful* sheep in the desert. What deep things that tells me!... You are *sure* of them, they cannot go astray now, for they are love's captives; so You deprive them of Your visible presence to bring Your consolations to sinners; or even if You do meet them upon Mt. Thabor, it is only for a few moments. O Lord, do with me as You please. And if You seem to forget me, very well. You are free to, since I am no longer mine but Yours.... You will sooner weary of keeping me waiting than I of waiting for You" (cf. T.C.J. *L*, 32,73,144,121,81).

I ask only one thing, my God : in this aridity let my love increase, and grant that I may remain faithful to You at all cost. May I love You more by the reality of deeds as my love becomes less sensible. Grant that the less joy my love gives to me, the more glory it may give to You. And if, in order to increase in love, I need to suffer, blessed be this trial; since You strike me to teach me, You mortify me to cure me and to lead me to a higher life.

158

LOVING ATTENTION TO GOD

PRESENCE OF GOD - O Lord, let Your presence be the light and strength of my soul, the aid and support of my prayer.

MEDITATION

1. If God invites the soul, by means of aridity, to a more simple and more profound form of prayer, it would be absurd to try to compel it to continue in meditation, which, moreover, it can no longer make. On the contrary, the soul ought to be encouraged to give up this form of prayer without scruple, and to apply itself to remaining calmly in the presence of God, attentive to Him by means of a simple glance of faith and love. It should stay there and keep Him company, glad to be with Him, even if it has no feeling of His presence. The soul will see that it is gradually becoming accustomed to this new way of prayer and will notice that it is in contact with God in a way which is substantially better than that which it formerly had.

The thought that it no longer knows how to love should not disturb the soul. Of course, it can no longer love as tenderly as before, when the mere thought of God's love for it could arouse its feelings; however, the soul must remember that the supernatural love of charity is not sensible love, but a love of the will, which does not have to be felt. It consists solely in a decision of the will by which the soul gives God preference over all creatures and wills to consecrate itself entirely to His service. This in the real love which leads to the " sense of God. " Moreover, St. John of the Cross teaches that it is precisely in this period of obscure, initial contemplation, entered by way of the sufferings of purifying aridity, that there begins to develop in the soul what he calls *infused passive love*, that is, the love by which the soul goes to God, no longer merely by a decision of the will, but also by a secret drawing by God Himself. This explains why its love, although not felt at all, is in reality stronger than before; it urges the soul to give itself to God with increasingly strong resolve. It is God Himself who, drawing it secretly to Himself, awakens love in it. When during prayer the soul suffers because of its powerlessness and aridity, and fears that it does not love God, let it gently examine itself on this point, that is, try to find out if, in spite of all the difficulties met with, it remains firmly resolved to give itself wholly to God. To make this decision more concrete, the soul should apply it to the different circumstances of its life, particularly those which cost it most. Because it no longer feels any love, it is impelled to give God concrete proofs of love, that is, good works and the virtues, which are practiced to please Him.

2. Treating here of initial contemplation, we note that the soul should not be completely passive. There is always the need for a certain application on the soul's part, which should consist in maintaining itself in the proper disposition for receiving the divine action. This is the teaching of St. John of the Cross : " Let the soul learn how to be still in God, fixing its *loving attention* upon Him, in the calm of the understanding, although it may think it is doing nothing " (*AS II*, 15,5). In fact, if the soul will content itself with keeping in the presence of God by a look of faith and love, its *loving attention* will go to meet the *loving knowledge* which God Himself communicates to it. In this way " knowledge may be united with knowledge and love with love " (J.C. *LF*, 3,34), and the soul will draw the greatest fruit from its prayer.

However, this loving knowledge which God infuses is tenuous and delicate. It never comes by way of clear, distinct concepts, but consists in a general, obscure " sense " of God, who secretly enamours the soul, without the assistance of feeling. This is why the soul, especially at first, cannot understand; and as it has been accustomed to proceed by way of reasoning and sensible affections, it has the impression that it is no longer doing anything. So strong is this sentiment, that the soul would often like to return to meditation, in which it felt that it did something. But St. John of the Cross puts it on guard; in spite of all its efforts it would gain nothing, and would only succeed in disturbing God's action within it. However, the Saint's words should not lead us to believe that the soul no longer needs to make use of some good thought or a little meditation. A delicate, attentive soul will know when it is in the presence of God, even in aridity; and that awareness will suffice for its prayer. On the contrary, it will see when it is rambling uselessly and needs some good thought to recollect itself in God.

COLLOQUY

" O God, my God, why hast Thou forsaken me? Far from my salvation are the words of my sins. O my God, I shall cry day by day, and Thou wilt not hear : and by night, and it shall not be reputed as folly in me. But Thou dwellest in the holy place, the praise of Israel. In Thee have our Fathers hoped : they have hoped, and Thou hast delivered them. They cried to Thee, and they were saved : they trusted in Thee, and were not confounded. But I am a worm and no man.... I am poured out like water; and all my bones are scattered. My heart has become like wax melting.... My tongue hath cleaved to my jaws " (*Ps* 21,2-16). When I would sing Your praises, my voice stops in my throat. O Lord, I have scarcely enough courage to raise my eyes to You, and yet it is my great desire to love You. I should like to tell You that I love You, but I dare not, for my heart is like stone, cold and hard as marble. What shall I do, O Lord, in such aridity? I shall disclose my misery to You; I shall show You my nothingness, my weakness, my lack of power, and I shall say to You : Remember, O Lord, that I am wretchedness and You are Mercy, I, the patient and You, the Physician! O Lord, do not permit the sight of my nothingness to cast me down, but let it draw me to You in humility, confidence, reverence and abandonment! O Lord, let me know myself that I may know You! Let me know myself, that I may despise myself, and know You, that I may love and bless You eternally.

Although I am an arid and desolate land, and in my heart there is not one drop of devotion, yet I wish to remain here in Your presence, here, near You, to tell You that, in spite of everything, I desire and want nothing but You alone. " O Lord, when I feel nothing, when I am incapable of praying or practicing virtue, then is the moment to look for small occasions, nothings, to give You pleasure. For example, a smile, a friendly word, when I should much prefer to say nothing at all or look bored.... When I find no occasions, at least I want to keep telling You that I love You; it is not difficult and it keeps the fire of love going; even if that fire were to seem wholly out, I should throw little bits of straw on the ashes, little acts of virtue and of charity; and I am sure that, with Your help, the fire would be enkindled again " (T.C.J. *L*, 122).

159

PRACTICAL CONDUCT

PRESENCE OF GOD - O Lord, may Your light always be my guide, so that I shall not go astray.

MEDITATION

1. During this period of transition from meditation to contemplation, it is very important for the soul to have a clear understanding of that " general, loving attention to God " mentioned by St. John of the Cross, in order to know how to act, and how to obtain from it the best fruit possible. In the Saint's opinion this new form of prayer results from the exercise of the theological virtues, aided by the secret, delicate influence of the gifts of the Holy Spirit. In other words, on the part of the soul it is a question of an exercise of faith and love so intense and simplified that, without having recourse to the continual repetition of distinct acts, the soul finds itself in an attitude of loving attention to God. Far from being idle, the soul fixes its gaze on God precisely by means of this prolonged act of faith and love. But it is not alone in this exercise. The Holy Spirit comes to meet it, and by a secret actuation of His gifts, orientates and attracts it to God, infusing in it a loving knowledge of Him. In this way the soul can persevere for a long time in this truly contemplative attitude; and because it is helped by the Holy Spirit, it " will take pleasure in being alone and waiting with loving attentiveness upon God, in interior peace, quietness, and rest, without making any particular meditation " (J.C. *AS II*, 13,4).

However, the influence of the gifts will not always be strong and pleasant enough to keep the soul peacefully occupied with God; often, especially at first, it will be weak and therefore the soul more arid. Generally in this the soul will not make steady progress; hence, in order to remain recollected in God, it will often have to use its own efforts. At this point, it will be very useful for the soul to apply itself principally to the occasional renewing of its acts of faith and love, simply because its part, in this kind of prayer, consists in an intense exercise of faith and of love.

2. In speaking of the passage from meditation to contemplation, St. John of the Cross remarks that it does not take place in the same manner in every soul, not only in the sense that it is not accomplished in all at an equal rate, but also because God does not call everyone to the contemplative state. In the *Ascent of Mount Carmel* (*II*, 13), he teaches that the soul should not give up meditation definitively until the habit of contemplation is formed; and referring to this, he remarks that many times the soul finds itself in contemplation from the very first moment of prayer, whereas at other times it needs to be helped in the beginning by meditation. He even expressly states : " As long as the soul can reason with pleasure in meditation, it should not stop doing so until it is in the peace and quiet...of loving attentiveness to God " (*AS II*, 13,2-4). Here we find a period of fluctuation more or less prolonged between meditation and contemplation. Thus, there are some souls whom God never completely takes away from meditative prayer.

This makes us understand that our arrival at initial contemplation does not dispense us from personal activity. First of all, we should make a very careful preparation for prayer, using a book, if necessary; if we cannot then fix our attention on what has been read, at least the reading will have helped to recollect the mind in God. Likewise, we must always begin our prayer by putting ourselves wholly in the presence of God, and then proceed according to the grace of the moment, being grateful to God if He recollects us quite simply in Himself, and diligent in helping ourselves by reflection or by means of a book when we feel that our thoughts are beginning to wander. We must also remember that even when the soul has entered into a state of loving attentiveness to God, the imagination may still roam here and there; for as St. John of the Cross says : " Even at times of great recollection, it can still be a wanderer " (*ibid.* 13,3). This activity of the imagination is not always a sign that the soul should return to meditation. Instead, it should try to become recollected above and beyond its thoughts, and if it sees that it remains in union with God, even in aridity, let it persevere thus, although the effort will be greater than when it had recourse to the reading of a pious book.

COLLOQUY

" O God, my God, to Thee do I watch at break of day. For Thee my soul hath thirsted; for Thee my flesh, O how many ways! In a desert land, and where there is no way, and no water " (*Ps* 62,2).

" Who will give me to rest in You? Who will make You enter my heart and inebriate it, so that I shall forget my misfortunes and embrace You, my only Good? What are You to me? In Your goodness, permit me to speak. What am I to You, that You enjoin me to love You, and are disturbed if I do not love You, and threaten me with all kinds of ills? If I do not love You, does that mean that I am slighting You? Poor creature that I am, tell me, in Your mercy, Lord, my God, tell me what You are to me? Say to my soul : ' I am your salvation! ' Say it so that I shall hear it. The ear of my heart is turned toward You. Open it, O Lord, and say to my soul : ' I am your salvation! ' I shall follow Your voice and adhere to You. Do not hide Your face from me....

" O Father, I do not know the road that will bring me to You. Show it to me; teach me the way. Give me whatever I need. If those who take refuge in You find You by faith, then give me faith; if they find You by virtue, give me virtue, and increase my faith and charity " (St. Augustine).

Give me an immovable faith, O Lord, and an ardent charity! Faith and love are the guide-posts which will take me by unfamiliar paths to the place where You hide Yourself. Grant that I may walk in faith and love, and await in faith and love Your visit to my soul. O Holy Spirit, You pray within me " with unspeakable groanings " (*Rom* 8,26); help my misery, illumine my faith and awaken charity in me. You penetrate " the depths of divine mysteries " (cf. 1 *Cor* 2,10); instruct me, be my teacher, help me to know my God. You who are the Spirit of Love, give me a loving knowledge of Him, so that I may always tend toward Him and be entirely captivated by love of Him.

160

THE LIFE OF PRAYER

PRESENCE OF GOD - O Lord, grant that I may seek You, not only at certain moments during the day, but also at every instant of my life.

MEDITATION

1. A soul who longs for a life of intimacy with God is not satisfied to limit its relations with Him to the time of prayer, but tries to extend them throughout the whole day. This is a rightful desire, for one who loves tries to prolong continuously his relations with the beloved. This is true, therefore, of a soul who loves God; and its desire is the more easily realized, since God Himself is always with us; He is always present and working in us. We are treating, it is true, of a presence which is spiritual and invisible; it is, however, *real* and not merely affective and moral, as is the presence of a loved one in the heart and mind of a lover.

If God is always with us, why can we not be always in continual contact with Him? This contact is realized by thought and love, but much more by the latter than by the former. In fact, it is impossible to be always thinking of God, partly because the mind becomes tired and partly because our many occupations demand all the application of our intellect, which cannot pay attention to two different things at the same time. The heart, on the other hand, can always love, even when the mind is busy elsewhere; and it never grows weary of tending toward the object of its love. Since supernatural love does not consist in sentiment, but in an intimate orientation of the will toward God, we know that this turning is possible, even during the performance of duties which absorb all our attention. The will can strengthen this orientation of itself toward God precisely by the desire to fulfill each duty for love of Him, to please Him and give glory to Him. St. Thomas says that the heart can always tend Godward by " the desire of charity, " that is, by the desire to love Him, to serve Him, and to be united to Him in every action. " Prayer is nothing but a desire of the heart; if your desire is continuous, your prayer is continuous. Do

you wish never to cease praying?   Then never cease desiring "
(St. Augustine).

2. Since prayer does not consist in thinking much but in
loving much, a life of continual prayer will consist much more
in love than in thought.   Nevertheless, a certain amount
of mental activity is necessary, either to direct the heart
toward God, or to maintain it in this direction.

The soul who applies itself well to mental prayer will
easily be able to collect in itself some good thoughts which
it can use during the day to keep its heart turned toward God.
Therefore, it will be useful for the soul to try to recall these
thoughts often in the midst of its occupations, and to apply
them practically to its life.

Thus, for example, if during prayer, we have been
considering God's infinite mercy toward us, we shall strive to
preserve this thought even during our occupations, recognizing
many signs of this mercy in the various circumstances in
which we find ourselves.   In fact, many happenings which,
from a purely human point of view, are unpleasant and
painful, hide, in reality, great mercies of the Lord who, by
means of the sorrows, fatigues, and the trials of life, wants to
detach us from creatures, make us practice virtue, and
advance in goodness.   Likewise, in our dealings with our
neighbor, we shall try to imitate God's mercy.   " Be ye
therefore merciful, as your Father also is merciful " (Lk 6,36).
Although our prayer was spent in aridity, without leaving us
any definite thought, but only a deeper realization of our
nothingness and the infinite greatness of God, we shall make
a treasure of it by attempting during the day to fulfill our
duties in a spirit of humility and homage to God.   We shall
rejoice if some opportunity occurs for humbling ourselves,
acknowledging our littleness—even before creatures—and
exalting the grandeurs of the Lord.

In this way prayer will not be an isolated item in our
day, but will permeate it, by conferring on each action and
circumstance the tone of continual prayer.

COLLOQUY

" O Lord, grant that my life may be the continual prayer
to which every rational creature is bound.   This prayer has

its origin in love; it is fire and true desire based on charity, which forces the soul to perform all its acts for love of You. Awaken charity in me, O Lord, so that I may always desire You, and always desiring, continually pray. Let my soul pray always in Your presence—everywhere, at all times, in everything I do, by the affection of charity " (cf. St. Catherine of Siena).

" O my God, if I were inebriated with love for You, I should seek in all creatures only a means of serving You more diligently and more perfectly; and by renouncing my own will in everything and for everything, I should force myself, in an outburst of love, to do henceforth only what will be more pleasing to You.

" Give me, O Lord, such great fervor and immense love that I shall see no difference between this or that life, this or that state, person, time, or place, but shall do what is most pleasing to You, whatever or wherever it may be, tending always to You by the affection of my soul. Grant that I may see all things in You, and nothing but You in them, ever eager and anxious to serve You in all things; and that, all on fire and burning with love, I may not take into consideration what is easiest and most agreeable for me, but only what is most pleasing to You.

" Grant, O Lord, that I may imitate the angelic spirits who, although they are with us, never interrupt their divine contemplation. May I treat and serve my brethren by seeing and enjoying You in them, and may I always assist my neighbor, offering my heart to You. If I should ever depart from this noble exercise, help me to return to it at once by doing all that is within my power to succeed, so that, with Your divine help, I may always live with my heart centered on You " (cf. St. Bonaventure).

161

GOD'S PILGRIMS

THIRD SUNDAY AFTER EASTER

PRESENCE OF GOD - Grant, O Lord, that the things of earth may not take hold of my heart and impede it from aspiring to heaven.

MEDITATION

1. Today the liturgy begins to direct our thoughts toward the coming Ascension of Jesus : " A little while, and now you shall not see Me...because I go to the Father. " The Gospel (*Jn* 16,16-22) which relates this passage is taken from the discourse that Our Lord made to the Apostles at the Last Supper. His purpose was to prepare them for His departure, before He went to His Passion; but the Church presents to us this farewell speech of Jesus today, before His Ascension. Having accomplished His mission, Jesus must return to the Father who sent Him. One day we shall have to do the same; earth is not our lasting dwelling, but the place of our pilgrimage. Jesus has said so : " A little while, and now you shall not see Me; and again a little while, and you shall see Me.... " These words which were enigmatic for the Apostles, who did not understand them, are now clear to us : " a little while "—that is our short lifetime, and very soon we too must leave the earth and follow Jesus to heaven where we shall see Him in His glory. Then, as our Lord said, " your heart shall rejoice; and your joy no man shall take from you. " However, before reaching this happy state, we have to endure the difficulties, struggles, and sufferings of life on earth. Although it is " short " compared with the " eternal weight of glory " (2 *Cor* 4,18) which awaits us, the Lord knows that for us, overcome as we are by the trials of life on earth, it is " much " and painful. He warns us, therefore, so that we shall not be scandalized : "—You shall lament and weep, but the world shall rejoice.... " The world rejoices and wants to rejoice at any cost, because it is immersed in the pleasures of this life, with no thought of what awaits it beyond. If it cannot escape the inevitable sufferings of life, it tries to stifle its sorrow in pleasure, by contriving to extract from

every fleeting moment all the enjoyment possible. A Christian does not do this; he imposes on himself a life of sacrifice and renunciation, in view of heavenly happiness : " You shall be made sorrowful, " said Jesus, " but your sorrow shall be turned into joy. "

2. The Epistle (1 *Pt* 2,11-19) likewise exhorts us to live on earth with our eyes turned toward heaven. " Dearly beloved, I beseech you as strangers and pilgrims, to refrain yourselves from carnal desires which war against the soul. " The pilgrim cannot delay to enjoy the pleasures and joys which he meets on the road, or he will endanger the success of his journey and may even run the risk of not reaching the end. So the Christian, God's pilgrim, cannot allow himself to be detained by the things of earth; he can use them and even enjoy them, if Providence puts them in his way, but only with a detached heart which immediately leaves them behind. Nothing can delay him, for he is in a hurry to reach the goal. The life of a Christian is like that of a traveler in a foreign land, who never delays because he is anxious to get back to his own country. The Secret of the Mass very aptly puts on his lips the following prayer : " May these mysteries, O Lord, quench the ardor of our earthly desires, and teach us to love only the things of heaven! " We need this prayer very much, for present satisfactions and goods, with their tangible, concrete character, may always make an impression on our senses and heart, even to the point of detaining us in our progress toward heaven, and of making us forget the emptiness of all earthly things. Another characteristic of the pilgrim is that he is never satisfied until he reaches his native land; this unrest throws a veil of sadness over his life. Thus, the Christian, God's pilgrim, can never be wholly content until he reaches heaven and possesses God. Today, sighing, he runs toward Him; he quickens his step, sustained by the hope of meeting Him " face to face " some day. His hope, however, is accompanied by a feeling of sadness, because he hopes for what he does not yet possess. His is the holy sadness of those who are seeking God. Let us thank God if He has made us experience this; it is a good sign; it is a sign that our heart has been captivated by His love, and that earthly things can no longer satisfy it. Once again the words of Jesus comfort us : " Your sadness shall be changed into joy. "

COLLOQUY

"O my Delight, Lord of all creatures and my God! How long must I languish for Your presence? O tedious, O painful, O dying life! What lonely, hopeless solitude! When then, O Lord, when, when.... What shall I do, my sovereign Good. What shall I do? Must I desire not to desire You? Ah! my God and Creator, You wound and do not heal; You strike but leave no wound; You kill to give more life! In a word, O my Lord, You do what You wish, because You are almighty! Let it be so, my God, because it is Your will; I have no other will than to love You.

"O Lord, my Creator, my anguish draws this complaint from me, making me speak of that for which there is no remedy until You provide one. My soul is in a narrow prison : it longs for liberty, yet would not move one slightest degree from Your will. O my Glory, either increase my pain or cure it altogether.

"O death, in you is life, and I know not why men dread you! Yet who that has not always loved God would not fear you? Since I am such a one, what do I desire and ask? Will death be the punishment which my faults have deserved? Do not permit it, O my Sovereign Good, for it cost You much to redeem me!

"O my soul, submit to the will of your God; it is best for you. Serve Him and trust in His mercy; when by penance you have won some little claim to pardon for your sins, He will ease your pain. Do not try to rejoice until you have suffered. But, O my true King and Lord, I am incapable even of this, unless You sustain me by Your power and majesty. With Your help, I can do all things " (T.J. *Exc*, 6).

162

PRACTICE OF THE PRESENCE OF GOD

PRESENCE OF GOD - O Lord, grant that I may always live in Your presence with my interior gaze fixed on You.

MEDITATION

1. The life of continual prayer becomes easier as the soul succeeds in preserving within itself, throughout the day, the awareness of the presence of God. We already know that God is always present within us, that we live, move, and have our being in Him; but while we try during the time of prayer to become more and more aware of this great truth, our consciousness of it gradually fades away in the course of our daily occupations, and we are often surprised to find ourselves acting as if God were no longer present within us.

The practice of the presence of God really consists in making strong efforts to keep God always present in our mind and heart, even when we are engaged in our daily tasks. We can do this in various ways : we can use external objects, such as an image or a crucifix which we wear or put on our worktable, the sight of which will often remind us of God; we also can use our imagination to picture " interiorly " the Lord near us. For, if the humanity of Jesus is not physically present, it is nevertheless always exercising an influence over us—even a physical one—in the communication of grace; hence we can truly " represent to ourselves " this action of Jesus within us. We can also keep a very vivid remembrance of God by using some truth of faith. For example, I can cultivate the thought of the continual presence of the Trinity within me, and try to perform all my actions in honor of my divine Guests; or else I can consider my duties as so many manifestations of the will of God, and so unite myself to this divine will as I perform them. Further, I can make it a practice to view all the circumstances of my life in the light of faith, and therefore, arranged by divine Providence for my good. This will incline me to accept them and to repeat continually to my heavenly Father : " I am content with everything You do. "

2. The practice of the presence of God, especially recommended by St. Teresa of Jesus to souls aspiring to divine intimacy, aims at keeping the soul in close contact with God, present within it. " We must retire within ourselves even during our ordinary occupations, " says the Saint. " If I can recall the companionship I have within me for so much as a moment, that is of great utility " (*Way*, 29).

One might object that this method is more suitable for those who live in solitude than for those who are in constant contact with others; yet St. Teresa applies it, simply and practically, to the latter : " If one is speaking, he must try to remember that there is One within him to whom he can speak; if he is listening, let him remember that he can listen to One who is nearer to him than anyone else. Finally, let him realize that, if he likes, he need never withdraw from this good companionship, and let him grieve when he has left his Father alone for so long, though his need of Him is so sore " (*ibid.*, 29).

Anyone who works, either mentally or manually, can adopt this method in all his relations with his neighbor. Nothing can hinder him from using it even inversely, that is, by applying it to the presence of God in the souls of others. If, unfortunately, God is not present at all times in all men by grace, He is present in essence, as the creator and conserver of their being.

Thus a teacher can always consider God present in his pupils; a doctor or a nurse, in their patients; a merchant or a dressmaker, in their customers, and so on. This thought will inspire in us sentiments of kindness, charity, and respect for all those with whom we come in contact; it will lead us to be interested in them and to serve them, neither for an advantage which we may reap by so doing, nor solely from a sentiment of duty, but as homage to God whom we recognize as present in them. It means, in short, to seek, serve, and love God present in our brethren. This practice, together with the one suggested by St. Teresa, will be very effective in maintaining our contact with God, whether we think of Him as present in our own soul, or in that of our neighbor. " If you become accustomed to having Him at your side, " says St. Teresa, " and if He sees that you love to have Him there and are always trying to please Him, you will never be able, as we put it, to send Him away " (*Way*, 26).

COLLOQUY

"Lord, may my motto be : Thou in me and I in Thee! How beautiful is Your presence within me, in the inmost sanctuary of my soul. May my continual occupation be to retire into myself, that I may lose myself in You, and live with You. I feel You so vividly in my soul, that I have only to become recollected to find You there within me, and in that I find all my happiness.

"O Lord, let me live with You as with a friend! Help me to live in the awareness of faith always, in order that I may be united to You no matter what happens. I bear heaven in my soul, since You, who satiate the blessed in the Beatific Vision, give Yourself to me in faith and mystery.

"Grant, O my God, that my soul may be a little heaven wherein You can rest with delight. In order that I may attain this end, help me to remove everything that might offend Your divine eyes, and then permit me to live always with You in this little heaven. Wherever I am or whatever I do, You never leave me alone; grant that I, too, may always remain with You. At every hour of the day and night, in joy or sorrow, in every work and action, may I always know how to find You within me!

"O my God, Blessed Trinity, be my dwelling, my rest, my Father's house which I shall never leave. Let me abide in You, not for a few fleeting minutes or hours, but permanently, habitually. May I pray in You, adore in You, love in You, suffer in You, work and act in You alone. Let me remain in You to offer myself to others through You, to attend to all my duties, while always penetrating further into Your divine depths. O Lord, grant that every day I may advance along the path of the abyss that leads me to You, that lets me slide down this slope with a confidence full of love" (cf. E.T. *L – I*, 1).

163

THE SPIRIT OF FAITH

PRESENCE OF GOD - Give me, O Lord, that spirit of faith which will keep me in contact with You in every occupation and circumstance of my day.

MEDITATION

1. There are two chief obstacles which hinder us from keeping in contact with God while we are at our daily tasks. First, there is the almost entirely worldly, material point of view with which we frequently consider persons and events; second, there is the opacity of creatures, and the painful, disconcerting, and sometimes evil aspect of many occurrences. As long as we are at Our Lord's feet in prayer, it is easy for us to believe that we can see Him in every creature, in every situation; but when we are face to face with certain persons, or difficulties, this idea vanishes and we founder in human reasonings which make us lose sight of God and His activities in the world. The remedy for this is to cultivate a deep spirit of faith.

Faith is not limited to knowing God in Himself as the Trinity; it makes us see Him also in all creatures, in all circumstances of our life, since He is always present everywhere by His providential action. God knows creatures as they exist in relation to Himself; and faith, showing creatures to us as dependent upon God, makes us, in this way, see and judge them somewhat as God Himself sees and judges them. Faith teaches us that nothing, absolutely nothing, happens in the world which is not subject to divine control. It is true that God cannot will evil; and therefore He does not will sin or its consequences, such as injustice, litigation, war; but He does permit them, simply to safeguard the liberty of His creatures. However, He sometimes intervenes in situations, even in those caused by sin, so as to make everything enter into His divine plan, which is ordained for His own glory and for the salvation and sanctification of souls. My spirit of faith must be so real that it will convince me that no circumstance, either in my private life or in my relations with others, escapes God's jurisdiction, which is so wise that it can draw good even out of evil. Consequently, I can see nothing apart from God; I can find Him in any person, in any situation.

2. A soul of faith meets God not only in prayer, but seeing Him in all things, in all things it finds Him; thus, it can keep itself in contact with Him, even in the midst of occupations. The spirit of faith makes it penetrate the opaqueness of creatures and occurrences so that it always finds God. Secondary causes become transparent to it, enabling it to discover at once the First Cause, God, who is present and operating everywhere. To be able to recognize and meet God in every creature, even in the ones that hurt us, offend us, or make us suffer, and in every happening, even the most disagreeable, painful, and disturbing ones—this is a great secret of the interior life. Then the world becomes an open book, on every page of which is written in large letters the one word : *God*. Before God, His will, His permission, His plans, everything else becomes secondary; we see how stupid it is to fix our gaze on creatures, which are, as it were, only a veil which hides the Creator. However, we need assiduous practice before we can reach such deep faith.

In my contacts with my neighbor—and how many people I do meet in the course of a day!—I can form the habit of greeting Our Lord, present in every creature. In the duties of my state in life and in the orders of my superiors, I can see the expression of God's will in all circumstances—great, small, or even minute—which cause me boredom, uneasiness, suffering, increase of labor, or change of plans. I must learn to see them as the many means which God is using to make me practice virtue—patience, generosity, charity. My hours of prayer must serve to show me all the details of my life in this supernatural light, so that I may laways be able to find Our Lord in them.

COLLOQUY

" O my God, Your divine presence is everywhere; it suntains, surpasses, rules, and penetrates all things; it is cofficient for all, and arranges all, so that it governs everything

with infinite love and power.   Before Your divine presence,
all the rest is as nothing; for it is so great and powerful that,
in reality, it absorbs everything else and makes it disappear.

" O Lord, grant that I may finally succeed in rising from
creatures to You, without losing myself in vain reflections
and idle thoughts about creatures; grant that I may do this
with simplicity and in a spirit of faith, a living and unshakable
faith.   You penetrate everywhere with Your goodness, Your
infinite personal love, and Your omnipotence.   This truth
simplifies everything; in it all becomes essentially and
substantially one; this truth surpasses, penetrates, and absorbs
all the rest, all that is created.   O my God, You are in
everything!   What a treasure!   Grant that I may live in this
truth as in my center and my place of rest, where nothing
can affect me or distract me from You, if I remain well
hidden there " (cf. Blessed M. Thérèse Soubiran).

Give me, O Lord, such a clear, penetrating glance of
faith, that beyond all human creatures and circumstances,
I may always see Your hand guiding and directing everything,
and continually inviting me to follow You and remain with
You.   Grant that I may see You more than creatures, You,
the Creator, present and operating in everything; teach me
to recognize You in each one of my neighbors, and to find
You in every event of my life.   Do not permit creatures
to occupy my mind or my heart; but while my duties oblige
me to occupy myself with them, may I tend more toward
You than toward them and live more with You than with
them.

O Lord, You are the first and great reality, the one,
absolute reality in which everything lives and moves!   Grant
that no human contingencies, which derive their existence
from You, may set themselves before my eyes in such a way
as to prevent me from seeing You, finding You, and uniting
myself to You through everything.

164

LITURGICAL PRAYER

PRESENCE OF GOD - O Jesus, Head of the Mystical Body, grant that while praying with the Church, I may unite myself to Your prayer.

MEDITATION

1. A Christian is not isolated. As man, he belongs to the great human family; as one baptized, he is grafted onto Christ and becomes a member of His Mystical Body, the Church. A Christian is, at the same time, a child of God and a child of the Church; it is precisely in the bosom of the Church that he becomes a child of God. Hence his whole spiritual life, even though it has a personal character which tends toward intimate contact with God, ought also to have a social, liturgical character, which shares in the life of the Church. In other words, the spiritual life of a Christian should be framed in that of the Church, his Mother; it should be associated to all that the Church does in union with Christ her Head to extend His sanctifying action in the world.

Just as our spiritual life is born, grows, and develops in the bosom of the Church, so our prayer, which is the highest expression of the spiritual life, should be inserted in the prayer of the Church, that is, in liturgical prayer. Liturgical prayer has a special excellence because it is not the prayer, however sublime and elevated, of individual souls, but is the prayer that the whole Church addresses to God, in union with Jesus, her Spouse and her Head. It is something like a prolongation of Jesus' prayer; indeed, it is a participation in those supplications which He Himself always offers to the Father. In the glory of heaven and in humble effacement on our altars, He praises Him in the name of all creatures and intercedes with Him for the needs of each one in particular. " The sacred liturgy is the public worship given to the Father by our Redeemer as Head of the Church; and it is the worship which the society of the faithful render to their Head and through Him, to the eternal Father " (Encyclical : *Mediator Dei*).

Whenever we feel the poverty of our own prayer, let us

offer to God the great prayer of Jesus and the Church, associating ourselves spiritually.

2. Because liturgical prayer is the public prayer of the Church, it necessarily gives a large place to acts of exterior worship, such as ceremonies, chants, collective prayers, all of which must be performed with great care. However, this would be insufficient unless accompanied by interior worship. "The sacred Liturgy requires that these two elements— exterior and interior worship—be closely united" (ibid.). Therefore, it is not enough to assist at sacred rites, to take part in ceremonies and collective prayers; this must all be vivified by personal interior prayer which raises the heart to God with the desire of knowing and of conversing with Him. Each soul in its own spiritual life is free to give a larger place to liturgical prayer or to private prayer, according to its own devotion; but these two kinds of prayer must never be opposed to one another. Rather, they must be united in such a way that the one penetrates and sustains the other. As liturgical prayer should be vivified by personal prayer, so personal prayer should be incorporated into liturgical prayer and nourished by it. In fact, as true children of the Church, we should try to sustain our personal prayer by the liturgy. Following the liturgical prayers—at least on feast days—by means of the texts in the Missal and Vesperal, we can attune our prayer life to the great mysteries of the life of Christ. The Church presents them to us at the various liturgical seasons, when she invites us not only to consider these mysteries, but also to associate ourselves with them. Thus, during Advent, our prayer will be centered on the mystery of the Incarnation; in Lent, it will be focused on the mysteries of the Passion and death of Jesus, and so on.

In this way, the liturgy becomes the central artery of our life of prayer and provides it with very substantial food. Our personal prayer, then, is submerged in liturgical prayer and vice-versa, since after we have contemplated in private prayer the mysteries presented to us by the liturgy, we return to liturgical prayer, better enabled to understand and relish it.

COLLOQUY

"O my God, how discouraged should I be by reason of my weakness and nothingness, if to praise, reverence, and glorify You, I did not have Jesus Christ, my only Good, who does this so perfectly! To Him I entrust my weakness, and I rejoice that He is all and I am nothing.... Yes, O Jesus, in You I possess everything; You are my Head and I am really one of Your members. You pray, adore, humble Yourself, and give thanks in me and for me, and I do the same in You, for the member is all one with the Head. Your holy, magnanimous life absorbs mine, which is so vile and mean" (cf. Bl. M. Thérèse Soubiran).

O Jesus, seated at the right hand of the Father, and interceding continually for us, deign to absorb into Your great prayer my very poor one.

"O Jesus, grant that I may adore the Father 'in spirit and in truth,' and in order that I may do so, permit me to adore Him by You and in union with You; for You are the great Adorer in spirit and in truth" (cf. E.T. I, 9). You alone are the real adorer, whose prayer and adoration are perfectly worthy of the infinite Majesty. You alone are the perfect praise of the Most Holy Trinity; You wish to associate with this praise the Church, Your Spouse and my Mother. You wish to associate me with it also, Your member and a child of the Church. Grant that by participating in the prayer of the Church, I may likewise participate in Your prayer. Do not look upon the poverty of my personal prayer, but see it united with the sublime, unceasing prayer of Your Spouse; see it joined to the perpetual chorus of praise and petition which Your priests, the souls consecrated to You, and all Your elect, are continually sending up to Your throne. Grant that my voice may not be discordant in this magnificent chorus. Help me then to pray with a real spirit of piety and with an attentive, devout soul, so that my heart will always accompany the movement of my lips, and my interior sentiments vivify every action, every chant, and every word.

165

HOLY MASS

PRESENCE OF GOD - Give me, O Lord, a better understanding of the value and meaning of Your Eucharistic Sacrifice.

MEDITATION

1. The heart of liturgical worship is the Mass. Just as the redemptive work of Jesus reached its culminating point on Calvary by His death on the Cross, so too, the liturgical action, which continues His work in the world, has its climax in the Mass, which renews and perpetuates on our altars the Sacrifice of the Cross. Jesus has willed that the precious fruits of redemption, which He merited on Calvary for the whole human race, be applied and transmitted to each of the faithful in a particular way by their participation in the Eucharistic Sacrifice. This fountain of grace which Jesus opened on Calvary continues to pour over our altars; all the faithful are obliged to approach it at least once a week by attending Sunday Mass, but we may approach it even daily, each time we are present at the Holy Sacrifice. Holy Mass is truly the " fountain of life. " By offering and immolating Himself continually on our altars, Jesus repeats to us, " If any man thirst, let him come to Me and drink " (*Jn* 7,37).

" The august Sacrifice of the Altar, " says the Encyclical *Mediator Dei*, " is not merely a commemoration of the Passion and death of Christ, but is a true and proper sacrifice, in which, by immolating Himself in an unbloody manner, the Great High Priest renews His previous act on the Cross. " The Victim is the same, so is the Priest; nothing but the manner of offering is different—bloody on the Cross, unbloody on the altar. If we do not see in the Mass, as Mary did on Calvary, the torn Body of Christ and the Blood flowing from His wounds, we do have, by virtue of the Consecration, the real presence of this Body and Blood. Moreover, as this divine presence becomes actualized under two distinct species, the bloody death on Calvary is mystically renewed by the real separation of the Body and Blood of the Savior.

2. The best way of assisting at Holy Mass is the one which makes us participate most in the sublime action taking place on the altar. The liturgical method is especially recommended; by having us recite the same prayers as the priest, it makes us follow more closely the various parts of the Holy Sacrifice. However, instead of being preoccupied with the exact rendering of the words, which is obligatory only for the priest, we should penetrate the meaning of the different prayers, especially those said at the principal parts of the Mass, such as the Offertory, Consecration, and Communion. Although the liturgical method is very good, it is not the only one; the Encyclical *Mediator Dei* expressly says, " The needs and dispositions are not the same in all souls, and they do not continue to remain the same in each one. " It is not uncommon, for example, that, after following the liturgical method for a long time with fruit, a particular soul might feel the need of closing the Missal in order to taste a little more profoundly the very substance of the Mass and to " penetrate " it further. This is not going backward but forward. Instead of focusing the attention in a special way on the various ceremonies and prayers, the soul feels the need of " getting into intimate contact with the High Priest " *(ibid.)*, in order to unite itself interiorly with His action, His offering, and His immolation. By doing this, she follows the Mass in a manner which is more contemplative than liturgical; we have the simple " loving attention " which is the characteristic of contemplative prayer. Without necessarily following the development of the Sacred Rite in all its various parts, the soul fixes the mind and heart upon the Mass drama with a general glance, made keen by love. Thus we advance in an ever clearer understanding of the Holy Sacrifice, and acquires a more profound " sense " of it, which in turn awakens in us a more efficacious desire of uniting ourselves with the Sacrifice. However, it will be well to return to the Missal from time to time, especially to follow the liturgy on Sundays and feasts; each time our soul does this we will find new light, and a new sense, which will help us to penetrate the very substance of the Holy Sacrifice.

COLLOQUY

"O eternal Father, permit me to offer You the heart of Jesus, Your beloved Son, as He offers Himself to You in the Holy Sacrifice of the altar. Accept, I beg You, this offering which I make You; accept all the desires, sentiments, affections, movements, and acts of His most sacred heart; they are all mine, because He sacrifices Himself for me, and I protest that I do not wish to have in the future any desires other than His. Accept them in satisfaction for my sins and in thanksgiving for all Your benefits; accept them, and grant me by Your merits all the graces necessary for me, especially the grace of final perseverance. Accept them as so many acts of love, adoration, and praise which I offer to Your divine Majesty, for they alone can worthily honor and glorify You.

"O my God, I offer You Your beloved Son, in thanksgiving for all Your goodness to me. I offer Him as my adoration, my petition, my oblation, my resolutions; I offer Him as my love and my all. Accept Him, O eternal Father, for all that You wish from me, for I have nothing worthy of You to offer, except Him whom You have given me with so much love" (St. Margaret Mary Alacoque).

" 'What shall I render unto the Lord for all that He has rendered unto me? I will take the chalice of salvation.' Yes, O my God, if I take this Chalice, crimsoned with the Blood of my Master, and in utterly joyous thanksgiving, mingle my blood with that of the sacred Victim, He will impart to it something of His own infinity, and it will give You, O Father, wonderful praise. Then my suffering will become a speech that proclaims Your glory. O Jesus, grant that I may become so identified with You that I may ceaselessly express You in the sight of Your Father. What were Your first words on entering the world? 'Behold I come to do Your will, O God!' May this prayer be like the beating of my heart. You made a complete offering of Yourself to accomplish the will of the Father; grant that will may be my food, and at the same time, the sword which immolates me. Thus, peaceful and joyous, I shall go to meet all sacrifices with You, my adored Master, rejoicing to be *known by the Father*, since He crucifies me with His Son" (cf. E.T. *II*, 7 - 14).

166

PARTICIPATING IN HOLY MASS

PRESENCE OF GOD - O Jesus, immolated at every moment of the day on our altars, let me share in Your Sacrifice.

MEDITATION

1. The Encyclical *Mediator Dei* exhorts all the faithful to "participate in the Eucharistic Sacrifice, not passively, carelessly, and with distractions, but with such ardor and fervor that we shall be closely associated with the High Priest." It is not enough to be present at Mass; we must take part, "participate" in it. In Holy Mass, Jesus continues to sacrifice Himself for us, and to offer Himself to His Father, in order to obtain divine blessings for us. It is true that Jesus offers Himself through the ministry of the priest, but the priest makes the offering in the name of all the faithful, and they, in union with him—as the words of the Canon indicate : "for whom we offer, or who offer up to You this sacrifice of praise." This means that the faithful also are invited to offer the divine Victim with the priest. *Mediator Dei* states it thus : "to unite their intentions of praise, petition, expiation, and thanksgiving with those of the priest, or better, the Sovereign Priest Himself." On Calvary, Mary did not take a passive part in the Passion of her Son; she united herself with His intentions, and offered Him to the Father. In the same way, when we are present at the Holy Sacrifice of the Mass, we, too, can offer the Father the divine Victim who is *ours*, because He offered and immolated Himself for all of us. Our praise, petitions, and expiations are only poor things; but if we give them to God united with those of Jesus and made valuable through His Sacrifice, we have the right to think that they will be acceptable to Him and will be heard because of the infinite dignity of the divine Victim Himself. Jesus, the Head of the Mystical Body, sacrificed Himself for us, His members; and being our Head, He belongs to us : *He is ours*. He is the Victim who, although He immolated Himself wholly on Calvary for our salvation, wills to perpetuate His immolation on our altars. Every day,

every hour, we have His offering at our disposal; daily we can offer it to the Father for our intentions.

2. " In order that the oblation by which the faithful offer the divine Victim to the heavenly Father may have its full effect, still one thing more is necessary; it is necessary that they immolate themselves as victims " *(Mediator Dei)*. This teaching, authorized by the Church, exhorts us to take part in the Holy Sacrifice, so far as to become, " together with the Immaculate Host, a victim acceptable to God the Father " *(ibid.)*. Jesus offered Himself as a Victim to the Father by accepting His will in everything, even to the point of willing to die on the Cross for His glory. We offer ourselves as victims to God when, renouncing everything that is contrary to His will, we study to conform ourselves to this divine will in everything, that is, in the exact fulfillment of our duties and in the generous acceptance of all that God permits in our regard. If a duty requires sacrifice, if our life includes suffering, we have the opportunity each morning in the Holy Mass to give the greatest possible value to our sacrifices by offering, as the *Mediator Dei* teaches, " ourselves as well as all our worries, troubles, sorrows, and misfortunes, together with our divine crucified Head. "

Jesus sacrificed Himself alone on Calvary for our salvation, but on the altar He wishes to associate us with His immolation; for, if the Head is sacrificed, the members must be sacrificed also. Let a poor creature offer in expiation to God his sacrifice and even his life. What value could this have? None, because we are nothing. But if this offering is united to Jesus' offering, then it becomes, with Him, by Him, and in Him, an acceptable sacrifice to God the Father. Then, when we return to our duties, the remembrance of the offering we have made in the morning will help us to be generous in accepting our daily trials, great or small. The thought that at every moment of the day and night Jesus is immolating Himself on our altars will urge us to continually unite our sacrifices with His, and will stimulate us to live as real victims in union with the divine Victim. What strength and generosity the soul will draw from this living, constant participation in the Holy Sacrifice of the Mass!

COLLOQUY

" O Jesus, grant that Your Sacrifice, the Holy Sacrifice of the Altar, may be the source and model of my sacrifice, for my life must also be a holy sacrifice. It certainly is a sacrifice, for life is all interwoven with mortification, detachment, and suffering.... But that my sacrifice be ' holy, ' like Yours on Calvary and in the Holy Mass, it must be vivified, offered, and consumed by love. O Jesus, give me a great love which will give value to my sacrifice and make it fruitful for the glory of the Father, the triumph of the Church, and the good of souls.

" O Jesus, divine Priest, what shall I offer You as matter for the sacrifice, as a victim of love who shares in Your Sacrifice? I offer You my heart, my will, my very love, to be entirely transformed into Yours. In fact, in Your Holy Sacrifice You give me an example of this perfect docility, this conformity to the divine will, and this abandonment. This is the offering which I too, make : a generous, total acceptance of every decree of divine Providence, of every divine wish " (cf. Sister Carmela of the Holy Spirit, O.C.D.). [1]

" O my Savior, in union with the offering and the sacrifice of Yourself which You made to the Father and in His honor, I offer myself to You to be a bloody victim of Your will, a victim immolated for Your glory and that of Your Father. Unite me to Yourself, O good Jesus, draw me into Your sacrifice, so that I may be sacrificed with You and by You. Since the victim must be sacrificed, slaughtered, and consumed by fire, make me die to myself, that is, to my vices and passions, to all that is displeasing to You. Consume me entirely in the sacred fire of Your divine love, and grant that hereafter my whole life may be a continual sacrifice of praise, glory, and love for Your Father and for You " (St. John Eudes).

---

[1] Sister Carmela of the Holy Spirit, a Discalced Carmelite of the Carmelite Monastery of St. Joseph, Via della Nocetta, Rome, died July 23, 1949. She was formerly the National Directress of Italian Catholic Action in Italy, and a soul of extraordinary interior life. Some of her writings were published by Fr. Gabriel of St. Mary Magdalen in 1950, in the *Revista di vita spirituale.* Her biography, together with some notes of direction from Fr. Gabriel, her spiritual director, was published by the Carmel in Rome in 1954. (Note of the translator of the French edition.)

167

THE DIVINE OFFICE

PRESENCE OF GOD - O Jesus, vouchsafe to associate my poor prayer with the great Prayer of the Church.

MEDITATION

1. The liturgy accompanies Holy Mass with the recitation of the Divine Office which, as *Mediator Dei* teaches " is the prayer of the Mystical Body of Christ, addressed to God in the name of all Christians and for their benefit, by priests, other ministers of the Church, and religious, who are assigned this task. " The great dignity of the Divine Office lies in the fact that it is not a private prayer, but the official public prayer of the Mystical Body of Christ, whose members do not pray alone, but with Christ their Head. " When the Word of God assumed human nature, He intoned in His earthly exile the hymn which is sung in heaven through all eternity. He joined to Himself the whole human community and united it with Himself in the chanting of this hymn of praise " *(ibid.)*. In the Divine Office, " Jesus prays with us as our Priest; prays in us as our Head.... Let us recognize then, " says St. Augustine, " our voice in His and His voice in us. " What a wonderful gift! Jesus, the Son of God, associates our poor, miserable prayers with His great precious Prayer.

Although the Divine Office is of obligation only for priests and religious who are charged with it by the Church, it can be said that it is the prayer of the whole Christian people, in the sense that it is addressed to God " in their name and for their benefit. " It is therefore highly praiseworthy for the laity to try to participate in it in some way; for example, the recitation of *Vespers* on feast days, as well as of *Prime* and *Compline*. Furthermore, they can offer to God at every hour of the day and night the great Prayer of the Church, for their own special intentions and individual needs. In this way they can make up for the deficiencies and the brevity of their own personal prayers. Even in the midst of daily occupations, each one can unite himself from time to time by pious aspirations with the " perpetual praise " which the Church sends up to God in the name of all Christians.

2. The Divine Office is made up, for the most part, of inspired texts taken from Holy Scripture. This is why we cannot find vocal prayers that are more beautiful and more suitable for praising the Divine Majesty; in the inspired word, the Holy Spirit Himself " asketh for us with unspeakable groanings " (*Rom* 8,26). Then, too, these prayers are so rich in doctrine and unction that they help greatly to nourish our personal piety. All these reasons make us understand that " the interior devotion of our soul must correspond to the lofty dignity of this prayer " *(Mediator Dei)*, in such a way that " our soul is in tune with our voice, " as St. Augustine says. Because the Divine Office is the prayer which the Church, together with Jesus, her Head, sends up to God, and because it is inspired by the Holy Spirit, it has great value in itself; but it will have no value for us, so as to increase our union with God and to draw divine blessings down upon us, if it does not become *our* prayer, if we do not accompany it with *our own personal* devotion. In the society of the faithful, the Church prays with the heart of her children, with *our* heart; and the more fervent and full of love this heart is, the more our prayer, the Prayer of the Church, will be pleasing to God.

Even if the obligation of reciting the Divine Office is not involved, and a few brief prayers only are taken from the Breviary, it is well for all interior souls to try to grasp the spirit of this liturgical prayer and to make it their own. It is a spirit of praise and adoration which desires to render to God perpetual worship in union with Christ and in the name of the whole Church, a spirit of solidarity with Jesus, our Head, and with all the faithful, our brethren; it is a universal spirit which embraces the needs of the entire world, and prays in the name of all Christianity. How the horizons broaden now with the intentions of our prayers! We no longer feel alone in prayer; we have become little orantes beside Jesus, the great Orante!

COLLOQUY

" O Lord, Your ears are not turned toward our lips, but toward our heart; they are not open to the speech, but to the life of him who praises You.

" I sing with my voice to awaken piety within me; I sing with my heart to please You.... Let not my voice be alone in praising You, but may my works also praise You. Grant that I may not cease to live a good life, so that I may praise You without interruption. If my tongue must be silent sometimes, let my life speak to You; Your ears will not be attracted by my voice, but may You attend to my heart.

" I shall not confine my praise to my voice, but I wish my praise to come from my whole being! Let my voice sing, let my life sing, let all my works sing. And if I must sigh, suffer, and be tempted here on earth, I hope that it will all pass away and the day will come when my praises will not fail. My voice may fail, but not my heart.

" It is better for me to use my strength in praising You, than to take breath to praise myself. It is impossible to faint in praising You. To give You praise is like taking food. The more I praise You, the stronger I become, because You are always giving me Your sweetness, You, the object of my praise.

" Help me, then, to praise You, by my voice as well as by my mind and by my good works, so that, as You exhort me in the Scriptures, I may sing to You a new canticle. To the old man, the old canticle; to the new man, the new canticle. If I love the things of the world, my song is old; I must love the things of eternity. Your love is ever new and eternal, ever new because it never grows old. Sin is what has made me grow old; rejuvenate me by Your grace " (St. Augustine).

168

THE GREAT PROMISE

FOURTH SUNDAY AFTER EASTER

PRESENCE OF GOD - O Jesus, prepare my heart to receive the Holy Spirit whom You have promised and merited for me.

MEDITATION

1. Since last Sunday, the Church has been preparing us for the Ascension of Our Lord. Today, taking up the subject again, she goes a step further. She mentions the coming of the Holy Spirit, and in so doing, makes use of a passage from Jesus' discourse after the Last Supper. Our Lord is speaking to the Apostles and preparing their souls for His departure. Sad and thoughtful, they listen to Him, without courage to question Him. Like a kind father, the Lord breaks the painful silence. " And now I go to Him that sent Me, and none of you asketh Me : ' Whither goest Thou? ' " He hastens to console them : " It is expedient to you that I go, for if I go not, the Paraclete will not come to you; but if I go, I will send Him to you " (*Gosp : Jn* 16,5-14). Only Jesus' death could merit this great gift for us, and it was not until after His Ascension into heaven that the Holy Spirit, the Envoy of the Father and the Son, could descend upon the Church. The Apostles were about to lose the sensible, physical presence of their adored Master. However, He would not leave them orphans and would continue to help them invisibly by His Spirit, who would take up His work with them. Jesus did His work in a visible manner in their midst; the Holy Spirit would do His in a secret, hidden way, but in one no less efficacious and real. Furthermore, as Jesus Himself said, the action of the Holy Spirit would complete His. " I have yet many things to say to you : but you cannot bear them now. But when He, the Spirit of Truth, is come, He will teach you all truth.... He shall receive of mine and shall show it to you. " The hearts of the Apostles, still dulled by sin, could not really comprehend these profound truths; it was necessary that Jesus, by dying

on the Cross, destroy sin—the great obstacle to the action
of the Holy Spirit—and then, when He had ascended into
heaven, He would send the divine Paraclete whom He
merited for them and for us by His Passion.

The sending of the Holy Spirit to our souls is the principal
fruit of the Passion of Jesus.

2. We can draw some practical applications from today's
Gospel. First of all, we must fervently prepare ourselves for
Pentecost, so that the coming of the Holy Spirit will be
renewed in us in all its plenitude. Since sin is the obstacle
to the outpouring of the Holy Spirit, our preparation must
consist in a very special purity of conscience. Sin must be
destroyed in us, not only in its actual manifestations, even
though they are slight, but also in its deepest and most
hidden roots.

We must be convinced, furthermore, that a certain
action of the Holy Spirit is never interrupted in a soul in the
state of grace; this is even more true of a soul who tries to
correspond faithfully to the divine motions. This action does
not necessarily have to be perceived and consoling. In aridity
and despondency the Holy Spirit also works in the faithful
soul; His action is secret and hidden, but also real and
effective. Its chief purpose is to purify the soul and dispose
it for union with God. If the soul is convinced of this, it will
remain confident, even in difficulties, and, if it neither
understands nor sees its path, it will trust in the Holy Spirit,
who sees and knows well the goal to which He is leading it.

Finally, today's Gospel invites us to invoke the action
of the Holy Spirit on the Church and on the whole world :
on the Church, to govern and direct her in the accomplishment of her mission; on the world, to convince it of the truth
which it rejects. " And when He is come, " said Jesus,
" He will convince the world of sin, and of justice, and of judgment, " that is, He will make it see that it is the slave of sin
because it has not believed in Christ. He will make it
understand that justice and sanctity are found only in Him,
the Redeemer, and He will show it that the devil, the " prince
of this world, " is henceforth overcome and condemned.

COLLOQUY

"Ah! eternal Word, tell me, I beg You, what prevents the Holy Spirit from accomplishing all His work in the soul? You tell me that the first impediment is malice; another impediment is the self-will of those who want to serve You, but in their own way. We want Your Spirit, but we want Him in the way that pleases us, and as much as pleases us; in this way we make ourselves incapable of receiving Him. At other times, lukewarmness is the hindrance; we think we are serving You and do not realize we are serving ourselves. But You, O Lord, want to be served with humility and sincerity, without self-love. Thus Your Spirit takes no rest but in a soul which He finds plunged in humility. Alas! O loving Word, I should like to know what I ought to do about these hindrances, for what good will it do me to understand them, if I do not know the cure for them? Now, I see plainly that the remedy for malice is a simple right intention; the remedy for self-will is a will so dead to self that it wills only what You will. The cure for lukewarmness is the ardor of charity, which like fire, comes into our hearts and burns up all tepidity " (St. Mary Magdalen dei Pazzi).

"Come, O Holy Spirit, sanctify me! Come, O Spirit of Truth, fill me! Your divine Wisdom will establish me in the truth. I am thirsting for truth, and wish it to rule over my mind, my words, my affections, and my actions, avoiding everything that is opposed to it, not only lies, but also dissimulation, duplicity, and lack of sincerity with myself.

"Come, O Spirit of Peace, bring me Your peace! That profound peace which dilates the soul and prepares it for Your operations, that peace which calms and dominates all the sensible part of the soul and even the superior part.

"Come, O Spirit of Charity, inflame me and inspire me with Your love, so that I can pour it out over the souls whom I would bring to You! Oh! transform me into love; only thus shall I be able to fully respond to Your call, and be of use to the Church " (Sr. Carmela of the Holy Spirit, O.C.D.).

169

MARY OUR GUIDE AND MODEL [1]

PRESENCE OF GOD - Under your protection I take refuge, O Mary; be the guide and model of my interior life.

MEDITATION

1. Month of May, month of Mary! The heart of every Christian turns spontaneously toward his heavenly Mother, with a desire to live in closer intimacy with her and to strengthen the sweet ties which bind him to her. It is a great comfort on our spiritual way, which is often fatiguing and bristling with difficulties, to meet the gentle presence of a mother. One is so at ease near one's mother. With her, everything becomes easier; the weary, discouraged heart, disturbed by storms, finds new hope and strength, and continues the journey with fresh courage.

" If the winds of temptation arise, " sings St. Bernard, " if you run into the reefs of trials, look to the star, call upon Mary. In danger, sorrow, or perplexity, think of Mary, call upon Mary. " There are times when the hard road of the " nothing " frightens us, miserable as we are; and then, more than ever, we need her help, the help of our Mother. The Blessed Virgin Mary has, before us, trodden the straight and narrow path which leads to sanctity; before us she has carried the cross, before us she has known the ascents of the spirit through suffering. Sometimes, perhaps, we do not dare to look at Jesus the God-Man, who because of His divinity seems too far above us; but near Him is Mary, His Mother and our Mother, a privileged creature surely, yet a creature like ourselves, and therefore a model more accessible for our weakness.

Mary comes to meet us during this month, to take us by the hand, to initiate us into the secret of her interior life, which must become the model and norm of our own.

---

[1] The meditations on Our Blessed Lady should be transferred according to the calendar of the year, so that they coincide with the month of May.

2. St. Thérèse of the Child Jesus, referring to certain discourses on the Blessed Virgin, said, " She is spoken of as unapproachable, whereas she should be represented as imitable " *(NV)*. Mary is inaccessible, it is true, in the sublime privileges which flow from her divine maternity, and it is right to consider these prerogatives in order to admire and contemplate them, to praise our Mother's greatness and hence always to love her more and more; but, at the same time, we must consider Mary in the concrete picture of her earthly life. It is a simple, humble picture, which never leaves the framework of the ordinary life common to all mothers; under this aspect, Mary is truly imitable. Our program for the month of May, then, will be to contemplate the grandeurs of Mary, that we may be stimulated to imitate her virtues.

We shall consider Mary especially as the ideal and the model of our interior life. No one has understood, as she did, the depth of meaning in the words of Jesus : " But one thing is necessary " *(Lk* 10,42), and no one has lived by these words better than she. From the very first moment of her life, Mary was entirely God's and lived only for Him. Consider the years spent in the Temple in silence and prayer, the months passed at Nazareth in recollection, and in adoration of the eternal Word incarnate within her, the thirty years lived in sweet intimacy with Jesus, her Son and her God; then the sharing of His apostolic life, the union with Him in His Passion, and finally, her last years with St. John, during which, by her prayers, she was the support of the infant Church. Although the scenes in which she moved changed in appearance, although the external circumstances varied, her life remained unchanged in its substance, in her interior search for the " one thing necessary, " and in her adherence to God alone.

The succession of events and her exterior activity did not hinder her from persevering in that attitude of continual prayer in which St. Luke presents her to us : " Mary kept all these words [the divine mysteries], pondering them in her heart " (2,19).

If, in imitation of Mary, our heart is firmly anchored in God, nothing can distract us from our interior occupation : to seek and love the Lord and live in intimacy with Him.

COLLOQUY

"O my soul, do you fear to approach God? He has given you Jesus as Mediator. Is there anything that such a Son could not obtain from His Father? The Father who loves Him will answer Him, because of the love He bears Him. But do you yet hesitate to approach Him? He made Himself your brother, your companion, and in everything, sin excepted, He willed to undergo all the humiliations of human nature, just to compassionate your miseries. Mary has given you this brother. But His divine Majesty still awes you, perhaps; for, although He is man, He does not cease to be God. Do you want an advocate with Him? Have recourse to Mary. Mary is a pure creature, pure not only because she is free from sin, but also because of her unique human nature. I am sure, O Mary, that your prayers will be heard because of the respect you deserve; your Son will certainly hear you because you are His Mother, and the Father will hear His Son. This is why my confidence is unshakable; this is the reason for all my hope! O Blessed Virgin, the Angel declared that ' you have found grace before God. ' You will always find grace, and I need only grace; I ask for nothing else " (St. Bernard).

"Draw me after you, O Virgin Mary, that I may run in the odor of your ointments. Draw me, for I am held back by the weight of my sins and the malice of your enemies. Since no one comes to your Son unless he is drawn by the Father, I dare to say that no one, so to speak, comes to Him if you do not draw him by your prayers. You teach true wisdom, you beg grace for sinners, you are their advocate, you promise glory to those who honor you, because you are the treasury of grace. You have found grace with God, O most sweet Virgin, you who have been preserved from original sin, filled with the Holy Spirit, and have conceived the Son of God. You have been given all these graces, O most humble Mary, not only for yourself, but also for us, so that you may be able to help us in all our necessities " (Ven. R. Jourdain).

170

THE HANDMAID OF THE LORD

PRESENCE OF GOD - O Mary, you who called yourself the handmaid of the Lord, teach me how to consecrate all my strength and life to His service.

MEDITATION

1. All the splendors—divine filiation, participation in divine life, intimate relations with the Trinity—which grace produces in our souls are realized in Mary with a prominence, a force, a realism, wholly singular. If, for example, every soul in the state of grace is an adopted child of God and a temple of the Holy Spirit, the Blessed Virgin is so par excellence and in the most complete manner, because the Triune God communicated Himself to her in the highest degree possible for a simple creature, to such a degree that Mary's dignity, according to St. Thomas, touches " the threshold of the infinite " (cf. I^a, q. 25, a. 6, ad 4). This can easily be understood when we think that, from all eternity, Mary was chosen by God to be the Mother of His Son. As the Incarnation of the Word was the first work of the mind of God, in view of which everything was created, so also Mary, who was to have such a great part in this work, was foreseen and chosen by God before all other creatures. It is fitting that the words of Sacred Scripture are applied to her : " The Lord possessed me in the beginning of His ways, before He made anything from the beginning " (*Prv* 8,22).

When Adam, deprived of the state of grace, was driven out of Paradise, only one ray of hope illumined the darkness of fallen humanity : " I will put enmities between thee and the woman, " God said to the serpent, " and...she shall crush thy head " (*Gn* 3,15). Here Mary appears on the horizon as the beloved Daughter of God, as she who will never be, for a single moment, a slave of the devil; as she who will always be spotless and immaculate, belonging wholly to God : as the Daughter whom the Most High will always look upon with sovereign complacency, and whom He will introduce into the circle of His divine Family by bonds of the closest intimacy with each of the three divine Persons : Daughter of the Father, Mother of the Incarnate Word, and Spouse of the Holy Spirit.

2. Mary lived her divine filiation in a profound sentiment of humble dependence and loving adherence to God's every will. We have the best example of this in her reply to the Angel's message : " Behold the handmaid of the Lord " (*Lk* 1,38). Mary was aware of her position as a creature in relation to the Creator, and although she had been raised to such high dignity that, " after God's, it is the greatest that can be imagined " (Pius XI), she could find no better way to express her relations with God than to declare herself His " handmaid. " This word describes the interior attitude of the Virgin toward God; it was not a passing attitude, but one that was permanent and constant throughout her whole life. Like Jesus, who, when He came into the world, announced, " I have come to do Thy will " (*Heb* 10,9), so Mary, who was to be the most faithful likeness of Jesus, offered herself to the will of her heavenly Father when she said, " Behold the handmaid of the Lord, be it done to me according to Thy word. " Faithful to her word, she would accept without reserve not only every manifest will of God, but also every circumstance permitted by Him : the long, inconvenient journey which would bring her far from home, just when she was about to bring into the world the Son of God; the poor, humble shelter of a stable; the flight into Egypt by night, the privations and inconveniences of exile, the labor and weariness of a life of poverty, the separation from her Son when He would leave her to begin His apostolate, the persecutions and insults He would endure and of which her maternal heart would be well aware, and finally, the disgrace of the Passion and death of her beloved Son on Calvary. We have good reason to believe that in each of these events, her interior dispositions were the same as on the day of the Annunciation : " Behold the handmaid of the Lord. " What an example for us of humble dependence on God, of absolute fidelity to His will, and of perseverance in our vocation, in spite of the difficulties and sacrifices we shall have to encounter.

COLLOQUY

O Mary, all pure and all holy, Paradise of God, His beloved Daughter, chosen by Him from all eternity to be the Mother of His only Son, preserved by Him from every shadow of sin, enriched by Him with all graces...how great and how beautiful you are, O Mary! " You are all beautiful, O Mary, and there is no stain of sin in you. You are the glory of Jerusalem, the joy of Israel, the honor of our people " (*Tota Pulchra*).

The Most High has always looked upon you with complacency and He willed to give Himself to you in a unique way. " The Lord is with you, O Mary! God the Father is with you, God the Son, God the Holy Spirit, the Triune and One God. God the Father, whose noble Daughter you are; God the Son, whose most worthy Mother you are; God the Holy Spirit, whose gracious Spouse you are. You are truly the Daughter of the sovereign, eternal God, the Mother of sovereign Truth, the Spouse of sovereign Goodness, the handmaid of the sovereign Trinity " (cf. Conrad of Saxony). But from all these titles, you choose the last, the humblest, and the lowest, and call yourself the handmaid of the Lord.

" Oh! how sublime is your humility, which never yields to the seductions of glory, and in glory knows no pride. You were chosen to become the Mother of God, and you call yourself servant! O Blessed Lady, how were you able to unite in your heart such a humble idea of yourself, with so much purity and innocence, and especially such plenitude of grace? O Blessed Lady, whence comes such humility? Truly, because of this virtue, you have merited to be looked upon by God with extraordinary love; and you have merited to charm the King with your beauty, and to draw the eternal Son from the bosom of the Father " (cf. St. Bernard).

O Mary, you proclaimed yourself to be the handmaid of the Lord, and you have truly lived as such, always humbly submissive to His will, always ready to respond to His call and invitation. Who more than you could say with Jesus : " My meat is to do the will of My Father " (cf. *Jn* 4,34)? O Mary, sweet Daughter of the heavenly Father, impress upon my heart a little of your docility, a little of your love for God's holy will, in order that I may serve Him less unworthily.

171

SPOUSE OF THE HOLY SPIRIT

PRESENCE OF GOD - O Mary, Spouse of the Holy Spirit, make me docile to His divine motions.

MEDITATION

1. " The Blessed Virgin Mary, " says St. Augustine, " was the only one who merited to be called the Mother and Spouse " of God. She became the Mother of God because she was the Spouse of the Holy Spirit : " the Holy Ghost shall come upon thee, and the power of the Most High shall overshadow thee " (Lk 1,35), said the Angel, explaining the mysterious, divine manner in which she would become a mother, the Mother of the Son of God. At that moment the Holy Spirit, who had already possessed Mary's soul from the first moment of her Immaculate Conception, came upon her with such exceptional plenitude that He formed within her the sacred Body of Jesus. Justly, therefore, does Mary deserve the name of Spouse of the Holy Spirit : she is His possession, His sanctuary, His temple.

The divine Paraclete may well say to her in the words of the Canticle : " My sister, my spouse, is a garden enclosed, a fountain sealed up " (4,12). Mary is a garden enclosed, because she was never defiled—even for an instant—by the shadow of sin, was never subject to the winds of unruly passions, never taken up with any affection for creatures. " The most glorious Virgin, our Lady, " says St. John of the Cross, " never had the form of any creature imprinted on her soul, and was never moved by any creature, but her actions were always inspired by the Holy Spirit " (AS III, 2,10). Filled with grace from her conception, Mary is always the faithful Spouse of the Holy Spirit, attentive and docile to all His impulses and inspirations.

If Mary's sublime privileges are reserved for her alone, we can, nevertheless, imitate her interior dispositions by keeping our heart, in imitation of hers, always attentive and docile to the action of the Holy Spirit.

2. Complete docility to the motion of the Holy Spirit is precisely the characteristic of the state of union with God. Mary was " raised to this lofty state from the beginning, " according to the teaching of St. John of the Cross *(ibid.)*; and this is evident if we consider that Mary was not only created in grace but that she had, from the very beginning, a degree of grace far superior to that attained by the greatest saints at the end of their lives. Therefore, this state of perfect union with God, which is our ideal and the goal of all our efforts, was Mary's portion from the dawn of life. Furthermore, by her free, faithful correspondence to grace, she advanced to towering heights in this lofty state.

Considering these truths, therefore, we can easily see that after Jesus the Virgin Mary is the surest model and guide for those who aspire to union with God; her very creaturehood makes her more accessible to us, and more easily imitable. Mary teaches us that the great secret of quickly reaching union with God is entire detachment from creatures, especially from that creature we love so much, ourself. Mary lived only for God. Studying her life in the Gospels, we never see her influenced by selfish motives or by reasons of personal interest; only one thing moves her : the glory of God and the interests of Jesus and of souls. In her humble, hidden life, in her work, in her poverty, in all the privations and sufferings she had to undergo, there was never a thought of self, never a complaint; rather, she was always ready to advance, totally oblivious of her suffering, wholly given to the fulfilling of the divine will. It was the Holy Spirit who guided her, who urged her, who sustained her, and her secret was to let herself be ruled and moved by Him in everything. Just as the Blessed Virgin conceived the Son of God by the operation of the Holy Spirit, so all her actions were begun by His inspiration. This is exactly how we should imitate Mary : eliminate from our life everything that is the fruit of our egoism, self-love, or pride, and do only the things that are inspired by grace, under the impulse of the Holy Spirit.

COLLOQUY

"O Mary, you are holy in body and mind. You can say in a special way : ' My conversation is in heaven ' (cf. *Phil* 3,20). You are the garden enclosed, the sealed fountain, the temple of the Lord, the sanctuary of the Holy Spirit; you are the wise Virgin who not only provided herself with oil, but filled her lamp with it. O Mary, how were you able to reach the inaccessible majesty of God, if you did not knock, ask, and seek? Yes, you found what you were looking for, and the Angel said to you, ' You have found grace before God. ' Yet, how could you, who were already full of grace, find more grace? Oh! you were truly worthy to find grace, because you were not satisfied with the fullness which you had, but asked for a superabundance of grace for the salvation of the world! ' The Holy Spirit will come upon you, ' said the Angel, and this precious balm was poured over you in such abundance that it flowed from you over the whole earth.... If heretofore the Holy Spirit was in you in the fulness of grace, now He *comes upon you*, as if to call attention to the superabundant plenitude of grace which He pours upon you. If in the past grace was present only in your soul, it now invades your breast also...the divine power makes you fruitful and you conceive of the Holy Spirit " (St. Bernard).

O Mary, faithful Spouse of the Holy Spirit, look upon my wretchedness and my weakness. God has placed in you the fullness of all His gifts so that I may understand that all hope, all grace, all salvation come from you! You see how hard my heart is, how dull my mind; help me, therefore, O faithful Virgin, to overcome the resistance of my pride, my selfishness and my cowardice, so that my soul may open itself fully to the invasion of grace, abandoning itself with docility to the action of the Holy Spirit, promptly following His impulses, inspirations and invitations.

172

THE MOTHER OF GOD

PRESENCE OF GOD - Holy Mother of God, make my heart one with yours, which was ever one with the Heart of God!

MEDITATION

1. The divine maternity is the source of all Mary's privileges. Mary, the Immaculate One, the beloved Daughter of the Father, is also the Spouse of the Holy Spirit, whose power overshadowed her because she had been chosen to be the Mother of the Incarnate Word. All Mary's greatness and glory are explained in the light of her divine maternity; furthermore, her very existence is explained by her predestination to this high office. If God had not decreed that the Incarnation of His Son should take place in the womb of a virgin, we should never have had that masterpiece of grace and loveliness, the Most Blessed Virgin; we should never have had her smile or her maternal caresses. Therefore, we love and honor Mary because she is the Mother of God, the Mother of Jesus; and loving her in her relation to God, our devotion to her only makes our love for God, for Jesus, deeper and more tender. " *Mater Dei, Mater Creatoris*, " Mother of God, Mother of our Creator, we invoke her in the litany. These two titles which seem to be contradictory, actually express a unique synthesis because Mary, although a creature, is really the Mother of her Creator, the Mother of God's Son to whom she has given a human body : the fruit of her flesh and blood is the Son of God in whom and by whom all things were created. Here we understand more than ever how Mary's dignity reaches the threshold of the infinite. " God could make a bigger world or a wider sky, but He could not raise a pure creature higher than Mary, for the dignity of Mother of God is the highest dignity that can be conferred on a creature " (St. Bonaventure).

To anyone who wonders why so little is said about Mary in the Gospel, St. Thomas of Villanova replies : " What more do you want? Is it not enough for you to know that she is the Mother of God? It would have been sufficient

to say, ' *De qua natus est Jesus,* ' Jesus was born of her. "
In fact, O Mary, all I need to know, in order to love you,
is that you are the Mother of my God.

2. Although God, from all eternity, had predestined
Mary to be the Mother of His Son, He would not have her
unaware of this, and so, when the time came for carrying
out His plan, He asked the humble Virgin's consent.   The
Angel's message revealed to Mary the sublime vocation which
God had reserved for her : " Behold thou shalt conceive
in thy womb, and shalt bring forth a Son; and thou shalt
call His name Jesus " (*Lk* 1,31).   Mary asked and the Angel
explained the mystery of the divine maternity which would
take place in her, without prejudice to her virginity.   What
could God have asked that Mary would have refused?
It was not the first time that she gave up her own will for
God's : from the beginning of her existence, she had lived
in the state of perfect union with God, and her chief
characteristic was simply this full conformity of her human
will with the divine will.   That is why Mary gave her
consent with all the love of her soul, said her *fiat*, accepted
voluntarily, and voluntarily abandoned herself to God's
action.   From this moment the mystery was accomplished,
and the Virgin Mary bore God present within her, not only
spiritually—like all souls who are in the state of grace—but
also physically.   St. Peter Damien says that the Word of
God was present in her " by identity, " since He was one
with her, as the child is one with its mother : identity of
nature by flesh and blood, and by the life of the body which
Mary communicated to her Son; identity of grace by the
abundance of supernatural life which the Son communicated
to His Mother; identity of affections, desires, and sentiments
which the Heart of Christ implanted in the Heart of Mary.
No one could ever say more truly than Mary : " I live,
now not I, but Christ liveth in me " (*Gal* 2,20).

Immense, marvelous mystery!   And in the depths of
this mystery we find the *yes* of a humble, human creature.
God has created man free, and that is why, although He
wants to work great things in him, He will not do so without
his consent.   God wants to transform us by His grace and
to sanctify us, but before He does so, He waits for our assent.
When this *yes* is complete and total, as Mary's was, God will
accomplish His work in us.

COLLOQUY

"I give You thanks, O Lord God, from the depths of my heart, because You condescended, for love of us unworthy creatures, to take upon Yourself our human nature. Born of a Virgin, You were nourished by her milk, cradled in her bosom; You were submissive to her, You who preserve and direct everything that exists. And You have deigned to enlighten me, a miserable creature, so that I might know that You have a Mother; You permit me, unworthy as I am, to be able and to dare to address her. . . . Oh! with what devotion should I not give my heart to you, O Virgin Mary! My mouth should be filled with wonderful sweetness when I speak to you, sweet and gentle Lady, and when I bless the fruit of your womb. Oh! when I address you, how is it that I am not so filled with delight that I forget everything but you and the fruit of your womb? What greeting is more welcome than the one which recognizes you as the Mother of God? You wish men to rejoice in you, so that their love will always reach your divine Son; therefore, you wish to be called and recognized as the Mother of God. Hail, then, O Mary, and truly hail! O wonderful *Ave*, that drives the demons away, frees sinners, and makes your children rejoice. . . . The Angel congratulates you, O Virgin; the Word took flesh in your womb, and you became the Mother of God. Every creature sings an endless *Ave* to you! With how great reverence, honor, and devotion should we salute you, O Blessed Virgin, because you seek those who approach you reverently and devoutly. You love them, you nourish them, and adopt them as your children. Oh! blessed is he who has the joy of having you for Mother, who embraces you lovingly and imitates you in his works! Oh! blessed is he who does all he can to conform himself to you, O Mother of God! Certainly he is one who, despising every creature, attaches himself to God alone, his only love, and, crucified with Christ, sighs for the salvation of souls" (cf. St. Bonaventure).

173

OUR MOTHER

PRESENCE OF GOD - O Mary, since you are really my Mother, make me your true and worthy child.

MEDITATION

1. When she consented to become the Mother of the Son of God, Mary bound herself by very close bonds not only to the person of Jesus, but also to His work. She knew that the Savior was coming into the world to redeem the human race; hence, when she agreed to become His Mother, she also agreed to become the closest collaborator of His mission. In fact, by giving us Jesus, the source of all grace, Mary collaborated most effectively and even directly in the diffusion of grace in our souls. " If Jesus is the Father of our souls, " St. Alphonsus says, " Mary is their Mother, for, in giving us Jesus, she gave us true life; and later, by offering on Calvary the life of her Son for our salvation, she brought us forth to the life of divine grace. "

As one woman, Eve, had cooperated in the losing of grace, so by a harmonious disposition of divine Providence, another woman, Mary, would cooperate in the restoration of grace. It is true that all grace comes from Jesus, who is the *only source* of grace and the *one and only Savior;* but, inasmuch as Mary gave Him to the world, and was intimately associated with His whole life and work, we can truly say that grace also comes from Mary. If Jesus is its source, Mary, according to St. Bernard, is its channel, the aqueduct which carries it to us. Since Jesus willed to come to us through Mary, so all grace and all supernatural life come to us through her. " This is the will of Him who decreed that we should have *everything* through Mary " (St. Bernard). *All* that Jesus merited for us by strictest right, *condignly,* Mary has merited for us fittingly, *congruously.* The Blessed Virgin is then truly our Mother. When she brought forth Jesus, she brought us forth at the same time to the life of grace; we can address her in all truth : " Hail, holy Queen, *Mother* of mercy; our *life,* our sweetness, and our hope! "

2. " From the moment that the Blessed Virgin Mary became the Mother of the Savior, she loved us so much, and she devoted herself so completely to obtaining our salvation that, " St. Bernardine of Siena tells us, " from that moment she carried us in her bosom like a most loving mother. " Even as the redemptive mission of Jesus, begun at the moment of His Incarnation, was consummated on Calvary, where His death merited supremely for us, so too, Mary's maternity found its fullest expression at the foot of His Cross. While Jesus was dying in the midst of the most atrocious torments, His loving Heart was preparing a truly exquisite gift for us. On earth, His dearest possession had been His Mother; now He would leave her to us as a most precious inheritance. " Behold thy Mother " (*Jn* 19,27), He said to St. John, thus giving her to the Apostle who, at that moment, represented the whole human race. These words of Jesus expressed the great truth which had had its beginning at the first moment of His Incarnation in the Virgin's womb and which now was fulfilled at the foot of the Cross : this is the truth of Mary's spiritual motherhood of all mankind. Mary saved our souls together with Jesus, for as He was offering Himself in sacrifice for us, Mary was offering Him, her Son, as the divine Victim for our redemption. As co-redemptrix, she procured the life of grace for us; therefore, she is the woman who in the supernatural order gives us life : she is our Mother.

" God so loved the world that He gave His only-begotten Son for our salvation, " says the Evangelist (cf. *Jn* 3,16), and similarly, St. Bonaventure declares, " it can be said that Mary so loved the world that she gave her only Son, in order that, through Him, all might have eternal life. " See at what price Mary has become our Mother and we have become her children. Because it has cost her so much to give us birth, she very rightly desires us to live as her true children, worthy of the life of grace, which flows from the pierced side of her Jesus and from her maternal heart, pierced by the sword of sorrow.

COLLOQUY

" Oh blessed confidence, O sure refuge, you, the Mother of God, are my Mother! How can I fail to hope, since my salvation and my sanctity are in the hands of Jesus, my Brother, and Mary, my Mother? " (Cf. St. Anselm).

" O Mary, Mary, bearer of the fire of love, and dispenser of mercy! Mary, co-redemptrix of the human race, when you clothed the Word with your flesh, the world was redeemed. Christ paid its ransom with His Passion, and you paid it with the sorrows of your body and soul " (St. Catherine of Siena).

" O Mary, you are that garden enclosed, which contains the Giver of Life; God Himself is within you, with heaven and all creatures. The whole world is saved by the Blood received from you. Without you, O Mary, there would be no paradise for me; without you, there would be no God for me. . . .

" O Mary, how countless are the gifts and graces which you wish to bestow on creatures! And who would not want to receive them? It is perseverance in desiring them which is lacking; you, most loving Mother, do not offer gifts to your children when you see that they would not appreciate them and would throw them away; for you know that the guilt thus incurred would have to be punished later. O Mary, you want to grant me your gifts, but I deprive myself of them, because I want to mingle my gifts with yours. I should like to have your graces, but I want my own will at the same time, and so I cannot have them. I should like to have your good will, but also the love and kindness of creatures. I cannot have both. I want your love and my self-love, but this combination is impossible. I want to live under your mantle, but also under the mantle of my own comfort. Yet, it is not fitting to be delicate members of a thorn-crowned head; neither is it fitting for your children to seek their comfort under your mantle, O sweet Mother, when you had so little regard for your own comfort.

" O Mary, what can I offer and give you that will please you? If I offer you my will, I fear that you will not accept it, because it is not conformed to God's will. If I offer you my intellect, it is not enlightened; if I give you my affection, it is not pure. I offer you the Heart of your only Son! and a greater gift I cannot offer " (St. Mary Magdalen dei Pazzi).

174

THE MARIAN LIFE

PRESENCE OF GOD - O Mary, I wish to live with you as a child with its mother.

MEDITATION

1. The high place which Mary, as the Mother of God, occupies in the work of our sanctification fully justifies our desire to live intimately with her. As children love to be near their mother, so we as Christians want to live with Mary, and in order to do this, we resort to little means of keeping her in our thoughts. For instance, we may have her picture before us and greet her affectionately every time we look at it. Then, with a glance of faith, we can go beyond the picture, and reach Mary *living* in glory, Mary who, by means of the Beatific Vision, sees us, follows us, knows all our needs, and helps us with her maternal aid. By means of this our faith, our soul remains in continual contact with Mary. Spontaneously throughout the day, we increase our little pious practices in her honor, our prayers and ejaculations; all these combine to intensify our relations with Mary. Saturdays, the month of May, the several feasts of Mary are for us so many occasions of remembering her especially, of meditating on her prerogatives, contemplating her beauty, and continually increasing our love for her. In fact, it is impossible to bear the sweet picture of Mary in our mind and heart without feeling moved to love her, without feeling the need of showing her the reality of our love by trying to please her, that is, by living like true children of hers. In this way the " Marian " life, or the life of intimacy with Mary, can penetrate the whole of our " Christian " life and make us more faithful in the fulfillment of all our duties, for nothing can please Mary more than to see us accomplishing with love her Son's will. Furthermore, Christian life lived under Mary's maternal eye acquires that special gentleness and sweetness which arise spontaneously from the constant companionship of a most loving Mother who lavishes attention on us.

2. Another aspect of the Marian life is the imitation of Mary. Jesus alone is the " Way " that leads to the Father, He is the only *model;* but who is more like Jesus than Mary? Of whom more than of Mary can it be said that she has the same thoughts as Christ? " O Lady, " exclaims St. Bernard, " God lives in you and you live in Him. You clothe Him with the substance of your flesh, and He clothes you with the glory of His Majesty. " While Jesus dwelt in the Virgin's pure womb, He clothed her with Himself, communicated His infinite perfections to her, filled her with His sentiments, desires, affections, and divine wishes; and Mary, who gave herself up entirely to His action, was completely transformed into Him, so that she became a faithful copy of Him. The liturgy says that " Mary is the most perfect image of Christ, formed truly by the Holy Spirit. " The Holy Spirit, the Spirit of Jesus, took full possession of Mary's pure, gentle soul, and traced in it, very delicately and perfectly, all the features and characteristics of the soul of Jesus. Therefore we can well say that to imitate Mary is to imitate Jesus. This is why we choose her for our model. We do not love Mary for herself alone, but because she is the Mother of Christ; likewise, we do not imitate Mary for herself, but for Christ, whose most faithful image she is. Jesus is the one Way which leads us to the Father, and Mary is the surest and easiest way to reach Jesus. By incarnating in Himself the perfections of the Father, Jesus made it possible for us to imitate them; by retracing Jesus' perfections in herself, Mary has made them more accessible to us, has brought them within our very reach. None can say as well as she : " Be ye followers of me, as I also am of Christ " (1 *Cor* 4,16). Since Jesus came to us through Mary, it is wholly appropriate that we should go to Jesus through her.

COLLOQUY

" O my most sweet Mother, you call me and say to me : ' If anyone is a little one, let him come to me. ' Children always have their mother's name on their lips, and they call her whenever they are in danger, fright, or difficulty. O sweet Mother, O loving Mother, you want me, like a little child, to call upon you always and to have unceasing recourse to you.... Permit me then to invoke you constantly and to say : ' O Mother, loving Mother! ' Your name consoles me, moves me tenderly, and reminds me of my obligation to love you. Your name encourages me to confide myself to you. ' My Mother, ' thus I call you, and thus I want to call you always. After God, you are my hope, my refuge, and my love in this vale of tears. O my sweet Lady and Mother! by the love you show your children you ravish their hearts. Ravish also, I beg you, my poor heart which so greatly desires to love you. You, O Mother, charmed God with your beauty, and drew Him from heaven into your womb; and I, shall I live and not love you? No, I shall have no rest without the assurance that I have a true love for you, my Mother, a constant, tender love. Yes, I want to love you, O sweet Mother, but I fear, at the same time, that I do not love you, for I have heard it said that love makes a lover resemble the loved one.... I know how different I am from you! Could this be a sign that I do not love you? You are so pure, and I so impure! You are so humble, and I am so proud! You are so holy, and I so wicked! But this is what you ought to do, O Mary, since you love me : make me like you. You have the power to change hearts; then take mine and transform it. Show all the world how great is your power in favor of those you love! Sanctify me and make me worthy of being your child " (cf. St. Alphonsus).

175

EFFICACIOUS PRAYER

FIFTH SUNDAY AFTER EASTER

PRESENCE OF GOD - O Jesus, make me understand that my prayer is of no avail unless it is made in Your Name; that my faith is vain unless I convert it into works.

MEDITATION

1. In today's Gospel, taken again from the discourse of Jesus after the Last Supper (*Jn* 16,23-30), the Church

continues to prepare us for the Ascension and Pentecost. " I came forth from the Father and am come into the world, " Jesus said, " again I leave the world, and I go to the Father. " Thus He announces His approaching Ascension. Having reached the end of His ministry on earth, Jesus presents it in synthesis as a long journey from the Father to the world and from the world to the Father. These words repeat the idea of " pilgrimage, " which every Christian should apply to his own life, considering it as " a night spent in a bad inn " (T.J. *Way*, 40), a " night " during which his heart is turned toward the radiant tomorrow of eternal life.

" The hour cometh when I will no more speak to you in proverbs, but will show you plainly of the Father. " Jesus is now referring to Pentecost, to the intervention of the Holy Spirit by whom Jesus will enlighten His Apostles, giving them a clear understanding of the divine mysteries, so that the Father will no longer be unknown to them. All that we can study and learn about the things of God is a dead letter if the Holy Spirit does not enlighten us concerning them. Our need for Him is absolute; our desire for His coming should be unbounded.

Yet another subject is brought to our attention in today's Gospel. Jesus had spoken to the Apostles many times about prayer and the way they should pray; today He reveals the secret of efficacious prayer : " If you ask the Father anything in My Name, He will give it you. " Jesus is going, but He leaves the Apostles an unfailing means of approach to the Father : to present themselves in His own Name, the Name of the God-Man who, because He sacrificed Himself for the glory of His Father and for our salvation, deserves to be " *heard for His reverence* " (*Heb* 5,7).

2. To pray " in the Name of Jesus " establishes the conviction that our prayers, as well as all our good works, have no value unless they are founded on the infinite merits of Jesus. We must be persuaded that, however much we do or pray, we are always " unprofitable servants " (*Lk* 17,10); we have no sufficiency in ourselves, but all our sufficiency comes from the Crucified. Consequently, the first condition of prayer made " in the Name of Jesus " is humility, an ever deeper and more realistic sense of our nothingness. It must be complemented by the second condition, a boundless confidence in the merits of Jesus, which surpass all our

poverty, misery, necessities, needs. In view of Jesus' infinite merits, we can never ask too much in His Name; we can never be too bold in imploring the plenitude of divine grace for our souls, in aspiring to that sanctity which is hidden, perhaps, but genuine. There is no fault, no want of fidelity, no evil tendency, no sin, which, if sincerely detested, cannot be cleansed, purified, and pardoned by the Blood of Jesus; there is no weakness which He cannot cure, strengthen, and transform. Moreover, there is no creature of good will, no matter how weak and insignificant, who, in the Name of Jesus, cannot aspire to sanctity.

However, in order to make our prayer effective, a third condition is required : our life must correspond to our prayer, our faith must be translated into good works. " Be ye doers of the word and not hearers only, deceiving your own selves. For if a man be a hearer of the word and not a doer, he shall be compared to a man beholding his own countenance in a glass. For he beheld himself, and went his way, and presently forgot what manner of man he was. " This strong exhortation of St. James, which is found in today's Epistle (1,22-27), is an urgent reminder of the practical character of the Christian life. Vain is our prayer, vain our confidence in God, if we do not add our generous efforts to perform all our duties, to live up to our high vocation. We can, and we should, hope for everything in the Name of Jesus, but He expects a constant effort on our part to be entirely faithful to Him.

COLLOQUY

" Almighty God, Father of our Lord Jesus Christ, You who are so merciful, be merciful to me, for whatever I can find that is most precious, I devoutly offer You; I present in humble supplication all that is dear to me. I have nothing that I have not offered to Your Majesty; I have nothing more to add, since I have sent You my Hope, my Advocate : Your beloved Son. I have sent Your glorious Son as a Mediator between You and me; I have sent Him as an Intercessor, by whom I hope to obtain pardon. I have sent that Word whom You sent to atone for my guilt, and I show You the Passion which Your Son suffered for me. He is the Sacred Victim whom I offer to appease You, so that You will look favorably upon me. Great, indeed, is my wrong-doing, but my Savior's justice is much greater. Even as God is superior to man, so is my wickedness inferior to His goodness, in quality as well as in quantity.

" What fault committed by man has not been expiated by the Son of God made man? What pride can be so immeasurably inflated, that it could not be brought down by such humility? Truly, O my God, if we were to weigh both the offenses committed by sinners, and the grace of God the Redeemer, we would find that the difference equaled not only the distance between east and west, but the distance between hell and the highest heaven. O wonderful Creator of light, by the terrible sorrows of Your Son, pardon my sins! Grant, O God, that His goodness may overcome my wickedness, that His meekness may atone for my perversity, that His mildness may dominate my irascibility. May His humility make amends for my pride; His patience, for my impatience; His benignity, for my harshness; His obedience, for my disobedience; His tranquillity, for my anxiety, His sweetness, for my bitterness; may His charity blot out my cruelty! " (St. Augustine).

176

MARY'S HUMILITY

PRESENCE OF GOD - O Mary, humblest of all creatures, make me humble of heart.

MEDITATION

1. St. Bernard says : " It is not hard to be humble in a hidden life, but to remain so in the midst of honors is a truly rare and beautiful virtue. " The Blessed Virgin was certainly the woman whom God honored most highly, whom He raised above all other creatures; yet no creature was so humble and lowly as she. A holy rivalry seemed to exist between Mary and God; the higher God elevated her, the lowlier she became in her humility. The Angel called her

" full of grace, " and Mary " was troubled " (*Lk* 1,28.29). According to St. Alphonsus' explanation, " Mary was troubled because she was filled with humility, disliked praise, and desired that God only be praised. " The Angel revealed to her the sublime mission which was to be entrusted to her by the Most High, and Mary declared herself " the handmaid of the Lord " (*ibid.*, 38). Her thoughts did not linger over the immense honor that would be hers as the woman chosen from all women to be the Mother of the Son of God; but she contemplated in wonder the great mystery of a God who willed to become incarnate in the womb of a poor creature. If God wished to descend so far as to give Himself to her as a Son, to what depths should not His little handmaid abase herself? The more she understood the grandeur of the mystery, the immensity of the divine gift, the more she humbled herself, submerging herself in her nothingness. Her attitude was the same when Elizabeth greeted her, " Blessed art thou among women " (*ibid.*, 42). Those words did not astonish her, for she was already the Mother of God; yet she remained steadfast in her profound humility. She attributed everything to God whose mercies she sang, acknowledging the condescension with which He had " regarded the humility of His handmaid " (*ibid.*, 48). That God had performed great works in her she knew and acknowledged, but instead of boasting about them, she directed everything to His glory. With reason St. Bernardine exclaims : " As no other creature, after the Son of God, has been raised in dignity and grace equal to Mary, so neither has anyone descended so deep into the abyss of humility. " Behold the effect that graces and divine favors should produce in us : an increase of humility, a greater awareness of our nothingness.

2. " If you cannot equal Mary's absolute purity, " says St. Bernard, " at least imitate her humility. The virtue of chastity is admirable, but humility is essential. A simple invitation calls to the first : ' He that can take, let him take it '; for the second, we have an absolute command : ' Unless you become as little children, you shall not enter into the kingdom of heaven. ' Chastity, therefore, will be rewarded; humility will be demanded. We can be saved without virginity, but not without humility. Even Mary's virginity would not have been pleasing to God without humility.

Mary certainly pleased God by her virginity, but she became His Mother because of her humility. "

The greatest qualities and gifts, such as the spirit of penance or of poverty, virginity, the call to the apostolate, a life consecrated to God, even the priesthood, are sterile if they are not accompanied by sincere humility. Furthermore, without humility, they might be a source of danger for the soul. Lucifer was pure but not humble and pride was his downfall. The higher the place we occupy in the Savior's vineyard, the higher the life of perfection we profess, and the more important the mission which God has entrusted to us, the deeper we need to plant the roots of humility. Mary's maternity was the fruit of her humility : *humilitate concepit*, she conceived in humility. Even so, the fruitfulness of our interior life, of our apostolate, will depend on our humility and will always be proportioned to it. Only God can accomplish great things in us and by us, but He will not do so unless He finds us completely humble. Humility alone is the fertile ground in which God's gifts fructify, while it is always humility which draws down upon us divine graces and favors. " No queen, " says St. Teresa of Jesus, " forces the King of heaven to give Himself, as does humility. It was humility that drew Him down from heaven into the Virgin's womb " (*Way*, 16).

COLLOQUY

" O Virgin! glorious stem, to what sublime height do you raise your corolla? Straight to Him who is seated on the throne, to the God of Majesty. I do not wonder, since you are so deeply rooted in humility. Hail, Mary, full of grace! You are truly full of grace, for you are pleasing to God, to the angels, and to men : to men, by your maternity; to the angels, by your virginity; to God, by your humility. It is by your humility that you attract the glance of God, of Him who regards the humble, but looks at the proud from afar. As Satan's eyes are fixed on the proud, so God's eyes are on the lowly " (St. Bernard).

O Mother most humble, make me humble, so that God will deign to turn His eyes toward me. There is nothing in my soul to attract Him, nothing sublime, nothing worthy of His complacency, nothing truly good or virtuous; whatever

good there is, is so mixed with wretchedness, so weak and
deficient that it is not even worthy to be called good. What,
then, can attract Your grace to my poor soul, O Lord?
" Where will you look, but on him who is poor and humble,
and contrite of heart? " (cf. *Is* 66,2). O Lord, grant that
I may be humble; make me humble, through the merits of
Your most humble Mother.

" O Mary, had you not been humble, the Holy Spirit
would not have come upon you, and you would not have
become the Mother of God... " (cf. St. Bernard). Similarly,
if I am not humble, God will not give me His grace, the Holy
Spirit will not come to me, and my life will be sterile,
unfruitful. Grant, then, O Holy Virgin, that your humility,
which is so pleasing to God, may obtain pardon for my pride,
and a truly humble heart.

177

MARY'S FAITH

PRESENCE OF GOD - O my Mother, show me how to have firm faith
in God and how to entrust myself entirely to Him.

MEDITATION

1. Using St. Elizabeth's words, the Church says in
praise of Mary : " Blessed art thou that hast believed, because
those things shall be accomplished that were spoken to
thee by the Lord " (*Lk* 1,45). Great things indeed were
to be accomplished in Mary; and she had the great merit
of believing in them. On the word of God as announced
by the Angel, she believed that she would become a mother
without losing her virginity; she, who was so humble,
believed that she would be truly the Mother of God, and that
the fruit of her womb would really be the Son of the Most
High. She adhered with entire faith to all that had been
revealed to her, accepting, without the least hesitation,
a plan that would upset the whole natural order of things :
a virgin mother; a creature, Mother of the Creator. She

believed when the Angel spoke to her; she continued to
believe even when the Angel left her alone and she found
herself in the condition of an ordinary woman who knows
that she is about to become a mother. "The Virgin,"
St. Bernard says, "so little in her own eyes, was magnanimous
in her faith in God's promise! She, who considered herself
nothing but a poor handmaid, never had the least doubt
concerning her vocation to this incomprehensible mystery,
to this marvelous change, to this inscrutable sacrament;
she firmly believed that she would become the true Mother
of the God-Man."

The Blessed Virgin teaches us to believe in our vocation
to sanctity, to divine intimacy. We did believe in it when
God revealed it to us in the brightness of interior light, and
the words of His minister confirmed it; but we should also
believe in it when we find ourselves alone, in darkness, amid
difficulties that tend to disturb and discourage us. God is
faithful, and He does not do things by halves : He will
finish His work in us, provided we have complete confidence
in Him.

2. It would be very far from the truth to think that the
divine mysteries were so revealed to Mary, and the divinity
of Jesus was so evident to her that she had no need of
faith. Excepting the Annunciation and the events surrounding the birth of Jesus, we do not find any extraordinary
manifestations of the supernatural in her life. Mary lived
by pure faith, trusting in God's word even as we must.
The divine mysteries which took place in her and around
her remained habitually hidden under the veil of faith,
assuming an outward appearance common to the various
circumstances of ordinary daily life. Hence, they were often
concealed under obscure, disconcerting aspects such as,
the extreme poverty in which Jesus was born, the necessity
of fleeing into exile in order to save Him, the King of heaven,
from the wrath of an earthly king, the toil undergone to
procure for Him the strict necessities, and the lack of even
these, perhaps. Yet Mary never doubted that this weak,
helpless Child, who needed her maternal care and protection
just like any other child, was the Son of God. She always
believed, even when she did not understand. Witness for
example, the unexpected disappearance of the twelve-year-old
Boy who had remained in the Temple without His parents'

knowledge. St. Luke relates that when Jesus explained His action, giving as a reason that He was carrying out the mission entrusted to Him by His heavenly Father, Mary and Joseph " did not understand His words " (cf. 2,50). Although Mary knew that Jesus was the Messiah, she did not know how He was to accomplish His mission; at this time, therefore, she did not see the connection between the divine will and His remaining behind in the Temple. Nevertheless, she questioned Him no further. She believed that Jesus was her God, and that was enough for her; she was certain, absolutely certain of Him.

Sometimes in our spiritual life, we come to a halt because we insist on understanding and searching into God's plans for our soul. A faithful soul, on the other hand, does not linger to inquire about God's actions; even though not fully understanding them, it believes, following blindly, if necessary, the manifestations of the divine will. This is pleasing to God who does not ask us to understand, but only to believe with all our strength.

COLLOQUY

" O Mary, overshadow me and I shall be calm and confident. Accompany me on my way and lead me by secret paths. I shall not be spared suffering, but you will arouse in me a real hunger for it, as for an indispensable food. Mary! Your name is sweet as honey and balm to my lips. Hail, Mary! who can resist you? Who can be lost if he says, ' Hail, Mary? ' You are the Mother of the little ones, the health of the sick, the star in storms.... Oh! Mary! If I am helpless, without courage, without consolation, I run to you and cry : Ave Maria! You are the comfort of slaves, the courage of little ones, the strength of the weak, Ave Maria! When I say your name, my whole heart is inflamed, Ave Maria! Joy of angels, food of souls, Ave Maria! " (cf. E. Poppe).

Yes, O Mary, lead me by the short route of complete confidence in God. You who are blessed because you have believed, increase my faith; give me a strong, unshakable, invincible faith. We are indebted to your faith for the accomplishment of God's promises; therefore, help me to share your faith, making me believe in Him, in His words, promises, and invitations, without any shadow of doubt, hesitation, or uncertainty. Doubt delays me, hesitation paralyzes me, uncertainty clips my wings.... O Mary, help me to have complete faith, so that I can give myself wholly to God, adhere to all His plans, accept with my eyes closed every disposition of divine Providence. Make me believe so that I shall be able to face storms with courage, abandon myself entirely to God's action, and advance with confidence along the road to sanctity. If you are with me, O Mary, I shall have no fear. The strength of your faith will be the support and refuge of mine, so weak and languid.

178

MARY'S HOPE

PRESENCE OF GOD - O Mary, Mother of Good Hope, teach me the way of complete confidence in God.

MEDITATION

1. In the *Magnificat*, the canticle which burst forth from Mary's heart when she visited her cousin Elizabeth, we find an expression which specially reveals Mary's interior attitude. " My soul doth magnify the Lord...because He hath regarded the humility of His handmaid " (*Lk* 1,46-48). When Mary spoke these words, they revealed the " great things " which God had done in her; but, considered in the framework of her life, they expressed the continual movement of her heart, which, in the full awareness of her nothingness, would turn always to God with the most absolute hope and trust in His aid. No one had a more concrete, practical *knowledge* of her nothingness than Mary; she understood well that her whole being, natural as well as supernatural, would be annihilated if God did not sustain her at every moment. She knew that whatever she was and had, in no way belonged to her, but came from God, and was the pure gift of His liberality. Her great mission and the marvelous privileges which she had received from the Most High did not prevent

her from seeing and feeling her " lowliness. " But far from disconcerting or discouraging her in any way—as the realization of our nothingness and wrechedness often does to us—her humility served as a starting point from which she darted to God with stronger hope. The greater the knowledge of her nothingness and weakness became, the higher her soul mounted in hope. That is why, being really poor in spirit, she did not trust in her own resources, ability, or merits, but put all her confidence in God alone. And God, who " sends the rich away empty, and fills the hungry with good things " (cf. *Lk* 1,53), satisfied her " hunger " and fulfilled her hopes, not only by showering His gifts on her, but by giving Himself to her in all His plenitude.

2. Mary's hope was truly *absolute*. We have a typical example of it in her attitude toward Joseph at the time when he, aware of her approaching maternity (of whose origin he knew nothing), " was minded to put her away privately " (*Mt* 1,19). Mary certainly perceived something of the state of mind of her pure spouse and of the doubts he was experiencing. She knew, likewise, the risk she was incurring of being " put away, " because the Angel had said nothing which could have reassured her on this delicate point. However, completely confident in God's help, she did not reveal her secret in any way. " In silence and in hope shall your strength be " (*Is* 30,15), said the Holy Spirit, through the mouth of His prophet. These words were to have their most beautiful realization in Mary's attitude. She remained silent, and did not try to justify herself in Joseph's eyes; she was silent because she was filled with hope in God and absolutely certain of His help. Silence and hope permitted her to rely entirely upon God; strong with His strength, she remained serene and tranquil in an extremely difficult and delicate situation.

We also hope in God, but our hope is not absolute like Mary's. Lacking her complete reliance on the divine assistance, we always feel the need of resorting to many little personal expedients to obtain some security, some human support. However, everything human is uncertain; if we base our hopes on these things, it is quite natural that we shall be constantly disturbed and anxious. By her silent hope, the Virgin Mary shows us the only way to real security, serenity, and inner peace, even in the most difficult circumstances : the way of total confidence in God. " *In te, Domine, speravi, non confundar in aeternum,* " In Thee, O Lord, have I hoped, let me not be confounded forever *(Te Deum)*. No, God will never disappoint us if we hope in Him; just as He sent an Angel to Joseph to reveal the mystery of Mary's maternity, He will always find a way to help and sustain a soul who entrusts itself wholly to Him.

COLLOQUY

" O Mother of holy love, our life, our refuge, and our hope, you well know that your Son Jesus, not satisfied with being our perpetual advocate with the eternal Father, has willed that you also, should implore divine mercy for us. I turn to you, then, hope of the unfortunate, hoping by the merits of Jesus and by your intercession, to obtain eternal salvation. My confidence is so great, that, if I had my salvation in my own hands, I should yet place it in yours, for I trust in your merciful protection more than I do in my own works. O my Mother and my hope, do not abandon me! The pity you have for sinners and your power with God are greater than the number and the malice of my faults. If all should forget me, do not you forget me, Mother of the omnipotent God. Say to God that I am your child and that you protect me, and I shall be saved

" Do not look for any virtue or merit in me, my Mother; look only at the confidence I place in you and my desire to improve. Look at all that Jesus has done and suffered for me and then abandon me, if you have the heart to do so. I offer you all the sufferings of His life : the cold He endured in the stable, His journey to Egypt, the Blood He shed, His poverty, His sweat, His sadness and the death He endured for love of me in your presence, and do you, for the love of Jesus, pledge yourself to help me. O my Mother, do not refuse your pity to one for whom Jesus did not refuse His Blood!

" O Mary, I put my trust in you; in this hope I live and in this hope I long to die, saying over and over : ' *Unica spes mea Jesus, et post Jesum virgo Maria,* ' My only hope is Jesus, and after Jesus, Mary " (St. Alphonsus).

179

THE ASCENSION OF OUR LORD

FORTY DAYS AFTER EASTER

PRESENCE OF GOD - O Jesus, who ascended into heaven, grant that I, too, may live there in spirit.

MEDITATION

1. The central idea in the liturgy today is the raising of our hearts toward heaven, so that we may begin to dwell in spirit where Jesus has gone before us. " Christ's Ascension " says St. Leo, " is our own ascension; our body has the hope of one day being where its glorious Head has preceded it " *(RB)*. In fact, Our Lord had already said in His discourse after the Last Supper, " I go to prepare a place for you. And if I shall go and prepare a place for you, I will come again and will take you to Myself; that where I am, you also may be " *(Jn* 14,2.3). The Ascension is, then, a feast of joyful hope, a sweet foretaste of heaven. By going before us, Jesus our Head has given us the right to follow Him there some day, and we can even say with St. Leo, " In the person of Christ, we have penetrated the heights of heaven " *(RB)*. As in Christ Crucified we die to sin, as in the risen Christ we rise to the life of grace, so too, we are raised up to heaven in the Ascension of Christ. This vital participation in Christ's mysteries is the essential consequence of our incorporation in Him. He is our Head; we, as His members, are totally dependent upon Him and intimately bound to His destiny. " God, who is rich in mercy, " says St. Paul, " for His exceeding charity wherewith He loved us...hath quickened us together in Christ...and hath raised us up... and hath made us sit together in the heavenly places through Christ Jesus " *(Eph* 2,4-6). Our right to heaven has been given us, our place is ready; it is for us to live in such a way that we may occupy it some day. Meanwhile, we must actualize the beautiful prayer which the liturgy puts on our lips : " Grant, O almighty God, that we, too, may dwell in spirit in the heavenly mansions " *(Collect)*. " Where thy

treasure is, there is thy heart also " (*Mt* 6,21), Jesus said one day. If Jesus is really our *treasure*, our heart cannot be anywhere but near Him in heaven. This is the great hope of the Christian soul, so beautifully expressed in the hymn for Vespers : " O Jesus, be the hope of our hearts, our joy in sorrow, the sweet fruit of our life " *(RB)*.

2. Besides the hope and the joyful expectancy of heaven so characteristic of the Ascension feast there is a note of melancholy. Before the final departure of Jesus, the Apostles must have been very much disturbed : each felt the distress of one who sees his dearest friend and companion going away forever, and finds himself alone to face all the difficulties of life. The Lord realized their state of mind and consoled them once more, promising the coming of the Holy Spirit, the Comforter : " He commanded them, " we read in the Epistle (*Acts* 1,1-11), " that they should not depart from Jerusalem, but should wait for the promise of the Father... you shall be baptized with the Holy Ghost, not many days hence. " But even this time the Apostles did not understand! How much they needed to be enlightened and transformed by the Holy Spirit, in order to accomplish the great mission which was to be entrusted to them! Jesus continued : " You shall receive the power of the Holy Ghost coming upon you and you shall be witnesses unto Me...even to the uttermost part of the earth. " For the moment, however, they were there, around the Master, weak, timid, frightened, like little children watching their mother leave for a distant, unknown land. In fact, " while they looked on, He was raised up, and a cloud received Him out of their sight. " Two angels came to distract them from their great amazement and to make them realize what had happened. Then, placing their trust in the word of Jesus, which would henceforth be their only support, they returned to Jerusalem where, in the Cenacle, they awaited in prayer the fulfillment of the promise. It was the first novena in preparation for Pentecost : " All these were persevering with one mind in prayer with...Mary, the Mother of Jesus " (*ibid.* 1,14).

Silence, recollection, prayer, peace with our brethren, and union with Mary : these are the characteristics of the novena we too should make in preparation for the coming of the Holy Spirit.

COLLOQUY

" O my God, O my Jesus, You are going away and leaving us! Oh! what joy there will be in heaven! But we have to remain here on earth. O eternal Word, what has Your creature done for You, that You should do so much for him and then ascend into heaven to glorify him even more? Tell me, what has he done for You, that You should love him so much? What has he given You? What do You look for in him? You love him so much that You give Yourself to him, You who are all things, and besides whom there is nothing. You want from him his entire will and intellect, because when he gives them to You, he gives You all that he has. O infinite Wisdom, O supreme Good, O Love, O Love so little known, little loved, and possessed by so few! Oh! our ingratitude, cause of every evil! O Purity, so little known and so little desired! O my Spouse, now that You are in heaven, seated at the right hand of the eternal Father, create in me a pure heart and renew a right spirit within me " (St. Mary Magdalen dei Pazzi).

" Alas! how long this exile is, O Lord, and how the desire to see You makes it seem longer still! O Lord, what can an imprisoned soul do?... I want to please You. Behold me, Lord! If I have to live longer in order to serve You further, I refuse none of the crosses which may await me on earth. But alas, Lord, alas! These are but words; I am capable of nothing else. Permit my desires, at least, to have some value in Your sight, O my God, and do not regard my lack of merit!

" Ah! my works are poor, my God, even if I could perform many! Then why should I remain in this life, so full of misery? Only to do Your will. Could I do anything better than that? Hope, therefore, my soul, hope. Watch carefully, for you know not the day nor the hour. Everything passes quickly, even though your desire makes a short time seem very long. Remember that the more you struggle, the greater the proofs of love you will be giving to your God, and afterwards the more you will enjoy your Beloved in happiness and felicity without end " (T.J. *Exc*, 15).

180

THE GROWTH OF CHARITY IN MARY

PRESENCE OF GOD - O Mary, Mother of fair love, teach me the secret of steady growth in charity.

MEDITATION

1. We must not think that the Blessed Virgin Mary was excused from all personal activity and progress because she had been established from the beginning in a higher degree of sanctity than that which even the greatest saint could ever hope to attain. Quite the contrary! For her, as for us, life on earth was a " way " where progress in charity was always necessary, where personal correspondence with grace was expected. The excellence of our Lady's merit consisted in her heroic fidelity to the immense gifts she had received. The privileges of her Immaculate Conception, of the state of sanctity in which she was born, and of her divine maternity were, unquestionably, pure gifts from God; still, far from accepting them passively, as a coffer receives the precious things put into it, she received them freely, as one capable of willingly adhering to the divine favors by means of a complete correspondence with grace. St. Thomas teaches that although Mary could not merit the Incarnation of the Word, by the grace she received she did merit that degree of sanctity which made her the worthy Mother of God (cf. IIIª, q. 2, a. 11, ad. 3), and she merited this precisely because of her correspondence with grace. Hence, even in Mary, we can consider progress in sanctity, a progress which did not depend solely on the new abundance of graces which God gave her at certain special times in her life—at the moment of the Incarnation for example—but also on her personal activity, wholly informed by grace and charity, by means of which she brought to fruition the treasure entrusted to her by God. Mary, in the truest sense of the word, is the " faithful Virgin, " who knew how to increase a hundredfold the talents she received from God. Yes, the greatest amount of grace ever given to a creature was freely bestowed on her by the divine liberality, in view

of the sublime mission for which she was destined, but she corresponded to it with the greatest fidelity possible to a creature. Thus there was plenitude of grace on God's part, and complete fidelity on Mary's, so that, as St. Alphonsus says, " Without ever stopping, her beautiful soul soared toward God, continually growing in love of Him. "

2. Theology teaches that the increase of grace and charity in us is the result of meritorious works, that is, good works performed under the influence of charity. When one does good works " with his whole heart, " the merit acquired —always an increase of grace and of charity—is immediately given to him, and as a result, his spiritual life immediately grows in intensity. With this doctrine in mind, we can readily see at what rate the capital of charity and grace which God had placed in Mary's soul at the very first moment of her existence must have developed. When we think, as St. John of the Cross points out, that Mary's soul was never moved, and therefore never retarded, by any attachment to creatures, and that consequently, she never had any secondary motives, or any pettiness caused by selfishness, but always acted under the impulse of the Holy Spirit, we must conclude that she was ever growing in grace, and that charity in her became a veritable abyss. This explains how Mary, although sanctified and established in union with God from the first moment of her life, was able to advance continually in sanctity, the constituent elements of which are grace and charity. It was the generous, faithful ardor with which she replied to the divine invitations, entered into every manifestation of God's will, accepted all the dispositions of divine Providence, and fulfilled all her daily duties, which put her in that magnificent state of incessant and most rapid progress in love. May Mary's shining example encourage us to apply ourselves with all our heart to God's service, so that we, too, may grow rapidly in charity.

COLLOQUY

" O Mary, you understood the gift of God; you never lost a particle of it. You were so pure, so luminous, that you seemed to be light itself: *Speculum justitiae*, mirror of justice. Your life was so simple, so lost in God, that there is scarcely anything to say about it. *Virgo fidelis :* the faithful Virgin, ' who kept all things in her heart ' " (E.T. *I*, 10).

O Mary, how marvelous to see your soul continually growing in love, to watch it scale the heights of sanctity without ever halting! Nothing retarded the divine action in you; no obstacle hindered the growth of charity. " Who is this that cometh up from the desert, flowing with delights, leaning upon her Beloved? " (*Ct* 8,5). It is you, O Mother, you who, under the guidance of the Holy Spirit and sustained by Him, ever rose from grace to grace, from virtue to virtue. O Mother of fair love, full of grace, O faithful Virgin, help me to correspond with fidelity to the gifts of God! Do not permit that my misery render sterile the grace within me. Help me, O Mother, to overcome the innumerable resistances of my weak, cowardly nature; draw me by the sweet charm of your example, so that I may follow you with ardor in the way of perfect charity.

" O my Mother, you who were ever on fire with love for God, give me at least a spark of that love. You appealed to your Son on behalf of the bride and bridegroom whose wine gave out, saying : ' *vinum non habent,* ' they have no wine; and will you not pray for me, lacking as I am in love for God, and yet owing Him so much? Say to Him : ' *amorem non habet,* ' he has no love. And ask this love for me. No other grace do I ask of you but this one. O Mother, by your love for Jesus, hear me. Show me what great favor you have with Him by obtaining for me a divine light and a divine flame so powerful that it will transform me from a sinner into a saint, and, detaching me from every earthly affection, will inflame me wholly with divine love. O Mary, you have the power to do this. Do it for love of the God who made you so great, so powerful, and so merciful " (St. Alphonsus).

181

MARY AND FRATERNAL CHARITY

PRESENCE OF GOD - O Mother, whose love for man was so great, teach me how to fulfill, in all its perfection, the precept of fraternal charity.

MEDITATION

1. Charity is *one* in its essence, because of the oneness of its object : God loved in Himself, God loved in the neighbor. Hence, the more a soul loves God, so much the more does it love its neighbor. Now if charity toward God reached its peak in Mary, we must also say that her charity toward her neighbor was boundless. This is the peculiar quality of true love of God; far from narrowing the soul of one who possesses it, charity dilates the soul, that it may pour out on others the wealth it has accumulated. Such was the characteristic of Mary's charity. Although she was completely filled with the love of God, wholly recollected in the contemplation of the divine mysteries which were taking place in and around her, her recollection did not hinder her from giving attention to her neighbor; on the contrary, we see her always gracious and attentive to the needs of others. Furthermore, her own interior wealth urged her to desire to share with others the great treasures which she possessed. This is the attitude described in the Gospel, when, immediately after the Annunciation, she undertook a journey " in haste, " as St. Luke says, to visit Elizabeth. It would have been very pleasant for her to remain at Nazareth, adoring in solitude and silence the divine Word incarnate in her womb, but the Angel had told her of the imminent maternity of her aged cousin; this was enough for her to feel obliged to go to Elizabeth and offer her humble services. We can say, therefore, that Mary's first act after becoming the Mother of God was an act of charity toward her neighbor. God gave Himself to her as a Son, and Mary, who gave herself to Him as His " handmaid, " wished also to give herself as the " handmaid " of others. The close union which exists between charity toward God and charity

toward the neighbor is singularly evident here. Her act
of charity toward Elizabeth is in perfect accord with the
act of sublime love in which Mary gave herself wholly to
God when she pronounced her "*fiat.*"

2. At the birth of Jesus, it was the same. Mary, in
ecstasy, contemplated Him, her divine Son, but this did
not prevent her from offering Him to the adoration of the
shepherds. Here is Mary's supreme charity to men : giving
Jesus to them almost as soon as He gives Himself to her.
She does not wish to be the only one to enjoy Him, but
would with all men share her joy. And just as she offered
Him to the shepherds and to the Magi who came to adore
Him, she would later offer Him to the executioners who
would crucify Him. Jesus was everything to Mary; yet,
because of her great charity, she did not hesitate to immolate
Him for the salvation of men. Can we imagine any more
exalted, or more generous charity? Next to Jesus, surely
no one loved mankind more than Mary.

Another aspect of her charity toward others is evidenced
in her tactfulness. When Mary found Jesus in the Temple
—after three days of anxious searching and keenest suffering—
she concealed her own sorrow behind that of Joseph's :
"Behold Thy father and I have sought Thee sorrowing"
(*Lk* 2,48). Delicate charity toward her spouse made her
profoundly sensitive to his grief and she put it before her
own deeper grief. The marriage in Cana gives us another
example of Mary's delicacy. While all were occupied
with the feast, she alone, although so recollected, noticed the
embarrassment of the bridal couple when the wine gave out,
and handled the matter so delicately that it passed unobserved,
even by the chief steward.

Mary teaches us that when our love of God is really
perfect, it flows at once into generous love of our neighbor,
because, as St. Thomas says, one who loves God, loves all
that God loves. If then, we have to recognize that in
dealing with our neighbor we are not very charitable, nor
very kind to him, nor attentive to his needs, we must conclude
that our love for God is still very weak.

COLLOQUY

"O Mary, with what sweetness and humility of heart you went to Elizabeth! You, the Queen, go to the servant; You, the Mother of God, visit the mother of the precursor.... And at Cana how graciously you went to the aid of the bridal couple! You took pity on their embarrassment, because you are merciful and kind. Can anything but tenderness come forth from the fountain of tenderness? Is it strange that a heart so full of kindness should produce kindness? If we hold in our hand a fragrant fruit for half a day, does not our hand retain the fragrance for the rest of the day? With how much virtue, O Mary, did not infinite Goodness fill your heart during the nine months He reposed within you! I know infinite Goodness filled your heart before entering your womb, and even when He left it, He did not leave your soul" (St. Bernard).

O holy Virgin, it is just this charity, the fruit of your intimate union with God, which you pour out upon all mankind, condescending to receive them in the wide embrace of your immense love. This same charity, which fires you with love for the Eternal, also inflames you with love for men, for you see them, not in themselves, but in God, considering them as His creatures and His children. This charity which has consecrated you to the service of the Most High, has also vowed you to the service of humanity, and so you have loved every creature, even me, despite my wretchedness.

It is true, O Mary, that on the day of my baptism the Holy Spirit diffused His charity in me; but my self-love has halted its growth, and I, who have so little love for my God, have likewise very little love for my neighbor. O most loving Mother, see how I need to have my heart dilated with charity! Stir up, then, and nourish that virtue in me and grant that, having given myself to the service of God, I may also give myself to that of my neighbor, with kindness and humility, promptness and generosity.

182

WAITING

PRESENCE OF GOD - Grant Lord, that my heart may ever be turned toward heaven where You await me.

MEDITATION

1. This Sunday is like a prolongation of the Feast of the Ascension. The Introit reflects the feelings which the Apostles must have experienced during the time between the departure of Jesus and the descent of the Holy Spirit : " Hear, O Lord, my voice calling to You.... I seek Your face, O Lord, do not hide Your face from me. " As on the day of the Ascension, the eyes of the Apostles are turned toward heaven, where they saw their Master disappear, and their hearts sigh after Him. As long as we are on our earthly pilgrimage, far from God, He must be the constant yearning of our souls. But we should not remain idle while we are waiting to go to our fatherland. In the Epistle of the day (1 Pt 4,7-11), Peter teaches us what we must do to make our life on earth a real preparation for our meeting with God : " Watch in prayers. But before all things, have a constant mutual charity among yourselves. " This is exactly what the Apostles did as they waited for the Holy Spirit : together in the Cenacle they were persevering in prayer in the unity of fraternal love. God does not look with favor on the prayers and sacrifices of one who does not love his neighbor—no matter who he may be—with sincere benevolence. Jesus has expressly said : " If therefore thou offer thy gift at the altar, and there thou remember that thy brother hath anything against thee; leave there thy offering...and go first to be reconciled to thy brother " (Mt 5,23.24). Prayer alone will not suffice to draw down divine graces, nor will it acquire eternal life for us. Fraternal charity, the surest pledge of the sincerity of our love for God, is an absolute requisite. The Holy Spirit, who is the spirit of charity, who is substantial love, cannot enter a heart

which is narrow and mean in its relations with its neighbor; lack of charity is one of the greatest obstacles to His action, because it is directly opposed to His essence. Just as water paralyzes the action of fire, so does lack of charity paralyze the action of the Holy Spirit. Furthermore, as long as we live on earth, we are all liable to fall; all of us, therefore, need pardon; " charity, " says the Epistle, " covers a multitude of sins. "

2. In today's Gospel (*Jn* 15,26.27 – 16,1-4) Jesus reiterates His promise concerning the descent of the Holy Spirit : " When the Paraclete cometh, whom I will send you from the Father...you shall give testimony [of Me]. " As on the day of His Ascension, He connects the coming of the Holy Spirit with the mission of the Apostles, that mission which will consist essentially in giving testimony of Christ. " You shall receive the power of the Holy Spirit...and you shall be witnesses unto Me...even to the uttermost part of the earth " (*Ep* : Feast of the Ascension). Today's Gospel explains the scope of this testimony which the Apostles, as well as all future Christians, will be called upon to give. " They will put you out of the synagogues : yea, the hour cometh that whosoever killeth you, will think that he doth a service to God. " Jesus died on the Cross to give testimony to the Father; His disciples will have to suffer, undergo persecution, and even death itself, to give testimony to Him. We cannot follow a road different from the one which Jesus has trodden : " If any man will come after Me, let him... take up his cross and follow Me " (*Mt* 16,24), He repeats to us. A calm, tranquil testimony, which is made without facing danger—still less of risking life—will always have only relative value and ordinarily gives no guarantee of its genuineness or its strength; on the contrary, the more it costs, the greater its value in proving the fidelity of him who renders it. To witness to Christ, without regarding the difficulties, sufferings or struggles that may be encountered, is the program of the true Christian. But who will give us courage? To us as to the Apostles, courage will come from the Holy Spirit, from His gift of fortitude; it will come from assiduous meditation on the example which Christ has given us; it will also come from His own words, spoken of coming persecutions : " I have told you these things, that you may not be scandalized in Me. "

COLLOQUY

O Lord, make me worthy to give testimony of You, not only in words, but especially in deeds, in spite of the difficulties and sufferings I may encounter. The Apostles gave testimony of You to the extent of facing death for love of You; grant that I may give testimony of You at least by a life worthy of You.

To give testimony of You, O Lord, " I would travel the world over to preach Your name, O my Beloved, and raise on heathen soil the glorious standard of the Cross! One mission alone would not satisfy my longings. I would spread the Gospel in all parts of the world, even in the farthest isles. I would be a missionary, but not for a few years only. Were it possible, I should wish to have been one from the world's creation and to remain one till the end of time. But the greatest of all my desires is to win the martyr's palm. . . .

" When I think of the fearful torments awaiting Christians at the time of Antichrist, my heart thrills within me and I wish that these torments could be reserved for me. Open, O Jesus, the book of life in which are written the deeds of all Your saints; each one of those deeds I long to accomplish for You. . . . Great deeds are forbidden me; I can neither preach the Gospel nor shed my blood. . .but what does it matter? My brothers labor in my stead while. . .I remain close to the throne and love You for all those who are in the strife " (cf. T.C.J. *St*, 13).

Yes, O Lord, grant me a true love, so that I may always be faithful to You in little things, since it is not given me to perform great ones. Grant especially that I may always give You the testimony of a sincere profession of faith, of behavior which is wholly conformed to Your law, no matter where or in what circumstance I may be, never letting myself deviate through human respect.

183

MARY'S PRAYER

PRESENCE OF GOD - O Mary, faithful adorer of God, show me how to make my life a continual prayer.

MEDITATION

1. In order to have even a slight understanding of Mary's prayer, we must try to penetrate the sanctuary of her intimate union with God. No one has ever lived in closer intimacy with Him. Let us reverently observe this intimacy from the viewpoint of the divine maternity. Who can imagine the secret communications between Mary and the Incarnate Word while she carried Him in her virginal womb? Although there was nothing to distinguish her exteriorly from other women in the same condition, yet, in the secrecy of her heart she led a life of the closest possible union between God and a mere creature. " *Omnis gloria ejus ab intus*"; all her glory is from within (cf. *Ps* 44,14). All Mary's glory and grandeur were interior. In this true sanctuary which concealed the Holy of Holies, Mary, living ciborium of the Incarnate Word, was aflame with love, absorbed in adoration. Carrying within her the " burning furnace of charity, " how could Mary not remain all inflamed by it! The more she was inflamed with love, the more she understood the mystery of love which was taking place within her. No one ever penetrated the secrets of Christ's heart as Mary did, or had a greater knowledge of the divinity of Christ and of His infinite grandeur. No one ever felt, as Mary did, the consuming need to give herself to Him, to lose herself in Him like a little drop in the immensity of the ocean. This was Mary's unceasing prayer : to adore perpetually the Word made Flesh within her; to unite herself closely with Christ; to be immersed in Him and completely transformed in Him by love; to join the infinite homage and praise which ascended continually from the heart of Christ to the Trinity, and to offer this praise unceasingly as the only homage worthy of the divine Majesty. Mary lived in adoration of her Jesus and, in union with Him, in adoration of the Trinity.

There is one moment in the day when we, too, can share in this prayer of Mary in a most excellent way : the moment of Holy Communion, when we receive Jesus, real and living, into our heart. How we need Mary to help us profit from this ineffable gift! She teaches us to submerge ourselves with her, in her and our Jesus, that we may be transformed in Him; she teaches us to unite ourselves to that adoration which ascends from the heart of Jesus to the Trinity, and she offers it with us to the Father, thus supplying for the deficiencies in our adoration.

2. Mary spent thirty years in Bethlehem and Nazareth in sweet family intimacy with Jesus. He was her center of attraction, the object of her affections, her thoughts and solicitude. The life of Mary was centered on Him; she took care of Him, always seeking new ways of pleasing, serving, and loving Him with the greatest devotion. Her will vibrated in unison with His; her heart beat in perfect harmony with His. She " shared the thoughts of Christ and His secret wishes, in such a way that it can be said that she lived the very life of her Son " (Pius X : *Ad Diem Illum*). Like Mary's life, her prayer was ever *Christocentric*, and Christ bore it to the Blessed Trinity. It was really the mystery of the Incarnation which brought Mary into the fullness of the Trinitarian life. Her unique relations with the three divine Persons began when the Angel told her that she was to be the Mother of the *Son of the Most High* and would be so by the power of *the Holy Spirit*. She was, from that moment, the beloved Daughter of the Father, the Spouse of the Holy Spirit, and the Mother of the Word. These relations were not limited to the time when Mary carried within her the Incarnate Word, but were to continue throughout her whole life, throughout eternity. Thus Mary is the temple of the Trinity. " Nearer than all to Jesus Christ, although at a distance that is infinite, " Mary is, " the great ' praise of glory ' of the Blessed Trinity " (E.T. *II*, 15).

In Mary, we find the most perfect model for the souls aspiring to intimacy with God; at the same time, she is the surest guide for them. She leads us to Jesus and teaches us to concentrate all our affections on Him, to give ourselves entirely to Him, until we are completely lost and transformed in Him. Then, through Jesus, she guides us to the life of union with the Trinity. By reason of sanctifying grace, our soul is also a temple of the Trinity, and Mary teaches us how to abide in this temple as a perpetual adorer of the three divine Persons who dwell therein. " I do not need to make any effort, " said Sister Elizabeth of the Trinity, " to enter into the mystery of the divine indwelling in the soul of our Lady; my soul seems to abide there habitually, in the same attitude that was hers : adoring the God hidden within me " *(L)*. May it also be given to us to live, under Mary's direction, in this attitude of continual adoration of the Trinity dwelling within our soul.

COLLOQUY

" O Mary, I can imagine how you must have felt when, after the Incarnation, you had within you the Word made flesh, the Gift of God! In what silence, what adoring recollection, must you have withdrawn into the depths of your soul to embrace the God whose Mother you were! Your attitude, O Blessed Virgin, during the months preceding the Nativity of Jesus, seems to be the model for interior souls, for those whom God has chosen to live *within*, deep in the unfathomable abyss. What peace and recollection accompanied your every action! You made ordinary things divine, because through them all, you remained the adorer of the Gift of God " (cf. E.T. *L – I*, 10).

" O Mary, you are the throne of God, the ostensorium of His love. You are the living monstrance of Jesus, and when I adore Jesus within you, it is as if I am really adoring the Blessed Sacrament exposed, *adoratio in ostensorio*, adoration in the monstrance. O Mary, all theology confirms your beautiful title : Ostensorium of Christ! Ostensorium of Christ at Bethlehem, at the Presentation, at Cana, on the Cross, in the Eucharist, in heaven. Yes, even in heaven. Do we not say : ' After this our exile show us *(ostende)* Jesus, the blessed Fruit of your womb? '... O Mary, teach me to see and love Jesus as you see and love Him. Teach me to long for Him with your love, to give myself to Him, to be wholly His as you are, and to adore Him with your own sentiments. O sweet Mother, teach me how to find Jesus and to pray to Him; fill me with Jesus, transform me into Him. O Mary, show me how to contemplate the life, the work and the divinity of your Son. Be the way which

leads me to Jesus, the bond which unites me to Him, and
which, with Him and in Him, unites me to the Most Blessed
Trinity " (cf. E. Poppe).

184

MARY'S APOSTOLATE

PRESENCE OF GOD - O Mary, Queen of Apostles, obtain for me the
heart of an apostle.

MEDITATION

1. Mary is, at the same time, the model of both
contemplative and apostolic souls. Furthermore, by combin-
ing in herself the highest contemplative life with the highest
apostolic life, she teaches us that contemplation and the
apostolate, far from being opposed to each other, complement,
support, and maintain each other. When the contemplative
life—considered as an assiduous seeking after union with
God—is really fervent, it cannot fail to enkindle in the soul
the burning fire of the apostolate. One who has experienced,
in an intimate contact with God, the ineffable reality of
His love for men, cannot fail to burn with the desire to win
all to that love. So it was with the Blessed Virgin, but in
the most sublime way. Having enjoyed and penetrated
God's love, and being more on fire with it than any other
creature, Mary desired more than anyone else to bring all
mankind to God. Indeed, no one has collaborated more
with Christ in saving the human race. Hers was an intimate
and profound collaboration, for by her blood, she supplied
the Son of God with the humanity which made it possible
for Him, the eternal Word, to become one of us, and to
suffer and die for us on the Cross. Mary's collaboration
was of the highest value, since she was willingly, knowingly
the Mother of the Savior. She gave her consent, knowing
well from the Sacred Scriptures that the Messiah was to be
the Man of Sorrows, immolated for the redemption of the
world. By consenting to become His Mother, she thereby

consented to link her fate with His and share in all His sufferings. To give a Redeemer to the world, to be willing to see her beloved Son die in torment, was Mary's sublime apostolate, born of her immense love of God.

The greater the love for God, the greater and more effective the apostolate which is derived from it. The reverse is equally true. Every apostolic work which is not animated by charity is *nothing*. " If I should distribute all my goods to feed the poor, " says St. Paul, " and if I should deliver my body to be burned, and have not charity, it profiteth me nothing " (1 *Cor* 13,3).

2. Intimately associated with the redemptive work of Jesus, Mary accomplished a universal, apostolic mission for the benefit of all mankind. Her apostolate, however, was a quiet one, free from ostentation; it was accomplished in the most humble, hidden and silent way. Mary gave the Redeemer to the world, but in the dark of night, in a poor stable. She shared the whole life of Jesus, but in the obscurity of the little house at Nazareth where she performed the lowly household tasks, amidst the difficulties and sacrifices of a life abounding in unusually toilsome and trying conditions. Even when Jesus, during the three years of His apostolic life, appeared publicly to accomplish the mission entrusted to Him by His Father, Mary remained in obscurity, although she followed Him and took part in all that happened. She never appeared when her Son was teaching the multitude, nor did she take advantage of her maternal authority to approach Him. On one occasion, when she sought to speak to Him while He was teaching the people in a house, she humbly waited outside (cf. *Mt* 12,46). Mary's apostolate was wholly interior, an apostolate of prayer and, above all, of hidden sacrifice, by means of which she adhered with great love to the will of God. He would ask her to separate herself from her Son after thirty years spent in sweet intimacy with Him, to withdraw apart, as if to leave to the Apostles and the crowd the place near Jesus which belonged to her as His Mother. Thus in obscurity and silence, Mary shared in the apostolate and sufferings of her Son : Jesus had no sorrow which Mary did not feel and live over again within herself. Her greatest sacrifice consisted in seeing Him, her beloved Son, persecuted, hated, condemned to death, and finally crucified on Calvary.

Her mother's heart felt the profound bitterness of all this, but at the same time she accepted everything for love, and offered it all for the salvation of souls. It was precisely through her hidden immolation, animated by *pure love*, that Mary reached the uttermost heights of the apostolate. " A little pure love, " says Saint John of the Cross, " is more precious in the eyes of God...and of more value to the Church...than all other works put together (*SC*, 29,2).

Mary shows us how far we are from the truth when, pressed by the urgency of our works, we make our apostolate consist solely in exterior activity, underestimating the interior apostolate of love, prayer, and sacrifice, on which the fruitfulness of our exterior acts depends.

COLLOQUY

" O Mary, you are our life, our sweetness, and our hope! You alone have taken away the world's universal guilt, for you alone gave birth to the Savior. You are the Mother of mercy, the Mother who washes away the stains of our sins. You pacified us when we cried in our cradle, you fed us and carried us in your arms. You are not only our Mother, but you also want to be the remedy for all our ills....

" In addition, O Mary, you became for us a sea of bitterness because of the pity you felt for your crucified Son and for all men.... Why, O Mary, have you loved us so much? Why do you overwhelm us with your love? Why do you overwhelm us with our God? Why, I ask, do you inebriate us with love for your Son, while we are unable to repay you in any way? What benefit is it to you, O lover of souls, if we love you, as well as your Son, with great love? Are not the things of heaven enough for you? Why do you seek earthly hearts, which are soiled and fetid? Take us, huntress of souls, take us and gather us into the bosom of your grace. Who can escape the rays of your goodness? No one can avoid the fire of your love, for heaven and earth are full of your favors...always and everywhere you lay the snares of your kindness. We cannot flee very far from you, O most sweet Mother, but we rest always in the bosom of your kindness " (cf. Saint Bonaventure).

" O Mary, you are more mother than queen! When I meditate upon your life, as the Gospel presents it to me, so humble and simple, I do not fear to approach you. I see you living in poverty and obscurity, with no transports or ecstasies, no splendid miracles or brilliant deeds. You show me that I, too, can follow your steps and climb the rough road of sanctity by practicing the hidden virtues. Close to you, O Mary, I like to remain little, and I get a better view there of the vanity of human greatness " (cf. T.C.J. *NV — Poems*).

O Mary, you gave Jesus to the world in silence and retirement; unnoticed, you shared His whole life, His works, His Passion. Teach me the secret of the interior apostolate of prayer and hidden sacrifices, known to God alone.

185

MARY OUR MEDIATRIX

PRESENCE OF GOD - O Mary, since Jesus willed to come to us through you, grant that I may go to Him through you.

MEDITATION

1. The Church teaches us to invoke Mary as *Mediatrix of all graces*. This title summarizes what the Blessed Virgin is for us, in our relations with her beloved Son : the Mediatrix of grace, of mercy, the treasurer of all the graces which Jesus merited for us. " By the communion of sorrows and of will between Christ and Mary, " says St. Pius X, " she merited to become the dispenser of all the benefits which Jesus acquired for us by shedding His Blood " (Encyclical : *Ad Diem Illum*). Mary, who was associated in the closest and most intimate way with the life, the work, and the Passion of her Son, cooperated with Him in our redemption to such an extent that the grace, which Jesus alone could merit for us *condignly*, was merited also by Mary, although in a secondary way and by *congruity* only. Thus Mary obtained real power over all the supernatural treasures acquired by her Son; and since she obtained them together

with Him, she also distributes them to us with Him. Leo XIII says, " It may be affirmed that, according to God's will, nothing comes to us without going through Mary's hands. Just as no one can approach the Almighty Father except through the Son, so no one can approach Christ except through His Mother " (Encyclical : *Octobri Mense*). After Jesus, who is the *only Mediator*, Mary is the Mediatrix : as Jesus continually intercedes with the Father in heaven on our behalf, so Mary intercedes with Jesus for us; she obtains and dispenses to us all the graces we need. The Introit of the Mass for the Feast of Mary Mediatrix of All Graces very fittingly applies to Mary the words spoken by St. Paul about Jesus : " Let us approach the throne of grace with confidence, to obtain mercy and pardon. " Next to Jesus, Mary is really the " throne of grace, " and she can obtain *everything* for us from her Son. She is the *omnipotentia supplex*, the all-powerful intercessor : all-powerful in her prayer as Mother.

2. Mary is the Mediatrix between her Son and us for a twofold reason : she *gives* Jesus to us and she *brings us* to Him. The Gospel tells us this several times, showing us the typically maternal attitude of Mary as she brought Jesus to mankind. Our Lady offered the Infant Jesus to the adoration of the shepherds and the Wise Men; she took Him to the Temple and presented Him to Simeon; by her intercession at Cana, she obtained the first miracle from her Son. On Calvary, Mary received into her arms the martyred, lifeless Body of her beloved Son, whom she offered to mankind as the price of its redemption. In the Cenacle, she begged the plenitude of the Holy Spirit for the Apostles and, from that day to the day of her Assumption, she sustained the infant Church by her prayers and maternal encouragement. To find Mary is to find Jesus. This is the whole reason for her existence and her mission : to give Jesus to the world and to souls, and with Jesus, to give His grace and blessings. As St. Bernard says, Mary is truly the channel which carries the living water of grace to mankind; furthermore, she brings Jesus, the very source of grace.

As Mediatrix, Mary also leads men to Jesus by teaching them the way to her Son and by showing them how to please Him. We are always poor little children incapable of making presentable gifts to God, but Mary our Mother, with maternal delicacy, arranges and embellishes our gifts, our acts, our prayers and sacrifices, and offers them with her own hands to her divine Son. She, like a true mother, gives particular attention to our hearts, which she desires to make pleasing to Jesus : Mary wants to form in each one of us a heart which is pure, full of love and goodness, a heart which can beat in unison with the heart of her Son. Let us then, place our hearts in Mary's hands, that she may fill them " with grace and truth, life and virtue " *(RM)*.

COLLOQUY

"O Blessed Lady, most holy Mother of God, full of grace, inexhaustible ocean of the intimate divine liberality and gifts of God, after the Lord of all, the Blessed Trinity, you are Lady of all; after the Paraclete, you are the new Consoler of all; and after the Mediator, you are the Mediatrix for the entire world. Behold my faith and my desire inspired by heaven; do not despise me although unworthy, neither let the ugliness of my sins suspend the immensity of your mercy, O Mother of God, O name which surpasses all my desire!" (St. Ephraem of Syria).

"O Mary, God has given you the plenitude of all His benefits, to show us that all hope, all grace, all salvation come from your superabundance. Grant, therefore, O Mary, you who have found grace and have given us life, that through you we may approach your divine Son, O Blessed Mother of Salvation! Grant that through you we may receive Him who was given to us through you. Let your spotless purity excuse before His eyes the faults of our malice. May your humility, so pleasing to God, obtain pardon for our pride! May your immense charity cover the multitude of our sins, and may your glorious fruitfulness make our good works fruitful!

"O Lady, our Mediatrix and our advocate, reconcile us with your Son, recommend us to your Son, present us to your Son! You are blessed by the grace you have found, by the privileges you have merited, by the mercy you have brought to the world. Obtain for us that Jesus, who through you deigned to share our infirmity and our wretchedness, may grant us also through you a share in His glory and in His beatitude " (St. Bernard).

186

THE HOLY SPIRIT

PRESENCE OF GOD - O Holy Spirit, teach me to know You, to want You, to love You, and to prepare myself to second Your action in my soul.

MEDITATION

1. The approach of Pentecost reminds us to turn our mind and heart to the Holy Spirit; with His help, we want to know Him better so as to love Him more ardently, invoke Him more fervently, and dispose ourselves in the best manner possible for the furtherance of His action in our soul.

The catechism teaches us that there are three Persons, equal and distinct, in God : the Father, the Son, and the Holy Spirit. *Ab aeterno* the Father, knowing Himself, generates His *Word*, the perfect, substantial Idea in whom the Father is expressed and to whom He communicates all His goodness, lovableness, divine nature and essence. The Father and the Word, mutually beholding Their infinite goodness and beauty, love each other from all eternity, and the expression of this unitive love is a third Person, the Holy Spirit. As the Word is generated by the Father by way of knowledge, so the Holy Spirit proceeds from the Father and the Son by way of love. The Holy Spirit is, therefore, the terminus, and the effusion of the reciprocal love of the Father and the Son, an *effusion* so substantial and perfect that it is a Person, the third Person of the Most Holy Trinity, to whom the Father and the Son, by the sublime fruitfulness of their love, communicate their very own nature and essence, without losing any of it Themselves. Because the Holy Spirit is the effusion of divine love, He is called " Spirit, " according to the Latin sense of the word which means *air, respiration, the vital breath.* In us, respiration is a sign of life; in God, the Holy Spirit is the expression, the effusion of the life and love of the Father and the Son, but a substantial personal effusion, which is a *Person.* It is in this sense that the third Person of the Blessed Trinity is called the " Spirit of the Father and the Son, " and also " the Spirit of love in God, " that is, the

" breath " of love of the Father and the Son, the " breath " of divine love. It was in this sense that the Fathers of the Church called the Holy Spirit " *osculum Patris et Filii,* " the kiss of the Father and the Son, a " sweet, but secret kiss, " according to the tender expression of St. Bernard.

Let us invoke the Holy Spirit, the Spirit of love, so that He may come to enkindle in our hearts the flame of charity.

2. According to our human concept, a person is a being who is *complete* and *distinct* from other beings; a *subsistent* being, existing by itself; an *intelligent* being, free and capable of willing; and an *affectionate* being, capable of loving. All this is verified in the Holy Spirit in the most perfect manner : He, the breath of love of the Father and the Son, is a Person, and a divine Person. He is a *complete* being. He is God, and wholly God, not a part of God; although absolutely equal to the other two divine Persons, He is *distinct* from them; He is *subsistent* in Himself, *knowing* and *loving.* Because the Holy Spirit is a divine Person, we can have relations with Him just as we do with the Father and the Son. The Church invites us to do so proposing to us many beautiful invocations to the Holy Spirit, especially in the hymn *Veni Creator Spiritus,* in which she mentions all the titles by which the divine Paraclete can be addressed with confidence. The hymn begins by calling the Holy Spirit " Creator Spirit, " reminding us that He, together with the Father and the Son, is one only God, our Creator. Then, she invokes Him as our Sanctifier, that is, as the One who diffuses grace in our souls : *Imple superna gratia, quae tu creasti pectora,* fill with heavenly grace the souls which You have created. Although all the external acts of God—such as creation, sanctification of souls, redemptions—are common to the three divine Persons, " by a certain relation and, as it were, an affinity which exists between the exterior works and the character proper to each Person, these works are attributed to one Person rather than to another " *(Divinum Illud).* Thus the work of sanctification, which is a work of love, is especially attributed to the Holy Spirit, who is the breath of divine love. Leo XIII teaches : " The Holy Spirit gives a sweet, strong impulse, and puts, so to speak, the final touch to the noble work of our eternal predestination " *(ibid.).* Under this special aspect of Sanctifier, then, the Church urges us to invoke the Holy Spirit. *Altissimi donum Dei, fons vivus, ignis, caritas et spiritalis*

unctio, gift of the Most High God, gift given to our souls to lead them to sanctity; living fount of grace, fire, divine love, spiritual sweetness. And again : *Septiformis munere, digitus paternae dexterae*, dispenser of the seven gifts by which He makes our spiritual life perfect, finger of the right hand of the Father which indicates to us the road to sanctity. With what joy, love, and desire we should invoke the Holy Spirit, the Sanctifier!

COLLOQUY

" O marvelous union in heaven, marvelous on earth, marvelous and most secret, perfect bond of the divine nature, by which the Holy Spirit, the bond of love, in an ineffable manner, unites the divine Persons! Oh, how He unites in perfect unity the Holy Trinity : unity of essence, of substance, and of love! You, O Holy Spirit, are its sweet bond! O divine Spirit, with the same bond by which You join and bind eternally the Father and Son in perfect union, You also unite the soul with God, in a way similar to that divine union. You do so by freeing its faculties so perfectly that because of its close union with God, it neither wishes nor is able to wish, to recall, know, or desire anything but divine charity. Oh! how happy would the soul be, if, like the blessed in heaven, it could nevermore be freed from such a close and blessed bond!

" O Holy Spirit, You come to us by a loving operation of grace...like an overflowing fountain in the soul, wherein the soul is submerged. As two rivers join and unite their waters so that the smaller one loses its name and takes that of the larger, so do You, O divine Spirit, come into the soul to unite Yourself to it. But it is necessary that the soul, which is the lesser, lose its name and leave it to You, O Holy Spirit, that it may be transformed in You, so as to become one spirit with You.

" Holy Spirit, I see You coming down into the soul like the sun which, finding no obstacle, no impediment, illumines everything; I see You descending like a fiery thunderbolt which, in falling, goes to the lowest place it finds and there it reposes, never stopping on the way nor resting on the mountainous or high places but rather in the center of the earth. Thus You, O Holy Spirit, when You come down from heaven with the fiery dart of Your divine love, You do not repose in proud hearts or in arrogant spirits, but You make Your abode in souls that are humble and contemptible in their own eyes " (St. Mary Magdalen dei Pazzi).

187

THE SPIRIT OF CHRIST

PRESENCE OF GOD - O Holy Spirit, You who had complete dominion over the holy soul of Jesus, deign to direct my poor soul.

MEDITATION

1. In Sacred Scripture, the Holy Spirit is called " the Spirit of Christ " (*Rom* 8,9), an expression that is pregnant with meaning. Christ is the Incarnate Word. Although He became Man, He remains the Word, the Son of God. From Him, as from the Father, the Holy Spirit proceeds; therefore, the Holy Spirit is properly termed the Spirit of Christ, because the Person of Christ is none other than that of the Word. When we speak of Christ, however, we do not speak of Him as God only, but also, and especially, as Man, that is, as the *Incarnate* Word. In this sense too, it can be said that the Holy Spirit is the Spirit of Christ. We know, in fact, that the divine Paraclete, with the Father and the Son, dwells in every soul that is in the state of grace, and not only does He dwell there, but He delights to abide there. The higher the degree of grace He finds in a soul, the greater is His delight, for wherever grace is more abundant, there is a more intense and luminous reflection of God's nature and goodness. This is why the Holy Spirit took such great complacency in the soul of the Blessed Virgin, who, although she was full of grace, continually grew from plenitude to plenitude. Yet the grace possessed by Mary was but a pale reflection of the grace which filled the soul of Jesus, grace which theologians call " infinite. "

If, then, Jesus possessed grace in an infinite manner, it can be said that the Holy Spirit took complacency in the soul of Christ in an infinite manner and dwelt there as in His temple of predilection. This idea is expressed in the Encyclical *Mystici Corporis*, when it says that the divine Paraclete " finds His delight in dwelling in the soul of the Redeemer as in His favorite temple. " And if we can say that the Holy Spirit is *ours* because He dwells in our souls sanctified by grace, with infinitely greater reason can we say that He is " Christ's, " whose sacred soul possesses grace in an immeasurable degree.

2. The Holy Spirit is the Spirit of Christ and dwells in Him as in His chosen temple. The Holy Spirit is in the soul of Christ to bear it continually to God, to direct it in the accomplishment of its redemptive mission and to the fulfillment of the will of the heavenly Father. We see this in the Gospel where St. Luke, after describing Jesus' baptism, when the Holy Spirit " descended in a bodily shape, as a dove, upon Him " (3,22), adds : " Jesus, being full of the Holy Ghost, returned from the Jordan, and was led by the Spirit into the desert " (4,1). This is an explicit statement of the immeasurable plenitude with which the Holy Spirit dwelt in the soul of Jesus; without doubt, this plenitude existed from the first moment of the Savior's life, but God wished to make it sensibly manifest at the time of His baptism. It is also a striking example of the unceasing operation of the Holy Spirit in Jesus' soul, inspiring all His actions and guiding Him to the accomplishment of His redemptive mission. According to St. Paul : " By the Holy Ghost, [Christ] offered Himself unspotted unto God " (*Heb* 9,14). If we wish a more profound understanding of this mysterious action of the divine Paraclete in the sacred soul of Jesus, it will suffice to think of what He accomplishes in a soul who has reached the transformation of love. St. John of the Cross teaches that, in this very exalted state, the Holy Spirit invades the soul, henceforth totally docile to His motions; He directs it and moves it in all its acts, impelling it unceasingly toward God by a perfect adherence to His divine will. The Holy Spirit accomplished immeasurably more in the soul of Christ which was supremely capable of docility and correspondence to His inspirations. The divine Spirit encountered the sublime creature, the soul of Jesus; He invaded it, directed it, guided it in the accomplishment of its mission and brought it to God with

unparalleled transports, because it was completely under His sway.

COLLOQUY

"O Holy Spirit, only Your clemency and ineffable love could have held the Son of God nailed to the wood of the Cross, for neither nails nor cords would have been able to hold Him there without the bonds of love. And then, when Christ returned to His Father at His Ascension, You, O Holy Spirit, were sent into the world with the power of the Father, the wisdom of the Son, and Your own mercy, to strengthen the way of the doctrine which Christ left in the world.... O Holy Spirit, come into my heart; by Your power, draw it to You, true God; grant me charity with fear, guard me from every evil thought, warm me, inflame me with Your most sweet love, so that every pain will seem slight to me. O Holy Father and my sweet Lord, help me now in all my actions" (St. Catherine of Siena).

"O Jesus, I offer You my poor love, placing it in the arms of Your ardent Spirit, in the furnace enkindled by Your love. O my Beloved, by Your divine power prepare me for spiritual warfare with the weapons of Your Spirit, since I do not rely upon myself, but on Your goodness alone. By Your unfathomable charity, root out of me anything that is not wholly Yours, so that, by the grace of Your love, invited and restored by Your loving sweetness, I may love You alone. The sweet outpourings of Your Spirit make the burden of life seem brief and light. Deign to cooperate with my works, so that my soul may magnify You eternally. May my life be consecrated to You, and may my spirit rejoice in You, my Savior; then every thought and act will be praise and thanksgiving to You" (St. Gertrude).

O Holy Spirit, You who worked with such plenitude in the most holy soul of Jesus, deign to operate also in my poor soul and take it entirely under Your direction, so that every act, interior as well as exterior, may be according to Your inspirations, Your choice, Your good pleasure.

188

SWEET GUEST OF THE SOUL

PRESENCE OF GOD - O Holy Spirit, You who deign to dwell in me, help me to open my soul completely to Your action.

MEDITATION

1. The Encyclical *Mystici Corporis* states that " the Holy Spirit is the soul of the Church. " Because soul means " principle of life, " this statement equivalently says that the divine Paraclete is the One who gives life to the Church. As the soul is the principle of life in the body, so the Holy Spirit is the principle of life in the Church, the Mystical Body of Christ (cf. *Divinum Illud*).

We have seen that the Holy Spirit was in Christ's soul to direct Him in the accomplishment of His redemptive mission. Jesus could have carried out this mission alone, but He wished the Church to participate in it. Since the Church continues Christ's work, she needs the same impetus which guided His soul; she needs the Holy Spirit. Jesus merited His Spirit for us on the Cross; by His death, He atoned for all sin, the chief obstacle to the action of the Holy Spirit, and when He had ascended into heaven, He sent Him to the Apostles, who represented the whole Church. Now, seated in glory at the right hand of the Father, He intercedes continually for us, He is always sending the Holy Spirit to the Church, as He promised. The Holy Spirit operates in the Church now, just as He once did in the blessed soul of Christ. He gives her impulse, moves her, and drives her to accomplish God's will, thus enabling her to fulfill His mission, the continuation down through the ages of the redemptive work of Christ. With reason, then, did the early Fathers call the Holy Spirit the Soul of the Church; the Church herself invokes Him in the *Credo* : " *Dominum et vivificantem!* " Lord and life-giver. As the soul vivifies the body, the Holy Spirit vivifies the Church. He is the impulse of love who kindles in her zeal for the glory of God and the salvation of souls; He gives light and strength to her shepherds, fervor and energy to her apostles, courage and invincible faith to her martyrs.

2. The Church, because she is the " society " of the faithful, is constituted by their union : it is the faithful, it is we ourselves, who form the Church. Hence, to say that Jesus merited the Holy Spirit for His Church is equivalent to saying that He merited Him for us; to say that Jesus, together with the Father, has sent and continues to send His Spirit to the Church, is equivalent to affirming that He has sent and continues to send Him to us. The Encyclical *Mystici Corporis* asserts that the Holy Spirit " is communicated to the Church abundantly, so that she herself and *each one of her members* may become, day by day, more like our Redeemer. " Thus the Holy Spirit exercises His influence not only in the Body of the Church, but also in each soul in which He dwells as the " sweet Guest. " He is in us : to take possession of our souls, to sanctify them, to form them in the likeness of Christ, and to urge us to continue His redemptive mission; He is that impulse of love which urges us to do God's will, guides us towards the glorification of the Most Holy Trinity, and brings us to God.

But if the Holy Spirit is an impulse of love that comes into us to sanctify us and bring us to God, why do we not all become saints? The mystery of human responsibility enters here. The Holy Spirit, with the Father and the Son, has created us free beings and He wishes us so; therefore, in coming to us, He respects our liberty and does no violence to it. Although He is eager to enter our souls and to possses it, He will not act thus unless we give Him free access. It is an example of the great principle on which St. Teresa of Jesus liked to insist : " God does not force anyone, He takes what we give Him; but He does not give Himself wholly to us, until we give ourselves wholly to Him " (*Way*, 28). If we do not become saints, it is not because the Holy Spirit does not will it—He was sent to us and comes to us for this very purpose—but it is because we do not give full liberty to His action. This is the point in which we fail : we do not use our liberty to wholly yield our soul to His powerful, loving invasion. If our will would open the doors wide, the Holy Spirit would take us under His direction, and, with His help, we would become saints.

COLLOQUY

"O Holy Spirit, You formed our Redeemer in the pure womb of the Virgin Mary; You gave life to Jesus, and directed Him in all He thought, said, did, and suffered during His earthly life, and in the sacrifice He Himself offered to the Father for us on the Cross. When Jesus ascended into heaven, You came upon earth to establish the Mystical Body of Christ, the Church, and to apply to this Body the fruits of the life, Blood, Passion, and death of Christ. Otherwise, Jesus would have suffered and died in vain. Furthermore, O Holy Spirit, You descended to us at holy baptism to form Jesus Christ in our souls, to incorporate us into Him, to give us birth and life in Him, to apply to us the effects and merits of His Blood and of His death, to animate and inspire us, and to guide and direct us in all that we should think, say, do, and suffer for God. What, then, should our life be? Oh! it should be completely holy, divine, and spiritual, according to the words of Jesus : ' that which is born of the Spirit is spirit! '

"O Divine Spirit, I give myself entirely to You. Take possession of my soul, direct me in everything, and grant that I may live as a true child of God, as a true member of Jesus Christ; grant that, born of You, I may totally belong to You, be totally possessed, animated, and directed by You" (St. John Eudes).

"O Holy Spirit, Soul of my soul, I adore You. Enlighten me, guide me, fortify me, console me. Tell me what I should do, give me Your orders. I promise to be submissive to all that You ask of me and to accept everything that You permit to happen to me" (Cardinal Mercier).

189

THE DESCENT OF THE HOLY SPIRIT

PENTECOST SUNDAY

PRESENCE OF GOD - Come, Holy Spirit, fill my heart and enkindle in it the fire of Your Love.

MEDITATION

1. Pentecost is the plenitude of God's gift to men. On Christmas Day, God gives us His only-begotten Son, Christ Jesus, the Mediator, the Bridge connecting humanity and divinity. During Holy Week, Jesus, by His Passion, gives Himself entirely for us, even to death on the Cross. He bathes us, purifying and sanctifying us in His Blood. At Easter, Christ rises, and His Resurrection, as well as His Ascension, is the pledge of our own glorification. He goes before us to His Father's house to prepare a place for us, for in Him and with Him, we have become a part of the divine Family; we have become children of God, destined for eternal beatitude. But the gift of God to men does not end there; having ascended into heaven, Jesus, in union with the Father, sends us His Spirit, the Holy Spirit. The Father and the Holy Spirit loved us to the point of giving us the Word in the Incarnation; the Father and the Word so loved us as to give us the Holy Spirit. Thus the three Persons of the Trinity give Themselves to man, stooping to this poor nothing to redeem him from sin, to sanctify him, and to bring him into Their own intimacy. Such is the excessive charity with which God has loved us; and the divine gift to our souls reaches its culminating point in the gift of the Holy Spirit, who is the Gift par excellence : *Altissimi Donum Dei*, Gift of the Most High God. The Holy Spirit, the bond and pledge of the mutual love of the Father and the Son, He who accepts, seals, and crowns their reciprocal gift, is given to our souls through the infinite merits of Jesus, so that He will be able to complete the work of our sanctification. By His descent upon the Apostles under the form of tongues of fire, the Holy Spirit shows us how He, the Spirit of love, is given to us in order to transform us by His charity, and having transformed us, to lead us back to God.

2. The gift of the Holy Spirit is not a temporary gift, but a permanent one; in fact, for a soul who lives in charity, He is the sweet Guest who dwells within it. " If anyone love Me, " says Jesus in the words of today's Gospel (*Jn* 14,23-31), " ...We will come to him and will make Our abode with him. " However, this indwelling of the Trinity—and hence of the Holy Spirit—in the soul which is in the state of grace, is a gift which can and should increase; it is a continual giving. The first donation was made when we were baptized; it was renewed later, *confirmed*, in a special way, by the Sacrament of *Confirmation*, the Sacrament that is, so to speak, the Pentecost of every Christian soul. Progressive renewals of this gift were made with every increase in charity. And what of the present? The Holy Spirit, in union with the Father and the Son, continues to give Himself to the soul more completely,`more profoundly and possessively. Today's Gospel speaks very forcefully about charity, which is at the same time both the condition for and the result of the indwelling of the Holy Spirit in our souls. It is the condition, because, according to Jesus Himself, the three divine Persons dwell only in a soul who loves; it is the result, because " the charity of God is poured forth in our hearts by the Holy Ghost, who is given to us " (*Rom* 5,5). Divine love completely preceded us at baptism; without merit on our part and solely through the merits of Jesus, the Holy Spirit was given to us, and His charity was gratuitously diffused in us. Thereafter, each time we corresponded to the divine invitations, by making generous acts of charity, He renewed His invisible visit to our soul, giving us always new grace and charity. Thus our supernatural life has developed under the action of the Holy Spirit; it is caught up in the life-giving transforming current of His love. In this way we understand how the Feast of Pentecost can and should represent a new out-pouring of the Holy Spirit in our souls, a new visit in which He fills us with His gifts :

Veni, Creator Spiritus — mentes tuorum visita,
Imple superna gratia — quae tu creasti pectora.

Come, Holy Ghost, Creator blest,
And in our hearts take up Thy rest,
Come with Thy grace and heavenly aid,
To fill the hearts which Thou hast made.

COLLOQUY

" O Holy Spirit, substantial Love of the Father and the Son, uncreated Love dwelling in the souls of the just, come down upon me like a new Pentecost and bring me an abundance of Your gifts, of Your fruits, and of Your grace; unite Yourself to me as the most sweet Spouse of my soul.

" I consecrate myself entirely to You; invade me, take me, possess me wholly. Be the penetrating light which illumines my intellect, the gentle motion which attracts and directs my will, the supernatural energy which gives energy to my body. Complete in me Your work of sanctification and love. Make me pure, transparent, simple, true, free, peaceful, gentle, calm, serene even in suffering, and burning with charity toward God and my neighbor.

" *Accendat in nobis ignem sui amoris et flammam aeternae caritatis*, kindle in me the fire of Your love and the flame of eternal charity. Multiply in me these holy transports of love which will bring me rapidly to transforming union.

" Make not only my will, but all my senses and faculties completely submissive to Your divine will, so that I shall no longer be ruled by my pride, but solely by Your divine impulse. Then everything in me will be moved by love, in love, in such a way that when I work, I shall work through love, and when I suffer, I shall bear everything through love. Grant that the supernatural may become the ' natural ' atmosphere in which my soul moves.

" Make me docile and prompt to follow Your inspirations. Grant that I may never neglect even one, but may always be Your faithful little spouse. Make me ever more recollected, more silent, and more submissive to Your divine action, more alert to receive Your delicate touches. Draw me into the inmost depths of my heart where You dwell, O sweet, divine Guest, and teach me to ' watch continually in prayer. '

" Come, O life-giving Spirit, to this poor world and renew the face of the earth; preside over new organizations and give us Your peace, that peace which the world cannot give. Help Your Church, give her holy priests and fervent apostles. Fill with holy inspirations the souls of the good; give calm compunction to sinful souls, consoling refreshment to the suffering, strength and help to those who are tempted, and light to those in darkness and in the shadow of death " (Sr. Carmela of the Holy Spirit, O.C.D.).

190

THE ACTION OF THE HOLY SPIRIT

PRESENCE OF GOD - O Holy Spirit, make me realize Your action in my soul; teach me to recognize it and correspond with it.

MEDITATION

1. Just as the Holy Spirit dwelt in the most holy soul of Christ in order to bring it to God, so He abides in our souls for the same purpose. In Jesus He found a completely docile will, one that He could control perfectly, whereas in su He often meets resistance, the fruit of human weakness; therefore, He desists from the work of our sanctification because He will not do violence to our liberty. He, the Spirit of *love*, waits for us to cooperate *lovingly* in His work, yielding our soul to His sanctifying action freely and ardently. In order to become saints, we must concur in the work of the Holy Spirit; but since effective concurrence is impossible without an understanding of the promoter's actions, it is necessary for us to learn how the divine Paraclete, the promoter of our sanctification, works in us.

We must realize that the Holy Spirit is ever active in our souls, from the earliest stages of the spiritual life and even from its very beginning, although at that time in a more hidden and imperceptible way. However, His very precious action was there, and it consisted especially in the preparing and encouraging of our first attempts to acquire perfection. By giving us grace, without which we could have done nothing to attain sanctity, the Holy Spirit inaugurated His work in us : He elevated us to the supernatural state. Grace comes from God; it is a gift from all three Persons of the Blessed Trinity : a gift created by the Father, merited by the Son in consequence of His Incarnation, Passion, and death, and diffused in our souls by the Holy Spirit. But it is to the latter, to the Spirit of love, that the work of our sanctification is attributed in a very special manner. When we were baptized, we were justified " in the name of the Father and of the Son and of the Holy Spirit"; nevertheless, Sacred Scripture particularly attributes this work of regeneration and divine filiation to the Holy Spirit. Jesus Himself pointed out to us that Baptism is a rebirth " of...the Holy Spirit " (*Jn* 3,5), and St. Paul stated : " For in one Spirit were we all baptized " and " the Spirit Himself giveth testimony to our spirit, that we are the sons of God " (1 *Cor* 12,13 – *Rom* 8,16). Therefore, it is the Holy Spirit who has prepared and disposed our souls for the supernatural life by pouring forth grace in us.

2. Besides this, in order to enable us to perform supernatural acts, the Holy Spirit comes to strengthen our powers—the intellect and the will—by the infused virtues : charity, together with the other theological virtues of faith and hope, and the moral virtues. Thus, through His intervention, we become capable of performing supernatural acts. But the Holy Spirit does not stop there; like a good teacher, He continues to help us in our work, urging us to do good and sustaining our efforts. He invites us by His interior inspirations, as well as by exterior means, especially Sacred Scripture and the teachings of the Church. Sacred Scripture is the word of God, written by men under the inspiration of the Holy Spirit. It is the divine Paraclete who speaks to us therein, enlightening our intellects with His light and spurring our wills by His motions; hence, meditation on the sacred texts is somewhat like " attending the school " of the Holy Spirit. Furthermore, the Holy Spirit continually teaches us and stimulates us to do good by the living word of the Church, since all those in the Church who have the mission to teach are under His influence when they expound sacred doctrine to the faithful. If we listen to the inspirations of the divine Paraclete, and accept His invitations, He unites Himself to us, aiding us by actual graces, so that we are able to perform virtuous acts. It is clear, therefore, that even when the spiritual life is in its first stages, and is concentrated on the correcting of faults and acquiring of virtues, the activity of the soul is entirely permeated and sustained by the action of the Holy Spirit. We give too little attention to this truth and therefore, in practice, we tend to ignore the constant work of the divine Spirit in our souls. Let us give thought to this, lest His inspirations and impulses go unheeded. " By the grace of God, I am what I am, " said St. Paul, and he could add : " His grace in me hath not been void " (1 *Cor* 15,10).

COLLOQUY

" O Holy Spirit, divine Guest of our souls, You are the noblest and most worthy of all guests! With the agility of Your goodness and love for us, You fly rapidly to all souls who are disposed to receive You. And who can tell the wonderful effects produced by You when You are welcomed? You speak, but without noise of words, and Your sublime silence is heard everywhere. You are always motionless, yet always in movement, and in Your mobile immobility, You communicate Yourself to all. You are always at rest, yet ever working; and in Your rest You perform the greatest, worthiest, and most admirable works. You are always moving, but You never change Your place. You penetrate, strengthen, and preserve all. Your immense, penetrating omniscience knows all, understands all, penetrates all. Without listening to anything, You hear the least word spoken in the most secret recesses of hearts.

" O Holy Spirit, You stay everywhere unless You are driven out, because You communicate Yourself to everyone, except to sinners who do not want to rise from the mire of their sins; in them You can find no place to rest, nor can You endure the evil emanating from a heart which obstinately persists in wrong-doing. But You remain in the creatures who, by their purity, make themselves receptive to Your gifts. And You rest in me by communication, operation, wisdom, power, liberality, benignity, charity, love, purity; in short, by Your very goodness. Diffusing these graces in Your creature, You Yourself prepare him suitably to receive You " (St. Mary Magdalen dei Pazzi).

191

THE INITIATIVES OF THE HOLY SPIRIT

PRESENCE OF GOD - O Holy Spirit, come and direct my soul in the way of sanctity.

MEDITATION

1. Although our soul is supernaturalized by sanctifying grace, our powers strengthened by the infused virtues, and our actions preceded and accompanied by actual grace, still the manner of our acting always remains human, and is therefore incapable of uniting us perfectly with God, of bringing us to sanctity.   In fact, our intellects, although invested with the virtue of faith, are always inadequate in regard to infinite Being, and are always incapable of knowing God as He really is.   Even following the truths of revelation, which tell us that God is One and Three, the ideas which we form about the Most Holy Trinity, the three divine Persons, and the perfections of God, always remain far short of the reality.   As long as we are on earth, we shall know God " through a glass in a dark manner "; only in heaven shall we see Him " face to face " (1 *Cor* 13,12).   The inadequacy of our knowledge of God extends equally to our ideas of sanctity; the same short-sightedness that characterizes our view of divine things affects our notions of the way of perfection.   In many cases we cannot even discern what is more perfect, and despite our good will, we often make mistakes, believing some things to be good and holy which really are not.

However, complete union with God, which is sanctity, requires a perfect orientation toward Him, according to the first and greatest commandment of Jesus : " Thou shalt love the Lord thy God with thy whole heart, and with thy whole soul, and with thy whole mind " (*Mt* 22,37); we have seen that this perfect orientation exceeds our powers, precisely because our knowledge of God and of the way which leads to Him is far too imperfect.   Must we then renounce sanctity? Not at all!   God, who wants our sanctification, has provided us with the means of attaining it : He has given us the Holy

Spirit. Jesus said : " You shall receive the power of the Holy Ghost coming upon you " (*Acts* 1,8).

2. The Holy Spirit, who " searcheth...the deep things of God " (1 *Cor* 2,10), has a perfect knowledge of the divine nature and mysteries; He who penetrates all things and knows perfectly the delicacy and secrets of the highest virtue, as well as the needs and deficiencies of our souls, comes to take us by the hand and lead us to sanctity. As long as we advance by our own initiative, our orientation toward God will always be imperfect and incomplete, because we shall be acting in a *human manner*, but when the divine Spirit intervenes, He operates as God, in a *divine manner;* that is why He draws us and directs us completely toward Himself. In human actions, thought precedes the determination of the will, and since our capacity for thought is so limited, our actions are, of necessity, limited too. This is especially true in regard to divine things. But when the Holy Spirit intervenes, He acts directly on the will by drawing it to Himself. He inflames our heart and enlightens our mind. This is the genesis of that " sense of God " which is impossible for us to express, but which makes us know God and taste Him; it directs us toward Him, more than any reasoning on our part could ever do. Then we feel that God is " the only One, " that all creatures are infinitely distant from Him, that He is worthy of all our love—which is nothing compared with His infinite, divine lovableness; we feel that any sacrifice, even the greatest, is but a trifle when made for such a God. This is how the Holy Spirit guides us on the road to sanctity. At the same time, He helps us to overcome actual difficulties. For example, we very often find ourselves struggling against a fault which we seem unable to overcome, or trying unsuccessfully to acquire a certain virtue, or endeavoring to solve some problem; but at a certain point, without our knowing how, things change : our former doubt is resolved and we are able to accomplish with ease what at first seemed impossible. This, too, is the result of the action of the Holy Spirit in our soul; it explains why His initiatives are so precious for us, and why we should desire Him and invoke Him with so much confidence.

COLLOQUY

" O Love of the eternal God, sacred communication between the omnipotent Father and His blessed Son, all-powerful Paraclete, most merciful Consoler of the afflicted, penetrate the innermost depths of my heart with Your powerful virtue; brighten with Your shining light any dark corners of that neglected dwelling of my soul. Visit it, fructifying with the abundance of Your dew, all that a long period of drought has dried up and choked. Pierce with the dart of Your love, the depths of my soul; penetrate the very center of my enervated heart and inflame it with Your salutary fire; strengthen Your creature by illumining, with the light of Your holy fervor, the inmost depths of my mind and heart.

" I believe that each time You come into a soul, You prepare there a dwelling for the Father and the Son. Blessed is he who is worthy to have You as Guest! Through You, the Father and the Son establish their dwelling in him. Come then, most benign Consoler of suffering souls, Protector in all circumstances and Support in tribulations. Come, Purifier of faults, Healer of the wounded. Come, Strength of the weak, Restorer of those who fall! Come, Master of the humble, rejecter of the proud! Come, O charitable Father of orphans, merciful Judge of widows! Come, hope of the poor, strength of the weak! Come, guiding star of sailors, harbor of the shipwrecked! Come, O unique beauty of all the living, and only salvation of the dying!

" Come, O Holy Spirit, come and take pity on me! Clothe me with Yourself, and graciously hear my prayers, that, according to the multitude of Your mercies, my littleness may be pleasing to Your greatness, and my weakness to Your strength, through Jesus Christ, my Savior, who, with the Father, lives and reigns in unity with You, forever and ever. Amen " (St. Augustine).

192

OUR COOPERATION

PRESENCE OF GOD - O Holy Spirit, make me docile to Your action and always willing to be guided and directed by You.

MEDITATION

1. In what concerns sanctity, we are always like school children, apprentices who, having only a rudimentary knowledge of the art they are learning, are always in need of direction and suggestions from their teacher. Our Teacher of sanctity is none other than the Holy Spirit; Jesus, speaking of Him, said, " He will teach you all things, and bring...to your mind, whatsoever I shall have said to you " (*Jn* 14,26). He teaches us what we must do in order to love God with all our strength; He teaches us all that we do not know, whether about God, or about the spiritual life; and to perfect His teaching, He guides us in the accomplishment of it. Actually, by directly influencing our wills, He strengthens them, attracts them, impels them forcefully to God, orientating them perfectly toward Him. In this way the Holy Spirit " helpeth our infirmity " (*Rom* 8,26), which being *constitutional*—inherent in our human nature—causes us to be continually in need of Him. In truth, He never leaves us : our whole spiritual life is enveloped in His action. We have seen how, from the very beginning, He comes to help us by preparing and encouraging our own personal initiatives; but then, if He finds us docile to His invitations, He Himself takes the initiative. That is why the whole work of our sanctification may be reduced to a question of docility to the divine Paraclete. Before all else, we must be very attentive and docile to His invitations : " *Utinam hodie vocem ejus audiatis; nolite obdurare corda vestra,* " Oh, today, if you shall hear His voice, harden not your hearts! (*Ps* 94,8). The promptings of the Holy Spirit can come to us in the words of Sacred Scripture, preaching, the teachings of the Church, the various circumstances of life, good thoughts and holy inspirations. Let us cooperate with them at once, proving our good will by our ready acceptance of and obedience to them.

2. But very often, alas! our will still remains hard, stubborn, and intractable because it is so attached to creatures, especially to that one creature, the " ego, " which we blindly cherish. Hence, to cooperate with the action of the Holy Spirit, the first requirement is the painstaking effort to detach ourselves from everything, especially from ourselves. Detachment will free us from numerous bonds which, like cords, tie us to creatures, making our docility and submissiveness to the Holy Spirit an impossibility. Let us be mindful of the fact that a fine thread, that is, any little attachment, is sufficient to bind our souls to creatures. " It comes to the same thing whether a bird be held by a slender cord or a stout one; since, even if it be slender, the bird will be as well held as though it were stout, for so long as it breaks it not it cannot fly away " (J.C. *AS I*, 11,4). Detachment breaks the thread which fastens us to earth, and our soul, thus freed, can follow every slightest impulse of the Holy Spirit, who will then take possession of it and direct it according to His good pleasure.

We have said that the Paraclete is not content simply to invite us to what is good, but He wishes to take the initiative, impelling us more effectually toward God. However, He respects our liberty, and will not make Himself Master of our will unless we are disposed to give it to Him freely. And here we can set up another obstacle to His action : the Holy Spirit would like to elevate us and bring us to God, but we do not accept His initiative and our lack of generosity retards the divine work. Perhaps we cooperate partially, giving Him something of what He asks, but we do not give Him " all. " We must, therefore, cultivate the spirit of " totality " which puts no limits to our giving. We must have a magnanimous heart and not retard the work of the Holy Spirit, who wills to bring us, not only, to good actions but to generous, heroic, saintly ones.

COLLOQUY

" O merciful God, my sweetness and my love, send Your Holy Spirit from paradise and create in me a new heart and spirit. Your unction teaches me everything, because I have chosen You among thousands and I love You above all else, more than my own soul. O Holy Spirit, God of love, receive me into Your sweet, merciful charity, so that, during the whole course of my life, I may have You as Master, Teacher, and sweet Lover of my heart " (St. Gertrude).

"O Holy Spirit, teach me to value even Your slightest inspiration. The smallest, were it only to refrain from a word or a glance, is more precious in fact than the entire world, for it is a call, an invitation to enter more deeply into divine intimacy. By faithfully corresponding to it, I grow in grace and love. O Holy Spirit, make me understand well that perfection consists in saying " Amen " every time You ask anything of me through the voice of obedience or by Your inspirations. Help me to avoid every slight infidelity or hesitation, to refuse You nothing; then Your light will grow in me continually and love will become an unfathomable abyss. But, O Holy Spirit, I know very well that I shall often fall, and that I shall commit faults; O my God, let them not be voluntary! However, You teach me that, even in this event, I must rise at once and, by an act of love, place myself under Your influence again. You do not want me to be troubled or discouraged by my infidelities, for Your Spirit is all sweetness. 'Oh! how sweet is Your Spirit, O Lord!' and 'where the Spirit of the Lord is, there also is liberty, ' joy, and peace in the Holy Spirit " (cf. Sr. Carmela of the Holy Spirit, O.C.D.).

193

CONFORMITY WITH CHRIST THROUGH THE ACTION OF THE HOLY SPIRIT

PRESENCE OF GOD - O Holy Spirit, make me conformable to Jesus, make me an " *alter Christus,* " another Christ.

MEDITATION

1. The Holy Spirit is given to us to sanctify us, but how will He accomplish His mission? The Encyclical *Mystici Corporis* tells us that the divine Paraclete " is communicated to the Church...so that she and each of her members may

become daily more and more like to our Savior. " The Holy
Spirit comes into our souls to make us conformable, and even
assimilated to Christ : this is the immediate end of His action
in us, this is the way by which He will lead us to sanctity.

All the elect are predestined by God " to be made
conformable to the image of His Son " (*Rom* 8,29) : we shall
be saints according to the degree of our resemblance to Christ.
The Holy Spirit has been given to us that He may imprint
in us the traits of this divine resemblance, and make us
" daily more and more like to our Savior. " Oh! how
necessary it is that no day should ever pass without some
increase in this likeness! Sister Elizabeth of the Trinity,
profoundly impressed by this truth, used to pray to the Holy
Spirit to make of her " an added humanity wherein He may
renew all His mystery " (E.T. *III*). If Jesus is the model
to whom we should all be conformed, there is no presumption
in aspiring to become so like Him that our life may be a
" prolongation " of His, and that He may continue in us His
work of unceasing adoration and glorification of the Father,
as well as that of the redemption of mankind.

Of ourselves, we are unable to reach such perfect
conformity with Christ, but the divine Spirit is in us to bring
it about. Christ is the *Holy One* par excellence. In order
to make us like Him, the Holy Spirit initially communicates
to us Christ's sanctity by pouring grace into us; this grace
penetrates our being, our activity, and our life in such a way
that it makes of each one of us an *alter Christus*, another Christ.
Let it be noted that the grace given to us by the Holy Spirit
is identical in its nature with the grace that sanctifies the soul
of Jesus : although it is given us in an infinitely lesser degree—
Christ possessing it " without limit "—it is the same seed, the
same principle of sanctity. This is why the full development
of grace can really bring us to identification with Christ, to
becoming other images of Him. To the degree of our
transformation in Him corresponds the degree of our participation in His sanctity and also in His work. Christ will
renew His mystery in us : in us He will continue to glorify the
Most Holy Trinity and to save souls.

2. The norm of life for Jesus was His Father's will, and
we have seen how the Holy Spirit guided Him continually
in the accomplishment of that will. In the same way, the
Holy Spirit wishes always to guide us further along the way

traced out by the will of God. Practically speaking, " sanctity consists in conformity to the divine will " (Benedict XV), in a conformity so complete that, as St. John of the Cross teaches : " there may be naught in the soul that is contrary to the will of God, but that, in all and through all, its movement may be that of the will of God alone " (*AS I*, 11,2). It is not easy to reach this point, and we shall never be able to do so without the help of the Holy Spirit. Furthermore, we must not forget that conformity to the divine will finds its expression in a " continual, exact fulfillment of the duties of one's state in life " (Benedict XV). Now, to be always faithful to duty, in all things and everywhere, is no small matter. It requires continual sacrifice, generosity, and constancy. Let us look at Jesus on the Cross, and we shall understand what the perfect accomplishment of our duty and God's will can exact. This is the way we must follow, constantly renewing our efforts and realizing, at the same time, that however much good will we may have, we are so weak, so inconstant, so deeply attached to ourselves, and so limited in our strength, that we will not always succeed in keeping ourselves to the perfect fulfillment of our duties; we often fall, and do not even know how to rise. Let us humble ourselves then, and make use of these falls to realize better our impotence and frailty : humility, yes; discouragement, never! Instead of weeping over ourselves, let us turn our eyes toward the Holy Spirit, call upon Him to come to our aid, and begin again humbly and confidently. When the Holy Spirit sees us renewing our efforts, He will come to meet us, take us by the hand, and in an instant will lead us to a degree of perfection which we have not been able to reach even after years of effort. We can be sure of this, for Jesus merited it for us, and sends us His Spirit " in a most copious outpouring. "

COLLOQUY

" My beloved Jesus, I desire to follow with You the rule of love, the rule of the will of God, by which I can renew and spend my whole life in You. Place it in the care of Your Holy Spirit, so that at all times I shall be most prompt to keep Your commandments and fulfill all my duties. I am only a poor twig, planted by You. Of myself, I am nothing, and less than nothing, but You can make me flourish in the abundance of Your Spirit. What am I, O my God, life of my soul? Ah! how far away from You I am! I am like a speck of dust, raised and blown away by the wind. Oh! by virtue of Your charity, by the breath of the Holy Spirit, and at the pleasure of Your Providence, may the violent wind of Your omnipotent love cast me into You with such force that I may really begin to die to myself in order to live solely in You, my sweet love. Make me lose myself in You, abandoning myself so completely that no trace of self will remain in me, just as an invisible speck of dust disappears without being noticed. Transform me wholly in the tenderness of Your love, that, in You, all my imperfection will be reduced to nothingness and I shall have no life outside of You" (St. Gertrude).

"O consuming Fire, Spirit of Love! Come down into me and reproduce in me, as it were, an incarnation of the Word; that I may be to Him an added humanity, wherein He may renew all His mystery!" (E.T. *III*).

194

THE WAY OF THE CROSS

PRESENCE OF GOD - O Holy Spirit, teach me the value of suffering, so that I may esteem it and love it as a means of sanctification.

MEDITATION

1. We must be thoroughly convinced that if the Holy Spirit works in our souls to assimilate us to Christ, He can do so only by opening to us the way of the Cross. Jesus is Jesus Crucified; therefore, there can be no conformity to Him except by the Cross, and we shall never enter into the depths of the spiritual life except by entering into the mystery of the Cross. St. Teresa of Jesus teaches that even the highest contemplative graces are given to souls only in order to

enable them to carry the Cross. "His Majesty," says the Saint, "can do nothing greater for us than to grant us a life which is an imitation of that lived by His beloved Son. I feel certain, therefore, that these favors are given to us to strengthen our weakness, so that *we may be able to imitate Him in His great sufferings*" (*Int C VII*, 4). Yes, conformity to Jesus Crucified has more value and importance than all mystical graces! The whole spiritual life is dominated by the Cross and, as the Cross is the central point in the history of the world, so it is the central point in the history of every soul. The Cross gave us life; it will imprint upon our souls the traits of the most perfect resemblance to Jesus; the more we share in His Cross, the more shall we resemble Him and cooperate in the work of Redemption.

In order to attain sanctity, it is evident that we need the Cross. To accept God's will always and in every circumstance implies the renouncement of one's own will; it is impossible to be conformed to Jesus in everything, "who in this life had no other pleasure, nor desired any, than to do the will of His Father" (J.C. *AS I*, 13,4), without renouncing one's own selfish pleasures. And all this means : detachment, crosses, sacrifice, self-denial. It means setting out steadfastly on the way indicated by Jesus Himself : "If any man will come after Me, let him deny himself, and take up his cross and follow Me" (*Mt* 16,24). This is the path which the Holy Spirit urges and invites us to follow. Whenever we find ourselves looking for things that are easier, more commodious, or more honorable; whenever we notice that we are satisfying our self-love, our pride, or see that we are attached to our own will, let us remind ourselves that all this is far removed from the inspirations of the Holy Spirit and, what is worse, it is an obstacle to His action in us.

2. By courageously practicing self-denial, we begin the way of conformity to Jesus Crucified; but here, too, our initiatives are disproportionate to the end to be attained; the acts of mortification and self-denial which we make are wholly insufficient to strip us of the old man and clothe us with Christ, with Christ Crucified. That is why the Holy Spirit, after setting us on the road of the Cross by His inspirations—which tend to make us accept, for the love of God, all that is hard and painful to nature—takes it upon Himself to complete our purification. He does this by

sending us trials, both exterior and interior. " We must know, " says St. John of the Cross, " that this divine fire of love. . .is wounding the soul, and destroying and consuming in it the imperfections of its bad habits; this is the operation of the Holy Spirit wherein He prepares it for divine union and the transformation of love in God " (*LF*, 1,19). Therefore, we must not imagine that the Holy Spirit's action will always be consoling—quite the contrary! Suffering is necessary for our purification and, flowing from this, our participation in the redemptive work of Jesus. The farther we advance along the road of the Cross, the more we shall be sanctified and the more fruitful the apostolate we shall exercise in the Church. It is evident then, that in order to sanctify us the Holy Spirit cannot lead us by any way other than that of the Cross. It is for us to second His action, primarily by willingly accepting everything hard and painful that comes to us in our daily life. Often we neglect the Cross of daily trials and prefer one that is far away, and which perhaps, may never be sent to us. We must not seek the Cross in these extraordinary sufferings, seldom, if ever, encountered; we must look for it in the duties, the life, the difficulties, and the sacrifices of each day and each moment. Here we shall find unfathomable treasures, recognizing them by the light of faith, by the aid of the Holy Spirit who urges us to embrace these daily crosses, not merely endure them— to *accept them and offer them* willingly, saying with all our heart : " Yes, I want this, even though it seems to crush me! "

COLLOQUY

" O Spirit of truth, make me know Your Word; teach me to remember all He has said; enlighten me, guide me, make me comformable to Jesus as an ' *alter Christus,* ' another Christ, by giving me His virtues, especially His patience, humility, and obedience; let me take part in His redemptive work by making me understand and love the Cross.

" O Holy Spirit, I come before You like a little green fruit which will ripen in the sun, like a bit of straw which is to be burned, like a drop of dew to be absorbed by the sun, like an ignorant child who must be taught. O Holy Spirit, giving Yourself to little souls, poor and humble, I present myself to You as one of these, and in this disposition I invoke

You : ' *Veni, Sancte Spiritus, sanctifica me!* ' Come, Holy Spirit,
sanctify me! My desire for holiness is so great! Sanctify
me Yourself; make haste to make me holy and a great saint,
without my knowing it, in the self-effacement of my daily
life.

"I wish to cast myself into You, O Holy Spirit, divine
Fire, so that You will complete my purification, destroy my
miserable self-love and transform me wholly into love. It is
for this that I beseech You to *come upon me* and direct me
according to Your good pleasure. ' *Dirige actos nostros in
beneplacito tuo.* ' Direct our actions according to Your good
pleasure.

"O consuming Fire, divine Love in person, inflame me,
burn me, consume me, destroy all self-love in me, transform
me entirely into love, bring me to the ' nothing ' that I may
possess the ' All '; bring me to the summit of the ' mountain '
where dwells only the honor and glory of God, where all is
' peace and joy ' in You, O Holy Spirit! Grant that here
below—through suffering and loving contemplation—I may
arrive at the most intimate union with the Blessed Three,
until I go to contemplate Them in the face-to-face vision of
heaven, in the peace, joy, and security of the ' perpetual
banquet ' " (Sr. Carmela of the Holy Spirit, O.C.D.).

195

THE GIFTS OF THE HOLY SPIRIT

PRESENCE OF GOD - O Holy Spirit, develop Your gifts in me, so that
I may respond generously to Your divine motions.

MEDITATION

1. We have already seen that it is impossible to arrive
at perfect union with God, at sanctity, without the help of
the Holy Spirit. This help is not reserved for privileged
souls; it is offered to every Christian. In fact, each soul
receives at Baptism, together with sanctifying grace, the
infused virtues and the gifts of the Holy Spirit. The infused

virtues are supernatural principles of activity, whereby we are enabled to act virtuously, from a supernatural, rather than from a human point of view; thus we can perform meritorious acts and apply ourselves actively to the acquisition of holiness.   The gifts, on the other hand, are supernatural principles, permanent dispositions with which God has enriched our faculties; they prepare and enable us to receive the help of the Holy Spirit, to recognize His inspirations, and follow them.   St. Thomas compares them to the sails of a boat : just as the ship, by means of its sails, can be driven by the wind, so our souls, by means of the gifts, have the capacity to be moved and directed by the Holy Spirit.   If a mariner sets the sails on his boat, he intends to move it not only by rowing, but also by the force of the wind.   In like manner, when God infuses the gifts of the Holy Spirit into our souls, He wishes them to advance, not alone by an active practice of the virtues, but also by the intervention of the Holy Spirit.   And while the sailor can hoist the sails on his ship but cannot stir up a breath of wind, God, on the contrary, has not only bestowed on us the gifts of the Holy Spirit, but He also has the power to put them into action when and as He wills.   The very fact that God has willed to put the gifts into our spiritual organism, is the most evident proof that He wishes to intervene in the work of our sanctification, and to grant us the help of the Holy Spirit.

2. The Encyclical *Divinum Illud* teaches : " The just man, who is already living the life of grace and acting with the aid of the virtues, needs these seven gifts which are rightly attributed to the Holy Spirit.   By means of them, man becomes both more docile and stronger in following with greater readiness and promptness the divine impulse. "   This " divine impulse " is nothing but the inspiration and motion of the Holy Spirit.   Now man, though by his very nature endowed with the keenest intellect and possessing good will, is incapable of understanding and following this impulse. " The sensual man " says St. Paul " perceiveth not these things that are of the Spirit of God; for it is foolishness to him, and he cannot understand " (1 *Cor* 2,14).   See then, how the gifts of the Holy Spirit have been given us precisely to make us aware of this " *divine impulse* "; without them we could not receive the motions of the Holy Spirit.   This fact should deepen our understanding of the great value of these gifts,

and hence, of the importance of their growth in us in all their plenitude. In fact, the gifts we have received as a seed, at Baptism, are intended, like sanctifying grace and the infused virtues, to grow and develop until we die. It is a very consoling thought that, due to the profound unity of our supernatural organism, grace, the virtues, and the gifts increase simultaneously with and in proportion to the growth of charity. If we want the gifts to be fully developed in our soul, we must practice charity constantly, for with every advance in divine love, there will be a corresponding new development of the gifts. They are the sails of the soul, but these sails can be let down, weighted by our egoism, our self-love and attachment to ourselves and to creatures. Charity, on the contrary, frees them from every impediment and turns them toward the gentle breeze of the Holy Spirit. The more open and full the sails are, the better they will be able to receive the least impulse of the divine Paraclete.

COLLOQUY

" I behold You, O God, Father, Word, and Spirit, and I know You are looking for Your creature with sovereign wisdom and eternal goodness; so that it seems that You have no glory or pleasure except in Your creature who is yet so vile. Your Spirit is the love by which You try to attract him. And his heart which receives this Spirit is like the bush that Moses saw, burning but not consumed. With supreme purity, it burns with the desire that God may never be offended, and it is consumed with the desire that God be honored, although it does not seem to be consumed.

" Come, come, Holy Spirit! Come, union of the Father, contentment of the Word, glory of the angels. O Spirit of Truth, You are the reward of the saints, the refreshment of souls, light in darkness, wealth of the poor, treasure of those who love, abundance of food for the hungry, comfort of pilgrims, and in a word, the One who contains all treasures.

" O Holy Spirit, with everlasting wisdom you gently urge rational creatures who want to receive Your gifts, but You do not take away their liberty. You knock at all hearts, but You knock gently, urging each one to prepare to receive these gifts. Softly singing, You are the source of sweet tears. Rejoicing and lamenting, You strive ardently that everyone may be disposed to receive You. May the intellect admire, the will and memory understand Your immense goodness, O Holy Spirit, in infusing Yourself and all Your gifts into the soul! O Spirit proceeding from the Father and the Word, You infuse Yourself into the soul so gently that it does not understand You, and, not being understood, Your ineffable gift is esteemed by few. Yet besides Your goodness, You infuse into the soul the power of the Father, and the wisdom of the Son. The soul, having thus become powerful and wise, is made fit to bear You within itself as a sweet Guest, cherishing You, that is, behaving in such a way that You take pleasure in it and do not leave it " (St. Mary Magdalen dei Pazzi).

196

FEAST OF THE MOST HOLY TRINITY

FIRST SUNDAY AFTER PENTECOST

PRESENCE OF GOD - " I return thanks to You, O God, one and true Trinity, one sovereign divinity, holy and indivisible unity. *(RB).* "

MEDITATION

1. From Advent until today, the Church has had us consider the magnificent manifestations of God's mercy toward men : the Incarnation, the Redemption, Pentecost. Now she directs our attention to the source of these gifts, the most Holy Trinity, from whom everything proceeds. Spontaneously, there rises to our lips the hymn of gratitude expressed in the Introit of the Mass : " Blessed be the Holy Trinity and undivided Unity; we will give glory to Him, because He has shown His mercy to us " : the mercy of God the Father, " who so loved the world that He gave it His only-begotten Son " (cf. *Jn* 3,16); the mercy of God the Son, who to redeem us became incarnate and died on the Cross; the mercy of the Holy Spirit, who deigned to come down into our hearts to communicate to us the charity of God and to

make us participate in the divine life. The Church has very fittingly included in the Office for today the beautiful antiphon inspired by St. Paul : " *Caritas Pater est, gratia Filius, communicatio Spiritus Sanctus, O beata Trinitas!* "; the Father is charity, the Son is grace and the Holy Spirit is communication : applying this, the charity of the Father and the grace of the Son are communicated to us by the Holy Spirit, who diffuses them in our heart. The marvelous work of the Trinity in our souls could not be better synthesized. Today's Office and Mass form a veritable paean of praise and gratitude to the Blessed Trinity; they are a prolonged *Gloria Patri* and *Te Deum.* These two hymns—one a succinct epitome, and the other a majestic alternation of praises—are truly the hymns for today, intended to awaken in our hearts a deep echo of praise, thanksgiving, and adoration.

2. Today's feast draws us to praise and glorify the three Persons of the Blessed Trinity, not only because of the great mercy They have shown to men, but also and especially in Themselves and for Themselves : first, by reason of Their supreme essence which had no beginning and will never have an end; next, because of Their infinite perfections, Their majesty, essential beauty and goodness. Equally worthy of our adoration is the sublime fruitfulness of life by which the Father continually generates the Word, while from the Father and the Word proceeds the Holy Spirit. The Father is not prior to, or superior to the Word; nor are the Father and the Word prior to or greater than the Holy Spirit. The three divine Persons are all co-eternal and equal among Themselves : the divinity and all the divine perfections and attributes are one and the same in the Father, in the Son, and in the Holy Spirit. What can man say in the presence of such a sublime mystery? What can he understand of it? Nothing! Yet what has been revealed to us is certain, because the Son of God Himself, " who is in the bosom of the Father, He hath declared Him " (*Jn* 1,18). But the mystery is so sublime and it so exceeds our understanding, that we can only bow our heads and adore in silence. " O the depth of the riches of the wisdom and of the knowledge of God! How incomprehensible are His judgments, and how unsearchable His ways! " exclaims St. Paul in today's Epistle (*Rom* 11,33-36). He who, having been " caught up into paradise, " could neither know nor say anything except that

he had " heard secret words which it is not granted to man to utter " (2 *Cor* 12,2-4). In the presence of the unspeakable mystery of the Trinity the highest praise is silence, the silence of the soul that adores, knowing that it is incapable of praising or glorifying the divine Majesty worthily.

COLLOQUY

" O eternal Trinity, You are a deep sea in which the more I seek the more I find, and the more I find, the more I seek to know You. You fill us insatiably, because the soul, before the abyss which You are, is always famished; and hungering for You, O eternal Trinity, it desires to behold truth in Your light. As the thirsty hart pants after the fount of living water, so does my soul long to leave this gloomy body and see You as You are, in truth.

" O unfathomable depth! O Deity eternal! O deep ocean! What more could You give me than to give me Yourself? You are an ever-burning Fire; You consume and are not consumed. By Your fire, You consume every trace of self-love in the soul. You are a Fire which drives away all coldness and illumines minds with its light, and with this light You have made me know Your truth. Truly this light is a sea which feeds the soul until it is all immersed in You, O peaceful Sea, eternal Trinity! The water of this sea is never turbid; it never causes fear, but gives knowledge of the truth. This water is transparent and discloses hidden things; and a living faith gives such abundance of light that the soul almost attains to certitude in what it believes.

" You are the supreme and infinite Good, good above all good; good which is joyful, incomprehensible, inestimable; beauty exceeding all other beauty; wisdom surpassing all wisdom, because You are Wisdom itself. Food of angels, giving Yourself with fire of love to men! You are the garment which covers our nakedness; You feed us, hungry as we are, with Your sweetness, because You are all sweetness with no bitterness. Clothe me, O eternal Trinity, clothe me with Yourself, so that I may pass this mortal life in true obedience and in the light of the most holy faith with which You have inebriated my soul " (St. Catherine of Siena).

197

THE VIRTUES AND THE GIFTS

PRESENCE OF GOD - Teach me, O Holy Spirit, to remain in an attitude of continual attention to Your inspirations, and of perpetual dependence upon Your impulses.

MEDITATION

1. St. Thomas teaches that the gifts of the Holy Spirit are given to us as a help to the virtues : " *dona sunt in adjutorium virtutum.* " This is a very meaningful expression : note that we receive the gifts to *help* the virtues, *not* to substitute for them. If the soul does its best, seriously applying itself to the practice of the virtues, the Holy Spirit, by means of the gifts, will complete the soul's work. To make the gifts operative then, personal activity and application are essential. The whole Catholic tradition places them at the starting point, for " if a soul is seeking God, its Beloved is seeking it much more.... He attracts the soul and causes it to run after Him " (J.C. *LF*, 3,28).

Although the assiduous practice of the virtues will not suffice to bring the soul to God, the manifestation of good will implied by this practice is very necessary. The sailor who is anxious to reach the port does not lazily wait for a favorable wind, but begins at once to row vigorously; similarly, the soul who seeks God, while waiting for Him to attract, it, does not abandon itself to indolence; on the contrary, it searches fervently on its own initiative : making efforts to overcome its faults, to be detached from creatures, to practice the virtues and to apply itself to interior recollection. The Holy Spirit perfects these efforts by activating His gifts. Thus we see how erroneous is the attitude of certain souls who remain too passive in the spiritual life, failing to exert their own initiative to advance in holiness and to meet God. These souls are wasting their time and easily exposing themselves to deception. It is necessary to take up the task vigorously, especially at the beginning of the spiritual life. Only by so doing can one hope to have the aid of the Holy Spirit.

2. Generally, at the outset of the spiritual life, the influence of the gifts, although never wanting, is rather hidden and rare. At this time, the soul's initiative—the active exercise of the virtues and prayer—must naturally predominate. But as the spiritual life develops, according to the measure of charity, the influence of the gifts increases too. If the soul is faithful, this influence gradually becomes stronger and more frequent until the soul's own initiative is eclipsed by it. Thus, under the direction of the Holy Spirit, the soul attains sanctity.

From the foregoing it can readily be seen why, from the very beginning, we must acquire the habit of being both *active* and *passive* in our journey toward God, making efforts, yes, but at the same time trying to be attentive and obedient to the whisperings of the Holy Spirit. In fact, if there are some souls who are too passive, there are others who err on the active side by making everything consist in their plans for spiritual reform, in their good resolutions, and spiritual exercises, as if sanctity depended solely upon their own industry. They depend too much on their own strength and too little on the help of God. Such souls run the risk of misunderstanding the inspirations of the Holy Spirit, of stifling His impulses, and consequently, of getting tired without reaching the goal. Tractability, docility, and surrender are needed : their minds must become more *tractable* in order to recognize the interior inspirations of the Holy Spirit; their wills must become more *docile* that they may carry them out. They need the spirit of *surrender* in order to let themselves be led by paths which are obscure, unknown, and contrary to their own liking. No one can be his own teacher of sanctity; there is only one Teacher, the Holy Spirit. To remain in His school and to be wholly dependent upon Him implies a twofold task : the active striving to correct our faults and to acquire virtue, and the interior attentiveness to His inspirations. Herein lies the true purpose of the gifts. The Lord " wakeneth my ear, that I may hear Him as a master, " says Isaias, " The Lord hath opened my ear, and I do not resist : I have not gone back " (50,4.5). This should be the interior attitude of a soul who wishes to let itself be guided by the Holy Spirit.

COLLOQUY

" O Holy Spirit, God of love, bond of love of the Blessed Trinity, You remain with the children of men and find Your delight in them, in that holy chastity which, under the influence of Your power and attraction, flourishes on earth like the rose among thorns. Holy Spirit! Love! Show me the way that leads to this delightful goal, that path of life that ends in the field made fertile by the divine dew, where hearts burning with thirst may find refreshment. O Love, You alone know this road which leads to life and truth. In You is consummated the wonderful union of the three divine Persons of the Holy Trinity. The most precious gifts are diffused in us by You, O Holy Spirit. From You come the fertile seeds which produce the fruits of life. From You flows the sweet honey of the delights which are found only in God. Through You descend upon us the fertilizing waters of the divine blessings, the precious gifts of the Spirit.

" O Holy Spirit, You are the Font for which I sigh, the desire of my heart. O overflowing ocean, absorb this stray little drop which wishes to leave itself and enter You. You are the only real substance of my heart, and I cling to You with all my might. Oh! what a wonderful union! Truly, this intimacy with You is more precious than life itself; Your perfume is a balm of propitiation and of peace.

" O Holy Spirit of love, You are the most sweet kiss of the Blessed Trinity, uniting the Father and the Son. You are that blessed kiss which royal divinity gave to humanity by means of the Son of God. O sweet embrace, clasp me, a poor little speck of dust; hold me tight in Your embrace, that I may become completly united with God. Let me experience what delights are in You, O living God. O my sweet Love, let me embrace You and unite myself to You! O God of love, You are my dearest possession, and I hope for nothing, want and desire nothing in heaven or on earth but You " (St. Gertrude).

198

THE HOLY SPIRIT AND PRAYER

PRESENCE OF GOD - O Holy Spirit, Spirit of piety, come and pray in me; come to regulate my filial relations with the heavenly Father.

MEDITATION

1. Our relations with God are essentially filial ones, trustful and confident, for we are not strangers, but " domestics of God " (*Eph* 2,19) : we belong to God's family. Our prayer then ought to express the feelings of a happy child who enjoys talking heart to heart with his father, and can throw himself into his father's arms with complete abandon. Unfortunately, we are always poor sinners, and the knowledge of our wretchedness and unfaithfulness may paralyze this filial affection, causing a certain fear to arise in our souls, a fear which, sometimes, spontaneously puts on our lips Peter's cry : " Depart from me, O Lord, for I am a sinful man, " (*Lk* 5,8). This happens especially when the soul is going through dark periods of struggle, temptations, and difficulties, all of which tend to throw it into agitation and confusion, impeding, in spite of its efforts, that confident outpouring of the heart which submerges all its worries in God. Then one day, during prayer, the soul becomes recollected under the influence of a new light which drives away all fear, not a new thought, but an intimate realization of truth never before experienced : God is my Father, I am His child. It is the influence of the gift of piety, set in motion by the Holy Spirit. St. Paul speaking to the first Christians told them : " You have not received the spirit of bondage again in fear; but you have received the spirit of adoption of sons, whereby we cry : Abba, Father. For the Spirit Himself giveth testimony to our spirit, that we are the sons of God " (*Rom* 8,15.16). Hence it is the Holy Spirit who infuses into the soul this strong feeling of filial piety, of full confidence in its heavenly Father; furthermore, He Himself, with unspeakable groanings, whispers within it : " Father! " " God hath sent the Spirit of His Son into your hearts, crying : Abba, Father! " (*Gal* 4,6). Thus the soul feels itself transformed, and its relations with God become filial.

2. Interior prayer is intimate converse of the soul with God. But who will teach man, so coarse and earthly minded, the delicacy required to converse intimately with the King of heaven and earth? There will never be a ritual nor a devout book capable of regulating the intimate relations of friendship between the Creator and His creature. But there is one Master, whose ability is fully proportioned to His aim, and whose instruction is within the reach of every Christian soul.

This Master is the Holy Spirit. " The Spirit also helpeth our infirmity, for we know not what we should pray for as we ought; but the Spirit Himself asketh for us with unspeakable groanings " (*Rom* 8,26). This is a consoling truth for the soul which feels its powerlessness, its inability to treat with God, its need of a prayer which is fully suitable to the sovereign Majesty, the infinite transcendency of the Most High. This is how the Holy Spirit alternates in the soul sentiments of complete confidence and of profound adoration, of loving friendship and of recognition of God's supreme greatness. He repeats within us : " *Pater,* " and also, " *Tu solus Sanctus, Tu solus Dominus, Tu solus Altissimus.* " Thou alone art holy, Thou alone art God, Thou alone art the Most High. Even when we are in a state of aridity, when our heart is cold and our mind in darkness, the Holy Spirit is praying within us, and we can always offer His prayer to God—prayer that is the truest and the most precious, prayer which will most certainly be heard, because the Holy Spirit cannot inspire sentiments and desires contrary to the divine will, but " He asketh for us according to God " (cf. *ibid.* 8,27).

COLLOQUY

" Come, Holy Spirit, send down from heaven a ray of Your light. Come, Father of the poor; come, Dispenser of gifts; come, Light of hearts! O perfect Comforter, sweet Guest of the soul, delicious refreshment. You are rest in toil, shelter from burning heat, consolation in sorrow! O blessed light! Fill with Your light the depths of my heart! Without Your powerful help, nothing in me is good, nothing is without imperfection. Cleanse what is soiled, water what is dry, heal what is wounded. Soften what is hard, warm what is cold, guide him who has gone astray. Give me, who trust in You,

Your seven gifts. Give reward to virtue, save me and bring me to eternal joy " (cf. Sequence of the Holy Spirit).

" Come, Holy Spirit, be my interior Master. Give me a true filial spirit toward our heavenly Father, great confidence in His paternal goodness, total adherence, both active and passive, to His will, and immense gratitude for His graces. Come and advise me in all things, reminding me of all that Jesus said; guide me, take upon Yourself the direction of my whole being, strengthen my weakness, supply for all my deficiencies. Come and fulfill in me my mission of continual prayer, for what would my prayer be worth unless it were inspired and given value by You? ' No man can say : the Lord Jesus, but by the Holy Ghost. ' O Divine Spirit, pray then in me and through me. I ought to think that it is You who are praying and praising God in me, even when weariness or aridity or distractions prevent me from being recollected. I should remain, then, in a humble attitude of prayer, confident that You will draw from me the praise and glory which I do not know how to give, but which I desire to give to my God " (Sr. Carmela of the Holy Spirit, O.C.D.).

199

THE HOLY SPIRIT AND ACTIVITY

PRESENCE OF GOD - O Holy Spirit, inspire my actions, direct my activity.

MEDITATION

1. An interior soul gradually arrives at the point where its whole life—prayer as well as activities—is under the direction of the Holy Spirit. Jesus Himself has told us that He would " teach us *all things* and bring *all* things to our minds " (cf. *Jn* 14,26). Let us first consider the activity which is so closely connected with the spiritual life and which consists in trying to carry out, in the course of the day, the prayerful resolutions made daily and also during our annual retreats, our monthly days of recollection, and our weekly

confessions.   Sometimes we make this an almost exclusively
" moral " work, and not sufficiently a " theological " one;
that is, we try to correct our faults and practice the virtues
with the intention of pleasing God, while remaining, as it
were, aloof from Him.   We labor alone, almost forgetting
that there is Someone within us who cannot only help us,
but can do the work better than we can.   Our activity
resembles that of a sailor who is so busy rowing that he pays
no attention to the direction of the wind, and thus receives
no help from it.   Certainly personal efforts are not to be
neglected, but they should be expended in a more interior
manner, that is, in a *theological* way, depending more upon
God and the action of the Holy Spirit.   Rather than aim
directly at correcting a fault or acquiring a virtue, it would
be much more profitable for us to maintain a continual
dependence on the interior Teacher, and to act only after
listening to His intimate, silent voice.   In short, it is a
question of acting always in conformity with the interior
movement of grace, with the inspirations of the Holy Spirit;
thus we transfer the reins of our interior life from our hands
to His, entrusting it completely to His direction.

2. In our relations with others, in the performance of our
daily duties, in our professional activity, as well as in our
apostolic work, we should let ourselves be guided by the Holy
Spirit.   He should direct all our actions.   In order that He
may do so, we must first of all maintain a continual contact
with Him, even in the midst of activity.   It will help us to
pause for a few moments, from time to time, to strengthen
this contact, or to re-establish it, when excessive activity or
the movements of our passions have interrupted it in one way
or another.   " I do nothing of Myself, " Jesus said, " but as
the Father hath taught Me, these things I speak " (*Jn* 8,28).
This was the norm of the conduct of Jesus, and it should also
be ours : to act with continual dependence on God, who will
suggest to us, through His Spirit, everything we should do.
In this respect, however, it is very necessary to know how to
distinguish the inspirations of the Holy Spirit from the
movements of nature and the suggestions of the evil spirit.
Without this prudent discretion, we may easily expose
ourselves to illusions and errors, taking for divine inspiration
what is, on the contrary, the result of the more or less
unconscious impulses of our defective nature, of our passions.

A practical, easy way to recognize true inspirations of the Holy Spirit is to see if they maintain us, or rather, make us enter ever more fully into the plan of God's will, in accordance with the commands of our superiors, the rules to which we are subject, and the duties of our state in life; or if, on the contrary, they make us leave, or even only sidestep this course. In the latter case, there would be reason to fear, for the Holy Spirit can urge us only to the accomplishment of God's will. Anything contrary to obedience and our duties cannot be inspired by Him. In doubtful cases, we should seek the advice of an enlightened, prudent person and then, if we are really being led by the Holy Spirit, we will follow that person's opinion with docility, even if it is contrary to our own.

The Holy Spirit, said Jesus, " shall abide with you and shall be in you " (*Jn* 14,17); what unpardonable folly it would be to act independently of Him who has been given us to be our guide, our sanctifier!

COLLOQUY

" O Holy Spirit, You are the dispenser of the treasures contained in the Father's bosom; You are the treasurer of the counsels of the Father and the Word. You show us what we should do in order to please the Trinity : You teach us in the intimacy of our hearts by Your inspirations, and exteriorly in our lives by the preaching and advice of Your ministers. The gates of heaven are always open so that grace may come down to us, but we do not open our hearts to receive it. Oh! send down this grace, O eternal Father, send it down, O most pure Word, since You deign to send Your loving Spirit, the Spirit of goodness. O Holy Spirit, how generous You are to us and blessed are they who welcome You! You bring us the Father's power, the ardent love of the Word!" (cf. St. Mary Magdalen dei Pazzi).

" O Lord, show me the path I must follow to reach You, teach me to do Your will, and let Your Spirit guide me on the right path. Create in me, O God, a clean heart, and infuse into me Your Spirit, the Spirit of uprightness and of truth. O my God, let me not depart from Your presence, and take not Your Holy Spirit from me, for without Him I should be deprived of life and grace. Sustain me, O God, by Your magnanimous Spirit, without whom I can do nothing" (cf. *Ps* 142-50).

O Holy Spirit, Spirit of truth, You who speak to souls and instruct them interiorly, make me attentive to Your teaching and docile to Your inspiration.

THE FEAST OF CORPUS CHRISTI

TO

THE NINTH SUNDAY

AFTER PENTECOST

THE HOLY EUCHARIST — THE SACRED HEART OF JESUS —
THE MOST HOLY TRINITY — THE DIVINE
PERFECTIONS — THE THEOLOGICAL
VIRTUES.

200

FEAST OF CORPUS CHRISTI

THURSDAY AFTER THE FEAST OF THE MOST HOLY TRINITY

PRESENCE OF GOD - " The eternal tide flows hid in living bread. That with its heavenly life too be fed... " (J.C. *Poems*).

MEDITATION

1. We have gone, step by step, in the course of the liturgical year, from the consideration of the mysteries of the life of Jesus to the contemplation of the Blessed Trinity, whose feast we celebrated last Sunday. Jesus, our Mediator, our Way, has taken us by the hand and led us to the Trinity; and today it seems as though the three Persons Themselves wish to take us back to Jesus, considered in His Eucharist. " No man cometh to the Father but by Me " (*Jn* 14,6), Jesus said, and He added, " No man can come to Me except the Father...draw him " (*ibid.* 6,44). This is the journey of the Christian soul : from Jesus to the Father, to the Trinity; from the Trinity, from the Father, to Jesus. Jesus brings us to the Father, the Father draws us to Jesus. A Christian cannot do without Christ; He is, in the strictest sense of the word, our *Pontiff*, the great Bridge-builder who has *spanned the abyss* between God and us. At the end of the liturgical cycle in which we commemorate the mysteries of the Savior, the Church, who like a good Mother knows that our spiritual life cannot subsist without Jesus, leads us to Him, really and truly present in the Most Holy Sacrament of the altar. The solemnity of the *Corpus Domini* is not just the simple memorial of an historical event which took place almost two thousand years ago at the Last Supper; rather, it recalls us to the ever-present reality of Jesus always living in our midst. We can say, in truth, that He has not " left us orphans, " but has willed to *remain permanently* with us, in the integrity of His Person in the fullness of His humanity and His divinity. " There is no other nation so great, " the Divine Office enthusiastically sings, " as to have its gods so near as our God is present to us " *(RB)*. In the Eucharist, Jesus is really Emmanuel, God with us.

2. The Eucharist is not only Jesus actually living among us, but it is Jesus become our Food. This is the chief aspect under which today's liturgy presents the mystery to us; there is no part of the Mass which does not treat of it directly, or which does not, at least, make some allusion to it. The Introit refers to it when it mentions the wheat and honey with which God once fed the Hebrews in the desert, a miraculous food, and yet a very poor representation of the living, life-giving Bread of the Eucharist. The Epistle (1 Cor 11, 23-29) speaks of it, recalling the institution of this Sacrament, when Jesus " took bread, and giving thanks, broke, and said, ' Take ye, and eat; this is My Body ' "; the Gradual chants, " The eyes of all hope in You, O Lord, and You give them meat in due season. " The very beautiful Sequence, *Lauda Sion*, celebrates it at length, and the Gospel (*Jn* 6,56-59), echoing the Alleluia, cites the most significant passage in the discourse when Jesus Himself announced the Eucharist. " My Flesh is meat indeed, and My Blood is drink indeed. " The Communion Hymn repeats a sentence of the Epistle, and reminds us that we receive the Body of the Lord worthily. Finally, the Postcommunion tells us that Eucharistic Communion is the pledge of eternal communion, in heaven. But in order to have a better understanding of the immense value of the Eucharist, we must go back to the very words of Jesus, most opportunely recalled in the Gospel of the day, " He that eateth My Flesh and drinketh My Blood, abideth in Me and I in him. " Jesus made Himself our food in order to assimilate us to Himself, to make us live His life, to make us live in Him, as He Himself lives in His Father. The Eucharist is truly the sacrament of union and at the same time it is the clearest and most convincing proof that God calls us and pleads with us to come to intimate union with Himself.

COLLOQUY

" O God, O Creator, O Spirit of life overwhelming Your creatures with ever new graces! You grant to Your chosen ones the gift which is ever renewed : the Body and Blood of Jesus Christ!

" O Jesus, You instituted this Sacrament, not through any desire to draw some advantage from it for Yourself, but solely moved by a love which has no other measure than to be without measure. You instituted this Sacrament because Your love exceeds all words. Burning with love for us, You desired to give Yourself to us and took up Your dwelling in the consecrated Host, entirely and forever, until the end of time. And You did this, not only to give us a memorial of Your death which is our salvation, but You did it also, to remain with us entirely, and forever.

" My soul, if you wish to penetrate the depths of this mystery, your gaze must be illumined by love! You need to see and understand! Contemplate the Last Supper : see Jesus who knows that He will soon be separated from the body of His humanity, and yet wishing to be united to us forever; contemplate the love by which He institutes this Sacrament which permits Him to be corporeally and forever united to mankind. O inextinguishable love! O love of Christ! O love of the human race! What a true furnace of love! O Jesus, You already saw the death which awaited You; the sorrows and atrocious tortures of the Passion were already breaking Your Heart, and yet You offered Yourself to Your executioners, and permitted them, by means of this Sacrament, to possess You forever as an eternal gift, O You, whose delights are to be with the children of men!

" O my soul, how can you refrain from plunging yourself ever deeper and deeper into the love of Christ, who did not forget you in life or in death, but who willed to give Himself wholly to you, and to unite you to Himself forever? " (St. Angela of Foligno).

201

THE REAL PRESENCE

PRESENCE OF GOD - " Hidden God, devoutly I adore Thee, truly present beneath these veils : all my heart subdues itself before Thee, since all before Thee faints and fails " (cf. *Adoro Te Devote*).

MEDITATION

1. " *Verbum caro factum est* " (*Jn* 1,14). The Incarnation of the Word, the ineffable mystery of the merciful love of God,

who so loved man that He became " flesh " for his salvation, is, in a way, prolonged and extended through the ages, and will be until the end of time, by the Eucharist, the Sacrament by means of which the Incarnate Word became Himself our " food. "   God was not content with giving us His only Son once for all, willing Him to take flesh in the womb of a Virgin — flesh like ours, so that He might suffer and die for us on the Cross—but He wished Him to remain with us forever, perpetuating His real presence and His sacrifice in the Eucharist. Aided by the Gospel narrative we can reconstruct and relive in our heart the sweet mysteries of the life of Jesus. Had we nothing but the Gospel, however, we would have only nostalgic memories; Jesus would no longer be with us, but only in heaven at the right hand of the Father, having definitively left the earth on the day of His Ascension.   With what regret we would think of the thirty-three years of our Savior's earthly life passed centuries ago!   Oh, how different the reality!   The Eucharist makes the presence of Jesus with us a permanent one.   In the consecrated Host we find the same Jesus whom Mary brought into the world, whom the shepherds found wrapped in swaddling clothes and lying in a manger; whom Mary and Joseph nurtured and watched over as He grew before their eyes; the Jesus who called the Apostles to follow Him, who captivated and taught the multitudes, who performed the most startling miracles; who said He was the " light " and " life " of the world, who forgave Magdalen and raised Lazarus from the dead; who for love of us sweat blood, received the kiss of a traitor, was made one enormous wound, and died on the Cross; that same Jesus who rose again and appeared to the Apostles and in whose wounds Thomas put his finger; who ascended into heaven, who now is seated in glory at the right hand of His Father, and who, in union with the Father, sends us the Holy Spirit.   O Jesus, You are always with us, " yesterday, and today, and the same forever! " (*Heb* 13,8).   Always the same in eternity by the immutability of Your divine Person; always the same in time, by the Sacrament of the Eucharist.

2. Jesus is present in the Eucharist with all His divinity and all His humanity.   Although His humanity is present " *per modum substantiae*, " that is, in substance and not in corporeal extension, it is whole and entire in the consecrated Host—body and soul, and this latter with its faculties of

intellect and will. Therefore our Eucharistic Lord knows and loves us as God and as Man. He is not a passive object for our adoration but He is *living;* He sees us, listens to us, answers our prayers with His graces. Thus we may have, with the gentle Master of the Gospel, living, concrete relations which, although imperceptible to our senses, are similar to those which His contemporaries had with Him. It is true that in the Eucharist not only His divinity but even His humanity is hidden; however, faith supplies for the senses, it substitutes for what we do not see or touch; " *sola fides suffícit,* " says St. Thomas, faith alone is sufficient *(Pange Lingua)*. As Jesus, disguised as a traveler, once taught the disciples of Emmaus, and inflamed their hearts, so too, Jesus hidden under the Eucharistic veil illumines our souls, inflames them with His love and inclines them ever more effectively toward sanctity.

Jesus is there, in the consecrated Host, true God and true Man; as He became incarnate for us, so for us too, has He hidden Himself under the Sacred Species. There He waits for us, longs for us, is always ready to welcome and listen to us. And we need Him so much! God, pure Spirit, is present everywhere, it is true; and in His Unity and Trinity, He even deigns to dwell within our souls, vivified by grace. Nevertheless, we always have need of contact with Jesus, the Word made Flesh, God made Man, our Mediator, our Savior, our Brother, and we find Him present in the Eucharist. Here on earth we are never closer to Him than when we are in the presence of the Blessed Sacrament of the altar.

COLLOQUY

" O Lord, wealth of the poor, how admirably You can sustain souls, revealing Your great riches to them gradually and not permitting them to see them all at once. When I see Your great Majesty hidden in so small a thing as the Host, I cannot but marvel at Your great wisdom.

" O my God, if You did not conceal Your grandeur, who would dare to come to You so often, to unite with Your ineffable Majesty a soul so stained and miserable? Be forever blessed, O Lord! May the angels and all creatures praise You for having deigned to adapt Your mysteries to our weakness, so that we might enjoy Your treasures without being frightened by Your infinite power.   Otherwise, poor, weak creatures like ourselves would never dare to approach You.

" How would I, a poor sinner, who have so often offended You, dare to approach You, O Lord, if I beheld You in all Your Majesty?   Under the appearances of bread, however, it is easy to approach You, for if a king disguises himself, it seems as if we do not have to talk to him with so much circumspection and ceremony.   If You were not hidden, O Lord, who would dare to approach You with such coldness, so unworthily, and with so many imperfections?

" Besides, I cannot doubt at all about Your real presence in the Eucharist.   You have given me such a lively faith that, when I hear others say they wish they had been living when You were on earth, I laugh to myself, for I know that I possess You as truly in the Blessed Sacrament as people did then, and I wonder what more anyone could possibly want " (T.J. *Life*, 38 – cf. *Way*, 34).

202

THE MYSTERY OF FAITH

PRESENCE OF GOD - O Jesus, I believe that You are present in the Blessed Sacrament of the altar, and I adore You.   Increase my faith.

MEDITATION

1. In the Canon of the Mass, the Eucharist is called " *Mysterium fidei*, " *the Mystery of faith*; indeed, only faith can make us see God present under the appearances of bread. Here, as St. Thomas says, the senses do not help at all—sight, touch, and taste are deceived, finding in the consecrated Host only a little bread.   But what matters?   We have the word of the Son of God; the word of Christ, who declared : " This is My Body... This is My Blood, " and we firmly believe in His word.   " *Credo quidquid dixit Dei Filius, nihil*

hoc verbo Veritatis verius. " I believe everything the Son of God has said; nothing can be truer than this word of Truth *(Adoro Te Devote)*. We firmly believe in the Eucharist, we have no doubts about it; unfortunately, however, we must admit that our faith is often weak and dull. Although we may not live far from a church, although we may perhaps dwell under the same roof with Jesus in the Blessed Sacrament, it is easy to become rather indifferent, or even cold, in the presence of this great reality. Alas, our coarse nature gradually grows accustomed to even the most sublime and beautiful realities, so that they no longer impress us and have no power to move us, especially when they are near at hand. Thus it happens that while we believe in the ineffable presence of Jesus in the Blessed Sacrament, we pay little or no attention to the greatness of this reality, and we fail to have the lively, concrete appreciation of it which the saints had. Let us then repeat, very humbly and confidently, the Apostles' beautiful prayer : " *Domine, adauge nobis fidem,* " Lord, increase our faith! *(Lk* 17,5).

2. When Jesus announced the institution of the Eucharist, many of His hearers were scandalized, and some of His disciples, who had been following Him up to that time " went back and walked no more with Him " *(Jn* 6,67). But Peter, in the name of the Apostles, gave this beautiful testimony of faith : " Lord... Thou hast the words of eternal life. And we have believed and have known, that Thou art the Christ, the Son of God " *(ibid.* 6,69.70). Belief in the Eucharist, therefore, seems to be the touchstone of the true disciples of Jesus, and the more intense this belief, the more it reveals a profound and intimate friendship with Christ. Anyone who like Peter firmly believes in Christ, also believes and accepts all His words, all the mysteries of His life, from the Incarnation to the Eucharist. We know that faith is first of all a gift of God. In the discourse in which He promised the Eucharist—which is, more than any other mystery, a mystery of faith because, more than any other mystery, it transcends every natural law—Jesus repeatedly affirmed the necessity and gratuity of faith, declaring to the incredulous Jews that no one could come to Him, or believe in Him, " except the Father...draw him " *(ibid.* 6,44). He added : " And they shall all be taught of God " *(ibid,* 45). To have a living faith in the Eucharist, as in every

other mystery, we must have that " attraction, " and that " interior instruction " which can come from God alone. Nevertheless, we can and should dispose ourselves, both by asking for this grace in humble, trusting prayer, and by an active practice of faith. In fact, since God infused this theological virtue into us at Baptism, and since faith is a *voluntary* adherence of the intellect to revealed truth, we can make acts of faith whenever we wish : it depends on us to will to believe and to put into this act all the strength of our will. In the measure that our faith increases, it will enable us to penetrate the depths of the Eucharistic mystery, to have vital contact with Jesus in the Host, and to enjoy His presence. The more intense our faith, the more it will appear in our attitude toward the Blessed Sacrament. Then when Jesus looks upon us from the tabernacle, He will never be able to make the sad reproach He several times made to the Apostles : " Ye of little faith! " (*Mt* 8,26), one which so many Christians in our day deserve, because they have so little respect for His divine presence. May our conduct in the presence of the Blessed Sacrament always be a living testimony of our faith.

COLLOQUY

" Praise and thanks to you, O blessed faith! You tell me with certitude that the Blessed Sacrament of the altar, the heavenly Manna, is no longer bread, but my Lord Jesus Christ who is wholly present there for love of me.

" One day, O Jesus, full of love and of goodness, You sat beside the well to await the Samaritan woman, that You might convert and save her. Now, You dwell on our altars, hidden in the consecrated Host, where You wait and sweetly invite souls, to win them to Your love. From the tabernacle you seem to say to us all : ' O men, why do you not come to Me, who love you so much? I am not come to judge you! I have hidden myself in this Sacrament of love only to do good and to console all who have recourse to Me '; I understand, O Lord; love has made You our prisoner; the passionate love You have for us has so bound You that it does not permit You to leave us.

" O Lord, You find Your delight in being with us, but do we find ours in being with You? Especially do we, who have the privilege of dwelling so near Your altar, perhaps even in Your very own house, find our delight in being with You? Oh! how much coldness, indifference, and even insults You have to endure in this Sacrament, while You remain there to help us by Your presence!

" O God, present in the Eucharist, O Bread of Angels, O heavenly Food, I love You; but You are not, nor am I, satisfied with my love. I love You, but I love You too little! Banish from my heart, O Jesus, all earthly affections and give place, or better, give the whole place to Your divine love. To fill me with Yourself, and to unite Yourself entirely to me, You come down from heaven upon the altar every day; justly then, should I think of nothing else but of loving, adoring, and pleasing You. I love You with my whole soul, with all my strength. If You want to make a return for my love, increase it and make it always more ardent! " (St. Alphonsus).

203

THE INVITATION TO THE BANQUET

SECOND SUNDAY AFTER PENTECOST

PRESENCE OF GOD - O Jesus, grant that I may always answer Your invitation and participate worthily in Your banquet.

MEDITATION

1. Today's Gospel (*Lk* 14,16-24) fits in perfectly with the feast of *Corpus Christi*. " A certain man made a great supper, and invited many. " The man who makes the supper is God; the great supper is His kingdom where souls will find full abundance of spiritual blessings while on earth, and eternal happiness in the next life. This is the real meaning of the parable, but we can also interpret it more specifically, seeing in the supper and in the man who prepares it a figure of the Eucharistic banquet and of Jesus, inviting men to partake of His Flesh and Blood. " The table of the Lord is set for us, " sings the Church, " Wisdom [the Incarnate

Word] has prepared the wine and laid the table" *(RB)*. Jesus Himself, when announcing the Eucharist, addressed His invitation to all : " I am the Bread of life! He that cometh to Me shall not hunger, and he that believeth in Me shall never thirst.... Your fathers did eat manna in the desert, and are dead. This is the bread which cometh down from heaven; that if any man eat of it, he may not die " *(Jn* 6,35.49.50). Jesus does not limit Himself, like other men, to preparing the table for a supper, inviting many, and serving delicious food; His is an unheard-of procedure, which no man, however rich and powerful he might be, could ever imitate. Jesus offers Himself as Food. St. John Chrysostom said to those who wanted to see Christ in the Eucharist with their bodily eyes, " Behold, you do see Him; you touch Him, you eat Him. You would like to see His garments; He not only permits you to see Him, but also to eat Him, to touch Him, and to receive Him into your heart.... He whom the angels look upon with fear, and dare not gaze upon steadfastly because of His dazzling splendor, becomes our Food; we are united to Him, and are made one body and one flesh with Christ " *(RB)*.

2. Jesus could not offer men a more precious banquet than the Eucharist. Yet, how do men answer His invitation? Many, like the unbelieving Jews, shrug their shoulders and turn away, with a skeptical smile on their lips : " How can this man give us his flesh to eat? " *(Jn* 6,53). However, it is not want of faith alone that keeps us from the Eucharist. Very often this is accompanied by, or sometimes derived from, the moral disorders which are mentioned in today's Gospel : " I have bought a farm and I must needs go out and see it; I pray thee, hold me excused, " replies one. Another says : " I have bought five yoke of oxen, and I go to try them; I pray thee, hold me excused. " Excessive preoccupation with earthly goods and attachment to them, total absorption in business affairs cause many people to refuse Jesus' invitation. There is still another reason : " I have married a wife, and therefore I cannot come, " replies a third, representing those, who, being immersed in the pleasures of the senses, have lost their taste for the things of the spirit, and go their way, not even asking to be excused.

We cannot help shuddering at the terrible blindness of a man who prefers the things of earth and the vile pleasures of the senses, which vanish as quickly as mist before the sun, to Christ's Gift, the Bread of Angels and the pledge of eternal life. And yet, how easily can a shadow of this blindness cover the eyes and hearts even of those whom Christ has invited to follow Him, and whom He has called by the sweet name of friend. They do not refuse His invitation, but they often accept it coldly, almost through force of habit. Is it not true that we pay very little attention to preparing ourselves each day as worthily as we can for the Eucharistic banquet, while we allow ourselves to be absorbed in so many other things : our work, family and friends? Perhaps Jesus comes to us every morning, but does He always get a warm, delicate, attentive, loving welcome? Alas, too often He finds the hearts of His friends filled with a thousand thoughts, trifles, and worldly affections, while there is so little room for Him, the divine Guest! Yet everything should be reserved for Jesus. The thought of our daily meeting with Jesus in the Eucharist should dominate every other thought!

COLLOQUY

"O Sacrament of mercy! O seal of unity! O bond of charity! He who wishes to live, finds the home and the dwelling where he can live. O Lord, I approach Your table with faith, there to become incorporated in You in order to be vivified by You.

"Grant, O Lord, that I may be inebriated with the riches of Your house, and let me drink from the torrent of Your delights. Since You are the fountain of life, there with You, and not elsewhere, is the source of my life. I will drink of it in order to live; I will not rely upon myself and be lost; I will not be satisfied with what I have and die of thirst; I will approach the source of the spring where the water never fails.

"I will do away with vain excuses and draw near to the banquet which will enrich me interiorly. Let me not become haughty through pride, and do not permit illicit curiosity to draw me away from You! May sensual pleasure never prevent me from enjoying spiritual joy!

"Permit me to approach You and be refreshed. Allow me to come, a beggar, weak, crippled, and blind, for the wealthy and strong scorn Your banquet; they consider themselves on the right path and believe their sight is sure. They are presumptuous, and so much the more incurable the prouder they are. Although a beggar, I come to You because You invite me; You, who being rich became poor for me, so that Your poverty would make me rich. Weak as I am, I shall draw near, for it is not the healthy who need the physician, but the sick. I shall approach you like a cripple and say : ' Set my feet in Your paths. ' I shall come like a blind person and say : ' Give sight to my eyes, that I may never sleep the sleep of death ' " (St. Augustine).

204

MYSTERY OF HOPE

PRESENCE OF GOD - Let me hunger for You, O Bread of Angels, pledge of future glory.

MEDITATION

1. Jesus said : " I am the living bread which came down from heaven. If any man eat of this bread, he shall live forever, and the bread that I will give is My Flesh, for the life of the world. " The Jews disliked this speech; they began to question and dispute the Master's words. But Jesus answered them still more forcefully : " Amen, amen, I say unto you, except you eat the Flesh of the Son of man and drink His Blood, you shall not have life in you " (*Jn* 6,51-54). These are definitive words which leave no room for doubt; if we wish to *live*, we must eat the *Bread of Life*. Jesus came to bring to the world the supernatural life of grace; and this life was given to our souls in Baptism, the Sacrament which grafted us into Christ. Thus it is a gift of His plenitude, but we must nourish it by a deeper penetration into Christ. To enable us to do so, He Himself willed to give us His complete substance as the God-Man, making Himself the Bread of our supernatural life, the Bread of our union with Him. St. John Chrysostom says, " Many mothers entrust the children they have borne to others to nurse them, but

Jesus does not do that. He feeds us with His own Blood and incorporates us into Himself completely. " Baptism is the Sacrament which engrafts us into Christ; the Eucharist is the Sacrament which nourishes Christ's life in us and makes our union with Him always more intimate, or rather, it transforms us into Him. " If into melted wax other wax is poured, it naturally follows that they will be completely mixed with each other; similarly, he who receives the Lord's Flesh and Blood is so united with Him that Christ dwells in him and he in Christ " (St. Cyril of Jerusalem).

2. By nourishing us with Christ's life, the Eucharist nourishes in us a life which has no end. By uniting us to Him who is Life, it frees us from death. In fact, Jesus has said, " He that eateth My Flesh and drinketh My Blood, hath everlasting life, and I will raise him up in the last day " (*Jn* 6,55). Notice that He said, " *hath* everlasting life, " not *will have*, because the Eucharist, by giving us an increase of grace—the seed of glory—becomes the pledge of eternal life for us, life not only for the soul but also for the body. " The sacred Host communicates the seed of future resurrection; Christ's immortal Body plants within us the seed of immortality which will grow and some day bring forth fruit " (Pope Leo XIII : *Mirae Caritatis*). From this point of view, the Eucharist is truly the Sacrament of hope : hope of celestial glory, of the beatific vision, where our " communion " with Christ will have no end. Our eternal " communion " begins here on earth precisely in the Eucharistic communion which is its prelude, pledge, and even, in a slight degree, its foretaste. But the Blessed Sacrament is a source of great hope and confidence in our present life, too, especially in what concerns our spiritual progress; for, by increasing grace in us, it also increases our charity, and with the growth in charity, our passions are subdued. St. Augustine says, " The increase of charity is the decrease of passion, and the perfection of charity is the absence of passion. " If, then, the struggle against a certain fault or temptation sometimes becomes very violent and difficult; if in spite of all our efforts, we do not succeed in overcoming nature, let us have confidence in the Blessed Sacrament. When Jesus comes to us, He can calm any storm and give us strength to win any kind of battle. " The chaste Flesh of Jesus, " says St. Cyril of Alexandria, " checks the insubor-

dination of ours; by dwelling in us, Christ effectively overcomes the law of the flesh which rages in our members. "
The Eucharist, therefore, is our hope both for this life and
for the life to come; it sustains us in adversity, fortifies us in the
struggle for virtue, saves us for eternal life and brings us
to heaven by providing us with the food necessary for our
journey.

COLLOQUY

" O heavenly Father, You gave us Your Son and sent
Him into the world by an act of Your own will. And You,
O my Jesus, did not want to leave the world by Your own
will, but wanted to remain with us for the greater joy of
Your friends. This is why, O heavenly Father, You gave
us this most divine Bread, the manna of the sacred humanity
of Jesus, to be our perpetual food. Now we can have
it whenever we wish, so that if we die of hunger, it will be
our own fault.

" O my soul, you will always find in the Blessed Sacrament, under whatever aspect you consider it, great consolation
and delight, and once you have begun to relish it, there will
be no trials, persecutions, and difficulties which you cannot
easily endure.

" Let him who wills ask for ordinary bread. For my part,
O eternal Father, I ask to be permitted to receive the heavenly
Bread with such dispositions that, if I have not the happiness
of contemplating Jesus with the eyes of my body, I may at
least contemplate Him with the eyes of my soul. This is
Bread which contains all sweetness and delight, and sustains
our life " (T.J. *Way*, 34).

" All graces are contained in You, O Jesus in the Eucharist, our celestial Food! What more can a soul wish when it
has within itself the One who contains everything? If I wish
for charity, then I have within me Him who is perfect charity,
I possess the perfection of charity. The same is true of faith,
hope, purity, patience, humility, and meekness, for You form
all virtues in our soul, O Christ, when You give us the grace
of this Food. What more can I want or desire, if all the
virtues, graces, and gifts for which I long, are found in You,
O Lord, who are as truly present under the sacramental
species as You are in heaven, at the right hand of the Father?

Because I have and possess this great wonder, I do not long for, want, or desire, any other!" (St. Mary Magdalen dei Pazzi).

205

MYSTERY OF LOVE

PRESENCE OF GOD - O Jesus, help me to penetrate the mystery of Your infinite love, which constrained You to become our Food and Drink.

MEDITATION

1. All God's activity for man's benefit is a work of love; it is summed up in the immense mystery of love which causes Him, the sovereign, infinite Good, to raise man to Himself, making him, a creature, share in His divine nature by communicating His own life to him. It was precisely to communicate this life, to unite man to God, that the Word became incarnate. In His Person the divinity was to be united to our humanity in a most complete and perfect way; it was united directly to the most sacred humanity of Jesus, and through it, to the whole human race. By virtue of the Incarnation of the Word and of the grace He merited for us, every man has the right to call Jesus his Brother, to call God his Father and to aspire to union with Him. The way of union with God is thus opened to man. By becoming incarnate and later dying on the Cross, the Son of God not only removed the obstacles to this union, but He also provided all we need to gain it, or rather, He Himself became the *Way*. Through union with Jesus, man is united to God.

It is not surprising that the love of Jesus, surpassing all measure, impelled Him to find a means of uniting Himself to each one of us in the most intimate and personal manner; this He found in the Eucharist. Having become our Food, Jesus makes us one with Him, and thus makes us share most directly in His divine life, in His union with the Father and with the Trinity.

By assuming our flesh in the Incarnation, the Son of God united Himself once and for all with the human race.

In the Eucharist, He continues to unite Himself to each individual who receives Him. Thus we can understand how the Eucharist, according to the mind of the Fathers of the Church, may really be " considered as a continuation and extension of the Incarnation; by it the substance of the Incarnate Word is united to every man " *(Mirae Caritatis)*.

2. The plan of Divine Love, that is, the desire to bring men to God and to communicate the divine nature and life to them, finds its supreme realization in the Blessed Sacrament. In the consecrated Host, we have not only Christ's Body, Blood, and Soul, but also the divinity of the Son of God and, therefore, God Himself. What more potent means could God use to unite us to Himself and to make us share His nature and life? Where could we find a more life-giving food than the Body of Christ, which through its personal union with the Word, is the source of all life and grace? By giving Himself to us, Jesus nourishes us with His substance, assimilates us to Himself, and personally communicates divine life to us. Jesus also gives us grace and thereby communicates the divine nature to us by means of the other Sacraments too; but in them, we have His action only, and that, only during the reception of the Sacrament. For example, when the priest absolves us from our sins, Jesus produces grace in us by His operative power; in the Eucharist, however, it is Jesus Himself who is the Sacrament, coming to us personally in the integrity of His Person, that of the God-Man. When we receive the Sacred Host, we not only receive Christ's *action* in our soul, but we actually possess His *Person*, really and physically present. We are given not only an increase of grace, but Jesus, the very source of grace. We not only enjoy a new participation in divine life, we possess the Incarnate Word, who takes us with Himself to the heart of the Trinity.

Furthermore, whereas *material food* is assimilated by the one who eats it and is changed into that person's body and blood, Jesus, the *Living Bread*, has the power to assimilate and change into Himself those who partake of Him. " Holy Communion, the Body and Blood of Christ, tends to transform us into what we eat, " says St. Leo, and St. John Chrysostom notes : " Christ has united Himself to us and infused His Body into us, that we may be one thing with Him as a body is fitted to its head. Such is the union of those on fire with love " *(RB)*.

COLLOQUY

"O eternal Trinity! O fire and abyss of charity! How could our redemption benefit You? It could not, for You, our God, have no need of us. To whom then comes this benefit? Only to man. O inestimable charity! Even as You, true God and true Man, gave Yourself entirely to us, so also You left Yourself entirely for us, to be our food, so that during our earthly pilgrimage we would not faint with weariness, but would be strengthened by You, our celestial Bread. O man, what has your God left you? He has left you Himself, wholly God and wholly Man, concealed under this whiteness of bread. O fire of love! Was it not enough for You to have created us to Your image and likeness, and to have re-created us in grace through the Blood of Your Son, without giving Yourself wholly to us as our Food, O God, Divine Essence? What impelled You to do this? Your charity alone. It was not enough for You to send Your Word to us for our redemption; neither were You content to give Him to us as our Food, but in the excess of Your love for Your creature, You gave to man the whole divine essence. And not only, O Lord, do You give Yourself to us, but by nourishing us with this divine Food, You make us strong with Your power against the attacks of the demons, insults from creatures, the rebellion of our flesh, and every sorrow and tribulation, from whatever source it may come.

"O Bread of Angels, sovereign, eternal purity, You ask and want such transparency in a soul who receives You in this sweet Sacrament, that if it were possible, the very angels would have to purify themselves in the presence of such an august mystery. How can my soul become purified? In the fire of Your charity, O eternal God, by bathing itself in the Blood of Your only-begotten Son. O wretched soul of mine, how can you approach such a great mystery without sufficient purification? I will take off, then, the loathsome garments of my will and clothe myself, O Lord, with Your eternal will!" (St. Catherine of Siena).

206

THE SACRAMENT OF UNION

PRESENCE OF GOD - O Jesus, You who nourish me with Your Body and Blood, grant that I may live by You, live of Your Life.

MEDITATION

1. In His discourse on the " Bread of Life, " Jesus Himself spoke of the Eucharist as the Sacrament of our union with Him. " He that eateth My Flesh and drinketh My Blood, abideth in Me and I in him " (*Jn* 6,57). It is a true inter-penetration : Christ is in us and we are in Christ. Of course, His life and ours, His person and ours, remain distinct; and yet, He so penetrates us with His life, with His Spirit, with His divinity, that we remain immersed in Him and He in us. St. Hilary affirms that " having received, the Body and Blood of Christ, we are in Christ and Christ is in us.... He Himself is in us by His Flesh and we are in Him, and—O marvelous consequence!—with Him, all that we are is in God. " We are never so close to Jesus, so penetrated by Him, transformed, deified, and plunged into the divinity as at the moment of sacramental Communion : " with Him, all that we are is in God. "

By faith and grace we are united to Christ and are in Him as His members, but this union which began at Baptism, is increased each time we receive the Eucharist worthily. By this Sacrament, Jesus " desired even to make Himself one with us; so that not by faith only but in every deed He makes us His own Body " (St. John Chrysostom). Our union with Christ by faith and grace is a real union, but in Holy Communion we have, in addition, physical union with Christ. Then, at least for a few moments, we have Him within us, as the Blessed Virgin had Him in her pure womb for nine months. And if, to this physical union is joined moral union, consisting in the full conformity of our will and our aspirations to God's will and good pleasure, Holy Communion actually becomes the moment of closest union with God that we can reach on earth.

2. But Jesus speaks of a union which transcends even this physical-moral union, and to explain this close bond established between Him and the soul of the communicant, He does not hesitate to compare it to His union with the Father : " As the living Father hath sent Me, and I live by the Father, so he that eateth Me, the same also shall live by Me " (*Jn* 6,58). Jesus lives because the Father communicates life to Him : He lives by the Father alone; He has no life other than that which He shares with the Father. Similarly, one who is nourished by the Eucharist, lives by the life Christ communicates to him, that is, by Christ's own life. This life which the soul has already received through Baptism or Penance is increased principally by the devout reception of Holy Communion, for at that time Christ comes Himself in Person, to communicate His life and even to live this life within the soul. Jesus lives by the Father, because the Father is the one and only source of His life; the communicant lives by Jesus, because Jesus, by becoming his Food, becomes the source of his life in the most direct, profound, and intimate manner. But we can also take another meaning from the words of Jesus. Having received His whole life and all His existence from the Father, Jesus also lives by the Father in the sense that He lives solely for His glory, making use of everything He has received from the Father to accomplish the mission entrusted to Him and to do the Father's will. So too for the communicant : he should not live for himself, leading a selfish life that is concerned only with earthly cares and interests; but he should *live for Jesus*, for His interests, for His glory; he should *live by Jesus*, the source of his life; he should *live in Jesus*, who by nourishing him daily with His Flesh, binds him and unites him more closely to Himself; he should *live for Jesus*, by employing all his strength, all his abilities for Him, giving himself totally to His service. This divine life which Jesus communicates to us should find in our souls a favorable ground for complete development, a ground cleared of pride, egoism, and attachment to creatures, one suitable for producing works worthy of Jesus and agreeable to Him. Just as Christ lived for the glory of the Father, " who sent Him " (*ibid.* 7,18), so must we live for the glory of Christ who, by making Himself our Food, shares His life with us.

COLLOQUY

"O Lord, how far has love brought You? It has brought You even so far as giving Yourself to Your creature, leaving Your Body and Blood for his Food and Drink. And for how long? Oh! my God, You Yourself have said it : " until the consummation of the world, " so that we can possess You not only once, not once a year, once a month, or once a week, but every day, every morning that we wish we can receive You, we can have You within us and remain with You as much as we like. O infinite bounty of the Word, my Spouse! How wretched I am! I have so many riches and I draw so little fruit from them! Still more miserable is he who does not know this gift, who cares not if he is deprived of it for many years, or who receives it in the state of mortal sin, so that the Bread of Life becomes for him the food of death. For these souls I pray, O Lord; do not look upon their sins, but only upon Your own goodness; convert them so that they may realize the great wrong they are doing to themselves, and to Your infinite bounty.

"But O Lord, when a soul receives You with the right dispositions, may it not be said of it as was said of the Virgin Mary : ' Blessed art thou, because thou bearest within thee Him whom the heavens cannot contain! ' Like unto Mary, a soul who receives You is clothed with the sun, for You are the Sun, the Sun of Justice, Christ, our God.

"As for me, O Lord, I think I am more obliged to You because You have left Yourself to me as my Food, than because You have created me, for what would I have done if You had created me, but had not given Yourself to me? In the Eucharist, You show how much You wanted to communicate Yourself to us, for You were not content to give Yourself to men only during the thirty years You were on earth; in addition to this, You wanted to leave us Your Body and Blood, so that we might be continually in You and You in us. Thus when You are in a soul, You deify it, so to speak, transforming it into Yourself; You communicate Yourself to it unceasingly, and keep it united to Yourself" (St. Mary Magdalen dei Pazzi).

207

LET US PREPARE FOR UNION

PRESENCE OF GOD - O Jesus, grant that I may derive great profit from the grace of union with You, which You offer me daily in Holy Communion.

MEDITATION

1. The Eucharist unites us to Christ directly; this physical union is the same for all who partake of His Body and Blood. However, it does not produce the same effects in everyone. This is so true that the Sacràment may even become a cause of damnation for those who approach it unworthily : " Whosoever shall eat this bread or drink the chalice of the Lord unworthily, " says St. Paul, " eateth and drinketh judgment to himself " (1 *Cor* 11,27-29). But even in those who receive worthily, the effects of the Eucharist are different, for they are always proportioned to the excellence and perfection of one's interior dispositions.

Jesus penetrates me, transforming me into Himself only in the measure that I place no obstacles in His way, and insofar as I am disposed to receive the special grace of the Eucharist, the grace of " union with Christ. " Although the physical union with Jesus offered to me in Holy Communion is a tremendous gift, it is, nonetheless, directed to my *spiritual* union with Him and to my transformation in Him by love. The more perfect the dispositions with which I approach the Holy Table, the more complete this union and transformation will be. These dispositions consist in preparing my heart for an ever greater union with the Lord, a union which requires conformity of aspirations, tastes, sentiments, and wills. How can I enjoy the visit of a friend and spend moments of sweet intimacy with him, moments of real union, if differences of desires, affections, and will separate us? This, then, will be the best preparation for my Communion : to rid myself of everything in my life, no matter how trivial it may be, that might be in disagreement with the divine will, with the sentiments and dispositions of the heart of Jesus. " Let this mind be in you, which was also in Christ Jesus" (*Phil* 2,5), St. Paul tells me; this must be the program of my remote preparation for Holy Communion.

2. In order that the Eucharist may produce its full fruit in me and be the occasion of very close, intimate union with Jesus, it is not enough, as St. Augustine says, for me to eat His Body materially; I also need to eat it "spiritually," that is, my spirit must be well disposed and prepared to receive the Body of Christ, to let itself be invaded and transformed by Christ. If when Jesus comes to me, He finds my heart, will, affections and sentiments entirely conformed to His own, nothing can prevent Him from giving Himself to me in the most complete manner. His spirit, His life, His divinity will penetrate the innermost fibres of my being and transform me into Him. Then I shall be able to say in all truth with St. Paul : "I live, now not I; but Christ liveth in me" (*Gal* 2,20).

When I receive Holy Communion, my heart must be enlarged by love, so that it will be wide open for the coming of Jesus, and ready to let itself be penetrated and transformed by Him. In addition to the physical presence of Jesus, and because of this presence, each Communion brings me a new increase of grace and charity, but even this increase will be in proportion to my capacity for receiving it. If my heart is closed by selfishness and pride, if it is bound by attachment to creatures, or is too much engrossed by worldly affections and affairs, it will be unable to make room for an increase of divine love, and Jesus will be, so to speak, forced to lessen the outpouring of His charity and to diminish His gifts. Yes, in Holy Communion, Jesus gives Himself completely—His entire Person as God and Man—and He unites Himself entirely to me; but, if I do not give myself entirely to Him, He cannot wholly pour Himself into me, as a friend into the heart of a faithful friend. Every day Jesus offers me in Holy Communion an actual grace to love Him more, to unite myself more closely to Him. Every day I must offer Him a heart always more open to love and union. Intense acts of faith in the real presence of Jesus in the Eucharist will help to arouse my love and make me *actually love* Him, and precisely during this actuality of love, Jesus will pour out the increase of His charity, the living flame of His infinite love.

COLLOQUY

"O my soul, when you receive Holy Communion, try to reanimate your faith, do all you can to detach yourself from exterior things and retire with the Lord into the interior of your being where you know He is abiding. Collect your senses and make them understand the great good they are enjoying, or rather, try to recollect them so that they may not hinder you from understanding it. Imagine yourself at Our Lord's feet, and weep with Magdalen exactly as if you were seeing Him with your bodily eyes in the house of the Pharisee. These moments are very precious; the Master is teaching you now; listen to Him, kiss His feet in gratitude for all He has condescended to do for you, and beg Him to remain always with you. Even should you be deprived of sensible devotion, faith will not fail to assure you that Our Lord is truly within you.

"If I do not want to act like a senseless person who shuts his eyes to the light, I can have no doubt on this point. O my Jesus, this is not a work of the imagination, as when I imagine You on the Cross or in some other mystery of Your Passion, where I picture the scene as it took place. Here, it concerns Your real presence; it is an undeniable truth. O Lord, when I receive Holy Communion, I do not have to go far to find You; as long as the accidents of bread are not consumed, You are within me! And if, during Your mortal life, You healed the sick by a mere touch of Your garments, how, if I have faith, can I doubt that You will work miracles, when You are really present within me? Oh, yes! when You are in my house You will listen to all my requests, for it is not Your custom to pay badly for the lodging given You, if I offer you good hospitality!

"O Lord, if a soul receives Communion with good dispositions, and if, wishing to drive out all coldness, it remains for some time with You, great love for You will burn within it and it will retain its warmth for many hours" (T.J. *Way*, 34-35).

208

FEAST OF THE MOST SACRED HEART OF JESUS

PRESENCE OF GOD - O Jesus, grant that I may penetrate the secrets hidden in Your divine Heart.

MEDITATION

1. After we have contemplated the Eucharist, a gift crowning all the gifts of the love of Jesus for men, the Church invites us to give direct consideration to the love of the Sacred Heart of Jesus, the source and cause of all His gifts. We may call the Feast of the Sacred Heart of Jesus the feast of His love for us. " Behold this Heart which has so loved men, " Jesus said to St. Margaret Mary; " Behold this Heart which has so loved men, " the Church repeats to us today, showing us that it is truly " in the Heart of Christ, wounded by our sins, that God has deigned to give us the infinite treasures of His love " (cf. *Collect*). Today's liturgy inspired with this thought, reviews the immense benefits we owe to the love of Christ and sings a hymn in praise of His love. " *Cogitationes cordis ejus*, " chants the Introit of the Mass : " The thoughts of His Heart " — the Heart of Jesus — " are to all generations : to deliver them from death, to feed them in time of famine. " The Heart of Jesus is always in search of souls to save, to free from the snares of sin, to wash in His Blood, to feed with His Body. The Heart of Jesus is always living in the Eucharist to satisfy the hunger of all who long for Him, to welcome and console all those who, disillusioned by the vicissitudes of life, take refuge in Him, seeking peace and refreshment. Jesus Himself is our support on the hard road of life. " Take up My yoke upon you and learn of Me, because I am meek and humble of heart, and you shall find rest for your souls, Alleluia. " It is impossible to eliminate sorrow from our life; yet if we live for Jesus we can suffer in peace and find in the Heart of Jesus repose for our weary soul.

2. Today's Gospel and Epistle lead us to consider the Sacred Heart of Jesus even more directly. The Gospel (*Jn* 19,31-37) shows us His Heart pierced with a lance : " One of the soldiers opened His side with a spear, " and St. Augustine offers this comment : " The Evangelist says... *opened*, to show us that thereby the door of life was thrown open, through which the Sacraments of the Church flow forth. " From the pierced Heart of Christ, symbol of the love which immolated Him on the Cross for us, came forth the Sacraments, represented by the water and the Blood flowing from the wound, and it is through these Sacraments that we receive the life of grace. Yes, it is eminently true to say that the Heart of Jesus was *opened* to bring us into life. Jesus once said, " Narrow is the gate... that leadeth to life " (*Mt* 7,14); but if we understand this gate to be the wound in His Heart, we can say that no gate could open to us with greater welcome.

St. Paul, in his beautiful Epistle (*Eph* 3,8-19), urges us to penetrate further into the Heart of Jesus to contemplate His " unsearchable riches " and to enter into " the mystery which hath been hidden from eternity in God. " This is the mystery of the infinite, divine love which has gone before us from all eternity and was revealed to us by the Word made flesh; it is the mystery of the love which willed to redeem us and sanctify us in Christ " in whom we have... [free] access to God. "

Again Jesus presents Himself as the door which leads to salvation. " I am the door. By Me if any man enter in he shall be saved " (*Jn* 10,9). This door is His Heart, which, wounded for us, has brought us into life. By love alone can we penetrate this mystery of infinite love, but not any kind of love will suffice. As St. Paul says, we must " be rooted and founded in charity. " Only thus shall we be able " to know... the charity of Christ which surpasseth all knowledge, that [we] may be filled unto all the fullness of God. "

COLLOQUY

" O Jesus, by a divine decree, a soldier was permitted to pierce Your sacred side. As the blood and water came forth, the price of our salvation was poured forth, which flowing from the mysterious fountain of Your Heart, gives

power to the Sacraments of the Church to bestow the life of
grace, and becomes for those who live in You, a saving drink
of living waters, bubbling up to life eternal.   Arise, my soul,
beloved of Christ, watch unceasingly, place your lips there,
and quench your thirst in the Savior's fount.

" O Jesus, now that I have been brought into Your most
sweet Heart, and it is a great good to be here, I do not want
to let myself be easily torn away from it.   Oh! how good and
pleasant it is to dwell in Your Heart!   Your Heart, O good
Jesus, is a rich treasure, it is the precious pearl which I have
found in the secret of Your pierced Body, as in a furrowed
field.   Who would cast aside this pearl?   Rather I will give
all the pearls in the world, I will exchange for it all my
thoughts and affections and I will purchase it for myself.
I shall entrust all my cares to Your Heart, O good Jesus,
and without fail it will support me.   I have found Your Heart,
O Lord, O most benign Jesus : the Heart of my King, my
Brother, my Friend!   Hidden in Your Heart, what is there
that I shall not ask of You?   I shall ask that *Your* Heart be
mine also.   If You, O Jesus, are my Head, can I not say that
it is mine as well as Yours?   Are not the eyes of my head
also   mine?   Then   the   Heart   of   my   spiritual   Head
is *my* Heart.   What joy for me!   You and I have but one
heart.   Having found this divine Heart which is Yours
and mine, O most sweet Jesus, I beseech You, O my God :
receive my prayers in that sanctuary where You are attentive
to them and, even more, draw me entirely into Your Heart "
(St. Bonaventure).

209

DEVOTION TO THE   SACRED HEART OF JESUS

PRESENCE OF GOD - O Sacred Heart of Jesus, teach me how to know You and to love You.

MEDITATION

The object of devotion to the Sacred Heart is, properly speaking, the physical Heart of Jesus which is worthy of adoration, because it is a part of His sacred humanity, hypostatically united to the Word.   However, the ultimate object of this devotion is the love of Jesus, the symbol of which is His Heart.   In other words, " beneath the symbolic image of the Heart, we contemplate and venerate our divine Redeemer's immense charity and generous love " (Pius VI).   This is the real meaning of the devotion to the Sacred Heart by which the Church asks us to honor the Heart of Jesus as the visible representation of His invisible love.   " Your charity has allowed You to be wounded by the visible blow of the lance, " the liturgy of the feast sings, " so that we may venerate the wounds of Your invisible love " *(RB)*.   Therefore, the principle object of this devotion is the love of Jesus, an uncreated love with which He, as the Word, together with the Father and the Holy Spirit, loved us from all eternity, and from all eternity willed to become incarnate for our salvation.   It is also the created love of charity with which, as Man, He loved us even to the death of the Cross, meriting for us by His love that same charity by which we are enabled to love Him in return.   Here we find the most profound significance of devotion to the Sacred Heart. St. Teresa Margaret of the Heart of Jesus had such a thorough understanding of this meaning that she made this devotion the center of her life.   The process for her canonization says that the Saint " saw the Heart of Jesus as the center, the source of the love with which the divine Word, in the bosom of the Father, loved us from all eternity, and merited for us in time the power to love Him in return, on earth and in heaven, by our sharing in this love. "

2. Other devotions to Our Lord have for their object the mysteries or special aspects of His life, as for example, the Incarnation, the hidden life, the Passion. Devotion to the Sacred Heart, on the contrary, has a more general object, the love of Jesus, which constitutes the profound, essential reason for all His mysteries, the love that is the first and only cause of all He has done for us. In this sense, devotion to the Sacred Heart touches, as it were, the mainspring of all the mysteries of the Redeemer, the essential raison d'être of His life, His Person. It is the love which explains the Incarnation of the Word, the life of the Man-God, His Passion, His Eucharist. We cannot possibly understand the mystery by which the Son of God became Man, died on the Cross to save mankind, and then became their Food, if we do not admit this infinite love which compelled God the Creator, the Most High, to find a way to give Himself entirely for the salvation of His creatures. The Church gives expression to this interpretation in the hymn at Matins : " *Amor coegit te tuus mortale corpus sumere.* " " Thy love has impelled Thee "—or rather, has *constrained* Thee, if we accept the Latin word in its full sense—" to assume a mortal body, so that as the new Adam, Thou wouldst restore what the old Adam had lost. " The hymn continues, now praising the eternal love of the Word, now the human love of Jesus; two loves which, in fact, cannot be separated, just as the sacred humanity of Jesus cannot be disassociated from the Word which assumed it. Jesus is both God and Man, hence His love is both divine and human. He loved us and continues to love us as God and as Man. His human, created love is made sublime by the eternal love of the Word, or rather, it becomes the very love of the Word who makes it His own, just as all the sentiments and acts of Christ as Man are raised to a supreme dignity. Thus, His divine love becomes sensible, comprehensible, and tangible to us by means of the manifestations of His human love. It is always the humanity of Jesus which reveals His divinity to us, and just as we know the Son of God through His sacred humanity, so do we know His divine love through the human love of Jesus.

COLLOQUY

"For this, O Jesus, was Your sacred side pierced, that it might give us an easy entrance. Your Heart was opened that we might dwell there, safe from exterior disturbances. In addition to this, You were pierced by a spear, so that through the visible wound, we could see the invisible one which love inflicted on You, for he who burns with love, is wounded by love. What better evidence of Your ardent love could You have given us than by permitting the lance to pierce, not only Your Body, but even Your Heart? The wound in Your flesh then shows forth the wound in Your spirit.

"Who will not love that Heart so deeply wounded? Who will not return love to One who so loved us? Who will not embrace a Spouse so chaste? Certainly the soul loves You in return, O Lord, who, knowing itself to be wounded by Your love, cries to You : Your charity has wounded me! We too, pilgrims in the flesh, love as much as we can, and embrace the One who was wounded for us, whose hands, feet, side, and Heart were pierced. Let us love and pray : ' O Jesus, deign to bind our hearts, still so hard and unrepentant, with the chain of Your love and wound them with its dart ' " (St. Bonaventure).

"O Jesus, a soldier opened Your side with his lance, so that, through the gaping wound, we might know the charity of Your Heart, which loved us unto death, and that we might enter into Your unutterable love through the same channel by which it came to us. Approach, then, O my soul, the Heart of Christ, that magnanimous Heart, that hidden Heart, that Heart which thinks of all things and knows all things; that loving Heart, all on fire with love. Make me understand, O Lord, that the door of Your Heart was forced open by the vehemence of Your love. Allow me to enter into the secret of that love which was hidden from all eternity, but is now revealed by the wound in Your Heart " (St. Bernardine of Siena).

210

MERCIFUL LOVE

THIRD SUNDAY AFTER PENTECOST

PRESENCE OF GOD - O Jesus, reveal to me the infinite treasures of mercy contained in Your Heart.

MEDITATION

1. Today's liturgy is a warm invitation to confidence in the merciful love of Jesus. Even from the beginning of the Mass, the Church has us pray thus : " Look toward me and have pity on me, O Lord, for I am desolate and unhappy. See my misery and my sadness, and pardon all my sins " *(Introit)*; then in the Collect we add : " O God... pour out upon us Your mercy, " and a little later we are exhorted : " Cast your care upon the Lord, and He will support you " *(Gradual)*. But how can we justify all this confidence in God, since we are always poor sinners? The Gospel *(Lk* 15,1-10) explains the grounds for this justification by relating two parables used by Jesus Himself to teach us that we can never have too much confidence in His infinite mercy : the story of the lost sheep and the account of the missing drachma. First He shows us the good shepherd who goes in search of the lost sheep; it is a picture of Jesus coming down from heaven to search for poor human beings lost in the dark caves of sin. In order to find them, rescue them, and bring them back to the sheepfold, He does not hesitate to undergo the greatest sufferings and even death. " And when he hath found it...[he lays] it upon his shoulders, rejoicing : and coming home, [he calls] together his friends and neighbors, saying to them : ' Rejoice with me for I have found my sheep that was lost. ' " This is the story of the love of Jesus for all mankind and especially for every individual soul. The story has a beautiful symbolism in the tender figure of the good shepherd, to which Jesus likened Himself. We might say that the image of the good shepherd—which was so greatly loved in the early days of the Church—is the equivalent of that of the Sacred Heart; both are living, concrete expres-

sions of the merciful love of Jesus, and they urge us to go
to Him with complete confidence.

2. " I say to you, that even so there will be joy in
heaven over one sinner who repents, more than over ninety-
nine just who have no need of repentance. " Here we have the
underlying idea of all three parables about mercy—the lost
sheep, the missing drachma, and the prodigal son—each
expressing this thought in a different way. This insistent
repetition tells us how earnestly Jesus would inculcate the
profound lesson of His infinite mercy, a mercy which is the
exact opposite of the hard, scornful attitude of the Pharisees
who murmured, saying, " He [Jesus] receives sinners and
eats with them. " The three parables are the Master's
answer to their mean and treacherous insinuations.

It is not easy for finite creatures with a limited spiritual
outlook to understand this ineffable mystery completely; not
only is it difficult to understand in respect to others, but it
presents a problem even in what concerns ourselves.
However, Jesus said and repeated : " There will be joy in
heaven over one sinner who repents, more than over ninety-
nine just " thus giving us to understand what great glory
a soul gives to God when, after many falls, it comes back
to Him, repentant and confident. The message of this
parable applies not only to great sinners, those converted
from serious sin, but also to those who turn from venial
sins, who humble themselves and rise again after faults
committed through weakness or lack of reflection. This
is our everyday story : how many times we resolve to overcome our impatience, our quick temper, our sensitiveness, and how many times we fall again ! But the Heart of
Jesus " thrills with joy when, humbly acknowledging our
fault, we come to fling ourselves into His arms, imploring
forgiveness; then, He loves us even more tenderly than before
we fell " (T.C.J. *L-C*).

The liturgy repeats in the Communion hymn the last
verse of the Gospel : " I say to you, there shall be joy before
the angels of God over one sinner doing penance. " Let us
ask Jesus, when He comes to us in Holy Communion, to help
us penetrate the secrets of His infinite, merciful love.

COLLOQUY

" In whom, Lord, can Your mercies shine forth as in me, who with my evil deeds have thus obscured the great favors which You had begun to show me? Alas, my Creator! If I would make an excuse, I have none, and no one is to blame but I. For had I cooperated even a little with Your love which You had begun to show me, I would not have been able to love aught but Yourself Lord...but as I have not deserved this...may Your mercy be availing for me.

" Yet even from me some good has been brought forth by Your infinite goodness, and, the greater have been my sins, the more has the great blessing of Your mercies shone forth in me. How many reasons have I for singing of them forever! I beseech You, my God, that it may be so : may I sing of them, and that without end, since You have deigned to work such exceeding great mercies in me that they amaze those who behold them, while as for me, I am drawn out of myself continually, that I may be the better able to sing Your praise. For so long as I am in myself, my Lord, and without You, I can do nothing but be cut off like the flowers in this garden, and this miserable earth will become a dunghill again as before. Permit it not, Lord. Let it not be Your will that a soul which You have purchased with so many trials should be lost, when You have so often redeemed it anew and have snatched it from the teeth of the horrible dragon " (T.J. *Life*, 4-14).

" O Jesus, I know that Your Heart is more grieved by the thousand little imperfections of Your friends than by the faults, even grave, which Your enemies commit. Yet, it seems to me, that it is only when those who are Your own are habitually guilty of thoughtlessness and neglect to seek Your pardon, that You can say : ' These wounds which you see in the midst of My hands I have received in the house of those who love Me. ' But Your Heart thrills with joy when You have to deal with all those who truly love, and who after each little fault come to fling themselves into Your arms, imploring forgiveness. You say to Your angels what the prodigal's father said to his servants : ' Put a ring upon his finger, and let us rejoice. ' O Jesus, how little known is the merciful love of Your Heart! " (cf. T.C.J. *L-C*).

211

RETURNING LOVE FOR LOVE

PRESENCE OF GOD - O Jesus, You have loved me so much; enable me to repay Your love.

MEDITATION

1. In the Encyclical *Annum Sacrum*, Leo XIII declares, " The Sacred Heart is the symbol and image of the infinite charity of Jesus Christ, the *charity which urges us to give Him love in return.* " Indeed, nothing is more able to arouse love than love itself. " Love is repaid by love alone, " the saints have repeatedly said. St. Teresa of Jesus wrote : " Whenever we think of Christ, we should remember with what love He has bestowed all these favors upon us...for love begets love. And though we may be only beginners...let us strive ever to bear this in mind and awaken our own love " (*Life*, 22).

The Church offers us the devotion to the Sacred Heart of Jesus in order to stir up our love. After reminding us, in the Divine Office proper to this feast, of the measureless proofs of Christ's love, this good Mother asks us anxiously, " Who would not love Him who has loved us so much? Who among His redeemed would not love Him dearly? " (*RB*). And in order to urge us more and more to repay love with love, she puts on the lips of Jesus the beautiful words of Holy Scripture : " I have loved thee with an everlasting love; therefore have I drawn thee, taking pity on thee "; and again, " *Fili, praebe mihi cor tuum,* " Son, give Me thy heart (*ibid.*). This, then, is the substance of true devotion to the Sacred Heart : to return love for love, " to repay love with love, " as St. Margaret Mary, the great disciple of the Sacred Heart, expresses it; " to return love unceasingly to Him who has so loved us, " in the words of St. Teresa Margaret of the Heart of Jesus, the hidden but no less ardent disciple of the divine Heart.

2. The attitude we take in our spiritual life depends greatly upon the idea we have of God. If we have a poor, impoverished concept of God, like the slothful servant

in the Gospel (*Mt* 25,14-30), instead of being impelled
to love Him and to give ourselves generously to His service,
we shall be cold, indolent, calculating; and burying the talent
we have received from the Master, we shall not trouble
ourselves to use for God the benefits we have received from
Him. Unfortunately, many Christians live this kind of life;
they serve Him like slaves, and if they do not commit sin,
it is only through fear of being punished; if they pray or
perform some good work, it is for their own personal interest
and is devoid of generosity and love. When, on the other
hand, our soul begins to understand that " *Deus caritas est,* "
God is charity (1 *Jn* 4,8), when we penetrate even slightly the
mystery of the infinite love that surrounds us, realizing
God's love in the love which Jesus has for us, then
everything changes spontaneously, because " love calls to
love. " Devotion to the Sacred Heart, which is devotion
to the infinite love of Jesus, should produce this particular
effect in us : it should give us an ever increasing comprehension
of " the charity of Christ which surpasseth all knowledge "
(*Eph* 3,19). In our meditation, our contemplation of the
Heart of Jesus pierced for love of us, we shall learn the science
of love, a science which no book on earth can teach us,
because it is a science that can be acquired only from the
open book of the Heart of Christ, our one and only Teacher.
" He taught me a science most delectable " (J.C. *SC*, 27,2),
sings the joyful soul who has been introduced into the secrets
of His divine Heart. Then the answer to His love is easy :
He " loved me and delivered Himself for me...and I most
gladly will spend and be spent myself for Him and for the
souls that are His treasure " (*Gal* 2,20 – cf. 2 *Cor* 12,15).
Behold the love that raises us above all calculation, all
self-love.

COLLOQUY

    " Awake, O my soul. How long will you remain asleep?
Beyond the sky there is a King who wishes to possess you;
He loves you immeasurably, with all His Heart. He loves you
with so much kindness and faithfulness that He left His
kingdom and humbled Himself for you, permitting Himself to
be bound like a malefactor in order to find you. He loves
you so strongly and tenderly, He is so jealous of you and has

given you so many proofs of this, that He willingly gave up His Body to death. He bathed you in His Blood and redeemed you by His death. How long will you wait to love Him in return? Make haste, then, to answer Him.

"Behold, O loving Jesus, I come to You. I come, drawn by Your meekness, Your mercy, Your charity; I come with my whole heart and soul, and all my strength. Who will give me to be entirely conformed to Your Heart, in order that You may find in me everything You desire?

"O Jesus, my King and my God, take me into the sweet shelter of Your divine Heart, and there unite me to Yourself in such a way that I shall live totally for You. Permit me to submerge myself henceforth in that vast sea of Your mercy, abandoning myself entirely to Your goodness, plunging into the burning furnace of Your love, and remaining there forever....

"But what am I, O my God, I, so unlike You, the outcast of all creatures? But You are my supreme confidence, because in You can be found the supplement or rather, the abundance of all the favors I have lost. Enclose me, O Lord, in the sanctuary of Your Heart opened by the spear, establish me there, guarded by Your gentle glance, so that I may be confided to Your care forever : under the shadow of Your paternal love I shall find rest in the everlasting remembrance of Your most precious love " (St. Gertrude).

212

CONSECRATION TO THE SACRED HEART OF JESUS

PRESENCE OF GOD - O Jesus, make me worthy to consecrate myself to Your loving Heart and to truly live this consecration.

MEDITATION

1. Because devotion to the Sacred Heart arouses in us a need to return His infinite love, it expresses itself spontaneously in an Act of Consecration by which the creature gives itself entirely to the God who has loved it so much. Conse-

cration to the Sacred Heart, says Leo XIII, " means a giving
of oneself, a binding of oneself to Jesus Christ, since all
respect, all homage, and all devotion to the Sacred Heart
are really addressed to Jesus Himself" *(Annum Sacrum)*.
Pius XI explains what this act consists of : " By this Act of
Consecration, we offer to the divine Heart of Jesus, ourselves
and all we possess, acknowledging that we have received it
all from the eternal charity of God" *(Miserentissimus
Redemptor)*.

To love is to give oneself : " To love is to give all and
to give oneself, " sang St. Therese of the Child Jesus. When
love is real it must make a gift of everything, and in this total
gift to God the loving soul finds its peace and rest. The
ardent cry of St. Paul : " *Caritas Christi urget nos,* " ends with
his triumphant cry : " *ut non sibi vivant, sed ei qui pro ipsis
mortuus est*"; the charity of Christ presseth us.... that we
may not now live to [ourselves] but unto Him who died
for [us]. (2 *Cor* 5,14.15).

One who consecrates himself to a person gives himself
entirely to that person; he no longer belongs to himself;
henceforth he cannot live for himself; his tastes, interests,
and desires must give way to those of the one to whom he
has given himself, and to whom he now belongs. This is the
profound meaning of Consecration to the Sacred Heart,
a Consecration which, far from being reduced to the recitation
of a mere formula, involves and must involve our whole
person, life, and abilities so that we use our complete being
and all we possess in the service of the divine Heart.

2. This Consecration to the Sacred Heart is not the same
as that contained in the three vows of religion, which is
reserved for certain souls, but we speak of the total consecration which Jesus Himself, in the Gospel, suggested to everyone
and which each one is obliged to carry out according to his
state in life. Jesus said to us : " Thou shalt love the Lord
thy God, with thy *whole* heart, and with thy *whole* soul,
and with thy *whole* mind, and with thy *whole* strength "
(*Mk* 12,30). By repeating the word " whole, " He asks for a
total love, and thus for a *total gift* of self; that is, He
asks us to give ourselves to Him and to His service, not by
halves, but entirely. Jesus shows us how to respond to His
appeal, urging us to prove by deeds the truthfulness of
our love and our complete gift : " If you love Me, keep My

commandments " (*Jn* 14,15). Therefore, we need not seek in distant places for ways and means of actualizing our Consecration to the Sacred Heart; nor should we make it consist in exceptional, extraordinary things, but should realize that the means are right at hand in our practical, everyday life.

To consecrate oneself totally to the Sacred Heart means preferring His commandments, will, desires, and tastes, as the norm of one's life, being ready to renounce one's own will and desires when they are contrary to His. Many Christians consecrate themselves to the Sacred Heart, but very few actually live their Consecration in its totality. Most people live it by halves; they prefer the will of Jesus to their own when to act otherwise would be to commit a grave sin; but when it is a question of venial sin, or more often, of imperfections, they have no scruple about displeasing the Sacred Heart and doing as they please. Jesus, however, seeks faithful souls, souls who live their Consecration to such a point that they *never* prefer their own desires and personal tastes to His. Should we not wish to be one of these? " My child, give Me thy heart, " Jesus says, and might add, " Give it to Me in its totality by living entirely according to My Heart. "

COLLOQUY

" Adorable Heart of my most loving Jesus, what good have You found in me to make You love me without limit, even though my heart, stained by a thousand faults, was so cold and indifferent toward You? The great proofs of love which You have shown me, even when I did not love You, give me hope that You will now find acceptable the proofs of my love. Receive then, my loving Savior, my desire to consecrate myself entirely to the honor and glory of Your Sacred Heart; accept the gift of all that I am. I consecrate to You my person, my life, my actions, my pains and sufferings, desiring to be in the future a victim consecrated to Your glory, on fire at this moment, and one day to be entirely consumed by the holy flames of Your love. I offer You then, my Lord and my God, my heart with all its desires, that during my whole life it may be perfectly conformed to Yours. I belong, then, wholly to Your Heart, I am entirely Yours. O my God, how great are Your mercies toward me!...

My adorable Savior, accept my consecration also in reparation
for the offenses which I have not ceased to commit against
You until now, by corresponding so badly to Your love.
I am giving You very little, I know, but at least I wish to
give You all that is in my power and all You wish, for that
You desire from me; therefore, by consecrating my heart to
You, I give it to You never to take it back.

" Teach me, O loving Savior, perfect forgetfulness of
self, for that is the one way by which I can enter Your adorable
Heart; and since in the future I shall do everything for You,
grant that all I do may be worthy of You.   Teach me what I
must do to arrive at the purity of Your love, but also give me
this love, give me a most ardent, generous love.   Give me
that profound humility without which no one can be pleasing
to You, and accomplish in me all Your holy will "
(St. Margaret Mary).

213

REPARATION

PRESENCE OF GOD - Heart of Jesus, wounded for love of us, make
me worthy to make reparation for all the wounds our sins have
inflicted upon You.

MEDITATION

1. We find in the hymn for First Vespers of the Feast
of the Sacred Heart the following words : " Lo, the proud,
insolent procession of our offenses has wounded the
innocent Heart of God. "   And even more realistically it
continues : " The lance which the soldier wielded was
directed by our sins " (RB).   These lines recall to our minds
the words addressed by Jesus to St. Margaret Mary : " Behold
this Heart which has so loved men...but which, in return
for its infinite love, finds only ingratitude; it meets only
with forgetfulness, indifference, and outrages, and all this
at times even from souls bound closely to it by the bonds of a
very special love. "   A soul that loves God cannot remain

indifferent to these complaints; it wants to expiate, repair and console, having " the most powerful motives, " as Pius XI teaches, " of justice and of love : of justice, in order to expiate the injury done to God by our sins...and of love, in order to compassionate the suffering Christ, patient and covered with opprobrium, and to bring Him insofar as our human weakness permits, some comfort in His sufferings " *(Miserentissimus Redemptor)*. It is easy to understand that we must make reparation for our own sins, but sometimes we do not see as clearly that reparation should also aim at consoling the Heart of Jesus. " But indeed, can acts of expiation console Christ who now reigns happily in heaven? " asks Pius XI " ' Give me a lover and he will understand what I say ' " *(ibid.)*, replies the great Pope in the words of St. Augustine. In fact, a soul who lovingly penetrates the mystery of Jesus will realize that when, in Gethsemane, He saw all our sins, He also saw the good works we would do in order to comfort Him. What we do today with this intention consoled Him then in reality. This thought spurs us on to further acts of reparation, so that Jesus finds no reason to complain sorrowfully to us : " My Heart hath expected reproach and misery...I looked for one that would comfort Me, and I found none " *(Mass of the Sacred Heart)*.

2. The idea of reparation brings to mind that of " victim of reparation " well-known to lovers of the Sacred Heart, and officially recognized by the Church in the Encyclical of Pius XI on reparation. This venerable document explains what should be done by one who intends to offer himself as a victim : " Such a one assuredly cannot but abhor and flee all sin as the greatest of evils. He will also offer himself wholly and entirely to the will of God and will strive to repair the injured divine Majesty by constant prayer, by voluntary penances and by patiently bearing all the misfortunes which may befall him; in a word, he will so organize his life that in all things it will be inspired by the spirit of atonement " *(Miserentissimus Redemptor)*. This is far from the fantastic idea of victim which some souls adopt. Under the pretext of being obliged to take upon themselves extraordinary immolations, they avoid the reality of ordinary, daily life and imagine they are capable of enduring all kinds of suffering, whereas actually, they try to escape the sacrifices which present themselves every day. The idea of a

victim of reparation offered by the doctrine of the Church is, on the contrary, something very serious, concrete, and realistic. The victim soul should make reparation for sin; and it will accomplish this by always doing what is contrary to sin. Sin is an act of rebellion against God and His will, as manifested by the commandments and the arrangements of divine Providence. Therefore, to do what is contrary to sin will consist in a total adherence to God's will, by accepting it with our whole heart in all its manifestations, in spite of the repugnances we may feel. This, then, is the program of a victim soul : not only to avoid sin, even the smallest one, but to embrace God's will in such a way that He can really do all that He wants with it. To this docility, the soul will add prayer and voluntary mortifications, which will have value only because they are offered by a heart entirely submissive to the divine will. And let us note that the first penitential act mentioned in the Encyclical is " the patient endurance " of the adversities of life.

COLLOQUY

" O God, why can I not bathe with my tears and blood all the places where Your Heart has been insulted? Why am I not permitted to make reparation for so many sacrileges and profanations? Why is it not given to me to be the mistress of the hearts of all men for a single moment, in order to atone, by the sacrifices I would make, for the neglect and folly of all those who have not wished to know You, or who, even knowing You, have loved You so little? But, O my adored Savior, what covers me with confusion and what most grieves me is that I myself have been one of these ungrateful souls. You, my God, see the depths of my soul; You see how I suffer because of my ingratitude and the unworthy treatment I have given You. Behold me, O Lord, my heart broken with grief, humbled and prostrate, ready to accept from Your hand all that it pleases You to ask of me in reparation for so many outrages " (St. Margaret Mary).
    " You know, my God, that my one desire is to be a victim of Your Sacred Heart, wholly consumed as a holocaust in the fire of Your holy love. Your Heart will be the altar on which I shall be consumed by You, my dear Spouse,

and You will be the Priest who will consume this victim by the fires of Your most Sacred Heart. But, O my God, how ashamed I am to see how guilty is this victim and how unworthy to have her sacrifice accepted by You! But I am confident that all will be consumed by this divine fire!

" By offering my whole self to You, I understand that I am giving You my free will, so that henceforth, You alone will be the Master of my heart and Your will alone will regulate my actions. Therefore, dispose of me always according to Your good pleasure; I am content with everything, since I wish to love You with a love that is patient, mortified, wholly abandoned to You, an active love, a strong, undivided love and, what is more important, a persevering love " (T.M. *Sp*).

214

THE HEART OF JESUS OUR MODEL

PRESENCE OF GOD - Sacred Heart of Jesus, teach me to model the affections of my heart on Yours.

MEDITATION

1. A soul consecrated to the Sacred Heart, a soul given to reparation, must feel the need of modeling its life on that of Jesus. How can we say that we are really consecrated to the Sacred Heart, how can we say that we are His victim of reparation, when we retain in our heart feelings, desires, and attractions which are opposed to His?

It is clear that in order to model our heart on the Heart of Christ we cannot limit ourselves to eliminating this or that fault, to acquiring such and such a virtue; rather, we must strive to reform our whole life. However, when the divine Master offered us His Heart as a model, He spoke of two virtues in particular, meekness and humility : " Learn of Me because I am meek and humble of heart " (*Mt* 11,29). Not without reason has He spoken thus, knowing that when we have removed all movements and feelings of

pride and self-love from our heart, we will also have
suppressed all our other faults; and when we have acquired
a profound humility, we will have acquired all the other
virtues as well. Let us pause, then, to consider this great lesson
of the Heart of Jesus.

First, Jesus speaks to us of meekness. This is
the virtue by which man is enabled to master everything
that falls under the heading of " anger. "   Meekness gives
the power to restrain and dominate all those passionate
movements—even slight ones—which sometimes make us
exceed just limits, and lose sight of the divine Guide. Since
the guide of a soul desirous of giving itself to the service
of God, is God Himself, is the Heart of Jesus, we must never
lose sight of Our Lord or withdraw from Him, even for a
short time; if we do, we will end by following our own
self-love and trivial passions.   Meekness, however, gives
us self-mastery, enabling us to dominate every kind of
irritation.   If we examine ourselves carefully, we shall see
that these irritations are almost always caused by some
little hurt to our pride; the irascible appetite has been
aroused by something which has wounded our " ego. "
Meekness, as we can see, is closely connected with humility.

2. Our Lord joins the lesson of meekness to that of
humility precisely because the immediate foundation of
meekness is humility.   It takes only a small amount of pride,
of self-love, of attachment to our own way of seeing or doing
things to make us unable to stand opposition.   Then
in the face of the shocks inevitably arising from the common
life, we lose, to a greater or lesser extent, our serenity,
our interior and exterior peace. If serenity is lost, calmness
of judgment is also lost; therefore, we are no longer able
to see clearly the divine light showing us which path to
follow in order to give Our Lord what He is asking of us.
Our soul wavers, loses its vigor, and allows itself to be
ruled somewhat by passion.   As long as any traces of pride
and self-love remain in us, there will always occur circumstances in which we will lose some of our control and
self-mastery; consequently, we shall lack meekness.   To
profit by the lesson of the Heart of Jesus, and to model
our heart on His, we must work assiduously to uproot
every trace of pride and self-love.   It is a task to which we
must give our attention day by day, always beginning

again, and never allowing ourselves to be discouraged by the constant recurrence of the attractions and resentments of our "ego." We can only win this battle by never giving up the struggle.

To arouse our courage, let us remind ourselves that our strivings are not only good for our own soul but useful also to others, for, as Pius XI says, "the more we have sacrificed our self-love and passions, the more abundant will be the fruits of propitiation and expiation which we shall reap for ourselves and for others" (*Miserentissimus Redemptor*). The battle against self-love and the practice of humility are both part of the program of a soul consecrated to the Sacred Heart, of one who has offered itself to Him as a victim of reparation.

COLLOQUY

"O most Sacred Heart of Jesus, You desire so ardently to shower Your favors upon the unfortunate, and to teach those who want to advance in the school of Your love; You continually invite me to be meek and humble of heart like You. For this reason, You convince me that in order to gain Your friendship and to become Your true disciple, I can do nothing better than to try henceforth to be truly meek and humble. Grant me, then, that sincere humility which keeps me subject to everyone, which makes me bear little humiliations in silence, which even makes me accept them willingly and with serenity, without excuse or complaint, remembering that I really deserve more and greater ones than I receive.

"O Jesus, permit me to enter Your Heart as I would a school. In this school teach me the science of the saints; in this school I shall listen attentively to Your sweet words : ' Learn of Me, for I am meek and humble of heart, and you will find rest for your souls. ' I can see that the storms I fear arise solely from my self-love, my vanity, my attachment to my own will. Defend me, O Lord, protect the peace of my soul ! Your Heart is an abyss in which I find everything and, above all, it is an abyss of love in which I must submerge every other love, especially love of self with its fruits of human respect, vain complacency and egoism. By drowning all these tendencies in the abyss of Your love I shall find there all the riches my soul needs. O Jesus, if I feel in

myself an abyss of pride and vainglory, I shall plunge it
immediately into the profound humiliations of Your Heart
which is an abyss of humility.   If I find in myself an abyss of
agitation, impatience or anger, I shall fly to Your Heart
which is an abyss of meekness.   In every circumstance, at
every encounter, I want to abandon myself to Your Heart,
the ocean of love and charity, and I will not leave it until
I am all penetrated by its divine fire " (cf. St. Margaret
Mary).

215

THE HEART OF JESUS OUR REFUGE

PRESENCE OF GOD - O Jesus, deign to take me into Your Sacred
Heart.   Grand that it may be the sanctuary where I may be
recollected, sheltered, and find my rest.

MEDITATION

1. The liturgy of the Feast of the Sacred Heart presents
to us the Heart of Jesus as the ark of salvation, our shelter
and our refuge.   " O Heart of Jesus, ark...of grace, pardon
and mercy, O Heart, inviolable sanctuary of the New Law,
Temple more sacred than the ancient ark!...Who would not
want an eternal home in this Heart? " (RB).   " Close to
these blessed wounds in the Heart of Christ, " exclaims
St. Peter Canisius, " I shall find refuge; in them I shall
build my nest in full security. "   This has always been the
hope of contemplative souls, of interior souls : to take refuge
in the Heart of Christ as in their chosen asylum.   St. Teresa
Margaret of the Heart of Jesus wrote in her last resolutions :
" My God, I wish to enclose myself now and forever in Your
most loving Heart as in a desert, to live there in You, with
You, and for You, a hidden life of love and sacrifice " (Sp).
The soul who wishes to sound the depths of the mysteries of
Christ and to understand something of His infinite love,
will find no better way than to enter within His Heart or,
as St. John of the Cross says, " to hide itself in the breast of

its Beloved, for to these clefts He invites it in the Canticle of Canticles saying : ' Arise, and make haste, my love, my fair one, and come into the clefts of the rock, and into the cavern of the enclosure " (*SC* 31,5). Let us take refuge then, in the Heart of Christ and contemplate His mysteries and His love, but seek there, too, a shelter for our interior life. This is a place of retreat which is always at our disposal and we can retire there even in the midst of occupations and duties. When rumors, curiosity, gossip, and the vanities of the world threaten to overwhelm us, let us quickly retire by a swift interior movement to the Heart of Jesus; there we shall always find recollection and peace.

2. In every temptation, we must fly to the Heart of Christ, reflecting on His goodness and charity, comparing them with our " vileness, malice, infidelity, and pride " (St. Peter Canisius). The Heart of Jesus will be our surest refuge in temptation; if we wish to escape Satan's wiles and our own evil tendencies, we must take shelter in the Heart of Him who conquered Satan, and healed our ills by His wounds. Jesus triumphed over evil; if we take refuge in Him, we will have nothing to fear. Tempests may still rage around us, but our soul will be guarded and protected from shipwreck. No matter what kind of struggles we have to undergo, no matter how bitter or humiliating they may be, if we keep intact our confidence in this divine Heart, it will be our salvation. " Heart of Jesus, salvation of those who trust in Thee, " the Church puts on our lips in the litany of the Sacred Heart.

We must have unshaken confidence in this meek Heart in spite of all our faults and daily infidelities. " Cast all your faults into the abyss of His charity with great confidence and you will immediately be free of them, " says St. Peter Canisius. And St. Bernard declared even more forcefully, " I have committed a great sin. My conscience will be troubled but will not despair because I remember the wounds of my Lord. For indeed, He was wounded for our iniquities. What sin is there so deadly that it cannot be remitted through the death of Christ? " With such confidence we, too, must seek the Heart of Jesus as a sure refuge in all our falls. We will often commit some fault through weakness or surprise in spite of all our good will. Let us then humble ourselves profoundly, acknowledge our weakness with humility, but we must not let this experience separate us from the Heart of Jesus. We should return to Him like the prodigal son to his Father and ask His pardon while kissing His sacred wounds, and renew our resolution to take up our abode in His Heart so full of goodness and mercy.

COLLOQUY

"O most sweet Jesus, the treachery of my sins would forbid my entering Your Heart. But since an inconceivable charity enlarged Your Heart, and since You, who alone are holy, can purify what is defiled, cleanse me from my faults, O good Jesus, and deliver me from my sins. When I am purified by You, I can approach You, O purest One, and enter and abide in Your Heart all the days of my life, to know and to do what You wish me to do " (St. Bonaventure).

"Truly, where is there sure and lasting safety and rest for one who is weak if not in Your wounds, O my Savior? I dwell there all the more securely as You are powerful and can save me.

"The world rages around me, the body weighs upon me, the devil lays snares for me, but I do not fall because I am founded on You, the firm rock.... If then, O Christ, the thought of Your wounds comes to my mind, if I recall such a powerful and efficacious remedy, I can no longer be terrified by the fear that any harm may befall me. Filled with confidence, I shall take what I need from Your Heart, O Lord, for mercies abound there, and Your wounds are open to permit these mercies to flow forth. They pierced Your hands and Your feet, they opened Your side with a spear; and through these clefts I am able...to taste and see how sweet You are, O Lord!...

"The blade pierced Your soul and reached Your Heart so that You might know compassion for my infirmities. Through the wounds in Your Body, the secret of Your Heart, that great mystery of love, was revealed; the inmost heart of Your mercy was opened, through which You came to us from the heights of heaven. Where then can we see more clearly than in Your wounds, O Lord, that You are sweet, gentle and full of mercy? No one indeed shows greater mercy than He who gives His life for the condemned, for those sentenced to death. Hence, all my hope lies in Your mercy, O Lord, and I shall never be deprived of it so long as You are merciful " (St. Bernard).

216

THE SACRED HEART AND THE EUCHARIST

PRESENCE OF GOD - Sacred Heart of Jesus, teach me how to live with You through the Sacrament of Your love.

MEDITATION

1. Devotion to the Sacred Heart should bring us to a life of intimate union with Jesus who, we know, is truly present and living in the Eucharist. The two devotions—to the Sacred Heart and to the Eucharist—are closely connected. They call upon one another and, we may even say, they require each other. The Sacred Heart explains the mystery of the love of Jesus by which He becomes bread in order to nourish us with His substance, while in the Eucharist we have the real presence of this same Heart, living in our midst. It is wonderful to contemplate the Heart of Jesus as the symbol of His infinite love, but it is even more wonderful to find Him always near us in the Sacrament of the altar. The Sacred Heart which we honor is not a dead person's heart which no longer palpitates, so that we have only the memory of him, but it is the Heart of a living Person, of One who lives eternally. He lives not only in heaven where His sacred humanity dwells in glory, but He lives also on earth wherever the Eucharist is reserved. In speaking of the Eucharist, Our Lord says to us, " Behold, I am with you all days, even to the consummation of the world " (*Mt* 28,20). In Holy Communion, then, this Heart beats within us, it touches our heart; through the love of this Heart, we are fed with His Flesh and with His Blood, so that we may abide in Him and He in us. " In the Eucharist, " said Benedict XV, " this divine Heart governs us and loves us by living and abiding with us, so that we may live and abide in Him, because in this Sacrament...He

offers and gives Himself to us as victim, companion, viaticum, and the pledge of future glory. "

2. The Eucharistic presence of Jesus in us is limited to the brief moments while the sacred species last, and ceases as soon as these disappear. However, Jesus expressly said, " He that eateth My Flesh and drinketh My Blood *abideth* in Me and I in him " (*Jn* 6,57). Now the word " *abide* " does not signify a passing visit, but is expressive of a stable, permanent state. Hence, from Our Lord's own words, we can see that our union with Jesus continues even after the sacred species are consumed. And this is the literal truth. First, union with the divinity of Jesus does not cease, since the three divine Persons dwell continually in souls in the state of grace; but there is also a certain enduring union with His humanity. Even when Christ in His sacred humanity is no longer substantially present in the one who has received Holy Communion, He is there by the influence of His operative presence and by the effusion of His grace. The Heart of Christ is no longer with us sacramentally when the appearances of bread and wine have disappeared, but He still abides with us spiritually by the irradiation of His love and His vivifying action, since we receive through the medium of the sacred humanity all that is given to us in the supernatural order. This spiritual union with Jesus, with His Sacred Heart, does not necessarily require Holy Communion; the state of grace suffices. Nevertheless, the Eucharistic Bread nourishes, consolidates, and strengthens this union, making it more profound in the sense that Jesus always exerts greater influence over the soul of the communicant, and His divine Heart radiates more completely His love and all His virtues in the hearts of those who receive Him in this Sacrament. Hence, it is not extravagant to aspire to an effective, permanent union with Jesus and His Sacred Heart; on the contrary, this is the union which the Church bids us ask for every day in the beautiful prayer before the Communion of the Mass : " *a te numquam separari permittas,* " never permit me to be separated from You.

COLLOQUY

"Lord Jesus Christ, Son of the living God, who, by the will of the Father and the cooperation of the Holy Spirit, hast by Thy death given life to the world, deliver me by this Thy most sacred Body and Blood from all my sins and from every evil. Make me always adhere to Thy commandments and never permit me to be separated from Thee" *(RM)*.

"O what a wonderful and intimate union is established between the soul and You, O lovable Lord, when it receives You in the Holy Eucharist! Then the soul becomes one with You, provided it is well disposed by the practice of the virtues, to imitate what You did in the course of Your life, Passion, and death. No, I cannot be perfectly united to You, O Christ, or You to me in Holy Communion, if I do not first make myself like You by renouncing myself and practicing the virtues most pleasing to You, and of which You have given us such wonderful examples.

"My union with You in Holy Communion will be more perfect to the degree that I become more like You by the practice of the virtues" (cf. St. Mary Magdalen dei Pazzi).

"O Jesus, You alone do I love and desire, for You alone do I hunger and thirst, in You I wish to lose myself and be consumed. Envelop me in the flame of Your charity and make me cling so closely to You that I can never be separated from You!

"O Lord Jesus, O immense ocean, why do You wait to absorb this little drop of water in Your immensity? My soul's one desire is to leave myself and enter into You. Open, O Lord, open Your loving Heart to me, for I desire nothing but You and I wish to cling to You with all my being. O wonderful union! This intimacy with You is, in truth, of more value than life itself! O my Beloved, permit me to embrace You in the depths of my soul so that, united to You, I may remain there, joined to You by an indissoluble bond!" (St. Gertrude).

217

FIRM CONFIDENCE

FOURTH SUNDAY AFTER PENTECOST

PRESENCE OF GOD - O Lord, make me understand that I am nothing, that I can do nothing by myself, and that only in You can I accomplish anything.

MEDITATION

1. Two ideas dominate the liturgy of today's Mass : great confidence in God and an acute awareness of human misery and insufficiency. These two ideas are closely connected, for it is the consciousness of our nothingness which leads us to put all our confidence in God, and the greater this confidence becomes in us, the more convinced we are of our nothingness.

The Mass begins with a cry of unshakable hope : " The Lord is my light and my salvation; whom shall I fear? " *(Introit)*. The Lord is with me in the Blessed Sacrament of the altar, the Lord comes to me in Holy Communion. What can separate me from Him? What can make me fear?

Yet I know my weakness; I have ever before my eyes the remembrance of my failures and infidelities. How great, then, is my need to humbly repeat the beautiful prayer of the Gradual : " Save us, O Lord, and pardon our sins.... Help us, O God, our Savior, for the glory of Your Name. " Yes, in spite of the continual help of divine grace, in spite of so many confessions and communions, I have to acknowledge new failures every day; daily, I must begin anew. The struggle is arduous and painful, but in today's Epistle *(Rom 8, 18-23)*, St. Paul reminds us that " the sufferings of this time are not worthy to be compared with the glory to come that shall be revealed in us. " This thought is one of consolation, hope and confidence; it does not, however, prevent us from longing for freedom and complete redemption. This is what the Apostle experienced when he said : " We also, who have the first fruits of the Spirit, even we ourselves groan within ourselves, waiting for the adoption of the sons of God, the redemption of our body in Christ Jesus. " The more we suffer because of our wretchedness, the more we should run to Jesus, with full confidence in the power of His Redemption.

2. Today's Gospel (*Lk* 5,1-11) is a practical demonstration of the words of Jesus : " Without Me, you can do nothing " (*Jn* 15,5). Simon and his companions had been fishing all night and had caught nothing; that is all they had been able to do by themselves. If we have had some little experience in the spiritual life, we will recognize that this is often our situation too. How many efforts we have made to rid ourself of this or that attachment, to forget injuries, to adapt ourself to our neighbor's way of doing things, to subject our will to another's! And yet, after all these attempts, we find our hands empty, like Peter's nets. Let us not be discouraged; if we can humbly acknowledge our failure instead of feeling annoyance because of it, the failure itself will turn into victory. So it happened to Peter after he had admitted publicly that he had " taken nothing. " St. Thérèse of the Child Jesus comments : " Had the Apostle caught some small fish, perhaps our divine Master would not have worked a miracle; but he had caught *nothing*, and so through the power and goodness of God his nets were soon filled with great fishes. Such is Our Lord's way. He gives as God, with divine generosity, but He insists on *humility of heart* " (*L*).

In spite of our good will to advance in virtue, Our Lord will not permit us to have any success until He sees that we are thoroughly convinced of our own weakness and inability; to give us this conviction, He lets us, as He let Peter, " work all night without catching anything. " But afterwards, as He sees our growing awareness of our poverty and our willingness to admit it openly, He will come to our aid. We must, then, have great faith in Him, never allowing ourselves to give up through lack of success. Every day, relying " on His word, " we must begin anew. If we have learned not to trust in our own strength, we must also learn to have complete confidence in the divine aid. If we have caught nothing until now, perhaps it is our lack of unshakable confidence that is the cause, and this deficiency, besides being displeasing to Jesus, paralyzes our spiritual life. Then let us repeat with Peter in a similar cry of confidence : " *in verbo tuo laxabo rete,* " Lord, at Thy word, I will let down the net. And let us repeat it every day, every moment, without ever growing weary.

COLLOQUY

" O Lord, You are my light and my salvation; whom shall I fear? You are the protector of my life; of whom shall I be afraid?... If armies in camp should stand together against me, my heart shall not fear. If a battle should rise up against me, in this will I be confident. One thing do I ask of You, O Lord, that I may dwell in Your house all the days of my life.... Then, in the day of evils, You will protect me in the secret place of Your tabernacle, You will exalt me upon a rock....

" Hear, O Lord, my voice with which I have cried to You : have mercy on me and hear me.... Turn not away Your face from me; decline not in Your wrath from Your servant; be my helper, forsake me not; do not despise me, O God my Savior. Although my father and my mother should abandon me, I am sure that You will never abandon me.... O my soul, expect the Lord, do manfully, and let your heart take courage, and wait for Him " (*Ps* 26).

" O Lord, You have done great things in me, and the greatest of all is that you have shown me my littleness, and how of myself I am incapable of anything good.

" Lord, You see how often I fail, but I am never astonished at it... I enter into myself and say : ' Alas, I am once more at the first step as before! ' But I say this in great peace without sadness, because I know that You know perfectly how fragile is our nature and You are always ready to help us. What, then, shall I fear? As soon as You see me fully convinced of my nothingness, You stretch out Your hand to me; but if I should try to do something great, even under the pretext of zeal, You desert me. So all I have to do is to humble myself, to bear with meekness my imperfections. Herein lies, for me, true holiness " (T.C.J. *St*, 9 – *NV – C*).

218

ABIDING IN CHRIST

PRESENCE OF GOD - O Jesus, teach me not only how to live with You, but how to live in You, to abide in You.

MEDITATION

1. On the evening of the Last Supper Jesus said : " Abide in Me and I in you " (*Jn* 15,4) and shortly afterwards He instituted the Eucharist, the Sacrament whose specific purpose is to nourish our life of union with Him. When Jesus comes to us, He does not depart without leaving on our soul " the impress of grace, like a seal pressed on hot wax...which leaves its impression after it has been removed. Thus the virtue of this sacrament, the warmth of divine charity, remains in the soul " (St. Catherine of Siena). Jesus said, " I am come to cast fire on the earth, and what will I but that it be kindled? " (*Lk* 12,49), and where will He light the fire of His love if not in the soul of the communicant who has the great privilege of giving Him hospitality? Each time we approach the Eucharistic table, Jesus, through the power of this Sacrament, rekindles in us the fire of His love and leaves the imprint of His grace; by this love and grace we remain spiritually united to Him. Even if we do not think of it, this reality is accomplished and is, of itself, very precious. However, Jesus wishes us to be aware of it, that we may live our union with Him in its fullness. Note that in speaking of our union with Himself, Jesus always presupposes our action before His own : " He that eateth My Flesh...abideth in Me and I in Him, " " Abide in Me, and I in you " (*Jn* 6,57 – 15,4); not that our action is the more important—for Jesus always precedes us with His grace, without which any union with Him would be impossible—but He would have us understand that we shall be united to Him in proportion to our correspondence with grace. Each Communion, of itself, brings us a new grace of union with Christ and therefore offers us the possibility of greater intimacy with Him, but we will live this union only according to the measure of our good will and our interior dispositions.

2. If we wish to " abide " in Christ throughout the day—having been nourished by Him in Holy Communion—we must, first of all, keep our heart recollected. If as soon as we leave the Church we forget that we have received the Lord and we submerge ourselves in " other business and occupations and worldly hindrances " says St. Teresa of Avila *(Way,* 34), we will never be able to remain united to Christ. Further, the Saint would tell us that by acting in such a way we seem " to be making all possible haste to prevent the Lord from taking possession of the house which is His own " *(ibid.).* The state of grace suffices, it is true, to keep us spiritually united to Christ, but how much more fruitful this union would be for us, if we tried to live it actually! Therefore, even in the midst of our daily occupations, let us try to remain under the influence of our morning Communion, that is, under the influence of Jesus, of His love, and His unceasing action in our soul. We should return often, at least in spirit, to the tabernacle to keep ourselves in contact with the Eucharist. If our duties oblige us to go out, let every church we pass or see from a distance, be a sweet reminder of the Lord we have received that day or will receive on the following day; let it be the occasion for a quick but fervent impulse of our heart toward Jesus in the Blessed Sacrament, or a rapid return to the sanctuary of our soul, there to renew our interior contact with the Lord. We should try to make a visit to the Blessed Sacrament every day, in such a way that it will be a real heart-to-heart visit with Jesus. If we truly *hunger* after Him we should feel an urgent need of keeping ourselves under the influence of the Eucharist; we should make use of all possible means to profit as much as we can from the grace of union with Christ, which has been offered to us in Holy Communion. By doing this, our sacramental Communion will be prolonged throughout the day by means of a continual spiritual Communion with Jesus. Then we will be really living by Him, for as He said, " He that eateth Me, the same also shall live by Me " *(Jn* 6,58).

COLLOQUY

" O Jesus, unite my heart to Yours, and consume everything in it that is displeasing to You; unite all that I am to all that You are, that You may supply for everything I lack. Unite my prayers and praises to those You address to Your Father from the Blessed Sacrament of the altar, so that Your prayer may supply for the deficiencies of mine.

" In order to make myself like You, who on the altar are obedient to every priest, good or bad, I will obey promptly and will put myself in the hands of my superiors as a victim to be immolated, so that dying to all my own wishes, inclinations, passions, and repugnances, I can be disposed of by my superiors as they see fit, without showing any repugnance. And as Your life in the Blessed Sacrament is completely hidden from the eyes of creatures, who see nothing but the poor appearance of the bread, so I shall strive, for love of You, to live so hidden that I shall always be veiled under the ashes of humility, loving to be despised, and rejoicing to appear the poorest and most abject of all.

" In order to be like You, who are always alone in the Blessed Sacrament, I shall love solitude and try to converse with You as much as possible. Grant that my mind may not seek to know anything but You, that my heart may have no longings or desires but to love You. When I am obliged to take some comfort, I shall take care to see that it be pleasing to Your Heart. In my conversations, O divine Word, I shall consecrate all my words to You so that You will not permit me to pronounce a single one which is not for Your glory. . . . When I am thirsty, I shall endure it in honor of the thirst You endured for the salvation of souls. . . . If by chance, I commit some fault, I shall humble myself, and then take the opposite virtue from Your Heart, offering it to the eternal Father in expiation for my failure. All this I intend to do, O Eucharistic Jesus, to unite myself to You in every action of the day " (cf. St. Margaret Mary).

219

FROM THE EUCHARIST TO THE TRINITY

PRESENCE OF GOD - O Jesus, lead me to the Trinity; help me to live
with the Trinity.

MEDITATION

1. Jesus came to us from the bosom of the Father to
bring us to the Trinity; this was the purpose of the Incarnation
and it is also that of the Eucharist, which prolongs the
mystery of the Incarnation in time.   In the Eucharist Jesus
continues to be the Mediator between the three divine
Persons and ourselves, holding out His hand to lead us to
Them. It is by coming to us in Holy Communion that He
continually puts us in more direct contact with the Blessed
Trinity; for He then comes in the integrity of His Person
as God and Man, humanity and divinity; and as God,
as the Word, He is always indissolubly united to the Father
and to the Holy Spirit.   Jesus can repeat from the consecrated
Host what He once said while He was on earth : " He that
sent Me is with Me, and He hath not left Me alone, " and
more explicitly : " I am in the Father and the Father [is]
in Me " (*Jn* 8,29 – 14,11).   Therefore, when He comes to us in
Holy Communion, He does not come alone, but with Him
come the Father and the Holy Spirit, because the three
divine Persons, although distinct one from another, are
inseparable.   The presence of the Trinity in our soul is not
limited to the moments when Jesus is sacramentally present
within us, for the three divine Persons dwell permanently in
a soul that is in the state of grace.   It is true, however,
that the Trinity is present in a very special way in Christ,
the Incarnate Word, the one Man personally united to the
Trinity and in whom dwells all the fullness of the divinity :
" *In quo habitat omnis plenitudo divinitatis* " (Litany of the
Sacred Heart).   Hence, it is certain that wherever Christ
is—and therefore in our soul at the time of Communion—
there the Trinity is also present in a very special way.

2. The Blessed Trinity is never so fully present to our souls as in the few moments when we have the sacramental presence of Jesus within us. The three divine Persons are not only present there but are pleased to remain there. The Father takes pleasure in His beloved Son who dwells within us and whom He has given to us in the Eucharist; the Word takes delight in the sacred humanity of Jesus which is wholly and forever His; the Holy Spirit rejoices in Christ, His chosen temple and, because of Him, is pleased to dwell within us. The entire Trinity, finding Jesus in us, abides in our soul with joy, looks on us with special love, and each Person diffuses Himself into us more fully. Thus each Communion nourishes our life of union not only with Jesus, but also with the entire Trinity; each Communion increases our capacity to welcome the three divine Persons and to live in " company " with Them in an increasingly intimate and profound relationship. The prayer of Jesus : " As Thou, Father, in Me and I in Thee, that they also may be one in Us...I in them, and Thou in Me, that they may be made perfect in one " (*Jn* 17,21.23), finds its most perfect realization in the precious moments when Jesus in the Eucharist is living within us. But even when His sacramental presence has gone, its effect remains; namely, this more intimate union with the Blessed Trinity.

Furthermore, we are never able to offer the Trinity a more worthy dwelling place than our soul during the moments when Jesus is sacramentally present within it; and not only a dwelling place, for we can also offer gifts, praises, supplications, and adoration worthy of God's infinite Majesty. In fact, we can offer Jesus present within us, because it is the Trinity, the three divine Persons Themselves, who have given Him to us, and He has given Himself to us with His whole substance : Jesus, the perfect praise of the Blessed Trinity, the beloved Son in whom the three divine Persons take all Their delight and complacency. Together with Him, we offer the love, the adoration, supplication, praise, and reparation of His Sacred Heart. How rich we are when we have Jesus within us! By Him and in Him we can fittingly honor, exalt, and glorify the Most Holy Trinity.

COLLOQUY

" O Jesus Christ, true God and true Man! My soul rejoices to find You in the Blessed Sacrament, You, the uncreated God who became man, a creature! In this Sacrament, O Christ, I find both Your humanity and Your divinity; from Your humanity I rise to Your divinity, and from it I go back to Your humanity. I see Your ineffable divinity which contains all the treasures of wisdom, of knowledge, of incorruptible riches. I see the inexhaustible fountain of delights which alone can satisfy our intelligence. I see Your most precious soul, O Jesus, with all the virtues and gifts of the Holy Spirit, a holy and unspotted oblation; I see Your sacred Body, the price of our redemption; I see Your Blood, which purifies and vivifies us; in brief, I find treasures which are so precious and so great that I cannot comprehend them.

" This Sacrament really contains You, O my God, You whom the Angels adore, in whose presence the Spirits and mighty Powers tremble. Oh! if we could only see You as clearly as they do, with what reverence would we approach this Sacrament, with what humility would we receive You.

" O Most Holy Trinity, You instituted this Sacrament in order to obtain the object of Your love, that is, to attract to Yourself the soul of Your creature, and detaching it from all earthly things, to unite it to Yourself, the uncreated God. In doing this, You make it die to sin and give it spiritual life, eternal life. O Blessed Trinity, this Sacrament was instituted by Your infinite goodness that we might be united to You and You to us; that we might receive You into ourselves and be received by You; that at the same time we might hold You within ourselves and be held by You " (St. Angela of Foligno).

220

THE MYSTERY OF THE TRINITY

PRESENCE OF GOD - O my God, Trinity whom I adore, teach me to know You and to love You.

MEDITATION

1. We had no right, as creatures, to know the mystery of the Most Blessed Trinity, which is the mystery of God's intimate life. However, God has made it known to us, for He did not wish to leave us in our natural state, that of a simple creature, but willed to raise us to the dignity of sons, of friends. The Son of God said, " I will not now call you servants; for the servant knoweth not what his lord doth. But I have called you friends, because all things whatsoever I have heard of My Father, I have made known to you" (*Jn* 15,15). The " all things " is precisely the mystery of the Most Blessed Trinity which Jesus, the Son of God, has seen and heard in the bosom of the Father.

In the Old Testament we find some references to this mystery, but its perfect revelation belongs to the New Testament, to the Testament of Love; and we might say that God wanted to reserve this manifestation for Himself. He did not reveal it to us by the prophets but by His only-begotten Son, who is one with Him. " No man hath seen God at any time, " says the Evangelist; " the only-begotten Son who is in the bosom of the Father, He hath declared Him " (*Jn* 1, 18). Jesus came to reveal to us the mystery of the intimate life of God; He spoke of Himself as the Son of God, equal to the Father in all things : " He that seeth Me, seeth the Father also, " because " I am in the Father and the Father [is] in Me " (*ibid.* 14,9.11). He spoke to us of the Holy Spirit, without whom we cannot attain eternal life : " Unless a man be born again of water and the Spirit, he cannot enter into the kingdom of God " (*ibid.* 3,5), and He promised us that He Himself, with the Father, would send us the Spirit who proceeds both from Him, the Word, and from the Father : " It is expedient to you that I go. For...if I go, I will send Him to you " (*ibid.* 16,7); " I will ask the

Father and He shall give you another Paraclete...the
Spirit of truth " (*ibid.* 14,16). Jesus often repeated these
ideas, thus teaching us that it is good for us to fix our gaze
on the sublime mystery of the Blessed Trinity : to admire,
to praise, and to return love to this One Triune God, who
loves us so much that He wishes to bring us into the secrecy
of His own intimate life.

2. God, the sovereign, infinite Good, is self-sufficient.
He finds all His happiness in knowing and loving Himself.
Because He is the infinitely perfect Being, knowledge and love
are essentially fruitful in Him, and from this fecundity comes
the mystery of His intimate life, the mystery of the Trinity.
The Father knows Himself perfectly from all eternity, and
knowing Himself, He generates the Word, the substantial
Idea in which the Father expresses, and to whom He
communicates, His whole essence, divinity and infinite
goodness. Thus the Word is " the brightness of the glory
and the figure of the substance " of the Father (*Heb* 1,3);
but He is a substantial brightness and figure, because He
possesses the same nature and the same perfections as the
Father. From all eternity, the Father and the Son contemplate and love each other infinitely, by reason of the
infinite, indivisible perfection which they have in common.

In this eternal love, there is a mutual attraction, a mutual
giving of Themselves, one to the other, diffusing Their whole
nature and divine essence into a third Person, the Holy
Spirit, who is the terminus, the pledge, and the substantial
gift of Their mutual love. Thus the same nature, the same
divine life circulates among the three divine Persons :
from the Father to the Son, and from the Father and the
Son to the Holy Spirit. The mystery of the Most Blessed
Trinity is therefore the mystery of the intimate life of God,
a mystery surging from the most perfect operations of knowledge and love by which God knows and loves Himself.

More than any other mystery, that of the Trinity
shows us our God as the *living* God, as One whose life is
essentially fruitful, so fruitful that the whole divine nature
and essence can be communicated by the Father to the Son,
and from the Father and the Son to the Holy Spirit without
any loss or diminution, all Three thereby possessing the
same infinite perfection. This mystery, above all others,
reveals to us the perfection of God's goodness. It tells us

that God is good, not only because He is the infinite Good, but also because this infinite good that He is is communicated : from the Father to the Son, and from the Father and the Son to the Holy Spirit. Whereas in works *outside* Himself God communicates His good only partially, in the bosom of the Trinity He communicates it integrally and necessarily, so that His intimate life consists precisely in this eternal, necessary and absolute communication of His whole good, His whole Being. The mystery of the Trinity teaches us that in God there is a boundless, inexhaustible ocean of goodness, love, fruitfulness and life. Precious knowledge this, because more than any other, it enables us to develop a sense of the infinite greatness of God.

COLLOQUY

" O incomprehensible God, Your greatness is eternal, and Your goodness ineffable. I see the three divine Persons flowing one into another in an indescribable, inscrutable way, and I rejoice in this sight. The Father flows into the Son, the Son into the Father, and the Father and the Son flow into the Holy Spirit. Eternal God, You are unspeakably good, You who, out of goodness, communicate to a creature, aware of its nothingness, some knowledge of Your eternal Being; but although this communication is wonderful, it might be called in all truth a mere nothing, in comparison with what You really are " (cf. St. Mary Magdalen dei Pazzi).

" O sovereign, eternal good, what has moved You, O infinite God, to enlighten me, Your finite creature, with the light of Your truth? You Yourself, O Fire of Love, You are the cause. For it is love which has constrained You and which always constrains You to be merciful to us, giving immense and infinite graces to Your creatures. O goodness which surpasses all goodness! You alone are He who is sovereignly good! You have given us the Word, Your only-begotten Son, that He might dwell among us who are nothing but wretchedness and darkness. What is the reason for this gift? Love, for you loved us before we ever were.

" O eternal Trinity! Who can reach You to thank You for the immeasurable gifts and unlimited favors You have showered upon me, as well as for the doctrine of the truth

You have taught me? Answer me, O Lord!... Enlighten me with Your grace, so that by this very light, I may thank You " (St. Catherine of Siena).

221

IN THE PRESENCE OF THE TRINITY

PRESENCE OF GOD - The knowledge of Your mystery, O Most Holy Trinity, creates in me profound humility, blind faith, and ardent love.

MEDITATION

1. What Jesus has revealed to us, and what the Church, relying on His word, teaches us about the Trinity, is sufficient to prove the existence of this mystery, but it does not suffice to enable us to understand it. Furthermore, it is the mystery of our faith which is least accessible to human reason, making us realize more than ever the infinite disproportion between our intelligence and the divine mysteries, giving us a vivid awareness of the vast distance which separates us, mere creatures that we are, from God, the Supreme Being, the Most High. All this is good—very good—because it makes us take, with regard to God, an attitude truly proper to creatures : an attitude of humility, of humble acknowledgement of our insufficiency, of respectful self-abasement, of reverent adoration. Thus, when we put ourselves in the presence of the great mystery of the Trinity, we feel the need to repeat humbly, " *Nihil sumus, nihil possumus, nihil valemus.* " We are nothing, we can do nothing, we are worth nothing (St. John Eudes), while at the same time praising the inaccessible greatness of our God : " *Sanctus, sanctus, sanctus, Dominus Deus Sabaoth!* " Holy, holy, holy, Lord God of hosts! Thou only art holy, Thou only art almighty, Thou only art worthy, Thou alone art He who is.

Unaided reason is blinded by the greatness of the mystery, but this same reason enlightened by faith is not misled. It admits its limitations, and submitting itself to divine revelation, it believes. This act of faith is all the more meritorious and supernatural, the less it leans on human reasoning. It gives greater honor to God the more blind its adherence to His word. St. Teresa of Jesus says, " The less of a natural foundation these truths had, the more firmly I held them and the greater was the devotion they inspired in me. I saw I had every reason for praising God " (*Life*, 19). This is the faith of a humble soul in the presence of the mystery of the Most Blessed Trinity.

2. Consideration of the mystery of the Trinity inspires us not only with an attitude of humble reverence and blind faith, but also with one of deep filial love. " This is the characteristic of friendship, " says St. Thomas, " that the friend confides his secrets to another. " This is also characteristic of the love of God for us, because by revealing to us the mystery of the Trinity, He has unveiled to us the secret of His intimate life, toward which we had no right to turn our gaze. If we had no other proofs of the love of friendship which God has for us, the revelation of this mystery would be more than enough to convince us of it. He has confided to us the secrets of His Heart; He has opened to us the mystery of His personal life and has admitted us into intimacy with Himself. All this justly strengthens our conviction of the *exceeding* charity with which God has loved us, especially since, not being satisfied to reveal this mystery, the three Persons of the glorious Trinity willed to give Themselves to us as well! The Father gave Himself to us by bringing us into existence and by sacrificing His only-begotten Son for our salvation; the Son gave Himself to us by becoming Incarnate, by dying for us on the Cross and by making Himself our Food; the Holy Spirit gave Himself to us by coming to dwell in our souls, by infusing grace and charity in us. If the three divine Persons have offered Themselves to us to this degree, it is to elevate us to the status of sons and to bring us, as sons, into Their divine family.

All through the Gospels we see the entire Trinity bending over man to redeem him and to make him share in Their divine nature and eternal beatitude. We see the Father enveloping us in His paternal mercy and providence; the Son becoming man and shedding His Blood for us; the Holy Spirit sanctifying our souls by filling them with grace and love.

Yes, in the presence of the Trinity, we always remain tiny creatures, infinitely distant from the divine Majesty; yet, the Trinity has stooped to us and drawn us, loving us with an eternal love. " *In caritate perpetua dilexi te, ideo attraxi te miserans tui,* " I have loved thee with an everlasting love, therefore have I drawn thee, taking pity on thee (*Jer* 31,3).

COLLOQUY

" My faith invokes You, O Blessed Trinity, with a clear, sincere voice, that faith which has been nourished by You since my birth, illumined unceasingly by the light of Your grace, and increased and confirmed in me by the doctrine of our Mother, the Church.

" I call upon You, O supremely happy Trinity, one, blessed, and glorious, Father, Son, and Holy Spirit; God, Lord, and Paraclete; charity, grace, and communication.

" O three divine Persons, equal and co-eternal; One, true God, Father, Son, and Holy Spirit, dwelling alone in eternity and in inaccessible light. By Your power You created the world, and by Your prudence You rule the terrestrial orb; holy, holy, holy, Lord God of Hosts, terrible and mighty, just and merciful, admirable, lovable, and worthy of all praise!

" I implore You, one, indivisible Trinity, open to me who invoke You.... I am knocking at Your door, O sovereign Father. You have said. ' Knock, and it shall be opened to you '; bid that it be opened for me. I am knocking at Your door, O most merciful Father, by the desires of my eager heart, my cries, and my tears. O Father of mercies, hear the groaning of Your child and hold out to me Your helpful hand.... I know, O Lord, I know and I confess, that I am unworthy to be loved by You but You are indeed worthy to be loved by me. I am not worthy to serve You, but You are most worthy to be served by Your creature. Give me, then, O Lord, what You are worthy of, and I shall be made worthy of that which I do not now deserve.

" I beseech You, O Blessed Trinity, come to me and make me a temple worthy of Your glory. I pray to the Father through the Son, and to the Son through the Father; I pray to the Holy Spirit through the Father and the Son, to take away all my vices and to implant all the virtues in me " (St. Augustine).

222

THE TRINITY WITHIN US

PRESENCE OF GOD - O Most Holy Trinity, who art pleased to make my soul Your dwelling place, deign to share with me Your divine life.

MEDITATION

1. Jesus came not only to reveal the mystery of the Blessed Trinity, but also to establish ties of the closest friendship between our souls and the three divine Persons. He is not only the Revealer of the Trinity, but the Mediator, the Way, the Bridge, leading us to the Triune God and uniting us with Him. In the beginning God willed to give Himself to our first parents who had been created in the state of grace, as Creator, and even more, as Trinity. However, sin cut off this intimate communication of friendship, by which God would have wished to treat man not only as a creature, but as a son, a friend for whom He would unveil the mystery of His intimate life in order to share it with him. All this would indeed be given back to man, but only after the Incarnation of the Word, when Jesus, as the God-Man, would restore what had been lost by becoming the Mediator between God and man. By cleansing us in His precious Blood, Jesus endowed our souls anew with the capacity of receiving the divine gift of sanctifying grace. We could once again participate in the divine nature and life; thus Jesus restored us to our original dignity as living temples of the glorious Trinity. Because He redeemed us, He could make this wonderful promise : " If anyone love Me...My Father will love him, and We will come to him, and will make Our abode with him " (*Jn* 14,23). These words reveal to us the mystery of the indwelling of the Trinity in our souls, an indwelling which implies a very special presence of God within us. It is realized only in a soul who loves, in a soul who lives in charity and grace, because, as St. John says, " He that abideth in charity abideth in God, and God in him " (1 *Jn* 4,16).

God dwells in a soul in the state of grace as friend delighting to be with friend, conversing with him in sweet familiarity. " Behold, " says the Lord, " I stand at the gate and knock; if any man shall hear My voice and open to Me the door, I will come in to him and will sup with him, and he with Me " (*Ap* 3,20).

2. If we are in the state of grace, God not only dwells in us, but since He is the living God, He lives in us : He lives His intimate life, the life of the Trinity. The Father is living in us, continually generating His Son; the Father and the Son are living in us, and from Them the Holy Spirit unceasingly proceeds. Our soul is the little heaven where this magnificent divine life, the life of the Blessed Trinity, is always unfolding. Why do the three divine Persons live in us, if not to give us a share in Their life, bringing us into this endless stream of divine life?

The Father begets His Son in us and gives Him to us in order to make us share in His divine Sonship, to make us His adopted child; and He does this because of His only-begotten Son who became incarnate for us. The Father and the Son breathe forth the Holy Spirit within our soul, and give Him to us, so that He who is the terminus and bond of Their love and union, may also be the bond of our love and union with Them.

The divine Persons are within us; we receive Them and participate in Their divine life through faith and charity. By faith we *believe* in Them, by charity we are *united* to Them. When we are one with the Father, He receives us into His paternal embrace, sustains us by His almighty power, and draws us with Himself to contemplate and love His Son, according to the words of Jesus Himself : " No man can come to Me except the Father draw him " (*Jn* 6,44). When we are joined to the Son, He clothes us with His splendor, penetrates us with His infinite light, teaches us to know the Father, and covers us with the merits He acquired for us by becoming Incarnate. He takes us with Him to love and praise the Father, thus verifying His word : " No man cometh to the Father but by Me " (*ibid.* 14,6).

When we are united with the Holy Spirit, He infuses within us the grace of the adoption of the children of God, and pours into our soul an ever-increasing participation in the divine life. He thus draws us with Him into an ever more intimate communion with the Father and the Son, so that, as Jesus said, we may be " made perfect in one " (*ibid.* 17,23).

" O souls created for these grandeurs and called thereto! What are you doing? " exclaimed St. John of the Cross. " Wherein do you occupy yourselves? " (*SC*, 39,7). The Most Blessed Trinity desires to share Its divine life with us, and shall we turn our gaze elsewhere?

COLLOQUY

" O eternal Trinity, One God, One in essence and Three in Persons, You created man to Your image, so that by the three powers of his one soul he would resemble Your Trinity and Unity. Through this likeness he is united with You; that is, by His memory, he is joined to and resembles the Father, to whom power is attributed; by his intellect, he resembles and is united to the Son, to whom wisdom is attributed; by his will, he resembles and becomes one with the Holy Spirit, the love of the Father and the Son, to whom mercy is attributed.

" O Father, grant that I may unite my memory to You by always remembering that You are the beginning from which all things proceed. O Son, unite my intellect to Yours and grant that I may perfectly judge all things according to the order established by Your wisdom. O Holy Spirit, grant that I may unite my will to You by loving perfectly that mercy and love which are the reason for my creation and for every grace given to me, without any merit on my part.

" O mighty, eternal Trinity, may You be thanked for all the love You have shown us in forming and sweetly endowing our soul with its powers : an intellect to know You, a memory to remember You, a will to love You above all things! It is reasonable that knowing You, O Infinite Goodness, I would love You; and this love is so strong that neither the devil nor any other creature can take it from me against my will.

" O power of the eternal Father, help me; wisdom of the Son, illumine the eye of my intellect; sweet mercy and love of the Holy Spirit, inflame my heart and unite it to Yourself.

" O eternal Trinity, my sweet Love, You who are Light, give me light; You who are Wisdom, give me wisdom;

O supreme Fortitude, give me strength. O eternal God, You are the calm ocean where souls dwell and are nourished, and where they find rest in the union of love " (St. Catherine of Siena).

223

EFFUSION OF THE TRINITY IN THE SOUL

PRESENCE OF GOD - O Most Holy Trinity, deign to renew Your visit to my soul.

MEDITATION

1. At the very moment of our Baptism, the three Persons of the Blessed Trinity take up Their abode in our soul. Yet the Church teaches us in the " *Veni, Sancte Spiritus,* " *Come, Holy Spirit,* to ask continually for the coming of the Holy Spirit and consequently, of the Blessed Trinity; for, by reason of Their indivisible unity, no one of the three divine Persons comes to us without the others. But, if the three divine Persons are within us already, how can They come again? A soul needs to have only a single degree of grace in order to have God—who is already present in it as Creator—present also as Friend, inviting it to live in intimacy with Himself. However, this friendship, this intimacy, has different degrees. It becomes closer and more profound according as the soul, growing in grace and charity, acquires a greater capacity for entering into a deeper relationship with the Blessed Trinity. Something similar is effected between two persons who are friends, and who live in the same house. When their mutual affection increases, their friendship becomes more intense; thus, although they were already present to each other, their reciprocal presence takes on a new aspect, one that is proper to the presence of a very dear friend. Likewise, the Trinity already inhabits the souls of the just, but the presence of the divine Persons can always be made stronger in terms of a more intimate affection; that is to say, They can always enter into deeper

relations of friendship with the soul. This is realized progressively as the soul acquires additional degrees of grace by advancing in charity. Since these new effusions of the Trinity in the souls of the just present aspects and produce effects which are always new, we can rightly call them new comings, new visits of the divine Persons. But, in reality, They are always present in the soul; Their visit does not come from without but from within the soul itself, where They dwell and give Themselves; and even, to a certain degree, reveal Themselves to the soul according to the words of Jesus : " He that loveth Me, shall be loved of My Father and I will love him and will manifest Myself to him " (*Jn* 14,21). Never are we given a better opportunity to understand the great reality contained in the words of the Gospel : " The kingdom of God is within you " (*Lk* 17,21), than when we are in the presence of this ineffable mystery.

2. The first visit or effusion of the Blessed Trinity in our soul took place on the day of our Baptism. The Father sent us His Son; the Father and the Son sent us the Holy Spirit, and because of the indissoluble unity of the Three, without being sent the Father Himself came. Now this visit is renewed every time we acquire an additional degree of grace—through the reception of a Sacrament or by advancing in charity. The promise of Jesus : " If anyone love Me...We will come to him and will make Our abode with him " (*Jn* 14,23), is never exhausted; it is always new, always ready to be actualized every time the conditions for it are renewed, that is, every time we love more intensely. This divine gift which is offered so generously to us, ought to spur us on to generosity and to constant progress in love, for only thus can we have full fruition of it. The Blessed Trinity will set no limits to the effusion of charity and grace in our soul, provided we place no obstacle to their development. Our horizon is broad and boundless, because the model proposed to us by Jesus for our life of union with the Blessed Trinity, is that very union that exists between the three divine Persons Themselves. Even in His priestly prayer on the evening of the Last Supper, Jesus asked His Father to give us a like union : " As Thou, Father, in Me, and I in Thee; that they also may be one in Us " (*ibid.* 17,21). It is evident that as creatures we can never be united to the Trinity as the three divine

Persons are united to one another; yet, Jesus did not hesitate
to offer us, and to ask for us, a similar union, in order to
urge us on to ever higher levels, and to make us understand
that if we do not fail in our correspondence to grace, the
three Persons of the Holy Trinity will never cease to diffuse
Themselves into our souls nor to unite us to Themselves
until we are made " perfect in one " (*ibid.* 17,23).

Only in heaven where we shall contemplate the Trinity
unveiled, face to face, will our union with the divine Persons
be perfect; but here on earth, we must hasten by faith and
love toward the wonderful goal which will be our happiness
for all eternity.

COLLOQUY

" O Trinity, most high God, merciful, beneficent,
Father, Son, and Holy Spirit, one God, my hope is in You.
Teach me, direct me, sustain me.

" O Father, by Your infinite power, fix my memory in
You and fill it with holy and divine thoughts.

" O Son, enlighten my intellect with Your eternal
wisdom, give me the knowledge of Your supreme truth and
of my wretchedness.

" O Holy Spirit, Love of the Father and the Son, by
Your incomprehensible goodness, draw my will to Yourself
and inflame it with the fire of Your charity which can never
be extinguished.

" O my Lord and my God, O my beginning and my end,
O sovereignly simple, calm, and lovable Essence! O abyss
of sweetness and delights, O my amiable light, supreme
happiness of my soul, ocean of ineffable joy, perfect plenitude
of all good things, my God and my All, what is lacking
to me when I possess You? You are my one, immutable
treasure. I do not have to seek or desire anything outside of
You. You alone do I seek and desire. Lord, draw me to You.
I knock, O Lord : open to me. Open to a little orphan
who implores You. Plunge me into the abyss of Your divinity.
Grant that I may be one spirit with You, so that I may
possess Your delights within me " (St. Albert the Great).

" O holy Father, by that love with which You cast on
me a reflection of the light of Your countenance, give me
grace to advance in You by holiness and virtue.

" O my Lord Jesus Christ, by the love which induced You to redeem me with Your Blood, clothe me with the purity of Your most holy life.

" O divine Paraclete! You, whose power equals Your holiness, by the love which made You bind me to Yourself, grant me the grace to love You with my whole heart, to adhere to You with my whole soul, and to use all my strength to love and serve You, so that I may live according to Your inspirations " (St. Gertrude).

224

FRATERNAL HARMONY

FIFTH SUNDAY AFTER PENTECOST

PRESENCE OF GOD - O Lord, teach me to live in perfect harmony with my neighbor, so that my prayers and offerings will be pleasing to You.

MEDITATION

1. This Sunday could well be called the Sunday of *Fraternal Charity*, a virtue so necessary to preserve proper relations with our neighbor. " Be ye all of one mind, " says St. Peter in his first Epistle (3,8-15), " having compassion one of another, being lovers of the brotherhood, merciful, modest, humble. " The Apostle speaks to us in a very practical and realistic way. He realizes that with our weakness and frailty we cannot preserve peace if we have no compassion for the faults of others, if we do not know how to be kind to those who displease us, and if we cannot bear blame with humility. Anyone who pretends that in achieving a life of perfect harmony with others, he need never suffer any annoyance or displeasure, and that he need never be contradicted or upset, has very little experience of the reality of life and forgets that, far from being pure spirits, we are limited by matter; he forgets that " we are mortal, frail, and weak, bearing about our bodies like vessels

of clay, a source of friction for one another " (St. Augustine),
even as clay jars carried in the same vehicle strike against
and jostle each other.   By reason of our limitations we have
mentalities, tastes, desires, and interests that differ from those
of others, and thus we do not always succeed in understanding
one another.

It even happens that sometimes, without wishing it and
without even the shadow of a bad intention, we work against
one another.   The remedy for these inevitable failures,
when the limitations of our nature are the cause of mutual
distress, is that suggested by St. Augustine : " *dilatentur
spatia caritatis,* " let more room be given to charity.   In other
words, let us enlarge our hearts by greater love, in order
that we may better understand and sympathize with one
another. Let us likewise practice greater humility, in order
to overcome the resentments of our self-love.   Even if someone
does act against us with ill will, we should know how to
forgive him, according to the words of the Apostle : " Not
rendering evil for evil, nor railing for railing, but contrariwise,
blessing. . . .   But if also you suffer anything for justice'
sake, blessed are ye. . . .   Sanctify the Lord Christ in your
hearts. "

2. The Gospel (*Mt* 5,20-24) repeats and intensifies the
same instruction.   First of all Jesus tells us : " Unless your
justice abound more than that of the scribes and Pharisees,
you shall not enter into the kingdom of heaven. "   This is a
clear allusion to the new law, the law of love, given to us by
Jesus Himself and far surpassing the simple law of justice.
We cannot content ourselves, as the Pharisees did, with
simply not doing harm to our neighbor; we must practice
toward him a positive, fraternal charity.   It is not enough
" not to kill " in order to escape " the judgment, " the Master
teaches, but " whosoever is angry with his brother, shall
be in danger of the judgment. "   Another aspect of the new
law proposed by Jesus concerns our interior dispositions.
It is useless to make an exterior display of goodness if this
does not proceed from a good conscience, a sincere heart.
It does not suffice to avoid giving outward offense to our
neighbor; we must avoid, or rather, repress our inner resentment.   The Pharisees, with their materialistic interpretation
of the law, had completely lost its spirit; they had forgotten
that the eyes of the Lord are always upon us and that He

sees our intentions as well as our acts.   Anger and resentment
that smolder in our heart do not escape Him.   At the
same time, Jesus asks great delicacy of us in all our exterior
dealings with our neighbor.   He demands that we avoid
not only offensive acts but even words that might hurt
another.   Charity and fraternal harmony meant so much
to Him that He did not hesitate to tell us : " If therefore
thou offer thy gift at the altar, and there thou remember
that thy brother hath anything against thee, leave there thy
offering before the altar, and go first to be reconciled to thy
brother. "   How much Our Lord loves us!   St. John Chrysostom remarks very aptly : " He does not take account
of His own honor, when He requires us to love our neighbor.
' Let My worship be interrupted, ' He says, ' but reestablish
your charity. ' "   Indeed, how can our prayers and sacrifices
be pleasing to God when something interferes with perfect
harmony between ourselves and our neighbor?

COLLOQUY

    " O Jesus, as I meditated on Your divine words,
I understood how imperfect was my love for my sisters in
religion and that I did not love them as You do.   Now
I know that true charity consists in bearing all my neighbor's
defects, in not being surprised at mistakes, but in being
edified at the smallest virtues.   Above all else I have learned
that charity must not remain shut up in the heart, for ' No
man lighteth a candle and putteth it...under a bushel; but
upon a candlestick, that they who come in may see the
light. '   This candle, it seems to me, O Lord, represents
that charity which enlightens and gladdens not only those
who are dearest to me, but likewise all those who are of the
household.
    " O Lord, how often it is said that the practice of charity
is difficult.   I should rather say that it *seems* difficult, for
' The yoke of the Lord is sweet and His burden light. '
And when we submit to that yoke we at once feel its sweetness
and can exclaim with the Psalmist : ' I have run in the way
of Your commandments since You have dilated my heart. '
O Jesus, ever since its sweet flame consumes me, I run with
joy in the way of Your new commandment, and I desire
so to run until that glorious day when with Your retinue

of virgins I shall follow You through Your boundless realm, singing Your new canticle—the Canticle of Love " (T.C.J. *St*, 10).

"O Lord Jesus Christ, if I had no other reason to love my neighbor—not only he who loves me but even he who does not—I should resolve to do so solely because of the commandment You have given us to love one another as You have loved us. Just as You, infinite beauty, goodness and perfection, love me, full of evil, and do not reject me because of my faults, so do I, for love of You, wish to love all my brethren " (Ven. John of Jesus Mary).

225

LIVING WITH THE TRINITY

PRESENCE OF GOD - O Father, Son, and Holy Spirit, take me into Your embrace and deign to admit me to intimacy with You.

MEDITATION

1. If we wish the great gift of the indwelling of the Blessed Trinity to bear its full fruit of intimate friendship with the three divine Persons, we must become accustomed to living with the Trinity, since it is impossible to have a real bond of friendship with someone if, after offering him the hospitality of our home, we immediately forget him. In order to live with the Trinity, it is not necessary to feel God's presence within us; this is a grace which He may give or withhold. It is sufficient to be grounded in the faith by which we know with certitude that the three divine Persons are dwelling within us. By relying on this reality which we cannot see, feel, or understand, but which we know with certainty because it has been revealed by God, we can direct ourselves toward a life of true union with the Blessed Trinity.

First, we should consider the three divine Persons present within us, in Their indivisible unity. We already know that everything done by the Trinity " ad extra, " that is, outside the Godhead, is the work of all three divine Persons without distinction; hence, this applies to Their action in our soul. All Three dwell equally in us. They are there simultaneously and They all produce the same effects in us. All Three diffuse grace and love in us; They enlighten us, offer us Their friendship and love us with one and the same love. Still this does not prevent each of Them from being present in our soul with the characteristics proper to His Person : the Father is there as the source and origin of the divinity and of all being; the Word is present as the splendor of the Father, as light; the Holy Spirit, as the fruit of the love of the Father and of the Son. Each divine Person, then, loves us in His own personal way and offers us His special gift. The Father offers us His most sweet paternity; the Son clothes us with His shining light; the Holy Spirit penetrates us with His ardent love. And we, insignificant creatures, should try to realize that we have such great gifts, so that we may fully profit by them.

2. You may have special relations with each of the three divine Persons, relations which correspond to Their particular characteristics. When you think of the Father, you will feel a need to live close to Him like a loving and devoted child, trying to please Him in all things, and desiring to do His will alone. At the same time, especially in moments of difficulty and anguish, you will hasten to take refuge in Him, finding in His omnipotence, His greatness and infinite goodness, a support and a remedy for your insufficiency, littleness and wretchedness.

When you contemplate the Word present in your soul, you will have the desire to allow yourself to be penetrated by His light, to be taught by Him who is the Word of the Father, that He may bring you to a true knowledge of the divine mysteries, and show you how to judge everything as God does. You will feel the need of seeking Him in His Incarnation where you find Him more accessible to your humanity, of taking refuge in His Redemption by which He gives you life, makes Himself your Brother and presents you to the Father as His child.

When you consider the Holy Spirit, the delightful fruit of the love of the Father and the Son, a more ardent desire will arise in you to assist His work of love in your soul;

therefore, you will be willing to follow His inspirations
with more docility; you will let yourself be guided by Him
in all things and, finally, you will allow yourself to be seized
by His divine motion, so that He can bring you with Himself
into the bosom of the Father and the Son.

In this way you will realize in yourself that very lofty end
for which God has created and redeemed us, that is, " that
our fellowship may be with the Father and with His Son
Jesus Christ " (1 *Jn* 1,3). This will not be accomplished
through your own merits but only through the infinite
merits of Christ, who has shared with you His glory as the
Son of God, who has made you participate in the love with
which the Father loves Him, who has given you His Spirit,
and has become your Food in order to nourish your life of
union with the Most Holy Trinity in the most direct manner
possible.

COLLOQUY

" O my God, Trinity whom I adore! Help me to
become wholly forgetful of self, that I may be immovably
rooted in Thee, as changeless and calm as though my soul
were already in eternity. May nothing disturb my peace
or draw me forth from Thee, O my unchanging Lord, but
may I, at every moment, penetrate more deeply into the
depths of Thy mystery!

" Establish my soul in peace; make it Thy heaven, Thy
cherished abode, and the place of Thy rest. Let me never
leave Thee alone, but remain ever there, all absorbed in
Thee, in living faith, plunged in adoration, and wholly
yielded up to Thy creative action!

" O my Christ whom I love! Crucified for love! Would
that I might be the bride of Thy heart! Would that I might
cover Thee with glory and love Thee...even until I die
of love! Yet I realize my weakness and beseech Thee to
clothe me with Thyself, to identify my soul with all the
movements of Thine own. Immerse me in Thyself; possess
me wholly; substitute Thyself for me, that my life may be
but a radiance of Thy life. Enter my soul as Adorer, as
Restorer, as Savior!

" O eternal Word, Utterance of my God! I long to
spend my life in listening to Thee, to become wholly

' teachable, ' that I may learn all from Thee! Through all darkness, all privations, all helplessness, I yearn to keep my eyes ever upon Thee, and to dwell beneath Thy great light. O my beloved Star! so fascinate me that I may be unable to withdraw myself from Thy rays!

" O consuming Fire, Spirit of Love! Come down into me and reproduce in me, as it were, an incarnation of the Word, that I may be to Him a super-added humanity, wherein He may renew all His mystery! And Thou, O Father, bend down toward Thy poor little creature and overshadow her, beholding in her none other than Thy beloved Son in whom Thou art well pleased.

" O my ' Three, ' my all, my beatitude, infinite solitude, immensity wherein I lose myself! I yield myself to Thee as Thy prey. Immerse Thyself in me that I may be immersed in Thee, until I depart to contemplate in Thy light the abyss of Thy greatness! " (E.T. *III*).

226

THE GLORY OF THE MOST HOLY TRINITY

PRESENCE OF GOD - O most Holy Trinity, You who have created me for Your glory, grant that I may give You all the glory of which I am capable.

MEDITATION

1. The mystery of the Most Blessed Trinity is the root and center of all the other mysteries of our holy faith : the root from which they all spring and upon which they depend, the center about which they gravitate. For example, the great work of creation and the love-filled work of Redemption are the gifts of the Blessed Trinity, the free, gratuitous outpouring of infinite goodness and love, yet, at the same time, ordered for the glory of the august Trinity. " We have been predestined in Christ, " says St. Paul, " according to the purpose of Him who worketh all things according to the counsel of His will, that we may be unto the praise of His glory " (cf. *Eph* 1,11.12). The work of

Redemption, which bestowed the greatest of divine benefits on us, and which far exceeds the work of Creation, is, as the Apostle says again, " unto the praise of the glory of His grace " (*ibid.* 1,6), that is, of the infinite goodness of God. If inanimate things, if the heavens and the earth " show forth the glory of God " (*Ps* 18,1) because they testify to His power, wisdom, and infinite beauty, the works which effected our elevation to the supernatural state sing the glory of the Blessed Trinity because they are the most glorious manifestation of His goodness.   This goodness is so great that it has impelled God, not through necessity, but solely through love, to impart to us, His little creatures, something of His own sovereign good, of His divine nature, of His eternal felicity.   It also caused Him to reveal to us the mystery of His life in the Trinity and to share this divine life with us. All this was done, not through any merit on our part, nor through any need God had for us in His infinite beatitude, in the felicity and glory which He enjoys in Himself, but solely because of His goodness.   Who, then, more than man, should be " the praise of God's glory, " man, whom He endowed, not only with natural, but also with supernatural beauty, making him like to Himself, and a partaker in His own divine life?

2. By the mere fact that all God's works are a proof of His omnipotence, His wisdom, and His infinite goodness, they all redound to His glory, just as a work of art always gives honor to the artist who made it, because it is an expression of his genius.   But whereas man can direct his works to the glory of another being who is superior to himself, God cannot.   He is the Supreme Being, the sovereign Good; therefore, He must necessarily work for His own glory. However, because God is infinitely good, He wishes to glorify Himself by working for the happiness and good of His creatures.

As a matter of fact, God is not content with glorifying Himself by works which, though great and beautiful, are incapable, because inanimate or unknowing, of enjoying their own beauty; but He desires above all to glorify Himself in creatures like angels and men, to whom He has given the power of enjoying His gifts and whom He has destined to share in His eternal happiness.   This truth gives us a clearer understanding of the overwhelming goodness of

God, who has willed to find His greater glory precisely in those things which turn more to the advantage and honor of His creatures. For example, nothing glorifies the Blessed Trinity more than the Incarnation of the Word and yet, at the same time, nothing is more advantageous or honorable for us.

God, in His infinite goodness, willed that His glory should be identified with our good and our happiness. Should we not, then, try to make our good and our happiness one with His glory, by seeking them in whatever gives the most glory to Him and to His holy Name? All the wonderful gifts showered on us by the Trinity should contribute to the honor of God, and bear fruit for His glory. And, whereas the heavens sing the glory of God all unknowingly, we should sing it from the depths of a being that is informed by knowledge and love. Have we not understood that it is truly right and just that our whole life and all our works should be a hymn of glory to the Blessed Three who, although infinitely happy and glorious in Themselves, wish to be glorified in Their poor little creatures!

COLLOQUY

" O Most Holy Trinity, I adore You, I bless You and glorify You in all Your mysteries, uniting myself to all the mutual love and praise of Your divine Persons. I offer You all the glory You have in Yourself, rendering You infinite thanks together with the whole Church : ' *Gratias agimus tibi, propter magnam gloriam tuam.* ' We give You thanks, because of Your great glory. O my God and my Father, how I rejoice to see that Your Son and Your Holy Spirit love You and praise You from all eternity and for all eternity with a love and praise worthy of Your greatness! O only-begotten Son of God, my soul exults when it sees the infinite love and glory You receive from Your Father and from Your Holy Spirit! O Holy Spirit, my heart rejoices at the thought of the love and the praises unceasingly given You by the Father and the Son! O Most Holy Trinity, how great is my joy, my exultation, my gladness, to know that You possess indescribable glory, inconceivable beatitude, and an infinite number of incomparable treasures and splendors!

" How joyful I am too, knowing that You, Most Holy Trinity, already infinitely glorious in Yourself, do not look with disdain upon the glory which this wretched creature can give You, but rather, that You have created me precisely for Your glory! Therefore, I consecrate and sacrifice myself entirely to You. If I possessed all creation, the lives of all the angels and of all men, if millions of worlds were in my power, I would be ready to sacrifice them all for Your honor. O my God, exercise Your infinite power and goodness to take me and possess me entirely, so that I may be consecrated to You forever, O my God, and may immolate myself totally for Your glory " (St. John Eudes).

227

THE DIVINE PERFECTIONS

PRESENCE OF GOD - Grant, O Lord, that I may understand something of Your infinite perfections.

MEDITATION

1. Jesus has said, " Be you therefore perfect, as also your heavenly Father is perfect " (*Mt* 5,48), thus turning our attention to God's infinite perfection. Here on earth, we can see some pale reflection of this infinite plenitude through the consideration of the limited perfections that we find in creatures, but we cannot know it in itself, for the human mind is incapable of embracing and comprehending the infinite. Our ideas tell us something about God and His infinite perfections, but they cannot show Him to us as He really is. " God, " says St. Paul, " inhabiteth light inaccessible " (1 *Tm* 6,16) : light which infinitely exceeds the capacity of the human intellect, light too bright and dazzling to be gazed at directly by the eye of our mind, even as the sun, which in the full power of its summer brilliance so far exceeds the capacity of our sense of sight that no human eye can look at it fixedly.

Yet on several occasions when Jesus spoke about the divine perfections, He invited us to raise our eyes to these heights. He taught us that although we can understand very little about them, this little will not be useless, but rather, of great value. In fact, the more a soul advances in the knowledge of God, the more it understands that what it knows about Him is nothing compared with what He is in reality. Far beyond its ideas—however lofty and beautiful they may be—there is an infinite ocean of splendor, beauty, goodness, and love which no human intellect can ever fathom. This awareness of God's immensity, which infinitely surpasses the capacity of our mind, is a great grace. St. John of the Cross says : " One of the greatest favors God can bestow on a soul in this life is to give it to understand clearly and to sense manifestly that He cannot be entirely known or sensed " (*SC* 7,9). This is a precious grace, because it infuses into the soul an ever deepening realization of God's immensity and infinite transcendence; and, by contrast, it also gives it a greater understanding of its own nothingness and the extreme limitation of any human perfection.

2. Only in heaven shall we be permitted to see the divinity " face to face, " without the intermediary of ideas. As St. Paul says, " We see now through a glass in a dark manner.... Now I know in part; but then I shall know even as I am known " (1 *Cor* 13,12). This partial knowledge of God, which is all we can have on earth, reaches us through the " glass " of creatures; they give us, it is true, a reflection of His infinite perfections—His goodness, wisdom, justice, and beauty—but a reflection which is very imperfect and limited. For example, there is no man so learned that he knows everything that exists; no man is so good that he does not sometimes fail in goodness because of his frailty; no man is so just that he is not sometimes unjust through too great severity. Only by stripping the perfections that we find in creatures of the defects and limitations that are always found therein, shall we be able to form a vague idea of the divine perfections. God is good : He is always good, infinitely good. " One is good, God " (*Mt* 19,17), said Jesus, meaning that He alone possesses goodness pre-eminently; rather, He is goodness itself, unlimited goodness which never diminishes or fails.

We should reflect, then, how we err when we become attached to any creature. However beautiful, good, or wise it may be, its goodness, beauty, and wisdom are nothing in comparison with the perfections of God. St. John of the Cross goes even further when he says : " All the beauty of creatures, compared with the infinite beauty of God, is the height of deformity.... All the goodness of the creatures of the world, in comparison with the infinite goodness of God, may be described as wickedness.... Therefore, the soul that sets its heart on the good things of the world is supremely evil in the eyes of God. And, as deformity cannot attain to beauty and as wickedness comprehends not goodness, even so, such a soul cannot be united to God who is supreme goodness and beauty " (cf. *AS I*, 4,4). Thus we can understand that if we wish to unite ourselves to God, we cannot allow our heart to be held by the beauty or good qualities of any creature and that we must place our affection and our hope in God alone, without fear of being deceived.

COLLOQUY

" When shall we reach You, O fount of wisdom, indefectible light, inextinguishable brilliance, and see You, no longer as in a mirror and darkly, but face to face? Then our desires will be satisfied, since we shall no longer be able to desire anything but You, O Lord, the supreme good. In You, we shall see and love and praise; in Your glory we hall see Your light, for near to You is the fountain of life, an d in Your light we shall see the light.

" What light? An immense, incorporeal, incorruptible light; an indefectible, inextinguishable, inaccessible light; an uncreated, true, divine light, which enlightens the angels and gladdens the eternal youth of the saints; light which is the source of all light and life, which is You, O Lord, my God! You are the light in whose light we shall see the light, that is, You in Yourself, in the splendor of Your face, when we shall see You face to face.

" To see You is all the compensation, all the reward, and all the joy we wait for. This is eternal life, that we know You, the only true God.... Then shall we have what we seek, when we shall see You the only true God, the true, living, omnipotent, simple, invisible, unlimited, incomprehensible God.

"O Lord, my God, do not permit me to be distracted any more from You, but take me away from exterior things and make me interiorly recollected. Give Yourself to me, so that I may give You my heart forever. I have sought Your face, O Lord, and I shall seek it, the face of the Lord of Hosts, in which consists the eternal glory of the blessed, in whose sight consists eternal life and the eternal glory of the saints" (St. Augustine).

"Make me understand, O Lord, that beauty and all other gifts of creatures are but dust; that their charm and attractiveness are only smoke and wind, and that I must esteem them for what they are, so as not to fall into vanity. In all these things help me to direct my heart to You, joyfully and cheerfully, remembering that You are, and have in Yourself, all beauties and graces in a most infinite degree; You are infinitely high above all created things, for, as David says, ' They are all like a garment which shall grow old and pass away,' and You alone remain immutable forever '" (cf. *AS III*, 21,2).

228

THE DIVINE ESSENCE

PRESENCE OF GOD - O my God, purify and enlighten my mind so that I shall be able to contemplate You.

MEDITATION

1. To the question : "Who is God?" the catechism answers : "God is the Supreme Being, infinitely perfect, the Creator of heaven and earth." In the first place it says that God is the *Supreme Being;* this is His foremost perfection, the one which distinguishes Him radically from creatures. "I am who am," God said to Moses, and added : "This is My name forever, and this is my memorial unto all generations" (*Ex* 3,14.15). This name by which God called Himself expresses His very essence, and tells us that He is *Being itself*, the eternally subsistent Being, who had

no beginning and will have no end, the self-existing Being, who finds the cause of His Being in Himself. St. John Damascene says : " God possesses Being itself as a kind of sea of substance, infinite and shoreless. " God revealed Himself to St. Catherine of Siena under this aspect, when He said to her : " I am He who is, and you are she who is not. " All creatures are nothing! " My substance is as nothing before Thee, " says the Psalmist, " I am withered like grass. But Thou, O Lord, endurest forever " (*Ps* 38,6 – 101,12.13). The creature receives his being from God, while God is the cause of His own Being. A creature exists only so long as God maintains it in existence; God, however, *is* His own existence, because He possesses Being by His very nature, and does not receive it from anyone. A creature is always a limited being in every respect—vitality, strength, ability; God, on the contrary, is the infinite Being, who knows no limits, who has all power and virtue. A creature bears within himself the seeds of death and destruction; in God all is life; He is Life : " I am...the life " (*Jn* 14,6), said Jesus.

Only God, the infinite Being, eternal Life, can communicate life, can give existence. Would it be too much, then, for us to consecrate our whole life and being to His service and glory? If we are living for God, we are living for life; if we live for ourselves, we are living for nothing, for death.

2. God is Being, the infinitely perfect Being who possesses all perfections, without defects and without limits. God is the infinitely good, beautiful, wise, just, merciful, omnipotent Being. All these perfections are not accidental qualities in Him, as they are in man, who may be more or less beautiful, good or wise, without ceasing to be a man. In God, however, these perfections are essential; that is, they belong to the very nature of the divine Being, or rather, they are one same thing with it. In order to speak of the divine perfections, we are obliged to enumerate them one after another, whereas, in reality, they are but one infinite perfection : goodness is identified with beauty; goodness and beauty, with wisdom; and these three, with justice; justice is identified with mercy, and so on. There is no multiplicity in God, but only one absolute unity. We need many words to speak of God, but God is not many things; He is the *One* Being, par excel-

lence : One in the Trinity of His Persons, One in the multiplicity of His perfections, One in the variety of His works, One in His thought, will, and love.

Therefore, you who have been created to the image and likeness of God ought to tend to unity. Your spiritual life is weak because it lacks unity. Examine your heart and see what a multiplicity of affections and preoccupations fill it : yes, you love God, but, together with Him, you also cherish your pride, comfort, and interests. You love God, but, at the same time, you love some creature with a disordered affection, that is, in a way and in a measure that does not please God. You are attached to these people, to these things—objects, money, occupations—which give you satisfaction... and all these affections, these attachments weigh upon you, drive you in a thousand different directions, dispersing your strength and preventing you from seeking the one thing necessary : " to love God and serve Him only " (*Imit. I*, 1,3). The more you lack profound unity—unity of affections, desires, and intentions—the weaker you will be and the more greatly will they endanger your interior life, for, as Jesus said, " Every kingdom divided against itself shall be brought to desolation " (*Lk* 11,17). Look, then, at God, the sovereign Unity, and beseech Him to help you to have unity in yourself.

COLLOQUY

" O eternal God, I rejoice that You are He who is, and that nothing can exist without You. I beg You, illumine the eye of my soul, that it may know the Being which You possess by Your essence, and the non-being, which I have by my nature, so that my whole life may gravitate around the axis of these two firm and immutable truths. O eternal God, who said, " I am who am, " I rejoice at the eminence of that Name, so much Your own that it cannot be applied to anyone but You. O venerable, ineffable Name, hidden from Abraham, Isaac, and Jacob, and made known to Moses as a testimony of love! O my God, reveal the inestimable riches of that Name to me, so that I will revere You, adore, love and serve You as You deserve. O my soul, if God alone is *He who is*, containing all the perfections of Being, why do you not join yourself to Him, so that your

being will find nobility and strength in His?   Why do you
give yourself to creatures, which lack substance and being,
since they cannot give you what you want, not having it in
themselves?   Henceforth, O my God, I will regard everything
as worthless, waste and harm, nothing and vanity, that
I may unite myself to You, to love and serve You for all
eternity " (Ven. Louis Du Pont).

 " O Lord, my days are vanished like smoke...and I am
smitten as grass.... But Thou, O Lord, endurest forever :
and Thy memorial to all generations.... In the beginning,
O Lord, Thou foundedst the earth, and the heavens are the
works of Thy hands.   They shall perish, but Thou remainest;
and all of them shall grow old like a garment.   And as a
vesture Thou shalt change them, and they shall be changed.
But Thou art always the selfsame and Thy years shall not
fail.... All creatures have received life from Thee, all
expect of Thee that Thou give them food in season....
But if Thou turnest away Thy face, they shall be troubled;
Thou shalt take away their breath, and they shall fail, and
shall return to their dust, but Thou remainest forever.

 " I will extol Thee, O God, my King, and I will bless Thy
Name forever!... Great is the Lord, and greatly to be
praised; and of His greatness there is no end " (*Ps* 101 –
103 – 144).

229

DIVINE SIMPLICITY

PRESENCE OF GOD - O Lord, Thou who art infinite simplicity,
simplify my mind and my heart, that I may serve Thee in simplicity
of spirit.

MEDITATION

 1. God is the unique simple Being because He is *one* in
His essence and in all His perfections.   When St. Thomas
speaks of God's simplicity, he presents it as the absence of all
that is composite.   In God there are not quantitative parts

as there are in us who are composed of body and soul.   God
is simple because in Him there is no matter; He is pure spirit.
Angels are also pure spirits; but angels are composite beings
because their essence is like ours, distinct from their existence.
The angelic essence does not exist by itself but has only the
capacity to exist; in fact, no angel, as likewise no man,
can exist if God does not call him to life.   In God, on the
contrary, there is supreme simplicity, infinitely superior
to that of the angels : in Him essence and existence are
identical.   His essence exists of itself; He is the eternally
subsistent Being.

Neither do the innumerable perfections of God create
in Him any multiplicity : God is not composed of goodness,
beauty, wisdom, justice, but He is, at the same time, the
infinitely good, beautiful, wise, and just Being.   There is no
distinction in Him between substance and quality, because
all is substance; His infinite perfections *are* His very substance.
God contains in one, unique and most simple perfection,
the perfection of His divine Being, all the multiple perfections
we find divided among creatures in addition to thousands
and thousands of others, somewhat as a million dollars
contains the value of many dollars.   God's simplicity is not,
then, poverty, but infinite riches, infinite perfections which
we ourselves ought to reflect.

Consider how rich God is in innumerable perfections
and how He possesses them all in the same degree.   Consider,
on the other hand, how poor you are in virtues and if you
have any at all, how limited they are, how mixed with
faults!   Moreover, for one virtue which you possess in
some slight degree, how many others you lack!   God is
simple; you, on the contrary, are complicated!   Contemplate
the divine simplicity and try to imitate it by means of true
simplicity of soul.

2. In God, *being* is not distinct from *acting;* there is no
difference between potency and act.   He *is* pure act, the
act of an infinite intellect which always subsists and embraces
all truth; at the same time, He is the act of a will which
always subsists and desires the good.   There is no admixture
of error in God's eternal thought; there are no deviations
toward evil in the eternal will of God.   In God, there is no
succession of thoughts, but only one single, eternal, immutable,
subsistent thought which comprehends all truth.   In God,

there are not separate acts of the will which follow one
another, but one single act, perfect and immutable, always
willing the good with a most pure intention, and if it permits
evil, it does so only with a view to a greater good.

If we wish to approach in some way to divine simplicity,
we must avoid every form of duplicity. We must avoid
duplicity of mind by a passionate search for the truth,
loving and accepting the truth even when it exacts sacrifice,
or if by revealing our defects and errors it is not to our
credit. We must also cultivate the most candid sincerity,
fleeing from every form of falsehood. Jesus said : " Let
your speech be yes, yes, no, no " (*Mt* 5,37). Even before
this simplicity appears in our words it should shine in
our thought and mind, for " If thy eye be evil, thy whole
body shall be darksome " (*ibid.* 6,23). Our thought is the
eye which directs our acts; if our thoughts are simple,
upright, and sincere, all our acts will be so too.

We will avoid duplicity of the will by rectitude of
intention : this will lead us to act solely to please God.
Then even in the multiplicity of our acts, there will be
simplicity and profound unity. Then we will not halt
between two sides : between love of self and love of God,
between creatures and the Creator, but we will walk on
one road only, the straight road of duty, of God's will and
good pleasure.

COLLOQUY

" O most high God, in Your one and simple Being
You are all the virtues and grandeurs of Your attributes;
for You are omnipotent, wise, good, merciful, just, strong,
and loving, and You possess other infinite attributes and
virtues of which we have no knowledge. You are all these
things in Your simple Being.

" O wondrous excellence of God! O abyss of delights,
which are the more abundant in proportion as Your riches
are all contained in the infinite simplicity and unity of
Your sole Being, so that each one is known and experienced
in such a way that the perfect knowledge and absorption
of the other is not impeded thereby, but rather each grace
and virtue that exists in You is light for some other of Your
grandeurs, so that through Your purity, O divine Wisdom,

many things are seen in You when one thing is seen "
(J.C. *LF*, 3,2.17).

" O divine Essence, bottomless and boundless abyss
of wonders! O unfathomable ocean of greatness, O Unity
of my God, O Simplicity, O Eternity without beginning
and without end, to whom everything is continually present!
O Immensity, which fills all things and contains all things!
O Infinity, which embraces all imaginable perfections,
O Immutability, O Immortality, O inaccessible Splendor!
O incomprehensible Truth, O abyss of Knowledge and
Wisdom, O Truth of my God.... O divine Power, creating
and sustaining all things! O divine Providence, governing
all! O Justice, O Goodness, O Mercy, O Beauty, O Glory,
O Fidelity!... O great God, in You I adore all the grandeurs
and perfections which I have been contemplating, as well
as all the innumerable and inconceivable others which are,
and will remain, unknown to me. I adore You, praise You,
glorify and love You for all that You are. Oh! how my
heart rejoices to see You so great, and so overflowing with
every kind of treasure and splendor! Certainly, if I possessed
all these grandeurs and You had none of them, I would
want to strip myself of them at once and give them to You "
(St. John Eudes).

230

THE IMMUTABILITY AND ETERNITY OF GOD

PRESENCE OF GOD - O God, grant that my life on earth may be a
continual preparation for the eternity which awaits me.

MEDITATION

1. All created things are subject to change, to variation,
to progress, to decline, and finally to death. An ignorant,
helpless child who requires so much help, and who would
perish if no one took care of him, gradually grows and
develops, becomes first a sturdy youth, then a strong, mature
man, capable of great undertakings. But then, beneath

the weight of years, his vigor decreases, gives way to the weakness of old age, and is eventually extinguished by death. This is the path followed by every creature; every life has its dawn, its noontide, its sunset.

Only in God, the uncreated, eternal Being, is there " no change, nor shadow of alteration " (*Jas* 1,17). God does not change and cannot change, because He is infinite and eternal. Being infinite, He possesses being and every perfection without limit; in Him there is no limit, no beginning or end. Our souls, although created, will not die with our bodies; therefore, they are immortal, but not eternal, for they had a beginning; this, however, is not true in regard to God, who always was and always will be. Every perfection in man is subject to further development and progress; God, on the contrary, possesses every perfection in the highest degree, that is, in an absolutely infinite degree, to which nothing can be added.

Man, precisely because he is limited, is very much subject to change and variation : his ideas, his mind, his opinions, tastes, desires, and his will, all change. The very thing we had so ardently desired, soon wearies us, and no longer satisfies us; that very idea which seemed so beautiful and clear, corresponding so well to truth, soon appears to us so imperfect and inexact that we regret we cherished and defended it so much. The very good we wanted so eagerly and enthusiastically, sometimes leaves us cold and indifferent, perhaps even disgusted. In God there is nothing of all this : " For I am the Lord, and I change not " (*Mal* 3,6). His mind does not change because His infinite wisdom is immutable, embracing at once all truth, and only truth. His will does not change because it is an infinite will for good, always and indefectibly willing good, the greatest, absolute, infinite good.

How much we need to unite our inconstant and change-able will to the immutable will of God! The more we try to will only what God wills, to love only what He loves, the more will our will be freed from its inconstancy and become fixed in good.

2. St. Augustine says : " God was in the past, is in the present, and will be in the future. He *was* because He never was not; He *will be* because He will never cease to exist; He *is* because He always exists. " This is a beautiful com-

mentary on the simple catechism answer : " God always was and always will be; He is the Eternal. " God's eternity is the possession of a full, perfect, interminable life, without any change : a full perfect life which subsists by itself, subsists with infinite power, vigor, and perfection; an interminable life which has no beginning and no end; a life without any change, that is, one which is not susceptible to any succession, mutation, or progress. In other words, God possesses the fullness of His infinite life " *tota simul*, " all at the same time, without beginning and in an eternal now.

The immutability and eternity of God are not, then, something materially static and motionless, like fixed matter, which indicates negation rather than affirmation of life. Rather, they are the characteristics of the greatest vitality; they are the fullness of an infinite, most perfect life in which there is no possibility of change or variation, because it has in itself all possible perfection.

We, as limited, changeable, mortal beings, live in time, and are subject to the succession of time; yet we are not created for time, but for eternity. God has destined us to share some day His divine immutability and eternity, although in a relative, not absolute, manner. Therefore, let us live with our eyes fixed on eternity, " *sub lumine aeternitatis*, " under the light of eternity, not allowing ourselves to be captivated and delayed by anything that is passing and contingent.

The passing moment should be lived in view of the eternity which awaits us. Let us not waste our time gathering treasures that " the rust and moth consume " (*Mt* 6,19), but let us lay up treasures which will remain in eternity; let us accumulate grace and love, which will be the measure of our eternal glory.

Furthermore, in adhering to God alone, the immutable and eternal One, the soul finds that stability, peace, and security which it would seek in vain in changeable, transitory creatures.

COLLOQUY

" O God, You are always the same and Your years have no end. Your years neither go nor come. Ours, on the contrary, flow on that they may reach the end. Your

years stand firm because they are lasting. Your years
are as one day, O Lord, and not a day to be renewed little
by little, but an immutable day, a today without a yesterday
or a tomorrow.

"My years pass in groanings, while You, O Lord,
my comfort, my Father, are eternal. I am dispersed and
scattered in the succession of time, and my thoughts are
broken in a continual and tumultuous movement. It is the
same with the interior of my soul, until, having been purified
by the flame of Your love, I shall cast myself irrevocably
in You.

"O my God, I give You thanks for having willed that
the day of this life should be brief and uncertain. What
length of time is long if it has an end? I cannot call back
yesterday; today is closely followed by tomorrow. In this
short space of time, grant that I may live a good life, in
order to be able to go to that place beyond which there
is no passing. Even as I am speaking, I am on my way
to it. As my words run on, flying from my lips, so do my
acts, my honors, my happiness, my unhappiness. Everything
passes!

"But it is not thus with You who are immutably eternal.
O God, he who understands exalts You, and he who does
not understand, exalts You likewise. Oh! how high You are!
yet, in the humble of heart is Your home. You raise up the
fallen, and those whose crown you are, do not fall"
(St. Augustine).

231

THE COMPASSION OF JESUS

SIXTH SUNDAY AFTER PENTECOST

PRESENCE OF GOD - O Jesus, my Lord and Father, have pity on my poor soul and sustain it by Your grace.

MEDITATION

1. One thought emerges from today's liturgy in a special way and dominates all : God is a merciful Father who takes pity on us and nourishes our souls. Our souls are always famished, we are always in need of nourishment to sustain our supernatural life.

God alone can give us the proper nourishment as the Church tells us in the beautiful prayer of the day : " O God of all power and might, the giver of all good things; implant in our hearts a deep love of Your name; increase in us true religion and sincere virtue; nourish us with all goodness and...keep us in Your loving care " (Collect). The heavenly Father graciously hears our plea and answers by directing us to His divine, only-begotten Son whom He sent into the world that we might have life in Him. In the Epistle (*Rom* 6, 3-11), St. Paul reminds us that as " we are baptized in Christ Jesus...in His death...so we also may walk in newness of life, " that in Him we may " live unto God. " It is in Jesus and in His Redemption that we find everything we need for the nourishment and life of our souls; it is in Him that we shall find the grace, love, faith, and the encouragement to virtue which we have petitioned in the Collect. It is a great joy for us to hear again that we are reborn in Christ to " newness of life "; it is a great comfort for our weakness. One point, however, remains obscure. How does it happen that we are always falling? Why are we always so miserable? A more attentive reading of the Epistle will reveal the reason : because we are not yet wholly " dead " with Christ, because the " old man " in us has not yet been " crucified " to the point of our no longer being " slaves of sin. " In a word, if we wish to live fully the life that Christ acquired for us by His death, we must first die with Him. As this does not mean material death of the body but spiritual death to our faults and passions, this death must be continually renewed : " *Quotidie morior,* " I die daily (*I Cor* 15,31). The weakness of our spiritual life is caused by the insufficiency of this death to self.

2. In the Gospel (*Mk* 8,1-9) we hear the words of Jesus, so full of kindness : " I have compassion on the multitude. " Jesus has compassion on us, our weakness, our cowardice, our unstable wills. He sees that our souls are weary, hungry, in need of help, and as He spoke to the crowds who gathered to hear Him, so He repeats to us : " I have compassion! " Jesus pities first of all our spiritual needs. Although His Passion and death have abundantly provided for them, He still continues to take care of us every day in the most direct and personal way—by offering Himself as food for our souls. The Gospel speaks to us about the second multiplication of the loaves. However, we are more fortunate than the people of Palestine; Jesus has reserved for us a bread infinitely more nourishing and precious : the Eucharist.

Fascinated by the words of Jesus, the crowd had followed Him, forgetting even their necessities; three days they remained with Him and had nothing to eat. What a lesson for us who are often much more solicitous for our material food than for our spiritual nourishment! And Jesus, after having provided abundantly for the needs of their souls, thought also of their bodily needs. His disciples, however, were astonished : " From whence can anyone fill them with bread here in the wilderness? " They had already assisted at the first multiplication of the loaves, but here they seemed to have no remembrance of it and remained distrustful. How many times have we too seen miracles of grace and the wonders of divine Providence! And yet, when we are placed in new, bewildering, or difficult circumstances, how often we remain hesitant; it seems as if we doubted God's almighty power. Let us think, for example, of our spiritual life : there are still things to be overcome or surmounted...we have tried so many times, and perhaps we no longer have the courage to begin again. Oh! if our faith were only greater, if we would only cast ourselves upon God with more confidence! One good act of total abandonment might be all we need to win the victory! Jesus is looking at us and saying, " I have compassion on the multitude" and His compassion is not sterile, but is vital action, help, and actual grace for our soul : why, then, do we not have more confidence in Him?

COLLOQUY

" Ah! my Lord, Your help is absolutely necessary for me; without You I can do nothing. In Your mercy, O God, do not allow my soul to be deceived and to give up the work it has begun. Give me light to know that my whole welfare depends on perseverance.

"Make me understand that my faith in You must rise above my misery, and that I must never be alarmed if I feel weak and fearful. I must make allowance for the flesh, remembering what You said, O Jesus, in Your prayer in the garden : ' The flesh is weak... ' If You said that Your divine and sinless flesh was weak, how can I expect mine to be so strong that it does not feel afraid? O Lord, I do not wish to be preoccupied with my fears nor to be discouraged at my weakness. On the contrary, I wish to trust in Your mercy, and to have no confidence whatever in my own strength, convinced that my weakness comes from depending on myself" (T.J. *Int C II*, 1 – *Con*, 3).

" In You, O Lord, have I hoped; let me never be confounded; deliver me in Your justice. Bow down Your ear to me; make haste to deliver me! Be unto me a God, a protector, and a house of refuge to save me. For You are my strength and my refuge; and for Your Name's sake You will lead me and nourish me. Into Your hands I commend my spirit; You have redeemed me, O Lord, the God of truth. I will be glad and rejoice in Your mercy. For You have regarded my humility, You have saved my soul out of distress. And You have not shut me up in the hands of the enemy : You have set my feet in a spacious place. I have put my trust in You, O Lord, save me in Your mercy. Let me not be confounded, O Lord, for I have called upon You. How great is the multitude of Your sweetness, O Lord, which You have hidden for them that fear You, which You have wrought for them that hope in You. Have courage, and let your heart be strengthened, all you that hope in the Lord " (*Ps* 30).

232

GOD'S INFINITE GOODNESS

PRESENCE OF GOD - O my God, You alone are good; deign to clothe me with Your goodness!

MEDITATION

1. When Moses asked God to show him His glory, God replied : " I will show thee all good " (*Ex* 33,19), as if to say that His glory is infinite goodness, the good that He possesses in such plenitude that all good is in Him and no good exists independently of Him.   God possesses good, not because He has received it from anyone, but because He Himself is, by His nature, the sovereign good, because His Being is infinite goodness.   If creatures are good, they are so, only because God has communicated to them a little of His goodness.   Of itself, the creature cannot even exist, therefore it cannot possess any good of its own. That is why Jesus said to the young man who had called Him " Good Master, " " Why callest thou Me good?   None is good but one, that is God " (*Mk* 10,18).   Not even Jesus as man possessed goodness as His own; but He possessed it only because the divine nature, which was hypostatically united to His human nature, communicated it to Him. Only of God can it be said that He is good, in the sense that He is goodness itself, that goodness belongs to Him by nature, as divinity belongs to Him by nature; and just as it is impossible for His divinity to be lessened, so it is impossible for His goodness to be lessened.   Heaven, earth, and the ages will pass away, but the goodness of God will never pass away.   Man's wickedness may accumulate sin upon sin, evil upon evil, but over all, God's goodness will remain unchangeable.   The shadow of evil will not mar it; instead, God who is always benevolent, will bend over the evil to change it into good, and to draw a greater good from it. Thus infinite Goodness stooped over man, the sinner, and made an immensely superior good come from Adam's fall : the redemption of the world through the Incarnation of His only-begotten Son.   This is the distinctive character

of God's goodness : to will the good, only the good, even to the point of drawing good from evil.

2. God, who is supremely good in Himself, is also good in all His works; from Him, infinite Goodness, only good works can come. " And God saw all the things that He had made, and they were very good " (*Gen* 1,31); thus Holy Scripture concludes the account of creation. Everything that has come from the hand of God bears the imprint of His goodness. The sun which illumines and warms the earth is good, the earth which brings forth flowers and fruit is good, the sea is good, the sky is good, the stars are good : everything is good because it is the work of God, who is essential, infinite, and eternal goodness. But God has willed that among His creatures there should be some, such as man, who besides being good because He created them so, might also be good because of the adherence of their free will to that goodness which He has diffused in them. This is the great honor given by God to man : not only has He created him good, as He created heaven and earth good, but He has desired that man's goodness should result from the free concurrence of his will, as if God made him owner of the goodness He had placed in him. This is just why God has given man the great gift of liberty. See, then, how far you withdraw from goodness when you use your free will to choose not good, but evil! Consider the enormous difference between you and God : God is infinite goodness to the extreme of drawing good even out of evil, whereas your profound malice is capable of changing even what is good into evil, of making use of the good of your liberty to follow your egoism, your pride, your self-love. Yet, it would not be hard for you to be good if you adhered to that interior impulse toward good which God has placed within you, if you allowed the good He has infused into your heart to develop. God created you good; He desires you to be good. It is true that your malice—the consequence of sin—is great, but His infinite goodness immensely surpasses it. He can cure it or destroy it altogether, provided you want Him to do it and trust in His goodness.

COLLOQUY

" If a soul understood Your goodness, O God, it would
be moved to work with all its strength to correspond to it;
it would run quickly to meet You who are pursuing it
and entreating, ' Open to Me, My friend! '

" What advantage does a soul receive from understanding
Your goodness?   The advantage of being clothed with
Your goodness.   Oh! if we would only open our eyes and
see how great it is!   But sometimes we are blind and do
not see.   The precious Blood of Christ is the only remedy
which can open, not only our eyes, but also our heart,
and make our soul understand the immensity of God's
goodness. . . .   O my God, You reveal Your infinite goodness
to me as a great river flowing over the earth, into whose
waters all creatures are immersed and nourished like the
fish in the sea.   I am absorbed in the contemplation of this
great river; but when I look around and see human malice
so opposed to Your goodness, I grieve exceedingly.   O
infinite Goodness, my soul desires to honor You in two ways;
first by praise—recounting Your splendors, thanking You,
blessing You unceasingly for all the gifts and graces You are
always bestowing, and narrating all Your grandeurs; and
then by my works—not spoiling Your image in me, but
keeping it pure and spotless as You created it from the
beginning " (cf. St. Mary Magdalen dei Pazzi).

" O Lord, I want to trust always in Your goodness
which is greater than all the evil we can do.   When, with
full knowledge of ourselves, we desire to return to friendship
with You, You remember neither our ingratitude nor our
misuse of the favors You have granted us.   You might well
chastise us for these sins, but You make use of them only
to forgive us the more readily, just as You would forgive
those who have been members of Your household, and who,
as they say, have eaten of Your bread.   See what You have
done for me, who wearied of offending You before You
ceased forgiving me.   You are never weary of giving and
never can Your mercies be exhausted : let us not grow
weary of receiving " (T.J. *Life*, 19).

233

GOD'S INFINITE GOODNESS IS DIFFUSIVE

PRESENCE OF GOD - O infinite Goodness, continually communicated to creatures, teach me how to imitate You.

MEDITATION

1. Goodness is not confined within itself; its characteristic is to diffuse itself, that is, to communicate itself to others, " *bonum diffusivum sui,* " good is diffusive of itself; the greater the good, the more it tends to diffuse itself. God is the supreme good; therefore, He diffuses Himself sovereignly. He diffuses Himself first in Himself, in the bosom of the Blessed Trinity : the Father communicates to the Son all His divinity—essence, life, goodness and divine beatitude; the Father and the Son together communicate this to the Holy Spirit. The mystery of the Blessed Trinity, the intimate life of God, consists precisely in this essential, total, unceasing, and absolute communication. In it we have the supreme expression of the axiom : " *Bonum diffusivum sui.* " Good is diffusive of itself.

But infinite Goodness wills to pour itself out exteriorly also; thus, God calls into existence an immense number of creatures to whom He communicates, in varying ways and degrees, some of His own goodness. God creates creatures, not because He has need of them, for they can add nothing to His beatitude and essential glory; but He creates them solely to extend His infinite goodness outside Himself. God wills creatures not because of any goodness or loveliness already in them, but because in creating them, He gives them a share in His own good and makes them lovable. God communicates Himself to creatures only because He is good and rejoices in sharing His good with other beings. His goodness is so great that it can communicate itself to an infinite number of creatures without being diminished; it is so diffusive that it makes all it touches good. This goodness is the cause of your being and of your life : when you were created, it left its imprint on you, and it is always and unceasingly penetrating and enveloping you. Has your heart retained the seal of the divine goodness? Examine your thoughts, feelings, actions and see if there shines in them the reflection of the infinite goodness of God.

2. God's goodness is so gratuitous that it gives itself to creatures without any merit on their part; it is so liberal that it always precedes them and never fails to impart its light to them even when, by abusing their liberty, they show themselves unworthy of it. God's goodness is so patient that it does not stop at the ingratitude, the resistance, or even the crimes of His creatures, but His grace always pursues them. God could, in all justice, requite man's sins by depriving him of life and all the other good things He has bestowed upon him, but His infinite goodness prefers to shower upon man new gifts and new proofs of His kindness. Has He not said : " I desire not the death of the wicked, but that the wicked turn from his way, and live " (*Ez* 33,11)?

Consider now your goodness, and see how weak, narrow, calculating, and self-interested it is, when compared with the goodness of God. How often you act like the publicans of whom the Gospel speaks, " who love only those who love them " (cf. *Mt* 5,46). You are good to those who are good to you, you help those who will help you in return; but many times you are hard and miserly with your gifts to those from whom you can expect no recompense. Does it not often happen that you are sweet and benevolent toward those who approve of you and share your opinions, but harsh and unkind toward those who oppose you? In the presence of coldness, ingratitude, insults, or even a trifling lack of consideration, your good nature is offended, closes up, and withdraws into itself and you are no longer capable of benevolence toward your neighbor. See what need you have to meditate on the words of Jesus, inviting you to imitate His heavenly Father's goodness : " Love your enemies, do good to them that hate you, and pray for them that persecute and calumniate you, that you may be the children of your Father who is in heaven, who maketh His sun to rise upon the good and bad, and raineth upon the just and the unjust " (*Mt* 5,44.45).

COLLOQUY

"O eternal Father! O fire and abyss of charity! O eternal clemency, O hope and refuge of sinners! O eternal, infinite good! Have you any need of your creature? You must have, since You act as if You could not live without her, You, the life of every creature, without whom nothing lives. Why, then, do You act in this way? Because You are in love with Your work, and You delight in it, as if You were overcome with the desire of its salvation. Your creature flees from You and You go looking for her; she moves away, and You draw near. You could come no closer than You did when You took upon Yourself her humanity.

"What shall I say? I must cry with Jeremias : ' Ah! Ah! ' because I cannot say anything else, my limited words cannot express the affection of my soul which so greatly desires You. I ought to repeat St. Paul's words : ' Tongue cannot tell, nor ear hear, nor eye see, nor hath it entered into the heart of man to know what I saw. ' What did I see? ' *Vidi arcana Dei,* ' I saw the ineffable mysteries of God. And what can I say? I, with my dull feelings, can add nothing more; I only say to you, my soul, that you have tasted and have seen the abyss of the sovereign, eternal Providence. Now I thank You, O eternal, sovereign Father, for the unlimited goodness You have shown me, so wretched and unworthy of every grace.

"Can I ever thank You sufficiently for the burning charity which You have shown to me and to all creatures? No! But You, O sweet, loving Father, will be grateful for me, that is, the affection of Your charity itself will return thanks to You, for I am she who is not. If I said I could do something by my own power, it would not be true, for You alone are He who is. My being and all other good things have come from You, who give them to me unceasingly because You love me, and not because You owe me anything.

"O infinite goodness, inestimable love, wonderful are the marvels You have worked in Your rational creature! " (St. Catherine of Siena).

234

INFINITE WISDOM

PRESENCE OF GOD - O my God, infinite Wisdom, enlighten my mind and teach me the secret of true wisdom.

MEDITATION

1. God is infinite wisdom who knows Himself and all things perfectly. In God wisdom is not distinct from being as it is in us, but it is the very Being of God. Therefore, God's Being is supreme wisdom; it is a luminous, resplendent, eternally subsistent ray of intelligence which embraces and penetrates all the divine essence, and at the same time sees in it, as in their cause, all things which have existed or ever can exist. Divine wisdom, says Holy Scripture, " reacheth everywhere by reason of her purity.... She is a vapor of the power of God, and a certain pure emanation of the glory of the almighty God.... She is the brightness of eternal light, the unspotted mirror of God's majesty, and the image of His goodness " (*Wis* 7,24-26).

Divine wisdom is, before all, perfect knowledge of God. No creature, not even the angels or the blessed in heaven, can know God to the point of exhausting the depths of the infinite greatness of His Being : God alone knows Himself perfectly. Divine wisdom alone can exhaust the infinite profundity of His essence and of His mysteries. Although we are incapable of knowing God as He really is, it is an immense joy for us to contemplate the infinite wisdom which penetrates all the divine mysteries, and an immense comfort to invoke this infinite wisdom and entrust ourselves to it, that it may be our light and guide in the knowledge of God.

Divine wisdom is, therefore, a perfect knowledge of everything that exists; there can be no error in it, since it is eternal, immutable truth. Nothing is hidden from it nor can anything be a mystery to it : because it has created all things and it penetrates their inmost essence. There is nothing new which it can learn because from all eternity it sees everything in an eternal present; nothing, however minute, can escape its most brilliant light. " The very hairs of your head are numbered " (*Mt* 10,30), Jesus has said. God knows us much better than we know ourselves; the most secret movements of our hearts, even those which escape our control, are perfectly manifest to Him. Let us ask Him for the grace to know ourselves in His light, in His eternal truth.

2. Divine wisdom knows all things in God, in reference to Him, who is their first cause. It sees all things as depending upon God and ordained by Him to His glory; therefore, it does not judge them according to their outward appearances, but solely according to the value, place, and meaning they have in God's eyes. Consequently, the judgments of divine wisdom are vastly different from our short human judgments which stop at the purely material aspect of things : " O the depths of the riches of the wisdom and knowledge of God! " St. Paul exclaims, " How incomprehensible are His judgments, and how unsearchable His ways! " (*Rom* 11,33). They are all the more incomprehensible to us the more we are accustomed to judge them from a point of view opposed to that of divine wisdom.

To know created things in their relation to God, and to esteem them according to the value they have in His eyes, is true wisdom, which we should try to acquire in the reflected light of eternal wisdom. How far we are from it when we judge creatures and events only from a human standpoint, basing our judgment solely on the joy or displeasure they give us. This is the wisdom of the world and it is " foolishness with God " (1 *Cor* 3,19), precisely because it evaluates things according to their relation to man, and not to God, it judges them according to their appearances and not according to their reality. Only by accustoming ourselves to ignore our human view, which is too subjective and self-interested, will we be able to see beyond the appearances of things, to discover, in the light of faith, the significance and value they have in the eyes of God. Then we will clearly see that everything that the world greatly esteems—such as great talents, success, the esteem of creatures —are as nothing in the eyes of divine wisdom, which deems as far superior the slightest degree of grace, the least act of supernatural charity. Let us consider how wrong we are when we preoccupy ourselves more about our success in worldly affairs than about our progress in virtue. How mistaken we are when we judge our neighbor by his natural qualities, considering the feelings of congeniality or antipathy which he arouses in us, rather than his super-natural worth. May the humble consideration of our foolishness make us feel more keenly than ever the need of invoking divine Wisdom : " O Wisdom who camest forth from the mouth of the Most High, come and teach us the way of prudence " *(RB)*.

COLLOQUY

" O divine Wisdom, in you is the spirit of under-standing : holy, one, manifold, subtle, eloquent, active, undefiled, sure, sweet, loving that which is good, quick, which nothing hindereth, beneficent, gentle, kind, steadfast, assured, secure, having all power, overseeing all things, and containing all spirits, intelligible, pure. You are more active than all active things : and reach everywhere and penetrate everything by reason of your purity. You are a vapor of the power of God, and a certain pure emanation of the glory of Almighty God, and therefore, no defiled thing comes into you. You are the brightness of eternal light and the unspotted mirror of God's majesty and the image of His goodness. And being but one, you can do all things; and remaining in yourself the same, you renew all things, and through nations you convey yourself into holy souls, and make friends of God and the prophets.... You are more beautiful than the sun, and above all the order of the stars; being compared with the light, you are found before it. For after this comes night, but you are never overcome by evil. You reach, therefore, from end to end mightily, and order all things sweetly.

" God of my Fathers and Lord of mercy...with You is Your Wisdom who knows Your works, who also was present when You made the world, and knew what was agreeable to Your eyes, and what was right in Your com-mandments.... Send her out of Your holy heaven and from the throne of Your Majesty, that she may be with me and may labor with me, that I may know what is acceptable to You. She knows and understands all things, and shall lead me soberly in my works, and shall preserve me by her power.... O Lord...hardly do we guess aright at things that are upon earth; and with labor do we find the things that are before us. But the things that are in heaven, who shall search out? And who shall know Your thought, except You give wisdom, and send Your Holy Spirit from above? " (cf. *Wis* 7,22-30 – 9,1-17).

235

INFINITE LOVE

PRESENCE OF GOD - O my God, my only love, kindle in me the fire of Your charity.

MEDITATION

1. Sacred Scripture tells us : " *God is charity* " (1 *Jn* 4,16). God is love, eternal, infinite, substantial love. Just as everything in God is beautiful, good, perfect, and holy, so also everything in God is love—His beauty, wisdom, power, providence; even His justice is love. Love is perfect and holy when it turns with all its strength toward the sovereign good, and prefers it to every other good. This is the love with which God loves Himself, precisely because He is the one supreme and eternal Good, to which no other good can be preferred. The infinite love which God has for Himself is therefore, by its very nature, completely holy and has nothing in common with what we call self-love or egoism, that disordered love by which we prefer ourselves— more or less, and sometimes wholly—to God the supreme good. We are egoists because we have a tendency to love ourselves to the exclusion of every other affection, but God is so free from every shadow of egoism that, even though He loves Himself infinitely and is wholly satisfied with His infinite good, He tends by nature to diffuse His love outside Himself. It is thus that God loves creatures; He does not love them because there is some good in them which attracts Him, but it is He Himself who, loving them, creates good in them. " The love of God, " says St. Thomas, " is the cause which infuses and creates good in creatures " (Iª, q. 20, a. 2, co.). See, then, how God loves us, with love entirely

gratuitous and free, with love supremely pure, with love
that is both benevolence and beneficence : *benevolence* which
desires our good, *beneficence* which *does* us good.   By loving
us, God calls us to life, He infuses His grace in us, invites
us to do good, urges us to be saints, draws us to Himself
and gives us a share in His eternal happiness.   Everything
we are and have is the gift of His infinite love.

2. God " first loved us, " exclaims St. John the Apostle
(1 *Jn* 4,10); and, in fact, He has loved us from all eternity.
Even when we were not yet in existence, we were already
in the mind of God, and seeing us, He loved us and willed
to call us into existence in preference to innumerable other
beings.   " I have loved thee with an everlasting love; therefore, have I drawn thee, taking pity on thee " (*Jer* 31,3).
This is how God reveals to us the story of our life, which
is simply the story of His love for us.   This story, once begun,
never ends, because God's love has no end; sin alone has
the sad possibility of interrupting it, but even then God
never ceases to love us with an infinite, eternal, immutable,
most faithful love.   He loves us when He consoles us, but
He loves us too when He sends us trials and leaves us in
distress; He loves us when He gives us joy in abundance,
as well as when He afflicts us with sorrow.   His consolations
are love; so too are His chastisements and trials.   In all the
circumstances of our life, even the saddest and most painful,
we are always encompassed by His love.   God's love can
will nothing but good; even when He leads us by the harsh,
rough road of suffering, He is infallibly willing our good.
God " makes us die and makes us live....   He scourges
us and He saves us " (cf. 1 *Sm* 2,6 – *Tb* 13,2), always because
of His love.   Thus it is not rare that He strikes hardest those
whom He loves most, for, as the Holy Spirit says, " ...accept-
able men [are tried] in the furnace of humiliation " (*Sir* 2,5).
St. Teresa of Jesus says : This suffering " is what the Father
gave to Him whom He loved most of all [Jesus]....   These,
then, are His gifts in this world.   He gives them in proportion
to the love He bears us.   He gives more to those He loves
most and less to those He loves least " (*Way* 32).
To believe in God's love, to believe in it strongly even
when He strikes us in what we hold most dear : such is the
program of the soul who wishes to entrust itself blindly
to infinite love!

COLLOQUY

" Teach me, O Lord, how to love You; wretched as I am, I will love You with my whole heart and soul, because You loved me first. I exist because You created me; You willed from all eternity to number me among Your creatures. Whence does this blessing come to me, O most benign Lord, Most High God, most merciful Father; for what merits of mine, what grace of mine, did it please Your Majesty to create me? I did not exist and You created me; I was nothing and from nothing You drew me and gave me being. Not the existence of a drop of water, of fire, a bird, a fish or any other irrational animal...but You created me a little lower than the angels, since, like them, I have been given reason by which I may know You, and knowing You, can love You. And I, O Lord, by Your grace, can become Your son, which is impossible to other creatures. Only Your grace, only Your goodness has done this, so that I may share in Your sweetness. Give me then, the grace to be grateful, O You who have created me out of nothing! " (St. Augustine).

" O my God and my infinite Wisdom, without measure and without bounds, high above all the understanding both of angels and of men! O Love, You who love me more than I can love myself or conceive of love! What amazes and bewilders me, considering what we are, is the love You had for us and still have. I am so astounded that I am beside myself.

" How could my will not incline to love You? O Lord, I have received from You so many signs of love and I want to repay You, at least in some small way. I am especially moved by the thought that You, because You truly love me, never leave me but go with me everywhere and give me being and life. I know that I can never have a better friend " (T.J. *Exc*, 17 – *Con*, 2 – *Int C II*, 1).

236

INFINITE MERCY

PRESENCE OF GOD - Teach me, O Lord, the secrets of Your mercy, that I may fully profit by them.

MEDITATION

1. God's love for us assumes a very special character, one that is adapted to our nature as frail, weak creatures : the character of mercy.   Mercy is love bending over misery to relieve it, to redeem it, to raise it up to itself.   It almost seems that God, in loving us, is attracted by our weakness, not because it is lovable, but because being infinite goodness, His compassion stoops to compensate for it by His mercy. He wants to heal our imperfection by His infinite perfection, our impurity by His purity, our ignorance by His wisdom, our selfishness by His goodness, our weakness by His strength. God, the supreme, eternal good, wants to be the remedy for all our ills, " for He knoweth our frame, He remembereth that we are dust " (*Ps* 102,14).

Since our greatest evil—rather, the only real evil—is sin, infinite mercy would be the remedy.   Assuredly, God hates sin, but, although He is forced to withdraw His friendship, that is, His grace, from the soul of the sinner because of the offense, His mercy still finds a way of continuing to love him. If He can no longer love him as a friend, He loves him as a creature, as the work of His hands; He loves him for the good that is still in him and which gives hope of his conversion. God's mercy is so immense that no misery, however great, can exhaust it; not even the most infamous sin, provided it is repented of, can halt it.   This sad power is reserved to one thing only : the proud will of man by which he disdainfully shuts himself up in his wickedness, not wishing to admit how great is his need of God's infinite mercy.   In such a case, in spite of the immensity of divine mercy, the solemn words of the Gospel are fulfilled : " God hath scattered the proud in the conceit of their heart, He hath put down the mighty from their seats...the rich He hath sent empty away " (cf. *Lk* 1, 51-53).

2. There is no limit to God's mercy. He never rejects us because of our sins, He never grows weary of our infidelities, He never refuses to forgive us, He is always ready to forget all our offenses and to repay our ingratitude with graces. He never reproaches us for our offenses, even when we fall again immediately after being forgiven. He is never angered by our repeated failures or weakness in the practice of virtue, but always stretches out His hand to us, wanting to help us. Even when men condemn us, God shows mercy to us; He absolves us and sends us away justified, as Jesus did the woman taken in adultery. " Go, and now sin no more " (*Jn* 8,11). By His words and example, Jesus has shown us the inexhaustible depths of God's mercy : let us think of the prodigal son, the lost sheep, Magdalen, and the good thief. But He has also said to us : " Be ye therefore merciful, as Your Father also is merciful " (*Lk* 6,36). How far does our mercy go? How much compassion do we have for the faults of others? The measure of our mercy toward our neighbor will be the measure of God's mercy toward us, for Jesus has said, " With what measure you mete, it shall be measured to you again " (*Mt* 7,2).

God does not require us to be sinless that He may shower upon us the fullness of His mercy, but He does require us to be merciful to our neighbor, and moreover, to be humble. In fact, to be sinners is not enough to attract divine mercy; we must also humbly acknowledge our sins and turn to God with complete confidence. " What pleases God, " said St. Thérèse of Lisieux, " is to see me love my littleness and poverty; it is the blind hope I have in His mercy. This is my sole treasure " (*L*, 176). This is the treasure which supplies for all our miseries, weaknesses, relapses and infidelities, because by means of this humility and confidence we shall obtain the divine mercy. And with this at our disposal, how can our wretchedness discourage us?

COLLOQUY

" Bless the Lord, O my soul, and never forget all He has done for you. No, I shall never forget that You have forgiven all my faults, healed all my diseases, crowned me with mercy and compassion and satisfied my desire with good things.

" O Lord, You are compassionate and merciful,
long-suffering and plenteous in mercy. You will not always
be angry, nor will You threaten forever. You have not dealt
with me according to my sins nor rewarded me according
to my iniquities. For according to the height of the heavens
above the earth, Your mercy surpasses my merits. As a
father has compassion on his children so have You compassion
on them that fear You. For You know our frame, You
remember that we are dust. Everything will pass; but Your
mercy, O Lord, is from eternity unto eternity to them that
fear You " (cf. *Ps* 102).

" O Lord, since it has been given me to realize the love
of Your heart, all fear has been driven from my heart. The
remembrance of my faults humiliates me, leads me never to
rely on my strength, which is only weakness; but this remembrance, O Lord, speaks to me still more of Your mercy and
Your love. How could my sins fail to be consumed completely
if I cast them with wholly filial confidence into the burning
furnace of Your love?

" O Lord, even if I had committed every possible crime,
my confidence would remain unshaken, for I should then
feel—after sincerely repenting of them—that all the multitude
of my offenses would vanish as a drop of water in a fiery
furnace.

" O Jesus, would that I could tell all little souls of Your
ineffable condescension! I feel that if, by any impossibility,
You could find a soul weaker than mine, I believe You
would take delight in showering upon it still greater favors,
if it abandoned itself with perfect trust to Your infinite
mercy " (cf. T.C.J. *L*, 220 – *NV* – *St*, 13).

237

INFINITE JUSTICE

PRESENCE OF GOD - O Lord, reveal to me the beauty of Your justice, teach me to love it ardently and trustfully.

MEDITATION

1. Although justice does not seem to resemble mercy, it is, like the latter, an aspect of the sanctity of God, of His goodness, and of His infinite perfection. Justice and mercy are, to be more exact, two different—but inseparable—aspects of that one love with which God loves His creatures.　Mercy is love, infinite love of the good, and justice is equally so.　Mercy and justice penetrate each other.　" Precisely because He is just, God is also compassionate, " says St. Thérèse of the Child Jesus " (*L*, 203). God is merciful because He is just, and He is just because He is merciful; so, knowing our wretchedness, He bends down to us with infinite mercy.　Nevertheless, justice is distinct from mercy, or better, justice is God's love which gives us all we need for our good, for the attainment of our last end; and mercy, on the other hand, is God's love which gives us much more than we need.　But justice is never separated from mercy; it rather presupposes it.　Could God, for example, provide for the needs of our life—and this is the work of justice—if He had not first created these needs in us when He called us into existence—this being the work of mercy?　Justice, then, is always accompanied by mercy, for God invariably gives us much more than our due. As created beings, we are only entitled to a state of natural happiness, but God has willed to call us to a state of supernatural happiness.　We could live as children of God with the help of grace alone, but God has given us in addition the great gift of the Eucharist.　One drop of the Blood of Jesus would have sufficed to redeem the world from sin, but He willed to die on the Cross.　This is mercy, which ever accompanies and surpasses justice.　They are always interrelated, since God would not be infinite Justice if He were not infinite Mercy, and vice versa.

2. Mercy is the effusion of the sovereign Good who communicates His goodness to creatures; justice is zeal defending the rights of that sovereign Good who ought to be loved above all things. In this sense, justice intervenes when the creature tramples on God's rights and offends Him instead of loving and honoring Him. The punishment of the sinner is the fruit of justice, but at the same time it is the fruit of mercy, for " whom the Lord loveth, He chastiseth " (*Prov* 3,12). God does not punish a sinner in order to destroy him but to convert him. In this life the means used by divine justice are always directed by mercy, insofar as their purpose is always to put the sinner in such conditions as to profit by the divine mercy. Therefore, God is always merciful even when He punishes; His chastisements are not merely punishments, but they are also, and above all, remedies to cure our souls from sin, except in the case of those who refuse to be converted.

In our spiritual life, mercy and justice are continually alternating and intertwining. God's mercy offers us His divine friendship; but, in justice, He cannot receive as an intimate friend anyone who retains the slightest attachment to sin and imperfection. Therefore He subjects us to purifying trials for a twofold purpose : to make us atone for our faults—which is the aim of justice—and to destroy in us the last roots of sin that we may be disposed for union with God—and this is the aim of mercy. Hence, we must accept our trials humbly, realizing that we deserve them. We must accept them with zeal and a love of justice, wishing to avenge in ourselves God's rights, rights which we too often forget and ignore. We ought to accept them too with love, for every trial is a great mercy on the part of God, who wants to make us advance in the way of sanctity.

COLLOQUY

" O God, You have manifested to me Your infinite mercy, and in this resplendent mirror, I contemplate Your other attributes. There each appears radiant with love—Your justice perhaps more than the rest. What a sweet joy, O Lord, to think that You are just, that You take into account our weakness and know so well the frailty of our nature. What then need I fear? You, the God of infinite justice, who deigned to pardon lovingly the sins of the prodigal son, will You not also be just to me who am always with You?

" I know that one must be most pure to appear before You, the God of all holiness, but I know, too, that You are infinitely just; and it is this justice, which terrifies so many souls, that is the basis of my joy and trust. . . . O Lord, I hope as much from Your justice as from Your mercy; precisely because You are just, You are compassionate and merciful, long-suffering and plenteous in mercy " (T.C.J. *St*, 8 – *L*, 203).

" What will become of me who have so many faults with which to reproach myself? But where sin abounds, grace also abounds. And as Your mercy, O God, is eternal, I shall sing Your goodness forever, Your goodness, Your justice, not mine. I have only Yours because You are my justice. Should I fear that it will not be enough for both of us? But Your justice is infinite and remains forever and it will cover both of us with its immensity. In me it will cover the multitude of my sins, while in You, O Lord, it will only conceal the treasures of Your goodness which await me in the wounds of Christ. Here I shall find Your infinite sweetness, hidden, it is true, and only for those who are willing to surrender themselves " (cf. St. Bernard).

238

THE FRUITS OF LIFE

SEVENTH SUNDAY AFTER PENTECOST

PRESENCE OF GOD - Help me, O Lord, not to be satisfied with words, but to bring forth fruits of sanctity.

MEDITATION

1. Both the Epistle (*Rom* 6,19-23) and the Gospel (*Mt* 7,15-21) for today speak of the true fruits of the Christian life and invite us to ask ourselves what fruit we have produced

so far. " When you were the servants of sin, " says St. Paul,
you brought forth the fruits of death, " but now, being made
free from sin and become servants of God, you have your
fruit unto sanctification. " Our sanctification should be
the fruit of our Christian life, and we must examine ourselves
on this point. What progress are we making in virtue?
Are we faithful to our good resolutions?

Every Christian may consider himself a tree in the
Lord's vineyard; the divine gardener, Jesus Himself, has
planted it in good, fertile, productive ground in the garden
of the Church, where it is watered by the living water of
grace. He has given it the most tender care, cut off its
useless branches by means of trials, cured its diseases by
His Passion and death, and watered its roots with His
precious Blood. He has taken such good care of it that He
can say : " What is there that I ought to do more to My
vineyard, that I have not done to it? " (Is 5,4). After all
this solicitude, one day Jesus comes to see what kind of
fruit this tree is bearing, and by its fruit He judges it, for
" a good tree cannot bring forth evil fruit, neither can an
evil tree bring forth good fruit. " Before the Redemption,
mankind was like a wild tree which could bring forth only
fruits of death; but with the Redemption, we have been
grafted into Christ, and Christ, who nourishes us with His own
Blood, has every right to find in us fruits of sanctity, of eternal
life. This is why words and sighs and even faith are not
enough, for " faith...if it have not works, is dead in itself "
(Jas 2,17). Works as well as the fulfillment of God's will are
necessary, because " not everyone that says to Me ' Lord,
Lord! ' shall enter into the kingdom of heaven, but he that
doth the will of My Father who is in heaven. "

2. In the Gospel of the day, Jesus directs our attention to
the " false prophets " who appear " in the clothing of sheep,
but inwardly are ravening wolves. " There are many who
claim to be teachers in spiritual or moral matters, but they
are false teachers because their works do not correspond
to their words. It is easy, in fact, to speak well, but it is
not easy to live well. Sometimes false doctrines are offered
to us, even though they may not seem false at first because
they have the appearance of truth. Thus any doctrine
which, in the name of an evangelical principle, offends
other doctrines is false : for example, that which in the name

of compassion for individuals does harm to the common good, or that which in the name of charity sanctions injustice or leads to a neglect of obedience to lawful superiors. Equally false is any doctrine which tends to make us lax, disturbs peace and harmony, or under the pretext of a greater good, brings about dissension between superiors and subjects, or does not submit to the voice of authority. Jesus would like us to be as " simple as doves, " averse to criticism and severe judgments of our neighbor; but He also wants us to be as " wise as serpents " (*Mt* 10,16), so as not to let ourselves be deceived by false appearances of good which hide dangerous snares.

Furthermore, it is not given to all to be teachers, nor is it expected of all; but of everyone—learned and ignorant, teachers and pupils—Our Lord asks the practice of the Christian life in the concrete. What good would it do us to possess profound, lofty doctrine if, at the same time, we should not live according to this doctrine? Before we begin to instruct others, we must try to instruct ourselves, pledging ourselves to follow all the teachings of the Gospel in imitation of Jesus, " who began to do and to teach " (*Acts* 1,1). The genuine fruit which proves the worth of our doctrine and of our life is always that indicated by Jesus : the fulfillment of His will. This fulfillment means total adherence to the laws of God and of the Church, loyal obedience to our lawful superiors, fidelity to duty—and all these in every kind of circumstance, even at the sacrifice of our own ideas and will.

COLLOQUY

" O eternal God, when man was only a tree of death, You made him a tree of life by grafting Yourself onto him! Nevertheless, many people bring forth only fruits of death, due to their sins and to their refusal to be grafted onto You, O eternal life. Many remain in the death of their sins and do not come to the fountain from which Christ's Blood flows to water their tree...and thus it is seen that You created us without our help but You will not save us without it.

" What great dignity, O God, does the soul receive which has been grafted onto You and what excellent fruits it produces! How does this tree bear these fruits, if, by itself, it is sterile and dead? It bears them in You, O Christ, for if You had not been grafted onto it, it could produce no fruit by its own power, for it is nothing.

" O eternal truth, inestimable love! You brought forth for us, O Christ, fruits of fire, love, light, and prompt obedience, by which You ran like a Lover to the ignominious death of the Cross; You gave us these fruits by grafting Your divinity onto our humanity. Thus, a soul who has been grafted onto You cares for nothing but Your honor and the salvation of souls : it becomes faithful, prudent, and patient. Be ashamed, my soul, that you deprive yourself of so much good on account of your faults! The good I do is of no use to You, O God, and the evil of which I am guilty cannot harm You, but You are pleased when Your creature brings forth fruits of life because she will reap infinite good from them and attain the end for which You created her.

" O God, Your high, eternal will desires only our sanctification; therefore, a soul who desires to sanctify itself, strips itself of its own will and clothes itself with Yours. O my sweet Love, I think this is the true sign of those who have been grafted onto You; they fulfill Your will according to Your pleasure and not according to their own, so that they become clothed in Your will " (cf. St. Catherine of Siena).

239

DIVINE PROVIDENCE

PRESENCE OF GOD - O my God, You order and dispose everything according to Your own exalted purposes; teach me to trust fully in Your divine Providence.

MEDITATION

1. Divine Wisdom, says Holy Scripture, "reacheth...from end to end mightily and ordereth all things sweetly " (*Wis* 8,1). Divine Wisdom is thus identified with divine Providence,

which orders, disposes, and directs everything to the attainment of a well-defined end : the ultimate and supreme end which is the glory of God, the proximate and secondary end which is the good and happiness of creatures. Nothing exists without a reason, nothing in the world happens by chance; everything, everything without the least exception, is part of the magnificent plan of divine Providence. In this plan every creature, even the lowest, has its definite place, its end, and its value; every event, even the most insignificant, has been foreseen from all eternity and regulated even to its slightest detail. In this plan, as vast as it is wonderful, all creatures, from the most sublime—such as the angels—to the humblest—like the dewdrops and the blades of grass—are called upon to contribute to the harmony and good of the whole.

If certain situations seem to us incomprehensible, if we cannot see the reason why particular circumstances and creatures make us suffer, it is because we do not see the place they occupy in the plan of divine Providence in which everything is ordered for our ultimate good. Yes, even suffering itself is ordered for our good, and God, who is infinite goodness, neither wills nor permits it except for this purpose. We believe all this in theory but we easily forget it in practice, so much so, that when we find ourselves in obscure, painful situations which upset or interfere with our plans and wishes, we are disturbed and our lips formulate the anguished question : " Why does God permit this? " However, the answer, as universal and infallible as divine Providence itself, is always the same : God permits it solely for our good. We need to be firmly convinced of this so that we may not be scandalized by the trials of life. " All the ways of the Lord are mercy and truth, to them that seek after His covenant and His testimonies " (*Ps* 24,10); we can mistrust ourselves, our goodness and our faithfulness, but we cannot mistrust God who is infinite goodness and faithfulness.

2. Having created us, God has not left us to care for ourselves but, like a tender mother, He continues to help us and provide for all our needs. " Can a woman forget her infant?...and if she should forget, yet will not I forget thee " (*Is* 49,15). Each soul can, in all truth, consider these words as addressed to itself for, in actual fact, God's Providence is so immense and powerful that, while it embraces

the whole universe, it simultaneously takes care of each individual creature, even the least. Jesus showed us the Providence of our heavenly Father when He said, " Not one [sparrow] shall fall to the ground without the permission of your Father...Fear not, therefore : better are you than many sparrows " (*Mt* 10,29-31). Since God does not create us *en masse*, but creates individually the soul of every man that comes into the world, so too, His divine Providence is not limited to aiding us as a totality, but it assists each one of us, knowing well our needs, our difficulties, and even our desires; it is fully cognizant of what is most suitable for our ultimate good. The most attentive mother may be unaware of some need of her child, she may forget or make a mistake in providing for it, or she may find it impossible to help the child at all. But this can never happen with God, whose Providence knows, sees, and can do all things. Not even the tiniest bird is forgotten, nor is the humblest flower of the field neglected. " Consider the lilies of the field, " Jesus said, " ...they labor not, neither do they spin, yet I say to you, not even Solomon in all his glory was arrayed as one of these. And if the grass of the field, which is today, and tomorrow is cast into the oven, God doth so clothe, how much more you, O ye of little faith? " (*Mt* 6,28-30). God's Providence surrounds us completely; in it we live and move and have our being. Nevertheless, how slow we are to believe in it, how distrustful we are! What need we have to open our hearts to a greater, unlimited confidence, for divine Providence has no limits!

COLLOQUY

" O God, having created the world, You govern it with admirable order. You give life to the plants and make them grow; the flowers bloom and the fruits ripen in their season. You control the sun, the moon, and the planets; You have created the universe in perfect order for the benefit of mankind. You have made man for Yourself alone, and Your desire is to live in him; You want him to find no rest or peace outside of You. You have no need of Your creature, yet in him You deign to seek Your rest, so that hereafter he may enjoy You eternally, seeing You face to face, with all the blessed in heaven.

" Your divine Providence, O God, takes care of all Your creatures as though they were but one, and it takes care of each one as though all others were contained in it. Oh! if Your Providence were only understood, everyone would forget the things of this world to be united to it " (St. Mary Magdalen dei Pazzi).

" Lord, You are good to all and Your tender mercies are over all Your works. Let all Your works praise You, O Lord! Let Your saints bless You.... The eyes of all hope in You, and You give them meat in due season. You open Your hand and fill with blessings every living creature, You execute judgment for them that suffer wrong, and give food to the hungry. You loose them that are fettered, and enlighten the blind. You lift up them that are cast down; You love the just, O Lord. You heal the broken of heart and bind up their bruises. You cover the heavens with clouds, and prepare rain for the earth; You make grass to grow on the mountains. You give to beasts their food and to the young ravens that call upon You. O Lord, at the remembrance of Your immense goodness, all creatures break forth in praise and acclaim Your liberality " (cf. *Ps* 144 – 145 – 146).

240

DIVINE OMNIPOTENCE

PRESENCE OF GOD - O God, use Your almighty power to convert me entirely to Your love.

MEDITATION

1. " I am the Almighty God " (*Gen* 17,1). With these words God revealed Himself to Abraham. God is all-powerful because He can do all that He wills; and this He can do as He wills, when He wills, without any limitations. " Whatsoever the Lord pleased, He hath done, in heaven, in earth, in the sea, and in all the deeps " (*Ps* 134,6). Nothing can impede His action, nor oppose His will; nothing is

difficult to Him. Our works, even the simplest, require time, fatigue, material adaptation, and collaboration; God's works, even the greatest, are performed in one instant by a simple act of His will. God is so omnipotent that with a single word He has brought all things out of nothing : "*fiat*" and light, the heavens, the earth, the seas, and the whole universe were made. Our words are often empty sounds; they are dispersed in the air, producing no effect. God's word, on the contrary, is omnipotent, creative, operative, and effective, so that it infallibly produces whatever it expresses. God is so mighty that, after creating man free, He rules and directs him according to His good pleasure, without prejudicing man's liberty in any way. God is so omnipotent that He can change men, the children of sin, into His adopted sons, called to share His divine life. He is so omnipotent that He can draw good even from evil. The omnipotence of God is always active and working, without ever stopping; and this magnificent, infinite, eternal omnipotence is completely at the service of His infinite goodness, or better, is infinite goodness itself, which can do all the good it wishes. How much we need the help of this omnipotence, we who are so weak that, even seeing and willing the good, we are very often incapable of doing it!

2. God alone is omnipotent; He is the only One who possesses power by nature; we, on the contrary—like all other creatures—are without power, incapable of doing anything. Without the concurrence of divine omnipotence, the sun cannot shine, fire cannot burn nor can the flowers bloom; and man cannot perform even the slightest act. This is the great truth which Jesus taught us : " Without Me you can do nothing " (*Jn* 15,5).

Our power and ability do not have their principle in us, but in God alone : " Our sufficiency is from God " (2 *Cor* 3,5), says St. Paul. This is a thought which should keep us very humble : if there is something we can and know how to do, it is only because God has shared His divine power with us. Left to ourselves, we could not even formulate a thought or utter a word. On the other hand, this our radical impotence should not discourage us, because God, infinite goodness, has communicated being to us, as well as His goodness and His power, and He is disposed to communicate these to us in greater measure, the more humble He sees us to be, and the more convinced we are of our impotence. Thus God delights in choosing the humble, " the base things of the world, and the things that are contemptible...and the things that are not " (1 *Cor* 1,28), to accomplish the most magnificent works. St. Teresa of Avila could rightly say, " Teresa alone can do nothing but with Jesus she can do all things, " and St. Paul adds : " I can do all things in Him who strengtheneth me " (*Phil* 4,13). The reason for so many of our failures in the works of the apostolate and in our progress in virtue is to be found in the fact that we do not rely sufficiently on the divine onmipotence. We count too much on human means and too little on the help of almighty God. Certainly, we are not to remain idle awaiting God's help; we must do all that is in our power. Nevertheless, we must never hope for success from our own efforts and labors but only from the help of divine omnipotence.

COLLOQUY

" Your omnipotent hand, O God, created the angels in heaven, and on the earth the worms, and it was not superior in creating the former, nor inferior in creating the latter for no other hand but Yours could create an angel, and no other could create a worm either; as no other could create heaven, so no other could create the tiniest leaf of a tree, nor any substance. Only Your hand could do these things, Your hand, to which everything is possible. It is no easier for You to create a worm than an angel, but You have done all that You wished in heaven and on earth, in the seas and in all the abysses.

" You created all things from nothing; this You did by Your will alone. You possess each one of Your creatures without difficulty; You govern them without labor; You rule them without tedium, and nothing either above or below can disturb the order of Your kingdom. You are not the author of evil; of this You are incapable, although there is nothing which You cannot do. You have never regretted what You have done; no storm or disturbance of soul can trouble You, nor the perils of the whole earth endanger You " (St. Augustine).

" I rejoice, O God, because Your omnipotence is in the hands of Your just and loving will; and everything that comes

from that will and power, will be good and useful for me
and will redound to the glory of Your Name. O God,
One and Triune, who are as wise as You are powerful and as
powerful as You are good, and in all things infinite, illumine
my intellect by Your wisdom, make my will good by Your
sovereign goodness, strengthen my faculties by Your wonderful
power, so that I may know You, love You, and serve You
with fortitude " (Ven. L. Du Pont).

241

FAITH

PRESENCE OF GOD - O Lord, grant that I may understand the great
value of faith.

MEDITATION

1. " Without faith, it is impossible to please God "
(*Heb* 11,6) because faith is the foundation of all our relations
with Him.   For the man without faith, God has neither
meaning, nor value, nor place in his life.   On the other hand,
the more lively our faith is, the more God enters into our life,
until finally He becomes our all, the one great reality for
which we live, and the One for whom we courageously
face sorrow and death.   It is only when faith has deeply
penetrated a soul that it can exclaim with St. Paul, " For
whether we live, we live unto the Lord, or whether we die,
we die unto the Lord " (*Rom* 14,8).   We do not lack faith,
but it is not sufficiently alive and practical to make us see God
in everything and over everything, thus giving us the sense
of His essential, transcendent, and eternal reality, which
infinitely surpasses all the immediate, contingent, and passing
realities of this life.   Faith does not depend upon data received
through the senses, on what we can see and touch, nor is it
reduced to what we can understand with the intellect,
but surpassing all this, it makes us share in God's own
knowledge, in His thoughts, in His understanding.   Having
raised us to the state of divine sonship, God has made us

capable of sharing His intimate life, His life of knowledge
and love. For this purpose He has given us the theological
virtues together with grace. Faith allows us to share His
life of knowledge, and charity, His life of love.

Faith enables us to know God as He knows Himself,
although certainly not exhaustively. God knows Himself
not only as the Creator, but also as the Trinity and as the
Author of grace; it is under these aspects that faith presents
Him to us. By faith we know creatures as He knows them,
that is, in relation to Him and dependent upon Him. Our
intellect can give us only natural light on God and creatures;
faith, on the contrary, gives us the supernatural light that
is a participation in the light of God, in the knowledge God
has of Himself and of creatures.

2. St. Thomas says that " faith is a habitual disposition of
soul by which eternal life begins in us, " it is a " beginning
of eternal life " (II^a, II^{ae}, q.4, a.1, co.). In fact, by faith we
begin to know God as we shall one day know Him in heaven.
There we shall know Him unveiled in the light of glory;
here below we know Him dimly by means of the truths
which faith proposes to us to believe, truths which give us,
however, the very same God. Faith and the beatific vision
are like two phases of the same knowledge of God : faith
gives us an initial, obscure, imperfect knowledge; the beatific
vision, where faith will end, will give us full, clear, perfect
knowledge. Now " we know in part " as St. Paul says,
referring to our knowledge by faith, " but when that which
is perfect is come, " that is, the beatific vision, " that which
is in part shall be done away " (1 *Cor* 13,9.10). St. John
of the Cross gives us a pleasing comparison to make us understand that faith already contains the germ of the beatific
vision. He refers to the episode, narrated in Scripture,
of Gideon's soldiers who had " lamps in their hands, which
they saw not, because they had them concealed in the darkness
of the pitchers; but, when these pitchers were broken, the
light was seen. In like manner, faith, which is foreshadowed by those pitchers, contains within itself divine light; which,
when it is ended and broken, at the ending and breaking of
this mortal life, will allow the glory and light of the divinity,
which was contained in it, to appear " (*AS II*, 9,3).

The more lively our faith is, the more we shall enjoy here
below an anticipation of the knowledge of God which we

shall possess in heaven. The more lively our faith and the more imbued with love it is, the higher will be our degree of glory and hence, of our vision of God. Today's faith must prepare us for the beatific vision of tomorrow; it should make us enter, even on earth, into communion with the thought and the knowledge of God. In this way, faith elevates us immeasurably above our human reasonings, our human thoughts.

COLLOQUY

" O faith of Christ, my Spouse, I turn to You who enclose and conceal within yourself the form and beauty of my Beloved. You are the clear, limpid fount, free from error, from which the waters of all spiritual good flow to the soul. Did You not assure the Samaritan woman, O Christ, that in those who believe in You would surge a fountain whose waters would spring up into everlasting life?

" O faith, such is the likeness between yourself and God, that there is no other difference, save that which exists between seeing God and believing in Him. For even as God is infinite, so You set Him before us as infinite; and as He is Three and One, so You set Him before us as Three and One; and as God is darkness to our understanding, even so do You blind and dazzle our understanding. And thus, O Lord, by this means alone, You manifest Yourself to the soul in divine light which passes all understanding. Increase, then, O Lord, my faith, for the stronger my faith is, the more closely shall I be united to You.

" O my soul, as God is inaccessible, do not concern Yourself with how much your faculties can comprehend and your senses can perceive, that You be not satisfied with less than God, and lose not the swiftness that is needful to attain to Him. But walk in naked, pure faith, which alone is the proximate and proportionate means to your union with God " (J.C. SC 12,1-3 – AS II, 9,1 – SM 1, 52).

" O infinite Wisdom, O eternal, infinite God, You want to be understood by Your creature because You are the sovereign Good. It can do so, understanding You in the way You show Yourself to it under the veil of faith. It is indeed a veil, but it is translucent, since Your word illumines and gives light to the humble. Nevertheless, just as it is impossible for You not to be God, so it is impossible for Your creature to understand You fully. He who wishes to attain to the sublime state of union with You, O Lord, must have great faith. Being the sovereign, infinite, immense, and unsearchable Good, You can be understood only by Yourself. But the more the soul believes in You, so much the more will it come to unite itself to You and participate in Your grandeur " (cf. St. Mary Magdalen dei Pazzi).

242

THE OBSCURE LIGHT OF FAITH

PRESENCE OF GOD - Teach me to believe, O Lord, even in darkness and obscurity; teach me to believe by relying only on Your word.

MEDITATION

1. Through its own efforts, the human mind is able to attain to a knowledge of God the Creator by considering created things; it can know His existence and even some of His perfections, but it cannot attain to the mystery of His intimate life which is beyond the knowledge of creatures, if God Himself does not raise it to this knowledge. God alone knows the mysteries of His intimate life, of the communication of this life to man, and He alone can reveal it. Divine revelation enables us to " know " with certainty that such realities exist, and yet, it does not enable us to " see " them; it tells us that God is Triune, but it does not show us the Trinity. It makes us know that God gives us grace, but we cannot see grace. Precisely because we do not see, to adhere to divine mysteries we must believe trustingly in God who has revealed them to us; and this is just what constitutes the act of faith. Faith is certain because it relies on the word of God, who can neither deceive nor be deceived; in this sense we can say that faith is *clear*, " free from errors " (J.C. *SC*, 12,3), admitting no doubt, since no one can doubt God's word. But at the same time, it remains *obscure*, because it does not show us the truths which it proposes for our

belief and, therefore, they remain mysteries to us. Let us remember the pitcher that contains a lighted but invisible lamp. This obscure side of faith is, at the same time, both painful and glorious for us. It is painful because we cannot see what we believe, painful because an act of faith often exacts a leap in the dark, a thing repugnant to human nature which likes to be in control, to know what it is doing, and to proceed on known facts. The more elevated supernatural realities are, the greater is their obscurity—even darkness—to the intellect, which is incapable of proceeding without the aid of the senses, and incapable of embracing the infinite. On the other hand, however, it is this very obscurity which constitutes the merit and glory of our act of faith : merit, because it is a wholly supernatural act based not on what we can see and verify, but solely on what God has revealed to us; glory, because our act of faith gives all the more glory and honor to God, the more it relies solely on His word.

2. My intellect does not need the concurrence of my will to believe that two and two make four. The truth is evident and I see it. In the case of divine truths, on the contrary, my intellect remains free to give its assent or not, simply because these truths are not evident to me; and I believe only because I *will* to believe. In the case of natural truths that I can verify, such as mathematical truths, my adherence to them depends upon the power of my intellect : the deeper my knowledge and comprehension of them, the stronger is my conviction. But in the presence of supernatural truths, my adherence depends upon the power of my will : the intellect is moved by the will. A free upright will, which loves its God, fully believes all that He reveals, not with a cold acceptance, but with a loving adherence which involves all the powers of the soul.

However, since evidence is lacking, doubt may always arise in the mind, and I should not be astonished at this. It is natural for the human intellect to doubt what it does not see and does not understand. Sometimes doubts are caused by ignorance, in which case we have a duty to seek further instruction; but at other times they will be mere temptations which must be overcome by an act of the will : Lord, I believe because I want to believe; I believe, even if I am in darkness, if I cannot see or understand; I believe

solely on Your word. This is the way we should act when
we experience temptations against faith. Instead of losing
ourselves in reasoning about them or becoming discouraged,
we must simply adhere by an act of the will. St. Thérèse
of the Child Jesus wrote at the time of her bitter trials against
faith : " I try to live by faith, even though it affords me
no consolation. I have made more acts of faith during the
past year than in all the rest of my life " (*St*, 9). These
painful trials strengthen our faith and make it purer, more
supernatural; the soul believes, not because of the consolation
that faith gives it, not because it trusts in its feelings or
enthusiasm, nor even in the little it does understand of the
divine mysteries, but it believes only because God has spoken.
When the Lord wishes to lead souls to a more intimate union
with Himself, He almost always makes them undergo such
trials; then is the moment to give Him testimony of our faith
by throwing ourselves, with our eyes closed, into His arms.

COLLOQUY

    " O blessed faith, you are certain but you are also
obscure. You are obscure because you make us believe
truths revealed by God Himself, and which transcend all
natural light. Your excessive light, radiance of the divine
truths, becomes for me thick darkness because the greater
overwhelms the lesser, even as the light of the sun overwhelms
all other lights and even exceeds my power of vision.
    " You are dark night for the soul and, as night, you
illumine it like that dark cloud which lighted the way in the
night for the children of Israel. Yes, although you are a
dark cloud, your darkness gives light to the darkness of my
soul. So I too can say : the night will be my illumination
in my delights. In the way of pure contemplation and union
with God, your night, O faith, will be my guide.
    " Make me comprehend, O Lord, that to be joined in
union with You I must not walk by understanding, neither
may I lean upon experience or feeling or imagination,
but I must believe in Your infinite Being, which is not
perceptible to my understanding nor to any other sense "
(cf. J.C. *AS II*, 3,1-6 – 4,4).
    " O faith, you are the great friend of our spirit, and to
the human sciences which boast that they are more evident

than you are, you can well say what the Spouse said to her
companions : ' I am black but beautiful. ' You are black
because you are in the obscurity of the divine revelations,
which, having no apparent evidence, make you appear
black, and almost unrecognizable; but yet you *are beautiful*
in yourself because of your infinite certainty " (cf. St. Francis
de Sales).

" Only the beautiful light of faith can light my way to
You, O God. The Psalmist sings, ' You made darkness Your
covert ' and then, in another place he seems to contradict
himself by saying, ' You are clothed with light as with a
garment. ' This apparent contradiction seems to me to mean
that I must plunge into the sacred darkness, keeping all my
powers in night and emptiness; then I shall meet You, O my
Master, and the light that clothes You as a garment will
envelop me also; for You desire Your bride to be shining
with Your light, and Yours alone " (E.T. *II*, 4).

243

THE POWER OF FAITH

PRESENCE OF GOD - " I do believe, Lord; help my unbelief; increase
my faith " (*Mk* 9,23 – cf. *Lk* 17,5).

MEDITATION

1. Jesus has said : " All things are possible to him that
believeth " (*Mk* 9,22). It would seem that before an act
of living faith, blind, unconditional faith, God does not know
how to resist and considers Himself almost obliged to grant our
requests. The Gospel tells us this on every page : before Jesus
performed a miracle, He always asked for an act of faith.
" Do you believe that I can do this unto you? " (*Mt* 9,28);
and when faith was sincere, the miracle took place immediately. " Be of good heart, daughter, " He said to the
woman who was troubled with an issue of blood, " thy faith
hath made thee whole " (*ibid.* 9,22). Jesus never said, " My

omnipotence has saved you, has cured you, " but *your faith,*
as if to make us understand that faith is the indispensable
condition that He requires if we are to benefit from His
omnipotence.   He, the Almighty, will use His omnipotence
only for the benefit of those who firmly believe in Him.
This is why the divine Master refused to perform in Nazareth
the many miracles He performed elsewhere.   The more
lively our faith, the more powerful it is with the very power
of God.   " If you have faith as a grain of mustard seed, "
Jesus affirmed, " you shall say to this mountain, ' Remove
from hence hither, ' and it shall remove; and nothing shall
be impossible to you " (*ibid.* 17,19).   These words are true,
literally true, like everything in the Gospel; if they are
not effectual for us, it is only because our faith is very weak.
How many difficulties we meet with in life which are for us
real mountains to move!   Difficulties in the spiritual life :
faults we cannot overcome, virtues we cannot seem to acquire;
difficulties in our everyday life : insufficient means of support,
duties which surpass our ability or our strength. . . .   And we
stop, discouraged, at the foot of these mountains : " It is
impossible, I cannot do it! "   It would take only a little faith
like a grain of mustard seed, which is very tiny indeed.   But
provided that faith is living, capable of sprouting like the
mustard seed, provided that faith is certain, resolute, supernatural, and that it counts only on God and trusts in His
Name alone, this faith will confront every difficulty whatsoever with courage.   Oh! if we could only have such faith!
" Nothing is impossible to him that believeth. "

2. Although the difficulties we encounter may be serious
ones, discouragement is never justified.   We become discouraged because we reflect on our powerlessness : on one side,
we remember our past failures, and on the other, we place
before ourselves the prospect of situations which are beyond
our strength, making them appear like insurmountable
mountains which crush, smother and paralyze us.   But a
soul who has faith in God, who is sure of its God, well knows
how to find a way to escape from these straits, and makes use
of its own impotence and difficulties as a springboard to
plunge into God by a strong, determined act of faith.

God sometimes permits us to find ourselves in very
difficult situations which cannot be solved by human means.
He permits us to undergo painful spiritual trials, resulting in

states of real anguish, and He permits this for the sole purpose
of forcing us to practice the virtue of faith, which in certain
cases can and must become heroic. If then, God visits us
with similar trials, we must believe that it is not because He
has abandoned or rejected us, nor that He wants to discourage or destroy us; He acts thus to make us strong, yes,
even heroic in our faith. We must believe in Him, in His
all-powerful omnipotence; believe in His word. Perhaps God
delays to come to our help only because we are not yet
to make an act of complete faith! He asks us, as he asked
the two blind men in the Gospel : " Do you believe that I can
do this? " (*Mt* 9,28); and we do not yet know how to answer
a strong determined *yes*, without uncertainty, without any
if or *but*. Yet, even if our faith were strong, God could
still test it as Jesus did that of the Canaanite woman. If He
does, we must imitate her : we must not give up, nor cease to
believe, but believe even more firmly, so that He will be forced
to answer us as He did that humble woman : " Great is thy
faith; be it done to thee as thou wilt " (*ibid.* 15,28).

COLLOQUY

" O my Lord and my God, so weak is our faith that we
desire what we see more than what faith tells us—though
what we actually see is that people who pursue these visible
things meet with nothing but ill fortune.
" If then, grave difficulties appear, oh! how the devil
rejoices—if for no other reason than to weaken our faith and
to persuade us not to believe, O Lord, that You are powerful
and can do works which are incomprehensible to our
understanding.
" May You be blessed, O my God! I acknowledge
Your great power. If You are mighty, as indeed You are,
what is impossible to You who can do all things? Miserable
though I am, I firmly believe that You can do what You will;
and the greater the marvels I hear of You, the stronger
grows my faith, and the more do I reflect that You can
work others yet greater. How can I wonder at what is
done by the Almighty? " (T.J. *Int C II*,1 – *VI*, 3 – *Exc*, 4).
" Not to believe in You, O my God, requires more faith than
to believe in You! Your love for me is so great that I no longer
need faith to believe in it " (St. Mary Magdalen dei Pazzi).

" O my God, You are love and omnipotence. You know all, You can do all, You will all, and You guide all for Your own glory and for our advantage. What faith I draw from these truths! What confidence, peace, and love they give me! I know that even when You are not giving me anything tangible, You are still my God, always providing lovingly for the work of Your hands. Hence, I hide myself in You with faith, to withstand the violence of the storm, certain that, when it pleases You, by Your divine omnipotence, You will make the dead rise again " (cf. Bl. M. Thérèse Soubiran).

No, my God, the strength of Your arm is not lessened. If you do not perform miracles in my favor, it is only because my faith is weak. Help my incredulity, O Lord : increase my faith!

244

FAITH IN PRACTICE

PRESENCE OF GOD - O Lord, grant that in every circumstance of my life, I may be guided by the light of faith.

MEDITATION

1. Faith ought to be the light which envelops not only our moments of prayer but our whole life as well. In prayer we say, " I believe in God, the Father almighty "; but a few minutes afterwards, in the face of some difficult task, a tiresome person, or something which upsets our plans, we forget that these have all been willed and planned by God for our good. We forget that God is our Father, and therefore is more concerned about our welfare than we are ourselves. We forget that God is all-powerful and can help us in every difficulty. In losing sight of the light of faith, which makes us see everything as dependent upon God and ordered by Him for our good, we lose ourselves in merely human considerations and protests, as if God had nothing to do with our life or had very little place in it.

We give way to discouragement as though we had no faith. Yes, we believe in God, the Father Almighty, but we do not believe to the point of seeing His will, or at least His permission, in every circumstance. And yet, until faith becomes such a factor in our life that it makes us see all things in relation to God, and as dependent upon Him, we will not be able to say that the light of faith is the guide of our life. It is, of course, but only partially. How often this true light, which participates in the very light of God, remains hidden under the bushel of a mentality which is still too human, too earthly! Jesus said, " Neither do men light a candle and put it under a bushel, but upon a candlestick, that it may shine to all that are in the house " (*Mt* 5,15). The light of faith was enkindled within us at Baptism; we must hold it aloft, above all our thoughts and reasonings, so that it may illumine our whole life, our whole house, that is, the interior dwelling of our soul and the exterior world in which we live, with all its persons, places, and things.

2. One who lives by faith can repeat the beautiful words of Sr. Elizabeth of the Trinity : " Everything that happens is a message to me of God's great love for my soul. " To attain this living and profound gaze of faith, we must accustom ourselves, in our relations with creatures, to pass over secondary causes in order to reach the first cause, God, who by His Providence rules and orders everything for His own holy ends. Since we know and believe that He who directs all things is our Father, we will entrust ourselves to His direction with absolute confidence, and thus we will remain serene even in adversity, strong in the conviction that He can make use of evil, of man's errors, and even of sins and malice for the good of the elect. " To them that love God, all things work together unto good! " (*Rom* 8,28). The gaze of faith is most comprehensive and real, because it takes into account the *total* reality of creatures and events, considering them not only in their material entity, but also in relation to their dependence on God. The more we know how to look at everything in this light, so much the more closely will we approach the eternal thought and infinite wisdom of God, judging everything according to God's infallible truth. With this view of faith it will be easier for us to accept the painful situations and hardships of life, for

we will be able to see in them God's paternal hand ordering everything for our sanctification. If, judging things from a human point of view, we are tempted to protest, to bring forward our own reasons and our rights, to rebel against treatment which in itself is unjust; we should raise our eyes to God, and consider that He permits all this for the exercise of virtue and to spur us on to sanctity. Then we would find the strength to accept everything peacefully, and to maintain a kindly attitude toward those who make us suffer. But at the same time, we should remember that faith is a light that is obscure to our intellect, and therefore, it very often asks us to believe in God's wise, loving guidance, even when we do not understand and are inclined to think that everything is going wrong. This is precisely what constitutes the true life of faith, and " the just man liveth by faith " (*ibid.* 1,17).

COLLOQUY

" My God, to give You pleasure and to obtain much from You, I have only to believe in Your love, Your power, and in the sweetness of Your gifts; I should believe that You have an ardent desire to give them to me and that Your desire far exceeds my great longing to receive them. I should believe it because the just man lives by faith. I want to be like an affectionate child who has no desire either to see or to know what means You will choose to shower it with Your ineffable gifts; I must only believe, because the just man lives by faith.

" O Lord, You penetrate everywhere with Your goodness, Your personal, infinite love, and Your omnipotence. Give me a very simple faith by which, without reflection, I can move and remain in this truth as in my center, a haven of peace where nothing can touch me if I remain well hidden within it. O God, You love me more than I can love myself and You can do everything; You desire my well-being above all else; I ought to believe that You desire it more than I do. I place myself constantly before You, because I know that acts of perfect adoration and total abandonment are more true, humble, and simple when devoid of any feeling; they are made with the help of faith alone. . . especially when my soul, in its inferior part, sees and touches a profound void in time and in eternity. Then O Lord, grant that in this state,

I may remain by faith, more present than ever before You.
O wonder of wonders! When it pleases Your divine goodness,
the soul, in its superior part can feel itself inundated with
peace, even while the tempest continues. O ineffable peace,
which surpasses all expression! You take away forever our
taste for sensible things and make us run to pure faith as to
the one source of the divine good whose ineffable and thousand
times blessed fruit you are " (cf. Bl. M. Thérèse Soubiran).

   " O Lord, it is so sweet to serve You in darkness and in
the midst of trial, for we have only this life in which to live by
faith " (T.C.J. C).

245

OUR RICHES

EIGHTH SUNDAY AFTER PENTECOST

PRESENCE OF GOD - Teach me, O Lord, to be a faithful, wise adminis-
trator of Your goods.

MEDITATION

   1. Today again, as last Sunday, St. Paul, in the Epistle
of the Mass (*Rom* 8,12-17), compares the two lives which
always struggle within us : the life of the old man, a slave to
sin and the passions, from which come the fruits of death,
and that of the new man, the servant, or better, the child of
God, producing fruits of life. " If you live according to the
flesh, you shall die, but if, by the spirit, you mortify the
deeds of the flesh, you shall live. " Baptism has begotten
us to the life of the spirit, but it has not suppressed the life of
the flesh in us; the new man must always struggle against
the old man, the spiritual must fight against the corporeal.
Baptismal grace does not excuse us from this battle, but it
gives us the power to sustain it. We must be thoroughly
convinced of this so that we will not be deceived or disturbed
if, after many years of living a spiritual life, certain passions,
which we thought we had subdued forever, revive in us.

This is our earthly condition : " The life of man upon earth is a warfare " (*Jb* 7,1), so much so that Jesus said : " The kingdom of heaven suffereth violence " (*Mt* 11,12). But this continual struggle should not frighten us; for grace has made us children of God, and as such, we have every right to count on His paternal help. " You have not received the spirit of bondage again in fear, " says St. Paul, " but you have received the spirit of adoption of sons, whereby we cry : Abba, Father. " To increase our belief in this great truth, he adds, " The Spirit Himself giveth testimony to our spirit, that we are the sons of God. " It is as though the Apostle would like to say to us : " It is not I who tell you this, but the Holy Spirit who says it and testifies to it within you. " The Holy Spirit is in us; in us He supplicates the heavenly Father, and in us He arouses confidence and trust. " You are not slaves, " He says to us, " but children; of what are you afraid? " This is our great treasure : to be children of God, co-heirs with Christ, temples of the Holy Spirit.

2. Today's Gospel (*Lk* 16,1-9) teaches us by means of a parable—which at first sight seems a little disconcerting—how to be wise in administering the great riches of our life of grace. When Jesus spoke this parable, He certainly had no intention of praising the conduct of the " unjust " steward who, after wasting his master's goods during his whole stewardship, continued to steal even when he learned that he was to be discharged. However, Jesus did praise him for the clever way he made sure of his own future. The lesson of the parable hinges on this point : " The children of this world are wiser in their generation than the children of light. And I say to you : Make unto you friends of the mammon of iniquity; that when you shall fail, they may receive you into everlasting dwellings. " Jesus exhorts the " children of light " not to be less shrewd in providing for their eternal interests than the " children of darkness " are in assuring for themselves the goods of earth.

We also, like the steward in the parable, have received from God a patrimony to administer, that is, our natural gifts, and more particularly, our supernatural gifts, and all the graces, holy inspirations, and promptings to good which God has bestowed upon us. The hour for rendering an account will come for us too, and we shall have to admit that we have often been unfaithful in trafficking with the gifts of God, in making the treasures of grace fructify in our soul. How can we atone for our infidelities? This is the moment to put into practice the teaching of the parable by which, as St. Augustine says, " God admonishes all of us to use our earthly goods to make friends for ourselves among the poor. They, in turn, becoming the friends of their benefactors, will be the cause of their admission into heaven. " In other words, we must pay our debts to God by charity toward our neighbor, for Sacred Scripture tells us, " Charity covereth a multitude of sins " (1 Pt 4,8). This does not mean material charity alone, but also spiritual charity and not in great things only, but in little ones too—yes, even in the very least things, such as a glass of water given for the love of God. These little acts of charity, which are always within our power, are the riches by which we pay our debts and put in order " our stewardship. "

COLLOQUY

" O Lord, it is Your Spirit which combats within me. You gave it to me to destroy the deeds of the flesh. Moved by Your Spirit, I keep up the struggle because I have a powerful helper; my sins have slain, wounded and humbled me; but You, my Creator, were wounded for me, and by Your death You overcame mine. I bear within myself human frailty and the chains of my former slavery; in my members there is a law which opposes the law of the spirit and would drag me into the slavery of sin; my corruptible body still weighs upon my soul. Although I am made strong by Your grace, as long as I continue to carry Your treasure in this earthen vessel, I shall always have to suffer because of my frailty. You are the stability which makes me firm against all temptations; if they increase and frighten me, You are my refuge. ' You are my hope, my inheritance in the land of the living. '

" Oh! how much I owe You, my Lord God, who redeemed me at so great a price! Oh! how much I ought to love, bless, praise, honor, and glorify You who have loved me so much! I shall give praise to Your Name, O God, who made me capable of receiving the great glory of being Your son. I owe to You all I have, all that is of use for my life, all that I know and love. Who possesses anything that is not Yours? Bestow Your gifts on me, O Lord our God, so that made rich by You, I may serve and please You, and every day return thanks to You for all that Your mercy has done for me. I cannot serve You or please You without making use of Your own gifts to me " (cf. St. Augustine).

246

HOPE

PRESENCE OF GOD - O Lord, strengthen my hope, for he who hopes in You will never be confounded.

MEDITATION

1. Faith makes us know God; we believe in Him with all our strength but we do not see Him. Our faith, therefore, needs to be supported by the certitude that some day we will see our God, that we will possess Him and will be united to Him forever. The virtue of hope gives us this certitude by presenting God to us as our infinite good and our eternal reward. Faith tells us that God is goodness, beauty, wisdom, providence, charity, and infinite mercy; and hope adds that this God so great, so good, belongs to us. He wants to be not only our eternal possession and our eternal beatitude, but even here below He wishes to be possessed by us through charity and grace, even *now* He invites us to live in intimate union with Him.

We look at the infinite God who is perfect and immensely higher than ourself, a weak, miserable creature, and we wonder : How can I ever reach Him and be united with Him, who is so infinitely beyond my capacity? And hope replies : You can, for God Himself wishes it; it was for this reason that He created you and raised you to the supernatural state, giving you all the help necessary for such an arduous undertaking. The Council of Trent affirms that we should all have " a very firm hope—*firmissimam spem*—in the help of God, " help which He has formally promised to those who love Him and have recourse to Him with confidence :

" Ask and it shall be given you, " Jesus said; " Seek and you
shall find; knock and it shall be opened to you.... If you
then, being evil, know how to give good gifts to your children,
how much more will your Father who is in heaven, give
good things to them that ask Him? " (*Mt* 7,7.11).   The
" good things " promised by Jesus are those contained
in the act of hope : " eternal life and the graces necessary to
attain it "; this is the object of hope and what we must ask
for before everything else.

2. When we place ourselves in the presence of God with
the intention of uniting ourselves to Him, we sense immediately that the great obstacles which seem to separate us from
Him are our sins, our frailty, and our wretchedness, all of
which make it so difficult for us to live in a manner worthy of
God.   But hope comes to assure us, on the part of infinite
mercy, of both the pardon of our sins and the grace necessary
to live a good—and even more—a holy life.

The pardon of our sins removes the obstacles to our
union with God; grace brings us close to Him and finally
consummates the union.   What consolation floods our soul
when we think that, in spite of the weakness which prevents
us from avoiding all sin, God wants us to be certain of
His forgiveness!   Yes, every time we acknowledge our
faults, being sincerely repentant, He pardons us by the
merits of Jesus, and our sins are forgotten forever.   Of this
we must be certain and we may not doubt it, because
we cannot and may not doubt God's mercy and promises.
" If your sins be as scarlet, " said the Lord, " they shall be
made as white as snow " (*Is* 1,18).   In addition, God wants us
to be equally sure that He will give us all the graces necessary
to lead a good life, overcome our temptations and our
faults, and to advance in virtue.   Thus we will attain
to union with Him, not only in heaven, but even on earth.
Our ideal, the ideal of sanctity, *can* be realized!   God wills
to expect all this from Him, not because of our merits,
but because He is infinitely good, because He is the *omnipotentia auxilians*, the helping omnipotence, always ready to
come to our aid.   Of course, it would be rash to hope that
God will save and sanctify us without our cooperation;
but if, on our part, we do all we can to avoid even the
slightest faults, and to practice virtue generously, we can hope
with *certainty* that He will do for us what we, in spite of all

our efforts, can never succeed in doing.   God wants us to be
certain of this.   Certitude is a quality of perfect hope, and
God wants us to practice this virtue to perfection.

COLLOQUY

"Clothe me, O God, with the green garment of hope.
A living hope in You gives the soul such ardor, so much
courage and longing for the things of eternal life that, by
comparison with what it hopes for, all things of the world
seem to it to be, as in truth they are, dry, faded, dead,
and without value.   Give me then, a strong hope, O my God,
so that it may strip me of all the vanities of the world, that
I may not set my heart upon anything that is in the world, nor
hope for anything, but live clad only in the hope of eternal
life.   Let hope be the helmet of salvation which will protect
my head from the wounds of the enemy, and will direct my
gaze to heaven allowing me to fix my eyes on You alone,
my God.   As the eyes of the handmaid are set upon the
hands of her mistress, even so are my eyes set upon You,
until You take pity on me because of my hope.   Grant that
I may set my eyes on naught but You, nor be pleased with
aught but You alone.   Then You will be pleased with me,
and I shall be able to say in all truth that I receive from
You as much as I hope for" (cf. J.C. *DN II*, 21,6-8).

"In order to understand the greatness of Your divinity,
O Lord, I need faith; and in order to accomplish anything,
I need hope, for if I did not have hope of possessing You some
day, I would not have the strength to labor here below.
I no longer desire the things of earth, although I have never
hoped in them.   I do have a lively hope of obtaining, not
the things of earth upon which worldly people usually set
their hopes, but only You, my God.

"O God, give me a firm hope, for I cannot be saved
unless this virtue is firmly rooted in my soul.   I need it
in order to implore pardon for my sins and to attain my end.
What delight hope gives to my soul, making it hope for what
it will one day enjoy in heaven, and by permitting it a partial
taste here on earth of what it will savor, understand, and
possess eternally, which is You, my God" (St. Mary Magdalen
dei Pazzi).

247

THE MOTIVE FOR HOPE

PRESENCE OF GOD - Make me understand well, O Lord, that my hope must be founded on You, on Your infinite merciful love.

MEDITATION

1. If we had to base our hope on our own merits and on the amount of grace we possess, it would be very insecure, because we cannot be certain that we are in the state of grace, nor can we be certain about our good works which are always so full of defects. But our hope is *sure* because it is founded, not on ourselves, but on God, on His infinite goodness, on His salvific will which desires " all men to be saved " (1 *Tm* 2,4), and on His sanctifying will that wants us not only to be saved, but also to be saints : " This is the will of God, your sanctification " (1 *Thes* 4,3).

God wishes the certitude of our hope to rest upon Him alone. Although He demands our cooperation and our good works, He does not want us to base our confidence on them; in fact, after having urged us to do all that is in our power, Jesus added : " When you shall have done all these things that are commanded you, say : we are unprofitable servants " (*Lk* 17,10). Souls who are accustomed to depend on their own strength and who delude themselves, thinking they can enter more deeply into the spiritual life by their own personal resources, find this lesson hard to understand. That is why when the Lord wills them to progress, He makes them go through painful states of powerlessness, permitting them to feel the rebellion and repugnance of nature that they may be convinced of the vanity of placing their confidence in themselves. There is here a delicate point : to know how to accept this experience without falling into discouragement. If in the past, we have relied upon ourselves, and now, in certain difficulties and trials of our interior life, we see our strength reduced to nothing, let us thank God. In this way He is detaching us from the too great confidence we had in ourselves, and is forcing us to practice a purer, more supernatural hope, one stripped of every human element and support. If, however we cannot place our hope in ourselves, this is reason for despair; rather, it should impel us to place our hope in God alone and force us to throw ourselves upon Him with full confidence like a child who takes refuge in its mother's arms with more trust, the weaker and more powerless it feels itself to be.

2. The certitude of our hope is derived from the certitude of our faith. " For I know whom I have believed, " says St. Paul, " and I am certain that He is able to keep that which I have committed unto Him against that day " (2 *Tm* 1,12), that is, unto life eternal. This certitude is not of the intellect, but rather of the will and the heart; it is the certitude which gives us full confidence in Someone who we know loves us. And who loves us more than God? Who has given us more proofs of His love than God? Let us look at Jesus on the Cross and repeat with St. Paul : " The Son of God...loved me and delivered Himself for me " (*Gal* 2,20). Now " greater love than this, no man hath, that a man lay down his life for his friends " (*Jn* 15,13).

This is the basis for the certitude of our hope. We must hope to come to the beatifying possession of God in eternity and to union with Him on this earth, not so much because we have always done our duty, or because we feel we are good, virtuous, and well-disposed...but because we know that in spite of our misery and our weakness, God is always ready to help us, provided we humbly acknowledge our nothingness and place all our trust in Him. St. Thérèse of the Child Jesus said : " Holiness does not consist in this or that practice; it consists in a disposition of heart which makes us humble and little in the arms of God, well aware of our feebleness, but *boldly confident in our Father's goodness* " (T.C.J. *NV*). If we withdraw into ourselves after our falls and weaknesses, we clip the wings of hope and only sink more deeply in our misery; but if, on the contrary, we go to God in an act of complete confidence, then our weakness will be fortified and sustained by His helping omnipotence. If, in the face of difficulties and sacrifices imposed on us by our duties, we stop to calculate our strength, we will draw back and be tempted to give up; but if, on the contrary, we stop looking at ourselves and turn our eyes to God, to His infinite love, the certitude of His help will give us the strength to go on. Firm hope in Him will make us strong, courageous, and generous; it will be the lever of our life.

COLLOQUY

"Almighty, omnipotent Lord, show me my poverty so that I may confess it. I said that I was rich and that I needed nothing; I did not know that I was poor, blind, naked, wretched, and miserable. I believed that I was something and I was nothing. I said, ' I shall become wise, ' and I became foolish; I thought that I was prudent, but I deceived myself. And I see now that wisdom is Your gift, that without You we can do nothing, for if You, O God, do not keep the city, he watches in vain that keeps it. You taught me this that I might know myself; You abandoned me and you tried me...so that I would know myself. You had hardly gone a short distance from me when I fell. Then I saw and knew that You were guiding me; if I fell, it was my own fault, and if I rose again, it was by Your help.

"O my God, I could despair on account of my great sins and my innumerable negligences...but I dare not because I, who was at one time Your enemy, have been reconciled to You by the death of Your Son; and not only reconciled, but I have been saved by Him. That is why all my hope and the certitude of my confidence is in His precious Blood which was shed for us and for our salvation. Living in Him, trusting in Him, I hope to come to You, not because of my justice, but through the justice which comes to me from Your Son, Our Lord Jesus Christ.

"Thus, in the weariness of this struggle, I raise my eyes to You, Lord Jesus. Let the enemy do what he will to me. I shall not fear because You are a strong defender. I have good reason to hope in You, for I shall never be confounded.

"Now, as long as I am in the body, I am far from You, since I journey by faith and not by vision. The time will come when I will see that which I now believe without seeing and I shall be happy. Then I shall see the reality which I now hope for. I live content in my hope because You are true to Your promises; nevertheless, because I do not possess You as yet, I groan beneath the weight of desire. Grant that I may persevere in this desire until what You have promised comes to pass; then my groaning will be over and praise alone will resound " (St. Augustine).

248

THE TEST OF HOPE

PRESENCE OF GOD - Give me, O Lord, invincible hope; teach me to hope against all hope, teach me to hope with all my strength.

MEDITATION

1. We prove the firmness of our faith by persevering in it in spite of its obscurity; we prove that our hope is strong by continuing to hope in spite of adversity and even when God seems to have abandoned us. As an act of faith made in the midst of darkness and doubts is more meritorious, so is it with the act of hope uttered in desolation and abandonment. The three theological virtues are the most appropriate and fitting means of uniting us to God; in fact, the purer, more intense, and supernatural are our faith, hope, and charity, the more closely they unite us to Him. To help us reach this point, God leads us through the crucible of trials. The story of Job is re-enacted in some way in the life of every soul dear to God; he was tried in his property, his children, his own person, deserted by his friends, and ridiculed by his wife. He who had been rich and esteemed, found himself alone on a dunghill, covered from head to foot with horrible sores. But if God is good, if it is true that He desires our good, why does He permit all this? Why does He let us suffer? " For God made not death," says Sacred Scripture, " neither hath He pleasure in the destruction of the living.... It was the wicked who with hands and words invited death " (*Wis* 1,13-16). Death and suffering are the consequences of sin, which God has not prevented because He has willed to leave man free. And yet not only sinners suffer, but the innocent also. Why? Because God wishes to try them as gold is tried in the furnace, purifying them and raising them to a good, to a state of happiness immeasurably superior to the goods and the happiness of earth. Thus God permits the sufferings of the innocent, and even uses the consequences of sin—wars, disorders, social and personal injustices—for the greater good of His elect. It is often true, however, that when we are

undergoing a trial we neither see nor understand the reason for it. God does not account for His actions nor does He reveal His plans to us; therefore, it is difficult to endure in faith and hope—difficult, but not impossible, for God never sends us trials which are beyond our strength, just as He never abandons us unless we first abandon Him.

2. The least act of hope, of trust in God, made in the midst of trials, in a state of interior or exterior desolation, is worth far more than a thousand acts made in times of joy and prosperity. When we are suffering in mind or body, when we are experiencing the void of abandonment and helplessness, when we find ourselves a prey to the repugnances and rebellions of nature which would like to throw off the yoke of the Lord, we cannot pretend to have the comforting feeling of hope, of confidence; often we may even experience the opposite sentiment, and yet, even in this state we can make acts of hope and of confidence which are not felt but willed. The theological virtues are practiced essentially by the will. When they are accompanied by feeling, the practice of them is pleasant and consoling; but when the act must be made by the will alone, then this exercise is dry and cold, but is not for this reason of less merit; on the contrary, it is even more meritorious and therefore gives more glory to God. We should not, therefore, be disturbed if we do not *feel* confidence; we must *will* to have confidence, *will* to hope, to hope at any cost, in spite of all the blows God may inflict on us by means of trials. This is the moment to repeat with Job : " Although He should kill me, I will trust in Him " (*Jb* 13,15). We must not deceive ourselves, thinking we can go through these trials without having to fight against discouragement, against temptations to distrust, and perhaps even to despair; this is the reaction of nature which rebels against that which wounds it. The Lord knows our weakness; He does not condemn us, He pities us. These feelings do not offend God, provided we always try to react gently by making acts of confidence with our will. Every time a wave of discouragement tries to carry us away, we must react against it by anchoring ourselves in God by a simple movement of trust; even if our spiritual life should be reduced, for certain periods, to this exercise alone, we will not have lost anything, but we will have gained much. It is precisely by going through these trials that we reach the

heroic practice of faith and hope; and the heroism of the
virtues is necessary for the attainment of sanctity.

COLLOQUY

" Save me, O God, for the waters have come in even unto
my soul.   I stick fast in the mire of the deep, and there is no
sure standing.   I am come into the depth of the sea, and a
tempest hath overwhelmed me.   I have labored with crying;
my jaws are become hoarse; my eyes have failed, whilst
I hope in my God. . . .   But my prayer is to Thee, O Lord,
for the time of Thy good pleasure. . . .   In the multitude of
Thy mercy, hear me, in the truth of Thy salvation.   Draw
me out of the mire that I may not stick fast; deliver me from
them that hate me, and out of the deep waters.   Hear me,
O Lord, for Thy mercy is kind; look upon me according
to the multitude of Thy tender mercies.   Turn not away
Thy face from Thy servant. . .   Save me, since Thou art
my patience; O Lord, my hope, O Lord, from my youth. . . .
I have always hoped in Thee. . . .   O God be not Thou
far from me, make haste to help me. . . .   I suffer, but I will
always hope, and will add to all Thy praise. . . .   What
great troubles hast Thou shown me, many and grievous;
and turning, Thou hast brought me back to life, and hast
brought me back again from the depths of the earth.   Thou
hast multiplied Thy magnificence, and turning to me,
Thou hast comforted me " (Ps 68 – 70).

" O hope, sweet sister of faith, you are that virtue which
with the keys of the Blood of Christ unlock eternal life to us.
You guard the city of the soul against the enemy of confusion,
and when the devil tries to cast the soul into despair by
pointing out the seriousness of its past sins, you do not slacken
your pace, but full of energy, you persevere in fortitude,
putting on the balance the price of Christ's Blood.   You place
on the brow of perseverance the crown of victory, for you have
hoped to obtain it by the power of His Blood " (St. Catherine
of Siena).

249

BOUNDLESS HOPE

PRESENCE OF GOD - Sustain my hope in Thee, O Lord, so that it may be without measure.

MEDITATION

1. St. Thomas teaches us that " man can never love God as much as He should be loved; neither can he believe and hope in Him as much as he ought " (Iᵃ IIᵃᵉ, q.64, a.4, co.). That is why we can say that the measure of hope in God is to hope without measure. Our hope, our confidence in God can never be excessive or exaggerated, because it is founded on God's mercy which has no limits. If we sincerely try to do everything we can to please God, we need not fear that our hope in Him can be too great. His helpful power and His desire for our good, for our sanctification, infinitely exceed our most ardent hopes. This blind, unlimited hope is so pleasing to God that the more hope we have, the more He overwhelms us with favors : " The more the soul hopes, the more it attains " (J.C. *AS III*, 7,2). St. Thérèse of the Child Jesus, making this thought her own said : " We can never have too much confidence in the good God who is so powerful and so merciful. We obtain from Him as much as we hope for " (*St*, 12).

The more wretched, weak, and powerless we find ourselves, the more we should hope in God. If we cannot, and should not, expect to reach sanctity by our own power, we should hope to reach it through the strength of Him who is omnipotent, through the infinite mercy of Him who loves to bend over souls aware of their frailty, who loves, as our Blessed Lady said, " to exalt the humble and to fill the hungry with good things " (cf. *Lk* 1,52.53). The knowledge of our weakness ought to make us keenly aware of our need for God; indeed, our weakness itself ought to be an incessant cry, begging with complete confidence for His all-powerful aid. The more our soul expands with hope and trust in God, the wider it will open to His sanctifying action. God's mercy is waiting to come to us, to purify and sanctify us, but it will not come until we open the doors of our heart by an act of complete confidence.

2. A soul that endeavors to apply itself with all the strength of its will to the practice of the virtues and the fulfillment of every duty, a soul that is determined to refuse nothing to Our Lord, should strive to maintain itself in an attitude of total trust in Him, in spite of inevitable falls. Yes, we should have complete confidence that God will come to sanctify us, regardless of our past faults, our present miseries, the aridity of our soul, the repugnances of nature, or the state of weariness and depression in which we may find ourselves.

God loves us, not because we are without sin, but because we are His children, in whom He has diffused His grace. We should never insult God by refusing to believe in His forgiveness; neither should we become discouraged because of the faults which escape us in spite of our good will. If we become discouraged, it is because we are seeking perfection not for God's glory alone, but for our own satisfaction as well, and also because we would prefer to find security in ourselves rather than to rely upon God alone. All this, in reality, is the result of a subtle pride. Instead of becoming disturbed and irritated by our imperfections, we must acknowledge them humbly, present them to God as a sick man shows his wounds to his doctor, ask pardon, and then immediately renew our efforts with great confidence. We must learn to make use of our miseries and failings to plead our cause, to show God how much we need His help, and to increase our confidence in Him. Hope in God is the great anchor of salvation for our poor soul, tossed by the billows of human frailty. With this in mind, St. Paul exhorts us to advance " according to the power of God, who hath delivered us and called us by His holy calling, not according to our works but according to His own purpose and grace, which was given us in Christ Jesus " (2 *Tm* 1,8.9). Far from concluding that our good works are useless, Christian hope calls for the greatest diligence in doing good and fleeing from evil; but then it carries us far beyond our poor works into the arms of God and His infinite mercy.

COLLOQUY

" O Jesus, how can a soul as imperfect as mine aspire
to possess the plenitude of love? O Jesus, my first, my only
Friend, You whom I love solely, tell me, then, what mystery
is this? Why do You not reserve these infinite longings
for lofty souls, for the eagles that soar in the heights?...
I see myself as a feeble little bird with only a light down to
cover me; I am not an eagle, yet I have an eagle's eyes and
an eagle's heart; for, notwithstanding my extreme littleness,
I dare to gaze on the divine Sun, the Sun of Love, and I burn
to fly to You, resplendent Sun, who attract my gaze.   I
would imitate the eagles I see soaring to the divine home of
the Most Blessed Trinity...but alas, I can only flutter
my little wings; it is beyond my feeble power to soar.
     " What then, is to become of me? Must I die of sorrow
because of my helplessness? Oh, no! I will not even grieve.
With daring confidence, I shall remain here, gazing on my
divine Sun.   Nothing can frighten me, neither wind nor rain;
and should impenetrable clouds come to conceal you from
my eyes, O Jesus, I shall not change my place, knowing that
beyond the dark clouds Your love shines always and that its
splendor cannot be eclipsed for a single moment. Sometimes,
it is true, my heart will be assailed by the tempest and
I may feel as if I believe that beyond this life there is only
the darkness which envelops me.   This would be the hour
of perfect joy...what happiness to remain here at all costs,
to fix my gaze on the invisible Light which hides itself
to my faith.
     " Yet should You remain deaf to my plaintive cries,
if You still veil Yourself...well then, I am content to remain
benumbed with cold, and so I rejoice in such well-merited
suffering.
     " O Jesus, how sweet is the way of love. True, one may
fall and be unfaithful to grace, but love knows how to draw
profit from everything, and quickly consumes whatever may
be displeasing to You, leaving in the heart only a deep and
humble peace " (T.C.J. *St*, 13-8 – L).

250

CHARITY

PRESENCE OF GOD - O Lord, grant that by charity I may really participate in Your life of love.

MEDITATION

1. Faith makes us adhere to God by means of knowledge; hence, it is especially related to our intellect. Hope makes us adhere to God by the conviction that we will one day possess Him in heaven, and therefore, it is related to our desire for happiness. But charity seizes our entire being, and by means of love, casts it into God. Faith tells us who God is, and reveals the mystery of His intimate life which we are called to share; hope tells us that this God wills to be our Good for all eternity, but charity enables us to attain this immediately by the unitive force proper to it. St. Thomas says : " Charity makes man tend to God by uniting his affection to God in such a way that man no longer lives for himself, but for God " (IIª IIªᵉ, q.17, a.6, ad 3).

But what is this charity which has the power to unite us to God, to make us live in such intimate relationship with Him that " he that abideth in charity, abideth in God, and God in him " (1 Jn 4,16)? It is a created participation in the charity, the infinite love with which God loves Himself, that is, the love with which the Father loves the Son, with which the Son loves the Father, and by which each loves the other in the Holy Spirit. Through charity we are called to enter into this divine current, into this circle of eternal love which unites the three Persons of the Blessed Trinity to one another.

Faith has already brought us into the intimacy of the divine life by making us share in the knowledge God has of Himself; but charity makes us penetrate even further by inserting us, as it were, into that movement of love, of incomparable friendship which exists in the bosom of the Blessed Trinity. Charity plunges us into the very center of God's intimate life; it enables us to share in the infinite

love of the three divine Persons : in the intimate love of the
Father for the Son, and of the Son for the Father; it enables
us to love the Father and the Son in the love of the Holy
Spirit.

2. By the love of *concupiscence* we love God, but we love
Him chiefly as our good, as the source of our happiness;
we love Him for the help and assistance we expect from Him.
Charity, on the contrary, makes us capable of loving God
for Himself, because He is goodness, beauty, infinite
wisdom—in a word, because He is God. Although the love
of concupiscence which accompanies hope is very precious,
it is still imperfect, because by it we love God not for Himself
alone, but for the benefits which we hope to receive from Him.
The love of charity, however, is perfect because it is pure love
of *complacency*, of *benevolence*, that is, love which takes compla-
cence in the infinite good of God, and desires this good,
not for any personal advantage, but for God Himself, for
His felicity, His glory. Charity elevates our love and makes
us capable of really loving God as He loves Himself, although
not with the same intensity. God loves Himself with infinite
complacency and benevolence : the Father takes infinite
pleasure in the infinite good of the Son and He desires that
good infinitely; the Son delights equally in the infinite good
of the Father and infinitely desires it, and this same movement
is true of the Father and the Son in regard to the Holy
Spirit, and vice versa. There is, therefore, a very pure,
affectionate love of friendship among the three divine
Persons, by which each one of Them delights in the good and
happiness of the others, and each desires the glory of the
others. Charity makes us capable of loving God with this
love of friendship, so as to love Him above all for Himself,
for His glory and His happiness. It is true, of course, that
we, poor insignificant creatures, can add nothing to God's
felicity and intrinsic glory; nevertheless, charity urges us to
try with all our strength to please Him, to obtain for Him,
if we may use the expression, the joy of seeing us correspond
fully to His love; it urges us to seek His will, His interest, and
His glory, before everything else, by renouncing our own
will and personal interests. Now we understand better
St. Thomas' sentence : " Charity unites man's affection to
God in such a way that he no longer lives for himself, but for
God. "

COLLOQUY

"Oh my soul, reflect upon the great delight and the great love which the Father has in knowing His Son and the Son in knowing His Father and the ardor with which the Holy Spirit unites Them, and how none of These can cease from this love and knowledge since They are one and the same. These sovereign Persons know each other, love each other and delight in each other. What need, then, have They of my love? Why do You seek it, my God, or what do You gain by it?

"O love, in how many places would I fain repeat this word, for it alone makes me bold enough to say with the spouse in the Canticle : ' I have loved my Beloved. ' It allows me to think that You, my God, my Spouse and my Good, have need of me.

"But love must not be wrought in our imagination but must be proved by works.... Oh Jesus, what will a soul inflamed with Your love not do? Those who really love You, love all good, seek all good, help forward all good, praise all good, and invariably join forces with good men and help and defend them. They love only truth and things worthy of love. It is not possible that one who really and truly loves You can love the vanities of earth; his only desire is to please You. He is dying with longing for You to love him, and so would give his life to learn how he may please You better.

"O Lord, be pleased to grant me this love before You take me from this life. It will be a great comfort at the hour of death to realize that I shall be judged by You whom I have loved above all things. Then I shall be able to go to meet You with confidence, even though burdened with my debts, for I shall not be going into a foreign land but into my own country, into the kingdom of Him whom I have loved so much and who likewise has so much loved me " (cf. T.J. *Exc*, 7 – *Con*, 4 – *Int C III*, 1 – *Way*, 40).

251

THE LOVE OF FRIENDSHIP

PRESENCE OF GOD - Grant, O Lord, that I may live my life in Your divine friendship.

MEDITATION

1. The highest expression of human love is friendship, and St. Thomas teaches that charity is specifically the love of friendship between man and God.   Friendship, however, requires a certain equality, community of life and of goods; it demands reciprocity of affection and mutual benevolence. But what equality and community of life can there be between a creature who is nothing and God, who is the Supreme Being?   None, from a natural point of view.   However, God willed to raise man to the supernatural state by giving him a share in His nature and divine life.   It is true that man always remains a creature—though divinized by grace— and God remains the inaccessible, transcendent Being; but in His infinite love He has found a way to raise man to the level of His divine life.   The first fruit of God's love for us is precisely this form of equality and community of life which He has willed to establish between Himself and us by means of grace.   God has preceded us, not only by His love as Creator by which He has given us existence, but also by His love as Father by which He permits us to participate in His divine life.

"Love either finds or makes equal those who love each other... " and God has loved us so much that He has made us like unto Himself, that He may admit us into the circle of His divine friendship, that friendship which exists in the bosom of the Trinity between the three divine Persons. Furthermore, just as a friend desires to live with his friend, and always seeks his presence, his nearness, in the same way God has willed to make Himself so present to us and so intimate with us that He has established His abode in our souls : " We will come to him, and will make Our abode with him " (*Jn* 14,23).   Can we imagine any greater community of life between God and us than this continual communion with the divine Persons who dwell in our soul and with whom, by means of charity, we can enter into true relations of friendship?

2. Friendship demands reciprocal love. God in His love of friendship has gone before us; He loved us first, and by loving us, He infused in us grace and charity, thus enabling us to return His love. We return God's love not with our human, natural love which would be inadequate, but with the love of charity which the Holy Spirit has infused into our hearts, and which is a participation in that infinite love with which God loves Himself. God infuses into us this most precious gift, and we should accept it with a pure, free heart, so that we may adhere to it with all the strength of our will and affection.

By offering us His friendship, God has made us like to Himself, transforming our natural being into a supernatural one, and we, in response to His friendship, should strive to make ourselves like Him by transforming our will into His. Real friendship leads to a oneness of thought, will, affections, desires, and interests. A true friend espouses the interests and wishes of his friend; he thinks as his friend thinks, loves what he loves and wants what he wants. We must do the same with God if we really wish to be His friend.

Jesus said, " You are My friends, if you do the things that I command you, " and " If anyone love Me, he will keep My word " (*Jn* 15,14 – 14,23). On our side, therefore, friendship with God, that is, charity, requires a continual striving to conform our thoughts, our will, and our desires to the thought and will of our divine Friend. Our friendship with God will be perfect when there is no longer anything in us which is contrary to the divine will, when we are conformed to it in everything; then our union with Him will be perfect. " The state of this divine union consists in the soul's total transformation according to the will, into the will of God, so that there may be naught in the soul that is contrary to the will of God, but that, in all and through all, its movement may be that of the will of God alone " (J.C. *AS I*, 11,2). Perfect charity, perfect friendship, perfect union with God : this is the end toward which we must tend, advancing speedily by the steps of love.

COLLOQUY

" My God, You know that I have ever desired to love
You alone, that I seek no other glory.   Your love has gone
before me from the days of my childhood.   It has grown with
my growth and now it is an abyss, the depth of which I cannot
sound.   Love attracts love, and mine darts toward You.
It would like to fill to the brim the abyss which draws
it; but alas! my love is not even a drop in that ocean!   To
love You as You love me, I must borrow Your own love
—thus only can my desire be satisfied.

" Love—that is all You ask of us.   You do not need our
works, but only our love.   You Yourself, who declared that
You have no need to tell us if You are hungry, did not
hesitate to beg for a little water from the Samaritan
woman...You were thirsty...But when You said, ' Give
Me to drink, ' You, the Creator of the universe, were asking
for the love of Your poor creature; You thirsted for love!
O Jesus, I feel that You are thirstier than ever.   You meet
with nothing but indifference and ingratitude among the
disciples of this world, and among *Your own*, how few are the
hearts that surrender themselves without reserve to the
infinite tenderness of Your love.

" Your merciful love is ignored and rejected on every side.
The hearts on which You would lavish it turn to creatures,
rather than cast themselves into Your arms, into the ecstatic
fires of Your infinite love.   O my God, must that love which
is disdained lie hidden in Your heart?   It seems to me that
if You could find souls offering themselves as a holocaust
to Your love, You would consume them rapidly, and would
be pleased to set free those flames of infinite tenderness now
imprisoned in Your heart. . . .   O Jesus, permit that I may
be that happy victim—consume Your holocaust with fire
of divine love. . . . .   Your love surrounds and penetrates me;
at every moment it renews and purifies me, cleansing my soul
from all trace of sin " (T.C.J. *St*, 12 – 13 – 8).

252

CORRESPONDENCE WITH GRACE

NINTH SUNDAY AFTER PENTECOST

PRESENCE OF GOD - O Lord, grant that Your grace in me may not be void.

MEDITATION

1. Today the liturgy invites us to consider the grave problem of our correspondence with grace. It does this by showing us the sad picture of the sufferings of Israel, the chosen people, upon whom God had showered His benefits, whom He had surrounded with graces, protected with jealous care, and who, in spite of all this, were lost through their own infidelity. In the Epistle (1 *Cor* 10,6-13), St. Paul, after mentioning certain points about Israel's unfaithfulness, concludes : " Now all these things happened to them in figure, and they are written for our correction.... Wherefore, he that thinketh himself to stand, let him take heed lest he fall. " This is a strong call to vigilance and humility. If God has gone before us with His graces, if He has called us to a more intense interior life and to closer intimacy with Himself, all this, far from making us presumptuous, should deepen our humility of heart. God's gifts are preserved beneath the ashes of humble mistrust of self. Woe to us if we consider ourselves henceforth free from the weaknesses which we meet and, perhaps, condemn in others! Rather let us humbly say : " Lord, help me, or I shall do worse. " At the same time that he exhorts us to be humble, St. Paul also urges us to have confidence, because " God is faithful, who will not suffer you to be tempted above that which you are able : but will make also with temptation issue, that you may be able to bear it. " The Apostle is telling us that the knowledge of our weakness should not discourage us, because God is always ready to sustain us with His grace. God knows our weaknesses, the struggles we have to undergo, and the temptations that assail us; and for each of them He gives us the measure of grace we need in

order to triumph over them. It is very true that when the
storm is raging we can feel only the impact of the struggle,
and the grace that God is giving to help us remains completely
hidden; nevertheless, this grace is there and we should be
certain of it, because " God is faithful. "   " God has always
helped me.... "   St. Thérèse of the Child Jesus said, " I
count on His aid.   My sufferings may reach even greater
heights, but I am sure He will not abandon me " *(St)*.

2. The Gospel (*Lk* 19,41-47) continues the same subject of
the Epistle and shows us Jesus weeping over Jerusalem.
The Creator, the Lord, the Redeemer weeps over the ruin
of His creatures, the people whom He has loved with predilection, even choosing them as the companions of His earthly
life, and whom He had desired to save at any price.
"Jerusalem, Jerusalem...how often would I have
gathered together thy children as the hen doth gather her
chickens under her wings, and thou wouldst not! " (*Mt* 23,37).
This was the constant attitude of Jesus toward the holy city,
but it always remained blind to every light, deaf to every
invitation, and the Savior, shortly before going to His Passion,
broke forth into His last sorrowful admonition : " If thou also
hadst known and that in this thy day, the things that are to
thy peace! "   But again the city resists, and Jesus, after
having loved it so much, and after having wept over it as a
mother weeps over her son who has gone astray, predicts
its ruin : " Thy enemies...shall not leave in thee a stone
upon a stone, because thou hast not known the time of thy
visitation. "
Do you know how to recognize the moments in which
Our Lord visits your soul?   A word read or heard, perhaps
even by chance, an edifying example, an interior inspiration,
a new light which makes you see your faults more clearly
and opens new horizons of virtue and of good—all are visits
from Jesus.   And you, how do you correspond?   Is your
soul sensitive to these lights, to these admonitions?   Do you
not sometimes turn your gaze away, fearing that the light
you have glimpsed may ask you for sacrifices which are too
painful for your self-love?
Oh! if you had always recognized the moment in which
the Lord visited you!   If you had always been open to His
action!   Try then to begin again today, resolve to commence
anew each time that you happen to give in to nature.   " The

things that are to your peace, " your good, your sanctification, are precisely here, in this continual adherence to the impulses of grace.

COLLOQUY

" As I have already confessed to You, O glory of my life, O Lord God, strength of my salvation, I have sometimes placed my hopes in my own virtue, which was no virtue; and when I attempted to run, thinking I was very strong, I fell very quickly and went backward instead of forward. What I expected to reach, disappeared, and thus, O Lord, in various ways You have tested my powers. With light from You, I now see that I could not accomplish by myself the things that I wanted to do most. I said to myself : ' I shall do this, I shall finish that, ' and I did not do either the one or the other. The will was there but not the power, and if the power was there, my will was not; this because I had trusted in my own strength. Sustain me then, O Lord, for alone I can do nothing. However, when You are my stability, then it is true stability; but when I am my own stability, then it is weakness " (St. Augustine).

" O Lord, teach me to be always docile to Your grace, to say ' yes ' to You always. To say ' yes ' to Your will as expressed in the commandments, to say ' yes ' to the intimate inspirations by which You invite me to a more intense union, to more generous self-denial and more complete detachment. Grant that I may always be ready to open the door of my will to You, or rather, to keep it open always, so that You can enter there, and thus I shall not miss a single one of Your visits, a single one of Your delicate touches; not one of Your requests will escape me.

" Make me understand well that true peace does not consist in being exempt from difficulties or in following my own wishes, but in total adherence to Your will, and in docility to the inspirations of the Holy Spirit " (cf. Sr. Carmela of the Holy Spirit, O.C.D.).

253

THE PRECEPT OF CHARITY

PRESENCE OF GOD - O Lord, teach me to love You truly, with my whole heart, my whole soul, and with all my strength.

MEDITATION

1. " Virtue lies in the golden mean . " This maxim which is so exact for the moral virtues, cannot be applied to the theological virtues, which, having an infinite object, can have no limit. The measure of our faith, hope, and charity is to believe, to hope, and to love without measure. However much we love God, we can never love Him too much, nor can we love Him as much as He is lovable. By its very nature then, the precept of charity admits of no limit and we could never say, " I shall love God up to a certain point and that will be enough, " for by doing so, we would renounce tending toward the perfection of charity, which consists in loving God in a way that is as nearly proportionate as possible to His infinite lovableness. This is why it is necessary never to stop in the practice of charity, employing all our strength that it may continually increase in our soul. Because the precept of charity concerns the love of God—the infinite, supreme Good—it possesses an absolute character : " Thou shalt love the Lord thy God with thy *whole* heart, and with thy *whole* soul, and with thy *whole* mind, and with thy *whole* strength " (*Mk* 12,30). If we, so little and so limited, do not employ in the love of God all the little that we have and are, how can we truly tend toward the perfection of charity? If it is not in our power to love God as much as He deserves to be loved, it is, however, possible for us to strive to love Him with our whole strength, and this is exactly the perfection of love which God asks of us.

Furthermore, even human love is by its nature " totalitarian. " The more intimate and intense a friendship, the more it demands the exclusive gift of the heart; and when a friend begins to make reservations or to give his affection to others, the friendship loses its vigor, grows cold, and may even vanish. Therefore, we must guard against any coldness in our friendship with God, being careful to keep for Him alone the first fruits of our heart and to employ ourself wholly in loving Him with all our strength. It is true that only in heaven will we be able to love God with all our strength and in such a way that our love tends *always* and *actually* toward Him. Although this absolute totality and stability in love is not possible to us here on earth, it is possible for us to make an act of love each time that we will to do so. It is always in our power to unite our whole being—heart, affections, will, and desires—to God by an act of love.

2. Jesus has said : " He that loveth father or mother more than Me, is not worthy of Me " (*Mt* 10,37) ; hence, the precept of charity commands us to love God above all things. However, this precept can be interpreted in two ways. To love God more than any creature to the point of being ready to give up everything rather than offend God gravely is the first degree of charity. It is indispensable for all who desire to be friends of God and to possess His grace, and therefore, it is required of all. But in a more profound sense, to love God above all things means to prefer Him to everything else, not only to what might be an occasion of mortal or venial sin, but even to all that does not fully correspond to His good pleasure. This is the degree of perfect charity toward which every soul aspiring to intimate friendship with God must tend. This degree requires absolute renouncement and absolute purity, that is, the total absence of every shadow of sin or attachment to creatures. The exercise of perfect charity requires, therefore, a work of total purification, a work that is accomplished only by charity : " Charity causes emptiness in the will with respect to all things, since it obliges us to love God above them all " (J.C. *AS II*, 6,4).

We should be convinced that here on earth the practice of charity is closely united with that of renouncement, each being proportionate to the other; the more perfect and intense is charity, the more total is the renunciation required; but this is so precisely that the soul may attain to loving God with all its strength : " The strength of the soul, " says the mystical doctor, " consists in its faculties, passions, and desires, all of which are governed by the will. Now when these faculties, passions, and desires are directed by the will toward God, and turned away from all that is not

God, then the strength of the soul is kept for God, and thus
the soul is able to love God with all its strength " (*AS III*, 16,2).
This is the great function of renouncement in respect to
charity : to free the powers of the soul so entirely that they
can be wholly employed in loving and serving God alone.
If we really want to love God with our whole heart, we must
be very generous in renunciation and detachment.   This
in itself is an exercise of love because it disposes the soul for
perfect charity.

COLLOQUY

" O Lord God, was it not enough to permit us to love
You without its being necessary to invite us to do so by
exhortations, even obliging us to do so by commanding it?
Yes, O divine Goodness, in order that neither Your greatness
nor our lowliness, nor any other pretext could prevent us
from loving You, You have commanded us to do so.   O my
God, if we could only comprehend the happiness and honor of
being able to love You, how indebted we should feel to You,
who not only permit but command us to love You!   O my
God, I do not know whether I should love more Your infinite
beauty which Your divine goodness commands me to love,
or this goodness of Yours which commands me to love such
infinite beauty!   O beauty of my God, how lovable you are,
being revealed to me by Your immense goodness!   O
goodness, how lovable you are, communicating to me such
eminent beauty!

" O Lord, how sweet is this commandment.   If it were
given to the damned, they would be instantly freed from their
sufferings and supreme misfortune, for the blessed enjoy
beatitude only by complying with it.   O celestial Love!
how amiable You are to our souls!   O divine Goodness, may
You be blessed eternally, You who so urgently command us to
love You, although Your love is so desirable and necessary for
our happiness that, without it, we could only be unhappy!

" O Lord, in heaven we shall need no commandment to
love You, for our hearts, attracted and ravished by the vision
of Your sovereign beauty and goodness, will necessarily love
You eternally.   There our hearts will be wholly free of
passions, our souls will be completely delivered from distractions, our minds will have no anxieties, our powers will have

no repugnances, and therefore we shall love You with a perpetual, uninterrupted love. But in this mortal life, we cannot achieve such a perfect degree of love, because, as yet, we do not have the heart, the soul, the mind, or the powers of the blessed. Nevertheless, You desire us to do in this life everything that depends on ourselves to love You with all our heart and all the strength we have; this is not only possible, but very easy, for to love You, O God, is a sovereignly lovable thing " (cf. St. Francis de Sales).

254

THE EXCELLENCE OF CHARITY

PRESENCE OF GOD - Make me understand, O Lord, the preeminence of charity, that I may apply myself to it with all my heart.

MEDITATION

1. The three theological virtues, having God for their immediate object, are superior to the moral virtues which are directed to the government of our conduct; but among the three theological virtues, charity holds the primacy. It holds the primacy because, being inseparable from grace, it is the constitutive and indispensable element of our supernatural life. Where there is no charity there is neither grace nor life, but only death. " He that loveth not, abideth in death, " and contrariwise, " He that abideth in charity, abideth in God, and God in him " (1 Jn 3,14 – 4,16). Faith and hope can subsist in a soul which has lost grace, but charity cannot. It is so *vital* that it cannot co-exist with the death that is caused by sin. Furthermore, it is so vital that it is imperishable and will remain unchanged for all eternity. In heaven, faith and hope will cease because they bear with them some imperfection : faith makes us know God without giving us the vision of Him, and hope lets us hope in Him without giving us possession of Him. Hence, " when that which is perfect is come, " that is, the beatific vision, these two virtues will have no further reason for existing. However, it is not the same with charity which implies no imperfection,

since by it, we love God either in the obscurity of faith,
or in the clarity of vision, and therefore St. Paul says,
" Charity never falleth away. "   Here on earth, to adhere
to God, " these three remain : faith, hope, and charity :
but the greatest of these is charity " (1 *Cor* 13,8.13).

Faith and hope are incomplete virtues, because without
charity they cannot unite us to God and produce the works of
eternal life.   The faith and hope of a sinner, one who has lost
charity, are inactive and inoperative; they remain in him,
it is true, but they are there as if dead.   " Faith without
works is dead " (*Jas* 2,26), and only " faith that worketh by
charity...availeth anything " (*Gal* 5,6), and this to the
extent, that " if I should have all faith so that I could remove
mountains, and have not charity, I am nothing " (1 *Cor* 13,2).
It is charity that gives the warmth and strength of eternal
life to faith and hope; it is charity that infuses vigor into these
virtues, for only he who loves is capable of abandoning
himself to God with eyes closed.

2. The moral virtues can make a man honest and
virtuous, and can regulate his actions according to reason,
but they can in no way bring him into friendship with God or
even give him the possibility of meriting eternal life.   Without
the life-giving breath of charity, everything is dead, sterile,
cold; without charity, man is confined to the natural level;
he cannot be a child of God, nor His friend; he cannot live in
intimacy with the three divine Persons.   Charity is the
principle, root, source, and measure of our supernatural life.
The more we love, the more the life of grace increases in us
and the more we live in God : " We know that we have
passed from death to life, because we love " (1 *Jn* 3,14).

It is a truly impressive thought : the greatest and most
beautiful works, such as the apostolate, works of beneficence,
and even martyrdom, are of no value without charity.   " If
I should distribute all my goods to feed the poor, and if I
should deliver my body to be burned, and have not charity, it
profiteth me nothing " (1 *Cor* 13,3).   But when charity is
present, everything changes in appearance, like a landscape
under the sun's caress, and with the change in appearance,
the value also changes; even the lowliest works, the most
secret acts of virtue, if performed out of love for God, acquire
value for eternal life.   This is the miracle worked by charity,
which St. Thomas calls with good reason, the " form and

mother " of all the virtues. " It is love alone which gives value to all things, " says St. Teresa, " and the most needful thing is that it be so great that nothing can hinder its operation " (*Exc*, 5). All this enables us to understand that charity is truly " the greatest and the first commandment, " on which " the whole law " depends (*Mt* 22,38.40). The soul that has understood this great truth, is no longer preoccupied with so many more or less accessory practices and exercises in its spiritual life, but aims straight at the heart, at the center of this life, at charity. This soul's only concern is to use all its strength in the exercise of love, to increase this love, to live as much as possible in continual, actual love; therefore, it strives in all things to work for the sole purpose of pleasing God and giving Him glory.

COLLOQUY

" Clothe me, O Lord, with the purple garment of charity which not only adds grace to faith and hope, but causes the soul to rise to so lofty a point that it is brought very near You and becomes very beautiful and pleasing in Your eyes. It is the virtue which most attracts Your love, protects the soul against pride and gives value to the other virtues, bestowing on them vigor and strength, grace and beauty so that they may please You, for without charity no virtue has grace before Your eyes.

" O sweetest love of God, how little are You known! He who has found Your fountain has found rest. You remove from the affections of the will whatever is not God and set it upon Him alone, and then you prepare this faculty and unite it to God through love.

" O God, teach me to use all my powers to love You, so that all the faculties of my soul and body : memory, understanding, and will, inward and outward senses, desires of the sensual part and of the spiritual part, will work in love and for the sake of love. Grant that all that I do I may do with love, and all that I suffer I may suffer with the pleasure of love, and that in this way, my God, I may keep all my strength for You " (J.C. *DN II*, 21,10.11 – *SM I*, 16 – *SC*, 28,8).

" I resolve, O my God, to have no other purpose but love in all my actions, interior as well as exterior, always saying

and asking myself : What am I doing now?   Am I loving my
God?   And if I see that there is any obstacle to pure love,
I shall reproach myself, remembering, O Lord, that I must
return You love for love.   Well do You make me understand
that the more I love You, the more diligent I shall be in the
observance of all Your holy laws " (cf. T.M. *Sp*).

255

THE ACT OF LOVE

PRESENCE OF GOD - O Lord, grant that I may love You for Yourself
and not for my own consolation, and that in loving You, I may
always seek Your will, not mine.

MEDITATION

1. To love a person is to *desire* his *well-being*.   We understand, therefore, that the essence of love is in the act of the
will by which we *wish good*.   This does not take away from the
fact that the act may often be accompanied by sensible
affection, making our love both an act of the will and of the
sensibility.   Nevertheless, it is clear that the substance of
real love is not to be found in the emotions but in the act
of the will.   Charity does not change our manner of loving,
but penetrates it, supernaturalizes it, making the will and
the sensibility capable of loving God.   Yes, even sensible
affection can be engaged in the act of supernatural love;
God does not despise this humbler and less lofty manifestation
of our love for Him, because He has commanded us to love
Him not only with our whole mind and our whole soul,
but also *with our whole heart*.   All our powers—intellectual,
volitive, and affective—are engaged in the act of love, and
yet the substance of this act is not found in the feelings but
in the will.   Therefore, when our emotions are cold in
our love of God, and we " feel " nothing, there is no reason
for us to be disturbed; we will find less satisfaction in
our love—for it is much more pleasant for us to feel that
we are loving—but our act of love will be equally true

and perfect. Even more, lacking the impetus and pleasure which come from our feelings, we will be obliged to apply ourself more resolutely to the act of the will and this, far from harming it, will make it more voluntary, and therefore, more meritorious. Precisely because the substance of love is in the act of the will that wishes good to God, in order to make our love purer and more intense, Our Lord will often deprive us of all consoling feelings; we will no longer feel that we love God—and this will give us pain—but in reality, we will love Him in the measure that we will with determination what He wills, and want His good pleasure and delight above all things. Besides, it is not in our power to feel love but it is always in our power to make voluntary acts of love; it is always in our power to *wish good* to God, striving with all our strength to live for Him and to please Him.

2. St. John of the Cross says : " It is by an act of the will that the soul is united to God; this act is love. Union with God is never wrought by feeling or exertions of the desire, for these remain in the soul as aims and ends " *(L)*. The operation of the will is the act of love by means of which we wish good to God and conform our will to His. This operation properly ends in God, and is the true means of uniting us to Him. The feeling of love, on the contrary, is only a subjective impression sometimes produced in our sensibility by the act of love. It ends in the soul which experiences it and is a source of consolation, but we can clearly see that of itself it has no power to unite the soul to God. However, the soul can and should make use of it to give itself to God with more generosity, and in this sense, the feeling of love intensifies the operation of the will. Unfortunately, as we are so eager to seek satisfaction even in the most sacred things, the soul may easily stop at the sweetness of these feelings, and then it ceases to tend toward God with all its strength.

Therefore, it is very expedient for us that God should make us go through periods of aridity, thus forcing us to go to Him by the pure operation of our will. " Then, " says the mystical doctor, " the soul sets on God alone its affection, joy, contentment, and love, leaving all things behind and loving Him above them all. " And he adds, " He would be very ignorant who should think that, because spiritual delight and sweetness are failing him, God is failing him, and he should rejoice and be glad because he has them and think that for this reason he has God " *(ibid.)*. No, true love and union with God do not consist in this, but in the pure operation of the will, which seeks God and His will above everything. Therefore, if we really want to love God and be united to Him, we must " hunger and thirst for God's will alone, " that is, seek His will alone, preferring it always to our own. This way of loving takes us completely out of ourself, out of what is deepest in our *ego*, our own will, and plunges us wholly into the will of God. If we truly realize that to attain perfect union with God, our whole life must be enclosed in His will, we will feel the need of being constantly generous in order to go out of our own will at every moment and abide in God's will.

COLLOQUY

" Ah, my God and Lord, how many there are who seek in You their own consolation and pleasure, and desire favors and gifts from You; but those who long to give You pleasure, *please You* and to give You something at their own cost, setting their own interests last, are very few.

" Give me the grace, O God, to follow You with a real love and a spirit of sacrifice, so that I may never seek for consolation or pleasure either in You or in aught else. I do not desire to pray to You for favors, for I see clearly that I have already received enough of these, and all my anxiety is set upon rendering You some service such as You merit, although it cost me much. O my Beloved, all that is rough and toilsome I desire for myself, and all that is sweet and delectable I desire for You " (J.C. *DN II*, 19,4 – *SM II*, 52).

" O God, how necessary it is that we should learn to love You without any motive of self-interest : To walk along the road of love as one should, we must have the one desire of serving You, O Christ crucified; therefore, I neither ask for consolations nor desire them, and I beg You not to give them to me in this life.

" No, my God, love consists not in interior favors but in the firmness of our determination to please You in everything, and to endeavor in all possible ways not to offend You, and in praying for Your greater honor and glory. It consists especially in perfect conformity to Your will, so that I too want—and steadfastly—all that I know You will, accepting the bitter and the sweet with equal joy. O strong love of God! I really think nothing seems impossible to one who loves " (T.J. *Int C IV*, 2 – 1; *F*, 5; *Con*, 3).

256

THE LIFE OF LOVE

PRESENCE OF GOD - Grant, O Lord, that even while I am here on earth, I may love You as I shall love You in heaven.

MEDITATION

1. If it may be said that by faith " eternal life begins in us " (St. Thomas, II^a II^{ae}, q.4, a.1, co.), the same may be said—and with greater reason—of charity, which will remain unchanged even in heaven. Eternal life will be essentially a life of love, of love which has reached its greatest height, for when we know God perfectly by the beatific vision, we shall finally be able to fulfill with absolute perfection the precept of loving God with all our strength. On this earth such perfection is possible only relatively; nevertheless, even now we possess the same charity with which we shall love God in heaven. Therefore, we can begin even now that life of love which will flower completely in eternity. Our love in heaven will have the characteristics of completeness and absolute continuity, with the impossibility of its ever failing. We cannot attain this while we are on earth, but we can strive for it by the exercise of a pure, intense love, a love that is, as far as possible, always in action. These, then, are the qualities our love for God should have : purity, intensity, continuity.

Our love for God will be pure when we love Him so much that we seek only His glory and the accomplishment of His will : " Hallowed be Thy name...Thy will be done " (*Mt* 6,9.10). This is the only real good that we, poor creatures, can wish for our God. All the glory we can

possibly give Him consists in saying a wholehearted *yes*
to His holy will, in rivalling the angels and blessed in heaven
by carrying out His will here on earth with such great love
and completeness : " Thy will be done on earth as it is in
heaven " *(ibid.)*.   The purity of our love should consist in
seeking God's glory alone, His will alone, completely forgetting
ourself, in being ready to sacrifice every wish, desire, and
interest for Him.

Therefore, even in the spiritual life, our first thought
should be, not our own perfection, progress, and consolation,
but always God's delight, good pleasure, and glory.   It is
thus that we will serve our own interests better, for he
who gives himself to God, completely forgetting himself,
draws down upon himself the fullness of divine love.   What
greater good could come to us than being loved by Infinite
Love?

2. But then it is necessary that our love for God be
intense and vigorous, because in this way the inclination of
our will toward Him will always grow stronger.   " *Amor
meus pondus meum,* " St. Augustine says, love is the weight
which draws me, which draws my entire being, all my will,
all my life, into God.   And it is necessary that this weight
increase, so as to draw us into God with an ever-increasing
speed.   St. John of the Cross says that one degree of love is
sufficient for a soul to be in its center, which is God, but the
more degres of love it has, the deeper it goes into its center,
and hence, " the strongest love is the most unitive love "
(*LF* 1,13).

Love becomes stronger and increases by exercise,
provided the exercise is generous and intense, making use
of all the powers of the soul.   When we perform our
actions, not carelessly or negligently, but with our whole
heart, that is, with all the good will of which we are capable,
our love immediately increases, and with every act there
is a corresponding growth in charity.   In this way our love
will always continue to grow, it will become strong and
mature, and will be able to draw us wholly into God.
Let us try, then, to make as many acts of love as possible during
the course of our day so that we will be able to live—as far
as is attainable in this life—in continual, actual love.   But
there is one time in the day which is especially intended to
make us more fervent in charity, and this is the time of

prayer, prayer understood as an intimate encounter of our soul with God by love, as an intercourse of friendship between God and us. It is especially then that we must endeavor to recollect ourself; we should renew the resolution of our will to give ourself entirely to God, to seek His will always, and to fulfill His good pleasure above everything else. We should pray to find God, to remain near Him as friend with Friend. Let us ask Him humbly, but with gentle insistance, to teach us how to love Him as we will love Him one day in heaven. Just as human friendship is strengthened by the frequent meeting of friends, so divine friendship—charity—is strengthened in the same way; charity grows stronger in prayer, which is the friendly, loving meeting of the soul with God.

COLLOQUY

" O Lord, You teach me that without love even the most perfect gifts are as nothing, that charity is the most excellent way, for it leads directly to You. That is why I wish for no science but the science of love, and having given all the substance of my house for love, I count it as nothing. I understand so clearly that love alone can make me pleasing in Your sight, that my sole ambition is to acquire it.

" My occupation is to gather flowers, the flowers of love and sacrifice, and to offer them to You, my God, to give You pleasure. I wish to labor for Your love alone—with the sole aim of pleasing You, of consoling Your Sacred Heart, and of saving souls who will love You through eternity " (T.C.J. St, 13 – Act of Oblation).

" O God, my love for You ought to be total, infinite in desire, because You will not give Yourself entirely to a soul unless it gives itself wholly to You. I must not cling to any attachment, nor admit even a single voluntary imperfection, nor refuse You anything. Grant that I may give myself to You in a continual, uninterrupted donation, moment by moment, seeking in all things Your greater glory, always trying to please You, always wanting Your will alone, doing each action with all my heart and with all my love.

" My love for You must be delicate. Help me to reach that exquisiteness and delicacy, that regard for details which You appreciate so much, which delights You.

" My love for You should be strong and generous, and prove itself in sacrifice, in seeking sacrifice in the offering and the smiling acceptance of suffering. O God, for love of You, I want to take advantage of the little opportunities so that I may be strong in the big ones " (Sr. Carmela of the Holy Spirit, O.C.D.).

THE TENTH TO THE EIGHTEENTH SUNDAY
AFTER PENTECOST

FRATERNAL CHARITY — THE MORAL VIRTUES —

THE GIFTS OF THE HOLY SPIRIT —

THE BEATITUDES.

257

FRATERNAL CHARITY

PRESENCE OF GOD - Grant, O Lord, that I may understand the depth of meaning in the precept of fraternal charity.

MEDITATION

1. Jesus has given us as the foundation of all law, not only the precept of the love of God, " the greatest and the first commandment, " but also the precept of the love of neighbor, and He expressly said that it is " like " to the first (*Mt* 22,38.39). That the precept of the love of God should be the basis of all Christian life is easy to understand, but it is not so easy to see that the same holds true of the precept of fraternal charity. However, Jesus has bound these two commandments so closely that the one cannot subsist without the other. He did not say that all is based on the first commandment, that of love of God, but " on these *two commandments* [the love of God and of neighbor] dependeth the whole law and the prophets " (*ibid*. 22,40). Why did He put the love of neighbor so close to the love of God as to make of it, with the latter, the one foundation of all Christianity? Because the virtue of fraternal charity is not love of the creature in itself and for itself, but it is love of the creature " *propter Deum*, " that is, for God's sake, because of its relation to God. In other words, we must clearly understand that God commands us to love Him not only in Himself, but also in His rational creatures whom He has been pleased to create to His image and likeness. Just as a father wants to be loved and respected not only in his own person, but also in that of his children, so God wants to be loved in His creatures as well as in Himself, and He desires this to such an extent that He considers anything done to one of His creatures as done to Him. Jesus has said : " Amen I say to you, as long as you did it to one of these my least brethren, you did it to Me " (*ibid*. 25,40). Fraternal charity is of great importance, because it is in reality an extension of our charity toward God, an extension which embraces all men in relation to God, their Creator and their Father. For this

reason, the precept of the love of neighbor is inseparable from the precept of the love of God.

2. God is so insistent upon being loved in the neighbor that He makes this love the essential condition of our eternal salvation. When Jesus speaks to us of the last judgment, He gives no other reason for the justification of the good and the condemnation of the wicked than the doing of, or the omission of, works of mercy toward our neighbor. " Come, ye blessed of My Father, possess the kingdom prepared for you from the foundation of the world. " Why? " For I was hungry, and you gave Me to eat; I was thirsty, and you gave Me to drink... " (*ibid.* 25,34.35). I was hungry in the poor, I thirsted in your neighbor. If it is very consoling to know that God considers works of charity done to our neighbor as done to Himself, and rewards them as such, it is a matter of serious reflection to know that He also considers failures in charity toward our neighbor as if done to Himself, and so will punish them accordingly. Jesus, who is the personification of the goodness and infinite mercy of our heavenly Father, does not hesitate to pronounce the sentence of eternal damnation against those who have not loved, or helped, or consoled their neighbor. Why? Because : " Amen I say to you, as long as you did it not to one of these least, neither did you do it to Me " (*ibid.* 25,45). God requires the concrete proof of our love for Him to be shown in the way we behave toward our neighbor. We cannot delude ourselves into thinking that we love God if we do not love our fellow men, who, like us, are the living images of our heavenly Father. What difference does it make if this image is sometimes disfigured by faults, by sin, or even by vices? It always remains the image of God which charity ought to make us recognize, venerate, and love in every man, regardless of his condition. We cannot be satisfied with an idealistic love for God. Our love must be realistic and actualized in our dealings with our neighbor : this is the unfailing proof of our love for God.

COLLOQUY

" O charity, you are as great as my God Himself, for God is Charity. You are so exalted that you reach the throne of the Blessed Trinity. There you enter the bosom of the eternal Father, and from the Father's bosom, you go to the heart of the Incarnate Word, where you take your rest and are nourished. Thus the soul who possesses you seeks its nourishment and rest in God alone, after which it returns to earth, for you reach even to our neighbors, O charity, loving them not only as creatures, but as beings created by God to His own image and likeness. You do not stop at loving their bodies, that is, their exterior appearance, but you penetrate to the interior of their souls, which you love more than all else. You do not stop at God's gifts, but soar to the Giver and love all men only in Him.

" O charity, you are so sublime that you unite us to God! You can do all things and in the Church you form a trinity, as it were, similar to the Blessed Trinity; because just as the Father is God, the Son is God, the Holy Spirit is God, and all three are united and are one and the same Being, so, by your virtue, O charity, this union reaches us, because you unite the soul to God, and one soul to another; in this invisible way, you form in the Church a kind of trinity. He who possesses you, O charity, nourishes himself with God, to such a point that he becomes like God through grace and participation.

" O my God, give me such perfect charity that I may know how to yield to my neighbor, helping and relieving him in all his needs, weaknesses, and troubles. May I know how to have prudent compassion for the faults of others " (St. Mary Magdalen dei Pazzi).

258

THE MOTIVE FOR FRATERNAL CHARITY

PRESENCE OF GOD - O Lord, teach me how to love You in my neighbor and to love my neighbor in You and for You.

MEDITATION

1. There are not two virtues of charity, one the love of God and the other love of the neighbor; for the charity by which we love God and the neighbor is one and the same. We love God because He is infinitely lovable, and we love the neighbor because faith teaches us to recognize in him a reflection of the lovableness of God. The motive for fraternal charity is the same as the motive for loving God, as we must always love God either directly in Himself or indirectly in the neighbor. Because fraternal charity has God for its ultimate object and last end, it is identical with the theological virtue by which we love God. Certainly God holds the first place! To Him, the infinite Good, we owe absolute preference above all other loves. The love of God, however, includes love of the neighbor, so that we love him in and for God, that is, because of his relation to God, and because he belongs to God. " God is the motive for loving the neighbor, " says St. Thomas, " which proves that the act by which we love God is the same as that by which we love the neighbor. Hence the virtue of charity does not stop at the love of God, but it also includes love of neighbor " (IIª IIae, q.25, a.1, co.). When one truly loves God, the neighbor is also loved, just as he is, in spite of his faults and the annoyance and trouble which he may sometimes cause; for instead of regarding these things, one looks much further and tries to see God in the brethren. With one's glance fixed on Him, and because of Him *(propter Deum)*, all are loved without distinction or restriction.

Such a soul readily understands the profound logic of the Apostle's words : " If any man say, I love God, and hateth his brother, he is a liar. For he that loveth not his brother whom he seeth, how can he love God whom he seeth not? And this commandment we have from God, that he who loveth God, love also his brother " (1 *Jn* 4,20.21).

2. If I love my neighbor because he is congenial, renders me service or sympathizes with me, or because I enjoy his friendship, if I love him because of his fine qualities and pleasing manners, my love is merely human, and is not the love of charity. If I am good to my neighbor and help him because I am sorry for him or feel bound to him by human ties, my love may be called sympathy or philanthropy, but it cannot yet be called charity, because the characteristic of charity is to love one's neighbor " *propter Deum,* " for God. My love becomes the virtue of charity only to the degree in which the love of God enters into it, only insofar as this love for my brethren is inspired by my love for God. The more my love is based on human motives alone—like congeniality, natural gifts, ties of blood—the more it is simply human love which has nothing of the merit and value of charity. " Love of neighbor is not meritorious if the neighbor is not loved because of God " (St. Thomas II^a II^ae, q.27, a.8). This is what St. Paul meant when he said : " If I should distribute all my goods to feed the poor...and have not charity, it profiteth me nothing " (1 *Cor* 13,3).

It is easy to deceive ourselves, thinking we have great charity because we love those who love us, because we are very thoughtful and full of attentions toward those who think as we do, or who are close to us, while, in reality, it is a question of purely natural love into which the love of God hardly enters. " If you love [only] them that love you, " Jesus said, " what reward shall you have?... Do not also the heathens this? " (*Mt* 5,46.47). If I want my love for my neighbor to be charity, I must transcend the natural and contemplate my neighbor in God, loving him in relation to God and because of God. Only in this way will my love for my neighbor be an act of the theological virtue of charity, the same act with which I love God; only thus shall I fulfill the precept of fraternal charity.

COLLOQUY

" As You, O God, have created man to Your image and likeness, so You have commanded us to love men with a love similar to that due to Your divinity. The reason why we love You, O Lord, is Your sovereignly high and infinite goodness, and the reason why we love men is because they have all been created to Your image and likeness, so that we love them as holy, living images of Your divinity.

" The same charity with which we love You, O Lord, is the source of the acts with which we love our neighbor. One same love holds for You, my God, as for our neighbor; it elevates us to the union of our spirit with You, my God, and it brings us back to loving society with our neighbor, but in such a way that we love him because he is created to *Your image and likeness*, created to share in Your divine goodness, to participate in Your grace and enjoy Your glory.

" To love our neighbor with the love of charity is to love You, my God, in man, and man in You; it is to love You alone for the love of Yourself, and to love creatures for love of You.

" O God of goodness! When we look at our neighbor created to Your image and likeness, should we not say one to another : See how much this person resembles the Creator? Should we not embrace him, caress him, and weep with love over him? Should we not give him many blessings? And why? For love of him? No, certainly not, for we do not know whether he, of himself, is worthy of love or of hatred. Then why? For love of You, O Lord, who created him to Your image and likeness, and made him capable of participating in Your goodness, grace, and glory. Therefore, O Love Divine, You have not only commanded us many times to love our neighbor, but You Yourself instill this love in our hearts " (St. Francis de Sales).

259

CHARITY AND HUMILITY

TENTH SUNDAY AFTER PENTECOST

PRESENCE OF GOD - Give me, O Lord, humility with love; let humility guard charity in me, and may charity increase according to the measure of Your will.

MEDITATION

1. In the texts of today's Mass, the liturgy sketches the features of the Christian soul in its fundamental lines. First St. Paul shows us in the Epistle (1 *Cor* 12,2-11) a soul vivified by the Holy Spirit, who diffuses His gifts in it. The Apostle mentions charismatic gifts, that is, those special graces, such as the gift of tongues, of knowledge, of miracles, bestowed by the Holy Spirit with great generosity upon the primitive Church. Although these are very precious gifts, they are inferior to sanctifying grace and charity, which alone give supernatural life to the soul. Whereas charismatic gifts may or may not accompany sanctifying grace, they neither increase nor decrease its intensity thereby. St. Thomas notes that while grace and charity sanctify the soul and unite it to God, these miraculous gifts, on the contrary, are ordered for the good of another and can subsist even in one who is not in the state of grace. St. Paul also—and in the same letter from which the passage in today's Mass is taken—after enumerating all these extraordinary gifts, concludes with his famous words : " ...all this, without charity, is nothing. " Charity is always the " central " virtue, the fundamental characteristic of the Christian soul, and is also the greatest gift the Holy Spirit can give us. If the divine Paraclete did not vivify our soul by charity and grace, no one, not even the most virtuous, could perform the slightest act of supernatural value. " No man can say the Lord Jesus but by the Holy Ghost, " the Apostle says. Just as a tree cannot bring forth fruit if it is deprived of its life-giving sap, so the soul which is not vivified by the Holy Spirit cannot perform acts of supernatural value. Note once again the great importance of

grace and charity; the smallest degree of them is worth more than all the extraordinary gifts which, although they can dispose souls to good, can neither infuse nor increase divine life in us.

2. The Gospel (*Lk* 18,9-14) presents us with another fundamental characteristic of the Christian soul : humility. Charity, it is true, is superior to it because it gives us divine life; yet, humility is of great importance because it is the virtue which clears the ground to make room for grace and charity. Jesus gives us a vivid and concrete example of this truth in today's parable of the Pharisee and the publican. The Gospel tells us explicitly that Jesus was speaking to some who " trusted in themselves as just and despised others. " The Pharisee is the prototype, the perfect representative of this group. See him! how convinced of his justice, how puffed up by his own merits : I am neither a thief nor an adulterer, I fast and pay tithes. What more can one expect? But this proud man does not see that he lacks the greatest of all things, charity, so much so that he inveighs against others, accuses and condemns them : " I am not as the rest of men, extortioners, unjust, adulterers, as also is this publican. " Having no charity for his neighbor, he cannot have charity toward God. In fact, having gone into the Temple to pray, he is incapable of making the least little act of love or adoration, and instead of praising God for His blessings, he does nothing but praise himself. This man is really unable to pray because he has no charity, and he cannot have any because he is full of pride. " God resisteth the proud, and giveth grace to the humble " (*Jas* 4,6). Therefore, the Pharisee returns home condemned, not so much by God who always loves to show mercy, as by his own pride which impedes the work of mercy in him.

The attitude of the publican is entirely different. He is a poor man who knows he has sinned, and he is aware of his moral wretchedness. He does not possess charity either, because sin is an obstacle to it, but he is humble, very humble, and he trusts in the mercy of God. " O God, be merciful to me, a sinner! " And God who loves to bend down to the humble, justifies him at that very moment; his humility has drawn down upon him the grace of the Most High. St. Augustine has said : " God prefers humility in things that are done badly, rather than pride in those which are done

well!" We are not justified by our virtues and our good
works, but by grace and charity, which the Holy Spirit
diffuses in our hearts, "according as He wills," yes, but
always in proportion to our humility.

COLLOQUY

"O good Jesus, how often after bitter tears, sobs, and
indescribable groanings, You have healed the wounds of my
conscience by the unction of Your mercy and the oil of Your
joy! How often after I have begun my prayer without hope,
I have found my joy again in the hope of forgiveness! Those
who have experienced this know that You are a real physician,
who heals contrite hearts and solicitously tends their wounds.
Let those who as yet have not had this experience, believe,
at least, in Your words : ' The Spirit of the Lord hath anointed
Me; He hath sent Me to preach to the meek, to heal the
contrite of heart. ' If they still doubt, let them approach
You and learn, and they will understand what Your words
mean : ' I will have mercy and not sacrifice. '

"O Lord, You said, ' Come to Me, all you that labor
and are burdened, and I will refresh you. ' But what path
should I take to reach You? The path of humility, for only
then will You console me. But what consolation do You
promise to the humble? Charity. In fact, the soul will
obtain charity in proportion to its humility. O what sweet,
delicious food is charity! It sustains us when we are weary,
strengthens us when we are weak, and comforts us when
we are sad. O Lord, give me this charity which makes
Your yoke sweet and Your burden light " (St. Bernard).

260

THE EXTENT OF FRATERNAL CHARITY

PRESENCE OF GOD - O Lord, make me understand that true charity allows of no exceptions, but embraces with sincere love our neighbor, whoever he may be.

MEDITATION

1. If charity were based on our neighbor's qualities, on his merits or his worth, if it were based on the consolation and benefits we receive from him, it would be impossible to extend it to all men. But since it is founded on the neighbor's relation to God, no one can be legitimately excluded from it, because we all belong to God—we are, in fact, His creatures, and, at least by vocation, His children, redeemed by the Blood of Christ and called to live in " fellowship " with God (cf. 1 *Jn* 1,3) by grace here on earth and by the beatific vision in heaven. Even if some, by their sins, have become unworthy of God's grace, as long as they live, they are always capable of being converted and of being readmitted to loving intimacy with their heavenly Father.

In the Old Testament, the great mystery of the communication of divine life to men was not revealed. Because Jesus had not yet come to establish these new relations between God and men, the law of fraternal charity did not demand this universal bond; the ancients would not have understood it. But since Jesus has come to tell us that God is our Father who wishes to communicate His divine life to us; since Jesus has come to offer us the grace of adoption as sons of God, the precept of charity has acquired a new breath. " You have heard that it hath been said, Thou shalt love thy neighbor and hate thy enemy. But I say to you : Love your enemies; do good to them that hate you and pray for them that persecute and calumniate you : that you may be the children of your Father who is in heaven, who maketh His sun to rise upon the good and bad, and raineth upon the just and the unjust " (*Mt* 5,43-45). This is how Jesus Himself gave us the motive of universal charity : we should love all men because they are the children of our heavenly Father; thus, we imitate His universal love for all those who are His creatures, chosen by Him to be His adopted children. Jesus also tells us to love our neighbor " *propter Deum,* " for God's sake.

2. We very often find it difficult in practice to fulfill the precept of universal charity because our love for our neighbor is almost exclusively personal and subjective, and therefore, egoistic. In other words, instead of basing our love for our neighbor upon his relation to God, we make it depend upon his relation to ourselves. If our neighbor likes and respects us, shows consideration for us, lends us his services, we find no difficulty in loving him; or rather, we enjoy it and seek pleasure in it. But it is a very different thing if our neighbor is hostile toward us, or does not get along with us, if, even involuntarily, he causes us displeasure, if he does not think as we do, or does not approve of our actions. Judging by this conduct, we must admit that we have erred from the beginning, substituting for God, who is the true motive for loving our neighbor, our miserable self with our egoistic exigencies. We must also admit that in regard to fraternal charity, we are, unfortunately, almost always *egocentric* and very seldom *theocentric.* If our relations with our neighbor were really centered in God, we should know how to overcome our egocentric point of view, that is, our personal selfish one; and even though suffering from the wrongs, want of delicacy and rebuffs we might have received from our neighbor, we would never claim this as a motive for refusing him our love. Basically, it is always selfishness which leads us astray, and in this case, it closes the way to the practice of theological charity.

We should, therefore, conquer our selfishness and immediately go beyond the limited horizons of a love based on our own personal interests. Let us look higher; let us look at God, who repeats to us, as He did to St. Catherine of Genoa, " He who loves Me, loves all that is loved by Me. " If our charity is arrested by the difficulties encountered in dealing with our neighbor, it is evident that our relations with our brethren are not regulated by our love of God, but by our love of self.

COLLOQUY

"O Jesus, I know I have no enemies; but I do have my natural likes and dislikes : I may feel drawn toward one sister, and may be tempted to go a long way in order to avoid meeting another. However, You tell me that this last is the sister I must love and pray for, even though her manners might lead me to believe that she does not care for me. 'If you love them that love you, what thanks are to you? For sinners also love those that love them.' And You teach me more, that it is not enough to love; we must also prove our love. We take a natural delight in pleasing friends, but that is not charity; even sinners do the same.

"From all this I conclude that I ought to seek the companionship of those sisters for whom I feel a natural aversion and try to be their good Samaritan. It frequently takes only a word or a smile to impart fresh life to a despondent soul. Yet it is not merely in the hope of bringing consolation that I wish to be kind; if it were, I should soon be discouraged, for often well-intentioned words are totally misunderstood. Consequently, in order that I may lose neither time nor labor, I shall try to act solely to please You, O Jesus, by following this precept of the Gospel : 'When thou makest a dinner or a supper, call not thy friends nor thy brethren, lest perhaps they also invite thee again, and a recompense be made to thee.'

"O Lord, what can I offer to my sisters but the spiritual feast of sweet and joyful charity? Teach me to imitate St. Paul who rejoiced with those who rejoiced. It is true he also wept with those who wept, and at the feast which I desire to provide, tears must sometimes fall, but I shall always do my best to change them into smiles, since Thou, O Lord, loveth the cheerful giver" (T.C.J. *St*, 10 – 11).

261

THE MEASURE OF FRATERNAL CHARITY

PRESENCE OF GOD - O Lord, make me understand the full meaning of Your words : " Thou shalt love thy neighbor as thyself " (*Mt* 22, 39).

MEDITATION

1. When Jesus gave the precept of fraternal charity, He Himself set its measure : " Thou shalt love thy neighbor as thyself " (*Mt* 22,39). This measure is so great that it would be difficult to exceed it, when we consider how much every man is inclined to love himself. The good that each of us desires for himself is so great that if we could succeed in desiring just as much for our neighbor—for any neighbor— our charity would be truly magnanimous. Jesus has said, " And as you would that men should do to you, do you also unto them in like manner " (*Lk* 6,31), which, in practice, signifies that we treat others exactly as we wish to be treated ourselves; for example, showing, toward our neighbor, the same consideration of thought, word, and deed, as we would desire for ourselves; serving and pleasing others, accommodating ourselves to their wishes, as we ourselves would wish to be served, pleased, and condescended to. Alas! our self-love incites us, instead, to use two different measures : one, very large—even exaggerated—for ourselves; the other, very small—even miserly—for our neighbor. The attentions we receive from others always seem to be so trifling, and how easily we complain that we are treated thoughtlessly! Yet how very far we are from showing such thoughtfulness toward our neighbor; although in retrospect, we always think we have done too much. We are very sensitive to the wrongs done us; and even when, in reality, they are slight, we consider them as almost unbearable; whereas we consider as mere nothings the things by which we offend others so freely. The greatest enemy of fraternal charity is self-love, which makes us too sensitive and demanding in what refers to ourselves, and very careless in what refers to others. For the sake of virtue we should force ourselves to cultivate the same thoughtfulness toward

our neighbor as we instinctively feel is due to us, and this, not so much for our neighbor himself, as for God, who wills that we act in this way and whom we must see in our neighbor. If we were really convinced that God is present in our brethren and that in them He is awaiting the delicacy of our love, how could we think it too much to love them at least as much as we love ourselves?

2. The love which each one of us bears to himself is not a theoretical nor abstract love, but a very definite and concrete one. It includes our person with all its peculiarities, needs, tastes, and feelings. We are so ingenious in justifying our own way of thinking, in maintaining our rights, in defending our cause, and in excusing our faults : how much understanding and sympathy we show in this realm! Yet, this is the attitude we should have toward our neighbor also. To love others for God does not mean that we confine ourselves to a general, platonic love, embracing them altogether as a group, without taking into account individual persons. No, it is necessary to love each one individually, in the actuality of his own personality, adapting ourselves to his feelings, tastes, and mentality, compassionating his faults, and concealing them just as carefully as we do our own. We must desire and seek his good, not by words alone but by deeds, just as we do for ourselves. And as we do not cease to love ourselves even though we have defects, so our love for our neighbor should be such as not to be lessened by the deficiencies we may find in him.

The first and greatest good we should wish for our neighbor is that which we should wish for ourselves : eternal salvation, sanctity, grace, and the ineffable joy of being a child of God, of sharing in His divine life, and enjoying Him in Heaven for all eternity. We should have a real, practical desire for this good, not contenting ourselves with simply sighing for it, but working with all our strength to obtain it—more by prayer, hidden sacrifice, and good example, than by words alone.

However, our first duty of striving for our neighbor's spiritual welfare should not be an easy excuse for dispensing ourselves from our obligation to help him in his material needs.

How often, alas! at the sight of the needs of others, our charity is limited to empty words and sterile compassion!

Whereas, to carry out the command of Jesus, we must translate our charity into practical, effective help, as we would wish to be helped in our personal needs. " All things therefore whatsoever you would that men should do to you, do you also to them. For this is the law and the prophets " (*Mt* 7,12). How we need to penetrate the profound meaning of these words, in order to apply them to all our relations with our neighbor, excluding no one!

COLLOQUY

" O most merciful Lord Jesus, love for our neighbor is well-ordered when he is loved for Your sake, because You have created him and have commanded that he should be loved with a proper, well-regulated love. If we love our parents and the members of our family more than we love You, our love is not well-ordered, and anyone who loves like this is unworthy of You. We have received a twofold commandment : to love God and to love our neighbor; but although the commandment is twofold, only one love is prescribed, for the love with which You are loved is not different from the love with which our neighbor is loved for Your sake; nor can he love You who errs in the way he loves his neighbor.

" O Lord Jesus Christ, if I want charity to be well ordered in me, I must love both You and my neighbor; I must love You with all my heart, all my soul, all my mind, and my neighbor as myself, in such a way that I shall not do to others what I would not want to have done to myself and I shall give to others the same benefits that I desire for myself.

" Teach me, O most benign Lord, to meditate on these truths, to remember them, and to practice them with all my strength. By my love for my neighbor I shall know whether I love You, O Lord, for he who is neglectful in loving You, does not know how to love his neighbor either. O most merciful Lord Jesus Christ, what shall I say and what shall I do, who on account of the hardness of my heart do not love my neighbor for Your sake; I have often sinned, trying to get something I thought I needed for myself or in trying to avoid something disagreeable. Thus there is no true love in me. Deign to help me, O merciful Lord Jesus Christ, You who are the source of charity and true love, genuine love; pardon my sins and in Your mercy give me a share in Your immense clemency. Oh! help me to be converted entirely to You, so that I may live with You in ordered charity, eternally! (Ven. Raymond Jourdain).

262

THE NEW COMMANDMENT

PRESENCE OF GOD - O Jesus, grant me the grace to understand Your new commandment, the commandment of fraternal charity.

MEDITATION

1. The commandment " Thou shalt love thy neighbor as thyself" (*Mt* 22,39), requires strong, solid virtue, but it does not yet reach the greatest perfection of love. The highest ideal was proposed to us by Jesus shortly before His death, in those last moments in which He recommended to His dear ones what He had most at heart : " A new commandment I give unto you... as I have loved you, that you also love one another.... This is My commandment, that you love one another, as I have loved you " (*Jn* 13,34 – 15,12). In these words, Jesus raised the precept of charity to a truly new perfection : that of loving others, not only as we love ourself, but as He loves us and as He loves them. This perfection was so dear to Him that He called it *His* commandment, the commandment which He most loved and the observance of which was to be the unfailing mark of His closest friends : " By this shall all men know that you are My disciples " (*ibid.* 13,35). With a master stroke, Jesus made us pass from one standard of charity to the other—from the high, certainly, but still too human one, based on our love of self to the divine standard based on God's infinite love for us. It is no longer a question of fixing our eyes on the love we have for ourself, in order to nourish a similar love for our brethren, but one of fixing our gaze infinitely higher, on the heart of Christ, the heart of God, to penetrate the secret of His infinite love for men that we might emulate it. Our fraternal charity will not

be perfect until it becomes the reflection, or better still, the continuation of the love of Jesus for each of His creatures. We must try to love each one of our companions—even the least congenial, even those who do not love us—as Jesus loves him. And Jesus loves him so much that He has given His life for him; so much, that every day He renews this immolation for him on the altar, and for him remains truly present in the Eucharist, ever ready to nourish him with His immaculate Flesh. What excuse can we find for our lack of charity toward our neighbor when we compare it with the charity of Jesus?

2. Considering the " new commandment, " St. Thérèse of the Child Jesus said, " Oh! how dearly do I cherish it, since it proves to me that it is Thy will, O Lord, *to love in me* all those Thou dost bid me love " (*St,* 10). The Saint understood that we would not reach the perfection of fraternal charity if we did not try to love our neighbor as Jesus loves him; but sensing how difficult this might be for us, she rejoiced, thinking that if Jesus gave us this commandment, it is because He wishes to lead us to such heights. And, in fact, this is so, provided we leave Him free to work in us, provided we offer Him all the energy of our heart, pure and entire, that He may use it to surround our brethren with the same delicate attentions He once gave the people of Palestine. He did it personally then; today He wishes to do it by means of us. In this way our love for our neighbor will truly become a renewal of the love of Jesus; we shall communicate to each person with whom we come in contact something of the infinite tenderness of the heart of Christ. But to reach this, we must cleanse our heart from every trace of egoism, every feeling of personal like or dislike. We must also try to fathom more and more the depths of the mystery of the love of Jesus for us. Jesus loves us just as we are, in spite of our faults, our dull minds and our stubborn wills; He loves us in spite of our sins. Furthermore, He became incarnate for us, sinners as we are, and died on the Cross for us. Our lack of natural gifts, our faults, even our sins, never make Him reject us; He is always seeking us, always surrounding us with His grace, always entreating, inviting us to become saints. Even the souls of the greatest sinners are dear to Him; He is continually pursuing them with His love. He surrounded the traitor, Judas, with the tenderness

of His love until the very end.   He called him by the sweet
name of friend and received his kiss.   Jesus loves us, not
because we are perfect, but because we are the children of
His heavenly Father; not because we are good, but because
in us, His creatures, the lambs of His flock, He sees the image
of His Father.   Then, how can we be satisfied to love only
those who are good, whose company is agreeable and whose
friendship gives us pleasure?   If Jesus treated us as we treat
others, we would have very little hope of enjoying His
understanding, His mercy, and His friendship.

COLLOQUY

   " In the Old Law, when You told Your people to love
their neighbor as themselves, You had not yet come down
upon earth, and knowing full well man's strong love of self,
You could not ask anything greater.   But when You gave
Your Apostles a new commandment—*Your commandment*—
You not only required us to love our neighbor as ourselves,
but would have us love even as You do, and as You will do
until the end of time.
   " O my Jesus!   You never ask what is impossible :
You know better than I how frail and imperfect I am;
You know that I shall never love my sisters as You have
loved them, unless You love them Yourself within me, my
Jesus.   It is because You desire to grant me this grace, that
You have given a new commandment, and dearly do I
cherish it, since it proves to me that it is Your will *to love in me*
all those that You bid me love!
   " When I show charity toward others I know that it is
You who are acting within me, and the more closely I am
united to You, the more dearly I love my sisters "
(T.C.J. *St*, 10).
   " O Christ, Your words form a new canticle : ' A new
commandment I give unto you! '   And what else does this
Your commandment contain but love and charity; You
wish us to love others as You, who are Love, love them!
You say to us, ' Love them as I have loved you, ' not ' as
I love Myself, ' for whereas You exercised justice upon
Yourself, You have loved us in an act of mercy, meekness,
and infinite compassion; and You wish us to love others
in the same way " (St. Mary Magdalen dei Pazzi).

263

JUDGE NOT

PRESENCE OF GOD - O Lord, keep me from judging and criticizing my neighbor; give me kind, loving thoughts about everyone.

MEDITATION

1. " Judge not, that you may not be judged " (*Mt* 7,1). Charity to our neighbor begins with our thoughts, as many of our failings in charity are basically caused by our judgments. We do not think highly enough of others, we do not sufficiently consider their manifest good qualities, we are not benevolent in interpreting their way of acting. Why? Because in judging others, we almost always base our opinion on their faults, especially on those which wound our feelings or which conflict with our own way of thinking and acting, while we give little or no consideration to their good points.

It is a serious mistake to judge persons or things from a negative point of view and it is not even reasonable, because the existence of a negative side proves the presence of a positive quality, of something good, just as a tear in a garment has no existence apart from the garment. When we stop to criticize the negative aspect of a person or of a group, we are doing destructive work in regard to our own personal virtue and the good of our neighbor. To be constructive, we must overlook the faults and recognize the value of the good qualities that are never wanting in anyone.

Moreover, do we not also have many faults, perhaps more serious ones than those of our neighbor? " And why seest thou the mote that is in thy brother's eye, and seest not the beam that is in thy own eye "? (*ibid.* 7,3). Let us seriously study these words of Jesus, for very often, in spite of our desire to become saints, some remnant of that detestable spirit of criticism remains hidden in our heart. In considering our faults and those of others, we still retain something of this twofold measure which makes us judge the faults of others differently from the way in which we judge our own. What great progress we should make in fraternal charity, in attaining our own perfection, if instead of criticizing

the faults seen in others, we would examine ourselves to see
if there is not something similar—or perhaps worse—in us,
and would apply ourselves to our own amendment!
St. Teresa of Jesus said to her nuns, " Often commend
to God any sister who is at fault and strive for your own
part to practice the virtue which is the opposite of her fault
with great perfection " (*Way*, 7). This is one of the best
ways of helping others to correct themselves.

2. Judgment belongs to God; it is reserved to Him alone,
for He alone can see into our hearts, can know what motives
and intentions make us act as we do. " Man sees the face,
but God sees the heart " (1 *Sm* 16,7). Therefore, anyone who
judges another—unless he is obliged to do so by his office,
as superiors are—usurps, in a sense, God's rights and puts
himself in the place of God. To presume to judge one's
brethren always implies a proud attitude toward God and
toward the neighbor. Besides, one who is quick to judge
others lays himself open to committing great errors, because
he does not know the intentions of others and has not the
sufficient prerequisites for formulating a correct judgment.

In the face of an act which is blameworthy in itself,
we are evidently not obliged to consider it good; nevertheless,
we must excuse the intention of the one who committed it
and not simply attribute it to a perverse will. " If our
neighbor's acts had one hundred facets, we should see only
the best one; and then, if the act is blameworthy, we should
at least excuse the intention " (T.M. *Sp*).

Every day I too commit many faults; I too fall into
many defects, but this does not signify that all these stem
from bad will. My faults are often committed inadvertently,
through frailty; and because I detest these failings of mine,
the Lord continues to love me and wants me to retain complete
confidence in His love. He regards others the same as He
does me; therefore, I have no right to doubt my neighbor's
good will simply because I see him commit some faults,
nor have I the right to diminish, for this reason, my love
and esteem for him. Perhaps that person who seems so
reprehensible has already abhorred his faults and wept over
them interiorly far more than I have over mine; God has
already forgiven him and continues to love him. Should
I be more severe than God? On this point it will be well
to remember that God will treat me with the same severity

that I show to others, for Jesus has said, " For with what judgment you judge, you shall be judged, and with what measure you mete, it shall be measured to you again " (*Mt* 7,2).

COLLOQUY

" O Jesus, You are my Judge! I shall try always to think leniently of others, that You may judge me leniently—or not at all, since You say : ' Judge not, that you may not be judged. ' This is why, when I chance to see a sister doing something seemingly imperfect, I do all I can to find excuses and to credit her with the good intentions she no doubt possesses.

" O Jesus, You make me understand that the chief plenary indulgence, which is within reach of everyone, and can be gained without the ordinary conditions, is that of charity, which ' covereth a multitude of sins ' " (cf. T.C.J. *St*, 10 – 11 – *C*).

" Teach me, O Lord, not to judge my neighbor for any fault I may see him commit, and if I should see him commit a sin, give me the grace to excuse his intention which is hidden and cannot be seen. But even if I should see that his intention was really bad, give me the grace to excuse my neighbor because of temptation, from which no mortal is free " (St. Mary Magdalen dei Pazzi).

" O Lord, help me not to look at anything but at the virtues and good qualities which I find in others and to keep my own grievous sins before my eyes so that I may be blind to their defects. This course of action, though I may not become perfect in it all at once, will help me to acquire one great virtue—to consider all others better than myself. To accomplish this, I must have Your help; when it fails, my own efforts are useless. I beg You to give me this virtue " (T.J. *Life*, 13).

264

BE YE MERCIFUL

PRESENCE OF GOD - O Lord, may the consideration of Your infinite mercy dilate my heart, that I may learn how to treat others mercifully.

MEDITATION

1. Jesus revealed to us the mystery of His heavenly Father's merciful love not only for our own consolation and personal benefit, not only to give us absolute confidence in God, but also to teach us to be merciful to our neighbor. " Be ye therefore merciful, as your Father also is merciful " (*Lk* 6,36). Good attracts good, goodness engenders goodness, kindness inspires kindness; therefore, the more a soul penetrates the mystery of infinite mercy, the more it will be incited to emulate it. When we feel irritated with someone and little disposed to indulgence and pardon, we ought to plunge with all our strength into the consideration of the infinite mercy of God, in order to stifle all harshness, resentment, and anger in ourselves. If we had but the slightest experience of our own wretchedness, it would not be difficult for us to realize that there is no moment of our lives in which we do not need the mercy of God. Our merciful Father is so forbearing that He never casts us off despite all our falls, never reproaches us about the many times He has forgiven us, never refuses us His paternal embrace of love and peace. Nothing softens a soul more, making it full of good will toward others, than this consideration. Oh! if others could see in our attitude toward them a reflection of God's infinite mercy!

Peter had not yet completely understood the deep mystery of merciful love when he asked Jesus if it were enough to pardon his neighbor seven times. Jesus' reply must have sounded like an exaggeration to him : " I say not to thee, till seven times, but till seventy times seven times " (*Mt* 18,22). Later, Peter's heart was completely changed when he experienced the goodness of Jesus, who, without a single word of reproach, forgave him his threefold denial so generously. This man, who was so impetuous, so quickly

moved to anger, and so ready to threaten, was later to
give to the primitive Church this gentle exhortation to
goodness and pardon : " Be ye all of one mind, having
compassion one on another, being lovers of the brotherhood,
merciful...not rendering evil for evil, nor railing for railing,
but contrariwise, blessing : for unto this are you called "
(1 *Pt* 3,8.9). How can we fail to hear in these words an
echo of the words of Jesus : " Love your enemies, do good
to them that hate you " (*Mt* 5,44)?

2. We notice in the Gospel how the words of Jesus,
generally so mild and loving, even when addressed to the
greatest sinners—like Mary Magdalen, the woman taken
in adultery, and even Judas—become exceptionally severe
and almost harsh, when He speaks of failures in fraternal
charity. God loves us infinitely, and He has but one desire :
to pour out upon our souls the torrents of His boundless
mercy; yet His love and mercy seem to vanish and are
replaced by severity in the measure that He finds us harsh
and exacting toward our neighbor. We need God's mercy so
much; we have such need of His mild judgment, His pity,
forgiveness, and mercy. Why, then, do we not do as much
for others? Perhaps because they have offended us, have made
us suffer? And have we never offended God? Have we not,
by our sins, contributed to the most bitter Passion of Jesus?
Too often we are like the cruel servant in the parable who,
having received pardon from his master for a big debt,
was not willing to pardon a trifling debt which one of his
companions owed to him, but cast him into prison until
he could pay the last cent. How can we expect mercy and
forgiveness from God if we are so exacting with our neighbor?
Let us not forget the words we repeat every day in the
Our Father : " Forgive us our trespasses, as we forgive those
who trespass against us. " Let us act in such a way that these
words will not be our own condemnation, for Jesus has said,
" For if you will forgive men their offenses, your heavenly
Father will forgive you also your offenses. But if you will not
forgive men, neither will your Father forgive you your
offenses " (*ibid.*, 14.15). It depends, therefore, on ourselves,
whether we shall one day be judged with more or less mercy.

" In the evening of life, we shall be judged on love "
(J.C. *SM I*, 57), that is, we shall be judged on our love for
God and for our neighbor.

COLLOQUY

" O Jesus, how much You esteem this mutual love of ours for one another! You could have taught us to say, ' Forgive us, Lord, because we are doing a great deal of penance, we pray often, we fast, or because we have left all things for Your sake and we love You greatly, ' or ' Forgive us because we would lose our life for Your sake ' or other words of the same kind; but You said only, ' *Forgive us, as we forgive!* '

" This is a truth which we should consider carefully. You, O Lord, have willed to bind a grace so great—in such a serious and important matter as pardoning our sins which have merited eternal fire—to such a simple condition as our forgiveness of others. But what about one as poor as I, who have had so few occasions for forgiving others and so many for being forgiven? O Lord, take my desire to do so, for I believe I would forgive any wrong if You would forgive me. But at this moment I see that I am so guilty in Your sight that I feel that those who injure me are treating me too well.

" As I have so few even of these trifling things to offer You, O Lord, Your pardoning of me must be a free gift : here is abundant scope for Your mercy!

" But are there, perhaps many others who are like myself and have not yet understood this truth? If there are any such, I beg them in Your Name, O Lord, to remember this truth often and to pay no heed to little things about which they think they are being slighted. Sometimes we get to the point of thinking that we have done something wonderful because we have forgiven a person for some trifling thing. Then we ask You, O Lord, to forgive us as people who have done something important, just because we have forgiven someone. Ah, Lord! grant us to understand how little we understand ourselves and how empty our hands are! Deign to pardon us, but only by Your mercy! " (T.J. *Way*, 36).

265

THE MANTLE OF CHARITY

PRESENCE OF GOD - O Lord, teach me to cover the defects and faults of others with the mantle of charity.

MEDITATION

1. " Do not speak against one another, my brethren. He that speaks against a brother...speaks against the law " (*Jas* 4,11), that is, he contradicts the evangelical law of fraternal charity. To speak evil of our neighbor does not necessarily mean that we spread unjust suspicions about him or accuse him of faults and wrong deeds which he has not committed. It is sufficient to mention needlessly the faults of others, even though they be real and known to all. To do this is to act contrary to charity, because it fixes our own attention, and that of others, on the imperfections of the neighbor, rather than on his good qualities. As a result, we lessen in the mind of the listener the esteem due to our neighbor. Quite different is the behavior of charity, which as Holy Scripture says, " covereth all sins " (*Prv* 10,12), and tries to hide the failings of others rather than draw attention to them. How instinctively we hide our own faults and blunders, not wishing them to be a subject of conversation. We should employ the same skill in concealing the faults of others. We are so sensitive about things said against us; how can we think that it is a wholly indifferent thing to speak with so much liberty about our neighbor's faults, under the pretext that what we say is true and already known? Are not our faults equally true, perhaps, and evident to all who approach us?

Fraternal charity means loving our neighbor for God's sake, because he belongs to God and is the work of His hands. As a mother does not care to have her children's faults spoken of, nor an artist like to have his works criticized, neither is God pleased to have us talk about the faults of His creatures. Therefore, we must not only strictly refrain from speaking about the faults of others, but we must also avoid paying attention to those who do talk about them.

St. John of the Cross says, " Never listen to the weaknesses of others, and, if anyone complains to thee of another, thou mayest tell him humbly to say naught of it to thee " (*SM II*, 61, 7).

2. St. Teresa of Jesus wrote to her daughters : " To be glad when your sisters' virtues are praised is a great thing, and when we see a fault in someone, we should be as sorry about it as if it were our own and try to conceal it from others " (*Int C V*, 3). This is the true attitude of a delicate fraternal charity. Besides, it is what we do spontaneously for our friends. Why should we not try to do it for everyone, since charity is universal. But, very often the devil, the enemy of charity, stirs up conflicts within us and tries to make us do the opposite. Even the saints have had temptations of this kind; but whereas we succumb to them so frequently, they reacted courageously and made of them an opportunity to practice charity more zealously. This was the strategy which St. Thérèse of the Child Jesus used : " Should the devil bring before me the defects of a sister, I hasten to look for her virtues and good motives. I call to mind that though I may have seen her fall once, she may have gained many victories over herself which in her humility she conceals, and also that what appears to be a fault may very well, owing to the good intention that prompted it, be an act of virtue " (*St*, 10).

If we feel a natural aversion toward any person, or if a certain person has done us some wrong, we see that person's defects far more easily than we see his virtues; the former are magnified in our eyes and the latter minimized. It will also be easy for us to put a wrong interpretation on whatever he says or does. This is the time to be especially watchful, to fight against the malevolent thoughts that spontaneously come into our mind, and not to permit ourselves to speak of them to others. We should oppose these thoughts, too, by positive acts of charity : praying particularly for this person, seizing every possible opportunity to render him some service, and acting in an especially kind and friendly manner toward him. The mantle of charity must be wide enough to cover, not only the faults of our friends, but even those of our enemies, and those who annoy us. Charity makes no distinction of persons, but has equal good will for all, because it sees and loves only God in all.

COLLOQUY

"If I wish to know whether I possess true charity, I must examine myself and see if when I speak about any of my neighbors, I am more ready to mention his virtues than his faults. Even if I do not speak ill of him, it is very wrong, nevertheless, to listen to detraction, because by remaining silent, I show my approval of what I hear. Therefore, O my God, whenever anyone comes to tell me some fault of another, I will not listen, but will tell him to pray for that person, and for me—that I may correct my own faults. Then it will be easier to speak about it to the guilty person than to talk about it to others; otherwise, instead of remedying it, I would be committing many more faults, and graver ones than those of the person spoken about.

"If my eye were pure, O Lord, I would very easily see how I ought to practice love toward my neighbor. If I knew that both of us had the same fault, I should go to him and ask his advice as to how I could correct it. In order to advise me correctly, he would think about this fault and would soon see that he too was guilty of it, and in this way we should both learn how to correct it. One whose eye is pure knows how to deal lovingly with his neighbor.

"O Lord, if I love my sister, then even when I am singing Your praises, I should interrupt them to help her when she needs help. If this is my duty as to her physical welfare, how much more is it my duty when it is a question of her spiritual needs? If I am obliged to take care of her for a night or two when she is ill, is it not more important for me, if I have real charity, to forget my weariness, and keep vigil a night or two, weeping for my sister's faults, even though they are slight? I must also pray that she will have all the virtues and strive to help her acquire them. Besides virtue and health of soul, I must also pray that she will gain much merit, and by Your grace, O Lord, become completely transformed in You" (St. Mary Magdalen dei Pazzi).

266

BAPTISMAL GRACE

ELEVENTH SUNDAY AFTER PENTECOST

PRESENCE OF GOD - Grant, O Lord, that the grace of holy Baptism may reach its full development in me.

MEDITATION

1. The healing of the deaf-mute, as narrated in today's Gospel (*Mk* 7,31-37), is a figure of baptismal grace. We, too, were once taken before Jesus in a condition similar to that of the poor man in Galilee. We were deaf and dumb in the life of the spirit, and Jesus, in the person of the priest, welcomed us lovingly at the baptismal font. The priest made the same gesture over us and said the same word as did the divine Master in the Gospel : " *Ephpheta,* " " Be thou opened! " From that moment the hearing of our soul was opened to faith and our tongue was loosed to give praise to God. We were enabled to listen to the voice of faith—to the exterior voice of the teaching Church and to the interior voice of the Holy Spirit, urging us to do good; from that moment, we could open our lips in prayer : in praise, adoration, and petition. But later the noise of the world deafened and distracted us; likewise, the tumult of our passions deadened our capacity to listen to the voice of God. Then, too, idle conversations about worldly things and great anxiety over various events in our life have left us unable to pray sincerely and earnestly. But Jesus wishes to renew the grace of our Baptism today and to repeat the all-powerful word " *Ephpheta.* " How greatly we need Him to reopen our ears to His voice and to make us more attentive and sensitive to His call! " In the morning He wakeneth my ear that I may hear Him as a master; I do not resist, I have not gone back, " says Isaias (50,4.5). This is the grace we must ask of Our Lord today, that we may not only hear His voice, but may follow it, without resistance. The more faithfully we follow it, the more sensitive we shall become to its slightest whisper. At the same time let us ask

for the grace of always being ready to give praise to the Lord, to call upon His mercy, to ask His pardon humbly, accusing ourselves of our faults sincerely and with sorrow.

2. Those who were present when Jesus performed this miracle wondered at it, saying, " He hath done all things well; He hath made both the deaf to hear and the dumb to speak. " Certainly, Jesus has done all things well; He has arranged everything in the best way possible for our sanctification. He has prepared for us all the graces we need, and not only in sufficient measure, but even superabundantly. Unfortunately, however, we do not always cooperate with His grace; many times pride, egoism, and all our other uncontrolled passions turn to evil what God has planned for our good. If we had accepted lovingly and with resignation that difficulty, that trial, or disappointment which God had permitted for the sole purpose of providing us with an opportunity to practice virtue, we should have made great progress; but by giving way to impatience, by protesting and complaining, we rather added to our failures and infidelities. We should cooperate with grace more readily and strive to maintain our soul in an attitude of open docility to all the invitations to virtue which God is continually sending us by means of the different circumstances of life.

Today's Mass, and especially the Epistle (1 *Cor* 15,1-10), offers us a splendid model of cooperation with grace. It is St. Paul, the Apostle, who in his humility calls himself " the least of the Apostles, " who says most sincerely : " By the grace of God, I am what I am, and His grace in me hath not been void. " St. Paul realizes that, if he became an Apostle, instead of the persecutor which he had been, it was not because of his own merits, but solely by the grace of God; he attributes nothing to himself, but all to God. At the same time, he is conscious of his personal correspondence, the correspondence which is always the fruit of grace, but which also includes, as an indispensible element, our free adherence to it. Consequently, we must have an attitude of profound humility as the basis of our correspondence to grace; that is, we must clearly realize that whatever good is in us is due only to God. This attitude of humility must be accompanied by a voluntary, continual assent of our will to God's invitations. We cannot give this assent without the help of grace, and yet it depends on us; it is entirely in our hands. Therefore, like

St. Paul, we can attribute nothing to our own merits, but should say with him, " By the grace of God, I am what I am. " Our willing adhesion to grace, however, will give us the right to add, " and His grace in me hath not been void. " But only steady, faithful, generous adhesion will give us that right.

COLLOQUY

" Henceforth, O Lord, it is You alone whom I love, follow, seek, and serve; You alone have the right to command, and to You alone do I wish to be subject. Command, I beg You, and demand of me anything You wish; heal and open my ears, that I may hear Your commands; cure and open my eyes, that I may see the signs of Your will; take away my dullness that I may be able to contemplate You, and thus, I hope, accomplish faithfully whatever You ask of me.

" O God and most merciful Father, receive this Your fugitive child. All that I have had in the past has been sufficient for me; I have had enough of being the plaything of vain, deceitful things. Now I am running away from this tyranny; receive me as Your servant, as they received me when I ran away from You to them. I know I need to return to Your house; behold me knocking at the door; open to me; show me how to reach You. I have nothing but my will : I know only one thing—that I must despise the ephemeral and trivial and seek the immutable and eternal.

" My desire is to return to You, and I ask You for the means to obtain my desire. If You abandon us, we perish, but You do not abandon us; for You are the Sovereign Good, and no one has ever truly sought You and not found You. . . . O Lord, You know that I have the will but not the power, and I cannot even will what is good without You, nor can I do what I will to do if Your power does not help me; and what I can do, I often do not wish to do, unless You make Your will triumph on earth as in heaven. I implore but one thing of Your sovereign mercy : that You convert me entirely to You and keep me from resisting the grace which leads me to You " (St. Augustine).

267

BEAR YE ONE ANOTHER'S BURDENS

PRESENCE OF GOD - Give me, O Lord, prompt, attentive charity for the needs of others, a charity which, for the love of You, knows how to make itself all things to all men.

MEDITATION

1. Everyone has some burden, more or less heavy, to bear : physical or moral weakness, the press of duties and responsibilities, fatigue or other troubles which weigh on his shoulders. Everyone feels the need of a friendly hand to help him carry this weight. This hand should be held out to him in fraternal charity, which for the love of God, knows how to be all things to all men. " Bear ye one another's burdens, and so you shall fulfill the law of Christ " St. Paul exhorts us (*Gal* 6,2). A Christian knows that he is not isolated, but is a member of a unique body, the Mystical Body of Christ. " So we being many, are one body in Christ, and every one members one of another " (*Rom* 12,5). This knowledge of his solidarity with the brethren makes a Christian live, not enclosed in the tiny circle of his own interests, but with his heart open to the needs and interests of others. The mystery of our incorporation in Christ is more than an individual fact; by its very nature, it is a social fact. Incorporation in Christ by grace and charity connotes reciprocal incorporation among brethren, like the branches of a vine, which, sprung from the same stock, are so closely united one to another that they live, grow and develop together. Love for Christ is the vital expression of our union with Him; the closer this union becomes, the more our love increases; so too, fraternal charity is the vital expression of our reciprocal union with the brethren in Christ, to such a point that if this charity were not living and operative, we could have to say that our union in Christ and with Christ was very weak or even absolutely null.

If charity and grace unite us to Christ in such intimate and vital relations, it is evident that we must live this union, first with Him who is our Head, and then with our brethren, who like us have also been engrafted into Christ. Hence there will be a supernatural affection which will bind us to one another and make us one heart and one soul, ready to labor and suffer for one another, to help and sustain one another. " Rejoice with them that rejoice; weep with them that weep " (*Rom* 12,15). Thus the Apostle teaches us to share the joys and sorrows, the cares and anxieties of others as if they were our own. They are, in fact, our own, because they are the joys, sorrows, cares, and anxieties of that one Mystical Body of Christ to which we belong and which, therefore, is *ours*.

2. Bearing one another's burdens also means enduring the faults of others calmly and kindly. Faults are the inevitable consequence of human limitations. The *Imitation of Christ* tells us, " what a man cannot amend in himself or others, he must bear with patience till God ordains otherwise " (I, 16,1). In the last months of her life, St. Thérèse of the Child Jesus wrote, " Now I know that true charity consists in bearing all my neighbor's defects, in not being surprised at mistakes, but in being edified at the smallest virtues " (*St*, 10).

Not without reason does St. Paul say, " charity beareth all things, believeth all things, hopeth all things, endureth all things " (1 *Cor* 13,7). Charity always believes in the good will of others, even though it may be accompanied by faults; it always hopes in the good which it knows how to discover in every creature, although it may be eclipsed by many deficiencies. What is more important, charity supports everything, never finding any burden too heavy. To support, according to the etymology of the word, means " to place oneself under a weight to carry it. " Charity feels that it must stoop with love to take up the burdens of others, particularly those burdens which all avoid because they are troublesome. St. Thérèse of the Child Jesus notes that certain people are left alone because of their natural imperfections, such as sensitiveness, or lack of judgment or education. " Defects of this kind are, I know, incurable.... From all this I conclude that I ought to seek the companionship of those sisters for whom I feel a natural aversion, and try to be their good Samaritan " (*St*, 11). Behold the charity which, instead of fleeing, seeks out those who are suffering through natural and moral imperfections, and busies itself with them so lovingly that they never guess how painful the effort is, nor how troublesome their defects are to others. Charity bears all things, endures all things with a smiling, serene face, never showing itself annoyed or crushed by the burden it bears.

COLLOQUY

" O Lord, teach me to love my neighbor with all my heart, not merely as myself, but more than myself, thus obeying Your commandment : ' Love one another, as I have loved you. '

" Just as You, O Lord, have always preferred us to Yourself, and do so still, making Yourself our Food in the Blessed Sacrament, so You wish us to have such great love for one another that we always prefer our neighbor to ourselves; and as You have done all that You could for us, so You want us to do all we can for one another. Grant, then, O Lord, that, without giving You any offense, my love for my neighbor may be so firm, cordial, and strong, that I will never refuse to do or endure anything for his sake. Teach me to love him with my deeds, obtaining for him all the good I can, both for his soul and for his body, to pray for him, and to serve him lovingly whenever I have the opportunity. If my love were to consist only in pleasant words, it would amount to very little, and I would not be really loving my neighbor as You have loved us. To attain the perfection of love, it is not enough for me to work for my neighbor; I must also do what he wants in the way that pleases him, without showing any displeasure. By doing this, I shall acquire greater merit, because I shall be practicing the highest degree of self-renunciation " (St. Francis de Sales).

268

CHARITY IS NOT SELFISH

PRESENCE OF GOD - O God, who hast loved me from all eternity and always lovest me in a disinterested way, teach me to love without calculation or measure.

MEDITATION

1. Charity "seeketh not her own" (1 *Cor* 13,5). Attention to the needs and sorrows of others, with a constant readiness to give one's help, is no justification for expecting a like return. "Do good, and lend, hoping for nothing thereby; and your reward shall be great, and you shall be the sons of the Highest; for He is kind to the unthankful and to the evil" (*Lk* 6,35). Charity does not give in order to receive; it gives without counting the cost and without measure, for it knows that the honor of serving and loving God in His creatures is ample reward. Charity loves, serves, gives, and spends itself lavishly, solely for the sake of loving and serving God in others, for the joy of imitating His infinite generosity, for the joy of feeling itself the child of the heavenly Father who bestows His favors upon all without distinction. What greater reward can there be than to be able to call ourselves, and to be in all truth, children of God! To enjoy this reward, charity seeks to fly from every earthly recompense and hides the good it does. "Let not thy left hand know what thy right hand doth" (*Mt* 6,3). It seeks by preference to benefit those from whom it can expect nothing in return : "When thou makest a dinner or a supper, call not thy friends, nor thy brethren...lest perhaps they also invite thee again and a recompense be made to thee. But when thou makest a feast, call the poor, the maimed, the lame, and the blind; and thou shalt be blessed, because they have not wherewith to make thee recompense" (*Lk* 14, 12-14). How the logic of the Gospel differs from the logic of human calculations!

Whenever a strong desire to give ourselves to God arises in our heart, it is accompanied by a similar longing to give ourselves to others solely for love of God. Then we no longer distinguish between serving God and serving others : we see God in everyone, we give ourselves to them in order to give ourselves to God, and we give ourselves to all as we would give ourselves to God. This was the attitude in the heart of St. Paul when he exclaimed : " But I most gladly will spend and be spent myself for your souls, although loving you more, I be loved less " (2 *Cor* 12,15).

2. " Charity is patient, is kind...is not provoked to anger " (1 *Cor* 13,4.5). Charity is never wearied, is never impatient with the ungrateful, is not irritated when repulsed, but perseveres in loving and doing good. Charity does not look for gratitude, is not ungracious. It is not offended when it meets with a lack of refinement or consideration; but, in spite of the coldness and hostility which it may encounter, it continues its one work : to give itself, and to give itself always, for the love of God. At the same time, however, charity is not insensible to ingratitude and offenses; on the contrary, the more a heart is refined in love, the more sensitive it is to everything which is opposed to love.

But it does not make use of its sensitiveness to defend its own rights, to protest against the ingratitude of others, or to demand some degree of justice; it sacrifices all these to God for the benefit of those who have caused its suffering. This is the characteristic of charity : it does not permit itself to be " overcome by evil, " but it " overcomes evil by good " (*Rom* 12,21).

We all know, however, how difficult this is, how hard for selfish, demanding nature. Sometimes, just when one is about to perform an especially delicate act of charity for another, a strong feeling of antipathy toward that person arises from the sensitive part of the soul because of the absence of some sign or token of respect or consideration. This is manifestly a temptation which must be overcome as soon as it appears, that it may not take root. Anyone who would yield to these feelings and act accordingly, under the pretext of justice or of teaching a lesson, would soon become very exacting to the great detriment of charity. In community life especially, patient charity must be practiced, the charity which knows how to pass over wrongs, little or great, misunderstandings and offenses; one which knows how to accept calmly every pinprick, without even appearing to feel it or trying to show others that they have hurt us.

With the help of God's grace and by struggling against the resentments of self-love, we shall attain to that charity which is completely forgetful of self; then we shall be good to those around us, " not justices of the peace, but angels of peace " (T.C.J. *C*).

COLLOQUY

" O eternal God, the soul who truly loves You spends itself for its neighbor and cannot do otherwise, for its love for You and its love of neighbor are one and the same thing; the more the soul loves You, the more it loves its neighbor, because love of neighbor has its source in You.

" You have given us this means of proving and practicing virtue, O Most High God, so that, since we cannot benefit You, we can benefit others. Therefore, a soul in love with You, most amiable Lord, never ceases to spend itself in doing good to others, striving to discover their needs and hastening to help them.

" O God, eternal Trinity, You ask us to love You with the same love with which You love us. This we cannot do, for You loved us when we were as yet Your enemies; and however great our love for You, we would always owe You this love, as due to You; it is therefore, not gratuitous, because You loved us first. As it is impossible for us to give You the love You desire, You have given us our neighbor, that we may do for him what we cannot do for You, that is, love him without having been loved by him—gratuitously—without expecting any benefit from it.

" Teach me, O Lord, to love my neighbor even when not loved by him, to love him with no concern for my own benefit, but solely because You love me, solely to repay Your gratuitous love. Then I shall fulfill the commandment of the law : to love You above all things, and my neighbor as myself " (cf. St. Catherine of Siena).

269

CHARITY ADAPTS ITSELF TO EVERYONE

PRESENCE OF GOD - O God, who adapted Yourself to my misery to the point of becoming man, teach me to adapt myself to others.

MEDITATION

1. Charity has no rigid requirements; it does not expect, and even less pretend, that others should adapt themselves to it, but it is always ready to accommodate itself to the neighbor. God adapted Himself to us when He became man; yet, we do not know how to come down from the little pedestal of our personality to adapt ourselves to the mentalities, preferences, and needs of our brethren. We excuse ourselves by saying, " They are wrong; they are rude and ungrateful, they do not understand my needs, my sensibilities.... " How we deceive ourselves! How petty we are in our demands on others! Let us look at the Son of God, the eternal Word, who did not disdain to put Himself on our level, to the extent of taking on our mortal flesh and living a human life in the midst of us. During His earthly life, He did not choose for His companions intellectual men of refined education; He chose ignorant fishermen of rude mentality, men of simple tastes who knew very little about the refinements of life. He lived with them and adopted their ways quite naturally, without any singularity aside from His unlimited charity.

Certainly, we cannot conform to the desires of our neighbor when there is question, however slight, of something in opposition to the honor of God and the observance of His law. To do so in such cases would be culpable weakness. But there are many other occasions when it is simply a matter of not insisting upon our personal feelings, our point of view, our own tastes, but of effacing ourselves, and considering the mentality and tastes of others. Then condescension is solid virtue, and far from being weakness, it is a beautiful proof of moral strength, of that strength which knows how to overcome self and sacrifice its ego for the love of God. Lasting charity and perfect harmony are not possible without this flexibility which makes us capable of adapting ourselves to others. When we have firmly resolved to overlook all differences of temperament, mentality, education and tastes, when we are determined to give up our own ideas to accommodate ourselves to the ideas and desires of others, then only can it be said that the goal of fraternal charity has been attained.

2. We find in the Gospel most beautiful examples of this condescension. " And if a man will contend with thee in judgment, and take away thy coat, let go thy cloak also unto him. And whosoever will force thee one mile, go with him other two. Give to him that asketh of thee, and from him that would borrow of thee turn not away " (*Mt* 5,40-42). The divine Master strongly exhorts us to patience, meekness, and the renouncement of our rights, so as to put ourselves humbly at the service of our neighbor, sacrificing ourselves generously for him, for his interests and his joy. Instead of quarreling and arguing with a troublesome person, Jesus teaches us to yield always, even if that person's demands are unreasonable. St. Thérèse of the Child Jesus comments on this passage in the Gospel : " It seems to me that to give up one's cloak is to renounce every right, and look upon oneself as the slave of all.... Hence, it is not enough for me to give to the one who asks, I ought to anticipate the wish; I should show myself honored by the request for service, and if anything set apart for my use be taken away, I should appear glad to be rid of it " (*St*, 10). However, the Saint has no illusions : she knows very well that our being asked in a tactless way or with a pretentious, commanding tone to render some service, to do a favor, or to give some object, will bring forth resentment and protests from our self-love, " There is an inward rebellion unless we are perfect in charity. We find no end of reasons for refusing " *(ibid.)*. But he who wishes to have perfect charity does not yield to these interior rebellions; doing violence to himself, he graciously places himself at the disposal of his neighbor.

If we frequently refuse to do what is asked of us, it is a sign that our charity is still very weak. We should not easily take refuge in excuses : " I have no time...this is an unreasonable request...she ought to learn to do things for herself, " and the like. Sometimes it is necessary to refuse to render a service because we really cannot do it or because it would prevent us from fulfilling our duties. Even in these circumstances, however, charity should make us avoid all discourteous ways which would mortify and humiliate others. " When charity has taken root in the soul, it shows itself outwardly, and there is always a way of refusing so graciously what one cannot give, that the refusal affords as much pleasure as the gift itself " (ibid.).

COLLOQUY

" O my God, it is impossible for me not to love Your creatures, since You have commanded me to do so. You are Love, and love made You create man, so that he, too, might share Your love. We were all created out of love, by love, and with love, so that we might enjoy You, O God, who are Love. How then can I help loving this neighbor of mine?

" Tell me, I beseech You, O Christ, in what way should I love my neighbor. You give me the lofty ideal of loving him as You Yourself have loved him. For human creatures You left, at least in appearance, Your Father's bosom; You left, or rather, You hid, Your power, wisdom, and infinite purity to live in contact with the impurity of creatures. And I also, for my neighbor's sake, must leave myself and my love for creatures, and be ready to shed my blood for their salvation if necessary.

" O charity! How beautiful and pleasing to God you are! Like the pelican, you give your own blood, not only for your children, but even for your enemies. Yet, in truth, he who possesses you considers no one his enemy but esteems them all as his dearest friends and would give his very life for the soul of his neighbor if he sees it necessary.

" O love of neighbor so little known! O God, who can read our hearts, You know whether they are filled with love or hate when we pretend to love our neighbor while we offend him. Oh! how different Your judgments are from ours! You teach me that, for love of my neighbor, I ought to know how to sacrifice my comfort, listen to the little and the poor in their bodily and spiritual needs, and answer them peacefully and with meekness " (St. Mary Magdalen dei Pazzi).

270

MILDNESS

PRESENCE OF GOD - O Lord, who art mildness itself, teach me meekness of heart and mildness in my dealings with others.

MEDITATION

1. Mildness is the flower of charity, a participation in that infinite sweetness with which God guides and governs all things. There is no one who has a greater desire for our good, for our sanctification, than God; yet He never uses harshness, severity, or violence. With a sovereignly gentle power He sustains our efforts, always respecting our liberty, always waiting for our acceptance of grace with infinite patience and mildness. The Gospel describes the mildness of Jesus in these words : " He shall not contend, nor cry out, neither shall any man hear His voice in the streets. The bruised reed He shall not break : and the smoking flax He shall not extinguish " (*Mt* 12,19.20). The Pharisees murmured because they saw Him eating with publicans and sinners. He said to them : " Go then and learn what this meaneth : I will have mercy and not sacrifice. For I am not come to call the just, but sinners " (*ibid.* 9,13). The Apostles were ready to call down fire from heaven upon the Samaritans who rejected the Master, but He rebuked them, saying, " You know not of what spirit you are. The Son of Man came not to destroy souls, but to save " (*Lk* 9,55.56). And to souls fighting against their miseries, feeling the weight and weariness of the daily struggle, He says : " Come to Me, all you that labor, and are burdened, and I will refresh you...for My yoke is sweet, and My burden light " (*Mt* 11,28.30). Our Lord's infinite charity makes His yoke sweet and His burden light, radiating as it does, sweetness and mildness everywhere.

Fraternal charity should expand in this spirit of sweetness and soothe the wounds of others rather than aggravate them. It should facilitate the accomplishment of duties, making them easier rather than more difficult. Charity uses this mildness with everyone, even with those who are stubborn, or slow in their response to kindness, and with the weak who fall repeatedly into the same faults. Given but a little good in a person, we must surround this little with the loving care that will help it develop, for one who has learned the mildness of Jesus " will not extinguish the smoking flax. "

2. Our charity is sometimes put to a hard test in our contacts with others; and the irritating behavior of some individuals can arouse feelings of anger and indignation despite our resolutions to be mild. We should not allow ourselves to become discouraged, as these spontaneous reactions are very often independent of our will. We are not, however, justified in giving way to them under the pretext that it is too hard to resist and that we are carried away in spite of ourselves. We can always subdue these impulses of passion; and the quicker, more energetic and mild our reaction is, the greater will be our success in overcoming them. St. Thérèse of the Child Jesus taught a novice : " Whenever anyone exasperates you, even to the point of making you angry, the way to regain peace of soul is to pray for that person and to ask God to reward her for giving you an opportunity to suffer. " And she suggested that the novice forestall these occasions by trying to " soften her heart in advance. "

Furthermore, if we reply angrily to another's anger, we shall only be fanning the flames, when we should be making every attempt to extinguish them by mildness and meekness. Mildness, however, is not condescension to evil, and much less, connivance with it. There are times, as the Gospel teaches, when fraternal correction is required; in such cases it becomes a real act of charity. But to make it truly so, it must never be done with the intention of humiliating, of mortifying, and still less, of offending the guilty one; nor should it ever be inspired, even indirectly, by personal reasons : to insure respect for our rights or opinions, or to revenge ourselves for some previous slight given to us. In these cases, the correction, far from being an act of charity, is completely contrary to this virtue; and instead of doing good, it will rather produce the opposite effect. Only a sincere dispassionate desire for the good of others can make fraternal correction charitable and efficacious; it should be made with so much kindness that the person concerned feels our love for him far more than the humiliation of being corrected. This is the way Jesus treated sinners; all were cured by His love and mildness.

COLLOQUY

"O Lord Jesus, when You died on the Cross Your heart was so filled with kindness toward us and You loved us so tenderly, even though we ourselves were the cause of Your death, that You had but one thought : to obtain pardon for Your executioners, even while they tortured You and cruelly insulted You. Help me, I beg You, to endure my neighbors, faults and imperfections with kindness.

To those who despise me or murmur against me, teach me to reply with humility, mildness, and a steadfast kindness of heart, never defending myself in any way. For love of You, I desire to let everyone say what he wishes, because words are not of value but love is, and he who loves more will be more loved and glorified. Help me, then, my Jesus, to love You; help me to love creatures for love of You, especially those who despise me, without letting myself be disturbed by their contempt, but applying myself to the practice of humility and mildness; then You will be my reward.

"Teach me to comport myself always with mildness and sweetness, and never to disrupt peace with anyone. All that I can do and obtain with love I will do, but what I cannot do or procure without a dispute, I will let it be. Help me to make use of the repugnances and aversions I encounter in my contacts with others to practice the virtue of mildness, and to show myself loving with all, even with those who are opposed to me, or who are a cause of aversion.

"Finally, I purpose with Your help, O most lovable God, to apply myself to acquire kindness of heart toward my neighbor by thinking of him as Your creature, destined to enjoy You some day in Paradise. Those whom You tolerate, O Lord God, it is but just that I, too, tolerate them tenderly and with great compassion for their spiritual infirmities" (St. Francis de Sales).

271

LOVE OF NEIGHBOR AND LOVE OF GOD

PRESENCE OF GOD - Make me understand, O Lord, that the surest sign of my love for You is a sincere love for my neighbor.

MEDITATION

1. A soul who lives for God sometimes needs to be reassured that its love for Him is not an illusion. What criterion will give it the greatest certitude? St. Teresa of Jesus says, " We cannot be sure if we are loving God, although we may have good reason to believe that we are, but we can know quite well if we are loving our neighbor. And be certain that, the farther advanced you find you are in this, the greater the love you will have for God " (*Int C V*, 3). This is an indisputable argument because the virtue of charity is but one; and while it is difficult to verify our love for God, it is impossible to deceive ourselves about our love for our neighbor. We have no need of any great insight to know whether we are charitable, patient, forgiving, and kind to others, and precisely from the way we behave toward them can we deduce the measure of our love for God.

Sometimes we can deceive ourselves thinking we love God very much because we experience certain spiritual joys during the time of prayer. We believe that we are ready to confront any sacrifice for the love of God because we feel ardent desires arising within us. St. Teresa of Avila, with keen psychological insight, warns souls of the pitfalls into which they may fall and puts them on their guard : " No, sisters, no; what the Lord desires is works. If you see a sick sister to whom you can give some help, never be affected by the fear that your devotion will suffer, but take pity on her : if she is in pain, you should feel pain too; if necessary, fast so that she may have your food, not so much for her sake as because you know it to be your Lord's will " (*ibid.*). This is real love, and it was exactly in this sense that St. John the Evangelist said in his first epistle, " We know that we have passed from death to life, because we love the brethren " (3,14). He did not say, *because we love God*, but *because we*

love the brethren, for fraternal charity is the most certain sign
of true love for God.

2. St. Teresa of Jesus wrote : " So dearly does His
Majesty love us that He will reward our love for our neighbor
by increasing the love which we bear to Himself, and that
in a thousand ways : this I cannot doubt " *(ibid.)*. Here
is a beautiful affirmation, and one worthy of faith, which
will incite us to practice fraternal charity enthusiastically;
it will make us sense with what good reason the Saint
said : " If you understood the importance of this virtue
to us all, you would strive after nothing but gaining it "
(ibid.).

A soul that really loves God has but one desire : to grow
in love for Him; and the infallible means of doing so is to
practice fraternal charity with great care. Such soul ardently
aspires to be united with God, and here is the royal way :
union with the brethren. We should always remember
that the virtue of charity is a certain participation not only
in the infinite charity with which God loves Himself, but
also in the immense love which He has for His creatures.
The more we love the brethren, the more do we enter into
that stream of love with which God surrounds all men, and still
more do we participate in His attitude of benevolence,
goodness, and infinite charity. This is how charity unites us
with Him who is charity by essence : *Deus caritas est,* " God is
charity, and he that abideth in charity, abideth in God,
and God in him " (1 *Jn* 4,16). On the other hand, when we
are at fault in fraternal charity, we withdraw from God,
from His attitude of infinite charity, which is the same thing
as withdrawing and even separating ourselves from Him.
Therefore, the Apostle exhorts us : " Dearly beloved, let us
love one another, for charity is of God. And everyone that
loveth is born of God, and knoweth God. He that loveth not,
knoweth not God; for God is charity. He that loveth not,
abideth in death " *(ibid.* 4,7.8 – 3,14). Supernatural love
for our neighbor is vastly different from love that is merely
human. Far from drawing us away from divine love, it
impels us toward God with ever increasing force, and unites
us more and more closely to Him.

COLLOQUY

" O Lord, the surest sign of my love for You is the degree of perfection with which I keep the commandment of charity toward my neighbor.   As this is most important, I must strive to know myself better, even in the very smallest matters, taking no notice of all the fine plans that come crowding into my mind when I am at prayer, and which I think I will carry out and put into practice for the good of my neighbor, in the hope of saving even one soul.   If my later actions are not in harmony with these plans, I can have no reason for believing that I should ever have put them into practice.   Nor should I, my God, imagine that I have attained to union with You, and love You very much, because of the devotion and spiritual delights which I may have had in prayer.   I ought rather to ask You to grant me this perfect love for my neighbor and then allow You to work.   If on my side I use my best endeavors and strive after this love in every way I can, doing violence to my own will so that the will of others may be done in everything, even foregoing my own rights; if I forget my own good in my concern for theirs, however much my nature may rebel; if I try to shoulder some trial, should the opportunity present itself, in order to relieve my neighbor of it, You certainly will give me even more than I can desire.   But I must not suppose that it will cost me nothing.   Besides, Lord, did not the love You had for us cost You, too?   To redeem us from death, You died such a grievous death as the death of the Cross " (T.J. *Int C V*, 3).

272

PRUDENCE

PRESENCE OF GOD - Show me, O Lord, the way of true prudence.

MEDITATION

1. If we wish to attain union with God, our whole life should be directed toward Him; and as our life is made up of many acts, we should see that each one is a step forward on the way that leads to Him. Supernatural prudence is that virtue which suggests to us what we should do and what we should avoid in order to reach the goal we have set for ourselves. If we wish to reach union with God, prudence tells us to conform ourself in everything to His will, to detach ourself from all things, even the least, if it be contrary to His divine will. If we wish to become a saint, we must perform these acts of charity and generosity without recoiling from the sacrifice. If we wish to become a soul of prayer, we must strive to be recollected, to avoid useless conversation, to mortify our curiosity, and to apply ourself diligently to prayer. Thus prudence prescribes what we ought to do and what we ought to avoid, whether in view of our final end—union with God, sanctity—or in view of an immediate goal—such as the acquisition of particular virtues—which, however, always must be ordered to our final end.

The parable of the wise and foolish virgins effectively demonstrates the need of this virtue. They all slept while waiting for the bridegroom to come; when he arrived, the first five were admitted into the banquet hall, the other five were refused simply because they had not had the prudence to provide themselves with sufficient oil to fill their lamps. And the parable concludes : " Watch ye therefore, because you know not the day nor the hour " (*Mt* 25,13). Supernatural prudence counsels us first of all to make good use of the time God gives us and the opportunities He offers us to practice virtue, because " the night cometh, when no man can work " (*Jn* 9,4). When, through indolence or carelessness, we miss an opportunity to do a good deed, it is lost forever; others may present themselves later, it is true, but that one will never return again.

2. The future is in the hands of God; all we have at our disposal is the present moment with its actual circumstances. Therefore, true supernatural prudence consists in setting the highest value on each fleeting moment in view of our eternal goal. Human prudence values time as a means to accumulate earthly goods; supernatural prudence values it as a means to accumulate eternal goods. " Lay not up to yourself treasures on earth...but lay up to yourselves treasures in heaven, where neither the rust nor moth doth consume.... Seek ye therefore first the kingdom of God, and His justice, and all these things shall be added unto you " (*Mt* 6,19.20.33). These are the chief rules of prudence, dictated by Jesus Himself.

St. Thérèse of the Child Jesus said to a religious who told her that she disliked doing a certain act of charity which required a great spirit of sacrifice, " I would have been glad to do it, since we are on earth to suffer. The more we suffer, the happier we are. Oh! how little you know about regulating your affairs! " *(Unedited Souvenirs)*. Supernatural prudence teaches us exactly how to regulate our affairs, not in view of earthly happiness, but of eternal beatitude; not in view of our own selfish interests, but in view of our progress in the way of perfection; and above all in view of the glory of God and the good of souls.

Supernatural prudence does not judge things according to their human value, according to the pleasure or displeasure they give us; but it evaluates them in the light of faith, in the light of eternity. " *Quid hoc ad aeternitatem?* " (St. Bernard). " *Quod Deus non est, nihil est* " (*Imit. III*, 31,2). What is this worth in the light of eternity? Whatsoever is not God, is nothing.

Christian prudence is opposed to the prudence of the flesh, which resolves everything with an eye to earthly happiness, without any regard for the law of God. " The wisdom of the flesh is an enemy to God; for it is not subject to the law of God, neither can it be " (*Rom* 8,7). Supernatural prudence far surpasses natural prudence which is not bad, but which is incapable of directing our actions to their supreme end, since it looks only to earthly goals.

COLLOQUY

"O my God, a soul who loves You listens no more to the suggestions of human prudence. Faith and love alone influence her, making her despise all earthly things, holding them to be worthless, as indeed they are. She cares not for any earthly good, being convinced that all is vanity. When she finds that by doing something she can serve You better, she listens to no objections but acts at once, for she understands that her profit consists entirely in this" (cf. T.J. *Con*, 3).

"O Lord, if I wish to be a saint, I must live entirely on a supernatural plane, always remembering that '*whatsoever is not God, is nothing*,' as the author of the Imitation says; consequently, I must leave all things or make use of all to come to You.

"If I do not watch over myself, I can materialize even spiritual things by considering everything superficially, under its human aspect. Alas! O Lord, I know that at times I have acted in this way.

"Oh no! a life spent for You is so great, so beautiful! But it is not great because of any extraordinary deeds, but rather because of the love and fidelity with which I must inform even the least important duties, which transforms these least actions, as well as all my daily occupations; it is great because of the apostolic intentions which vivify my prayers and sacrifices. Teach me, O Lord, to give the greatest amount of love to each instant, to make eternal every passing moment, by giving it the added value of charity" (cf. Sr. Carmela of the Holy Spirit, O.C.D.).

273

THE GOOD SAMARITAN

TWELFTH SUNDAY AFTER PENTECOST

PRESENCE OF GOD - O Lord, impress upon my heart Your commandment of charity and the example You gave of it.

MEDITATION

1. " A certain man went down from Jerusalem to Jericho,
and fell among robbers, who also stripped him, and having
wounded him, went away, leaving him half dead " (*Lk* 10,
23-37). That unfortunate man represents each one of us.
We too have encountered robbers on our way. The world,
the devil, and our passions have stripped and wounded us.
Who can say that he does not have in his own soul some
wound, more or less deep, left by temptation or sin? But,
on our route, there was also a good Samaritan, rather the
Good Samaritan par excellence, Jesus, who, moved by
compassion for our state, brought us help. With infinite
love He bent over our open wounds, curing them with the oil
and wine of His grace. The oil represents its gentleness
and the wine its vigor. Then He took us in His arms and
brought us to a safe place, that is, He entrusted us to the
maternal care of the Church, to which He has consigned the
price of our ransom, the fruit of His death on the Cross.

The parable of the good Samaritan thus delineates
the story of our redemption, a story which is ever in action
and which is renewed every time we draw near to Jesus,
humbly and regretfully showing Him the wounds of our
souls. It is actuated in a very special way in the Mass,
where Jesus presents to the Father the price of our salvation,
and renews His immolation for our benefit. We should go to
Mass in order to meet Him, the Good Samaritan, to invoke
and receive His sanctifying action. The more we recognize
our own misery and our need of redemption, the more
will Jesus apply the fruits of redemption to us. When He
comes to us in Holy Communion, He will heal our wounds,
not only our exterior wounds, but our interior ones also,

abundantly pouring into them the sweet oil and strengthening wine of His grace.

This is how Jesus treats us, this is how He has treated mankind, which, by sin, had become a stranger, yes, an enemy to Him and even rejected Him, the Son of God!

2. Jesus, who by His redemptive work, had given us the highest example of a most merciful and compassionate charity, could fittingly conclude the parable of the good Samaritan with these words : " Go, and do thou in like manner "; and He might have added, as He did to His Apostles on the evening of the Last Supper : " For I have given you an example, that as I have done to you, so you do also " (*Jn* 13,15).

To the scribes and Pharisees, the word *neighbors* meant friends, or at most, the Israelites, but never the pagans or the Samaritans. However, the Savior went beyond this narrow interpretation and suggested an act of charity to an enemy as a concrete example of the charity which was commanded by the law. The good Samaritan brought help to a poor Jew who had been left unaided and abandoned by a priest and a levite, his own fellow countrymen; he did not take into account the hatred the Jews had for his people. This universal charity is to be the distinctive mark of the new religion established by Christ. St. James wrote : " Religion clean and undefiled before God and the Father is this : to visit the fatherless and widows in their tribulation " (1,27). There is no true religion without charity toward our neighbor, and above all toward a suffering neighbor. The scribes and Pharisees, and even their priests, who had reduced religion to mere exterior formalism while neglecting the duties of charity with such unconcern, found themselves condemned by the parable of the good Samaritan. Unfortunately, even among Christians, there are found devout persons who are scrupulous about omitting a single exercise of piety but have no hesitation about abandoning those who suffer; they have not grasped the real inner meaning of religion, but have stopped at the exterior practices. Religion gives us an intense realization of our relationship with God : He is our Father and we are His children; but if we are all children of the same Father, how is it that we do not consider ourselves brothers? True piety consists in the realization of our divine sonship and of our brotherhood with all men, without exception. And he who truly feels himself a brother will never be heedless of the needs and sufferings of others.

COLLOQUY

"O Lord, the more I understand the love You have for us, the more shall I be willing to put aside my own pleasure and profit in order to please You by serving my neighbor.

"Then I shall not consider at all what I may lose : I shall have my neighbor's good in mind and nothing else. In order to give You greater pleasure, my God, help me to forget myself for others, and if need be, even give up my life as did many martyrs" (T.J. *Con*, 7).

"O charity, you are the sweet, holy bond uniting the soul to its Creator : you unite God to man and man to God. You kept the Son of God nailed to the wood of the holy Cross. You unite those whom discord keeps apart. You enrich with virtue those who are poor, because you give life to all the virtues. You bring peace and suppress hatred and war. You give patience, strength and perseverance in return for every good and holy work. You are never weary, you never turn aside from the love of God and neighbor, either because of weariness, pain, contempt, or insult.

"O Christ, sweet Jesus, give me this holy charity, that I may persevere in doing good and never give it up; for he who possesses charity is founded on You, the living rock, and by following Your example, he learns from You how to love His Creator and his neighbor. In You, O Christ, I read the rule and doctrine which are right for me, for You are the way, the truth, and the life. If I read You, I shall follow the right path and shall occupy myself solely with the honor of God and the salvation of souls" (St. Catherine of Siena).

274

PRUDENT JUDGMENT

PRESENCE OF GOD - Help me, O God, to judge with rectitude so that I may be able to act accordingly.

MEDITATION

1. The first duty of prudence is to help us choose the best means for attaining our final end. Many times the choice is easy, and presents itself spontaneously to a mind accustomed to making judgments and acting in the light of eternity. At other times, however, it is difficult and perplexing, as for example, when it concerns choosing one's vocation or profession, or solving complicated problems in which elements independent of one's own will must be considered. In these cases we must take time to examine everything carefully and to consult prudent, experienced persons; to act hastily would show a want of prudence. In the Gospel, Jesus Himself tells us about the prudent man who " having a mind to build a tower, first *sits down* and reckons the charges that are necessary, whether he have wherewithal to finish it " (*Lk* 14,28). The time spent in these examinations and calculations as dictated by prudence is not time wasted. Quite the contrary! When facing serious decisions, we must realize that God Himself often wants us to wait patiently until circumstances clearly manifest His will to us. In this waiting we should give a large place to prayer, begging Our Lord for the light which our own prudence cannot give us. In fact, prudence, even though it is an infused supernatural virtue, is always a virtue exercised by human faculties and, therefore, is affected by human limitations; however, to help it, God has given us a special gift of the Holy Spirit, the gift of counsel, the actuation of which does not depend on us but is obtainable by prayer.

After using all the means suggested by supernatural prudence, we arrive at a decision. Prudence then commands us to put it into effect with courage and diligence, without needless delays on our part and without being discouraged by the difficulties we may meet.

2. In order that our judgments and choices may be prudent, we must know how to free them from elements which are too subjective, such as our personal attractions and interests, our natural likes and dislikes. Sometimes we can deceive ourselves into thinking that we are judging a situation or deciding to do something solely for the glory of God or for the good of our neighbor, when, in fact, if we examined ourselves thoroughly, we would perhaps see that the motives which prevailed in our judgment or in our deliberations were egoistic and dictated by our own personal interests. Hence, even prudence requires that we cleanse our hearts from all these human motives, and that we practice detachment and renunciation. After Jesus had spoken of the prudence necessary for the man who wished to build a tower, and for the king who was about to make war against another king, He said : " So likewise everyone of you that doth not *renounce* all that he possesseth, cannot be My disciple" (*Lk* 14,33). In other words, the prudence needed by one who wishes to be a true follower of Christ, consists in the renunciation of all that can be an obstacle to the attainment of eternal life; it consists in that renunciation of self which frees the heart from selfish personal impulses. Only this renunciation will permit the soul to triumph over the spontaneous reactions of self-love, the impulses of egoism, thus allowing it to form right judgments and impartial decisions.

Above all, in the case of important judgments or decisions which would affect our neighbor or about which we have a personal bias, prudence requires a conscientious examination as to whether we are really moved by supernatural motives, independent of human considerations. Finally, when something has greatly disturbed us, prudence will teach us to suspend all judgment and deliberation until calm has returned; otherwise, we would be exposing ourselves to act by passion rather than by a sincere love of the good.

" Love is prudent, circumspect, upright, " says the *Imitation of Christ* (*III*, 5,7), which means that prudence is the indispensable characteristic of all genuine virtue.

COLLOQUY

" O God, one work performed with prudence is more pleasing to You than many done carelessly and imprudently, for this virtue thoroughly examines and weighs every action so that it may be turned to Your honor and glory.

" True and supernatural prudence belongs to You and is in You, O Lord. Few there are in whom we find it, because many seek it through cunning, using their own wisdom to scrutinize Your designs; thus they lose their time and find nothing. Anyone who really desires to possess prudence must come to You, the Incarnate Word; he will find it in You, together with all the other virtues, but vastly different from human prudence, which tends to what exalts and not to what abases. In You he will find the prudence which teaches us to humble and abase ourselves, as You willed to humble and abase Yourself, in order to show us the way which leads to salvation. You, O Lord, have said : ' If you wish to be My disciple, renounce yourself, take up your cross and follow Me. ' Oh! this is prudence in the highest degree! Yet to human prudence it looks like utter madness. For, O crucified Christ, to the wise ones in this world it is the height of madness to take up one's cross and follow You! But You teach me that the foolishness of the cross is supreme wisdom, and to deny oneself is supreme prudence. What wiser folly can there be than to take up the cross with You and follow in Your footsteps? And what greater prudence can there be than to die to self in order to find life in You, from whom everything receives life? " (St. Mary Magdalen dei Pazzi).

275

PRUDENCE AND RECTITUDE

PRESENCE OF GOD - Teach me, O my God, the prudence which leads to You by the straight path of duty and truth.

MEDITATION

1. Prudence is not limited to suggesting good works to be done in order to attain sanctity, but it remains with us while we do these works, and enlightens us as to the best

conduct to observe therein, according to the circumstances of the moment. For example, prudence tells us when to speak and when to be silent, when to act and when to wait, when to yield and when to resist, when and how to practice this or that virtue. Thus prudence is the great regulator of our whole life; it has been well termed the " *auriga virtutum*, " as it directs the exercise of all the other virtues. Prudence regulates the moral virtues that we may always observe a golden mean in our conduct by avoiding culpable excess in either direction—too much assurance or overtimidity, excessive activity or passivity, seeking our ease or performing penances which ruin our health. On the other hand, in the case of the theological virtues, for which there is no question of a golden mean, it is the task of prudence to direct us as to when and in what way they are to be practiced. Thus, for example, prudence will point out the dangers that threaten our faith and the way to avoid them; it will show us how we can have complete confidence in God, without fear of being presumptuous; it will teach us how to love God with all our heart, without prejudice to fraternal charity or the fulfillment of our duties; finally, it will tell us how to practice fraternal charity with great devotedness, avoiding any harmful imprudences.

We can truly say, therefore, that prudence is extremely useful and necessary in all things; it is the salt that ought to season all our acts. A soul detached from itself, centered on God alone, a recollected soul that does not let itself be distracted by the noise of the world, will easily and almost spontaneously follow the path of supernatural prudence, and by so doing, will reach God by a straight path, without deviations or loss of time.

2. " True, perfect prudence counsels, judges, and commands with *rectitude*, having in view the final end of the whole of life " (St. Thomas, II^a II^{ae}, q.47, a.13, co.). The great difference between supernatural prudence and worldly prudence lies, not only in the vast divergence of the ends aimed at, but also in the choice of means to be used. While the latter does not scruple to use illicit means or to follow the tortuous path of falsehood, trickery, or deceit, Christian prudence repudiates immediately any means which, even in the slightest degree, is contrary to God's law, and it follows the path of rectitude. Christian prudence

may also suggest that we delay to a more suitable time the execution of a plan, good and holy in itself; it may caution us to refrain from revealing our intentions to everyone or to keep silence about certain things.   However, it will never ask us to fail in our duty or to trifle with the truth.   When Jesus said that " the children of this world are wiser than the children of light " (*Lk* 16,8), He certainly meant to remind us to be more prudent and circumspect in doing good, but He had no intention of encouraging us to use the illicit means which the children of darkness use so freely.   We should not think that our prudence is outdone by the prudence of the world because we make use of honorable means only. In opposing the intrigues and deceptions which we can in no wise reciprocate, we have at our disposal a much more powerful means, one which will always be victorious : recourse to God by prayer and sacrifice.

When Jesus sent His disciples out into the world which was full of the ambushes of evil, He told them, " Be ye therefore, wise as serpents and simple as doves " (*Mt* 10,16). By mentioning the two virtues, prudence and simplicity, together, He clearly shows that they must never be separated from one another, nor should one be used as a pretext for failing in the other.   Prudence should never lack simplicity—and here is meant the exclusion of all those means based on untruthfulness—but at the same time, simplicity should never lack prudence.

COLLOQUY

" O prudence, you are like a high mountain.   Those whom the mountain shelters, live a healthy life and enjoy its pure air.   From its height, they see and foresee everything they should do.   So also, my God, the prudence which proceeds from You keeps the soul high above the clouds of passion and human considerations; it invigorates her virtue, and causes her to honor You in all her works, making her foresee everything, so that she can arm herself against temptation.   O my God, give me this true upright prudence, which will lead me to union with You.   Let it guide me in such a way that I shall never fail to perform Your works out of any motive of human respect or regard for any creature " (St. Mary Magdalen dei Pazzi).

" Create a clean heart in me, O God, and renew a right spirit within me. Teach me Your ways, that I may follow Your truth. Give me temperance and prudence, justice and fortitude, for nothing is more profitable to men " (cf. *Ps* 50 – *Wis* 8,7).

" O Jesus, supreme Goodness, I ask You to give me a heart so enamored of You that nothing on earth can distract it...a free heart, never seduced or enslaved, an upright heart which never goes astray " (St. Thomas Aquinas).

276

DILIGENCE

PRESENCE OF GOD - O God, make me diligent in Your service, diligent and prompt in every duty!

MEDITATION

1. A prudent man is also diligent; he carefully examines and selects the means best suited to his sanctification, and diligently makes use of them. " He hath done all things well, " St. Mark said of Jesus (7,37). Speaking absolutely, such praise belongs only to Jesus, whose care and diligence in accomplishing the mission He had been given by His heavenly Father, were most perfect and totally free from the smallest defect. Nevertheless, in due proportion, we should be able to say the same of a diligent person; in fact, this should be the program of his life : to do all things well. It is not enough to do good works; we must do them well, that is, not in a half-hearted sort of way, but with care, solicitude, and promptness—in a word, diligently. What distinguishes saints is not so much their great works or the important position they may occupy in the Church, but their perfect diligence in the performance of every duty, even the humblest.

It often happens, for example, that in a group of people who lead the same kind of life, have the same duties, practice the same exercises of piety, austerity, and mortification, and perform the same apostolic works, some will reach a high degree of charity and union with God, while others will lead a mediocre life, the difference depending on the degree of diligence, greater or less, with which each one applies himself to the fulfillment of his duties. Diligence makes the soul attentive and alert in what is good, so that all its acts are vivified by charity and accomplished with great exactness in every detail. " He that feareth God neglecteth nothing " (*Eccl* 7,19). When this fear is not servile, but the fruit of love which avoids everything that might be displeasing to God, it makes the soul so much the more diligent as it is the more loving.

2. " Diligence is the application of the soul in the prompt performance of good works. It makes man like the angels who fly with wonderful speed to fulfill God's commands " (Ven. John of Jesus Mary,). Promptness in doing good works is a special characteristic of diligence.

A negligent person goes to his work unwillingly, slowly, and with needless delay, whereas the diligent man hastens to it cheerfully, with promptness and concern. The prompt doing of a thing that should be done, even when it would be more convenient to do something else, is the fruit of diligence. Above all, one who is bound to a definite rule of life, either privately or in a community, must observe it punctually and exactly. In fact, any rule which has been approved by one who represents God, is, for the soul who is bound to it, a manifestation of the divine will, which must be carried out without delay or postponement. Punctuality exacts self-discipline and detachment; it often asks us to interrupt some interesting, pleasant work in order to give ourselves to another kind, perhaps less attractive or less important. However, it would be a great mistake to esteem our duties and to dedicate ourselves to them according to the attraction we have for them or according to their more or less apparent importance. All is important and beautiful when it is the expression of the will of God, and the soul who wishes to live in this holy will at every minute of the day, will never omit the slightest act prescribed by its rule of life. To prolong what we are doing beyond the prescribed time, or to dispense ourselves from a duty without a serious reason, is to abandon the will of God; it shows an attachment to our own will, and often enough, to our own convenience.

"In carefulness not slothful. In spirit fervent, serving the Lord" wrote St. Paul to the Romans (12,11); and to the Ephesians he recommended, "See therefore, brethren, how you walk circumspectly : not as unwise, but as wise : redeeming the time.... Wherefore, become not unwise, but understanding what is the will of God" (5,15-17).

COLLOQUY

"O Lord, meditating in Your presence, I understand that the best remedy for carelessness and laxity in performing my duties is charity. I must strive to do everything for love, with the special intention of pleasing You.

"How gracious of You, my God, and how fortunate for me, a poor nothing, to be able to work in order to please You! This thought makes me want to sacrifice everything with joy. O Lord, Your words console me and renew my youth as an eagle's! Yes, sometimes I succeed better and more surely by repeating to myself : ' Do this because it is pleasing to God, ' instead of simply saying, ' It is my duty. '

"O Lord, all I can do is already owed to You, and will always be less than what I should do. Yet Your divine goodness likes to give me the consolation of thinking that I am acting freely and generously when I work diligently in order to please You, not only in carrying out my duties, but also in works of supererogation and perfection, in great and important things as well as in small and unimportant ones, for nothing that can be offered to You is negligible.

"O Lord, I wish to show You continually how great are my desires and my love, by performing all my actions with loving diligence. The more generous and liberal I am in serving You, the more will I receive the fruits of Your generosity" (cf. Bl. M. Thérèse Soubiran).

277

JUSTICE

PRESENCE OF GOD - Teach me, O Lord, to love justice and to hate all that is opposed to it.

MEDITATION

1. When with clever astuteness, the Pharisees asked Jesus if it were lawful to pay tribute to Caesar, He replied : " Render to Caesar the things that are Caesar's, and to God, the things that are God's " (*Mt* 22,21). By this simple reply, Jesus gave us clearly and precisely a description of the virtue of justice : to give to everyone what is his due. " Justice, " says St. Thomas, " is the perpetual, constant will to give to everyone what is due to him " (IIa IIae, q.58, a.1, co.). To God, we give the worship which is due Him as our Creator, Lord, and Father : adoration, honor, glory, gratitude, faithful observance of His laws, and humble, devout service. To our neighbor, we owe respect for his rights, taking into account our various obligations toward him, according to whether He is our superior, equal, or inferior.

Certainly, a soul striving for perfection, cannot be satisfied to remain within the limits of justice; charity will urge it to give and do more. However, justice is always the necessary foundation of charity, without which charity itself could not subsist. Charity toward God can and ought to incite us to do something more than what is strictly prescribed; but this *more* will not be pleasing to God if it causes us to neglect some duty of obligation. Thus a professional man cannot devote himself to apostolic works to the prejudice of his professional duties, nor can a religious undertake works of supererogation, if they prevent him from observing some point of his rule. In the same way, charity toward our neighbor can and should urge us to give alms, but this will not be pleasing to God if it is done with money which rightfully belongs to someone else, as for instance, money which should be used as wages for workmen, or for the paying of debts. A failure in justice—that is, in what is of obligation—cannot be considered an act of charity, either

toward God or toward our neighbor.   Only by starting from
the solid, indispensable foundation of justice, will charity
be able to mount to sure and lofty heights.

2.   "Thou hast loved justice and hated iniquity;
therefore, God, thy God, hath anointed thee with the oil of
gladness " (*Ps* 44,8), the Psalmist says in praise of the just man.
God gives His joy and peace to the soul which respects
justice and fulfills with great exactness all the duties required
by it, even at the cost of sacrifice.   Actually, it is not infrequent
that respect for the rights of others calls for the sacrifice
of our own ease and comfort, and sometimes even our
personal interests; but the soul aiming for perfection must be
generous at all times and never fail, through selfishness, to
fulfill the duty of justice toward its neighbor.   One of the
things which scandalizes and most antagonizes those in the
world is to see pious people who, in their relations with others,
have no scruple about failing in justice, who close their eyes
to the rights of others when they interfere with their own personal interests.   The more we aspire to perfection, the more
we should cultivate the virtue of justice, and sincerely
detest all that is even slightly opposed to it.   Such conduct
is a source of peace for ourself and others.   "Justice and peace
have kissed " (*Ps* 84,11), says Holy Scripture, because peace
can reign only where there is justice, whereas all attempts
at peace and harmony will be useless where justice is not
respected.   Our God is the God of peace; who, more than a
soul who wishes to live in intimacy with Him, should be the
bearer of peace to all?   But only if we observe justice will
we radiate peace.   In fact, it is futile to exhort others to
peace if we refuse to give to everyone what is his due.
As the observance of justice is a fount of peace and joy
for our own conscience, so it also brings peace and joy to our
family, to our community, to each person with whom we
come in contact in our daily life, and to society in general.

COLLOQUY

" O justice, thou art the precious pearl which makes the
soul shine brightly; thou givest peace and light to creatures;
thou keepest them in holy fear and dost unite their hearts.
If thy light failest, we are immediately plunged into confusion

and surrounded by the darkness of injustice " (St. Catherine
of Siena).

O God, Thou alone can infuse true justice in me, for
Thou alone art infinite Justice, " Thou who art just in all
Thy ways and holy in all Thy works " (*Ps* 144,17).

" Thou art just, O Lord : and all Thy judgments are
right.   Justice and fidelity are in Thy testimonies.   Thy
justice is justice forever; Thy law is an eternal law.   Give me
understanding of Thy commandments, and I will live by them.
Teach me to keep Thy law and to observe it with all my
heart.   Lead me by the paths of Thy laws, for they are my
delight.   Incline my heart to Thy precepts, and not to the
love of money.   Teach me to love justice and to hate iniquity,
that I may enjoy Thy blessings for all eternity " (cf. *Ps*
118 – 44).

278

HUNGER AND THIRST AFTER JUSTICE

PRESENCE OF GOD - Give me, O God, a strong efficacious desire for
justice, that I may draw near You, O infinite Justice.

MEDITATION

1. " Blessed are they who hunger and thirst after justice "
(*Mt* 5,6), Jesus said, speaking of justice in general, which
inclines man to live in perfect harmony with God's will,
to the extent of desiring that sacred will as the one indispensable food of his spiritual life.   However, these words may
also be applied to the special virtue of justice, without which
there will never be any harmony with God's will, and therefore, no sanctity.   If we wish to live in union with God,
who is infinite Justice, we must hunger and thirst for justice
in all our actions and in all our relations with others.
Hunger and thirst indicate imperious needs which cannot
be suppressed; it is a question of life or death.   As food and
drink are absolutely essential to the life of the body, so

justice is absolutely necessary for a life of virtue, and its duties are so compelling that no motive can exempt us from fulfilling them. If an act of charity for the neighbor should impose on us great inconvenience or cause us serious harm, we would not be obliged to do it, but the same inconvenience or harm could not excuse us from fulfilling a duty of justice. Serious motives can sometimes authorize us to postpone the fulfillment of such a duty, but the obligation always remains; although we might be prevented from acquitting it ourselves in a material way, we must supply for it, at least morally. It is thus appropriate to speak of *hunger* and *thirst* for justice, not in the sense of vindicating rights, but in the sense of cultivating in ourselves such a lively desire and imperious need for justice in all our relations with others, that we do not feel satisfied until we have completely fulfilled all the duties stemming from this virtue.

2. Justice, like all the other virtues, has bitter enemies in our passions, particularly in egoism. When not thoroughly mortified and subdued, egoism always finds a way to make certain duties required by justice seem too burdensome; it can always invent excuses and subterfuges to exempt itself from them. In addition to being an attachment to our personal interests and rights, egoism sometimes appears under the special aspect of jealousy, and even here, it is the cause of injustice. The jealous person—or worse still, the envious person—is almost unconsciously inclined to belittle the merits of others, to criticize and find their way of acting defective. Thus they rob others of the esteem which, in all justice, they should have from their superiors, equals, and inferiors. All this is contrary to justice as well as to charity.

Another source of injustice is partiality or preference for one particular person to the great detriment of others who have identical rights. Very often this is done under the mask of charity, but there can be no question of charity when, to favor, defend, or sustain one person or to be more generous to him, one fails in justice toward others and sometimes perhaps toward an entire community. A soul that hungers and thirsts after justice will watch over itself very carefully to prevent even the slightest fault of this kind, from insinuating itself into its conduct. As long as we have passions—and we shall always have them—we have reason to be fearful of ourselves, and we should be diligent in examining the

motives of our acts.   It is necessary to have a great love for
justice, for truth, and for the common good together with
a great sincerity if we are to succeed in unmasking all those
little passions that might cause us to deviate, however slightly,
from the path of justice.   Let us look at our justice in the
mirror of infinite justice, and we shall always find something
to correct or improve.   " Blessed are they who keep judgment
and do justice at all times, " sings the Psalmist, for " the
righteous will behold His countenance " (*Ps* 105,3 – 10,7).
The desire to be united to God, who is infinite Justice,
will lead us to practice this virtue ever more perfectly.

COLLOQUY

   " O Lord, increase my hunger and thirst for justice,
so that I may lovingly fulfill all the duties of justice, every
obligation to You and to others, neglecting none, but doing
them all willingly, even if they are unpleasant to nature.
This hunger presses me to always make more progress in the
virtues, considering as very little what I have already obtained,
and as very much, what I still lack.   May this hunger and
thirst give me a most ardent desire for Your grace and a
fervent love for the holy Sacraments especially the Sacrament
of the Altar, so that I may nourish myself with You, O Jesus,
who are my Justice.
   " O Jesus, Your hunger after justice was so great that You
no longer felt bodily hunger, and one day when You were
very tired and in need of refreshment, You said to Your
disciples : ' My meat is to do the will of Him who sent Me. '
You had such an ardent thirst for justice that You burned
with desire to taste the bitter chalice of Your Passion, even to
the point of saying : ' I have a baptism wherewith I am to be
baptized, and how am I straightened until it be accomplished! '
   " O my beloved Redeemer, inflame me with the fire of
Your love, the source of this hunger and thirst; may I continually use this hunger and thirst to serve You, as You did
to redeem me " (cf. Ven. L. Du Pont).

279

PERFECT JUSTICE

PRESENCE OF GOD - O Lord, You who are just and love what is just, teach me how to practice justice perfectly.

MEDITATION

1. The justice of a soul aspiring to perfection is not cold and dry, not insistent about receiving all that is its due, but it is broad, liberal, generous, and vivified by the expansive breath of charity. Hence it reaches far beyond material justice, which does not come from the heart but limits itself to exterior acts. Primarily, the former is interior justice, that is, uprightness of heart and mind, justice in thoughts, desires, feelings, and intentions. The soul who possesses it has not listened in vain to the words of Jesus : " Unless your justice abound more than that of the scribes and Pharisees, you shall not enter into the kingdom of heaven " (*Mt* 5,20). The justice of the Pharisees was insufficient, because it was limited to a purely exterior observance of the law. They had no scruple about secretly trampling upon their most sacred religious duties. These men covered their public conduct with the cloak of justice, without troubling themselves to make it the motive of their private conduct, their affections and the desires of their hearts.

What good, then, is the outer display of justice if its interior spirit is lacking? For example, what use is it to pose in public as a defender of the rights of the people, if in private life a man does not pay workmen a just wage, or is dishonest in commerce, in business, in exercising his profession? What use is it to pour out fine words and promises —or even gifts—on anyone, when we are not willing to recognize and respect his rights?

The soul that thirsts for justice has a horror of all such proceedings, and, far from being satisfied to appear just in acts which can be judged by others, wants to be just in all actions, even those which are not seen by others, but are known only to God. He seeks above all justice of heart and of mind, for exterior justice proceeds solely from interior justice.

2. If we ourselves should fulfill justice rigorously in all our actions, interior as well as exterior, this does not give us the right to demand justice from our neighbor.   More than anyone, Jesus brought justice into the world, yet no one was more gentle and kind than He.   Even when it is our duty to safeguard or establish justice in specific circumstances, we should be careful not to be severe, but to act with kindness, trying to persuade rather than to impose.   If we attempt to administer justice by force, we shall obtain nothing, or at most, a strained situation which will soon collapse. Following the example of Jesus, we must try to make justice penetrate into souls and into society by means of charity, love, and an understanding of the weaknesses of others. If we want to be realistic, we must remember that, no matter how much we do, we shall never, even under the best of circumstances, obtain absolute justice in this world.   Perfect justice is found only in heaven; even Jesus bore with the unjust acts of Judas and the Pharisees.   Although He could have acted otherwise, He did not wish the cockle to be uprooted from the field until the time of the harvest.   We then, must be very patient and merciful, especially when the injustice is aimed against ourselves.   For a soul aspiring to sanctity, it can well be said that the greatest justice consists in bearing patiently and humbly all the injustices of which it is the target, for it would be absurd to think of reaching perfection without following in the footsteps of Jesus.   If He, Innocence itself, suffered so much injustice without complaining, is it not just that we who are sinners should, at least, suffer something without posing as victims, but remaining calm and serene?   Justice itself, then, urges us to bear injustices.   Thus, this virtue which begins by enjoining us to give to everyone his due, reaches its culmination in making us enter fully upon the path of sanctity and union with God.

COLLOQUY

"Justice comes from You, O God; its eye is always turned toward You, and it gives to each one his due.   But what is this justice and what does it mean to say that it always looks at You?   Oh! justice is one of Your perfections, and properly speaking, justice is Yourself, O God!   And he who reflects this virtue in himself, has his glance turned toward You, because he resembles You and wants to be like You in all his actions, always acting without deceit or fraud. A soul who looks upon You, O Incarnate Word, sees that You are so just that, rather than fail in justice, You preferred to take on Yourself the punishment for all our sins; therefore, this soul also wishes to do justice to itself for all its faults. But it sees, too, that justice and mercy are united in You, so much so that You give Yourself, O Christ, as Food to Your redeemed; You nourish them with Your words, Your deeds, Your example, but still more with Your Precious Blood " (St. Mary Magdalen dei Pazzi).

" O God, the perfume of Your justice is everywhere; it is so pervasive that You are not called simply the Just One, but Justice itself, even justifying Justice, and the more You can justify the more You are inclined to pardon. Therefore, all who, hating their sins, hunger and thirst for justice, can hope in You, who justify the impious.

" No one is so presumptuous that he thinks his justice or holiness is enough to assure his salvation. For this reason I hasten to You, O Jesus : Your Passion is my supreme refuge and sole remedy! It comes to help us when our wisdom fails, when our justice is weak, and the merits of our holiness are useless. When my strength grows weak, I shall not be discouraged. I know what I must do : ' I shall take the chalice of salvation and call upon the name of the Lord. ' Open my eyes, O God, that I may always know what is pleasing to You and then I shall be wise. Pardon the faults of my youth and ignorance, and I shall be just. Lead me, O God, on Your path, and I shall be holy. But if Your Blood does not intercede for me, I shall not be saved " (St. Bernard).

280

THE TEN LEPERS

THIRTEENTH SUNDAY AFTER PENTECOST

PRESENCE OF GOD - O Jesus, my Savior, I need You; heal me, have pity on me!

MEDITATION

1. In the cycle of the Sundays after Pentecost, the Church brings to our attention, sometimes under one aspect, sometimes under another, the merciful action of Jesus on our souls. Two weeks ago she told us about the deaf-mute; last Sunday, the kindness of the good Samaritan; today, the touching scene of the ten lepers whom Jesus cured. It is in this way that the Church tries to awaken in us humble consideration of our misery and to show us the immense need we continually have of the redemptive work of Jesus; at the same time, she wants to make us feel that this work is always in action and that we are living under its influence every day, every moment. The passage in the Gospel (*Lk* 17,11-19) chosen for today's Mass is especially effective in making clear the chief purpose of the Redemption : the healing of souls from the leprosy of sin. From ancient times leprosy has been considered the most fitting figure to represent the hideousness of sin, and indeed it would be difficult to picture anything more horrible and repulsive. Yet, while everybody has such a great dread of leprosy of the body, how indifferent and easy-going even Christians are in regard to leprosy of the soul. How far we are from the deep realization that the saints had of what an offense against God really is! " Oh! " St. Teresa of Avila exclaimed, " why can we not realize that sin is a pitched battle fought against God with all our senses and the faculties of the soul; the stronger the soul is, the more ways it invents to betray its King " (*Exc*, 14). One of the fruits of today's Gospel is that of awakening in us a great horror of sin, of arousing again in our souls a lively and efficacious repentance for the sins we have committed and a

feeling of profound humility upon recognizing our misery.
Let us go with the ten lepers to Our Lord and cry out :
" Jesus, Master, have Mercy on us! "

2. Today's Gospel shows us the remedies for sin. The
first of these is the sincere humility which recognizes one's
own misery. However, humility is not enough; it needs to be
accompanied by confident recourse to God. The poor
lepers, knowing their miserable state, put their trust in Jesus,
and full of faith made their plea to Him; this was the first
step toward their cure. Some people bewail their misfortunes
and are distressed because of them; still, they never succeed
in being cured because they do not have recourse to Jesus,
the only physician capable of healing them. The remembrance of their past sins holds them back; they hardly dare to
approach Him or to trust in His mercy. Such persons do
not understand that it is just because we are sinners that
we should go to Jesus, and that " they that are whole, need
not the physician, but they that are sick " (*Lk* 5,31).
    The divine Master did not cure the poor lepers imme-
diately, but sent them to the priests : " Go, show yourselves
to the priests. " They obeyed at once, without arguing
or doubting, and " as they went, they were made clean. "
Jesus acts in the same way with us; it is always He who
heals us, but He usually wills to do so through the mediation
of the priest. Some persons do not have enough faith in the
words and works of God's minister. Their faith in the efficacy
of the sacraments and in the sacramental absolution is not
sufficiently strong; and therefore, they live in a state of
continual anguish. When one has sincerely revealed the
state of his conscience to a priest, that is, with no intention of
deceiving him, he should be at peace and submit wholly to
the judgment of the priest. In such a case, to doubt the word
of God's minister, to doubt the absolution he has given,
is to doubt Jesus Himself, for it is He who is acting through
His representative.
    Only one of the ten lepers who were cured felt the need
to return and thank Our Lord. " Blessed is the soul, "
St. Bernard comments, " who every time he receives a gift
of grace from God, returns to Him, to Him who responds to
our gratitude for the favors we have received by giving
us new favors. The greatest hindrance to progress in the
spiritual life is ingratitude, for God counts as lost the graces we

receive without gratitude, and He refrains from giving us new graces. "

COLLOQUY

" O Lord, physician of my soul, heal me, that I may acknowledge Your gifts, O health of my soul, and thank You with all my heart for the favors You have showered upon me since my youth, and will continue to shower upon me unto old age. In Your goodness, do not abandon me, I beseech You. You made me when I did not exist; You willed to redeem me when I was perishing and was dead. You came down to him who was dead; You put on mortality; a King, You came to the servant to redeem him and gave Yourself that he might live; You endured death and conquered it, and humbling Yourself, You restored me.

" I was perishing, far away, immersed in my sins; You came for me to redeem me and You loved me so much that You shed Your Blood for me. You loved me, Lord, more than Yourself, for You willed to die for me. For so high a price, You brought me back from exile; You freed me from slavery, You drew me out of torments, gave me Your Name and marked me with Your Blood, so that I would always remember You and keep You in my heart. Your love for me made You accept the Cross. You anointed me with the oil with which You were anointed, so that by You, O Christ, I might be called a Christian. Your grace and mercy have always gone before me. You have often rescued me from grave dangers, O my Deliverer. When I strayed from the right path, You brought me back to it; when I lay in ignorance, You instructed me; when I sinned, You corrected me; when I was sad, You consoled me; when I was in despair, You strengthened me; when I fell, You lifted me up; when I stood up, You supported me; when I journeyed, You guided me on my way; when I came to You, You received me; when I slept, You watched over me; when I invoked You, You answered me " (St. Augustine).

281

JUSTICE AND RELIGION

PRESENCE OF GOD - Help me, O God, by Your grace, to render You all the homage of which I am capable.

MEDITATION

1. Justice leads us to render to each one what is his due. But when it is a question of justice to God, we can never succeed in giving Him all that we owe Him, in making Him a suitable return for all His gifts, in paying Him the worship and homage which are due His infinite Majesty. We can fulfill our obligations to others according to justice, but we cannot do so with regard to God. However much man does, it will always be far less than what justice demands. Therefore, justice to God creates in us an urgent need to give ourselves to Him without reserve, without measure, without calculations, in other words, to make a complete gift of ourselves to God, in an attempt to render Him all the homage of which He, by His grace, has made us capable.

Because our justice is insufficient, we should have recourse to Jesus " who of God is made unto us...justice " (1 *Cor* 1,30), not only in the sense that He justified us from sin, but also in that He came upon earth to give the Father, in the name of all mankind, the worship worthy of Him. Therefore, we should seek in Jesus, in His wounds and His precious Blood, all that will make up for our insufficiency, and pay our debt to God; and we shall find it superabundantly. Even though we have consecrated ourselves to the service and worship of God, we are always useless servants, always His great debtors; this, however, should not discourage us, but should serve to stimulate us never to lessen, never to draw back in our dedication to God. At the same time, it ought to urge us to appeal with immense confidence to Jesus, our Savior and Mediator.

2. The virtue of religion makes us give to God the homage and worship which are His due; in this sense, it is related to the virtue of justice; however, it can never completely

fulfill the requirements of justice, but it approaches these as closely as possible. Our religion can honor God worthily only when it becomes part of Christ's religion, that is, insofar as it is united with the homage, adoration, praise, and offering which are continually rising up from the heart of Christ to His heavenly Father. Jesus was the perfect religious, in the sense that all His affections, His activity and His will were so directed to the glory of the Father and to His service that His whole life was one continual act of worship and religion. " Did you not know that I must be about My Father's business? " (*Lk* 2,49). This was the fundamental attitude of His spirit. Jesus, who in the secret of His heart incessantly adored the Trinity, who so often expressed His prayer even externally, raising His eyes to Heaven and calling upon His Father, who passed a good part of the night in solitary conversation with Him, who went punctually to the temple at Jerusalem for all the acts of external worship prescribed by the law, who died on the Cross to offer to the Triune God a sacrifice worthy of Him—yes, Jesus has shown us in what the true virtue of religion consists. It is interior worship, because " God is a spirit, and they that adore Him must adore Him in spirit and in truth " (*Jn* 4,24); but it is also exterior, because our whole being, including our bodies, must take part in the homage we render to God.

Religious who are wholly consecrated to the service of God by their vows practice the virtue of religion in the highest degree, provided they fulfill their obligations " in spirit and in truth. " But even those who are not bound by vows should try in all their acts to have the intention of performing them for the glory, honor, and service of God; therefore, they should do them in such a way that they can be presented to Him as acts of homage, offering, and sacrifice. Thus the virtue of religion is not confined to the hours of prayer; it embraces our whole life, transforming it into one continual act of homage to God, in imitation of the life of Jesus and in union with it.

COLLOQUY

" What return shall I make to You, O God, for all You have given me? Reason and human justice require me to give myself entirely to You from whom I have received all that I am, and they enjoin me to love You with all my strength. But faith teaches me that I should love You still more than this because Your gifts are greater than I am. You have given me not only my being, but also, by grace, Your being.

" If, because You created me, I ought to give myself entirely to You, what should I add in exchange for my redemption? When You created me, You gave me myself; when You redeemed me, You gave me Yourself, and by so doing, You gave me back to myself. Given and then returned, I owe myself to You in exchange for myself; I owe myself twice. But what can I give You, my God, in return for Yourself? Even if I could give myself to You a thousand times, what am I compared with You?

" I will love You, O Lord, my strength, my support, my refuge, my redeemer. I will love You for Your gifts, according to my measure, which certainly will be less than the just measure, but will not be less than my capacity for loving You. Doubtless I shall know how to love You more when You deign to give me more love, and yet I shall never be able to love You as much as You deserve. Your eyes have seen my imperfection, but the names of those who have done all that they could are written in Your book, even if they could not do all they should " (St. Bernard).

" I invoke You, omnipotent Father, by the charity of Your omnipotent Son; nor do I know of any other intercessor, if not this One who made Himself a propitiation for our sins. I beseech You through Him, the High Priest, true Pontiff and Good Shepherd, who offered Himself as a sacrifice and gave His life for His flock; I pray to You through Him who is seated at Your right hand interceding for us, to give me the grace to bless You and praise You and glorify You together with Him, with intense compunction of heart, with many tears, and with great reverence. He is my advocate with You, God the Father; He is the sacred Victim, pleasing to You, perfect, offered in the odor of sweetness and acceptable to You " (St. Augustine).

282

PIETY AND DEVOTION

PRESENCE OF GOD - O God, our Father, infuse into my soul the true spirit of piety and devotion.

MEDITATION

1. The Christian religion is not limited to the simple relations of the creature with the Creator, relations which, given the infinite distance between them, would remain only within the sphere of reverence and homage, without any character of intimacy, without any confidential impetus toward God. A Christian knows that he is bound to God for other reasons than those of creation, strong though these may be—he has been redeemed from sin and raised to a supernatural state. A Christian is conscious of the fact that he is not only a creature, but a child of God, redeemed by Christ; and this gives to all his relations with God that quality of filial piety, which is the very soul of his religion. Let us contemplate Jesus in His relations with God; He knows He is a *Son*, a *Son* who lives for the Father who has given Him existence. " The Father hath sent Me...and I live by the Father " (*Jn* 6,58) ; a *Son* who has no other ideal than to do His Father's will, to which He adheres with all the strength of His Heart : " Yea, Father, for so hath it seemed good in Thy sight " (*Mt* 11,26) ; a *Son* who in all His actions, seeks only to please His Father : " I do always the things that please Him " (*Jn* 8,29). Jesus, the only-begotten of the Father, the only Son of God by nature, has by grace made us sharers in His divine filiation, so that " we should be called and should be the sons of God " (1 *Jn* 3,1). If we are sons of God, then it is right that we, too, strive to share Christ's dispositions of filial piety toward His heavenly Father. For it is this which truly characterizes our religion as given to us by our divine Master : " Thus, shall you pray : Our Father, who art in heaven " (*Mt* 6,9). He wishes us to consider and invoke God as *our Father :* the *Father* who provides for all our needs; the *Father* who wishes us to pray to Him in secret, and who in secret will hear our prayers;

the *Father* who sees all our actions, even the most hidden ones, and who is preparing a reward for them; the *Father* who wishes us to honor Him by keeping His commandments, and who is pleased to make His abode in the souls of those who love Him. The divine paternity is the center of the Christian religion, and to this paternity should correspond, on our part, an attitude of deep filial piety. We should love God as a child loves its father, trying to please Him in all things. Piety is truly the heart of our religion.

2. If God has wished to raise us to the dignity of being His children, we should live as such and not like servants. The servant does only what is strictly necessary to obtain his salary and retain his position; the son, however, does not consider the reward, but loving his father dearly, puts himself at his disposal unreservedly, without restriction. The servant is lazy and selfish; he tries to spare himself as much as he can, and does not wish to give his employer anything more than what has been agreed upon. Not so the son; for him it is not a question of a time for work and a time for rest; nothing is too laborious when it is a question of giving pleasure to his father; he is always ready to carry out his orders, always attentive to his wishes, he is happy to be able to repeat at every moment, " Behold, I come...to do Thy will " (*Heb* 10,7). Similarly, in our relations with God, filial piety flows into *devotion*, which according to St. Thomas, is " the will to do promptly all that pertains to the service of God " (II^a II^{ae}, q.82, a.1, co.). Piety as well as devotion can be very much alive in the soul, although in the sensible part it feels cold and dry; and this to the extent that all its exercises of prayer and virtue are performed without the feeling of any sweetness or consolation, but rather with great repugnance.

This should not alarm us : St. Thomas teaches that devotion is an *act of the will*, that this act can very well exist in spite of aridity, coldness, repugnance, and even rebellion in the inferior part of the soul. St. Paul himself, although raised to the third heaven, was still not entirely free from these miseries, and confessed : " I am delighted with the law of God, according to the inward man : but I see another law in my members, fighting against the law of my mind " (*Rom* 7,22.23). Now as St. Paul—in spite of this resistance in the sensible part of his soul—was not deprived of true piety and true devotion, so neither is the soul deprived of them if it remains firm in the decision of its will to give itself promptly to God's service, in spite of everything. *Devotion*, which is derived from the Latin word *devoveo*, means precisely consecration to the divinity; and the soul gives itself entirely to God, not by bursts of enthusiasm in its feelings, but by an act of the will. Furthermore, when devotion is deprived of relish for the things of God, " it has a double worth, because the soul both fulfills its duty and governs its sensitive appetite by a strong act of the will " (Ven. John of Jesus Mary).

COLLOQUY

O Most High God, You have willed to be my Father; grant that I may really be Your child, a loving, devoted child, attentive and docile to every manifestation of Your will, desiring to serve and please You in everything. O You, who have a Father's heart for me, create in me the heart of a child, a heart free from servile fear, but rich in filial fear, a disinterested, generous heart which has but one fear : the fear of offending You, and but one desire : that of pleasing You.

" May Your will be my will, my passion, my honor! Grant that I may seek it, find it, and accomplish it. Show me Your ways, point out to me Your paths. O Father, You have Your designs over me. Show them to me clearly and grant that I may follow them so as to obtain the salvation of my soul. Apart from You, may every joy be bitter to me. May I have no desire or rest but in You. May every work undertaken for You be sweet.

" Let my piety not be merely mechanical, but a continual impulse of my heart... and grant that my spirit, which is incapable of not knowing You, be ardent in seeking You, and know how to find You, O most loving Father.

" Ah! let not my words displease You! Grant that, trustful and calm, I may await Your answer, relying on Your word! " (St. Thomas).

Receive me, O Father, in Your embrace; admit me to intimacy with You! Grant, I beseech You, that my heart may never wander when You leave it in darkness and distress; but sustained with Your grace, may it persevere in seeking and serving You with good will.

283

GRATITUDE

PRESENCE OF GOD - O my God, give me a grateful heart, that I may sing Your praises forever.

MEDITATION

1. Incapable as we are of paying our debts to God according to justice, we should at least try to supply for them by our gratitude. Even the poorest beggar, having nothing to give in return for the alms he has received, can always acknowledge a kindness by showing gratitude to his benefactor. This is our position in regard to God : we have nothing of our own; all that we are and have comes from Him, and in return for His infinite generosity, we can do nothing but use His gifts to express our gratitude to Him. " In all things give thanks : for this is the will of God in Christ Jesus concerning you all " (*Thes* 5,18). God, who showers blessings upon us with infinite generosity, has a perfect right to expect gratitude from us. Yet this, a natural need of a humble, delicate soul, is a duty so often neglected even by good people, even by those who have received the most favors from God. Jesus complained of this neglect when only one of the ten lepers whom He had cured returned to thank Him : " And where are the nine? Is there no one found to return and give glory to God, but this stranger? " (*Lk* 17,17.18). It is significant that the nine ungrateful ones were the nine Jews, who, being fellow-citizens of Jesus, were in a more privileged position than the stranger. Sometimes those whom Jesus has called to be His close friends, those upon whom He has bestowed a privileged vocation, are the very ones who show Him the least gratitude.

It is almost as though the multiplicity of the graces which they have received dulls their sensitiveness to the divine gifts; it seems they no longer regard the greatness of these gifts, nor the fact that they are totally gratuitous; gratitude seems to have dried up in their hearts. " Oh! " exclaims St. Teresa, " how the very greatness of His favors condemns those who are ungrateful! " (*Exc*, 3). Ingratitude

always redounds to the disadvantage of the soul. Let us
think, for example, of the irreparable loss of the nine lepers
who, not returning to give thanks for the healing they had
received, forfeited the joy the one grateful leper had of
hearing Jesus say : " Thy faith hath made thee whole "
(*Lk* 17,19). Their want of gratitude deprived them of
health of soul, a grace immeasurably more precious than the
health of the body.

2. St. Bernard says, " Ingratitude is the enemy of the
soul, the destroyer of merit and virtue, causing the loss of
favors. It is a burning wind which dries up the fountain
of piety, the dew of mercy, the torrents of grace. " Gratitude,
on the contrary, attracts new graces, new gifts; it draws
down upon souls the infinite liberality. But this gratitude
should be sincere and cordial, and should extend to all of
God's gifts. " Every gift of God, whether great or small,
should be gratefully acknowledged; not even the least
grace should be forgotten " *(ibid.)*. This sincere gratitude
flourishes only in a heart that is humble, convinced of its own
poverty, and thoroughly aware that it is nothing and can do
nothing without continual help from God. It is not
impossible, in fact, to thank God with the lips, while in the
heart, one attributes the graces received to one's own merits.
Such was the false gratitude of the Pharisee when he said :
" O God, I give Thee thanks that I am not as the rest of men "
(*Lk* 18,11). The context clearly shows that this proud
man was far from recognizing his own nothingness and
attributing to God alone the little good that might have been
in him. A humble man has an entirely different attitude :
if he has done some good, or practiced virtue, he is convinced
that all is the fruit of grace, and therefore, not only God's
great gifts to him, but even the least of the good works he
performs, are opportunities for giving continual thanks
to God, whom he recognizes as the source of all good.
Who, then, can express his gratitude for every Mass, for
every Communion, for every confession? Each one of these
graces even if renewed a thousand times finds this gratitude as
lively and alert, as if it were a question of an entirely new gift.
And in reality, it is : each sacrament, each divine succor,
each actual grace, each spiritual or material help, brings
with it newness of grace, of spiritual life, of love; blessed
the soul who realizes this and praises God for it! If the

multitude of divine benefits do not produce in us proportionate fruits, the reason probably lies in our want of gratitude, and if we want to look more deeply for the root of this evil, almost always we shall find that it is a lack of humility.

COLLOQUY

" I give You thanks, O eternal Father, because You have not despised Your creature, nor turned away Your face from me, nor ignored my desires. You, who are light, did not despise my darkness; You, who are life, did not go far away from me who am death; nor did You, the physician, fail to heal my wounds.... Your wisdom, mercy, and infinite goodness have not looked with scorn at all these and the infinite number of other evils and faults that are in me. What forced You to love me and to grant me so many graces? It was not my virtues but only Your charity. May I always keep Your favors in mind, and may my will burn with the fire of Your charity.

" O inestimable Love, how admirable are the things You have done in Your creature! O my wretched, blind soul, where is your cry of gratitude, where are the tears you should shed in the sight of your God who is unceasingly calling to you? Where are all my yearning desires in the sight of divine mercy? They are not in me because I have not yet lost myself, for if I were lost and had sought only You, my God, only the glory and the praise of Your Name, my heart would have thrilled in a hymn of gratitude.

" Thanks be to You, O eternal, most high Trinity! I am she who is not and You are He who is. Glorify Yourself by enabling me to praise You. Pardon me, O Father, pardon me who am miserable, and ungrateful to You for the immense benefits I have received. I confess that Your goodness has preserved me, Your spouse, although because of my many defects I have often been unfaithful to You " (St. Catherine of Siena).

284

SINCERITY

PRESENCE OF GOD - Give me, O Lord, an open, sincere heart, loving the truth, seeking and desiring it at any cost.

MEDITATION

1. " Lord, who shall dwell in Thy tabernacle, or who shall rest in Thy holy hill? " asks the Psalmist. And he gives the answer : " He that walketh without blemish, and worketh justice " (*Ps* 14,1.2).

God is truth, and no one can be admitted to His intimacy who does not strive as much as he can, to live in truth and to be sincere in all his actions. First of all, we must seek to possess truth in the depths of our heart, that we may know ourselves as we really are in the eyes of God, stripped of all disguise and artificiality. To do this we must accept, not only the truths which please us, but also those which are painful and wound our pride to the quick, revealing our faults and evil tendencies. A person who is sincere never closes his eyes to these truths, but values them, even if they are humiliating, knowing that humiliation which reveals the truth is worth more than illusion which flatters pride and keeps us in error. Sometimes God permits difficult circumstances which are especially hard and trying for the practice of virtue, that we may see the truth and know ourselves as we really are. Under the onset of contradiction, we experience movements, hitherto unknown, surging up within us : movements of anger, rebellion, selfishness, from which perhaps we had had the illusion that we were free. In such cases, instead of turning our gaze away, it is necessary to have the courage to recognize these faults and confess them, humbly and frankly. St. John of the Cross speaks of certain pious souls who, in confession, " palliate [their sins] and make them appear less evil, and thus...excuse themselves rather than accuse themselves " (cf. *DN I*, 2,4). A soul that loves the truth is very far from acting in this way; even if it has only venial sins and imperfections of which to accuse itself in confession, it exposes them all very sincerely, without magnifying or minimizing them, never blaming circumstances, but only itself for all that is faulty.   Sincerity in confessing our faults is the first step toward freeing ourselves from them.

2. A soul can be insincere in its interior life and its relations with God, but it can never deceive Him, and its lack of sincerity will only redound to its own disadvantage.   But with respect to our neighbors it is not so; a want of sinceritly can easily harm them, or at least deceive them.   Hence, not only charity, but also justice demands that we conduct ourselves with the greatest sincerity in our relations with our neighbor.   " Wherefore putting away lying, " St. Paul exhorts, " speak ye the truth every man with his neighbor, for we are members one of another " (*Eph* 4,25).   Because of the natural ties, and still more, the supernatural ones, which bind us to our neighbor, he has every right not to be deceived either by our words or by our actions.

To be sincere, our words must, first of all, correspond to our thoughts.   To be convinced of one thing and to affirm another, with the intention of deceiving someone, is directly contrary to truth and, therefore, an offense against God, who is infinite Truth.   Such an act is absolutely inadmissible in any soul, and especially in one who aspires to union with God : How can falsehood hope to be united to supreme Truth?   And yet under a more subtle form certain deficiencies in sincerity are not wholly absent from the conduct of devout souls—little subterfuges, words spoken in such a way that they ward off a just rebuke, conceal a mistake which one does not wish to admit, or even attract a little praise or admiration... and all this through vanity or human respect, in order to avoid humiliation or suffering.   These are mean ways of acting, unworthy of a sincere, noble spirit. Any want of sincerity, however small, in a soul who has consecrated itself to God, is very displeasing to Him, and is a serious obstacle to its spiritual progress.   St. Margaret Mary writes : " If I should see a soul adorned with all the virtues except sincerity, and if I knew that she had been favored with great graces, it would all seem to me but deceit and illusion. "

It is not sufficient to be sincere in our words; we must also be sincere in our actions and conduct.   Sincere conduct is that which makes us appear just as we are, with no affectation, and no desire to appear to be what we are not. Our words and actions should express the truth which has been sought and loved interiorly. Sincerity does not require us to reveal all that we think or know to everyone; this would be contrary to prudence and to other virtues. It does, however, demand that everything we do reveal, by word or act, or even by silence, corresponds to truth.

COLLOQUY

" O Lord, if I wish to reach You, who are the Way, the Truth, and the Life, I must travel the road of truth, without any pretense or dissimulation, renouncing reason that has been darkened by self-love and human respect. I must act with simplicity, wholly dying to myself and to creatures. Teach me, O eternal Truth, how to act sincerely and frankly. Let my soul, simple as a dove, fly to You to build its nest in Your heart, and nourish itself with the knowledge of You and of itself; thus despising its own malice, it will find nothing in itself to satisfy it, and therefore, it will be unable to stay far away from You, not finding where to repose outside of You. Teach me to walk in the straight path of truth without stopping, but always advancing, hurrying and running swiftly, in order to follow You, eternal Truth, my guide and my way " (St. Mary Magdalen dei Pazzi).

" O Lord, let Thy truth teach me, let Thy truth guard me, and keep me till I come to a happy end. Let the same deliver me from all evil affections. I confess my sins to Thee with great compunction and sorrow; never permit me to esteem myself for my good works. I am indeed a sinner, subject to, and entangled with many passions. I always tend to nothing, I fall quickly, I am quickly overcome, easily disturbed and discouraged. I have nothing in which I can glory, but many things for which I ought to humble myself, for I am much weaker than I am able to comprehend.

" Teach me, O Lord, to admire Thy eternal truth, and to despise my own exceeding vileness " (*Imit. III*, 4,2-4).

285

SIMPLICITY

PRESENCE OF GOD - O Lord, give me a simple heart, free from duplicity and deceit, a heart which goes to You with childlike simplicity.

MEDITATION

1. Simplicity is a virtue very much like sincerity, its indispensable foundation, but one which surpasses it when perfect, embracing man's whole moral life and reducing it to unity. Simplicity excludes every form of duplicity and complication stemming from egoism, self-love, or attachment to self and to creatures; hence it impels the soul in one direction only : to God, to live for Him, to please Him, and to give glory to Him. The whole spiritual life consists in this progressive simplification which proceeds at an equal pace with interior purification. When a soul is perfectly purified from every passion and attachment, then is it reduced to perfect simplicity, that simplicity which makes it live only in God and for God. To reach this goal, we must, during our whole life, let ourselves be guided in everything by one light alone; we must rely on one power alone, and seek but one end : God.

A soul who wishes to acquire holy simplicity accepts no light but that which comes from God, which is God Himself; therefore, it puts aside its selfish and egoistic point of view; it rejects the deceptive voice of the passions and the blinding but false maxims of the world, knowing that all is darkness and illusion except the light of truth which can come from God alone, from His law, from the Gospel. It judges all things in the light of faith, seeing the hand of God in every circumstance and happening, even the most painful. It makes use of everything to go to Him, without wasting time in reasoning about the conduct of creatures, for to do so would complicate its life and create obstacles to the practice of virtue. Nothing holds it back in its rapid pace, because it finds in God, not only the light by which to see the right path, but also the strength to pursue it. A simple soul leans on God at every moment, at every step of its life, seeking in Him its sole support and strength. In whatever difficulty it finds itself, it immediately looks to God for help, and with complete confidence, convinced that only in Him will it find the strength necessary to sustain its weakness, and that this strength will never be refused. It is not prevented, however, from seeking the help of wise, prudent persons, but it does so with detachment, and does not become troubled or disturbed when God permits it to be deprived of this help.

2. In everything, a simple soul considers but one end, God, and has but one intention, to serve God and to please Him. Therefore, it watches very carefully lest any secondary intention arising from self-love ever insinuate itself into its actions, as, for example, a desire of making a good appearance, of procuring the esteem of others, or of satisfying its own curiosity or love of ease. These secondary intentions are like the little foxes of which the Canticle of Canticles speaks; they stealthily penetrate into the blossoming vine of the soul and destroy the flowers and fruits of our good works. How many good actions begun out of love for God, lose at least half their value because, before they are completed, they are contaminated by some secondary intention not sufficiently suppressed or rectified! And how many others which also began well are transformed into evil by lack of rectitude in the intention. The simple soul has declared war on all such deviations and repeats with St. Francis de Sales : " My God, if I knew that even one fibre of my heart did not beat for You, I would tear it out at once and throw it far from me. " Purity of intention makes all its words and actions simple, clearly reflecting its thoughts and intentions. Its language is simple : " Yes, yes; no, no " (*Mt* 5,37); its conduct is simple : it does what it should without pretense or dissimulation. It fears nothing because it is seeking only God and His approval, it acts with the holy liberty of the children of God, without human respect, without preoccupying itself with the judgment and approval of creatures : " He that judgeth me is the Lord, " it says with St. Paul (*1 Cor* 4,4), and continues on its way, looking only at God. Thus, free from all cares and useless preoccupations, the simple soul goes straight to God, as rapidly and as directly as an

arrow. The one light, the one strength, the one end of its life is God, and because of this, its whole life attains a purity, a strength, and an enchanting unity—a pale reflection of the divine perfections.

COLLOQUY

" O Lord, would that I could go to You by the straight path of truth and simplicity! Grant to my soul that right intention, that simple gaze which desires to please You alone and pays no heed to the interpretations put on its actions by others.

" Teach me to see with the eyes of faith, to see You alone in my superiors, so that my relations with them will be marked by frankness, respect, esteem, confidence, obedience and docility. As for myself, grant that I may go right to the center of my nothingness and remain there without preoccupations about myself, eliminating all scruples and melancholy, all disturbance. Teach me to go straight to the inmost depths of my soul, where You abide.

" Grant that, when dealing with my neighbor, I may always follow the straight path of the love of pure benevolence, loving You in him and not seeking any natural satisfaction.

" In the midst of the vicissitudes and unexpected events of life, teach me to go directly where Your will calls me, without any curiosity or distraction. Teach me to follow the straight path of love, which knows no delay; of simplicity, which knows no deviation; of truth, which knows no deceit; of obedience, which knows no objections; of purity, which knows not the fascination of creatures; of recollection, which knows not distractions.

" This is the path which pleases You, O Jesus, the one You wished to call the straight path : ' *Ego sum via rectissima,* ' I am the straightest way (*Imit. III*, 56,1). This is the way which leads to the Father, for You have said, ' No man goes to the Father but by Me. ' This is the way by which the Holy Spirit guides us, for Wisdom leads the just man by straight ways! '

" Therefore, I beseech You, O God, with a fervent, trustful desire, to create in me a pure heart and to renew in me Your Spirit. May Your good Spirit guide me by the straight path! " (Sr. Carmela of the Holy Spirit, O.C.D.).

286

FORTITUDE

PRESENCE OF GOD - Teach me, O Lord, to act courageously, trusting in You.

MEDITATION

1. " The kingdom of heaven suffereth violence, and the violent bear it away " (*Mt* 11,12).   Neither good resolutions nor good desires suffice to make a saint.   These must be translated into action; but precisely in the accomplishment of this work, great difficulties are encountered, causing many to stop in discouragement or actually to turn back from the way they have begun.   These are weak souls who become frightened in the face of fatigue, effort, and struggle.   They lack the virtue of fortitude, or at least, are deficient in it.   This virtue enables us to face and bear whatever difficulty, whatever hardship or sacrifice we may encounter in the fulfillment of duty.   Difficulties and sacrifices will never be wanting for, although " wide is the gate and broad is the way that leadeth to destruction...narrow is the gate and strait is the way that leadeth to life " (*ibid.* 7,13.14).   Hence, it would be an illusion to pretend that the way to sanctity is easy and agreeable, as it would equally be an illusion to think that one can could persevere in it without constantly practicing the virtue of fortitude.   On the contrary, the greater the perfection to which a soul aspires, the stronger and more courageous it must be, because the difficulties it has to face will be greater.

When Jesus wished to praise the Precursor, He said, " What went you out into the desert to see?   A reed shaken with the wind? " (*ibid.* 11,7).   No, John the Baptist was not a weak man who could be shaken by the wind of difficulties; his was the strength of one who, to uphold the law of God, did not fear to incur his king's displeasure and to courageously face martyrdom.   Elsewhere, speaking of the victory over sin and the devil, Jesus praised the strong man : " When a strong man armed keepeth his court, those things are in peace which he possesseth " (*Lk* 11,21).   This is a picture of the soul that possesses the virtue of fortitude : it is well armed and cannot be frightened by any struggle, temptation, or other obstacle; rather, in the midst of all this, it remains in peaceful security because its strength comes from God Himself.

2. " His Majesty, " writes St. Teresa of Avila, " desires and loves courageous souls if they have no confidence in themselves but walk in humility " (T.J. *Life*, 13). Christian fortitude is neither rashness nor presumption because of one's own strength; it is based on God and the great gifts He has lavished on man. If man is nothing in himself, he is, however, great because of what God has done for him and given to him, and by reason of the exalted dignity God has conferred upon him. In fact, in the natural order, man has been appointed to rule the world; all other creatures have been subjected to him, and he should use them to know and love God better. In the supernatural order, he has been given the high vocation of being a child of God, called by Him to participate in His life and in His eternal beatitude. To attain this end, he has received grace, which is not only supernatural life and light, but also divine strength, strength infused into him precisely to cure the weakness of his nature, to strengthen his will, thereby making him capable of fulfilling all the duties inherent in his vocation. At Baptism, together with the other infused virtues, he has received the virtue of fortitude, a participation in the divine strength which has been placed in his soul like a seed, capable of developing into full perfection. Christian fortitude has its foundation, therefore, in the natural and supernatural gifts received from God, and in the exalted dignity to which man has been raised by God.

If we are weak, it is not due to the insufficiency of the divine gifts, but to our own insufficiency—because we have not properly developed the gifts of nature and grace which God has given us. And if we are strong, it is due, not to our own merits, but to the work God has done in us. The Christian is humble in his strength because he knows that it does not spring from him as its source, but from the gifts God has given him. He always lives in dependence upon God, both in the consideration of his nothingness and in that of his greatness, both in his humility and in his strength. Behold why the Lord, loving courageous souls, wants them, nevertheless, to be humble and always distrustful of self;

behold why the Holy Spirit says, " Let thy heart take courage, and wait thou for the Lord " (*Ps* 26,14).

COLLOQUY

" O God, You have seen the weakness of our human nature; You know how weak, frail and miserable it is; therefore, You, the sovereign Provider, who in all things have provided for all the needs of Your creatures, You, the perfect Repairer, who have given a remedy for all our ills, You gave us the rock and fortitude of will to strengthen the weakness of our flesh. This will is so strong that no demon or creature can conquer it if we do not will it, that is, if our free will, which is in our own hands, does not consent.

" O infinite Goodness, where does such great strength in Your creature's will come from? From You, sovereign, eternal Strength because it shares the strength of Your will. Hence, we can see that our will is strong to the degree in which it follows Yours, and weak to the degree in which it deviates from Yours because You created our will to the likeness of Your will, and therefore, being in Yours, it is strong.

" In our will, O eternal Father, You show the fortitude of Your will; for if You have given so much fortitude to a little member, what should we think Yours to be, O Creator and Ruler of all things?

" It seems to me that this free will which You have given us is fortified by the light of faith, for in this light it knows Your will, which wishes nothing but our sanctification. Then our will, fortified and nourished by our holy faith, gives life to our actions, which explains why neither good will nor lively faith can exist without works. Faith nourishes and maintains the fire of charity, because it reveals to our soul Your love and charity to us, and thus makes it strong in loving You " (St. Catherine of Siena).

287

THE TWO KINGDOMS

FOURTEENTH SUNDAY AFTER PENTECOST

PRESENCE OF GOD - Give strength to my weakness, O Lord, so that I may come to possess Your kingdom.

MEDITATION

1. We find the central thought of today's Mass synthesized in the Collect : " O Lord...because the frailty of man without Thee cannot but fall, keep us ever by Thy help from all things hurtful, and lead us to all things profitable to our salvation. " Behold the position of man in respect to the spiritual life : he is like a child who finds himself at a crossroad : he cannot go on alone, and he does not know which road leads to his home. Two roads open up before the Christian : one leads to the kingdom of the spirit, the kingdom of God; the other to the kingdom of the flesh, the kingdom of Mammon; which of the two will he choose? Evidently, he wishes to give the preference to the one leading to the kingdom of God, the calm, peaceful kingdom described by Jesus in today's Gospel (*Mt* 6,24-33). Unfortunately, however, the kingdom of Mammon also has attractions and tries to seduce his heart. The Epistle (*Gal* 5,16-24) tells us that we must struggle against these allurements. " For the flesh lusteth against the spirit, and the spirit against the flesh; for these are contrary one to another, so that you do not the things that you would. "

The struggle is hard sometimes, even in souls that are decidedly advanced in the things of God. Why? Because the path that leads to the kingdom of God is rough and tiring; it is often shrouded in dense darkness, rendering it impossible for the soul to discern the progress already made. Then the soul must proceed in the night, believing and hoping. Meanwhile, its gaze falls on the other road, which is broader and more comfortable, strewn with sensible goods which can be seen and touched, gathered and enjoyed immediately, by merely stretching out one's hand. The soul feels the temptation and realizes that alone it could not resist, but if it takes refuge in God, if it yields to the guidance of the Spirit, it will be saved, although not without sacrifice. " I say then, walk in the spirit, " continues St. Paul, " and you shall not fulfill the lusts of the flesh. . . . Now the works of the flesh are manifest. . ." and the Apostle gives a very unattractive list of them. It is always true : material goods present themselves like flowers, attractive, yes, but doomed to quickly vanish and decay; it is not worthwhile to stop to enjoy them. That is why " they that are Christ's have crucified their flesh, with the vices and concupiscences. "

2. The Gospel again puts us on our guard against the attractiveness of earthly goods. First it affirms that no man can simultaneously serve two masters, God and Mammon, any more than one can follow the two roads at the same time : the one leading to the kingdom of God and the other to worldly pleasure. Anyone giving himself to God must have the courage to give himself entirely, with no regrets, no backward glance—however fleeting—at the things of the world. The soul who, after choosing the path of perfection, does not go forth generously, with its whole heart, will never be contented. It will neither experience the joy of knowing that it belongs entirely to God, nor will it have the satisfaction of being able to follow all the attractions of the world; the first will be impeded by the soul's unfaithfulness, the second by the fear of God which it still possesses. Such a soul is unhappy, torn between the two and in continual struggle with itself. But what keeps it from seeking the kingdom of God with its whole heart? Jesus gives us the answer in today's Gospel : too much solicitude about material things, about ease and security in this present life. Even though we have the will to live according to the spirit, as long as we are pilgrims here below and in a mortal body, we shall always have to face the possibility of becoming engrossed in worldly cares : " What shall we eat? What shall we drink? Wherewith shall we be clothed? " Precisely to relieve us of such anxieties, Jesus presents to us the marvelous picture of divine Providence. " Behold the birds of the air, for they neither sow nor do they reap, nor gather into barns; and your heavenly Father feedeth them. Are not you of more value than they? " These are words that give us wings and fill us with a desire to cast aside all vain preoccupations

about earthly things and concentrate on seeking the kingdom of God. "Seek ye therefore first the kingdom of God, and His justice, and all these things shall be added unto you." Oh, if we only had greater faith in divine Providence, how much freer we would be to attend to the things of our soul! Although obliged to occupy ourselves with earthly affairs, we would not remain entrapped by them, but would know how to attend to them with complete liberty of spirit.

COLLOQUY

"O Lord, as the desires of the flesh are opposed to those of the spirit, and the desires of the spirit are opposed to those of the flesh, the struggle is a mortal one; I do not do the things I would like to do, for I would like to free myself from concupiscence, but this is impossible. Whether I will it or not, I cling to it; it flatters, tempts, importunes, always trying to raise up its head. It can be restrained but not suppressed.

"O Lord, my God, Your commandments are weapons. By the Holy Spirit, You have given me the possibility of keeping my members under control; therefore, all my hope is in You. Grant that I may do what You command, and then command what You will.

"I do not want to be a friend of this world, O Lord, for if I were, I should be Your enemy. I want to make a ladder of all created things, by which I may mount to You, for if I love creatures more than You, I shall not possess You. Of what benefit would an abundance of created things be to me, if I did not have You, the Creator of all things?

"Why do I work so much for the love of riches? The desire for gain imposes fatigue, dangers, and tribulations; and I, unhappy that I am, submit to them. I accept them in order to fill my coffers, and so I lose my tranquillity.

"But You, what do You command me to do, O my God? To love You. If I love gold, I try to seek it but am not able to find it; but You are always with those who seek for You. I desire honor, and I may not receive it; but can anyone love You and not reach You? All I have to do is love You, and love itself will bring You near me. Is there anything sweeter than such love? You, O Lord, are my love! I love

You with all the ardor of my heart, and I trample underfoot all earthly attractions, resolving to pass them by " (St. Augustine).

288

COURAGE

PRESENCE OF GOD - O Lord, make me strong and courageous in Your service.

MEDITATION

1. The more a soul loves God, the more courageous it will be in undertaking any work, no matter how laborious, for love of Him. Fear of fatigue, of suffering, and of danger, is the greatest enemy of fortitude; it paralyzes the soul and makes it recoil before duty. Courage, on the contrary, is invigorating; it enables us to confront anything in order to be faithful to God. Courage, therefore, incites us to embrace death itself, if necessary, rather than be unfaithful to duty. Martyrdom is the supreme act of Christian fortitude, an act which is not asked of all, yet one which it is well not to ignore as a possibility. Every Christian is, so to speak, a potential martyr, in the sense that the virtue of fortitude, infused into him at Baptism and Confirmation, makes him capable, if necessity requires it, of sacrificing even his life for the love of God. And if all Christians are not actually called upon to render to the Lord this supreme testimony of love, all should, nevertheless, live like courageous soldiers, accustoming themselves never to desert any duty, little or great, through fear of sacrifice.

It is true that the virtue of fortitude does not exempt us from the fear and alarm which invade our nature when faced with sacrifice, danger, or above all, the imminent danger of death. But fortitude, like all the other virtues, is exercised by the will; hence, it is possible to perform courageous acts in spite of our fear. In these cases, courage has a twofold function : it conquers fear and faces the difficult task. Such

was the supreme act of fortitude Jesus made in the Garden
of Olives when He accepted to drink the bitter chalice of His
Passion, in spite of the repugnance of His human nature.
It is by uniting ourselves to this act of our Savior that we
shall find strength to embrace all that is painful in our lives.

2. Grace can give courage even to those who are naturally
timid; but we must not expect grace to do this without our
cooperation.   The virtue of fortitude has been given to all
Christians, and in this sense is an infused virtue; however,
it remains for us to activate it by practice, and in this sense it
becomes an acquired virtue.   Furthermore, the same is true
of all the theological and moral virtues which are infused
into the soul with grace.   They are like capital which will
increase only if we invest it with good will to make it
productive.

We become humble by making acts of humility; likewise,
we become strong and courageous by performing courageous
acts.   It is not within our power to suppress the sensible
fear which we inherit with our fallen nature and which we
feel in spite of ourselves, but we can prevent it from taking
possession of our will and paralyzing our acts.   We must act
energetically, forcing ourselves in the name of God to do
what we should, and not stopping to argue with fear.   " Many
souls say, ' I have not the strength to accomplish such an act. '
But let them begin and put forth some effort! The good God
never refuses the initial grace which imparts courage to act.
After that, the heart is strengthened, and the soul goes on
from victory to victory " (T.C.J. *NV*).   This is true.   To
become courageous, we must make up our minds to act in
spite of our natural cowardice and fear.   This is particularly
necessary at times when, because of physical weakness or
because of the privation of the support of actual grace,
even the smallest difficulties seem like mountains and everything frightens us.   If we were to wait until we felt courageous,
we should never undertake anything.   " What does it matter
if we have no courage, " said the Saint of Lisieux to a novice,
" provided we act as though we were really brave? " *(C)*.
Courageous acts performed when we have no courage are
purer and more supernatural : they are purer, because they
afford no place for feelings of pride; they are more supernatural because they are based, not on the resources of
nature, but on those of grace.   On the contrary, acts of

courage which we perform according to our natural dispositions are often simply human acts; they can easily become
food for self-love.   Therefore, one who is brave by nature
must learn not to rely on his own strength but to depend on
God's grace, without which all human strength is mere
weakness.

COLLOQUY

"O Lord God of hosts, You said in Your Gospel, ' I am
not come to bring peace but the sword '; provide me then
with strength and weapons for the battle.   I burn with
desire to fight for Your glory, but I beseech You, strengthen
my courage.   Then with holy King David I can exclaim :
' You alone are my shield, O God; it is You who prepare
my hands for war. '

"O my Jesus, I will fight for You as long as I live,
and love will be my sword.   My weakness should never
discourage me; when in the morning I feel no courage or
strength for the practice of virtue, I must look upon this
state as a grace, for You teach me that it is the very moment
to put the axe to the root of the tree, counting only on Your
help.

"What merit would there be in fighting only when I feel
courage?   What does it matter even if I have none, provided
that I act as if I had?   O Jesus, make me understand that
if I feel too weak to pick up a bit of thread, and yet do it for
love of You, I shall gain much more merit than if I had
performed some nobler act in a moment of fervor.   So
instead of grieving, I ought to rejoice seeing that You,
by allowing me to feel my own weakness, give me an occasion
of saving a greater number of souls " (cf. T.C.J. *Prayer* –
L, 40 – *C*).

289

MAGNANIMITY

PRESENCE OF GOD - O Lord, give me a generous heart, capable of undertaking great things for You.

MEDITATION

1. Whoever aspires to sanctity should have a generous, magnanimous heart, which is not satisfied with doing little things for God, and tiny acts of virtue, but is eager to do great things and give great proofs of love. Just as there is no sanctity without heroic virtue, so it is impossible to attain to heroism without performing great acts of virtue.

Some think there is pride and delusion of the devil in fostering great desires, or in wanting to do great things for God. There would be, certainly, if in this we sought honor for ourselves, or praise from others, or if, in trying to do great things, we were to neglect the small details of our daily duties. The virtue of magnanimity, on the contrary, inclines the soul to do great things for God, but never to the detriment of obedience, humility, or the fulfillment of duty. Generous souls, precisely in this domain, will often meet with arduous, difficult things which call for much virtue, but which usually remain hidden from the eyes of others. In circumstances such as these we are often tempted to give up, under the pretext that it is not necessary to push virtue to such extremes; we excuse ourselves, saying that we are neither angels nor saints. St. Teresa of Jesus says, " We may not be; but what a good thing it is for us to reflect that we can be if we will only try, and if God gives us His hand!" (*Way*, 16). The Saint strongly insists that those who have dedicated themselves to the spiritual life should not nourish petty desires, but generous ones, nor should they fear to emulate the saints; she affirms with authority, " I have never seen any courageous person hanging back on this road, nor any soul that, under the guise of humility, acted like a coward, go as far in many years as the courageous soul can in a few " (*Life*, 13).

2. The contrary of magnanimity is pusillanimity, or faintheartedness, a defect which prevents souls from accomplishing great things through excessive fear of failure. Certainly, of our own volition, we should not rashly attempt to do what is beyond our strength. This too, is a defect, evincing imprudence and presumption which displease God. But when, in particular circumstances, and after sufficient examination, we see clearly that Our Lord wishes of us certain acts of virtue or some special work, we should not refuse, however difficult it may seem to be. Can God not give us the strength to do what He asks? Why do we doubt Him? A pusillanimous person who withdraws on such occasions, under the pretext that he does not feel capable of doing so much, may believe that he is humble; but in reality he is a coward, proud, and lacking trust in God. He is a coward because, overly preoccupied with himself, he fears failure, he is afraid to expose himself to the criticism of others, he dreads fatigue and sacrifice. He is proud because he relies more on his own erroneous judgment than on God and His grace. The humble soul, on the contrary, although conscious of his nothingness, trusts in God; convinced of his weakness, he is still more convinced that God can make use of him to accomplish great things. The truly humble person is never pusillanimous, but always magnanimous : he is not afraid to encourage himself to attempt great things for God, and this very attitude helps him greatly to make progress. " The soul may not have the strength to achieve these things at once, " says St. Teresa of Jesus, " but if it takes its flight it can make good progress, though like a little unfledged bird, it is apt to grow tired and stop " (*Life*, 13). It is natural to our weakness to stop, but if we have great confidence and great love, we shall soon know well how to spread our wings. The more confidence we have in God, the stronger we shall become with His divine strength. The more intense our love, the greater will become our capability of doing arduous things for God. " Perfect love, " says St. Thomas, " undertakes even the most difficult things " (III Sent. D. 29, q.1, a.8). Sustained by confidence and love, we shall be able to soar very high without fear of dangers or falls.

COLLOQUY

"O strong love of God! I really think that nothing seems impossible to one who loves! O happy soul that has obtained Your peace, O my God! It has become mistress over all the trials and perils of the world, and it fears none of them when there is question of serving You.

"It is a characteristic of the true servant of God, to whom His Majesty has given light to follow the true path, that when beset by these fears, his desire not to stop only increases. Teach me, then, O my God, always to go straight ahead, to fight with courage, and to parry the blows of the devil who is trying to frighten me.

"For what can a man accomplish, my Lord, who does not wholly abase himself for Your sake? How far, O, how far, how very far—I could repeat it a thousand times—am I from doing this! How many imperfections do I find in myself! How feebly do I serve You! Sometimes I could really wish I were devoid of sense, for then I should not understand how much evil is in me. May He who is able to do so, grant me succor! We must have great confidence for it is most important that we should not cramp our good desires but should believe that, with God's help, if we make continual efforts to do so, we shall attain, though perhaps not at once, to that which many saints have reached through His favor.

"How true it is, O Lord, that everything is possible in You; I realize too, that of myself I can do nothing. Therefore, I beseech You with St. Augustine : ' Give me, Lord, what You command me and then command what You will ' " (T.J. *Con*, 3 – *Way*, 21 – *Life*, 39 – 13).

290

GENEROSITY

PRESENCE OF GOD - Fill my heart with Your spirit of generosity, O Lord, so that I may know how to give myself wholly to Your service.

MEDITATION

1. Generosity is very similar to magnanimity but has a wider scope, including not only great things, but anything which concerns the service of God. It urges the soul to do all with the greatest devotion. Generosity is the virtue which teaches us to spend ourselves, without counting the cost, without ever saying, " It is enough "; it teaches us to give ourselves completely, and to work with the maximum of love, not only in great things but also in little ones, even the least. Only when we are not hampered by the bonds of selfishness can we be really generous, that is, capable of giving ourself wholly to the service of our ideal, to the accomplishment of our mission, without thinking of self, without letting ourself be detained by personal preoccupations. If we really understood that our vocation comes from God, and that He has prepared for us all the graces we need to correspond with it most perfectly, we should not allow ourselves to be disheartened by the sacrifices it requires. Selfishness, preoccupation with self, and discouragement are all enemies of generosity; they are " earth and lead " which weigh down our spiritual life, making it more fatiguing and keeping us from soaring to the heights. Why should we reduce ourselves to walking at " a hen's pace " (T.J. *Life*, 13) when God has made us capable of flying like the eagle? St. Teresa laughs somewhat mischievously at those who are afraid of doing too much for God, and under pretext of prudence, measure their acts of virtue with a yardstick : " You need never fear that they will kill themselves; they are eminently reasonable folk! Their love is not yet ardent enough to overwhelm their reason. How I wish ours would make us dissatisfied with this habit of always serving God at a snail's pace! As long as we do that we shall never get to the

end of the road.   Do you think that if we could get from one
country to another in a week, it would be advisable to take a
year over it? " (*Int C III*, 2).   The quickest way to reach
our goal is generosity, which is the fruit of love and at the
same time the generator of love.

2. To become generous, we must first learn to forget
ourselves, our own interests, our convenience, our own
rights, making no account of weariness or pain.   We must
have but one thought : to give ourselves entirely to God
and to souls.   " God's good pleasure, the welfare of others,
not my own; for me the most unpleasant things, in order to
please God " (Bl. Marie Thérèse Soubiran).   Such is the
program of the generous soul.   It desires nothing but to
spend life, strength, and talents in serving God, knowing
that it is in the total gift of self that the greatest love
consists.   " To love is to give all and to give oneself " (T.C.J.
Poems).

To become generous, we must learn to do with our
whole heart, not only what is a duty, but also what, though
not obligatory, will give more glory to God.   St. Teresa
gives us a golden rule for this : the " first stone " of our
spiritual edifice must be the decision to " strive after the
greatest possible perfection " (*Way*, 5).   The proposal may
seem too arduous, but the Saint is not talking at random.
Even if at first the soul does not succeed in discerning or in
doing always what is most perfect, yet this resolution, if it is
sincere and accompanied by humility and trust in the help
of grace, will be a great stimulus to desire always to do
better, always to do a little more; it will prevent us from
settling down in a tranquil mediocrity.   It is very important
for those who would be intimate with God to cultivate
these dispositions; in this way, little by little, we will be able
to make the complete gift of ourself, the gift God awaits
before giving Himself completely.   " God does not give
Himself wholly until He sees that we are giving ourselves
wholly to Him " (*ibid.*, 28).   God wants to give Himself to
us in this life, but He proportions His gift to ours; it will
depend upon our generosity in giving ourselves to Him.

COLLOQUY

" O Lord, how little we do for You! Indeed we cannot consider as signs of great virtue and mortification, these little acts which are of no weight or bulk, like grains of salt which a bird might carry in its beak. Sometimes we attribute importance to trifling things we do for You which, however numerous they may be, cannot be considered of much value. I am like that myself and I forget Your favors at every moment. I do not say that in Your great mercy, You do not value these little acts of virtue; but I have no wish to set store by them myself, or even to notice when I do them, since they are nothing.

" Forgive me, then, O Lord, and blame me not if I try to take comfort from anything I do, since I am of no real service to You : if I served You in great matters, I would set no store by these nothings. Blessed are they who serve You by great deeds! If merely envying them and desiring to imitate them counted in my favor, I should not be wanting in pleasing You! But I am of no worth, my Lord; do You put value into what I do, since You have such love for me.

" O my God, grant that I may no longer be content with serving You in a small way, but let me do so to the greatest extent of my powers. Help me to make You a complete gift of my soul, emptying it of everything, so that You may take out and put in just what You like, as You would with something of Your own. You refuse to force our will, You take what we give You, but You do not give Yourself wholly until we give ourselves wholly to You. You like everything to be done in order, and You do not work within a soul unless it is wholly Yours, and keeps nothing back " (T.J. *Life*, 39 – 20 – *Way*, 28).

" O most loving Word of God, teach me to be generous, to serve You as You deserve : to give and not to count the cost, to fight and not to heed the wounds, to toil and not to seek for rest, to labor and not to ask for any other reward save that of knowing that I do Your holy will " (St. Ignatius).

291

FORTITUDE AND PATIENCE

PRESENCE OF GOD - Teach me, O Lord, to bear my sufferings with fortitude and patience.

MEDITATION

1. Although courage is needed to face or to undertake hard tasks, it is even more necessary in order to persevere in them, above all when they are unpleasant or of long duration, and it is impossible to avoid or change them. In this sense, St. Thomas teaches that the principal act of fortitude is not to attack but to stand firm in the midst of dangers, and to endure struggles, opposition, privations, and persecutions with a virile spirit.

In the spiritual life we meet not only difficulties which can be surmounted and overcome once and for all by a strong act of courage, but we encounter—and this much more frequently—difficult, painful situations from which it is impossible to escape, and which willingly or unwillingly we must face. There are physical ailments which exhaust us, and prevent us from extending our activity as we would wish; there are moral sufferings caused by our own temperamental deficiencies or by contact with persons who are opposed to us or do not understand us; or again, there is the pain of seeing our loved ones suffer without our being able to relieve them; there is the experience of separation from our friends, and loneliness of heart. There are also spiritual troubles due to aridity, interior darkness, weariness of mind, temptations, and scruples. In addition to these, there are all the problems, fatigue, and difficulties inherent in our everyday duties. We know that all these things are planned by God for our sanctification and our good; nevertheless, that does not prevent us from feeling the weight of them; suffering is never pleasant, and though we will to accept all for the love of God, we are sometimes tempted to react, to give up, to shake off the yoke, or we are weighed down by sadness and discouragement. What remedy is there? There is the one which Jesus suggested to the Apostles after telling them of the persecutions they would have to endure : " *In patientia vestra possidebitis animas vestras,* " in your patience you shall possess your souls (*Lk* 21,19). Patience is the virtue which permits us to live in a state of suffering, hardship and privation without losing our serenity. It enables us to remain firm amid storms, contradictions, and dangers, without becoming irritated or despondent, without being deterred by them.

2. Christian patience is not the forced resignation of the fatalist or the philosopher who submits to suffering because he cannot escape it, nor is it the attitude of one who submits because he is not able to react through lack of strength and resources; it is the voluntary acceptance of suffering in view of God and eternal happiness, an acceptance sustained by the knowledge that suffering is absolutely necessary to purify us from sin, to atone for our faults, and to prepare us to meet God. Christian patience incites us to accept suffering serenely, and gradually to esteem and love it, not because we see it as an end in life, but rather as a necessary means for attaining the end, which is love of God and union with Him. If Jesus willed to live a life of martyrdom and to die on the Cross in order to kindle the fire of charity in us and restore us to friendship with God, how can we expect to attain the plenitude of love and intimacy with God if we do not follow in His footsteps? " Christ, therefore, having suffered in the flesh, be you also armed with the same thought, " cries St. Peter (1 *Pt* 4,1). Let us embrace suffering, then, with the same sentiments which Jesus had : to do the heavenly Father's will, to atone for sin, and to give Him proof of our love.

Christian patience is not merely a passive attitude in the face of suffering; it is also active and voluntary. The latter is the more important because it is this which makes suffering meritorious. A patient man is passive because he wills to be passive, because he uses his free will to submit to all the sufferings which he meets on his way, because he voluntarily bows his shoulders under the yoke of suffering, just as Jesus bowed His under the weight of the Cross, because He willed to do so, " *quia ipse voluit* " (*Is* 53,7). A Christian is not a forced Cyrenean, but a willing one, not in the sense that he goes spontaneously in search of suffering — this would not be feasible for all, and sometimes would be imprudent —

but in the more modest sense whereby he accepts willingly all the suffering which he encounters on his way, recognizing in this the Cross offered him by God for his sanctification.

COLLOQUY

" O Jesus, the duty of souls admitted to Your intimacy is to suffer with You, to raise the Cross on high, not to allow it to leave their hands, whatever the perils in which they find themselves, and not to let themselves be found wanting in suffering.

" Now that You have shown me what a signal blessing it is to suffer trials and persecutions for Your sake, I find I cannot cease from desiring trials; for those who follow You must take the way which You took, unless they want to be lost. Blessed are their labors which, even here in this life, have such abundant recompense!

" O Jesus, what greater proof of Your love could You give me than to choose for me all that You willed for Yourself? To die or to suffer : this is what I should desire " (T.J. *Way*, 18 – *Life*, 33 – 11).

" O Christ crucified, You are sufficient for me; with You I wish to suffer and to take my rest! Grant that I may be crucified with You inwardly and outwardly, and may live in this life in the fullness and satisfaction of my soul, possessing it in patience.

" Teach me to love trials and repute them of small account to attain Your favor, O Lord, who hesitated not to die for me. O my Beloved, all that is rough and toilsome I desire for myself, and all that is sweet and delectable I desire for You " (J.C. *SM II*, 13,8,15,52).

292

THE PRACTICE OF PATIENCE

PRESENCE OF GOD - O Lord, give me greater patience that I may be able to endure more for Your love.

MEDITATION

1. Patience is a virtue of primary importance and daily necessity. As we need bread to live, so every day, even every moment, we need patience, because every day and every moment brings with it its own trial. We become patient by making acts of patience, that is, by accustoming ourselves to accept peacefully all that contradicts us and makes us suffer. If, however, instead of accepting annoyances, we use every means possible to avoid them, we shall never acquire patience. For example, we may at our work come in contact with someone who clashes with us, or we may be given a difficult or disagreeable task; if under these or similar circumstances we do our utmost to free ourselves as soon as possible, asking for a change, we are depriving ourselves of a precious opportunity prepared for us by God Himself to make us practice the virtue of patience. In certain cases it is lawful and even a duty to represent our problems to our superiors and to ask humbly for a solution, but we should never insist on obtaining one at all costs. On the contrary, we should think that divine Providence has arranged these circumstances to help us acquire the patience we do not yet possess. St. Philip Neri once complained to Our Lord because he had to deal with an extremely insulting, disagreeable person. Our Lord replied to him interiorly, " Philip, you have asked for patience. Here is the means of acquiring it. "

God will surely give us the virtue we ask of Him, but only on condition that we make use of the means He gives us, and apply ourselves to practice that virtue with the help of His grace. Whoever wishes to become a saint will not be anxious to avoid opportunities for practicing patience, but will welcome them, recognizing in them the means offered by God for his sanctification. And how can a mere creature dare wish to make any change in what has been ordered " in measure, and number, and weight " (*Wis* 11,21) by God's infinite wisdom?

2. God can draw good out of evil; therefore, He can, and in fact does, use our faults and even our sins and the sins of others, to make us practice patience : patience with ourselves, seeing ourselves so frail, so imperfect, so prone to fall, yet humbly recognizing our faults and bearing their consequences peacefully; patience with others, being indulgent toward their frailties, compassionating the weaknesses of each one, and accepting without irritation the discomfort and sufferings caused by their faults. For example, when anyone disturbs or provokes us, we must not stop to consider his manner of behaving, for that would rouse our indignation, making it more difficult to practice patience. Instead, we should turn our gaze away from the creature to fix it upon God who permits this contradiction to make us advance in virtue. We should also avoid complaining about our sufferings to others, or even to ourselves. Complaints always make the heart bitter, rendering it ill-disposed to accept trials calmly. " To suffer and be silent for You, my God " (T.M.) is the motto of the patient soul who wishes to conform its conduct to that of Jesus in His Passion : " He was offered...and He opened not His mouth " (*Is* 53,7). If we feel the need of a little help in bearing a trial, let us speak of it only to those who will encourage us to suffer for the love of God, and not to those who will give us merely human consolation and sympathy, thereby nourishing our resentment toward those who make us suffer.

All the saints were eager for the occasions of suffering which we so eagerly avoid. Let us consider St. Jane Frances de Chantal who chose to live for many years in her father-in-law's house, amidst the disrespect and calumnies of a servant who also attempted to endanger her children's welfare. Let us think of St. John of the Cross who being free to choose the monastery in which he would spend his last days, gave the preference to one whose superior was hostile to him. These are examples of the heroism of the saints, to be sure — but heroism from which no soul of good will is excluded and to which everyone is called by God, heroism for which we too, if we really wish to be generous, must prepare ourselves by lovingly accepting everything which causes us suffering.

COLLOQUY

" O Lord, we want to serve and please You, yes, but we do not want to suffer anything. Yet we must be much more pleasing to You when after Your example and out of love for You, we endure suffering in Your service. Suffering is so noble and precious, O eternal Word, that when You were in the bosom of the Father, superabounding in all the riches and delights of Paradise but unadorned with the robe of suffering, You came to earth in order to clothe Yourself with it. You are God and cannot be deceived; since You have chosen stark suffering, I too desire it for love of You. I beseech You, therefore, Lord, to permit me to experience this suffering which is unmixed with any consolation, and by the confidence I have in Your goodness, I trust that You will grant me this grace before I die.

" But in order to obtain profit from tribulations, teach me to accept them in total conformity to Your will; otherwise, they will be a great and unbearable burden. When, however, a soul abandons itself entirely in the arms of Your will, then it finds strength in the midst of its sorrows, and even if You leave it in darkness for a time, very quickly will its sadness be changed into joy, so that, for no delight in the world would it exchange this suffering.

" O blessed, happy, and glorious is he who suffers for love of You, O eternal Word, for—shall I dare to say it?—as long as we are here below, it is a greater thing to suffer for You than to possess You, because possessing You, we can still lose You, but if we suffer for love of You, it will admit us to eternal life where we can never lose You " (St. Mary Magdalen dei Pazzi).

293

PERSEVERANCE

PRESENCE OF GOD - Grant, O Lord, that by Your grace I may persevere unto the end.

MEDITATION

1. To become a saint, it is not enough to be courageous and patient and to practice the other virtues for a few days or a few months, or even for a few years. We must *persevere* in these dispositions to the end of our life, never yielding to fatigue, discouragement, or laxity. This is the crucial point for, as St. Thomas says, " to apply oneself for a long time to a difficult task—and virtue is almost always difficult— constitutes a special difficulty " (II^a II^ae, q.137, a.1, co.); and it is only by overcoming this difficulty that we shall be able to reach perfection. We are not angels, we are human beings. The angel, a pure spirit, is stable by nature; if he makes a resolution, he holds to it; but this is not the case with us. We, being composed of spirit and matter, must suffer the consequences of the instability and fluctuations of the latter. As stability is characteristic of spirit, so insta- bility is characteristic of matter; hence it becomes so difficult for us to be perfectly constant in the good. Although we have formed good resolutions in our mind, we always feel handicapped by the weakness of the sensible part of our nature which rebels against the weariness of sustained effort, and seeks to free itself from it, or at least to reduce it to a minimum. Our bodies are subject to fatigue; our minds are disturbed by emotions which are always fluctuating. That which at one moment fills us with enthusiasm may, at the next, become distasteful and annoying to such a point that we think we can no longer endure it. This is our state while on earth and no one can escape it. However, God calls us all to sanctity, and since sanctity requires a continual practice of virtue, He, who never asks the impossible, has provided a remedy for the instability of our nature by giving us the virtue of perseverance, the special object of which is the sustaining of our efforts. Though fickle by nature, we can by the help of grace become steadfast.

2. There are two types of perseverance. The first is so perfect that it never wavers, it is always inflexible, maintained even in the most difficult and unexpected circumstances. This is the perseverance of heroic virtue, of souls who have reached the state of transforming union, who habitually live under the influence of the Holy Spirit. It is the beautiful goal to which we can and should aspire, though we cannot attain to it by the practice of virtue alone; only the continual intervention of the gifts of the Holy Spirit can completely overcome the instability of our nature.

The second type is the perseverance practiced by fervent or even perfect souls who do not as yet enjoy the habitual motions of the Holy Spirit, and whose perseverance, therefore, shows some fluctuations, more or less slight, according to the degree of perfection of the soul. In this case perseverance does not consist in remaining perfectly stable in good, but rather in constantly beginning again as soon as any failure is recognized. Sometimes just a momentary inattention, an unexpected happening, a little weariness or emotion, is enough to make us commit some fault that we had sincerely resolved to avoid at any cost, and here we have failed again! This, however, is no reason for being discouraged or sad; rather it is a motive for humbling ourselves, for recognizing our weakness and begging more insistently for God's help to rise at once and begin again. Because our human nature is so unstable, our perseverance will usually consist in continually beginning again. This is the perseverance to which we should all attain, because it depends on our good will, in the sense that God has infused this virtue in our soul, giving us at every moment sufficient grace to practice it. It is not in our power to free ourselves from this instability of our nature, and therefore we cannot avoid every slackening in virtue, every negligence, weakness, or fault; but it is within our power to correct ourselves as soon as we perceive that we have failed. This is the kind of perseverance that God demands of us, and when we practice it faithfully, and are always prompt in rising after each fall, He will crown our efforts by granting us the supreme grace of final perseverance.

COLLOQUY

" O Lord, I shall certainly be saved if I persevere to the end, but my perseverance must be virtuous if it is to merit salvation; from You comes the virtue which will save me; it is You who make me persevere until I attain salvation.

" At present I am still engaged in battle : the struggle from without against false virtue, the struggle from within against my concupiscence. When I think of the number of little faults which I commit every day, even if only in thought and word, I realize that their number is very great, and that this great number of little failings makes an immense heap. O unhappy that I am! Who will deliver me from the body of this death? You will deliver me, O God, by Your grace, through the merits of Jesus Christ, Your Son and Our Lord. In the toil of this battle, then, I shall look to Your grace and, in the heat and burning thirst which I feel, I will beg for Your life-giving shade.

" Help me, O Lord Jesus, by saying to me : ' Do not tire of the narrow way : I walked it before you, I am the way itself; I am the guide, and I carry those whom I lead and bring them to Myself at the last ' " (St. Augustine).

" O eternal God, grant me the virtue of perseverance; without it, no one can please You nor be acceptable to You. This virtue brings to the soul an abundance of charity and the fruit of every effort. Oh! how happy I should be, Lord, if You would give me this virtue, because even here on earth it will make me enjoy a pledge of eternal life. But Your light reveals to me that I cannot attain it unless I suffer much, because this life cannot be lived without suffering. He who would escape suffering would deprive himself of holy perseverance " (St. Catherine of Siena).

294

JESUS OUR LIFE

FIFTEENTH SUNDAY AFTER PENTECOST

PRESENCE OF GOD - O Jesus, life of my soul, make me rise each day to a new life of charity and fervor.

MEDITATION

1. In the Mass of today there is a dominant thought, so often repeated in the liturgy and so dear to our hearts : Jesus is our life. Whatever good there is in us is the fruit of His grace, by which we remain steadfast in good *(Collect)* and live in the Spirit *(Ep)*; by His grace we rise from sin *(Gosp)*, and eating His flesh, we nourish His life within us *(Communion)*. Without Jesus we would abide in death; without Him we could never live the glorious life of the Spirit described by St. Paul in today's Epistle *(Gal* 5,25.26 – 6,1-10).

It would be well to glean a few thoughts from this. " Let us not be made desirous of vainglory, provoking one another. For if any man think himself to be something, whereas he is nothing, he deceiveth himself. " True humility is presented here as the basis of fraternal charity; anyone who is proud carries about with him a hotbed of discord for, preferring himself to others, he will often be provocative, envious, haughty, and disdainful of those whom he considers his inferiors.

" If a man be overtaken in any fault, you, who are spiritual, instruct such a one in the spirit of meekness. " One who wishes to scale the heights must never be critical of him whose way is not so high, nor be scandalized at the faults of another. If duty requires us to admonish anyone, we should do so with sweetness and kindness. This sweetness is another fruit of humility, because when we correct others, we should always take heed to ourselves : " lest thou also be tempted. "

" And in doing good, let us not fail; for in due time we shall reap, not failing. " We must not allow ourselves to be discouraged by difficulties in the spiritual life, even when we

do not succeed in overcoming them. God does not ask us to
succeed but to continually renew our efforts, although the
results may not be apparent. " In due time, " that is,
when God wills and in the way that pleases Him, we shall
reap the fruit, provided we " fail not. "

2. The thought that Jesus is *our Life* shines forth even
more in the Gospel (*Lk* 7,11-16). The Master meets the sad
funeral procession of a young man. His mother is walking
beside the bier, weeping. " And the Lord, seeing her, had
compassion on her, and said to her : Weep not. And He
came near and touched the bier.... And He said : Young
man, I say to thee, arise.... And He gave him to his
mother. " Jesus is our Savior who sympathizes with us in
our trials and uses His divine omnipotence to alleviate them.
Today we see Him work a miracle in order to console a
widowed mother; He restores her dead son to life. This
was an expression of the delicacy of His love for us; but how
many others, less visible perhaps but no less full of love and
life, have surged from His heart! " The Gospel speaks of
three who were dead and who were visibly restored to life by
Our Lord, " St. Augustine tells us, " but He has restored
thousands invisibly. " When writing these words, the Saint
must have recalled with ineffable gratitude the much greater
miracle Jesus had wrought for him, making him rise from the
death of sin.

St. Augustine and many other saints have been restored
to life. If the saints who led lives of innocence attract us so
much, those who were brought back from sin have still
greater power to encourage us in our struggles. It may be a
laborious task for us to overcome pride, sensuality, and all
the other passions, but it was no easier for them. They
too knew our temptations, struggles and falls; if they overcame
them, why cannot we do the same?

Thanks be to God, it is not always a question of having
to rise from a life of serious sin, but there is always occasion
for a resurrection from our little daily infidelities; if they are
not corrected, our fervor in the spiritual life will gradually
weaken. In this regard, we need to rise every day, indeed
every hour; yet so many times we lack the strength for it.
But if we beseech Jesus, *our Life*, He will touch us with His
grace as He once touched the bier of the young man of
Naim; He will give us fresh vigor and will put us back again,

full of courage, on the way to perfection. The resurrection of the young man was implored by his mother's tears; let ours be implored every day by the tears of our hearts, by our compunction, humility, and trust.

COLLOQUY

" O Lord, my God, I had reached the gates of death, but You placed Yourself between them and me, so that I could not pass through them. O my Savior, You have often rescued me from bodily death when I was seriously ill or exposed to danger. You knew, Lord, that if death had surprised me then, my soul would have been cast into hell and I should have been damned forever. Your mercy and Your grace prevented me, and saved both my body and soul from death. You have done all this and much more for me, O Lord, my God!

" Now, O light of my soul, my God, life by which I live, I give You thanks : to You do I offer my thanks, though I am poor and worthless and unworthy to receive Your benefits.

" I was once among the sinners whom You saved. To give others an example of Your most benign mercy, I shall declare Your great favors. You saved me from the deepest pit of hell once, twice, thrice, a hundred times, a thousand times. I was ever tending toward hell, and always You drew me back when, if You had so willed, You could have justly damned me a thousand times; You did not will to do so, because You love souls and dissimulate the sins of men so that they may do penance, O Lord, most merciful in all Your ways.

" Now I see and by Your light I know all this, O Lord my God, and my soul faints away when it considers the greatness of Your mercy. My whole life, which was perishing in my misery, has been revived by Your mercy. I was wholly dead and You restored me wholly to life. May all that is in me be Yours then, henceforth, for I give myself wholly to You! " (St. Augustine).

295

PERSEVERANCE AND CONFIDENCE

PRESENCE OF GOD - O Lord, increase my confidence in Your help and grant that in this confidence, I may always find courage to begin again.

MEDITATION

1. What most distresses souls of good will who are seriously trying to live a spiritual life, is to find themselves falling so many times, despite their continual and sincere resolutions. When they begin a program of asceticism, they are usually very brave and have no doubts concerning their success; but being still inexperienced, and not having yet faced the demands of more advanced virtue, they know nothing of the struggles that await them on this way. And herein lies the danger : meeting with new difficulties, they fall; they rise and fall again; again they rise, and shortly after, find themselves prostrate once more until they are, at a certain point, attacked by that most dangerous temptation : to give up the undertaking which henceforth seems impossible. How many souls have fervently begun the ascent of the mount of perfection, but discouraged by their continual falls, have stopped halfway up or even turned back, because they lacked the courage to begin anew every day and every moment.

Humility is needed for the exercise of courage; we must be convinced that in spite of our lofty aspirations, we are fallible men like all the rest. Sacred Scripture affirms that the " just man shall fall seven times and shall rise again " (*Prv* 24,16); how, then, can we, who are not just, pretend never to fall?

The real evil is not so much in falling as in failing to rise. The distinguishing mark of fervent souls, and even of saints, is less their lack of faults, than their promptness in rising after each fall. The annoyance felt by so many souls when they see themselves continually falling, is not the fruit of humility but of pride. They are not yet convinced of their own misery and are astonished to experience it so constantly. They rely too much on themselves, and God, who wishes to lead them to the full realization of their nothingness, permits them to fall again and again. In the plan of divine Providence these falls are for the definite purpose of convincing us that we are miserable creatures. If we wish to adhere to the divine plan, we have but one thing to do : to humble ourselves. But if, on the contrary, we become discouraged, and give up what we have begun, we shall be going farther away from our goal, to our very great loss.

2. Some souls justify their discouragement saying that they cannot bear to offend God. That is well, for the first condition required for sanctity is a hatred for sin and a firm determination to avoid even the slightest sin, at the cost of any sacrifice. However, we must make a distinction : if we cultivate the sincere disposition not to tolerate in ourselves the slightest offense against God, it signifies our intention to make no truce with the faults and failings which, in spite of our good will, escape us. However, if we do fall, notwithstanding all our efforts, this disposition does not authorize us to become so discouraged that we are unable to rise. It is just because we do not wish to tolerate in ourselves anything displeasing to God that we should never surrender in the struggle, but begin again vigorously, in order to avoid future falls. On this field, he who surrenders is already conquered. In fact, if even when we are fighting without respite, we are liable to fall, what will happen if we surrender our arms? It will always be better to fight maimed and wounded, than not to fight at all.

But to have the courage to persevere in the struggle, especially when we fall repeatedly—either as a result of our imperfection and frailty, or because God permits it in order to humble us more—we must join to humility an immense confidence in the divine help. Having experienced our own misery we know that we cannot rise relying on our own strength, but there still remains to us a much more powerful resource : trust in the help of God. We shall find the strength to keep beginning again, precisely in trust. God alone can give us this strength, and He will give it in the measure of our confidence : the more trust we have in Him, the stronger we shall be. The more convinced we are that God is calling us to sanctity, and that our personal resources are insufficient for attaining it, so much the more should we be convinced that God will furnish us with the help needed to answer His call.   There is nothing illogical in God : if He asks something from us, He cannot refuse us the help needed to give it to Him.   Not finding this strength in ourselves, we shall surely find it in Him, in His omnipotent help.

" He that shall persevere unto the end, he shall be saved " (*Mt* 10,22), said Jesus.   He who will persevere unto the end is not he who will never fall, but he who after every fall will humble himself and rise again, relying on the infinite strength of God.

COLLOQUY

" O Jesus, You see I am a very little soul and can offer You only very little things : I frequently miss the opportunity of welcoming these small sacrifices which bring so much peace; but I am not discouraged—I bear the loss of a little peace and I try to be more watchful in the future.   You are so good to me that it is impossible for me to fear You.

" If it is Your will that throughout my whole life I should feel a repugnance to suffering and humiliation; if You permit all the flowers of my desires and good will to fall to the ground without producing any fruit, I shall not be disturbed.   I am sure that if I persevere in my good efforts, in the twinkling of an eye, at the moment of death, You will cause rich fruits to ripen on the tree of my soul " (cf. T.C.J. *St*, 11 – C).

" O God, I am very weak in ability, poor in strength, and full of poverty, but if Your eye will look upon me, I shall be lifted up from my low estate, my head shall be exalted, and many will glorify You.

" Grant that I may be steadfast in Your covenant, and be conversant therein, and grow old in the work of Your commandments.   I will trust in You and persevere in what I am doing, for it is easy for You to suddenly make the poor man rich.   Your blessing will be my reward, and in a swift hour my efforts will bear fruit " (cf. *Sir* 11,12-24).

296

TEMPERANCE

PRESENCE OF GOD - Teach me, O Lord, to mortify my flesh, in order
that I may live fully the life of the spirit.

MEDITATION

1. We may fail in our duty either because of the hardships
and sacrifices we encounter, or because of the allurements
of pleasure. Our help in the first case is the virtue of fortitude;
in the second, the virtue of temperance. Temperance is the
virtue which moderates in us the inordinate desire for sensible
pleasure, keeping it within the limits assigned by reason
and faith. Sin has produced in us the great discord by which
the inferior part tends to rebel against the superior, and
craves that which is contrary to the spirit. We shall never be
able to defend ourselves against the attractions of pleasure
without the help of this virtue, which has been infused
by God into our souls for the express purpose of enabling
us to regulate our disordered tendency to pleasure. As
fortitude, with its accompanying virtues of magnanimity,
patience and perseverance, is a sustaining power for our
weakness, in like manner, temperance, with the virtues
which spring from it—sobriety, chastity, continence,
modesty—controls our concupiscence. Nevertheless,
although this virtue is a check, it has not only a negative task,
to temper, restrain, and moderate the disordered love of
pleasure, but it has also a positive one : that of regulating
our passions and permitting us to use our senses in perfect
harmony with the requirements of the spirit, in such a way
that they do not disturb our spiritual life. In this way
temperance, together with grace and the other virtues, heals
and elevates our nature by reestablishing in us the harmony
which was destroyed by sin. However, this cannot be realized
without our cooperation which, in regard to temperance,
consists above all in the mortification of our passions and
senses. St. Paul says : " If you live according to the flesh you
shall die; but if by the spirit you mortify the deeds of the
flesh, you shall live " (Rom 8,13). The virtue of temperance

has been infused into us to " mortify the deeds of the flesh ";
this mortification is not an end in itself, but it is an indispensable condition for the life of the spirit.

2. The beauty of the virtue of temperance lies in the
fact that it helps us to turn back on the down-hill path
taken by our first parents in consequence of their sin.   In
order to reestablish perfect harmony between spirit and
matter, we have to ascend an arduous path.   Just as a hor-
seman, before setting out on a race, bridles his spirited horse,
so we, to take this road, must impose on our flesh the strong
bridle of mortification, so as to bring under control all its
appetites and movements.

One easily understands how important mortification is
in the realm of chastity : it is an illusion to think we can live
chastely without bodily mortification, for neither the virtue
nor the vow of chastity changes our nature, or makes us
insensible to the allurements of the senses, the world, and the
devil.   The need of mortification of the sense of taste, however,
is less understood.   In this matter, even souls striving for
perfection are quite free in admitting sensible pleasure,
considering it a wholly innocent pleasure and of no consequence for the spiritual life.   This is not so, since everything
inordinate—even to the slightest degree—in the life of the
senses eventually impairs, more or less, the life of the spirit
and weakens it.   In fact, there is disorder in the use of food
and drink every time we allow the amount we use to be
determined in any way by the pleasure we find in it, taking
more than is necessary if we like it, or if we do not like it,
showing displeasure or refusing to take it.   This too is being
a slave to our senses, and allowing ourselves to be dominated
by sensible pleasure; it is to open a door to the rebellion of the
senses against the spirit.   St. Paul warns us : " Be not
deceived...for what things a man shall sow, those also
shall he reap.   For he that soweth in his flesh, of the flesh also
shall reap corruption.   But he that soweth in the spirit,
of the spirit shall reap life everlasting " (*Gal* 6, 7.8).   He who
in this life sows sensible pleasures of any kind whatsoever,
sows corruption, because all that is of the senses is destined to
perish and leads us astray.   Then how can a soul that aspires
to a deeply spiritual life, subject itself, even though it be in a
slight matter, to sense satisfactions?   " Weary not yourself, "
says St. John of the Cross, " for you shall not enter into

spiritual delight and sweetness if you give not yourself to
mortification of all this that you desire " (*SM I*, 38)

COLLOQUY

"I am not astonished, O Lord, at human defection,
for You have wounded my heart with Your perfect charity,
and have protected it with the guard of purity.   Oh! if
only blind mortals would taste the delights and sweetness of
Your holy love!   I think they would immediately hate the
pleasures of the senses and would be filled with loathing
and disgust for them.   Thirsty and anxious, they would
hasten to drink from the fountain of Your sweetness.   Why
do they not run in the odor of Your perfumes?

" I understand, eternal Truth.   If they meditated and
considered attentively, they would engrave in their memory
the immense favors You bestow upon them daily, they would
easily allow themselves to be drawn by the ineffable sweetness
of Your love, and they would hasten with eagerness and
longing to take delight in the fragrance of Your sweetness! "
(St. Catherine of Siena).

" I have but one desire, Lord : to seek You!   And while
I seek You, I will never stop to pluck the flowers that I may
find on my way; that is, I will not pause to enjoy the pleasures
which may be offered to me in this life, because they would
delay me on my journey.   I will not apply my heart to riches
and worldly goods, neither will I accept the pleasures and
delights of my flesh, nor rest in the sweetness and consolations
of my spirit, in order not to be kept from seeking You,
my God and my love, over the mountains of virtues and labors.
Grant, O Lord, that my soul may really be enamored of You,
that it esteem You above all else; and then, trusting in Your
love and in Your help, I shall have the strength to cast far
from me the desires of sense and all natural affections "
(cf. J.C. *SC*, 3,5-10).

297

MEEKNESS

PRESENCE OF GOD - Jesus, meek and humble of heart, make my heart like unto Thine.

MEDITATION

1. Temperance makes man master of himself by controlling the passions of concupiscence; meekness makes him master of himself by controlling the impulses of anger. The great value of this virtue lies in the fact that it assures the soul of that inner peace which is so necessary in order to fulfill serenely all its duties toward God and toward the neighbor. The soul, when upset by resentments and anger, is unable to see things in their true light, to form unbiased judgments, to make wise decisions, or to keep words and actions within the limits of courtesy and kindness. A person's manner becomes brusque, unrestrained, and often unjust, provoking displeasure in others; charity is cooled and harmonious relationships are disturbed. Unrestrained anger clouds the mind, preventing it from recognizing God's will, and thus making the soul swerve from the line of duty to follow the impulses of the passions. It is the task of meekness to moderate and calm all such movements of passion by giving the soul mastery of itself, enabling it to remain tranquil, even in difficult or irritating circumstances. " Let us be very meek toward everyone, " exhorts St. Francis de Sales, " and take care that our heart does not escape from our hands; therefore, let us place it every morning in an attitude of humility, meekness and tranquillity. Perfect equanimity, meekness and unalterable graciousness are virtues more rare than perfect chastity and are most desirable. " In order to keep our heart free from the movements of anger, we should be prompt in restraining them as soon as they appear, because if we favor them, even a little, they will at once gain strength, and it will be much more difficult for us to overcome them. Constant fidelity in repressing every feeling of anger will gradually bring us to the enjoyment of the sweet fruit of meekness : " The meek shall inherit the land, and shall delight in abundance of peace " (Ps 36,11).

2. Meekness has a very special importance in the development of a life of prayer and union with God. How can a soul, agitated by the storms of anger, apply itself to recollection and intimate conversation with God?   In vain will it try to apply itself to prayer : its mind and heart will escape it, following after the imaginations aroused by passion. " *Non in commotione Dominus,* " The Lord is not in the earthquake (3 *Kgs* 19,11); God does not let Himself be found nor does He show Himself in the midst of disturbance and excitement, but only in interior peace and calm.   When we are disturbed, even slightly, by impulses of anger, we are unable to perceive the delicate impulses of grace or to hear the gentle whisper of divine inspirations : the noise of our unbridled passions prevents us from listening to our interior Master, and losing our guide, we no longer act according to God's good pleasure, but allow ourselves to be carried away by the whims of our own impulsiveness, which will always cause us to commit faults.

Our interior soul knows very well that everything that happens to us, however painful, is permitted by God for our sanctification; yet in moments of rising anger, this thought vanishes and we no longer see anything but the creature, which has injured us and against which we wish to react If we wish our life to remain always under the inspiration of the Holy Spirit, our actions to be always directed by grace and conformed to God's will, we should never permit ourselves to yield to the impulses of anger, not even under the pretext of good.   Rather, in these moments we should use our energy to suspend every judgment and every act, striving to reestablish in our heart the peace necessary to judge things in the light of God.

Our Lord teaches His ways to the meek, because only one who has silenced all resentments and feelings of anger is ready to be instructed by God, to listen to His voice and to follow it.

COLLOQUY

" O Jesus, meekest Lamb, who being cursed did not curse, who suffering injuries did not threaten, who receiving the greatest contempt, answered with divine meekness or preserved an admirable silence, help me to follow Your

example, to repress my anger, to embrace meekness, and
armed with patience, to suffer willingly any labor so that
I may come to enjoy eternal repose with You " (Ven.
L. Du Pont).

" O Lord, with Your help, I desire especially to practice
meekness and resignation to Your will, not so much in
extraordinary matters as in the events and vexations of
everyday life.

" As soon as I notice anger rising within me, I will
gather my strength, not impetuously but gently, not violently
but sweetly, and I will endeavor to restore peace to my
heart.   But knowing well that I can do nothing by myself,
I will take care to call upon Your aid as the Apostles did
when they were harassed by the tempest and buffeted by the
angry waters.   O Lord, would You allow me to invoke
You in vain?   Deign to hasten to help me at such times;
command my passions to subside, raise Your hand in blessing,
and a great calm will follow.   Teach me to be meek toward
all, with those who offend or oppose me, and even with
myself, not becoming angry with myself because of my
frequent relapses and defects.   When I find that I have
fallen, in spite of my efforts, I will meekly rise again and
say, ' Come, my poor heart.   Behold, we have fallen again
into the ditch which we have so often resolved to avoid.
Let us rise now, and leave it forever.   Let us have recourse
to God's mercy; let us place our hopes in it, and it will help
us. '   Trusting in You, O Lord, I will begin again, and keep
to the path of humility and meekness " (St. Francis de Sales).

298

SPIRITUAL PROGRESS

PRESENCE OF GOD - Help me, O Lord, to advance rapidly in the path of virtue.

MEDITATION

1. " Be ye holy, because I the Lord your God am holy " (*Lv* 19,2) : this is the will of God, this is our vocation, the object of all our desires and efforts. Created to the likeness of God, we do not wish His image in us to be dimmed by our sins and passions, but to shine forth clear and pure, reflecting His sanctity as far as possible. In order to make us like Himself, God has infused into our soul, together with grace, the moral and theological virtues, the purpose of which is to reproduce in us to some degree His infinite perfections; and as a father delights to find in his children some traces of resemblance to himself, so God greatly desires to see us grow in virtue. St. John of the Cross says, " The virtues cannot be wrought by the soul alone, nor can it attain to them alone without the help of God, neither does God work them alone in the soul without its cooperation " (*SC*, 30,6). In fact, although God has infused the virtues into us at Baptism without any merit on our part, He does not make them grow without our collaboration; it remains for us, always with the help of grace, to put into practice the virtuous principles he has given us. Only in this way shall we acquire good habits of virtue and facility in practicing them.

Therefore, if we desire to cooperate with the action of God who wishes to make us like to Himself, we should apply ourselves with great zeal to the practice of the virtues. We should concentrate particularly on the virtue that we see is most necessary in order to correct our faults, or to overcome our dominant passion. This should be the special subject of our resolutions, of our examinations of conscience, and of the account given to our spiritual director. We should not think that this exercise is only for beginners, for " the obligation to advance in the love of God—and therefore, in all the other virtues as well—lasts even unto death " (St. Francis de Sales). No one, however advanced in the spiritual life, can consider himself dispensed from the practice of the virtues.

2. St. Teresa of Jesus in describing the high states of the life of union with God, often digresses to urge the practice of virtue. " You must not build, " she wrote to her daughters, " upon the foundation of prayer and contemplation alone, for unless you strive after the virtues and practice them, you will never grow to be more than dwarfs " (*Int C VII*, 4); and elsewhere she expressly says that, by means of the virtues, " even though not greatly given to contemplation, people who have them can advance a long way in the Lord's service, while, unless they have them, they cannot possibly be great contemplatives " (*Way*, 4,). It is not essential that God should lead us by the path of high contemplation in order to make us saints; besides, this does not depend upon our will. What does depend upon us, and is essential, is that we maintain the practice of virtue. Whether God wills for us a family life or one dedicated to the duties of a professional life, whether He calls us to the apostolate or to the contemplative life, in each case we shall become saints only in the measure in which we practice virtue.

The more we apply ourselves to the practice of virtue, the easier and more natural it will become; but to attain this facility which is the mark of mature virtue, we must have sufficient courage to persevere a long time in the struggle against our faults, and in the effort to acquire the opposite virtues. However, we shall never reach perfect, much less heroic, virtue unaided by the gifts of the Holy Spirit, the end of which is precisely to perfect the virtues. Although the task of practicing the virtues is ours, it is only God who can actuate the gifts, and ordinarily He does this in proportion to our zeal in practicing virtue. The assiduous practice of the virtues opens our soul wide to God's action, rendering it apt to receive and follow the motions of the Holy Spirit. Let us devote ourselves to this exercise with great generosity, and the Holy Spirit will not delay to come to us with His gifts; then we shall make rapid progress toward perfect, heroic virtue, toward sanctity.

COLLOQUY

"O Lord, You said, ' Be ye holy because I am holy. '
I think this was the wish You expressed on the day of creation
when You said, ' Let us make man to our image and likeness. '
It is Your continual desire to associate and identify Yourself
with Your creatures.... How can I better satisfy Your
desire than by keeping myself simply and lovingly turned
toward You, so that You can reflect Your own image in me,
as the sun is reflected through pure crystal?... But if
I am to reflect Your perfections, I must first put off the old
man before I can put on the new man created by You in
justice and holiness of truth. The path is traced for me.
To walk therein as You intend, I have but to deny myself,
to die to self, to lose sight of self " (E.T. *II*, 9 – *I*, 7).

Help me, O God, to combat my faults and to put off
the old man; help me to practice virtue in order to put
on the new man. You have far greater esteem for the practice
of virtue than for magnificent deeds or the fame of a great
name.

" You would rather see in me the least degree of purity
of conscience than all the works that I could do.

" You desire of me the least degree of obedience to all
the services I might think to render You.

" You esteem my acceptance of aridity and of suffering
for love of You more than all the spiritual consolations
I could have " (J.C. *SM I*, 12-14).

299

THE GIFT OF FEAR

PRESENCE OF GOD - O Lord, grant that I may fear but one thing :
that of displeasing You and being separated from You.

MEDITATION

1. The Holy Spirit invites us to His school : " Come,
children, hearken to me : I will teach you the fear of the
Lord " (*Ps* 33,12). This is the first lesson the divine Paraclete
teaches the soul desiring to become a saint. It is fundamental
and most important because, infusing into the soul hatred of
sin, which is the greatest obstacle to union with God, it
insures the development of the spiritual life. In this sense
Holy Scripture says, " The fear of the Lord is the beginning of
wisdom " (*Sir* 1,16).

To educate us in the fear of the Lord, the Holy Spirit,
instead of placing before our eyes pictures of the punishment
and pains due to sin, instead of representing God as a stern
judge, shows Him to us as a most loving Father, infinitely
desirous of our good, and He presents us the touching picture
of God's favors and mercies. " I have loved thee with an
everlasting love; therefore, have I drawn thee, " whispers the
Holy Spirit in the depths of our soul; " You are not servants,
but my friends, my children " (cf. *Jer* 31,3 - cf. *Jn* 15,15).
Captured by love for such a good Father, the soul has but
one desire, to return Him love for love, to give Him pleasure
and to be united with Him forever. Consequently, it
fears nothing but sin, which offends God and alone can
separate it from Him. What a difference there is between
this filial fear, which is the fruit of love, and servile fear,
which arises from the dread of punishment! It is true that
the fear of judgment and the divine punishment is salutary
and in certain cases can serve greatly to hold a soul back
from sin; but if it does not change gradually into filial fear,
it will never be sufficient to impel the soul on to sanctity.
Fear that is merely servile contracts the soul and makes it
petty, whereas filial fear dilates it and spurs it on in the way
of generosity and perfection.

2. The gift of fear perfects at the same time the virtues of hope and of temperance. The object of hope is the possession of God and eternal beatitude. The gift of fear, by making us carefully avoid even the slightest offense against God, establishes us in the disposition best suited to maintain our hope for the beatific union of heaven and to receive the graces necessary to obtain it.

Temperance restrains our passions and the attractions of sense pleasure. The gift of fear perfects this virtue by making us more generous in mortifying our senses and passions. Impelled by this holy fear, we become more vigilant than ever, lest we be seduced by the desire for pleasure; we are eager to renounce anything rather than displease our heavenly Father in even the slightest degree. " It is much better to displease myself than to be displeasing to God, " says the soul under the influence of this gift.

The Holy Spirit, rather than have us fear God, incites us to fear ourselves, with our evil dispositions and passions. These, being the source of sin, may put us in danger of offending God and of being separated from Him, or at least, of not living in complete union with Him. However, this fear should not give rise to anxiety or scruples; if it is accompanied by confidence and love, it will urge us to place ourselves unreservedly in God's hands, that He may keep us from every shadow of sin. While the gift of fear causes us to throw ourselves into the arms of the heavenly Father with great confidence, it infuses into the soul at the same time, a sense of respectful reverence toward His infinite Majesty. The soul feels that God, because of His immense dignity, is most distant from it; but it feels too, that through His merciful love He has made Himself so near that He invites it to live in intimacy with Him. Between these alternations of filial reverence and trustful confidence, the gift of fear matures and blossoms into perfect love. " When the soul attains to perfect possession of the spirit of fear, it has likewise in perfection the spirit of love, since that fear which is the last of the seven gifts, is filial, and the perfect fear of a son proceeds from the perfect love of a father " (J.C. *SC*, 26,3).

COLLOQUY

"My God, although I desire to love You, and although I know the vanities of the world and prefer to serve You rather than them, I can never be sure while I am here below, that I shall never again offend You. Since this is true, what can I do but flee to You and beg You not to allow my enemies to lead me into temptation? How can I recognize their treacherous assaults? Oh! my God! how I need Your help! Speak, O Lord, the word that will enlighten and strengthen me. Deign to teach me what remedy to use in the assaults of this perilous struggle! You Yourself tell me the remedy is love and fear. Love will make me quicken my steps; fear will make me look where I set my feet so that I shall not fall. Give me both, O Lord, for love and fear are two strong castles from the height of which I shall be able to conquer every temptation. Sustain me, O God, so that for all the gold in the world, I may never commit any deliberate venial sin, however small" (cf. T.J. *Way*, 39 – 40 – 41).

"My Lord and my God, all my good consists in being united to you and placing all my hope in You. If my soul were left to itself, it would be like a puff of wind, which goes away and does not return. Without You I can do no good, nor can I remain steadfast. Without You I cannot love You, please You, or avoid what is displeasing to You. Therefore, I take refuge in You, I abandon myself to You, that You may sustain me by Your power, hold me by Your strength, and never permit me to become separated from You" (cf. St. Bernard).

300

BLESSED ARE THE POOR IN SPIRIT

PRESENCE OF GOD - O Holy Spirit, show me the way which leads to true poverty of spirit and give me strength to walk therein to the end.

MEDITATION

1. When we cooperate with the action of the gifts of the Holy Spirit, they produce in us fruits of virtue so exquisite that they give us a foretaste of the eternal beatitude of which they are a sweet pledge. For this reason, we call them *beatitudes*. For each gift there is a corresponding beatitude : the beatitude which corresponds to the gift of fear is poverty of spirit : " Blessed are the poor in spirit, for theirs is the kingdom of heaven " (*Mt* 5,3).

The gift of fear, the purpose of which is to liberate the soul completely from sin, tends to extinguish in us the desire for earthly things, which is the principal cause of sin. Therefore, it urges us to a life of total self-detachment so that, stripping us of all selfish proud desires, of all cupidity and concern as to worldly things, it gradually establishes us in perfect poverty of spirit. In the face of all that life can offer us in the way of honors, satisfactions, affections of creatures, comforts, and riches, the Holy Spirit repeats in the depths of our heart the words of Jesus : " If thou wilt be perfect, go sell what thou hast...and come, follow Me " (*ibid.* 19,21). This means, not only to desire nothing more than what one has, but to give up even this; not to be eager for riches, pleasures, consolations, fame, nor earthly affections, but to sacrifice all these things which fill the heart with the world, and prevent it from being filled with God.

The Holy Spirit spurs the soul on to material poverty, teaching it to be content with little, curbing its desires for the necessities of life, but He urges it even more to poverty of spirit, for without this, the former is of no worth. " The lack of things, " says St. John of the Cross, " implies no detachment on the part of the soul if it retains a desire for them, that is, if it is still attached to them.... The things of this world neither occupy the soul nor cause it harm, since they enter it not, but rather the will and the desire for them, for it is these that dwell within it " (*AS I*, 3,4).

2. Poverty of spirit includes detachment not only from material goods, but also from moral and even spiritual goods. Whoever tries to assert his own personality, seeking the esteem and regard of creatures, who remains attached to his own will and ideas, or is too fond of his independence, is not poor in spirit, but is rich in himself, in his self-love and his pride. " If thou wilt be perfect, " says St. John of the Cross, " sell thy will...come to Christ through meekness and humility; and follow Him to Calvary and the grave " (*SM III*, 7).

In like manner, one who still seeks the affection of creatures, and the joy and satisfactions which they can give him, is not poor in spirit; neither is he who goes in search of consolations and spiritual delights in his devotions and relations with God. Poverty of spirit consists in being entirely stripped and empty of all these pretensions, so that the soul seeks and desires only one thing : to possess God, and to be thus content, even when God lets Himself be found only in darkness, aridity, anguish, and suffering. Here is that perfect poverty of spirit which frees the soul from all that is not God; this very freedom constitutes the reason for our happiness, because " the soul that strips itself of its desires, either to will or not to will, will be clothed by God with His purity, joy, and will " (J.C. *SM II*, 19). The beatitude promised to the poor in spirit is the possession of God, a possession which will clothe them with His infinite riches. This is the goal to which the Holy Spirit desires to lead us; let us second His action by responding with docility to His invitation to detachment and total despoliation. The more generously we renounce all that is not God, the more we shall enjoy the beatitude promised to the poor in spirit.

COLLOQUY

" O Jesus, our book of life and our salvation, Your first companion on earth was extreme, continual, perfect poverty. You, the Almighty, the Lord of all things, willed absolute poverty in order that we might unite love and poverty as one. You became poor in everything : poor in material things, poor in Your own will, poor in spirit, beyond anything that we can possibly imagine, infinitely poor, because Your love for us was infinite. You were poor like those who possess nothing, who do not even ask for what they need. You were poor in possessions, in friends, in power and human wisdom, poor in reputation for sanctity, in worldly honors, poor in everything that exists.

" You also wished to glorify poverty by Your words and You said ' blessed are the poor, ' and that the poor would judge the world.

" But, oh! shame and sorrow! Today, O Lord, this poverty of spirit which You taught and exalted so highly, is rejected and fled from by almost all men, and even those who preach it and glorify it by their words, in reality, deny it in will, desire, and actions.

" Oh! truly blessed is he who, following Your example, O Christ, has chosen poverty for his companion! Truly blessed, as You said, is he who, not only by his words, but by his will and by his life, embraces poverty of earthly goods, poverty of friends and relatives, of consolations and vain knowledge; blessed is he who shuns honors, dignities, and the reputation for sanctity.

" O Lord, if I cannot strip myself materially of all earthly things, at least permit me, I beseech You, to become detached at least in spirit, and not once only, but every day and every moment. Oh! truly blessed is such a poor one, for the kingdom of heaven is his! " (St. Angela of Foligno).

301

THE CHARACTERISTICS OF A CHRISTIAN

SIXTEENTH SUNDAY AFTER PENTECOST

PRESENCE OF GOD - Grant, O Lord, that my soul may be deeply rooted in charity and in humility.

MEDITATION

1. The Epistle (*Eph* 3,13-21) which we read in today's Mass is one of the most beautiful passages in the letters of St. Paul. In it we find the famous counsel of the Apostle addressed to the Ephesians, which summarizes in three parts, the whole of the spiritual life.

" That the Father of Our Lord Jesus Christ...would grant you...to be strengthened by His Spirit with might unto the inward man. " The inward man is the human spirit regenerated by grace; it is the spiritual man who has renounced all material things and the pleasures of the senses. This man is in each one of us and should be strong in order to keep up the struggle against our lower nature, which will always be a part of us while we are on earth, and is always trying to drag us down. The Apostle rightly asks this fortitude of the Holy Spirit, because the strength of our virtue is not sufficient unless it is supported by what the Holy Spirit infuses into us through His gifts.

" That Christ may dwell by faith in your hearts. " Christ with the Father and the Holy Spirit already dwells in the soul in the state of grace, but His presence can always become more profound. And the more profound His presence, the more deeply will the soul be penetrated with divine charity, until it becomes truly " rooted and founded " in love. If we wish to grow in love we should keep ourselves in contact with the fount of love, with God living in our soul.

" That you may be able to comprehend...the charity of Christ, which surpasseth all knowledge. " To comprehend the mystery of God's love, insofar as it is possible to our limitations, is the summit of the spiritual life. Christianity is all love : we are Christians in the measure that we live in

love, in the measure that we understand God's love. Yet this
mystery always leaves us a little incredulous, a little skeptical.
Oh! if we could see as the blessed do, that God is love
and wishes nothing but love; that the way to go to Him is
the way of love; that suffering, mortification and humility
are only means to reach perfect love, and to correspond
with the love of the God who is Charity! Then indeed
we would be " filled unto all the fullness of God. "

2. St. Paul in the Epistle has exhorted us to be rooted in
love, and in the Gospel (*Lk* 14, 1-11) Jesus exhorts us to be
rooted in love and in humility.

Despite the tacit disapproval of the Pharisees, caused by
their narrowness of mind and heart, Jesus cured a man of
dropsy on the Sabbath, thus teaching us again the great
importance of love of neighbor. In vain would we believe
that we were rooted in the love of God if we failed in our
love of neighbor. How could one think that an act of
fraternal charity might be in opposition to the law for sanctifying the Sabbath? Such are the aberrations of one who
pretends to love God while paying attention solely to his
own interests, without any thought for the needs of others.
This is not Christianity, but Pharisaism and the destruction
of charity.

To be rooted in love, we must also be rooted in humility,
for only he who is humble is capable of really loving God and
his neighbor. The Gospel continues with a practical lesson in
humility, condemning those who seek the first places. We
should not think that this refers only to material places;
it refers also to those places which our pride seeks to occupy
in the esteem and regard of others. It is really humiliating
to note how our self-love always tries to make us take a
higher place than that which is due us, and this to our own
confusion, for " he that exalteth himself shall be humbled. "
" Let us always take the lowest place, " says St. Bernard,
" there is no harm in humbling ourselves and believing
that we are less than we really are. But there is exceeding
harm and great evil in wishing to elevate ourselves, even if
only a finger's breadth, above what we are and in preferring
ourselves to even one. There is no danger in stooping too
much to pass through a low doorway, whereas there would
be great danger in lifting our head even an inch above the
lintel, as we would strike against it and injure our head;

similarly, we should not be afraid that we shall humble ourselves too much, but should fear and abominate the slightest movement of presumption. " Let us, like the saints, ask God to send us a humiliation every time our pride tries to raise us above others; this will be the surest way to become rooted in humility. At the same time, we shall be rooted in charity and shall thus possess the two fundamental characteristics of a Christian soul.

COLLOQUY

" O Lord, increase my faith in Your love, so that I may be able to say to You in all truth : ' I have known and have believed the charity which God hath to me. ' It seems to me that this is the greatest act of our faith, the most beautiful way to render You love for love; in it is the hidden secret of which St. Paul speaks, a secret which my soul longs to understand, because in understanding it, I shall thrill with joy. Make me capable of believing in Your exceeding love for me. Then I shall not stop at preferences or feelings. It will matter little if I feel Your presence or not, whether You send me joy or suffering. I shall believe in Your love and that will suffice. Grant, O God, that my soul may penetrate into Your depths and remain there, rooted and founded in love.

" O Lord, when I ponder within myself Your immensity, Your faithfulness, the proofs of love You have shown me, and Your benefits, and then look at myself and see how I have outraged You, I can only turn upon my soul with a profound feeling of contempt; yet this self-contempt is not strong enough to cast me down as low as I would wish. O Lord, plunge me into humility! It seems to me that to be plunged into humility is to be plunged into You; for, living in You who are the Truth, I cannot fail to realize my nothingness. The humble soul is the chosen recipient, the vessel capable of receiving Your grace, and only into it do You wish to pour Your grace. Grant then, O Lord, that I may be humble, and make me understand that the humble soul will never put You high enough or itself low enough " (cf. E.T. I, 6 – II, 8 – I, 9).

302

THE GIFT OF FORTITUDE

PRESENCE OF GOD - O Holy Spirit, You know how weak I am;
make me strong with Your divine fortitude.

MEDITATION

1. Under the influence of the gift of fear, the soul puts
itself completely into the hands of God and has but one
desire, that of never being separated from Him. The gift of
fortitude comes to strengthen it so that it may be always
more and more courageous in serving God.

In the measure that the soul advances in the spiritual
life, it should follow God's initiative, and let itself be
guided by the Holy Spirit, rather than proceed according to
its own ideas; however, its activity is necessary here too,
consisting as it does in a prompt, docile adherence to
the promptings of the divine Paraclete, accepting and
willing all that He does for it and in it. Thus this gift
comes to help and to perfect the virtue of fortitude, which,
in spite of our good will, is always weak and too often fails us,
especially when we are faced with the rigorous demands
of a more perfect spiritual life. We need courage to remain
faithful to God's law and the duties of our state—even at the
cost of great sacrifice—and to endure patiently the difficulties
of life. We need it even more to second the action of God
in our soul, to follow faithfully the inspirations of the Holy
Spirit, and not be frightened by the trials God makes us
undergo. He is a kind, gentle Master, but at the same
time, a very exacting one, because He cannot lead us to
sanctity without asking us for *all*. And this is just where we
most experience our frailty : we feel intuitively what God
wants from us, perhaps we see it very clearly, and yet we are
not capable, we lack the strength to do it. This is a great
grief for a soul of good will, not yet fully matured. It is the
condition of human weakness which actual grace and the
infused virtue of fortitude can do much to relieve, but which
they cannot completely cure, acting as they do by means of
our limited faculties. The direct intervention of God Himself

is necessary and God does intervene by putting the gift of fortitude into action.

2. The virtue of fortitude and the gift of fortitude have the same end, to strengthen us in the spiritual life, but they differ as to the manner in which they act. The virtue acts in us by means of our own efforts, sustained, certainly, by grace, but yet these efforts are always human efforts; hence, even though they are supernatural, they must necessarily adapt themselves to our human way of acting; consequently, they will always be affected by our limitations. On the other hand, the gift—like all the gifts of the Holy Spirit—is supernatural not only in itself, but also in its activation. In fact, instead of being put into action by us—as is the case with the virtue—it is activated by God Himself. By means of the virtue and using our good will, the little sister of grace, it is we who try to acquire fortitude to make ourselves strong; by means of the gift, however, it is the Holy Spirit who fortifies us interiorly, communicating to us something of His omnipotence, something of His infinite fortitude. Between the fortitude acquired by our own efforts and that infused by the Holy Spirit, there is a difference similar to that which exists between the work of an inexperienced student and that of a skillful artist, or rather, between man's capacity and power, and God's. " You shall receive the power of the Holy Ghost coming upon you, " Jesus said to the Apostles, "and you shall be witnesses unto Me in Jerusalem " (*Acts* 1,8). Indeed, those poor fishermen full of fear, who did not have the courage to accompany Jesus to Calvary, became as brave as lions after the coming of the Holy Spirit, ready to face every danger, even death itself. This shows us how necessary is the gift of fortitude; without it, we would always be vacillating, always uncertain, always inconstant. But the Holy Spirit wills that we should be disposed to receive this gift by practicing the virtue. Our efforts, repeated with humility and constancy, are in themselves a tacit plea for the gift of fortitude. Through these efforts we unfurl the sails of our souls to the breeze of the Holy Spirit. It remains for Him to choose the moment to move us, but He will not do this unless He finds us disposed to welcome His divine impulse, that is, applying ourselves to the practice of virtue.

COLLOQUY

"O eternal God, You are Fortitude and You give fortitude to the soul, making it so strong that neither the devil nor any other creature can take this strength away unless it consents. It will never do so if it clothes itself with Your will, because it is only its own will that weakens it. O eternal God! inestimable love! I, Your creature am wholly incorporated into You, and You into me by creation, by the force of Your will, by the love with which You have created me!" (St. Catherine of Siena).

"*Veni, Spiritus fortitudinis, robora me!*" Come, O Spirit of fortitude, strengthen me! Grant me the gift of fortitude, to confront with courage, to support with patience, difficult and painful things, overcoming all obstacles. I am in great need of this Your gift, because I am little and weak, and I tire as easily as a child. 'But You do not tire, grow weary, and Your wisdom is unsearchable. Give strength to the weary; and to those who have little, increase their strength and vigor. Youths shall faint, and young men shall fall by infirmity. But they that hope in You shall renew their strength, they shall take wings as eagles, they shall run and not be weary; they shall walk and not faint!' (cf. *Is* 40,28-31).

"O Holy Spirit, sustain me and then I shall become strong with Your strength. If You are my strength and my salvation, what shall I fear? My own power cannot sustain me, but I can do all things in You who strengthen me! Come to my aid, and in spite of my weakness, I shall overcome temptations and obstacles; I shall accomplish great things, and strong with Your strength, I shall bear suffering with patience and joy.

"O Holy Spirit, with all my heart I beg this gift; let it make me generous, fearless, loving in sacrifice, virile, desirous of tending to perfection resolutely and wholeheartedly" (Sister Carmela of the Holy Spirit, O.C.D.).

303

BLESSED ARE THEY THAT HUNGER
AND THIRST AFTER JUSTICE

PRESENCE OF GOD - O Holy Spirit, may I no longer hunger for the things of earth, but for heavenly things alone.

MEDITATION

1. When the Holy Spirit becomes master of a soul and takes entire control of it, He communicates to it an invincible strength which sweeps away and overcomes all obstacles, enabling it to bear all kinds of suffering. As the strong are not easily satisfied, but are always aspiring to greater things, so in the measure in which the Holy Spirit strengthens a soul, He makes ever increasing desires to spring up in it, longings for justice and virtue and sanctity, so ardent and impelling that they may well be called hunger and thirst. Under the influence of the gift of fortitude, the soul hungers and thirsts after justice. This explains how the fourth beatitude corresponds to the gift of fortitude. " Blessed are they that hunger and thirst after justice, for they shall have their fill " (*Mt* 5,6). The word *justice* must be taken in the very broad sense, signifying perfection, sanctity, and a total gift of self to God and to souls; it is in this sense that the Holy Spirit impels the soul, revealing to it ever wider horizons, calling it to ever more perfect works and to an increasingly generous and complete gift of self. Such a soul can no longer reserve anything for itself : the Holy Spirit will not permit it; it must give itself wholly. " The charity of Christ presseth us " (2 *Cor* 5,14), the soul repeats with St. Paul. It is consumed by a burning thirst for God's will, which it seeks even as the miser searches for gold. It is an ardent thirst for sanctity which will not tolerate the slightest infidelity to grace; the soul always thinks itself to be doing too little for God, and " if it were lawful for it to be destroyed a thousand times for Him it would be comforted " (J.C. *DN II*, 19,3); it has a burning thirst for souls, and continually spends itself for them, without ever sparing itself; it thirsts for God's glory and has no thought of rest, but is

always ready for new sacrifices and labors. Whence comes such courage and zeal? Not from its own strength and energy, as it well knows, but it springs from the power of the Holy Spirit, from trust in Him and docility to His inspirations. The soul can truthfully say : " I can do all things in Him who strengtheneth me " (*Phil* 4,13).

2. Just as a starving person rejoices when he can satisfy his hunger with bread, so the soul living under the influence of the gift of fortitude rejoices when it is able to satisfy its hunger for justice and sanctity. It is happy when able to immerse itself in God's will, the only food which can satiate it; it rejoices when it can quench its thirst for immolation by sacrificing itself for God and for souls. The soul is delighted when it can appease its hunger for God by receiving Him in the Eucharist, or by immersing itself in Him in the intimacy of prayer. This is a pure joy, because it is not sought after, but is the fruit of the fulfillment of duty, the joy of the soul gravitating toward its center, God, and conscious of giving itself more and more to Him, of belonging entirely to Him. But to taste this joy, the soul must be firmly resolved not to want, seek, or admit any other. St. Teresa of Jesus says : " Anyone whose sole pleasure lies in seeking God and who cares nothing for her own pleasure, will find our life a very good one " (*Way*, 13).

If we do not taste this joy, it is because we do not hunger after justice sufficiently : together with this holy hunger we still nourish, perhaps, eagerness for the things of the world; and our hunger for earthly things and earthly joys weakens our hunger for justice, making us turn aside in search of human satisfactions. But what can creatures give us? They will never be able to satiate our hunger, but will always leave us unsatisfied. Let us, therefore, ask the Holy Spirit to extinguish in us all hunger for earthly things and to make our hunger for sanctity increase. This hunger is still very weak in us and, above all, it is inconstant. How many times, after making great resolutions, we have relapsed, and remained discouraged, perhaps even resigned to doing no better. The Holy Spirit, through the gift of fortitude, wishes to make our hunger for sanctity stronger and more persevering, that it may never be extinguished, leaving us to die of starvation, but may satiate us with imperishable goods : with God's will, with justice, with sanctity. He who has the power to awaken this hunger in us, has also the power to satisfy it even to satiety, and with this satiety we shall be blessed forever.

COLLOQUY

" O God, ocean of sacred love and sweetness, come and give Yourself to my soul.   Grant that I may continually long for You with my whole heart, with absolute desire and burning love, and that I may live in You.   O my true supreme joy, may I prefer You to all creatures, and for Your sake, renounce all transitory pleasures!

" O Lord, nourish this starving beggar with the influx of Your divinity, and delight me with the desired presence of Your grace.   This I long and beg for, so that Your vehement love may penetrate, fill, and transform me into You.

" O loving Redeemer, make me burn with love for You, making no account of myself, and finding my delight in You alone; may I know and enjoy no one but You.   O overflowing abyss of the divinity!   draw me, and immerse me in You!   Take all the love from my heart and apply it to Yourself, so that I may be dead to all other things.

" My soul calls You, and seeks You with indescribable love, O delight of loving embraces!   Come, my Beloved, come, You whom I desire above all, that I may possess You within me, and that my soul may embrace You and hold You close!   Come into my soul, O sovereign sweetness, and let me taste Your sweetness, and delight and rest in You alone.

" O my Beloved, Beloved of all my desires, let me find You and then hold You and press You close in a spiritual embrace.   I desire You, I sigh for You, O eternal Beatitude! Oh! give Yourself to me, unite me closely to You, and inebriate me with the wine of Your love! " (Bl. Louis de Blois).

304

THE GIFT OF PIETY

PRESENCE OF GOD - O Holy Spirit, Spirit of piety, give to my heart the spirit of filial love.

MEDITATION

1. By means of the gift of piety, the Holy Spirit gives a new touch to our spiritual life, a touch of delicacy and sweetness which perfects and simplifies our relations with God and our neighbor. Basically these relations are regulated by justice, the virtue which inclines us to fulfill every duty and to give to each one his due. But if we were guided in our lives by justice alone, our path would be very arid, and fidelity, difficult. When, however, a sense of *filial piety* toward our heavenly Father is developed in us by the action of the Holy Spirit—a sense which, in practice, is expressed in ardent desires to please Him in all things—then we pass beyond the limits of justice—always a little rigid—and devote ourselves wholeheartedly to the service of God. Incited by that profound cry of " Father! " (*Gal* 4,6) which the Holy Spirit repeats within us, we rise toward heaven, longing to win God's heart and to behave in all things as His true children; then the most difficult, laborious tasks become easy and sweet. This is how the gift of piety helps the virtue of justice as well as the virtue of religion. By this gift, " the Spirit Himself giveth testimony to our spirit, that we are the sons of God " (*Rom* 8,16); and this truth becomes a living, personal experience, capable of elevating us to God with entirely new filial ardor, ardor which will make our prayer easier, transforming it into an intimate heart-to-heart talk with our heavenly Father.

Therefore, if we aspire to live in close union with God, it is right for us to desire and pray for this gift. Under its influence our prayer will become more affectionate, more filial, and we shall attend with greater facility to all that concerns divine worship. Let us ask for this gift, especially when we seem to be very dry and cold, so that in times of trial and interior suffering by its help we shall go to God as a child to its Father. Furthermore, our diligent, constant application to prayer, notwithstanding the lack of sensible devotion, is one of the best dispositions for bringing upon us the life-giving breath of the gift of piety.

2. The gift of piety perfects justice in our relations with others by helping us to smooth over differences and overcome the feelings of reserve and coldness which, in spite of ourselves, may remain in our conduct, particularly toward those who are disagreeable and unfriendly. The gift of piety inspires a sense of the divine paternity, not only in respect to ourselves, but also in respect to others; it makes us realize that this same paternity extends, not only to ourselves, but to all men, near or far away, friends or enemies, since there is only " one God and Father of all, who is above all " (*Eph* 4,6). The knowledge that God is the Father of us all must not be confined to our thoughts, but should penetrate our life in a practical way and sweetly influence our relations with others, giving them warmth and ease. This is just what the Holy Spirit wishes to accomplish in us by means of the gift of piety, by which He inclines us to meekness, indulgence, and kindness to all because we are all children of the same Father. The Holy Spirit teaches us that our supernatural kinship is a stronger bond between ourselves and others than the bond of flesh and blood, because the former springs not from the will of man, but from the will of our heavenly Father, who " before the foundation of the world...hath predestinated us unto the adoption of children through Jesus Christ unto Himself " (*ibid.* 1,4.5). By means of this bond, the Holy Spirit urges us to overcome all the difficulties we may meet with in dealing with others, treating them all, not as strangers, but as brothers.

If we wish to respond to the inspirations of the gift of piety, we must make every effort to be kind and gentle, and to form the habit of seeing in everyone, even in those who may be opposed to us, a child of God and our brother. When we find it very difficult to do this, instead of becoming discouraged, let us appeal more insistently to the Holy Spirit, begging Him to accomplish in us what we cannot do by ourselves.

COLLOQUY

" O Holy Spirit, guide my soul, because all who are led by the Spirit of God, are truly the sons of God. You teach me that I have not received the spirit of bondage to live in fear, but the spirit of adoption of sons, whereby I can cry to God : ' Abba, Father! ' You Yourself give testimony to my spirit that I am a child of God and a joint-heir with Christ : because, if we suffer with Him, we shall also be glorified with Him " (cf. *Rom* 8,14-17).

" My God, send forth Your light and Your truth, that they may shine upon the earth : for I am like land that is dry and barren, awaiting Your light. Pour forth Your grace from above; water my heart with the dew of heaven; send down the waters of devotion to wash the face of the earth, to bring forth good and perfect fruit. Lift up my mind oppressed with the weight of my sins, and raise all my desires toward heavenly things, that having tasted the sweetness of supernal happiness, I may have no pleasure in dwelling on the things of this earth.

" Draw my heart to You, and deliver me from all vain human consolations, none of which can fully satisfy my desires or make me happy. Unite me to Yourself by the inseparable bond of Your love; for You alone are sufficient for the soul that loves You, and without You, all is vain and of no value " (*Imit. III*, 23,9.10).

O Holy Spirit, create in me the heart of a child toward its heavenly Father, a heart that seeks Him always, loving and serving Him with good will. Create in me the heart of a brother toward all my neighbors, so that I may overlook all differences and be kind, gentle, and meek with all.

305

BLESSED ARE THE MEEK

PRESENCE OF GOD - O Holy Spirit, diffuse in my heart an increase of
the spirit of piety and meekness.

MEDITATION

1. By the gift of fortitude the Holy Spirit strengthens our
heart; by the gift of piety He makes it meek and gentle.
When we practice the virtue of meekness, we are doing our
part—as we should do at all costs—to acquire that meekness
of heart which Jesus has so strongly recommended and which
He Himself tells us brings interior peace as its fruit. " Learn
of Me, because I am meek and humble of heart, and you shall
find rest to your souls " (*Mt* 11,29). However, we have not
yet acquired a sustained habitual meekness and the continual
peace that accompanies it, if when we meet with unexpected
trials, contradictions, injuries, or offenses, our meekness
fails and our peace of heart vanishes, at least momentarily.
These daily experiences, although painful and humiliating,
are salutary, because, far more than any reasoning, they make
us realize the insufficiency of our efforts and the extreme
need we have of God's help. This help He has already
willed to give us by infusing into our soul the gift of piety.
When the Holy Spirit moves us through this gift, He quenches
in us every trace of ill-feeling toward our neighbor; He
softens our hardness and, so to speak, takes our heart in His
hands to establish it in meekness and habitual peace.

As long as this poor heart remains in our own hands,
we shall never succeed in being wholly master of it; but even
if, in spite of all our frequently renewed resolutions, we fail
in meekness every day, we should not on this account desist
from our undertaking, but cheerfully renew our efforts and,
at the same time, beg God's help with humble persistence.
" *Veni, Sancte Spiritus, flecte quod est rigidum, fove quod est frigidum,
rege quod est devium* " (*Sequence*). Come, Holy Spirit, bend the
stubborn heart and will, melt the frozen, warm the chill,
guide the steps that go astray.

2. The beatitude which corresponds to the gift of piety is the reward promised to those who have attained perfect meekness by making use of their own efforts and the help of the Holy Spirit. "Blessed are the meek, for they shall possess the land" (*Mt* 5,4). What land? First of all, that of their own heart since, St. Thomas says, "Meekness makes a man master of himself" (IIª IIᵃᵉ, q.157, a.4, co.). Without this interior control of all our impulses—feelings of animosity, of antipathy, indignation, anger—we might be able to present an appearance of meekness as worldlings do when it is opportune, but we will never have that profound meekness which calmly faces all the trials of daily living. Furthermore, this complete self-control is what Jesus said would enable us to possess the land in a broader, more beautiful sense, that is, to possess the hearts of others. If we wish to be of service to our brethren, winning their hearts and orientating them to goodness and truth, that is, to God, we must not use force or an authority which exasperates others and arouses opposition, but rather, meekness, patience, and forbearance. This is the method used by Jesus who Himself announced His mission as one of meekness : " The Spirit of the Lord is upon Me, wherefore He hath anointed Me to preach the gospel to the poor; He hath sent Me to heal the contrite of heart. . . to set at liberty them that are bruised " (*Lk* 4,18.19).

The " Spirit of the Lord, " the Holy Spirit, has also been given to us, and our hearts have been anointed with the oil of piety and meekness, to enable us to continue the mission of Jesus in the world. To this He invites us saying : " Go : Behold I send you as lambs among wolves " (*ibid.* 10,3); and He commands us, as He commanded the Apostles, to go without staff or arms of defense, though we know that we shall meet opposition, struggles, and enemies.

Jesus, the Lamb of God, conquered the world by His meekness; so we too shall win the hearts of others to the degree in which, overcoming ourselves, we become lambs of meekness, ready, like Him, to suffer rather than to assert ourselves and defend ourselves by force.

COLLOQUY

" O Jesus, Savior of the world, in the midst of Your sufferings, persecutions, and revilings, You did not utter any threat or malediction; You did not defend, excuse, or avenge Yourself! You were spat upon, but You did not turn Your face away; Your hands and arms were stretched upon the Cross, but You did not draw them back; in all things You surrendered Yourself to the will of Your executioners, in order to accomplish the work of the Redemption. This is a mystery of infinite mercy, but it is also an example. Thus, O Lord, You give us an example of meekness and patience in tribulations and adversities; You teach us not to render evil for evil, but, on the contrary, to render good for evil.

" Read then, O my soul, read again in this book of life which is Christ crucified! Read the infinite meekness of God! How can you still protest and murmur against tribulations, against those who make you suffer, when your God has immolated Himself for you as the meekest of lambs? " (St. Angela of Foligno).

" O Holy Spirit, give me a simple heart which will not retire within itself to savor its own sorrows, a heart magnanimous in giving itself, easily moved to compassion, a faithful, generous heart, which does not forget any favor received, nor hold resentment for any injuries done to it. Make my heart meek and humble, quick to forgive and capable of bearing tranquilly all opposition, a heart which will love without expecting love in return, content to vanish in the hearts of others, sacrificing itself before the heavenly Father, a great and indomitable heart, that no ingratitude can close and no indifference can weary, a heart tormented by the glory of Jesus Christ, wounded by His love, with a wound which cannot be healed except in heaven " (Leonce de Grandmaison, S.J.).

306

THE GIFT OF COUNSEL

PRESENCE OF GOD - Come, O Spirit of Counsel, make my heart attentive to all Your inspirations!

MEDITATION

1. " The Holy Ghost whom the Father will send in My name, He will teach you all things, and bring all things to your mind, whatsoever I shall have said to you " (*Jn* 14,26). This promise made by Jesus is valid for all Christians, including ourselves. The Holy Spirit dwells within our souls to counsel us, to recall to us the instructions of Jesus and to apply them to the actual circumstances of our life. But how can we poor creatures who are so dull, and accustomed to the clamor of human language, perceive the light murmur of the divine inspirations? God has provided for this with a special gift, the gift of counsel, which enables our soul to understand the quiet interior voice of the Holy Spirit, and to distinguish it from all other voices.

The gift of counsel is a powerful aid to the virtue of prudence. Guided by this virtue, we try to understand how we ought to behave in the various circumstances of life so as to be pleasing to God. However, not always seeing clearly, we often remain doubtful in concrete cases, asking ourselves if this or that action will be more conformable to God's will. Am I really moved by supernatural motives in this deliberation, or does nature enter in, or self? The question remains; often even the counsels of wise persons are not sufficient to dissipate our perplexity, to give us that light whereby we may act with security. We need God Himself to enlighten us within, we need the Holy Spirit who, by activating the gift of counsel, brings His divine light to our soul. The gift is like an antenna which permits us to detect the counsels of the Holy Spirit, most precious and most simple counsels which, overstepping the labyrinth of our reasonings, show us with luminous clarity which road to follow, and make us understand God's will in an instant. The more this gift develops in us, the more our soul will open to the voice of the Holy Spirit, and will become more responsive to His inspirations. Because of this gift, although we are but weak creatures, we can address to the Almighty this humble, but daring prayer : " Speak, Lord, for Thy servant heareth " (1 *Sm* 3,9).

2. There is no doubt that the Holy Spirit, by means of the gift of counsel, wishes to be our counsellor in the way of sanctity. Why, then, are we so seldom aware of His divine reminders? First of all, because we are distracted; our soul is deafened by the voices of creatures, and filled with the noises of the world. Holy Scripture compares the voice of the Holy Spirit to the " whistling of a gentle air " (1 *Kgs* 19,12). Therefore, we must be silent, silent exteriorly, but, even more so, interiorly, if we wish to be able to perceive this voice so tenuous and sweet. Only in silence can He be heard who manifests Himself " in divine silence " (cf. J.C. *SM I*, 26).

Another cause of our failure to receive the counsels of the Holy Spirit is attachment to our own judgment, to the limited counsels of our own mind. A little of this attachment, a little obstinacy in holding to our own ideas, is sufficient to immure the soul within itself and make it incapable of detecting the divine inspirations. Let us not deceive ourselves : this happens even when it is a question of obstinacy in good things, because attachment to our own opinions is never good; it never indicates the action of grace, but rather that of a self-love which has not been overcome. When a soul is not attentive nor submissive to the external voice of obedience which tries to dissuade it from its tenacity, so much the less will it be able to heed the interior silent voice of the Holy Spirit. As a boat which, although furnished with sails, cannot be moved by the wind as long as it is moored, so the soul attached to its own opinions is unable to enjoy the precious influence of the gift of counsel; it possesses this gift, but it remains powerless, as if paralyzed, like the sails of a ship anchored in the harbor. St. John of the Cross advises us : " Renounce thy desires and thou shalt find that which thy heart desires. How knowest thou if thy desire is according to God? " (*SM I*, 15).

By cultivating interior recollection, and detaching ourselves from our own judgment, we shall be truly, as Jesus said, " *docibiles Dei,* " that is, we shall have the necessary dispositions for being instructed by God and receiving the counsels of the Holy Spirit.

COLLOQUY

" ' Speak, Lord, for Thy servant heareth. ' I am Thy servant, give me understanding that I may know Thy testimonies. Incline my heart to the words of Thy mouth, let Thy speech distil as the dew. Heretofore, the children of Israel said to Moses : ' Speak thou to us, and we will hear; let not the Lord speak to us, lest we die. ' It is not thus, O Lord, it is not thus I pray; but rather with the prophet Samuel, I humbly and earnestly entreat Thee : ' Speak, Lord, for Thy servant heareth. ' Let not Moses, nor any of the prophets, speak to me; but speak Thou rather, O Lord God, who art the inspirer and enlightener of all the prophets; for Thou alone without them canst perfectly instruct me; but they without Thee will avail me nothing.

" They may indeed utter fine words, but they give not the spirit. They speak well; but if Thou be silent, they inflame not the heart. They give the letter, but Thou disclosest the sense. They publish the mysteries, but Thou unlockest the meaning of the things signified.

" They declare the commandments, but Thou enablest us to fulfill them. They show the way, but Thou givest strength to walk in it. What they can do is only from without, but Thou instructest and enlightenest the heart. They water outwardly, but Thou givest the increase. They cry aloud in words, but Thou givest understanding to the hearing.

" Speak then, O Lord, for Thy servant heareth; for Thou hast the words of eternal life. Speak to me, that it may be for me some comfort to my soul, and for the amendment of my whole life, and also to Thy praise and glory, and everlasting honor " (*Imit III*, 2,1-3).

307

BLESSED ARE THE MERCIFUL

PRESENCE OF GOD - O Holy Spirit, make my heart merciful in imitation of the heart of Jesus.

MEDITATION

1. By the gift of counsel, the Holy Spirit wishes to take over the practical direction of our life that He may lead us to sanctity, because all Christian perfection, which was the object of the teaching of Jesus, is likewise the object of the gift of counsel, of the inspirations of the Holy Spirit : " He will teach you all things...whatsoever I shall have said to you " (*Jn* 14,26), the Master declared. Just as in the teaching of Jesus there is a *dominant* note, love, which He calls *His* commandment, so among the inspirations of the gift of counsel there is one which is generally recognized as the *proper effect* of this gift, and it is *mercy*.

When Jesus gave His commandment, He said : " Love one another, as I have loved you " (*ibid.* 15,12); now the fundamental characteristic of His love, of the love of God for men, is precisely mercy. All creatures are misery in the eyes of God, misery incapable of subsisting without the continual intervention of His action. And we men, what are we? Not only misery incapable of subsisting, but misery capable of sinning : of ourselves " we are nothing, we can do nothing, we are worth nothing, we possess nothing except sin " (St. John Eudes). We are misery in the fullest sense of the word. Therefore, when God loves us, His love is essentially and necessarily an act of mercy; that is, it is love which stoops to our misery to elevate, sustain, and enrich it with His infinite riches. This is what the Holy Spirit proposes especially to accomplish in us by means of the gift of counsel : to teach us to imitate that mercy which is the chief characteristic of God's love for us. The Holy Spirit wishes to bring us to the perfect observance of the commandment of Jesus, to the imitation of the merciful love of His divine heart : " Love one another as I have

loved you "; and to bring us to reproduce the infinite mercy
of the heavenly Father : " Be ye therefore merciful, as your
Father also is merciful " (*Lk* 6,36).

2. God is infinitely merciful, because He knows the
depths of our misery; we are far from being merciful because
we know too little about it.   By the gift of counsel, the Holy
Spirit enlightens us on this point, particularly in regard
to our own personal wretchedness.   In our failures and in
our falls, He repeats in the depths of our heart the warnings
of Jesus : " Without Me you can do nothing.... You are
unprofitable servants " (*Jn* 15,5 – *Lk* 17,10).   This lesson
gradually becomes more and more vivid and effective
through experience, and it penetrates our souls more deeply;
we do not need long reasonings to persuade us of our insufficiency, our nothingness : we see it and touch it.   The gift of
counsel has opened our eyes to it.

This comprehension of our own personal misery makes
us equally understanding of the misery of others.   How can
one who is really convinced of his own frailty, weakness,
and inconstancy, dare to condemn others?   " He that is
without sin among you, let him first cast a stone " (*Jn* 8,7),
the Holy Spirit whispers to us interiorly when, annoyed by
the faults of others, we may perhaps be tempted to imitate
the cruel conduct of the Pharisees toward the woman taken
in adultery.   The Holy Spirit wishes to chisel the features
of Jesus in us, transforming us into living images of the Savior;
therefore, He gently and unceasingly urges us to be merciful.
He puts into our hearts a love for the miserable : for those who
are wretched both in the material and in the moral sense,
so that, like Jesus, we may go in search of them, ready to
sacrifice ourselves for the salvation of their souls.   Above all,
He spurs us on to seek those who, because they have made us
suffer, have a special claim to our mercy.   We can no longer
be satisfied with forgiving them and treating them with
kindness, but we must experience the need of doing good to
them if we are to fully carry out the teaching of Jesus :
" Do good to them that hate you " (*Mt* 5,44).

This is the goal toward which the Holy Spirit wants
to lead us by the gift of counsel, and in this way He will
establish us in that perfect mercy of which our divine Master
has said : " Blessed are the merciful, for they shall obtain
mercy " (*ibid.*, *6*, 7).   Consider this most prudent advice of the

Holy Spirit : be merciful, because " With what judgment you judge you shall be judged " (*ibid.* 7,2).

COLLOQUY

" O Lord, I run to You because You are so good and merciful and because I know that You did not despise the poor nor hate the sinner. You did not reject the thief who confessed his sins, nor the weeping Magdalen, nor the supplicant Canaanite woman, nor the woman taken in adultery, nor the tax collector sitting at his counter, nor the publican who implored Your mercy, nor the Apostle who denied You, nor even those who crucified You. I am drawn by the perfume of Your graces.

" I have inhaled the fragrance of Your mercy and I come to You to be strengthened by it. Blessed is the man who, following Your example, has a heart filled with compassion for the unfortunate. Blessed is he who is merciful and quick to help those who are in need, he who remembers that it is more blessed to give than to receive, who is quick to forgive and slow to anger, who never takes revenge, but in all circumstances considers the needs of others as though they were his own. O Lord, pour into my soul the dew of Your mercy, fill my heart with charity, that I may know how to be all things to all men and be so dead to myself that I live only for the good of others. Teach me to distil the sweet perfume of mercy, which is composed of the needs of the poor, the anguish of the oppressed, the anxieties of the afflicted, the failures of sinners, and finally, all the pains of those who suffer, even if they be my enemies. All these things are repugnant to my nature, but the fragrance one draws from them surpasses all other odors, because, as You have said, it has the power to give eternal life : ' Blessed are the merciful, for they shall find mercy. ' O Lord, grant that I may pour out this perfume, not only on Your head and on Your feet, but on Your whole body, which is the Church, so that it will lessen the sorrows of all Your suffering members " (cf. St. Bernard).

308

FRATERNAL UNION

SEVENTEENTH SUNDAY AFTER PENTECOST

PRESENCE OF GOD - O my God, give me the grace to preserve union with my neighbor by the bonds of charity and peace.

MEDITATION

1. As Jesus during His earthly life never ceased to recommend fraternal charity and union, so the Church in the Sunday Masses continually preaches this virtue. She does it today by making use of a passage in St. Paul's Epistle to the Ephesians (4,1-3). " I, therefore...beseech you, that you walk worthy of the vocation in which you are called, with all humility and mildness, with patience, supporting one another in charity, careful to keep the unity of the Spirit in the bond of peace. " The call which we have received is the vocation to Christianity, which is to say, the vocation to love. God, infinite Charity, adopts us as His children, that we may so emulate His charity that love becomes the bond which unites us all in one heart, as the Father and Son are united in one Godhead by the bond of the Holy Spirit. " As Thou, Father, in Me, and I in Thee; that they also may be one in Us " (*Jn* 17,21), was the prayer of Jesus for us.

To " keep unity in the bond of peace " is easy and difficult at the same time. It is easy because when the heart is truly humble, meek, and patient, it bears everything with love, carefully trying to adapt itself to the feelings and desires of others, rather than asserting its own. It is difficult because, as long as we are here below, self-love, even when mortified, always tends to rise and assert its rights, thus creating continual occasions of clashes, the avoidance of which calls for much self-renunciation and much delicacy toward others. We should be persuaded that all that disturbs, weakens, or worse still, destroys fraternal union, does not please God; it does not please Him even if done under pretext of zeal. We should always prefer to renounce our own ideas—although they be good—rather than dispute with our neighbor,

308 - FRATERNAL UNION

except when it is a question of fulfillment of duty or respect for the law of God. An act of humble renunciation for the sake of union and peace among our brethren gives much more glory to God than a glorious deed which might cause discord or disagreement.

2. Very often the cause of division among good people is excessive self-assertion : the desire to do things one's own way. Given our limitations, there can be nothing so absolute in our ideas that it cannot give way to the ideas of others. If our ideas are good, upright, and brilliant, those of others may be equally good, or even better. Therefore, it is much wiser, more humble and charitable to accept the views of others and to try to reconcile our views with theirs, rather than to reject them, lest we be obliged to give up our personal ways and views. This individualism is the enemy of union; it is a hindrance to good works as well as to spiritual progress.

In today's Epistle, St. Paul puts before us all the reasons why we should preserve union with our neighbor. Be " one body and one spirit; as you are called in one hope of your calling. One Lord, one faith, one baptism, one God and Father of all. " If God has willed to save and sanctify us all in Christ, uniting us in Him in one body, giving us one same vocation, one faith, and one hope, and being Himself the Father of all, how shall we pretend to save and sanctify ourselves if we are not united with one another? If we do not wish to frustrate God's plan and endanger our salvation and sanctification, we should be ready to make any personal sacrifice whatsoever in order to maintain and strengthen union. Let us bear in mind that Jesus has asked for us not only union, but perfect union : " That they may be made perfect in one " (*Jn* 17,23).

Today's Gospel (*Mt* 22,34-46) also strengthens this exhortation to union, since in it Jesus repeats that the commandment to love our neighbor is, together with the commandment to love God, the basis of " the whole law, " that is, of all Christianity. Let us not turn a deaf ear to these repeated appeals for charity and union; the Church insists on these points because Jesus has insisted on them, and because charity is " the precept of the Lord; if this only is done, it is enough " (St. John the Evangelist).

COLLOQUY

" O Word, Son of God, You look with more complacency on one work done in fraternal union and charity than on a thousand done in discord; one tiny little act, like the closing of an eye, performed in union and charity, pleases You more than if I were to suffer martyrdom in disunion and without charity. Where there is union, You are present, for You call Yourself charity : ' *Deus caritas est,* ' God is charity. You call Yourself the God of peace and union : ' *Deus pacis,* ' God of peace. You are the source of all peace, and without You there can be neither true peace nor union. False is the peace and union among sinners; it cannot last long, because as their hearts are dominated by the tyranny of sin and of passions, the bond which unites them quickly breaks; it is a weak bond no stronger than a thread of tow. Therefore, from You alone, O God, comes perfect union, and where there is disunion, confusion reigns because of sin and the devil. With what great desire should we seek this union and love it with all our heart! Where there is union, there is all good, there is an abundance of all things, of all celestial and terrestrial riches.

" O Most Holy Trinity, give us, then, the grace to live always united with one another, preserving union of spirit, having one will and opinion, imitating the indivisible unity which exists among the three divine Persons " (St. Mary Magdalen dei Pazzi).

"Where charity and love are, You are there also, O Lord! Your love, O Christ, has united us in one body and one heart; grant, then, that we may love one another with a sincere heart. Keep far from us all quarrels and contentions; grant that our hearts may be always united in You, and do You dwell always in our midst" (The Liturgy).

309

THE GIFT OF KNOWLEDGE

PRESENCE OF GOD - O Holy Spirit, teach me the nothingness of earthly things.

MEDITATION

1. By the gifts of fear, fortitude, piety, and counsel, the Holy Spirit regulates our moral life; whereas, by the other gifts—knowledge, understanding, and wisdom—He governs our theological life more directly, that is, our relations with God. The first four gifts perfect the moral virtues especially; the last three perfect the theological virtues. They are the so-called gifts of the contemplative life, that is, of the life of prayer and union with God.

In our ascent toward God we find one great obstacle : creatures which impress and allure us by their attractions, tempting us to stop at them and thus drawing us away from God, the infinite good, who transcends human experience. It is not easy for us who live in the realm of sense to believe that God is all, that He is the only good, the only happiness, and to place our hope in Him alone, while He is veiled from sight. We find it difficult to believe that creatures are nothing, to be convinced of their vanity, while they present themselves to us so alluringly. It is true that faith comes to our aid, and in its light we have often reflected on these truths, yet in practice, our reasonings have often failed. Confronted with the attractions of creatures, we forget and perhaps even betray our Creator. Therefore we need more powerful help, a divine light, which illumines from within, without the need of passing through our reasonings, so limited and rude : it is this light that the Holy Spirit infuses into our soul by means of the gift of knowledge. This gift does not make us reason on the vanity of things; but it gives us a living, concrete experience of them, an intuition so clear that it admits no doubt. Under the influence of this gift, Francis of Assisi suddenly left his merry companions to espouse Lady Poverty, and when his indignant father drove him out of his house, he exclaimed

in the fervor of his spirit, " Henceforth I will not call Peter
Bernardone my father, but our Father who is in heaven! "

Under the impulse of this gift, Teresa of Avila wrote
these words : " All things pass, God never changes.　He who
has God, finds he lacks nothing : God alone suffices ";
and the dying words of Blessed Maria Bertilla were : " One
must work only for Jesus.　All else is nothing. "

2. Inspired by the gift of knowledge, St. John of the
Cross traced the famous way of the " nothing, " the way
which, leaving aside all created goods, goes quickly and
directly up the mount of perfection, on whose summit the
soul finds God.　" Nothing, nothing, " the saint repeats,
" neither this, nor that, neither the goods of earth, nor the
goods of heaven, " that is, not even spiritual joys and consolations, but God alone.　So much renunciation, so much
sacrifice, so much stripping of self terrifies poor human
nature.　But the soul illumined by the Holy Spirit understands :
nothing at all, because " all is vanity, except to love God and
serve Him alone " (*Imit. I*, 1,3).　In the measure that the gift
of knowledge develops in the soul, it understands and tastes
the " nothingness " of creatures, which makes it relish the
" all " of God and feel the need of escaping from creatures to
plunge into Him.　This is the first step toward contemplation.

" All the being of creation, then, compared with the
infinite Being of God, is nothing " (J.C. *AS I*, 4,4).　The
wonders of creation are nothing, the most marvelous works
of human genius are nothing, the knowledge possessed by the
most learned men is nothing : God is the only reality,
and it is He who gives value to all things, either because
they are the works of His hand, or because they are works done
by man for His glory.

In the midst of our most beautiful undertakings and our
solicitude for earthly things, the Holy Spirit reminds us of the
words of Jesus : " For what shall profit it a man, if he gain the
whole world, and suffer the loss of his soul? " (*Mk* 8,36).
And again, " Thou art careful and art troubled about many
things : but one thing is necessary " (*Lk* 10,41.42).　Thus
He teaches that our adherence to God is what is essential;
all the rest is accessory and very often fruitless.

In evaluating the beauty of created things, the gift of
knowledge, while revealing the essential nothingness of
these things, does not deny the relative perfections to be

found in them, but shows them only as vestiges, reflections of the infinite perfection of God. It is this light that changes creatures from an obstacle into a ladder leading us to God, because " the soul is strongly moved to love her Beloved, her God, by the consideration of the creatures, seeing that these are things that have been made by His own hand " (J.C. *SC*, 4,3).

When a soul is profoundly enlightened by the gift of knowledge, creatures no longer hinder its ascent to God, for whether considering their nothingness or the beauty with which God has endowed them, whether in giving them up or in using them through necessity, they always urge the soul on to God, inspiring it to seek Him and love Him, the one infinitely beautiful Being.

COLLOQUY

" My God, here on earth all is vanity. What can I seek and desire to find here below where nothing is pure? All is vain, uncertain, and deceptive, except to love You, O Lord, and do good works. But I cannot love You perfectly unless I despise myself and the world.

" O my soul, do not think it hard to leave your friends and acquaintances; they often stand in the way of divine consolations. Where are the companions with whom you played and laughed? I do not know; they went away and abandoned me. And where are the things you were interested in yesterday? They have vanished. Everything has gone. Then only he who serves You, O Lord, is wise, because he despises the earthly life with all its charms.

" Keep me, O my God, from seeking the joys of the world. I conjure you, remove from my heart every attachment to earthly vanities. Lift me up to the height of the Cross; grant that I may follow You wherever You precede me. Poor and stripped of all, an exile on earth, and unknown, I willingly remain with You " (Thomas à Kempis).

" Remove from me, O my God, everything that leads me away from You; give me everything that will bring me nearer to You. Enrapture me, so that I will live wholly and always for You " (St. Nicholas of Flüe).

" O Lord, grant that the sweet, burning power of Your love may draw my heart away from all earthly delights,

so that I may die for love of You as You deigned to die for
love of me " (St. Francis of Assisi).

310

BLESSED ARE THEY THAT MOURN

PRESENCE OF GOD - Grant, O Lord, that I may shed only such tears
as are pleasing to You and that will help me to grow in Your love.

MEDITATION

1. The Beatitude : " Blessed are they that mourn, for they
shall be comforted " (*Mt* 5,5), corresponds to the gift of
knowledge. Blessed are they who, thoroughly enlightened
by the Holy Spirit as to the nothingness of creatures, weep for
the time they have spent seeking them, and mourn over the
energy and affection they have wasted on the vanities of the
world. These are the burning tears of St. Augustine who,
in his *Confessions*, continually laments : " Late have I loved
Thee, O Beauty ever ancient, ever new, late have I loved
Thee.... Thou wert with me, but I was not with Thee;
creatures kept me far from Thee. " These are the tears of the
penitent Magdalen, and of St. Peter weeping over his fall;
blessed tears, cleansing souls from sin and disposing them for
friendship with God. These are the tears of souls determined
to seek God in preference to all creatures, but who still,
because of their frailty, have to reproach themselves daily
for some weakness, some slight return to futile earthly satisfactions. The gift of knowledge does not permit us to close
our eyes to our infidelities, however slight, but it makes us
hate them and weep for them with tears of compunction.
One who lives under the influence of this gift will never be
careless or superficial in his examinations of conscience;
his confessions, though peaceful, will always be sorrowful and
accompanied by true contrition. Such were the confessions
of the saints, who with the most lively sorrow accused
themselves of their slightest imperfections.

The Holy Spirit does not want us to be scrupulous, but He does want us to be very delicate in our fidelity to God. He is not satisfied that we despise the vanities of the world in general, but He wants us to despise them in their most subtle manifestations, such as slight retaliations of self-love, little self-complacencies, or concern for the affection and esteem of others. Blessed the soul who knows how to recognize all its miseries and weep for them, not with tears of discouragement or anxiety, but with tears of profound sorrow, which instead of contracting its heart in fear, will dilate it in repentant love, and cast it into God's arms, with a heart renewed by love and sorrow.

2. The gift of knowledge, making us clearly realize the vanity of creatures, convinces us that they are perishable and full of defects; hence, it incites us to place all our hope in God. In this sense, the gift of knowledge perfects and strengthens the virtue of hope so that, without further hesitation, our heart anchors itself in God, recognizing in Him our only strength and support, our only happiness.

The more we hope in God and the beatific possession of Him which awaits us in eternal life, so much the more are we disposed, not only to renounce the happiness and satisfaction which creatures can offer us, but also to embrace all the sacrifices necessary to reach eternal life. Many sacrifices are necessary because we cannot go to God except by following the path traced by the Son of God to lead us to Him : the way of the Cross. But even though it suffers, the soul who lives by hope can repeat the words of St. Paul : " We faint not...for that which is at present momentary and light of our tribulation, worketh for us above measure exceedingly an eternal weight of glory " (2 *Cor* 4, 16.17). The gift of knowledge helps us judge our present sorrows as light when compared with eternal beatitude, in view of which it incites us to bless them, even should they cost us our blood. This is why the Apostle rejoiced and gloried in his tribulations (cf. *Rom* 5,3), and St. Francis of Assisi sang, " The joys I hope for are so great that all pain is dear to me. "

Under the influence of the gift of knowledge, the soul understands the blessedness of tears, that is, the blessedness of suffering embraced for the love of God. This gift does not make us insensible to physical and moral pain; so true is this that the beatitude speaks expressly of " tears, " but although it does not keep us from weeping, it does sanctify our weeping and makes us more resigned to God's will, preferring these tears to the vain joys of the world and regarding them as a means of becoming more like unto Christ crucified.   What a difference between such tears and those shed through pride, because we will not submit to God's will, or because of the capricious resentments of self-love.

When a soul has reached the point where it prefers blessed tears shed at the foot of the Cross to the joys of earth, it can hope in the beatitude promised by Jesus : " Blessed are they that mourn, for they shall be comforted. "

COLLOQUY

" O Lord, the peace You give us in this world is full of anxieties, tribulations, and persecutions; but then You bring us to a quiet, tranquil peace.   I can even say that in the midst of these difficulties You give us Your peace, because the Spirit attests in this way that we are Your children.   This means, ' Blessed are they that mourn, for they shall be comforted. '   Not only will You comfort us in the future, but You turn our very tears into consolation, and war itself into peace.   He who loves You, O Lord, finds in the most burning fire of tribulation the cool breeze and the dew of heavenly consolation " (St. Mary Magdalen dei Pazzi).

" Blessed are You, O my God, because You have not demanded from us as the price of Your kingdom, a long period of suffering, but a very brief one, as brief as life, a moment compared with an eternity of happiness!   Truly, if for love of You, we had to endure for hundreds of thousands of years, sufferings a thousand times harder, more painful and severe, we should have accepted Your decree with immense joy and longing, and thanked You on our knees with our hands joined.   How much more then, should we thank You now that, in Your mercy, You have deigned to give us the shortest time possible of suffering, a time as short as life! Short as an instant, as nothing, because life is nothing compared with eternity.

" Come then, come, O children of God; let us hasten to the Cross of Christ, to sorrow, contempt, and poverty!

Grant, O Lord, that I may love You as You have loved me, with that absolute fidelity, purity, and love which reserves nothing for self, which gives itself wholly and therefore runs to pain and suffering, seeing and feeling in all things nothing but love " (St. Angela of Foligno).

311

THE GIFT OF UNDERSTANDING

PRESENCE OF GOD - Come, O Spirit of understanding, and enlighten me!

MEDITATION

1. As we advance toward God, we encounter many difficulties, not only because of creatures obstructing our path, but also because of the impenetrability of the divine mysteries. To enable us to surmount the former, the Holy Spirit comes to our aid with the gift of knowledge; to overcome the latter, He comes to our aid with the gift of understanding.

Our intellect is incapable of seizing the infinite. Although gifted with faith, its manner of understanding is always human, proceeding by means of ideas and limited concepts, which are totally inadequate to express the divine realities. Revelation itself comes to us in human language; therefore, it cannot tell us what God is in Himself, nor manifest to us the intimate essence of revealed truths. Proceeding with the virtue of faith alone, we are constrained to stop, so to speak, at the surface of the divine mysteries. We know with certitude that they have been revealed by God; we adhere to them with all our strength and yet we do not succeed in penetrating them. However, what faith alone cannot do, it is able to do with the help of the gift of understanding. This gift surpasses our human way of comprehension and enlightens us in a divine way; it makes us " *intus legere,* " that is, " read within " the divine mysteries, with the light, with the understanding of the Holy Spirit Himself.

It is a swift, deep penetration which, while adding
nothing new to what we already know from revelation,
does make us understand the inner meaning of the revealed
truth.   The gift of understanding tears off, so to say, the
outer coverings of the propositions and human concepts,
allowing us to see the substance of the divine mysteries.
Faith tells us that God is Trinity; the gift of understanding
tells us nothing more, it does not make us see, nor does it
explain this mystery to us, but it does make us penetrate it.
Under the influence of this gift, the soul not only believes
that God is One and Three, but it has the intuition that the
mystery of the Trinity is essential to the divine nature
and that it reveals better than anything else the perfection,
the power, and the infinite love of God.

2. Only the Holy Spirit, who is God, can make us
penetrate the divine mysteries.   St. Paul expressly says so :
That which " eye hath not seen nor ear heard...to us God
hath revealed...by His Spirit.   For the Spirit searcheth
all things, yea, the deep things of God....   So the things
also that are of God, no man knoweth, but the Spirit of God.
Now we have received not the spirit of this world, but the
Spirit that is of God; that we may know the things that
are given us from God " (1 *Cor* 2,9-12).   And this is the
wonderful work that the Holy Spirit performs in us by the
gift of understanding.   He communicates a share of His
knowledge of the divine mysteries to souls united to Him by
love.   Therefore, it is clear that the more closely united we are
to the Holy Spirit by perfect charity, the more capable we
shall be of receiving this precious communication.   Then the
gift of understanding will not be inactive in us, but will
intervene with its light to illumine our studies and our meditations on divine things, making us penetrate into their
depths, making us " see " the intimate sense of the sacred
texts and giving us a correct understanding of God's
commandments and counsels.   In this way, the Holy Spirit
introduces the soul to a form of prayer more simple and
profound : the mind no longer needs to reason or to look for
convincing motives; under the illuminating touch of the
Holy Spirit, the soul's gaze is arrested and fixed on truth.
This simple contemplative gaze reveals God to the soul
better than any theological study; it feels itself engulfed in
God; it senses a bottomless abyss into which it is glad to

plunge. It does not see, does not distinguish, cannot describe anything with precision, but it feels God, feels that it is in contact with Him. What a difference in our comprehension of the same mystery when we meditate on it by the light of faith only and when, on the contrary, we have the grace to penetrate it by the light derived from the gift of understanding! Then we no longer look at the exterior, but at the interior; we no longer stop at the words which express it, but we penetrate the secret meaning hidden within the words.

COLLOQUY

Come, Holy Spirit, come light divine!

" O light that sees no other light, light that obscures all other light, light which is the source of all other light, brightness compared with which all other brightness is darkness, and all other light obscurity; supreme light, not darkened by blindness, not clouded by darkness, not obscured by shadows; light that no obstacle impedes, no shade divides; light illuminating all things together and forever, absorb me in the ocean of your brilliance, that I may see You in Yourself, and myself in You, and all things beneath You " (St. Augustine).

" How can I approach You, O Holy Spirit? You dwell in inaccessible light, and are Yourself all light, knowledge and splendor, while I dwell in a place of darkness and am nothing but ignorance and rudeness.

" Meanwhile, O divine Spirit, I beg You with confidence to illumine me. Reveal to me the divine greatness and the divine mysteries, so that I may adore and acknowledge them. Disclose the wiles of the devil and of the world, that I may avoid them and never fall again; reveal to me my miseries and my weaknesses, my errors, my prejudices, my obstinacies, the artifices of my self-love, so that I may hate and correct them. But, O beneficent light, above all illumine my soul, that it may know what You wish of me : make me understand well the charm of Your attractions and of Your grace, and all that I must do to merit the beneficent influence of Your goodness, so that I may correspond with complete fidelity; O loving Spirit, sustain me in this fidelity unto death " (Fr. Aurillon).

312

BLESSED ARE THE CLEAN OF HEART

PRESENCE OF GOD - O Lord, purify my heart and my mind, that I may learn to know You better.

MEDITATION

1. The beatitude : " Blessed are the clean of heart, for they shall see God " (*Mt* 5,8), corresponds to the gift of understanding. There is a purity of heart which is the indispensable condition for receiving an abundant inflowing of the gift of understanding; it is the purity that results, not only from the absence of sin, but also from the absence of the slightest earthly affection. In fact, God does not communicate Himself fully to a creature whose heart is not absolutely pure; that is, one whose entire capacity for affection is not reserved for Him. As long as we have any attachment to creatures, any seeking for the affection of others, any complacency in feeling that we are loved by them, our heart is not pure enough to enjoy the divine communications. Therefore, before allowing a soul to penetrate His divine mysteries, God subjects it to a purification of the affections by means of detachments and sacrifices, sometimes at the cost of blood, but which, if generously accepted, will eventually detach the heart from creatures and leave it entirely free for its Creator. If God makes us pass through this trial, let us not draw back or try to evade His action, but let us cooperate with it, being fully persuaded that He reserves the fullness of His gifts and of His light for those souls alone who are free from any shadow of creatures, those hearts which belong entirely to Him. In this sense it may well be said that the sight of God is the reward promised to the pure of heart. In fact, if the heart retains any attachment, even slight, to creatures, the intellect remains clouded, and " has no more capacity for receiving enlightenment from the wisdom of God than has the air, when it is dark, for receiving enlightenment from the sun.... Oh! " exclaims St. John of the Cross, " if men but knew how great is the blessing of divine light whereof they are deprived by this blindness

which proceeds from their affections and desires!" (*AS I,* 8,2.6). Indeed, when the heart is pure, then the intellect, like a clear glass, can be completely penetrated by the light of the Holy Spirit.

2. There is another purity of heart which is not just a disposition to receive the gift of understanding, but is the fruit of this gift. Here the word " heart " is used in its broader meaning of spirit and mind, which is its usual meaning in Holy Scripture.

Our minds are so dull that we can always err in understanding divine things, either by imagining them in a material way, measuring them by worldly standards, or by interpreting them according to our personal views, considering only one aspect, and ignoring others which are essential, and so on. This dullness of mind, unfortunately, has been the source of many heresies in the Church. The gift of understanding, giving us the light of the Holy Spirit Himself, purifies our minds from these errors and frees them from the illusions of the imagination, as well as from other false interpretations. By means of this purity of mind, the gift of understanding insures the integrity of our faith, enabling us to penetrate the objective reality of the divine mysteries, and giving us the real meaning of God's law, of the commandments, and the counsels. On the other hand, this gift, which allows us to penetrate the divine mysteries by the infused light of the Holy Spirit, makes us clearly understand that God cannot be enclosed in our dull imaginations nor in our limited ideas, but that He is infinitely superior to anything we can think or imagine about Him. St. John of the Cross says, " Since God is inaccessible, see that thou concern not thyself with how much thy faculties can comprehend and thy senses can perceive, that thou be not satisfied with less and that thy soul lose not the agility that is needful for one that would attain to Him " (*SM I,* 52).

If we wish to respond to the motions of the gift of understanding, we must be detached from our own ideas and ready to renounce them even though very dear to us; we must not be too sure about our way of understanding the things of God, but must seek the guidance of the Church. Above all, we must humbly pray for the gift of understanding because it will free us from errors and give us a right understanding of divine things.

If the Holy Spirit finds us pure in heart, He will enlighten us more and more; greater purity will lead to greater light, and vice versa; thus, from clarity to clarity, we shall arrive at a more profound penetration of the divine mysteries, which will give us a kind of foretaste of the beatific vision. " Blessed are the clean of heart, for they shall see God! "

COLLOQUY

" O Lord, give me right sentiments about You and grant that I may seek You with simplicity of heart. My heart says to You, ' I will seek Your face. ' When my heart seeks You, O Lord, it is Your presence it is seeking. Your home is where You dwell, and where do You dwell, if not in Your temple? My heart is Your temple : teach me how to welcome You there. You are spirit, and I must adore You in spirit and in truth. Come into my heart, and all the idols shall fall.

" Now I shall listen to Your voice and learn to long for You and to prepare myself to see You. Blessed are all who see You! And if they do see You, it is not because, while they were on earth, they were poor in spirit, or because they were meek or merciful, or because they mourned or hungered and thirsted after justice, but because they were clean of heart. Humility is good for attaining the kingdom of heaven; meekness is good for possessing the land; tears are good for receiving consolation; hunger and thirst after justice, for being filled; mercy is good for obtaining mercy, but only purity of heart permits us to see You.

" My desire is to see You; what I desire is great, but it is You who tell me to wish for it. Help me to purify my heart, because what I desire to see is pure but my means of seeing it, impure. Come to me, O God, and purify me by Your grace; purify my heart with Your aid and strength. If I receive You into my heart during this present life, after my death You will admit me into Your presence" (St. Augustine).

" Come, Holy Spirit, speak to my heart; or at least, if You wish to remain silent, may Your very silence speak to me, because without You I am always in danger of following my own errors and confusing them with Your teachings" (cf. St. Bernard).

313

THE GIFT OF WISDOM

PRESENCE OF GOD - Come, O Spirit of Wisdom, draw me!

MEDITATION

1. The gift of understanding enables us to penetrate God's mysteries; the gift of wisdom takes us further : it lets us taste them and gives us a delightful knowledge of them. This is the *savory knowledge* of which St. Bernard speaks, the untranslatable " *dulce sapere* " invoked by St. Thomas in the *Adoro Te Devote*; it is the precious gift which the Holy Spirit offers us in the words : " *Gustate et videte quam bonus sit Dominus* " (*Ps* 33,9). " Taste and see that the Lord is sweet. " It is not by chance that it is first said *taste*, and then *see*, for by the gift of wisdom we know God by the experience of the heart which " tastes " the object loved.

There are two ways of knowing : a speculative, intellectual way, and an experimental way, resulting from a kind of " connaturality " with the object of our knowledge. The latter is not so clear, but it is much deeper than the former, and grasps the inner substance of things. Thus, for example, because of the affinity of thought and affection that binds a mother to her child, she knows its heart much better than any other person. Similar to this is the knowledge of divine subjects which we acquire by means of the gift of wisdom. Between God and us there is a certain " connaturality, " a certain similarity, produced by the love which unites us to Him and in some way assimilates us to Him; even more, St. Paul does not hesitate to say that " He who is joined to the Lord, is one spirit " (1 *Cor* 6,17).

The gift of wisdom enables us to know God and divine things precisely through this " connaturality, " and therefore gives us a delightful experience of them through the love which is its source. This experience seizes the soul in its very center, that is, in the will, forcibly drawing it to God and at the same time, inundating the intellect with floods of light. The gift of wisdom acts somewhat like the rays of the sun which give heat and light at the same time. Its

warmth quickens charity in the soul, and through this
enkindling of love, the soul is enlightened concerning the divine
realities and is enabled to judge of them, because it knows
intuitively their infinite goodness and their absolute superio-
rity over all created things. "Oh, the depth of the riches
of...God!" (*Rom* 11,33). This is the cry of the soul
inflamed and illumined by the gift of wisdom.

2. All the gifts of the Holy Spirit are closely connected
with charity, for they abound only in souls who possess
charity, and they develop in the measure that charity
increases. However, the gift of wisdom has a very special
relationship to the love of charity, primarily because it is set
in action by means of charity. St. Thomas says, "The
cause of the gift of wisdom is found in the will, and it is
charity" (II^a II^{ae}, q.45, a.2, co.); therefore, the more a soul
loves God, the more capable it becomes of receiving the
motions of this gift. In addition, the delightful knowledge
of God derived from the gift of wisdom is a most powerful
means of increasing charity. How can we fail to love the
Lord more after having tasted His sweetness? In the measure
that the gift of wisdom invades a soul, charity increases
and so does its unitive force, by which the soul adheres ever
more closely to God.

This gift leads to a more profound prayer than that
experienced when the gift of understanding alone intervenes :
the soul feels "seized" and drawn by God in an irresistible
way; it feels truly united to the Lord and tastes Him in
this union—not in a sensible manner but spiritually—and
by intuition, it knows Him in the most intimate way possible
here below. The soul emerges from this prayer inflamed
with love, a love which it expresses above all by the
perfect conformity of its will with God's in all the happenings
of life; it comes from this prayer so full of God that, upon
returning to its ordinary duties, it sees and considers
everything in relation to God. In this way the gift of wisdom
extends its influence even into our practical life and teaches
us to judge all things in the light of God.

In order to receive the actions of the gift of wisdom
—the most sublime of all the gifts—we should gently prepare
our heart for the plenitude of love, and at the same time
apply ourselves to the acquiring of a profound humility,
because as Jesus has said : "Thou hast hid these things

from the wise and prudent, and hast revealed them to little ones " (*Mt* 11,25).

" And those alone acquire the wisdom of God who are like ignorant children, and, laying aside their knowledge, walk in His service with love " (J.C. *AS I*, 4,5).

COLLOQUY

" Come, O divine Spirit, and take possession of my heart; dissipate all the darkness that the folly of the world calls wisdom, and grant me in its place the gift of heavenly wisdom. You alone can teach me to despise what the world loves, that is, what delights and flatters. You alone can teach me to enjoy the things of God, the virtue, piety, and love which You came to kindle on earth in order that the world might be inflamed " (Anonymous).

" O God, who by Your essence are uncreated Love, infinite Love, boundless Love, not only loving, but Love itself; O God, from whom proceeds the love of all the seraphim and of all creatures, why do I not love You? Why am I not consumed in this burning furnace of love, which embraces the whole universe?

" O God, essential goodness, You by whom all goodness is good, who are the source of the goodness of all creatures, just as the sea is the source of all waters, You whose goodness is so excellent that nothing in heaven or on earth can be called good in respect to it, why do I not love You, since goodness is the object of love?

" O most holy Father! O most merciful Son! O most loving Holy Spirit! When will You, O Father, be most deeply hidden in the innermost depths of my soul and fully possess me? When shall I be all Yours and You all mine? When will You be my King? When will that day come? Oh! When? Oh, it will surely come! Do You believe that I shall see it? Why such delay! How painful this waiting! Hasten, O Jesus, hasten, delay no longer! " (Ven. Louis of Granada).

314

BLESSED ARE THE PEACEMAKERS

PRESENCE OF GOD - O Holy Spirit, help me to establish my heart in peace.

MEDITATION

1. A soul who has tasted God, under the influence of the gift of wisdom, looks at the world with the eyes of God, and therefore is able to judge all things " *secundum rationes divinae* " (St. Thomas II^a II^{ae}, q.45, a.3, ad 3) by divine principles, according to supernatural motives, and not according to limited human reasoning. These are the truly " wise " judgments that we can never formulate without the help of the Holy Spirit. In fact, " the sensual man [the man of the senses and of natural reason] perceiveth not these things that are of the Spirit of God; for it is foolishness to him, and he cannot understand, because it is spiritually examined. But the spiritual man [the man of faith guided by the Holy Spirit] judgeth all things " (1 *Cor* 2,14.15). He judges all things in relation to their supreme Cause, God; therefore, he directs all his acts and orders everything in his life according to God. From this order—the only true order—comes peace, the fruit of the wise direction of the gift of wisdom; hence, the man who habitually lives under the influence of this gift is a *peaceful* man par excellence. His heart is established in peace, there is no longer anything disordered in it; all his affections and desires, all his thoughts and acts, are completely ordered according to God, being wholly submitted and conformed to His laws, to His will, to His good pleasure. One who possesses peace, disseminates peace. A *peacemaker*, in the etymological sense, is one who makes peace, cultivates peace, and spreads it about him. This is why the gift of wisdom corresponds to the beatitude of peace, " Blessed are the peacemakers. " Only one who lives under the influence of this gift can truly judge and regulate everything according to God, so that nothing, not even suffering, can disturb his interior peace, for he knows that even the most painful

happenings are permitted and ordered by God for the good of His elect. " To them that love God, all things work together unto good " (*Rom* 8,28).

In this way the gift of wisdom gives a note of sweetness, not only to our prayer, but also to our practical life : " Under the influence of this gift, " says St. Thomas, " what is bitter becomes sweet, and weariness becomes repose " (II^a II^{ae}, q.45, a.3, ad 3).

2. The gift of wisdom leads us to peace : the interior peace of the soul who, having tasted God, gives itself to Him without reserve, in complete surrender to His divine will; the serene peace of one who, seeing God in all things, accepts the hardships of life without being disturbed, adoring God's providence in all; finally, it is the social peace of him who, considering all men in relation to God, as His creatures and His children, loves them all and wishes to live in peace with all. The more perfect it becomes, the more will this peace bring us to taste the reward promised by Jesus : " Blessed are the peacemakers, for they shall be called the children of God " (*Mt* 5,9).

All Christians are children of God by grace, but here we are considering the special reward which we might call a superabundance of the grace of adoption, an experience by which the soul not only knows, but even *feels and tastes* that it is a child of God. It is the savory sense of divine filiation which is born in the soul under the influence of the gift of wisdom. " The Spirit Himself giveth testimony to our spirit, that we are the sons of God " (*Rom* 8,16); these words of St. Paul become a living reality, a delightful experience; the soul feels itself called a child of God, not by men, but by God Himself; no audible voice speaks to it, but the more it feels drawn by God and enjoys Him in intimate union, so much the more does it feel that He is its Father and that, in very truth, it is His child.

Our God is the God of peace; therefore, it is perfectly right that the peaceful man, he who possesses and diffuses peace, should feel in a very special way that he is God's child. If men generally do not feel themselves to be children of God, it is because they are so little disposed to peace, so ready for disputes, quarrels and war. They talk about peace but do not make peace, for they do not accept the guidance of the Spirit of wisdom. In their

ignorance they prefer to be guided by themselves, and
as a result they are dominated by pride, self-interest, and
cupidity; they live in disorder and they sow disorder around
them.

The more our soul becomes firmly established in peace,
and the more we become messengers of peace, to that degree
will the Holy Spirit infuse into us this delightful sense of our
divine sonship, and this will become for us a source of immense
happiness, a true prelude of eternal beatitude.

COLLOQUY

" O Holy Spirit, give us Your wisdom to teach and guide
us and to bring all things back to You, from whom they came.
Oh! if we could really return to You as we came out from You,
like waves returning to the ocean whence they came! Oh!
If we could only make this complete return to You, we should
be in perpetual happiness and perpetual peace!

" Your wisdom is the perfection which orders all things in
relation to You who are their end. It considers the past,
looks at the present, and scans the future always in relation
to You. From this orientation, peace, the sweet fruit of
wisdom, is born in our hearts. He who possesses this peace
is always serene : he is not troubled by the past or the present,
and he looks peacefully toward the future, because he knows
that everything is permitted and arranged by Your sovereign
goodness.

" O eternal Father, give us light to know this peace, the
cause of so many blessings, and without which we fall into
so many faults and evils!

" Oh! why can I not communicate this peace to every
creature? If I were what I should be, I certainly could
diffuse it everywhere! O Lord, give me Your peace, the
peace of a heart which lives united to You, for of myself
I can have no good and without You I cannot have peace "
(St. Mary Magdalen dei Pazzi).

" O most benign Jesus, give me above all desires the
desire to rest in You, and in You let my heart find peace.
You are the true peace of the heart; You are its only refuge;
without You all things are difficult and troubled. In this
peace, then, that is, in You, the one sovereign eternal Good,
I will sleep and take my rest " (*Imit. III*, 15,4).

315

THE POWER AND LOVE OF JESUS

EIGHTEENTH SUNDAY AFTER PENTECOST

PRESENCE OF GOD - O Jesus, grant me the grace to correspond always with the gifts of Your love.

MEDITATION

1. A poor paralytic is presented to Our Lord; he probably had himself brought there to ask for bodily health, but in the presence of the purity and holiness which emanates from the Person of Jesus, he realizes that he is a sinner and remains confused and humiliated before Our Lord. Jesus has already read his heart, and seeing his faith and humility, He does not even wait for him to speak, but suddenly says to him with infinite kindness : " Be of good heart, son, thy sins are forgiven thee " (*Gosp : Mt* 9,1-8). The first and the greatest miracle has taken place : the man is no longer a slave of Satan; he is a child of God. Jesus, who came to save souls, rightfully healed the soul before the body.

This miracle, however, does not please the scribes who, not believing in the divinity of Jesus, begin immediately in the secret of their hearts to accuse Him of blasphemy. But the Master, who had read the soul of the paralytic, also reads theirs. " Why do you think evil in your hearts? " If Jesus had seen there even a little humility and faith, He would have been as ready to heal them as He was to heal the heart of the paralytic; but unfortunately, He found nothing but pride and obstinacy. However, He wishes to use every means to soften them, so He gives them the strongest proof of His divinity. " But that you may know that the Son of Man hath power on earth to forgive sins — then He said to the man sick of the palsy — ' Arise, take up thy bed, and go into thy house. ' And he arose and went into his house. " The miracle was striking and instantaneous. The word of Jesus effected immediately what it expressed. The words of God alone could have such power. But the scribes will not admit that they are defeated :

when the heart is proud and obstinate, not even factual evidence is capable of moving it.

Let us never say our faith is weak because we do not see or touch with our hand the truth which is proposed for our belief; let us rather admit that it is weak because our heart is not sufficiently docile to grace, nor entirely free from pride. If we want to have strong faith, let us be as humble and simple as children; if we wish to share in the grace of sanctification which was given to the paralytic, let us offer ourselves to Our Lord with contrite, humble hearts, thoroughly convinced that we need His help and forgiveness.

2. The Gospel presents Jesus to us in all the splendor of His divine personality, possessing all the powers proper to God. The Epistle (1 *Cor* 1,4-8) shows Him in the act of putting His divinity at our service, as it were, to sanctify us and make us divine. Jesus continues to do for our souls what He did for the soul of the paralytic, and today's Epistle is a beautiful synthesis of His action in us, an action far-reaching and complete, embracing our whole being. Contemplating this action, St. Paul bursts forth in a hymn of gratitude : " I give thanks to my God always for you, for the grace of God that is given you in Christ Jesus, that in all things you are made rich in Him, in all utterance, and in all knowledge...so that nothing is wanting to you in any grace. " Yes, every grace, every gift comes to us from Jesus, and through them our person and our life are sanctified. By means of sanctifying grace, He sanctifies our soul; through the infused virtues, He sanctifies our faculties; and by actual grace, He sanctifies our activity, enabling us to act supernaturally. Yet even this does not satisfy His liberality : He is not content with setting us on the road to God, supernaturalized by grace and the virtues, but He wishes to substitute His divine way of acting for our human way; therefore, He enriches us with the gifts of the Holy Spirit, which make us capable of being moved by God Himself. All this is the gift of Jesus to us, the fruit of His Passion. The Holy Spirit is also His gift, the Gift par excellence, which He merited for us by His death on the Cross, the Gift which He and the Father are continually sending to us from heaven to enlighten and direct our souls.

It seems as if Jesus, the true Son of God, is not jealous of His divinity or His prerogatives, but seeks every possible means to make us share by grace what He possesses by nature.   How true it is that the characteristic of love is to give oneself and to place those one loves on a plane of equality with oneself!

Let our hearts be filled with gratitude; let us correspond to the infinite love of Jesus and always keep ourselves under its influence, for He wills to " confirm us unto the end without crime, in the day of His coming" (cf. 1 *Cor* 1,8).

COLLOQUY

" O Jesus, You have taken away my death by giving me Your life; You have taken my flesh to give me Your Spirit; You have charged Yourself with my sins to bestow grace on me.

" Thus, O my Redeemer, all Your pains are my treasure and my wealth.   You clothe me with Your purple, You honor me with Your crown, Your sorrows are a gift to me, Your grief sustains me, Your wounds heal me, Your Blood enriches me, Your love inebriates me.

" You are the repose, the fire, and the desire of my soul. You are the Shepherd, and the Lamb who takes away the sins of the world.   You are the eternal Pontiff, powerful to appease the wrath of the supreme Father.   Who would not praise You, O Lord?   Who would not love You with all his heart?   O benign Jesus, inflame my soul with this love, show me Your beautiful countenance, make my eyes happy because they see Yours, and refuse not the kiss of peace to one who loves You.   You are the Spouse of my soul; it seeks You and calls You tearfully.   You, O Holy One, have delivered it from death by Your death, and, wounding it with Your love, You have not despised it.   Why does my misery not feel the sweetness of Your presence?   Listen, my God and Savior, give me a heart that will love You, for there is nothing sweeter than to burn always with Your love ." (Ven. Louis of Granada).

316

OUR MEETING WITH THE HOLY SPIRIT

PRESENCE OF GOD - Come, Holy Spirit, invade me with Your action.

MEDITATION

1. Considering the gifts of the Holy Spirit and the beatitudes which are their fruits, we arrive at a better understanding of the marvelous riches God has bestowed upon us. Every Christian possesses these gifts from the day of his Baptism; hence, there is no temerity in the desire that they attain their full maturity in us, so that our soul may be completely invaded by the action of the Holy Spirit. Furthermore, by this desire, we respond to a like desire on the part of God, who has given us these gifts that we may be moved and directed by His Spirit, " for whosoever are led by the Spirit of God, they are the sons of God " (*Rom* 8,14). And if we desire to be true children of God, does not our heavenly Father, who for this very purpose created us and raised us to the state of grace, desire it infinitely more?

Let us, then, nourish great desires in our souls. It is not too much, it is not rash, it is not presumptuous : God wills it. " *Voluntas Dei sanctificatio vestra* " (1 *Thes* 4,3); this is the will of God, your sanctification! If, however, our desires are to be effective, we must apply ourselves with ever-increasing generosity to dispose our soul for the action of the Holy Spirit. Let us be persuaded that before we can *experience* God and His divine union, the divine Paraclete must accomplish in us a work of thorough purification, for, as the green wood cannot be penetrated by the fire unless it is first dried and freed of all moisture, neither can our soul be invaded and transformed by the fire of divine love if it is not first purified of all its imperfections. Let us then prepare ourselves to undergo this indispensable purification courageously; or rather, let us try ourselves to anticipate it by mercilessly cutting all the ties which still bind us to earth, especially those which attach us to our self-love, our pride. " O humility, humility!... " exclaims St. Teresa of Jesus, " it is the lack of this... which prevents us from making progress, for the foundation of the whole [spiritual] edifice is humility, and, if you have not true humility, the Lord will not raise it very high for it lacks solidity. " (*Int C III*, 1-2 – *VII*, 4).

2. Generosity, detachment, and humility, must be united to fervent prayer to implore the action of the Holy Spirit. Let us send our supplications up to Him in the words of the Church :

> *Veni, Creator Spiritus. . .*
> *Accende lumen sensibus,*
> *Infunde amorem cordibus,*
> *Infirma nostri corporis,*
> *Virtute firmans perpeti.*

> Come, Creator Spirit. . .
> O guide our minds with Thy blest light,
> With love our hearts inflame,
> And, with Thy strength which ne'er decays,
> Confirm our mortal frame.

We need interior light because of the darkness of our senses; may the divine Spirit come and enkindle this flame within us, making us know God through loving contemplation. We need charity; may He come and pour it into our hearts, so often cold and dry because they are full of self-love and egoism. " The charity of God is poured forth in our hearts by the Holy Ghost " (*Rom* 5,5), and only from Him can we receive it. We need fortitude to conquer ourselves, to face difficulties, to keep ourselves serene and generous. May He come and sustain us with His gifts, and we shall no longer follow the foolish demands of self-love; we shall no longer let ourselves be frightened and affected by suffering and difficulties; we shall not so easily lose our peace in the midst of contradictions; but, strong in His strength, we shall maintain our interior composure with a serenity which will permit us to be generous always, and to be ever careful to give ourselves wholly to God.

> *Hostem repellas longius,*
> *Pacemque dones protinus.*

> Drive far from us our deadly foe,
> And grant us Thy true peace to know.

When the Holy Spirit has brought us to that perfect equilibrium which is sanctity itself, we shall no longer have anything to fear from the devil; he will flee far away, and if sometimes he succeeds in disturbing us, he will not be able to go beyond the threshold of our sensibility. Under the powerful protection of the Holy Spirit, the depths of our soul will remain in peace.

Perfect stability and lasting peace are the characteristics of the life of union with God. The Holy Spirit will introduce us to this union and cause us to advance in it, until He brings us into the sanctuary of the intimate life of God, into the very life of the Trinity. This is the most beautiful fruit of His action in our souls : an exquisite fruit, a pledge of eternal glory, a fruit which will attain perfect maturity in heaven, in the beatific vision of the God whom we love.

COLLOQUY

" O Holy Spirit, You have taken, so to speak, a clear, luminous ray from the glory of the Father and from the Incarnate Word, a glowing dart of love to illumine and to obscure, to wound and to heal, to inflame and to cool, to cast down or to blind, in order to glorify the creatures who receive You into their hearts and to help them advance with love. Who can ever tell the quality and number of Your inspirations? They are innumerable.

" But where do You pour out Your gifts and graces? In souls that You find ready to accept them. You renew those souls and bring them to the knowledge of God. What then, O my God, deprives the soul of Your Spirit? It is perverse self-love, the source and origin of every sin. Alas! I well see that the world remains wholly submerged and drowned in self-love! Some persons are sunk in it by their intellect, some by their memory, some by their will and some, with their whole soul, submerge themselves in it. What is most displeasing to You, O God, is that this perverse self-love dwells even in Your priests and in Your spouses. The disorder of our self-love, of our attachment to our own will is no small thing. It does not require mountains of enormous sins to block the course of this rapid stream, this ocean of love; the sands of our defects, which we think trivial, but which are not, suffice to do so.

" O Holy Spirit, purify the whole world, purify my soul of self-love, and do not permit it to return!" (St. Mary Magdalen dei Pazzi).

" O Holy Spirit, the Sanctifier, omnipotent God, essential Love of the Father and the Son, adorable bond of the august Trinity, I adore You and I love You with all my heart. Inexhaustible fountain of grace and love, enlighten my mind, sanctify my soul, and inflame my heart. God of goodness and mercy, come to me, visit me, fill me, abide in me, and make my heart a living temple and sanctuary where You can receive my adoration and worship and where You can find Your delight. Fountain of living water, springing up to eternal life, water my soul and quench its thirst for justice. Sacred Fire, purify me, make me burn with Your flames and never let them be extinguished in me. Ineffable Light, illumine me; perfect Sanctity, sanctify me. Spirit of Truth, without You I am in error; Spirit of Love, without You I am cold; Spirit of Unction, without You I am in aridity; life-giving Spirit of Life, without You I am dead.

" O divine Spirit, do gentle violence to my heart, and force it to desire You, to seek You, to obey You, to love You, and to possess You in time and in eternity. Amen" (Fr. Aurillon).

THE NINETEENTH TO THE LAST SUNDAY
AFTER PENTECOST

THE APOSTOLATE : DUTY, FORMATION, PREPARATION, PRACTICE

— UNION WITH GOD : PURIFICATION OF THE SPIRIT,

DEVELOPMENT OF LOVE, UNION OF WILL,

COMPLETE UNION.

317

ZEAL FOR SOULS

PRESENCE OF GOD - O Jesus, You who gave Yourself without reserve for the salvation of the world, enkindle in my heart an ardent zeal for the salvation of souls.

MEDITATION

1. According to the measure in which the love of God takes possession of our heart, it creates and nourishes in us an ever increasing love for our neighbor; this love, being supernatural, seeks only the supernatural good of our fellow men and thus becomes zeal for the salvation of souls.

If we have little love of God, we shall have little love for souls, and vice versa; if our zeal for souls is weak, this means our love of God is also weak. In fact, how could it be possible to love God sincerely without loving those who are His children, the object of His love, of His care, and of His zeal? Souls are, as it were, God's treasure; He has created them to His image and likeness by an act of love; and by an even greater act of love He has redeemed them with the Blood of His only-begotten Son. " For God so loved the world as to give His only-begotten Son, that whosoever believeth in Him may not perish, but may have life everlasting " (*Jn* 3,16). One who has penetrated the mystery of God's love for men, cannot remain indifferent to their fate : by the light of faith, he has understood that all that God does in the world is for man's good and for his eternal happiness. He longs to have some share in this action, knowing that he can do nothing which will be more pleasing to God than to lend his humble collaboration for the salvation of those who are so dear to Him. This was always the ardent desire of the saints, a desire which impelled them to perform heroic acts of generosity to benefit even one soul. St. Teresa of Jesus writes : " This is an inclination given me by Our Lord; and I think He prizes one soul which, by His mercy and through our diligence and prayer, we may have gained for Him, more than all the other services we can render Him " (*F*, 1).

It is true that the primary end of God's action is His own glory, but He who is infinitely good wills to obtain this glory especially through the salvation and the happines of His creatures.   In fact, nothing exalts His goodness, love, and mercy more than the work of saving souls.   Therefore, to love God and His glory means to love souls; it means to work and sacrifice oneself for their salvation.

2. Zeal for souls finds its source in charity and in the contemplation of Christ crucified.   His wounds, His Blood, the excruciating sufferings of His agony, all tell us how much God values souls and how dearly He loves them.   But this love is unrequited, and it seems that ungrateful men strive more and more to elude His action.   It is this sad spectacle of all the ages which is renewed even today, as though men wished to insult Jesus and renew His Passion. " The world is on fire.   Men try to condemn Christ once again, as it were, for they bring a thousand false witnesses against Him.   They would raze His Church to the ground " (T.J. *Way*, 1).   If Teresa of Jesus could speak these words in her century which was troubled by the Protestant heresy, how much more can we say it in ours, when the struggle against God and the Church has increased immeasurably, and has now spread over the entire world.   Happy shall we be if we can say with the Saint : " It breaks my heart to see so many souls traveling to perdition.   I would the evil were not so great. . . .   I felt that I would have laid down a thousand lives to save a single one of all the souls that were being lost " (*ibid.*).   But it is not a question of merely formulating desires; we must work, act, and suffer for the salvation of our fellow men.

St. John Chrysostom affirms : " Nothing is colder than a Christian who does not care about the salvation of others. " This coldness comes from a very languid charity.   Let us kindle and revive our charity and it will inflame us with zeal for the salvation of souls.   Then our apostolate will no longer be merely a duty which is imposed from without, one which we are obliged to attend to because of the obligation of our state in life, but it will be an exigency of love, an interior flame of charity which burns spontaneously.

Devoting ourselves to the spiritual life does not mean shutting ourselves up in an ivory tower to enjoy God's consolations undisturbed, with no concern for the welfare of others. It means concentrating all our powers on seeking God, working for our own sanctification in order to please God, and thus acquiring a power of action and impetration capable of obtaining the salvation of many souls.

COLLOQUY

"O my dear Lord, how much oppressed You are by those to whom You have shown so much good! It seems as though these traitors would send You to the Cross again and that You would have nowhere to lay Your head. My heart cannot conceive this without being sorely distressed!

"O eternal Father! Surely all these scourgings and insults and grievous tortures will not be forgotten. How, then, my Creator, can a heart as loving as Yours endure that an act which was performed by Your Son in order to please You the more and to obey Your commands (for He loved You most deeply, and You commanded Him to love us) should be treated as lightly as the heretics treat the most Holy Sacrament today, destroying His tabernacles and demolishing His churches? Could it be that Your Son failed to do something to please You? Has He not fulfilled everything? . . . Has this most loving Lamb to pay once more whenever we relapse into sin? Permit it not, my sovereign Lord! Let Thy Majesty be appeased! Look not upon our sins, but upon our redemption by Thy most sacred Son, upon His merits and upon those of His glorious Mother and of all the saints and martyrs who have died for You!

"Alas, Lord, who is it that has dared to make this petition in the name of all? . . . When this sovereign Judge sees how bold I am, it may well move Him to anger, as would be right and just. But behold, Lord, You are a God of mercy; have mercy upon this poor sinner, this miserable worm who is so bold with You. Behold my desires, my God, and the tears with which I beg this of You; forget my sins, for Your name's sake, and have pity on all these souls who are being lost, and help Your Church " (T.J. *Way*, 1 - 3).

318

THE DUTY OF THE APOSTOLATE

PRESENCE OF GOD - O Jesus, You who have accepted me as a member of Your Mystical Body, grant that I may not be in it as a stranger, but that I may work for the good of all my brethren.

MEDITATION

1. Regardless of the degree of charity to which a soul may have attained and of its particular vocation, there is for every Christian a duty of apostolate based on the very fact of his being a Christian, that is, a member of the Mystical Body of Christ. " So we being many, are one body in Christ, and every one members one of another " (*Rom* 12,5); for as in our body each member is interested in the welfare of the other members, " and if one member suffer anything, all the members suffer with it; or if one member glory, all the others rejoice with it " (1 *Cor*, 12,26), so every Christian is bound to be concerned about the welfare of others.

" If a thorn, " says St. John Chrysostom, " gets into the sole of the foot, the whole body feels it and is solicitous for it : the back bends, the hands reach down to draw it out, the head is lowered, and the eyes watch very carefully and anxiously. " As the back, the hands, the head, and the eyes do not disregard the good of the foot, nor say, ' What is this to me? ' but each, in its own way, hastens to help the suffering member, so no Christian can be unconcerned about his brother, but is obliged, according to his ability, to work for the good of his neighbor's soul, and this by reason of his Baptism, which constitutes him a member of the Mystical Body, making him one with the other members, so that the good of others is his good, the suffering of others is his suffering.

" The cause of all evils lies in the fact that we consider as alien the things that concern our own body [the Mystical Body of Christ]. No one is fulfilling his own duty if he ignores his neighbor's salvation. If you dare to contend that you have nothing in common with your fellow member; if you think you have nothing in common with your brother, then neither have you Christ for your Head. " These strong words of St. John Chrysostom remind us that the apostolate is not *an extra*, it is not something optional, left to the free will and generosity of individuals; it is the express duty of every Christian, a duty which comes from the very nature of Christianity, a duty so binding that one cannot be a true Christian without complying with it.

2. As St. Paul to the early Christians and St. John Chrysostom to the Church at Antioch, so today the Vicar of Christ raises his voice to inculcate in the faithful throughout the world the great duty of the apostolate. Jesus by His death on the Cross merited grace for us, and " It was possible for Him personally, immediately to impart these graces to men; but He wished to do so only through a visible Church that would be formed by the union of men, and thus through that Church every man would perform a work of collaboration with Him in dispensing the graces of Redemption. The Word of God willed to make use of our nature, when in excruciating agony He would redeem mankind; in much the same way throughout the centuries He makes use of the Church that the work begun might endure " (Pius XII : *Mystici Corporis*). The Church is the society of the faithful; *we* are the Church; therefore, it is incumbent upon each one of us to cooperate in the diffusion of grace in souls. Unquestionably, the first place in carrying out this work belongs to the bishops and priests, but next to them and under their direction, every Christian is called upon to take part in it. " Not only the sacred ministers and those who have consecrated themselves to God in the religious life, but also all the other members of the Mystical Body of Jesus Christ have the obligation of working hard and constantly for the upbuilding and increase of this Body " *(ibid.)*.

Jesus wills to make use of His members, that is, all Christians, to continue His redemptive work in the world. Being infinite omnipotence, He can sanctify souls without help from anyone, just as He created everything out of nothing; but He wills to *need* us and our poor works, and He invites us and begs us to sacrifice ourselves with Him for the salvation of others. " A tremendous mystery, " exclaims Pius XII, " and one which can never be sufficiently meditated upon : that the salvation of many depends on the prayers and voluntary mortifications undertaken for this end by the members of the Mystical Body of Jesus Christ and on the cooperation of the pastors and of the faithful " *(ibid.)*. To be apostles means to lend Christ our talents and activity, so that He may continue to redeem and sanctify souls through us.

COLLOQUY

" O Lord, turn Your merciful eyes upon Your people and upon Your Mystical Body, the Holy Church, since You will receive more glory from pardoning many souls than You will by pardoning only me, a wretched creature who has offended You so often.   I beseech You, therefore, divine eternal Charity, to avenge Yourself on me and be merciful to Your people; I shall never depart from Your presence until I see that You have shown mercy to them.   How could I be happy if I had eternal life and Your people were condemned to death?...   Therefore, I wish, and as a favor I implore You, to show mercy to Your people by that same charity which moved You to create man to Your image and likeness, so that He might have a share in You and in Your life.

" O Lord, I offer You my life now and forever, whenever it shall please You to take it, and I offer it for Your glory, humbly beseeching You, by the merits of Your Passion, to cleanse and purify Your Spouse, the Church, from every defect; delay no longer!...   I turn my gaze in another direction and I see the lost souls of countless sinners.   My heart is broken at the sight of them, or rather, it is dilated by the force of bitter regret.   I am overcome with compassion, and I cannot help weeping for their misery, as if I found myself—like them—soiled with the mire of their guilt.

" Lord, during Your mortal life, You bore the weight of two crosses by carrying in Your body the heavy burden of our sins.   In order that I may be conformed to You, You have burdened me with the weight of two crosses : one crushes my body with infirmities and other distresses, the other transfixes my soul which grieves for the perdition and blindness of so many poor, obstinate sinners " (St. Catherine of Siena).

319

GOD'S COLLABORATORS

PRESENCE OF GOD - Take me, O Lord, and make me worthy of collaborating with You in the work of extending Your kingdom.

MEDITATION

1. St. Paul, speaking of the work of the apostolate, says : " *Dei sumus adjutores* " (1 *Cor* 3,9); we are God's coadjutors, collaborators with Him.

The apostolate, therefore, is not merely a personal activity, the more or less praiseworthy result of our own resources and initiatives; nor is it an activity which we can carry on according to our own ideas, and much less by our own powers. Every type of apostolate is a *collaboration* in the one work of redemption and sanctification which God has been developing through the centuries. No one but God, who is Sanctity itself, the Creator and Source of all grace, has the power to redeem and sanctify. " There is one Mediator of God and men " (1 *Tm* 2,5); one alone is the Redeemer and Sanctifier : Jesus, the Incarnate Word. All others, the greatest saints, and even our Blessed Lady, are apostles only insofar as they collaborate in Christ's work. As St. Paul teaches, we do nothing but lend God our activity : " I have planted, Apollo watered, but God gave the increase. Therefore, neither he that planteth is anything, nor he that watereth; but God that giveth the increase " (1 *Cor* 3,6.7).

The field certainly must be cultivated before it can produce fruit, but the farmer's work is not enough; there must be rain and sunshine, and the season must be favorable. Similarly, in the plan established by God for the salvation of men, the activity of the apostle is necessary, but not sufficient; only God can give the increase. As only God can cause the sun to shine or send the rain to make the fields fruitful, so God alone can give the grace to make the field of the apostolate fructify. St. Paul was so thoroughly convinced of this fact that, when speaking to the Corinthians he exclaimed, " *Dei agricultura estis, Dei aedificatio estis* " (*ibid.* 3,9);

You are God's husbandry; you are God's building. And
although he was the first to bring them to the faith, he does
not say, you are my children, you are my field, but " you
are God's field, you are God's building. " The apostolate
is not a human but a divine work, to which man lends his
collaboration as a humble instrument.

2. If the apostle is God's instrument, he is not, however, a
material one such as a pen in a writer's hand. He is a living,
personal instrument endowed with intellect and will; therefore,
he should put these powers at the service of the divine Artist,
trying to harmonize, or better, to synchronize his way of
thinking, willing and acting with the divine way, that is to
say, with the divine order and will. Each one of us will be
an apostle in the measure in which we are docile instruments
in God's hands, ready to be used as He wishes.

Here again, we ought to fix our eyes on Jesus, whose
humanity was the instrument which the Word used to redeem
the human race. The humanity of Jesus possesses no
personality of its own; His will, intellect, affections, and
body are instruments of the Word, which He used with the
most complete freedom and by which He accomplished
His work of love for the salvation of men.

In an analogous way the apostle—although he has his
own personality which always remains distinct from God,
even in the highest states of mystical union—should give
himself up to God as a docile instrument, as a pure
capacity placed wholly at His disposal. The apostle should
freely offer to God all he has received from Him—his intellect
and will, his natural and supernatural gifts—for Him to use
as He pleases for the extension of His kingdom. It matters
little whether God employs him in great and brilliant works
or in humble, hidden ones, whether He uses him to preach
His word publicly or to enlighten souls privately, whether
He engages him in intense activity or immolates him in prayer
and silence, provided his whole life and all his strength
be spent in the service of souls.

Like the work of personal sanctification, so also the
work of the sanctification of others, that is, the apostolate,
can be reduced to a matter of docility, of openness to grace and
to God's will; in other words, of death to self and to everything
in one's thought, will, and actions that might be even slightly
contrary to God's thought, will and action.

COLLOQUY

" O my God, I know that You have no need of anyone to accomplish Your work, but just as You permit a clever gardener to cultivate rare and delicate plants, providing him with the necessary skill to accomplish it, so You wish to be helped in the divine cultivation of souls.... Oh! how many souls might attain great sanctity if only they were directed aright from the start!

" My God, the greatest honor You can do a soul is not to give it much but to ask much of it. Therefore, when You make me suffer for the salvation of souls, You are treating me like one of Your privileged friends! Was it not by suffering and dying that You redeemed the world? O Jesus, I aspire to the happiness of sacrificing my life for You, but I know that martyrdom of the heart is no less fruitful than the shedding of one's blood, and even now this martyrdom is mine. How beautiful, O Lord, is the part You have reserved for me, a part worthy of an apostle!

" O Lord, I desire to work with You for the salvation of souls; I have only the single day of this life in which to save them and thus give You proofs of my love. The morrow of this day will be eternity; then You will return me a hundred-fold for the joys I am sacrificing for You.

" How sweet it is, O Jesus, to offer You our slight sacrifices to help You save the souls which You have redeemed at the price of Your Blood, and which await only our help in order not to fall into the abyss.

" How happy I would be if, at the hour of my death, I could have a single soul to offer You! There would be a soul snatched from the fire of hell to bless You for all eternity " (T.C.J. *L*, 184,171,23).

320

ONE WITH THE MIND OF CHRIST

PRESENCE OF GOD - Grant, O Jesus, that I may have for souls sentiments like those of Your own divine Heart.

MEDITATION

1. Efficacious collaboration always demands a certain unity of purpose and method between the promoter of a work and his collaborators. This unity must be all the more profound if the work to be accomplished is not material, but spiritual. An apostle, working with God for the good of souls, must live in intimate *spiritual union* with Him, so as to enter as far as possible into His views and plans for the salvation of the world.

Only by penetrating to the depths of the mystery of God's love for mankind can the apostle cooperate in the actual diffusion of love and grace. He must keep in close contact with God by means of the theological virtues, and must try to grasp the profound inspirations of His love. By faith we know that God brought men into existence through the promptings of His infinite goodness. He willed to extend the goodness outside Himself, to communicate to others something of His own goodness, happiness, and life. Grace, the creation of His love, makes man participate in His divine nature. When man cut himself off from God by sin, and became unworthy of His gift, God did not renounce His loving plan; and in order to restore to man what he had culpably lost, He sacrificed His only-begotten Son " who for us men and for our salvation came down from heaven " (*Credo*).

The apostle must thoroughly understand that God's action on souls is entirely the action of love : it is the action of the Father who goes in search of the prodigal son, of the shepherd who seeks the sheep that has gone astray; it is the action of a God who offers His friendship to men to make them happy, to be able to welcome them into His Home, to admit them to His intimacy, to make them blessed with His eternal beatitude. An apostle should try to put his own heart into contact with the Heart of God, that it may be filled with God's love and share in His charity toward men. The apostle should, as it were, have the *mind* of God, the *mind* of Christ, that is, he should cultivate deep sentiments of love for the brethren, a pale reflection of the love of God for men.

2. Not only at prayer, but in the very exercise of the apostolate, the apostle should strive to keep in contact with God and with the mystery of His love for men, in which he should humbly collaborate. He will seek this contact by an intense practice of faith, which will give him a deeper understanding of the mystery of the Redemption and enable him to recognize the fulfillment of this mystery in the various circumstances of his life and in every event of time. This spirit of faith will help him to make his humble activity a part of the great action of God. In this way, even while making use of human means or when occupied with material affairs, the apostle will live in a supernatural atmosphere. He will never lose sight of the goal of his activity, but will always be very keenly aware that he is collaborating with Christ for the salvation of souls.

To faith, an apostle must unite ardent charity, for contact with God and response to His love are realized by means of love. Charity, by the power of intuition proper to it, will permit the apostle to penetrate more deeply into the mystery of the Redemption and to savor the sweet reality of the infinite Love manifested therein; it will urge him to live in close communion with this Love, whose collaborator and instrument he should be. Then his example and words will testify to the truth savored and experienced in his intimate contact with God, the truth that is not only believed in theory, but lived in practice. Then the apostle can say with St. John : " We have known, and have believed the charity which God hath to us " (1 *Jn* 4,16), and again : " That...which we have seen with our eyes, which we have looked upon, and our hands have handled, of the Word of life...we bear witness...[we] declare unto you " (*ibid.* 1, 3).

By faith and love the apostle will attain to an ever increasing spiritual affinity with the mystery of the Redemption and with Jesus, who accomplished it; he will be able to make the sentiments of Jesus his own, according to the words of St. Paul : " For let this mind be in you,

which was also in Christ Jesus" (*Phil* 2,5). Having the "mind
of Christ," which means loving and willing in unison with
the divine Heart, sharing its immense love for God and
souls, is the secret of every apostolate.

COLLOQUY

"O Jesus, Son of God, if I think how You died to save
souls, how can I fail to want to die for them also? And if I
think of men trampling upon Your Blood, how can I tolerate
such an insult to You, my Lord? How can I say I love
You and long for Your love, if when I see Your picture
thrown in the mud, I do not try to pick it up? Why then,
do I not devote myself entirely to prayer, and wear myself
out trying to make Your Name known and honored, so that
by converting souls, I may gather the fruits of Your Blood?

"My God, even if I knew I would never enjoy Your
presence, I would, nevertheless, be willing to die for each
sinful soul, in order to honor You; in this way, I would
undergo as many deaths as there are sinners in the world,
so that they might obtain grace now and glory hereafter.
But I would do it all the more willingly if I knew that I
would attain glory with them!" (St. Bonaventure).

"Lord, I have but one thing to do during the night of
this life, this single night which will come but once, and
that is to love You with all the strength of my heart and
to save souls for You that You may be loved.

"O Jesus, at the sight of Your precious Blood falling
to the ground, with no one caring to treasure it as it falls,
my heart is torn with grief. I resolve to remain continuously
in spirit at the foot of the Cross, that I may receive the
divine dew of salvation and pour it forth upon souls.

"Your cry, ' I thirst! ' resounds incessantly in my heart,
kindling within it new fires of zeal.... O my Beloved,
to give You to drink is my constant desire; I am consumed
with an insatiable thirst for souls, and I long at any cost to
snatch them from the everlasting flames of hell.... To
obtain this, I wish to employ all the spiritual means I can
think of, but knowing that of myself I can do nothing, I
offer You, O my Savior, Your own infinite merits together
with all the treasures of Holy Church" (T.C.J. *L*, 74 - *St*, 5).

THE SOUL OF THE APOSTOLATE

PRESENCE OF GOD - O Lord, make me understand that only union with You, only love, can make my apostolate fruitful.

MEDITATION

1. Unless our life is one of intimacy with God and His Son Jesus, we cannot be His collaborators, docile instruments in His hands; unless we have an intense interior life, we cannot have the mind of Christ and be associated with His love and His work for the salvation of souls.

By means of prayer and the struggle against sin, by self-renunciation, and the practice of the virtues, the interior life progressively rids the soul of all that is defective, thus favoring in it the growth of grace and love, that is to say it vivifies the soul with divine life, since grace and love are a participation in the very life of God. It follows, therefore, that the more a soul cultivates the interior life, the nearer it will come to God, and having become like Him by grace and love, will be able to live in intimacy with Him, enjoy His friendship, penetrate His mysteries and participate in them. Who, then, will be better able to understand the great mystery of the Redemption and contribute his share to it, than one who by means of a fervent interior life, lives in intimate friendship with God?

The first degree of friendship with God, which consists in the absence of serious sin, does not suffice to fulfill the purposes of the apostolate. A deeper friendship is required, one which creates such uniformity of will, desire and affection that the apostle is enabled to act according to God's Heart; he is moved not by his own impulses, but by the impulse of grace, by God's will, and the inspirations of the Holy Spirit. It is a very significant fact that Jesus made His apostles live for three years in intimacy with Him, treating them like dear friends, before sending them out to convert the world : " I will not now call you servants...but I have called you friends " (*Jn* 15,15). Friends, not only because He shared the treasures of His divine life with them, but also because He wanted them to be the collaborators, and in a certain sense, the successors of His mission as Redeemer.

Only if we are friends of God can we be apostles; God Himself invites us to this friendship, but we must correspond by living an intense interior life, one which makes our relations with God ever more intimate and richer in love.

2. Only friendship with God, and the charity which unites us to Him, can produce that supernatural strength which makes any form of the apostolate effective. The more a soul is united to God, the more it shares in the power of God Himself; and hence, its prayers, sacrifices, and works undertaken for the salvation of souls, are efficacious and attain their end.

But where will an apostle obtain this love which, uniting him to God, gives him such power? Undoubtedly from God Himself : " The charity of God is poured forth in our hearts by the Holy Ghost, who is given to us " (*Rom* 5,5). In a single moment, the moment of our justification, God infused charity into us without any cooperation on our part, but He does not preserve this gift, much less increase it, unless we remain united to Him by living an interior life. The purpose of the struggle against our passions, the practice of the virtues, recollection, prayer, the practice of the presence of God, and frequent reception of the Sacraments, is to foster union with God and the growth of charity. The interior life is a secret hearth where a soul in contact with God is inflamed with His love, and precisely because it is inflamed and forged by love, it becomes a docile instrument which God can use to diffuse love into the hearts of others. Therefore, it is very important to recall frequently this great principle : *the interior life is the soul of the apostolate.* A deep interior life will generate intense love and intimate union with God, and, therefore, from it will spring a fruitful apostolate, a true sharing in Christ's work of saving souls; on the other hand, a mediocre interior life can produce only a feeble love and union with God; hence, the resultant apostolate cannot have an efficacious influence on souls. Where there is little or no interior life, charity and friendship with God are in danger of being extinguished; and if this interior flame be extinguished, then the apostolate will be emptied of its substance and reduced to mere external activity which may make a great noise, but will not bring forth any fruit.

St. John of the Cross says, " It is to hammer vigorously and to accomplish little more than nothing, at times nothing at all; at times, indeed, it may even be to do harm " (J.C. *SC*, 29,3).

COLLOQUY

" Draw me, Lord, we will run!...

" O Jesus, I beg You to draw me into the fire of Your love and to unite me so closely to You that You may live and act in me.   The more the fire of Your love consumes my heart, the more frequently shall I cry, ' Draw me! ' and the more also will those souls who come in contact with mine run swiftly in the sweet odor of Your perfumes, my Beloved.

" We shall run—yes, we shall run together, for souls that are on fire can never remain inactive.   Mary Magdalen sat at Your feet listening to Your sweet and burning words, but though appearing to give You nothing, she gave far more than Martha, who was ' troubled about many things. '

" O my Jesus, there is no need then to say : In drawing me, draw also the souls that I love.   The words ' draw me ' suffice.   When a soul has been captivated by the odor of Your perfumes she cannot run alone : as a natural consequence of her attraction toward You, all those whom she loves are drawn in her train.

" As a torrent bears down to the depths of the sea whatsoever it meets on its way, so likewise, my Jesus, does the soul that plunges into the boundless ocean of Your love bring with it all its treasures!   O Lord, my treasures, as You well know, are the souls it has pleased You to unite with mine, and which You Yourself have confided to me.

" The end cannot be reached without adopting the means, and since You, O Lord, have made me understand that it is through the Cross You will give me souls, the more crosses I encounter the stronger becomes my attraction to suffering " (T.C.J. *St*, 12 – 7).

322

THE DIVINE INVITATION

NINETEENTH SUNDAY AFTER PENTECOST

PRESENCE OF GOD - O my God, give me the sovereign grace to respond to all Your invitations with generosity.

MEDITATION

1. Today's Gospel (*Mt* 22,1-14) outlines the sad story—so true even today—of human ingratitude which rejects God's mercy, and is indifferent to His gifts and invitations.

" The kingdom of heaven is likened to a king, who made a marriage for his son, and he sent his servants to call them that were invited to the marriage; and they would not come. " The king is God the Father, the son is the eternal Word who, becoming incarnate, espoused human nature in order to redeem and sanctify it. God invites all men to the great banquet of the divine nuptials at which they will find their salvation; but submerged in the materialism of earthly things, they reject the invitation and the messengers. " Jerusalem, Jerusalem, thou that killest the prophets and stonest them that are sent unto thee " (*ibid.* 23,37), will one day be the lament of the Son of God as He denounces before the world, not only the obstinate resistance of the chosen people, but also that of all souls who have stubbornly and ungratefully rejected His love and His grace. The prophets, St. John the Baptist, and the apostles are the " servants, " the messengers sent by God to call men to the banquet of the Redemption, but they were all taken and killed. They " laid hands on his servants, and having treated them contumeliously, put them to death, " the Gospel says. Today's parable ends there, but unfortunately, human ingratitude has gone much further : not only the servants and messengers were killed, but even God's very Son. Yet God's mercy is so great that it cannot be vanquished; He still invites all men to His feast, and even offers this divine Son whom they have killed, to be their Food. The banquet is prepared; Jesus, the divine Lamb has been

immolated for the redemption of mankind and, if many
fail to accept the invitation, others will be invited. " The
marriage indeed is ready, but they that were invited were not
worthy. Go ye therefore into the highways, and as many
as you shall find, call to the marriage. "

We too have been invited. How have we responded
to the invitation? Have we not also shown more interest
and concern for earthly matters than for the things of God?
Have we not been like the men in the parable who " neglected,
and went their way, one to his farm, and another to his
merchandise? "

2. Today's parable delineates primarily the invitation
to the Christian life, the invitation which, being rejected
by the Jewish people, is offered to all nations. But we can
also see in it a special invitation to follow a particular
vocation : a call to the priesthood, to consecration to God
either in the cloister or in the world, to the apostolate, or to a
certain mission. In order to respond to this invitation,
our assent must be more than nominal. It must involve
the sincere and profound commitment of our whole soul.
The parable tells us of one man who did not refuse the
invitation, but who accepted it in an unworthy manner,
appearing at the marriage feast without the wedding garment.
This is a figure of those who respond to Our Lord's invitation
in a material way only, without embracing it heart and soul,
and without striving, by their works, to live in a manner
worthy of their vocation. Such souls seriously endanger their salvation, for God will not be mocked. He
cannot be deceived by appearances; no uniform or external
decorations can conceal from Him the true state of a soul.
More clearly than the king in the parable, He takes note of
those who are not clothed in a nuptial garment, that is,
in the robe of grace and virtue befitting their vocation.
Sooner or later the day will come when He will pronounce
for each one of them the terrible words : " Bind his hands and
feet, and cast him into exterior darkness. "

Without going to these extremes, however, we can still
remain far from complete correspondence to the divine call.
It is well to remember that the problem of corresponding
to a vocation is not one that can be resolved once and for all
on the day that we embrace a particular state of life; it is a
question that arises every day, because each day our vocation

calls for a new response, a fresh adherence adapted to the
circumstances and grace of the moment. A vocation attains
its full realization only by our continual fidelity to God's
invitations. These invitations follow one another without
interruption and reveal to the attentive soul ever new horizons,
presenting new duties, new opportunities for generosity, and
new aspects of perfection and immolation. The parable ends
with this grave sentence : " Many are called but few are
chosen. " Why are only a few chosen? Because there are
few who know how to correspond day by day with the grace
of their vocation; because there are few who know how to
accept all the consequences and demands of the divine call,
and who always answer *yes* to the solicitations of grace.

COLLOQUY

" O Lord, this is what You say to my soul : ' Why are you
so far away from Me, detained by useless pursuits? Why do
you not hasten to prepare a beautiful wedding garment?
I suffered death to take you for My spouse. I became man for
you, to preserve your life from corruption, I preferred your
salvation before all My works. I prepared a nuptial couch
for you in heaven, and I commanded the angels to serve you.
Would you despise Me, your heavenly Spouse? And whom
would you prefer to Me, who in My mercy saved the whole
human race? What father could give you life as I have?
What father or what spouse can love you as much as I? '
" O my God, what shall I answer You?
" Pardon me, save me, O patient, long-suffering Lord!
Save me, O Christ, Son of God, who alone are without sin!
Grant that my heart may have no desire but to respond
to Your invitations, and that with the help of Your grace,
I may always do Your will, and be prompt and willing
to carry out Your orders, so that, with the talents I have
received from You, I may be able to trade and acquire the
good things of Your kingdom. Grant that I may praise You
trustfully and tell You joyfully when I see You : ' I am
blessed because You have come to clothe me with the
worthy nuptial garment which Your grace has purchased
for me. '
" I shall light the lamp, O Christ, given to me by Your
grace and bounty. I shall meet You joyfully, blessing,

praising, and glorifying You, O my immortal Spouse "
(St. Ephrem).

323

THE APOSTOLIC IDEAL

PRESENCE OF GOD - Enkindle in me, O Lord, the fire of the apostolate
and feed it with Your love.

MEDITATION

1. Just as a seed cannot produce a stalk which will bear
a new ear unless it first buries its roots deep in the ground,
so we cannot bear fruit for the apostolate if we do not first put
forth the roots of a deep interior life, enabling us to draw
from God Himself the sap which will make us fruitful. The
interior life is the vital principle, the force, and the flame of
the apostolate; but on the other hand, the apostolate brings
its contribution to the interior life, helping to make it more
generous and more intense. When a soul is fired with zeal for
the apostolic life, its very desire to win other souls for God
impels it to devote itself with greater generosity to prayer,
mortification, and the practice of the virtues, with the
intention of making itself more capable of a fruitful apostolate.
Thus, while the interior life is the soul of the apostolate,
the apostolate in its turn is a very powerful mainspring
urging the soul on to union with God, to perfection, to sanctity.
The apostolic ideal is of its very nature a generator of spiritual
energy and a spur to a generous, holy life. St. Teresa of
Jesus, moved by an ardent desire to counteract the great
havoc wrought by the Protestant heresy in her times, stamped
the reform she initiated with a seal of particular austerity
and organized the life of her daughters in such a way as to
engage them in a continual exercise of prayer, sacrifice,
and self-giving for the salvation of souls (cf. *Way*, 1). The
rule of life of the Teresian Carmel, a contemplative
life of profound intensity, was thus born of a great apostolic
ideal.

The same ideal has recently given rise to a new state of perfection in the Church, the Secular Institutes, in which souls desiring to consecrate themselves to God for the salvation of souls, pledge themselves to a life of evangelical perfection in the world. " The specific end [of the apostolate] seems of necessity to demand and even to create the generic end [of perfection] " (Pius XII : *Primo Feliciter*).

When the apostolic ideal is alive and well understood, it does not plunge souls headlong into activity; it rather guides them to a deeper interior life, to the total gift of self, to sanctity, for we ourselves must be holy before we can make others holy. " And for them do I sanctify Myself " (*Jn* 17,19).

2. An interior life in which the apostolic ideal does not shine, can never be full and vigorous. This is because of the nature of grace and charity, which, of themselves, are expansive and apostolic. Although grace remains in an intimate, incommunicable manner in the soul on whom it is bestowed, it should, nevertheless, be beneficial to the whole Christian community. The dogma of the Communion of Saints tells us precisely that the grace and holiness of one of Christ's members necessarily redounds to the advantage of all the other members. Likewise, charity, the inseparable companion of grace, is by nature expansive, and when it embraces God, it embraces all creatures in God. It gives the soul a twofold impetus : toward God and toward its neighbor; if either one is repressed, charity is stifled in its very essence. This virtue develops and reaches maturity only when its two aspects, love of God and love of neighbor, are fully efficient. If we exclude or diminish fraternal charity, the highest expression of which is the apostolate, our love for God will inevitably be diminished also.

Therefore, a cold spiritual life, indifferent to the good of souls, is necessarily dwarfed; it is nothing more than a mean, petty and selfish form of piety; it has lost its vital heat, the warmth of charity, and does not even deserve the name of life. On the contrary, where the fire of the apostolate burns brightly, one's interior life becomes more vigorous than ever and makes one capable of great generosity. Is it not true perhaps that sometimes our desire for perfection is not strong enough to make us courageous in accepting certain sacrifices or renunciations which are costly to nature? But when we think that the salvation of other souls may depend on our generosity, our fidelity to grace, or our immolation, then we can refuse nothing to Our Lord, and we find the strength to accept even what is most bitter and painful.

In this way the apostolic ideal becomes a powerful lever for our own personal sanctification, and enriched by a more fervent interior life, can bring to this ideal new energy and fecundity.

COLLOQUY

" O Lord, there come to me desires to serve You with impulses so strong that I cannot describe them, and with a distress caused by the realization of my own unprofitableness.... I think I should like to cry aloud and tell all souls how important it is for them not to be contented with just a little in Your service, and how many blessings there are which You will give us if we prepare to receive them.

" O my God, I experience very deep distress because of the great number of souls who are bringing damnation upon themselves, especially of those who were members of the Church through Baptism, and I greatly desire to labor for their salvation, so much so that I really believe that, to deliver a single one of them from such dreadful torments, I would willingly die many deaths.... Who could bear to look upon souls condemned for eternity to endless suffering? Even earthly suffering which, after all, has a limit and will end with death, moves us to deep compassion. And that other suffering has no limit : I do not know how we can look on so calmly and see the devil carrying off as many souls as he does daily.

" Thou knowest, my God, how grieved I am to see how very many are lost. Save at least one, Lord, at least one who can give light to many others, and this not for my sake, Lord, for I do not merit it, but for the merits of Thy Son. Look upon His wounds, Lord, and as He forgave them who inflicted them upon Him, so do Thou pardon us.

" My God, I want nothing but Your will; submission to it has such power over me that my soul desires neither death nor life. But then, if such be Your will, I desire to live, in order to serve You better. If, through my intercession, I could do anything to make a single soul love and praise You more, and that only for a short time, it would seem to me of greater moment than my being in glory" (T.J. *SR*, 1 – *Life*, 32 – *Exc*, 11 – *SR*, 6).

324

VARIOUS FORMS OF THE APOSTOLATE

PRESENCE OF GOD - O Jesus, teach me to pray, suffer, and work with You for the salvation of souls.

MEDITATION

1. When we speak of the apostolate, we think almost exclusively of external activity; this is certainly necessary, but it is not the only kind of apostolate. We must always bear in mind that Jesus saved us not only by the activity of the last three years of His life, which were dedicated to the evangelization of the multitudes and the formation of the first nucleus of the Church, but also by prayer, suffering, vigils—by His whole life. Jesus was always an *apostle*, always the *one sent* by the Father for our salvation. His apostolate began at Bethlehem in the dreariness of a cave; as a tiny Babe wrapped in swaddling clothes, He was already suffering for us; it continued during the thirty years spent at Nazareth in prayer, in retirement, in the hidden life; it took an external form in His direct contact with souls during His public life, and reached its culmination in His agony in the Garden of Olives and His death on the Cross. Jesus was an apostle in the stable of Bethlehem, in the shop of St. Joseph, in His anguish in Gethsemane and on Calvary no less than when He was going through Palestine, teaching the multitudes or disputing with the doctors of the law.

Our apostolate consists in associating ourselves with what Jesus has done for the redemption of mankind; therefore, it is not limited to external activity, but it also consists, and essentially so, in prayer and sacrifice. Thus one clearly sees that there are two fundamental forms of apostolate : the interior apostolate of prayer and immolation, which is a prolongation of the hidden life and of the Passion of Jesus; and the exterior apostolate of word and of work, which is a prolongation of His public life. Both are a participation in the redemptive work of Jesus, but there is a great difference between them. The interior apostolate is the indispensable foundation of the exterior apostolate; no one, in fact, can hope to save souls by exterior works which are not sustained by prayer and sacrifice. On the other hand, there are cases where external works can be dispensed with, without, on that account, lessening the interior apostolate of prayer and sacrifice, which can still be very intense and fruitful. Every Christian is an apostle, not only in virtue of the activity in which he engages,, but principally because of his partici-pation in the prayer and sacrifice by which Jesus has redeemed the world.

2. The interior apostolate can subsist by itself; in fact, there are states of life that justify the absence of an exterior apostolate. One of these is the purely contemplative life, which has always flourished in the Church. Like a mother, she jealously defends it against the attacks of those who condemn it as an escape from the field of action. Those who follow God's call and retire from active works to give themselves to this kind of life are not deserters; if they leave the ranks of the external apostolate, they do this only in order to give themselves to a more intensive apostolate, that of prayer and continual immolation.

" Those in the Church who perform the function of prayer and continual penance, contribute to the growth of the Church and the salvation of the human race to a *greater degree* than those who cultivate the Lord's field by their activity; for, if they did not draw down from heaven an abundance of divine grace to irrigate the field, the evangelical workers would certainly receive less fruit from their labors " (Pius XI : *Umbratilem*). This authorized statement of a great Pope can leave no doubt as to the immense apostolic value of the contemplative life; but, on the other hand, it is but just to remark that such value is realized only when contemplatives engage themselves with all their strength in prayer and continual immolation. In other words, it is not any kind of prayer or sacrifice that will result in such great fruitfulness,

but only the prayer and sacrifice that come from an extremely
pure and generous heart, a heart wholly given to God and
which, day by day, renews and lives its immolation with
ever greater freshness and intensity. When the contemplative
life is lived with such intensity it is, in an eminent way, an
apostolic life.

It is in this sense that Pope Pius XII has defined the
vocation to a cloistered life as " a universal, apostolic
vocation...a fully and totally apostolic vocation, not limited
by boundaries of place, time, and circumstances, but always
and everywhere, zealous for everything that in any way
relates to the honor of the heavenly Spouse or the salvation of
souls " (Apostolic Constitution : *Sponsa Christi*). Furthermore,
contemplative monasteries, by the simple example of their
hidden life, their prayer and penance, are a continual
reminder for all to be detached from earthly things and to
seek those that are heavenly : union with God and sanctity.

COLLOQUY

" What can I do, O Jesus, to save souls? You answer
me with the words You once addressed to Your disciples,
pointing to the fields of ripened corn : ' Lift up your eyes and
see the countries; for they are already white for the
harvest.... The harvest indeed is great, but the laborers are
few. Pray ye, therefore, the Lord of the harvest that He send
forth laborers. '

"How mysterious it is! O Jesus, are You not all powerful?
Do not creatures belong to You who made them? Why
then do You say, ' Pray ye the Lord of the harvest to send
laborers? ' Why? O Jesus, because You have so incomprehensible a love for us that You want us to have a share
with You in the salvation of souls, You want to do nothing
without us. You, the Creator of the universe, wait for the
prayer of a poor little soul to save other souls redeemed like
it at the price of Your blood.

" My vocation is not to go harvesting in the fields of ripe
corn; You do not say to me : ' Lower your eyes, look at the
fields, and go and reap them '; my mission is still loftier.
You tell me : ' Lift up your eyes and see.... See how in
heaven there are places empty; it is for you to fill them...you
are to be My Moses praying on the mountain; ask Me for

laborers and I shall send them, I await only a prayer, a sigh from your heart! '

" Behold, O Lord, the mission You have entrusted to me, to contribute by prayer and sacrifice to the formation of evangelical workers who will save millions of souls whose mother I shall be " (cf. T.C.J. *L*, 114).

325

APOSTOLIC PRAYER

PRESENCE OF GOD - Accept, O Lord, my humble prayer that Your kingdom may come.

MEDITATION

1. When Jesus died on the Cross for us, the redemption of mankind became an accomplished fact. Thereafter, every one coming into this world is already redeemed, in the sense that the precious Blood of Jesus has already merited for him all the graces necessary for his salvation and also for his sanctification. What still remains to be done is the application of these graces to each individual soul; and it is for this that God wishes our collaboration. He wants it so much that He has made the granting of certain graces, necessary for our salvation and that of others, dependent upon our prayers. In other words, by the merits of Jesus, grace—God's infinite mercy—is ready to be poured out abundantly into men's souls, but it will not be poured out unless there is someone who raises supplicating hands to heaven, asking for it. If prayer does not ascend to the throne of the Most High, grace will not be granted. This explains the absolute necessity for apostolic prayer and its great efficacy. " This kind [of devil] is not cast out but by prayer and fasting " (*Mt* 17,20), Jesus has said. There is no substitute for prayer, because prayer draws grace directly from its source, God. Our activity, our words and works can prepare the ground for grace, but if we do not pray, it will not come down to refresh souls.

In the light of these truths we can better appreciate the importance of the insistent exhortations of Jesus in respect to prayer : " We ought always to pray and not to faint.... Ask and it shall be given you; seek and you shall find; knock and it shall be opened to you " (*Lk* 18,1; 11,9). We can never be certain that all our prayers will be answered according to our expectation, for we do not know if what we ask is conformable to God's will; but when it is a question of apostolic prayer which asks for grace and the salvation of souls, it is a very different matter.   In fact, when we pray for the aims of the apostolate, we are fitting into the plan prearranged by God Himself from all eternity, that plan for the salvation of all men which God desires to put into action infinitely more than we do; therefore, we cannot doubt the efficacy of our prayer.   Because of this effectiveness, apostolic prayer is one of the most powerful means of furthering the apostolate.

2. If God has willed the distribution of grace in the world to depend upon the prayers of men, and if people today pray so little—many indeed, and perhaps most of them, not at all—it is extremely necessary to have in the Church souls who are totally consecrated to prayer.   By their lives of continual prayer, adoration and unceasing praise to the Most High, these souls supply for the negligence and carelessness of many, and thus they re-establish in the world the balance between God's rights and man's duty, between action and contemplation.   Praying and supplicating for all, they are in Christ's Mystical Body the hidden but precious organs whose task is to make the sap of divine grace flow to each of its members.   In the Church they are " powerhouses " of supernatural energy, energy derived from and accumulated by prayer, and diffused by it to the utmost bounds of the earth. The prayer of contemplatives is the secret and guarantee of victory for those who struggle in the world, even as the prayer of Moses was the secret and guarantee of victory for Israel. " My brothers labor in my stead, " wrote St. Thérèse of the Child Jesus, " while I...stay close to the Throne, and *love* Thee for all those who are in the strife " (*St*, 13); I *love*, that is, I pray, suffer and sacrifice for them.

The prayer which contemplatives unceasingly send up to God in the name of all Christians does not dispense the rest of the faithful from this great duty.   Above all, those who dedicate themselves to the external apostolate should give sufficient place in their lives to prayer. But, unfortunately we often put more trust in our work, our diligence, our technique, than in our prayer; we have not enough faith in its efficacy, in the help which God will surely give those who invoke Him from their heart, and as a result, we consider wasted the time we give to prayer. This basic error springs from a lack of faith and humility; it is an error which explains the sterility of so many works. " Let those, then, who are great actives, " admonishes St. John of the Cross, " that think to girdle the world with their outward works and their preachings, take note here that they would bring far more profit to the Church, and be far more pleasing to God (apart from the good example they would give) if they spent even half of this time with God in prayer " (*SC*, 29,3).

COLLOQUY

" O eternal Father, I offer You the Blood shed by Your Son with such deep love and ardent charity for the salvation of men.

" O Jesus, I offer You the innumerable drops of Blood which You shed so freely at Your dreadful scourging, and as You shed it for all Your members, so do I offer it to You for all the members of holy Church, whose Head You are. I offer It to You so that Your " Christs, " your priests, may once again be the light of the world, that Your virgins may not be of the number of the foolish virgins, that infidels and heretics may return to your fold and that all souls may be saved.

" O eternal Word, I want to speak to You as You did to us. In truth, I say to You that I would sacrifice a thousand lives, if I had them, to help save these souls. I do not want to depart from this life until You have enlightened some one of them. But I am not worthy to be heard. Hear not one who is so presumptuous, but answer Your own Blood. You cannot fail Yourself; hear then, O Jesus, the voice of Your Blood.

" O eternal Father, that love which moved You to create men, urges You also to infuse Your light into them. I well know that You do infuse it, but they do not accept it. What is the reason for this? My ingratitude. I know,

O my God, my ingratitude, but I have not plumbed its depths. Punish me for their offenses; punish me for their sins. Oh! how wretched I am to be the cause of so much ingratitude and wickedness.

" If I could, I would take all men and lead them to the bosom of Your Holy Church, so that she could cleanse them of all their infidelities, regenerate them like a mother, and then nourish them with the sweet milk of the holy Sacraments " (St. Mary Magdalen dei Pazzi).

326

APOSTOLIC IMMOLATION

PRESENCE OF GOD - O Jesus, immolated for my salvation, make me worthy to immolate myself with You for the salvation of souls.

MEDITATION

1. Apostolic prayer must be accompanied by sacrifice, as we learn from the prayer which Jesus made to His Father in the Garden of Olives and on the Cross. Love should urge those who pray to " *active sacrifice* which does not allow them to rest calmly in prayer as long as pain and suffering have not all but reached the limits of endurance Then, consumed by the ardor of charity and the vehemence of desire, they are no longer persons who pray but *living prayers* " (Pius XII, January 17, 1943). There is a close connection between prayer and sacrifice, since they both flow from one source : love, which spurs the soul on to prayer and incessant immolation for the glory of God and the salvation of souls. The contemplative life, therefore, is synonymous with an austere, penitential life; it is a continual " sacrifice of praise. " The more prayer is nourished and accompanied by sacrifice, the more efficacious it becomes; indeed, it attains its maximum efficacy when sacrifice is total.

Every contemplative soul should be " an altar worthy of the presence of His Majesty " (J.C. *AS I*, 5,7), an altar from which prayer rises, and on which the sacrifice is immolated. The apostolate of Jesus reached its climax and was consummated in the annihilation of death on the Cross; not until He had been scourged, pierced with nails, abandoned by God and man, could He say, " Consummatum est, " it is consummated (*Jn* 19,30). It will be the same with us; only when we have really sacrificed ourselves for souls, when we have willingy immolated ourselves with Jesus for their salvation, shall we be able to repeat with Him : " It is consummated. " Our participation in the apostolate of Jesus attains its fulfillment in the sacrifice of ourselves—not an imaginary, hypothetical sacrifice, but one that is real and concrete. The form and measure of this sacrifice will be made known to us by God Himself, through the circumstances of our life, the events permitted by His divine Providence, the orders of our superiors, and the duties of our state in life. When, for the salvation of souls, we are disposed to live in continual sacrifice of our own will, in continual renouncement of self; when we are disposed to let ourselves be crucified in whatever way the holy will of God ordains, in order to win other souls to His love, then we shall have reached the apex of the apostolate and hence of apostolic fruitfulness.

2. Many souls are lost because there is no one to pray and make sacrifices for them. Without the tears and sufferings of a St. Monica, it is probable that the Church would never have had a St. Augustine. Blessed, then, are those souls who make apostolic immolation the reason for, and the object of, their life. " Oh, my sisters in Christ! " St. Teresa of Jesus wrote to her daughters, " Help me to entreat this of the Lord, who has brought you together here for that very purpose [the salvation of souls]. This is your vocation, this must be your business, these must be your desires, these your tears, these your petitions.... If your prayers and desires, your disciplines and fasts are not performed for the intentions of which I have spoken, reflect (and believe) that you are not carrying out the work or fulfilling the object for which the Lord has brought you here " (*Way*, 1 – 3). Contemplatives, not having an exterior apostolate, are especially bound to concentrate all their powers in prayer and sacrifice; only by so doing will they make the great contribution which the Church expects from them and thus

fulfill their vocation. They are called in a special way to generously fill up in their flesh, for the benefit of His Mystical Body, the Church, what is lacking in Christ's Passion. This is accomplished by the penances entailed by community life and by the observance of an austere, humble life, subject to obedience in all things and deprived of all human satisfaction (cf. Apostolic Constitution : *Sponsa Christi*).

St. Thérèse of the Child Jesus declared : " I have come to Carmel to save souls" (*St.* 7); and after she had consumed and offered all her energies for this end, she even offered for sinners the prayers which were offered for her during the sufferings of her last illness that she might obtain a little relief.

Contemplatives should be " specialists " in the apostolate of sacrifice which, however, cannot and should not be wanting, in one form or another, in the life of every apostle. Christ has purchased our souls at the price of His precious Blood; and whoever wishes to collaborate with Him in the salvation of mankind, should be willing to unite to the most precious Blood of Christ some drops of his own blood. Souls cost dearly, and an apostle must pay *with himself* for those he wants to win. The apostolate is true and fruitful in the measure in which it is imbued with suffering, which is the fruit of immolation.

COLLOQUY

" Lord, my heart rejoices when I consider that You have deigned to associate me to the great work of Redemption, that in me You may undergo, as it were, an extension of Your Passion. You have taken me, and You will that I be as another humanity in which You can still suffer for Your Father's glory and for the needs of Your Church.

" How glad I should be, my adored Master, if You asked me also to shed my blood for You. But what I ask of You, above all, is that martyrdom of love that consumed the saints.... Since You...have said that the greatest proof of love is to give one's life for the one loved, I give You mine, to do with it as may please You; and if I am not a martyr unto blood, I want to be a martyr by love.

" How I rejoice when I think that from all eternity we were known by the Father, and that He wished to find Your image in us, O Crucified Christ! How necessary suffering is then, if Your work is to be accomplished in me! You desire to enrich me with Your graces, but it is I who set a limit to Your gift, and determine its measure by the generosity with which I let myself be immolated by You.

" O Lord, You called the hour of Your Passion ' *Your hour*, ' the hour for which You had come, the hour You welcomed with all Your desires. When a great or even a very small sacrifice presents itself to me, I want to think quickly that this is ' *my hour*, ' the hour in which I can give a proof of my love to You, who have loved me ' exceedingly ' " (E.T. *L*).

327

THE APOSTOLATE OF EXAMPLE

PRESENCE OF GOD - O Lord, grant that all my actions may glorify You and may draw many souls to Your love.

MEDITATION

1. In addition to prayer and sacrifice, there is another powerful arm of the apostolate which is accessible to everyone, the apostolate of a good, holy life. All cannot be preachers, all do not have the duty to admonish or exhort others, not all can attend to apostolic works, but there is no one who cannot contribute to the spiritual good of his neighbor by giving the example of a life which is integrally Christian : holding to the principles one has professed and faithfully fulfilling one's duties. " Everyone can help his neighbor if he does his duty, " says St. John Chrysostom, and he adds : " There would be no pagans if Christians were real Christians, if they really kept the commandments. A good life sounds clearer and louder than a trumpet. " A good life speaks for itself, it has an authority and exercises an attraction greatly superior to that of words.

For a soul who seeks the truth, who seeks virtue, there is no difficulty in finding books and teachers who will present it in an attractive form, but there is much difficulty in finding persons whose lives give practical testimony to it. The modern mind, thirsting for experimental knowledge, has special need of such examples, capable of offering not only beautiful theories of the spiritual life, but, above all, of being concrete incarnations, as it were, of virtue, of the ideal of sanctity and union with God. Souls are attracted far more by thoughts and ideals that are lived than by ideas alone. Was this not the course that God Himself followed in revealing Himself to men? The eternal Word became incarnate and through the concrete reality of His human life on earth, He manifested the infinite perfections of God and His tremendous love for us. Jesus, who possessed the divine perfections, could tell us : " Be you therefore perfect, as also your heavenly Father is perfect " (*Mt* 5,48); and speaking thus, He not only showed us the supreme ideal of sanctity, but He also offered Himself as our model. An apostle must follow the same path that Jesus trod, incarnating in his life the ideal of sanctity that he wishes to propose to others. Only if he does this can we say of him, as was said of Our Lord, " coepit facere et docere " (*Acts* 1,1), he began (first) to do and (then) *to teach*. By this way alone can the apostle repeat, in deeds rather than in words, the daring sentence of St. Paul : " Be ye followers of me, as I also am of Christ " (1 *Cor* 4,16).

2. Jesus, who taught us to pray, to fast, and to give alms in secret, so that only our heavenly Father would know of it and reward us, also taught us to act in such a way that our good works might be a silent encouragement toward good for those who see them. " So let your light shine before men that they may see your good works, and glorify your Father who is in heaven " (*Mt* 5,16). St. Gregory explains how to reconcile these two instructions of Our Lord : " Let the action be public, " he says, " while the intention remains hidden; thus we shall give our neighbor the example of a good work and, at the same time, by our intention which is directed only toward God, we shall please Him alone in secret. " There is a great difference between one who makes a big display of his good acts, hoping to call forth praise from others, or perhaps to gain a reputation for sanctity, and one who, acting with the right intention of pleasing God alone, is by his conduct a light and guide for those around him. When we have a right intention, that of giving

glory to God and drawing others to His service, we should not fear lest our good works be seen; on the contrary, we should feel it a duty to edify others by our conduct.

Every soul who lives an interior life, trying to please God alone, should also endeavor to be an apostle by his good example. His life of sincere piety, solid virtue, and union with God, should shine before men, inspiring them to pray, to be recollected, to seek after the things of heaven. This is possible in every walk of life. The professional man in the world can exercise this apostolate among his colleagues, pupils, or clients; the wife and mother, in her family circle; religious, in their own community, and priests, in their sphere of activity.

A truly interior soul is, of itself, an apostle, and as Jesus said, " a city seated on a mountain [which] cannot be hid "; it is a burning light set " upon a candlestick that it may shine to all that are in the house " (*Mt* 5,14.15). The more deeply interior a soul is, the more brightly will its light shine upon other souls and bring them to God.

COLLOQUY

" O my God, there is nothing colder than a Christian who has no interest in the salvation of others! I cannot use poverty as a pretext to dispense myself from it. Peter said, ' Silver and gold I have none '; Paul was so poor that he often suffered from hunger. I cannot allege my humble state, for neither were they of the nobility, nor were their ancestors.

" I cannot give ignorance as an excuse, Lord, because they, too, were ignorant. Even were I a fugitive slave, I could perform my task; Onesimus was such. I cannot object that I am sick, for Timothy was often ill.

" O Lord, You teach me that I can help my neighbor if I fulfill my duty. I will do this by observing Your laws, especially the law of love by which we teach goodness to those who offend us. Good example has more influence on worldly people than miracles, and You tell me that there is nothing better than charity and love of one's neighbor. Help me, then, O Lord, to lead a holy life and to do good works, so that those who see me may praise Your Name " (cf. St. John Chrysostom).

"O Lord, grant that I may believe with my heart, profess with my mouth, and put into practice Your words, that others, seeing my good works, will glorify You, our Father who art in heaven, through Jesus Christ, Our Lord, to whom be glory forever and ever. Amen" (Origen).

328

APOSTOLIC WORKS

PRESENCE OF GOD - O my God, make me worthy to collaborate with You in spreading Your kingdom of Love.

MEDITATION

1. The interior apostolate of prayer and suffering in virtue of its intrinsic efficacy and fruitfulness possesses a preeminence over all other forms of the apostolate, to such a degree that, even without any exterior activity, it is sufficient to make those who practice it eminent apostles. Nevertheless, works are also necessary in society and in the Church; God wills them, and indeed He ordinarily intervenes in the world through the activity of His apostles. Side by side with the interior apostolate of contemplatives, the exterior activity of pastors and the faithful is needed for the diffusion of the life of grace in souls. The ministry of the priesthood is necessary for the administration of the Sacraments; missionaries are needed to convert infidels; we must have schools and teachers for the Christian formation of youth; to christianize society, we need social works and workers, professional men and women who will be apostles in their own walks of life. In the field of the apostolate, as St. Paul says, there are many duties, many offices of varied importance and value, but they all proceed from one and the same spirit, the Holy Spirit, who "divides to everyone according as He will," and at the same time, orders them all to one end : the growth of the Mystical Body of Christ (1 *Cor* 12,11). Just as one member of the human body has need of the others, "and the eye cannot say to the hand, I need not thy help, nor again the head

to the feet, I have no need of you " (*ibid.*12, 21), so neither can contemplatives say to those in the active life, " Your works are not necessary "; nor can the latter say to the former, " Your prayer is of no avail. " Neither can the supporters of the various kinds of apostolic activity consider one to be more important than others; but with mutual appreciation, all should work in a spirit of solidarity, helping one another, each one trying to carry out his own functions with the greatest possible perfection. From the love with which each one discharges his own duties and, at the same time, remains united to the others, will result the universal good of the Church, which the apostle should seek above and beyond any of his own personal works or interests.

2. The first place in the apostolic ministry belongs, beyond all doubt, to the Bishops who are the direct successors of the Apostles, to whom Jesus officially entrusted the charge of evangelizing the world : " Going, therefore, teach ye all nations, baptizing them in the name of the Father, and of the Son, and of the Holy Ghost, teaching them to observe all things whatsoever I have commanded you " (*Mt* 28,19.20). Next to this apostolate of the Hierarchy, reserved for the clergy, there is the apostolate of the laity, who are invited by the Church to collaborate with the Hierarchy. The Bishops guide, govern, draw up the plans; and under their direction the faithful are called upon to lend their assistance. It is evident, therefore, that the authentic apostolate, the only one which is in accord with God's plan for the salvation of mankind, is that which is exercised in harmony with the directives of the Church. He who wants to work in the Lord's vineyard, independently of those whom God has chosen to direct and govern it, is not worthy to be called an apostle. Activity of this kind would not only fail to further the ends of the apostolate, but it would also be prejudicial to them.

First on the list of collaborators with the Hierarchy are the persons consecrated to God by the vows of religion, that is, religious men and women dedicated to the works of the apostolate, and the members of Secular Institutes. Next are the members of Catholic Action groups, and finally, there is a place for all Christians who, privately or as members of a group, practice some form of the apostolate. It was not by chance that Pius XII, in the Encyclical *Mystici*

Corporis, speaking of the collaboration of the faithful in the apostolate, made special mention of fathers and mothers of families; indeed every Christian who works to bring the spirit of the Gospel into his own sphere of action—whether it be the home, the school, the office, or the hospital—is a true collaborator with the Hierarchy. Furthermore, the same Pope declared : " This apostolic work, performed according to the spirit of the Church, consecrates a layman as a kind of minister of Christ; this is what St. Augustine meant when he wrote : ' O brethren...you, too, in your own way, ought to be ministers of Christ by leading a good life, giving alms, and preaching His name and His doctrine. In this way the father of a family also will fulfill his duty as a cleric in his own home, and to some degree the duty of a bishop, serving Christ, in order to be with Him in eternity ' " (Encyclical : *Summi Pontificatus*). It was in this sense that St. Peter, addressing himself to the faithful, did not hesitate to say : " You are a chosen generation, a kingly priesthood " (1 *Pt* 2,9).

COLLOQUY

" O my God, grant that I may no longer think whether I am to gain or lose, but let my one aim be to serve and please You. Knowing Your love for us, I willingly renounce all my pleasure in order to please You alone, by serving my neighbor and proclaiming to others the truths which will do good to their souls. I shall not worry about any loss I may suffer; I wish to have only my neighbor's good in mind and nothing further. In order to give You more pleasure, my God, I want to forget myself for others, and I am ready, if need be, even to give up my life, as did many martyrs.

" This, I think, must be one of the greatest comforts on earth, to see good coming to souls through one's own agency. Happy are they, O Lord, to whom You grant these favors! " (T.J. *Con*).

" My God, fortunate is he who has tasted how sweet it is to work for the salvation of souls! He is not afraid of cold or heat, hunger or thirst, offenses or insults, no, not even of death.

" O Lord, give me crosses and thorns, persecutions of all kinds, if only I can save souls, and my own among them.

Da mihi animas, coetera tolle : give me souls, Lord, and take all the rest.

" Only when I know that the devil has given up plotting against souls, shall I cease trying new ways of saving them from his deceits and snares.

" O Lord, I wish to make a complete sacrifice of my life to You, to work for Your glory until I draw my last breath, bearing patiently all adversities and contradictions in my work. Help me to spend all my strength for the salvation of souls " (St. John Bosco).

329

THE ROAD TO OUR ETERNAL HOME

TWENTIETH SUNDAY AFTER PENTECOST

PRESENCE OF GOD - O Lord, teach me the way to come to You.

MEDITATION

1. The liturgy of the last Sundays after Pentecost has a special note, warning us of the approaching end of all things. In fact, the liturgical year is almost at its close, and, as it ends, it invites us to consider the uncertainty of the present life and to turn our eyes toward the eternal life awaiting us. Spontaneously we stop to reflect on the condition of our own soul : How have we employed the time that God has given us? In the Introit we find the humble confession : " O Lord, we have sinned against Thee, we have not obeyed Thy commandments, " and in the Collect we pray to obtain forgiveness : " Grant unto Thy faithful people pardon and peace, we beseech Thee, merciful Lord. " In the Epistle (*Eph* 5,15-21) St. Paul counsels us to use the time that remains to us in the best possible way, to attain eternal glory. " See, therefore, brethren, how you walk circumspectly, not as unwise, but as wise, redeeming the time, because the days are evil. " The Apostle then explains what the nature of our wisdom should

be : " Become not unwise, but understand what the will
of God is. " It would be the height of folly and imprudence
to go through life following our own whims and desires.
This is a most dangerous way and one which will never
lead us to our destination. The only road that takes us to
our eternal home is that of the will of God. Anyone who
sincerely seeks God's will and follows it, will be guided,
not by his own spirit, but by God's Spirit, the Holy Spirit,
and can be sure that he will not go astray. " Be ye filled
with the Holy Spirit, " exhorts St. Paul, " speaking to yourselves in psalms and hymns and spiritual canticles, singing
and making melody in your hearts to the Lord...being
subject one to another. " When a soul allows itself, with
childlike docility, to be led by the Holy Spirit, He takes
complete possession of it, filling it entirely with Himself;
and from this plenitude, the spirit of prayer, virtue, humble
submission and fraternal love spontaneously blossoms
forth. To follow God's will under the direction of the Holy
Spirit is the quickest and safest way of reaching our heavenly
home.

2. It is impossible to discover and walk in the way of
God's will without faith; today's Gospel (*Jn* 4,46-53)
expressly treats of this faith and the qualities it must have
in order to be pleasing to God.

A certain ruler, having heard of the marvelous cures
performed by Jesus, went to Him and begged Jesus to come
to his house and " heal his son, for he was at the point of
death. " This man had faith in the miraculous power of the
Master, but he was far from believing that He was the Son
of God. Jesus knew this and replied : " Unless you see
signs and wonders, you believe not. " These words, which
historically were addressed to the ruler and his companions, were meant for all whose faith depends on what
they see and hear. There are very few who believe with
simplicity in the Gospel, in Revelation, in the teachings
of the Church; most people remain indifferent and are moved
only in the presence of something unusual which strikes
their senses. It is true that the Lord can use such things to
help our weakness, but this is not the faith which pleases
Him. " Blessed are they that have not seen and have
believed " (*ibid.* 20,29), He said to Thomas, who would not
believe unless he saw the place of the nails and put his finger

into His wounds. True faith is not based on our experience, on what we see and touch, but on the authority of God. God has revealed Himself; He can neither deceive nor be deceived; and we believe firmly on His word. To believe on the word of God is supernatural faith, the pure faith which is pleasing to God.

Jesus, who wished to lead the ruler to this true faith, said to him : " ' Go thy way, thy son liveth. ' The man believed the word which Jesus said to him, and went his way. " It was not yet supernatural faith in the Son of God; nevertheless, it was an act of faith in the Master's word, and although it was imperfect, it brought forth fruit : his son was cured. God does not demand more than each one can give Him, and when He sees our good will, our sincere efforts, He Himself intervenes to perfect the work. Thus the ruler's imperfect and still human faith was rewarded by his son's cure, and as a result, his faith became supernatural. He believed in Jesus, no longer as a simple prophet or wonder-worker, but as the Son of God; " and himself believed and his whole house. "

In this life we walk toward God, not by vision, but by faith. The purer our faith is and the more free from human elements, the more pleasing it will be to God, and the more it will enable us to know His holy will and to accomplish it with love.

COLLOQUY

" Be propitious to Your children, O divine Master, Father and Lord. Grant that we who keep Your command-ments may reflect Your image; may we experience, according to our strength, Your goodness, and not the severity of Your judgment.

"Grant that we may all live in Your peace and be admitted to Your kingdom after struggling against the waves of sin without being shipwrecked. In great tranquility, may we be drawn by the Holy Spirit, Your ineffable Wisdom, and guided by Him day and night, unto the perfect day. Grant that, until our last hour, we may be grateful in prayer and prayerful in gratitude to the one Father and Son, Son and Father, the Son our Teacher and Master, together with the Holy Spirit " (Clement of Alexandria).

" Lord, You know what is best; let this or that be done as You will. Give what You will, as much as You will, and when You will. Do with me as You know best, as will most please You, and will be for Your greater honor. Put me where You will, and do with me in all things according to Your will. Lo, I am Your servant, ready to obey You in all things; for I do not desire to live for myself, but for You : Oh, that I could do so in a faithful and perfect manner!

" O most loving Jesus, grant me always to will and desire that which is most acceptable to You, and which pleases You best. Let Your will be mine, and let my will always follow Yours, and agree perfectly with it. Let my will be one with Yours in willing and in not willing, and let me be unable to will or not will anything but what You will or do not will " (*Imit. III*, 15,2.3).

330

THE FORMATION OF APOSTLES

PRESENCE OF GOD - Jesus, divine Teacher, deign to accept me in Your school, so that, under Your direction, I may prepare myself for the apostolate.

MEDITATION

1. No special preparation is necessary before giving oneself to the interior apostolate, for, if a soul dedicates itself to prayer and sacrifice, not only will it help others, but at the same time it will draw great profit for its own sanctification. In fact, the practice of the interior apostolate coincides perfectly with the fundamental exercises of the spiritual life. However, the same cannot be said of the external apostolate which, by its very nature, involves cares and occupations beyond those required for one's personal progress. One who is just setting out in the spiritual life is not capable of attending to his own sanctification and the sanctification of others simultaneously; he should first have time to concentrate all his powers on his own spiritual formation.

Furthermore, since the effectiveness of the apostolate corresponds to the degree of love and union with God which the apostle has attained, it is evident that a beginner will not be capable of exercising a very fruitful apostolate. Hence, if he engages in the active apostolate prematurely, he will dissipate his energy uselessly, with consequent harm to his own interior life and to the fruitfulness of his apostolate.

Jesus Himself spent thirty years in prayer and retirement although, being God, He had no need to do so. It was as if He wanted to show us that before we plunge into the work of the exterior apostolate, we must have reached a certain spiritual maturity by the exercise of the interior life. He treated the Apostles in a similar way : the three years they spent with Jesus were years of true formation for them. Our Lord instructed and admonished them, taught them how to pray and to practice virtue. Only occasionally, and then with precaution, did He entrust some mission to them, in order to give them experience. Finally, before He sent them out to conquer the world, He wished to strengthen their spirit by nourishing them with His Body, calling them to witness His Passion, and reuniting them in the Cenacle to await the coming of the Holy Spirit. Thus true Catholic tradition demands that, before apostles go out into the field of battle, they must prepare themselves by the practice of an intense interior life, which will make them qualified, fruitful instruments for the good of souls.

2. The great necessity for apostolic works, which is growing in urgency today, cannot justify a hasty preparation for the apostolate. What advantage would it be to send a greater number of apostles into the fray if, from lack of formation, they would not only be incapable of making any headway, but could not even withstand the attacks of the enemy?

Enthusiasm and good will are not enough. A vigorous interior life, maturity of thought and judgment, and a spirit of sacrifice and union with God are also necessary; if these are wanting, no good will be accomplished, and the spiritual life of the apostles themselves will be endangered. The urgency of the apostolate must be answered by intensifying the formation of those who are to dedicate themselves to it, because only souls who are firmly anchored in God by an intense interior life will be able to withstand

the constant pressure of external activity, and to vivify this
activity with the fire of love.

St. Teresa of Jesus says, " A single one who is perfect
will do more than many who are not " (*Way*, 3). It is,
therefore, of the greatest importance that those who give
themselves to the apostolate strive earnestly for perfection
and sanctity, for only thus can they give God to souls and
bring souls to God. The entire history of the Church is a
practical demonstration of this principle : " St. Paul was
only one, yet how many he attracted!... If all Christians
were like St. Paul, how many worlds would be converted! "
(St. John Chrysostom). The holy Curé of Ars had very few
human resources, yet he converted an immense number of
souls by the power of his own holiness, love, and union
with God.

The pressing demands of the external apostolate focus
our attention more than ever upon the need of well-formed
apostles, apostles of deep interior life, saintly apostles.
Therefore, even when the formative period has ended,
we must always take care that external activity in no way
diminishes our interior life. It is necessary to continually
maintain the balance between prayer and work in such
a way that we do not exhaust our spiritual energies, but
allow sufficient time to renew them, to revive and to sustain
our intimate contact with God.

COLLOQUY

" O Lord, my whole yearning is that, as You have so
many enemies and so few friends, these last should be trusty
ones. Therefore I am determined to do the little that is in
me : namely, to follow the evangelical counsels as perfectly
as I can, and...to pray for those who are defenders of the
Church, and for the preachers and learned men who defend
her. O Lord, since I am not strong enough to defend Your
Church myself, I want to strive to live in such a way that
my prayers may be of avail to help these servants of Yours,
who, at the cost of so much toil, have armed themselves with
learning and virtue and have labored to defend your Name.

" O my God, I wish to try to live in such a way as to
be worthy to obtain two things from You : first, that there
may be many of these very learned and religious men who

have the qualifications for their task, and that You may prepare those who are not completely prepared already; for a single one who is perfect will do more than many who are not. Secondly, that, after they have entered upon this struggle, You may have them in Your hand so that they may be delivered from all the dangers that are in the world, and, while sailing on this perilous sea, may shut their ears to the song of the sirens. If I can prevail with You, my God, in the smallest degree about this, I shall be fighting Your battle even while living a cloistered life.

" I beseech Your Majesty to hear me in this; miserable creature that I am, I shall never cease to beg You for this, since it is for Your glory and the good of Your Church, and on these my desires are set. The day that my prayers, desires, disciplines and fasts are not performed for the intentions of which I have spoken, I shall not have fulfilled the object for which You, O Lord, called me to the contemplative life " (cf. T.J. *Way*, 1 – 3).

331

SANCTIFICATION IN THE APOSTOLATE

PRESENCE OF GOD - Give me light, O God, that I may recognize the graces You have prepared for me to lead me to sanctity; help me to correspond with them.

MEDITATION

1. It is the saints who are the most efficient apostles. Must we then be saints before devoting ourselves to the apostolate? Theoretically, this is the ideal, but in practice, it is impossible. To think that the formative years—those spent in the seminary or novitiate, for example—suffice to make us saints is a misconception. It is equally wrong to exempt ourselves from apostolic work, when charity or our duty imposes it on us, under the pretext that we have not yet arrived at sanctity. We must therefore conclude that when the period allotted exclusively to preparation is over, we

must combine our own personal efforts toward sanctity with
the exercise of the active apostolate. In other words, apostles
must sanctify themselves in the apostolate and by means
of it. "To sanctify yourself in view of and by means of the
apostolate : these should be the marching orders of a diocesan
priest.... We would be giving the lie to the Church,
to the life of Jesus, and the lives of all the saints, if we said
that the exterior apostolate is incompatible with personal
sanctity." These words, spoken by the servant of God,
Don Poppe, to priests, are equally true for all apostles,
cleric or lay, religious or secular. Every apostle should
be convinced that precisely in his own field of labor—and
nowhere else—will he find all the graces necessary to sanctify
himself, to attain intimate union with God. When a person
gives himself to the apostolate, not by his own choice, nor because of a natural attraction for activity, but solely in answer
to a call from God, he can be certain that, since God has
willed him to engage in the apostolate, and as He also *wills*
him to be a saint, that the apostolate will provide him with
the means to become one. God cannot condemn to mediocrity one who, in order to do His will, and out of love for
Him, is burdened with apostolic labors and responsibilities.
"No, brethren," Don Poppe continues, "the active life is
not a night in which the light of the ideal is extinguished.
If so many apostles have lost their light, you should not
lose confidence, but *humble yourselves* profoundly because of
your weakness, and then more abundant grace will surely
bring you success. Do you not know that difficulties and
obstacles are sometimes transformed into helps under the
wonderful action of grace, and may contribute greatly to
good? ' *Certus sum,* ' you can say with St. Paul : I am certain
that no creature in the world has the power to draw me away
from the road to sanctity." In the measure that an apostle is
docile and faithful to grace, God will purify him, refine
him, and sanctify him, precisely by means of his apostolic
labors.

2. The conviction that we can sanctify ourselves in the
midst of our work does not prevent us from having that silent
longing for recollection, that desire for solitude and intimacy
with God which often accompanies an apostle in his activities,
becoming so keen at times that it casts a veil of nostalgia
over his life. Anyone who has tasted, even in a slight degree,

the infinite beauty and goodness of God, cannot fail to experience an overwhelming longing and need for Him. This is a good sign : it means that the apostle has not permitted himself to be pervaded and distracted by exterior occupations, and that, although living in the world, he is not of the world, but really tends toward God. Even if this longing should at times become painful, the apostle must not be disturbed nor believe that he has mistaken his way. This pain will purify him and lead him to God. Moreover, he should not think that the mere desire for deeper recollection and union with God necessarily indicates a call to the contemplative life, which is characterized especially by the need of a radical dedication and self-immolation. An insistent call to a deeper interior life should be considered rather as a grace given to protect the apostle against the dangers of the exterior life. It is the bulwark, the enclosure wall of his spiritual life.

However, the desire for God should be satisfied; in addition to the daily hours of prayer and silence, the apostle must have sufficient pauses in his work. Monthly and yearly retreats are indispensable, and even more leisure for recollection must be taken after periods of intense activity. It would be a fatal error to allow oneself to become so absorbed in work that time could no longer be found for concentration on God in intimate heart-to-heart conversation with Him. Not even from the standpoint of greater generosity should an apostle renounce his hours of prayer.

But at the same time, he must go to his work calmly and confidently, ever mindful of the fact that, until he has attained to full maturity in the spiritual life, he will not be able to escape the conflict between action and contemplation : action which tries to draw him away from contemplation, and contemplation which would like to prolong itself beyond the appointed time. He must make every effort to maintain an equilibrium, avoiding both extremes, and unifying his life by means of love. Before the conflict is settled in perfect harmony, a long road must be traversed, where it is absolutely necessary to give oneself to activity with great prudence, and to be very faithful to prayer, being careful not to allow the time allotted for it to be encroached upon.

COLLOQUY

" O my God, how few saintly apostles there are! How rare are Your real friends! O Lord, I am on fire with longing for the coming of Your kingdom in the souls of apostles; I am on fire, but I am so poor that I shall be consumed before this kingdom comes!

" O Lord, make me a holy apostle, because a saint can accomplish more with one word than an ordinary worker can with a whole series of speeches. Without sanctity, I am like sounding brass or a tinkling cymbal, and You, O God, speak only through the mouths of the saints. Give me sanctity then, as it alone can enlighten minds, move hearts, and renew them. O my God, do not permit me to deal in tinsel or to be an empty vessel!

" It is hard to sanctify oneself in the apostolate; there are many obstacles and dangers to be encountered. Shall I then retire in discouragement? No, my God, because if my will is good, I shall always be aided by Your grace, and where there is grace, the way which leads to the end, to sanctity, will always be found! Then what have I to fear? Your grace is with me; You Yourself are with me and in me. And if You, O God, enter the battle with me, what can I call an obstacle? Would it be tribulation or sorrow, hunger or nakedness, danger, persecution, or the sword? I shall overcome all these difficulties with Your help, for You love me, and will not abandon me. Leaning on You, O Lord, I am certain that nothing in the world has the power to separate me from the way of sanctity. I am certain because You want apostles to be saints, because You are infinitely good, infinitely powerful, and faithful to Your promises, and because You are infinitely merciful " (Don Poppe).

332

A RIGHT INTENTION

PRESENCE OF GOD - O God, remove from my heart all secondary intentions and all movements of self-love, so that I may seek only Your glory.

MEDITATION

1. Difficulties encountered in the apostolate often arise because apostolic activity is not exercised under conditions which are required by its very nature, conditions which are indispensable if this activity is to be transformed into an intense exercise of the spiritual life. There is question here of a certain disorder, arising from the more or less natural motives which insinuate themselves into the work and cause it to descend from the supernatural to the natural level. Thus it becomes an occasion for deviation and lukewarmness in the interior life, which in turn, makes the soul feel dissatisfied and uneasy. Pope Pius XII, in his Motu proprio *Primo Feliciter*, expressed very clearly the necessary conditions for a holy activity. He said : " The apostolate should always be exercised in a saintly manner, with such purity of intention, such interior union with God, such generous forgetfulness and abnegation of self, and with so great a love for souls that it [the apostolate] flows from the interior spirit which informs it and at the same time nourishes and renews this same spirit. " Examining our apostolate in the light of these words, we shall be able to detect its weak points, to discover the defects to be avoided and the remedies to be applied. There are four conditions proposed : purity of intention, union with God, self-abnegation, love for souls. They are so important that while guaranteeing a fruitful apostolate, they constitute an efficacious means of spiritual progress. Striving to realize them, we shall simultaneously raise the level of our activity and of our interior life.

Let us first consider purity of intention. If no one can " serve God and Mammon " (*Mt* 6,24), much less can the apostle give himself to apostolic works with the double intention of serving God and his own self-love, of pleasing

God and the world, of being zealous for the interests of souls and for his own personal interests. Strength, peace, and life come from unity; dividing one's forces especially in the realm of the spirit, can only lead to weakness, conflict, and ultimately to death. An apostle whose heart is torn between opposing intentions will look in vain for peace in his work; he will always be disturbed and dissatisfied.

2. There can be a lack of right intention in a way that easily escapes one's notice; it may be so subtle that to a distracted soul, it passes wholly unobserved. In order to discover the least secondary intentions which, like little foxes, creep in secretly to destroy apostolic activity, an atmosphere of recollection and prayer is necessary. In his moments of quiet at the feet of Our Lord, the apostle will discover that often, in the course of his daily occupations, he loses sight of the supernatural end which should animate his activity, and that in its place secondary ends appear, becoming the immediate motive of many of his decisions and acts. This means that his intention has not remained directed solely toward God and souls, but has often deviated under the influence of self-love. Sometimes it is a question of seeking praise and glory, more or less unconsciously, or it may be preoccupations concerning his personal advantage or material interests : keeping a position, obtaining some promotion, being favored by superiors, or selected for more attractive or remunerative work.... In short, the apostle should realize that, side by side with his love for God and souls there is still much self-love and egoism. This is not a very consoling picture, but he should not be discouraged by it; instead, he should humbly recognize his own misery and thank God who has revealed it to him in order that he may correct it. On the other hand, he must not think that everything he does is merely the fruit of pride. No, when a person has consecrated himself to the apostolate with a sincere desire of doing God's will and winning other hearts for Him, he should acknowledge that he is animated by love for God and souls, but that his love is not strong enough yet to triumph completely over human passions. Therefore, the apostle should not give up the struggle against the manifestations of self-love, no matter how trivial. He must not yield to them under the pretext that they are natural tendencies, but must correct, mortify, repress, and

cut them off without pity, and must always rectify his intentions. A long, thorough purification is necessary to overcome completely the dualism between God and " self, " between love for souls and love of self. The apostle must ask Our Lord for the grace of this total purification and dispose himself to receive it, profiting by every occasion for detachment, renunciation, sacrifice, and humiliation, which apostolic activity offers in abundance to all who seriously dedicate themselves to it. If the apostle does this, he will find in his work an excellent means of spiritual progress, and instead of becoming entangled in the dangers which abound in external activity when self-love is not mortified, he will be purified by the very exercise of his apostolate.

COLLOQUY

" When I desire to pray or work for the good of others, I must first of all turn the eyes of my mind toward You, O eternal Light, and to Your splendor, so that You will give me light, strengthen my spirit, and help me to withdraw, as much as possible, from external things in order to turn wholly toward that which is interior. Grant that I may see only the interior man in my neighbor, paying attention to the exterior only insofar as it helps the interior, so that everything else will be put aside as vanity and I may not be attracted by vain things.

" O my God, grant that I may be drawn to the apostolate, to prayer, and to giving good example, not by vainglory, ambition, human complacency, or any worldly interest, but only by the desire to save souls. You alone, O my crucified Christ, do I wish to seek! I want to inebriate souls with Your Blood, and not with vain curiosities, in order that they may desire You alone. I would say to each one of them, ' I know only Jesus Christ and Him crucified. ' Hence I not only have no desire of worldly advantages or of being pleasing to men; I do not even judge myself as knowing anyone or anything but You, Christ crucified.

" O Lord, inebriate me so thoroughly with Your love that, if anything else but You presents itself to my sight or taste, to my hearing or any other sense, I shall consider it as nothing, so much so that I shall not take my delight, nor my glory, nor my rest except in Your Precious Blood, toward which I desire to be completely turned. Grant that my eyes may not be filled with the things of earth, but only with Your sufferings; grant that my mouth may not be filled with vain words, but with what concerns Your Passion, and may it be the same with all my other senses " (cf. St. Bonaventure).

333

SELF-FORGETFULNESS AND ABNEGATION

PRESENCE OF GOD - O Lord, You who give Yourself to us even to becoming our food, teach me to give myself to souls even unto total forgetfulness of myself.

MEDITATION

1. Another condition necessary for making our activity holy is " generous forgetfulness and abnegation of self " (Pius XII); what is more, without forgetfulness of self, it would be impossible to have rectitude of intention. Many secondary intentions steal into our actions precisely because we are so wrapt up in ourselves, so occupied and preoccupied with our *ego*, our interests, our conveniences, so anxious to be admired and to win applause and esteem. " We must go forth from ourselves and from creatures, " says St. John of the Cross, go forth especially from this creature whom we love more than every other, *ourself*. If the Saint indicates to us the way of " the nothing " with a view to the contemplative ideal of union with God, we may assert that the apostolic life does not require less; it too exacts total abnegation of self which can only be brought about by constantly reminding ourselves : nothing, nothing, nothing.

To realize his vocation, the missionary must leave his homeland, his parents, his friends; he must give up the language, habits, and customs of his country in order to conform to those of his adopted land; likewise, due proportion being made, every apostle must renounce many things, even when working in home surroundings, his place of employment, or among his neighbors. Tastes, habits, personal demands of culture, education, sensibility must be generously put aside, that the apostle may adapt himself to the mentality and to the demands of others; quiet, rest, relaxation, must yield their place to the service of souls. The apostle should not go about seeking interesting conversations, consoling friendships, pleasant occupations, satisfying results. Occasionally it may happen that he will meet these things on his way, but even then, he may not stop to enjoy them selfishly, but must use them as means for the apostolate; in any case, they may never and must never rule his activity. The apostle is sent to " give " and not to " receive, " to sow and not to reap; therefore, he ought to know how to give his time, his work, his energies, and his very self, even in situations which offer nothing consoling, and even to those souls from whom he receives neither satisfaction nor gratitude.

2. St. Paul teaches that the priest " is ordained for men " (*Heb* 5,1), and the same can be said of every apostle. The apostle does not exist for himself, for his career, for his own advantage, but for souls, for the advantage of others and for all that concerns their spiritual good. Even if the apostolate confers on him some authority, some dignity, it is not for his honor, for his utility, but only for the service of his fellow men. The only personal advantage that he can and should derive from the exercise of his apostolate is his own sanctification. Such is the only right that the apostle is entitled to, the sole benefit he can seek for himself; all the rest must be generously sacrificed for God and for souls.

A soul truly *given* to the apostolate no longer belongs to himself : his strength, his talents, his time, his health, his life belong to God and his neighbor, and having *given* himself, he can no longer take himself back, nor dispose of himself. It can be said that he has lost the right of ownership over all that he is and all that he has. To give himself by forgetting himself, and to forget himself that he may give himself even more : such is his program; and this, not only in moments of enthusiasm, on bright days, when souls respond to his care, when his works flourish, and he himself is strong and vigorous, but also in moments of darkness, on gray days, when all seems to crumble under the impact of difficulties, when his tired body claims a little rest, when the work is heavy and energy declines and, with the onrush of internal and external struggles, it becomes very difficult to remain at his post.

Yes, even in hours of abandonment and trial, the apostle must continue to give himself with equal constancy and generosity. If he does not do so cheerfully, that is, with a true spirit of sacrifice, it will be impossible for his conduct not to betray his ill humor, discontent, aversion, or impatience; and all this is very prejudicial to his work and the influence he could exercise. But where can the strength be found for this complete and continual gift of self? In the Holy Eucharist. In it, Jesus gives Himself to us even to becoming our food. If the apostle, called to extend the mission of the Master, cannot imitate Him by giving himself literally as food to souls, he can nevertheless follow His example by putting himself at their disposal to the point of allowing himself to be " eaten " by them, that is to say, by allowing himself to be consumed in their service.

COLLOQUY

" O Lord, help me to understand well that my work has eternal value only in proportion to the love with which I do it, and not to the success or failure it may or may not have. Even if I do not see the fruits, what does it matter as long as You see them? You want me to work in the spirit of faith, without seeking personal satisfaction.

" I feel that I am a mother of souls, and I must sacrifice myself for them with the greatest generosity because the salvation of many souls may depend on my correspondence to grace. I am a poor little nothing, Lord, but I offer You all. Father, I offer You Your divine Son. Take me and dispose of me for Your greatest glory.

" O Lord, with insistence You are constantly urging me to an ever more generous and total sacrifice. I feel the need to give myself to You, no longer to reserve anything for myself. I wish, then, to renew my offering to You in order that You may take me wholly, that You may transform me, that You may use me for Your glory, for the salvation of souls, and that You may complete in me what is lacking to Your Passion for Your Body which is the Church. I am happy to find so many practical occasions in the course of my day to realize this offering " (Sr. Carmela of the Holy Spirit, O.C.D.).

" O Jesus, my whole strength lies in prayer and sacrifice : these are my invincible weapons, and experience has taught

me that the heart is won by them rather than by words "
(T.C.J. *St*, 11).

334

HUMILITY IN THE APOSTOLATE

PRESENCE OF GOD - Impress in me such a deep sense of my poverty,
O Lord, that I may look to You for everything and attribute to You,
to You alone, all that is good.

MEDITATION

1. Humility is the indispensable foundation of the whole
spiritual life; hence it is the basic condition of every apostolate and constitutes the principal part of the program of
abnegation and forgetfulness of self which the apostolate
requires.   Because the apostle is placed, as it were, on
a candlestick, he needs more than others to protect himself from
pride and vainglory by a deep humility.   In glancing through
the Gospels, it is significant to note how much Jesus insisted
on this point relative to the training of His Apostles.   While
they were debating among themselves who would be the
greatest in the messianic kingdom, the Master answered :
" Unless you be converted and become as little children,
You shall not enter into the kingdom of heaven " (*Mt* 18,3).
On another occasion, when the mother of James and John
asked the first places for her sons, Jesus replied : " He that
will be first among you shall be your servant " (*ibid.* 20,27).
And on the evening of the Last Supper, while washing the
feet of the Apostles, He showed them to what extent they
should make themselves *servants :* " If then, I, being your
Lord and Master, have washed your feet, you also ought to
wash one another's feet " (*Jn* 13,14).   Finally, before sending
them into His vineyard to bear " much fruit, " He repeatedly
told them, " Without Me you can do nothing " (*ibid.* 15,5).

Yes, the apostle is the friend of Jesus, chosen by Him and
destined to evangelize the world.   Some have been appointed
by Him to govern the Church, clothed with the dignity

of the priesthood, with the power " to loose and to bind. " All—cleric or lay—have been elevated to the dignity of collaborators with the Hierarchy in the work of saving souls. But at the base of all these privileges, all these honors, are found the great words : " You must become as little children.... Without Me you can do nothing. " Oh! If we were truly convinced that, although God may will to make use of us, He alone possesses the power to make our action fruitful, He alone can produce fruits of eternal life, He alone can give grace to souls, and we are nothing but instruments! In fact, the smaller we make ourselves by acknowledging our poverty, the more qualified we become to be used as a means for the salvation of others. What glory can a brush claim if a skillful artist uses it to perfect a work of art? Can the marble used by Michelangelo to sculpture his Moses boast of any merit? " You have not chosen Me, " Jesus said to His Apostles, " but I have chosen you; and have appointed you, that you should go and should bring forth fruit " (*Jn* 15,16).

2. " Without Me you can do nothing. " How many ambitions and points of honor, how much vain self-complacency, how many desires for applause and for advancement in recognition of our personal worth are broken, like waves on the rocks, by these words! Jesus does not tell us that " without Him we can do little, " but, *nothing*, absolutely *nothing*, and if in appearance the works flourish, admirers increase, churches and halls are filled, in reality not the least atom of grace can descend into hearts if God does not intervene.

Poor apostle, at times so satisfied, so inflated by success! Despite your abilities, your talent, your brilliant style, your attractive conversation, your titles, your successes—in relation to the apostolate, you are smaller and more powerless than an ant before a very high mountain. Recognize your nothingness, take refuge in God, keep yourself closely united to Him, for only from Him will you draw the fruitfulness of your works.

Charged with the education of the novices, St. Thérèse of the Child Jesus exclaimed : " You see, Lord, that I am too small to feed Your little ones, but if through me You wish to give to each what is suitable, then fill my hands, and without leaving the shelter of Your arms, or even turning

my head, I will distribute Your treasures to the souls who
come to me asking for food " (*St* 11).   Such should be the
attitude of every apostle; and what is more, the higher his
mission, the more important and delicate it is, the more
necessary is this humble consciousness of his personal misery,
this confident recourse to God, this constant union with Him.
If God does not use us to accomplish great works, is it because,
being insufficiently convinced of our nothingness, we would
take to ourselves the glory due to Him alone, attributing our
success to our own merits?   If our apostolic activity produces
few fruits, is it because, relying too much on ourselves, we do
not constantly strive to keep close to God by means of humility
and prayer?

"Abide in Me, " Jesus repeats to us.   " As the branch
cannot bear fruit of itself, unless it abide in the vine, so
neither can you, unless you abide in Me " (*Jn* 15,4).   It does
not suffice for the apostle to be united to Jesus through the
state of grace; he must remain united to Him, plunged in
profound humility which makes him realize that he can do
nothing, absolutely nothing, without continual help.

COLLOQUY

"O Lord, You wish that in my apostolate I may feel
and recognize my nothingness, but at the same time You
want me to let myself be taken and carried by You to
accomplish the mission that You confide to me, and then
enter again into obscurity and silence, boasting of nothing
and saying only : ' *servi inutiles sumus* '; I am a useless servant,
without You I can do nothing.

"O Lord, help me to flee praise and the applause of
creatures; help me to act always with an upright intention,
seeking only Your good pleasure.   I beg You to put far from
me those defects which could distract me from working
only to please You : ostentation, compliments, adulation,
the desire of making a good appearance, of being agreeable
to others.   Grant that I may never seek my glory but only
yours.   All to please You, nothing to satisfy myself "
(Sr. Carmela of the Holy Spirit, O.C.D.).

"I beg You, Lord, to direct the heart and the will of
Your apostles to Yourself so that they may follow You,
immolated Lamb, poor, humble, and meek, by the way of the

Holy Cross, in Your way and not in their way. Dispel the darkness of their hearts and give them Your light; take from them all self-love and kindle in them the fire of Your charity. Make them close the faculties of their souls, shutting their minds to vain delights and earthly benefits, leaving them open only to Your benefits, that they may love nothing outside of You, but love You above all things, and everything else according to Your will; may they follow You alone.

" Grant that, with well ordered charity, they may seek the salvation of all, disposing themselves to give their life for the good of souls. And may they be angelic creatures, earthly angels in this life, and burning lamps in the Holy Church! " (cf. St. Catherine of Siena).

335

HUMAN QUALITIES AND APOSTOLIC CHARITY

PRESENCE OF GOD - Melt my heart, Lord, in the flame of Your charity.

MEDITATION

1. The apostolate is the expression and the fruit of *caritas apostolica*, that is to say, of love of God and neighbor, which has increased until it has become zeal for souls. But besides this essential aspect of the charity which must animate the apostle, there are secondary aspects; we might almost say human ones, that are, nevertheless, of great importance, since they permit the apostle to exercise influence over souls. We here speak of such qualities as affability, thoughtfulness, courtesy, sociability, sincerity, understanding, which although human gifts in themselves, acquire supernatural value when elevated by grace and placed at the service of the apostolate. It is a matter, in substance, of those qualities which St. Paul attributes to love : " Charity is patient, is kind...is not provoked to anger, thinketh no evil...rejoiceth with the truth " (1 *Cor* 13,4-6).

It is not sufficient to love souls in the secret of our heart, working and sacrificing ourselves for them; this love must also be manifested exteriorly by an agreeable and pleasant manner, in such a way that those who approach us may feel themselves loved, and consequently encouraged to confidence and to trust. A rude, brusque, or impatient manner might cause some to go away offended, and perhaps, even scandalized. The apostle may well have a heart of gold, rich in charity and zeal, but if he maintains a rough and sharp exterior, he closes access to souls, and considerably diminishes the good he could realize. The saints, while being very supernatural, never neglected these human qualities of charity. St. Francis de Sales liked to say that, as more flies are attracted with a drop of honey than with a barrel of vinegar, so more hearts are conquered by a little sweetness than by rough manners. And St. Teresa of Jesus, who wished her daughters to be united by the bond of pure supernatural charity, did not believe it superfluous to make recommendations of this kind : "The holier you are, the more sociable you should be with your sisters. Although you may be sorry if all your sisters' conversation is not just as you would like it to be, never keep aloof from them if you wish to help them and to have their love. We must try hard to be pleasant, and to humor the people we deal with" (*Way*, 41). This is very useful advice for anyone who wishes to win souls for God.

2. Concerning natural qualities employed in the service of apostolic charity, we can meditate fruitfully on the exhortation addressed by Pius XII to a group of religious men : " Before the young religious (and this could be said of the apostle) becomes a shining example, let him study to become a perfect man in the ordinary everyday things.... Let him learn, then, and show by his works, the dignity proper to human nature and to society; let him regulate his countenance and bearing in a dignified manner and be faithful and sincere; let him keep his promises; let him govern his acts and his words; let him have respect for all and not harm the rights of others; let him endure evil and be sociable.... As you well know, the virtues called natural are raised to the dignity of the supernatural life chiefly when a man practises them and cultivates them in order to become a good Christian and a worthy herald and

minister of Christ " (September, 1951). There is, therefore, no reason to believe that an antagonism exists between the plenitude of the supernatural life, union with God, and the plenitude of human virtue, deriving from a right development of the natural virtues. We must remember that grace does not destroy nature, but elevates it. The struggle against nature making way for grace, tends to mortify and to destroy only what is defective in nature, leaving intact the good qualities and powers to be raised and transferred to the supernatural plane. Grace, and consequently the Christian life, greatly respects and uses all human values; moreover, how could we believe that the supernatural destroys nature when the latter, no less than the former, is the work of God, the fruit of His wisdom and of His infinite goodness?

In raising man to the supernatural plane, God did not intend to destroy in him what had already been created, but only to sublimate and to elevate it. In the light of these principles, we understand why it has been said that the apostle, as well as the priest, must be a " perfect gentleman " (Cardinal Newman). We also grasp why the saints are the more perfect men, in the sense that they have carried the natural virtues to their highest perfection and sublimation. It follows that the saints are more capable than others of surrounding men with amiability, delicacy, and understanding, while loving them with a purely supernatural love; thus they more easily win their hearts. This perfect courtesy, ever self-possessed, even with the importunate, and even in moments of weariness, can only flow from great supernatural virtue and delicate charity.

COLLOQUY

O Lord, " if I speak with the tongues of men and of angels, and have not charity, I am become as sounding brass, or a tinkling cymbal...if I should have the gift of prophecy and should know all mysteries and all knowledge, and if I should have all faith, so that I could remove mountains, and have not charity, I am nothing. And if I should distribute all my goods to feed the poor, and if I should deliver my body to be burned, and have not charity, it would profit me nothing.

" Grant me charity, then, O my God, for charity is patient, is kind : charity envieth not, dealeth not perversely; is not puffed up; is not ambitious, seeketh not her own, is not provoked to anger, thinketh no evil; rejoiceth not in iniquity, but rejoiceth with the truth; beareth all things, believeth all things, hopeth all things, endureth all things " (cf. 1 *Cor* 13,1–7).

Grant, O Lord, that in consecrating myself to Your service, my tenderness toward my neighbor may not diminish, but may grow in my heart, and may become ever more pure, more supernatural. Teach me to love tenderly all who draw near to me. Make me gentle, affable, agreeable, not to attract to myself the affection of creatures, but to conquer their hearts for You.

O Jesus, if the apostle should be a copy of You, not only in broad lines, but even in details, how shall I be such if I do not try to imitate the gentleness of Your heart? O Jesus, meek and humble of heart, make my heart like unto Yours.

336

FORGIVENESS

TWENTY-FIRST SUNDAY AFTER PENTECOST

PRESENCE OF GOD - O Lord, as You are so generous in forgiving me, teach me to forgive others generously.

MEDITATION

1. " The kingdom of heaven is likened to a king who would take an account of his servants. " Today's Gospel (*Mt* 18,23-35) refers to the account which all men will one day be called upon to give. It is a serious thought, which makes us reflect, as we did last Sunday, on the state of our conscience. Yet, as we continue the reading of this parable, our hearts are comforted. God, represented by the king, manifests such kindness, mercy, and compassion to the poor

servant who cannot pay his debt; He forgives him everything
and sets him free.

The debt of that servant was not a trifling one : ten
thousand talents; our debts to God are much greater
and cannot be computed in talents, nor in silver and gold;
they must be reckoned according to the price of our
redemption, the most precious Blood of Jesus. Our debts are
our sins which needed to be washed away in the Blood of a
divine Victim. In spite of our good will, we increase these
debts each day, to a greater or lesser extent, if only by
faults of frailty and weakness. Is there one who can say
at the day's end that he has not contracted new debts with
God? If, at the end of life, God should place before us an
exact account of our *deficit*, we should find ourselves in a
much more embarrassing position than that of the servant
in the parable. But God, being infinite goodness, knows
and has pity on our misery; each time we place ourselves
before Him and humbly acknowledge our faults with sincere
repentance, He immediately pardons us and cancels all our
debts. God is magnificent when He pardons : He does not
reproach us for the faults over which we have already wept,
nor does He keep any account of them; His pardon is so
generous, so great and complete, that it not only annuls our
debts, but destroys even the memory of them, as if they had
never existed. It is enough for Him to see us repentant;
then every wound, even the most grievous and repugnant,
is completely healed by the precious Blood of Jesus. Christ's
Blood is like an immense sea which has the power to cleanse
and destroy the sins of all mankind, provided they are
sincerely repented of. Every minute of every day we can
take the burden, heavy or light as it may be, of our sins and
infidelities and make it disappear in this ocean of grace
and love, certain that not one trace of it will remain.

2. The second part of the parable speaks of our forgiveness
of others. Returning home, the fortunate servant whose
debts had all been cancelled, met one of his fellow servants,
who owed him a hundred pence, a very small sum
compared with the ten thousand talents which had been
cancelled for him. Yet he who had been treated with so
much mercy, showed none to his fellow servant; he would
neither listen to his pleadings, nor heed his tears, but " went
and cast him into prison, till he paid the debt. "

A few moments ago we were moved by the master's kindness; now the servant's cruelty makes us indignant. Yet, even though we blush, we ought to recognize that, just as the kindheartedness of the master is the image of the mercy of God, ever ready to pardon, so the cruelty of the servant is the figure of our own hardheartedness and miserliness in forgiving our neighbor. Unfortunately, it is all too true : we who need God's forgiveness even more than we need our daily bread, are so hard, so demanding toward our fellow men; we find it difficult to be indulgent and forgiving. Yet what are the debts that our neighbor may owe us compared with what we owe to God? Certainly, infinitely less than a few pence compared with ten thousand talents, since it is a matter of an offense committed against a mere creature compared with one committed against the infinite majesty of God. But what a contrast! God pardons, forgets, and entirely cancels all our heavy debts; He does not cease to love us and bestow favors upon us in spite of our continual want of fidelity. We, on the contrary, find it very difficult to forgive some little slight; even if we do forgive, we cannot entirely forget it, and we are ready to reproach the other person at the first opportunity. How would we act if our neighbor committed against us each day the numerous infidelities and faults that we commit against God? Oh! how miserable and constrained is our way of pardoning others!

The parable describes the punishment inflicted on the cruel servant by his master : " And his lord being angry, delivered him to the torturers until he paid all the debt "; and the conclusion follows : " So also shall My heavenly Father do to you, if you forgive not your brothers from your hearts. " If we wish God to be generous in pardoning us, we must be generous in forgiving others; we shall be forgiven according to the measure in which we forgive, which means that we ourselves give to God the exact measure of the mercy He is to show to us.

COLLOQUY

" Is there anyone, O Lord, who is not in debt to You? Is there anyone who has not someone in debt to him? In Your justice You have determined that Your rule of conduct toward me, Your debtor, should be that followed by me in regard to my debtors. Therefore, because I also have sinned—and how often!—I must be indulgent with him who seeks my pardon. In fact, when the time of prayer comes, I should be able to say to You, ' Forgive me, O Lord, my trespasses, ' and how? The condition is laid down by me, I myself fix the law : ' Forgive me my trespasses as I forgive those who trespass against me. '

" O Lord, You have set down in the Gospel two short sentences : ' Forgive and it shall be forgiven you; give and it shall be given to you. ' This is my prayer : I ask pardon of You for my sins, and You will that I should pardon others.

" Just as the poor beg from me, so I, Your poor little beggar, stand at the door of my Father's house; rather, I prostrate myself there, begging and groaning, longing to receive something, and this something is You. The beggar asks me for bread, and what do I ask of You, if not Yourself, for You have said, ' I am the living bread that came down from heaven? '

" In order to obtain forgiveness, I shall forgive; I shall pardon others, and I shall be pardoned. Because I wish to receive, I shall give, and it shall be given to me.

" If it is hard for me to forgive someone who has offended me, I shall have recourse to prayer. Instead of repaying insults with more insults, I shall pray for the guilty one. When I feel like giving him a harsh answer, I shall speak to You, O Lord, in his favor. Then I shall remember that You promise eternal life, but You command us to forgive others. It is as if You said to me, ' You who are a man, forgive other men, so that I, who am God can come to you ' " (St. Augustine).

337

EDUCATION AND CULTURE AT THE SERVICE OF THE APOSTOLATE

PRESENCE OF GOD - Teach me, O Lord, to put into the service of the apostolate all the talents I have received from You.

MEDITATION

1. Together with the natural virtues placed at the service of apostolic charity, it is also necessary to consider the other human qualities which give the apostle an ascendency in his field of activity, not for his personal gain, but for the benefit of the Christian ideal. To say that notwithstanding his culture and abilities, the apostle can do nothing without the help of God, is not a condemnation of these natural values; is merely the statement that, of themselves, these qualities are insufficient to attain the essential end of the apostolate, that is, the communication of grace to souls, an end which only the divine action can effect. However, that which does not suffice in itself, can become in the hands of God a most excellent means for procuring the good of souls. The brush of itself can do nothing, but in the hands of a skillful master, it can be used to create great works of art.

The apostle should be conscious of the radical insufficiency of his gifts and talents; but at the same time, he should cultivate these gifts and make these talents bear fruit, so as to put them at the disposal of God for apostolic ends. It is therefore necessary that apostles foster their intellectual formation, together with the interior life. Certainly sanctity is always the more important element; however, when learning is united to sanctity, the results will be better. St. Teresa of Jesus was of this opinion, and she did not hesitate to say concerning spiritual direction : " The director ought to be a spiritual man, but if he has no learning, it is a great inconvenience " (*Life*, 13). This is true, not only in the direction of souls, but in any form of apostolate, for " learning is a great help in giving light upon everything " (*Way*, 5); furthermore, it is impossible to gain entrance into certain circles without sufficient culture. It is therefore a duty of the apostle to procure an intellectual preparation adequate to the apostolate which he must exercise. It is not a question of seeking knowledge which inflates, nor of cultivating one's intellect in order to make a display of oneself, but of putting into use for the good of souls all the talents received from God. Under the vivifying influence of charity, such things as education, culture, doctrine, technical capabilities, — everything, in fact, is transformed into means of furthering the apostolate.

2. Those who are called to exercise the apostolate in professional life have, more than others, the duty of training themselves and of developing the technical skill required for their profession. A teacher who does not carefully prepare his courses, who does not keep abreast of the times, or give himself with zeal to teaching, will never deeply influence his pupils; any apostolic endeavor among them is doomed to failure. Only good professional competence can obtain for the Catholic that authority which, going beyond the limits of his profession, often embraces the moral and religious field, permitting him to exercise an efficacious influence over those who approach him; in this way he can do immense good, and his word is sometimes more readily heeded than that of the priest. It is noteworthy that Pope Pius XII counseled Catholic laymen not to " be inferior to others in scientific and professional competence, but to do what they could to become better professionals, better jurists, scholars, physicians, engineers " (to the Catholic Laureates, March 20, 1941); and this, not in view of financial profit, but in order to acquire for apostolic ends a wider and more authoritative influence. In proportion to their professional competence, Catholics will be called upon to occupy positions of command in society; they will in this way be able to cooperate more effectively in organizing a civil world in harmony with the principles of the Gospel, thus making it more receptive to divine grace.

Before devoting himself to other forms of the apostolate, the layman should first exercise it by the perfect fulfillment of his professional duties. For, as sanctity should be sought above all in the fulfillment of the duties of one's state in life, so the apostolate should be developed primarily through the perfect accomplishment of professional duties, which are precisely those of one's state of life. To become a saint and an apostle by means of his ordinary everyday life, that is, by the fulfillment of his professional duties, should be the program of the Catholic layman. This practical program is within the reach of all; nevertheless, it requires an eminent spirit of sacrifice, of faith and of love, to transform arduous professional labor into an apostolic force. But apostolic charity is capable of great things. In the name of God it can do all things, because it "beareth all things, hopeth all things " (1 *Cor* 13,7).

COLLOQUY

O Lord, I do not desire knowledge that inflates, but the humble learning which comes from You, enlightening minds and enkindling hearts.

" You, O Lord, are He who teaches men knowledge, and to little ones You give a clearer understanding than can be taught by man. If You speak to me, I shall become learned in a short time and will make great progress in the spiritual life.

" It is You, O Lord, who in an instant so enlighten the humble mind that it comprehends more of eternal truth than could be learned by ten years in the schools, You who teach without noise of words or clash of opinions, without contention of arguments " (*Imit. III*, 43,2.3).

Give me this knowledge, O Lord, and I shall be able to enter into study and work without any danger of vainglory. I want to use the intelligence You have given me by employing it in Your service; I want to make it fructify for Your glory and for the good of souls. Everything that I have received from You—intelligence, will, physical and moral energies—should be used for this end, for the apostle must be completely devoted to the fulfillment of his mission, always at his post for the defense and the glory of Your Name.

Sanctify, Lord, my studies, my work, the practice of my profession; grant that love may transform all into a means of apostolate.

" Remember, Lord, that You declared to me, ' I have come for the salvation of souls. ' I offer You, then, my life, now and forever; grant that it may be pleasing to You; I offer it for Your glory, humbly begging You by virtue of

Your Passion, to purify and to sanctify Your people"
(St. Catherine of Siena).

338

APOSTOLIC HOPE

PRESENCE OF GOD - O Jesus, I place all my hope for the souls that
You have entrusted to me, in Your power, in Your infinite love,
and in Your Passion.

MEDITATION

1. In his work the apostle needs to be sustained by a
strong hope. The moments of enthusiasm are brief, success
is quickly followed by failure, difficulties are numerous, the
struggle waged by enemy forces is sharp and incessant,
and if the apostle is not firmly anchored in God by solid
theological hope, he will end, sooner or later, by giving
up the enterprise in discouragement. " I have overcome
the world" (*Jn* 16,33), Jesus declared, and sending the
apostles to continue His victorious mission, He assured
them, " I am with you all days, even to the consummation
of the world" (*Mt* 28,20). The foundation of apostolic
hope is the victory of Christ and His continual help. Yes, He
is with us *all days*, even on the dark days, when the horizon is
black without a ray of light, when the enemy triumphs,
when our friends forsake us, and when, humanly speaking,
one does not see any possibility of success. If we had to
rely upon our own resources, our ability, our works, we
should have every reason to give up in despair; this, however,
is not the case. We hope and we are certain in our hope,
because God is omnipotent, because He wills all men to be
saved, because Christ has redeemed us with His Precious
Blood, and because He has died for us and for us has risen
again; and finally, because His promises—the promises
of a God—are infallible : " Heaven and earth shall pass,
but My words shall not pass" (*ibid.* 24,35).

Relying on the salvific will of God, on His infinite power, and on the redemption of Christ, the apostle should nourish the certain hope that grace will triumph in the end. But at the same time, he should have no delusions; he should realize that he will not attain victory except by passing through Calvary. " Neither is the apostle greater than He that sent him " (*Jn* 13,16). If Jesus reached the triumph of the Resurrection only after His Passion and most painful death, the apostle cannot seek another way. For him also, there will necessarily come hours of darkness, but rather than being a sign of defeat, they will be the prelude to victory; rather than being a sign of abandonment on the part of God, they will be a proof that God is with him, precisely because He is leading him by the very same way along which He led His divine Son.

2. Jesus also has known failure : after His discourse in the synagogue of Nazareth, His fellow citizens were indignant. " They brought Him to the brow of the hill... that they might cast Him down headlong " (*Lk* 4,29). On two other occasions when the Jews were scandalized by His words, they " took up stones to stone Him " (*Jn* 10,31). The Pharisees conspired against Him and treacherously plotted His death; Judas betrayed Him; His own abandoned Him. He was made the laughingstock of the soldiers; He was scourged, crowned with thorns, clothed as a mock king, blindfolded, spat upon; Barabbas was preferred to Him. He was led to Calvary and crucified between two thieves. Humanly speaking, one could well say that the apostolate of Jesus terminated in absolute failure, with His death as a malefactor. All this should be deeply impressed on the mind of the apostle, so that he may not be scandalized if something similar should happen in his own life : " If they have persecuted Me, they will also persecute you " (*ibid.* 15,20).

By means of persecutions, humiliations and failures, the apostle will learn not to trust in his own strength; he will consider himself a useless servant even after he has labored much; he will be convinced of his own insufficiency and of the insufficiency of all human means; hence, he will place all his hope in God. He will learn to work solely for the love of God, without seeking the consolation of success, renouncing even the legitimate satisfaction of seeing the results of his labors. He will learn to be detached from the opinions and judgments of men, to act independently of their approval or disapproval, and to look only to the judgment and approval of God. The contradictions and troubles that the apostle encounters in his work constitute his dark night, comparable to that of contemplatives, a night that is painful but very precious, because its purpose is to purify the soul of every remnant of self-love, of egoism, of vanity, of attachment to creatures and to their esteem. This night, if generously accepted, will gradually lead to an ever greater interior purity, and therefore, to an ever closer union with God. The apostle should remain steadfast in hope, notwithstanding struggles, difficulties, and failures. He should be assured of success, not only where the salvation of the souls entrusted to him is concerned, but also in relation to his own personal sanctification. Even if God should permit his success to remain hidden and all his work to end, as did that of Jesus, in apparent failure, the apostle will find strength in the wounds and Blood of the divine Crucified to persevere in hope, and to hope against all hope.

COLLOQUY

" O Lord, I wish to draw down Your mercy on this poor world, not only by the generosity of my sacrifice and my detachment, but also by the generosity of my confidence. I want to believe against all evidence, hope against all hope; I want to believe with unshakable confidence, even when things seem to become ever more painful and difficult to resolve. I want to touch Your heart, O Lord, by the firmness and generosity of my confidence!

" I know and firmly believe that You love me, that You permit all for Your greater glory and for my greater good; I know that I can cooperate in the salvation of souls, and that the sufferings of time have no proportion with future glory; I know that to become a saint it is necessary to suffer much, and that one reaches pure love through pure suffering; I know that all is possible to me in You, who are my support. Even if I were fatigued, oppressed by darkness, anguish, and agony, by looking at You, O Jesus Crucified, I should always taste an intimate supernatural joy, since You admit me to share Your sufferings in order to conform me to Your

Passion and to permit me one day to participate in Your glory.

"I can always rejoice in the face of any suffering, humiliation, trial, interior or exterior pain, by reflecting that You, O Jesus, do me the honor of inviting me to participate in Your Passion, in Your redemptive work for souls. Therefore, far from considering these sorrows as evils, teach me to embrace them and to welcome them as favors and precious means for my sanctification, vivifying them through love and a peaceful, total adherence to Your will. O Lord, it is in this spirit that I intend to offer You my prayer, my mortification, my daily renunciation, my continual acceptance of the sufferings You send me, to draw down graces on the whole Church and to save souls" (Sr. Carmela of the Holy Spirit, O.C.D.).

339

PROGRESS IN THE APOSTOLATE

PRESENCE OF GOD - Unite me to You, O Lord, and may the power of Your charity enkindle in my heart true apostolic fire.

MEDITATION

1. St. Thomas teaches that love is like fire. It produces a flame, and the flame of love is zeal. If the fire burns intensely, then the flame will also be intense and devouring. True apostolic zeal is the spontaneous result, the normal fruit of intimate contact of the soul with God through love. The more a soul is united to God by love, the more it becomes enveloped in the flame of His charity, participating in His infinite love for men, in His eternal zeal for their salvation; thus it *necessarily* becomes *apostolic*.

It would be an exaggeration to say that one could not be an apostle before being thus intimately enraptured by divine love, but it is evident that the fullness of the apostolate, and therefore of apostolic fecundity, will not be attained without this interior flame which is born of union with God. Until we attain this, we must consider ourselves beginners in the apostolate, like apprentices who apply themselves to an art, executing this or that work without yet being sustained or led by personal inspiration. Beginners must act as such, that is, with caution, giving themselves to the apostolate with prudence and measure, because not having attained that spiritual maturity in which the flame of zeal burns spontaneously within them, they have not as yet those reserves of grace which serve to defend the soul from the dangers of a too intense external activity, and which, at the same time, have the power to make all their labor fruitful. St. Teresa asserts that " as yet the soul is not even weaned, but is like a child beginning to suck the breast. If it be taken from its mother, what can it be expected to do but die? That, I am very much afraid will be the lot of anyone to whom God has granted this favor, if he gives up prayer; unless he does so for some every exceptional reason, or unless he returns to it quickly, he will go from bad to worse " *(Int C IV, 3)*. Let us remark that the Saint is not speaking of souls who are taking the first steps in the interior life, but of those who have attained to the prayer of quiet and could well be called proficients; yet it is no exaggeration to say that, in respect to the apostolate, they are still beginners.

2. St. Teresa shows us a soul at the moment in which —in consequence of the charity which unites it to God— there is born in it the interior flame of the apostolate. Through love and abandonment, it has becomed so submissive to the will of God that " it neither knows nor desires anything save that God shall do with it what He wills "; and God who " takes it for His very own...seals it with His seal " and infuses into it a most lively sorrow for the sins of men and an ardent desire to immolate itself for their salvation *(Int C V, 2)*. In this soul charity has increased to such a point as to enable it to renounce effectively its own will in order to conform itself in all things to the divine will. Even when confronted with difficult and unforeseen circumstances which require a great spirit of sacrifice it puts aside every natural repugnance and resentment, all personal views and desires, in order to adhere entirely to the divine will, whether this presents itself under the aspect of daily duties or by means of the external voice of obedience, the interior voice of the Holy Spirit, or even by the circumstances of life.

Then, when the soul is truly united to God by love, truly *given* to Him, God *takes* it and sends it forth in the service of the Church and souls. He wills to make use of it to realize His plan for the salvation and sanctification of humanity.

Immense desires of the apostolate, in no wise comparable to those it had nourished before, awaken in the soul. It feels that it no longer belongs to itself, that its life is necessarily bound to that of the divine Redeemer, and that, in imitation of Him, it should dedicate its life to souls and let it be wholly consumed in their service. Even those who apparently live isolated from the world and from external contact with men—religious in their cloisters, contemplatives in hermitages and deserts—become eminently apostolic when they have reached this state. Their whole life of prayer and sacrifice is orientated toward one ideal : to make reparation for the sins of mankind, to save souls. Whereas contemplatives give vent to this apostolic zeal by redoubling their hidden immolation, active souls, given to exterior works, find in the interior flame blazing forth from their union with God the impulse, the strength, the support, the fecundity of their apostolate. Once again we must come to the conclusion that to the way to attain to the greatest apostolic efficicacy is the solitary and silent way of union with God.

COLLOQUY

" O my God, how fervent and strong is the charity of a soul who is united with You by love! Those whom You have taken to Yourself in this way, cannot confine themselves to their personal advantage, and be satisfied with it. Nor would it suffice for them to go to heaven alone, but with solicitude and affection wholly celestial, and with utmost diligence, they endeavor to lead many others with them. Grant, O Lord, that my love for You may have this same effect on me " (cf. J.C.).

" O Lord, when once a soul is resolved to love You and has resigned itself into Your hands You will have nothing else save that it desire and seek to contribute to Your greater glory.

" Oh! the charity of those who truly love You! How little rest will they be able to take if they see they can do anything to help even one soul to make progress and love You better, or to give it some comfort or save it from some danger! How insupportable would their rest become for them!

"Even if I can do nothing for others by my actions, I can do a great deal by means of prayer, importuning You, O Lord, for the many souls the thought of whose ruin causes me such grief. I would lose my own comfort, and look upon it as well lost, for I am not thinking of my own pleasure but of how better to do Your will.

"O my God, as time goes on, my desires to do something for the good of some soul grows greater and greater, and I often feel like one who has a large amount of treasure in her charge and would like everyone to enjoy it, but whose hands are tied, so that she cannot distribute it.... Unable to contain myself any longer...I call upon You, O Lord, beseeching You to find me a means of gaining some soul for Your service" (T.J. *F*, 5 – 1).

340

APOSTOLIC MATURITY

PRESENCE OF GOD - Your love, O my God, matures my soul and renders it capable of giving itself fully to the service of souls.

MEDITATION

1. We may ask if the apostle can devote himself freely to the apostolate when he has reached the degree of union with God in which the flame of zeal bursts forth spontaneously. The fact is that, at this point, he cannot and should not evade the gift of self. Whether he is consecrated to contemplation or to action, whether he lives in the cloister or in the midst of the turmoil of the world, his life consists henceforth in giving himself unceasingly : in giving himself to God for the good of his neighbor, in giving himself to his neighbor for the glory of God. To stifle this tendency would be to retrogress and to impoverish his own spiritual life; the time has come when the soul should be enriched by the gift of self lived in the exercise of an intense apostolate,

interior or exterior as the case may be. However, the saints teach that prudence is still necessary, and one must not cease to be vigilant, since to have received the interior grace of the apostolate does not signify that one has been confirmed in grace. St. Teresa says this expressly : " I have known people of a very high degree of spirituality who have reached this state, and whom, notwithstanding, the devil with great subtlety and craft, has won back to himself" (*Int C V*, 4). " How many are called by the Lord to the apostleship, as Judas was, and enjoy communion with Him...and afterwards, through their own fault, are lost! " (*ibid.*, 3). Spontaneously one recalls the cry full of humility and distrust of self that burst forth from the heart of St. Paul, the Apostle who had been rapt to the third heaven : " Lest perhaps, when I have preached to others, I myself should become a castaway " (1 *Cor* 9,27). As long as we are on earth, we have reason to fear; we always have, alas, the sad possibility of not corresponding with grace, of separating ourselves, even in small things, from the will of God—and herein lies our ruin—thus, little by little we fall back. " Christian souls whom the Lord has brought to this point on your journey, " exclaims St. Teresa of Jesus, " I beseech you, for His sake, not to be negligent, but to withdraw from occasions of sin "; and she adds, " For this purpose [the downfall of an apostle] the devil will marshall all the powers of hell, for as I have often said, if he wins a single soul in this way, he will win a whole multitude " (*Int C V*, 4). On the contrary, if the apostle remains faithful to the grace of the apostolate, he will not only be an instrument for the salvation of many, but his own interior life will be deeply enriched.

2. In order not to be unfaithful to the grace of the apostolate, three cautions are particularly necessary. First of all, one must always have a jealous care for humility, defending oneself against the flattering voices of praise and success and confronting them with the picture of one's misery, the poor figure so often made, as well as of one's blunders and failures in the apostolate. If Lucifer—a pure spirit—fell through pride, it is not unthinkable that an apostle, too, is subject to such a fall, being man and weighed down by matter. Constant vigilance is necessary, then, to maintain intimate contact with God, for just as iron becomes red hot

and glows only when it is in contact with fire, so the apostle radiates the divine light and warmth only if he keeps himself united to Him who is their only source.

Lastly, it is of the greatest importance to persevere in perfect detachment from one's own will and judgment. In regard to this, St. John of the Cross warns us that " among the many wiles used by the devil to deceive spiritual persons, the most ordinary is that of deceiving them under an appearance of what is good, not under an appearance of what is evil : for he knows that if they recognize evil, they will scarcely touch it " (*P*, 10). Therefore, in order not to fall into his snares, the Saint warns us never to undertake any action " however good and full of charity " (*ibid.*, 11) it may seem to be, without the sanction of obedience. This advice is good not only for religious but for all who work in the apostolate, because all should be submissive to ecclesiastical authority. For even if such a work, such an initiative, such a method of apostolate should obtain excellent results, from the moment that ecclesiastical authority does not approve of it, for whatever reason, the apostle should immediately renounce it, without criticism, complaint, or murmuring, by which he might try to make his own point of view prevail.

Protected by deep humility and sincere detachment, sustained by intimate union with God, the apostle can go through the paths of the world without fear for his spiritual life.

COLLOQUY

" O Lord, the souls who were closest to You, as were Your most holy Mother and Your glorious Apostles, were those who suffered and labored the most for You, giving themselves no rest.

" O my God, how little should the soul that lives closely united to You think about resting! How far it ought to be from wishing to be esteemed in anything! If it is occupied with You, as it is right it should be, it will forget itself; its whole thought will be concentrated upon finding ways to please You, and seeing in what things and in what ways it can show You its love. You teach me, O Lord, that this is the aim of prayer, and that union with You tends to this : to produce good works and good works alone.

"If I fix my eyes on You, my crucified Lord, everything will become easy to me. Since you have shown me Your love by doing and suffering such amazing things, why should I content myself with words alone? Oh! make me know how to give myself to You as Your slave, so that branded as such with Your sign, which is the sign of the Cross, You can sell me as a slave to the whole world. Let me see what it means to become truly spiritual.

"Unite me to You, O divine Strength, that I may share in Your strength as the saints shared in it, so that with great zeal, I may work for Your glory, and suffer and die for You, and thus win many souls for You" (*Int C VII*, 4).

341

SPIRITUAL PATERNITY AND MATERNITY

PRESENCE OF GOD - O my God, unite me to Yourself by a bond of fervent love; grant that by this union I may bring You many souls.

MEDITATION

1. God has bestowed on man the great honor of willing that he be His collaborator in a work which is proper to Himself, as God, which belongs essentially to Him alone, that is, the communication of life, and not only of natural life but of supernatural life also. On the natural level, which we may call the plan of creation, the fathers and mothers of families are His collaborators, having been entrusted with the high mission of communicating life to new human beings, of rearing and educating them for the glory of God. On the supernatural level, that of Redemption, God's collaborators are all those who, by dedicating themselves to the apostolate, have an even more noble and vast mission, that of communicating to men the life of grace, without which they are unhappy creatures, and in a certain sense, are unable to attain eternal life. In his Encyclical *Menti Nostrae*, Pope Pius XII declares, "The priest is...the organ of the

communication and increase of life in the Mystical Body of Christ. Far from losing the gift and the office of paternity because of his celibacy, the priest increases them immeasurably, since if he does not beget children for this passing life on earth, he begets them for that life which is heavenly and eternal. " In due proportion, the same can be said of every apostle; for the final end of the apostolate is precisely to engender souls to the supernatural life.

" My little children, of whom I am in labor again, until Christ be formed in you, " exclaimed St. Paul in a letter to the Galatians (4,19). Every apostle has an equal right to feel himself both father and mother of the souls for whom he sacrifices himself entirely—a paternity and a maternity which are a reflection of, or rather, a sharing in the paternity of God. In the natural order, God has arranged that fecundity, the source of life, should be the result of the union of two creatures. In the supernatural order also, fecundity is born of union, but of an immensely superior and wholly spiritual union : the union of the soul with God. The more a soul is united to God by love, the greater is its participation in His inexhaustible fecundity, which has for its end the communication of the divine life to men. Therefore, consecrated souls, who have renounced natural fecundity, have not impoverished and stifled their lives, condemning them to sterility; through their union with God, these souls have been raised to a paternity, to a maternity, of a far superior nature.

2. To be a father or mother of souls is not limited to those who work in the external apostolate; it extends also to those who have dedicated themselves to the contemplative life. Although completely separated from the world, St. Thérèse of the Child Jesus felt an ever increasing spiritual maternity grow in her heart, and in the solitude of Carmel she writes : " To be Your spouse, O Jesus, and by my union with You, to be the mother of souls! " (T.C.J. *St*, 13). This is the fundamental aspiration of her spirit, the ideal that attracted her, sustaining and urging her on to a life of continual and painful immolation. She is ever conscious that she must give herself, sacrifice herself for souls; like a loving mother she must be constantly at the complete disposal of her children. One day, seeing a novice sauntering listlessly to her work, the Saint teasingly reproved her :

" Is that the way people hurry when they have children and are obliged to work to procure them food? " (T.C.J. *C*).

The earnest apostle, ever conscious of having children to *nourish*, realizes that he should spend his whole life for them, that he has to *maintain* them by his toil, his prayers, his weariness, and above all by his love. Precisely from love—from this same love which unites him to God—does he draw the strength to sacrifice himself for them, and draws even that spiritual fecundity by which he becomes God's collaborator in communicating to them the life of grace. As love increases, union with God becomes deeper, and this, in turn, gives rise to greater fecundity and more power in communicating divine life to an immense number of souls. Who can estimate the extent of the spiritual paternity and maternity of the saints?

There is no interior life, no real sanctity which is not crowned with the aureole of spiritual paternity or maternity. But as in the natural realm, the mother brings forth her children in sorrow, so in the supernatural order, there is no paternity or maternity of souls without suffering.

It was by dying on the Cross that Jesus brought us forth to divine life. From Him we learn that if we wish to share in His redemptive work, we must not fear either persecutions, or mockeries, or scourgings, or thorns, or nails, or the cross; we must be ready to give for souls all that we have and are, even our very life, that they may be nourished with our blood.

COLLOQUY

" O eternal Father, You cannot fail to know that poor sinners are Your creatures and belong to You by the supreme title of creation.

" O eternal Son, blessed King, You cannot deny that these wretched beings belong to You, since You gained them for Yourself by the incomparable title of Redemption. Listen to me, O most obedient Son, listen to me and show Yourself propitious to my prayers, because when I present myself to the eternal Father with the pledge of Your Blood and Your Passion in my hand, He cannot drive me far away from Him without first hearing my requests.

" Come to my aid, O eternal Holy Spirit! No matter
how abominable these sinners may be by the enormity of
their sins, they still belong to You, since You made them
Yours by admitting them to a share in Your goodness.

" O Lord, my only comfort is to see souls converted
to You; and for this alone I suffer patiently Your absence.
If You do not grant me this comfort, what can I do? Do
not drive me away, most merciful Lord!

" You are resolved and already disposed to hear me,
since in Your compassionate glance toward me, I perceive,
clothed with Your light, my spiritual sons and daughters,
my brothers and sisters and all those whom I strive to
win to You day by day. May they always remain faithful
to You.

" O sovereign and eternal Father, I recommend to You
my beloved children, whom You have confided to me;
I beg of You to visit them with Your grace, to make them
live as dead to the world that they may enjoy clear and
perfect light, and be united among themselves with the
sweet bond of charity. I pray You, O eternal Father,
that none of them be taken from my hands, and I beg You to
pardon us all our offenses. I offer and commend to You
my beloved children, because they are my very soul "
(St. Catherine of Siena).

342

MARTHA AND MARY

PRESENCE OF GOD - Grant, O Lord, that I may love You with the
heart of Mary, while serving You with the devotedness of Martha.

MEDITATION

1. There are two great attractions in a soul which has
given itself seriously to God : the attraction to solitary,
silent prayer where, immersed in God, the soul listens to
His voice, penetrates His mysteries, and above all unites

itself more intimately with Him; and correspondingly,
the attraction to the apostolate, to active, generous sacrifice
for the salvation of souls.   To recollect itself in God
" the soul would like to flee from other people, and greatly
envies those who live, or have lived, in deserts.   On the
other hand, it would like to plunge right into the heart of
the world, to see if by doing this it could help one soul to
praise God more " (T.J. *Int C VI*, 6).   Such is the double
movement of charity which, fusing the love of God and the
love of neighbor into one and the same love, urges the soul
equally to union with God and to the service of its neighbor.
If one of these movements is lacking, charity will not be
complete.   The development of the interior life requires
this double attraction which is both a sign and a means of
progress; it is at the same time, a torment for the soul that
has not yet found the just mean between the two tendencies.
To which of the two will it give the preference?   To
action or to contemplation?   In practice, the problem
must be solved on the basis of the requirements and the
duties of one's state in life, the directions of obedience,
and the particular circumstances permitted by God.   A
desire for contemplative prayer which distracts, or withdraws the soul from the fulfillment of duty would not be
in conformity with the will of God; God has every right to
ask us to renounce such a desire, that He may send us to
serve our neighbor.   Magdalen rejoiced when she finally
found Jesus, her Risen Lord; she longed to remain at His
feet, but He commanded her : " Go to My brethren "
(*Jn* 20,17); and she, with docility, left Him to announce His
Resurrection.   On the other hand, the contrary is also true.
Jesus said to His Apostles on their return from preaching :
" Come apart into a desert place and rest a little " (*Mk* 6,31),
thereby inviting them to suspend their apostolic activity
and to reinvigorate their spirit in silence and in prayer,
alone with Him.   The best way, which steers a middle course
deviating neither to right nor left, is always the way of duty,
of the will of God, of interior inspiration, under the guidance
of one who has the authority to direct the soul.

2. To harmonize interiorly this double attraction to the
active apostolate and to union with God in prayer, there is
need of a deeper solution, one which can come only from the
interior.   This solution consists in a greater progress in the

interior life leading to an ever greater degree of love. Love is the only root from which blossom both action and contemplation; it is the only force which, nourishing these two activities simultaneously, finally succeeds in blending them into perfect harmony, thus enabling them to bear the best fruit. Springing from the same stem of an advanced love, action and contemplation are fused only in perfect love.

Perfect charity makes the soul, while recollected in contemplation at the feet of the Lord, more operative and fruitful than ever for the good of others. " A very little of this pure love " (solitary love which flourishes in intimate contact with God) " is more precious in the sight of God and the soul, and of greater profit to the Church, even though the soul appear to be doing nothing, than are all other works together.... Therefore, " declares St. John of the Cross, " if any soul should have aught of this degree of solitary love, great wrong would be done to it and to the Church, if, even for a brief space, one should endeavor to busy it in active or outward affairs of however great moment " (*SC* 29,2.3).

In the regions of pure love, that is, of perfect charity, contemplation and the apostolate become identified; they complete and require one another. At this point, the contemplative soul is eminently apostolic. Its greatest activity for the benefit of its fellow men is precisely its solitary prayer, nourished by love, sacrifice and immolation. On the other hand, the soul occupied in apostolic works becomes, through perfect charity, more contemplative, more united to God than ever. Love has so fixed the soul in God that, even during work, its interior gaze is always turned toward Him, to nourish itself with His divine presence, to reflect in its own conduct His infinite perfections, and to govern itself at all times according to His good pleasure. Thus at the summit of the spiritual life, action and contemplation become fused in perfect unity and harmony. " Believe me, " wrote St. Teresa of Avila, " Martha and Mary must work together when they offer the Lord lodging, and must have Him ever with them, and they must not entertain Him badly and give Him nothing to eat...His food consists in our bringing Him souls, in every possible way, so that they may be saved and may praise Him forever " (T.J. *Int C VII*, 4). From this we can understand how all the great contemplatives were at the same time great apostles, and the great apostles, great contemplatives.

COLLOQUY

" O Lord, the desire to listen to Your divine Word, the need to be silent is sometimes so strong that I would wish not to know how to do anything else save to remain at Your feet, like Magdalen, in order to penetrate ever more deeply into that mystery of love which You came to reveal to us. But You teach me that if the soul never separates itself from You, it can always remain absorbed in contemplation, even though apparently it is carrying out Martha's functions. In this way, O Lord, I intend and wish to exercise my apostolate : I shall radiate You, I shall give You to souls, provided I do not separate myself from You, O divine Source. Help me, sweet Master, to come very near You, to commune with Your Soul, to identify myself with all Your operations, and then to go forth like You to do the Father's will.

" What a wonderful influence over souls has the apostle who never leaves the source of living waters! Grant me, O Lord, to be one of these. Then the spring of water will fill my soul and overflow it without danger of its becoming empty, for it will find itself in continual communication with You, the Infinite.

" My God, deign to invade all the faculties of my soul; grant that everything within me may become divine and marked with Your seal, so that I may be another Christ working for Your glory.

" Lord, how I long to labor for Your glory! I long to give myself entirely to You, to be pervaded by Your divine life; be the life of my life, the soul of my soul, and grant that I may always remain under the influence of Your divine action " (E.T. *L*).

343

OUR DUTIES

TWENTY-SECOND SUNDAY AFTER PENTECOST

PRESENCE OF GOD - Teach me, O Lord, to fulfill all my duties in homage to Your sovereign Majesty.

MEDITATION

1. The teachings contained in the Mass of this Sunday can be synthesized in the well known statement of Jesus, which we read in the Gospel (*Mt* 22,15-21) of this day : " Render...to Caesar the things that are Caesar's, and to God, the things that are God's "; in other words, fulfill with exactness your duties toward God and toward your neighbor, by giving to each one his due.

The Epistle (*Phil* 1,6-11) presents St. Paul to us as a model of charity toward those whom God has confided to his care. " I have you in my heart, " writes the Apostle to the Philippians, " for that in my bands and in the defence and confirmation of the Gospel, you all are partakers of my joy. " St. Paul is keenly aware of his spiritual paternity toward the souls he has begotten in Christ; even from a distance, he feels responsible for their success, is preoccupied with their perseverance in good, sustains them with his fatherly affection and wise counsels : " Being confident of this very thing, that He, who hath begun a good work in you, will perfect it unto the day of Christ Jesus. " He does not want them to be frightened because he is far away from them : he is nothing but a poor instrument, God alone is the true guide of souls, and He will complete the work begun. As for him, they may be certain that he does not cease to love them : " For God is my witness how I long after you all in the heart of Jesus Christ. "

St. John Chrysostom asserts that the heart of Paul is the heart of Christ because of the great love for souls which makes him so like the Redeemer; thus should it be possible to say of the heart of every apostle. When God has put us in contact with a soul and has asked us to occupy ourselves with it, we can no longer be disinterested; this soul is henceforth bound to ours, we should feel responsible for it, and bound to help it even to the end.

After having spoken to us of the solicitude we should have for those confided to our care, the Epistle reminds us also of charity toward our neighbor in general : " That your charity may more and more abound in knowledge and in all understanding : that you may approve the better things. " He speaks of a charity increasingly delicate in its understanding of the souls of others, adapting itself with an ever more refined tact to the mind, the demands, the tastes of others; a charity which must urge us, as St. Paul says, to " approve "—and therefore, to do—" the better things, " in order that we " may be sincere and without offence unto the day of Christ. "

2. The Gospel outlines, clearly and distinctly, the position of the Christian toward civil authority. The insidious question : " Is it lawful to give tribute to Caesar, or not? " gives Jesus the occasion to solve the problem of the relation between religious and civil duties. He asks for a coin and says : " Whose image and inscription is this? They say to Him : Caesar's. Then He saith to them : Render, therefore, to Caesar the things that are Caesar's, and to God, the things that are God's. "

There is no opposition between the rights of political power and the rights of God, since " there would be no power unless it were given from above " (cf. *Jn* 19,11) : political authority, legitimately constituted, comes from God and must be respected as a reflection of the divine authority. This is precisely the reason why every Christian is bound to fulfill all the duties of a good citizen, and, consequently, must obey political authority, unless its orders are opposed to the law of God; for, in this case, it would no longer represent divine authority and then, as St. Peter says, " We ought to obey God rather than men " (*Acts* 5,29).

We must not believe that because we are vowed to the apostolate or dedicated to religious works, we are, by this fact, dispensed from civic duties; on the contrary, even in this domain Catholics should be in the front rank. Emperors, kings, statesmen, soldiers, whom the Church honors as saints, tell us that sanctity is possible everywhere and for everyone, that it can be realized by those who dedicate themselves

to the service of the State, because even here it is a question
of serving God in His creatures.

By telling us to render to Caesar what is Caesar's, Jesus
teaches us to give to the State all that falls under its jurisdiction, that is, everything that concerns temporal order and
the public good. But Jesus does not stop there, He says more :
" Give to God what is God's. " If the coin which bears the
image of Caesar should be restored to Caesar, with much
greater reason should our soul, which bears the image of God,
be restored to God. To say that we must give our soul to
God, is to say that we owe Him *everything*, because, as a
matter of fact, we have received everything from Him.
In this sense, to fulfill our duties toward our neighbor,
toward our equals or our inferiors, toward our ecclesiastical or civil superiors, is to fulfill our duty toward God;
it is to restore to Him everything He has given us, by
submitting our freedom to His law, by putting our will in the
service of His will.

COLLOQUY

" O my God, since I am Yours for so many reasons,
and have so many obligations to serve You, permit no longer
that sin, or Satan, or the world, usurp, even in the slightest
degree, that which is entirely Yours. But, if it please You,
take complete and absolute possession of my being and of my
life. Here I am, O my God, I give myself entirely to You, protesting to You that I do not wish to exist but for You, and that
I do not want to think, or say, or do, or suffer anything
but for Your love, today, tomorrow, and always " (St. John
Eudes).

" O my Lord Jesus, You gave Yourself to me and You
ask only for my heart. But, O my Lord, what is this poor
heart of mine when You are all? If my heart were worth
more than those of all the children of men combined, and
all the love of the angels, and if its capacity were so great
that it could contain more than all the empyreal heaven,
I would consecrate it wholly to You. It would be a very
poor gift, and even almost nothing, to so great a Lord.
But, how much more shall I not give You, and wholly
repose in You, this little spark of a heart which I find in
myself! Because this is for me a very great thing, that You

should deign to keep my heart. Would it not be folly if I should consecrate it henceforth to some creature, when my God wills it for Himself? I do not want it to remain any longer in me, but to repose entirely in You, who have created it to praise You. It is better that I place my heart in eternal joy, in divine majesty and in immense goodness, rather than in my frailty; that I place it in Your deity, rather than in my iniquity " (St. Bonaventure).

344

THE HOLY SPIRIT AND THE APOSTOLATE

PRESENCE OF GOD - O Holy Spirit, take possession of my soul and transform it into a chosen instrument for the glory of God and the salvation of souls.

MEDITATION

1. The heart of the apostolate is love. St. Thérèse of the Child Jesus understood this well; after having passed in review all possible vocations, and recognizing that they would not suffice to appease her immense apostolic desires, she exclaimed : " My vocation is found at last—*my vocation is love*!... In the heart of the Church, my Mother, *I will be love!* Thus shall I be all things " (T.C.J. *St*, 13). Where can we obtain such a complete and transforming love? We must never forget that the source of charity is the Holy Spirit, who is the personal terminus of the love of the Father and of the Son, the eternal breath of Their mutual love. This Spirit " has been given " to us, He is " ours "; He dwells in our hearts precisely to pour forth in them that supernatural love which makes us burn with love for God and for souls. " The charity of God is poured forth in our hearts by the Holy Spirit who is given to us " (*Rom* 5,5). By communicating the flame of divine charity to men and associating them to His infinite love, the Holy Spirit is the secret animator and sustainer of all apostolate; " It is He, " Pius XII teaches, " who through His heavenly breath of life

is the source from which proceeds every vital and efficaciously
salutary action...in the Mystical Body of Christ" *(Mystici
Corporis)*. He is the soul of the Church. Do we wish to
become apostles? Let us open our hearts wide to the outpourings of the Holy Spirit, in order that His love may invade
and penetrate us to the point of absorbing our poor love into
Himself. When the love of a soul is united to " the living
flame of love " which is the Holy Spirit, so as to " become
one thing with it " (cf. J.C. *LF*, 1,3), then it becomes a
vivifying love in the heart of the Church. This is the only
way to realize the magnificent ideal : " In the heart of the
Church I will be love. Thus I shall be everything "
(T.C.J. *St*, 13). To attain to this supreme summit of love and
of the apostolate, we must follow, day by day, moment by
moment, the motions of the Holy Spirit, open ourselves
submissively to His action, and allow ourselves to be directed
and governed by Him. Above all, we must yield ourselves
to His infinite love which diffuses itself totally in the
Father and the Son, and then overflows on souls, to draw
them all into the Blessed Trinity.

2. The apostolate was inaugurated in the Church on the
day of Pentecost when the Apostles " were all filled with
the Holy Spirit, and they began to speak with divers tongues,
according as the Holy Spirit gave them to speak " *(Acts* 2,4).
Before that, the twelve were poor men, dull, weak, full of
fear. But once the Holy Spirit took possession of them,
He transformed them into men of fire, ready to give their
lives to witness to the Lord.

In our day too, the Holy Spirit can renew that great
miracle. As in former times, He can—or rather, He wills—
to take possession of poor men, of weak women, in order to,
transform them into ardent apostles. What is the condition
that He requires? A total *self-surrender*, a docility so sensitive,
so delicate, that the apostle becomes wholly amenable
to His operative presence, to His motions, to His inspirations.
To attain this, the apostle must have a true sense of his complete dependence on the divine Paraclete, a sense which
must manifest itself practically by diligent care to maintain,
even in the midst of activity, a continual contact with Him,
always attentive to His inspirations, and quick to follow
them. Like the wind " the Spirit breatheth where He will;
and thou hearest His voice, but thou knowest not whence

He cometh, and whither He goeth " (*Jn* 3,8). His inspirations may surprise us in the midst of activity no less than in prayer; it is essential, therefore, to learn to speak interiorly with Him even while exteriorly we are occupied with creatures. This attitude is particularly necessary in our direct contact with souls; then, more than ever, the apostle should invoke the Holy Spirit, keep himself under His influence, and allow himself to be directed by Him. Souls belong to God and they should be directed, not according to one's own spirit, but according to the Spirit of God. Complete submission demands great faith and great confidence in the omnipotent and transforming action of the Holy Spirit. Only in this way will the apostle have the courage to follow His lead in any form of activity, while remaining fully aware of his own insufficiency. Only thus will he have the courage to face any sacrifice with generosity, while feeling all his own weakness. The Holy Spirit has not been given to us in vain; He is within us, and provided we give ourselves wholly to Him, He can transform us into " chosen instruments " for the glory of God and the salvation of souls.

COLLOQUY

" Pardon me, my Jesus, if I venture to tell You of my longings, my hopes that border on the infinite; and that my soul may be healed, I beseech You to fulfill all its desires. To be Your spouse, O my Jesus...and by my union with You, to be the mother of souls, should not all this content me? Yet other vocations make themselves felt, and I would wield the sword, I would be a priest, an apostle, a martyr, a doctor of the Church.... O Jesus, my Love, my Life, how shall I realize these desires of my poor soul?

" You make me understand that all cannot become apostles, prophets, doctors; that the Church is composed of different members; that the eye cannot also be the hand.... You teach me that all the better gifts are nothing without love, and that charity is the most excellent way of going in safety to You.

" At last I have found rest.... Charity gives me the key to my vocation. I understand that since the Church is a body composed of different members, she could not lack the most necessary and most nobly endowed of all the bodily organs. I understand, therefore, that the Church has a heart—and a heart on fire with love.

"I see too, that love alone imparts life to all the members, so that should love ever fail, apostles would no longer preach the Gospel and martyrs would refuse to shed their blood. And I realize that love includes every vocation, that love is all things, that love is eternal.... O Jesus, my Love! my vocation is found at last—my vocation is love! I have found my place in the bosom of the Church, and this place, O my God, You Yourself have given to me : in the heart of the Church, my Mother, I will be love. Thus shall I be all things and my dream will be fulfilled" (cf. T.C.J. *St*, 13).

345

UNION WITH GOD

PRESENCE OF GOD - My God, Thou hast created me for Thyself; grant that I may return to Thee and unite myself to Thee by love.

MEDITATION

1. The whole life of man is a return journey to God : he came from God and must go back to Him. The more complete this return, the more intimate his union with God will become and the better will he have attained the end for which he was created : he will be perfect and eternally happy. St. Thomas teaches that a being is perfect when it attains its end; thus the perfection of man consists in rejoining God and uniting himself to Him, his last end. Man finds in union with God all that he can desire : he finds his peace, the assuaging of his hunger for the infinite, of his thirst for love and imperishable felicity. "Thou hast made us for Thyself, O Lord, and our heart is restless until it rests in Thee" (St. Augustine). Man finds his eternal happiness in union with God; and the life of heaven is nothing else than this union carried to its ultimate perfection, wherein

man gives God the greatest glory and the greatest love which, in turn, redounds to man's own eternal beatitude.

The soul that truly loves God does not resign itself to waiting for heaven in order to be united to Him, but desires ardently to anticipate this union here below. Is this possible? Yes, Jesus has said so : " If anyone love Me, he will keep My word, and My Father will love him; and We will come to him and will make Our abode with him " (*Jn* 14,23). Our Lord Himself tells us in these words the condition for living united to Him : love. " He that abideth in charity, abideth in God, and God in him " (1 *Jn* 4,16). Love is the great power which unites us to God even in this life, where, imprisoned in matter, we cannot yet enjoy the direct contact, the face to face vision of Him.

" The end of the spiritual life, " says St. Thomas, " is that man unite himself to God by love " (II^a II^{ae}, q.44, a.1, co.). By steps of love, *gressibus amoris*, we advance toward our last end : union with God. Such is the great ideal which should illumine and direct our whole life, the great goal which, with the divine assistance, we can attain even here below, as far as is possible in our state as pilgrims.

2. St. John of the Cross explains wherein union of love with God consists. It is not a question of the *substantial union* which always exists between God and everything created and by means of which He is preserving their being. That kind of union is *natural* and can never be lacking in any creature, not even in the greatest sinner. The union of love, however, is *supernatural* and only takes place in souls " when there is produced that likeness that comes from love, " that is, in souls that are in the state of grace. The Saint says : " Although...God is ever in the soul, giving it, and through His presence conserving within it, its natural being, yet He does not always communicate supernatural being to it. For this is communicated only by love and grace, which not all souls possess; and all those that possess it have it not in the same degree; for some have attained more degrees of love and others fewer. " He concludes : " God communicates Himself most to that soul that has progressed farthest in love " (*AS II*, 5,3.4).

The state of grace is the point of departure for the union of love with God. The goal is the full development of grace, so that the soul remains totally supernaturalized, and all its powers, its entire will, all its affections are concentrated in God, neither desiring nor loving anything henceforth but what God wills and loves. Grace is the life of God in us, a life which develops through progress in love. The more the soul loves, the more grace increases in it, with the result that its participation in the divine life becomes more profound, leading it to an ever more intense and perfect union with God. Grace and love are the precious seeds of union with God; they put the soul in intimate communion with Him : communion of life, of thought and of will. God always remains God, distinct from His creature; the creature always keeps its own personality, and yet the soul becomes so permeated with divine life, God so " communicates to it His own supernatural Being that it seems to be God...rather than a soul " (*ibid.*, 7).

Such is the ultimate end of union with God upon earth, a sublime end, but one which it is not rash to desire, since each of us has already received in baptismal grace the seed of union with God.

COLLOQUY

" O Jesus, who will give me the grace to form one only spirit with You? Rejecting the multiplicity of creatures, I desire indeed, O Lord, Your unity alone! O God, You are the only One, the sole unity necessary for my soul! Ah! dear friend of my heart, unite this poor soul of mine to Your singular goodness! You are entirely mine, when shall I be all Yours? The magnet draws iron and holds it fast to itself; Lord Jesus, my Beloved, be the magnet of my heart : draw, hold fast, unite forever my spirit to Your paternal heart! Oh, since I was made for You, how is it that I am not in You? Submerge this drop, which is the spirit You have given me, in the sea of Your goodness, from which it proceeds. Lord, seeing that Your heart loves me, why do You not lift me up to You, as I so much desire? Draw me, and I will run in the odor of Your ointments until I cast myself into Your arms and never move from thence forever. Amen " (St. Francis de Sales).

" O Lord, who could describe how great a gain it is to cast ourselves into Yours arms and make an agreement with You : You will take care of my affairs and I of Yours

" For what am I, Lord, without You? What am I
worth if I am not near You? If once I stray from Your
Majesty, be it ever so little, where shall I find myself?

" O my Lord, my Mercy and my Good! What more
do I want in this life than to be so near You that there is no
division between You and me?

" O Lord of my life, draw me to Yourself, but do it in
such a way that my will may ever remain so united to You
that it shall be unable to leave You " (T.J. *Con*, 4 – 3).

346

THE WAY OF UNION

PRESENCE OF GOD - Lord, give me light and strength to root out
of my heart all that hinders me from being united to You.

MEDITATION

1. " God communicates Himself most to that soul that
has progressed farthest in love : namely, that has its will in
closest conformity with the will of God " (J.C. *AS II*, 5,4).
In ordinary life, true love is manifested in willingness to do
what pleases the person loved; in conforming oneself to his
desires, tastes and will, not willing anything which could
displease him. The soul unites itself to God in the measure
in which it is truly conformed to His will. It is evident
that this union cannot be perfect as long as the soul resists
the divine will, be it only in very small things, or does not
accept it readily, or as long as it retains desires and tastes
which, even in a very slight way, are not in harmony with
the will of God. The whole spiritual ascent to divine union
consists in a double movement, very simple but essential :
despoiling oneself of all that is displeasing to God, and
renouncing all that is in opposition to His will, by conforming
oneself to that will and fulfilling it with the greatest love.
It is an extremely simple movement, but at the same time
an all-embracing one, because it extends to every circumstance
of life, without exception, so that in all things, the greatest

as in the least, the soul acts in a manner that is in perfect conformity with the divine will. It is also a very profound movement which must reach even to the most secret recesses of the spirit, in order to free it from the least residue, the last resistances of egoism and pride, not only eliminating their manifestations but undermining their very roots. As long as this work of total purgation is incomplete, the soul's will cannot be totally conformed to that of God; its numerous imperfections and imperfect habits are still opposed to this entire conformity. Only " the soul that has attained complete conformity and likeness of will is totally united and transformed in God supernaturally. It needs, then, only to strip itself of these natural dissimilarities and contrarieties..." *(ibid.)*.

2. If we examine ourselves attentively, we shall see that our will is still very dissimilar to God's will. God wills only the good, and He wills it in the most perfect manner. We, on the contrary, often will evil together with the good; moreover, we lack the strength to do the good that we will, and we realize it only imperfectly. Every time we commit any fault, even a simple imperfection, we desire something that God cannot will : these faults include slight acts of slothfulness, negligence, impatience; they may involve a subtle seeking of self or the affection and esteem of creatures; there could be numerous secondary motives which secretly insinuate themselves into our actions. To attain to divine union all these must be eliminated.

St. John of the Cross says expressly that it is not only beginners on the spiritual road, but even the " proficients " who are subject to many imperfections and still retain imperfect habits, proceeding especially from a subtle pride and spiritual egoism. As they have exercised themselves for a long time in the interior life, a certain presumption and self-assurance may easily creep in, through which these souls are exposed to failings in humility and reverence in their relations with God, while in their relations with their neighbor, they often fall into the weakness of desiring to be esteemed as perfect. Furthermore, as they are not entirely detached from themselves, they stop to enjoy, a bit egoistically, the spiritual consolations they receive in prayer; thus they distract themselves from seeking God alone, retard their union with Him, and even expose themselves to falling into the snares of imagination or of the devil (cf. *DN II*, 2,2).

All this proves how deeply pride and egoism are rooted in us. Scarcely have we detached our hearts from earthly vanities and material goods, than we are immediately ready to attach ourselves to spiritual goods. Yet we must not despair of attaining divine union; we must seize the occasion of our misery to beg with greater insistence that Our Lord may deign to complete the work of our purification. Moreover, He desires it more than we ourselves, and if He does not effect it as He would, it is only because He finds us refractory, impatient, little disposed to accept in good part what humbles and mortifies us to the core. Yet this alone is the way to reach union with God.

COLLOQUY

"As long as my will desires that which is alien to the divine will, has preferences for one thing or another, I remain like a child; I do not walk in love with giant strides. The fire has not yet burnt away all the dross, and the gold is not yet pure. I am still seeking myself. O Lord, You have not yet done away with all my resistance to You. But when the crucible has consumed all tainted love, all tainted pain, all tainted fear, then love is perfect, and the golden ring of our union is wider than heaven and earth.

"But in order to attain this I must die daily to myself. O Jesus, I wish to die, to decrease, to deny myself daily more and more, in order that You may grow and be exalted in me. As a ' little one ' I dwell in the depths of my poverty; I see my nothingness, my penury, my weakness; I see that I am incapable of progress, of perseverance; I appear to myself in all my destitution; I prostrate myself in my wretchedness, and recognizing my state of dire need, I spread it out before You, my divine Master.... As far as my will—not my feelings—is concerned, I set my joy in everything that can humble me, immolate me, destroy self in me, for I want to give place to You, O Lord.... I no longer wish to live by my own life, but to be transformed in You, so that my life may be more divine than human, and that, inclining unto me, the Father may recognize Your image, the image of His beloved Son, in whom He is well pleased " (E.T. *I*, 2 – 3).

347

THE NIGHT OF THE SPIRIT

PRESENCE OF GOD - Pour forth, O Lord, into my soul greater love and greater courage, that I may willingly accept Your purifying action.

MEDITATION

1. The difficult and bitter purification called the *night of the spirit* is necessary to extirpate the roots of imperfect habits. The purification of the soul begins with the *night of sense*, which, by putting the soul into obscurity and depriving it of all sensible consolation, frees it from attachment to creatures and to material goods; but this night is completed only by the *night of the spirit*, which, annihilating the soul in its spiritual faculties, succeeds in destroying in it every imperfect habit. St. John of the Cross remarks very appositely that after having passed through the *night of sense*, " there still remain in the spirit the stains of the old man, although the spirit thinks not that this is so, neither can it perceive them " (*DN II*, 2,1); these stains are so deep and hidden that the soul has difficulty in recognizing them.

Consider, for example, one who is detached from creatures and earthly goods, advanced in prayer and virtue, a soul, therefore, who has already gone through the stages of the purgative and illuminative ways; nevertheless, when put to the test, it is easy to discover in it a certain attachment to its good works—works of the apostolate, exercises of penance or devotion—so that if obedience or the service of its neighbor oblige it to leave these works or substitute others for them, the soul is troubled, offers a certain resistance, and only with much reluctance does it succeed in submitting. This happens precisely because there are still within it the roots of imperfect habits and, above all, those of pride and egoism, whence spring all the other faults and imperfections. Of what use is it to suppress faulty actions if their roots remain in the spirit? Cut off only superficially, these roots, sooner or later, send forth shoots in a new direction.

No one can be freed from the roots of his faults without passing through the painful night of the spirit. Comparing this night with the night of sense, St. John of the Cross says that the difference between one and the other " is the difference between the root and the branch, or between the removing of a stain which is fresh and of one which is old and of long standing " *(ibid.)*. Although the operation is very arduous and painful to undergo, it is nevertheless indispensable, because the stains of the old man are removed only " with the soap and strong lye " of the purgation of the spirit, without which the soul " will be unable to come to the purity of divine union " *(ibid.)*.

2. In order to enter the *night of sense* a good measure of courage is necessary, for it is a matter of renouncing " every pleasure that presents itself to the senses, if it be not purely for the honor and glory of God " (J.C. *AS I*, 13,4). To enter the *night of the spirit*, much more is required, since it is necessary to renounce not merely material things, but spiritual things as well. It is a matter, for example, of blinding one's own reason, of renouncing one's own will or the asserting of one's personality, not only in what concerns material goods but even in regard to moral and spiritual goods. In the night of the spirit the soul must walk in darkness, it must be placed in emptiness with respect to the senses and also with respect to its spiritual faculties. In this night God " strips their faculties, affections, and feelings, both spiritual and sensual, both outward and inward, leaving the understanding dark, the will dry, the memory empty and the affections in the deepest affliction, bitterness and constraint, taking from the soul the pleasure and experience of spiritual blessings which it had aforetime " (J.C. *DN II*, 3,4).

Such desolation and such privation of everything should not discourage us; they are not ordered to death, but to life and even to the fullness of life, which is union with God by love. Therefore, the soul that loves is neither frightened nor alarmed; its ideal is divine union and it desires to reach it at any cost; no sacrifice seems too hard, provided it reach its goal. On the other hand, if we had the least conception of the infinite perfection of God and were even dimly aware of our own profound misery, we should have to admit that no purification, however severe or painful, could ever be exaggerated when it prepares us, unworthy and wretched as we are, for union with Him who is Goodness, Purity, and Infinite Beauty; nor could the sufferings which this purification imposes on us ever seem insupportable when compared with the immense good which they will procure for us. The soul enamoured of its God repeats with St. Francis : " So great is the good which awaits me that all pain is delightful to me "; and it is here below that it awaits this good, because it knows that God does not refuse to admit to union with Himself the spirit which is well disposed, that is, totally purified.

COLLOQUY

" O my soul, when will you be delivered from your passions and vicious tendencies and changed for the better? When will the root of all evil be dried up within you? When will every trace of sin in You be effaced? Oh, if only you would love your God ardently! If only you were indissolubly united to your Sovereign Good!

" Good Jesus, tender Shepherd, my sweet Master, King of eternal glory, when shall I appear before You without stain and truly humble? When shall I truly despise all that is of earth for Your love? When shall I be entirely detached from myself and all things? For if I were really free of all worldly attachment I would no longer have any will of my own, nor would I any longer groan under the yoke of my passions and ill-regulated affections; I would no longer seek self in anything. The lack of this absolute, total detachment is the only real obstacle between You and me, the only thing which keeps me from taking flight freely toward You. When, then, shall I be despoiled of all? When shall I abandon myself without reserve to Your divine will? When shall I serve You with a pure, humble, calm, serene spirit? When shall I love You perfectly? When, after receiving you into my heart, will my soul unite itself delightfully to its Beloved? When shall I leap up to You with tender and ardent desire? When will my negligence and imperfections be absorbed in the immensity of Your love? O my God, my life, my love, my sole desire! My treasure, my good! My beginning and my end! My soul longs for Your tender embrace, it languishes and faints with desire

to unite itself to You, to be held close to You by the bond
of a sweet, holy and indissoluble love! What have I in
heaven? What do I desire upon earth? The God of my
heart, the God who is my portion forever!" (Bl. Louis de
Blois).

348

PURIFYING LOVE

PRESENCE OF GOD - O Lord, help me to open my heart wide to the
outpouring of Your purifying love.

MEDITATION

1. One of the greatest graces God can give a soul is
that of introducing it into the painful desolation of the night
of the spirit, for it is in this way that He prepares and disposes
it for union. Although to the soul who experiences its
distressing pains, this night seems to be a chastisement from
God, it is, on the contrary, a gift of His merciful love, by
means of which, He wills to disentangle the soul from the last
snares of its imperfections. St. John of the Cross declares
expressly that this night is the work of " the loving wisdom
of God," which purifying the soul "prepares it for the union
of love" (*DN II*, 5,1). But if this is the work of love, why
is it is so painful? The soul has become like a piece of
green wood placed in the fire; material fire, acting upon
wood, first of all begins to dry it by driving out its moisture,
and "to make it black, dark, and unsightly, and even to make
it give forth a bad odor; and, as it dries it little by little, it
brings out and drives away all the dark and unsightly accidents which are contrary to the nature of fire. Finally, it
begins to kindle it externally, to give it heat, and at last
transforms it into itself, making it as beautiful as fire."
Likewise divine Love, " before it unites and transforms the
soul into itself, first purges it of all its contrary accidents.
It drives out its unsightliness, and makes it black and dark, so

that the soul seems worse than before, and more unsightly and abominable than it was wont to be " (*ibid.*, 10,1.2). One easily understands that under the weight of such purifications the soul must suffer; nevertheless, all this is the work of Love. The loving Wisdom of God invading the yet imperfect soul must necessarily begin in it a work of destruction, of purification, and only after having freed it from everything contrary to divine love, will He unite it to Himself and transform it in Himself. Then the work of Love will no longer be grievous to the soul, but very sweet and delightful; however, as long as it is not completely purified, this work of purgation cannot fail to be afflictive. O blessed affliction which disposes the soul for so great a good! St. John of the Cross cries out : " O souls that seek to walk in security and comfort in spiritual things! If ye did but know how necessary it is to suffer and endure in order to reach this lofty state of security and consolation...ye would in no way seek consolation, either from God or from creatures, but would rather bear the cross, and having embraced it, would desire to drink pure vinegar and gall, and would count this a great happiness " (J.C. *LF*, 2,28).

2. The more deeply convinced we are that purification is the work of Love, the more eager we shall be to welcome it gladly, and to embrace it courageously, even when it costs us dear. Moreover, the general law of perfect love—even of human love—does not tolerate sharing the heart. Love will not admit rivals and cannot endure a lack of harmony between those who love. If human love, so limited and weak, demands such totality, why should we not accord the same rights—or rather, infinitely superior ones—to divine Love?

Love by its very nature tends to equality : it either finds or it makes those who love one another equal; and God, seeing a soul of good will, wanting to give itself entirely to Him, loves it to the point of making it like Himself, by stripping it of all that is contrary to His infinite perfection; and in the measure that He strips it, He clothes it with Himself, with His own divine Life.

By its very nature, love also tends to unity : it desires complete fusion of hearts; and God, who infinitely loves the soul that sincerely seeks Him, desires nothing more than to unite it to Himself; therefore He purifies it of every stain that would impede perfect union with His infinite purity.

Jesus Himself, at the Last Supper, expressed the supreme desire of His love for us by asking for this perfect union : " As Thou, Father in Me, and I in Thee; that they also may be one in Us " (*Jn* 17,21). But because we were radically incapable of this union, vitiated by sin and full of every misery, He took our sins upon Himself and washed them away in His Blood. The Passion of Jesus tells us how much our purification has cost the sinless Son of God. And if it has cost Him, Innocence itself, so much, is it not just that we should suffer a little, too, we who are culpable, having so often offended God, and having so many times, by our willfulness, put obstacles to the outpouring of His love in our souls? And now that this divine Love, instead of abandoning us as we deserve, comes to us in order to purify us, shall we flee from its action? No, this cannot be! Just as purifying sufferings are the work of God's love for us, so we want our acceptance of them to be the work, the proof, of our love for Him. " To love is to labor to detach and strip ourselves for God's sake of all that is not God " (J.C. *AS II*, 5,7).

COLLOQUY

" O Lord, be mindful of me, who dwell in darkness and in the shadow of death, and quicken Your creature with Your love, which is the very breath of my life. Make the divine fire of Your love consume in me every desire for earthly affection, and may there remain in my heart but one love alone, entirely directed to Your infinite beauty and goodness.

" O Jesus, Your immense love, drawing me to union with Yourself, awakens in me a great longing to love You in return. Therefore, from the very depths of my heart I cry to You, and beg You, by the flames of the boundless charity with which You loved me and became incarnate for me, to send me the Holy Spirit, that divine Fire which inflames the Church, my Mother and Your Spouse, that He may enlighten and convert me and thus revivify my soul.

" O sweetest Son of God, let that divine Spirit come. I open wide my heart to Him so that, disfigured as I am by sin, He may, transform me according to Your beautiful form and grace.

" This, O Lord, is my request, and to obtain it I surrender myself to the fire and water of tribulations, and to all the pains of this life. For this I rise early to forestall You with prayer and to sacrifice myself to You in the morning watches. For this I supplicate You in the silence of the night and knock at the door of Your mercy. By their tears my eyes speak to You, and I shall not take any rest until You have satisfied my desire.

" If You condescend to hearken to me by sending me Your Fire, I will sacrifice to You the firstfruits of my affections, and I will never serve strange gods.   I will praise You in public and in secret. I will sing Your mercies eternally and acclaim the victories of Your love " (Ven. John of Jesus Mary).

349

TOWARD COMPLETE PURIFICATION

PRESENCE OF GOD - Help me, O Lord, that I may have the courage set out myself by my own initiative toward complete purification.

MEDITATION

I. " The soul desirous of reaching this high state of union with God is greatly impeded when it clings to any understanding or feeling or imagination or appearance or will or manner of its own, or to any other act or to anything of its own, and is unable to detach and strip itself of all these " (J.C. *AS II*, 4,4). This profound and radical detachment is effected in the soul by the night of the spirit. If then, we wish to enter this night, which will bring such good to our soul, we must try as far as in us lies, to deny ourselves in everything, especially in those things to which we are most attached. We must be disposed to renounce our plans, our projects, and our views, not only regarding material things, but even spiritual ones, for we must go to God, not by a way of our own choosing or taste, but only by the way which He Himself has prepared for us. We must be disposed to renounce divine consolations and to walk in darkness and aridity for as long as Our Lord wills, to renounce our most cherished works, our most legitimate affections, our most holy friendships, even the very support of the one who understands and guides us in the ways of God.

There are few who enter effectively into the night of the spirit precisely because " there are few who can enter, and desire to enter, into this complete detachment and emptiness of spirit " (*ibid.*, 7,3).

Even among spiritual persons, few are persuaded that the way which leads to union with God " consists only in the one thing that is needful, which is the ability to deny oneself truly, according to that which is without and that which is within, giving oneself up to suffering for Christ's sake, and to total annihilation " (*ibid.*, 7, 8). We must be convinced of this, and act in all things with the greatest detachment, without detaining ourselves through a spirit of ownership or by vain complacency, either in material or in spiritual goods. We must look at Jesus on the Cross : He was truly despoiled, stripped of all things, and " annihilated in everything, that is, with respect to human reputation; since, when men saw Him die, they mocked Him rather than esteemed Him; and also with respect to nature, since His nature was annihilated when He died; and further, with respect to the spiritual consolation and protection of the Father, since at that time, He forsook Him " (*ibid.*, 7,11). From this we should understand the way to unite ourselves to God; we should realize that the more completely we annihilate ourselves for love of Him, the more completely will we be united to Him.

2. The generous practice of total renunciation is not the only thing we can do in order to enter the night of the spirit; there is another, no longer negative but eminently positive : the intense exercise of the theological virtues. Faith, hope and charity must be our support and guide in the obscurity of the night and, at the same time, help us to purify the faculties of our soul—the understanding, the memory and the will—so that they may cling to God alone.

" Faith, " writes St. John of the Cross, "causes an emptiness and darkness with respect to the understanding "

(*AS II*, 6,2).   Indeed, in proposing for our belief truths which we cannot understand because of their sublimity, faith teaches us that instead of depending upon our own manner of reasoning and understanding, we ought rather to despoil ourselves of this—thus placing our intellect in emptiness—in order to unite ourselves to God.   The greater our progress in faith, the more detached we shall be from our shallow ways of thinking, not only in what concerns the divine mysteries and our direct contacts with God, but even with respect to the events of life, which we shall learn to judge only in relation to God.

Hope, on its part, " renders the memory empty and dark with respect both to things below and to things above " (*ibid.*, 6,3).   If we hope earnestly, it means that we await blessings which we do not yet enjoy and are not content with those already possessed.   If we place all our hope in God, it means that we no longer hope in the things of earth, that possession of them does not satisfy us; thus the remembrance of them becomes less lively, less frequent, so that our memory remains empty, and capable of applying itself solely to what concerns God and His service.   If we exercise ourselves intensively in the hope of heavenly goods, we shall forget earthly ones; if we hope in God alone, we shall no longer be occupied with the remembrance of creatures.

" Charity causes emptiness in the will with respect to all things, since it obliges us to love God above them all; which cannot be unless we withdraw our affection from them all in order to set it wholly upon God " (*ibid.*, 6,4).   If we wish to attain to detachment and to total renunciation we must love much.   The more we grow in divine love, and the more readily we detach ourselves from earthly things and also from ourselves, the more capable we become of renouncing our own will and annihilating our ego in all things.

If we walk in faith, hope, and love, we shall go forward in the night of the spirit, without going astray in the obscurity and darkness that is encountered, for these virtues will keep us strongly anchored in God.

COLLOQUY

" O Lord, make possible to me by Your grace what seems impossible to me by nature.   You know that I can bear but little and that I am quickly discouraged by a small adversity. Let every trial and tribulation become agreeable to me, for Your name's sake; for to suffer and to be afflicted for You is very beneficial to my soul.

" Be with me, O Lord Jesus, in all places and at all times. Let this be my consolation, to be willing to be without all human comfort. And if Your comfort also be withdrawn, let what You will and ordain for my trial be to me as the greatest of comforts. ' For You will not always be angry, nor will You threaten forever. '

" Lord, provided that my will remain but right and firm toward You, do with me whatever pleases You. For whatever You shall do with me can only be good. If You wish me to be in darkness, I shall bless You; and if You wish me to be afflicted, I shall still bless You forever.

" Lord, I shall suffer willingly for Your sake whatever You wish to send me. I will receive with indifference from Your hand both good and evil alike; keep me from all sin, and I will fear neither death nor hell. Do not cast me out forever, nor blot me out of the book of life, and whatever tribulation befalls will not harm me " (*Imit. III*, 19,5 – 16,2 – 17,2.4).

350

DESIGNS OF PEACE AND LOVE

TWENTY-THIRD SUNDAY AFTER PENTECOST

PRESENCE OF GOD - O Lord, fulfill in me Your designs of peace and love, making me rise to a life of complete fervor.

MEDITATION

1. In spite of our sublime ideal, our ardent desire for sanctity, we always find ourselves full of miseries, always indebted to God. Our souls often tremble with fear in His presence, and we ask ourselves : How will He receive me? Will He turn me away? But the answer

is quite different from what we would expect : " The Lord saith : I think thoughts of peace and not of affliction. You shall call upon Me and I will hear you, and I will bring back your captivity from all places. " These consoling words, which we read in the Introit of today's Mass, open our hearts to the sweetest hopes. God loves us in spite of all. He is always and everywhere our Father, and He desires to free us from the servitude of our passions and from our weaknesses. Then spontaneously the humble invocation of the Collect rises to our lips : " Grant, O Lord, that by Your goodness we may be delivered from the bonds of sin which by our frailty we have committed. " Humility and the sincere acknowledgment of our wrongdoing is always the starting point for conversion.

In the Epistle (*Phil* 3,17-21–4,1-3) St. Paul speaks to us of conversion : " For many walk, of whom I have told you often, and now tell you weeping, that they are enemies of the Cross of Christ...who mind only the things of earth. " Every time that we shun a sacrifice, that we protest against suffering, that we seek selfish pleasures, we behave, in practice, like enemies of the Cross of Christ. Thus our lives become too earthly, too much attached to creatures, too heavily burdened to rise toward heaven. We must be converted, we must practice detachment, and remember that " our conversation is in heaven "; to this end, we must willingly embrace the hardships of the return journey to our heavenly homeland. As an encouragement, St. Paul places before our eyes the glory of our eternal life : " Jesus Christ will reform the body of our lowness, made like to the body of His glory. " These are the " thoughts of peace, " the great designs of love which our heavenly Father outlines for us : to free us from the bondage of sin, and conform us to His own Son, making us sharers in His glorious resurrection. They are marvelous designs but they will be realized only with our cooperation. " Therefore, " the Apostle beseeches us, " my dearly beloved brethren, and most desired, my joy and my crown : so stand fast in the Lord. " Stand fast, that is, persevere in your conversion, strong in humility, confidence, and love of the Cross.

2. Today's Gospel (*Mt* 9,18-26) gives a striking example of the transformation which God desires to accomplish in us. It also shows how He realizes His thoughts of peace in those who approach Him with a humble and trustful heart. First,

let us consider the woman troubled with an issue of blood. Her malady was incurable, she had been suffering from it for twelve years, and she had found no remedy. The poor woman, ashamed and humiliated, did not dare, like the other sick persons, to present herself directly to Jesus. However, her faith was so lively that she said within herself : " If I shall touch only His garment, I shall be healed. " Furtively drawing near to Him she touched the hem of His garment. Jesus noticed that light touch and turning around said : " Be of good heart, daughter, thy faith hath made thee whole. " No petition, no spoken request—but what moved the Lord was the prayer of that humble, trustful heart, so full of faith.

As Jesus healed the woman with the issue of blood, so does He wish to heal our souls, but He expects of us dispositions similar to hers. Too often we are content to pray with our lips while our hearts are cold and distant; Jesus, however, looks to the heart; He wants the prayer of the heart, a cry of humility and confidence, a cry which goes straight to His own divine Heart. On the other hand, how much more fortunate are we than that poor sick woman! She succeeded only once in touching the hem of His garment, whereas our souls in Holy Communion may be daily united with His very Body and Blood. Oh! if we only had faith like a grain of mustard seed!

The second miracle followed. The daughter of Jairus was not simply ill, she was dead; but it was no more difficult for Jesus to restore a dead person to life than to heal one who was sick. He, the true Lord of life and death, " took her by the hand and the maid arose. " Jesus is our Resurrection not only for our eternal life when, at a signal from Him, our body will rise glorious and be reunited to our soul; but He is our Resurrection even in this life : our Resurrection from the death of sin to the life of grace, our Resurrection from a lukewarm life to a fervent and holy life.

Let us draw near to Jesus with the humility and confidence of the woman cured of the issue of blood. Let us beg Him with all our hearts to realize in us His designs of love, by drawing us away from the sluggish mediocrity of a spiritual life still entangled in the snares of egoism, and by giving us a strong, determined impetus toward sanctity.

COLLOQUY

" O Lord, how ill is Your friendship requited by those
who so soon become Your mortal enemies again! Of a
truth, Your mercy is great; what friend shall we find who is so
long-suffering?   If once such a cleavage takes place between
two earthly friends, it is never erased from the memory
and their friendship can never again become as close as
before.   Yet how often has our friendship for You failed in this
way, and for how many years do You await our return to You!
May You be blessed, my Lord God, who bear so compas-
sionately with us that You seem to forget Your greatness and
do not punish such treacherous treason as this, as would
only be right " (T.J. *Con*, 2).

" O Jesus, You are my peace; for through You I have
access to the Father, since it has pleased the Father to grant
peace through the Blood of Your Cross to all in heaven
and on earth.

" This is Your work as regards every soul of good will;
it is what Your immense, Your exceeding charity urges
You to do in me.   You desire to be my peace. . . .   By the
Blood of Your Cross, You will make peace in the little
heaven of my soul. . . You will fill me with Yourself, You will
bury me in Yourself, and You will make me live again with
You, by Your Life.

" O Jesus, even though I fall at every moment, in
trustful faith I shall pray You to raise me up, and I know
You will forgive me, and will blot out everything with jealous
care.   More than that : You will despoil me, deliver me from
my miseries, from everything that is an obstacle to Your
divine action; and will draw all my powers to Yourself,
and make them Your captive. . . .   Then I shall have
passed completely into You and shall be able to say : It is no
longer I that live; my Master liveth in me " (E.T. *II*, 12).

351

PASSIVE PURIFICATION

PRESENCE OF GOD - My God, illumine my way, that I may not go astray in the midst of the darkness of tribulation.

MEDITATION

1. Although it is possible for us to enter the night of the spirit by a generous practice of total renunciation and an intense exercise of the theological virtues, we will never be able to penetrate into its deepest part if God Himself does not place us there. Only He can deepen the darkness which envelops us in this night, so that we may be reduced to nothingness in all, to the point of attaining the purity and poverty of spirit which are required for union. Far from taking the initiative, our task is then reduced to accepting with love, to enduring with patience and humility all that God disposes for us.

In order not to resist the divine action, we should remember that God generally purifies souls through the ordinary circumstances of life. In the life of every Christian, every apostle, every religious, there is always a measure of suffering sufficient to effect the purification of the spirit. These are the sufferings which God Himself chooses and disposes in the way best suited to the different needs of souls; but, unfortunately, few profit by them because few know how to recognize in the sorrows of life the hand of God who wishes to purify them. Illness, bereavement, estrangement, separation from dear ones, misunderstandings, struggles, difficulties proceeding sometimes from the very ones who should have been able to give help and support, failure of works that were cherished and sustained at the price of great labor, abandonment by friends, physical and spiritual solitude —these are some of the sufferings which are met with more or less in the life of every man, and which we will find in ours. We must understand that all such things are positively willed or at least permitted by God precisely to purify us even to the very inmost fibers of our being. In the face of these trials, we must never blame the malice of men, or stop to examine whether or not they are just; we must see only the blessed hand of God who offers us these bitter remedies to bring perfect health to our soul. St. John of the Cross writes : " It greatly behooves the soul, then, to have patience and constancy in all the tribulations and trials which God sends it, whether they come from without or from within, and are spiritual or corporal, great or small. It must take them all as from His hand for its healing and its good, and not flee from them, since they are health to it " (*LF*, 2,30).

2. Let us consider how great a spirit of faith is necessary to accept from the hand of God all the circumstances which afflict and humble, contradict and mortify us. It will sometimes be easier to accept heavy trials which come directly from Our Lord, such as illness and bereavement, than other lighter ones where creatures enter into play, and for which, perhaps, we experience greater repugnance. The immediate action of creatures, especially if their malice has a share in it, makes it more difficult for us to discover the divine hand. A greater spirit of faith is necessary here, that we may pass beyond the human side of circumstances, the faulty way of acting of such and such a person, and find, beyond all these human contingencies, the dispositions of divine Providence, which wills to use these particular creatures, and even their defects and errors, to file away our self-love and destroy our pride.

The counsel given by St. John of the Cross to a religious will be very useful for us in such cases : " Thou must know that those (who are in the convent) are no more than workers whom God has placed there only that they might work upon and chisel at thee by mortifying thee. And some will cut at thee through words...others in deed...others by their thoughts, neither esteeming nor feeling love for thee... and thou must be subject to them in all things, even as an image is subject to him that fashions it and to him that paints it and to him that gilds it " (*P*, 15). Profoundly convinced that God guides and disposes all for the good of those who love Him, the soul of faith sees in every person a messenger from our Lord, charged by Him to exercise it in virtue, particularly in that which it lacks most. Instead of rebelling and being indignant because of some want of consideration or even some really unjust treatment, it bows its head and accepts all humbly, as the most suitable treatment for curing its faults and imperfections. This must be our conduct, if we wish to draw profit from all the trials that God places in our path. In each instance we must keep ourselves from posing as a victim, from protesting, from complaining, or from retaliating. Whatever suffering may come to us from creatures has only one true explanation : Our Lord wishes to purify us, and is beginning to do it precisely through these exterior tribulations. Let us be persuaded that all serves greatly for our spiritual progress, because before attaining to union with God, it is necessary to be reduced to nothingness, that is, to be established in profoundest humility.

COLLOQUY

" Teach me, my God, to suffer in peace the afflictions which You send me that my soul may emerge from the crucible like gold, both brighter and purer, to find You within me. Trials like these, which at present seem unbearable, will eventually become light, and I shall be anxious to suffer again, if by so doing I can render You greater service. And however numerous may be my troubles and persecutions...they will all work together for my greater gain though I do not myself bear them as they should be borne, but in a way which is most imperfect " (T.J. *Life*, 30).

" O grandeur of my God ! All the temptations and tribulations which You permit to come upon us, absolutely all, are ordered for our good, and if we have no other thought, when we are tried here below, than that of Your goodness, this will suffice for us to overcome every temptation.

" O Word of God, my sweet and loving Spouse, all power in heaven and on earth is Yours. You confound and put to flight every enemy. As for me, I am extremely weak; I cannot see, being filled with misery and sins; but by Your slightest glance, O Word, You put all these enemies to flight, like bits of straw in the wind; first, however, You permit them to give battle to Your servants, to make these, Your servants, more glorious. And the greater the grace and light You want to give Your servants, that they may love and know You better, the more do You try them by fire and purify their hearts like gold, so that their virtues may shine like precious stones.

" By Your power, O divine Word, You confer strength for the combat, and he who wishes to fight manfully for Your glory must first descend into the most profound knowledge of self, yet all the while raising his heart to You, that he may not be confounded " (St. Mary Magdalen dei Pazzi).

352

INTERIOR TRIALS

PRESENCE OF GOD - O Lord, purify me as gold in the crucible; purify me and do not spare me, that I may attain to union with You.

MEDITATION

1. If Our Lord finds you strong and faithful, humble and patient in accepting exterior trials, He will go on little by little to others that are more inward and spiritual " to purge and cleanse you more inwardly. . . to give you more interior blessings " (J.C. *LF*, 2,28). The passive night of the spirit culminates precisely in these interior sufferings of the soul, by which God " destroys and consumes its spiritual substance and absorbs it in deep and profound darkness " (J.C. *DN II*, 6,1) in order that it may be completely reborn to divine Life. We are, in fact, so steeped in miseries and faults, which adhere so closely to our nature, that if God Himself did not take our purification in hand, renewing us from head to foot, we should never be delivered from them. Jesus, too, spoke of this total renovation, of this profound spiritual rebirth : " Unless a man be born again of water and the Spirit, he cannot enter into the kingdom of God " (*Jn* 3,5) ; the kingdom of God here below is the state of perfect union with Him, to which no one attains if he be not first totally purified.

St. John of the Cross explains at length how this work of purification is accomplished by the Holy Spirit, who, invading the soul with the living flame of His Love, destroys and consumes all its imperfections. So long as this divine flame purifies and disposes the soul, says the Saint, it " is very oppressive...the flame is not bright to it, but dark, and if it gives any light at all, it is only that the soul may see and feel its own faults and miseries " (J.C. *LF*, 1,19). Although the soul finds itself under the direct action of the Holy Spirit, this action is not agreeable but painful, because its first fruit is precisely to show it all its weaknesses and miseries that it may conceive a horror for them, detest them, humble itself for them and be sorry for them. The penetrating light of the " living flame of Love " lifts the thick veil which hides from the soul the roots of its evil habits. The soul suffers at such a sight, not only because it feels humbled, but also because it fears being rejected by God; indeed, seeing itself so miserable, it feels itself dreadfully unworthy of divine love, and, at certain times, it even seems as if God in anger had cast it off from Himself. This is the greatest torment the soul can suffer, but a precious one, because it purifies the soul of all residue of self-love and pride, and deepens within it the profound abyss of humility which calls to and draws down the abyss of divine mercy.

2. If the Holy Spirit did not make you understand and experience your wretchedness, you could not be delivered from it, for in your ignorance you could not further the work of purification which He wills to accomplish in you. Therefore, when the divine light shows you the depths of your depravity through the failures of your spiritual life, the powerlessness of your spirit, or the struggles and rebellions of nature, you must support the sight humbly, recognizing and confessing your weaknesses without excusing them, without blaming adverse circumstances, without turning your gaze elsewhere. These are the moments in which, more than ever, you must humble yourself " under the mighty hand of God " (1 *Pt* 5,6), who shows you what you really are in His sight. But, on the other hand, the sight of your miseries, however ugly and detestable they may be, should not plunge you into discouragement, for this is not the end for which the Holy Spirit reveals them to you; rather, it is to divest you of every trace of secret self-esteem and to extinguish in your heart—in case it were there—any claim to meriting divine gifts and favors. Neither should you

believe that you have become worse than formerly. You have always borne these miseries within you! Hitherto you were ignorant of them, whereas now the divine light shows them to you clearly, not that they may overwhelm you but that you may be delivered from them. Therefore, despite all the suffering that you may experience at the sight of your misery, you must remain confident and certain that God will never abandon you. You have been unfaithful to Him, it is true; you have not corresponded to His love as you should have done, and the services which you have rendered Him are very little in comparison with what God deserves; nevertheless He who is infinitely good does not despise your contrite and humble heart. God loves you and, far from rejecting you, He desires to unite Himself to you; but first He wants to make you perfectly aware that you are wholly undeserving of this great grace. God communicates Himself only to humble souls, and only the humble are filled with His gifts; that is the reason for the purifying sufferings of the night of the spirit : it is impossible to be entirely humble without passing through the bitter anguish of this night in which God Himself undertakes to humble the soul. But when finally He will have reduced it to the center of its nothingness, then He will exalt it, drawing it to Himself in the perfect union of love.

COLLOQUY

" O my soul, if you are wounded by sin, behold your physician, ready to cure you. His mercy is infinitely greater than all your iniquities. This I say, not that you may remain in your misery, but that by doing your utmost to overcome it, you may not despair of His clemency and pardon.

" Your God is sweetness itself, mildness itself; whom will you love, whom will you desire except Him?

" Let not your imperfections discourage you; your God does not despise you because you are imperfect and infirm; on the contrary, He loves you because you desire to cure your ills. He will come to your assistance and make you more perfect than you would have dared to hope, and adorned by His own hand, your beauty will be unequalled, like His own goodness.

" O my Jesus, tender Shepherd, gentle Master, help me, lift up Your dejected sheep, extend Your hand to sustain me, heal my wounds, strengthen my weakness, save me; otherwise I shall perish. I am unworthy of life, I confess, unworthy of Your light and help; for my ingratitude has been so great; Your mercy, however, is greater still. Have pity upon me, then, O God, You who love men so much! Oh, my only hope! Have pity upon me according to the greatness of your mercy " (Bl. Louis de Blois).

" One abyss calleth upon another. It is there, my God, at the bottom that I shall meet You : the abyss of my poverty, of my nothingness, will be confronted with the abyss of Your mercy, the immensity of Your All. There I shall find strength to die to myself and, losing every trace of self, I shall be changed into love " (E.T. *I*, 1).

353

DESOLATION AND DARKNESS

PRESENCE OF GOD - Come to my aid, O Lord, that I may not be overwhelmed by the storm.

MEDITATION

1. Seeing its wretchedness so clearly, the soul senses the infinite distance separating it from God; and, while desiring even more to be united to Him, it realizes that it is farther from Him than ever, absolutely incapable of bridging the chasm which divides them. This recognition causes pain as well, for the lover ardently desires union with the beloved. The suffering sometimes becomes so intense that it seems to the soul that there no longer exists any hope of holiness, of union with God, or even of eternal salvation for it.

There is nothing exaggerated, much less feigned in this desolation. The Holy Spirit, under whose action the soul finds itself, cannot inspire it with anything not entirely conformable with truth. It is quite true that between us, poor creatures that we are, and God, sovereign and infinite perfection, there is a distance, an incalculable distance; it is quite true that, by our own strength, we are radically incapable of elevating ourselves to God; again it is true that considering our actions—even the best of them—there is nothing in us which merits either union with God or eternal life. If many souls are not convinced of this, thinking that they are able of themselves to do something to advance toward God and holiness, it is because they have not yet been enlightened as to the depths of their own nothingness.

If we are, then, utterly unworthy of God, of His love, of union with Him, of His eternal glory, it is equally true that God Himself, in His merciful love, has desired to bridge the distance that separates Him from us. He has stooped down to us to the point of clothing us with His divine Life and calling us to his intimacy. What is impossible to our misery is entirely possible to the omnipotence and infinite mercy of God. He wills to do this work in us, yet He wants us to realize that it is His work alone.

In those moments when the soul is tempted to despair of attaining to God and eternal salvation, it must remain firm in unshakable hope. However justifiable may be its mistrust of itself and all its efforts, there is even more reason to await all from God, whose love and goodness infinitely surpass both its poverty and its expectation. In this way the desolation of the night of the spirit will achieve its end—that of establishing the soul in a deeper humility, in a purer and more perfect hope, because now the soul trusts only in the merciful love of God.

2. St. John of the Cross writes : " And thus at this time the soul also suffers great darkness in the understanding.... And in its substance the soul suffers from abandonment and the greatest poverty. Dry and cold, and at times hot, it finds relief in naught, nor is there any thought that can console it, nor can it even raise its heart to God " (J.C. *LF*, 1,20). Yet another cause of spiritual distress is the aridity in which the soul finds itself : the inability to think of God, to find help by reflecting upon divine things. It seems to the soul as if a very high wall had risen up between God and itself, preventing its cries from reaching Him. It is deep night, in which the soul cannot go forward except by leaning upon pure, naked faith, clinging with all its strength to the

belief that God is infinitely good, that He loves it and listens
to its cries, that He knows its torment, and allows it to suffer
only to purify it.   It is not surprising that the soul in this
state may experience strong temptations against faith, like
those which afflicted St. Thérèse of the Child Jesus in the last
period of her life.   She writes : " Our Lord allowed my soul
to be plunged in thickest gloom, and the thought of heaven,
so sweet from my earliest years, to become for me a subject of
torture " (*St*, 9).   She adds, however : " God knows how I
try to live by faith, even though it affords me no consolation.
I have made more acts of faith during the past year than in all
the rest of my life " (*ibid.*).   Alluding to her poems on the
happiness of heaven, she confesses : " When I sing... of the
happiness of heaven and of the eternal possession of God,
I feel no joy; I sing only of what *I will to believe* " (*ibid.*).
This is exactly how the soul must conduct itself : *believing
because it wills to believe*, not relying on what it feels or
experiences, but relying solely upon the word of God.
These acts of pure faith, stripped of all consolation,
independent of any feeling whatsoever, are truly heroic
acts; they honor God more purely, the more they are
based only on divine revelation; and they unite the soul
to God, the more stripped they are of all human support.
The darkness of the night of the spirit has precisely this end :
to accustom the soul to walk by pure faith, by heroic faith.

COLLOQUY

   " O Jesus, King of peace, whose presence heaven and
earth long for, how have You gone so far away from me!
How are all my riches and strength lacking!   O loss more
painful than mortal wounds, O truly bitter separation,
worse than the anguish of death!
   " Why have You hidden Yourself, my gentle Spouse,
and by Your absence cast me into this night full of thick
shadows and dark desolation?   Who will help me in this
utter abandonment, in this solitude?   Oh! how great are
the sufferings of love, how great is the anxiety of the heart
which knows not nor can do anything but love, while
possessing not Him whom it loves!
   " I have no other remedy, O most kind King, than to
sigh for You.   I cry to You from the bottom of my heart and

speak to the tenderness of Your love. Remember me, O my hope; see my desolation at the thought of Your refusal, and the bitter abandonment consuming me.

" Do not abandon me, O gentle Son of the Virgin, because mercy was born, together with You, from the womb of Your Immaculate Mother. See, Lord, how all my strength is failing, and how, bereft of You, I am oppressed by the horror and shadow of death.

" Have pity on me, my Friend, because all my strength being consumed, I have only lips and tongue left to cry to You. O immortal life and fountain of living water, do not deprive me of Your presence with so much rigor, for it is dearer to me than life. I shall not rest, O gentle Son of God, nor ever cease my sighs and supplications until You show me Your Face " (Ven. John of Jesus Mary).

354

CONFIDENCE AND ABANDONMENT

PRESENCE OF GOD - Into Your hands, O Lord, I abandon myself with all confidence.

MEDITATION

1. " There are many who desire to make progress [in the spiritual way] and constantly entreat God to draw them and let them advance to this state of perfection [the state of union], but when it pleases God to begin to bring them through the first trials and mortifications, as is necessary, they are unwilling to pass through them, and flee away, to escape from the narrow road of life and to seek the broad road of their own consolation " (J.C. LF, 2,27). This is the reason why many souls do not reach union with God; they are not willing to tread the way of the Cross, the only way which leads to it.

You also desire to arrive at divine union, but perhaps you, too, think to reach it by a broad, sunny, pleasant way, by the way of success, where one goes from victory to victory, where one enjoys abundant spiritual consolations, where one finds the applause, support, and esteem of creatures. But by now you must certainly have understood that it is necessary to take quite another way : the narrow and obscure way where the soul discovers all its misery, experiences all its powerlessness, where consolation from God and men is wanting. You know, too, that you must accept having to walk on this road for as long as it will please God. How many months or years will suffice? Only God knows. He often keeps souls a long time in the dark night of the spirit, and it might even be said that, in general, even after the principal stages have been passed, there is always a little of the night as long as one lives upon earth. The wisest course to take is to surrender yourself completely to the divine will of God, without setting limits either to the duration or the nature of your trials. God knows what is best for you; He, who knows so well the weaknesses and necessities of your soul, will know how to prescribe exactly the treatment to cure your evils. Do not be hasty, but, on the contrary, have much patience, and you will not expose yourself to deception. Let your patience be long-suffering and trustful because, although you truly suffer, these sufferings do not come to you from an enemy but from your greatest Friend, from God, who loves you much more than you could love yourself, who wills your good, your happiness, your sanctification much more than you could ever desire them. Hope in Him and you will never be confounded; entrust yourself to Him blindly and you will have nothing to fear.

2. The most suitable moments to prove to God that you trust Him blindly, that you wish to abandon yourself to Him without reserve, are undoubtedly those of the dark night of the spirit. Even if it seems to you that all gives way under your feet, even if the tempest engulfs you to the point of making you feel tempted against faith and hope, you have nothing to fear, because in this night you are, in a very special way, under the action of the Holy Spirit. It is He who, by the living flame of His Love, lays waste your soul to purify it, but at the same time He Himself covers it with His shadow, secretly pouring into it the strength to resist, and measuring the suffering in such a way as not to exceed your capacity. Do not be afraid; you are in good hands : you are protected by the shadow of the Almighty, and no

evil can befall you, provided you adhere voluntarily and with docility to His purifying action. Accept, and continually repeat your "fiat"; this is what Our Lord wants of you in this state, and this you can and should do, even in the midst of the most violent tempests. This pure, simple adhesion of your will to God, will unite you to Him and anchor you in Him, keeping you from shipwreck. What does it matter if you can neither say nor do anything more, if you are incapable of long prayers; even Jesus, in the Garden of Olives, did nothing but repeat this one protestation: "Father...Thy will be done" (*Mt* 26,42). Let this be your prayer too, prayer rising more from your heart than from your lips, rising from a profound attitude of pure adherence to the will of God, in which you submerge yourself with all the powers of your soul. This adherence must become so strong, so complete, so filial and confident as to transform itself into a prolonged act of abandonment: "Father, into Thy hands I commend My spirit" (*Lk* 23,46). Jesus Himself formulated this act in the midst of anguish and desolation infinitely more intense than anything you could ever experience. Unite yourself to the agonizing Jesus; lean upon Him, and in Him you will find the necessary strength to accept and to resist. Keeping your eyes fixed upon Jesus Crucified, who has reconciled and united the human race to His divine Father by His Passion and death, you will understand ever more perfectly that union with God " consists not in refreshment and in consolations and spiritual feelings, but in a living death of the Cross, both as to sense and as to spirit—that is, both inwardly and outwardly " (J.C. *AS II*, 7,11).

COLLOQUY

" O my God, where is the sun of Your grace? It seems to me that it is darkened. You seem to have wholly withdrawn Your goodness from my soul. I am abandoned now, like a body which, deprived of its members, cannot help itself, or like a sterile tree trunk, for, Your grace being taken away, I can do nothing. O my God, stretch out Your right hand to me and give me strength.

" O eternal Father, if Your Word is with me, who can be against me? What can move me, cast me down, or vanquish me? Storms will beat against me exteriorly, but will not touch my inmost heart. They may make me suffer, and I accept it willingly because You so will, but they can never trouble my soul, ever abandoned to Your divine good pleasure. I shall still every storm, thinking that these sorrows come by Your will, and I shall immerse myself in the lowliness of my being. If these troubles swallow me up in hell, I shall raise myself up again to heaven with Your help, and in Your name I shall overcome every conflict.

" Nevertheless, I know my weakness and during this trial, which may be long or short according to Your good pleasure, while many battles rage, I know well what I must do; I shall trust in You and I shall never be moved " (St. Mary Magdalen dei Pazzi).

" Blessed Master, grant that the divine good pleasure may be my food and daily bread; may I let myself be immolated according to the Father's every wish, after Your example, O adored Christ. If at times what He wills is more crucifying, no doubt I may say with You : ' Father, if it be possible let this chalice pass from me, ' but I shall immediately add : ' not as I will, but as Thou wilt '; and calmly and steadfastly I shall climb my calvary with You, singing in my inmost soul, sending up to the Father a hymn of thanksgiving. For those who tread that Way of Sorrows are those ' whom He foreknew and predestined to be made conformable to the image of His divine Son, ' who was crucified for love! " (E.T. *I*, 3 - 8).

355

THE DEVELOPMENT OF LOVE

PRESENCE OF GOD - My God, from all eternity You have gone before me with Your infinite love; increase my love for You.

MEDITATION

1. " What shall prevent God from doing that which He will in the soul that is resigned, annihilated, and

detached? " (J.C. *AS II*, 4,2). This statement of St. John of the Cross makes you understand that God has an immense desire to work in your soul, to lead you to sanctity and to union with Himself, provided you commit yourself into His hands, despoiled of every attachment, annihilated in your self-love, entirely docile, malleable, and adaptable to His action. The Lord comes to your assistance with purifying trials in order to empty you of self, to detach you from creatures, to immerse you in true humility, but at the same time He helps you to grow in love, the strong bond which must unite you to Him. All the work which God accomplishes in your soul is done in view of making you advance in this virtue; exterior and interior trials, humiliations, powerlessness, aridity, struggles, and tempests are meant in the divine plan to extinguish the illusory fires of self-love, pride, earthly affections, and all other irregular passions, so that only one fire may burn within you, ever more intensely and strongly, the fire of charity.

The more the Lord purifies you, the more your heart will be freed from all dross and become capable of concentrating all its affection upon Him. Walk, then, in this way by accepting purification in view of a deeper love, and by orientating your whole spiritual life toward the exercise of love. What you suffer, suffer for love, that is, suffer it willingly, without rebellion or complaint, and then, in the measure that your soul is humbled, despoiled, and mortified, it will also be clothed with charity. The trials which God sends you have the purpose not only of purifying your heart, but also of dilating it in charity. They aim at deepening your capacity for love; not, certainly, a sensible love, but a powerful love of the will, which tends toward God through pure benevolence, independent of all personal consolation, its sole pursuit being His glory and good pleasure.

2. By means of purifying trials, " God secretly teaches the soul and instructs it in the perfection of love " (J.C. *DN II*, 5,1). Above all, He teaches it to love independently of all happiness and joy, even depriving it of that joy, though legitimate and spontaneous, which proceeds from the consciousness of its own love. The soul that is not yet wholly purified could become attached to this joy, so God withdraws it entirely; in the thick darkness the soul feels that it no longer loves; dry aridity extinguishes all joy and

sweetness, and it is constrained to go forward by a pure act of the will. Instead of taking complacency in its own love, which henceforth it no longer feels, the soul is profoundly afflicted by the tormenting doubt that it no longer knows how to love, and to combat this doubt, it can only apply itself with all its might to performing the works of love, that is, embracing generously every labor, every sacrifice that may please God. In this way, its love matures, becoming purer and stronger : purer, because it is not mixed with any personal consolation; stronger, because it urges the soul to more generous labors. In this state, the soul adheres to God by a simple act of the will, and herein the substance of love consists : it *wills good* to God solely because He is the supreme, infinitely lovable Good; it desires Him alone and serves Him alone, fulfilling all His divine will without any return on self, without seeking any joy or spiritual consolation. The soul is no longer preoccupied with enjoying His love, or with receiving; its one solicitude is to give, to give itself, to give pleasure to God. From this we understand how aridity and darkness, instead of stifling love, make it grow in a wonderful manner, provided the soul is disposed to seek only God's good pleasure and forget itself completely.

"Learn to love as God desires to be loved, and lay aside your own temperament" (*SM* I, 57) St. John of the Cross tells you; that is, learn to love God by a pure, strong act of the will, without being preoccupied with what is sentiment, consolation and joy of heart. Perhaps your manner of loving is still a little too dependent upon feeling; so be grateful to God if He makes you walk in darkness and aridity : it is thus that He will help you deliver yourself from this weakness.

COLLOQUY

"O Lord of my soul and my only Good! When a soul has resolved to love You, and forsaking everything, does all in its power toward that end, so that it may the better employ itself in Your love, why do You not grant it at once the joy of ascending to the possession of this perfect love? But I am wrong : I should have made my complaint by asking why we ourselves have no desire so to ascend, for it is we alone who are at fault in not at once enjoying so great a dignity.

"If we attain to the perfect possession of this true love of God, it brings all blessings with it. But so niggardly and so slow are we in giving ourselves wholly to God that we do not prepare ourselves as we should to receive that precious love which it is His Majesty's will that we should enjoy only at a great price.

"There is nothing on earth with which so great a blessing can be purchased; but if we did what we could to obtain it, if we cherished no attachment to earthly things, and if all our cares and all our intercourse were centered in heaven, I believe there is no doubt that this blessing would be given us very speedily.... But we think we are giving God everything, whereas what we are really offering Him is the revenue or the fruits of our land while keeping the stock and the right of ownership of it in our own hands.... A nice way of seeking His love! And then we want it quickly and in great handfuls, as one might say.

"O Lord, if You do not give us this treasure all at once, it is because we do not make a full surrender of ourselves. May it please You to give it to us at least little by little, even though the receiving of it may cost us all the trials in the world.

"No, my God, love does not consist in shedding tears, in enjoying those consolations and that tenderness which for the most part we desire and in which we find comfort, but in serving You with righteousness, fortitude of soul, and humility. The other seems to me to be receiving rather than giving anything....

"May it never please Your Majesty that a gift so precious as Your love be given to people who serve You solely to obtain consolations" (T.J. *Life*, 11).

356

THE LOVE OF ESTEEM

PRESENCE OF GOD - O my God, sovereign and infinite Good, grant that I may esteem nothing more than You and prefer nothing to You.

MEDITATION

1. Our Lord once said to St. Teresa : " Knowest thou what it is to love Me in truth? It is to realize that everything which is not pleasing to Me is a lie " (Life, 40). Without sound of words, the Holy Spirit gives this lesson to every soul that lets itself be formed and purified by Him. The more He enlightens it on the truth of its own misery and that of all creatures, the more the soul remains disinclined toward them; it withdraws all its hope from them and comes truly to esteem God above all things and to prefer Him to everything else. The attitude of this soul becomes very like that of St. Paul, who exclaimed : " I count all things to be but loss for...Jesus Christ, my Lord, for whom I have suffered the loss of all things and count them but as dung, that I may gain Christ " (Phil 3,8).

The love of esteem which the Holy Spirit pours into the soul through the purifying darkness is so strong that the soul is disposed to accept any sacrifice whatsoever, to confront every obstacle, to undergo every humiliation and suffering that it may win its God. St. John of the Cross says : " The love of esteem which it has for God is so great, even though it may not realize this, and may be in darkness, that it would be glad, not only to suffer in this way, but even to die many times over in order to give Him satisfaction " (DN II, 13,5). Let us note that the soul does not feel nor take pleasure in its own love, this love is not accompanied by enjoyment and sweetness; nevertheless, it is a love so real that it leads the soul effectively to the accomplishment of the most difficult things " if thereby...it might find Him whom it loves " (ibid.). We sould also note that it is not a question of impulses, of inoperative desires which immediately give way before concrete opportunities for sacrifice, but, on the contrary, of a strong determination of the will which nothing can shake. Once the soul has understood that a certain action is necessary in order to unite itself to God, it pays no attention to anything, neither to the repugnances of nature, nor to the voice of self-love or egoism, nor to what others might say or think; it plunges headlong with great courage.

2. A further effect of this great love of esteem for God is that " the greatest sufferings and trials of which [the soul] is conscious in this night are the anguished thoughts that it has lost God, and the fears that He has abandoned it " (J.C. *DN II*, 13,5). Just as it is not concerned about acquiring any possession except the possession of God, neither is the soul concerned about any loss, if it be not the loss of God. Everything can be taken from it : health, riches, honors, esteem, trust, the affection of the most cherished creatures, and these creatures themselves; but never could the soul endure that God should be taken from it, or that it should be prevented from loving Him. Thus have the saints thought and acted. In her immense desire to love God, St. Teresa Margaret Redi declared that she was ready to suffer even the pains of hell to obtain that grace; and to one who asked how she would be able to support such unspeakable torments she replied : " I think that love would render them bearable for me and perhaps even sweet, for of itself love makes all things else seem as naught " (T.M. *Sp*). That is also what St. Teresa of Jesus thought when she wrote to her daughters these beautiful lines : " Let your desire be to see God; your fear, that you may lose Him; your sorrow, that you are not having fruition of Him; your joy, that He can bring you to Himself " (*M*, 69). Such is the characteristic of true love : to create but one preoccupation in the soul, one fear, one desire, and one joy,—all of which are concentrated on God alone.

If you wish to see how far your love of esteem for God has reached, examine your conduct, and try to discover the ultimate motive of your preoccupations, fears, desires, and joys; if this motive is not God, but creatures, your own interests and satisfaction, you ought to acknowledge humbly that you have not yet succeeded in esteeming God above all things; for you weigh " in the balance against God that which...is at the greatest possible distance from God " (J.C. *AS I*, 5,4). Searching your heart more deeply, you will see that you frequently place on the same plane your will and the will of God, your tastes and His good pleasure, your interests and His glory, your convenience and His service. Furthermore, although in theory you protest that you esteem God above all things, in practice you very often give the preference not to His will, desires, and interests, but to your own, and that is why you fall into so many imperfections.

Be convinced that " where there is true love of God, there enters neither love of self nor that of the things of self" (J.C. *DN II*, 21,10).

COLLOQUY

" Most amiable Son of God, I confess to You my fault. I know not by what spirit I was led when I allowed my heart, created for You, to be ensnared by affection for creatures and sullied by the profane conversations of earth. I let myself be deceived, not by reality, but by the appearance of a love artfully represented, and I withdrew far from You and from the sweet law of Your true and only love. But now that Your light has drawn me out of my darkness, I renounce all worldly beauty and I choose You, Son of God and of the Blessed Virgin, that I may love You by a pact of eternal love.

"Without You, infinite Beauty and Goodness, no creature can possess true good, and outside of You my soul finds no satisfaction. For You have given it so great a capacity and such a hunger for the infinite, that it can neither will nor seek any other good than You. When I consider the earth, and all things, O Son of the Most High, they seem small and imperfect compared with You. If all the dignities of the world, all created beauties, all the comforts of life were given to me; if I had at my disposal all that is great, honorable, rich, and admirable in the world and could enjoy all these things together for all eternity, I would never change what I have chosen, but I would sing with ardent love : Your Face, O Lord, I seek and I shall seek it forever.

" Close my heart, Lord, that no human affection may enter there. Grant that I may not see, nor feel, nor taste, anything created, and may no creature attach itself to me, to the detriment of Your pure love. You alone, O my infinite Good, suffice to fill to the brim all my desires and to satisfy this hunger which tortures me; no other good, not even all other goods combined would be able to satisfy me; rather, after having tasted them all, I would be left dying with hunger, languishing in extreme abandonment, deprived of You " (Ven. John of Jesus Mary).

357

THE GRAIN OF MUSTARD SEED

TWENTY-FOURTH SUNDAY AFTER PENTECOST
SIXTH AFTER EPIPHANY

PRESENCE OF GOD - May Your kingdom come, O Lord, in the whole world and in my heart.

MEDITATION

1. The parable of the mustard seed emerges from the text of today's Mass; it is brief, but rich in meaning : " The kingdom of heaven is like to a grain of mustard seed which a man took and sowed in his field; which is the least indeed of all seeds, but when it is grown up, it is greater than all herbs and becometh a tree, so that the birds of the air come and dwell in the branches thereof" (Gosp : Mt 13,31-35). Nothing was smaller or more humble in its beginnings than " the kingdom of heaven, " the Church : Jesus, its Head and Founder, was born in a stable; He worked for the greater part of thirty years in a carpenter's shop, and for only three years unfolded His mission to a poor people, preaching a doctrine so simple that all, even the unlettered, could understand. When Jesus left the earth, the Church was established by an insignificant group of twelve men, gathered about a humble woman, Mary; but this first nucleus possessed so powerful a vitality that in a few years it spread into all the countries of the vast Roman Empire. The Church, from a very tiny seed, sown in the hearts of a Virgin Mother and of poor fishermen, became little by little through the centuries a gigantic tree, extending its branches into all regions of the

globe, with peoples of every tongue and nation taking shelter in its shade.

The Church is not merely a society of men, but of men who have for their Head, Jesus, the Son of God; the Church is the whole Christ, that is, Jesus and the faithful incorporated in Him and forming one Body with Him. The Church is the Mystical Body of Christ of which each of the baptized is a member. To love the Church is to love Jesus; to work for the extension of the Church is to work for the increase of the Mystical Body of Christ, so that the number of His members may be filled up and each may contribute to the splendor of the whole. All this is summarized and asked of the Father in the brief invocation : " *Adveniat regnum tuum.* "

Perhaps there is but little that we can do for the extension of the Church. Let us, at least, do that little; let us contribute our insignificant labor, as a veritable mustard seed, toward the growth of this wonderful tree, beneath whose shadow all men are called to find salvation and repose.

2. The parable of the mustard seed makes us consider not only the expansion of the kingdom of God in the world, but also its development in our hearts. Has not Jesus said : " The kingdom of God is within you " (*Lk* 17,21)? Yes, in us too this wonderful kingdom began as a tiny seed, a seed of grace : the sanctifying grace which, in a hidden and mysterious way, was sown in us by God at Baptism, and the actual grace of good inspirations and of the divine word—" *semen est verbum Dei* "—which Jesus the heavenly Sower, has scattered plentifully in our souls. This little seed has germinated slowly, it has sent down ever deeper roots, it has grown progressively, penetrating our whole spirit, until it has entirely conquered us for God, until we have felt the need of saying : Lord, all that I have, all that I am, is Yours; I give myself wholly to You. I want to be *Your kingdom.*

To be entirely the *kingdom of God*, so that He is the only Sovereign and Ruler of the heart, so that nothing exists in it which does not belong to Him or is not subject to His rule, is the ideal of a soul that loves God with perfect love. But how can we attain to the full development of this kingdom of God within us? The second parable which we read in today's Gospel tells us : " The kingdom of heaven is like to leaven which a woman took and hid in three measures of meal,

until the whole was leavened. " Here is another very beautiful image of the work grace must accomplish in our souls :
grace has been placed in us like leaven which little by little
must increase until it permeates our whole being and divi-
nizes it entirely. Grace, the divine leaven, has been given to
purify, elevate, and sanctify our entire being, with all its
powers and faculties; only when this work will have been
brought to completion, shall we be entirely the *kingdom of God*.

Let us reflect further on the great problem of our correspondence with grace. This divine seed, this supernatural
leaven, is within us; what can prevent it from becoming a
gigantic tree, capable of giving shelter to other souls; what
can impede the leaven from fermenting the whole mass, if we
remove all the obstacles opposed to its development, if we
respond to all its motions and requirements?

" *Adveniat regnum tuum!* " Yes, let us pray for the absolute
coming of the kingdom of God in our hearts.

COLLOQUY

" O Lord, my God, who created me to Your own image
and likeness, grant me this grace which You have shown
to be so great and necessary for salvation, that I may overcome
my very evil nature that is drawing me to sin and perdition.
For I feel in my flesh the law of sin contradicting the law
of my mind and leading me captive to serve sensuality in
many things. I cannot resist the passions if Your most holy
grace warmly infused into my heart does not assist me.....

" O Lord, without grace I can do nothing, but with its
strength I can do all things in You.

" O grace, truly heavenly, without which our merits are
nothing and no gifts of nature are to be esteemed! O most
blessed grace, which makes the poor in spirit rich in virtues,
which renders him who is rich in many good things humble
of heart, come descend upon me, fill me quickly with your
consolation lest my soul faint with weariness and dryness of
mind.

" Let me find grace in Your sight, I beg, Lord, for Your
grace is enough for me, even though I obtain none of the
things which nature desires. If I am tempted and afflicted
with many tribulations, I will fear no evils while Your grace
is with me. It is my strength. It gives me counsel and

help. It is more powerful than all my enemies and wiser than all the wise.

"Let Your grace, therefore, go before me and follow me, O Lord, and make me always intent upon good works, through Jesus Christ, Your Son" (*Imit. III*, 55).

358

COURAGEOUS AND IMPATIENT LOVE

PRESENCE OF GOD - May Your love, my God, make me intrepid in seeking You, and impatient to possess You.

MEDITATION

1. Although the soul subjected to interior purifications by the Holy Spirit is profoundly conscious of its own misery and unworthiness, it is nevertheless " sufficiently bold and daring to journey toward union with God " (J.C. *DN II*, 13,9). Whence comes such audacity? From the love which is ever growing within it; indeed, " the property of love is to desire to be united, joined, and made equal and like to the object of its love " *(ibid.)*. Therefore, the more love increases in the soul, the greater is the longing for union with God. Even if its love is still imperfect—since it has not yet brought the soul to union—nevertheless, it is sincere and thanks to " the strength set by love in the will, " the soul experiences " hunger and thirst for that which it lacks, which is the union " to which love tends *(ibid.)*. Besides, how could the soul which has grasped something of the infinite beauty and immense love of God not aspire to unite itself to Him? That same divine light which reveals to it the abyss of its own nothingness and that of creatures, enlightens it, by contrast, as to the infinite transcendence of God, so that the soul remains seized and captivated, while God Himself, in the measure that He purifies it, draws it to Himself by infusing new love in it.

Humbled by the knowledge of its own unworthiness, but emboldened by the love which is growing within, and by the invitation which God Himself addresses to it, drawing it secretly to Himself, the soul dares to aspire to this supreme good which is divine union.   It is humble in its audacious desire, because it knows that it does not merit such a gift; but it is also daring, because it feels that God Himself wills to give this union, and because its hunger and thirst for God are so great that it cannot live apart from Him. " Why should not the confiding soul venture toward the One whose noble image and glorious likeness it is conscious of bearing within itself? " exclaims St. Bernard.   God's love has gone before it, willing to render it like unto Himself by creation and by grace.   This divine resemblance, natural and supernatural, best expresses the desire of God to unite the soul to Himself and, at the same time, constitutes the basis of such union.   God, who has established this basis, certainly wills to bring His work to completion; and to do it He only waits for the soul to concur with His action, letting itself be purified, despoiled of self, and clothed completely with divine Life.

2. The soul, famished and athirst for God, seeks Him without respite, " for, being in darkness, it feels itself to be without Him and to be dying of love for Him " (J.C. *DN II*, 13,8).   Love makes the soul impatient to find the Lord, and it seeks Him with great solicitude, like Magdalen, who, after the death of Jesus, gave herself no peace, but, rising early, ran to the sepulcher, and finding the sacred Body no longer there, went in search of it, questioning all whom she met.   " I will rise and go about the city, " says the spouse in the Canticle, " in the streets and in the broad ways I will seek Him whom my soul loveth " (3,2).   This is the attitude of the soul who does not turn back or resign itself to being vanquished; indeed, it desires at any cost to find this God whom it loves more than its very self.   In this state, says St. John of the Cross, " the soul now walks so anxiously that it seeks the Beloved in all things.   In what-soever it thinks, it thinks at once of the Beloved.   Of whatsoever it speaks, in whatsoever matters present themselves, it is speaking and communing at once with the Beloved.   When it eats, when it sleeps, when it watches, when it does aught soever, all its care is about the Beloved " (*DN II*, 19,2).

Oh! if you, too, were so solicitous in seeking your God! From all eternity His love has gone before you; created to

His image and likeness, you, also, have been clothed with divine life, and God has invited you to divine union. Why then, do you go about the world, not in quest of God, but of yourself; anxious, not for His love, but for the love of creatures? Is there not, perhaps, more anxiety and solicitude in you for the wretched things of earth than for the things of heaven, than for God?

Oh! how much need you still have of detachment, of renunciation and purification! Do not resist the divine invitations; open your heart wide to the purifying action of the Holy Spirit; He alone can finally disengage you from all earthly cares and solicitude. If you are attentive and faithful to the inspirations of the divine Paraclete, He will send you new, more subtle and delicate ones which will incline you ever more and more to leave the vanities of earth, to seek and love God alone.

COLLOQUY

" O Lord, my life and my strength, one of the greatest of the divine mercies which You have bestowed upon me is that of deigning to invite a creature so sinful and ungrateful as I am to love Your Majesty. In Your presence the heavenly seraphim veil their faces, dazzled by the splendor of the divinity and the fire of Your love. I am honored by such liberality and at the same time impelled to love You in return for Your love and for the desire which You have to unite me to Your heart, that sweet refuge, to which I long to fly that I may find repose therein.

" Let others look after their affairs and worldly pretensions; as for me, I shall occupy myself with You alone and shall importune You to grant me Your love. I know not, nor can I ask anything but You alone : I love You and seek You; I shall love You and always seek Your Face, that I may be drawn and captivated by its divine beauty.

" Cast me not away from You, most amiable Lord! You, who have ever been most liberal and divinely merciful, even toward those who have not asked it of You, be not severe with me, who implore from the bottom of my heart the kindness and sweetness of Your love.

" May it please Your most tender Heart, O Son of the Most High, to accept me for Your service, to number me

among the servants of Your house, who suffer, labor, bear
the burden of the day, and desire no other recompense
than You Yourself.

"But my desire goes further still, for I aspire to unite
myself to You by an indissoluble bond. O Beauty full of
majesty which ravishes hearts with an infinite power, and
makes them like unto Yourself, realize this transformation
in me, I implore, so that I may no longer live in myself
but in You. May the most sweet law of Your grace and the
power of Your love direct all my thoughts, words, and works "
(Ven. John of Jesus Mary).

359

HUMBLE AND REVERENT LOVE

PRESENCE OF GOD - O God, who art so great, deign to lift up my
soul, so small and miserable, to Yourself.

MEDITATION

1. The love which audaciously urges the soul on to the
conquest of divine union is, at the same time, full of reverence
and respect, for the soul understands, much better than
before, how sublime and lofty is the majesty of God. If,
on the one hand, love makes it impatient to be united to
Him, on the other, the clear and continual consciousness
of its misery renders it more eager than ever to keep strict
watch over its conduct, so that nothing may be found in it
which could displease such great majesty.

"The soul," says the Mystical Doctor, "immediately
perceives in itself a genuine determination and an effective
desire to do naught which it understands to be an offense
to God, and to omit to do naught that seems to be for His
service. For that dark love cleaves to the soul, causing
it a most watchful care and inward solicitude concerning
that which it must do, or must not do, for His sake, in order
to please Him. It will consider and ask itself a thousand
times if it has given Him cause to be offended " (*DN II*, 16,14).

Evidently there is question here of something far exceeding mere flight from sin : it is the firm resolution to shun every imperfection, omission, or voluntary negligence; and since the soul knows from experience that, in spite of all its good will, many of these faults may escape it, either through inadvertence or through frailty, it desires to intensify its vigilance in order to avoid even these as far as is possible.

This solicitude proceeds from love and not from scruples, a truly loving anxiety, like that which made St. Teresa Margaret continually repeat : " What am I doing now, in this action? Am I loving my God? " *(Sp)*, or that which St. Angela of Foligno expressed in these burning words : " See, O Lord, if there is anything in me which is not love! "

If you would have a sure sign of your love of God, test the firmness of your resolution to fly from every least thing which might displease Him. This resolution must be so deeply rooted in your will that not only is it continually present to you—as are the things you really care for—but is also strong enough to withdraw you from every imperfection as soon as you become aware of it. This is absolutely indispensable, because, as St. John of the Cross teaches, " for the soul to come to unite itself perfectly with God through love and will...it must not intentionally and knowingly consent with the will to imperfections, and it must have power and liberty to be able not to consent intentionally " *(AS I*, 11,3).

2. Knowledge of its lowliness helps keep the soul humble in its love, driving away all presumption. Far from relying on its own merits and good works, it sees clearly that however much it might accomplish, it is as nothing in comparison with the exalted majesty of God. " Wherefore it considers itself useless in all that it does and thinks itself to be living in vain " (J.C. *DN II*, 19,3). The words of the Gospel : " We are unprofitable servants, " are for it a living actuality, and they express very well its habitual state. The light poured forth in the soul by the Holy Spirit is too great to let it fall into any illusion concerning its own worth, or to allow it to take complacency in its works. Even more, the soul " considers itself as being, most certainly, worse than all other souls : first, because love is continually teaching it how much is due to God; and secondly, because, as the works which

it here does for God are many and it knows them all to be faulty and imperfect, they all bring it confusion and affliction, for it realizes in how lowly a manner it is working for God, who is so high " *(ibid.)*. It is wonderful to see how this profound humility is not only the fruit of light but also of love : love makes the soul esteem God so highly that, while ardently desiring to possess Him, it is profoundly convinced of being absolutely incapable of reaching Him. On the other hand, although humble and reverent, love maintains its characteristic audacity and the soul does not cease to aspire to divine union. Precisely in this spirit St. Thérèse of the Child Jesus wrote : " Notwithstanding my littleness, I dare to gaze upon the divine Sun of love " *(St,* 13). The Saint, who in all simplicity compared herself to a downy little bird, incapable of taking its flight, well understood that of herself she could never soar so high; nevertheless, she did not lose her confidence. If she could not count on her own strength, she knew that she could rely upon the love of Jesus, the divine Word, who became incarnate precisely to come and seek us, poor sinners that we are, who willed " to suffer and to die, in order to bear away each single soul and plunge it into the very heart of the Blessed Trinity, Love's eternal home " *(ibid.)*. St. Thérèse had the certitude that one day Jesus would be touched by her weakness, and would swoop down to make her the " prey " of His love : " I am filled with the hope that one day Thou wilt swoop down upon me, and bearing me away to the source of all Love, wilt plunge me at last into its glowing abyss " *(ibid.)*.

Yes, Jesus is ready to meet all souls of good will, to come to your soul and raise it to the much desired union, but He would have you know how to await Him with fidelity, fully and generously devoted to His service.

COLLOQUY

" O eternal Word! O my Savior! Thou art the divine Eagle whom I love and who allurest me. Thou who, descending to this land of exile, didst will to suffer and to die, in order to bear away each single soul and plunge it into the very heart of the Blessed Trinity—Love's eternal home! Thou who, returning to Thy realm of light, dost still remain hidden here in our vale of tears under the semblance of the white Host.... O eternal Eagle, it is Thy wish to nourish me with Thy divine substance, a poor little being who would fall into nothingness if Thy divine glance did not give me life at every moment....

"Forgive me, O Jesus, if I tell Thee that Thy love reacheth even unto folly, and at the sight of such folly, what wilt Thou but that my heart should leap up to Thee? How could my trust know any bounds?

"I know well that for Thy sake the saints have made themselves foolish—being "eagles" they have done great things. Too little for such mighty deeds, my folly lies in the hope that Thy love wilt accept me as a victim....

"O my divine Eagle! As long as Thou willest, I shall remain with my gaze fixed upon Thee, for I long to be fascinated by Thy divine eyes, I long to become Love's prey. I am filled with the hope that one day Thou wilt swoop down upon me, and bearing me away to the source of Love, wilt plunge me at last into its glowing abyss, that I may become forever its happy victim " (T.C.J. *St*, 13).

360

STRONG AND ACTIVE LOVE

PRESENCE OF GOD - Lord, grant that my love for You may not be content with words, but prove itself in generous deeds.

MEDITATION

1. "Love is never idle" (T.J. *Int C V*, 4). When true love of God enters the soul it gradually begets in it an interior dynamism so strong and forceful that it spurs it on to seek ever new ways of pleasing the Beloved, and makes it diligent in devising fresh means of proving its fidelity to Him. Love, in fact, is not nourished by sweet sentiments or fantasies, but by works. "This love," says St. Teresa, "is also like a great fire which has always to be fed lest it should go out. Just so with these souls [in which God Himself kindles the

flame of charity]; cost them what it might, they would always want to be bringing wood, so that this fire should not die " (*Life*, 30). The soul that truly loves does not stop to examine whether a task is easy or difficult, agreeable or repugnant, but undertakes everything in order to maintain its love. It even chooses by preference tasks which demand more sacrifice, for it knows that love is never truer than when it urges the sacrifice of self for the One loved. Hence, through love, " there is caused in the soul a habitual suffering because of the Beloved, yet without weariness. For, as St. Augustine says, ' Love makes all things that are great, grievous, and burdensome to be almost naught. ' The spirit here has so much strength that it has subjected the flesh and takes as little account of it as does the tree of one of its leaves. In no way does the soul here seek its own consolation or pleasure, either in God, or in aught else " (J.C. *DN II*, 19,4).

This explains the attitude of the saints, who not only embraced wholeheartedly the sufferings with which God strewed their paths, but sought them with jealous care, as the miser seeks gold. St. John of the Cross replied to Our Lord, who had asked him what recompense he desired for the great services he had rendered Him : " To suffer and to be despised for Your love. " And St. Teresa of Jesus, seeing her earthly exile prolonged, found in suffering embraced for God the only means of appeasing her heart, athirst for eternal love; and she entreated : " To die, Lord, or to suffer! I ask nothing else of Thee for myself but this " (*Life*, 40).

In heaven we shall have no further need of suffering to prove our love, because then we shall love in the unfailing clarity of the beatific vision. But here below, where we love in the obscurity of faith, we need to prove to God the reality of our love.

2. " If our love is perfect, it has this quality of leading us to forget our own pleasure in order to please Him whom we love "; it has the power to make us accept our trials with joy " and take the bitter with the sweet, knowing that to be His Majesty's will " (T.J. *F*, 5). Evidently, a love like this cannot be the fruit of our own human nature, which has such repugnance for suffering; it cannot be acquired, for it greatly surpasses the capacity of our nature, so poor

and weak. God alone can infuse it little by little into souls who allow Him to guide them by the narrow way of interior purification. Yes, in aridity, in solitude of heart, in the privation of all light and consolation, the Holy Spirit enkindles in them this flame of charity, a flame which invades them increasingly as it finds them well disposed, that is, purified of everything contrary to love. When all resistances have been overcome, all dross eliminated, the flame of love will blaze up irresistibly and give to the soul the strength of a giant. The flame of love, St. John of the Cross explains, " causes [the soul] to go forth from itself, and be wholly renewed and enter upon another mode of being " (SC, 1,7). While formerly the soul feared and fled suffering, now it embraces it courageously.

The soul strongest in suffering is also the strongest in love. No creature in the world loved, nor will love God more than the most Blessed Virgin Mary, and none was, nor ever will be, stronger than she in suffering. See her at the foot of the Cross : she is a Mother, and she voluntarily assists at the terrible agony of her Son; she sees the nails being driven into His Flesh; she hears the heavy blows of the hammer; she beholds His Head crowned with thorns, vainly seeking a little repose on the hard wood of the Cross; she sees the Cross raised and her Son hanging on it, suspended between heaven and earth, disfigured by suffering, without the least consolation. Mary's heart was pierced; nevertheless, she repeated her *fiat* with the same fullness of consent with which she had pronounced it at the joyous annunciation of her maternity. In her love, she found courage to offer her well-beloved Son for the salvation of His executioners. What mother could rival Our Lady in strength? Yet her sacrifice immeasurably surpassed that of any other mother because only she could say : The Son whom I immolate is my God.

Let us learn the secret of strong love at the foot of the Cross beside Mary, Queen of Martyrs, through love and suffering.

COLLOQUY

" He who truly loves You, Lord, has only one ambition, that of pleasing You. He dies with desire to be loved by You, and so will give his life to learn how he may please You better. Can such love remain hidden? No, my God, that is impossible! There are degrees of love, for love shows itself in proportion to its strength. If it is weak, it shows itself but little. If it is strong, it shows itself a great deal. But love always makes itself known, whether weak or strong, provided it is real love.

" O Lord, grant that my love be not the fruit of my imagination but be proved by works. What can I do for You, who died for us and created us and gave us being, without counting myself fortunate in being able to repay You something of what I owe You?

" May it be Your pleasure, O Lord, that the day may finally come in which I shall be able to pay You at least something of all I owe You. Cost what it may, Lord, permit me not to come into Your presence with empty hands, since the reward must be in accordance with my works. Well do I know, my Lord, of how little I am capable. But I shall be able to do all things provided You do not withdraw from me.

" It is not You that are to blame, my Lord, if those who love You do no great deeds; it is our weak-mindedness and cowardice. It is because we never make firm resolutions but are filled with a thousand fears and scruples arising from human prudence, that You, my God, do not work Your marvels and wonders. Who loves more than You to give, if You have anyone that will receive; or to accept services performed at our own cost? May Your Majesty grant me to have rendered You some service and to care about nothing save returning to You some part of all I have received " (T.J. *Way*, 40 – *Int C III*, 1 – *Life*, 21 – *F*, 2).

361

UNITIVE LOVE

PRESENCE OF GOD - My God, You have infused love into my soul. Grant that it may increase until it brings me to union with You.

MEDITATION

1. " God continues to do and to work in the soul by means of this night, illumining and enkindling it divinely with yearnings for God alone and for naught else whatever " (J.C. *DN II*, 13,11). In proportion as it detaches itself from earth, leaving aside all affection and desire for creatures, the soul climbs " the secret ladder " of love which raises it step by step even unto its Creator, " for it is love alone that unites and joins the soul to God " (*ibid.*, 18,5).

This enkindling of love is not perceived in the beginning of the purification, because then " this divine fire is used in drying up and making ready the wood (which is the soul), rather than in giving it heat. But, as time goes on, the fire begins to give heat to the soul, and the soul then very commonly feels this enkindling and heat of love " (*ibid.*, 12,5). The flames of love can produce great spiritual delight; there are moments of unspeakable joy in which the soul receives a foretaste of its approaching union with God, a joy which compensates fully for all the pain and anguish suffered in the obscurity of the night, and one which encourages it to accept wholeheartedly whatever it must still undergo to attain perfect union with God. Nevertheless, it is well to remember that the enkindling of love does not consist in the joy the soul may experience, but rather in the firm determination of the will to give itself entirely to God. Moreover, " this is wrought by the Lord, who infuses as He wills, " that is, who can infuse love, either " leaving the will in aridity " (*ibid.*, 12,7) or inflaming it with sweet ardor.

Be that as it may, what matters is not the enjoyment of love, but our rapid advancement in it, for love is the only power that can unite us to God. St. John of the Cross, developing this topic, states precisely : " It is to be observed, then, that love is the inclination of the soul and the strength and power which it has to go to God...and thus, the more degrees of love the soul has, the more profoundly does it enter into God and the more is it centered in Him " (*LF*, 1,13). As a stone in its fall is drawn toward the center of the earth by gravity, so the soul is drawn to God by the power of love. The stronger the love, the more powerfully will the soul be drawn to God and entirely united to Him : " the strongest love is the most unitive love " *(ibid.).* How, then, could a soul that sincerely desires union with God fail to exert all its efforts to grow in love?

2. A degree of imperfect love bears a corresponding degree of imperfect union, whereas perfect union corresponds to perfect love. " For the soul to be in its center, which is God, it suffices for it to have one degree of love, since with one degree alone it may be united with Him through grace. If it have two degrees of love, it will be united and have entered into another and a more interior center with God, and so forth " *(ibid.).* We may compare these degrees of union to a stone which by its weight is drawn to the center of the earth ; the heavier it is and the less impeded by obstacles, the more rapidly will it reach the center, and even the deepest part of it. Love is the weight which draws us into God, and, conversely, love draws God into our souls, for Jesus has said : " If anyone love Me, he will keep My word...and We will come to him and will make Our abode with him " (*Jn* 14,23). A single degree of love, shown by the observance of the divine law, guarantees that we are in the state of grace and that God is present in the soul, making His abode there; consequently, we can live united to Him. But it is evident that a very imperfect union with God corresponds to this first degree of love and grace. In this state the soul is already in its center, that is, in God, and it already lives united to Him who deigns to dwell in it by grace; however, it still has a long way to go before reaching its deepest center, before penetrating into the depths of God and living intimately with Him, perfectly united to Him. The stages of this road are marked by progress in love; the more the soul loves, the more it immerses itself in God; and, on the other hand, God Himself, making good His promise, becomes ever more present to it by grace, inviting it to an increasingly more intimate friendship and union.

Finally, the day comes when "if it attain to the last degree [of love], the love of God will succeed in wounding the soul even in its remotest and deepest center—that is, in transforming and enlightening it as regards all its being and power and virtue such as it is capable of receiving, until it be brought into such a state that it appears to be God" (J.C. *LF*, 1,13).

Love accomplishes the great miracle; it draws God into the soul that loves Him and immerses the soul in Him; by means of love, a miserable creature comes to the embrace of its Creator and is united to Him so intimately and perfectly that it abides there entirely transformed and divinized. Could God have granted us a greater gift than that of creating us in love and filling us with love, the great power capable of uniting us to Himself?

COLLOQUY

"O most loved King of peace, desired by all generous hearts in heaven and upon earth, who ask me with infinite sweetness to love You with all my heart, my mind, and my strength; despise not my sighs and yearnings.

"Beloved King, You came into the world to reign in the hearts of men by Your sweet law of charity, grant that I may love You with all my heart, and all the strength of my mind. Grant, most amiable Lord, that I may live no longer in myself but in You, who are my life; transform me into Yourself by love's activity. Communicate to me that sweet fire which burns in Your Heart and grant that in all things I may seek You alone, You who are the true peace and center of my soul. I await but one thing from You : kindle Your eternal fire within me and let it beget in my heart such great desire for You that I may seek You always, night and day; let this longing constrain me to use everything, to seize every occasion, to find ever new ways of pleasing You and of inducing all creatures to serve You, to love You, and to unite themselves to You by the bond of charity.

"Come within me, O sweet Spouse of my soul, O ardent Heart, desirous of my own. Enter Your dwelling as absolute Lord, and govern there irresistibly by the power of Your omnipotent love. This very day I wish to be drawn to You,

O generous Son of God; let my soul be transformed in Yours, and, after that, You will be my soul, my life, the one comfort of my afflicted heart, and my only consolation " (Ven. John of Jesus Mary).

362

UNION OF WILL

PRESENCE OF GOD - O Lord, take my entire will and transform it into Your own.

MEDITATION

1. The first and most important result of the unitive power of love is the perfect union of man's will with the will of God. As love develops, it so empties the soul of everything opposed to the divine will, so impels it to love and desire only that which God Himself loves and desires, that little by little, the weak human will becomes fully conformed and united to the divine will of God; the two wills are made into one, " namely, into the will of God, which...is likewise the will of the soul " (J.C. *AS I*, 11,3). In all its deliberate actions, the soul is no longer guided by its personal will, so frail and inconstant; it is directed and moved solely by the will of God, wherein its own has been lost, lost through love. " He that shall lose his life for My sake shall find it, " Jesus declared (*Mt* 16,25). Captivated by love for God, the soul has, for His sake, entirely renounced its own will; it has voluntarily lost in Him all desire, all inclination; and now, the loss has become the greatest of all gains, because the soul finds its will, now entirely transformed in the divine will of God. Could one hope for a more advantageous exchange? St. John of the Cross writes : " The state of this divine union consists in the soul's *total* transformation, according to the will, in the will of God" (*AS I*, 11,2). This transformation is total, and not merely in part, nor is it merely in things of greater importance, but even in very

small, minute things, so that the divine will truly becomes the unique motive force of the soul : whatever it does, says and thinks is " in all and through all . . . the will of God alone " *(ibid.).* A sublime state, which lifts a creature to the heights of the Creator, which takes it from the level of human life to that of the divine! To achieve this it was worthwhile for the soul to have undergone the bitter purification by which it was " stripped and denuded of its former skin " (J.C. *DN II,* 13,11), that is, of its own imperfect will; it was worthwhile to have renounced itself and everything created!

2. Speaking of perfect union with the will of God, St. Teresa of Jesus writes : " This is the union which I have desired all my life; it is for this that I continually beg Our Lord; it is this which is the most genuine and the safest " *(Int C V,* 3). The Saint, who had experienced the efficacy and sweetness of the mystical graces of union, wherein the soul " cannot possibly doubt that God has been in it and it has been in God " *(ibid.,* 1), does not hesitate to prefer to such delights perfect union with the will of God. Actually, the essence of sanctity consists solely in this union, whereas mystical graces are only a means toward its attainment, a very precious means, because a more rapid one, but always a means and not an end. The end consists solely in perfect conformity of one's own will with the will of God. Besides, it does not depend upon us to choose the " shortcut " of mystical graces, rather than to follow the ordinary way of generous and persevering effort. The choice depends upon God alone, who is Master of His gifts and " gives when He wills, and as He wills, and to whom He wills . . . and this is doing no injury to anyone " *(ibid. IV,* 1).

What is of the greatest importance is to know that union with God is not reserved for a small number of privileged souls; God calls every soul of good will to union with Himself, regardless of the way by which He chooses to lead it. Hence, the ordinary way, " the little way, " as St. Thérèse of the Child Jesus called it, or the " carriage road, " according to St. Maria Bertilla, leads just as surely to divine union. Instead of preoccupying ourselves about *the way,* let us rather concern ourselves with striving to be completely generous, for only souls who give themselves wholly to God reach union with Him. " But observe, my daughters, " writes St. Teresa of Avila, " that if you are to gain this [union with God], He would have you keep back nothing; whether it be little or much, He will have it all for Himself, and according to what you yourself have given to Him, the favors He will grant you will be small or great " (*ibid. V,* 1). The more generous our gift, the more God will anticipate us with His grace and sustain us by His omnipotent action. The ordinary way, though more hidden and less consoling than the way of mystical favors, is no less genuine or efficacious. Whether God chooses to lead us by one way or by the other, we shall never lack the necessary divine help to attain to union with Him.

COLLOQUY

" Lord, what power this gift has! If it be made with due resolution, it cannot fail to draw You, the Almighty, to become one with our lowliness and to transform us into Yourself and to effect a union between the Creator and the creature.

" The more resolute we are in soul and the more we show You by our actions that the words we use to You are not words of mere politeness, the more and more do You draw us to Yourself and raise us above all petty earthly things, and above ourselves, in order to prepare us to receive great favors from You, for Your rewards for our service will not end with this life. So much do You value this service of ours that we do not know for what more we can ask, while You never weary of giving.

" Not content with having made this soul one with Yourself, through uniting it to Yourself, You begin to cherish it, to reveal secrets to it, to rejoice in its understanding of what it has gained and in the knowledge which it has of all You have yet to give it. You begin to make such a friend of the soul that not only do You restore its will to it, but You give it Your own also. For now that You are making a friend of it, You are glad to allow it to rule with You. So You do what the soul asks of You, just as the soul does what You command, only in a much better way, since You are all-powerful and can do whatever You desire, and Your desire never comes to an end.

" O my God, how precious is the union which the soul attains with You, after having established itself in submission to Your will. Oh, how much to be desired is this union, in which we resign our wills to the will of God! Happy the soul that has attained to it, for it will live peacefully both in this life, and in the next, for, apart from the peril of losing You, O Lord, or of seeing You offended, there is nothing that could afflict it, neither sickness nor poverty nor even death, for this soul sees clearly that You know what You are doing better than it knows itself what it desires! " (T.J. *Way*, 32 – *Int C V*, 3).

363

DIVINE ASSISTANCE

PRESENCE OF GOD - O Lord, You anticipate, accompany, and sustain me with Your grace. Grant that it may not remain sterile.

1. " If a soul is seeking God, its Beloved is seeking it much more; and, if it sends after Him its loving desires...He likewise sends after it the fragrance of His ointments, wherewith He attracts the soul and causes it to run after Him " (J.C. *LF*, 3,28). The soul is never alone in its efforts to attain union : God goes to meet it, giving it His helping hand and drawing it to Himself by means of the holy inspirations which enlighten its mind, and the interior touches which inflame its will. These inspirations and divine touches are none other than the actuation of the gifts of the Holy Spirit, by which God directs the soul and works within it, first to purify and dispose it for union, and then to unite it effectively to Himself by love. It is most consoling to consider that this wealth of divine help enters into the normal course of the development of the life of grace, and hence is encountered even in the ordinary way of holiness. This is the heritage which God has prepared for every soul, provided it is generous in giving itself to Him.

With St. John of the Cross we must conclude that if souls which actually reach perfect union are so few, "it is not because God is pleased that there should be few raised to this high spiritual state, " or that He is sparing of His help;

" it is rather that He finds few vessels which can bear so high and lofty a work " (*LF* 2,27).

If after many years of the spiritual life we find ourselves still far from union with God, we cannot attribute this to the insufficiency of divine help; rather, we should blame our own lack of generosity and fidelity to grace. St. Teresa emphatically declares : " True union can quite well be achieved with the favor of Our Lord, if we endeavor to attain to it by not following our own will but by submitting our will to whatever is the will of God. " And, while recognizing that one does not attain this except by painful labor, she assures us, " You must not doubt the possibility of this true union with the will of God " (*Int C V*, 3).

2. " We do not require extraordinary favors from the Lord before we can achieve this [union]. He has given us all we need in giving us His Son to show us the way " *(ibid.)*. Jesus suffices for us! He has not only shown us the way to divine union, but has likewise procured for us the means of obtaining it.

Jesus washes and purifies our souls in His Blood; He nourishes them with His Flesh, instructs them by His doctrine; every day, and many times a day, He renews His sacrifice upon the altar on our behalf; Jesus, glorious at the right hand of the Father, is always interceding for us, obtaining grace and dispensing it to us according to our need. Jesus sends us the Holy Spirit, *His* Spirit, that He may guide us on the road to sanctity. Jesus gives us His Mother, the most Holy Virgin Mary, that she may be our Mother, our refuge, our support in time of trial. What more could we desire? Should we consider these graces less precious because they form part of the " ordinary " graces accorded to all souls? Oh! if we were truly convinced of the great efficacy of these means of sanctification, we would not seek others; instead of waiting for some extraordinary favors in order to give ourselves wholly to God, we would work at corresponding with great fidelity to the grace which He offers each day with wonderful largesse, and thus we would surely achieve our end.

" Let us beg the Lord, " St. Teresa exhorts us, " that, since to some extent it is possible for us to enjoy heaven upon earth, He will grant us His help so that it will not be our own fault if we miss anything " (*ibid. V*, 1). The heaven which we can enjoy here below is precisely the state of union with God in which the soul, perfectly conformed to the divine will, enjoys great peace, even amid the inevitable sorrows of life, because it abandons itself always into the hands of divine Providence. We can all reach this happy state, provided we are determined to follow the way which Jesus Himself has marked out for us : " If anyone love Me he will keep My word.... You are My friends if you do the things that I command you " (*Jn* 14,23 – 15,14). It is the way that Jesus Himself travelled, desiring no other food than the Father's will and doing always the things that pleased Him. Let us follow Jesus, entrusting ourselves to His guidance, and He, who is the way, the truth and the life, will lead us to the union we so desire.

COLLOQUY

" O Jesus, in those words by which You told us that Your food was to do the Father's will, You have shown us that Your will was His, and His will was Yours, and, having but one will with Him, You have declared to us that You are equal to the Father, and one with Him. Further, You have taught us how we, too, can become by grace, in a certain manner, equal to God and one with Him. We can do this by accomplishing His will, which should be the rule and pole toward which our will, like a magnetized needle, ceaselessly tends; and when we deviate, be it ever so slightly, from the divine will, we will lose this equality and union.

" O Lord, deign to unite me entirely to Yourself as a bride. Take from me my will and all my desires, so that I may neither will nor desire anything except what You will. Make my will so conformed and united to Yours that I may no longer will anything of myself, being preoccupied neither with living nor dying, but only willing what You will.

" My God, when I shall have offered You my will in all and for all, You will return it to me, for, when it is no longer mine, but I shall have given it entirely to You, then You will be content that I follow it in all things, since it will not be mine but Yours " (cf. St. Mary Magdalen dei Pazzi).

" Receive, O Lord, all my liberty; take my memory, my understanding and my will. All that I am and have,

You have given to me.   I give it all back to You to dispose
of according to Your will.   Give me Your love and Your
grace.   With these I am rich enough and have nothing
more to desire " (St. Ignatius Loyola).

364

THE END OF THE WORLD

LAST SUNDAY AFTER PENTECOST

PRESENCE OF GOD - My God, in the evening of life You will judge
me according to my love.   Help me to grow in love each day.

MEDITATION

1. The Mass for today, the last Sunday of the liturgical
year, is a prayer of thanksgiving for the year that is ending,
and one of propitiation for that which is about to begin;
it is a reminder that the present life is fleeting, and an
invitation to keep ourselves in readiness for the final step
which will usher us into eternity.

In the Epistle (*Col* 1,9-14), St. Paul prays and gives
thanks in the name of all Christians : " We...cease not to
pray for you and to beg that you may be filled with the
knowledge of His will...that you may walk worthy of God,
in all things pleasing; being fruitful in every good work. "
This is a beautiful synthesis of the task which the interior
soul has endeavored to accomplish during the whole year :
to adapt and conform itself to God's holy will, to unite
itself to it completely, and, being moved in all things by
that divine will alone, to act in such a manner as to please
Our Lord in everything.   God be praised if, thanks to His
help, we have succeeded in advancing some steps along that
road which most surely leads to holiness.   Making our own
the sentiments of the Apostle, we should give thanks to " the
Father who hath made us worthy to be partakers of the lot
of the saints in light. "   The lot, the inheritance of the saints,
of those who tend toward holiness, is union of love with

God—here below in faith, hereafter in glory. This heritage is ours because Jesus has merited it for us by His Blood, and because in Jesus " we have redemption, the remission of sins "; thus, cleansed from sin and clothed in grace by His infinite merits, we also can ascend to that very lofty and blessed state of union with God.

If, with God's help, we have succeeded in making some progress, there still remains more and greater work to be done. The Church, therefore, has us ask in the Collect : " Stir up, we beseech Thee, O Lord, the wills of Thy faithful people, that by more earnestly seeking the fruit of good works, they may receive more abundantly the gifts of Thy loving kindness. " So it is : the more we correspond to grace, the greater the graces Our Lord will grant us; the more we press on toward Him, the more He will draw us to Himself, so that the result of this continuous interplay of the divine assistance and our correspondence will be the sanctification of each one of us.

2. With the description of the end of the world and the coming of Christ to judge the living and the dead, the Gospel (*Mt* 24,15-35) reminds us that just as the liturgical year passes and comes to an end, so does the life of man on earth. Everything will have an end, and, at the end of all, will come the majestic epilogue : " Then shall appear the sign of the Son of Man in heaven [the Cross] : and then shall all tribes of the earth mourn; and they shall see the Son of Man coming in the clouds of heaven with much power and majesty. " Jesus who once came upon earth in poverty, hiddenness and pain, to teach us the way to heaven and to redeem our souls, has every right to return glorious at the end of time, to gather the fruit of His labor and His Blood. He will be our judge, and will judge us, as He Himself has said, according to our love : " Come, ye blessed of My Father, possess the kingdom prepared for you.... For I was hungry and you gave Me to eat...thirsty and you gave Me to drink.... As long as you did it to one of these My least brethren, you did it to Me " (*Mt* 25,34.35.40). His sweet precept of love, love of God and of neighbor, will be the law by which we shall be examined. Blessed shall we be if we have loved, and loved much! " Many sins are forgiven her, because she hath loved much " (*Lk* 7,47), Jesus said, referring to the sinful woman. The greater and deeper our

love, the more effectively will it efface all the sins, miseries, and faults into which, despite our good will, we fall daily.

" For this reason it is a great thing, " says St. John of the Cross, " for the soul to exercise itself constantly in love, so that, being perfected here below, it may not stay long, either in this world or in the next, without seeing God face to face " (*LF*, 1,34). The Saint is alluding to a soul inflamed with divine love and longing anxiously for heaven in order to see its God face to face and be able to love Him more. Only an intense exercise of love, however, can of itself lead to union with God, both here on earth and in a blessed eternity. Happy the soul who, at the end of life, after having exercised itself much in love, can be immediately admitted to the beatifying union of heaven. Then it will have nothing to fear from the judgment of Jesus, for this judgment will be its eternal joy and happiness.

COLLOQUY

" Deign, O Lord, to grant me the experience of true love before You take me from this life, for it will be a great thing at the hour of my death to realize that I shall be judged by One whom I have loved above all things. I shall be able to meet You with security, certain that I shall not be going into a foreign land, but into my own country, for it belongs to the One whom I have loved so truly and who has loved me in return.

" How sweet will be the death of that soul who has done penance for all its sins and does not have to go to purgatory! It may be that it will begin to enjoy glory even in this world, and will know no fear, but only peace! " (T.J. *Way*, 40).

" To You, O Lord our God, we must always cling, that with Your continual help we may live in all holiness, godliness and uprightness. The weight of our weakness drags us down : but by Your grace, may we be enkindled and raised on high, may we be inflamed so as to climb from the depths, arranging in our hearts to ascend by steps. Let us, then, sing the song of ' ascents, ' burning with Your holy fire and journeying on toward You.

" Where are we going? On high, to the peace of the heavenly Jerusalem, as it is written : ' I rejoiced at the things that were said to me : we shall go into the house of the Lord. ' There, good will shall be so ordered in us that we shall have no other desire than to remain there eternally. So long as we live in this mortal body we are journeying toward You, O Lord; here below we have no lasting dwelling place, but seek one which is to come, since our home is in heaven. Therefore, with the help of Your grace, I enter into the secrecy of my heart, and lift up songs of love to You, to You, my King and my God! " (St. Augustine).

365

THE " YES " OF PERFECT CONSENT

PRESENCE OF GOD - Lord, grant that I may give You the free and full consent of my will.

MEDITATION

1. St. John of the Cross very aptly says that the characteristic of union of wills is the *yes* of the soul's " free consent " (*LF* 3,24) by which it gives itself entirely to God, surrendering itself completely to Him by the full and total gift of its will. In other words, the soul is henceforth so determined not to will anything but God and His good pleasure, that in every circumstance it only repeats its *yes*, by accepting with love all that He wills and does for it. This *yes* is effective, and not simply a desire; it is a *yes* by which the soul truly gives itself with all the generosity of which it is capable.

From the beginning of the spiritual life, the fervent soul should desire to give itself to God without reserve, always saying *yes* to Him. But in practice, being still hampered by the bonds of passions and attachment to creatures, it often happens that the soul's gift is not a complete one. Frequently, in the concrete instances of life, when faced with the bitterness of renunciation and interior conflict, its ideal *yes* is changed into a virtual *no*. In the state of union, however, this is no longer true. Here the soul is so surrendered to the holy will of God that it does not take back anything of its gift; its *yes* is so definitive and efficacious that it offers and unites the soul to God as a bride to her Bridegroom; that is why the mystics call this state " spiritual espousals. "

It is important to realize, that, on the part of the soul, the intensity of its union with God depends on the perfection of its *yes*; it should be a consent that is perfect in breadth and in depth : in breadth, because it should extend not only to what God commands, but even to all that He desires, to all that would give Him greater pleasure. Love must keep the soul so vigilant and attentive that it can discern in various circumstances what pleases God most, and this same love should make the soul generous enough to accomplish all without the least hesitation. The *yes* must be equally perfect in depth, because the soul should adhere to the divine good pleasure, not with negligence, niggardliness, nor even with the slightest bad grace, but with all the ardor of its will, happy to be able to give itself to God, whatever sacrifice this might entail.

2. The soul must apply itself to saying its *yes* perfectly, especially in the sense that Jesus has indicated to us in His great commandment of charity, which is the foundation, not only of the whole law, but of all sanctity. St. Teresa of Avila says expressly : " Here the Lord asks only two things of us : love for His Majesty and love for our neighbor. It is for these two virtues that we must strive, and if we attain them perfectly, we are doing His will, and so shall be united with Him " (*Int C V*, 3). But the attention of the Saint is immediately turned to charity toward our neighbor, because she sees in it the surest sign of the love of God, and also because she knows that this is a very vulnerable point. It is not uncommon that, after having said *yes* to Our Lord in the face of sacrifice, renunciation, or works of greater importance, some *no* is permitted to escape in connection with fraternal charity. Speaking of certain faults which insinuate themselves very secretly into the soul, and hinder it from attaining union, St. Teresa singles out, besides self-love and self-esteem, " criticism of our neighbors (even if only in small things), lack of charity toward them, and failure to love them as we love ourselves " (*ibid.*). As long as we find in ourselves

failings of this kind, however slight, it is a sign that **our** gift to God is not complete, that our *yes* is not perfect. God wants us to love our neighbor, whoever he may be, and to love him perfectly : " This is My commandment, " Jesus said, " that you love one another, as I have loved you " (*Jn* 15,12). How can we be united to the will of God, if we do not fulfill this commandment with great diligence?

" I tell you, " warns St. Teresa, " that doing what I have said [that is, practicing fraternal charity with perfection], you will not fail to obtain this union, but, if you find that you are lacking in this virtue [of fraternal charity], you should be persuaded that you will never reach it, although you may have devotion and consolation so that you think that you have attained it. " And she concludes with this beautiful assertion : " So dearly does His Majesty love us that He will reward our love for our neighbor by increasing the love we bear to Himself, and that in a thousand ways : this I cannot doubt " (*Int C V,* 3).

COLLOQUY

" O infinite God, I wish to offer and consecrate myself unceasingly to You on the altar of my heart. First of all, I offer You my soul, Your spouse, ransomed with Your precious Blood. I offer it as a place of repose for Your Majesty, that it may be transformed in You, no longer living of itself, but only with Your life.

" O divine Wisdom, I offer You my intellect avid for knowledge, that You may quench its thirst by enabling it to comprehend Your grandeurs! Enlighten my darkness, and let me taste You in that very sweet knowledge which inflames my heart with love.

" Next, O most beautiful Spouse of my soul, I offer You my will which seeks You above all else, to love You with an eternal ardor, and be united to You forever. Deign, O Lord, that my will may detach itself from all creatures and, soaring aloft, elevate itself to You; then, in the slumber of pure love, let it repose in the cavern of Your Heart. O delightful cavern, when shall I hide within You, and hear the pulsations of that Heart which gives me life and salvation?

" But why, O my God, do I offer You my soul with its faculties, when I am already all Yours by creation and, even more, by Redemption?   Is there some advantage for You, O most lovable Life, in this gift and offering which I would make to Your majesty and greatness?   No, certainly it is not for Your interest, but for mine, O immortal Life, that I offer and give myself to You, since I know with certainty that my happiness consists in uniting myself to You " (Ven. John of Jesus Mary).

366

THE RECIPROCAL GIFT

PRESENCE OF GOD - May I be all Yours, Lord, and You all mine.

MEDITATION

1. " God does not give Himself wholly to us until He sees that we are giving ourselves wholly to Him " (T.J. *Way*, 28). God respects man's liberty so much that, although desiring to have him share in His divine Life, He actually communicates Himself only in the measure of our consent; when this consent is total, He does not hesitate to give Himself wholly.   God responds to the perfect *yes* of the soul with the " true and entire *yes* of His grace " (cf. J.C. *LF*, 3,24). To the perfect gift of the will on the part of the soul corresponds the full communication of grace on the part of God; grace is granted in all its perfection, accompanied by the wealth of the infused virtues and the gifts of the Holy Spirit.   Grace and love necessarily go together, and as perfect adherence to the will of God is the sign of perfect love, it follows that God gives the superabundance of grace to the soul which is completely conformed to His divine will.

St. John of the Cross explains this lofty state yet more fully : " When the will of God and the will of the soul are as one in a free consent of their own, then the soul has attained to the possession of God through grace of will, insofar as can be, by means of will and grace; and this signifies that God has corresponded to the *yes* of the soul with the true and entire *yes* of His grace " *(ibid.)*. The soul has given itself entirely to God, and now it receives its reward : God gives Himself to it. The soul, says the Saint, possesses God " through grace of will, " that is, by reason of the perfect communication of grace, which is God's response to the total gift of the will. By this perfect communication, God gives Himself to the soul, allowing it to participate more and more in His supernatural Being and divine Life, and dwelling in it in a manner ever more intimate and profound.

This is the triumph of grace in the soul. That grace, which was communicated to it in germ at Baptism, and which has increased little by little in the course of the various stages of the spiritual life, reaches maturity when the soul has surrendered itself completely into the hands of God, giving Him its whole will. Not in vain has the soul died to itself; it has died in order to live in God and for God, to live by His life, by His love, by His will. " You are dead, " says St. Paul, " and your life is hid with Christ in God " *(Col* 3,3.).

2. With the authority of a Doctor of the Church, St. John of the Cross declares : " When in this way the soul voids itself of all things and achieves emptiness and surrender of them (which, as we have said, is the part that the soul can play), it is impossible, if the soul does as much as in it lies, that God should fail to perform His part by communicating Himself to the soul, at least secretly and in silence. It is more impossible than that the sun should fail to shine in a serene and unclouded sky; for as the sun, when it rises in the morning, will enter your house if you open the shutter, even so will God...enter the soul that is empty and fill it with divine blessings " *(LF* 3,46).

How long has Our Lord, the divine Sun, let the luminous ray of His grace shine upon your soul; how long has He knocked at your door : " Behold, I stand at the gate and knock " *(Ap* 3,20). Each confession, each Holy Communion, each Mass, each occasion for the exercise of virtue, each inspiration, each command or request of obedience : are not these God, knocking repeatedly at the door of your heart? And what are you doing? Why do you still keep Him waiting? Wake from your torpor, open your soul! " Lift up your gates...and be ye lifted up, O eternal gates, and the King of glory shall enter in! " *(Ps* 23,7). Do not be satisfied with opening the door half-way, or even three-quarters; open it completely. It is necessary to lift up the gates, to remove every obstacle : your God must enter in.

If you find it costly to deny your will in everything, consider how great a good it is to be guided in all things by the will of God. If you find it a burden to renounce self-love and earthly affections, think how joyous it is to possess the love of God. If you are reluctant to die to self, ponder how glorious it is to live to God. St. Teresa of Jesus cried out in a burst of enthusiasm : " What nothingness is all that we have given up, and all that we are doing, or can ever do, for a God who is pleased to communicate Himself in this way to a worm! If we have the hope of enjoying this blessing while we are still in this life, what are we doing about it, and why are we waiting? What sufficient reason is there for delaying even a short time instead of seeking this Lord, as the Bride did, through streets and squares? " (*Int C VI*, 4).

Our Lord wills to communicate Himself to your soul, to give Himself entirely; He wills to come and live with you : " If any man shall hear My voice and open to Me the door, I will come into him and will sup with him and he with Me " (*Ap* 3,20). Oh! may you not lose this immense gift through your own fault, your own negligence!

COLLOQUY

" O Lord of heaven and earth! Is it possible, while we are still in this mortal life, for us to enjoy You with such special friendship?... Oh! the joys which You bestow on souls who give themselves entirely to You! What endearments, what sweet words are these, one word of which would suffice to unite us to You. May You be blessed, O Lord, for so far as You are concerned we shall lose nothing. By how many paths, in how many manners, through how many means do You reveal Your love to us! By trials, by bitter death, by tortures, by affronts suffered daily, by Your forgiveness. And not by these alone, but by words that pierce the soul that loves You.

" So, my Lord, I ask You for nothing else in this life but that You should ' kiss me with the kiss of Your mouth '; and let this be in such a way, Lord of my life, that, even if I should desire to withdraw from this friendship and union, my will may be so completely subject to Yours that I shall be unable to leave You. May nothing ever hinder me, O my God and my glory, from being able to say : ' Better and more delectable than any other good is Your friendship and Your love. '

" For the love of the Lord, my soul, wake out of this sleep and remember that God does not keep you waiting until the next life before rewarding you for your love of Him. Your recompense begins in this life.

" O my Lord, my Mercy and my Good! What more do I want in this life than to be so near You that there is no division between You and me? And since Your love allows it, I will repeat without ceasing : ' My Beloved to me and I to my Beloved ' " (cf. T.J. *Con,* 3 - 4).

367

PERFECT UNION

PRESENCE OF GOD - I implore You, my God, to let nothing trouble my union with You.

MEDITATION

1. The *yes* of perfect consent has surrendered the whole human will to God, placing it completely under the vivifying influence of the divine will. Yet there are still found in the sensitive part of the soul disturbances which tend to withdraw it from the governance of God's will : this sensitive part is subjected to the spirit only with difficulty, in consequence of the disorder produced by original sin. Even while the soul is by its will entirely conformed and united to the divine will, the sensitive part is always pulling in its own direction, carrying the affections along with it, sometimes stirring up repugnances and difficulties which can render continual adherence to God's will painful and trouble the peace of the soul. Sensitiveness can still subject the soul to impressions and emotions which are a little too lively and expose it,

when it does not succeed in wholly dominating them, to commit faults through inadvertence or frailty. Nor is the devil excluded from making use of the movements of the sensitive part to assail the soul, to hinder its progress, or, quite simply, to make it turn back, which, unfortunately, is always possible as long as we are in this life. The soul suffers from these trials, and ardently sighs to be freed from them, for it sees how they can disturb its union with God, and it desires this union to be more intense and perfect than ever. Only God can re-establish in man the harmony destroyed by original sin, and He does not refuse this sublime grace to a soul which is truly faithful to Him. He grants it by means of a more intimate and complete union with Himself, wholly dominating the soul by His powerful influence, as if taking it into His possession. This is *total union*, called by the mystics " spiritual marriage, " the highest degree of union with God possible in this life.

Oh! with what fervor the loving soul longs for this sublime state in which it can give itself entirely to God, and can be wholly possessed and directed by Him, without being troubled by the turbulence of sensibility.

2. " Spiritual marriage, " writes St. John of the Cross, " is a total transformation in the Beloved, wherein on either side there is made surrender by total possession of the one to the other with a certain consummation of union of love " (*SC*, 22,3). It is a *total* transformation in God; that is, the transformation which at first—in the spiritual espousals—was realized only in the will, is now extended to the other faculties as a result of that mutual, perfect giving of God to the soul and of the soul to God. God gives Himself to the soul as if He were its possession; He establishes Himself in it as the active principle, not only of its will, but of its whole being, directing its entire life, and inspiring it in all that it does. This is the result of an ever more intense influence of the gifts of the Holy Spirit that pervades all the faculties of the soul, entering even into its sensitive part, which remains henceforth completely subject to the spirit. The soul possesses its God as One who vivifies, moves and governs it; it possesses Him as its principle of life, as its support, its strength, its all; it exclaims spontaneously with St. Paul : " I live, now not I; but Christ liveth in me " (*Gal* 2,20). It feels that its life is much more the

life of God than its own life; in fact, since God has given Himself wholly to the soul, it is precisely in virtue of the singular plenitude of the divine gift that the soul has given itself wholly to Him. It is no longer only the perfect gift of the will; it is the gift of the entire being, magnificently harmonized by the full actuation of the gifts of the Holy Spirit. This gift, this total surrender of the soul to the Beloved, effects, as it were, the transfer of the life of the soul into God, so that it lives more in Him than in itself, " more in Him whom it loves than in the body which it animates " (cf. J.C. *SC*, 8,3). Like the mystical spouse of the Canticle, the soul which has arrived at this state can repeat in all truth : " My Beloved to me, and I to Him " (2,16).

The union of the soul with God is henceforth so perfect, so full, that only the beatific union of heaven can surpass it. Total union is heaven anticipated, heaven offered to generous souls who spare neither pain nor sacrifice in order to give themselves wholly to God.

COLLOQUY

" Great is this favor, my Spouse, and this delectable feast, this precious wine that You give me, one drop of which makes me forget all created things, and withdraw from creatures and from myself, and no longer desire the satisfactions and joys which until now my senses have longed for. Great is all this and unmerited by me.

" Let worldlings come with all their possessions, their riches, their delights, their honors, and their feasts : even if all these could be enjoyed without the trials that they bring in their train, which is impossible, they could not in a thousand years cause the happiness enjoyed in a single moment by a soul whom You have elevated to this state.

" No, I do not see how it is possible to compare the base things of the world with these delights so sweet that no one could merit them, with this union so complete with You, my God, with this love so ineffably shown and so blissfully experienced " (T.J. *Con*, 4).

" O Lord my God, who is there that seeks Thee in pure and true love who does not find Thee to be the joy of his will? It is Thou who art the first to show Thyself, going forth to meet those who desire Thee.

" O my God, how sweet to me Thy presence, who art the sovereign Good. I will draw near to Thee in silence...I will rejoice in nothing till I am in Thine arms. O Lord, I beseech Thee, leave me not for a moment because I know not the value of my soul " (J.C. *SM I*).

368

THE TRIUMPH OF LOVE

PRESENCE OF GOD - Grant that there may be only love in me, my God; that all may proceed from love, and all revert to love.

MEDITATION

1. The life of the soul which has reached total union may be defined as one simple, continual, most intense exercise of love, by means of which it gives itself to God unceasingly. All its faculties, not only purified, but perfectly harmonized, are wholly employed in the divine service : " Its understanding [the soul] employs in the understanding of those things that pertain most nearly to His service in order to do them; its will, in loving all that pleases God and in having affection of the will for God in all things; and its memory and care in that which pertains to His service and will be most pleasing to Him " (J.C. *SC*, 28,3). Furthermore, even the sensual part, the body with all its senses, takes part in this magnificent concert of love, so that the soul can truly say that all its " possessions, " that is, all its spiritual and sensitive powers, are completely employed in the service of holy love. " For the body now works according to God; the inward and outward senses are directed toward Him in all their operations and all the four passions of the soul [that is, joy, hope, fear, and sorrow], it likewise keeps bound to God, because it neither has enjoyment save from God, nor has hope save in God, nor fears any save only God, neither does it grieve save according to God; and likewise all its desires and cares are wholly directed to God alone " (*ibid.*, 4).

The loving flame of divine Wisdom has taken possession
of this soul to such an extent, has so purified it and made
it love God alone, that its whole being and all its faculties
vibrate solely for Him, being engaged in nothing except in His
service and in giving Him pleasure.   It has no craving
but for Him, no other desire than to give itself and unite
itself to Him in perfect love; hence even the very first movements of this soul are movements of love : " The understanding,
the will, and the memory go straightway to God; and the
affections, the senses, the desires and appetites, hope, joy,
and all the rest of the soul's possessions are inclined to God
from the first moment " (*ibid.*, 5).   Love has become the
atmosphere in which the soul moves; it has become its
breath, its life.   The difficult sacrifices, the bitter struggles
and renunciations of the past, when its exercise of love
consisted " in stripping itself for God's sake of all that was
not God " (J.C. *AS II*, 5,7), seem to it as nothing now,
compared with the great good it has obtained; thus it repeats
enraptured : " Everything is little when it is a question of
acquiring pure and true love of God " (T.M. *Sp*).

2. The love of a soul completely surrendered to God is
truly pure love, because it has been purged of the least
affection for creatures and of all return on self; it is pure
love because it goes straight and swiftly to God through all
the circumstances of life, without stopping at anything
created.   The soul makes use of every happening, all its
duties, all its actions to love God, which simply means
that it gives itself to Him by serving Him in the way most
pleasing to Him.   It no longer needs to apply itself, as
formerly, to the practice of this or that virtue, since it has
acquired all of them in a perfect manner, and " whether its
commerce be with temporal things or whether its exercise be
concerning spiritual things, a soul in this case can ever
say that its exercise is now in loving alone " (J.C. *SC*, 28,9).
The soul no longer has need of the spur and stimulus
of an exterior law to guide it, because its law is now the great
love it bears within itself, which impels it in all things to seek
and to will the divine good pleasure.   " Love and do what
you will, " said St. Augustine; " For the just man there
is no law, " wrote St. John of the Cross at the summit of the
Mount of Perfection.   Far from implying that love dispenses
from the observance of the law, from duties and obedience,

these words signify rather, that love, when it is truly perfect, replaces and completes all law, having in itself the power to draw the soul to the highest perfection.

Of this perfect and most pure love, which concentrates upon God all the powers of the soul without anything being able to draw them away; of this love which wounds the heart of God directly, passing beyond all that is of earth, St. John of the Cross writes : " A very little of this pure love is more precious, in the sight of God and the soul, and of greater profit to the Church...than are all these [other] works together " (*SC*, 29,2). There cannot be, in fact, an activity more intense and more sublime than that which concentrates and employs in God all the energies and capacities of the creature. It is the eternal activity of the angels and saints in heaven; it is the activity which, even here below, souls who have attained to perfect union with God can enter upon in emulation of the Blessed. " Happy life and happy estate and happy the soul that arrives thereat, where all is now substance of love to it, and joy and delight of betrothal " (*ibid*, 28,10).

COLLOQUY

" Even as a maiden that is betrothed sets not her love upon another than her spouse, nor directs her thoughts or her actions to any other, grant, O Lord, that my soul may no longer have any affections of the will or acts of knowledge of the understanding, nor any thought or action which is not wholly turned to Thee. Grant that I may know naught save how to love Thee, O my divine Spouse, and seeing that Thou prizest nothing and art pleased with nothing besides love, help me to employ everything purely for love of Thee and to serve Thee perfectly.

" Permit not that I should seek my own gain nor pursue my own tastes nor busy myself in other things and in intercourse that has naught to do with Thee. May I have no other style or manner of intercourse save the exercise of love. May all in me be moved by and in love. In laboring, I wish to do all with love; in suffering I wish to endure all for love.

" Grant that I may repeat to Thee with the Spouse of the Canticle : ' All the fruits, the new and the old, my Beloved,

I have kept for Thee, ' which is as if she said : My Beloved,
I desire for Thy sake to have all that is hard and wearisome,
and all that is sweet and delectable I desire for Thee "
(J.C. *SC*, 27,7.8 – 28,2-10).

" O Jesus, I do not ask for riches or glory, not even for the
glory of heaven. . . . I ask only for love.   One thought is
mine, henceforth, dear Jesus, it is to love Thee!. . .   I love
Thee, I love my Mother the Church, and I bear in mind
that ' the least act of pure love is of more value to her than
all other works together. '   But does this pure love really
exist in my heart?. . .

" O Jesus, grant that love may surround and penetrate
me; that at each moment Thy merciful love may renew
and purify me, cleansing my soul from all trace of sin "
(T.C.J. *St*, 13 – 8).

369

TRANSFORMING LOVE

PRESENCE OF GOD - My God, may Your love inundate and penetrate
my soul until I am completely transformed in You.

MEDITATION

1. As the flame of a candle, united to the flame of an
immense fire, becomes one with it, burning and shining with a
single brightness, so that it is impossible to distinguish it from
the great fire in which it is immersed, similarly the soul united
to God by love loses itself in Him, remaining so enveloped
and transformed in Him as to appear to be God Himself,
and to be made " divine and become God by participation,
insofar as may be in this life " (J.C. *SC*, 22,3).   God is always
God, essentially distinct from the soul.   Love, however,
has so united and, as it were, merged the creature with
the Creator, that " there are two natures in one spirit and
love " *(ibid.)*.   By the perfection of charity and of grace the
Holy Spirit dwells with singular plenitude in such a soul,
and in this divine Spirit—the Spirit and bond of Love—the

soul lives completely united to the Blessed Trinity. Here is realized in the most perfect manner the burning desire and ardent prayer of Jesus : " As Thou, Father, in Me and I in Thee; that they also may be one in Us " (*Jn* 17,21).

United to God in this way, the soul remains transformed in Him by love, or rather, it is love which, uniting it completely to God, makes the soul so similar as to transform it wholly in Him. This transformation extends to all its powers : " The human understanding. . . becomes divine, through union with the divine, " and wholly enlightened with supernatural light; " the will is informed with divine love so that it is a will that is now no less than divine, nor does it love otherwise than divinely. . . . So, too, is it with the memory; and likewise the affections and desires are all changed and converted divinely, according to God " (J.C. *DN II*, 13,11). Further, the soul remains divinized not only in its being and its faculties, but also in its actions, for " it is God Himself who moves the faculties and commands them divinely, according to His divine Spirit and will; and the result of this is that the operations of the soul are divine " (J.C. *AS III*, 2,8). The plenitude of supernatural life communicated to the soul in the state of spiritual marriage realizes in it, in the highest degree, the prerogative of grace, which is precisely that of making man a " partaker of the divine nature " (2 *Pt* 1,4). We see here the marvelous continuity which exists between the development of grace in our soul and these elevated states which are its ultimate consequence and its refulgent crown. Why do we tarry amid the paltry things of earth, when God has created us for these divine grandeurs?

2. St. John of the Cross says : " The lover cannot be satisfied if he feels not that he loves as much as he is loved " (*SC**, 37,2). One who truly loves cannot endure being outdone in love, and the more he feels himself loved, the more he desires to love in return. But how can a creature, so weak and limited, equal God in love, that is, love Him as much as it is loved by Him? This holy and audacious ambition is realized precisely in the state of total transformation. As the will is completely transformed in that of God, " there is equality of love, " affirms the Saint, " for the will of the soul that is converted into the will of God. . . becomes the will of God. And thus the soul loves God with the will of God,

which is also its own will; and thus it will love Him even as much as it is loved by God, since it loves Him with the will of God Himself, in the same love wherewith He loves it, which is the Holy Spirit " *(ibid.)*. The Holy Spirit, the Third Person of the Blessed Trinity, terminus and subsistent bond of uncreated Love, who unites indissolubly the Father and the Son, has been given to us, so that, enkindling in our souls the fire of divine love, He may make us capable of loving God, not alone with our poor and very limited powers, but conjointly with Him, infinite Power and Love. The flame of charity was enkindled in our soul by the divine Paraclete on the day of our Baptism; it has grown since then, in proportion to our correspondence with grace. In the soul that has reached full transformation in God and has become one spirit with Him, this flame of charity is totally absorbed and loses itself in the infinite flame of the Holy Spirit. Then it truly loves God as it is loved by Him, because it loves Him together with the Holy Spirit. The capacity of the soul becomes in a certain sense and by participation, quasi infinite, and only in this way is its love assuaged because it can love God in return with parity of love. The Mystical Doctor again explains : " And thus the soul loves God in the Holy Spirit together with the Holy Spirit... by reason of the transformation... and He supplies that which it lacks by its having been transformed in love with Him " *(ibid.)*.

What joy and consolation for the soul, who suffers because of the extreme poverty of its love, compared with the infinite love of God and His infinite lovableness, to know that the Holy Spirit can and will supply for its insufficiency, provided that it let itself be completely seized and absorbed in the immense flame of His love.

COLLOQUY

" O my soul, created for these grandeurs and called thereto! What are you doing? Wherein do you occupy yourself? Your desires are base and your possessions misery. O wretched blindness of your eyes, which obscures so great a light! And why are you deaf to so clear a voice, seeing not that for as long as you seek grandeurs and glories you remain miserable and mean, and have become ignorant and unworthy of so many blessings? " (cf. J.C. *SC*, 39,7).

" O Holy Spirit, You serve as intermediary between the soul and God, moving it with such ardent desires that it becomes enkindled by that sovereign Fire, who is so near it.

" O Lord, what mercies are these that You bestow upon the soul! May You be blessed and praised forever, You who are so good a Lover! O my God and my Creator! Is it possible that there is any soul who does not love You? Unhappy that I am since for so long a time I myself loved You not!

" O my Lord, how good You are! May You be blessed forever! Let all things praise You, my God; You have so loved us that we can truly say that You have communication with souls even in this exile. O infinite Bounty, how magnificent are Your works!

" One whose understanding is not occupied with things of earth is amazed at being unable to understand such truths. Do You, then, grant these sovereign favors to souls who have so greatly offended You? Truly, my own understanding is overwhelmed by this, and when I begin to think about it I can go no farther. Where, indeed, would I go that would not be turning back? As for giving You thanks for these favors, there is no way of doing it... " (T.J. *Con*, 5 - *Life*, 18).

370

DIVINE INTIMACY

PRESENCE OF GOD - Grant, O Lord, that I may have perfect and lasting intimacy with You, that I may ever love You more and more.

MEDITATION

1. A soul enters upon the way of divine intimacy the moment that it resolutely determines to go forth from itself and from all created things, in order to set out with fervor in quest of God, living and present within it. The road

between this first step and profound intimacy, which will bind to God the soul that has reached complete union, is long and difficult. Progressively, the soul begins to walk toward that "sweet and delectable union" (J.C. *DN II*, 16,14) in the measure that, sustained by grace, it becomes detached from itself and creatures, delivered from its imperfections, despoiled of its own will so as to be clothed with the divine will alone, and permits the fire of love to be enkindled within it. Intimacy with God becomes more intense and loving, until, attaining the heights of transforming love, it becomes continual and perfect, a divine embrace which binds the creature to the Creator. Then the great promise of Jesus : " If anyone love Me...My Father will love him : and We will come to him and will make Our abode with him " (*Jn* 14,23), is realized as perfectly as is possible here below. St. John of the Cross affirms : " It must not be held incredible that in a faithful soul which has already been tried and proved and purged in the fire of tribulations and trials, and found faithful in love, there should be fulfilled that which was promised by the Son of God : namely, that, if any man loved Him, the Blessed Trinity would come to dwell within him and would abide in him. And this comes to pass when the understanding is divinely illumined in the Wisdom of the Son, and the will is made glad in the Holy Spirit, and the Father, with His power and strength, absorbs the soul in the embrace and abyss of His sweetness " (*LF*, 1,15). In the most sublime moments of transforming union, the soul is rendered conscious of God living, present, and working in it; it is conscious of His sweet paternal embrace which sustains it, of the splendor of His Wisdom which enlightens it, of the divine enkindling of His Love which penetrates it through and through. Even when the realization of the divine presence and action is less strong, and does not make the soul so blissful, it is still conscious of being profoundly united to God, of being moved and governed by Him. St. Thérèse of the Child Jesus attests : " I know that Jesus is within me, always guiding and inspiring me " (*St*, 8). The humble Saint, although not having experienced the extraordinary mystical graces, attained no less than her glorious Mother, St. Teresa of Jesus, to the profound intimacy with God which the soul enjoys in the state of perfect union.

2. Divine intimacy, especially in its highest degrees, is in itself a very joyous and blessed state; yet the enamored

soul does not desire this intimacy in order to enjoy it, but to love God more, to be totally united to Him, entirely possessed, moved, and governed by Him, that it may serve Him better and give Him glory in all its actions. St. Teresa of Avila says expressly that the end for which Our Lord communicates Himself to souls and gives them so many graces—even the highest mystical favors—is not merely to " give them pleasure, " or to console them, but " to strengthen their weakness that they may be able to imitate Him in His great sufferings, " and she adds, with her usual enthusiasm : " This is the aim of prayer, this is the purpose of the spiritual marriage, to give birth to good works and good works alone " (*Int C VII*).

The end of the sweetness and the joy of intimacy with God is to make the soul more courageous in the divine service, more generous in the gift of self, stronger in bearing the cross. As long as we are on earth, suffering will never be wanting, and it will be found even amid the delights of divine union, for we must be conformed to Jesus Crucified; we must follow Him on the way to Calvary, that we may be completely immolated with Him for the glory of the Father and the salvation of our brethren. The works which union with God should produce are precisely works of love; it is through the intense activity of pure love that the soul gives itself unceasingly to God, eager to draw with it an immense multitude of other souls. Therefore, the most fruitful apostolate springs spontaneously from divine intimacy, from perfect union with Our Lord, from pure love. " Their conception of glory " (that of souls who have arrived at spiritual marriage), says the ardent Teresa of Jesus, " is that of being able in some way to help the Crucified, especially when they see how often people offend Him, and how few there are who really care about His honor and are detached from everything else " (*ibid.*, 3).

The loving soul, truly forgetful of itself, thinks neither of enjoying nor of suffering, but only of loving and serving God, of contributing as much as it can to His glory by associating itself to the redemptive work of Jesus. And if it aspires to an ever more perfect and intimate union with God, as well today, on earth, as tomorrow in heaven, it is in order to love with the greatest intensity, and make Love loved by the greatest possible number of souls.

COLLOQUY

" O Lord God, my Love, if Thou art still mindful of my
sins, and wilt not grant my petitions, Thy will be done,
for that is my chief desire.   Show Thou Thy goodness and
mercy, and Thou shalt be known by them.   If it be that
Thou art waiting for me to do good works, that in them
Thou mayest grant my petition, do Thou give them and
work them in me; send also the penalties which Thou wilt
accept, and do Thou inflict them.   But if Thou art not
waiting for my good works, what art Thou waiting for,
O most merciful Lord?   Why tarriest Thou?   For if, at last,
it must be grace and mercy, and I pray for it in Thy Son,
do Thou accept my worthless offering, according to Thy will,
and give me this good also according to Thy will.

" Who can free himself from base and mean ways, if Thou,
O my God, will not lift him up to Thee in pure love?

" How shall a man raise himself up to Thee, for he is
born and bred in misery, if Thou wilt not lift him up with the
hand that made him?

" Thou wilt not take away from me, O my God, what
Thou hast once given me in Thy only-begotten Son, Jesus
Christ, in whom Thou dost give me all I desire.   I will
therefore rejoice; Thou wilt not tarry if I wait for Thee.
Wait in hope, then, O my soul, for from henceforth thou
mayest love God in thy heart.

" Mine are the heavens and mine is the earth; mine are
the people, the righteous are mine, and mine are the sinners;
the angels are mine, and the Mother of God, and all things
are mine; God Himself is mine and for me, because Christ
is mine, and all for me.   What dost thou, then, ask for,
what dost thou seek, O my soul?   All is thine, all is for
thee, do not take less, nor rest with the crumbs which fall from
the table of thy Father.   Go forth and exult in thy glory,
hide thyself in it, and rejoice, and thou shalt obtain all the
desires of thy heart " (J.C. *SM I*, Prayer of the Enamored
Soul).

IMMOVABLE FEASTS

371

THE PURIFICATION OF THE BLESSED VIRGIN MARY

FEBRUARY SECOND

PRESENCE OF GOD - O Lord, I come to You and beg You, through the intercession of the Blessed Virgin Mary, to purify my soul.

MEDITATION

1. Today's Feast, which marks the end of the Christmas season, is a feast both of Jesus and of Mary : of Jesus, because He is presented by His Mother in the Temple forty days after His birth, according to the requirements of the law; of Mary, because she submits herself to the rite of purification.

The liturgy celebrates, primarily, the entrance for the first time of the Infant Jesus into the Temple : " Behold the Lord, the Ruler, cometh into His holy Temple : rejoice and be glad, O Sion, and hasten to meet your God " *(RB)*. Let us, too, go to meet Him, emulating the holy sentiments of the old Simeon who " came by the Spirit into the Temple " *(Gosp : Lk* 2, 22-32), and filled with joy, received the Divine Child into his arms.

In order to celebrate this event more fittingly, the Church today blesses candles and gives them to us; with burning tapers, we enter the Temple in procession. The lighted candle is a symbol of the Christian life, of the faith and grace which should shine in our soul. It is also the image of Christ, the light of the world, " a light to the revelation of the Gentiles, " according to Simeon's canticle. The lighted candle reminds us that we must always bear Christ in us, the source of our life, the author of faith and grace. By His grace, Jesus Himself disposes us to go to meet Him with livelier faith and greater love. May our meeting with Him today be particularly intimate and sanctifying!

Jesus is taken to the Temple to be offered to the Father, although, being God, He was not subject to the prescriptions of the Jewish law as were the other firstborn of the Hebrews. He is the Victim who will be immolated for the salvation of the world.   His presentation in the Temple is, so to speak, the offertory of His life; the sacrifice will be consummated later, on Calvary.   Let us offer ourselves with Jesus.

2. Jesus was presented in the Temple by His Mother. Let us therefore contemplate Mary in her office of Co-Redemptrix.   Mary knew that Jesus was the Savior of the world, and through the veil of prophecy she sensed that His mission would be accomplished in a mystery of sorrow in which she would participate, in her role as Mother. Simeon's prophecy : " And thy own soul a sword shall pierce, " confirmed her intuition.   Deep in her heart, Mary at that moment must have repeated her *fiat :* " Behold the handmaid of the Lord; be it done to me according to Thy word " (*ibid.* 1,38).   At the same time that she offered her Son, she offered herself, being always closely united to His destiny.

But, before entering the Temple to present Jesus, Mary wanted to submit to the law of legal purification.   Although she knew she was a virgin, she put herself on the level of all the other mothers, and standing with them, humbly awaited her turn, carrying " a pair of turtle-doves, " the offering of the poor.   We see Jesus and Mary submitting themselves to laws by which they are not bound : Jesus does not need to be redeemed, nor Mary to be purified.   These are lessons in humility and respect for the law of God.

There may be some laws by which we are bound and from which our pride by false pretexts seeks to exempt us. Such dispensations are abuses sought in the name of rights which do not really exist.   Whereas Mary had no need to be purified, let us humble ourselves and acknowledge our extreme need of interior purification.

COLLOQUY

" O Jesus, You went to the Temple to offer Yourself. Who offered You?   The Virgin Mary, who has never had, and never will have, an equal.   You were offered by Mary who, through the mouth of Wisdom, was called by Your Father the ' all-beautiful, all-fair. '   To whom were You offered?   To God, the infinite Being, sublime in His creation, fruitful in His heritage, unfathomable in His designs, gracious and sweet in His love.   What did she offer?   She offered You, the eternal Word, substance of the divine essence, Son of the Most High, the Lawgiver of the universe, You, who have been called by so many great and beautiful names : O Key of David, O King of nations, O Emmanuel!

" What do You teach me, O Lord, offering Yourself thus in the Temple?   You show me respect for the law by Your willingness to observe it.   You teach me adoration, for You offered Yourself to the Father, not as His equal, which You really were, but as man.   Here You have given me a model of the respect which I owe to Your law, not only to the Ten Commandments, but also to my Holy Rule and Constitutions.   This law is all sweetness and delight for me, but I make it bitter when I do not renounce myself, for then, instead of my bearing it sweetly, the law is obliged to bear me " (St. Mary Magdalen dei Pazzi).

O Jesus, through the hands of Mary, I wish to offer myself today with You to the eternal Father.   But You are a pure, holy, and immaculate Host, while I am defiled with misery, and sin.   O Mary, my Mother, you were willing to be purified, although you were free from the slightest shadow of imperfection; purify, I beseech you, my poor soul, so that it may be less unworthy to be offered to the Father along with Jesus, who is your Son as well as His. O Virgin most pure, lead me along the way of a serious, and thorough purification; accompany me yourself, so that my weakness will not make me faint because of the roughness of the road.

372

ST. JOSEPH, SPOUSE OF THE BLESSED VIRGIN MARY, PATRON OF THE UNIVERSAL CHURCH

MARCH NINETEENTH

PRESENCE OF GOD - O glorious St. Joseph, under your patronage may my interior life grow and develop.

MEDITATION

1. Today the Church presents St. Joseph, the great Patriarch, to whose care God willed to entrust the most chosen portion of His flock, Mary and Jesus. Because Joseph was selected by God to be the guardian of the family of Nazareth, the nucleus of the great Christian family, the Church recognizes in him the Guardian and Patron of all Christendom. Herein lies the significance of today's Feast, which invites us to fix our attention on the mission entrusted to this great Saint in relation to Jesus and to the Church.

Aware of the great mystery of the Incarnation, Joseph's whole life gravitated about that of the Incarnate Word : for Him he endured worry, suffering, fatigue, labor. To Him he consecrated all his solicitude, his energy, his resources, his time. He reserved nothing for himself, but completely oblivious of any personal needs, desires, or views, he devoted himself entirely to the interests and the needs of Jesus. Nothing existed for Joseph except Jesus and Mary, and he felt that his life on earth had no other *raison d'être* than his care of them. In this way he participated fully, as a humble, hidden collaborator, in the work of the Redemption; if he did not accompany Jesus in His apostolic life and to His death on the Cross—as Mary did—nevertheless, he worked for the same end as the Savior.

Having been the faithful guardian of the Holy Family, it is impossible that from the heights of heaven St. Joseph should not continue to protect the great Christian family, the universal Church, which, confident of his protection, and relying on his assistance, prays thus : " Sustained, O Lord, by the protection of the spouse of Your holy Mother,

we beseech Your clemency...that by his merits and intercession You will guide us to eternal glory " *(RM)*.

2. St. Joseph's vocation to become the guardian of the
Holy Family was also an invitation to divine intimacy.   We
must not forget that he stood at the dividing line between
the Old and the New Testament.   The first part of his life
belonged to the Old Testament, the second, to the New.
Before the coming of Jesus, he, like all the patriarchs of the
Old Law, would certainly have followed the trend of his
time, and his relations with God would have been especially
influenced by the sentiment of reverent fear.   But as soon as
the Angel revealed to him the mystery of the Incarnation,
and he learned that Mary his Spouse was to be the Mother
of the Redeemer, everything in his life changed.   God, whom
he had always honored as the Most High, the Inaccessible,
the Thrice Holy, had now come near to him, so near that He
had taken flesh in the womb of his Spouse, and had chosen
him, Joseph, as His foster father.   As soon as Jesus was born,
He was placed in Joseph's arms and entrusted to his care;
later He would grow in his sight, be fed at his table, and
sleep under his roof.   What a life of intimacy!   And it was
not only an intimacy of external relations, but also one of
profoundly interior, spiritual relations, for Joseph knew by
faith that Jesus was his God.   Thus, together with Mary, this
great Saint was the first one to enter into that life of love
and intimacy with God, to which Jesus opened the door.
Let us, then, watch Joseph fulfill his mission, not only with
complete exterior dedication, but also with a heart filled
with Jesus, a heart in which a glorious life of divine intimacy
flourishes.   While he is devoting himself to the work required
by his position as foster father, he lives, in the secrecy of his
heart, in continual relations of love with his God, the Incarnate
Word.
     In the Church, each one of us has his mission to fulfill
for the good of souls and the glory of God.   This mission
requires work—often fatiguing work—and much sacrifice
and intense activity.   Like St. Joseph, we must give ourselves
generously and totally, without sparing, without reserve,
but, at the same time, we must also give ourselves to the
works of God with a heart filled with God, with a heart which
lives with Him in an intimacy nourished by the assiduous
exercise of prayer.   St. Joseph teaches us the blessed secret

of a life of combined activity and contemplation, so that, following his example, we may give ourselves to the active life without neglecting our life of intimate union with God.

COLLOQUY

" O St. Joseph, happy are you to whom it was given not only to see and hear that God whom so many desired to see and saw not, to hear and heard not, but even to carry Him in your arms, to embrace Him, to clothe Him, to watch over Him.... O St. Joseph, what others have only after death, you had while still living; like the blessed in heaven, you enjoyed God and lived close to Him. You clasped to your heart the Infant Jesus, you accompanied Him in the flight to Egypt, you sheltered Him under your roof " *(RB)*.

" Oh, how sweet were the kisses you received from Jesus! With what joy you heard the little one lisp the name of ' father, ' and how delightful to feel His gentle embrace! With what love did He rest on your knees, when His little body was worn out with fatigue! Love without reserve brought you to Him as to a most dear Son whom the Holy Spirit had given you through the Virgin, your Spouse " (St. Bernardine of Siena).

" O glorious Saint, it is a thing which truly astonishes me, the great favors which God has bestowed on me and the perils from which He has freed me, both in body and in soul, through your intercession. To other saints the Lord seems to have given grace to succour us in some of our necessities, but you succour us in them all.... If anyone cannot find a master to teach him how to pray, let him take you as his master and he will not go astray " (T. J. *Life*, 6).

May the life of the whole Church, as well as the interior life of every Christian, grow and prosper under your patronage, O Joseph. I place my spiritual life under your protection. You, who lived so close to Jesus, bring me to intimacy with Him, so that, following your example, I may serve Him with a heart full of love.

373

ST. JOSEPH'S LIFE OF FAITH

PRESENCE OF GOD - In your school, O glorious St. Joseph, I desire
to learn how to live by faith, guided in all things by divine
Providence.

MEDITATION

1. The fundamental disposition of St. Joseph's soul was
one of complete confidence and abandonment to God, which
had its source in his faith. St. Matthew called him " a just
man " (1,19); now Sacred Scripture teaches that " the just
man liveth by faith " (*Rom* 1,17), and it can well be affirmed
that no creature, after the Blessed Virgin, has lived as much
by faith as St. Joseph. In fact, having spent his whole life
within the orbit of the mystery of the Incarnation, he necessarily had to pass through all the obscurities which surrounded
the accomplishment of the great mystery. So Joseph needed
deep faith, a faith continually nourished by suffering and
tempered through anguish. The perplexity aroused in his
mind by Mary's mysterious maternity, the extreme poverty
and anxieties connected with Bethlehem, the privations
during the flight into Egypt, afflicted his sensitive soul
to such an extent that in the most serious crises he needed
the intervention of an angel, by whom he was sustained and
introduced into the depths of the divine mystery unfolding
before his eyes. Joseph allowed himself to be guided with
the docility and blind confidence of a child. The Gospel
relates four events which testify to this :

(1) An Angel put an end to his anguish by commanding
him to take Mary as his Spouse, " for that which is conceived
in her is of the Holy Spirit. " Joseph did not hesitate a
moment and did " as the Angel of the Lord had commanded
him " (*Mt* 1,20.24). (2) An Angel warned him to " take
the Child and His Mother and fly into Egypt " (*ibid.* 2,13).
Without delay, in the middle of the night, the Saint arose
and carried out the order. Objectively the flight presented
overwhelming difficulties : the great inconvenience and
dangers of the journey, extreme poverty, exile in a strange

land. But the Angel spoke and Joseph obeyed. (3) After Herod's death, an Angel ordered him to return into the land of Israel. (4) An Angel warned him to withdraw into Galilee (cf. *ibid.* 2,19.23).

Here we have four acts of faith and blind obedience. Joseph neither hesitated nor reasoned; he made no objection; for he had complete trust in God; he believed in Him fully, in His Word, in His divine Providence.

2. St. Joseph's whole life may be summed up as a continual adherence to the divine plan, even in situations which were very obscure and mysterious to him.

In our life, too, there is always some mystery, either because God is pleased to work in a hidden, secret manner or because His action is always incomprehensible to our poor human intelligence. Therefore, we need that glance of faith, that complete confidence which, relying on the infinite goodness of God, convinces us that He always and in all circumstances wills our good and disposes everything to that end. Only this loving trust will permit us, like Joseph, always to say our *yes* to every manifestation of the divine will, a humble, prompt, trustful *yes*, in spite of the obscurities, the difficulties, the mystery. . . . God made use of the angels to make His will known to Joseph; to manifest it to us He makes use of our superiors who, like the angels, are His messengers and envoys. Let us obey with the simplicity of St. Joseph, understanding that God can employ any person or circumstance to make us know and execute His divine will, just as He used Caesar's edict to bring Joseph to Bethlehem, where Jesus was to be born. The Roman Emperor had far different intentions, but God utilized this political act to carry out the plan of the Incarnation. God always governs and directs all things toward the fulfillment of His will.

Another characteristic of St. Joseph's life was his entire consecration to the mission entrusted to him by God. Joseph did not live for himself and his own interests, but only for God, whom he served in Jesus and Mary. Thus he is the true model of interior souls, of souls who desire to live totally for God and with God, in the accomplishment of the mission they have received from Him.

COLLOQUY

" O St. Joseph, how much I love you!   How much good
it does me to think of your humble, simple life!   Like us,
you lived by faith.   I contemplate you in the little house
at Nazareth, near Jesus and Mary, busy working for them.
I see you using the plane, and then wiping your forehead
from time to time, and hurrying to finish the work on time
for your customers.   Although you lived with the Son of God,
your life was very ordinary, for Jesus certainly did not
perform any useless miracles.   Everything in your life was
just as it is in ours.   And how many sorrows, fatigues and
dangers!   Oh! how astonished we should be if we knew all
that you suffered! " (cf. T.C.J. *C*, – *NV*).

" I do not know how anyone can think of the Queen of
Angels during the time that she suffered so much with the
Child Jesus, without giving thanks to you, O glorious
St. Joseph, for the way you helped them.   For this reason it
seems to me that those who practice prayer should have a
special affection for you always.

" I wish I could persuade everyone to be devoted to you,
for I have great experience of the blessings which you obtain
from God.   I have never known anyone to be truly devoted to
you and render you particular services who did not notably
advance in virtue, for you give very real help to souls who
commend themselves to you.   I have clearly seen that your
help has always been greater than I could have hoped for.
I do not remember that I have ever asked anything of you
which you failed to grant.   The Lord wishes to teach us that
as He was Himself subject to you on earth (for, being His
guardian and being called His father, you could command
Him), just so in Heaven He still does all that you ask "
(cf. T.J. *Life*, 6).

O dear St. Joseph, I place myself, then, with full confidence under your protection.   Teach me to live as you did,
in faith and abandonment to God; teach me to live solely
for Him, by consecrating myself entirely to His service.

374

THE ANNUNCIATION
OF THE BLESSED VIRGIN MARY

MARCH TWENTY-FIFTH

PRESENCE OF GOD - At your side, O Mary, I wish to learn how to repeat in every circumstance your " Ecce ancilla Domini! " Behold the handmaid of the Lord.

MEDITATION

1. Let us try, through the inspired narrative of St. Luke (*Gosp:* 1, 26-38), to enter into the dispositions of Mary's soul at the time of the Annunciation.

The Angel sent by God finds the Virgin recollected in solitude, and " being come in, " says to her : " Hail, full of grace, the Lord is with thee : blessed art thou among women. " At these words, according to the sacred text, Mary is " troubled "; we must not, however, take this phrase to mean real disturbance, which destroys the peace of the spirit; it means rather a profound astonishment at this unusual greeting, an astonishment so great as to cause a kind of fear. This is Mary's first reaction to the angelical message, a reaction arising from her deep humility, which makes her think this extraordinary eulogy very strange.

Meanwhile the Angel communicates to her his great message : God wishes her to become the Mother of the Redeemer. Mary had always lived under the continual direction of the Holy Spirit and under His inspiration had made a vow of virginity; therefore, she was convinced that she should remain a virgin and that this was God's will. But now God lets her know that He has chosen her to be the Mother of His Son, and she, humble handmaid that she is, is ready to adhere to the divine plan. However, she does not yet understand how she can be at the same time a mother and a virgin, and she questions the Angel on this point : " How shall this be done? " The Angel explains : " The Holy Spirit shall come upon thee and the power of the

Most High shall overshadow thee. " Her maternity will
be the direct work of the Holy Spirit and will respect her
virginity.

The will of God is then entirely clear to Mary, and
she, who during her whole life has always been moved by
the divine will alone, accepts it immediately, with an entire
adherence and a most intense pure love : " Behold the handmaid of the Lord, be it done to me according to Thy word. "
The total acceptance is accompanied by a total donation :
Mary accepts by offering herself, and she offers herself
by giving herself. She offers herself as a servant, or rather,
as a slave, if we take the word in the full sense of the Greek
text; she gives herself by abandoning herself as a prey to the
divine will, accepting by anticipation everything that God
may ask of her. Her adherence to Him is both active and
passive : Mary wills all that God wills, and she accepts all
that He does. Thus Mary appears as the model of a
soul completely united to God, fully given up to His divine
will.

2. The Angel's explanation does not prevent many
future events and circumstances from remaining hidden
and obscure to Mary. She finds herself face to face with
a mystery, a mystery which she knows intuitively to be rich
in suffering; for she has learned from the Sacred Scriptures
that the Redeemer will be a man of sorrows, sacrificed for
the salvation of mankind. Therefore, the ineffable joy of the
divine maternity is presented to her wrapped in a mystery
of sorrow : to be willing to be the Mother of the Son of God
means consenting to be the Mother of one condemned to
death. Yet Mary accepts everything in her *fiat :* in the joy,
as well as in the sorrow of the mystery, she has but one simple
answer : " Behold the handmaid of the Lord. " By this
acceptance, the Blessed Virgin becomes intimately associated
with the life of suffering of her Son Jesus, and, therefore,
with His work of Redemption, thus becoming the spiritual
Mother of the human race. This is the divine plan for
her, and Mary accepts it wholly, without reserve, precisely
because her will is wholly united to the will of God.

Every Christian receives a vocation from God, a mission
to fulfill, by means of which he is called to participate in the
redemptive work of Jesus. For souls consecrated to God,
this mission always finds its culminating point in a task of

spiritual paternity or maternity.   Oh, if every soul would respond to the divine appeal by as complete an acceptance as Mary's " *Ecce ancilla Domini...Fiat!* "   Behold the handmaid of the Lord.... Be it done!

Many times in the course of our life we have received invitations from the Lord—and we shall certainly continue to receive them—invitations to suffering, to sacrifice, to the gift of self.   How have we corresponded?   Perhaps the thought of the fatigue and suffering which we would have to embrace has held us back.   Let us try, in the future, to keep the eyes of our soul open to the light of faith, so that, like Mary, we shall understand that it is through suffering that God calls us to collaborate with Jesus in the sanctification of souls.

COLLOQUY

" Hail Mary, full of grace, the Lord is with thee!   Not only is God the Son with you, to whom you gave your blood, but also God the Holy Spirit, by means of whose operation you conceived, and also God the Father, who generated from all eternity Him whom you conceived.   The Father, who gives you His Son, is with you; the Son is with you, who, wishing to accomplish a prodigious mystery, conceals Himself in your maternal bosom without violating your virginal integrity; the Holy Spirit is with you, who, together with the Father and the Son, sanctifies you.   God is truly with you " (St. Bernard).

" O Mary, Mary, temple of the Trinity...O Mary, vessel of humility, you were pleasing to the eternal Father, and in His own singular love, He has captivated you and drawn you to Him.   By the fire of your charity, by the unction of your humility, you have drawn the Divinity to come within you.

" Did fear disturb you at the Angel's word, O Mary? It does not seem that it did, although you were astonished. At what, then, were you astonished?   At the great goodness of God, when, considering yourself, you knew you were unworthy of so great a grace.   You wondered at the sight of your unworthiness, your weakness and at God's ineffable grace...and thus you showed profound humility.   But there also appears today in you, O Mary, the dignity and liberty of man, for before the Word was made incarnate, the Angel was sent to ask your consent. The Son of God did not descend into your bosom before you had consented; He waited at the door of your will which you opened to Him, for although He wanted to come to you, He would never have entered if you had not opened to Him saying : ' Behold the handmaid of the Lord, be it done unto me according to Thy word....'

" O Mary, my sweet love, you opened to the eternal Divinity the door of your will, and the Word immediately became incarnate within you. By this you teach me that God, who created me without my help, will not save me without it...but knocks at the door of my will and waits for me to open it to Him " (St. Catherine of Siena).

O Mary, by the ineffable mystery which was accomplished in you I beg you to teach me and help me always to open wide the door of my soul to every divine appeal, to every solicitation of grace. At each manifestation of the divine will, may I repeat with you a humble, prompt, " Ecce, fiat! "

375

FEAST OF SS. PETER AND PAUL

JUNE TWENTY-NINTH

PRESENCE OF GOD - O Lord, grant that the Feast of these Apostles may strengthen my faith and my fidelity to the Church.

MEDITATION

I. The Feast of the Holy Apostles Peter and Paul, Princes of the Church, awakens in our souls a greater love for the Church and for our Holy Father the Pope.

The liturgy today gives the place of honor to St. Peter, the head of the Apostles; tomorrow it will speak to us of St. Paul, the Apostle to the Gentiles. Thus it presents to us those who have established the Church, not only by their labors, but even by their blood. The Gospel (*Mt* 16,13-19) recalls the scene at Caesarea, where Jesus, for the first time, proclaimed Peter as the foundation stone of the Church : " I say that thou art Peter, and upon this rock I will build My Church, " words which have had a magnificent repercussion down through the centuries, and which, even today, bear witness to the primacy of Peter and his successors over the whole of Christianity—not over a number of small churches, but over one great, unique Church, the One, Holy, Catholic, Apostolic, and Roman Church. One only Church, whose sole Founder and Head is Christ, who chose Peter to represent Him. " Where Peter is, there is the Church " (St. Ambrose). This means that wherever the Pope, Peter's successor, is, there the Church is. Rightly, then, should we consider the Feast of St. Peter as the Feast of the Church, the Feast of our Holy Father the Pope, and one which should awaken in every Christian soul a profound sense of belonging to the Church and of devotion to the Sovereign Pontiff. At the moment of her death, St. Teresa of Jesus repeated : " I am a daughter of the Church! " After having labored so much for God and souls, this was the only title that made her sure of the divine mercy. To be a child of the Church! This is our title to salvation, this is our glory, after that of being a child of God. Or rather, not *after*, but *together with*, for, as the Fathers of the Church say, " He cannot have God for Father who does not have the Church for Mother " (St. Cyprian). He is not a true Catholic who does not feel the joy of being a child of the Church, whose heart does not vibrate for the Church and for the Vicar of Christ upon earth, who is not ready to renounce his own personal views in order to " *sentire cum Ecclesia,* " to think with the Church, always and in all things.

2. Today's Communion antiphon repeats again the memorable words by which Jesus constituted Peter the foundation stone of the Church. " Thou art Peter, and upon this rock I will build My Church. " It is a renewed expression of honor to the Prince of the Apostles, but it is also a summons to us. Every Christian, in fact, ought to be a firm, solid rock which Jesus can use to sustain His Church. Evidently, the living rock, the cornerstone par excellence is Christ, and, next to Himself, He has placed His Vicar; next come all the faithful, from the Bishops down to the last

person to be baptized. We are all, as St. Peter says in his
first Epistle, " living stones built up, a spiritual house, a holy
priesthood " (2,5).

Whoever you may be—priest or lay person, religious or
father of a family, simple Christian or humble nun, you
also are called to support the Church, just as in a building,
not only the big blocks of granite, but also the smallest
bricks help to solidify the whole edifice. This profound
apostolic sense must not be wanting in any soul; it must
make us conscious of our degree of responsibility for the
growth of the Church. We must fulfill our part, first of
all, by our obedience and submission to the directives of the
Hierarchy; but this is not enough. If we are true children
of the Church, we cannot be indifferent to her needs, her
interests, and her sufferings. The Church today suffers
more than ever : she suffers in her Vicar, who, placed as a
sentinel for the whole Christian world, knows and estimates
better than anyone else the dangers and struggles threatening
her on all sides; the Church suffers in her Bishops, in her
persecuted martyred priests, who are rendered powerless;
she suffers in her children, abandoned and dispersed like
sheep without a shepherd; she suffers because of errors,
because of the calumnies which are hurled against her.
And you, her child, can you remain indifferent? Suffer with
your Mother; pray, work, and use your strength to serve and
defend her. Lay aside your own little personal interests
and consecrate yourself—your life, your works, your prayers,
your silent, hidden sacrifices—to the great interests of the
Church.

COLLOQUY

" O sovereign, ineffable God, I have sinned and am
unworthy to pray to You, but You have the power to make
me worthy. Lord, punish my sins and do not judge me
according to my faults. I have a body : I offer and give it to
You. If it is Your will, crush my bones and my marrow for
Your Vicar on earth, for whom I pray to You. . . . Give me
a heart that will continually grow in grace, a heart strong
enough to defend the banner of the Holy Cross, so as to bring
infidels to share like us in the Passion and Blood of Your
only-begotten Son, the Lamb without spot.

" O infinite, eternal Trinity, do not delay any longer, but through the merits of St. Peter, help Your Spouse, the Holy Church.... I cry to You today, O my Love, eternal God; show mercy to the world and enlighten Your Vicar, so that all will follow him.... Enlighten also the enemies of the Church who resist the Holy Spirit, that they may be converted to You, my God. Call them, stir up their hearts, O inestimable Love, and let Your charity constrain You to conquer their hardness. Bring them back to You, that they may not perish. And because they have offended You, O God of sovereign mercy, punish me for their sins. Take my body which I have received from You; I offer it to You. May it become an anvil for them, so that their sins may be destroyed " (St. Catherine of Siena).

" O Lord, in spite of my great misery I do not cease to beseech You to hear me : Your glory and the good of Your Church are at stake. All my desires are directed to this intention. Does it seem overbold of me to think that I can do anything toward obtaining this? Hear me not, O Lord, when I ask You for honors, endowments, money or anything that has to do with the world, but when I ask only for the honor of Your Son, why should You not hear one who would willingly forfeit a thousand honors and a thousand lives for You? Do not hear me, O Lord, for my own sake, for I do not deserve to be heard, but for the sake of the Blood of Your Son and for His merits " (T.J. *Way*, 3).

376

FEAST OF THE MOST PRECIOUS BLOOD OF OUR LORD JESUS CHRIST

JULY FIRST

PRESENCE OF GOD - O Jesus who redeemed me by Your Precious Blood, grant that it may produce all its fruit in me.

MEDITATION

1. In today's liturgy the majestic figure of Jesus stands before us as that of a king who presents himself to his people robed in his royal mantle. The first antiphon of Vespers says : " Who is this that cometh...with dyed garments? This beautiful one in his robe " *(RB)*. But the mantle Jesus wears is not beautiful by reason of fine linen or purple, but rather because it is sprinkled with *His* Blood, which was shed for our sins. " He was clothed in a robe sprinkled with blood, and His Name is called the Word of God " *(ibid.)*. That blood which the Word, when He became incarnate, took from our human nature, He gave back to us—every drop of it—as the price of our redemption. And He gave it back, not as if constrained by anyone, but freely, because He willed to, because He loved us. " Christ...hath loved us, " says St. John, " and washed us from our sins in His own Blood " *(Ap* 1,5). All the mysteries of our redemption are mysteries of love; and, therefore, all urge us to love. But the one on which we meditate today is especially moving, since it makes us consider the Redemption from its most terrible aspect : the shedding of the Blood of Jesus, which, from Calvary, flowed forth to crimson the whole world, to sprinkle all souls. Christ has redeemed us, " neither by the blood of goats or of calves, but by His own Blood, " St. Paul exclaims in the Epistle *(Heb* 9,11-15). This is a great truth which, if really understood, would more than suffice to make us genuine saints. We must have a " sense " of Christ's Blood, that Blood which He shed to the last drop for us, and which, through the Sacraments, especially Penance,

continually flows over our souls to cleanse them, purify them and enrich them with the infinite merits of the Redeemer. " Bathe in His Blood, immerse yourself in His Blood, clothe yourself in the Blood of Christ, " was St. Catherine of Siena's continual cry.

2. In the Office of the day, St. Paul earnestly invites us to correspond with Christ's gift. " Jesus...that He might sanctify the people by His own Blood, suffered outside the gate. Let us go forth therefore to Him...bearing His reproach. " If we want the Blood of Christ to bear all its fruit in us, we must unite our own blood with it. His alone is most precious, so precious that a single drop is sufficient to save the whole world; nevertheless, Jesus, as always, wants us to add our little share, our contribution of suffering and sacrifice, " bearing His reproach. " If we are sincere we will have to admit that we do all in our power to escape Christ's shame and disgrace. A lack of consideration, a slight offense, a cutting word, are all that it takes to arouse our passions. How can we say that we know how to share in Christ's humiliations? Behold our divine Master treated like a malefactor, dragged amidst the coarse insults of the soldiers outside the gate of Jerusalem and there crucified between two thieves! And we? What part do we take in His Passion? How do we share in His reproach?

To redeem us, " Jesus...endured the Cross, despising the shame... " and " you, " St. Paul reproaches us, " have not yet resisted unto blood, striving against sin " (*Heb* 12,2.4). Can we say that we know how to struggle " unto blood " to overcome our faults, our pride, our self-love? Oh! how weak and cowardly we are in the struggle, how self-indulgent and full of pity for ourselves, especially for our pride! Jesus, Innocence itself, expiated our sins even unto a bloody, ignominious death! We, the guilty ones, far from atoning for our faults unto blood, cannot even sacrifice our self-love. The blood which flows from sincere, total renunciation of self, from humble, generous acceptance of everything that mortifies, breaks, and destroys our pride : this is the blood which Jesus asks us to unite with His! The Precious Blood of Jesus will give us the strength to do so, " for the soul which becomes inebriated and inundated by the Blood of Christ, is clothed with true and genuine virtue " (St. Catherine of Siena).

COLLOQUY

" O sweet Jesus, my Love, to strengthen my soul and
to rescue it from the weakness into which it has fallen,
You have built a wall around it, and have mixed the mortar
with Your Blood, confirming my soul and uniting it to the
sweet will and charity of God! Just as lime mixed with
water is placed between stones to cement them together,
so You, O God, have placed between Your creature and
Yourself, the Blood of Your only-begotten Son, cemented
with the divine lime of the fire of ardent charity, in such
a way that there is no Blood without fire, nor fire without
Blood. Your Blood was shed, O Christ, by the fire of
love! " (St. Catherine of Siena).

" I adore You, O Precious Blood of Jesus, flower of
creation, fruit of virginity, ineffable instrument of the Holy
Spirit, and I rejoice at the thought that You came from the
drop of virginal blood on which eternal Love impressed its
movement; You were assumed by the Word and deified in
His person. I am overcome with emotion when I think of
Your passing from the Blessed Virgin's heart into the heart
of the Word, and, being vivified by the breath of the Divinity,
becoming adorable because You became the Blood of God.

" I adore You enclosed in the veins of Jesus, preserved
in His humanity like the manna in the golden urn, the
memorial of the eternal Redemption which He accomplished
during the days of His earthly life. I adore You, Blood of the
new, eternal Testament, flowing from the veins of Jesus in
Gethsemane, from His flesh torn by scourges in the Praeto-
rium, from His pierced hands and feet and from His opened
side on Golgotha. I adore You in the Sacraments, in the
Eucharist, where I know You are substantially present....

" I place my trust in You, O adorable Blood, our
Redemption, our regeneration. Fall, drop by drop, into the
hearts that have wandered from You and soften their hardness.
O adorable Blood of Jesus, wash our stains, save us from the
anger of the avenging angel. Irrigate the Church; make
her fruitful with Apostles and miracle-workers, enrich her
with souls that are holy, pure and radiant with divine
beauty " (St. Albert the Great).

377

THE VISITATION OF THE BLESSED VIRGIN MARY

JULY SECOND

PRESENCE OF GOD - O my Mother, most holy Virgin Mary, be always my model, my support, and my guide.

MEDITATION

1. " And Mary, rising up in those days, went into the hill country with haste into a city of Juda. " These words are from today's Gospel (*Lk* 1,39-47). Mary, in the exquisite delicacy of her charity, has such a profound sense of the needs of others, that as soon as she hears of them, she acts spontaneously and decisively to bring help. Having learned from the Angel Gabriel that her cousin was about to become a mother, she goes immediately to offer her humble services.

If we consider the difficulty of traveling in those days, when the poor, such as Mary, had to go on foot over difficult roads, or at best, by means of some rude conveyance, and also the fact that Mary remained three months with Elizabeth, we can readily understand that she had to face many hardships in performing this act of charity. However, she was in no way disturbed : charity urged her, making her wholly forgetful of herself, for as St. Paul says : " Charity seeketh not her own " (1 *Cor* 13,5). How many times, perhaps, have you omitted an act of kindness, not to spare yourself a hard journey, but only to avoid a little trouble. Think how uncharitable you are and how slow to help others. Look at Mary, and see how much you can learn from her!

Charity makes Mary forget not only her hardships but also her own dignity, which was greater than that given to any other creature. Elizabeth is advanced in years, but Mary is the Mother of God; Elizabeth is about to give birth to a man, but Mary will give birth to the Son of God. Nevertheless, before her cousin as before the Angel, Mary continues to look upon herself as the humble handmaid of the Lord, and nothing more. Precisely because she considers herself a handmaid, she comports herself as such, even in respect to her neighbor. In your case, perhaps, although you know how to humble yourself before God and recognize your lack of perfection in the secrecy of your heart, it displeases you to appear imperfect before your neighbor, and you quickly resent being treated as such. Are you not anxious to have your dignity, education, and ability recognized, as well as the more or less honorable offices or charges which have been entrusted to you? Your dignity is a mere nothing, and yet you are so jealous of it. Mary's dignity approaches the infinite, yet she considers herself and behaves as if she were the least of all creatures.

2. And Elizabeth cried out with a loud voice and said : " Blessed art thou among women, and blessed is the fruit of thy womb. And whence is this to me, that the Mother of my Lord should come to me? " Enlightened interiorly by the Holy Spirit, Elizabeth recognizes her young cousin as the Mother of God, and, deeply moved, breaks forth into words of praise and admiration. Mary makes no protest but listens with simplicity, knowing well that this praise is not due to her, but solely to the Almighty who has done great things in her. Immediately, her humble heart, by a sponta-neous movement, refers all Elizabeth's praises to God. " Elizabeth, " the Virgin says, " you glorify the Mother of the Lord, but ' my soul doth magnify the Lord. ' You say that, at the sound of my voice, the child in your womb leaped for joy, but ' my spirit doth rejoice in God, my Saviour.... ' You say : Happy is she who has believed, but the reason for her faith and happiness is the gaze which divine goodness has turned upon her. Yes, ' henceforth all generations shall call me blessed, because God hath regarded the humility of His handmaid ' " (St. Bernard). This beautiful para-phrase of the *Magnificat* gives us a vivid picture of the attitude of Mary's soul as she bows in humble confession of her nothingness, touching as it were the depths of her lowliness, and then, rising higher in God than she had previously abased herself, she is not afraid to acknowledge and praise the wonderful things He has accomplished in her, precisely because she sees perfectly that they are a pure gift on His part.

If you are still inclined to vain complacency about your successes, the praise of others, the graces which God has given you, it is because you have not yet touched, as Mary did, the depths of your lowliness, and have not gone deeply

enough into the consideration of your nothingness.   You are
not yet convinced of your radical insufficiency, your powerlessness, wretchedness, and frailty.   Ask Mary to obtain
for you the great grace of a clear, practical knowledge of
your nothingnesss.   Do not cherish any illusions here!
You have inherited the seed of pride from Adam; hence,
the road to self-knowledge is rough and hard; it is the road
of humiliations.   But Mary is your Mother; if she is with
you, helping you, everything will become easier and sweeter.

COLLOQUY

" O Mary, how great is your humility when you hasten
to serve others!   If it is true that he who humbles himself
will be exalted, who will be more exalted than you who have
humbled yourself so much?

" When Elizabeth caught sight of you she was astonished
and exclaimed : ' Whence is this to me that the Mother of my
Lord should come to me? '   But I am still more astonished
to see that you, as well as your Son, came not to be served,
but to serve. . . .   It was for this purpose that you went to
Elizabeth, you the Queen, to the servant, the Mother of God
to the mother of the Precursor, you who would give birth
to the Son of God, to her who would bring forth a mere man.

" But your profound humility in no way lessened your
magnanimity; the greatness of your soul was not opposed to
your humility.   You, so small in your own eyes, were so
magnanimous in your faith, in your hope in the Most High,
that you never doubted His promises, and firmly believed
that you would become the Mother of the Son of God.

" Humility did not make you fainthearted; magnanimity
did not make you proud, but these two virtues were perfectly
combined in you!

" O Mary, you cannot give me a share in your great
privileges as Mother of God; these belong to you alone!
But you want me to share in your virtues, giving me
examples of them in yourself.   If, then, sincere humility,
magnanimous faith, and delicate, sympathetic charity are
lacking in me, how can I excuse myself?   O Mary, O Mother
of mercy, you who are full of grace, nourish us, your poor
little ones, with your virtues! " (St. Bernard).

378

OUR LADY OF MOUNT CARMEL

JULY SIXTEENTH

PRESENCE OF GOD - O Mary, Beauty of Carmel, make me worthy of your protection, clothe me with your scapular, and be the teacher of my interior life.

MEDITATION

1. The Blessed Virgin is a Mother who clothes us with grace and takes our supernatural life under her protection, in order to bring it to its full flowering in eternal life. She, the Immaculate, full of grace from the first moment of her conception, takes our souls stained by sin, and with a maternal gesture, cleanses them in the Blood of Christ and clothes them with grace, which, together with Him, she has merited for us. We can truly say that the garment of grace was woven by the blessed hands of Mary, who day by day, moment by moment, gave herself entirely, in union with her Son, for our salvation. Legend tells of the seamless robe which the Blessed Virgin wove for Jesus; but, for us—and in reality—she has done much more. She has cooperated in obtaining the garment of our eternal salvation, the wedding garment in which we shall enter the banquet hall of heaven. How she longs that this robe be imperishable! From the moment we received it, Mary has never ceased to follow us with her maternal gaze, to safeguard within us the life of grace. Each time we are converted and return to God or rise again after falling into sin—be it great or small—each time we increase in grace, all, everything, is effected through Mary's mediation. The scapular, the *little habit*, that our Lady of Mount Carmel offers us, is only the external symbol of her unceasing, maternal care : the symbol, but also the sign, the pledge of eternal salvation. " My beloved son, " Mary said to St. Simon Stock, " take this scapular...whoever dies clothed in it will not suffer eternal fire. " The Blessed Virgin gives the assurance of the supreme grace of final perseverance to all who wear worthily her *little habit*.

" Those who wear the scapular," said Pius XII, " profess
to belong to Our Lady. " Because we belong to Mary she
takes special care of our souls. One who belongs to her
cannot be lost or be touched by eternal fire. Her powerful
maternal intercession gives her the right to repeat, for her
children, the words of Jesus : " Holy Father...those whom
Thou gavest Me have I kept; and none of them is lost "
(*Jn* 17,12).

2. Devotion to our Lady of Mount Carmel indicates a
strong call to the interior life, which, in a very special way,
is Mary's life. The Blessed Virgin wants us to resemble her
in heart and mind much more than in externals. If we
penetrate into Mary's soul, we see that grace produced
in her a very rich interior life : a life of recollection, prayer,
uninterrupted giving of herself to God, and of constant
contact and intimate union with Him. Mary's soul is a
sanctuary reserved for God alone where no creature has
ever left an imprint; here reign love and zeal for the glory
of God and the salvation of men.

Those who wish to live truly devoted to our Lady of
Mount Carmel, must follow Mary into the depths of the
interior life. Carmel is the symbol of the contemplative life,
of life wholly consecrated to seeking God and tending wholly
toward divine intimacy; and she who best realizes this very
high ideal is Mary, *Queen, Beauty of Carmel*. " Judgment
shall dwell in the wilderness and justice shall sit in Carmel.
And the work of justice shall be peace, and the service
of justice quietness and security forever. And my people
shall sit in the beauty of peace, and in the tabernacles of
confidence. " These verses, taken from Isaias (32,16-18)
and repeated in the Office proper to Our Lady of Mount
Carmel, delineate very well the contemplative spirit and, at
the same time, they are a beautiful picture of Mary's soul
which is a real " garden " (Carmel in Hebrew signifies
garden) of virtues, an oasis of silence and peace, where justice
and equity reign; an oasis of security completely enveloped in
the shadow of God, and filled with God. Every interior
soul, even if living amid the tumult of the world, must strive
to reach this peace, this interior silence, which alone makes
continual contact with God possible. It is our passions and
attachments that make noise within us, that disturb our peace
of mind and interrupt our intimate converse with God.

Only the soul that is wholly detached and in complete control of its passions can, like Mary, be a solitary, silent " garden " where God will find His delights. This is the grace we ask of Our Lady today when we choose her to be the Queen and mistress of our interior life.

COLLOQUY

" O Mary, flower of Carmel, fruitful vine, splendor of heaven, who brought forth the Son of God yet remained a Virgin, sweet and Immaculate Mother, grant the favors your children implore, O Star of the sea " (St. Simon Stock).

" O most Blessed Virgin : has anyone ever invoked your aid without being helped? We, your little children, rejoice with you for all your virtues, but particularly for your mercy. We praise your virginity, we admire your humility; but for the needy, mercy has even a sweeter savor. We have a more tender love for mercy, we recall it more often, and we invoke it more frequently. Truly your mercy has obtained the redemption of the world; together with your prayers, it has secured the salvation of all mankind. Oh Mary, who can measure the length, breadth, height and depth of your mercy? Its length reaches to the end of time, to help all who call upon it; its breadth encompasses the whole world, for all the earth is full of your goodness! The height of your mercy has unlocked the gates of the heavenly city and has obtained the redemption of those who dwell in darkness and the shadow of death. By you, O Mary, the erring are brought back to the right road and heaven is filled. Thus your most powerful and merciful charity is poured over us like a compassionate and helpful love " (St. Bernard).

379

THE ASSUMPTION OF THE BLESSED VIRGIN MARY

AUGUST FIFTEENTH

PRESENCE OF GOD - O most Blessed Virgin Mary, assumed into heaven, I beg you to purify my senses so that I may begin to enjoy God even while I am on earth.

MEDITATION

1. The Blessed Virgin Mary, whom we contemplate today assumed body and soul into heaven, reminds us very definitely that our permanent abode is not on earth but in heaven where she, with her divine Son, has preceded us in all the fulness of her human nature. This is the dominant thought in today's liturgy. " O Almighty and everlasting God, who hast taken up body and soul into heavenly glory the Immaculate Virgin Mary, Mother of Thy Son : grant, we beseech Thee, that, ever intent upon heavenly things, we may be worthy to be partakers of her glory " *(Collect)*.

The Feast of the Assumption is a strong appeal to us to live " ever intent upon heavenly things, " and not to allow ourselves to be carried away by the vicissitudes and seductions of the world. Not only was our soul created for heaven, but also our body, which, after the resurrection, will be welcomed into our heavenly home and admitted to a participation in the glory of the spirit. Today we contemplate in Mary, our Mother, this total glorification of our humanity. That which has been wholly realized in her, will be realized for us, as well as for all the saints, only at the end of time. This privilege was very fitting for her, the all-pure, the all-holy one, whose body was never touched by even the faintest shadow of sin, but was always the temple of the Holy Spirit, and became the immaculate tabernacle of the Son of God. It is a reminder to us to ennoble our whole life, not only that of the spirit, but also that of the senses, elevating it to the heights of the celestial life which awaits us. " O Mother of God and of men, " exclaims Pius XII in his beautiful prayer for the Assumption, " we beg you to

purify our senses, so that we may begin to enjoy God here
on earth and Him alone, in the beauty of creatures. "

2. Mary's Assumption shows us the route we must follow
in our spiritual ascent : detachment from the earth, flight
toward God, and union with God.

Our Lady was assumed body and soul into heaven
because she was Immaculate; she was all-pure—free not
only from every shadow of sin, but even from the slightest
attachment to the things of earth, so that she " never had the
form of any creature imprinted in her soul, nor was moved
by such, but was invariably guided by the Holy Spirit "
(J.C. *AS III*, 2,10).

The first requirement for attaining God is this total
purity, the fruit of total detachment. The Blessed Virgin, who
lived her earthly life in absolute detachment from every
created thing, teaches us not to allow ourselves to be captivated
by the fascination of creatures, but to live among them,
occupying ourselves with them with much charity, but
without ever letting our heart become attached to them,
without ever seeking our satisfaction in them.

In her Assumption Mary speaks to us of flight toward
heaven, toward God. It is not enough to purify our heart
from sin and all attachment to creatures, we must at
the same time direct it toward God, tending toward Him
with all our strength. The Church has us pray in today's
Mass, " O Lord, through the intercession of the Blessed
Virgin Mary who was assumed into heaven, may our hearts,
enkindled by the fire of Thy love, continually aspire toward
Thee " *(Secret)*. Our earthly life has value for eternal life
insofar as it is a flight toward God, a continual seeking
after Him, a continual adherence to His grace. When
this flight fails, the supernatural value of our existence
lessens.

Mary has been taken up to heaven because she is the
Mother of God. This is the greatest of her privileges, the
root of all the others and the reason for them; it speaks to us,
in a very special way, of intimate union with God, as the
fact of her Assumption speaks to us of the beatific union of
heaven. Mary's Assumption thus confirms us in this great
and beautiful truth : we are created and called to union with
God. Mary herself stretches out her maternal hand to guide
us to the attainment of this high ideal. If we keep our eyes

fixed on her, we shall advance more easily; she will be our guide, our strength, and our consolation in every trial and difficulty.

COLLOQUY

" O Immaculate Virgin, Mother of God and Mother of men, we believe with all the fervor of our faith in your triumphal Assumption, both body and soul, into heaven, where you are acclaimed as Queen by all the choirs of angels and all the legions of the saints. And we unite with them to praise and bless the Lord who has exalted you above all other pure creatures, and to offer you the tribute of our devotion and our love.

" We know that your gaze, which on earth watched over the humble and suffering humanity of Jesus, in heaven is filled with the vision of that humanity glorified, and with the vision of uncreated Wisdom; the joy of your soul in the direct contemplation of the adorable Trinity causes your heart to throb with overwhelming tenderness. We, poor sinners, weighed down by a body which hinders the flight of the soul, beg you to purify our hearts, so that while we remain here below, we may learn to love God and God alone in the beauty of His creatures.

" We trust that your merciful eyes may deign to look down upon our miseries and our sorrows, upon our struggles and our weaknesses; that your countenance may smile upon our joys and our victories; that you may hear the voice of Jesus saying to you of each one of us, as He once said to you of His beloved disciple : ' Behold thy son. ' And we, who call upon you as our Mother, take you, like John, as the guide, strength, and consolation of our mortal life.

" And from this earth over which we tread as pilgrims, comforted by our faith in the future resurrection, we look to you, our life, our sweetness, and our hope. Draw us onward by the gentleness of your voice, so that one day, after our exile, you may show us Jesus, the Blessed Fruit of your womb, O clement, O loving, O sweet Virgin Mary " (Pius XII).

380

THE NATIVITY OF THE BLESSED VIRGIN MARY

SEPTEMBER EIGHTH

PRESENCE OF GOD - O Mary, my Mother, teach me to live hidden with you in the shadow of God.

MEDITATION

1. The liturgy enthusiastically celebrates Mary's Nativity and makes it one of the most appealing feasts of Marian devotion. We sing in today's Office : " Thy Nativity, O Virgin Mother of God, brings joy to the whole world, because from you came forth the Sun of Justice, Christ, our God. " Mary's birth is a prelude to the birth of Jesus because it is the initial point of the realization of the great mystery of the Incarnation of the Son of God for the salvation of mankind. How could the birthday of the Mother of the Redeemer pass unnoticed in the hearts of the redeemed? The Mother proclaims the Son, making it known that He is about to come, that the divine promises, made centuries before, are to be fulfilled. The birth of Mary is the dawn of our redemption; her appearance projects a new light over all the human race : a light of innocence, of purity, of grace, a resplendent presage of the great light which will inundate the world when Christ, " lux mundi, " the Light of the World, appears. Mary, preserved from sin in anticipation of Christ's merits, not only announces that the Redemption is at hand, but she bears the firstfruits of it within herself; she is the first one redeemed by her divine Son. Through her, all-pure and full of grace, the Blessed Trinity at last fixes on earth a look of complacency, finding in her alone a creature in whom the infinite beauty of the Godhead can be reflected.

The birth of Jesus excepted, no other was so important in God's eyes or so fruitful for the good of humanity, as was the birth of Mary. Yet it has remained in complete obscurity. There is no mention of it in Sacred Scriptures and when we look for the genealogy of Jesus in the Gospel, we find only what refers to Joseph; we find nothing explicit about Mary's ancestry except the allusion to her descent from David. Our Lady's origin is wrapped in silence, as was her whole life. Thus, her birth speaks to us of humility. The more we desire to grow in God's eyes, the more we should hide ourselves from the eyes of creatures. The more we wish to do great things for God, the more we should labor in silence and obscurity.

2. In the Gospel the figure of Mary is, as it were, completely overshadowed by that of her divine Son; the Evangelists tell us only what is necessary to present the Mother of the Redeemer, and in fact, she enters on the scene only when the narrative of the Incarnation of the Word begins. Mary's life is confounded with, is lost in, the life of Jesus : truly she lived " hidden with Christ in God. " Let us note, too, that she lived in obscurity, not only during the years of her childhood, but also during the whole period of her divine maternity, yes, even during the triumphal moments in the public life of her Son, even when a certain woman, enthusiastic about the wonderful things that Jesus did, cried out in the midst of the crowd : " Blessed is the womb that bore Thee and the breasts that nursed Thee! " (*Lk* 11,27).

The Feast which we celebrate today is an invitation to the hidden life, to hide ourselves with Mary in Christ, and with Christ in God. Many times it is God Himself who, through circumstances or the decisions of our superiors, makes us live in obscurity. We should be very grateful for this, and take advantage of these opportunities to make more progress in the practice of humility and self-effacement. At other times, however, God gives us responsibilities, offices, apostolic works which bring us into prominence, but even in such circumstances we should try to efface ourselves as much as possible. Certainly we must not refuse the assignment, but we should know how to withdraw as soon as our activity is no longer needed for the success of the work entrusted to us. All the rest—praise, applause, the account of our success or the excuse for our failure—should not concern us. In the face of all this we should strive to remain wholly indifferent. An interior soul should long to hide itself as much as it can under the shadow of God, for, if it has been able to accomplish some little good, it is convinced that in reality all has been the work of God; therefore, it eagerly seeks that all may redound to His glory alone.

Let Mary's humble, hidden life be the model of ours, and if, in emulating her, we have to struggle against our ever-recurrent tendencies to pride, let us confidently seek her maternal aid, and she will help us to triumph over all vainglory.

COLLOQUY

" When I feel myself tossed about in the sea of this world amidst storms and tempests, I keep my eyes fixed on you, O Mary, shining star, lest I be swallowed up by the waves.

" When the winds of temptation arise, when I dash against the reefs of tribulations, I raise my eyes to you and call upon you, O Mary. When I am agitated by the billows of pride, ambition, slander or jealousy, I look to you and I invoke you, O Mary; when anger or avarice or the seductions of the flesh rock the fragile little barque of my soul, I always look to you, O Mary. And if I am troubled by the enormity of my sins, troubled in conscience, frightened at the severity of judgment, and if I should feel myself engulfed in sadness or drawn into the abyss of despair, again I raise my eyes to you, always calling on you, O Mary.

" In dangers, in difficulties, in doubts, I will always think of you, O Mary, I will always call on you. May your name, O Virgin Mary, be always on my lips and never leave my heart; in order that I may obtain the help of your prayers, grant that I may never lose sight of the example of your life. Following you, O Mary, I shall not go astray, thinking of you I shall not err, if you support me I shall not fall, if you protect me I shall have nothing to fear, if you accompany me I shall not grow weary, if you look upon me with favor, I shall reach the port " (St. Bernard).

381

FEAST OF THE BLESSED VIRGIN MARY OF THE ROSARY

OCTOBER SEVENTH

PRESENCE OF GOD - O most holy Virgin, may the Rosary be my spiritual armor and my school of virtue.

MEDITATION

1. Today's Feast is a manifestation of gratitude for the great victories won by the Christian people through the power of Mary's Rosary; it is also the most beautiful and authoritative testimony of the value of this prayer. The liturgy of the day is not only a commentary on the Rosary, but an amplification of it : the three hymns of the Office as well as the antiphons of Matins and Lauds, review its different mysteries; the lessons chant its glories, and the continual references to the Virgin, who " blossomed as it were, among the flowers, surrounded by roses and lilies of the valley, " are a clear allusion to the mystical crowns of roses which Mary's devoted children weave at her feet when they recite the Rosary. This Feast tells us that to honor the Rosary is to honor Mary, for the Rosary is simply a meditation on Our Lady's life, accompanied by the devout recitation of the Hail Mary. It is for this reason that the Church praises this practice and recommends it so insistently to the faithful. " O God, " she prays in today's Collect, " grant that meditating on the mysteries of the most Holy Rosary of the Blessed Virgin Mary, we may both imitate what they contain and obtain what they promise. " The Rosary, if recited well, is both prayer and instruction; its mysteries tell us that in Mary's life everything is judged in relation to God : her joy and consolation found in all that gives pleasure to God; her sorrows are, so to speak, the very sorrows of God, who being made man, willed to suffer for the sins of mankind. Mary's only joy is Jesus : to be His Mother, to clasp Him in her arms, to offer Him for the adoration of the world, to contemplate Him in the glory of His Resurrection,

to be united to Him in Heaven. Mary's unique sorrow
is the Passion of Jesus : to see Him betrayed, scourged,
crowned with thorns, and crucified by our sins. This, then,
is the first fruit which we must gather from the recitation
of the Rosary : to judge all the events of our life according to
their relation to God, to rejoice in what gives Him pleasure,
in what unites us to Him, to suffer for sin which separates us
from Him and is the cause of the Passion and death of Jesus.

2. The second fruit that we should derive from the daily
recitation of the Rosary is a penetration into Christ's
mysteries; by Mary and with Mary, who opens the door to
them for us, the Rosary helps us to penetrate the ineffable
grandeurs of the Incarnation, Passion, and glory of Jesus.
Who is there who has understood and lived these mysteries
as Our Lady did? And who better than she can make us
understand them? If, during the recitation of the Rosary,
we really know how to put ourselves in spiritual contact
with Mary and to accompany her in the various stages of
her life, we shall be able to perceive something of the sentiments of her heart concerning these great mysteries which
she witnessed, and in which she played such an important
part; this, in turn, will serve wonderfully to nourish our
souls. Thus, our Rosary will be transformed into a quarter
of an hour's meditation—we might almost say contemplation—under Mary's guidance. This is what Mary
desires, rather than many Rosaries recited with the lips,
while the mind wanders in a thousand directions! The
Hail Mary, continuously repeated, should express the
attitude of a soul who is striving to approach the Blessed
Virgin, hastening toward her in order to be captivated by
her and given insight into the divine mysteries. " Ave
Maria! " the lips say, and the heart murmurs : " Teach me,
O Mary, to know and love Jesus as you knew and loved
Him. "
Saying the Rosary in this way requires recollection.
St. Teresa of Jesus says that " before beginning to recite
the Rosary, let the soul think of whom it is going to address,
and who it is that is speaking, that it may speak to Him
with due respect " (cf. *Way*, 22). The Saint, with her
keen wit, laughs at those people " who are so fond of repeating
a large number of vocal prayers in a great hurry, as though
they were anxious to finish their task of repeating them daily "

(*ibid.*, 31). Rosaries recited in this way cannot really nourish our interior life; they will bring little fruit to the soul and little glory to Mary. On the other hand, if recited with a real spirit of devotion, the Rosary becomes an effective means of cultivating devotion to Mary and of bringing us into intimacy with Our Lady and her divine Son.

COLLOQUY

" O Mary, just as there is no saint who loves God more than you love Him, so we neither have, nor could we have, after God, anyone who loves us more than you, our most loving Mother. If it were possible to bring together the love of all mothers for their children, of all wives for their husbands, of all the saints and angels for those who have devotion to them, it would not equal the love you have for one single soul, and, therefore, for my soul too.

" O Mary, since you love me, make me resemble you. You have all power to change hearts : take my heart, then, and transform it. Make me a saint, make me your worthy child.

" Let others ask for what they will : health, riches, worldly advantages; I come to ask you, O Mary, for those things which you yourself desire for me and which are very dear to your heart. You, who were so humble, obtain for me humility and a love for contempt. You, so patient in the sorrows of this life, obtain for me patience in adversity. You who were filled with love for God, obtain for me the gift of pure, holy love. You were all charity toward your neighbor; obtain for me charity toward all, and especially toward those who are opposed to me. O Mary, you who are the holiest of all creatures, make me holy. You lack neither love nor power; you can and you will obtain everything for me. Only my failure to have recourse to you and my want of confidence in your aid can prevent me from receiving your favors " (St. Alphonsus).

382

FEAST OF THE MOTHERHOOD OF THE BLESSED VIRGIN MARY

OCTOBER ELEVENTH

PRESENCE OF GOD - O Mary, Mother of God, deign to accept my humble homage and grant that I, too, may enjoy the blessed fruits of your maternity.

MEDITATION

1. The Feast we celebrate today honors Mary under her most beautiful title and in her most glorious prerogative : Mother of God. This title and prerogative were solemnly proclaimed by the Council of Ephesus, to oppose the Nestorian heresy. Today the Church congratulates Mary for this supreme dignity, which raises her above all other creatures, even to the threshold of infinity, and makes her Queen, not only of men, but also of angels. This is the dominant theme throughout the Mass. The Introit repeats the prophecy of Isaias which, even in the Old Testament, had foretold the sublimity of our Blessed Lady, " Behold, a Virgin shall conceive, and bear a son, and His Name shall be called Emmanuel " (Is 7,14), that is, God with us. The Epistle (Sir 24,23-31), applying to Our Lady an extract from the book of Wisdom, sings the praises of her divine maternity : Mary is the fruitful vine which bore the fairest fruit, Jesus. Mary is " the mother of fair love " in whom is " all grace of the way and of the truth...all hope of life and of virtue, " since through her alone God gave to the world His only-begotten Son; through her alone men have had their Savior. He who wants Jesus must seek Him in Mary's arms; he who wishes to propitiate the Savior must have recourse to her who is His Mother. How sweetly, then, does her maternal invitation sound in our ears : " Come over to me, all ye that desire me, and be filled with my fruits. " Yes, let us go to Mary and we shall not be deceived; in her we shall find all we can desire, because Mary gives us Jesus, the Redeemer, Father and true Food of our souls. Not only

does she give Him to us, but, by the example of her wonderful life, she teaches us to love Him, to imitate Him, to follow Him, and to profit as much as possible from His redemptive, sanctifying work. Thus Mary extends her maternity to us too, fulfilling toward us the duties of a Mother, and we can repeat with full confidence the prayer which the Church puts on our lips today : " O Lord...grant that we who believe her to be indeed the Mother of God may be aided by her intercession with Thee " *(Collect)*.

2. The Feast of Mary's Maternity should awaken in our hearts confidence and trust in her who, because of her dignity as Mother, has the greatest influence with her divine Son. In praising the Mother of God, we beg her to use her maternal power in our behalf : " Holy Mary, Mother of God, pray for us sinners. " What greater advocate could we find? What more powerful Patroness? Jesus cannot resist His Mother's supplications, nor can Mary resist those who invoke her under her sweetest title : Mother. If every woman is touched when she hears herself called " Mother, " will not Mary be even more deeply touched when she is invoked as " Mother of God "? Then let us call her by that name, let us treat her as a mother—as the Mother of God first of all and then as our own Mother—since Jesus, when dying on the Cross, put at our disposal the treasures of her maternity. Our Lady has a maternal mission to accomplish in our souls. Jesus Himself has entrusted it to her; therefore, it is very dear to her, and she desires to fulfill it perfectly. Yes, Mary wishes to be our Mother, she wishes to use the privileges and treasures of her maternity for our advantage, but she cannot do so unless we entrust ourselves to her care like docile, loving children. Even among those who are consecrated to God, not all realize sufficiently the necessity of giving themselves to Mary as her children, of opening their soul to her maternal influence, of having recourse to her with complete confidence, of calling upon her aid in all their difficulties and dangers, and of placing their whole spiritual life under her patronage. In the natural order a child needs a mother, and suffers both morally and spiritually without one; so also in the supernatural order, souls need a mother, they need Mary, most holy. Without her and her maternal care, souls suffer, their spiritual life is stunted and often becomes lax, or, at least, is not as vigorous

as it should be.   On the other hand, when souls give themselves to Mary, seek Mary, and trust themselves to her,
their interior life progresses rapidly, their journey toward
God is more simple and swift; everything becomes easier
because there is a Mother's hand to sustain them, there is a
Mother's heart to comfort them.

COLLOQUY

"Your name, O Mother of God, is filled with every
divine grace and blessing.   You carried in your womb Him
whom the heavens could not contain.   You nourished Him
who feeds the whole world.   The Lord of the universe willed
to have need of you, for you gave Him the flesh which
He did not have before.   Rejoice, O Mother and Handmaid
of God!   Rejoice!   You have for debtor Him who gives
existence to all creatures; we are all debtors to God, but God
is debtor to you!

"O most holy Virgin, you have more goodness and
charity than all the other saints and you have greater access
to the throne of God than they, because you are His Mother.
I, then, who am celebrating your glories and praising your
immense goodness, beg you to be mindful of me and my
miseries " (St. Methodius).

"O great Mother of God, I, too, will say with
St. Bernard : ' Speak, O Lady, because your Son is listening
to you, and whatever you ask He will grant you! '   Speak,
then, speak, in my favor, O Mary, my advocate, wretched
as I am.   Remember it was for my benefit, too, that you
were given such power and dignity.   God willed to make
Himself your debtor by taking His human nature from you,
so that you might freely dispense the riches of His divine
mercy to the poor and wretched.

"If you, who are so immensely good, do good to all,
even to those who do not know and honor you, how much
more should we hope in your benignity, we who wish to
honor you and love you and who trust in your aid?   O Mary,
although we are sinners, you can save us, because God has
enriched you with mercy and power that surpasses all our
iniquity.   O most sweet Mother, to you I give my soul, that
you may purify it, sanctify it, and consecrate it wholly to
to Jesus " (St. Alphonsus).

383

FEAST OF OUR LORD JESUS CHRIST THE KING

LAST SUNDAY OF OCTOBER

PRESENCE OF GOD - O Jesus, Prince of Ages, King of Nations, be the sole Ruler of my mind and heart.

MEDITATION

1. The liturgy today is truly a triumphant hymn celebrating the Kingship of Christ. From the First Vespers of the Feast, the figure of Jesus is majestically portrayed, seated on a royal throne and dominating the entire world; " His Kingdom is an everlasting Kingdom, and all kings shall serve and obey Him.... He shall sit and rule and shall speak peace unto the nations. "

The Mass opens with the apocalyptic vision of this extraordinary King whose majesty is intimately linked to His immolation for the salvation of souls.... " The Lamb that was slain is worthy to receive power and divinity and wisdom and strength and honor. To Him belong glory and power forever and ever " (Introit).

In the Epistle (Col 1,12-20) St. Paul enumerates the titles which make Christ King of all kings : He is " the image of the invisible God, the firstborn of every creature; for in Him were all things created in heaven and on earth, visible and invisible. " These titles belong to Jesus Christ inasmuch as He is God, perfect image of the Father, exemplary cause of all earthly and heavenly creatures and, at the same time, Creator, together with the Father and the Holy Spirit, of all that exists, for nothing has existence without Him, but " all things were created by Him and in Him...by Him all things consist. "

Then come His titles to Kingship as Man : " He is the Head of the Mystical Body, the Church.... Through Him [God]...reconciled all things unto Himself, making peace through the Blood of His Cross. " He, who is already our King by reason of His divinity, is also King through

His Incarnation, which has constituted Him the Head
of all humanity, and through His Passion, by which at the
price of His Blood He has regained our souls, which
already belonged to Him as His creatures.

Jesus is our King in the full sense of the word : He has
created us, redeemed us, vivified us by His grace, He nourishes
us with His Flesh and Blood, He governs us with love, and
by love He draws us to Himself. In the face of such considerations, the cry of St. Paul rises spontaneously from our
heart : " Giving thanks to God the Father...who hath
delivered us from the power of darkness, and hath translated us into the kingdom of the Son of His love, in whom
we have redemption...the remission of sins. "

2. In today's Gospel (*Jn* 18,33-37) we have the
most authoritative proclamation of the Kingship of Christ,
since it comes from His own lips in that most solemn moment
during the trial which preceded His Passion. Pilate explicitly
questioned Him on the subject : " Art Thou the King of the
Jews? " Jesus did not reply directly to this first question;
actually, He is not King of any one determined nation;
His Kingdom has nothing to do with the kingdoms of earth.
But to Pilate's second and more precise question, " Art
Thou a King then? " Jesus replied unhesitatingly : " Thou
sayest it; I am a King. " He proclaims His Kingship in the
most formal manner before the highest civil authority in
Palestine; He proclaims it, not in the midst of an enthusiastic
crowd, nor in the triumph of His miracles, but bound with
chains, before him who is about to condemn Him to death,
before a crowd thirsting for His Blood, a few moments
before being dragged to Calvary where, from the heights
of the Cross, above His thorn-crowned head, will appear
for the first time the title of His royalty : " Jesus of Nazareth,
the King of the Jews " (*Jn* 19,19). He had fled when the
enthusiastic crowd wished to make Him their King; now He
proclaims Himself King in the midst of the unspeakable
humiliations of His Passion, thus affirming in the clearest
manner that His Kingdom is not of this world, that His
Kingdom is so sublime that no dishonor, no insults can
eclipse it. But by this act Jesus also tells us that He prefers
to manifest His Kingship far more as a conquest of His
Blood than as a title belonging to Him in virtue of His
divine nature.

We should go to meet this divine King with all the yearning of our soul. He presents Himself to us under an appearance so human, so loving, so welcoming, stretching out His arms on the Cross to invite all to come to Him, showing us the wound in His side as the symbol of His Love. Far from trying to escape His dominion, we should beseech Him to be the sole Ruler of our mind and heart, and the complete master of our will. We should submit ourselves and all that belongs to us to " His most gentle rule " *(Collect)*.

COLLOQUY

" You, my God, are an eternal King, and Yours is no borrowed kingdom.... When the Credo says : ' of Your Kingdom there shall be no end ' this phrase nearly always makes me feel particularly happy. Yes, I praise You, Lord, and bless You, for Your Kingdom will endure forever " (T.J. *Way*, 22).

" O divine King, most amiable Jesus, my Redeemer, my Savior, my Spouse, my Master and model, I renew today the total consecration of my being to You, begging You to take absolute dominion over me. Be my Sovereign, my Ruler, my Guide. Direct and govern me entirely, so that everything may turn to Your greater glory. Be King of my memory, of my intellect, of my will, of my emotions; I wish all to be completely subject to You and I invite You to reign in me.

" Your Kingdom is a kingdom of Truth, of Love, of Justice and of Peace.

" Grant that Your reign of *Truth* may be established in my mind, destroying all error, deceit and illusion. Enlighten me by Your divine Wisdom.

" Grant that Your reign of *Love* may be completely established in my will, to move it, draw it, and direct it always, so that I may no longer be moved by self-love, or by creatures but by Your Holy Spirit alone. Make this weak, mean, rebellious will of mine strong, generous, constant; make it grow stronger by the persevering exercise of virtue, and by the gifts of Your Spirit.

" Grant that Your reign of *Justice* may be established in all my actions, so that all I do, having this characteristic, may be a work of holiness, accomplished with purity of

intention and with the greatest fidelity in order to give You
pleasure and accomplish Your holy will.

" Grant that Your reign of *Peace* may be established, not
only in my soul but also in my sensibility, so that, in harmony
with the superior part of my soul, it may give You glory
and neither retard me nor be an obstacle to union with You "
(Sr. Carmela of the Holy Spirit, O.C.D.).

384

FEAST OF ALL SAINTS

NOVEMBER FIRST

PRESENCE OF GOD - Through the intercession of Your saints,
O Lord, may I tread the way of holiness courageously.

MEDITATION

1. Holy Mother Church, always solicitous and anxious
for our salvation, exults today with exceeding joy as she
contemplates the glory of her children who, having reached
their heavenly fatherland, are safe for all eternity, forever
delivered from the snares of the evil one, and now numbered
everlastingly among the elect, the people of God. Like a
mother, proud of the triumph of her children, she presents
them to the whole Christian world, inviting all the faithful
to share her maternal joy : " Let us all rejoice in the Lord,
celebrating a feast in honor of all the saints, at whose
solemnity the angels rejoice and give praise to the Son of
God " *(Introit)*.

The Epistle *(Ap* 7,2-12) offers us the apocalyptic vision
of the glory of the saints : " I saw a great multitude which
no man could number, of all nations and tribes and peoples
and tongues, standing before the throne and in the sight of the
Lamb, clothed in white robes, and with palms in their hands. "
Ranks of martyrs, apostles, confessors, and virgins, luminous
hosts who delight unceasingly in the vision of God, adore
Him continually and praise Him as they repeat : " Benediction

and glory and wisdom and thanksgiving and honor and power and strength to our God forever and ever. Amen. "

Who are these glorious saints? Men who have lived upon earth as we have, who have known our miseries, our difficulties, our struggles. Some of them we recognize easily, for the Church has raised them to the honors of the Altar, but the great majority are entirely unknown to us. They are humble people who lived obscurely in the accomplishment of duty, without display, without renown, whom no one here below remembers, but whom the heavenly Father looked upon, knew in secret, and, having proved their fidelity, called to His glory. The honorable positions occupied by some in this vast gathering, or the mighty deeds accomplished by others, no longer possess any value of themselves : eternal beatitude is not determined by the great things achieved here below. One thing only endures, for the humble and the great, the poor and the wealthy : the degree of love they had attained, to which corresponds the degree of glory which now renders them eternally happy.

2. While the Epistle gives us a glimpse of the life of the saints in heavenly glory, the Gospel (*Mt* 5,1-12), citing a passage from the beatitudes, unveils the life which was theirs upon earth : " Blessed are the poor in spirit...Blessed are the meek...Blessed are they that mourn...Blessed are they that hunger and thirst after justice...Blessed are the merciful...Blessed are the clean of heart...Blessed are the peacemakers...Blessed are they that suffer persecution. " Poverty, humility, detachment from earthly goods; meekness of heart, resignation and patience in sorrow, uprightness, hunger for justice; kindness and understanding toward one's neighbor; purity of mind and heart; peacefulness of spirit and bearer of peace; fortitude and generosity, which, for love of God, embrace every suffering and endure every injustice : such are the characteristics of the life led by the saints on earth, and such must be our program, too, if we wish to attain sanctity as they did.

We want to become saints, but in the easiest way possible, without effort, without fatigue or violence to ourselves; we should like to practice virtue, but only to a certain point, only when it does not ask for great sacrifice, or go too much against the grain. And so it happens that when faced with acts of virtue which exact greater self-renunciation, or the acceptance of difficult and repugnant things, such as quelling the resentments of self-love, renouncing an attempt to make our opinion prevail, submitting ourselves and meekly condescending to one who is opposed to us, very often—if not always—we refuse, thinking it unnecessary to go to such lengths.

Yet our progress in holiness depends precisely upon these acts which we hesitate to make; without them we shall always lead a mediocre life, we shall always remain on the same level, if indeed we do not lose ground. Let us beg the saints whom we honor today to help us overcome our laziness, our lassitude, our cowardice; let us ask those who have gone before us in the arduous way of sanctity to obtain for us the strength to follow them. " If such as these [have attained to sanctity], why not I? " (St. Augustine). God offers us the grace which He gave to the saints; but alas! what is lacking is our correspondence with it.

COLLOQUY

" O holy souls that now rejoice without fear of losing your joy and are forever absorbed in the praises of my God! Happy indeed, your lot! How right that you should employ yourselves ceaselessly in these praises! and how my soul envies you, free as you now are from the affliction caused by the grievous offenses which in these unhappy days are committed against my God! No longer do you behold all the ingratitude of men and their blindness nor the multitude of souls being carried away by Satan.

" O blessed, heavenly souls! Help us in our misery and intercede for us with the divine Mercy, so that we may be granted some part of your joy and you may share with us some of that clear knowledge which is now yours.

" And You, O my God, make us understand what it is that You give to those who fight manfully through the dream of this miserable life. Help us, O loving souls, to understand what joy it gives you to behold the eternity of your bliss and what delight to possess the certain knowledge that it will never end.

" O blessed souls, who knew so well how to profit by the gifts of God, and to purchase with this precious ransom so delectable and enduring a heritage, tell us how you won through Him such an eternal blessing! Assist us, since you are so near the Fountainhead. Draw water for those of us on earth who are perishing with thirst " (T.J. *Exc*, 13).

" O saints of heaven, I am the least of all creatures. I know my worthlessness, but I also know how noble and generous hearts love to do good. Therefore, O blessed inhabitants of the heavenly City, I entreat you to adopt me as your child. All the glory you may help me to acquire will be yours; deign, then, to hear my prayer and obtain for me...your love..." (T.C.J. *St*, 13).

385

COMMEMORATION OF ALL THE FAITHFUL DEPARTED

NOVEMBER SECOND

PRESENCE OF GOD - Grant, O Lord, eternal rest to the souls of the departed; and may the thought of death spur me on to greater generosity.

MEDITATION

1. " Holy Church, our good Mother, after having exalted with fitting praise all her children who now rejoice in heaven, strives also to help all those who still suffer in purgatory, and to this end intercedes with all her power before Christ, her Lord and Spouse, in order that as speedily as possible they may join the society of the elect in heaven. " These are the words of the *Roman Martyrology*.

Yesterday we contemplated the glory of the Church triumphant and implored her intercession. Today we consider the expiatory pains of the Church suffering and solicit for these souls the divine assistance : " Eternal rest grant unto them, O Lord. " This is the dogma of the Communion of saints put into practice. The Church triumphant intercedes for us, the Church militant; and we, in our turn, hasten to the help of the Church suffering. Death has

taken from us those we love; yet there can be no real
separation from those who have died in the kiss of the Lord.
The bond of charity continues to unite us, enfolding in one
embrace earth, heaven and purgatory, so that there circulates
from one region to another the fraternal assistance which
springs from love, which has as its end the triumph of love
in the common glory of Paradise.

The liturgy of the day is pervaded with sadness, but it is
not the grief of those " who have no hope " (1 *Thes* 4,12), for
it is resplendent with faith in a blessed resurrection, in
the eternal felicity which awaits us. The passages chosen
for the Gospels of the three Masses for the faithful departed
speak to us explicitly of all these consoling truths, and in a
most authoritative way, since they repeat to us the very
words of Jesus : " This is the will of the Father who sent Me;
that of all that He hath given Me, I should lose nothing,
but should raise it up again in the last day " (*Gosp*, 2nd Mass :
Jn 6,37-40). Could there be a more consoling assurance?

Jesus presents Himself to us today as the Good Shepherd
who does not want to lose even one of His sheep, nor does He
spare any pains to lead them all to salvation. As if in response
to the sweet promises of Jesus, Holy Mother Church, full of
gratitude and enthusiasm, cries out : " For with regard to
Thy faithful, O Lord, life is changed, not taken away; and the
abode of this earthly sojourn being dissolved, an eternal
dwelling is prepared in heaven " *(Preface)*. Rather than an
inexorable end, death is, for the Christian, a door opening
into eternity, a door which admits the soul into eternal
life.

2. All Souls' Day makes us mindful not only of the
death of our dear ones but also of our own. Death is a
punishment, bringing with it, of necessity, a feeling of pain,
of fear, of uncertainty. The saints experienced it, and
Jesus Himself willed to undergo it. Thus the Church puts
before us passages from Scripture most suited to encourage
us : " Blessed are the dead who die in the Lord...
henceforth they rest from their labors, for their works
follow them " (*Ep*, 3rd Mass : *Ap* 14,13). The life of the
body dies; the life of the spirit and the good deed accomplished during life remain; these deeds alone accompany
the soul in its journey from this life and render its death
precious.

" Precious in the sight of the Lord is the death of His saints. " This death has been justly defined : " *dies natalis,* " the day of birth to eternal life. Would that our own death might be such! A *dies natalis* which would bring us into the beatific vision, bring us to birth in the indefectible love of heaven.

However, by inviting us to pray for the faithful departed, today's liturgy reminds us that between death and eternal beatitude there is purgatory. Because our works *do* follow us, and not all of them are good works, or, even if they are good, they are full of faults and imperfections, it is necessary for the soul to be purified of every blemish before being admitted to the vision of God. And yet, if we were perfectly faithful to grace, there would be no need of purgatory, for God purifies here below those who give themselves wholly to Him, who let themselves be fashioned and formed according to His good pleasure. Furthermore, purification accomplished on earth has the great advantage of being meritorious, that is, of increasing grace and charity in us, thus permitting us to love God more for all eternity; whereas in purgatory, one suffers without growing in charity. That is why we should desire to be purified during life. But let us have no illusions : even on earth total purification entails great suffering. If now we are not generous in suffering, if here on earth we do not know how to accept suffering, pure and unmitigated, as Jesus did on the Cross, our purification will of necessity have to be completed in purgatory.

May the thought of that place of expiation rouse our zeal to pray for the souls of the departed, and may it also make us more courageous in embracing suffering in reparation for our own faults.

COLLOQUY

" Grant, O Lord, that I may experience a reasonable sorrow at the death of those who are dear to me, shedding tears of resignation over our mortal condition, yet soon restraining them by this consoling thought of the faith : that in dying, the faithful have only withdrawn a little from us to go into a better world.

" May I not weep as do the pagans who are without hope. I may have reason to be sad, but in my affliction hope will comfort me. With hope so great, it is not fitting, O my God, that Your temple should be in mourning. You dwell there, You who are our Consoler; and You cannot fail in Your promises " (St. Augustine).

" O Master and Creator of the universe, Lord of life and death, You give our souls being and fill them with blessings : You carry out and transform everything by the work of Your Word, at the time foreordained and according to the plan of Your Wisdom; receive, today, our deceased brethren and give them eternal rest.

" May You welcome us, in our turn, at the moment pleasing to You, after having guided us and left us in the body for as long as You think useful and salutary.

" Made ready in Your fear, without trouble and without delay, may You receive us on the last day. Grant that we may not leave the things of this world with regret, like those who are too much attached to earth and the flesh; grant that we may advance resolutely and happily toward that blessed and unending life which is in Christ Jesus Our Lord, to whom be glory forever and ever. Amen " (St. Gregory Nazianzen).

386

THE PRESENTATION OF THE
BLESSED VIRGIN MARY

NOVEMBER TWENTY-FIRST

PRESENCE OF GOD - O Mary, present my offering and my life to Our Lord.

MEDITATION

1. Although Holy Scripture does not tell us anything about the presentation of the Most Blessed Virgin Mary in the Temple, this belief is based upon evidence authorized by a very ancient Christian tradition, and the Church has given it official recognition by making it the object of a special Marian feast. Mary, who leaves her home and parents in her most tender years in order to live in the shadow

of the Temple, speaks to us of detachment, of separation from the world, of complete dedication to the service of God, of virginal consecration to the Most High.   After her, countless virginal souls will present themselves in the Temple to offer themselves to God, but no offering will be as pure, as total, as acceptable as Mary's.

Our Lady is truly the privileged one among all creatures, who, from the first moment of her existence, heard the great call : " Hearken, O daughter, and see and incline thy ear, and forget thy people and thy father's house " (Ps 44,11). The Most High is enamored of her beauty and wills that she be wholly His.   Mary responds, and her answer is eminently prompt and complete.   The response of souls whom God calls to the Altar, to the religious life or to virginal consecration in the world, should resemble Mary's.   These souls must also be separated from the world, leave parents and friends; they must detach themselves from their people and their homes.   There cannot always be material separation, but there must always be a spiritual one, that is, a separation in the realm of the affections.   It is the heart which must be detached, be secluded, because the Lord's elect can no longer belong to the world : " they are not of the world " (Jn 17,14), Jesus said.   To live in the world without being of the world is not easy, but it is absolutely essential in order to answer the divine call.   There are virginal souls who fail in their consecrated vocation, or neglect to correspond fully, because they are still attached to the world—to its maxims, its vanities, its affairs, its comforts; they have not had the courage to effect a true separation, or at least, if they have undertaken it, they have not remained faithful.   This can happen not merely to souls living in the world but even to those in the cloister, for the world penetrates everywhere, and everywhere it invades hearts that are not entirely detached.

2. Corresponding to complete separation is oblation, total consecration.   Mary gave herself wholly to God, unreservedly, forever.   " Lord, in the simplicity of my heart I offer myself to You this day as Your servant for evermore, for Your homage and for a sacrifice of perpetual praise " (Imit IV, 9,1).   Such must have been the dispositions with which this holy child offered herself to the Most High, dispositions which were lived with a fullness and coherence incomprehensible to our wretchedness.

Never for a moment did Mary fail in her complete consecration; God was able to accomplish in her all that He willed, without meeting the least resistance. Circumstances of an exceedingly difficult and painful nature abounded in the life of our Blessed Lady : Joseph's doubt concerning the origin of her maternity; the hardships and inconveniences of the journey to Bethlehem; the bleak poverty in which she saw her Child born, the flight into Egypt, the life of privation at Nazareth, the hostility and malice of the Pharisees toward Jesus, the treason of Judas, the ingratitude of a people so favored and beloved, her Son's condemnation to death, the way to Calvary, the Crucifixion amid the insults of the populace. In vain would we scrutinize Mary's heart to find there a single movement of resentment, of protest; in vain would we seek to find upon her lips one single word of complaint. Mary gave herself wholly to God, allowing Him to exercise over her all His rights as Sovereign, Lord, and Master. She made no objections nor did she marvel that her immolation should reach such proportions : had she not offered herself without reserve? And when her offering was consummated she did nothing but repeat : " *Fiat! Ecce ancilla Domini!* "

What a contrast to our life as consecrated souls! How easily we take back the gift made to God! We take back our heart when we admit human affections; we take back our will when we refuse to submit to certain commands of obedience which mortify or contradict us, when we will not accept that which entails sacrifice, when we complain, protest or defend our rights. Yet the only true right of a soul consecrated to God is that of letting itself be used and consumed for His glory.

Let us ask Mary, presented in the Temple, to take our poor offering into her maternal hands, to purify and complete it by her offering, so pure, so perfect; to include and hide it in hers, so great and so generous, that being thus purified and renewed, it may be agreeable to God.

COLLOQUY

" O dearly Beloved of God, most amiable Child Mary, would that today I could offer you the first years of my life and consecrate myself to your service, my blessed and sweet

Lady, as you presented and consecrated yourself in the Temple for the honor and glory of God.... But time has slipped away and so many years have been spent in serving the world and my own caprice, as it were, forgetful of you and of God. Woe to the time when I did not love you! But better late than never. Behold, O Mary, I present myself to you today, offering myself entirely to your service, for the number of days, whether few or many, that are still left to me on earth. I renounce all creatures, as you did, and vow myself entirely to the love of my Creator. I consecrate to you, O my Queen, my intellect, that it may always think upon the love you deserve, my tongue, that it may praise you, my heart that it may love you. Accept, O Most Holy Virgin, the offering which this wretched sinner presents to you; accept it, I beg, by the consolation your heart felt when you gave yourself to God in the Temple. And if I am late in putting myself at your service, it is but fitting that I redeem the time lost by redoubling my devotion and my love.

" O Mother of Mercy, help my weakness by your powerful intercession, and obtain for me from your Jesus the strength to be faithful to you until death. Grant that after having served you always in this life I may go to praise you eternally in Paradise " (St. Alphonsus).

ANALYTICAL INDEX

ANALYTICAL INDEX

N. B. - The numerals in heavy print indicate the number of the Meditation, the other numerals (1,2), the points of the Meditation. This Index refers to the text of the Meditations, not to the Colloquies.

Abandonment — To God in suffering : **129**, 2; **130**, 2; **138**, 2; - and in the anguish of the night of the spirit : **354**, 2.

Abnegation — Is necessary that the soul may learn to renounce its own satisfaction and tendency to take pleasure : **80**,1; **81**,1,2; **82**,1,2.
See : RENUNCIATION; MORTIFICATION.

Activity — How to seek God in : **21**,1,2; - regulated by obedience, does not interfere with union with God : **21**,1; - to know how to interrupt it, to dedicate oneself to prayer : **21**,2; **59**,1; - perfect harmony between — and contemplation is only in the full maturity of the spiritual life : **331**,2; **342**,2; - the need to dedicate oneself to — and contemplation, according to the duties of one's state : **342**,1; - the need to give oneself to the works of God with a heart filled with God : **372**,2.

Affections — All — not in conformity with the Will of God draw the soul into the way of the imperfect spirit : **7**,2; - the soul who has not the courage to conquer all inordinate —, will not attain perfection : **90**,1; - to attain divine union, one must renounce all disordered — : **80**,2; - the heart filled with disordered — cannot love God with all its strength : **80**,1; **228**,2; - natural — play havoc in the heart consecrated to God : **90**,1; - the multiplicity of — waste the powers of the soul : **228**,2.
See : ATTACHMENTS.

Apostle — Rectitude of intention necessary for the — : **25**,2; **332**,1,2; - should continually die to self-love and vainglory : **25**,2; **332**,2; - purification of the — through the hardships of the apostolate : *ibid.;* **338**,2; - hindrances and trials which — meets with constitute his dark night : *ibid.;* - is collaborator with God : **319**,1,2; **341**,1,2; - should place himself at the complete disposal of God : **319**,2; - to share his love with all men : **320**,1; **339**,1; - to live in intimate affinity with Infinite Love, of which he is a humble collaborator and instrument : **320**,2; - to be the intimate friend of God by acting according to His Heart : **321**,1; - should be completely docile to the action of the Holy Spirit : **344**,2; - every Christian is an —, chiefly in the strength and participation of the sacrifice with which Jesus redeemed the world : **324**,1; - an interior soul is an — : **327**,2; - should dedicate sufficient time to prayer and recollection : **325**,2; **331**,2; **339**,1; - finds in his apostolate all means necessary for his sanctification : **331**,1; - seeking recollection is a grace which protects one against dangers of activity : **331**,2; - should seek to maintain balance between action and contemplation : *ibid.;* **342**,1; - should live the ideal of sanctity he proposes to others : **327**,1; - necessity of a serious formation of the — : **330**,1,2; - not for himself but for souls, for their spiritual advantage : **333**,2; - should spend himself completely for the benefit of souls : *ibid.;* **341**,2; - the true — is happy to have sons to nourish by his toil and prayers : *ibid.;* - should have deep humility : **334**,1,2; - knowledge of one's nothingness should keep one continually united to Jesus, whence comes all help : **334**,2; - to ever keep in mind humility, union with God, detachment from one's judgment and will : **340**,2; - should be a perfect gentleman : **335**,2; - should procure for himself an intellectual formation adequate for the apostolate in which he wishes to work : **337**,1; - should be convinced that victory is not attained except by Calvary : **338**,1; - should hope in spite of all the difficulties and failures he may meet with in the apostolate : **338**,2.

See : APOSTOLATE.

Apostolate — Is the duty of every Christian : **23**,1,2; **77**,2; **318**,1,2; **328**,2; - is the special duty of the soul consecrated to God : **23**,2; **61**,1; - is collaboration with the salvific work of Christ : **319**,1; **324**,1; - is the highest expression of fraternal charity : **323**,2; - Jesus wills that we should collaborate

with Him for the salvation of souls : **23**,1,2; **61**,1; **65**,2; **325**,1; - the salvation of many depends on our voluntary prayers and sacrifices : **23**,2; **318**,2; **323**,1;

the interior — of prayer and sacrifice : **24**,1,2; **184**,2; **324**,1,2; **325**,2; **326**,1,2; - is a prolongation of the hidden life and Passion of Jesus : **324**,1; - is the indispensable basis for the exterior — : *ibid.;* - has the pre-eminence over every other form of the — : **328**,1; - gives apostolic value to the contemplative life : **324**,2; **325**,2; **326**,1,2; - apostolic prayer is one of the most powerful means of the — : **325**,1,2; - should be accompanied by sacrifice : **326**,1; - has its culmination in the sacrifice of self for the salvation of souls : *ibid.;* - souls are paid for and saved by suffering : **326**,2; **341**,1; **374**,2;

the external — : **25**,1,2; - is a prolongation of the apostolic life of Jesus : **324**,1; - its necessity : **328**,1; - its fruitfulness derived from the love of God and union with Him : **25**,1; **184**,1; **321**,2; **330**,1,2; **340**,2; **341**,1; - of prayer and sacrifice : **25**,2; **184**,2; **324**,1; **325**,2; **326**,1,2; cannot consist solely in external activity : **184**,2; **324**,1; - God alone can make it fruitful : **319**,1; **334**,1,2;

the soul of the — is the interior life : **25**,1; **321**,2; **323**,1; - the — without the interior life is mere movement : **321**,2; - the soul cannot produce the fruits of the — if it is not first rooted in a deep interior life : **323**,1; **330**,1; - exterior activity should not diminish the interior life : **330**,2; **331**,2; **339**,1; - the urgency of apostolic work cannot justify a hurried preparation for the — : **330**,2; - those who give themselves to the — should be well advanced in perfection : *ibid.;* - the need of joining one's personal advance to sanctity with the exercise of apostolic activity : **331**,1; - until one has attained spiritual maturity, he should give himself to the — with caution and moderation : **339**,1; - though one has received the interior grace of the —, one should always be on one's guard : **340**,1,2; - zeal for souls is derived from the love of God : **184**,1; **317**,1; **344**,1; - and from union with Him : **339**,1; - and is a participation in God's love for men : *ibid.;* - the interior life should be orientated toward the salvation of souls : **317**,2; **323**,2 - the apostolic ideal urges the soul to a deeper interior life : **323**,1,2; - is a powerful lever for personal sanctification : **323**,2; - the — of example is accessible to all : **327**,1,2; - diverse functions in the field of the — : **328**,1,2; - spirit of solidarity in the various forms of the — : **328**,1; - collaboration of the faithful with the hierarchy : **328**,2; - the — should be carried on according to the directives of the Church : *ibid.;* **340**,2; - the perfect harmony between action and contemplation is found only in the full maturity of the spiritual life : **331**,2; **342**,2; - how to harmonize the attraction to the — with that of union with God : **342**,1,2; - the profound harmony comes only from perfect charity : **342**,2; - in the regions of perfect charity, contemplation and the — become identified, are complementary, and mutually help each other : *ibid.;* - secondary intentions can insinuate themselves into apostolic activity : **332**,2; - apostolic life calls for a total abnegation of self : **333**,1; - affability and courtesy in the service

of apostolic charity : **335**,1,2; - technical ability and professional competency as a means of the — : **337**,2; - a professional should practise the — above all in the perfect fulfillment of his professional duties : *ibid.;* - the basis of apostolic hope is the saving Will of God, His infinite Power, the Redemption of Christ : **338**,1; - the more a soul is united to God by love, so much the more apostolic it becomes : **339**,1,2; - in the soul that has attained union with God, there arise immense and irresistible longings for the — : **339**,2; **340**,1; - from total union with God, a very fruitful — spontaneously arises : **370**,2; - spiritual paternity and maternity derived from the — : **341**,1,2; - the Holy Spirit is the secret inspiration of the — : **344**,1,2; - necessary to direct souls, not according to one's own spirit, but according to the Spirit of God : **344**,2.

See : APOSTLE; ACTIVITY.

Aridity — To await the Lord in — : **8**,2; - notwithstanding —, to persevere in quest of God : **18**,2; - and in prayer : **153**,2; **156**,2; - caused by infidelity : **153**,1; **156**,2; - comes from physical and moral causes independent of the will : **153**,2; - permitted by God for the good of the soul : **155**,1,2; **157**,1,2; - means used by God to free soul from childishness of sensibility : **155**,1; - leads to purer love and deeper humility : **155**,1,2; - how to act in such — : **155**,2; - how to distinguish — coming from God from that due to other causes : **157**,1; - which the soul suffers in the night of the spirit : **353**,2; **355**,2; - in — arises the torturing pain of not loving God : **157**,2; **158**,1; **355**,2; - by — love

becomes purer : **255**,1,2; - God can inflame the soul even in — : **361**,1; - the Holy Spirit works in souls through — : **168**,2.
See : PRAYER.

Attachments — Every voluntary attachment hinders union with God : **79**,1; - the least attachment to sin and imperfection hinders union with God : **237**,2; - habitual — are bonds that bind one to earth : **79**,2; - attachment to riches is obstacle to salvation : **84**,2; **85**,1,2; - the root of every attachment is the disordered tendency to pleasure : **81**,1; **82**,1.
See : AFFECTIONS; IMPERFECTIONS.

Baptism — Engrafts and incorporates us into Christ : **43**,2; **48**,1; - has made us children of God : **71**,1; - and is the beginning of the Christian life and eternal beatitude : **71**,2; - consecrates the body of the Christian as the temple of God : **88**,1; - in — we have received the first visit of the Holy Spirit : **189**,2; - is a rebirth in the Holy Spirit : **190**,1; - in —, together with grace, we receive the infused virtues and the gifts of the Holy Spirit : **195**,1; - duty of living our — : **71**,1,2; - the grace of — does not exonerate us from struggle against the old man, but makes us able to withstand it : **245**,1; - grace of — foreshadowed in cure of deaf-mute : **266**,1.

Beatitudes — Are the fruit of the gifts of the Holy Spirit : **300**,1; - blessed are the poor in spirit : **300**,1,2; - blessed are they that hunger and thirst after justice : **303**,1,2; - blessed are the meek : **305**,1,2; - blessed are the merciful : **307**,1,2; - blessed are they that

mourn : **310**,1,2; - blessed are the clean of heart : **312**,1,2; - blessed are the peacemakers : **314**,1,2.
See : COUNSEL; FORTITUDE; UNDERSTANDING; PIETY; WISDOM; KNOWLEDGE; FEAR OF THE LORD.

Charity — Is inseparable from grace : **4**,2; **259**,1; - cannot subsist with the death caused by sin: **254**,1; - whoever possesses it shares in the life of God : **4**,2; - is the condition and the consequence of the indwelling of the Holy Spirit : **189**,2; - proportionately to —, the gifts of the Holy Spirit develop in our souls : **195**,2; - only — and grace confer supernatural life to the soul : **259**,1; - is the greatest gift the Holy Spirit can infuse in us : *ibid.;* - is the greatest virtue : **4**,2; **254**,1; - is the essence of Christian perfection : **100**,1; **106**,1; **145**,2; - has pre-eminence over all the virtues : **254**,1,2; - gives the warmth and strength of eternal life to hope : **254**,1; - nothing avails without — : **254**,2; - least act of — immensely superior to all human values : **234**,2; - and to all extraordinary gifts : **259**,1; - Christianity is all love : **301**,1; - a soul is holy in the measure that it is dominated by — : **4**,2; - by means of — the soul is always orientated toward God : **13**,2; **160**,1; - increase of — : **35**,2; **180**,2; - Jesus has commanded the exercise of this virtue in the greatest measure : **19**,1; - the precept of — has no limits : **53**,2; **253**,1; - is absolute : *ibid.;* - makes one share in the infinite love with which God loves Himself and creatures : **53**,1; **271**,2; - is a created participation in the love with which God loves Himself : **250**,1,2; **251**,2; - makes us enter

into the current of love existing in the Blessed Trinity : **250**,1,2; - is the love of friendship between God and man : **251**,1,2; - conquers all things : **63**,2; - spiritual life and consecration to God worth little if they do not lead to perfection of — : **70**,1; - end of spiritual life is the perfection of — : **145**,2; **301**,1; - perfection of — demands detachment from earthly goods; **86**,1; - perfect — requires absolute renunciation and purity : **253**,2 **355**,1,2; - empties the will of all things because it obliges it to love God above all things : **349**,2; - on earth absolute perfection of — not possible, but only relative perfection : **253**,1; **256**,1; - the foundation of — is humility : **106**,1; **259**,2; **301**,2; - is one because it has but one object, God, loved in Himself and in one's neighbor : **181**,1; **258**,1; - double movement of — toward God and neighbor; one repressed, the other cannot be perfect : **323**,2; **342**, 1 ; - is by nature expansive, apostolic : **323**,2; - action and contemplation born of love and established only in perfect love : **342**,2; - at the end of life we shall be judged on — : **364**,2.
See : LOVE OF GOD; LOVE OF NEIGHBOR.

Chastity — Souls consecrated to God obliged to perfect — : **75**,1; - vow of perfect — : **88**,2; - vow of — does not condemn souls to a sterile life, but uniting them to God, opens to them the sublime fruitfulness of the apostolate : *ibid.;* - the vow of — does not liberate the soul from temptations and struggles : **89**,1; - required of every Christian in conformity with his state of life : **88**,1; - of body, not sufficient, should include that of heart and

thoughts : *ibid.;* - of heart : **90**,1,2; - modesty, custodian of — : **89**,1,2.

Christian — Every — has the duty of the apostolate : **23**,1,2; **77**,2; **318**,1,2; - no one more cold-hearted than a — with no interest in the salvation of others : **317**,2; - no pagans, if — were what they should be : **327**,1; - every — who strives to make the spirit of the Gospel penetrate his own life is, in his own sphere, a collaborator with Christ : **328**,2; - should live for the glory of Christ : **32**,2; **40**,2; **206**,2; - is a new creature purified in the Blood of Christ : **36**,2; - should live in Christ : **43**,2; **48**,1; **65**,1; - is a member of the Mystical Body of Christ : **44**,1,2; **48**,2; **67**,2; **164**,1; **267**,1; - is *alter Christus* in measure in which he is influenced by Jesus and the inspirations of the Holy Spirit : **65**,1; - his life should be a prolongation of the life of Christ : **65**,2; - is called to participate in the redemptive work of Jesus : **374**,2; - is a child of God : **34**,2; **75**,1; **164**,1; **282**,1; - is a temple of the Holy Spirit : **47**,2; - should seek only the glory of God : **62**,2; - his riches are to be a child of God, heir of Christ, temple of the Holy Spirit : **245**,1; - should serve God, not as a servant, but as a son : **282**,2; - is a child of the Church : **67**,2; **164**,1; **375**,1; - his spiritual life should conform to the directives of the Church : **164**,1; - should contribute to the good of the Church : **357**,1; **375**,2; - the greatness of his vocation : **75**,1; - is great through gifts received from God : **286**,2; - is a tree in the vineyard of the Lord, lovingly cared for by the Divine Gardener : **238**,1; - should carefully manage the natural and supernatural patri-

mony received from God : **245**,2;
- should be deeply engaged in
struggle against sin, in himself
and in others : **100**,2; - should
impose upon himself a life of
sacrifice, in view of the happiness
of the next world : **161**,1; - is a
pilgrim anxious to reach the
fatherland of Heaven : **161**,2;
- cannot be completely satisfied
until he has reached Heaven :
ibid.; - many Christians serve God
merely for their own interests :
211,2; - should be aware of his
fellowship with his brethren :
267,1; - is a potential martyr :
288,1; - should not be a forced
Cyrenian, but a voluntary one :
291,2; - we are Christians in the
measure in which we live in love and
understand the mystery of the love
of God : **301**,1.

The Church — Society of the
faithful : **23**,1; **318**,2; - its beginning
and development : **357**,1; - Spouse
of Christ : **23**,1; **67**,1; - Mystical
Body of Christ : **44**,1; **67**,1; **68**,1;
69,1; **357**,1; - Christ makes — live
His own Life : **44**,1; **67**,1; -
continues the work of Christ :
ibid.; **188**,1; **318**,2; - sole depository
of the merits and doctrine of
Christ : **67**,2; - by means of the
sacraments, — nourishes the life of
its members : **69**,1; - love and
devotion to — and submission to
its directives : **67**,1,2; **328**,2; **357**,1;
- duty of contributing to the good
of — : **77**,2; **357**,1; **375**,2; - not a
true Catholic if he does not renounce
his personal views to *feel* with — :
375,1; - solidarity with — : **375**,2;
- our spiritual life should be
framed in that of — and associated
with it : **164**,1; - participation in
the universal prayer of — : **165**,2;
167,1,2; - prays through the hearts

of her children; the more fervent
they are, the more pleasing will
their prayer be to God : **167**,2;
- the Holy Spirit is the soul of — and
guides it to the fulfillment of its
mission : **188**,1; - Holy Spirit
illumines souls through the teaching
of — : **190**,2; - importance in — of
contemplative Orders : **324**,2;
325,1,2; **326**,1,2; - active and
contemplative Orders necessary for
the growth of — : **328**,1; - contacts
between — triumphant, — militant,
and — suffering : **385**,1.

Confession — Utility of frequent
— and dispositions to receive its
fruit : **73**,2; **104**,1,2; by means of
sacramental grace, — protects the
soul from sin : **3**,2; **104**,1; - accusation of the degree of willfulness
in our faults and motives : **104**,2;
- importance of sorrow : *ibid.;*
- sincerity in — : **284**,1; - accompanied by deep compunction :
310,1; - difficulties due to a lack
of the spirit of faith : **280**,2;
- to doubt absolution is to doubt
Jesus Himself : *ibid.*

Confidence — Too much self-
confidence prevents the soul from
having recourse to God with
full — : **63**,2; - God admits to His
intimacy only souls completely free
from self-confidence : **108**,2;
- — in God increases in the measure
of one's humility and diffidence in
self : *ibid.;* **21** ,1,2; - soul who
trusts itself is not mature in sanctity
and the apostolate : **135**,2; - should
have recourse to God with all — :
63,2; - unlimited — in the infinite
merits of Jesus : **175**,2; - and in
divine Providence : **239**,2; - we
should trust ourselves to God
because we are His children :
245,1; - to trust in God even to

not permit his heart to be bound to — : **227**,2; - in the measure that a soul separates herself from —, she climbs the secret ladder of love : **361**,1; - greatest folly to let the heart be bound to — who have no claim on it : **90**,1; - soul who wishes to live for God alone desires to be forgotten by — : **114**,2; - whoever seeks possession of — has not poverty of spirit : **300**,2; - to live in the midst of — and to be occupied with them without the heart being attached to them : **379**,2; - — not sufficient to satisfy our thirst for happiness : **143**,1; **303**,2; - vanity of — : **309**,1; **356**,1; - attractiveness of — easily makes one forget and even betray his Creator : **309**,1; - necessary to esteem God above all — : **356**,1; - are nothing in comparison with God : **227**,2; **228**,1; **229**,1; **309**,1,2; - exist only because God has created them and maintains them in existence : **228**,1; - are variable and changeable : **230**,1; - can do nothing without the help of God : **240**,2; - to the soul enlightened by the gift of knowledge, — become a ladder to God : **309**,2.

Cross — To follow Jesus necessary to carry the — : **126**,1; **129**,1; **193**,2; - the more we share in the — of Christ, the more we shall be like Him : **194**,1; - when we flee from sacrifice, we act as enemies of the — of Christ : **350**,1; - only the way of the — leads to union with God : **354**,1; - love of Jesus transformed the —, a horrible instrument of torture, to a most effective means for the glory of God and the salvation of mankind : **127**,2; - the — of Jesus is the greatest proof of His love for men : **132**,2; - Jesus reigns from the — :

133,1; - the victory of the — : **139**,1; - the daily — : **129**,1,2; **194**,2; - to bear the — with love : **129**,2; - is the great means of our sanctification : **132**,1; **194**,1; - is the instrument and work of love : **132**,2.

Death — Jesus in submitting to — has given us strength to accept it with love : **94**,1; - soul who tries to fulfill the Will of God with love can trust that God will grant her the grace to accept — with love : **95**,2; - — of love accessible to all souls of good will : *ibid.;* - to overcome the anguish of — by acts of adhesion to the Will of God and abandonment : **138**,2; - usefulness of the thought of — : **94**,1; - is never sudden for one who is ready : **95**,1; - will not be feared by one who is always faithful to grace : *ibid.;* - last visit of the Lord to the soul : *ibid.;* - door opened to eternity, which introduces us to eternal life : **385**,1; - happy the soul who at the end of life with no delay is admitted to the beatific union of Heaven : **364**,2; - at the end of life only love remains : **384**,1; - and the good works accomplished which render — precious : **385**,2.

Defects — Should not be too much at peace with our — : **295**,2. See : IMPERFECTIONS.

Despoilment — Of self and of all things in order to respond to the infinite love of God : **31**,1,2; - to love and despoil oneself for God of all that is not God : **31**,2; **348**,2; - need of despoiling self of all to attain true poverty of spirit : **300**,1; - the soul which strips itself of its appetites, its likings and dislikings will be clothed by the Lord with His own purity, His own joy, and His own will : **300**,2; - God rids the soul of its imperfections in order to clothe it with Himself : **348**,2.

Detachment — Necessity of — to find God : **11**,1,2; **13**,2; **81**,1,2; - the more a soul feels the need of God, the more she is detached from earthly things : **141**,1; - renders the soul docile to the inspiration and voice of the Holy Spirit : **192**,2; **306**,2; - a thread suffices to attach the soul to earth : **192**,2; - deep and radical — necessary to attain union with God : **349**,1,2; - — is the indispensable foundation of the spiritual life : **54**,2; - required of the soul consecrated to God : **76**,1,2; **88**,2; **386**,1; - total — is the logical consequence of the precept of charity : **80**,1; - essence of — consists in putting to death all disordered affections : **80**,2; - - relation between effective and affective — : *ibid.;* - not an end in itself, but a means to unite the soul with God : **81**,2; **82**,1; - its end is not to leave the soul in emptiness, but to raise it to God : **81**,2; - rules for — : **82**,1,2; - should be practised with generosity and discretion : **82**,2; - to practise — even in relaxation : *ibid.* See : ABNEGATION; MORTIFICATION; RENUNCIATION.

Devotion — Absence of sensible — causes aridity : **153**,1; - consists in the promptness of the will in the service of God : **153**,2; **282**,2; - is an act of the will and can subsist in spite of aridity and the rebellion of our lower nature : *ibid.;* - when it is deprived of relish, its value is doubled : *ibid.*

Discouragement — Due to pride and lack of confidence in God : **109**,1; **249**,2; **295**,1; - makes one recede in the path of perfection : **295**,1; - not to be discouraged by falls, but to humble oneself and begin again : **193**,2; **293**,2; **294**,1; **295**,1; - not to be discouraged by one's misery and impotence : **247**,2; **252**,1; - in temptations to — to react with an act of confidence in God : **248**,2.

Divine Office — Prayer of the Mystical Body of Christ : **167**,1,2; - universal prayer offered in union with Christ and in the name of the whole Church : *ibid.*

Doctrine — False — : **238**,2; - avails little to possess profound — if one fails to live in conformity to it : *ibid.;* - the fruit that should prove the worth of the — is the fulfillment of the Will of God : *ibid.;* - sanctity should be based on — : **337**,1.

Duty — Is the expression of the Will of God : **6**,2; - how to seek God in the fulfillment of our — : **13**,1,2; - conformity to the Will of God should be expressed in the fulfillment of our — : **193**,2; - perfect fulfillment of — leads to sanctity : **6**,2; - that which distinguishes the saints is perfection of diligence in fulfillment of — : **276**,1; - promptness and punctuality in the fulfillment of — : **276**,2; - — toward God takes the first place : **42**,2; **343**,2; - toward family : **42**,2; - perfect fulfillment of professional — as a means of the apostolate : **337**,2; - relation between civil and religious — : **343**,2; - every Christian is bound to fulfill every — of good citizenship: *ibid.;* - conflict between action and contemplation should be resolved by — of one's state : **342**,1.

Efforts — To react against difficulties without sacrificing one's peace : **63**,1; - God wills our —, but not that we should place our hope in them : **63**,2; - to continually renew our — with humility and confidence : **193**,2; - draw down the help of the Holy Spirit : *ibid.;* **197**,1; - are necessary to attain sanctity : *ibid.;* - God does not ask us to succeed but to continually renew our — : **294**,1.

Eternity — In — we shall be confirmed in degree of grace which we had at the moment of death : **35**,1; - present life should be seen in connection with — that awaits it : **230**,2.
See : HEAVEN.

Eucharist - Communion — Foreshadowed in miracle at the Wedding of Cana : **49**,2; - is the response of Jesus to the betrayal of men : **137**,1; - at the moment of — we, like Our Lady, hold Jesus truly living in our heart : **183**,1; **206**,1; - in the — we find the Sacred Heart living in the midst of us : **216**,1; - by means of — the Heart of Jesus comes to dwell within us : *ibid.;* - perpetuates the presence of Jesus within us : **200**,1; **201**,1,2; - in the — Jesus is not a passive object of our adoration but a living one : **201**,2; - living faith in the — : **202**,1,2; - behavior in the presence of the — : **202**,2; - in the — Jesus makes Himself our Food : **201**,1; **202**,2; **203**,1,2; **204**,1; - the — nourishes the life of Christ in us : *ibid.;* - in the — Jesus feeds us with His substance, assimilating us into Himself and personally communicating the

divine life : **205**,2; - by means of the other sacraments Jesus gives us His grace; by the — He gives Himself to us : *ibid.;* - he who nourishes himself by the — lives the life Jesus communicates to him : **206**,2; - is the sacrament of union : **200**,2; **206**,1,2; **207**,1; - by means of the — Jesus unites Himself to us in the most intimate manner : **205**,1,2; - union with Christ begun at baptism has its greatest fulness in the — : **206**,1; - special grace of the — is union with Jesus : **207**,1,2; **218**,1; - it strengthens permanent union with Jesus : **216**,2; **218**,1,2; - to remain throughout the day under the influence of the — : **218**,2; - is a pledge of eternal life : **204**,2; - is our hope for this life and the next : *ibid.;* - in the — the love of Jesus surpassed all measures : **205**,1; - the — crowns all the gifts of the love of Jesus : **208**,1; - coldness toward the — : **202**,1; **203**,2; - the reasons that keep some persons from the — : **203**,2; - the effects of the — are proportioned to the communicant : **207**,1; **218**,1; - every — produces an increase of grace and charity : **207**,2; **218**,1; - Jesus in the — continues to be mediator between us and the Trinity : **219**,1; - — strengthens the union of our soul with the Trinity : **219**,1,2; - special presence of the Blessed Trinity through the reception of the — : **219**,2; - sacramental presence of Jesus in our soul enables us to render worthy adoration to the Blessed Trinity : *ibid.*

Evil — To omit good is to do — : **112**,2; - tactics for overcoming — : *ibid.;* - from the double — of sin and suffering, God has drawn the great good of our Redemption :

127,1; - the infinite goodness of God draws good even from — : 232,1.

Examination of Conscience — Necessity and practice : 103,1,2; - need to examine oneself on the degree of willfulness in our failings : 103,2.

Extreme Unction — Perfects the purification of the soul in order to prepare it to meet God : 74,1; - necessity of receiving it with proper dispositions : 74,2.

Faith — Its necessity : 15,2; 18,1,2; 241,1; - is proximate and proportionate means to union with God : 18,1; - quest of God in — : 18,2; 141,2; - spirit of — makes one recognize God in all creatures : 20,1,2; 163,1,2; - to believe in the infinite love of God : 18,2; 19,1; 30,1,2; 63,1; 235,2; 301,1; - to believe in one's vocation to sanctity and intimacy with God : 177,1; - practice of — in darkness and temptation : 41,2; 147,2; 242,2; 243,2; - and in the dark night of the spirit : 353,2; - spirit of — in trials : 63,1; 119,2; 147,2; 163,1; 177,1; - conduct in temptations and doubts against — : 242,2; - by trials and difficulties — becomes purer and stronger : ibid.; 243,2; - naked and pure — the sole support of the soul in the dark night of the soul : 353,2; - makes one share in the knowledge of God : 53,1; 241,1; 250,1; - makes one see and judge things as God Himself does : 163,1; 241,1; 244,2; 349,2; - is an anticipation of the knowledge of God that we shall have in Heaven : 241,2; - makes us enter, while on earth, into communion with the thought and knowledge of God : ibid.; - the more we

judge things in the light of —, the nearer we draw to the Wisdom of God : 244,2; - examples of living — : 56,1; 91,2; - doubt of Thomas the Apostle strengthens our — : 147,2; - necessary to draw near to Jesus with the simplicity of a child : 147,1; - to have great —, necessary to have humility and simplicity of a child : 315,1; - — is the foundation of supernatural obedience : 124,2; - importance of — in relation to the Eucharist : 202,1,2; - spirit of — in suffering and difficulty : 128,2; 243,1; - in the providential government of God, who ordains all for our good and our sanctification : 163,1,2; 244,1,2; 351,2; - spirit of — recognizes God, His Will, or permission in every circumstance of life : 163,1,2; 244,1,2; 351,1,2; - spirit of — does not examine the Ways of God, but believes in Him and follows Him blindly : 177,2; - lack of — hinders us from overcoming many difficulties : 231,2; 243,1; - — should enlighten, not only hour of prayer, but our whole life : 244,1; - glance of — is most comprehensive and penetrating : 244,2; - to believe in the wise and loving government of God without understanding it : ibid.; - blessed are those who have no need of sensible signs to believe in God : 147,2; 329,2; - more than substitutes for the senses : 201,2; - is often smothered in a too natural mentality : 244,1; - purifies the understanding : 349,2; - value of — which clings blindly to God through every circumstance and personal experience : 147,2; 221,1; 242,1,2; 353,2; - is voluntary adherence of the intellect to revealed truth : 202,2; 242,2; - certitude and obscurity of — : 242,2; - obscurity of — constitutes the glory and the merit of the act of — : *ibid.* - profound motive of — is not our experience, but the authority of God : **329**,2; - the purer is —, the more free from human elements, the more pleasing it is to God : *ibid.;* - without works — is dead : **238**,1; **254**,1; - should be sustained by hope : **246**,1; - — without charity is incomplete : **254**,1; - in Heaven it will cease : *ibid.;* - is perfected by the gift of understanding : **311**,1; - the more lively — is, so much the more God enters into our life—the great reality in whom we live : **241**,2; - God uses His omnipotence in favor of one who firmly believes in Him : **243**,1; to believe in God at all costs and without uncertainty : **243**,2.

Fear — Of God which comes from love and makes the soul diligent : **276**,1; - difference between servile and filial — : **299**,1; - perfect filial — is the fruit of perfect love : **299**,2; - *Gift of Fear* : inspires hatred for sin which offends God : **299**,1, - perfects the virtues of hope and temperance : **299**,2; - inspires filial reverence for the majesty of God : *ibid.;* - to the Gift of — corresponds the beatitude of poverty of spirit : **300**,1.

Fervor — Sensible — makes spiritual exercises easy and pleasant : **153**,1.

Fidelity — To God in love : **22**,1; - in suffering : **105**,2; - in times of darkness : **139**,2; - in following the impulses of grace : **266**,1; - delicacy in — to God : **310**,1; - — of the soul is met with new invitations on the part of God : **76**,2.

Fortitude (Gift of) — Perfects the virtue of — : **302**,1; - by means of this gift the Holy Spirit communicates something of His infinite strength : **302**,2; - corresponds to the beatitude : blessed are they that hunger : **303**,1; - by the practice of the virtue of — we dispose ourselves to receive the gift : **302**,2.

Fortitude (Virtue of) — Makes one capable of facing sacrifices in the fulfillment of duty : **286**,1; - supreme act of — is martyrdom : **288**,1; - it is for us to exercise — infused in us at baptism : **288**,2; - principal act of — to stand firm in danger and to bear difficulties with virility : **291**,1; - is based on God and His great gifts given to men : **286**,2; - without grace, all human — is weakness : **288**,2; - the more confidence we have in God, the more we shall become strong in — : **289**,2; - our — insufficient if not strengthened by infused gift of the Holy Spirit : **301**,1; **302**,1,2; - should be joined to humility : **286**,2; - — and patience in inevitable difficulties of life : **291**,1,2.

Generosity — Consideration of the love of God urges to — : **30**,1; **150**,1; - the more a soul loves God, the more it feels the need of total — : **151**,2; - is the fruit and the generator of love : **290**,1; - love of souls urges to — : **323**,1,2; - in mortifications : **92**,2; **93**,2; - in despoilment : **300**,1,2; - in the practice of the apostolate : **333**,2; - necessary to attain union with God : **362**,2; - in accomplishing the mission God has entrusted to us : **372**,2; - God does not refuse His gifts to a generous soul :

144,1; - total — is the means by which to dispose ourselves to receive the divine gifts : **145**,1,2; **290**,2; - lack of — is an obstacle to the action of the Holy Spirit in our soul : **192**,2; - a soul who does not serve God with — will not be satisfied : **287**,2; - no need to fear doing too much for God : **289**,2; **290**,1,2; urges to do all with the greatest dedication without stint or calculation : **290**,1,2; - is short cut to reach goal quickly : **290**,1; - one becomes generous by forgetting self and always seeking what is most perfect : **290**,2.

Gifts of the Holy Spirit — Graces of light and love infused into our souls by the — : **143**,2; - activity of the — in prayer : **145**,1; **159**,1; - actuation of the — is the normal achievement of the soul who corresponds to grace : **145**,1; **316**,1; - no temerity to desire the — to develop into full maturity : *ibid.;* - are supernatural principles which make the soul capable of receiving the help of the Holy Spirit : **195**,1,2; - we receive them in baptism together with grace and the infused virtues, and they develop together : *ibid.;* - by means of the — God Himself intervenes in the work of our sanctification : **195**,1; - they grow in us with the growth of charity : **195**,2; - progressive influence of the — in the spiritual life : **197**,2; - they are given to perfect the virtues : **197**,1; **298**,2; - by the practice of the virtues the soul should dispose itself for the action of the — : **197**,1; - only under the habitual influence of the — can the instability of human nature be cured : **293**,2; - they are indispensable in attaining perfect virtue, sanctity : **298**,2;

- fear, fortitude, piety, and counsel perfect the moral virtues; knowledge, understanding, and wisdom perfect the theological virtues : **309**,1; - every gift corresponds to a beatitude : **300**,1.
See : COUNSEL; FORTITUDE; UNDERSTANDING; PIETY; WISDOM; KNOWLEDGE; FEAR OF THE LORD.

Glory — The Christian should not wish any — but that which comes from being a child of God : **62**,2; - if we admire and glorify ourselves, our — is nothing : *ibid.;* - the search for human — blinds one to the ways of the spirit : *ibid.*
Glory of God — Is the prime motive of all the works of God : **32**,1; **226**,2; **317**,1; - God, infinitely good, wishes to be glorified in procuring the happiness of His creatures : **226**,2; **317**,1; - we have been created and should live for the — : **32**,2; **226**,1,2; - we should seek the — in everything : **62**,2; - no waste to use gifts of God solely for His glory : **134**,1; - glory we can give God consists in being one with His Will : **256**,1; - need to seek perfection, not to enjoy it, but for the — : **132**,2; - first consideration should always be the — and His pleasure : **256**,1; - the soul, who after falling, turns to God with repentance and confidence, gives much glory to God : **210**,2.

God — Gave His only-begotten Son for the salvation of the world : **2**,1; **22**,1; **26**,1; **29**,1; **30**,2; **36**,1; **231**,1; **317**,1; - permits the fall of man in view of the redemptive Incarnation of the Word : **39**,2; - wishes all to be saved : **2**,1; - wishes all to be saints : **2**,2; **53**,1; **77**,2; **84**,1; **298**,1; - He calls at all hours : **77**,2; - — is Love : **4**,1; **26**,1,2; **29**,1; **235**,1; **271**,2; - He wills only love : **301**,1; - He has created us to communicate His goodness and His happiness : **4**,1; **26**,1; **233**,1; **320**,1; - His infinite love for us : **4**,1; **22**,1; **30**,1,2; **36**,1; **63**,1; **189**,1; **205**,2; **208**,2; **221**,2; **226**,1; **251**,1; **301**,1; **352**,2; **353**,1; **354**,1; **358**,1; - He has created us by an act of love : **26**,1; **233**,1; **235**,1,2; - He has redeemed us by a more striking act of love : **26**,1; **205**,1; **320**,1; - has made us His children and has resolved to make us share in His Nature, His intimate Life, and in His eternal beatitude : **26**,1; **205**,1; **251**,1; - all His actions in our favor are actions of love : **26**,1,2; **205**,1; **235**,1,2; **320**,1; - consideration of His infinite love urges to generosity and a return of love : **22**,1; **30**,1; **31**,1,2; **150**,1; **211**,1,2; **299**,1; - we are called to imitate His infinite perfections : **4**,1; **53**,1; **227**,1; **298**,1; - above all, we should imitate His Charity : **4**,1; **53**,2; - we should reflect His Unity, bringing about unity in ourselves : **228**,2; - His Simplicity, the means of our simplicity of spirit : **229**,1,2; - His Goodness, loving and benefiting all : **233**,2; - His Wisdom, judging all things in relation to Him : **234**,2; - His Mercy, showing mercy to our neighbor : **236**,2; **264**,1,2; - God invites the soul to intimacy with Himself : **10**,1,2; **141**,2; **321**,1; - and to union with Himself : **358**,1; - cannot admit to His intimacy a soul who retains even a slight attachment to sin or imperfection : **237**,2; - does not reject us because of our misery, but notwithstanding it, invites us to His intimacy : **352**,2; **353**,1; - the divine natural and supernatural

likeness God has imprinted on our souls expresses His desire to unite us to Himself : **358**,1; - to find — it is necessary to make use of all things and to recollect oneself in God : **11**,1,2; **12**,1,2; - how to seek Him in ourselves : **11**,1,2; **12**,1,2; **141**,2; **152**,1,2; - how to maintain contact with Him in the midst of occupations : **13**,1,2; **21**,1,2; **160**,1,2; **162**,1,2; **163**,1,2; - the quest for — : **18**,1,2; and *fol.;* **140**,2; and *fol.;* - if the soul is seeking —, much more is her loving Saviour seeking her : **19**,2; **197**,1; **363**,1; - we should live for the glory of — : **32**,2; **226**,2; **228**,1; - — alone suffices : **105**,2; - the soul should strive to please God alone : **115**,2; - — forces no one, but He gives Himself wholly to those who give themselves wholly to Him : **34**,1; **90**,2; **145**,2; **188**,2; **366**,1; - He does not give Himself wholly to the soul while it is not purified from everything that is contrary to His infinite perfections : **78**,1,2; - He does not sanctify us without our cooperation and our consent : **77**,2; **84**,1,2; **99**,2; **172**,2; **298**,1; - only — can sanctify us, but He does not do it without our concurrence : **119**,2; - Jesus is the only Way that leads to — : **38**,1,2; - — loves us and recognizes us as His adopted children only if He sees us grafted onto Christ : **43**,1; - — is not a tyrant who enslaves us, but a Father who tries us because He loves us : **63**,1; - — does not abandon us if we do not first abandon Him : *ibid.;* **119**,2; **248**,1; - — permits evil to put His servants to the test : **70**,2; — does not permit us to be tempted beyond our strength : **98**,2; **252**,1; - every circumstance, however painful, is permitted by

— for our good : **128**,2; **129**,2; **130**,2; **163**,1,2; **239**,1; **243**,2; **291**,1; **292**,1,2; - is faithful : **177**,1; **239**,1; **252**,1; - does not deceive our hope : **178**,2; - tries those whom He loves : **248**,1; **354**,1; - has the right to require renunciation of the affections that are most holy : **76**,1; - is jealous of the heart that is consecrated to Him : **90**,2; - not possible to serve — and Mammon : **85**,1; **287**,1; - — does not give us consolation for pleasure, but to make us more generous in suffering : **105**,2; - without — we cannot think or will any good : **107**,2; - — alone can satisfy us : **141**,1; **143**,1; **231**,1; - hunger and thirst for — : **141**,1; **231**,1; **358**,1,2; - our life is one continual seeking of — : **141**,2; **379**,2; - the seeking of — is the preoccupation of the loving soul : **142**,1,2; - transcendence of — : **142**,2; **227**,1; **251**,1, - — infinitely surpasses our understanding : **191**,1; **196**,2; **227**,1; - perfect orientation toward — impossible without the help of the Holy Spirit : **191**,1; **195**,1; - infinite distance between us and — : **353**,1; - while on earth we know — through the mirror of creatures : **191**,1; **227**,2; - perfections of creatures are nothing in comparison with those of — : *ibid.;* **228**,1,2; - our contact with — should be that of children : **198**,1; **245**,1; **282**,1,2; - we should consider — as a Father : *ibid.;* **299**,1; **304**,1; - — is our Father in spite of our miseries : **350**,1; - — is infinite Being eternally subsisting : **228**,1; - — possesses all perfections without defects or limits : **228**,2; **230**,1; - He is *ONE* in His myriad perfections : **228**,2; - He is Being absolutely simple, to the exclusion of all duplicity and multiplicity :

229,1,2; - He wishes good always and solely : **229**,2; **230**,1; **232**,1; - He is immutable; His thought and will do not change : **230**,1; - He is eternal; He possesses the fulness of His infinite life totally at the same time : **230**,2; - He is infinite Wisdom who knows all things in the most perfect manner : **234**,1; - He is infinite Goodness who wishes only good and who draws good even out of evil, even from sin : **232**,1; **244**,2; - all that comes from the Hand of — bears the impress of His goodness : **232**,2; - this infinite goodness immeasurably surpasses all human malice : *ibid.;* - goodness of — gratuitous and inexhaustible : **233**,2; - — is infinite Love; all that is in Him is love : **235**,1; - the love of — is the Cause that infuses and creates goodness in things : *ibid.;* - all that we have; all that we are, is the gift of His infinite love : *ibid.;* - He goes before us and continually accompanies us with His love : **235**,2; - He loves us when He consoles us and also when He afflicts us with sorrow : *ibid.;* - He loves us, not because we are without sin, but because we are His children : **249**,2; - He has loved us to the extent of becoming like to us, so that it is possible to admit us within the circle of the divine friendship : **251**,1; - and to unite us to Himself by love : **348**,2; **358**,1; - He has first loved us and made us capable of returning His love : **251**,2; - the love of — for us is merciful love : **236**,1; - — is merciful because He is just, and He is just because He is merciful : **237**,1; - in His mercy He gives as much as He can in accordance with justice : *ibid.;* - — does not demand more than one can give Him : **329**,2; - — is Providence that ordains and directs all for our good : **239**,1; **244**,2; - permits suffering only for our good : **239**,1; **248**,1; **292**,1; - has special care for each creature, even the least : **239**,2; - governs all things with infinite sweetness : **270**,1; - nothing can obstruct His omnipotence : **240**,1,2; - omnipotence of — is totally at the service of His infinite goodness : **240**,1; - — is helpful omnipotence always ready to come to our assistance : **246**,2.

See : GLORY OF GOD; MERCY; PRESENCE OF GOD; PROVIDENCE; TRINITY.

Goods of Earth — Attachment to — is an obstacle to perfection : **85**,1,2; - should not have a too great solicitude for — : **87**,1,2; - — are a temptation to allure the heart : **287**,1; - excessive solicitude for — hinders the total seeking for the kingdom of God : **287**,2; - poverty of spirit frees the soul from servitude to — : **85**,2; - the vow of poverty prohibits their free use : **86**,1,2.

Grace — Makes one a participant in the Divine Life : **3**,1; **251**,1; **321**,1; - seed of sanctity : **3**,1; **45**,2; - seed of glory : **44**,2; **105**,1; - vital principle of our likeness with Christ : **65**,1; - creation of the love of God : **320**,1; - is gratuitous gift lavished on us through the merits of Christ : **3**,2; - given only through Jesus : **38**,2; **43**,1; **45**,1,2; - continually communicated by Christ in proportion to the fidelity of the soul's union with Him by faith, charity, and good works : **43**,2; - — communicated to our souls is in essence identical with that which adorned the soul of Jesus : **45**,2; **58**,2; **193**,1; - every — comes

to us from the creative action of the Holy Spirit and the mediatory action of Christ : **47**,2; - is infused in the soul in proportion to its conformiy to the Will of God : **60**,2; **78**,1; - and its purity : *ibid.;* - communicated by the sacraments : **69**,1; - is inseparable from charity : **4**,2; **254**,1; - is destroyed by sin : **100**,1; - we cannot be certain that we are in the state of — : **247**,1; - transformation of soul by — : **49**,2; **78**,1,2; **105**,1; - — transforms and transfigures from glory to glory : *ibid.;* - full development of — leads to identification with Christ : **193**,1; - — respects and utilizes all human values to their utmost : **335**,2; - — has been given to us that our whole soul may be healed, elevated and sanctified; only when this is our goal shall we enter into the " Kingdom of God " : **357**,2; - we should collaborate with — that the fruits of the Redemption may be applied to our souls and to others : **61**,1; - — does not sanctify us without our collaboration : **73**,1; - resistance of our souls to — : **133**,2; **322**,1; - correspondence with — : **252**,1,2; **266**,2; **357**,2; **364**,1; **366**,2; - there are few who always respond to invitations of — : **322**,2; - to the perfect " Yes " of the soul, God replies with the true and complete " Yes " of — : **366**,2; - all is — : **63**,1; - God gives us — to overcome every evil tendency : **92**,1; - temptations : **98**,2; - weakness : **288**,2; - God does not refuse the first — which gives us the courage to act : *ibid.;* - the necessity of prayer to obtain — : **325**,1; - God has willed to have the distribution of — depend on the prayers of men : **325**,2; - necessity of actual — to perform any supernatural act : **107**,2; - without —

we cannot correspond with — :
266,2; - God is within us by — :
141,2; - by means of — God has
established between Himself and us
a certain community of life :
251,1; **345**,2; - only — and charity
sanctify the soul and unite it
with God : **259**,1; - by means
of — and love the soul becomes
like to God and enjoys His
friendship : **321**,1; - — and love
are the precious seeds of union
with God : **345**,2; - strength of — :
143,1; - the least degree of — is
immensely superior to great
achievements : **234**,2; - and to all
extraordinary gifts : **259**,1; - — is
not only light and divine life,
but also strength : **286**,1; - increase
of — : **180**,2; - development and
triumph of — : **357**,2; **366**,1;
- — of a member of Christ redounds
to the good of all the other
members : **323**,2.

Gratitude — Duties of — toward
God : **280**,2; **283**,1,2; - — draws
new benefits : **283**,2; - — flourishes
only in a humble heart : *ibid.;*
- sometimes the souls who have
received the most are the least
grateful : **283**,1.
See : INGRATITUDE.

Haughtiness — Has the sad
power of impeding the work of
the infinite mercy of God : **236**,1;
259,2; - God resists the haughty
and gives His grace to the humble :
ibid.; - hinders charity : **259**,2;
- he who is haughty is a seeding
ground of discord : **294**,1; - — is
an obstacle to faith : **315**,1.
See : PRIDE.

Heaven — Sufferings of this life
are nothing in comparison with the
glory of — : **161**,1; - our life should
be a continuous pilgrimage and

yearning for — : **161**,1,2; **175**,1;
179,1; **182**,1; **379**,1; - our citizenship
in — : **350**,1; - the soul inflamed
with love yearns for — to love God
more : **364**,2; - and to make Him
loved by as many souls as possible :
370,2; - ascension of Jesus has given
us the right to — : **179**,1;
- assumption of Mary is a plea to
live with our thoughts on — :
379,1,2; - only in — will an
absolute fulness and stability of
love be possible : **253**,1; **256**,1;
- in — we shall love God in the
clarity of the beatific vision : **360**,1
- glory of — corresponds with the
degree of love attained on earth :
384,1; - life of — is union with
God in its ultimate perfection :
345,1; - the happy soul who at the
end of life with no delay is admitted
to the beatific union of — : **384**,2;
- glory of the saints in — : **384**,1.

Hidden life — Imitation of the
— of Jesus : **114**,1; **116**,1,2; - and
of Mary : **380**,2; - practice of
remaining unobserved : **114**,1,2;
380,2; - to forget oneself and to
hide from oneself : **115**,1; - from the
— is derived a great disinterestedness, not only for human
recompense, but also for divine
consolations : **115**,2; - the more
we wish to do great things for
God, the more we should work
in silence and be hidden : **380**,1;
- to be very grateful to God when
He makes us live in obscurity :
380,2; - a soul of interior life
should be anxious to hide herself
under the shadow of God : *ibid.;*
- the positive aspect of the — consists
in being centered on God : **116**,1;
- the more a soul hides itself from
creatures, the more it is able to
live hidden with Christ in God :
116,1,2.

Holy Spirit — Is the soul of the Church : **44**,2; **188**,1; - given to the Church that each member may always become more like the Redeemer : **44**,2; **188**,2; **193**,1; - promised by Christ as comforter and support of the Apostles : **179**,2; **182**,2; - gives strength to render testimony to Christ in any difficulty : *ibid.;* **188**,1; - inflames in the Church zeal for glory of God and the salvation of souls : *ibid.;* - is the inspiration of every apostolate : **344**,1; - is the Spirit of Jesus : **47**,1; **187**,1; - dwells in Christ with a singular fulness of grace : **47**,1; - Soul of Christ is His chosen temple : *ibid.;* **187**,1; - His action in the Soul of Christ which is most docile to His impulses : **187**,2; - incorporated in Christ we receive the — : **48**,1; - we receive Him in a special way in confirmation : **72**,1,2; - Jesus merited Him for us and sent Him to continue His work in us : **168**,1; **188**,2; - the descent of the — is the fulness of the gift of God to men : **189**,1; - He is the substantial expression of the mutual love of the Father and the Son : **186**,1; - is the Third Person of the Blessed Trinity : **186**,2; - to Him particularly is attributed the diffusion of grace : **47**,1; **190**,1; **193**,1; - and the work of sanctification : **186**,2; **190**,1; - dwells in all souls in state of grace and is pleased the greater is their degree of grace : **187**,1; - immensely complacent in the most holy soul of Mary : *ibid.;* - is the sweet Guest of the soul : **188**,2; **189**,2; - His renewed and continual effusions in the soul : *ibid.;* - His continual and secret action in souls : **168**,2; **190**,1,2; - is in us to sanctify us : **188**,2; **189**,1; - cannot sanctify us if we do not respond

freely and fully to His action : **188**,2; **190**,1; **192**,2; - prepares souls for the supernatural life : **190**,1; - infuses charity in us : **189**,2; **190**,2; **259**,1; **344**,1; - invites the soul to good and sustains its efforts : **190**,2; - our whole spiritual life develops under His influence : **190**,2; **192**,1; - His initiative in us supplies for our insufficiency : **191**,2; **192**,1,2; - attracts us and orientates us completely toward God : **191**,2; **192**,1; - is Master of sanctity : *ibid.;* - Master sweet but exacting : **302**,1; - in us to conform us and assimilate us to Christ : **193**,1; - urges us to the way of the cross : **194**,1,2; - completes the soul's purification : **194**,2; **316**,1; **352**,1,2; - His action in the soul is not always consoling : **194**,2; **316**,1; **352**,1; - without His help impossible to attain sanctity : **195**,1; **298**,2; **316**,2; - acts in us by His Gifts : **195**,1,2; - infuses in us the sense of our divine sonship : **198**,1; **299**,1; **304**,1; - He teaches us to pray and He prays in us : **198**,2; - His influence in prayer : **143**,2; **145**,1; **159**,1; - He enlightens the soul on its own misery : **307**,2; **352**,1,2; **256**,1; - the full dominion over sensibility is the fruit of the — : **367**,2; - sin is great obstacle to action of the — : **168**,1,2; **188**,1; - cannot fill the soul lacking in fraternal charity ; **182**,1; - attachment to self and lack of generosity hinder His action : **192**,2; **306**,2; - to act only under the impulse of the — : **171**,2; - docility to His action and voice : **192**,1,2; **197**,2; **302**,1; **306**,2; **344**,1,2; - trustful recourse to the — : **193**,2; - the assiduous practice of virtue disposes the soul to receive the Gifts of the — : **197**,1; **298**,2; - the attitude of the soul to dispose itself for His action and to profit by it : **197**,1,2; **316**,2; - to place the whole spiritual life under His direction : **199**,1; - to act in continual dependence on Him : **199**,2; **344**,2; - how to recognize His inspirations : **199**,2; - to follow the Will of God guided by the — is the most secure way to the heavenly Fatherland : **329**,1; - commentary on *Veni Creator* : **186**,2; **316**,2.

See : BEATITUDES; GIFTS OF HOLY SPIRIT.

Honor — Attachment to points of — is obstacle to spiritual progress : **117**,1; - struggle against points of — : **117**,2.

Hope - As much as the soul hopes for, so much it obtains : **63**,2; **249**,1; - — in God's mercy is very pleasing to Him : **108**,2; - in spite of our misery, we should trust ourselves to God completely : **247**,2; **249**,1,2; - — in God is not excessive because it is based on His infinite mercy : **249**,1; - the more a soul is dilated by — in God the more it is open to His sanctifying action : *ibid.;* - in spite of its weakness and misery, the soul hopes to attain union with God : **359**,2; - our — is based on the Passion of Jesus : **126**,1; - we can — for all in the name of Jesus and in His infinite merits : **175**,2; - — has a sense of sadness, as we do not yet possess that which we — for : **161**,2; - in Heaven — will cease : **254**,1; - without charity, this virtue is incomplete : *ibid.;* - it is perfected by the gift of knowledge : **310**,2; - it purifies the memory, emptying it of all things : **349**,2; - our — in God is not complete as long as we still trust in creatures : **178**,2; - the

Holy Eucharist is a motive for great — and confidence : **204**,2; - object of — possession of God in Heaven : **246**,1; **299**,2; - we should have firm — that God will pardon our sins and give graces necessary for sanctification : **246**,1,2; - foundation of — is infinite goodness of God, His saving and sanctifying Will : **247**,1; - we should not base our — on our merits, on our works or resources, but in God alone : **247**,1,2; **249**,1,2; **338**,2; - certitude of — based on faith in infinite love of God : **247**,2; - in trials our — becomes more pure, supernatural, and intense : **247**,1; **248**,1,2; - stability of — measured by trial, desolation, abandonment : **248**,1; - least act of — in trial and desolation worth more than a thousand in joy and prosperity : **248**,2; - not necessary to have sentiment of —; it suffices to will to — : *ibid.;* - conduct in trials and temptations against — *ibid.;* - is the anchor of salvation for the soul tossed by the waves of human weakness : **249**,2; - unshakable — in anguish of purifying trials : **353**,1; - temerity to think God will save and sanctify us without our collaboration : **246**,2; - though God requires good works, God does not wish us to base our confidence in them : **247**,1; - Christian — requires good works, though it does not direct us to depend upon them, but upon God and His infinite mercy : **249**,2; - firm — necessary for an apostle : **338**,1,2; - to continue to — in spite of contradiction and failure in the apostolate : **338**,2. See : CONFIDENCE.

Humiliations — Are means of acquiring humility : **110**,1; **377**,2;

- — do not render one humble but by the way in which they are accepted : **110**,2; - — which show the truth are worth much more than illusions which lead to deception : **284**,1; - to ask for — whenever we are tempted to raise ourselves above others : **301**,2; - to share in the outrages and — of Jesus : **376**,2.

Humility — Means of preparing in our hearts the way of the Lord : **22**,2; - necessity of — to overcome enticements to self-love : **62**,2; - difficulty in obedience due to lack of — : **125**,2; - is difficult to humble oneself before one's neighbor : **377**,1; - in falls : **101**,2; **109**,1,2; **193**,2; **210**,2; **295**,1; - —, sincere and trustful, is the remedy for every fall and misery : **109**,2; **210**,2; **236**,2; **249**,2; - to humbly recognize one's own faults without excusing them and to accept correction : **118**,1; - the humble recognition of one's misery draws down the mercy of God : **236**,2; **259**,2; - — in things poorly done pleases God more than pride in things well done : **259**,2; - to recognize our own miseries is the first step toward freeing ourselves from them : **284**,1; **350**,1; - — is the foundation of our spiritual life : **106**,1; **316**,1; - and of charity : **106**,1; **259**,2; **294**,1; - the more a soul humbles itself, so much the more will God fill it with grace and sanctify it : **106**,2; **176**,2; **240**,2; **259**,2; **352**,2; - — gives us the capacity to receive gifts of God : **106**,2; - — is the virtue that makes us keep our place : **107**,1; **109**,2; - and which makes us take the lowest place : **113**,1,2; **301**,2; - fruitfulness and riches of the interior life always in proportion

to — : **176**,2; - we are nothing and can do nothing without the help of God : **107**,1,2; **240**,2; **307**,1; **334**,1,2; - though doing all we can, we should not expect success from our works, but solely from the help of God : **240**,2; - awareness of our insufficiency and impotence should keep us very humble : *ibid.;* - deep — necessary for an apostle : **334**,1,2; - Christian — does not depress, but lifts the soul to God : **108**,1; **240**,2; - relation between — and confidence : **108**,1,2; - humble soul does not trust self, but only God : **108**,2; - true — does not disquiet, but false — does : **109**,2; - lack of confidence in the mercy of God is not fruit of — : **109**,2; - to acquire — necessary to accept humiliations : **110**,1; - humble soul considers it just to be humiliated : *ibid.;* - the more one strives for humiliations on his own initiative, the more he should accept those that come from others : **110**,2; - importance and practice of — of heart : **111**,1,2; - — of heart is born of humble recognition of one's own misery : **111**,2; - practice of — in honors and posts of authority : *ibid.;* **113**,2; **176**,2; **377**,1; - the humble soul conceals all that could draw the attention of others : **114**,1,2; - it is great — to remain silent when unjustly accused : **118**,2; - attitude of — in contemplation : **144**,1; **145**,2; - practice of — in aridity : **155**,2; - — in prayer : **175**,2; - the higher the post one fills, the deeper should be — : **176**,2; **334**,1,2; - in gaining — the other virtues also gained : **214**,1; - the humble soul is grateful : **283**,2; - the humble soul is not pusillanimous, but magnanimous : **289**,2; - Jesus the Model of — : **111**,1; **113**,1; **114**,1; - for the followers of Jesus, the place of honor is the place of service : **113**,2; - — leads to the imitation of the hidden life of Jesus : **114**,1; - to imitate the silence of Jesus in the case of unjust accusations : **118**,2; - to imitate the — of Mary : **176**,1,2; **377**,1,2; **380**,2; - graces and divine favors should make us more humble : **176**,1; **252**,1; - Jesus, the Gift of God, wishes — of heart : **217**,2; - God permits failures that the soul may be convinced of its insufficiency : *ibid.;* - God permits falls that the soul may be persuaded of its misery : **295**,1; **307**,2; - the Holy Spirit illumines the soul on its own misery : *ibid.;* **352**,1,2; **359**,2; - by means of the night of the spirit, God Himself undertakes to humble the soul : **352**,2; - deep — that the soul attains in this night : **359**,2.

Imperfections — Every voluntary imperfection is contrary to the Will of God : **5**,2; **78**,2; **102**,1; - — hinder union with God : **78**,2; **79**,1; **102**,1; **359**,1; - habitual — are the most harmful and not only prevent union with God, but even progress in perfection : **79**,1,2; **102**,1; - voluntary — always come from a lack of effort and vigor : **102**,2; - the struggle against deliberate and semi-deliberate —: **103**,2; - voluntary — can lead to tepidity : **153**,1; - to recognize one's own — : **249**,2; - meaning of — : **102**,1; - diverse types of — : **102**,1,2; - — of proficients : **346**,2; **347**,1; - to extirpate the roots of habitual —, the night of the spirit is necessary : *ibid.;* - the firm resolution to avoid every imperfection is a sure sign of the love of God : **359**,1.

Imprudence — The greatest — to follow one's own whims and will : **329**,1.

Incarnation (Mystery of) — The greatest proof and manifestation of the infinite love of God for men : **22**,1; **26**,1,2; **27**,2; **28**,1; **29**,1,2; **30**,1,2; **32**,1; - greatest work of God accomplished in time : **28**,1; - was accomplished in obscurity and silence : **28**,2; - it glorifies the infinite goodness of God more than any other work : **32**,1; **226**,2; - purpose of the — is the glory of God : **32**,1; - leads man again to the Trinity : **219**,1.

Ingratitude — For favors received hinders reception of others : **280**,2; - is always harmful to the soul : **283**,1,2; - human — withholds divine mercy : **322**,1.

Intentions — Purity of intention often lacking in one who seeks the esteem of creatures : **114**,2; - purity of intention makes one act solely for God and one's spiritual profit : **115**,2; - when our — are right we should not fear that our good works may be seen : **327**,2; - secondary — contaminate good works : **285**,2; - the secondary — which can insinuate themselves in apostolic activity : **332**,2.
See : RECTITUDE.

Jesus Christ — His redemptive work : **2**,1,2; **24**,1,2; **38**,1,2; **39**,2; **61**,1; **64**,1; **67**,1; **154**,1; **210**,1; **222**,1; **238**,1; **273**,1; **280**,1; - has redeemed the world principally by the death of the Cross : **24**,1; **25**,2; **38**,2; **43**,2; **93**,1; **139**,1; **326**,2; - wishes our collaboration in His redemptive work : **23**,1,2; **61**,1; **65**,2; **93**,2; **318**,2; **325**,1; - dispositions to profit by His

383,2; - He reigns from the Cross : **133**,1; - He is the Head of the Mystical Body : **44**,1; **67**,1,2; **383**,1; - in — dwells the fulness of the Divinity : **39**,1; **219**,1; - as God He possesses the Divine Life as does the Father : **45**,1; **66**,1; - as man He receives the greatest plenitude of grace : **45**,1; **187**,1; - the power of the most holy humanity : **46**,1; - the Divinity acts through the Humanity of — : **46**,1; - as man He is our Way; as God He is our End : **66**,1,2; - we should " Abide " in Jesus : **43**,2; - our real and vital union with Christ our Head : **44**,2; **179**,1; **206**,1; - we should live and grow in Christ : **48**,1,2; **65**,1; - our spiritual rebirth in Christ : **147**,1; **231**,1; - our vital partici- pation in His mysteries, the consequence of our incorporation in Him : **179**,1; - to live in Christ we must first die with Him : **231**,1; - Jesus is our Resurrection, not only to eternal life, but also in this life : **350**,2; - the soul of — is the chosen Temple of the Holy Spirit : **47**,1; **187**,1; - by His death He has merited the Holy Spirit and together with the Father, He continually sends Him to us : **47**,2; **55**,2; **66**,2; **188**,1; **315**,2; - to live in — is to live in the Holy Spirit : **47**,2; - — continues His work in souls through the Holy Spirit : **168**,1; **175**,1; - the Master : **50**,1,2; and *fol.;* - as the Word, He is the substantial expression of the Father and contains and manifests all truth : **50**,2; - He, not only knows all truth, but He is Truth : *ibid.;* - characteristics of the teaching of — : **51**,1,2; **55**,1,2; - He reveals the Father : **52**,1,2; - whoever knows —, knows the Father : **52**,1; - He teaches us to

imitate the Heavenly Father and gives us the means : **53**,1; - — would have us engage in the struggle against sin : **54**,1,2; **100**,2; - He leads our soul to accept the truth and to put it into practice : **55**,1; - He infuses in us the light of faith and the flame of charity : **55**,1; - He interiorly instructs souls : **55**,2; - — reveals to us the love of God : **29**,1,2; **30**,1,2; **52**,2; - our Model : **57**,1,2; and *fol.;* - imitation of Jesus : **57**,1,2; - conforming ourselves to His image, we conform ourselves to the likeness of God : **57**,1; - His permanent and intimate union with the Father, model of our union with God : **25**,1; **58**,1; **61**,2; - His interior life and our participation in it : **58**,2; **116**,1,2; - His prayer : **59**,1,2; - our assimi- lation and conformation to — : **65**,1,2; **193**,1; - — wills to continue in us His life and His work : **65**,2; **93**,2; **193**,1; - conformity to — Crucified : **93**,1,2; **194**,1,2; - we cannot be His intimate friends if we do not suffer with Him : **93**,2; - — Model of humility : **111**,1; **113**,1; **114**,1; - His humility and humiliations : **27**,2; **31**,1; **36**,1; **42**,1,2; **62**,1; - His obedience : **42**,2; **121**,1; - His submission to the law : **36**,2; **371**,2; - Model of patience : **128**,1; **279**,2; - His meekness and mildness : **133**,2; **270**,1; **279**,2; - attitude of the Soul of — wholly immersed in the Trinity : **58**,2; **64**,1; **116**,1; - guides us to the Trinity : **116**,2; **219**,1; **222**,1; - He has revealed to us the mystery of the Trinity : **220**,1; - His infinite love for us : **64**,1; **132**,2; **136**,2; **137**,1,2; **139**,2; **209**,1,2; **210**,1; **238**,1; **262**,2; **273**,1; **315**,2; - the same love that binds Him to the Father makes Him love men as creatures of the Father :

64,1; - the yearning of His soul for the glory of the Father and for the salvation of men : **65**,1; - knows and loves each soul individually : **154**,2; - love unfolds the mystery of all that — has done for us : **209**,2; - — the Good Shepherd : **64**,1; **154**,1,2; **210**,1; - sower of the divine word in souls : **84**,1; - has overcome the demon and has paid the price of our victories : **112**,1; - — Fount of Living Water invites all to draw from its source : **143**,1; **144**,1; - — has compassion on our spiritual and material needs : **231**,2; **294**,2; - has every right to find the fruits of sanctity in us : **238**,1; - is the Good Samaritan Who tends and heals our souls : **273**,1; - — has founded His Church as the continuation of His work : **67**,1,2; - lives and works in His Church : *ibid.;* - if we wish to live according to His Spirit, we should let ourselves be guided by the Church : **67**,1; - He gives the sacraments their efficacy : **69**,1.

See : INCARNATION; PASSION; REDEMPTION; SACRED HEART.

Joseph (St.) — His obedience, spirit of faith, and humility : **28**,2; **373**,1; - his adhesion and abandonment to the Will of God and in the most obscure circumstances : **33**,2; **373**,2; - together with Mary, — was the first to enter into that life of intimacy and love to which Jesus opened the door : **372**,2; - — is the model of souls of the interior life : **373**,2; - His mission of guardian of the Holy Family and Patron of the Church : **372**,1; - —has participated in full as a humble hidden collaborator in the work of Redemption : *ibid.;* - — did not live for Himself,

but solely for Jesus and Mary : *ibid.;* **373**,2.

Joy — Of the soul who is completely given to God : **303**,2; - of the soul who has the foretaste of union with God : **361**,1.

Judas — Conduct of Jesus toward him : **134**,2; - represents the souls who by their infidelity have made themselves unworthy of the graces received : *ibid.*

Judgment — Last — : **1**,2; **364**,2; - in the last — God will judge on charity : **257**,2; **264**,2; **364**,2; - God will judge us with the same mercy which we have shown our neighbor : **264**,2; - necessary to judge things, not according to appearances, but according to their value in the sight of God : **234**,2.

Justice — Exterior — not sufficient : **224**,2; **279**,1; - necessity of fulfilling duties of — toward the neighbor : **277**,1,2; **278**,1; - we should not be satisfied until we have fulfilled all duties of — : **278**,1; - the enemies of — : **278**,2; - to maintain rectitude by not deviating from — : *ibid.;* - not lawful to fail in — under pretext of charity : **238**,2; **277**,1; - indispensable for charity : *ibid.;* - should be vivified by charity : **279**,1; - to uphold — not by strength but by charity : **279**,2; - is the constant will to give to each his due : **277**,1; - is source of peace : **277**,2; - in this world absolute — not possible : **279**,2; - for soul aspiring to sanctity greatest — is patient bearing of injustice : *ibid.;* - hunger and thirst for — corresponds to hunger and thirst for sanctity : **303**,1,2; - blessed are they who hunger and thirst for — : **303**,1; - is perfected by the gift of piety : **304**,1,2; - in our contacts with God we are always infinitely below what — exacts : **281**,1; - — to God impels one to give himself to God without measure : **281**,2; - in Jesus we are able to supply for the insufficiency of our — : **281**,1; - — and religion : **281**,2.

Justice of God — Presupposes mercy and is accompanied by it : **237**,1; - infinite — is the zeal which protects the rights of God **237**,2; - punishments of God are the fruit of the — and of His mercy : *ibid.*

Knowledge (Gift of) — Makes one understand the nothingness of creatures : **309**,1,2; - the soul who is enlightened feels the need of withdrawing from creatures : **309**,2; - under the influence of — creatures become a ladder to go to God : *ibid.;* - infuses contrition for sin : **310**,1; - perfects the virtue of hope: **310**,2; - to the gift of — corresponds the beatitude of mourning : **310**,1; - makes the soul understand the joy of sorrow embraced for love of God : **310**,2.

Law — To observe the divine — gives glory to God : **33**,1; - submission of Jesus and Mary to the — which did not bind them : **36**,1; **371**,2; - — to which we are bound and to which self-love would claim exemption under false pretexts : *ibid.*

Lent — Time for spiritual reform : **77**,1; - dedicated to the remembrance of the Passion of Jesus : **91**,1; - and to penance : **94**,2; - and to the struggle against sin : **98**,1; - Lenten program : **99**,1,2.

Liberty — Man is free to correspond with grace or to reject it : **34**,1; **73**,1,2; - God does not do violence to our — and will not sanctify us without our consent : **188**,2; - God is omnipotent and governs man without hindrance to his — : **240**,1; - to correspond with grace, our free consent is necessary : **266**,2; - — is the ability to adhere to the good without letting oneself be influenced by passion : **102**,1; - to refuse to do what is best under pretext of freedom is an abuse of — : *ibid.;* - it is an abuse of — to use it to will evil rather than good : **232**,2; - — of spirit permits the soul to concentrate itself wholly on God : **116**,2; - renunciation of — is greatest sacrifice man can offer God : **121**,2; - free immolation of — by the vow of obedience : **122**,1,2.

Life (Earthly) — Conditioned by continual flow of time : **35**,1; - happy the soul who at the end of — without delay can be admitted to the beatific union of Heaven : **364**,2; - the degree of glory we shall possess for all eternity will correspond to the degree of love attained at end of — : **384**,1; - — of the body dies, but life of the soul remains : **385**,2; - — is a pilgrimage to eternal life : **161**,1,2; **175**,1; - — should be a preparation for our meeting God : **182**,1; - it is a way of return to God : **345**,1; - while on earth we should long for God, for Heaven : **179**,1; **182**,1; - the worth of our — should be proved by the accomplishment of the Will of God : **238**,2; - — is a continual struggle : **245**,1; **287**,1; - greatest imprudence to be guided in our — by our own whims and self-will : **329**,1.

Life (Interior) — Is the soul of the apostolate : **25**,1; **321**,2; **323**,1; - should be orientated to the salvation of souls : **317**,1; - apostolic ideal urges the soul to a deeper — **323**,1; - an — indifferent to the good of souls is necessarily stunted and narrow : **323**,2; - deep — necessary for an apostle : **320**,1,2; - — is not genuine if not crowned with spiritual paternity or maternity : **341**,2; - whoever seeks the esteem of creatures and wishes to assert his rights cannot have a deep — : **114**,2; **117**,2; - — leads to intimate friendship with God : **321**,1; - is the secret hearth where the soul in contact with God is inflamed with His love : **321**,2; - the development of — calls for the twofold attraction of union with God and the apostolate : **342**,2.

Life (Spiritual) — To awaken fervor in — : **1**,2; **77**,1; - renewal of — : **140**,2; **141**,1; - in — there is daily need of beginning over again : **217**,1,2; - lack of deep unity renders — weak : **228**,2; - even after long years of — there can arise the struggle between the flesh and the spirit : **245**,1; **287**,1; - as long as one does not understand that God is infinite Love the — is only in bud : **30**,2; - hunger for God is a sign of an efficient — : **141**,1; - — depends much on the thought that we are working for God : **211**,2.

Love — Resembling God our supernatural life should be essentially — : **4**,1; - in every action we are impelled by the — of God, of creatures, or of self : **5**,2; - — is an act of the will : **19**,2; **255**,1; - — is repaid by —: **22**,1; - — overcomes every obstacle

in order to be united with the loved one : **31**,1; - — finds or renders lovers equal : **251**,1; **348**,1; - — tends by nature to unity : *ibid.*
See : LOVE OF GOD; LOVE OF NEIGHBOR; CHARITY.

Love of God — Is the power that unites the soul to God : **4**,2; **100**,1; **250**,2; **345**,1; **361**,1,2; - true — consists in doing the Will of God : **5**,1; **19**,1,2; **255**,1,2; **256**,1; - the perfection of — consists in full conformity to the Will of God : **6**,1; **120**,1; **251**,2; - pure — seeks only the glory of God and the fulfillment of His Will : **256**,1; - the soul who with all its strength believes that God is truly God will love Him very much : **19**,1; - — makes one taste and experience God : *ibid.;* - — confers on the soul the " sense of God " : **143**,2; **157**,2; **158**,1,2; - prayer is above all an exercise of — : **149**,2; **150**,1,2; - of — is born the loving knowledge of God : **150**,1; - — is reinforced by prayer : **256**,2; - love of charity is pure benevolence toward God : **19**,1; - — makes one love God for Himself as He loves Himself : **250**,2; - renders one capable of loving God with the love of friendship : *ibid.;* **251**,2; - makes man live no longer for himself but for God : *ibid.;* - infusing charity in us, God has made us capable of returning His love : *ibid.;* - our friendship with God will be perfect when there is nothing in us contrary to His Will : *ibid.;* - — does not consist in sentiment, but in the act of the will : **19**,2; **158**,1; **255**,1; **361**,1; - the love of charity does not consist in sentiment, but in the will to give God the preference over

1204

all things : **158**,1; **255**,2; - relations
between the feeling of — and the
act of — : **255**,1,2; - — is true
even when deprived of feeling :
255,1; **356**,1; - lacking the feeling
of love, one needs to apply oneself
with all one's strength to accomplish
its works : **355**,2; - one should
not seek enjoyment in —, but
should seek to make progress in it :
361,1; - to return with — the
infinite — for us : **22**,1; **30**,1;
31,1,2; **150**,1; **211**,1,2; **252**,1; - — is
a spur to generosity : **30**,1; **31**,1,2;
211,1,2; **290**,1; - and to the total
gift of self : **212**,1; **250**,2; **290**,2; - to
love and to despoil oneself of all
that is not God for God : **31**,2;
348,2; - the — and the cult of God
should always have the first place :
134,1; - when the — has taken full
possession of a soul there remains
no room for other loves : **142**,1;
356,1; **358**,2; - how the loving soul
seeks God : **142**,1,2; - the need to
love God above all things : **253**,2;
- generous and continuous exercise
of — : **256**,2; - only — can give
an intuition of the mystery of the
— for us : **208**,2; - the degree of
— attained on earth is the same as
that with which we shall love God
in Heaven : **35**,1; **256**,1; **384**,1;
only in Heaven shall we be able
to love God with absolute perfection
and stability : **253**,1; **256**,1; - to
increase in love, one must do good
works with all one's heart : **35**,2;
180,2; **256**,2; - necessary to keep
oneself in contact with God :
301,1; - however much we love
God, we shall not be able to love
Him to the extent of His lova-
bleness : **53**,2; **99**,2; **249**,1; **253**,1;
- measure of loving God is to love
without measure : **99**,2; **253**,1;
- — is inseparable from the love
of neighbor : **64**,2; **181**,1,2; **257**,1,2;

301,2; **323**,2; - the more a soul
loves God, the more it loves its
neighbor : **181**,1; **258**,1; - a soul
who loves God loves all that God
loves : **181**,2; **260**,2; - we cannot
be deceived about our — if we
love our neighbor : **257**,2; - the
best way to increase our — is
careful practice of fraternal charity :
271,2; - from — is born zeal for
souls : **317**,1; **344**,1; - reality of — is
shown by embracing suffering for
His love : **96**,1,2; **132**,2; **360**,1;
- the stronger the — the more it
enables the soul to embrace what
is painful and arduous for God :
288,1; **289**,2; **356**,1,2; **360**,1,2; - the
stronger the soul is in suffering, the
stronger is — : **360**,2; - — when it
is perfect, destroys sin more than
does purgatory : **100**,2; - — can
make any suffering a means of
sanctification : **127**,2; - whoever
works purely for the — seeks his
own interest in nothing : **115**,2;
256,1; **355**,2; **356**,2; - one degree of
pure — is more precious in the
sight of God and more useful to the
Church than all other works
combined : **342**,2; **368**,2; - — makes
the soul completely forgetful of
self, of one's consolations and
satisfactions : **355**,2; **356**,2; **360**,2;
370,2; - torturing pain not to love
God : **157**,2; **158**,1; - — is purified,
strengthened, and developed by
aridity : **255**,2; - and by the painful
trials of the night of the spirit :
355,1,2; - for the soul who loves
God, the fear of not loving Him is a
very great torment : **355**,2; - the
strong and appreciative — that the
Holy Spirit infuses into the soul
by purifying trials : **356**,1,2; - the
fire of love invades the soul so much
the more as it is purified from
everything contrary to it : **360**,2;
- — makes the ardent soul impatient

in its inspirations for union with God : **358**,1,2; - most careful to avoid the least offense against God : **359**,1; - — indomitable in fatigue and suffering for God : **360**,1,2; - — in proportion to its strength, unites the soul to God : **361**,1,2; - — draws God to the soul and the soul to God : **361**,2; - it is of the utmost importance to exercise oneself much in love in order to attain union with God while on earth and hereafter in a blessed eternity : **364**,2; - sublime exercise of — in the soul which has attained union with God : **368**,1,2; - — renders the soul so conformed to God as to transform it into Him : **369**,1; - in this state the soul loves God with the equality of love : **369**,2; - the enamored soul longs for union and intimacy with God, not for enjoyment, but to love Him always more : **370**,2.
See : LOVE; CHARITY.

Love of Neighbor — Is the precept of the Lord and it is sufficient : **32**,2; **308**,2; - — is distinctive of the disciples of Christ : **70**,1; **262**,1; - — is the commandment of the New Law : **224**,2; **260**,1; **262**,1; - the commandment of Jesus is to love one's neighbor as He loves him : **262**,1,2; **307**,1; - our charity will be perfect when it is the reflection of the love of Jesus for every creature : **262**,1,2; - — should extend to all, excluding no one : **56**,2; **258**,1; **260**,1; **265**,2; **273**,2; - it is necessary to overcome evil by love : **56**,2; **63**,2; **70**,2; **224**,1; - charity does not permit divisions, overcomes opposition, maintains peace : **70**,1; **224**,1; **308**,2; - greatest charity is practised toward those who do us harm and in bearing with the wicked : **70**,2; - to know

how to pardon : **70**,1,2; **224**,1; **264**,1,2; - to be good to all, even to the ungrateful and to enemies : **233**,2; **264**,1; - to overlook wrongs, misunderstandings, offenses : **268**,2; - and injustice : **279**,2; - charity shares in the sorrows and necessities of others and sacrifices itself for them : **64**,2; **267**,1,2; **273**,2; - — requires an understanding of the material needs of others : **119**,1; **261**,2; - — is the consequence and extension of the love of God : **64**,2; **181**,1,2; **257**,1; **268**,1; - — is strong and constant only when it stems from love of God : **64**,2; - when — is weak so also is the love of God : **181**,2; **317**,1; **323**,2; - — is the proof and the most certain sign of our love for God : **182**,1; **257**,2; **271**,1; **365**,2; - —, together with the love of God, is the foundation of Christian life : **257**,1; **308**,2; - recollection and union with God should not hinder the practice of — : **64**,2; **181**,1,2; - lack of — is one of the greatest obstacles to the action of the Holy Spirit : **182**,1; - God is not pleased with prayer that is not accompanied by charity : *ibid.;* **224**,2; - to cover our debts to God with charity : **245**,2; - — is an essential condition for eternal salvation : **257**,2; - there is no true religion without — : **273**,2; - — should be the fruit of Holy Communion : **137**,2; - duties of fellowship stemming from our incorporation in Christ : **267**,1; - — is love for creatures *propter Deum* : **257**,1; **258**,1,2; **260**,1; - the precept of — is inseparable from that of love for God : **257**,1; - God considers as done for Himself all that we do for our neighbor : **257**,1,2; - — is identical with the theological virtue with which we love God : **258**,1; - he who says he loves God and hateth his brother is a liar : *ibid.;* - — is charity only in the measure in which it is inspired by the love of God : **258**,2; - one who does not love his neighbor does not love God : **259**,2; **301**,2; **323**,2; - charity should not be based on the qualities of our neighbor, nor on our relations with him, but on his relation to God : **260**,1,2; - in recompense for our —, God will make our love for Him increase : **271**,2; **365**,2; - — is a created participation in the love which God has for His creatures : **271**,2; - practising — we unite ourselves to God; failing to do so, we alienate ourselves from Him : *ibid.;* - failures in — are obstacles to union with God : **365**,2; the foundation of charity is humility : **259**,2; **294**,1; **301**,2; - egoism hinders the practice of charity : **260**,2; - the greatest enemy of charity is self-love : **261**,1; - to love our neighbor as ourselves, treating him with the same delicacy and understanding that we would desire ourselves : **261**,1,2; **263**,2; **265**,1; - to love each one individually in his concrete personality : **261**,2; - it is not charity to give in order to receive, but to give without calculation or measure : **268**,1; - charity hides the good that it does, as it seeks no return : *ibid.;* - self-renunciation is the delicacy of charity in order to adapt oneself to one's neighbor : **269**,1,2; **308**,1,2; **343**,1; - charity is always mild and sweet : **270**,1; - the practice of mildness in difficult contacts with one's neighbor : **270**,2; - charity should be accompanied by affability and delicacy of manner : **335**,1,2; - perfect courtesy, always unvarying, is the fruit of a delicate charity : **335**,2; - the chief good we should

wish for our neighbor is his spiritual welfare : **261**,2; - it is a great mistake to judge persons and things only on the negative side : **263**,1; - rather than criticize the faults of others, we should try to correct the same in ourselves : *ibid.;* - to judge no one because judgment is reserved to God alone : **263**,2; - if it is not possible to excuse the action, at least excuse the intention : *ibid.;* - the defects of a neighbor should not lessen the esteem and benevolence for him : *ibid.;* **267**,2; - fraternal charity draws a veil over the faults of others : **265**,1; - to fight against thoughts and judgments lacking benevolence for one's neighbor : **265**,2; - true charity consists in bearing with the faults of others : **267**,2; - in contacts with one's neighbor, to imitate the mercy of our heavenly Father : **264**,1; **307**,1; - God will show us the same mercy that we have shown others : **264**,2; **336**,2; - fraternal correction is real act of charity if done with kindness : **270**,2; **294**,1; - charity is the best means of practising justice : **279**,2; - charity should be the bond that unites all : **308**,1; - necessary to be prepared for any personal sacrifice to preserve fraternal union : **308**,2; - the highest expression of fraternal charity is the apostolate : **323**,2. See : LOVE; CHARITY.

Love of Self — Heart occupied by — cannot be filled with God : **22**,2; - impossible to serve God and — at the same time : **117**,2; - until mortification attacks —, it does not attain its end : **97**,1; - struggle against demands of self-love : **117**,1,2; - assiduous labor to uproot all its germs : **214**,2; - to break all the binding threads of — :

316,1; - — leads us to excuse our failings : **118**,1; - cause of anger in face of opposition : **214**,2; - great enemy of fraternal charity : **261**,1; - — not mortified, disturbs fraternal union : **308**,1; - eliminating —, we eliminate all other defects : **214**,1; - often we believe we are acting for love of God when acting for — : **274**,2; - — makes us deviate from right intention : **332**,2.

Magnanimity — Inclines the soul to render great service to God embracing what is arduous and difficult : **289**,1; - — should be united to obedience, humility, and the fulfillment of duty : *ibid.;* - the truly humble are magnanimous : **289**,2.

Man — Does not exist and can do nothing without the help of God : **107**,1,2; **240**,2; **307**,2; - his insufficiency and limitations in comparison with God and sanctity **191**,1; **192**,1; **227**,1,2; **228**,1; **230**,1; - — is changeable and weak, affected by time : **230**,2; - immeasurable distance between — and God : **232**,2; - his powerlessness and insufficiency should keep him very humble : **240**,2; - — is by nature unstable : **293**,1; - all sufficiency comes from God : **107**,2; **240**,2; - — exists only inasmuch as God communicates life to him and maintains him in existence : **228**,1; - — is good only insofar as God communicates to him a reflection of His goodness : **232**,1; - experience of his own misery should direct him to God with full confidence : **249**,1; - — is nothing in himself but great through gifts God has given him : **286**,2; - his responsibility in view of invitations of God : **188**,2; - God has created — free;

therefore, freely he should respond to goodness infused in him : **232**,2; - weakness of human nature : **193**,2; **287**,1; **295**,1; **307**,1,2; - malice of — : **232**,1,2; - interior — is natural — regenerated by grace : **301**,1.

Mary — Her Immaculate Conception : **9**,1; **171**,1; - her sanctity from first instant of her conception : **9**,1,2; **180**,1; - elevated to the state of union with God from the first moment of her existence : **9**,2; **171**,2; **172**,2; - always and in everything moved by the Holy Spirit : **9**,2; **171**,1,2; **180**,2; **374**,1; - beloved daughter of the Father : **170**,1; - faithful spouse of the Holy Spirit : **171**,1; - her greatest dignity to be the Mother of God : **172**,1; **382**,1; - her interior life : **14**,1,2; **169**,2; **183**,1,2; **378**,2; - intimate contacts with the Trinity : **183**,2; - faith : **15**,2; **49**,1; **177**,1,2; - perfect adhesion and abandonment to the Will of God : **33**,2; **170**,2; **171**,2; **172**,2; **374**,1,2; - correspondence and fidelity to grace : **171**,2; **180**,1,2; - and to the call of God : **386**,1,2; - humility : **176**,1,2; **377**,1,2; - no one had such concrete and practical knowledge of her own nothingness : **178**,1; - the deeper her consideration of her nothingness, so much the more she was raised to God, seeing and praising Him for the great things He had done in her : **377**,2; - full confidence and hope in God : **178**,1,2; - fidelity in employing the talents received : **180**,1; - incessant progress in charity and grace : **180**,2; **187**,1; - strength in sorrow : **360**,2; - humble submission to the law : **371**,2; - judged all things in their relation to God : **381**,1; - gave herself to God and permitted Hir to exercise all His rights over her : **386**,2; - recollection and union with God did not prevent her from caring for the needs of her neighbor : **14**,2; **181**,1,2; - charity for her neighbor : *ibid.;* **377**,1; - charity makes her unmindful of discomfort and of her dignity : *ibid.;* - giving herself wholly to God, she is wholly given to her neighbor : **181**,1; - the apostolate derived from her love of God : **184**,1; - her apostolate characterized by retirement and silence : **184**,2; - attains the height of the apostolate by hidden immolation : *ibid.;* - mediatrix of all graces : **49**,1; **185**,1,2; - our Mother, comfort, support, and refuge : **169**,1; - after Jesus, the surest guide to union with God : **171**,2; - her maternity in our regard : **173**,1,2; **378**,1; **382**,1,2; - her maternity at the foot of the Cross : **173**,2; - all graces received through the hands of — : **173**,1; **185**,1; - — has loved us to the extent of sacrificing her Son for our salvation : **173**,2; **181**,2; - — is the easiest and most secure way to reach Jesus : **174**,2; - she guides us to Jesus and through Him to the Blessed Trinity : **183**,2; - she has given Jesus to us and she brings us to Him : **185**,2; **382**,1; - filial and confident recourse to — the Mother of Jesus and our Mother : **382**,1,2; - he who wishes Jesus, should seek Him in the arms of — : **382**,1; - we should trust ourselves to — as devoted and loving children : **382**,2; - she teaches us to practise the teachings of Jesus : **49**,2; - with her we ‸ould share in the Passion of **131**,2; - — model of souls ‸nterior life : **169**,2; life of intimacy - imitation of — :

169,1,2; **174**,2; **176**,2; **374**,2; **380**,2; - model for contemplative and apostolic souls : **184**,1; - model of souls totally united and given to the Will of God : **374**,1; - — is perfectly united to Jesus in the observance of His teaching : **112**,2; - her participation in the Passion of her Son : **131**,1,2; **184**,1,2; **185**,1; - the intimacy of her contacts with her Divine Son : **172**,2; **174**,2; **183**,1; - participation and association with the Redemptive work of her Son : **173**,1,2; **184**,1,2; **185**,1; **371**,2; **374**,2; - — is the most perfect image of Christ : **174**,2; - her birth is the dawn of Redemption : **380**,1; - her origin and her whole life wrapt in silence : *ibid.;* - — presented in the Temple is model of consecrated souls : **386**,1,2; - her conduct at the moment of the Annunciation : **374**,1,2; - her conduct at the wedding of Cana : **49**,1; - her Assumption tells us that we have no lasting dwelling here, but in Heaven : **379**,1; - and it indicates the itinerary of our spiritual life : **379**,2; - the Little Habit our Lady of Mount Carmel offers us in an external sign of her constant and maternal work for our souls : **378**,1; - devotion to our Lady of Mount Carmel implies a call to the interior life : **378**,2.

Mass — Is the center of liturgical cult : **165**,1; - how to assist at — : **165**,2; - with the priest to offer the Divine Victim : **166**,1; - to associate ourselves with the immolation of Jesus : **166**,2.

Meditation
See : PRAYER.

Meekness — Renders man capable of dominating anger : **214**,1;

297,1; - its foundation is humility : 214,2; - ensures the soul of interior peace : 297,1; - importance of — for a life of prayer and union with God : 297,2; - by gift of piety the Holy Spirit helps the soul to preserve — : 305,1; - blessed are the meek for they shall possess the land : 305,2; - the meek person possesses himself and gains the hearts of men : *ibid.*
See : MILDNESS.

Mercy — Of God in Redemption of man : 2,1; 26,2; - — characterizes love of God for us : 236,1; 307,1; - relations between the — of God and His justice : 237,1,2; - we have continual need of divine — : 264,1,2; - with infinite love God has willed to bridge the distance that separated us from Him : 353,1; - distrust in the — of God shows pride and diabolical temptation : 109,2; - we cannot trust too much in the — of God : 210,1; 249,1; - Jesus has inculcated in us a deep sense of the infinite — of God : 210,2; - — of God is so great that no repented sin can stop it : 236,1; - wrong to doubt the — of God and the pardon of sins : 246,2; - sins committed should not hinder our trust in divine — : 280,2; - — of God is not arrested by the ingratitude of men : 322,1; - magnificence and largesse of the — of God : 336,1; - God is always ready to pardon our sins : 336,1,2; - to draw down upon ourselves the divine —, God requires us to be merciful to our neighbor : 236,2; 264,2; 336,2; - and that we humbly recognize our misery : 236,2; 259,2; - God will treat us with the same — that we have shown our neighbor : 264,2; 336,2; - the consideration

of the — of God should render us merciful to our neighbor : 264,1,2; - we should imitate the infinite — of the heavenly Father : 307,1; - one who is convinced of his own misery is merciful to his neighbor : 307,2; - through the gift of counsel, the Holy Spirit establishes the soul in perfect — : *ibid.*

Mildness — Is the flower of charity : 270,1; - to overcome anger by — and mercy : 270,2; - more hearts are gained by a little kindness than by a harsh manner : 335,1.

Modesty — The practice of — in relation to chastity : 89,1,2.

Mortification — To prepare by — for the coming of the Lord : 8,2; - necessity of — that Christ may live in us : 65,1; 231,1; - — removes the obstacles to the development of grace : 143,2; - relaxation in — leads to tepidity : 153,1; - — of the senses : 16,1,2; 83,1,2; - importance and scope of corporal — : 92,1,2; 93,1,2; - necessity of — of the flesh in order to re-establish harmony between spirit and flesh : 296,2; - — of the taste : *ibid.;* - active — should be completed by passive — : 83,2; - voluntary — is a proof of love : 96,1; - — avails in the measure of love and generosity with which it is accomplished : 96,2; - spirit of — is complete only when it leads to self-renunciation : 97,1; - true spirit of — embraces all the occasions of suffering permitted by God in the circumstances of life : 97,2; - each day the need to die to self : 231,1.
See : ABNEGATION; DETACHMENT; PENANCE; RENUNCIATION.

Night of the Senses — Is the total mortification of the senses : **83**,1; **347**,1; - to enter the — it is necessary not to rest in sensible pleasure : **83**,1; - activity of soul to enter into the — : **83**,2; - God gives a great grace when He introduces the soul into the passive — : *ibid.*

Night of the Spirit — Uproots imperfect habits : **347**,1; - achieves in the soul a deep and radical detachment : **349**,1; - to enter the — there is need of renunciation of self, not only in regard to material goods, but also in regard to moral and spiritual goods : **347**,2; - need to exercise oneself intensely in the theological virtues : **349**,2; - anguish and darkness the soul suffers in this — : **353**,1,2; - its sole support is pure and naked faith : **353**,2; - one of the greatest graces God can grant a soul is to introduce it into the — : **348**,1; - this —, though very bitter, is the work of Divine Love : *ibid.;* - only God can lead the soul into the depth of this — : **351**,1; - the — culminates in interior pain in which God annihilates it in its spiritual faculties and destroys in it every imperfect habit : **352**,1; - in the — the soul is reduced to the center of its nothingness : **352**,2; - in this — the soul is in a special way under the influence of the Holy Spirit : **354**,2; - the obscure night of the apostolic life : **338**,2; - while we are on earth there will always be something of the — : **354**,1.

Nothing — The way of — leads to perfection : **7**,1,2; **81**,1,2; - only the way of — leads to the all of God :**7**,1,2; **31**,1; - to attain to union

with God it is necessary to go through the way of — : **54**,2; - the apostle should go by the way of — : **333**,1; - when a soul has gone so far as to be reduced to — she will then have attained union with God : **106**,1; - in attaining union with God, the soul is reduced to — : **351**,2; **352**,2; - awareness of our own nothingness : **217**,1,2; - to thank God when we see ourselves reduced to — : **247**,1.

Obedience — Gives the soul the security of dwelling in the Will of God : **21**,1; - makes one adhere to the Will of God expressed by the commands of superiors : **120**,1; - makes one abandon one's own will to embrace the Will of God : **120**,2; - the formal act of — consists in the free renunciation of self and the free adhesion to the Divine Will : **122**,1; - supernatural — places one in direct contact with the Will of God : **123**,2; - he who leaves the path of — leaves the secure road of the Will of God for the dangerous way of one's own will : **124**,2; - imitation of the — of Jesus : **42**,1; **121**,1; **125**,2; - — simple as that of a child : **49**,1; - motive of supernatural — : **123**,1; - confidence in the government of God through the commands of — : **123**,2; - — based on human motives has little value in the sight of God : *ibid.;* - blind — **124**,1,2; - life of — is wholly based on supernatural values and motives : **125**,1; - the more one considers in superiors the authority that comes from God, the more meritorious will be their — : *ibid.;* - God prefers — to penance : **92**,2; - and to anything else : **120**,1; - — is the shortest path to union with God : **122**,1; - the most

perfect way is always that of — : **123**,1; **124**,2; - the vow of — is greatest and most meritorious sacrifice : **121**,2; - the complete immolation of man in honor of God : *ibid.;* - and the free immolation of liberty : **122**,1; - fidelity to the — vowed to God : **122**,2; - lack of spirit of faith in — : **125**,1,2; - and lack of humility : **125**,2; - — to political authority : **343**,2; - necessary to obey God rather than man : *ibid.*
See : SUPERIORS.

Pardon — Of offenses : **70**,2; - magnificence and largesse of the — of God : **336**,1; - pettiness and narrowness of our — : **336**,2.

Passion of Jesus — Prediction of the — : **91**,1; - voluntary mortification, means of sharing in the — : **93**,1,2; - participation in the — : **126**,1; **132**,2; **376**,2; - to accompany Jesus in His Passion : **133**,1; - he who suffers with Jesus best understands the — **138**,1; - consideration of the — renders the soul generous in embracing suffering : **96**,2; - zeal for souls arises from the contemplation of Jesus Crucified : **317**,2; - the — tells us how great is the malice of sin and its destructive power : **100**,2; - the — is our salvation and our hope : **126**,1; - Jesus in His Passion has embraced the sufferings of all humanity : **128**,1; - attitude of Jesus facing His Passion : **135**,1; - He went to His Passion because He willed to go : *ibid.;* **136**,2; - His desolation, abandonment, and abjection : **136**,1,2; - Jesus is the Victim who immolates Himself with love and full liberty : **136**,2; - the Agony in the Garden of Olives : **138**,1;

- the arrest for crucifixion : **138**,2; - Jesus abandoned by the Father : *ibid.;* - the death of Jesus is not a defeat, but a victory : **139**,1; - Jesus proclaimed King in the midst of the unheard cruelties of His Passion : **383**,2; - the — is the greatest proof of the love of Jesus for us : **132**,2; **136**,2; **139**,2; - he who resists grace, resists the — : **133**,2.
See : JESUS.

Passions — Struggle against the predominant passion : **103**,2.

Patience — One learns — in considering Jesus all-patient : **128**,1; - progressive practice of — : **128**,2; **292**,1,2; - — enables one to live in a state of suffering without losing serenity : **291**,1; - is the willing acceptance of suffering in view of God and eternal beatitude : **291**,2; - one acquires — by sweetly accepting that which contradicts and causes suffering : **292**,1; - necessity of spirit of faith to exercise — in the difficulties of life : **128**,1; - — is humility in bearing injustice : **279**,2; **351**,2; - — in the painful trials of the purification of the spirit : **351**,1,2; **354**,1.

Peace — In what true — consists : **33**,1,2; - — promised to men of good will : **33**,2; - fruit of humility : **111**,2; - preoccupation of those concerned about their own rights makes them lose interior — : **117**,2; - gift of wisdom establishes the soul in — : **314**,1; - peacemaker is one who sows — and cultivates it *ibid.;* - little — in the world because man does not let himself be guided by the Spirit of Wisdom : **314**,2; - the reward of peacemakers is to be called children of God : *ibid.;* - the intentions of the Lord are intentions of — : **350**,1.

Penance — Sacrament of : **73**,1,2; - without obedience is the — of animals : **92**,2; - is a means of assimilation into Christ Crucified : **93**,1,2; - relation between corporal and spiritual — : **94**,2; - the most important — is the patient suffering of the trials of life : **213**,2.
See : CONFESSION; MORTIFICATION.

Perfection — God alone is infinitely perfect : **53**,1; - by stripping the — of the creature of all limits and defects, we can form a faint idea of the infinite — of God : **227**,2; - the Mount of — : **7**,1,2; - not to be satisfied with — already acquired : **53**,2; **99**,2; - precept to tend to — has no limits : **53**,2; - Christian — consists in union with God by charity : **100**,1; - few attain — because few welcome purification : **132**,1; importance of nourishing generous desires in order to attain — promptly : **289**,1,2; **290**,2; - a perfect man does much more than a great number of imperfect men : **330**,2; - the first thought should not be personal —, but the glory of God, His pleasure, and approval : **256**,1.

Perseverance — Necessity of — to derive fruit from the word of God : **84**,2; - — in prayer : **156**,1,2; - — in the struggle against one's defects and in the effort to acquire virtue : **298**,2; - remedy for the instability of human nature : **293**,1; - has for object endurance in effort : *ibid.;* - perfect — not possible without habitual intervention of the gifts of the Holy Spirit : **293**,2; - our — consists in continually beginning again : *ibid.;* **295**,2; - God will crown our efforts with the grace of final — : **293**,2; - he who after every fall humbles

himself and rises, relying on the infinite strength of God, will persevere : **295**,2.

Peter (St.) — Conduct of— in the Passion of Jesus : **135**,2; - — made the head of the Church : **375**,1; - where—is, there is the Church : *ibid.*

Piety (Gift of) — Infuses the sense of divine sonship and filial piety : **198**,1; - perfects the virtue of justice : **304**,1; - inspires the sense of filial piety toward God : *ibid.;* - under its influence prayer becomes more filial : *ibid.;* - it renders contacts with one's neighbor more brotherly and cordial : **304**,2; - beatitude of mercy corresponds to — : **305**,1,2.

Piety (Virtue of) — True — consists in the sense of sonship with God and brotherhood with all men : **273**,2; - filial — is the heart of religion : **282**,1; - and penetrates all devotion : **282**,2; - to imitate the filial — of Jesus for His Father : **282**,1.

Poverty — Imitation of the — of Jesus : **31**,2; - Jesus invites us to follow Him in — : **85**,1; - material — without the spirit of — has no value : **85**,2; **300**,1; - only the spirit of — frees the soul from slavery to earthly goods : **85**,2; - the spirit of — is fruit of the gift of fear : **300**,1; - spirit of — requires detachment from moral and spiritual goods : **300**,2; - to acquire — of spirit, it is necessary to despoil oneself of all that is not God : *ibid.;* - voluntary — is primary foundation for acquisition of perfect charity : **86**,1; - meaning and practice of voluntary — : **86**,1,2; - practice of the spirit of — : **87**,1,2; - the spirit of — is based on confidence in Providence : **87**,2.

Prayer — How to seek God in — : **12**,1,2; - to interrupt activity to give oneself to — : **12**,1; **59**,1; - apostolic activity should not absorb the time necessary for — : **325**,2; **331**,2; **339**,1; - — should be a prolongation of the — of Jesus : **59**,2; - — should be accompanied by sacrifice : *ibid.*; **326**,1; - continuity of — : **146**,1; - substance of every form of — is intimate contact with God : **146**,1,2; **198**,2; our — should be filial contact with God : **198**,1; - vocal — : **148**,1,2; - necessary always to unite vocal — with mental — : **148**,2; - liturgical — : **164**,1,2; - relationship between liturgical — and personal — : **164**,2; **167**,2; - Holy Mass is the center of liturgical cult : **165**,1,2; - Divine Office is the — of the Mystical Body : **167**,1,2; - efficacy of — made in the Name of Jesus : **175**,1,2; - — is vain if it does not correspond to one's life : **175**,2; - not granted by God to one without fraternal charity : **182**,1; - the more — is interwoven with sacrifice, the more efficacious it is : **326**,1; - Jesus wishes the — of the heart : **350**,1; - the Holy Spirit teaches us to pray and prays within us : **198**,2; - God has ordained that certain graces necessary for our salvation and that of others should depend upon our — : **325**,1,2; - apostolic — is one of the most potent means of the apostolate : **325**,1; - it is of the highest importance that there should be in the Church souls totally consecrated to — : **325**,2; - — and self-indulgence do not go together : **92**,2; - — places the soul in actual contact with God :

143,2; - God draws to Himself the soul who seeks Him in — : **145**,2; **151**,2; **151**,1; - the most precious knowledge of God does not come from reasoning but from the " sense " of God derived from the love and the action of the Holy Spirit : **143**,2; **157**,2; **158**,1,2; **191**,1; - vocal — : **148**,1,2; - difficulty in mental — produced by mobility of the imagination : **149**,1; - how to make use of reading in order to pray : **149**,2; - — consists much more in loving than in thinking : *ibid.*; **150**,1,2; - reflections and reasoning should serve to awaken love : *ibid.*; - to begin — by placing oneself in the presence of God : **150**,2; - mental — consists in an intimate contact with God : *ibid.*; **151**,1; - intimate conversation with God : **151**,1,2; - — of recollection based on the presence of God in the soul : **152**,1,2; - practice of recollecting the senses in — and withdrawing oneself with them into God : **152**,2; - method of meditation which disposes the soul to contemplation : **150**,1,2; - loving contemplative gaze : **151**,2; - it is absurd to wish to meditate when God invites the soul to a simpler — : **158**,1,2; - to recollect oneself in the presence of God by a simple glance of faith and love : **158**,1; - loving attention to God : **158**,2; **159**,1; - action of the Holy Spirit in this form of — : *ibid.*; - conduct of the soul in passage from meditation to contemplation : **159**,1,2; - — deepens under the influence of the gift of knowledge : **309**,2; - and understanding : **311**,2; - and of wisdom : **313**,2; - divers causes of aridity in — : **153**,1,2; - fidelity to — regardless of aridity : **153**,2; **155**,2; **156**,2; - it is a beautiful proof of our love to

persevere in — regardless of aridity and repugnancy : **153**,2; - to humbly welcome the torment of aridity in — **156**,2; - the resolute decision not to relax in — regardless of all difficulties which one may meet : **156**,1; - by means of aridity God raises the soul to a higher prayer **157**,1,2; - in aridity is born a "sense" of God : **157**,2; - soul should not be disturbed by her impotence and aridity in — : **158**,1; - to prolong — during the day : **160**,1,2; - to maintain oneself in intimate contact with God by means of — : **160**,1; - and by the practice of the presence of God : **162**,1,2.
See : ARIDITY; CONTEMPLATION.

Presence of God — In all creatures : **10**,1; **152**,1; - in the souls of the just : **10**,1,2; **152**,1; **160**,1; **251**,1; - God always with us, even when we do not advert to the — : **141**,2; - prayer based on the — in us : **152**,1,2; - continual contact with God present within us : **160**,1; **162**,1,2; - the — in us deepens in proportion to the measure of our love : **301**,1; - the practice of the — and its diverse forms : **162**,1,2; - consciousness of the — in us and in our neighbor : **162**,2; **163**,2; - to keep oneself in the — in the midst of daily occupations and difficulties : **163**,1,2.
See : TRINITY.

Pride — Struggle against — : **62**,2; - one conquers — by accepting what is humiliating : **98**,1; - humiliations are the remedy for — : **110**,1,2; - to make use of temptations to — to humble oneself : **111**,2; - to struggle against — even "unto blood" : **376**,2; - to have

recourse to Mary in the struggle against the ever-recurring tendencies to — : **380**,2; - — is an obstacle to grace and to the action of God in the soul : **106**,2; **259**,2; - —, egoism, and the other passions turn into evil that which God has disposed for our good : **266**,2 - — does not wish to recognize its own faults : **118**,1; - vexation of the soul finding itself always on the ground is the fruit of — : **295**,1; - imperfections arising from subtle spiritual — : **346**,2.
See : SELF-LOVE; HAUGHTINESS.

Priest - Priesthood — Function and dignity : **68**,1,2; - perpetuates among us the work of Jesus : **68**,2; - is organ of communication and increase in the life of the Mystical Body of Jesus : **341**,1; - duties toward — : respect, gratitude, and prayer : **68**,1,2; - call to — and correspondence : **75**,1; **76**,1,2.

Progress — The need to always make — in the spiritual life : **77**,1; **99**,1,2; - — not measured by the comfort the soul experiences : **153**,2; - — in the way of sanctity depends upon the generosity with which we renounce ourselves : **384**,2; - examen of conscience is a means of spiritual — : **103**,1,2.

Providence (Divine) — Confidence in — : **87**,2; **239**,2; **287**,2; - confidence in — frees the soul from anxiety for worldly goods : **87**,2; **287**,2; - and gives courage to bear their privation : **98**,1; - one who lets herself be guided by — does not flee from occasions of sufferings : **97**,2; - — permits and directs all for our good : **128**,2; **130**,2; **163**,1,2; **239**,1; **244**,1,2; - even suffering, evil, and its consequences : **248**,1; **292**,2; - nothing escapes the government of — : **163**,1; **239**,1; **244**,2; - — is so great that it embraces the universe and cares for each individual creature, even the least : **239**,2; - — makes use of our defects and falls to humble us and to make us understand our misery : **295**,1; - — makes use of the defects of others to exercise our virtue : **292**,1,2; - and to make manifest our self-love and to purify us of our imperfections : **351**,2; - — chooses and prepares the sufferings of this life for our purification : **351**,1,2. See : GOD.

Prudence — Necessary in order not to let oneself be deceived by false appearances : **238**,2; - shrewdness in providing for our eternal interests : **245**,2; **272**,2; - — tells us what to do and what to avoid in order to attain the end : **272**,1; - supernatural — consists in setting the utmost value on the present moment for the sake of our eternal end : **272**,2; - Christian — has nothing in common with — of the flesh : *ibid.;* **275**,2; - — in deliberations : **274**,1,2; - — is perfected by the gift of counsel : **274**,1; **306**,1; - in order that judgment and choice may be prudent, they should be free of selfish motives : **274**,2; - — is the guide of all the other virtues : **275**,1; - Christian — travels the straight way of duty and truth : **275**,2; - relationship between — and uprightness : *ibid.*

Punctuality — In the fulfillment of duty requires mortification and detachment : **276**,2.

Purgatory — Would not be necessary if we were perfectly faithful to grace : **385**,2; - in — one suffers without increasing in love,

though on earth purification is accomplished with an increase of grace and charity : *ibid.*

Purification — Necessity of — : **78**,1,2; **132**,1; **237**,2; **316**,1; **346**,1,2; **346**,1,2; **348**,1; **385**,2; - God fills the soul in the measure of its — from every stain of sin and imperfection : **78**,1,2; - few attain the fullness of the spiritual life because few accept the purifications : **132**,1; **354**,1; - the purpose of purifying trials is reparation for faults committed and the destruction of the last roots of sin : **237**,2; - a great — is necessary to overcome completely the dualism between the ego and God : **332**,2; - the painful — which is the night of the spirit is necessary to remove the roots of imperfect habits : **347**,1; **352**,1; - God alone can lead the soul to complete — : **83**,2; **132**,1; **194**,2; **351**,1; **352**,1; - though very painful, — is the work of God's love : **348**,1,2; **354**,1; - God purifies the soul of every stain that hinders its perfect union with His infinite purity : **348**,2; - God purifies the soul by the circumstances of life : **351**,1; - — of the soul is the work of the Holy Spirit : **194**,2; **316**,1; - with the Living Flame of His Love, He destroys and consumes all its imperfections : **352**,1,2; - how the soul suffers in this state : *ibid.;* and *fol.;* - patience and confidence in the pain of — : **354**,1; - purifying sufferings ordained for the development of love : **355**,1,2; - Holy Spirit fills the soul with the flames of His Charity when He finds it purified from all that is contrary to love : **360**,2; - by spiritual — God inflames the soul with yearnings for divine love : **361**,1; - by means of the struggle against pride and self-love : **316**,1; - to desire and ask for the grace of — : **346**,2; **385**,2; - we should welcome — to give God proof of our love : **348**,2; - loving, patient, humble acceptance of purifying sufferings : **351**,1,2; - if we do not know how to accept — in this world, we shall suffer it in purgatory : **385**,2.

See : ARIDITY; NIGHT OF THE SENSES; NIGHT OF THE SPIRIT; TRIALS.

Purity — Of heart enables one to understand divine subjects : **90**,2; - — of heart is necessary for penetration of the divine mysteries : **312**,1; - — of heart is the fruit of the gift of understanding : **312**,2; - first condition to reach God is total — which is the fruit of total detachment : **379**,2.

See : **Charity.**

Pusillanimity — Deters the soul from accomplishing great works from excessive fear of failure : **289**,2; - — is cowardice and pride : *ibid.*

Recollection — To await in — the coming of Jesus : **8**,2; - — should not hinder the practice of charity : **14**,2; **64**,2; **181**,1,2; - — and interior silence : **17**,1,2; **378**,2; - to keep — in activity : **21**,2; - — necessary to penetrate and practice the teaching of Jesus : **55**,2; **84**,2; - to perceive the counsels of the Holy Spirit : **306**,2; - — disposes the soul for contemplation : **145**,2; - prayer of — : **152**,1,2.

Rectitude — Of intention in the apostolate : **25**,2; **332**,1,2; - necessity of — of intention : **285**,2; - relation between prudence and — : **275**,2;

- — necessary in order not to deviate from justice : **278**,2.

See : INTENTION.

Redeemer and Redemption — Expectation of — : **1**,1,2; **22**,1,2; - our collaboration with the work of — : **23**,1,2; **24**,1,2; - from the twofold evil of sin and suffering God has drawn the great good of our — : **127**,1; - work of — is the most glorious manifestation of infinite goodness of God : **226**,1; - by — humanity has been grafted into Christ : **238**,1; - the work of — is always in action and we live under its influence : **273**,1; **280**,2; - all the mysteries of — are mysteries of love : **376**,1.

See : JESUS; INCARNATION; PASSION.

Religion (Virtue of) — Gives us a profound sense of our relations with God and with our neighbor : **273**,2; - filial piety is the characteristic, the heart of our — : **282**,1; - — urges us to give God the worship which is His due : **281**,2 - — honors God in the only way worthy of Him, inasmuch as it shares in the — of Christ : *ibid.* - the virtue of — makes our life a continuous act of worship of God : *ibid.*

Renunciation — Of self is indispensable foundation of spiritual life : **54**,2; - total — necessary in order to attain union with God : **79**,2; **80**,1; - when the soul has attained total — of self, it will acquire the precious pearl of divine union : **82**,1; - — places one on the path of conformity to Jesus Crucified : **194**,2; - — frees the soul so that it can use all its strength to love God : **253**,2; - — is an exercise of love : *ibid.;* - the way that leads

to union with God consists in abnegation of self : **349**,1; - — of anything that may not be for the honor and glory of God : **62**,2; - — of any satisfaction and affection that does not lead to God : **81**,1; - — of the satisfaction of taking account of one's interior progress : **115**,1; - — of defending one's rights : **117**,2; - — of one's own will by means of obedience : **120**,1,2; and *fol.;* - — of one's own views by acting according to God's view as manifested by orders of superiors : **124**,1; - — of one's own tastes and rights and ideas in favor of charity and fraternal union : **269**,1,2; **308**,1,2; - — necessary for soul consecrated to God : **76**,1.
See : ABNEGATION; DETACHMENT; MORTIFICATION.

Reverence — Before the majesty of God : **155**,2; **359**,1; - — infused by the gift of fear : **99**,2.

Rosary — Is the meditation of the life of Mary : **381**,1; - the — helps one to penetrate the mysteries of Christ : **381**,2.

Rule of life — Is a manifestation of the Will of God : **276**,2; - punctuality and exactness in keeping — : *ibid.*

Sacraments — The exterior rite accomplished by the Church — the interior effect produced by Christ : **69**,1; - working *ex opere operato* : **69**,2; - dispositions with which to receive the — : *ibid.*

Sacred heart of Jesus — The love of the — is the source and motive of all His gifts : **208**,1; **209**,2; - the — holds the mystery of the love of God for men : **208**,2;

- is the symbol and image of the love of Jesus : **209**,1; **210**,1; - chief object of devotion to the — is the love of Jesus : **209**,1; - devotion to the — touches the depths of all the mysteries of the Redeemer : **209**,2; - and aims to spur us to return His love : **211**,1,2; **212**,1; - contemplating the — one always understands His love better : **211**,2; **215**,1; - devotion to the — inspires reparation : **213**,1,2; - to model our heart on the — : **214**,1; - to imitate the meekness and humility of the — : **214**,1,2; - consecration to the — is the response to His love : **212**,1; - to consecrate oneself to the — signifies one's choosing His Will, His desires, and His tastes as the norm of one's own life : **212**,2; - the — is the abode of the soul living the interior life : **215**,1; - and its refuge in temptation : **215**,2; - confidence in the — in failings and infidelity : *ibid.;* - the — living in the Eucharist : **216**,1.
See : JESUS.

Sacred Scriptures — Inspired by the Holy Spirit : **167**,2; **190**,2; - to meditate on the — is to enter the school of the Holy Spirit : **190**,2.

Sacrifice — Is a most powerful means of the apostolate : **24**,1,2; **25**,2; **326**,1,2; - renders works fruitful : **36**,1; - — and prayer : **59**,2; - our sacrifices have value only inasmuch as they are offered in union with the — of Jesus : **166**,2; - when we avoid —, we act like the enemies of the Cross of Christ : **350**,1.
See : CROSS; SORROW; SUFFERING.

Salvation (Eternal) — God wills all to be saved : **2**,1; **247**,1; - God gives to all the grace necessary

of practicing patience : **292**,1; - it is necessary to persevere in good to the end : **293**,1; - and to do violence to oneself : **384**,2; - our insufficiency in the matter of — : **191**,1,2; **192**,1; - in the case of — we are always learners : *ibid.;* - the Holy Spirit Master of — : *ibid.;* - our sanctification is a question of docility to the Holy Spirit : *ibid.;* - necessity of the assistance of the Holy Spirit in order to attain — : **191**,1,2; **192**,1; **193**,2; **195**,1; **298**,2; **316**,1,2; - the Holy Spirit makes the soul hunger and thirst for — : **303**,1,2; - saints are the most perfect men, even from the human point of view : **335**,2; - they show us the way that leads to — : **384**,2.

Selfishness — Is the cause of voluntary imperfections : **102**,2; - — hinders the practice of charity : **260**,2; - only the soul free from — is fully generous : **290**,1; - imperfections due to subtle spiritual — : **346**,2.

Self-Knowledge — Knowledge of self and of our miseries should not be separated from knowledge of God : **109**,1.
See : HUMILITY.

Senses — Custody of the — : **16**,1,2; **17**,1; - to attain union with God total mortification of the — is necessary : **83**,1; - to use the — only in the measure required by duty : **89**,2; - mortification of the sense of taste : **296**,2; - every disorder, however slight, in the life of the — weakens the life of the spirit : *ibid.;* - how to recollect the — in prayer : **152**,2.
See : MORTIFICATION; NIGHT OF THE SENSES; RENUNCIATION.

Silence — Exterior and interior — : **17**,1,2; - interior — makes contact with God possible : **378**,2.
See : RECOLLECTION.

Simplicity — In suffering : **130**,1,2; - excludes all duplicity of mind and will : **229**,2; **285**,1; - perfect — makes one live solely for God and with God : *ibid.;* - the simple soul follows but one light, relies upon one strength, tends to but one end — God : *ibid.;* - — does not preoccupy itself with the judgment and favor of others : **285**,2; - relation between — and prudence : **238**,2; **275**,2.

Sin — Dishonors Christ and saddens the Holy Spirit who dwells within us : **48**,2; - — is in opposition to the infinite perfection of God : **54**,1; - ugliness and consequences of — : *ibid.;* **100**,1,2; **280**,1; - — caused the death of Jesus : **54**,1; - is the violence that separates man from God : **100**,1; - while grace transforms man from glory to glory, — disfigures those who are its victims : **105**,1; - — is an obstacle to the effusions of the Holy Spirit : **168**,2; **188**,1; - the slave of — produces death : **238**,1; **245**,1; - lack of harmony caused in us by — : **296**,1,2; - struggle against — : **54**,2; **98**,1; **100**,2; **101**,1,2; - need to destroy — in its roots and causes : **54**,2; **100**,2; **103**,2; - horror and hatred for — : **280**,1; **299**,1; - remedy for — is sincere humility and trustful recourse to God : **280**,2; - the real evil is not so much in falling as in not rising again : **295**,1; - Jesus dying on the Cross conquered — : **54**,2; **168**,1; - God willed to free us from the slavery of — : **350**,1; - in Jesus we have the remission

of — : **383**,1; - we all bear the
wounds of — : **273**,1; - our debts to
God are for our sins : **336**,1; - mercy
of God in pardoning — : **336**,1,2;
- we should be assured of the pardon
of — sincerely detested : **246**,2;
- and confessed : **280**,2; - the
first requisite for becoming saints
is to hate — : **295**,2; - the soul who
loves God fears nothing more
than — : **299**,1; - blessed are they
who weep for their sins : **310**,1;
- love destroys — : **100**,2; **364**,2.

Original Sin — its consequences :
2,1; **26**,2; **38**,1; **127**,1; - in consequence of original — man has lost
the dominion of the spirit over his
senses, his flesh : **92**,1.

Mortal Sin — is in complete
opposition to God : **54**,1; **100**,1;
- malice and consequences of
mortal — : **100**,1,2; - struggle
against mortal — : **100**,2; - God
clothes with His grace the soul
cleansed from mortal — : **78**,1.

Venial Sin — diminishes the vigor
of charity and hinders its development : **101**,1; - when venial — is
deliberate and habitual, it leads to
tepidity : *ibid.;* **153**,1; - venial
— always includes a transgression
more or less light of the law of God :
102,1; - conduct in case of venial
— caused by frailty or inadver-
tance : **101**,2.

Sincerity — A sincere soul
recognizes its defects : **140**,1; **284**,1;
- — with one's neighbor : **284**,2;
- — in words and actions should
express truth loved interiorly : *ibid.*

Solitude — Is necessary in order
to find God : **12**,1; - interior — :
13,2.

Sorrow — Is permitted by God
only for our good : **63**,1; - — being
the consequence of sin, has been

transformed by Jesus as means of
destroying sin : **127**,1; - it is
necessary to pass through the
crucible of suffering in order to
reach sanctity : **91**,1; - the gift of
knowledge shows — of present
life light in comparison with eternal
blessedness : **310**,2; - man is blind
in face of the mystery of — : **91**,2.
See : CROSS; SUFFERING.

Soul — Temple of the Holy
Trinity : **11**,1,2; **16**,1; **58**,2; **61**,2;
78,2; - the — totally free from
every attachment acts only
according to the Will of God :
5,2; - when the — is completely
purified, God transforms it into
Himself by means of grace and
love : **78**,1,2; - when the — does
what it can, God will not fail to do
His part and to communicate
Himself to it at least in secret and in
silence : **366**,2; - the — should open
itself to the action of God : *ibid.;*
- the first vineyard that we sould
cultivate is our — : **77**,2; - should be
fully resolved to practice renunciation : **82**,1; - dispositions the
— should have in order to draw
profit from the word of God :
84,2; - the — that seeks the esteem
of creatures does not live alone
with God alone : **114**,2; - the
— should forget itself to be
completely centered on Christ :
115,1; - the — living an interior life
should not act as a mercenary,
but as a child : **115**,2; - the
enamored — should give herself
exclusively to God giving up all
that she is and all that she has :
134,1; - the — who has given
herself seriously to God has two
great attractions : prayer and the
apostolate : **342**,1.

Spiritual Childhood — Attained
by rebirth in Christ : **147**,1.

Spiritual Consolation — Not an end in itself, but a maid to serve God with greater generosity and to give us more strength to carry the cross : **105**,2; **370**,2; - it is necessary to learn how to love God with a pure and strong act of the will above every feeling and consolation : **255**,1,2; - the loving soul longs for divine intimacy, not to enjoy it, but to increase in the love of God : **370**,2.

Spiritual Delights — To seek God rather than — : **18**,1,2; - he who seeks — does not love God with all his strength : **19**,2.
See : SPIRITUAL CONSOLATIONS.

Spiritual Espousals — The characteristic of — is the perfect " Yes " of the consent the soul gives to God : **365**,1; - to the perfect " Yes " of the soul, God replies with the true and complete " Yes " of grace : **366**,1.
See : UNION WITH GOD.

Spiritual Marriage — Is a total transformation in the Beloved : **367**,2; - is a union as perfect and full as is possible outside of the union of Heaven : *ibid.;* - love, fully uniting the soul to God, makes it so conformed to Him that it transforms it into Him : **369**,1; in its most elevated movements the soul adverts to the living God present and working within it : **370**,1; - in the state of — the sensibility of the soul is fully pacified : **367**,1; - the whole " capital " of the soul is employed in the practice of love : **368**,1; - even the first motions are those of love : *ibid.;* - its sole activity consists in loving : **368**,2; - it loves God with pure love : *ibid.;* - it loves God as it has been loved by

Him because it loves Him with the Holy Spirit : **369**,2; - it does not long for the divine intimacy to enjoy it, but to love God always more : **370**,2; - it tends to produce works and to work : *ibid.;* - the glory souls attain in this state is in their power to assist their Crucified God by working for the salvation of souls : *ibid.*
See : UNION WITH GOD.

Struggle — Of the flesh against the spirit : **245**,1; **287**,1; **301**,1; - not to relent in the — regardless of falls : **295**,2.

Suffering — Its value : **91**,1,2; **127**,1,2; - has value only when offered with Christ and for Christ : **93**,2; - value of — permitted by God in circumstances of life : **97**,2; **213**,2; - — is lovable only in view of the good attainable by means of it : **127**,1; - value and fruitfulness of — : **129**,1,2; **139**,1; **194**,2; - is impossible to attain eternal glory without — : **105**,1; **161**,1; - present — nothing in comparison with glory awaiting us : *ibid.;* **217**,1; **310**,2; - — in this world necessary in order to prove our love for God : **360**,1; - cannot fail to have — in this world : **370**,2; - we should be generous in — to expiate our faults : **385**,2; - any — can be made to harmonize with the ideals of a Christian : **127**,2; - charity makes us capable of bearing any — without becoming overwhelmed : *ibid.;* - to suffer for the love of Jesus, who has suffered for love of us : **128**,1; **291**,2; - our — is nothing in comparison with that of Jesus : **128**,1; **130**,1; - spirit of faith on occasions of — : **128**,2; **351**,2; - by — the soul gives glory to God

and shows its love : **132**,2; - only God can infuse love for — : **360**,2; - — is permitted for our sanctification : **128**,2; **129**,2; **291**,1; **351**,1; - the more God makes us suffer, the more will He sanctify us and love us : **132**,2; - God permits — for the good of His elect : **248**,1; - the gift of understanding makes us comprehend the beatitude of — embraced for the love of God : **310**,2; - necessity of — to attain union with God : **347**,2; **348**,1,2; - God chooses and disposes the — of life for our purification : **351**,1; - profit the soul receives from — embraced for love of God : **128**,2; **129**,2; - every — accepted from the hand of God is a means of sanctification : *ibid.;* - confidence and abandonment to God in — : *ibid.;* **130**,1,2; **138**,2; - self-forgetfulness and simplicity in — : **130**,1; - a simple soul is one who suffers with the greatest courage : *ibid.;* - necessity of — for our purification : **132**,1; **248**,1; **351**,1,2; - active — is not sufficient; passive — is necessary : **132**,1; - patience renders us able to bear daily — without losing serenity : **291**,1; - saints longed for occasions of — : **292**,2; **360**,1; - to suffer without complaining : **292**,2; - to suffer injustice with serenity : **279**,2.
See : CROSS; SORROW; TRIALS.

Superiors — Whoever obeys — obeys God : **120**,1; **124**,2; - to see God in — : **123**,1; **125**,1; - by orders of — God enables one to act according to His Will : **124**,1; - legitimate orders of — are a secure manifestation of the Will of God : **124**,2; - in — necessary to consider authority of God : **125**,1,2; - God governs us by — notwith-

standing their errors : **123**,2; - not to reason on the faults and lacks of — : *ibid;* **125**,1,2; - duties of — : **125**,2.
See : OBEDIENCE.

Temperance — Moderates the disordered desire of sensible joy : **296**,1; **299**,2; - helps to re-establish the harmony lost by sin : **296**,1,2; - — in regard to the sense of taste : **296**,2.

Temptation — Conduct to maintain in — : **98**,1,2; - every — is accompanied by grace sufficient to overcome it : **98**,2; **252**,1; - discouragement and want of confidence is most dangerous — : **295**,1.

Tepidity — Cause and consequences of — : **101**,1; - tepid soul does not advert to its need for God : **141**,1; - voluntary infidelity can draw a fervent soul into — : **153**,1.

Time — Good use of — : **35**,1,2; **329**,1; - — not used for our sanctification and for others is — lost : **61**,1; - — is from God : **36**,2; - Jesus will come at the end of — to gather the fruits of His work and Blood : **364**,2.
See : LIFE (Earthly).

Trials — Spirit of faith in — : **63**,1; - in — the need to have recourse to God with confidence : **63**,2; - fidelity to God in — : **105**,2; - humble acceptance of purifying — : **237**,2; **351**,2; - if the soul is strong in accepting exterior —, God purifies by interior — : **352**,1; - the greatest suffering of the soul in purifying — is to feel itself unworthy of the love

of God and the fear that it has been rejected by Him : *ibid.;* - the fear of not being able to attain union with Him : **353**,1,2; - the fear of not knowing how to love Him : **355**,2; - every trial is a great mercy of God : **237**,2; - God tries the souls He loves : **248**,1; - God does not try us beyond our strength : *ibid.;* - by purifying — God helps the soul to increase in love : **355**,1; - and trains the soul in the perfection of love : **355**,2.
See : ARIDITY; NIGHT OF THE SENSES; NIGHT OF THE SPIRIT; PURIFICATION.

Trinity — Indwelling in the soul in the state of grace : **10**,1,2; **11**,1; **16**,1; **152**,1; **183**,2; **222**,1; **223**,1; - the — lives in the soul in the state of grace by associating it with Its Life : **222**,2; - the divine Persons are present in the soul and each One communicates Himself to it according to His characteristics : *ibid.;* **225**,1; - progressive effusions of the — in the soul of the just : **223**,1,2; - three Persons of the Blessed — concurred in the work of the Incarnation : **26**,2; - all the external works of God are common to the three Persons of the — : **186**,2; **225**,1; - the Triune God gives Himself to man to redeem, sanctify, and introduce him to divine intimacy : **189**,1; **221**,2; **225**,1; - every gift comes from the — : **196**,1; **226**,1; - merciful work of the — for the benefit of our souls : **196**,1; **221**,2; - equality of the three divine Persons : **27**,1; - intimate life of the — : **186**,1; **196**,2; **220**,2; **250**,1,2; - sublimity of the Trinitarian mystery : **196**,2; - incomprehensibility of this mystery : *ibid.;* **221**,1; - the — has been revealed by Jesus : **220**,1;

- mystery of the — reveals more than any other mystery the perfection of the goodness of God : **220**,2; - revealing to us the mystery of the —, God has unveiled the secret of His intimate life : **221**,2; - the — is the source and center of all other mysteries : **226**,1; - life of intimate union with the — : **58**,2; **61**,2; **116**,2; **183**,2; **225**,1,2; - union with the — nourished by the Eucharist : **219**,1,2; - union with the — deepens in proportion to charity and grace possessed by the soul : **223**,1; - particular contacts with each of the divine Persons : **225**,2; - purpose of Incarnation and Redemption is to lead man to the — : **116**,2; **219**,1; **222**,1; **225**,2; - the end of the Christian life is to make us share in the life of the — : **116**,2; - all has been ordained for the glory of the — : **226**,1,2; - to live for the glory of the — : *ibid.;* - attitude of humility and faith in the presence of the — : **221**,1.

Truth — Excusing our faults, though it satisfy our pride, in reality blinds us, makes us incapable of seeing the — in our own case : **118**,1; - joy in the — : **140**,1; - doing the — in charity : *ibid.*
See : SINCERITY.

Understanding (Gift of) — Enables one to penetrate the divine mysteries : **311**,1; - introduces the soul to a prayer more simple and profound : **311**,2; - perfects the virtue of faith : **311**,1,2; - purifies the mind of errors : **312**,2; - to — corresponds the beatitude : blessed are the clean of heart : **312**,1,2; - purity of heart is necessary to become open to the influence of — : **312**,1; - purity of heart is the fruit of this gift : **312**,2.

Union with God — Calls for total conformity of will with the Will of God : **5**,2; **78**,2; **120**,1 **272**,1; **346**,1; **362**,1; - — not attained so much in the sweetness of prayer as in fully embracing the Will of God : **21**,1; - state of — consists in the soul being wholly transformed in the Will of God : **5**,2; **251**,2; **362**,1; - in this state the Will of God becomes the will of the soul : **7**,1; **362**,2; - measure of — is measure of conformity to His Will : **346**,1; - the power that unites the soul to God is love : **4**,2; **100**,1; **250**,1; **345**,1,2; **361**,1,2; - it is not the sentiment of love that unites the soul to God, but the act of love that seeks God and His Will : **255**,2; **345**,2; - the more a soul is united with God, the greater its progress in love : *ibid.;* **346**,1; - to a greater degree of love corresponds a greater — : **361**,1,2; - the greater the faith of a soul the greater will be its — : **18**,1; - the soul disposes itself for — by purity and love : **78**,2; - it attains — in proportion to its humility : **106**,1,2; - obedience the shortest way to — : **122**,1; - we are united to God by the theological virtues and in the measure of their purity and intensity : **248**,1; - — is indispensable for the efficacy of the apostolate : **25**,1; - — and dependence on Him in every work : **61**,2; - — and with one's neighbor is the secret of victory over evil : **112**,2; - blessed is the soul who is united to God by the observance of His doctrine : *ibid.;* - — requires union with our brethren : **271**,2; - the more a soul is united to God, the more it is inflamed with His charity and becomes apostolic, participating in His inexhaustible fecundity : **339**,1; **341**,1; - the soul cannot attain — if it keeps any attachment or imperfection : **78**,1,2; **79**,1; **80**,1,2; **82**,1; **346**,1,2; **359**,1; - a single voluntary imperfection is an impediment to — : **78**,2; **79**,1; **102**,1; - any disordered affection hinders — : **80**,2; **81**,1; **349**,1; - he who wishes — should not let his heart be bound to creatures : **227**,2; - lack of fraternal charity prevents — : **365**,2; - necessity of purification in order to attain — : **78**,1,2; **132**,1; **237**,2; **316**,1; **346**,1,2; **347**,2; **348**,1,2; - when the soul has attained renunciation of self in everything, God Himself will place in her hand the pearl of divine union : **82**,1; - no sacrifice is too great, no purification is too painful to attain — : **347**,2; **348**,2; **356**,1; **366**,2; **368**,1; - Divine Love before uniting and transforming the soul to God purifies it from every contrary quality : **348**,1; - how necessary it is to suffer before attaining — : **348**,1,2; and *fol.;* - God desires nothing more than to unite the soul to Himself, and therefore He purifies it of every stain of sin that can prevent perfect union with His infinite purity : **348**,2; - way that leads to — consists in interior and exterior self-abnegation and a willingness to suffer for Christ : **349**,1; - to attain — the soul must be reduced to the center of its nothingness : **351**,2; **352**,2; - many souls fail to attain — because they do not accept the pain of purification : **354**,1; - only the way of the cross leads to — : **354**,1,2; - — does not consist in joy and feeling, but in the living death of the cross : **354**,2; - as long as we are on earth, suffering will not be lacking, even in the midst of the delights of — : **370**,2; - — by means of charity is the essence of Christian

perfection : **100**,1; - end of man
is — : **345**,1; - the soul who truly
loves God longs to anticipate
his — while on earth : *ibid.; * **347**,2;
- the divine likeness, natural and
supernatural, which God has
imprinted on the soul, expresses
His desire to unite it to Himself
and is the foundation of this union :
358,1; - love makes the soul ardent
in its desire for — and impatient
to attain it : **358**,1,2; **359**,2;
- regardless of its weakness and
misery the soul hopes to attain
— relying on the help of Jesus :
*ibid.; * - Jesus has shown us the way
of — and procured for us the
means to attain it : **363**,2; - — is
our inheritance because Jesus has
merited it for us with His Blood :
364, 1.
Perfect Union of Will — **362**,1,2;
- is the essence of sanctity and is
to be preferred to all mystic graces :
362,2; - every soul of good will
can attain — if it is generous :
*ibid.; * **363**,1,2; - one can always
attain it by forcing one's will to
submit to the Will of God : **363**,1;
- characteristic of union of will
is the " Yes " which the soul gives
interiorly to God : **365**,1; - God
communicates Himself and His
gifts to the soul who has given
herself interiorly to Him : **366**,1,2.
Total Union — is total transformation in God : **367**,1,2; - in this
state the soul possesses God as its
principle of life : **367**,2; - is
completely employed in the exercise
of love and even its first movements
are motions of love : **368**,1;
- becomes God by participation as
much as is possible in this life :
369,1; - loves God with the same
love with which He loves her
because she loves Him with the
Holy Spirit : **369**,2; - she enjoys a
deep intimacy with God : **370**,1;
- spontaneously she becomes apostolic, desiring to draw with herself
an immense multitude of souls :
ibid.
See : SPIRITUAL ESPOUSALS;
SPIRITUAL MARRIAGE; WILL OF GOD.

Victim — Jesus is the — who
immolates Himself continually for
us : **166**,1; - the soul who offers
itself as a — to God when renouncing her own will is completely
conformed to God : **166**,2; **213**,2;
- — of reparation : *ibid.; * - not to
pose as a — in the face of unjust
treatment : **351**,1.

Virtue — Is strengthened by
difficulties : **63**,1; - — marked
by the cross flourishes in the midst
of difficulties : **128**,1; - no one
can perform the least act of
— without the aid of actual grace :
107,2; - however much the soul
practices —, it cannot count on
its strength **108**,2; the greatest
obstacle to the acquisition of — is
to believe it is already attained :
117,2; - the intense practice of — is
necessary to receive the divine
gifts : **145**,2; **197**,1; **298**,1,2; **302**,2;
- the infused virtues are capital
that will have increase only if we
know how to invest them by good
will : **288**,2; - one should not be
contented with tiny acts of —,
but should perform generous and
heroic acts : **289**,1; - God uses
every circumstance of life to invite
us to — : **163**,2; **266**,2; **292**,1;
- God will give us — only if we
apply ourselves to its exercise :
ibid. - the infused virtues are
supernatural principles of activity :
195,1; - God has infused — in us
without any merit on our part,
but He will not make it increase

without our collaboration : **298**,1;
- one cannot attain perfect
— without the help and the gifts
of the Holy Spirit : **298**,2.

Virtues (Theological) — Are the
means best adapted to unite us to
God : **248**,1; - if we practice them
by our will, it is not necessary to
have sentiment : **248**,2; - they
purify the three powers of the soul :
349,2.

Vocation — To the Christian life :
75,1; - to consecration to God :
ibid.; - privilege and gratuity
of — : **75**,2; - correspondence
to — : **76**,1,2; **322**,2; **386**,1;
- progressiveness of the divine call :
76,2; - each day requires a new
response, a new acceptance
according to the grace of the
moment : **322**,2; - infidelity to — :
134,2; **322**,2; - fidelity to — requires
the breaking of every attachment :
134,2; - cloistered — is an apostolic,
universal — : **324**,2.
See : CONSECRATION TO GOD.

Vows — To correspond with one's
vocation, it does not suffice to
make — : **76**,2; - vow of poverty :
86,1,2; - vow of chastity : **88**,2;
- vow of obedience : **121**,2; **122**,1,2.
See : CHASTITY; OBEDIENCE;
POVERTY.

Will of God — Is our sanctification :
2,1; **247**,1; - the — disposes the
events of our life for our sanctification : **36**,2; - the — is always
best for us : **56**,1; - conformity
to the — is the essence of sanctity :
5,1,2; **6**,2; **362**,2; - the happier
souls are in doing the —, the more
perfect they are : **5**,1; - the — is
the sole incentive for souls to be

perfect : **5**,2; **7**,1; **362**,1; - conformity to the — should be such that
there is nothing in the soul contrary
to It, but in all things the soul be
moved solely by the Divine Will :
5,2; **60**,2; **78**,1; **193**,2; **251**,2; - only
in the — shall we find our sancti-
fication : **36**,2; - the — should
become the sole motive of our
actions : **99**,2; - manifestations of
the — : **6**,1; **120**,1; **276**,2; -
conformity to the — by obedience :
120,2; - the — securely manifested
by orders of superiors : **123**,1,2;
124,1,2; - to attain full conformity
to the — it is necessary to undergo
purifications : **7**,2; **346**,1; - one of
the greatest obstacles to conformity
to the — is attachment to one's own
will : **120**,2; - one cannot embrace
the — without renouncing one's
own : **194**,1; - one cannot be united
with the — if one does not diligently
fulfill the commandment of fraternal
charity : **365**,2; - conformity to
the — is a source of peace : **33**,2;
36,2; **363**,2; - is the best preparation
for Communion : **207**,1,2; - and
reparation for sin : **213**,2;
- acceptance of the — : **36**,2;
112,2; - the — should be the rule
of our conduct : **60**,2; - the greater
the conformity to the —, the greater
the graces corresponding to it :
ibid.; **78**,1; - conformity to the
— corresponds to the degree of
purity of the soul : *ibid.;* - the soul
should be able to find satisfaction
only in doing the — : **81**,1; - Jesus
Crucified has told us how great is
the cost of fulfilling the — : **193**,2;
- the accomplishment of the
— should be the fruit of the
Christian life : **238**,2; - he who
travels by the way of the —,
instead of being guided by his
own spirit, is guided by the Holy
Spirit : **329**,1; - simple adhesion

to the — in the painful trials of the night of the spirit : **354**,2; - true love consists in seeking always the —, preferring it to one's own : **255**,2; **256**,1; - love leads the soul to the perfect conformity of its will with the — : **362**,1; - every soul of good will can attain to this state : **363**,1,2; - the perfect " Yes " to the — : **365**,1,2; - the soul of interior life should try to conform herself always more to the — : **364**,1.

See : UNION WITH GOD.

Will (Human) — Should in all things conform itself to the Will of God : **5**,1,2; - our stubborn, petty — is an obstacle to the action of the Holy Spirit : **192**,2; - to hold on to our inconstant — rather than to the immutable Will of God : **230**,1; - quality of good — : **33**,2; - importance of renunciation of one's own — : **120**,2; - sacrifice of one's own — the greatest and most meritorious act : **121**,2; - he who has consecrated to God his own will by promise or vow should be on his guard not to take back what he has offered : **122**,2; - he who is attached to his own — is not poor in spirit : **300**,2; - how our — differs from the Will of God : **346**,2.

Wisdom — Of the world is foolishness to God : **234**,2; - — to judge things as God values them : *ibid*.

Gift of Wisdom — makes one relish the things of God : **313**,1; - — actuates us by charity : **313**,2; - introduces the soul to the prayer of union : *ibid.;* - under its influence the soul judges all things according to the divine judgment : **314**,1; - to — corresponds the beatitude of the peacemakers : *ibid.;* - — establishes the soul in the peace of the children of God : **314**,2.

The Word (Second Person of the Most Blessed Trinity) — In every way is equal to the Father and the Holy Spirit : **27**,1; - Incarnate for love of us : **27**,2; - in order to communicate to us supernatural being : **39**,2; - becoming Incarnate — remains as He was : **27**,2; **52**,1; - becoming Incarnate — conceals His greatness and His Divinity : **31**,1.

See : JESUS; INCARNATION.

Works — The more — cost us, the more they are proofs of true love : **36**,1; - our good — are always full of defects : **247**,1 - our — should be to the edification of our neighbor : **327**,2.

Zeal
See : APOSTOLATE.

NOTES

NOTES

NOTES